THE ROUGH GUIDE TO

London

There are more than one hundred and fifty Rough Guide titles
covering destinations from Amsterdam to Zimbabwe

Forthcoming titles include
Devon & Cornwall • Madeira • Tenerife • Vancouver

Rough Guide Reference Series
Classical Music • Country Music • Drum 'n' bass • English Football
European Football • House • The Internet • Jazz • Music USA • Opera
Reggae • Rock Music • Techno • Unexplained Phenomena • World Music

Rough Guide Phrasebooks
Czech • Dutch • Egyptian Arabic • European Languages • French
German • Greek • Hindi & Urdu • Hungarian • Indonesian • Italian
Japanese • Mandarin Chinese • Mexican Spanish • Polish • Portuguese
Russian • Spanish • Swahili • Thai • Turkish • Vietnamese

Rough Guides on the Internet
www.roughguides.com

Rough Guide Credits

Text Editor:	Polly Thomas
Series Editor:	Mark Ellingham
Editorial:	Martin Dunford, Jonathan Buckley, Jo Mead, Kate Berens, Amanda Tomlin, Ann-Marie Shaw, Paul Gray, Helena Smith, Judith Bamber, Orla Duane, Olivia Eccleshall, Ruth Blackmore, Geoff Howard, Claire Saunders, Gavin Thomas, Alexander Mark Rogers, Joe Staines, Lisa Nellis, Andrew Tomičić, Richard Lim, Duncan Clark, Peter Buckley, Sam Thorne, Lucy Ratcliffe, Clifton Wilkinson, David Glen (UK); Andrew Rosenberg, Mary Beth Maioli, Stephen Timblin (US)
Online:	Kelly Cross, Anja Mutić-Blessing, Jennifer Gold, Audra Epstein (US)
Production:	Susanne Hillen, Andy Hilliard, Link Hall, Helen Ostick, Julia Bovis, Michelle Draycott, Katie Pringle, Robert Evers, Mike Hancock, Robert McKinlay, Zoë Nobes
Cartography:	Melissa Baker, Maxine Repath, Ed Wright, Katie Lloyd-Jones
Picture Research:	Louise Boulton, Sharon Martins
Finance:	John Fisher, Gary Singh, Edward Downey, Mark Hall, Tim Bill
Marketing & Publicity:	Richard Trillo, Niki Smith, David Wearn, Chloë Roberts, Birgit Hartmann (UK); Simon Carloss, David Wechsler (US)
Administration:	Tania Hummel, Demelza Dallow, Julie Sanderson

Acknowledgements

The author would like to thank Polly Thomas for her ruthless editing, Robert McKinlay for typesetting, Jennifer Speake for proofing, and Maxine Repath for cartography.

This fourth edition published January 2001 by Rough Guides Ltd, 62–70 Shorts Gardens, London WC2H 9AH.

Distributed by the Penguin Group:

Penguin Books Ltd, 27 Wrights Lane, London W8 5TZ.

Penguin Putnam, Inc. 375 Hudson Street, New York, NY 10014, USA.

Penguin Books Australia Ltd, 487 Maroondah Highway, PO Box 257, Ringwood, Victoria 3134, Australia.

Penguin Books Canada Ltd, 10 Alcorn Avenue, Toronto, Ontario M4V 1E4, Canada.

Penguin Books (NZ) Ltd, 182–190 Wairau Road, Auckland 10, New Zealand.

Printed in England by Clays Ltd, St Ives PLC

Typography and original design by Jonathan Dear and The Crowd Roars.

Illustrations throughout by Edward Briant.

ISBN 1-85828-684-0

THE ROUGH GUIDE TO

London

Written and researched by
Rob Humphreys

With additional contributions by
Sean Bidder, Charles Campion and Mel Steel

**ROUGH
GUIDES**

Help us update

We've gone to a lot of trouble to ensure that this fourth edition of *The Rough Guide to London* is accurate and up-to-date. However, things inevitably change, and if you feel we've got it wrong or left something out, we'd like to know: any suggestions, comments or corrections would be much appreciated. We'll credit all contributions and send a copy of the next edition – or any other Rough Guide if you prefer – for the best correspondence.

Please mark letters "Rough Guide to London Update" and send to:
Rough Guides, 62–70 Shorts Gardens, London WC2H 9AH or
Rough Guides, 4th Floor, 345 Hudson St, New York, NY 10014.

Email should be sent to:
mail@roughguides.co.uk

Online updates about Rough Guide titles can be found on our Web site at www.roughguides.com

The Author

Rob Humphreys joined Rough Guides in 1989, having worked as a failed actor, taxi driver and male model. He has travelled extensively in central and eastern Europe, writing guides to Prague, the Czech and Slovak Republics, and St Petersburg. He has lived in London since 1988.

Readers' letters

Many thanks to the readers of the last edition who took the time to write in with their comments and suggestions: Mairi Allan, Michelle Austin, Joan Craig, I. H. Davey, Bernadette Kowey, Ben Levy, Bo Lundin, Donald B. McKay, Klaus-Martin Meyke, Vanessa Mitchell, Jo Pascoe, Karen Reber, Jackie Ross, Bernadine E. Sperling and José Valverde-Bastán.

Rough Guides

Travel Guides • Phrasebooks • Music and Reference Guides

We set out to do something different when the first Rough Guide was published in 1982. Mark Ellingham, just out of University, was travelling in Greece. He brought along the popular guides of the day, but found they were all lacking in some way. They were either strong on ruins and museums but went on for pages without mentioning a beach or taverna. Or they were so conscious of the need to save money that they lost sight of Greece's cultural and historical significance. Also, none of the books told him anything about Greece's contemporary life – its politics, its culture, its people, and how they lived.

So with no job in prospect, Mark decided to write his own guidebook, one which aimed to provide practical information that was second to none, detailing the best beaches and the hottest clubs and restaurants, while also giving hard-hitting accounts of every sight, both famous and obscure, and providing up-to-the-minute information on contemporary culture. It was a guide that encouraged independent travellers to find the best of Greece, and was a great success, getting shortlisted for the Thomas Cook travel guide award, and encouraging Mark, along with three friends, to expand the series.

The Rough Guide list grew rapidly and the letters flooded in, indicating a much broader readership than had been anticipated, but one which uniformly appreciated the Rough Guides' mix of practical detail and humour, irreverence and enthusiasm. Things haven't changed. The same four friends who began the series are still the caretakers of the Rough Guide mission today: to provide the most reliable, up-to-date and entertaining information to independent-minded travellers of all ages, on all budgets.

We now publish 150 titles and have offices in London and New York. The travel guides are written and researched by a dedicated team of more than 100 authors, based in Britain, Europe, the USA and Australia. We have also created a unique series of phrasebooks to accompany the travel series, along with the acclaimed series of music guides, and a best-selling pocket guide to the Internet and World Wide Web. We also publish comprehensive travel information on our Web site: *www.roughguides.com*

Contents

Part Three: The Listings 495

Part Four: Contexts 639

Index 667

List of maps

MAP SYMBOLS

═══	Road	◖	Cave
═ ═ ═	Passageway	♛	Castle
▬▬	Railway	🏛	Stately home
～～	River/canal	♦	Museum
– – –	Ferry route	⊥	Public gardens
───	Chapter division boundary	⊠	Post office
♦	Point of Interest	▨	Building
⊖	Underground station	⊞	Church
○	Train station	✿	Synagogue
ⓘ	Tourist office	ℂ	Mosque
⊠	Gate	⁺⁺⁺	Christian cemetery
▲	Peak	▨	Park

Introduction

What strikes visitors more than anything about London is the sheer size of the place. With a population of just under eight million, it's Europe's largest city by far, spreading across an area of more than 620 square miles from its core on the River Thames. Londoners tend to cope with this by compartmentalizing the city, identifying with the neighbourhoods in which they work or live, and making occasional forays into the "centre of town" – the West End, London's shopping and entertainment heartland.

Ethnically, London is also Europe's most diverse metropolis, and for those without local roots the place can seem bafflingly diverse. With around two hundred languages spoken within its confines and all the major religions represented, London is more like an entire country than a single city. Over thirty percent of the population is made up of first, second- and third-generation immigrants, while some claim as many as 75 percent of white Londoners are in fact descended from French Huguenot refugees.

Despite Scottish, Welsh and Northern Irish devolution, London still dominates the national horizon, too: this is where the country's news and money are made, it's where the central government resides and, as far as its inhabitants are concerned, provincial life begins beyond the circuit of the city's orbital motorway. Londoners' sense

For a rundown on London's highlights, see "Introducing the city" (p.31).

Average daily temperatures in London

	Jan	Feb	March	April	May	June	July	Aug	Sept	Oct	Nov	Dec
°F	38	40	42	47	53	60	62	62	57	50	43	40
°C	3	4	6	8	12	15	17	16	14	10	6	4

Average monthly rainfall in London

	Jan	Feb	March	April	May	June	July	Aug	Sept	Oct	Nov	Dec
inches	1.9	1.6	1.6	1.7	1.9	2.1	2.3	2.3	2.2	2.4	2.3	2.1
mm	48	39	40	42	47	52	60	57	55	62	59	53

METRIC CONVERSION TABLE

LENGTH

1 mile = 1.61 kilometres	1 foot = 0.31 metres
1 yard = 0.91 metres	1 inch = 2.54 centimetres

MASS

1 ton = 1016 kilograms	1 pound = 0.45 kilograms
1 stone = 6.35 kilograms	

CAPACITY

1 gallon = 4.55 litres	1 pint = 0.57 litres

of superiority causes enormous resentment in the regions, yet it's undeniable that the capital has a unique aura of excitement and success – in most walks of British life, if you want to get on you've got to do it in London.

For the visitor too, London is a thrilling place – and since the beginning of the new millennium, the city has also been overtaken by an exceptionally buoyant mood. Thanks to the lottery and the millennium-oriented funding frenzy of the last few years, virtually every one of London's world-class museums, galleries and institutions has been reinvented, from the Royal Opera House to the British Museum. With the completion of the Tate Modern and the London Eye, the city can now boast the world's largest modern art gallery and Ferris wheel; there's also a new tube extension, a new tram system (albeit in the suburbs) and the first new bridge to cross the central section of the Thames for over a hundred years. And after sixteen years of being the only major city in the world not to have its own governing body, London finally has its own elected mayor and assembly.

In the meantime, London's traditional sights – Big Ben, Westminster Abbey, Buckingham Palace, St Paul's Cathedral and the Tower of London – continue to draw in millions of tourists every year. Monuments from the capital's more glorious past are everywhere to be seen, from medieval banqueting halls and the great churches of Sir Christopher Wren to the eclectic Victorian architecture of the triumphalist British Empire. There is also much enjoyment to be had from the city's quiet Georgian squares, the narrow alleyways of the City of London, the riverside walks, and the quirks of what is still identifiably a collection of villages. Even London's traffic pollution – one of its worst problems – is offset by surprisingly large expanses of greenery: Hyde Park, Green Park and St James's Park are all within a few minutes' walk of the West End, while, further afield, you can enjoy the more expansive parklands of Hampstead Heath and Richmond Park.

You could spend days just shopping in London too, hob-nobbing with the upper classes in Harrods, or sampling the offbeat weekend

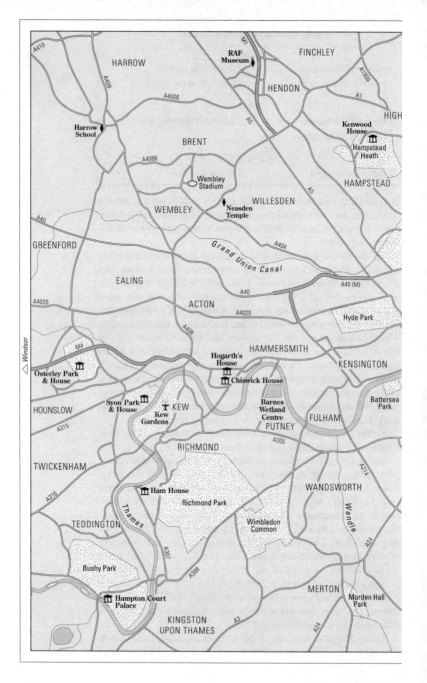

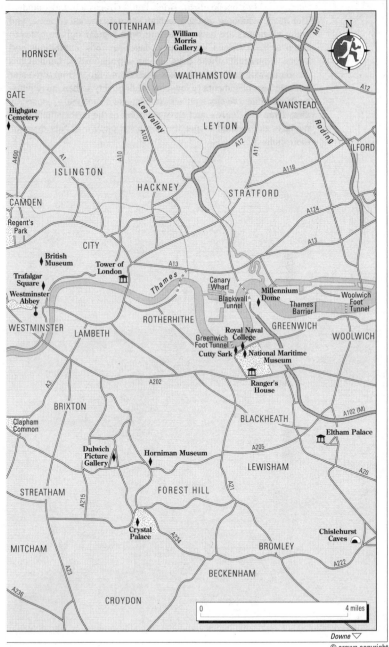

N

TOTTENHAM

William Morris Gallery

HORNSEY

WALTHAMSTOW

M11

GATE

A12

Highgate Cemetery

WANSTEAD

Lea Valley

LEYTON

A107

Roding

ILFORD

A400

A1

A10

A12

A11

ISLINGTON

HACKNEY

STRATFORD

A118

CAMDEN

A124

Regent's Park

CITY

A13

British Museum

Tower of London

A13

Trafalgar Square

Thames

Canary Wharf

Millennium Dome

Woolwich Foot Tunnel

Westminster Abbey

Blackwall Tunnel

Thames Barrier

ROTHERHITHE

Royal Naval College

GREENWICH

WESTMINSTER

LAMBETH

Greenwich Foot Tunnel

WOOLWICH

Cutty Sark

National Maritime Museum

A3

A202

Ranger's House

BRIXTON

BLACKHEATH

A102 (M)

Clapham Common

Eltham Palace

Dulwich Picture Gallery

Horniman Museum

A205

LEWISHAM

A20

STREATHAM

A215

FOREST HILL

A21

Crystal Palace

Chislehurst Caves

MITCHAM

A234

BROMLEY

A23

BECKENHAM

A222

A236

CROYDON

0   4 miles

Downe ▽

© crown copyright

markets of Portobello Road, Brick Lane, Greenwich and Camden. The music, clubbing and gay/lesbian scene is second to none, and mainstream arts are no less exciting, with regular opportunities to catch brilliant theatre companies, dance troupes, exhibitions and opera. Restaurants these days, are an attraction too. London has caught up with its European rivals, and offers a range from three-star Michelin establishments to low-cost, high-quality Indian curry houses. Meanwhile, the city's pubs have heaps of atmosphere, especially away from the centre – and an exploration of the farther-flung communities is essential to get the complete picture of this dynamic metropolis.

The Basics

Getting there from North America

All the major US and Canadian airlines run direct services from North America to London, Europe's busiest gateway city. Two of London's airports – Heathrow and Gatwick (see p.36) –

handle transatlantic flights, and in terms of convenience they are about equal.

Figure on around six hours' **flying time** from New York; it's an hour extra going the other way, due to headwinds. Most eastbound flights cross the Atlantic overnight, depositing you at your destination the next morning without much sleep, but if you can manage to stay awake until after dinner that night, you should be over the worst of your jet lag by the next morning. Some flights from the East Coast depart early in the morning, arriving late the same evening, but this lands you in London just as the city is shutting down – a recipe for a disorienting and expensive first night.

Shopping for tickets

Given the enormous volume of air traffic crossing the Atlantic, you should have no problem finding

---

MAJOR AIRLINES IN NORTH AMERICA

Aer Lingus ☎ 1-800/223-6537; *www.aerlingus.ie*. Daily flights from Boston, Chicago and New York (and every day except Wed from Newark) to London, via Dublin or Shannon.

Air Canada ☎ 1-800/263-0882 in Canada; *www.aircanada.ca*. Nonstop flights from Halifax, Montréal, Toronto and Vancouver.

American Airlines ☎ 1-800/433-7300; *www.aa.com*. Daily nonstop service from Boston, Chicago, Dallas/Fort Worth, LA, Miami, New York, Newark and Raleigh/Durham.

British Airways ☎ 1-800/247-9297; *www.british-airways.com*. Daily nonstop service from most US and Canadian gateway cities, plus Cancun and Mexico City.

Canadian Airlines ☎ 1-800/426-7000 in Canada; *www.cdnair.ca*. Daily nonstop flights from Montréal, Toronto, Calgary and Vancouver.

Continental Airlines ☎ 1-800/231-0856; *www.flycontinental.com*. Daily nonstop flights from Houston, Cleveland, Miami, Washington DC and Newark, with connecting flights from most other major cities in North America.

Delta Airlines ☎ 1-800/241-4141; *www.delta-air.com*. Daily nonstop flights from Atlanta and Cincinnati, with connecting flights from most major American cities.

Kuwait Airways ☎ 1-800/458-9248; *www.kuwait-airways.com*. Daily nonstop flights from New York.

Northwest/KLM Airlines ☎ 1-800/225-2525; *www.nwa.com*. Daily nonstop flights from Detroit and Minneapolis.

TWA ☎ 1-800/221-2000; *www.twa.com*. Daily nonstop flights from St Louis.

United Airlines ☎ 1-800/538-2929; *www.ual.com*. Daily nonstop flights from Boston, Chicago, LA, New York, Newark, San Francisco and Washington DC, with connecting flights from most major American cities.

Virgin Atlantic Airways ☎ 1-800/862-8621; *www.virgin.com*. Daily nonstop flights to London from Boston, Chicago, LA, New York, Newark, Miami, Orlando, San Francisco, Washington DC, plus flights from Las Vegas on Sundays and Thursdays.

---

a seat – the problem will be sifting through all the possibilities. Basic fares are kept very reasonable by intense competition; discounts by bulk agents and periodic special offers by the airlines themselves can drive prices still lower. Any local **travel agent** should be able to access airlines' up-to-the-minute fares, although in practice they may not have time to research all the possibilities – you might want to call a few **airlines** directly (see box on p.3).

The **Internet** is also an increasingly popular, and often more convenient, option for purchasing tickets. All of the above airlines, as well as most of the discount agents, consolidators and travel clubs listed opposite, have Web sites offering all sorts of ticket information, and can usually take your reservation online. Discount Airfares Worldwide (*www.etn.nl/discount.htm*) and International Travel Network/Airlines of the Web (*www.flyaow.com*) both specialize in online booking and have useful links to other sites that offer all sorts of travel information, including hotel and car rental booking.

The least expensive tickets widely available from the airlines are **Apex** tickets, which carry certain restrictions: you have to book – and pay – at least 21 days before departure, spend at least seven days abroad (maximum stay three months), and you tend to get penalized if you change your schedule. There are also winter **Super Apex** tickets, which are slightly less expensive than an ordinary Apex, but limit your stay to between seven and 21 days. Some airlines also issue **Special Apex** tickets to those under 24, often extending the maximum stay to a year. It's worth remembering that most cheap fares involve spending at least one Saturday night away, and that many will only give a percentage refund if you need to cancel or alter your journey, so make sure you check the restrictions carefully before buying a ticket.

Whatever the airlines are offering, however, any number of **specialist travel companies** should be able to beat it. These are the outfits you'll see advertising in the Sunday newspaper travel sections, and they come in several forms. **Consolidators** buy up large blocks of tickets that airlines don't think they'll be able to sell at their published fares, and sell them at a discount. Besides being inexpensive, consolidators normally don't impose advance purchase requirements (although at busy times you'll want to book ahead just to be sure of getting a ticket), but they

do often charge very stiff fees for date changes. Also, these companies' margins are pretty tiny, so they make their money by dealing in volume – don't expect them to entertain lots of questions. Some agencies specialize in **charter flights**, which may be even cheaper than anything available on a scheduled service, but again there's a trade-off: departure dates are fixed and withdrawal penalties are high. **Discount travel clubs** are another option for those who travel a lot – most charge an annual membership fee, which may be worth it for discounts on air tickets, car rental and the like.

Incidentally, don't automatically assume that tickets purchased through a travel specialist will be the least expensive on offer – once you get a quote, check with the airlines and you may turn up an even cheaper promotion. Be advised also that the pool of travel companies is swimming with sharks – exercise caution with any outfit that sounds shifty or impermanent, and never deal with a company that demands cash up front or refuses to accept payment by credit card.

Regardless of where you buy your ticket, **fares** will depend on the season, although the exact dates may vary from airline to airline and between flights from the US and Canada. If you want to make sure you're getting the best deal, always double check. That said, fares are generally highest from mid-June to the end of September plus the couple of weeks before Christmas; and lowest from the beginning of October to mid-December and from Christmas Day to the end of March. The rest of the year is the somewhat vague "shoulder season", when you can expect prices anywhere between the "high" and "low" rates.

Flights from the US

Many airlines fly nonstop to London from the major East and West Coast cities and Midwestern hubs. Flight time from the West Coast is around 9–10 hours, compared to around 6–7 hours from East Coast cities. There is heavy competition on these routes, and consolidators and discounters often have cheap, last-minute fares. The cheapest midweek, round-trip fares in, respectively, low and high season, cost around $350 or $660 from **New York**; $450 or $850 from **Chicago**; $560 or $770 from **Miami**; $420 or $820 from **Atlanta**; and $500 or $900 from **Los Angeles**. From the West Coast, some of the best fares are on flights connecting through Midwest and East Coast cities, but occasionally there will be sales on nonstops, so check around before assuming you'll have to take a connecting flight. It's also well worth checking out the charter and discount agents (see box below) who have been known to find flights to London, in the low and high season respectively, for as little as $290 or $430 from New York, and $450 or $600 from LA.

London is also a popular stop on **Round-the-World (RTW) tickets**. A few examples of possible RTW itineraries, with estimate prices are: New York–Bangkok–Kathmandu–London–New York for $1350; LA–London–Istanbul–Bangkok–Tokyo–LA for $1500; Toronto–London–Athens–Cairo–Bombay–Delhi–Kathmandu–Bangkok–Toronto for $1795; and Vancouver–London–Johannesburg–Sydney–Auckland–Fiji–Honolulu–Vancouver for $1995. All of the above tickets are available from RTW ticket specialists Airtreks.com, 442 Post St, Suite 400, San Francisco, CA 94102 ☎1-800/350-

0612 (*www.airtreks.com*). The Web site features an interactive database that lets you build your own RTW itinerary.

Flights from Canada

In Canada, you'll get the best deal flying to London from the big **gateway cities** of Toronto and Montréal, where competition between the major carriers drives midweek return fares as low as CDN$679 in the off season, or CDN$1533 in the high season; direct flights from Ottawa and Halifax cost only slightly more. From Vancouver, Edmonton and Calgary, flights start at CDN$957 in the off season, CD$1257 in the high season. It's also worth checking discount agents and consolidators, which can often find London flights from Toronto or Montréal for as low as CDN$575 low season, CDN$1200 high season, and from Vancouver or Calgary for CDN$850 low season and CDN$1150 high season.

DISCOUNT AGENTS, CONSOLIDATORS AND TRAVEL CLUBS

Air Brokers International, 150 Post St, Suite 620, San Francisco, CA 94108 ☎1-800/883-3273 or ☎413/397-1383; *www.airbrokers.com*. Consolidator and specialist in RTW tickets.

Air Courier Association, 15000 W 6th Ave, Suite 203, Golden, CO 80401 ☎1-800/282-1202 or ☎303/279-3600; *www.aircourier.org*. Low-cost courier fares to London and other parts of Europe.

Council Travel, Head Office 205 E 42nd St, New York, NY 10017 ☎212/822-2700 or ☎1-800/226-8624 to find the branch nearest to you; *www.counciltravel.com*. Specialist in student travel.

Educational Travel Centre, 438 N Frances St, Madison, WI 53703 ☎1-800/747-5551 or ☎608/256-5551; *www.edtrav.com*. Student /youth discounts.

Now Voyager, 74 Varick St, Suite 307, New York, NY 10013 ☎212/431-1616; *www .nowvoyagertravel.com*. Courier-flight broker and consolidator.

Skylink, 265 Madison Ave, 5th floor, New York, NY 10016 ☎1-800/247-6659 or ☎416-922-1000 in Canada. Consolidator with branches in Chicago, Los Angeles, Montréal, New York, Toronto and Washington DC.

STA Travel, 10 Downing St, New York, NY 10014 ☎212/627-311; 7202 Melrose Ave, Los Angeles, CA 90046 ☎323/934-8772; 429 S Dearborn St, Chicago, IL 60605 ☎312/786-9050; call ☎1-800/777-0112 to find the branch nearest you; *www.sta-travel.com*. Worldwide specialists in student/youth fares.

TFI Tours International, 34 W 32nd St, 12th Floor, New York, NY 10001 ☎1-800/745-8000 or ☎212/736-1140. Consolidator.

Travac, 989 6th Ave, 16th Floor, New York, NY 10018 ☎1-800/872-8800 or ☎212/563-3303; *www.thetravelsite.com*. Consolidator and charter broker.

Travel Avenue, 10 S Riverside Plaza, Suite 1404, Chicago, IL 60606 ☎1-800/333-3335 or ☎312/876-6866; *www.travelavenue.com*. Discount-travel company.

Travel CUTS, 187 College St, Toronto, ON M5T 1P7 ☎1-800/667-2887 or ☎416/979-2406; plus branches on most Canadian university campuses; call ☎1-800/954-2666 to find the branch nearest you; *www.travelcuts.com*. Student /youth discount agency.

UniTravel, 11737 Administration Drive, Suite 120, St Louis, MO 63146 ☎1-800/325-2222 or ☎314/569-250; *www.flightsforless.com*. Consolidator.

Packages and organized tours

Although you'll want to see London at your own speed, don't dismiss the idea of a **package deal**. Many agents and airlines put together very flexible packages, sometimes amounting to nothing more restrictive than a flight plus accommodation, and these can work out cheaper – and be less stressful – than the same arrangements made independently.

There are plenty of **tour operators** specializing in travel to London, and they can be contacted either directly or through travel agents – the cost is the same. Choose only an operator that is a member of the United States Tour Operator Association (USTOA) or has been approved by the American Society of Travel Agents (ASTA). Below are examples of deals offered by dependable tour operators, while the box below contains useful addresses; for a full but uncritical listing, contact the British Tourist Authority (see box on p.21). The prices quoted below are for packages from New York; for West Coast flights you'll pay an extra $260–280; for Chicago, it's around $160–180 extra; for Miami, add $80–100; for Toronto, add CDN$250–300; for Vancouver add CDN$350–400.

British Airways Holidays offers an assortment of tours from various British cities including London. The selection includes "A Taste of London", a four-day/three-night or seven-day/six-night tour for between $649 and $1489 including airfare, airport transfers, hotel and continental breakfast; alternatively, "Treasures of London", a seven-day/six-night package for $729–1809, includes a seven-day pass for unlimited use on buses and the Underground (tube) and a choice of tours such as Buckingham Palace, Greenwich, Windsor Castle, or a full-day cruise on the River Thames. "London on Stage", a four-day/three-night package costing $669–1369, includes two theatre tickets to shows such as *Chicago*, *Blood Brothers*, *Saturday Night Fever* and *Cats*, a backstage theatre tour and a three-day travel pass.

American Airlines Vacations sells a variety of packages and tours, including "Historic Pubs of London", a eight-day/seven-night package starting at $1022 for airfare, airport transfer, hotel, continental breakfast, a three-day pass to major museums and galleries, a seven-day travel pass and two passes good for a main-course lunch and a drink at a selection of London's pubs. "Best

---

NORTH AMERICAN TOUR OPERATORS TO ENGLAND

AESU Travel, 3922 Hicory Ave, Baltimore, MD 21211 ☎1-800/638-7640; *www.aesu.com*. Airline tickets, customized tours, and various "city stays" – packages that include air, hotel and a tour guide for a portion of your stay.

American Airlines Vacations, American Airlines, PO Box 619616, Dallas/Fort Worth Airport 75261-9616 ☎1-800/321-2121; *www .aavacations.com*. Independent and group itineraries.

BA Tours, 5728 Major Blvd, Suite 750, Orlando, FL 32819 ☎1-800/359-8722; *www.british -airways.com*. British Airways package-tour agents; see box on p.3.

British Travel International, PO Box 299, Elkton, VA 22827 ☎1-800/327-6097; *www .britishtravel.com*. Made-to-measure packages: air tickets, train and bus passes, hotels and flat and cottage rentals.

Contiki Holidays, 300 Plaza Alicante, Suite 900, Garden Grove, CA 92640 ☎1-800/CONTI-KI; *www.contiki.com*. Specific group tours for people aged 18–35.

Euro Vacations, 851 Southwest Sixth, Suite 1010, Portland OR 97204 ☎1-888/281-EURO; *www.eurovacations.com*. Rail Europe subsidiary offering BritRail products plus flight accommodation and package deals to London.

International Gay Travel Association, 4331 North Federal Highway, Suite 304, Ft. Lauderdale, FL 33308 ☎1-800/448-8550; *www.iglta.org*. Trade group with lists of gay-owned or gay-friendly travel agents, accommodation options and other travel-related services.

Select Travel Service, 99 Bauer Drive, Oakland, NJ 07436 ☎1-800/752-6787. Specialist in individualized group tours with a theme: history, literature, theatre, horticulture, sports, etc.

United Vacations, PO Box 24580, Milwaukee, WI 53224-580 ☎1-800/328-6877; *www.ual .com*. All-inclusive packages, fly-drives and sightseeing tours.

Virgin Vacations, 465 Smith St, Farmingdale, NY 11735. ☎1-888/937-8474. Virgin's package-tour division.

---

of London" is a seven-day/six-night package starting at $1186 for airfare, airport transfer, hotel, continental breakfast, theatre tickets, a London Bus Tour, a River Thames Dinner Cruise, tea at Harrods and a seven-day travel pass. AA Vacations can also arrange self-contained apartments in London starting at $283 per person for three nights.

Virgin Atlantic Vacations offers several set packages and customized itineraries. A four-night package, including flights and accommodation, costs from $649. Optional add-ons include theatre passes, a "Jack the Ripper Murder Mystery" bus tour and a "Discovering London" city bus tour. Other options include a three-night "London Jaunt" flight and accommodation package starting

around $539; or "Channel to Paris" which starts at $849, and includes three nights in London and three nights in Paris.

Contiki Holidays, which specializes in tours for people aged 18 to 35, runs a twelve-day "Great Britain" tour, starting at $925, which covers hotels, all meals, bus travel and sightseeing tours (but not flights). The trip begins in London, then moves on to Stonehenge, Stratford-on-Avon, the Lake District, Edinburgh and Wales.

Euro Vacations (BritRail's tour division) offers two- and five-night London packages starting at $428/$654 and including airfare, transfers and accommodation, with optional add-ons such as theatre tickets, museum vouchers and public transport passes.

Getting there from Australia and New Zealand

As London is a major destination for most international airlines flying out of Australia and New Zealand, the high level of competition ensures a wide choice of routes worldwide, with flights via Southeast Asia generally being the cheapest option.

If you're planning to visit London as part of a wider world trip, then **Round-the-World** tickets offer greater flexibility and are better value than a straightforward return flight. For example, prices for

a RTW ticket from Sydney or Auckland to Singapore or Bangkok, London, New York, Los Angeles, Auckland and back to Sydney start at around A$2399/NZ$2899; a ticket from Sydney to Auckland, Santiago, Rio, London, Paris, Bangkok, Singapore and back to Sydney starts at A$2499 /NZ$2999.

Regular return **fares** are seasonally adjusted – **low season** is from mid-January to the end of February and October to November; **high season** is mid-May to August and December to January, with the remainder of the year classed as **shoulder season**. Tickets purchased direct from the airlines tend to be expensive; travel agents generally offer much better deals, and have the latest information on limited special offers and stopovers. The best discounts are offered by companies such as Flight Centres, STA and Trailfinders (see box on p.10); these can also help with visas, travel insurance and tours. You might also want to have a look on the Internet; *www.travel.com.au* offers discounted fares online, as does *www.sydneytravel.com*.

Average return economy fares to London from eastern Australian gateways cost around A$1800 in the low season and A$2800 in the high season, and NZ$2000 and NZ$3000 respectively from Auckland. Fares climb by A/NZ$300 for each successive fare season.

Flights from Australia

Airfares from Australian east-coast gateways are all pretty much the same: common rated, with Ansett and Qantas providing a shuttle service to the point of international departure. Depending on the route and transfer time, flights between Australia and Britain take between 22 and 28 hours via Asia, 28 and 36 hours via Africa, and 25 and 30 hours via the US.

The cheapest scheduled flights are **via Asia**, and can involve a night's free overnight stop – often a needed break on long-haul flights – in the carrier's home city, with accommodation, meals and transfers included in the ticket price. Fares from Perth and Darwin cost around A$100–200 less than from eastern gateways via Asia and Africa, and A$400 more via the US and South

America. The best low-season bargains are with the newly formed Sri Lankan Airlines, at around A$1300 return; in the high season, the cheapest fares are usually offered by Garuda, Japan Airlines and Royal Brunei, all from A$1350 to A$2400. Virgin Atlantic has teamed up with Malaysian Airlines to offer no-frills London flights via Kuala Lumpur for around A$1600 in the low season, and around A$2600 in the high season, while of the rest of the carriers flying to London, Korean Airlines and Malaysia Airlines, are recommended; prices range from A$1899 to A$2600. More expensive but faster, entailing only a short refuelling stop or quick change of planes, are Thai Airways, Singapore Airlines, Cathay Pacific, Qantas, British Airways and Air New Zealand, at A$1900–A$2800. Many of these airlines also offer stopover and fly-drive packages in their hub cities and within Britain and Europe, as well as return domestic flights, which, if booked with your main ticket, can work out more economical than arranging everything independently.

AIRLINES IN AUSTRALIA AND NEW ZEALAND

Air New Zealand Australia ☎ 13/2476; New Zealand toll-free ☎ 0800/737 000, or ☎ 09/357 3000; *www.airnz.com*. Daily flights to London Heathrow from Sydney, Brisbane, Melbourne and Auckland, with a transfer in LA.

British Airways Australia ☎ 02/8904 8800; New Zealand ☎ 09/356 8690; *www .british-airways.com*. Daily flights to London Heathrow from Sydney either direct, or with a transfer in LA; twice weekly via Perth with either a transfer or overnight stop in Harare or Johannesburg; and daily from Auckland with a transfer in LA.

Canadian Airlines Australia ☎ 1300/655 767; New Zealand ☎ 09/309 0735; *www.cdnair.ca*. Several flights weekly to London Heathrow from Sydney, Melbourne and Auckland, with a transfer in Vancouver or Toronto.

Cathay Pacific Australia ☎ 13/1747 or ☎ 02/9931 5500; New Zealand ☎ 09/379 0861; *www.cathaypacific.com*. Several flights weekly to London Heathrow from Brisbane, Sydney, Melbourne, Perth, Cairns and Auckland, all with a transfer in Hong Kong.

Garuda Australia ☎ 1300/365 330; New Zealand ☎ 09/366 1855 or ☎ 1800/128 510. Several flights weekly from major cities in Australia and New Zealand to London Gatwick, with either a transfer or an overnight stop in Denpasar or Jakarta.

Japan Airlines Australia ☎ 02/9272 1111; New Zealand ☎ 09/379 9906; *www .japanair.com*. Daily flights to London Heathrow from Brisbane and Sydney, and several flights a week from Cairns and Auckland, all with either a transfer or overnight stop in Tokyo or Osaka. Code-share with Air New Zealand.

Korean Air Australia ☎ 02/9262 6000; New Zealand ☎ 09/307 3687; *www.koreanair.com*. Several flights weekly to London Heathrow from Sydney and Auckland, plus once a week from Christchurch with either a transfer or overnight stop in Seoul.

Malaysian Airlines Australia ☎ 13/2627; New Zealand ☎ 09/373 2741 or ☎ 0800/777 747; *www.malaysiaair.com*.Several flights weekly to London Heathrow from Sydney, Melbourne, Perth and Auckland with either a transfer or overnight stop in Kuala Lumpur.

Flights are pricier **via North America**, and all require a change of planes en route (via LA with United Airlines and Air New Zealand, and via Toronto or Vancouver with Canadian Airlines); expect to pay A$2100–A$3000. Flying **via South America** is expensive, with a normal return fare to London via Buenos Aires with Aerolineas Argentinas costing a flat rate of $3600 year-round. A more economical option is a Round-the-World ticket (see p.7).

Although fares are not as high as those via South America, there are no real bargains **via Africa**, and the choice of airlines is limited. Qantas/British Airways and South African Airways fares to Heathrow, with either a transfer or overnight stop in Johannesburg, are A$2300 to A$3000 from Sydney, and $2000 to A$2700 from Perth.

Flights from New Zealand

Most airlines fly out of Auckland; add between NZ$150 and NZ$300 to the following fares for flights from Christchurch and Wellington.

Fewer carriers fly from New Zealand than from Australia; however, routes are just as varied. Garuda, Japan Airlines, Malaysia Airlines, Thai Airways and Korean Air all fly from Auckland, with a transfer or overnight stop in the carrier's home city, for between NZ$2000 and NZ$2400; Qantas and British Airways, via Sydney, Bangkok or Singapore, are more expensive at NZ$2300 to NZ$3000, but will get you there faster.

The most direct route (though still requiring a change of planes) is **via the Pacific and North America**, with Air New Zealand and United Airlines flights via LA costing between NZ$2200 and NZ$3000. British Airways (via LA), and Canadian Airlines (via Vancouver), offer flights for about NZ$2499 to NZ$3000. Via South America, a normal return fare with Aerolineas Argentinas via Buenos Aires is quite expensive, with a year-round flat rate of NZ$3600; an RTW ticket is a better bet. Another option is to fly to an Australian gateway city and then on to

---

Qantas Australia ☎ 13/1313; New Zealand ☎ 09/357 8900 or ☎ 0800/808 767; *www.qantas.com.au*. Daily flights to London Heathrow from major cities in Australia, either direct (with a short refuelling stop) or with a transfer in Singapore or Bangkok, plus twice weekly via Perth with either a transfer or overnight stopover in Harare or Johannesburg; daily flights from major cities in New Zealand to London Heathrow via Sydney, and with a transfer in Singapore, Bangkok or LA.

Royal Brunei Airlines Australia ☎ 07/3221 7757 (no NZ office); *www.bruneiair.com*. Three flights weekly to London Heathrow from Brisbane, and two weekly from Darwin and Perth, all via Abu Dhabi and with a transfer or overnight stop in Brunei.

Singapore Airlines Australia ☎ 13/1011; New Zealand ☎ 09/303 2129 or ☎ 0800/808 909; *www.singaporeair.com*. Daily flights to London Heathrow from Brisbane, Sydney, Melbourne, Perth and Auckland, either direct or with a transfer in Singapore.

South African Airways Australia ☎ 02/9223 4402 or ☎ 1800 221 699; New Zealand agent ☎ 09/379 3708; *www.saa.com*. Several flights

a week to London Heathrow from major eastern Australian cities, via Perth and with either a transfer or overnight stop in Johannesburg or Harare. Code-share with Qantas.

Sri Lankan Airlines Australia ☎ 02/9244 2234; New Zealand ☎ 09/308 3353. Three flights a week to London Heathrow from Sydney, with a transfer or overnight stop in Colombo.

Thai Airways Australia ☎ 1300/651 960; New Zealand ☎ 09/377 3886; *www.thaiair.com*. Several flights a week to London Heathrow from Brisbane, Sydney, Melbourne, Perth and Auckland, with either a transfer or overnight stop in Bangkok.

United Airlines Australia ☎ 13/1777; New Zealand ☎ 09/379 3800; *www.ual.com*. Daily flights to London Heathrow from Sydney, Melbourne and Auckland, with a transfer in LA.

Virgin Atlantic Airways Australia ☎ 02/9244 2747; New Zealand ☎ 09/308 3377; *www.virgin-atlantic.com*. Daily flights to London Heathrow from Sydney, Melbourne and Adelaide, with a transfer or overnight stop in Kuala Lumpur. Code-share with Malaysia Airlines.

London; you'll get a greater choice of airlines and routes.

Package holidays

Competition among wholesalers is fierce, so there is little variation in package content or prices. As well as flights and B&B, hotel and apartment accommodation, all the operators listed in the box below offer the following: three- to seven-day London mini-breaks (combinations that usually include hotel accommodation, London Transport passes and pre-booked theatre tickets) from A\$325/NZ\$396; city sightseeing tours from A\$20/NZ\$25; and car rental from A\$40/NZ\$50 per day.

SPECIALIST AGENTS

Best of Britain, 352a Military Rd, Cremorne, Sydney ☎02/9909 1055. Flights, London accommodation (B&Bs and apartments as well as hotels), car rental and city tours.

Contiki, 35 Spring St, Bondi Junction, Sydney ☎02/9511 2200 or 1300/301 835; *www .contiki.com*. Specializes in tours for 18–35-year-old party animals.

European Travel Office, 122 Rosslyn St, West Melbourne ☎03/9329 8844; Suite 410, 368 Sussex St, Sydney ☎02/9267 7714; 407 Great South Rd, Auckland ☎09/525 3074. Flights, accommodation, car rental and tours.

Silke's Travel, 263 Oxford St, Darlinghurst, Sydney ☎02/9380 6244, toll-free ☎1800/807 860; *www.silkes.com.au*. Specially tailored packages for gay and lesbian travellers.

DISCOUNT TRAVEL AGENTS IN AUSTRALIA AND NEW ZEALAND

All of the agents listed below will sell you discount flights, as well as acting as retail agents for tour companies such as Creative, Insight and Contiki, which offer London accommodation packages, tours and car rental.

Anywhere Travel, 345 Anzac Parade, Kingsford, Sydney ☎02/9663 0411, ☎018 401 014: *anywhere@ozemail.com.au*.

Budget Travel, 16 Fort St, Auckland, plus branches around the city ☎09/366 0061, and toll-free 0800/808 040; *www.budgettravel.co.nz*.

Destinations Unlimited, 220 Queen St, Auckland ☎09/373 4033.

Flight Centres, Australia: 82 Elizabeth St, Sydney ☎02/9235 3522; plus branches nation-wide – for the nearest branch call ☎13 1600. New Zealand: 350 Queen St, Auckland ☎09/358 4310, toll-free ☎0200/354 448, plus branches nationwide; *www.flightcentre.com.au*.

Northern Gateway, 22 Cavenagh St, Darwin ☎08/8941 1394; *oztravel@norgate.com.au*.

STA Travel, Australia: 855 George St, Sydney; 256 Flinders St, Melbourne; other offices in state capitals and major universities; for nearest branch call ☎13 1776; fastfare telesales ☎1300/360 960. New Zealand: 10 High St,

Auckland ☎09/309 0458; for nearest branch call ☎0800/874 773; fastfare telesales ☎09/366 6673; plus branches in major cities and university campuses; *www.statravel .com.au*.

Student Uni Travel, 92 Pitt St, Sydney ☎02/9232 8444; plus branches in Brisbane, Cairns, Darwin, Melbourne and Perth; *sydney @backpackers.net*.

Thomas Cook, Australia: 175 Pitt St, Sydney ☎02/9231 2877; 257 Collins St, Melbourne ☎03/9282 0222; plus branches in other state capitals; for the nearest branch call ☎13 1771; for telesales call ☎1800/801 002. New Zealand: 191 Queen St, Auckland ☎09/379 3920; *www .thomascook.com.au*.

Trailfinders, 8 Spring St, Sydney ☎02/9247 7666; 91 Elizabeth St, Brisbane ☎07/3229 0887; Hides Corner, Shield St, Cairns ☎07 /4041 1199.

Usit Beyond, cnr Shortland Street and Jean Batten Place, Auckland ☎09/379 4224 or toll-free on ☎0800/788 336; plus branches in Christchurch, Dunedin, Palmerston North, Hamilton and Wellington; *www.usitbeyond .co.nz*.

Getting there from Ireland

The cheapest and fastest way of getting from Ireland to London is to fly. The only foot passengers likely to find ferries a more cost-effective way of doing the journey are students or under-26s – and even then, the extra cost of a flight is so little that it's probably worth paying for the added convenience.

Most airlines can offer budget return tickets **from Dublin** from around IR£90. Ryanair (☎01/609 7800; *www.ryanair.com*) flies to London from Dublin, Cork, Kerry and Knock, and is generally the cheapest – its best deals are on flights into Stansted. Aer Lingus (☎01/705 3333; *www.aerlingus.ie*) flies out of Dublin, Shannon and Cork into Heathrow and Stansted and offers similar budget fares, as do British Airways (☎1800/626747; *www.british-airways.com*), which flies into Gatwick from Dublin and Cork.

Another option is CityJet (☎01/844 5588) to London City Airport, with return fares starting at around IR£100.

Flying **from Belfast**, however, your best bet is British Midland (☎0345/554554; *www.iflybritishmidland.com*), which flies into Heathrow from Belfast International for around £80 return; British Airways (☎0345/222111) covers the same route, but is usually a little more expensive. EasyJet (☎0870/600 0000; *www.easyjet.com*) offers a few return flights to London Luton for as little as £40, but you can only book online. It's also worth checking with British European (☎08705/676676; *www.british-european.com*), which flies to Gatwick and Stansted from Belfast City Airport, and can usually match – if not undercut – the prices of their competitors.

Flying cuts out a long overland and ferry journey, but if you're keeping costs to a minimum, then take the **coach**. Eurolines (☎0870/5143219; *www.eurolines.co.uk*) offers return fares from Dublin to London from IR£40. Considering the distances involved, this is great value; the downside is that the trip, with an overnight ferry crossing to Holyhead, takes around eleven hours from Dublin (or up to 14 hours from elsewhere in Ireland).

Travelling to London **by train** is more comfortable, but equally time-consuming. You can buy a through ticket from any station in Ireland to London. If you're in Northern Ireland, you need to phone National Rail Enquiries (☎0845/

TRAVEL AGENTS

Aran Travel, 58 Dominick St, Galway ☎091/562 595; *arantvl@iol.ie*. General discount agent.

Joe Walsh Tours, 69 Upper O'Connell St, Dublin 2 ☎01/872 2555 (and branches across the city); 117 St Patrick St, Cork ☎021/277959. General budget fares agent.

Student & Group Travel, First Floor, 71 Dame St, Dublin 2 ☎01/677 7834. Student specialists.

Thomas Cook, 11 Donegal Place, Belfast ☎028/9088 3900; 118 Grafton St, Dublin 2 ☎01/677 0469; *www.thomascook.com*. Package-holiday and flight agent with occasional discount offers.

Trailfinders, 4–5 Dawson St, Dublin 2 ☎01/677 7888; *www.trailfinders.co.uk*. General discount agent.

USIT, 19 Aston Quay, Dublin 2 ☎01/677 8117; *www.usit.ie*; Fountain Centre, College St, Belfast BT1 6ET ☎028/9032 4073; *www .usitnow.com*; plus other branches across the country. Student and youth specialists for flights and trains.

FERRY COMPANIES

Norse-Irish Ferries Victoria Terminal 2, Westbank Rd, Belfast 3 ☎028/9077 9090; *www.norse-irish-ferries.co.uk*. Routes: Belfast–Liverpool.

Irish Ferries 2–4 Merrion Row, Dublin 2 ☎01/638 3333, 24hr information ☎01/661 0715; St Patrick's Bridge, Cork ☎021/551 995; *www.irishferries.com*. Routes: Larne–Cairnryan; Dublin–Holyhead; Rosslare–Pembroke.

Stena Sealink Line, Ferry Terminal, Dun Laoghaire ☎01/204 7777; Rosslare Harbour, Wexford ☎053/33115; *www.stenaline.com*. Routes: Dun Laoghaire–Holyhead; Rosslare–Fishguard; Larne–Stranraer.

Swansea Cork Ferries 52 South Mall, Cork ☎021/276000; *www.swansea-cork.ie*.

7484950); the best route is via Dublin and the Dun Laoghaire–Holyhead ferry. From the Republic, all through-tickets go via Dun Laoghaire–Holyhead; for more information phone Continental Rail (☎01/703 4095). A return ticket from Dublin to London will cost you around IR£70, or around £100 return from Cork. For the latest times and trains within the Republic, contact Irish Rail/Iarnrod Eireann (☎01/836 6222; *www.irishrail.ie*).

Driving is the other option, although taking your car on the ferry is expensive if you're travelling alone and can't split the fare, and driving around London is a nightmare. Fares on the ferries fluctuate wildly depending on the time of year and the length of your car, but expect to pay IR£200–300 return for a small vehicle and one driver between Dublin and Holyhead, IR£190–250 on the Rosslare–Pembroke route or IR£150–300 on the Cork–Swansea route. Note that as ferries from Belfast only go to Scotland, you're better off driving down to Dublin if you're travelling from Northern Ireland.

Visas, work permits, customs and tax

Citizens of all European countries – except Albania, Bosnia, Bulgaria, Croatia, Macedonia, Romania, Slovakia, Yugoslavia and all the former Soviet republics (other than the Baltic states) – can enter Britain with just a passport, for up to three months (indefinitely if you're from the EU). US, Canadian, Australian and New Zealand citizens can stay for up to six months, providing they have a return ticket and adequate funds to cover their stay. Citizens of most other countries require a visa, obtainable from the British consular or mission office in the country of application. A selection of overseas consulates in London is listed on p.636.

Note that visa regulations are subject to frequent changes, so it's always wise to contact the nearest British Embassy or High Commission before you travel. Visa regulations are also listed on the Foreign and Commonwealth Office's **Web site** (*www.fco.gov.uk*), from which you can download the full range of application forms and information leaflets. In addition, an independent charity, the **Immigration Advisory Service** (IAS), County House, 190 Great Dover St, London SE1 4YB (☎020/7357 6917; *www.iasuk.org*) offers free and confidential advice to anyone applying for entry clearance into the UK.

Longer stays and work permits

For stays of longer than six months, US, Canadian, Australian and New Zealand citizens can apply to the British Embassy or High Commission (see box on p.14) in person or by post for an **Entry Clearance Certificate**. If you want to **extend your visa**, you should write, before the expiry date given in your passport, to the Immigration and Nationality Dept, Lunar House, Wellesley Road, Croydon CR9 2BY (☎0870/606 7766).

Unless you're a resident of an EU country, you need a **work permit** in order to work legally in the UK, although without the backing of an established employer or company, these can be very difficult to obtain. Persons aged between 17 and 27 may, however, apply for a **Working Holiday-Maker Entry Certificate**, which entitles you to stay in the UK for up to two years, during which it is permissible to undertake work of a casual nature (ie, not in a profession, or as a sportsperson or entertainer). The certificates are only available abroad, from British Embassies and High Commissions, and when you apply you must be able to convince the officer you have a valid return or onward ticket, and the means to support yourself while you're in Britain without having to claim state benefits. Note, too, that the certificates are valid from the date of entry into the UK – you won't be able to recoup time spent out of the country during the two-year period.

In **North America**, full-time, bona fide college students can get temporary work permits through **BUNAC**, PO Box 430, Southbury, CT 06488 (☎1-800/GO BUNAC; *www.bunac.org*). Work permits cost $225 to arrange and are good for six months; BUNAC will give you possible employment contacts, help you find accommodation and arrange social events, but it's up to you to take the initiative. Completed applications should be processed in twenty-four hours. Note that Australians, New Zealanders and South Africans can also go through BUNAC, and obtain work permits valid for up to two years.

Commonwealth citizens, with a parent or grandparent who was born in the UK, are also entitled to work in Britain. If you fall into this category, you can apply for a Certificate of

Entitlement to the Right of Abode. If you're unsure about whether or not you may be eligible for one of these, contact your nearest British Mission (embassy or consulate).

The kind of work you can expect to find in London as a visitor is generally **unskilled employment** in hotels, restaurants, cleaning companies and fast-food joints. Working conditions may not be up to much, and as a casual employee you can be fired at short notice. Pay is poor, too (the legal minimum wage is currently £3.20 per hour for those aged 18 to 21, and £3.70 for those over 21), and will bring in barely enough to survive. So, unless you're desperate, try to save at home before travelling.

If you're between 17 and 27, you might also consider **working as an au pair**, though you must be a citizen of a country included in the Au Pair Scheme: Bosnia, Croatia, Cyprus, Czech Republic, Hungary, Macedonia, Malta, Slovakia, Slovenia, Switzerland and Turkey. This enables you to live for a maximum of two years with an English-speaking family. In return for your accommodation, food and a small amount of pocket money (say, £40 per week), you'll be expected to help around the house and to look after the children for a maximum of five hours each day. The easiest way to find au pair work is through a licensed agency. The Federation of Recruitment and Employment Confederation (REC), 36–38 Mortimer St, London W1N 7RB (☎020/7462 3260; www.rec.uk.com), will send you a list of reputable agents (ie, those that are vetted annually by the government) on receipt of an International Reply Coupon.

Customs and tax

Since the inauguration of the **EU Single Market**, travellers coming into Britain directly from another EU country do not have to make a declaration to customs at their place of entry. If you've bought the goods in a normal shop or supermarket within the EU, the limits are 90 litres of wine (of which no more than 60 litres should be sparkling), 20 litres of fortified wine, 10 litres of spirits, 110 litres of beer, 800 cigarettes or 1kg of tobacco. If you are travelling from a non-EU country, you can still buy tax- or **duty-free goods**, but within the EU, this perk no longer exists. The duty-free allowances are as follows:

• **Tobacco**: 200 cigarettes; or 100 cigarillos; or 50 cigars; or 250 grams of loose tobacco.

• **Alcohol**: 2 litres of still wine plus 1 litre of spirits, or 2 litres of fortified, sparkling or still wine.

BRITISH EMBASSIES AND HIGH COMMISSIONS ABROAD

Australia British High Commission, Commonwealth Ave, Yarralumla, Canberra ACT 2600 ☎1902/941555; www.uk.emb.gov.au.

Canada British High Commission, 80 Elgin St, Ottawa, ON K1P 5K7 ☎613/237-1530; www.britain-in-canada.org.

Ireland British Embassy, 29 Merrion Rd, Dublin 4, ☎01/205 3700; www.britishembassy.ie.

New Zealand British High Commission, 44 Hill St, Wellington ☎04/472 0889 or 472 6049; www.brithighcomm.org.nz.

USA British Embassy, 3100 Massachusetts Ave, NW, Washington, DC 20008 ☎202/462-1340; www.britain-info.org.

OVERSEAS EMBASSIES AND HIGH COMMISSIONS IN LONDON

US Embassy, 5 Upper Grosvenor St, W1X 9PG ☎020/7499 9000; www.usembassy .org.uk.

Australian High Commission, Australia House, Strand, WC2B 4LA ☎020/7379 4334; www.australia.org.uk.

Canadian High Commission, 1 Grosvenor Square, W1X 0AB ☎020/7258 6600; www .canada.org.uk.

Irish Embassy, 17 Grosvenor Place, SW1X 7HR ☎020/7235 2171; www.irlgov.ie.

New Zealand High Commission, New Zealand House, 80 Haymarket, SW1 ☎020/7930 8422; www.brithighcomm.org.nz.

- **Perfumes**: 60cc of perfume plus 250cc of toilet water.
- **Other goods** to the value of £145.

There are **import restrictions** on a variety of articles and substances, from firearms to furs derived from endangered species, none of which should bother the normal tourist. However, if you need any clarification on British import regulations, you should visit the **HM Customs and Excise** Web site: *www.hmce.gov.uk*. After decades of strict quarantine laws, **pets** are to be allowed into Britain from 2001, providing their owners obtain a pet passport; for more information, check the HM Customs Web site above.

Most goods in Britain, with the chief exceptions of books and food, are subject to **Value Added Tax** (VAT), which increases the cost of an item by 17.5 percent. Visitors from non-EU countries can save money through the **Retail Export Scheme**, which allows a refund of VAT on goods to be taken out of the country. (Savings will usually be minimal for EU nationals, because of the rates at which the goods will be taxed upon import to the home country.) Note that not all shops participate in this scheme (those doing so will display a sign to this effect) and that you cannot reclaim VAT charged on hotel bills or other services.

Money, banks and costs

The basic unit of currency in Britain is the pound sterling (£), a decimal currency divided into 100 pence (p).

Coins come in denominations of 1p, 2p, 5p, 10p, 20p, 50p, £1 and £2. **Notes** come in denominations of £5, £10, £20 and £50. The British have an innate mistrust of all high denomination notes, partly due to the large number of forgeries, and shopkeepers will carefully scrutinize any £20 or £50 notes. The quickest test is to hold the note up to the light to make sure there's a thin wire filament running through it from top to bottom; this is by no means foolproof, but it will catch most fakes. Very occasionally you may receive Scottish banknotes from £1 upwards:

they're legal tender throughout Britain, but if you have any problems, go to the nearest bank and get them changed for English currency. Approximate exchange rates at the time of writing were US$1.50, AUS$2.50, NZ$3.10, IR£1.20 or €1.60 to the pound.

Carrying Money

There are no exchange controls in Britain, so you can bring in as much cash as you like and change travellers' cheques up to any amount. You'll never be caught short – either for purchases or for cash withdrawals – if you carry your money in the form of **debit and/or credit cards**. Most hotels, shops and restaurants in London accept the major credit cards: Access/MasterCard, Visa/Barclaycard are the most popular, followed by American Express and, lastly, Diners Club. Your card will also enable you to get cash advances from certain ATMs – known in Britain as **cashpoint** machines; call the issuing bank or credit company to get full details. In addition, you should be able to make withdrawals straight from your own bank account back home using your **ATM cash card** – your bank's international banking department should be able to advise on this. Make sure you have a personal identification number (PIN) that's designed to work overseas.

Another possibility, is to take **Visa TravelMoney** (*www.visa.com*), a disposable debit card pre-paid with dedicated travel funds, which you can access from ATMs with a PIN which you select yourself. When your funds are depleted, you simply throw the card away (it's recommended you buy at least a second card in case your first is lost and stolen – up to nine cards can be bought to access the same funds). If you lose your card, you can get an emergency cash replacement immediately. To report stolen or lost cards, to check your balance or to find out more, you can call toll-free from North America (☎1-800 847 2399), Australia (☎1-800 125161), New Zealand (☎0-800 449149) and London (☎0800/963833).

It's a lot more hassle, but old-fashioned **travellers' cheques** are still the safest way to carry your money, and are available for a small commission (normally one percent) from any major bank. The most commonly accepted travellers' cheques are American Express, followed by Visa and Thomas Cook – most cheques issued by banks will be one of these three brands. You'll usually pay commission again when you cash each cheque, normally one percent or so, or a flat rate – though no commission is payable on Amex cheques exchanged at Amex offices.

Every area of London has a branch of at least one of the big four high-street **banks**: NatWest, Barclays, Lloyds and HSBC. The **opening hours** for most are Mon–Fri 9.30am–4.30pm, with some branches in central locations staying open half an hour later and some opening on Saturday mornings. Banks tend to give the best rates, and charge the lowest commission, and are therefore usually the best places to change money and cheques. Outside banking hours go to a **bureau de change**; these can be found at train stations and airports in most areas of the city centre. Try to avoid changing money or cheques in hotels, where the rates are normally the poorest on offer.

Emergencies

If you're using travellers' cheques, TravelMoney or credit cards, you should make a note of the **emergency phone number** given to you by your bank. However, the advantage of travellers' cheques over debit/credit cards is that if you keep a record of the cheque numbers as you cash them, you can get the value of all uncashed cheques refunded immediately should you lose them. Things can be a little trickier if you lose your cards, as you won't be provided with a replacement card until you get home. Your bank

Wiring Money

Moneygram (*www.moneygram.com*) International toll-free ☎00800/8971 8971; US ☎1-800/926-9400; Canada ☎1-800/933 3276; Australia ☎1800/230 100; New Zealand ☎0800/262 263.

Thomas Cook (*www.thomascook.com*) UK☎01733/318922; Ireland ☎01/677 1721; US & Canada ☎416/359 3764; Australia ☎02/9248 6100; New Zealand ☎09/379 3920.

Western Union (*www.westernunion.com*) UK ☎0800/833833; Ireland ☎1800/395395; US & Canada ☎1-800/325-6000; Australia ☎1800/649565; New Zealand ☎09/270 0050.

may be prepared to wire money from your account to you immediately in an emergency, but not all banks will – check before you travel. If they won't, it will take a couple of days for any money to be transferred from your account to a UK bank of your choice.

Assuming you know someone who is prepared to send you the money, the quickest way to have funds sent out to you in an emergency is to **wire the money**. However, it's an expensive way to send and receive money abroad, and should be considered only as a last resort. The money wired should be available for collection, in local currency, from the company's local agent within a few minutes of being sent via Western Union or Moneygram; both charge on a sliding scale, so sending larger amounts of cash is better value (US$1000 will cost about $75). Thomas Cook have a much cheaper flat rate, but it takes 1–2 days for the money to arrive. In Britain, you can arrange Western Union transfers from Going Places travel agents and some newsagents and chemists, Moneygram via Thomas Cook and American Express offices, Eurochange outlets and all post offices.

If you're in really dire straits, you can get in touch with your **consulate or High Commission**, who will usually let you make one phone call home free of charge, and will – in worst cases only – repatriate you, but will never, under any circumstances, lend money.

Costs

The strong pound, and the prohibitive cost of accommodation, makes London a very **expensive** place to visit. The minimum expenditure for a couple staying in a budget hotel and grabbing takeaway meals, pizzas or other such basic fare would be in the region of at least £50 per person per day. You only have to add in the odd better-quality meal, plus some major tourist attractions, a few films or other shows, and you're looking at **around £75** as a daily budget, even in decidedly average accommodation. Single travellers should budget on spending around sixty percent of what a couple would spend (single rooms cost more than half a double). For more detail on the costs of accommodation, transport and eating, see chapters 1, 14, 15, 16 and 17.

Tipping

There are no fixed rules for **tipping**. If you think you've received good service, particularly in restaurants or cafés, you may want to leave a tip of ten percent of the total bill (unless service has already been included). It is not normal, however, to leave tips in pubs, although bar staff are sometimes offered drinks, which they may accept in the form of money (the assumption is they'll spend this on a drink after closing time). Taxi drivers, on the other hand, will expect tips on long journeys – add about ten percent to the fare. The other occasion when you'll be expected to tip is in upmarket hotels where, in common with most other countries, porters, bellboys and table waiters rely on being tipped to bump up their often dismal wages.

Youth and student discounts

Various official and quasi-official youth/student ID cards are widely available, and most will pay for themselves in savings pretty swiftly. Full-time students over the age of 16 are eligible for the **International Student ID Card** (ISIC; *www.istc .org*), which entitles the bearer to special fares on local transport, and discounts at museums, theatres and other attractions; there's also a health benefit for Americans and Canadians (see p.18). The card costs US$20, CDN$15, AU$10, NZ$15 and £5 in the UK. It is available from branches of Council Travel, STA and Travel CUTS around the world (see boxes on pp.5 & 10).

You only have to be 25 or younger to qualify for the **Go-25 Card**, which costs the same as the ISIC and carries the same benefits. It can be purchased through Council Travel (see box on p.5) in the US, TravelCUTS (see p.5) in Canada and STA in Australia (see box on p.10). STA also sells its own ID card that's good for some discounts, as do various other travel organizations. A university photo ID might open some doors, too.

Insurance, health and emergencies

A typical travel insurance policy usually provides cover for the loss of baggage, tickets and – up to a certain limit – cash or cheques, as well as cancellation or curtailment of your journey.

Read the small print and benefits tables of prospective policies carefully; **coverage** can vary wildly for roughly similar premiums. Many policies can be chopped and changed to exclude coverage you don't need – for example, sickness and accident benefits can often be excluded or included at will. If you do take medical coverage, ascertain whether benefits will be paid as treatment proceeds, or only after you return home, and whether there is a 24-hour medical emergency number. When securing baggage cover, make sure that the per-article limit – typically under £500 equivalent – will cover your most valuable possession. If you need to make a **claim**, you should keep receipts for medicines and medical treatment, and in the event you have anything stolen, you must obtain an official statement from the police. Bank and credit cards often have certain levels of medical or other insurance included, and you may automatically get travel insurance if you use a major credit card to pay for your trip.

Americans and **Canadians** should also check that they're not already covered. Canadian provincial health plans usually provide partial cover for medical mishaps overseas. Holders of official student/teacher/youth cards are entitled to meagre accident coverage and hospital in-patient benefits, and students will often find that their student health coverage extends during the vacations and for one term beyond the date of last enrolment. Homeowners' or renters' insurance often covers theft or loss of documents, money and valuables while overseas, though conditions and maximum amounts vary from company to company.

Rough Guides Travel Insurance

Rough Guides now offers its own **travel insurance**, customized for our readers by a leading UK broker and backed by a Lloyds underwriter. It's available for anyone, of any nationality, travelling anywhere in the world, and we are convinced that this is the best-value scheme you'll find.

There are two main Rough Guide insurance plans: **Essential**, for effective, no-frills cover, starting at £10 for 2 weeks; and **Premier** – more expensive but with more generous and extensive benefits. Each offers European or Worldwide cover, and can be supplemented with a "Hazardous Activities Premium" if you plan to indulge in sports considered dangerous, such as skiing, scuba-diving or trekking. Unlike many policies, the Rough Guides schemes are calculated by the day, so if you're travelling for 27 days rather than a month, that's all you pay for. You can alternatively take out annual **multi-trip insurance**, which covers you for all your travel throughout the year (with a maximum of 60 days for any one trip).

For a **policy quote**, call the Rough Guides Insurance Line toll-free on UK ☎0800 015 0906, or, if you're calling from outside Britain on (+44) ☎1243 621 046. Alternatively, get an online quote at *www.roughguides.com/insurance*.

Medical matters

No **vaccinations** are required for entry into Britain. Citizens of all EU countries are entitled to free medical treatment at National Health Service hospitals; citizens of other countries will be charged for all medical services. **Health insurance** (see opposite) is therefore strongly advised for all non-EU nationals; citizens of Australia and New Zealand should note that Medicare has a reciprocal healthcare arrangement with the UK NHS.

Pharmacists can dispense only a limited range of drugs without a doctor's prescription. Most pharmacies are open standard shop hours, though some stay open later; Zafash, 233–235 Old Brompton Rd, SW5 ☎020/7373 2798 (Earl's Court tube) is open 24hrs, while Bliss, at 5–6 Marble Arch, W1 ☎020/7723 6116 (Marble Arch tube) and 149 Edgware Road, W2 ☎020/7723 2336 (Edgware Road tube) opens from 9am till midnight, seven days a week. To cater for emergencies, every police station keeps a list of all the late-opening pharmacies in its area.

Doctor's surgeries tend to be open Mon–Sat 9am–noon and then for a couple of hours on weekday evenings; outside surgery hours, you can turn up at the Accident and Emergency department of local hospitals for complaints that require immediate attention – unless it's an absolute emergency, in which case ring for an ambulance (☎999).

Police

Although the traditional image of the friendly British "bobby" has become tarnished over the years by incidences of corruption and institutionalized racism, in the normal run of events the **police** continue to be approachable and helpful. If you're lost in London, asking a police officer is generally the quickest way to pinpoint your destination – alternatively, you could ask a **traffic warden**, a species of law-enforcer much maligned in car-loving Britain. Traffic wardens are distinguishable by their security-guardish uniforms and by the fact that they are generally armed with a hand-set for dispensing parking-fine tickets; police officers on street duty wear a distinctive domed hat with a silver tip.

Like any other capital, London has its dangerous spots, but these tend to be obscure parts of the city where no tourist has any reason to be. The chief risk on London's streets is **pickpocketing**, and there are some virtuoso villains at work, especially on the big shopping streets and the Underground (tube). Carry only as much money as you need for the day, and keep all bags and pockets fastened. Should you have anything stolen or be involved in some incident that requires reporting, go to the local police station; the ☎999 number should only be used in emergencies.

Emergency services

For **Police**, **Fire Brigade** and **Ambulance** dial ☎999.

Information and maps

If you want to do a bit of research before arriving in London, contact the **British Tourist Authority (BTA)** in your home country – the addresses are given in the box opposite. The BTA will send you a wealth of free literature, some of it just rose-tinted advertising copy, but much of it extremely useful, especially the maps, guides and event calendars. You can also pick up maps and information from the tourist booths at the airports, ports and in central London.

The chief BTA office in London is the **British Visitor Centre**, at 1 Regent St (Mon 9.30am–6.30pm, Tues–Fri 9am–6.30pm, Sat & Sun 10am–4pm; June–Oct same times except Sat & Sun 9am–5pm; *www.bta.org.uk*). London has its very own **London Tourist Board** (LTB; *www.londontown.com*), too; for a full rundown of LTB offices in London, see p.38. In addition, some **London boroughs** run their own tourist information offices, and every London borough has its own tourism/leisure department, which can be consulted via the local council Web site. The address for Camden is *www.camden.gov.uk*; for other boroughs simply replace Camden with the relevant borough name. The only significant exceptions to the above rule are Kensington & Chelsea, which is *www.rbkc.gov.uk*, and Hammersmith & Fulham, which is *www.lbhf.gov.uk*.

The Internet

There's a vast quantity of useful London-related information on the **Internet**. Apart from the afore-mentioned tourist authority and local borough Web sites, there are some excellent sites which concentrate on specific areas, such as the site *www.london-se1.co.uk*, which gives a daily update (with maps and links) of events and attractions all along the south bank of the Thames. Most tourist sights have their own Web site (detailed after the opening hours in the text), and many hotels, B&Bs, shops and restaurants are following suit. Below are a few of the better general London Web sites.

www.24hourmuseum.co.uk A useful national Web site, with up-to-date information on virtually every single museum, large or small, in London.
www.infolondon.co.uk A news and transport site with some good features: it'll work out your route on the Tube and summon up a map.
www.londonnet.co.uk Lots of themed ways of looking at London – Diana's London, Literary London, Drugs London and so on – and lots of links.
www.s-h-systems.co.uk/tourism/london
Short for Smooth Hound Systems, this is an excellent tourist info site, which covers London in exhaustive A–Z categories.
www.streetmap.co.uk Call up an aerial map of any street in London.

Maps

The Geographers' **A–Z map** series produces a whole range of street-by-street maps of London, from pocket-size foldouts to giant atlases. The Nicholson **Streetfinder** series is similarly comprehensive. The maps in this book should be adequate for holiday purposes, but if you want something more detailed, the best investment is one of the spiral-bound notebook-sized atlases produced by Geographers' and Nicholson, costing around £5. These books mark and index every street in the city, down to the narrowest alleyway. Virtually every newsagent in London stocks one or the other of them, or you could pick them up from one of the shops listed opposite. Free maps of the Underground and bus networks can be picked up at tourist offices and London Transport information offices – see p.39.

BRITISH TOURIST AUTHORITY HEAD OFFICES

Australia Level 16, Gateway, 1 Macquarie Place, Sydney, NSW 2000 ☎ 02/9377 4400.

Canada 5915 Airport Rd, Suite 120, Mississauga, Ontario L4V 1TI ☎ 905/405 1840.

Ireland 18–19 College Green, Dublin 2 ☎ 01/670 8000.

New Zealand 17th Floor, Fay Richwhite Building, 151 Queen St, Auckland ☎ 09/303 1446.

US Floor 7, 551 Fifth Ave, New York, NY 10176 ☎ 1-800/GO 2 BRITAIN.

MAP OUTLETS

ENGLAND

Blackwell's Map and Travel Shop, 53 Broad St, Oxford OX1 3BQ ☎ 01865/792792; *http://bookshop.blackwell.co.uk.*

Heffers Map and Travel, 3rd Floor, Heffers Stationery Department, 19 Sidney St, Cambridge, CB2 3HL ☎ 01223/568467; *www.heffers.co.uk.*

Newcastle Map Centre, 55 Grey St, Newcastle upon Tyne, NE1 6EF ☎ 0191/261 5622; *www.newtraveller.com.*

Stanfords, 12–14 Long Acre, London WC2E 9LP ☎ 020/7836 1321; 29 Corn St, Bristol BS1 1HT ☎ 0117/929 9966; *www.stanfords.co.uk.*

Waterstone's, 91 Deansgate, Manchester, M3 2BW ☎ 0161/837 3000 (plus branches country-wide); *www.waterstones.co.uk.*

SCOTLAND

John Smith and Sons, 57–61 St Vincent St, Glasgow, G2 5TB ☎ 0141/221 7472; *www.johnsmith.co.uk.*

James Thin Melven's Bookshop, 29 Union St, Inverness, IV1 1QA ☎ 01463/233500; *www.jthin.co.uk.*

IRELAND

Eason's Bookshop, 40 O'Connell St, Dublin 1 ☎ 01/873 3811; *www.eason.ie.*

Waterstone's, Queens Bldg, 8 Royal Ave, Belfast BT1 1DA ☎ 028/9024 7355; 7 Dawson St, Dublin 2 ☎ 01/679 1415; 69 Patrick St, Cork ☎ 021/276 522; *www.waterstones.com.*

NORTH AMERICA

The Complete Traveller Bookstore, 199 Madison Ave, New York, NY 10016

☎ 212/685-9007; 3207 Fillmore St, San Francisco, CA 92123 ☎ 415/923-1511.

Elliott Bay Book Company, 101 S Main St, Seattle, WA 98104 ☎ 206/624-6600; *www.elliottbaybook.com.*

Open Air Books and Maps, 25 Toronto St, Toronto, ON M5R 2C1; ☎ 416/363-0719.

Rand McNally, 444 N Michigan Ave, Chicago, IL 60611 ☎ 312/321-1751; 150 E 52nd St, New York, NY 10022 ☎ 212/758-7488; 595 Market St, San Francisco, CA 94105 ☎ 415/777-3131; *www.randmcnally.com.*

World Wide Books and Maps, 552 Seymour St, Vancouver, BC V6B 3J5 ☎ 604/687-3320; *www.itmb.com.*

AUSTRALIA

The Map Shop, 16a Peel St, Adelaide ☎ 08/8231 2033; *www.mapshop.net.au.*

Worldwide Maps and Guides, 187 George St, Brisbane ☎ 07/3221 4330.

Mapland, 372 Little Bourke St, Melbourne ☎ 03/9670 4383; *www.mapland.com.au.*

Perth Map Centre, 1/884 Hay St, Perth ☎ 08/9322 5733; *www.perthmap.com.au.*

Travel Bookshop, Shop 3, 175 Liverpool St, Sydney ☎ 02/9261 8200.

NEW ZEALAND

Specialty Maps, 46 Albert St, Auckland ☎ 09/307 2217; *www.ubd-online.co.nz/maps.*

Mapworld, 173 Gloucester St, Christchurch ☎ 03/374 5399; *www.mapworld.co.nz.*

Post and phones

Almost all of London's post offices are open Mon–Fri 9am–5.30pm, Sat 9am–noon – the exception is the Trafalgar Square Post Office (24–28 William IV St, WC2N 4DL ☎020/7930 9580), which is open Mon–Fri 8am–8pm, Sat 9am–8pm. It's to this office that poste restante mail should be sent. Mail is held at the Enquiries Desk and is kept for one month; take a passport or other identification when collecting mail. In the suburbs you'll find sub-post offices operating out of shops, but these are open the same hours as regular post offices, even if the shop itself is open for longer.

Stamps can be bought at post office counters, from vending machines outside post offices, or from an increasing number of newsagents, although they usually only sell books of four or ten stamps. A first-class letter to anywhere in the British Isles currently costs 27p and should arrive the next day; second-class letters cost 19p, taking two to four days. **Postcards** to the rest of Europe cost 36p; to the rest of the world they cost 40p. **Airmail** letters of less than 20g (0.7oz) cost 36p to European countries; airmail letters of less than 10g (0.35oz) cost 45p to the US, Canada, Australia and New Zealand. Pre-stamped aerogrammes conforming to overseas airmail weight limits of under 10g cost 40p from post offices only. For more information about postal services, all of which are run by Royal Mail, call ☎0345/740740 or visit their Web site *www.royalmail.com.*

OPERATOR SERVICES

You can make a call to any of the following numbers – and any prefixed with ☎0800 – free of charge.

Domestic operator ☎100
International operator ☎155
Domestic directory assistance ☎192
International directory assistance ☎153

INTERNATIONAL CALLS

To call London from overseas dial the international access code (☎011 from the US and Canada, ☎0011 from Australia and ☎00 from New Zealand) followed by 44, the area code minus its initial zero, and then the number. To dial out of London, it's ☎00 followed by the country code, area code (without the zero if there is one) and subscriber number. Country codes are as follows:

Australia ☎61
Ireland ☎353
New Zealand ☎64
US and Canada ☎1

LONDON PHONE CODES

All London telephone numbers changed during 2000. The **new area code** is now 020, and all local numbers have become eight digits long: old 0171 numbers are now prefixed with a 7, old 0181 numbers with an 8. We have put the new area code before all numbers within the text, but when calling within London, you need only use the eight-digit numbers.

Public **payphones** are operated by a variety of companies, the largest of which is British Telecom (BT) – there should be one within ten minutes' walk of wherever you're standing. Virtually all pubs have a public phone too, though many eat your money pretty fast. Most payphones take all coins from 10p upwards, though some take only **phonecards** and credit cards, but an increasing number take all three. Phonecards are available from post offices and newsagents. Resist the temptation to use the phone in your **hotel** room – telephone surcharges in London hotels are among the most expensive in Europe, with hoteliers imposing a mark-up of around 800 percent in some instances.

Inland calls are cheapest between 6pm and 8am on weekdays, and all day at weekends. These times are also **reduced rate periods** for most **international calls**, though for Australia and New Zealand, calls are cheapest between midnight and 7am and 2.30 to 7.30pm daily.

Opening hours, holidays and entrance charges

Generally, shop opening hours are Mon–Sat 9am /10am to 5.30pm/6pm, with some in central London staying open till around 7pm, and later on Thursdays and Fridays (around 8 or 9pm), as well as on Sundays (usually noon–6pm). That said, there are still plenty of stores that close completely on Sundays, and numerous family-run corner shops that stay open late every day of the week. The big supermarkets tend to open Mon–Sat from 8am/9am to 9pm/10pm, Sun 10am/11am to 4pm/5pm. Note that many (gas/petrol) service stations in London are open 24 hours and have small shops.

Fee-charging **tourist attractions** and state **museums** are typically open Mon–Sat 10am–6pm, with shorter hours (often 10am or noon to 6pm) on Sundays and public Holidays (these are listed in the box on p.24). It's worth noting that most places are closed on December 25 and 26. Several state museums now have late-night openings until 9 or 10pm, typically one or two nights a week. Individual opening hours for all attractions are given in the main text of this guide.

A few of London's historic properties come under the control of the private **National Trust** (36 Queen Anne's Gate, London SW1H 9AS ☎020/7222 9251; www.nationaltrust.org.uk), or the state-run **English Heritage** (Keysign House, 429 Oxford St, London W1R 2HD ☎020/7973 3000; www.english-heritage.org.uk). These properties are denoted in the guide by "NT" or "EH" after the opening times. Both organizations charge an entry fee for the majority of their sites, and these can be quite high (around £5), especially for National Trust sights. **Annual membership** (NT £30, EH £28) allows free entry to their respective properties, though if you're only visiting London for a short time, it's hardly worth it. Many other old buildings, albeit rarely the most momentous structures, are owned by the local authorities, which are generally more lenient with their admission charges, and sometimes allow free access.

Admission charges to galleries and museums in London have been creeping ever higher, with a few great and notable exceptions, such as the British Museum, the Tate Modern and Tate Britain, and the National Gallery, all of which are still free. The Labour government has a manifesto commitment to eliminating admission charges for all state-funded national museums. At the time of going to print, children and senior citizens can enter free of charge; the government has pledged to reduce adult admission charges to £1, though it faces strong opposition from some of the museums concerned. Those affected by this change will be the Science, Natural History, V&A, National Maritime and Imperial War museums, plus HMS Belfast.

Apart from St Paul's Cathedral and Westminster Abbey, all religious institutions are open free of charge. That said, many churches have been forced to lock their doors outside of services, as a deterrent to vandals. As for sights run by the private sector, the trend towards the use of inter-active displays, dark rides, animatronics and other expensive trickery has pushed prices ever closer to the £10 mark, and expense is not necessarily an indication of quality.

Public holidays

January 1
Good Friday – late March/early April
Easter Monday – late March/early April
Spring Bank Holiday – first Monday in May
May Bank Holiday – last Monday in May
August Bank Holiday – last Monday in August
December 25
December 26
Note that if January 1, December 25 or December 26 falls on a Saturday or Sunday, the holiday falls on the following weekday.

The majority of fee-charging attractions in London extend **reductions** for senior citizens, the unemployed, full-time students and children under 16, with under-5s being admitted free almost everywhere. Proof of eligibility will be required in most cases, though even the flintiest desk clerk will probably take the age of a babe in arms on trust. The entry charges given in the guide are the full adult charges – as a rule, adult reductions are in the range of 25–35 percent, while reductions for children are usually around 50 percent.

The media

Most visitors will want to make use of the English press chiefly for its listings of events. The mainstay in this market is the weekly magazine *Time Out* (£1.95; *www.timeout.com*), whose listings cover just about everything going. The *Evening Standard* (35p; *www.thisislondon.com*), London's only daily paper, also has events listings. Another useful publication is the *Big Issue* (£1), a weekly magazine (published Monday) which contains detailed listings as well as focusing on homelessness, the "issue" of the title. *Big Issue* is not available in the shops, but must be bought from official vendors, who are themselves homeless, and to whom a large proportion of the cover price goes.

American and **European** newspapers are on sale in the West End, at well-stocked newsstands in Leicester Square and Piccadilly Circus and at specialist newsagents in Soho and Covent Garden. Australians and New Zealanders can get a résumé of the news from home, as well as information about jobs, accommodation and events in the capital, through the free weekly magazine *TNT*, distributed outside main tube stations.

The English press

English daily newspapers divide into two breeds: the broadsheets, or "quality" papers, which have extensive foreign coverage, as well as home news; and the tabloids (with a smaller page size), which concentrate – in some cases exclusively – on sex, sport, scandal and the royals (ideally in combination).

Politically, the national papers are predominantly right wing, with the Murdoch-owned *Times* and the staunchly Conservative *Daily Telegraph* dominating the "quality" end of the market, trailed by the *Guardian*, which inhabits a niche marginally to the left of centre, the *Independent*, which strives to live up to its self-righteous name, and the *Financial Times* business daily. At the opposite end of the scale in terms of intellectual weight and volume of sales is the pernicious *Sun*, the sleaziest occupant of the Murdoch stable; its chief rivals in the sex and scandal stakes are the *Daily Star*, the self-consciously ridiculous and pornographic *Daily Sport* and the *Daily Mirror*, which more or less consistently backs the Labour Party. The middlebrow tabloids – the *Daily Mail* and the *Daily Express* – are uniformly reactionary. The scene is a little more varied on a Sunday, when the *Guardian*-owned *Observer*, England's oldest **Sunday newspaper**, supplements the Sunday editions of the dailies, whose ranks are also swelled by the sleazy *People*, and the amazingly popular *News of the World*, a smutty rag commonly known as "The News of the Screws".

London's *Evening Standard*, which comes out in several separate editions every weekday, is good for events in the city, and saves commuters the trouble of having to talk to one another. In addition, each of the London boroughs has its own paper, usually printed twice weekly, covering local issues, but filled mostly with adverts. The most useful London-based publication for visitors is, as mentioned above, *Time Out*, which comes out every Tuesday evening. It carries critical appraisals of all the week's theatre, film, music, exhibitions, children's events and much more besides.

When it comes to **specialist periodicals**, London newsagents can offer a range covering just about every subject. The one noticeably poor area is current events: the only high-selling weekly commentary magazine is the right-leaning *Economist*, essential reading in City boardrooms. The left-leaning alternative, the *New Statesman*, is subsidized by a few socialist millionaires, and is complemented by the glossy monthly *Red Pepper*. The satirical biweekly *Private Eye* is a much-loved institution that prides itself on printing the stories the rest of the press won't touch, and on riding the consequent stream of libel suits.

Television

Currently England has five terrestrial **television** stations: the state-owned BBC (with two public

service channels) and the independent commercial channels ITV, Channel 4 and Channel 5.

The **BBC** is just about maintaining its worldwide reputation for quality in-house productions, ranging from expensive costume dramas to intelligent documentaries. BBC2 is the more offbeat and heavyweight BBC channel; BBC1 is avowedly mainstream. Various regional companies form the **ITV** network, united by a more tabloid approach to programme making – necessarily so, because if they don't get the advertising they don't survive. The London stations are Carlton (weekdays) and London Weekend Television (weekends); the latter is a bit more adventurous. **Channel 4**, a partly subsidized institution, is the most progressive of the bunch, with a reputation for broadcasting an eclectic spread of "arty" and minority-pleasing programmes, and for supporting small-budget movies. **Channel 5**, the most recent newcomer, is the self-consciously "young 'n' fun" alternative, distinguished by its amateur presenters and soft porn output.

Rupert Murdoch's multi-channel Sky network has a monopoly of the **satellite** business, presenting a blend of movies, news, sport, reruns and overseas soaps. It has an increasing number of rivals in the form of **cable** TV companies, which are making big inroads in London. Within a few years these commercial stations will probably be making life uncomfortable for the BBC and ITV networks, but for the time being the old terrestrial stations still attract the majority of viewers. All these services (and many more) can be accessed by means of the latest **digital** system, through which the BBC presents its News 24, Knowledge, Parliament and Choice channels.

Radio

Market forces are eating away rather more quickly at the **BBC radio** network, which has five national stations: Radio One (98.8FM) is almost exclusively pop music, with a chart-biased view of the rock world; Two (89.1FM) is golden oldies and chat; Three (91.3FM) is predominantly classical music; Four (93.5FM /198LW), a blend of current affairs, arts and drama; and Five (693 & 909 MW), a live sports and news channel. And last, but not least, you can even pick up the BBC World Service (648MW) in London. Radio One has **independent radio** rivals on all fronts, with Virgin FM (105.8FM/1215 MW) and Capital FM (95.8FM) attracting large sections of Radio One's target audience. Melody Radio (105.4FM) has whittled away at the Radio Two easy-listening market, as has Jazz FM (102.2FM), while Classic FM (100.9FM) has lured people away from Radio Three, by offering a less earnest approach to its subject. Finally Radio Five has to stay on its toes, due to competition from the Murdoch-sponsored Talk Sport (1053 & 1089MW). There are plenty more London-based channels on FM and MW, ranging from Spectrum (558MW), aimed at and presented by members of the city's ethnic communities, to dance music stations such as Kiss FM (100FM) and black music stations such as Choice (96.9FM); London's pirate FM radio stations also play a wealth of black music, from R&B to reggae; a random flick along your radio dial is bound to turn up a few.

Disabled travellers

London is getting better for disabled travellers, but the biggest problem still remains the public transport system. An ancient tube, bus and rail system, designed, for the most part, in the nineteenth century has had little investment put into facilities for those with mobility problems. The only exceptions are the Docklands Light Railway, the new Jubilee Line Extension and the Heathrow Express. For a more detailed rundown, get hold of London Transport's *Access to the Underground*, available free from LT information offices (see p.39), or from its Unit for Disabled Passengers (see box below).

Accommodation poses a similar problem, with modified suites found only at higher-priced establishments and the occasional B&B; one exception is the fully accessible Rotherhithe Youth Hostel (see p.499). The London Tourist Board publishes the *London for All* information news sheet on transport and hotels, which can be obtained from any LTB office (see p.38).

In view of this situation, you might consider approaching one of the growing number of **tour operators** catering for physically disabled travellers. For more information on these operators and on facilities for the disabled traveller, you

---

USEFUL CONTACTS FOR DISABLED TRAVELLERS

LONDON

London Transport's Unit for Disabled Passengers, 172 Buckingham Palace Rd, SW1 ☎ 020/7918 3312 or Minicom ☎ 020/7918 3015.

Mobility International, 228 Borough High St, SE1 1JX ☎ 020/7403 5688.

The Royal Association for Disability and Rehabilitation (RADAR), 12 City Forum, 250 City Rd, EC1V 8AF ☎ 020/7250 3222 or Minicom ☎ 020/7250 4119; *www.radar.org.uk*.

NORTH AMERICA

Mobility International, PO Box 10767, Eugene, OR 97440 (☎ 541/343-1284; *www.miusa.org*.

AUSTRALIA AND NEW ZEALAND

ACROD, PO Box 60, Curtain, ACT 2605 ☎ 06/6282 4333; *www.acrod.org.au*.

Barrier Free Travel, 36 Wheatley St, North Bellingen, NSW 2454 ☎ 02/6655 1733.

Disabled Persons Assembly, 173–175 Victoria St, Wellington ☎ 04/801 9100.

should get in touch with RADAR, the Royal Association for Disability and Rehabilitation, which publishes its own guide to holidays and travel abroad (see box opposite). There's also Mobility International, which, among other things, puts out a quarterly newsletter detailing current developments in disabled travel. Similar services are provided in North America, Australia and New Zealand by the organizations listed in the box opposite.

The essential **publication** for anyone with mobility problems is *Access in London,* a thoroughly researched guide with detailed information and maps covering access to everything from tourist attractions and transport to accommodation, and entertainment and sports venues, plus a section on wheelchair-accessible loos. It's available by post from Access Project, 39 Bradley Gardens, West Ealing, London W13 8HE (£7.95 donation requested, which includes postage).

Another valuable service is provided by **Artsline** (☎020/7388 2227; *www.artsline.org.uk*), who can give up-to-date information and advice by phone on access to arts venues and events in London: theatres, cinemas, galleries and concert halls.

The City

Chapter 1

Introducing the city

With a population of just under eight million, and stretching more than thirty miles at its broadest point, **London** is by far the largest city in Europe. It is also far more diffuse than the great cities of the Continent, such as Rome or Paris. The majority of London's sights are situated to the north of the **River Thames**, which loops through the centre of the city from west to east, but there is no single predominant focus of interest, for London has grown not through centralized planning but by a process of agglomeration – villages and urban developments that once surrounded the core are now lost within the amorphous mass of Greater London. Thus London's highlights are widely spread, and visitors should make mastering the public transport system, particularly the Underground (tube), a top priority.

One of the few areas which is manageable on foot is **Westminster and Whitehall** (Chapter 2), the city's royal, political and ecclesiastical power base for several hundred years. It's here you'll find the National Gallery and the adjacent National Portrait Gallery, and a host of other London landmarks: Buckingham Palace, Nelson's Column, Downing Street, Big Ben, the Houses of Parliament and Westminster Abbey. From Westminster it's a manageable walk upriver to the Tate Britain gallery, the nation's repository of British art (the modern art collection has now moved to Bankside in Southwark). The grand streets and squares of **St James's, Mayfair and Marylebone** (Chapter 3), to the north of Westminster, have been the playground of the rich since the Restoration, and now contain the city's busiest shopping zones: **Piccadilly**, Bond Street, Regent Street and, most frenetic of the lot, Oxford Street.

East of Piccadilly Circus, **Soho and Covent Garden** (Chapter 4) are also easy to walk around and form the heart of the West End entertainment district, where you'll find the largest concentration of theatres, cinemas, clubs, flashy shops, cafés and restaurants. Adjoining Covent Garden to the north, the university quarter of **Bloomsbury** (Chapter 5) is the traditional home of the publishing industry and location of the British Museum, a stupendous treasure

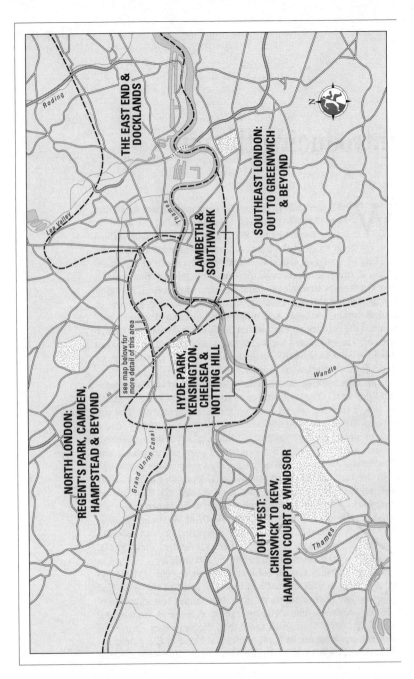

THE EAST END & DOCKLANDS

SOUTHEAST LONDON: OUT TO GREENWICH & BEYOND

LAMBETH & SOUTHWARK

see map below for more detail of this area

HYDE PARK, KENSINGTON, CHELSEA & NOTTING HILL

NORTH LONDON: REGENT'S PARK, CAMDEN, HAMPSTEAD & BEYOND

OUT WEST: CHISWICK TO KEW, HAMPTON COURT & WINDSOR

Roding

Lee Valley

Thames

Wandle

Grand Union Canal

A5

Thames

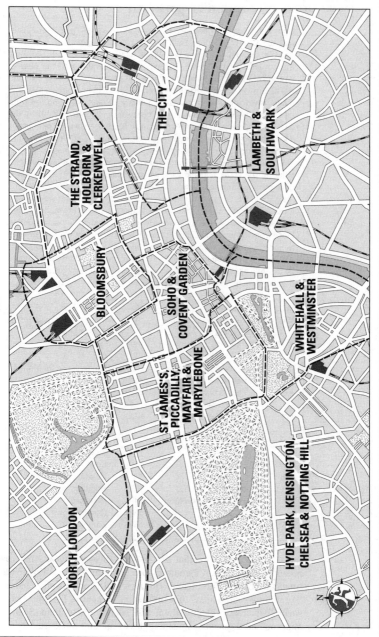

© crown copyright

NORTH LONDON

THE STRAND,
HOLBORN &
CLERKENWELL

THE CITY

LAMBETH &
SOUTHWARK

BLOOMSBURY

SOHO &
COVENT GARDEN

ST JAMES'S,
PICCADILLY,
MAYFAIR &
MARYLEBONE

WHITEHALL &
WESTMINSTER

HYDE PARK, KENSINGTON,
CHELSEA & NOTTING HILL

N

Boroughs, districts and postal codes

Greater London is divided into 31 **boroughs**, plus the City of Westminster and the City of London. Each borough has a population of between 150,000 and 300,000, making them too unwieldy to use as divisions for the purposes of this guide. Instead, we've generally used the **district names** by which Londoners designate the areas in which they live and work. Most of these districts take their names either from smaller boroughs which disappeared in the boundary changes of 1965, or from parishes or villages which have now been subsumed into the fabric of the city. Thus when we refer to Camden or to Greenwich, we are talking not about the present-day London boroughs of Camden or Greenwich, but about the core areas from which these districts take their names.

London is further divided into **postal areas**, which do not coincide with either of the above boundaries. Each street name is followed by a letter giving the geographical location of the street in relation to the City (E for "east", WC for "west central" and so on) and a number that specifies its location more precisely. Unfortunately, this number corresponds to the position of the first letter of the district in the alphabet, and not to its distance from the centre (as in most cities). So SE5, for example, is closer to the centre of town than SE3, and W5 lies beyond the remote-sounding NW10. Full postal addresses end with a digit and two letters, which specify the individual block, but these are only used in correspondence. Below is a list of some frequently occurring postcodes:

WC1	Bloomsbury	SW5	Earl's Court
WC2	Covent Garden, Holborn and Strand	SW7	Knightsbridge and South Kensington
EC1	Clerkenwell	SW11	Battersea
EC2	Bank, Barbican and Liverpool Street	SW19	Wimbledon
		SE1	Lambeth and Southwark
EC3	Tower Hill and Aldgate	SE10	Greenwich
EC4	St Paul's, Blackfriars and Fleet Street	SE16	Bermondsey and Rotherhithe
W1	Mayfair, Marylebone and Soho	SE21	Dulwich
		E1	Whitechapel and Wapping
W2	Bayswater		
W4	Chiswick	E2	Bethnal Green
W6	Hammersmith	E3	Bow
W8	Kensington	N1	Hoxton and Islington
W11	Notting Hill	N5	Highbury
SW1	St James's, Westminster and Belgravia	N6	Highgate
		NW1	Camden Town
SW3	Chelsea	NW3	Hampstead

house, attracting more than five million tourists a year, that has recently been expensively redeveloped. Welding the West End to the financial district, **The Strand, Holborn and Clerkenwell** (Chapter 6) are little-visited areas, but offer some of central London's most surprising treats, among them the eccentric Sir John Soane's Museum and the secluded quadrangles of the Inns of Court.

A couple of miles downstream from Westminster, **The City** (Chapter 7) – or the City of London, to give it its full title – is simultaneously the most ancient and the most modern part of London. Settled since Roman times, the area became the commercial and residential heart of medieval London, with its own Lord Mayor and its own peculiar form of local government, both of which survive (with considerable pageantry) to this day. The Great Fire of 1666 obliterated most of the City, and the resident population has dwindled to insignificance, yet this remains one of the great financial centres of the world, ranking alongside New York and Tokyo. Nowadays, the City's most prominent landmarks are the hi-tech offices of legions of banks and insurance companies, but the Square Mile boasts its share of historic sights, notably the Tower of London and a fine cache of Wren churches that includes the mighty St Paul's Cathedral.

The **East End and Docklands** (Chapter 8), to the east of the City, are equally notorious, but in entirely different ways. Impoverished and working-class, the East End is not conventional tourist territory, but to ignore it is to miss out a crucial element of the real, multi-ethnic London. With its abandoned warehouses converted into over-priced apartment blocks for the city's upwardly mobile, Docklands is the converse of the down-at-heel East End, with the Canary Wharf tower, the country's tallest building, epitomizing the pretensions of the 1980s' Thatcherite dream.

Lambeth and Southwark (Chapter 9) comprise the small slice of central London that lies south of the Thames. The South Bank Centre, London's little-loved concrete culture bunker, is enjoying a new lease of life – thanks, in part, to the London Eye, the world's largest ferris wheel, which hangs over the Thames nearby. Southwark, the city's low-life district from Roman times to the eighteenth century, is also a millennial renaissance, with a new pedestrian bridge linking St Paul's with Bankside, whose former power station is now home to the new Tate Modern gallery.

In the districts of **Hyde Park, Kensington and Chelsea** (Chapter 10) you'll find the largest park in central London, a segment of greenery which separates wealthy West London from the city centre. The museums of South Kensington – the Victoria and Albert Museum, the Science Museum and the Natural History Museum – are a must; and if you have shopping on your London agenda you may well want to investigate the hive of plush stores in the vicinity of Harrods, superstore to the upper echelons.

Some of the most appealing parts of **North London** (Chapter 11) are clustered around Regent's Canal, which skirts Regent's Park and serves as the focus for the capital's trendiest weekend market, held around Camden Lock. Further out, in the chic literary suburbs of Hampstead and Highgate, there are unbeatable views across the city from half-wild Hampstead Heath, the favourite parkland of thousands of Londoners. The glory of **Southeast London** (Chapter 12) is

Greenwich, with its nautical associations, royal park and observatory (not to mention its Dome). Finally, there are plenty of rewarding day-trips along the Thames from **Chiswick to Windsor** (Chapter 13), a region in which royalty and the aristocracy have traditionally built their homes, the most famous being Hampton Court Palace and Windsor Castle.

Arriving in London

Flying into London, you'll arrive at one of the five **international airports** in and around the capital: Heathrow, Gatwick, Stansted, Luton or City Airport, each of which is less than an hour from the city centre. If you're departing from either Heathrow or Gatwick, make sure you find out which terminal you need, as Heathrow has two separate train/tube stations, while Gatwick's train station is at South Terminal, connected to the North Terminal by monorail.

For more details of train services to and from London's airports, call National Rail Enquiries: ☎08457/ 484950.

Getting into London from **Heathrow** (☎0870/000 0123; *www.baa.co.uk*), twelve miles west of the city, couldn't be easier. The new BAA-run, high-speed **Heathrow Express** (☎0845/600 1515; *www.heathrowexpress.co.uk*) trains take between fifteen and twenty minutes to reach Paddington, with one station serving terminals 1, 2 and 3, and another serving terminal 4; trains depart every fifteen minutes between 5.10am and 11.40pm, tickets cost £12 each way (£22 return) and can be purchased on board the train; accompanied children under 16 travel for free. A much cheaper way to get into central London is on the **Piccadilly Underground line** (☎020/7222 1234) which connects the airport to numerous stations across central London; tickets cost just £3.50, and trains depart every few minutes between 5am and 11.30pm, taking about fifty minutes to reach the centre. If you plan to spend the rest of your arrival day sightseeing, buy a multi-zone One-Day Travelcard for £4.70 (see "Getting around the city", p.40). There is also a **National Express** service from Heathrow, direct to Victoria Coach Station (every 30min; daily 6am–9.30pm; 35min–1hr 10min depending on the traffic), which costs £6 single, £8 return. **Airbus #2** (☎0990/747777; *www.airlinks.co.uk*) also runs from outside all four Heathrow terminals (every 30min; daily 6am–10pm) to several destinations in the city, including Holland Park, Notting Hill, Queensway, Lancaster Gate, Marble Arch, Baker Street, Great Portland Street, Euston and King's Cross. Journey time is about an hour and tickets cost £7 single, £12 return, but can be worth the money if you have a lot of luggage to haul. From midnight, the night bus #N97 runs every half hour from Heathrow to Trafalgar Square; tickets are a bargain £1.50 and the journey takes roughly an hour and ten minutes. **Taxis** are plentiful, but will set you back around £35 to central London, and take around an hour (much longer in the rush hour); a slightly cheaper alternative is to book a **minicab** in advance from a local minicab firm, which will bring the price down to around £25.

Gatwick (☎01293/535353; *www.baa.co.uk*) is thirty miles to the south: the non-stop **Gatwick Express** (☎0990/301530; *www.gatwickexpress.co.uk*) trains run between the airport's South Terminal and Victoria, taking thirty minutes and costing £10.20 single, £19.50 return; trains depart every fifteen minutes at peak times, and every thirty minutes off-peak. A cheaper option is the **Connex South Central** service to Victoria, which costs £8.20 single, departs every thirty minutes, but stops a couple of times en route, bringing the journey time up to nearly forty minutes. **Thameslink** trains to King's Cross (among other places) run roughly every thirty minutes; tickets cost £9.50 and the journey takes fifty minutes. However, note that Connex and Thameslink don't run services in the very early hours of the morning. **Airbus #5** departs hourly from Gatwick's North and South terminals (daily 7am–8pm), arriving at Victoria Coach Station in approximately an hour and a half later; the journey costs £8 single, £10 return. A **taxi** ride will set you back £50 or more, and take at least an hour.

The Norman-Foster-designed **Stansted** (☎01279/680500; *www.baa.co.uk*), newest and swankiest of London's international airports, lies 34 miles northeast of the capital. It's served by the Stansted **Skytrain** to Liverpool Street, which takes 45 minutes and costs £12 single, £22 return; trains run every fifteen minutes during the day and every thirty minutes at other times and over the weekend. **Airbus #6** or **#7** runs every thirty minutes (daily 6am–7pm; £7 single, £10 return) from Stansted to Victoria Coach Station, usually calling at Hendon Central, Finchley Road and Marble Arch en route; journey time is 1hr 25min. A **taxi** ride will set you back £50 or more, and take at least an hour.

Used primarily by business folk, **City Airport** (☎020/7646 0000; *www.londoncityairport.com*), is situated in among the Royal Albert Docks, nine miles east of central London, and handles European flights only. **Shuttle buses** connect City Airport with Canning Town DLR (every 5min; journey time 5min; £2 single); with Canary Wharf DLR and tube (every 10min; journey time 10min; £2 single) and Liverpool Street station (every 10min; journey time 30min; £5 single). Another option is to take the **North London Line** (Mon–Sat every 15min, Sun every 30min) to Silvertown, which is ten minutes' walk from the airport. To get to the airport from the nearest DLR station, Prince Regent, you have to catch the local bus #473, which runs every fifteen minutes or so from outside the station. A **taxi** from the airport to the City's financial sector will cost around £15, and take half an hour or so.

Luton airport (☎01582/405100; *www.london-luton.com*) is roughly thirty miles north of the city centre, and mainly handles charter flights. Luton Airport Parkway station is connected by **rail** to

King's Cross and other stations in central London, with **Thameslink** running trains every fifteen minutes, plus one or two throughout the night; the journey takes thirty to forty minutes; the single fare is £9.50, return £16.90. **Green Line buses** (☎020/8668 7261; *www.greenline.co.uk*) run approximately every hour from Luton to Victoria Station, taking around an hour and a half, and costing £7.50 single, £12 return. A **taxi** will cost in the region of £70 and take at least an hour to central London.

Eurostar trains arrive at **Waterloo International**; trains from the Channel ports arrive at Charing Cross or Victoria, while boat trains from Harwich arrive at Liverpool Street. Arriving by **train** from elsewhere in Britain, you'll come into one of London's numerous mainline stations, all of which have adjacent Underground stations linking into the city centre's tube network. Coming into London by **coach**, you're most likely to arrive at **Victoria Coach Station**, a couple of hundred yards south down Buckingham Palace Road from Victoria train station and tube.

Information

The **London Tourist Board** (LTB; *www.londontown.com*) has a desk in arrivals at Heathrow Terminal 3 (daily 6am–11pm), and another in the Underground station concourse for Heathrow Terminals 1, 2 and 3 (daily: June–Sept 8am–7pm, Oct–May 8am–6pm). There are also offices in Victoria (Easter–April Mon–Sat 8am–7pm, Sun 8am–6pm; May Mon–Sat 8am–8pm, Sun 8am–6pm; June–Sept Mon–Sat 8am–10pm, Sun 8am–7pm; Oct–Easter daily 8am–7pm), Waterloo International (daily 8.30am–10.30pm) and Liverpool Street stations (daily: June–Sept 8am–7pm, Oct–May 8am–6pm). The main central office is the **British Visitor Centre**, near Piccadilly Circus at 1 Regent St (June–Oct Mon 9.30am–6.30pm, Tues–Fri 9am–6.30pm, Sat & Sun 9am–5pm; Nov–May same times except Sat & Sun 10am–4pm).

Individual boroughs also run tourist offices at various prime (and not-so-prime) locations. **Greenwich**'s is at 46 Greenwich Church St, SE10 (daily: April–Oct 10.15am–4.45pm; Nov–March 11am–4pm; ☎020/8858 6376; *www.greenwich.gov.uk*); **Islington** has one at 6 Clerkenwell Close, N1 (Mon–Sat 11am–5pm; ☎020/7253 7438; *www.islington.gov.uk*); **Richmond**'s is inside the Old Town Hall on Whittaker Ave (Mon–Sat 10am–5pm; Easter–Sept also Sun 10.15am–1.30pm; ☎020/8940 9125; *www.richmond.gov.uk*); **Southwark** information centre is at the south end of London Bridge (Mon–Sat 10am–6pm, Sun 10.30am–5.30pm; ☎020/7403 8299; *www.southwark.gov.uk*); and there's an information office run by the **Corporation of London** on the south side of St Paul's Cathedral (April–Sept daily 9.30am–5pm; Oct–March Mon–Fri 9.30am–5pm,

Sat 9.30am–12.30pm; ☎020/7332 1456; *www.cityoflondon.gov*
.uk).

The tourist offices of individual boroughs are the only ones that will answer **phone enquiries**. The best that the LTB can offer is **Visitorcall** (☎0839/123456), a spread of prerecorded phone announcements – these are a very poor service indeed, and the calls are charged at an exorbitant rate. Most of the above offices hand out a useful reference **map** of central London, plus plans of the public transport systems, but to find your way around every cranny of the city you need to invest in either an *A–Z Atlas* or a *Nicholson Streetfinder*, both of which have an index covering every street in the capital; you can get them at most bookshops and newsagents for under £5. The only comprehensive and critical weekly **listings** magazine is *Time Out*, which costs £1.95 and comes out every Tuesday evening. In it you'll find details of all the latest exhibitions, shows, films, music, sport, guided walks and events in and around the capital.

Getting around the city

Starved of public funding for the last two decades, **London Transport** (LT; *www.londontransport.co.uk*) is now the most expensive system in the world, and despite a never-ending modernization programme, it's still notoriously unreliable. That said, 1999 was a relatively good year for LT, witnessing the opening of the Docklands Light Railway (DLR) extension to Greenwich (see p.288) and beyond, and the much-awaited Jubilee Line Extension (see box on p.40). Even more remarkable was the return of the tram to London in the year 2000, in the form of the Croydon TramLink (see p.473).

Except for very small journeys, the Underground – or **tube**, as it's known to Londoners – is by far the quickest way to get about; the capital's famous red **buses** are fun to ride on, but tend to get stuck in traffic jams, which prevents them running to a regular timetable. The principal **LT travel information office**, providing excellent free maps and details of bus and tube services, is at **Piccadilly Circus tube station** (daily 9am–6pm); there are other desks at Heathrow (Terminals 1, 2, & 3), and Euston, King's Cross, Liverpool Street, Paddington and Victoria stations. There's also a 24-hour phone line for information on all bus and tube services (☎020/7222 1234). If you possibly can, avoid travelling during the **rush hour** (Mon–Fri 8–9.30am & 5–7pm), when tubes become unbearably crowded, and some buses get so full they literally won't let you on.

Travelcards

An essential investment to get the best value out of the public transport system is a **Travelcard**, which is available from machines and booths at all tube and train stations (and at some newsagents as well – look for the sticker), and is valid for the bus, tube, Docklands Light Railway, TramLink and the suburban rail networks.

One-Day Travelcards, valid on weekdays from 9.30am and all day at weekends, cost £3.90 for the central zones 1 and 2, rising to £4.70 for all zones (1–6, including Heathrow); the respective **Weekend Travelcards**, for unlimited travel on Saturdays and Sundays, cost £5.80 and £7. If you need to travel before 9.30am on a weekday, but don't need to use suburban trains, you can buy a **One-Day LT Card**, which costs from £5 (zones 1 & 2) to £7.50 (all zones). **Weekly Travelcards** are even more economical, beginning at £18.20 for zones 1 and 2; these cards can only be bought by holders of a **Photocard**, which you can get, free of charge, from tube and train station ticket booths on presentation of a passport photo.

Children under 5 travel free of charge; those aged 5 to 15 go for half price (or thereabouts). One-Day and Weekend Travelcards for children cost a standard £3, however many zones you want, while LT Cards cost from £2.50 (zones 1 & 2) to £3.30 (all zones). Children aged 14 and 15 must have a **Child Rate Photocard** to buy any child-rate ticket. Another option for those with kids is to buy a one-day **Family Travelcard**, which costs £2.60 for an adult (zones 1 & 2), rising to £3.10 (all zones), plus an additional 80p for each child (up to as many as four). Despite the name, the adults and children don't have to be related, they just have to travel together, and the restrictions are the same as for normal One-Day Travelcards (see opposite).

There are further **youth and student reductions** available on weekly and monthly Travelcards and passes for sixteen- and seventeen-year olds, and for students. Reductions for those over sixty are only available to London residents – **pensioners** who live here (women over 60 and men over 65) can obtain a Freedom Pass, a

---

Jubilee Line Extension

London's underground system is the oldest in the world, but in 1999 it took a quantum leap into the future with the long overdue opening of the **Jubilee Line Extension** (JLE; *www.jle.lul.co.uk*), twenty months late and £1.4 billion over budget. Whatever the merits of extending an existing line rather than building a new one, the new architecture has proved a big hit with the public. The underground station which has attracted the most attention from visitors is **North Greenwich** (gateway for the Dome, and, apparently, the largest in the world), with its giant concrete columns, peppered with cobalt blue tiles. Other JLE highlights include the fetching, gently curving glass canopy entrance at **Canary Wharf** station, designed by Norman Foster, the wall of blue glass by Alex Beleschenko in **Southwark** station, and the glazed drum that heralds **Canada Water**. The other surprises for first-time users are the smoothness and quietness of the ride, and the transparent platform edge doors, which should help prevent accidents and suicides that bedevil older lines.

yearly pass that allows free travel on all services within London; to find out more, contact your local council.

The tube

Eleven different **tube** lines cross much of the metropolis, although London south of the river is not very well covered. Each line has its own colour and name – all you need to know is which direction you're travelling in: northbound, eastbound, southbound or westbound (this gets tricky when taking the Circle Line). As a precaution, it's also worth checking the final destination displayed on the front of the train, as some lines, such as the District Line, have several different branches. Services operate from around 5.30am, Monday to Saturday, and from 7.30am on Sundays, until around midnight, and you rarely have to wait more than five minutes for a train between central stations. However, the reliability of connections to further-flung stations, especially on the notorious Northern Line, is not always what it should be, due to the endemic British problem of underfunded public services.

Tickets must be bought in advance from automatic machines or from a ticket booth in the station entrance hall; if you cannot produce a valid ticket for your journey, you will be liable for an on-the-spot Penalty Fare of £10. A single journey in the central zone costs an unbelievable £1.50. If this is the type of journey you'll be making once or twice a day, then it might be worth buying a **Carnet** of ten tickets for £11 instead, though if you're intending to travel about a lot, a Travelcard is by far your best bet.

Buses

Tickets for all bus journeys within, to or from the central zone costs a flat fare of £1; journeys outside the central zone cost 70p; children aged 5 to 15 pay a standard fare of 40p. Normally you pay the driver on entering; to find out how much you need to pay, simply state your destination; note that if you cannot produce a ticket valid for your entire journey, you will be liable for an on-the-spot Penalty Fare of £5. Some routes – especially those which traverse the West End – are covered by older Routemaster buses, which are staffed by a conductor and have an open rear platform. A lot of bus stops are request stops (easily recognizable by their red sign), so if you don't stick your arm out to hail the bus you want, it will pass you by.

While the majority of London's buses are still the distinctive red double-deckers, all routes are now run by private companies. The great majority accept Travelcards – look for the London Transport logo on the windscreen or door. Note that, in addition to the Travelcards mentioned above, a **One-Day Bus Pass** is also available, and, more importantly, it can be used before 9.30am; for zones 1 and 2 it costs £3 for adults and £1 for kids. You can also buy a **Saver 6**, a single card which gives you six £1 bus fares for the price of five.

Regular buses run between about 6am and midnight, and a network of **Night Buses** (prefixed with the letter "N") operate outside this period. Night bus routes radiate out from Trafalgar Square at approximately hourly intervals, more frequently on some routes and on Friday and Saturday nights. Fares are a flat £1.50 from central London; One-Day, Family and Weekend Travelcards aren't valid on them, but Weekly Travelcards are.

Suburban trains

Large areas of London's suburbs, particularly in the southeast, are not served by the tube and are impractical to reach by bus. The only way to reach these parts of London is by the **suburban train** network (Travelcards valid), which fans out from the main city termini. Wherever a sight can only be reached by overground train, we've indicated the nearest train station and the central terminus from which you must depart. Note that Travelcards are not valid as far out as Windsor, for which you must buy a separate train ticket.

If you're planning to use the railway network a lot, you might want to purchase a **Network Railcard**, which is valid for a year, costs £20, and gives you up to 33 percent discount on fares to destinations in and around the southeast. A couple of useful train lines that actually cross the capital are the **Silverlink** or **North London Line**, which runs between Richmond and North Woolwich via Hampstead, Camden and Islington (Mon–Sat every 15min, Sun every 30min), and the **Thameslink** service, which runs north–south via King's Cross, Blackfriars and London Bridge. To find out about a particular service, phone **National Rail Enquiries** on ☎08457/484950, or visit *www.britrail.co.uk*.

Taxis

*If you want to
book a black
taxi in
advance, call
☎020/7272
0272.*

If you're in a group of three or more, London's metered **black cabs** can be an economical way of getting around the centre – a ride from Euston to Victoria, for example, should cost around £10. The meter will show two amounts: one calculates distance and time, while the other is the fixed charge for passengers, luggage and any Sunday/bank holiday tariff – after these are totalled, a small tip is customary. A yellow light over the windscreen tells you if the cab is available – just stick your arm out to hail it. London's cabbies are the best trained in Europe; every one of them knows the shortest route between any two points in the capital, and they won't rip you off by taking another route. They are, however, a blunt and forthright breed, renowned for their generally reactionary opinions.

Minicabs are less reliable than black cabs, as their drivers are just private individuals rather than trained professionals; however, they

Sightseeing tours and guided walks

Standard **sightseeing bus tours** are run by several rival companies, their open-top double-deckers setting off every thirty minutes from Victoria station, Trafalgar Square, Piccadilly and other conspicuous tourist spots. The Original Tour (☎020/8877 1722; *www.theoriginaltour.com*) runs several buses on several routes; 24-hour tickets cost around £12, and you can hop on and off as often as you like. Alternatively, you can hop aboard one of the bright yellow World War II amphibious vehicles used by Frog Tours (☎020/7928 3132; *www.frogtours.com*), which offers a combined **bus and boat tour**. After fifty minutes driving round the usual sights, you plunge into the river and go on a half-hour cruise. Tours set off every half hour from 10am to dusk, with tickets costing £13. Another option is to save yourself the money and the inane commentary by hopping on a real London bus – the #11 from Victoria station will take you past Westminster Abbey, the Houses of Parliament, up Whitehall, round Trafalgar Square, along the Strand and on to St Paul's Cathedral.

Walking tours are infinitely more appealing and informative, covering a relatively small area in much greater detail, mixing solid historical facts with juicy anecdotes in the company of a local specialist. Walks on offer range from a literary pub crawl round Bloomsbury to a roam around the remains of the Jewish East End. You'll find most of them detailed, week by week, in *Time Out* (in the "Around Town" section); as you'd imagine, there's more variety on offer in the summer months. Tours tend to cost £4–5 and take around two hours; normally you can show up at the starting point and join a tour, though guides prefer you to phone ahead.

If you want to plan – or book – walks rather more in advance, you might contact one of the following companies direct:

Original London Walks (☎020/7624 3978; *www.walks.com*). The widest range of walks, and the most reliable and well-established company.

Stepping Out (☎020/8881 2933; *www.walklon.ndirect.co.uk*). Wide range of walks from a romp round the Inns of Court to a wander round Hampstead.

Historical Tours (☎020/8668 4019; *johnmuffty@dial.pipex.com*). Focuses on the City and Westminster, and also offers evening pub walks.

are often considerably cheaper, so you might want to take one back from a late-night club. Minicabs cannot be hailed, and touting is illegal. There are hundreds of minicab firms in the phone book, but the best way to pick is to take the advice of the place you're at, unless you want to be certain of a woman driver, in which case call Ladycabs (☎020/7254 3501), or a gay/lesbian driver, in which case call Freedom Cars (☎020/7734 1313). Most minicabs are not metered, so always establish the fare beforehand.

Cycling

Despite being a potentially lethal mode of city transport, **cycling** is increasingly popular in London, not least because – in the centre, at least – it's by far the fastest way to get around. If you also use the tubes and suburban trains, it can even be a good way to explore some

Getting
around the
city

Thames river services and boat trips

Despite the building and upgrading of several piers and all the talk about making more use of the river, **boat services** on the Thames still do not form part of an integrated public transport system, and Travelcards are currently not valid on the river. So for the moment at least, travelling by boat remains a leisure pastime rather than a commuting option.

Services are most frequent between **Westminster and Greenwich** (every 40min; 50min); typical fares are around £6 single, £7.50 return. If you're taking the DLR, it's worth finding out about Sail & Rail tickets (see p.288). There's also a new **Fast Ferry** service in central London, plying between Blackfriars, Canary Wharf, Greenwich and beyond. From April to October, you can take a boat from Westminster via Kew and Richmond **to Hampton Court** (journey time is 3hr–3hr 30min; £10 single, £14 return). Lastly, there are **circular cruise** boats, which bombard passengers with a loud multilingual commentary, as well as lunch and dinner cruises.

All services are keenly affected by demand, tides and the weather, and tend to be drastically scaled down in the winter months. **Timetables and services** are complex, and there are numerous companies and small charter operators – for a full list pick up the Thames River Services booklet from an LT travel information office, phone ☎020/7222 1234 or visit *www.londontransport.co.uk*.

of the suburbs. There are, however, restrictions on taking your bike on public transport; no bikes are allowed on any part of the system from Monday to Friday between 7.30am to 9.30am, and from 4pm to 7pm. Bikes are also only allowed on the District, Hammersmith & City, Metropolitan and Circle lines, plus the overground sections of tube lines. Bicycles are not allowed on the Docklands Light Railway, and restrictions on the suburban trains vary from company to company, so check before you set out.

Bike rental is available from Bikepark, 14 Stukeley St, Covent Garden (Mon–Fri 7.30am–7.30pm, Sat 10am–6pm; ☎020/7430 0083; *www.bikepark.co.uk*), which has a range of mountain bikes and hybrids, starting at around £10 for the first day, £5 for the second, and £3 a day thereafter, and also run a secure bike park (as their name suggests); the London Bicycle Tour Company, on the South Bank at 1a Gabriel's Wharf (Easter–Oct daily 10am–6pm; Nov–Easter phone for times; ☎020/7928 6838; *www.londonbicycle.com*), runs guided bicycle tours, but also has bikes for rent at similar prices.

Museums, monuments and sights

The list of major sights below is by no means exhaustive – for a more comprehensive list, scan the museums and palaces entries in the index. Opening hours and prices are the latest available, though bear in mind that some of the sights are prone to raising their charges dramatically from year to year. The new Labour government made a commitment to granting free entry to all national museums (those affected are marked with an asterisk); entry is currently free for all children and pensioners, but the final hurdle of free entry for adults (or entry for a nominal £1) may well prove impossible to surmount. At other museums, there is usually a concessionary rate available for card-holding students, senior citizens, under-18s and the registered unemployed. Under-5s get in free almost everywhere and many attractions offer discounted family tickets, though these are only really worthwhile if you have at least two adults and two children over five years old in your family unit. The South Kensington and Greenwich museums operate special tickets which allow you entry into a group of sights at a discount, and an increasing number of places now offer good-value season tickets for those wishing to make several visits to a particular sight.

BBC Experience (p.127) Mon 11am–4.30pm, Tues–Sun 10am–4.30pm; £7.50; ☎0870/603 0304; *www.bbc.co.uk/experience*.

British Museum (p.161) Mon–Sat 10am–5pm, Sun noon–6pm; free; ☎020/7636 1555; *www.thebritishmuseum.ac.uk*.

Buckingham Palace (p.71) Aug & Sept daily 9.30am–4.15pm; £10; ☎020/7930 4832; *www.royal.gov.uk*.

Courtauld Institute Galleries (p.196) Mon–Sat 10am–6pm, Sun noon–6pm; £4; free Mon 10am–2pm; ☎020/7848 2526; *www .courtauld.ac.uk*.

Hampton Court Palace (p.477) Mid-March to mid-Oct Mon 10.15am–6pm, Tues–Sun 9.30am–6pm; mid-Oct to mid-March closes 4.30pm; £10.50; ☎020/8781 9500; *www.hrp.org.uk*.

* Imperial War Museum (p.308) Daily 10am–6pm; £5.50; free after 4.30pm; ☎020/7416 5000; *www.iwm.org.uk*.

Kensington Palace (p.340) April–Sept daily 10am–6pm; Oct–March Wed–Sun 10am–5pm; £9.50; ☎020/7937 9561; *www.hrp.org.uk*.

Kenwood House (p.408) Daily: April–Sept 10am–6pm; Oct 10am–5pm; Nov–March 10am–4pm; EH; free; ☎020/8348 1286; *www .english-heritage.org.uk*.

Kew Gardens (p.464) Daily 9.30am to 7.30pm or dusk; £5; ☎020/ 8332 5000; *www.kew.org*.

London Aquarium (p.305) Daily 10am–6pm or later; £8.50; ☎020/7967 8000; *www.londonaquarium.co.uk*.

London Dungeon (p.321) Daily: April–Sept 10am–6pm; Oct–March 10.30am–5.30pm; £9.50; ☎0891/600 0666; *www.thedungeons .com*.

London Eye (p.304) Daily: April–Sept 9am–late evening; Oct–March 10am–5.30pm; £8.50; ☎0870/500 0600; *www.ba-londoneye.com*.

Museums, monuments and sights

A useful Web site for up-to-date information on London's museums is www.24hour museum.co.uk.

Museums, monuments and sights

London Transport Museum (p.153) Mon–Thurs, Sat & Sun 10am–6pm, Fri 11am–6pm; £5.50; ☎020/7836 8557; *www.ltmuseum .co.uk*.

London Zoo (p.389) Daily: March–Oct 10am–5.30pm; Nov–Feb 10am–4pm; £9; ☎020/7722 3333; *www.londonzoo.co.uk*.

Madame Tussaud's (p.132) Daily: June to mid-Sept 9am–5.30pm; mid-Sept to May 10am–5.30pm; £11.50; ☎0870/400 3000; *www .madame-tussauds.com*.

Museum of London (p.236) Mon–Sat 10am–5.50pm, Sun noon–5.50pm; £5; free after 4.30pm; ☎020/7600 3699; *www .museumoflondon.org.uk*.

National Gallery (p.53) Daily 10am–6pm (Wed till 9pm); free; ☎020/7747 2885; *www.nationalgallery.org.uk*.

* National Maritime Museum (p.433) Daily 10am–5pm; £7.50; ☎020/8858 4422; *www.nmm.ac.uk*.

National Portrait Gallery (p.65) Daily 10am–6pm (Thurs & Fri till 9pm); free; ☎020/7306 0055; *www.npg.org.uk*.

* Natural History Museum (p.360) Mon–Sat 10am–5.50pm, Sun 11am–5.50pm; £7.50; free Mon–Fri after 4.30pm, Sat & Sun after 5pm; free guided tours daily; ☎020/7942 5000; *www.nhm.ac .uk*.

* RAF Museum (p.415) Daily 10am–6pm; £7; ☎020/8205 2266; *www.rafmuseum.org.uk*.

St Paul's Cathedral (p.223) Mon–Sat 8.30am–4pm; £5; ☎020/7236 4128; *www.stpauls.co.uk*.

* Science Museum (p.356) Daily 10am–6pm; £6.95; free after 4.30pm; ☎020/7942 4455; *www.nmsi.ac.uk*.

Shakespeare's Globe Theatre (see p.315). Daily: May–Sept 9am–noon; Oct–April 10am–5pm; £7.50; ☎020/7902 1500; *www .shakespeares-globe.org*.

Tate Britain (p.96) Daily 10am–5.50pm; free; ☎020/7887 8000; *www.tate.org.uk*.

Tate Modern (p.311) Mon–Thurs & Sun 10am–6pm, Fri & Sat 10am–10pm; free; ☎020/7887 8000; *www.tate.org.uk*.

Tower Bridge (p.263) Daily: April–Oct 10am–6.30pm; Nov–March 9.30am–6pm; guided tour £6.25; ☎020/7378 1928; *www .towerbridge.org.uk*.

Tower of London (p.255) March–Oct Mon–Sat 9am–6pm, Sun 10am–6pm; Nov–Feb Mon & Sun 10am–5pm, Tues–Sat 9am–5pm; £11; ☎020/7709 0765; *www.hrp.org.uk*.

* Victoria and Albert Museum (p.346) Daily 10am–5.45pm (Wed also 6.30–9.30pm); £5; free after 4.30pm; ☎020/7942 2000; *www.vam.ac.uk*.

GoSee Card & London Pass

For the really serious museum addict, the **GoSee Card** (formerly known as the London White Card) gives you entry into the following museums and galleries: Apsley House (Wellington Museum), Barbican Art Galleries, BBC Experience, BFI London IMAX Cinema, Design Museum, Hayward Gallery, Imperial War Museum, London Transport Museum, Museum of London, National Maritime Museum, Royal Observatory Greenwich, Natural History Museum, Royal Academy, Science Museum, Shakespeare's Globe Museum, Theatre Museum, Tower Bridge and the V&A. The three-day card costs £16, though this gives you too little time to visit all the above; the seven-day card costs £26. Even better value is the Family Card, which covers two adults and up to four children and costs £32 for three days or £50 for seven. The cards are available from any of the above museums or galleries, and at LTB and LT offices; for more information, phone ☎020/7923 0807, or visit *www.london-gosee.com*.

An alternative to the GoSee Card is the new **London Pass**, which gives you entry to a mixed bag of attractions including Buckingham Palace, Chislehurst Caves, Chiswick House, the *Cutty Sark*, Downe House, Eltham Palace, the Estorick Collection, F.A. Premiership Museum, Fan Museum, HMS *Belfast*, Jewel Tower, Jewish Museum, London Aquarium, RAF Museum, Ranger's House at Greenwich, Saatchi Gallery, St Paul's Cathedral and Windsor Castle, but also throws in an All-Zone Travelcard, £5 worth of free phone calls and various other perks and incentives. The pass costs £22 for one day (£14 for kids), £49 for three days (£30 for kids), and £79 for six days (£42 for kids). However, the London Pass is currently in its infancy, and more sights need to be added to its portfolio if it's going to compete for value with the GoSee Card. The London Pass can be bought over the phone (☎0870/242 9988) or on the Internet (*www.londonpass.com*), and can also be purchased in person from Exchange International bureaux at Heathrow and Gatwick airports, and London's mainline train stations.

Westminster Abbey (p.86) Mon–Fri 9.30am–4.45pm, Sat 9.30am–2.45pm, also Wed 6–7.45pm; £5; ☎020/7222 5152; *www.westminster-abbey.org*.

Windsor Castle (p.485) Daily: March–Oct 9.45am–5.15pm; Nov–Feb 9.45am–4.15pm; £10.50; ☎01753/868286; *www.royal.gov.uk*.

Chapter 2

Westminster and Whitehall

Nearby Soho and Covent Garden are far better areas for pubs, cafés and restaurants, though you'll find good cafés in the National Gallery, St Martin-in-the-Fields church and the ICA on the Mall.

Political, religious and regal power has emanated from **WESTMINSTER** and **WHITEHALL** for almost a millennium. It was Edward the Confessor (reigned 1042–66) who first established Westminster as London's royal and ecclesiastical power base, some three miles west of the real, commercial City of London. The embryonic English parliament met in the abbey in the fourteenth century, and eventually took over the old royal palace of Westminster when Henry VIII moved out to Whitehall. In the nineteenth century, Whitehall became the "heart of the Empire", its ministries ruling over a quarter of the world's population. Even now, though the UK's world status has diminished, and its royalty and clergy no longer wield much real power or respect, the institutions that run the country inhabit roughly the same geographical area: Westminster for the politicians, Whitehall for the ministers and civil servants.

The monuments and buildings covered in this chapter also span the millennium, and include some of London's most famous landmarks – **Nelson's Column**, **Big Ben** and the **Houses of Parliament**, **Westminster Abbey** and **Buckingham Palace**, plus two of the city's finest permanent art collections, the **National Gallery** and the **Tate Britain** gallery. This area is a well-trodden tourist circuit for the most part, with few shops or cafés and little commercial life to distract you, but it's also one of the easiest parts of London to walk round, with all the major sights within a mere half-mile of each other, linked by two of London's most triumphant – and atypical – avenues, **Whitehall** and **The Mall**.

Until the westward expansion of the City of London in the seventeenth century, Westminster was a more or less separate city. Today, the modern borough of Westminster encompasses a much wider area than that covered in this chapter, including most of the West End and parts of the well-to-do districts of Mayfair and Belgravia, making its council one of the richest in the country. In the 1980s this

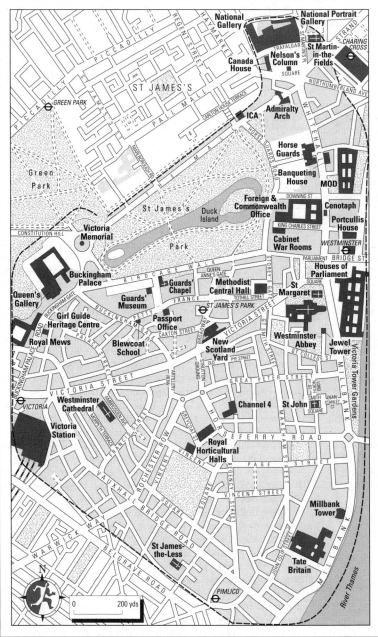

© crown copyright

was one of the Thatcher government's flagship right-wing councils, at the forefront of immoral and illegal privatization campaigns, closing down its hostels for the homeless, selling off its housing stock, even its cemeteries, and reducing spending and services to a minimum. Its leader was Dame Shirley Porter, heiress of the Tesco supermarket chain, who, with her colleagues, was found guilty of financial corruption on a scale hitherto unknown in local government.

Trafalgar Square

Despite being little more than a glorified, sunken traffic island, infested with scruffy urban pigeons, **Trafalgar Square** is still one of London's grandest architectural set pieces. John Nash designed the basic layout in the 1820s, but died long before the square took its present form. The Neoclassical National Gallery filled up the northern side of the square in 1838, followed shortly afterwards by the central focal point, **Nelson's Column**; the famous bronze lions didn't arrive until 1868, and the fountains – a real rarity in a London square – didn't take their present shape until the eve of World War II. The development of the rest of the square was equally haphazard, though the overall effect is unified by the safe Neoclassical styles of the buildings. The sheer volume of traffic thundering around Trafalgar Square has prompted a plan for partial pedestrianization of the north end, below the National Gallery.

Trafalgar Square is a major terminus for day and (usefully) night buses. The nearest tubes are Charing Cross and Leicester Square.

There's a distinct whiff of Empire in the juxtaposition of **South Africa House** (closed to the public), erected in 1935 on the east side of the square, complete with keystones featuring African animals, and **Canada House**, opposite, built in warm Bath stone as a gentlemen's club and home for the Royal College of Surgeons in the 1820s by Robert Smirke, who also designed the British Museum. Despite alterations over the years, Canada House retains much of its original Neoclassical interior. You can walk the entire length of the ground floor from north to south, taking in the excellent temporary exhibitions and the ornate entrance lobby to the south of the building en route. From the latter, you may also sit and listen to CDs, thumb through the Canadian press or browse online; Canadians can also send and receive emails from the folks back home.

Canada House is open Mon–Fri 10am–6pm; free; ☎020 /7258 6600.

As one of the few large public squares in London, Trafalgar Square has been both a tourist attraction and the main focus for **political demonstrations** for over a century. It was here that the Chartists assembled in 1848 before marching to Kennington Common. Countless demos and rallies were held over the next hundred years, including huge turnouts against nuclear disarmament and the Poll Tax, and a nonstop vigil outside the South African embassy during the 1980s and early 1990s. All of which would seem to justify the provision of a police phone box, purpose-built into one of the stone bollards in the southeast corner of the square, which once had a direct link to Scotland Yard.

On a more festive note, the square is graced each December with a giant Christmas tree covered in fairy lights, donated by Norway in thanks for liberation from the Nazis. And on **New Year's Eve**, thousands of inebriates sing in the New Year, though injuries and fatalities in recent years have meant that just about everything traditionally associated with the event – drinking, dancing and indiscriminate kissing of police officers – is now strictly forbidden.

Nelson's Column and the statues

Nelson's Column, raised in 1843 and now one of London's best-loved monuments, commemorates the one-armed, one-eyed admiral who defeated Napoleon at the Battle of Trafalgar in 1805, but paid for it with his life. The statue which surmounts the granite column is more than triple life-size but still manages to appear minuscule, and is coated in anti-pigeon gel to try and stem the build-up of guano. The acanthus leaves of the capital are cast from British cannons, while bas-reliefs around the base – depicting three of Nelson's earlier victories as well as his death aboard HMS *Victory* – are from captured French armaments. Edwin Landseer's four gargantuan **bronze lions** guard the column and provide a climbing frame for kids (and demonstrators) to clamber over. If you can, get here before the crowds and watch the pigeons take to the air as Edwin Lutyens' **fountains** jet into action at 9am.

Keeping Nelson company at ground level, on either side of the column, are bronze statues of Napier and Havelock, Victorian major generals who helped keep India British; against the north wall are busts of Beatty, Jellicoe and Cunningham, more recent military leaders. In the northeast corner of the square is an equestrian statue of George IV (bareback, stirrupless and in Roman garb), which he himself commissioned for the top of Marble Arch, now at the northeast corner of Hyde Park, but which was later erected here "temporarily". The **fourth plinth** in the northwest corner was earmarked for William IV, but remained empty until 1999 when a bizarre trio of statues took turns to fill the gap. Fittingly, the first statue, which greeted the new millennium, was Mark Wallinger's life-size Christ; the second was Rachel Whiteread's inverted cast of the plinth; the final one, Bill Woodrow's bronze of a tree, a book and a human head, comes down in May 2001. To find out the future of the plinth, visit *www.fourthplinth.com*.

Predating the entire square is the **equestrian statue of Charles I**, stranded on a traffic island to the south of the column. It was completed in 1633 and originally intended for a site in Roehampton, only to be confiscated and sold off during the Commonwealth to a local brazier, with strict instructions for it to be melted down. The said brazier, John Rivett, made a small fortune selling bronze mementoes, allegedly from the metal, while all the time concealing the statue in the vaults of St Paul's, Covent Garden (see p.152). After the

Restoration, Rivett resold the statue and it was placed on the very spot where eight of those who had signed the king's death warrant were disembowelled in 1660, and within sight of the Banqueting House in Whitehall where Charles himself was beheaded (see p.76).

Charles's statue also marks the original site of **Charing Cross**, from where all distances from the capital are measured. The original thirteenth-century cross was the last of twelve erected by Edward I, to mark the overnight stops on the funeral procession of his wife, Eleanor, from Nottinghamshire to Westminster Abbey in 1290. The cross was pulled down during the Civil War, though a Victorian imitation now stands amidst the taxis outside Charing Cross station, at the beginning of the Strand, to the east of the square.

St Martin-in-the-Fields

Church open to visitors Mon–Sat 10am–8pm, Sun noon–8pm; brass-rubbing centre Mon–Sat 10am–6pm, Sun noon–6pm; café in the crypt Mon–Sat 10am–8pm, Sun noon–8pm; ☎020/7930 0089; *www.stmartin-in-the-fields .org*. Leicester Square or Charing Cross tube.

At the northeastern corner of Trafalgar Square stands James Gibbs's church of **St Martin-in-the-Fields**, fronted by a magnificent Corinthian portico and topped by an elaborate, and distinctly unclassical, tower and steeple. The first church on this site was indeed built "in the fields", outside the city perimeters, while the present building, completed in 1726, was hemmed in on all sides for more than a century before the surrounding houses were demolished to make way for Trafalgar Square, giving the church a much grander setting. The interior is purposefully simple, though the Italian plasterwork on the barrel vaulting is exceptionally rich; it's best appreciated while listening to one of the church's free lunchtime concerts. St Martin's witnessed the marriage of John Constable, the christening of Charles II and the funerals of, among others, the latter's mistress, Nell Gwynne (buried in the former churchyard), the outlaw Jack Sheppard, French sculptor Roubiliac and furniture designer Thomas Chippendale. George I was a church warden (though he seldom turned up for duties), and the present church, as the official parish church for Buckingham Palace, maintains strong royal and naval connections – there's a royal box on the left of the high altar, and one for the admiralty on the right.

The St Martin's crypt café is a good-value sanctuary on Trafalgar Square.

The touristy souvenir market along the north wall of the church is just one of St Martin's many money-spinning exercises; more usefully, there's a licensed café in the roomy **crypt** – accessible via steps on the southern side – not to mention a shop, gallery and brass-rubbing centre. The set of steps by the market leads down to a subterranean "social care centre" and soup kitchen serving the burgeoning ranks of the West End homeless, for whom the church has consistently cared since the pioneering work of one of its vicars, Dick Sheppard, among the parish's homeless ex-soldiers after World War I. St Martin's is also the venue for the annual **Costermongers' Harvest Festival**, held in early October. Since Victorian times, Cockney market-stallholders and their families have converged on the church from all over London, dressed up in aid of charity as "Pearly Kings and Queens", their clothes studded with hundreds of pearly buttons.

The National Gallery

Daily 10am–6pm (Wed till 9pm); free. Guided tours daily 11.30am & 2.30pm, Wed also 6.30pm; free; ☎020/7747 2885; *www.nationalgallery.org.uk*. Leicester Square or Charing Cross tube.

Taking up the entire north side of Trafalgar Square, the sprawling Neoclassical hulk of the **National Gallery** houses one of the world's greatest art collections. Unlike the Louvre or the Hermitage, the National Gallery is not based on a former royal collection, but was begun as late as 1824 when the government reluctantly agreed to purchase 38 paintings belonging to a Russian émigré banker, John Julius Angerstein. Further paintings were bought by the gallery's wily directors or bequeathed by private individuals in lieu of death duty – in other words, to help the rich avoid paying taxes. These days, the gallery's budget can do little to compete with the private endowments of the Getty and other American galleries, though in times of emergency (for example when a painting is put up for sale by a stately home) the government has been known to step in with a one-off financial package.

The gallery's years of canny acquisition has produced a collection of more than 2200 paintings, but the collection's virtue is not so much its size, but the range, depth and sheer quality of its contents. A quick tally of the National's Italian masterpieces, for example, includes works by Uccello, Botticelli, Mantegna, Piero della Francesca, Paolo Veronese, Titian, Raphael, Michelangelo and

---

Boris Anrep's floor mosaics

One of the most overlooked features of the National Gallery are the mind-boggling **floor mosaics** executed by Russian-born Boris Anrep between 1927 and 1952 on the landings of the main staircase leading to the central hall. The *Awakening of the Muses*, on the halfway landing, features a bizarre collection of famous figures from the 1930s – Virginia Woolf appears as Clio (Muse of History), Greta Garbo plays Melpomene (Muse of Tragedy). The mosaic on the landing closest to the central hall is made up of fifteen small scenes illustrating the *Modern Virtues*: Anna Akhmatova is saved by an angel from the Leningrad Blockade in *Compassion*; T.S. Eliot contemplates the Loch Ness Monster and Einstein's Theory of Relativity in *Leisure*; Bertrand Russell gazes on a naked woman in *Lucidity*; Edith Sitwell, book in hand, glides across a monster-infested chasm on a twig in *Sixth Sense*; and in the largest composition, *Defiance*, Churchill appears in combat gear on the white cliffs of Dover, raising two fingers to a monster in the shape of a swastika.

Caravaggio. From Spain there are dazzling pieces by El Greco, Velázquez and Goya; from the Low Countries, van der Weyden, van Eyck, Memlinc and Rubens, and an array of Rembrandt paintings that features some of his most searching portraits. Poussin, Claude, Watteau and the only Jacques-Louis David paintings in the country are the early highlights of a French contingent that has a particularly strong showing of Cézanne and the Impressionists. British art is also represented, with important works by Hogarth, Gainsborough, Stubbs and Turner, though for twentieth-century British art – and many more Turners – you'll need to move on to the Tate Britain gallery on Millbank (see p.96).

The National Gallery's original collection was put on public display at Angerstein's old residence, 100 Pall Mall, until today's purpose-built edifice on Trafalgar Square was completed in 1838. A hostile press dubbed the gallery's diminutive dome and cupolas "pepperpots", and poured abuse on the Greek Revivalist architect, William Wilkins, who went into early retirement, and died a year later. Subsequent additions to the rear of the building over the next hundred and fifty years provoked little comment, but a similar barrage of abuse broke out in the mid-1980s over plans for the new **Sainsbury Wing**, endowed by the supermarket dynasty. The winning design, by Ahrends, Burton and Koralek, elicited the oft-quoted remark from Prince Charles about "a monstrous carbuncle on the face of a much-loved and elegant friend". Planning permission was, of course, not granted. Instead, the American husband-and-wife team of Robert Venturi and Denise Scott-Brown were commissioned to produce a softly-softly, postmodern adjunct, which playfully imitates elements of Wilkins' Neoclassicism and even Nelson's Column and, most importantly, got the approval of Prince Charles, who laid the foundation stone in 1988.

Visiting the gallery

Crivelli's Garden in the Sainsbury wing does moderately priced lunch or coffee, and there's a branch of the inexpensive Pret à Manger sandwich bar chain in the basement of the East Wing.

There are **three entrances** to the National Gallery: Wilkins' original elevated entrance on Trafalgar Square, the back entrance on Orange Street, and the new entrance on the ground floor of the Sainsbury Wing. All three entrances have cloakrooms, and both the Trafalgar Square and Sainsbury Wing entrances have a shop, a café/restaurant and an information desk, which hands out free plans.

More importantly, the two main entrances can also provide visitors with a **Gallery Guide Soundtrack**, a portable CD player, which has a brief audio commentary on each of the paintings on display. The soundtrack is available free of charge, though you may be asked for a "voluntary contribution": on the whole it's a useful introduction, though the commentaries tend to be descriptive rather than interpretive. The Sainsbury Wing also features the innovative **micro gallery** on the first floor, where a range of computer consoles allow you to plan – and print out – your own personalized tour; it's good for locating particular favourites, learning more about specific paintings and painters and for generally playing around on, but by no means essential if this is your first visit.

With over a thousand paintings on permanent display in the main galleries, you'll need visual endurance to see everything in one day. If you want to view the collection chronologically, begin with the Sainsbury Wing – this is the order our account follows. If you're after the late nineteenth-century works, go through the main, central entrance and head for rooms 43–46 in the East Wing. Another possibility is to join up with one of the gallery's free **guided tours**, which set off from the Sainsbury Wing foyer. The guides vary enormously in the politics and style of their art criticism and in their choice of paintings, but all try and give you a representative sample. In addition, there are free lectures and films in the gallery's three theatres, all listed in the monthly newsletter available from the information desks.

On any one visit, you're likely to discover at least one or two rooms that are in the process of being rehung, and therefore throw the account below into confusion. If so, you might find the missing paintings lurking in rooms B to F of the little-visited **Lower Floor Collection**, accessible from the stairs in room 13 and directly from the Orange Street entrance, though it's sometimes closed due to staff shortages. The gallery's reserve collection is also on permanently cramped display in room A.

Temporary exhibitions take place in the basement of the Sainsbury Wing but compare unfavourably with those in London's other public art galleries: the rooms are small, have no natural light, and there is sometimes an entrance fee. The temporary displays in the newly expanded **Sunley Room** in the main building, however, are always free; they often focus on the background to one of the gallery's works (and include a video on the subject), and host an annual exhibition by the gallery's artist in residence. Look out, too, for the programme of **free concerts** of chamber music, which take place in the Central Hall on Wednesday evenings.

Leonardo da Vinci

The first room you enter in the Sainsbury Wing (room 51) contains the earliest works in the collection, but also boasts **Leonardo da Vinci**'s melancholic *Virgin of the Rocks* (the more famous version hangs in the Louvre), and behind it, in a separate dimly lit shrine of its own, the "Leonardo Cartoon" – a preparatory drawing of *The Virgin and Child with St Anne and John the Baptist* for a painting which, like so many of Leonardo's projects, was never completed. Before the 1960s, the cartoon was known only to scholars – that is, until an American tried to buy the picture for £2,500,000. In 1987, it gained further notoriety when an ex-soldier blasted the work with a sawn-off shotgun in protest at the political status quo – hence the bulletproof glass behind which it now resides.

Giotto to Uccello

Appropriately enough, the early works in room 51 include one attributed to **Giotto**, considered, even by his contemporaries, to be "the
father of modern painting". He was one of the first painters to develop a softer, more three-dimensional approach to painting after the
flat, Byzantine-style paintings that had gone before. **Duccio**, a
Sienese contemporary of Giotto, maintained a more iconic approach,
but also introduced a new sense of movement and space to his nar-
rative paintings, several of which hang in room 52. The panels are
taken from his *Maestà* (a Sienese invention depicting the Madonna
enthroned as Queen of Heaven), which was carried in triumph from
the artist's studio to the cathedral in 1311 with virtually the whole of
Siena looking on.

Rooms 53 & 54

Room 53 features the extraordinarily vivid **Wilton Diptych**, a
portable altarpiece painted by an unknown fourteenth-century artist
for the boy king Richard II, who is depicted being presented by his
patron saints to the Virgin, Child and assorted angels. During
restoration, a minuscule map was discovered in the orb atop the banner, showing a green island, a white castle and a boat in full sail, sym-
bolizing Richard's island kingdom. Also in this room is a vast altarpiece by **Jacopo di Cione**, whose richly patterned canvases are like
gilded jewels, with the figures of Christ and Mary distinguished by
their white and gold robes. In Room 54, it's worth pausing to admire
the surprisingly realistic depiction of old age in the faces of the saints
who appear in the panels begun by Masaccio and completed by
Masolino.

Room 55

Paolo Uccello's blood-free *Battle of San Romano*, which dominates room 55, once decorated a Medici bedroom as part of a three-
panel frieze on the same theme. First and foremost, it's a commemoration of a recent Florentine victory over her bitter Sienese rivals,
but it's also an early essay in perspective: a foreshortened body, broken lances and pieces of armour are strewn across the foreground to
persuade the viewer that the picture is, in fact, three-dimensional.
The bucking white charger at the centre of the battle also appears in
Uccello's much smaller *St George and the Dragon*, one of the earliest surviving canvas paintings. Also in this room is another Medici
commission, *The Annunciation* by **Fra Filippo Lippi**, a beautifully
balanced painting in which the poses of Gabriel and Mary carefully
mirror one another, while the hand of God releasing the dove of the
Holy Spirit provides the vanishing point.

Jan van Eyck

Room 56

Room 56 switches to the beginnings of oil painting, which did away
with the painstaking overpainting of egg-based tempera and allowed
the artist to blend infinite gradations of pigment in the palette. The
possibilities of depicting the minutiae of life with oils were explored
by the likes of **Rogier van der Weyden** in *The Magdalen Reading*,

where even the nails in the floor are carefully picked out. But the master of early oil painting was **Jan van Eyck**, whose *Arnolfini Portrait* is an immensely sophisticated painting despite its seemingly mundane domestic setting: each object has been carefully chosen for its symbolism, from the dog, traditionally a symbol of fidelity, to the status-symbol orange tree that can be glimpsed through the window. The picture has often been interpreted as a depiction of a marriage ceremony – perhaps even a marriage certificate as, under Flemish law, a couple could marry without employing a priest – hence van Eyck's signature in Latin on the back wall, and his and another figure's appearance as witnesses in the mirror on the back wall (the dog alone acknowledges their presence). Such a marriage was only valid if the couple produced a child within a year, and this was thought to account for the apparently pregnant bride. However, the theory is now strongly criticized, and the bride is thought simply to be fashionably round-bellied, rather than actually pregnant. Whatever the truth, it is certainly one of the most intriguing paintings in the Sainsbury Wing.

Mantegna, Bellini, Botticelli and Raphael

It's back to Italian art in room 57, where one of **Mantegna**'s early works, *The Agony in the Garden*, demonstrates a convincing use of perspective, with one of the earliest successful renditions of middle distance; nearby, the dazzling dawn sky in the painting on the same theme by his brother-in-law, **Giovanni Bellini**, shows the artist's celebrated mastery of natural light. One of the most accomplished perspectivist paintings of the period was **Crivelli**'s *Annunciation*, an exercise in ornamentation and geometry, its single vanishing point the red hat of the man in the background standing before the window. *Room 57*

Botticelli's elongated *Venus and Mars* dominates room 58, with a naked and replete Mars in a deep postcoital sleep, watched over by a beautifully calm Venus, fully clothed and somewhat less overcome. His painting of the *Adoration of the Magi* hangs opposite, with the painter himself the best-dressed man at the Nativity, resplendent in bright red stockings and giving the audience a knowing look. The **Pollaiuolo** brothers' *Martyrdom of St Sebastian*, in room 59, reads like an anatomical textbook, with the three pairs of archers who surround the saint all striking different poses. Before moving on, don't miss the bloody excesses of **Piero di Cosimo**'s *Fight between the Lapiths and Centaurs*, apparently considered an entertaining subject for a marriage gift. *Rooms 58 & 59*

Room 60 contains the first batch of the National's nine works by **Raphael**, including the *Ansidei Madonna*, painted when the artist was a mere 21 years old, and another early work, *St Catherine of Alexandria*, whose sensuous "serpentine" pose is accentuated by the folds of her clothes. Room 61 has some fine examples of Mantegna's "cameo" paintings, which imitate the effect of classical *Rooms 60 & 61* stone reliefs, reflecting the craze among fashionable Venetian society for collecting antique engraved marbles and gems. The largest of them (painted to be viewed from below), *The Introduction of the Cult of Cybele*, was the artist's last work, and was commissioned by Francesco Cornaro, a Venetian nobleman who claimed descent from one of the greatest Roman families. The Venetian theme is continued with Bellini's *Doge Leonardo Loredan*, one of the artist's greatest portraits.

Bosch, Dürer, Memlinc, Bermejo and della Francesca

Rooms 62–64

The next three rooms, 62 to 64, take you away from Italy with a jolt; four manic tormentors (one wearing a dog's collar) bear down on Jesus in the National's one and only work by **Hieronymus Bosch**, *Christ Mocked*. Gerard David's *Christ Nailed to the Cross* is iconographically unusual in that Jesus (who shows no outward signs of pain) is being hammered onto his crucifix while flat on the ground. Look out, in room 63, for **Dürer**'s sympathetic portrait of his father (a goldsmith in Nuremberg), which was presented to Charles I in 1636 by the artist's home town.

In room 64 hangs **Memlinc**'s perfectly poised *Donne Triptych*, a portable (though rather heavy) altarpiece which features Memlinc himself peering from behind a pillar in the left-hand panel. In the same room, **Bartolomé Bermejo**'s masterly depiction of St Michael trouncing the devil is one of only twenty extant paintings by the Spanish artist. The devil looks like a giant cockroach, while the saint looks utterly resplendent in his shining armour and crumpled cloak – literally dressed to kill – the heavenly city reflected in his jewelled breastplate. Antonio Juan, the Lord of Tous, looks comically unmoved by the whole spectacle, casually leafing through the Book of Psalms, his sword still in its scabbard. The *cartellino* (scroll) on the floor beside the donor bears the painter's signature.

Room 66

At the far end of the wing, in room 66, it's back to Italy once more for **Piero della Francesca**'s monumental religious paintings: *The Nativity* and *The Baptism of Christ*, the latter one of Piero's earliest surviving pictures, dating from the 1450s and a brilliant example of his immaculate compositional technique. Blindness forced Piero to stop painting some twenty years before his death, and to concentrate instead on his equally innovative work as a mathematician.

Veronese, Titian and Giorgione

Room 9

The first main-building room you come to from the Sainsbury Wing is the vast Wohl Room (room 9), in the West Wing, containing mainly large-scale Venetian works. The largest of the lot is **Paolo Veronese**'s lustrous *Family of Darius before Alexander*, its array of colourfully clad figures revealing the painter's remarkable skill in juxtaposing virtually the entire colour spectrum in a single canvas. **Titian**'s even more colourful early masterpiece, *Bacchus and*

Ariadne, and his very late, much gloomier *Death of Actaeon*, separated by some fifty years, hang on either side of the far doorway, amply demonstrating the painter's artistic development and longevity. Also in room 9, *Madonna and Child* is a typical late work by Titian, with the paint jabbed on and rubbed in.

There are more Venetian works in room 10, including Titian's consummate *La Schiavana*, a precisely executed portrait within a portrait, and two typically perplexing paintings attributed to the elusive **Giorgione**, about whom very little is known. The octagonal room 11 contains all four of Veronese's slightly discoloured *Allegories of Love* canvases, designed as ceiling paintings, perhaps for a bedchamber.

Bronzino, Raphael and Michelangelo

In room 8, **Bronzino**'s strangely disturbing *Venus, Cupid, Folly and Time* is a classic piece of Mannerist eroticism, which suitably enough made its way into the hands of François I, the decadent, womanizing, sixteenth-century French king. It depicts Cupid about to embrace Venus as she, in turn, attempts to disarm him; above them Father Time tries to reveal the face of Fraud as nothing but a mask, while the cherub of Folly gets ready to shower the couple with roses; weirdest of all is the half-animal, half-human Pleasure, whose double-edged quality is symbolized by her honeycomb and the sting in her tail.

In the same room, **Raphael**'s trenchant *Pope Julius II* – his (and Michelangelo's) patron – is masterfully percipient, though the gallery's curators thought it was no more than a copy until it was cleaned in 1970. Here too is **Michelangelo**'s early, unfinished *Entombment*. Unlike earlier, static depictions, this painting shows Christ's body being hauled into the tomb, and has no fixed iconography by which to identify the figures – either of the women could be Mary Magdalene, for example, and it is arguable whether the man in red is John the Evangelist or Nicodemus. Michelangelo also provided drawings for the *Raising of Lazarus* by **Sebastiano del Piombo**, the largest painting in the room, which was originally commissioned for Narbonne cathedral.

One of the greatest portrait specialists of the Italian Renaissance was **Giovanni Moroni**, and several of his likenesses of the fashionably black-clad folk of Brescia and Bergamo can be seen in room 6. It has been suggested that Moroni's portrait of *The Tailor* was for services rendered, while Lorenzo Lotto's painting of his landlord and family was executed in lieu of a year's rent.

Holbein, Cranach, Bruegel and Gossaert

Room 4 contains several masterpieces by **Hans Holbein**, most notably his extraordinarily detailed double portrait, *The Ambassadors*. The French duo flank an open cabinet piled high with various objects: instruments for studying the heavenly realm on the upper shelf, those for contemplating the earthly life on the lower. The painting clearly demonstrates the subjects' wealth, power and intelligence, but also serves as an elaborate memento mori, a message underlined by the distorted skull in the foreground.

Among the other works by Holbein is his intriguing portrait *A Lady with a Squirrel and a Starling*, painted in 1527 during the artist's first visit to England. This striking portrait of the 16-year-old Christina of Denmark was part of a series commissioned by Henry VIII when he was looking for a potential fourth wife. The king eventually plumped for Anne of Cleves on the basis of Holbein's flattering portrait (now in the Louvre), though when he saw her in the flesh he was distinctly unimpressed with his "Flanders mare", after which Holbein fell from royal favour.

Holbein's contemporary, **Lucas Cranach the Elder**, made his name from slender, erotic nudes such as the model used for *Cupid Complaining to Venus*, a none-too-subtle message about dangerous romantic liaisons. Venus's enormous headgear only emphasizes her nakedness, while the German landscape, to the right, serves to give this mythological morality tale a distinctly "contemporary" edge.

Room 12

The gallery's only painting by **Bruegel**, *The Adoration of the Magi*, hangs round the corner in room 12, with some very motley-looking folk crowding in on the infant; only the Black Magus looks at all regal. Also in this room is the world's finest collection of works by the Flemish painter **Jan Gossaert**. The tiny *Virgin and Child* was only recently acknowledged as an original after a dendrochronologist dated the wood panel to 1501; it had been in storage for nearly seventy years. Despite the obvious power of the works by Bruegel and Gossaert, the painting that grabs most folks' attention is **Massys'** caricatured portrait of a grotesque old woman.

Vermeer and the Hoogstraten Peepshow

Rooms 16 & 17

The North Wing's seventeenth-century collection begins in room 16 with several austere church interiors by, among others, the chief specialist in the genre, **Emanuel de Witte**. Also in this small room is **de Hooch**'s classic *Courtyard of a House in Delft*, and two typically serene works by **Vermeer**, including *Young Woman Standing at a Virginal*, whose subject is now thought to be Vermeer's eldest daughter Maria, though nobody is quite sure of the relevance of the picture of Cupid holding a card that hangs above her. The darkened interior beyond room 17 is given over entirely to the seventeenth-century **van Hoogstraten Peepshow**, a box of tricks which perfectly illustrates the Dutch obsession of the time with perspectival and optical devices.

Turner, Claude and Poussin

Claude Lorrain's *Enchanted Castle*, in room 19, caught the imagination of the Romantics, supposedly inspiring Keats' *Ode to a*

Nightingale, while the English painter **J.M.W. Turner** left specific instructions in his will for two of his **Claude**-influenced paintings to be hung alongside a couple of the French painter's landscapes. All four now hang in the octagonal room 15, and were slashed by a homeless teenager in 1982 in an attempt to draw attention to his plight. Claude's dreamy classical landscapes and seascapes, and the mythological scenes of **Poussin** were favourites of aristocrats on the Grand Tour, and made both artists very famous in their time. Nowadays, though Poussin has a strong academic following, his works strike many people as empty and dull. Hardly surprising, then, that rooms 19 and 20, which are given over entirely to these two French artists, are among the quietest in the gallery.

The National Gallery

Rooms 15 & 18–20

The Yves Saint Laurent Room (room 18) is devoted to Parisian seventeenth-century paintings. Louis XIII's right-hand man, Cardinal Richelieu, is the subject of both the room's large, regal painting and of a triple portrait, both by **Philippe de Champaigne**.

Cuyp, Hobbema and Ruisdael

Rooms 21 & 22

Aelbert Cuyp's landscapes, a number of which hang in room 21, stand out due to the warm Italianate light which suffuses his views of his home town of Dordrecht. In room 22, the eye is drawn to the back wall, to one of the finest of all Dutch landscapes, **Hobbema**'s tree-lined *Avenue, Middleharnis*. The market for such landscapes at the time was limited, and Hobbema quit painting at the age of just thirty. **Jacob von Ruisdael**, Hobbema's teacher, whose works are on display nearby, also went hungry for most of his life.

Rembrandt, Rubens and van Dyck

Room 23

Room 23 is dominated by **Rembrandt**'s splendid equestrian portrait of Frederick Rihel, painted to commemorate the entry of William of Orange into Amsterdam in 1660. Elsewhere in the room, two of Rembrandt's searching self-portraits, painted thirty years apart, regard each other – the melancholic *Self Portrait Aged 63*, from the last year of his life, making a strong contrast with the sprightly early work. Similarly, the joyful portrait of Saskia, Rembrandt's wife, from the most successful period of his life, contrasts with his more contemplative depiction of his mistress, Hendrickje, who was hauled up in front of the city authorities for living "like a whore" with Rembrandt. The largest Rembrandt picture in the room is the highly theatrical *Belshazzar's Feast*, painted for a rich Jewish patron. The portraits of Jacob Trip and his wife are among the most painfully realistic depictions of old age in the entire gallery.

Several small rooms of Dutch painting follow, mostly genre and specialist stuff. In room 27, however, you'll find a striking *View of Delft*, painted as if through a fish-eye lens by **Carel Fabritius**, Rembrandt's greatest pupil, just two years before he died in the calamity depicted in **van der Heyden**'s *View of Delft after the Explosion of 1654*, which hangs in the same room.

Three adjoining rooms, known collectively as room 29, are dominated by the expansive, fleshy canvases of **Peter Paul Rubens**, the Flemish painter whom Charles I summoned to the English court; a prime example is his *Samson and Delilah*. The one woman with her clothes on is the artist's future sister-in-law, Susanna Fourment, whose delightful portrait became known as *Le Chapeau de Paille* (*The Straw Hat*) – though the hat is actually made of black felt and decorated with white feathers. At the age of 54, Rubens married Susanna's younger sister, Helena (she was just 16), the model for all three goddesses posing in the later version of *The Judgement of Paris*, painted in the 1630s. Also displayed here are Rubens' rather more subdued landscapes, one of which, the *View of Het Steen*, shows off the very fine prospect from the Flemish country mansion Rubens bought in 1635, earning himself the title Lord of Steen. Another Flemish painter summoned by Charles I was **Anthony van Dyck**, whose most familiar work here is his portrait of *Cornelius van der Geest*, a wealthy merchant from the painter's home town of Antwerp.

Velázquez, El Greco, van Dyck and Caravaggio

The cream of the National Gallery's Spanish works are displayed in room 30, among them **Velázquez**'s *Kitchen Scene with Christ in the House of Martha and Mary*, where Mary's choice of the contemplative life is held up for approval, though the sensuous pleasure of the painting, which focuses on moody Martha's domestic chores, might suggest the opposite. A less ambivalent sensuality pervades the startling *Rokeby Venus*, one of the gallery's most famous pictures, painted when Velázquez was court painter to Philip IV, himself the subject of two portraits displayed here. Despite being a religious fanatic, Philip owned several paintings of nudes, though with the Inquisition at its height they were considered a highly immoral subject. Velázquez is nonetheless known to have painted at least four in his lifetime, of which only the *Rokeby Venus* survives, an ambiguously narcissistic image that was slashed in 1914 by suffragette Mary Richardson, who loved the picture but was revolted by the way it was leered at. Slightly lost in this vast room is the diminutive masterpiece *Christ Driving Traders from the Temple*, by the Cretan painter **El Greco**. Its acidic colouring and angular composition are typical of his highly individual work.

Next door, amidst the formal state portraits in room 31, is **van Dyck**'s *Equestrian Portrait of Charles I*, a fine example of the work that made him a favourite of the Stuart court, romanticizing the monarch as a dashing horseman. Adjacent is the artist's double portrait of *Lord John and Lord Bernard Stuart*, two dapper young cavaliers about to set out on their Grand Tour in 1639, and destined to die fighting for the royalist cause shortly afterwards in the Civil War. Two huge canvases by Rubens can also be seen here, including *Peace and War*, which he presented to King Charles I in 1630 during his diplomatic mission on behalf of the Archduchess Isabella, Regent of the Spanish Netherlands.

Caravaggio's art is represented in room 32 by the typically salacious *Boy Bitten by Lizard*, and the melodramatic *Christ at Emmaus*. The latter was a highly influential painting: never before had biblical scenes been depicted with such naturalism – a beardless and haloless Christ surrounded by scruffy disciples. At the time it was deemed to be blasphemous, and, like many of Caravaggio's religious commissions, was eventually rejected by the customers.

From room 32, you enter the East Wing, which begins with a small room (33) of French art – including works by Fragonard, Boucher, Watteau and a spirited self-portrait by **Elizabeth Louise Vigée le Brun**, one of only three women artists in the whole National Gallery collection – before moving on into the Sackler Room (room 34), where most of the gallery's British art hangs. *Room 33*

Room 34

Turner to Tiepolo

When the Tate Gallery first opened on Millbank in 1897, the vast bulk of the National's British art section was transferred there, leaving a small but highly prized core of works behind. These include a number of superb late masterpieces by **Turner**, two of which herald the new age of steam: *Rain, Steam and Speed* and *The "Fighting Téméraire"*, in which a ghostly apparition of the veteran battleship from Trafalgar is pulled into harbour by a youthful, fire-snorting tug, a scene witnessed first-hand by the artist in Rotherhithe. Here, too, is **Constable**'s *Hay Wain*, probably the most famous British painting of all time, though it was just one of a series of landscapes that he painted in and around his father's mill in Suffolk, such as the irrepressibly popular *Cornfield*. There are also several works by **Thomas Gainsborough** – landscapes, as well as the portraits at which this quintessentially British artist excelled. The painting of the actress Sarah Siddons is one of his finest "grand ladies", and his feathery, light technique is seen to superb effect in *Morning Walk*, a double portrait of a pair of newlyweds. **Joshua Reynolds**' contribution is a portrait of *Lady Cockburn and her Three Sons*, in which the three boys clamber endearingly over their mother.

There are more works by Gainsborough and Reynolds in the neighbouring room (35), including the only known portrait of the former with his family, painted in 1747 when he was just 20 years old. On the opposite wall are the six paintings from **Hogarth**'s *Marriage à la Mode*, a witty, moral tale that allowed the artist to give vent to his pet hates: bourgeois hypocrisy, snobbery and bad (ie Continental) taste. Where Gainsborough excelled in his "grand ladies", his rival Reynolds was at his best with male sitters – as in the *Rooms 35 & 36* dramatic portrait of the extraordinarily effeminate Colonel Tarleton, displayed in the ornate, domed Central Hall (room 36).

Room 38 features **Canaletto**'s *Stonemason's Yard*, an unusual portrayal of everyday Venetian life compared to his usual glittery vistas of Venice (of which there are also several examples). In room 39, **Guardi**'s postcard snaps of Venice hang rather awkwardly alongside **Goya**'s gloomy portrait of the Duke of Wellington. Close by, in room 40, are examples of the airy draughtsmanship of **Tiepolo**, father and son, seen to best effect in the *Allegory with Venus and Time*, commissioned for the ceiling of a Venetian *palazzo*.

From David to Picasso

Room 41

In room 41, the only two paintings in Britain by the supreme Neoclassicist **Jacques-Louis David** hang alongside works by **Delacroix**, who was profoundly impressed by Constable's dappled application of paint. One of the most eye-catching pictures is **Ingres**'s elegant portrait of a wealthy banker's wife, *Madame Moitessier*, completed when the artist had reached the age of 76, having taken twelve years to finish. **Gustave Courbet**'s languorous *Young Ladies on the Bank of the Seine* looks innocent enough to the modern eye, but it caused a scandal when it was first shown in 1857 due to the ladies' "state of undress". Nowadays, the most popular of all the paintings in the room is **Paul Delaroche**'s slick and phoney *Execution of Lady Jane Grey*, in which the blindfolded, white-robed, 17-year-old queen stoically awaits her fate.

Rooms 42–46

Five magnificent rooms of Impressionist and early twentieth-century paintings close the proceedings, starring, in room 43, **Manet**'s unfinished *Execution of Maximilian*. This was one of three versions Manet painted of the subject and was cut into pieces during the artist's lifetime, then bought and reassembled by Degas after Manet's death. The fashionable crowd in Manet's *Music in the Tuileries Gardens* includes the poet Baudelaire and the artist Fantin-Latour. Other major Impressionist works usually displayed here include **Degas**'s *Miss La-La at the Cirque Fernando*, **Renoir**'s *Umbrellas*, **Monet**'s *Thames below Westminster* and his *Gare St Lazare*, for which he had the entire station cleared of commuters. There are also several townscapes from **Pissarro**'s period of exile, when he lived in south London, having fled Paris before the advancing Prussian army. In the tiny room (42) to the side of room 43, there's a mixed bag of smaller-scale works, including several landscapes by **Corot**, and, more surprisingly, a sentimental *Winter Landscape* by **Caspar David Friedrich**, one of the few works by the German Romantic painter on public display in this country.

The Courtauld Institute (p.196) also has a superb collection of Impressionists.

Seurat's classic "pointilliste" canvas, *Bathers at Asnières*, in room 44, is one of the National's most reproduced paintings, along with Pissarro's *Boulevard Montmartre at Night*. There's a comprehensive showing of **Cézanne** in room 45, with works spanning the great artist's long life. *The Painter's Father* is one of his earliest extant works, and was originally painted onto the walls of his father's house outside Aix. *The Bathers*, by contrast, is a very late work, whose angular geometry exercised an enormous influence on the Cubism of Picasso and Braque.

The
National
Gallery

Several late canvases by **van Gogh** also hang in room 45: the beguiling *Van Gogh's Chair*, dating from his stay in Arles with Gauguin, the trademark *Wheatfield with Cypresses* and *Long Grass with Butterflies*, which typifies the intense work he produced inside the asylum to which he was committed shortly before his suicide. The most famous of the lot, though, his dazzling *Sunflowers*, is just one of seven versions he painted, one of which became the most expensive picture ever sold when it was bought for over £24,000,000 in 1987 by a Japanese insurance company. Van Gogh himself sold only one painting in his lifetime, and used to dream of finding someone who would pay just £25 for his work.

Many of the National's early twentieth-century paintings have been loaned to the Tate in return for late nineteenth-century works, making 1900 the theoretical cut-off point between the two galleries. In reality, though, there's plenty of overlap; Monet's *Water-Lilies* (painted after 1916) currently hangs in the Tate Modern, while his *Irises* study, from as late as 1914, hangs in room 46 of the National. In the same room, you'll also find **Picasso**'s sentimental Blue Period *Child with a Dove*, Degas's luxuriant red-orange *La Coiffure* and Vuillard's *Young Girls Walking*, with its deliberately flat, decorative surfaces.

*For a more
comprehensive
display of
modern art,
visit the new
Tate Modern
on Bankside;
see p.311.*

The National Portrait Gallery

Daily 10am–6pm (Thurs & Fri till 9pm); free; ☎020/7306 0055; *www.npg .org.uk*. Leicester Square or Charing Cross tube.

Around the east side of the National Gallery lurks the **National Portrait Gallery** (NPG), which was founded in 1856 to house uplifting depictions of the good and the great. Though it undoubtedly has some fine works among its collection of ten thousand portraits, many of the studies are of less interest than their subjects. Nevertheless, it is interesting to trace who has been deemed worthy of admiration at any moment: aristocrats and artists in previous centuries, warmongers and imperialists in the early decades of this century, writers and poets in the 1930s and 1940s. The most popular part of the museum by far is the contemporary section, where the whole thing degenerates into a sort of thinking person's Madame Tussaud's, with photos and very dubious portraits of retired footballers, politicians and film and pop stars.

Visiting the gallery

There are two **entrances** to the NPG: disabled access is from Orange Street, while the main entrance is on St Martin's Lane, opposite the statue of Edith Cavell, the nurse who was accused of spying and shot by the Germans in 1915. Once inside, head straight for the bright, white new Ondaatje Wing, where you'll find the main information desk. To view the collection chronologically, as the account below does, take the escalator to the second floor, and work down. The gallery's **special exhibitions** (for which there is often an entrance charge) are well worth seeing – the photography shows, in particular, are often excellent.

You might like to avail yourself of the NPG's **Soundguide**, which gives useful biographical background information to many of the pictures. The service is provided free of charge, though you're strongly invited to give a "voluntary contribution". Before or after viewing the works, you can play around on a CD-Rom of the collection in the new mezzanine **IT Gallery**, or simply collapse in the nearby comfy chairs. There's a café on the ground floor, but if you want to splash out, the NPG's new **rooftop restaurant** serves pricey Modern British cuisine, and dishes out great views over Trafalgar Square, and down Whitehall to Big Ben.

The Tudor Galleries

Second Floor

The **Tudor Galleries** on the second floor kick off with a large painting of **Sir Thomas More** (based on an earlier one by Holbein), in which the martyr is surrounded by his soberly dressed ancestors. Beyond, in room 1, there are Tudor portraits of pre-Tudor kings, and a stout **Cardinal Wolsey** looking like the butcher's son he was. Holbein's larger-than-life cartoon of **Henry VIII**, a preparatory drawing for a much larger fresco in Whitehall Palace, shows the king as a macho buck against a modish Renaissance background. The composition is deliberately echoed in the nearby portrait of his sickly young son and heir, **Edward VI**.

In room 2 hangs the intriguing *Allegory of the Reformation under Edward VI*, in which the boy-king is depicted casting down the pope and burning religious images. By contrast, the future **Bloody Mary** looks positively benign in a portrait celebrating her reinstatement to the line of succession in 1544. The most eye-catching canvas, however, is the anamorphic portrait of the syphilitic **Edward VI**, Henry's only male heir. An illusionistic device (similar to that used on the skull in Holbein's *Ambassadors* in the National Gallery), the painting must be looked at from the side to be viewed properly.

Also in room 2 are several classic propaganda portraits of the formidable Elizabeth I and her various favourites. The only known painting of **Shakespeare** from life hangs in room 3, a subdued image in which the Bard sports a gold-hoop earring; appropriately enough, it was the first picture acquired by the gallery. Close by is the "rocky face" of his one-time rival playwright, **Ben Jonson**. The exquisite Tudor miniatures in this room also deserve attention.

The seventeenth century: the Stuarts

Leading personalities from the Jacobean court hang in room 4, including an outrageously camp full-length portrait of the **Duke of Buckingham** showing off his lovely long legs. A favourite of James I, he was deeply unpopular with everyone except the king, and was eventually assassinated at the age of just 36.

To keep to the chronology, you must turn left here into room 5, where the portraiture goes up a notch thanks to the appointment of van Dyck as court painter. Both sides of the Civil War are represented: **Oliver Cromwell** is depicted looking dishevelled but masterful, while the future **Charles II**, painted at four months old, appears dressed in drag and clutching a toy spaniel. Further on, in room 7, an overdressed, haggard adult Charles hangs alongside his long-suffering Portuguese wife and his most famous mistress, the orange-seller turned actress Nell Gwynne.

There's more romance in room 8, where you can view **Queen Anne**, her double chin, and her long-term lover, the cocky-looking Duchess of Marlborough.

The eighteenth century: the Georgian period

The eighteenth century begins in room 9, which is filled with members of the **Kit-Kat Club**, a group of Whig patriots – including Robert Walpole – who met in a pub run by one Christopher Cat. The club was formed to ensure the Protestant succession at the end of William's reign and painted by one of its members, Godfrey Kneller, a naturalized German artist, whose self-portrait can be found in room 10. Keeping company with Kneller is an energetic and determined **William Hogarth**, depicted in a terracotta bust by **Roubiliac**, the Duchess of Queensbery, a friend of the literati who died of "a surfeit of cherries", according to the caption, and Hogarth's nemesis, **Lord Burlington**, who strikes an arty pose with his cap and protractor.

Room 11 contains a hotchpotch of visionaries such as Blind **John Fielding**, who established the Bow Street Runners (see p.155), and **Jacobites**, including a juvenile-looking Bonnie Prince Charlie and his saviour, the petite Flora MacDonald. Among the various artists, writers and musicians in room 12 are several fine self-portraits: **George Stubbs** painted in monkish garb onto a Wedgwood plaque, a relaxed **Thomas Gainsborough** and a perplexed and youthful **Joshua Reynolds**.

Political figures dominate room 14, where the dramatic death of **Pitt the Elder** is depicted; he collapsed in the House of Lords having struggled in to denounce American Independence. **Captain Cook** can be seen in room 11, and close by, there's a mezzotint of his Tahitian lover, Omai, who caused a sensation when he was brought back to England in 1774. At this point, the first caricatures begin to creep into the collection, led by Gilray and Hogarth, though there are significantly more in room 17, where you'll find a bold likeness of

Lord Nelson, along with one of the many idealized portraits painted by the smitten George Romney of Nelson's mistress, Lady Emma Hamilton.

The Romantics get room 18 to themselves, with the ailing John Keats painted posthumously by Joseph Severn, in whose arms he died in Rome. Elsewhere, there's Lord Byron in Albanian garb, an open-collared Percy Bysshe Shelley, with his mother-in-law, Mary Wollstonecraft, above it, and a moody image of William Wordsworth by the historical painter Benjamin Haydon. Painted in response to Wordsworth's sonnet on another of Haydon's pictures, this portrait itself became the subject of Elizabeth Barrett Browning's sonnet, *Wordsworth on Helvellyn*.

Passing by the worthy inventors of the Industrial Revolution in room 19, you reach the final room on this level, room 20, where there's a portrait of George IV and, opposite, the twice-widowed Catholic woman, Maria Fitzherbert, whom he married without the consent of his father. His official wife, Queen Caroline, is depicted at the adultery trial in the House of Lords at which she was acquitted. Close by, Caroline is depicted again, with sleeves rolled up ready for her sculpture lessons, in an audacious portrait by Thomas Lawrence, who was called to testify on his conduct with the queen during the painting of the portrait.

The Victorians

First Floor

Down on the first floor are the Victorians: mostly stuffy royalty, dour men of science and engineering, and stern statesmen such as those lining the corridor of room 22. Centre stage, in room 21, is a comical statue of Victoria and Albert in Anglo-Saxon garb, while on the far wall there's the striking sight of rank upon rank of bronze busts of yet more Victorian worthies. Room 24, by contrast, concentrates on the arts, with one deteriorated and oddly affecting group showing the Brontë sisters as seen by their disturbed brother Branwell; you can still see where he painted himself out, leaving a ghostly blur between Charlotte and Emily. Nearby are the poetic duo, Robert and Elizabeth Barrett Browning, looking totally Gothic in their grim Victorian dress.

One of the most notable features on this floor is the emergence of photography as an art form. There's a snapshot of Queen Victoria with her Scottish manservant, John Brown, in room 23, and another of Queen Victoria with her Indian servant by her side at Frogmore, in the grounds of Windsor, in room 19. Several great early Victorian photographs are displayed further on in room 27: one, by Julia Margaret Cameron, showing the astronomer John Herschel looking like the proverbial mad professor; the other, of engineer Isambard Kingdom Brunel, perkily posed in front of colossal iron chains.

Before you abandon the Victorians entirely, it's worth popping into room 28, where there are some excellent John Singer Sargent

portraits, and room 29, where you can see work by the Slade students: **Augustus John**, looking very confident and dapper at the age
of just 22, his sister, **Gwen John**, **Walter Sickert** and **Philip Wilson
Steer**, who founded the New English Arts Club, at which the last two
portraits were originally exhibited.

The twentieth century

The twentieth-century collection begins in room 30, with a parade of
World War I generals and an effigy of **T.E. Lawrence**, better known
as "Lawrence of Arabia", rendered in concrete. The interwar years
are then generously covered in the large room 31, the final one on
this floor. The faces on display here change from time to time, but
there are always one or two genuine works of art, such as Jacob
Epstein's vigorously sculpted busts of **Ralph Vaughan Williams** and
T.S. Eliot. Augustus John portrays **Dylan Thomas** as a ruddy-lipped
Celt in a leopard-skin jumper, while Lucien Freud depicts Stephen
Spender as a friendly old queen. There's the odd surprise, too, such
as the very Deco-ish aluminium bust of **Edith Sitwell** by Maurice
Lambert, and the early hologram portrait from the 1960s of the
father of holography, Dennis Gabor. Finally, don't miss the unusual
oil and pencil self-portrait by the sculptor **Barbara Hepworth**, and a
equally arresting double portrait of her and her husband **Ben
Nicholson** (by the latter).

Out on the Balcony Gallery, the really popular display of who's
who (or was who) in postwar Britain begins in **Britain 1960–90**.
Even here, amid the photos of the Beatles and the Stones, there are
a few genuine works of art: Leon Kossoff's self-portrait, a superbly
sinister smudge of thick grey and cream impasto, the odd Andy
Warhol screen print and a gilded life mask of Francis Bacon. If you
want to find (or skip) the current **Royal Family**, they've been banished to the first floor landing of the old staircase.

Britain since 1990

The contemporary collection, **Britain since 1990**, on the ground
floor, is an unashamedly populist trot through the media personalities of the last ten years. The displays here are rearranged more often
than any others, according to the whims and tastes of the day, making it difficult to predict exactly what will be on show. In addition,
much of the space is used for the gallery's excellent temporary
exhibitions.

Ground Floor

Sadly, there are some pretty uninspired paintings here, epitomized
by Bryan Organ's obsequious renderings of the great and the good.
Amid the welter of publicity photos, you'll find oil paintings of the
most unlikely folk, from Germaine Greer to Bobby Charlton. One of
the more diverting pieces is a copper-sheet and plastic sculpture of
ballerina Lynn Seymour by the high priest of British camp, Andrew
Logan, which hangs from the ceiling of the central hall of room 36.

The Mall

The tree-lined sweep of **The Mall** – London's nearest equivalent to Haussmann's Parisian boulevards – was laid out in the first decade of the twentieth century as a memorial to Queen Victoria, and runs along the northern edge of St James's Park. The bombastic **Admiralty Arch**, most recently used as a hostel for the homeless, was erected to mark the entrance at the Trafalgar Square end of The Mall, while at the other end stands the ludicrous **Victoria Memorial**, Edward VII's overblown tribute to his mother: Truth, Motherhood and Justice keep Victoria company around the plinth, which is topped by a gilded statue of Victory, while the six outlying allegorical groups in bronze confidently proclaim the great achievements of her reign.

There has been a thoroughfare on the site of The Mall since the Restoration, though its most distinctive building is John Nash's Carlton House Terrace, whose graceful cream-coloured Regency facade stretches away into the distance beyond Admiralty Arch. Among other things, it serves as the unlikely home of the **Institute of Contemporary Arts** (ICA), London's official headquarters of the avant-garde, so to speak, which puts on a regular programme of provocative exhibitions, films, talks and performances. Many people pay the day membership simply for admission to the bar, which stays open till 1am most nights and has the unusual distinction of being a trendy gathering point with no style arbiters or bouncers on the door. There's also a good Italian-run café/restaurant and an arts bookshop with cutting-edge stock.

The Mall is best viewed on Sundays, when it's closed to traffic. The nearest tubes are Charing Cross, Green Park and St James's Park.

The ICA is open Mon–Sat noon–1am, Sun noon–10.30pm; day pass Mon–Fri £1.50, Sat & Sun £2.50; ☎020/7930 3647; www .ica.org.uk.

For Carlton House Terrace and the grand houses to the north of the park, see p.107.

St James's Park

St James's Park, on the south side of The Mall, is the oldest of London's royal parks, having been drained and enclosed for hunting purposes by Henry VIII and opened to the public by Charles II, who used to stroll through the grounds with his mistresses, and even take a dip in the canal. By the eighteenth century, when some 6500 people had access to night keys for the gates, the park had become something of a byword for prostitution: Boswell was, of course, among those who went there specifically to be accosted "by several ladies of the town". The park was finally landscaped by Nash into its present elegant appearance in the 1820s, in a style that established the trend for Victorian city parks.

Today, the tree-lined lake is a favourite picnic spot for the civil servants of Whitehall and an inner-city reserve for wildfowl. James I's two crocodiles have left no descendants, alas, but the pelicans (who have resided here ever since a pair was presented to Charles II by the Russian ambassador) can still be seen at the eastern end of the lake, and there are exotic ducks, swans and Canada geese aplenty. From the bridge across the lake there's a fine view over to Westminster and the jumble of domes and pinnacles along Whitehall; even the dull facade of Buckingham Palace looks majestic from here.

Buckingham Palace

Aug & Sept daily 9.30am–4.15pm; £10; advance booking on ☎020/7321 2233; general information ☎020/7930 4832; *www.royal.gov.uk*. Green Park tube.

The graceless colossus of **Buckingham Palace**, popularly known as "Buck House", has served as the monarch's permanent London residence only since the accession of Victoria. It began its days in 1702 as the Duke of Buckingham's city residence, built on the site of a notorious brothel, and was sold by the duke's son to George III in 1762. The building was overhauled by Nash in the late 1820s for the Prince Regent, and again by Aston Webb in time for George V's coronation in 1913, producing a palace that's about as bland as it's possible to be.

The Royal Standard flies from the roof of Buckingham Palace if the Queen is in residence. Her Majesty is not at home during public visiting months.

For ten months of the year there's little to do here, with the Queen in residence and the palace closed to visitors – not that this deters the crowds who mill around the railings all day, and gather in some force to watch the **Changing of the Guard** (see box on p.76), in which a detachment of the Queen's Foot Guards marches to appropriate martial music from St James's Palace (unless it rains, that is).

Until relatively recently, unless you were one of the select 30,000 invited to attend one of the Queen's three annual garden parties – the replacements for the society debutantes' "coming out" parties, which ceased to be royally sanctioned in 1958 – you had little chance of ever seeing inside Buckingham Palace. Since 1993, however, the hallowed portals have been grudgingly nudged open for two months of the year. **Tickets** are sold on-line or from the marquee-like box office in Green Park; queues vary enormously, but average around forty minutes, after which there's a further wait until your allocated visiting time. While you're waiting, take a moment to admire the unusual **Canadian Memorial**, beside the ticket office. Erected in 1994, it's a beautiful abstract work comprised of a huge piece of dark red granite from Nova Scotia, randomly scattered with maple leaf patterning and washed over with water.

The interior

Once inside, it's all a bit of an anticlimax, despite the voyeuristic pleasure of a glimpse behind those forbidding walls: of the palace's 660 rooms you're permitted to see around twenty, and as the Queen and her family decamp to Scotland every summer, there's little sign of life. The public entrance is via the **Ambassadors' Court** on Buckingham Palace Road, which lets you into the enormous **Quadrangle**, from where you can see the Nash portico, built in warm Bath stone, that looked over St James's Park until it was closed off by Queen Victoria. Through the courtyard, you hit the **Grand Hall**, site of the Duke of

Buckingham's original entrance hall and decorated to the taste of Edward VII in a frenzy of red carpets, gold and marble.

From the hall, Nash's winding, curlicued **Grand Staircase**, with its floral gilt-bronze balustrade, leads past a range of dull royal portraits, all beautifully lit by Nash's glass dome. Beyond, the small Guard Room, decorated with Gobelin tapestries and nineteenth-century sculpture, is a mere formality that leads into the **Green Drawing Room**, a blaze of unusually bright green silk walls, framed

---

The Royal Family

Tourists may still flock to see London's royal palaces, but over the last decade, the British public have become more critical of the huge tax bill that goes to support the **Royal Family** (*www.royal.gov.uk*) in the style to which they are accustomed. This creeping republicanism can be traced back to 1992, which the Queen herself, in one of her few memorable Christmas Day speeches, accurately described as her *annus horribilis* ("One's Bum Year" as a *Sun* headline pithily put it). This was the year that saw the marriage break-ups of Charles and Di, and Andrew and Fergie, and the second marriage of divorcee Princess Anne.

Matters came to a head towards the end of the year over who should pay the estimated £50 million cost of repairs after the fire at Windsor Castle (p.485). Misjudging the public mood, the Conservative government immediately offered taxpayers' money to foot the entire bill. After a furore, it was agreed that at least some of the cost would be raised from the astronomical admission charges to Windsor Castle and to Buckingham Palace. In addition, under pressure from public opinion polls, the media and even some Tory backbenchers, the Queen also offered to reduce the number of royals paid out of the Civil List, and, for the first time in her life, pay taxes on her personal fortune.

Estimates of the Queen's wealth range from a modest £50 million to £6.5 billion, a calculation famously dismissed by Prince Edward as "absolute crap". Whatever the truth, she's certainly not hard up, and public subsidy of the richest woman in the world doesn't stop at the Civil List, as millions more are spent by government departments on luxuries such as the Royal Train, not to mention the upkeep of the palaces. Given the mounting public resentment against the Royal Family, it was hardly surprising that public opinion tended to side with Princess Diana rather than Prince Charles during their acrimonious divorce proceedings. Diana's subsequent death, and the huge outpouring of grief that accompanied her funeral, further damaged the reputation of the royals, though her demise has also meant the loss of one of the Royal Family's most vociferous critics.

Despite the general disenchantment with the Royal Family, public appetite for stories about the adolescent princes (and their potential girlfriends, fox-hunting antics and so forth), or the status of the relationship between Charles and Camilla, shows little sign of abating. None of the political parties would dare to advocate abolishing the monarchy, though Buckingham Palace is now acutely aware of the volatility of public opinion, and its press officers currently work overtime at trying to minimize the gaffes that have characterized the monarchy in recent years.

---

by lattice-patterned pilasters, and a heavily gilded coved ceiling. It was here that the Raphael Cartoons used to hang, until they were permanently loaned to the V&A (see p.346). In the scarlet and gold **Throne Room**, there's an unusual Neoclassical plaster frieze, depicting the War of the Roses, two winged figures holding up the proscenium arch, but disappointingly, no regal throne – just two pink his 'n' hers chairs initialled ER and P.

Nash's vaulted **Picture Gallery**, stretching right down the centre of the palace, is more impressive, though the original spectacular hammerbeam ceiling was replaced by a rather dull glazed arched ceiling in 1914. On show here is a selection of the Royal Collection (see below) – among them several van Dycks, two Rembrandts and an excellent Vermeer. From the East Gallery, you are now allowed into the palace's vast **Ballroom**, where Prince Charles had his fiftieth birthday bash. It is here that the Queen holds her State Banquets, and where the annual Diplomatic Reception takes place, with 1500 guests present. The Ballroom is also the venue for Investitures, at which folk receive their honours and knighthoods. Having passed through several smaller rooms, you eventually reach the stultifyingly scarlet and gilt **State Dining Room** and, beyond, Nash's **Blue Drawing Room**, with thirty fake onyx columns, flock wallpaper, yet more gilt coving and an extraordinary Sèvres porcelain table made for Napoleon.

The best place from which to view the palace grounds is the enormous semicircular bow window of the domed **Music Room**, where the current royal offspring were all baptized with water brought from the River Jordan. The frothy gold and white Nash ceiling and priceless French antiques of the **White Drawing Room** form the incongruous setting for an annual royal prank: when hosting the reception for the diplomatic corps, the Queen and family emerge from a secret door behind the fireplace to greet the ambassadors – nobody seems clear why. Before you leave the palace, be sure to check out the Canova sculptures: *Fountain Nymph* at the bottom of the Ministers' Staircase, and *Mars and Venus* in the Marble Hall.

Queen's Gallery

Due to open February 2002; for more information phone ☎020/7930 4832 or visit *www.hrp.org.uk*. Victoria tube.

From spring 2002, the public will be able to view more of the monarch's art collection at the new, greatly expanded **Queen's Gallery** on the south side of the palace, designed at a cost of £15 million by John Simpson. Until recently, much of the Royal Collection – which is more than three times larger than the National Gallery's – has remained hidden from public view. Among the works on display will be paintings by Michelangelo, Reynolds, Gainsborough, Vermeer, van Dyck, Rubens, Rembrandt and Canaletto, as well as the odd Fabergé egg and heaps of Sèvres china.

The Mall

While on the subject of the Royal Collection, it's worth recalling that until 1979, the Surveyor of the Queen's Pictures was an ex-Russian spy, Anthony Blunt, KGB talent-spotter at Cambridge in the 1930s. This fact had been known to the British intelligence service, MI6, since 1964, when Blunt told all in a "keep it secret" deal with the Establishment, but it was not until fifteen years later that Parliament was informed. The press subsequently hounded Blunt, dwelling as much on his homosexuality ("the Queen's queen") as his espionage. He died shortly afterwards.

The Royal Mews

Mon–Thurs: Aug & Sept 10.30am–4.30pm; Oct–July noon–4pm; £4; ☎020/7930 4832; *www.hrp.org.uk*. Victoria tube.

There's more pageantry on show at the **Royal Mews**, further south on Buckingham Palace Road, built by Nash in the 1820s after the old mews were demolished to make way for Trafalgar Square. The horses – or at least their backsides – can be viewed in the stables, along with an exhibition of equine accoutrements, but it's the royal carriages, lined up under a glass canopy in the courtyard, that are the main attraction. The most ornate is the Gold Carriage, made for George III in 1762, smothered in 22-carat gilding and weighing four tons, its axles supporting four life-size figures. Eight horses are needed to pull it and the whole experience made Queen Victoria feel quite sick; since then it has only been used for coronations and jubilees.

The Girl Guide Heritage Centre

Mon–Sat 10am–5pm; £3; ☎020/7834 6242; *www.guides.org.uk*. Victoria tube.

Directly opposite the Royal Mews, at 17–19 Buckingham Palace Rd, is the **Girl Guide Heritage Centre**, housed in the headquarters of the movement, which has numbered the Queen and Princess Margaret among its members. The exhibition, whose entrance is round the back off Palace Street, is light on the history of the movement – it was founded in 1910, after an alarming number of girls turned up at the first ever Scout Rally the previous year, and subsequently run by Baden-Powell's sister, Agnes – but good on hands-on games for groups of girl guides.

The Wellington Barracks, Guards' Chapel and Museum

Guards' Museum: daily 10am–4pm; £2; ☎020/7414 3271. St James's Park tube.

Named for James I's aviary, which once stood here, Birdcage Walk runs along the south side of St James's Park, with the Neoclassical façade of the **Wellington Barracks**, built in 1833 and fronted by a parade ground, occupying more than half its length. Of the various buildings here, though, it's the modernist lines of the **Guards' Chapel** which come as the biggest surprise. Hit by a V-1 rocket bomb on the morning of June 18, 1944, killing 121 Sunday worshippers, the chapel was rebuilt in the 1960s. Inside, it's festooned with faded military flags, and retains the ornate Victorian apse, with Byzantine-style gilded mosaics, from the old chapel.

The Mall

In a bunker opposite is the **Guards' Museum**, which displays the glorious scarlet and blue uniforms of the Queen's Household Regiments (see box on p.76). The museum also attempts to explain the Guards' complicated history, and gives a potted military history of the country since the Civil War. Among the exhibits here are a lock of Wellington's hair, an impressive array of toy soldiers, and a whole load of war booty, from Dervish prayer mats plundered from Sudan in 1898 to items taken from an Iraqi POW during the Gulf War.

Whitehall

Whitehall, the unusually broad avenue connecting Trafalgar Square to Parliament Square, is synonymous with the faceless, pinstriped bureaucracy charged with the day-to-day running of the country. Since the sixteenth century, nearly all the key governmental ministries and offices have migrated here, rehousing themselves on an ever-increasing scale, a process which reached its apogee with the grimly bland **Ministry of Defence** building, the largest office block in London when it was completed in 1957. The statues dotted about Whitehall recall the days when this street stood at the centre of an empire on which the sun never set. Nowadays, with Scotland, Wales and Northern Ireland each having their own assemblies, Whitehall's remit is ever-decreasing.

During the sixteenth and seventeenth centuries, Whitehall was the permanent residence of the kings and queens of England, and was synonymous with royalty. The original **Whitehall Palace** was the London seat of the Archbishop of York, confiscated and greatly extended by Henry VIII after a fire at Westminster forced him to find alternative accommodation; it was here that he celebrated his marriage to Anne Boleyn in 1533, and here that he died fourteen years later. Described by one contemporary chronicler as nothing but "a heap of houses erected at diverse times and of different models, made continuous", it boasted some two thousand rooms and stretched for half a mile along the Thames. Little survived the fire of 1698, caused by a Dutch laundrywoman, after which, partly due to the dank conditions in this part of town, the royal residence shifted to Kensington.

WESTMINSTER AND WHITEHALL   7 5

Banqueting House

Mon–Sat 10am–5pm; £3.80; ☎020/7839 8918; *www.hrp.org.uk*. Charing Cross or Westminster tube.

The only sections of the palace that survived the 1698 fire are the **Banqueting House**, the first Palladian building to be built in England, begun by Inigo Jones in 1619, and Cardinal Wolsey's wine cellars, which now sit underneath the Ministry of Defence – sadly, the cellars are no longer open to the public. The Banqueting House opened in 1622 with a performance of Ben Jonson's *Masque of Angers*, with Jones providing the scenery and costumes; the entertainment took place in the main banqueting hall, which is still used for State occasions.

Other plays and masques were performed here until Charles I banned such shows in 1634 to prevent candle smoke damaging the ceiling paintings he had commissioned from **Rubens**, glorifying the Stuart dynasty. Sixteen years later, Charles walked through the room for the last time and stepped onto the executioner's scaffold from one of its windows. He wore several shirts in case he shivered in the cold, which the crowd would take to be fear; once his head was chopped off, it was then sewn back on again for burial in Windsor – a very British touch. The execution is still commemorated here on

---

The Changing of the Guard and royal parades

The Queen is colonel-in-chief of the seven **Household Regiments**: the Life Guards (who dress in red and white) and the Blues and Royals (who dress in blue and red) are the two Household Cavalry regiments; while the Grenadier, Coldstream, Scots, Irish and Welsh Guards make up the Foot Guards. The Foot Guards can only be told apart by the plumes (or lack of them) in their busbies, and by the arrangement of their tunic buttons. The three senior regiments (Grenadier, Coldstream and Scots) date back to the time of the Civil War, and all five still form part of the modern army as well as performing ceremonial functions such as the Changing of the Guard.

The **Changing of the Guard** takes place at two separate London locations: the two Household Cavalry regiments take it in turns to stand guard at the Horse Guards building on Whitehall (Mon–Sat 11am, Sun 10am), while the Foot Guards take care of Buckingham Palace (May–Aug daily 11.30am; Sept–April alternate days; no ceremony if it rains). A ceremony also takes place regularly in Windsor Castle (see p.485).

A considerably grander ceremony is the **Trooping of the Colour**, when one of the Household battalions presents its colour (flag) to the Queen for inspection, a spectacle memorably described by Labour minister Peter Mandelson as "lots of chinless wonders with bright scarlet uniforms". This takes place on the Saturday nearest the Queen's official birthday, June 6, with rehearsals (minus Her Majesty) on the two preceding Saturdays.

The ceremony takes place in Horse Guards' Parade, though you can watch the soldiers march to their destination along The Mall. If you want tickets for a seat in the stands around the parade ground, you'll need to reserve well in advance; phone ☎020/7414 2479.

---

the last Sunday in January with a parade by the royalist wing of the
Civil War Society.

Oliver Cromwell moved into the palace in 1654, having declared himself Lord Protector, and kept open table for the officers of his New Model Army; he died here in 1658. Two years later Charles II was welcomed here by the Lords and Commons for the Restoration, and kept open house for his adoring public – Samuel Pepys recalls seeing the underwear of one of his mistresses, Lady Castlemaine, hanging out to dry in the palace's Privy Garden. (Charles housed two mistresses and his wife here, with a back entrance onto the river for courtesans.) The weathervane on the north side of the roof was erected in 1686 by James II to warn of the foul "Protestant wind" that might propel William of Orange over the seas from Holland; it did little to protect James from the Glorious Revolution, however, and, after taking the throne in 1689, William and Mary came to live here until William's asthma forced them to move to Kensington.

The building continued to serve as the Chapel Royal until 1890, after which it was converted into a museum for the Royal United Services Institute. Then, in the 1960s, it was restored to something like its original condition. The one room open to the public has no original furnishings, but is well worth seeing for the superlative **Rubens** ceiling paintings, depicting the union of England and Scotland, the peaceful reign of James I and finally his apotheosis. The information boards posted in the room explain everything you need to know to appreciate the paintings; the video and the acoustophone commentary are not worth bothering with unless your English history is a bit thin and you want a rather formal remedy.

Horse Guards

Across the road, where Henry VIII had the palace cockfighting pit, tennis courts and a tiltyard, two mounted sentries of the Queen's Household Cavalry and two horseless colleagues, all in ceremonial uniform, are posted daily from 10am to 4pm. Ostensibly they are protecting the **Horse Guards** building, a modestly proportioned edifice begun in 1745 by William Kent, originally built as the old palace guard house, but now guarding nothing in particular. The mounted guards are changed hourly; those standing have to remain motionless and impassive for two hours before being replaced. Try to time your visit to coincide with the **Changing of the Guard** (Mon–Sat 11am, Sun 10am), when a squad of twelve mounted troops in full livery arrive from Hyde Park Barracks via Hyde Park Corner, Constitution Hill and The Mall. The main action takes place in the parade ground at the rear of the building overlooking Horse Guards' Parade. Alternatively, if you miss the whole thing, turn up at 4pm for the daily inspection by the Officer of the Guard, who checks the soldiers haven't knocked off early.

Downing Street and the Cenotaph

Further down this west side of Whitehall is London's most famous address, **10 Downing Street** (*www.number-10.gov.uk*), the terraced house that has been the residence of the Prime Minister or PM since it was presented to the First Lord of the Treasury, Sir Robert Walpole, Britain's first PM, by George II in 1732. With no. 11 – home of the Chancellor of the Exchequer since 1806 – and no. 12, home of the government's Chief Whip, it's the only remaining bit of the original seventeenth-century cul-de-sac, though all three are now interconnecting and, having been greatly modernized over the years, house much larger complexes than might appear from the outside. The public have been kept at bay since 1990, when Margaret Thatcher ordered a pair of iron gates to be installed at the junction with Whitehall, an act more symbolic than effective – a year later the IRA lobbed a mortar into the street from Horse Guards' Parade, coming within a whisker of wiping out the entire Tory cabinet.

Just beyond the Downing Street gates, in the middle of the road, stands Edwin Lutyens' **Cenotaph**, built in wood and plaster for the first anniversary of the Armistice in 1919, and rebuilt, by popular request, in Portland stone the following year. The stark monument, which eschews any kind of Christian imagery, is inscribed simply with the words "The Glorious Dead" – the lost of World War I, who, it was once calculated, would take three and a half days to pass by the Cenotaph marching four abreast. The memorial remains the focus of the Remembrance Sunday ceremony in November, with its "great awful silence", a two-minute silence once observed throughout the entire British Empire every year on November 11 at 11am.

Foreign & Commonwealth Office

Information centre: Mon–Fri 10am–5pm; free; ☎020/7270 1500; *www.fco .gov.uk*. Westminster tube.

The Cenotaph stands directly outside the front door of the colossal bulk of the **Foreign & Commonwealth Office**, designed in the style of an Italian palazzo in 1873 by Giles Gilbert Scott. As part of the new government's charm offensive, the FCO now has an **information centre**, where you can peruse their dull Web site, learn about the origins of the diplomatic corps' greyhound emblem, and watch a series of short documentaries on contemporary social and cultural issues in Britain. What you don't get to see, unfortunately, is any of the FCO's expensively refurbished interior, beyond a few tantalizing pictures. In order to admire Durbar Court, with its marble floor and glazed roof, and the ornate Grand Staircase, you need to enquire about one of the occasional open days (phone for details).

The Cabinet War Rooms

Daily: April–Sept 9.30am–6pm; Oct–March 10am–6pm; £5; ☎020/7930
6961; *www.iwm.org.uk*. Westminster or St James's Park tube.

In 1938, in anticipation of Nazi air raids, the basement of the civil
service buildings on the south side of King Charles Street were converted into the **Cabinet War Rooms**. Though these claustrophobic
suites were fragile in comparison with Hitler's bunker in Berlin (the
Führer's refuge was 50ft below ground, whereas Churchill's was protected only by a three-foot-thick concrete slab, reinforced with steel
rails and tramlines), it was here that Winston Churchill directed
operations and held cabinet meetings for the duration of World War
II. By the end of the war, the warren had expanded to cover more
than six acres, including a hospital, canteen and shooting range, as
well as cramped sleeping quarters; tunnels fan out from the complex
to outlying government ministries, and also, it is rumoured, to
Buckingham Palace itself, allowing the Royal Family a quick getaway
to exile in Canada (via Charing Cross station) in the event of a Nazi
invasion.

The rooms have been left pretty much as they were when they
were finally abandoned on VJ Day 1945, and make for an atmospheric underground trot through wartime London. To bring the
place to life, avail yourself of the museum's free acoustophone commentary (available in adult or child versions), which takes around 45
minutes to complete, and includes various eyewitness accounts by
folk who worked there. Along the way, you get to view Churchill's
secret telephone hotline direct to the American President, and his
emergency bedroom (though he himself rarely stayed there, preferring to watch the air raids from the roof of the building, or rest his
head at the *Savoy Hotel*). The Map Room, with its rank of multicoloured telephones and copious ashtrays, is lined with maps covering every theatre of war and showing the exact position of the front
line on VJ Day, 1945.

Parliament Square

Parliament Square was laid out in the mid-nineteenth century to
give the new Houses of Parliament and the adjacent Westminster
Abbey a grander setting. It has the dubious privilege of being one of
the city's first traffic roundabouts, though there are plans to pedes-
trianize the east side. Meanwhile, statues of notables – Abraham
Lincoln, Benjamin Disraeli and Jan Smuts, to name but a few – are
scattered amid the swirling cars and buses. Winston Churchill stoops
determinedly in the northeast corner of the central green.

Two other noteworthy statues punctuate nearby **Westminster
Bridge**: Boudicca (Boadicea), who led an uprising against the
Romans, can be seen keeping her horses and daughters under

control without the use of reins – Cowper's boast, "regions Caesar never knew, thy posterity shall sway", adorns the plinth – while on the south side of the bridge stands the Coade Stone Lion, made from a weather-resistant pottery, invented in the eighteenth century by Elizabeth Coade. Incidentally, Wordsworth's poem, *Lines Written upon Westminster Bridge* – "Earth has not anything to show more fair. . ." and so on – were addressed to the bridge's predecessor. The current one was only opened in 1862.

Right by Westminster Bridge stands the much criticized, but eco-friendly **Portcullis House**, designed by Michael Hopkins, unveiled in 1999 and topped by giant air ducts made to look like Victorian smokestacks. With parliament's MPs fighting for office space in the Palace of Westminster across the road (see below), more space was desperately needed; unfortunately, nobody considered the cheapest option: simply cutting the number of MPs from the present 659. Instead, £250 million of public money was spent building Portcullis House, whose name speaks volumes for the current administration's commitment to open government.

The Houses of Parliament

*The nearest
tube is
Westminster.*

The Palace of Westminster, better known as the **Houses of Parliament**, is London's best-known monument. The "mother of all parliaments" and the "world's largest building" – or so it was claimed – it is also the city's finest Victorian building, the symbol of a nation once confident of its place at the centre of the world. Best viewed from the south side of the river, where the likes of Monet and Turner

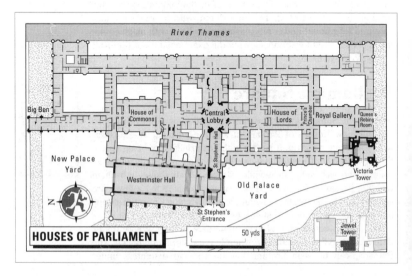

set up their easels, the building is distinguished above all by the ornate, gilded clock tower popularly known as **Big Ben**, which is at its most impressive when lit up at night. Strictly speaking, "Big Ben" refers only to the thirteen-ton main bell that strikes the hour (and is broadcast across the world by the BBC), and takes its name from either the former Commissioner of Works, Benjamin Hall, or a popular heavyweight boxer of the time, Benjamin Caunt.

The original Westminster Palace was built by **Edward the Confessor** in the first half of the eleventh century to allow him to watch over the building of his abbey. It then served as the seat of all the English monarchs until a fire forced Henry VIII to decamp to Whitehall. The Lords had always convened at the palace, but it was only following Henry's death that the House of Commons moved from the abbey's chapter house into the palace's St Stephen's Chapel, thus beginning the building's associations with parliament.

In 1834, the old palace burnt down after a fire, started by workmen setting alight wooden tally sticks, got out of hand. Save for a few pieces of the old structure buried deep within the interior, everything you see today is the work of **Charles Barry**, whose design had won the competition to create something that expressed national greatness through the use of Gothic and Elizabethan styles. The resulting orgy of honey-coloured pinnacles, turrets and tracery, somewhat restrained by the building's classical symmetry, is the greatest achievement of the Gothic Revival. Inside, the Victorian love of mock-Gothic detail is evident in the maze of over one thousand committee rooms and offices, the fittings of which were largely the responsibility of Barry's assistant, **Augustus Pugin**.

Westminster Hall

Virtually the only relic of the medieval palace is the bare expanse of **Westminster Hall**, on the north side of the complex. First built by William Rufus in 1099, it was saved from the 1834 fire by the timely intervention of the prime minister, Lord Melbourne, who had the fire engines brought into the hall itself, and personally took charge of the firefighting. The sheer scale of the hall – 240ft by 60ft – and its huge oak hammerbeam roof, added by Richard II in the late fourteenth century, make it one of the most magnificent secular medieval halls in Europe.

Unless you're on a guided tour, you can only peer down from St Stephen's Porch at the bare expanse that has witnessed some nine hundred years of English history. Nowadays, the hall is only used for the lying-in-state of members of the Royal Family and a select few non-royals, but until 1821 every royal coronation banquet was held here; during the ceremony, the Royal Champion would ride into the hall in full armour to challenge any who dared dispute the sovereign's right to the throne.

Parliament Square

Visiting the Houses of Parliament

From Monday to Wednesday, debates in the Commons – the livelier House – begin at 2.30pm and end no earlier than 10.30pm; on Thursday they start at 11.30am and finish at 7.30pm, and on Friday, they start at 9.30am and finish at 3pm. **Question Time** – when the House is at its most raucous and entertaining – lasts from 2.30pm until about 3.30pm from Monday to Wednesday, and from 11.30am to 12.30pm on Thursday; **Prime Minister's Question Time** is on Wednesday from 3pm until 3.30pm. To attend either Question Time you need a special ticket (see below). The House of Lords kicks off at 2.30pm from Monday to Wednesday, and from 3pm on Thursdays; if it sits on a Friday, it usually starts at 11am. Recesses (holiday closures) of both Houses occur at Christmas and Easter, and from August to the middle of October. If Parliament is in session a flag flies from the southernmost tower, the Victoria Tower, and at night there is a light above the clock face on Big Ben. If an MP wants a taxi, a little sign saying "taxi" flashes on the corner railings of Parliament Square.

To watch the proceedings in either the House of Commons or the Lords, simply join the queue for the **public galleries** (known as Strangers' Galleries) outside St Stephen's Gate. The public are let in slowly from about 4pm onwards from Monday to Wednesday, from 1pm on Thursdays, and from 10am on Fridays; the security checks are very tight, and the whole procedure can take an hour or more. To avoid the queues, turn up an hour or more later, when the crowds have usually thinned. If you just want to sit in on one of the evidence-taking sessions of the select committees, which take place throughout the day, you can usually jump the queue; phone ☎020/7219 4272 for more information or visit the parliamentary Web sites (*www.parliament.uk* or *www.explore.parliament.uk*). Full explanatory notes on the procedures (and warnings about joining in or causing a disruption) are supplied to all visitors.

To see Question Time, you need to book a **ticket** well in advance from your local MP (if you're a UK citizen) or your embassy in London (if you're not). To contact your MP, simply phone ☎020/7219 3000 and ask to be put through. For some of the 2000 summer recess (Aug to mid-Sept), public access was increased significantly, with five **guided tours** taking place from Monday to Saturday, costing £3.50, and lasting an hour and fifteen minutes. Visitors were required to book five days in advance by phoning ☎020/7344 9966. If the 2000 trial is deemed a success, it will be repeated, so phone ahead to find out. The rest of the year, it's still possible to tour the building in the morning from Monday to Thursday and on Friday afternoons; first off, however, you must obtain a **permit** from your MP or embassy. The full price of a guided tour (with a maximum of sixteen people) is £30, and while it used to be simple enough to join up with a pre-booked **guided tour**, for around £3 per person, this has become much more difficult since security measures have been tightened up. For individuals, the only alternative is to guide yourself around the building, once you've obtained your permit. Only those with a genuine specialist interest may visit **Big Ben**, either separately or before or after their tour; to find out more about access requirements, phone ☎020/7219 4862.

From the thirteenth to the nineteenth centuries the hall was used as the country's highest court of law: among the many tried here was **Guy Fawkes**, the Catholic caught in the cellars trying to blow up the House of Lords on November 5, 1605; he was later hanged, drawn and quartered in Old Palace Yard. **Charles I** was also tried in the hall, but refused to take his hat off, since he did not accept the court's legitimacy. **Oliver Cromwell**, whose statue now stands outside the hall, was sworn in here as Lord Protector in 1653, only to have his head stuck on a spike above the hall after the Restoration – it remained there for several decades until a storm dislodged it. It now resides in a secret location at Cromwell's old college in Cambridge.

St Stephen's Hall and the Central Lobby

From St Stephen's Porch, the route to the parliamentary chambers passes through **St Stephen's Hall**, designed by Barry as a replica of the chapel built by Edward I, where the Commons met for nearly three hundred years until 1834. The ersatz vaulted ceilings, faded murals, statuary and huge wooden doors do their best to conjure up the old medieval atmosphere, but they do nothing to conjure up the dramatic events that have unfolded here. It was into this chamber that Charles I entered with an armed guard in 1642 in a vain attempt to arrest five MPs – "I see my birds have flown," he is supposed to have said. Shortly afterwards, the Civil War began, and no monarch has entered the Commons since. St Stephen's also witnessed the only assassination of a prime minister, when in 1812 Spencer Perceval was shot by a merchant whose business had been ruined by the Napoleonic Wars.

After a further wait you're shepherded through the bustling, octagonal **Central Lobby**, where constituents "lobby" their MPs. In the tiling of the lobby Pugin inscribed in Latin the motto "Except the Lord keep the house, they labour in vain that build it." In view of what happened to the architects, the sentiment seems like an indictment of parliamentary morality – Pugin ended up in Bedlam mental hospital and Barry died from overwork within months of completing the job.

The House of Commons

If you're heading for the **House of Commons**, you'll be ushered into a small room where all visitors sign a form vowing not to cause a disturbance; long institutional staircases and corridors then lead to the Strangers' Gallery, rising steeply above the chamber. Everyone is given a guide to the House, which includes explanatory diagrams and notes on procedure, and a Points of Order sheet to help unravel the matters discussed. Protests from the Strangers' Gallery were once a fairly regular occurrence: suffragettes have poured flour, farmers have dumped dung, Irish Nationalists have lobbed tear gas, and gay women have abseiled down into the chamber. Rigorous security arrangements have unfortunately put paid to such antics.

Since an incendiary bomb in May 1941 destroyed Barry's original chamber, what you see now is a rather lifeless reconstruction by Giles Gilbert Scott, completed in 1950. Barry's design was modelled on St Stephen's Hall (see p.83), hence the choir-stall arrangement of the MPs' benches. Members of the cabinet (and the opposition's shadow cabinet) occupy the two "front benches"; the rest are "backbenchers". To avoid debates degenerating into physical combat, MPs are not allowed to cross the red lines – which are exactly two swords' length apart – on the floor of the chamber during a debate, hence the expression "toeing the party line". The chamber is at its busiest during Question Time, though if too many of the 659 MPs turn up, a large number have to remain standing, as the House only has 427 seats. For much of the time, however, the chamber is half-empty, with just a handful of MPs present from each party.

The House of Lords

On the other side of the Central Lobby, a corridor leads to the **House of Lords** (or Upper House), a far dozier establishment peopled by unelected Lords and Ladies, most of whom are appointed by successive PMs, plus a smattering of bishops. Their home boasts a much grander décor than the Commons, full of regal gold and scarlet, and dominated by a canopied gold throne where the Queen sits for the state opening of Parliament in November. Directly in front of the throne, the Lord Chancellor runs the proceedings from the scarlet Woolsack, an enormous cushion stuffed with wool, which harks back to the time when it was England's principal export. Once again, before ascending to the Strangers' Gallery here, you will be given a guide to the House, with explanatory diagrams and notes on procedure.

Nowadays, the Lords have little real power – they can only advise and review parliamentary bills, although a handful act as the country's final court of appeal. In 1999, the new Labour government took the bull by the horns and kicked out all but 92 of the 1000-plus hereditary Lords, who had, until then, the right to vote and debate in the House. The majority of the hereditary Lords were solidly Conservative – over a quarter went to Eton – but rarely bothered to turn up. Nevertheless, they could be (and were) called upon by the Conservatives in emergencies, to ensure a right-wing victory in a crucial vote. The future of the few who now remain in the House is as yet undecided.

The royal apartments

If the House of Lords takes your fancy, you can see more pomp and glitter by applying to go on a **guided or self-guided tour** (see p.82). You'll be asked to enter at the **Norman Porch entrance** below Victoria Tower, where the Queen arrives in her coach for the state opening. Then, after the usual security checks, you'll be allowed up the Royal Staircase to the Norman Porch itself, every nook of which is stuffed with busts of eminent statesmen.

Next door is the **Queen's Robing Chamber**, which boasts a superb coffered ceiling and lacklustre Arthurian frescoes. As its name suggests, this is the room where the monarch dons the crown jewels before entering the Lords for the opening of Parliament. Beyond here you enter the **Royal Gallery**, a cavernous writing room for the House of Lords, hung with portraits of the royals past and present, and two 45-foot-long frescoes of Trafalgar and Waterloo. Before entering the House of Lords itself, you pass through the **Prince's Chamber**, commonly known as the Tudor Room after the numerous portraits that line the walls, including Henry VIII and all six of his wives. The tour then takes you through both Houses, St Stephen's Hall and finally Westminster Hall (all described above), before ejecting you into New Palace Yard.

Sadly, the fourteenth-century crypt known as St Mary Undercroft, and the cloister beyond, are currently off limits, though there are plans afoot to open up more of the palace to the public. It's to be hoped that any new arrangements are more generous than the current ones concerning visits to the **Lord Chancellor's apartments**, for which you must book a year in advance. Ostensibly, the motivation for allowing access to the Lord Chancellor's apartments is to allow the public to view the selection of State-owned artworks that hang there. In reality, though, it's simply an exercise in damage limitation after the embarrassment caused to the government (though not to the unrepentant Lord Chancellor) by the £650,000 bill for refurbishing the rooms – the Pugin wallpaper alone cost British taxpayers £65,000 – for which, the Lord Chancellor famously opined, future generations would thank him.

Jewel Tower and the Victoria Tower Gardens

Daily: April–Sept 10am–6pm; Oct 10am–5pm; Nov–March 10am–4pm; EH; £1.50; ☎020/7222 2219. Westminster tube.

The **Jewel Tower**, across the road from parliament, is another remnant of the medieval palace. The tower formed the southwestern corner of the original exterior fortifications (there's a bit of moat left, too), and was constructed in around 1365 by Edward III as a giant strongbox for the crown jewels. Nowadays, its three floors house an excellent exhibition on the history of parliament, including a touch-screen tour of the palace and ending with a video on the procedural rigmarole that still persists there.

Alongside the Jewel Tower, the small stretch of lawn sporting a Henry Moore sculpture is a prime spot for TV interviews with MPs, with the Houses of Parliament as a backdrop. On the other side of the road are the rather more attractive and leafy **Victoria Tower Gardens**, which look out onto the Thames. A replica of Rodin's famous sculpture, *The Burghers of Calais*, makes a surprising appearance here, while nearby stands a statue of **Emmeline Pankhurst**, leader of the suffragette movement, who died in 1928, the same year that women finally got the vote on equal terms with men.

St Margaret's Church

Mon–Fri 9.30am–3.45pm, Sat 9.30am–1.45pm, Sun 2–5pm; free; ☎020/7222 5152. Westminster tube.

To the north of the Jewel Tower, and sitting in the shadow of Westminster Abbey, is **St Margaret's Church**, which has been the unofficial parliamentary church since the entire Commons tipped up here in 1614 to unmask religious Dissenters among the MPs. St Margaret's has also long been a fashionable church to get married in – Pepys, Milton and Shakespeare were followed this century by Churchill and Mountbatten – and it gets a steady stream of visitors simply by dint of being so close to the abbey (and because it's free). The present building dates back to 1523, and its most noteworthy furnishing is the colourful Flemish stained-glass window above the altar, which commemorates the marriage of Henry VIII and Catherine of Aragon (depicted in the bottom left- and right-hand corners). Constructed in 1526, the window was never intended for St Margaret's, and was only bought by the church in 1758. The west window commemorates Sir Walter Raleigh, who was beheaded in Old Palace Yard and buried in the old churchyard, Also interred here are the Czech engraver Václav Hollar; John Cleland, author of the saucy *Fanny Hill*; and William Caxton, who audited the parish accounts and set up the country's first printing press in the abbey close in 1476.

Westminster Abbey

Entry to the abbey is via the north door; exit is via the west door.

Mon–Fri 9.30am–4.45pm, Sat 9.30am–2.45pm, also Wed 6–7.45pm; £5; ☎020/7222 5152; *www.westminster-abbey.org*. Westminster or St James's Park tube.

The Houses of Parliament dwarf their much older neighbour, **Westminster Abbey**, which squats uncomfortably on the western edge of Parliament Square. Yet this single building embodies much of the history of England: it has been the venue for all but two coronations since the time of William the Conqueror, and the site of more or less every royal burial for some five hundred years between the reigns of Henry III and George II. Scores of the nation's most famous citizens are honoured here, too – though many of the stones commemorate people buried elsewhere – and the interior is cluttered with hundreds of monuments, reliefs and statues.

Legend has it that the first church on the site was consecrated by St Peter himself, who came down from heaven and was rowed across

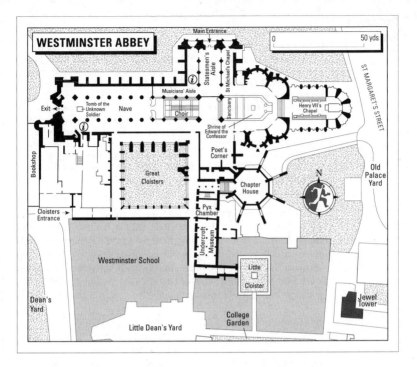

WESTMINSTER ABBEY

the Thames by a fisherman named Edric, who received a giant salmon as a reward. More verifiable is that there was a small Benedictine monastery here by the end of the tenth century, for which **Edward the Confessor** built an enormous church. Nothing much remains of Edward's church, which was consecrated on December 28, 1065, just ten days before his own death, though the ground plan is his, as is the crypt.

The following year two kings were crowned in the abbey, thus firmly establishing the tradition of royal coronation within the Confessor's church. In January 1066, Harold was crowned, and, on Christmas Day, William the Conqueror rode up the aisle on horseback. In 1161 there was a ceremony here to canonize Edward the Confessor, and it was again in Edward's honour that **Henry III** began to rebuild the abbey in 1245, in the French Gothic style of the recently completed Rheims Cathedral. Over the next 25 years the entire east end, both transepts and four bays of the nave were constructed, Henry bankrupting the royal coffers in the process.

Nothing more was done to the church until Richard II came to the throne one hundred years later; the vaulting had to wait until the reign of **Henry VII**, who contributed the single most significant addition to the church, the late Gothic masterpiece of the rebuilt Lady

Chapel at the east end (also known as the Henry VII Chapel). The
monks were kicked out during the Reformation, but the church's status as the nation's royal mausoleum saved it from anything worse. In
the early eighteenth century, Nicholas Hawksmoor gave the church
its quasi-Gothic twin towers and west front. In the niches above the
west door, you'll find a series of new statues representing twentieth-
century martyrs, from Dietrich Bonhoeffer to Martin Luther King.

Statesmen's Aisle and the north ambulatory

With over three thousand people buried beneath its flagstones and
countless others commemorated here, the abbey is, in essence, a
giant mausoleum. It has long ceased to be primarily a working
church, and admission charges are nothing new: Oliver Goldsmith
complained about being charged three pence in 1765. A century or
so later, so few people used the abbey as a church that, according to
George Bernard Shaw, one foreign visitor who knelt down to pray
was promptly arrested because the verger thought he was acting sus-
piciously. Despite attempts to prove otherwise – like the large signs
ordering visitors to "Shhhh!" – the abbey is now more a mass tourist
attraction than a House of God.

Once you've paid your admission charge, head over to the **information** desk and pick up a free plan. Locating some of the graves is
tricky unless your Latin is good, so if you have any questions as you
go round, ask the vergers in the red gowns. You are now standing in
the north transept, littered with overblown monuments to long-
forgotten empire-builders and nineteenth-century politicians, and
traditionally known as **Statesmen's Aisle**. It's worth noting that
many of those commemorated in the abbey, are not, in fact, buried
here. **Pitt the Elder** – immediately to the right as you pass the ticket
office – is one of the few in the Statesmen's Aisle who is, his statue
standing high above his extravagantly expensive tomb, lording it
over Britannia and Neptune. Another of those actually buried here is
the great Liberal leader **William Ewart Gladstone**, who, despite

being prime minister a record four times, is best known for his penchant for "saving" prostitutes.

The best funereal art in the north transept is to be found in the Nightingale or **St Michael's Chapel** to the east. This is sometimes closed to the public, but you can still look through and admire the remarkable monument to **Sir Francis Vere**, made out of two slabs of black marble, between which lies Sir Francis; on the upper slab, supported by four knights, his armour is laid out, to show that he died away from the field of battle. The most striking grave, by Roubiliac, is that in which Elizabeth Nightingale, who died from a miscarriage, collapses in her husband's arms while he tries to fight off the skeletal figure of Death, who is climbing out of the tomb.

From this point, you enter the **north ambulatory**, its two side chapels now containing ostentatious Tudor and Stuart tombs which replaced the altarpieces that had graced them before the Reformation. One of the most extravagant Tudor tombs is that of Lord Hunsdon, which dominates the **Chapel of St John the Baptist**, and, at 36ft in height, is the tallest in the entire abbey. More intriguing, though, are the sarcophagi in the neighbouring **Chapel of St Paul**: Thomas Bromley's features his eight children as "weepers", kneeling figures around the base of the tomb – the two holding skulls predeceased their parents – while the red-robed Countess of Sussex has a beautiful turquoise and gold porcupine (the family emblem) as her prickly footrest.

Henry VII's Chapel

Before you enter the main body of the Lady Chapel, better known as **Henry VII's Chapel**, pop into the chapel's north aisle, which is virtually cut off from the chancel. Here James I erected a huge ten-poster tomb to his predecessor, **Elizabeth I**. Unless you read the plaque on the floor, you'd never know that Elizabeth's Catholic half-sister, "Bloody Mary", is also buried here, in an unusual act of reconciliation. The far end of the north aisle, where James I's two infant daughters lie, is known as **Innocents' Corner**: Princess Sophia, who died aged three days, lies in an alabaster cradle, her face peeping over the covers, just about visible in the mirror on the wall; while Princess Mary, who died the following year at the age of 2, is clearly visible, casually leaning on a cushion. Set into the wall between the two is the Wren-designed urn containing the bones of the murdered princes, Edward V and his younger brother, Richard, whose remains were discovered under a staircase in the Tower of London during Charles II's reign.

The **main nave** of the chapel is the most dazzling architectural set piece in the abbey. Begun by Henry VII in 1503 as a shrine to Henry VI and as his own future resting place, it represents the final gasp of the English Perpendicular style, with its intricately carved vaulting, fan-shaped gilded pendants and statues of nearly one hundred saints,

installed high above the choir stalls. The stalls themselves are decorated with the banners and emblems of the Knights of the Order of
the Bath, to whom the chapel was dedicated by George I. **George II**,
the last king to be buried in the abbey, lies in the burial vault under
your feet, along with Queen Caroline – their coffins were fitted with
removable sides so that their remains could mingle. Close by lies the
son they both hated, **Frederick Louis**, who died after being hit in the
throat by a cricket ball.

Beneath the altar is the grave of Edward VI, the single, sickly son
of Henry VIII, while behind lies the chapel's *raison d'être*, the black
marble sarcophagus containing **Henry VII** and his spouse – their lifelike gilded effigies, modelled from death masks, are obscured by an
ornate Renaissance grille, designed by Pietro Torrigiano, who fled
from Italy after breaking Michelangelo's nose in a fight. **James I** is
also interred within Henry's tomb, while the first of the apse chapels,
to the north, hosts a grand monument by Hubert le Sueur to James's
lover, George Villiers, Duke of Buckingham, the first non-royal to be
buried in this part of the abbey, who was killed by one of his own soldiers. Le Sueur was also responsible for another overblown monument in the last of the apse chapels, to the south, in which four weeping caryatids hold a vast bronze canopy. The easternmost chapel is
dedicated to the RAF, and sports a modern stained-glass window
depicting airmen and angels in the Battle of Britain. Beneath it, a
plaque marks the spot where Oliver Cromwell rested, briefly, until
the Restoration, whereupon his mummified body was disinterred,
hanged at Tyburn and beheaded.

Before descending the steps back into the ambulatory, squeeze
your way around the south aisle of Henry VII's chapel. The first red-
robed effigy belongs to the Countess of Lennox, James I's grand-
mother, followed by James's mother, **Mary Queen of Scots**, whom
Elizabeth I beheaded. James had Mary's remains brought from
Peterborough Cathedral in 1612, and paid out significantly more for
her extravagant eight-postered tomb, complete with a terrifyingly
aggressive red lion, than he had done for Elizabeth's (see p.89); the
27 hangers-on who are buried with her are listed on the nearby
wooden screen. The last of the tombs here is that of **Lady Margaret
Beaufort**, Henry VII's mother, her face and hands depicted wrinkles
and all by Torrigiano. Below the altar, commemorated by simple
modern plaques, lie yet more royals: **William and Mary**, **Queen
Anne** and **Charles II**. To the left is a nautically flavoured monument
to **General Monck**, who, despite being Cromwell's commander-in-
chief, was the man responsible for the Restoration of the monarchy
in 1660.

The Coronation Chair and the south ambulatory

As you leave Henry VII's Chapel, you're invited to inspect Edward I's
Coronation Chair, a decrepit oak throne dating from around 1300.

The graffiti-covered chair, used in every coronation since 1308, was custom-built to incorporate the **Stone of Scone**, a great slab of red sandstone which acted as the Scottish coronation stone for centuries before Edward pilfered it in 1296, in a demonstration of his mastery of the north. The stone remained in the abbey for the next seven hundred years, apart from a brief interlude in 1950, when some enterprising Scottish nationalists managed to steal it back and hide it in Arbroath. Then, in a futile attempt to curry favour with the Scots in the run-up to the 1997 election, the Conservative government returned the stone to Edinburgh Castle, where it now resides.

Parliament Square

Behind the chair lies the tomb of **Henry V**, who died of dysentery in France in 1422, and was regarded as a saint in his day. Above him rises the highly decorative H-shaped Chantry Chapel, where the body of Henry's wife, Catherine of Valois, was openly displayed for several centuries – Pepys records kissing her on his 36th-birthday visit to the abbey. The chapel acts as a sort of gatehouse for the **Shrine of Edward the Confessor**, the sacred heart of the building, but now sadly closed to the public. With some difficulty, you can just about make out the battered marble casket of the Confessor's tomb and the niches in which pilgrims would kneel, praying to the saint for a cure to their ailments. Completely out of eyeshot, however, are some of the abbey's finest medieval royal tombs, which enclose the shrine. The only way to gain any notion of the treasures within is from the **south ambulatory**, from which you can admire the six remaining gleaming bronze "weepers" (out of the original fourteen) in the outer recesses of **Edward III's** tomb.

There are more bombastic Tudor and Stuart tombs in the side chapels of the south ambulatory, and, in the **Chapel of St Edmund**, the second of the two, a very fine effigy of a fourteenth-century knight, which the inscription claims is Bernard Brocas, "who had lands to the value of £400 in Hampshire", and who was beheaded in 1400 for his part in trying to restore the deposed Richard II to the throne. In actual fact, it is his father who is buried in the vault. Close by is the unusual statue of Elizabeth Russell, who died of consumption at the age of just 26, and is depicted seated, "not dead but sleeping" as the Latin inscription has it, with her right foot resting on a skull.

Poets' Corner

Nowadays, the royal tombs have been upstaged by **Poets' Corner**, in the south transept. The first occupant, **Geoffrey Chaucer**, was buried here in 1400, not because he was a poet, but because he lived nearby. His battered tomb, on the east wall, wasn't built for another hundred and fifty-odd years. When **Edmund Spenser** was buried here in 1599, his fellow poets – Shakespeare may well have been among them – threw their own works and quills into the grave. But it wasn't until the eighteenth century that this zone became an artistic Pantheon, since when the transept has been filled with tributes to all shades of talent.

Among those who are actually buried here, you'll find – after much searching – grave slabs or memorials for John Dryden, Samuel Johnson, Robert Browning, Lord Tennyson, Charles Dickens, Rudyard Kipling and Thomas Hardy (though his heart was buried in Dorset). Among the merely commemorated is the dandyish figure of William Shakespeare, erected in 1740 on one of the east walls, and thus starting a trend that has continued well into this century, with the maverick William Blake only receiving official recognition in 1957 with a sculpture by Jacob Epstein.

Among the non-poets buried here is the German composer **George Frideric Handel**, depicted in similar dandyish mode by Roubiliac, and directly opposite Shakespeare. Handel, who spent most of his life at the English court, wrote the coronation anthem, *Zadok the Priest*, which was first performed at George II's coronation, and has been performed at every subsequent one. Further along the same wall, the great eighteenth-century actor **David Garrick** is seen parting the curtains for a final bow. The one illiterate is old Thomas Parr, a Shropshire man who was brought to London as a celebrity in 1635 at the alleged age of 152, but died shortly afterwards, and whose remains were brought here by Charles II. The whole area is now so overcrowded that the abbey authorities claim to have called a stop to all burials here, the last one being that of the actor **Laurence Olivier**, who died in 1989.

The sanctuary and the south choir aisle

From the south transept, you can gain access to the central **sanctuary**, site of the coronations. On its north side are three wonderful fourteenth-century gabled tombs featuring "weepers" around their base, the last of them that of Edmund Crouchback, founder of the House of Lancaster. But the most precious work of art here is the **Cosmati floor mosaic**, which was constructed in the thirteenth century by Italian craftsmen. It depicts the universe with interwoven circles and squares of Purbeck marble, glass and red and green porphyry, though it is often covered by a carpet to protect it. The richly gilded high altar, like the ornately carved choir stalls, is, in fact, a neo-Gothic construction from the nineteenth century.

There are a few memorials to undeserving types in the **south choir aisle**, which nevertheless deserve closer inspection, though you may have to ask a verger to allow you to see them properly. The first is to **Thomas Thynne**, a Restoration rake, whose tomb incorporates a relief showing his assassination in his coach on Pall Mall by three thugs, hired to kill him by his Swedish rival in love. Further along lies **Admiral Clowdesley Shovell**, lounging in toga and wig. He was washed up alive on a beach in the Scilly Isles, after his crew got drunk and wrecked his ship, only to be killed by a fisherwoman for his emerald ring. Above Shovell is a memorial to the court portrait painter **Godfrey Kneller**, who declared, "By God, I will not be buried in Westminster . . . they do bury fools there." In the event, he has the honour of being the only artist commemorated in the abbey; the tomb is to his own design, but the epitaph is by Pope, who admitted it was the worst thing he ever wrote – which is just as well, as it's so high up you can't read it.

Parliament Square

The cloisters
Doors in the south choir aisle lead to the **Great Cloisters** (daily 8am–6pm; free via Dean's Yard entrance), rebuilt after a fire in 1298 and paved with yet more funerary slabs, including, at the bottom of the ramp, that of the proto-feminist writer **Aphra Behn**, upon whose tomb "all women together ought to let flowers fall", according to Virginia Woolf, "for it was she who earned them the right to speak their minds."

There's a small café in the north cloisters.

At the eastern end lies the octagonal **Chapter House** (daily: April–Sept 9.30am–5pm; Oct 10am–5pm; Nov–March 10am–4pm; £2.50 or £1 with an abbey ticket; free with an audio tour), which was built in 1255 for Henry III's Great Council or putative parliament. The House of Commons continued to meet here until 1395, though the monks were none too happy about it, complaining that the shuffling and stamping wore out the expensive tiled floor. Despite their whinging, the thirteenth-century decorative paving tiles have survived well, as have the remarkable apocalyptic wall-paintings, which were executed in celebration of the eviction of the Commons. Be sure to check out the Whore of Babylon riding the scarlet seven-headed beast from The Book of Revelation.

Tickets for the Chapter House also include entry to the neighbouring **Pyx Chamber** (daily 10.30am–4pm), east of the cloisters. This was the sacristy of Edward the Confessor's church and subsequently the royal treasury – hence the mighty double doors and panoply of locks – which was originally lined with human skin as a warning to thieves. The chamber takes its name from the trial of the pyx, a ceremony which was initiated here during the reign of Edward I, in which specimen gold and silver coins were tested for purity. It now displays the abbey's plate, boasts the oldest altar in the building, and contains a wonderful quarter-circle cope chest.

The same ticket covers entry to one of the few surviving Norman sections of the abbey, now the **Undercroft Museum** (daily 10.30am–4pm). There's a real mixed bag of exhibits here, from replica coronation regalia used during rehearsals to a second coronation chair, made for Mary II, who was jointly crowned with William III in 1689. The most bizarre items here, though, are the bald, royal death masks, including those of Edward III and Henry VII, and the wax funeral effigies of Charles II, William III and Mary, and Lady Frances Stuart, model for Britannia on the old penny coin, complete with her pet parrot, who died a few days after she did.

If you visit the cloisters on a Tuesday or Thursday, make your way via **Little Cloister**, where sick or elderly monks used to live, to the little-known **College Garden** (Tues–Thurs: April–Sept 10am–6pm; Oct–March 10am–4pm; free), a 900-year-old stretch of green originally used as a herb garden by the monastery's doctor. The garden now provides a quiet retreat and a croquet lawn for pupils of Westminster School (see p.95); brass band concerts take place here during July and August on Thursdays between 12.30 and 2pm.

The nave

It's only when you finally leave the cloisters that you get to enter the **nave** itself. Narrow, light and, at over a 100ft in height, by far the tallest in the country, the nave is an impressive space. The first monument to head for is the **Tomb of the Unknown Soldier**, by the west door, with its garland of red poppies commemorating the million British soldiers who died in World War I. Close by is a large floor slab dedicated to **Winston Churchill**, though he chose to be buried in his family plot in Bladon, Oxfordshire; Neville Chamberlain, his prime ministerial predecessor, lies forgotten in the south aisle.

A tablet in the floor near the Unknown Soldier marks the spot where **George Peabody**, the nineteenth-century philanthropist whose housing estates in London still provide homes for those in need, was buried for a month before being exhumed and removed to his home town in Massachusetts; he remains the only American to have received the privilege of burial in the abbey. On the pillar by St George's Chapel is a doleful fourteenth-century portrait of **Richard II**, painted at his coronation at the age of just 10, and the oldest known image of an English monarch painted from life. Above the west door, **William Pitt the Younger**, prime minister at just 23, teaches Anarchy a thing or two, while History takes notes.

In the north aisle is the florid memorial of Pitt's great rival, the hard-drinking, hard-gambling **Charles James Fox**, who lies in the arms of Liberty, a black American at his feet thanking him for his anti-slavery campaigning. **Clement Attlee**, the great prime minister of the postwar Labour government, is buried a short distance away, close to his foreign secretary, **Ernest Bevin**, and **Sidney and Beatrice Webb**, Fabians and founders of the left-wing journal *New Statesman*. Further along the north wall is the grave of poet and playwright **Ben Jonson**, who, despite being a double murderer, was granted permission to be buried here, upright so as not to exceed the eighteen square inches he'd been allowed; his epitaph reads simply, "O Rare Ben Jonson."

The so-called **Musicians' Aisle** lies to the east, beyond a barrier, so if you want to see a particular grave, you'll need to ask a verger. In fact, just two musicians of great note are buried here: Ralph Vaughan Williams and Henry Purcell, who served as the abbey's organist. Of the statues lining the aisle, only the tireless anti-slavery campaigner William Wilberforce, slouching in his chair, is actually buried in the abbey.

The dried and salted body of the explorer and missionary **David Livingstone** is buried in the centre of the nave – except for his internal organs, which, following the tradition of the African people in whose village he died, were buried in a box under a tree. In an alcove of the gilded neo-Gothic choir screen is a statue of **Isaac Newton**, who, although a Unitarian by faith, would no doubt have been happy enough to be buried in such a prominent position. Other scientists' graves cluster nearby, including **John Herschel**, **Lord Kelvin** and **Lord Rutherford**, who, when asked if electrons really existed, replied, "Not exist? Not exist! Why, I can see the little buggers as plain as I can see that spoon in front of me!" Last, but not least, despite being at loggerheads with the Church for most of his life over *On the Origin of Species*, non-believer **Charles Darwin** was given a religious burial in the abbey.

In the far corner of the south aisle, there's a monument to **John André**, who was hanged as a spy by the Americans, despite his plea to George Washington to be shot as a soldier; it was forty years before his body was brought back from America and given a proper funeral. Further along the wall are two huge marble memorials with statues by Roubiliac, one of which – **General Hargrave**'s – has the deceased rising from the grave in response to the Last Trumpet; at the time there was a public outcry that such an undistinguished man should receive such a vast memorial.

Around the abbey

On the other side of the abbey lies **Westminster School**, one of the country's top public (in other words, private) schools, with alumni ranging from Ben Jonson and Christopher Wren to Peter Ustinov and Andrew Lloyd-Webber. There are occasional **guided tours** around the school, which occupies the old medieval monastery complex. At other times, you can wander into Dean's Yard through the archway on Broad Sanctuary; it's now a car park, but was once the abbey farm, filled with crops and animals tended by the monks themselves. Through another archway, you can peek at Little Dean's Yard – the prettier of the school's two courtyards – whose buildings date back as far as the eleventh century. In Broad Sanctuary itself, outside the abbey's main entrance, is a modest column to old boys who lost their lives in the Crimean War.

To find out more about guided tours of Westminster School, phone ☎020/7963 1000.

In an attempt to avoid the Gothic of the abbey, and the Byzantine style of the Catholic cathedral, the Methodists opted for the Edwardian beaux-arts style of architecture for their national headquarters, the **Methodist Central Hall** (*www.wch.co.uk*), to the northwest of the abbey on Storey's Gate. It's an unusual building for London, looking something like a giant casino, which is hardly appropriate given the Methodists' views on gambling and alcohol.

Parliament Square

Venue for the inaugural meeting of the United Nations in 1946, it has been used over the years as much for political meetings as religious gatherings. You're free to wander down to the cheap "caff" in the basement (daily 10am–4.30pm), where there are also occasional exhibitions. For **guided tours** (£3) of the hall, including a chance to climb up to the stone balustrade atop the reinforced concrete dome, phone ☎020/7222 8010.

Millbank and Tate Britain

Running south from midway along the Victoria Tower Gardens, **Millbank** is dominated by the unprepossessing 1960s Millbank Tower, which reaches a height of 387ft and currently serves as the headquarters of the Labour Party. Behind and to the south of it, **Tate Britain** occupies the site of the old Millbank prison, built in the shape of a six-pointed star in 1821, according to the ideas of Jeremy Bentham. The prisoners were kept under constant surveillance, forbidden to communicate with each other for the first half of their sentence and put to work making mailbags and shoes – for its day, an extremely liberal regime. Nevertheless, very little natural light penetrated the three miles of labyrinthine passages, and epidemics of cholera and scurvy were commonplace. The prison closed down in 1890.

The green and beige postmodernist ziggurat across the water is the indiscreet headquarters of the British Secret Intelligence Service, **MI6**. Designed in the early 1990s by Terry Farrell at a cost of £260 million, it was no sooner completed than a huge refurbishment was started, allegedly costing a further £85 million, a large slice of which went on a tunnel under the river to Whitehall. It's a far cry from the days when MI6 was ensconced in a building whose unmarked front door was in the tasteful and terribly English terrace of houses on Queen Anne's Gate.

Tate Britain

Daily 10am–5.50pm; free; ☎020/7887 8000; *www.tate.org.uk*. Pimlico tube.

The Tate's international modern art collection is now displayed in the Tate Modern on Bankside (see p.311).

Founded in 1897 with money from Sir Henry Tate, inventor of the sugar cube, the original Tate Gallery on Millbank has recently undergone probably the biggest period of change in its hundred-year history. Having struggled to perform a difficult dual function as both the nation's chief collection of British art and, since 1916, its primary gallery for international modern art, the Tate has finally split into two. The new Tate Modern on Bankside now houses the twentieth-century international collection, while the old Tate is devoted exclusively to British art from 1500 to 2000, and has been renamed **Tate Britain**.

Inevitably, with the Tate Modern pulling in by far the biggest crowds, Tate Britain is going to struggle to compete. Still, the gallery

Visiting the Tate

The main entrance on Millbank leads up the steps to the information desk
under the glass-domed rotunda, where you can rent one of the gallery's
audioguides for £3. The Tate's Clore Gallery extension, which houses the
Turner Bequest, can be reached via the modern art galleries, but it also has
its own entrance, with its own information desk, to the right of the gallery
steps.

has a reputation for hosting some of London's best exhibitions (for
which there is usually an entrance fee), and, from spring 2001, will
have yet more gallery space and a new entrance on Atterbury Street.
In addition, every autumn Tate Britain will continue to stage the
Turner Prize – the country's most prestigious modern art competition – thereby virtually guaranteeing it widespread publicity. Works
by a shortlist of four artists, which can be in any medium, are displayed a month or two prior to the prize-giving, and the competition
is nothing if not controversial, since it tends to rake up all the usual
arguments about the value and accessibility of modern art.

British art from 1500 to 2000

With its first major re-hang in 2000, Tate Britain formally abandoned
the chronological approach to gallery displays, which had been its
hallmark for decades. Instead of inviting visitors to march through
the centuries from Tudor times to the present day, the gallery
grouped paintings according to themes such as War, the Portrait,
City Life and Home Life. The curators clearly had a lot of fun juxtaposing wildly contrasting works, placing the likes of Gilbert &
George in the same room as Joshua Reynolds. Others may find it
frustrating, however, and for the purposes of this guide, it is virtually impossible to say what artworks will be where. Whatever the merits of the current approach, it certainly forces you to consider paintings and periods that you might otherwise reject out of hand. And the
new-found space has allowed the Tate to show lots of seldom-seen
twentieth-century British artists' works. An element of chronology is
likely to be reintroduced in 2001, but a complete return to the days
of old has been permanently ruled out.

However the works are displayed, you're pretty much guaranteed
to get to see many of the Tate's best-known British paintings. **John
Constable**'s most famous work, *The Hay Wain*, hangs in the
National Gallery, though the same location – his native Stour valley
in Suffolk – features here in *Flatford Mill*. The first great British
artist, **William Hogarth**, usually gets a room more or less to himself,
where you'll usually find *O the Roast Beef of Old England*, a particularly vicious visual dig at the French, whom Hogarth loathed. There
are also bound to be one or two paintings by **George Stubbs**, for
whom "nature was and always is superior to art", and who portrayed

*Some of
Constable's
best-known
works hang in
the National
Gallery (p.63);
there's an even
larger collec-
tion of his
paintings in
the V&A
(p.346).*

animals – horses in particular – with a hitherto unknown anatomical precision.

Works by **Thomas Gainsborough** and **Joshua Reynolds** are sprinkled throughout the collection. Of the two, Reynolds, first president of the Royal Academy, was by far the more successful, elevating portraiture to pole position among the genres and flattering his sitters by surrounding them with classical trappings, as in *Three Ladies Adorning a Term of Hymen*. Gainsborough was equally adept at flattery, but rarely used classical imagery, preferring instead more informal settings, and concentrating on colour and light, as in the vivacious portrait of the ballerina Giovanna Baccelli. At the outset of his career, Gainsborough was also a landscape artist, often painting the Stour valley in Suffolk, where he was born.

One room in the gallery is regularly devoted to the visionary works by the poet **William Blake**, who was considered something of a freak by his contemporaries. He rejected oil painting in favour of watercolours, and often chose unusual subject matter, which matched his highly personal form of Christianity. He earned a pittance producing illuminated books written and printed entirely by himself, and painted purely from his own visions: "Imagination is My World; this world of Dross is beneath my notice," as he wrote. From illuminated books he moved on to do a series of twelve large colour prints on the myth of the Creation, now considered among his finest works, several examples of which are normally on display here. During the recent upheavals, Blake's works have been shifted about the gallery, though they were originally intended for the room decorated by Boris Anrep's floor mosaics, which are accompanied by quotes from Blake's poem *The Marriage of Heaven and Hell*.

The Tate is justifiably renowned for its vast collection of paintings by the **Pre-Raphaelites**, who formed their Brotherhood, the PRB, in 1848 in an attempt to re-create the humble, pre-humanist, pre-Renaissance world. The origins of the name lay in their aim to return to the method and spirit of artists who painted before Raphael. One of the first PRB paintings to be exhibited was **Rossetti**'s *Girlhood of Mary Virgin*, which was well received by the critics, but the following year, **Millais**'s *Christ in the House of His Parents* caused considerable outrage; Dickens described the figure of Jesus as "a hideous, wry-necked, blubbering, red-headed boy in a bed-gown". Millais also got into trouble for *Ophelia*, after his model, Elizabeth Siddal, caught a chill from lying in the bath to pose for the picture, prompting threats of lawsuits from her father. Siddal later married Rossetti, and is also the model in his *Beata Beatrix*, painted shortly after she died of an opium overdose in 1862. Other classics in the collection are Arthur Hughes' *April Love* and John William Waterhouse's *The Lady of Shalott*, both inspired by poems by Lord Tennyson, and Lord Leighton's *Bath of Psyche*, a typical piece of

Victorian soft porn, the likes of which made him by far the most successful artist of his generation.

You'll find works by leading twentieth-century and contemporary British artists displayed in both the Tate Modern and Tate Britain; the sculptors Barbara Hepworth and **Henry Moore**, and painters **Stanley Spencer** and Francis Bacon are just some of the better-known figures who crop up twice over. There's also a good selection of work in both venues by living artists such as Lucien Freud, **David Hockney**, R.B. Kitaj and Anselm Keifer. And throughout Tate Britain, the term "British" is very loosely applied, so that the canvases by the American **John Singer Sargent** – the Tate owns his well-known *Carnation, Lily, Lily-Rose* – and Frenchman André Derain, both of whom worked in London, are to be found here.

The Clore Gallery: the Turner Bequest

J.M.W. Turner (1775–1851), possibly the greatest artist Britain has ever produced, bequeathed over a hundred oil paintings to the nation, and by the time his relatives had donated their share of the spoils, the total came to three hundred, plus a staggering nineteen thousand watercolours and drawings. Hence the world's largest Turner collection is housed here, in the adjoining Clore Gallery, a surprisingly uninspiring building designed by arch-postmodernist James Stirling and opened in 1987.

As the Turner collection is rehung from time to time, it's impossible to predict which paintings will be in which rooms.

Turner was an extremely successful artist, exhibiting his first watercolours in the window of his father's barber shop in Maiden Lane, Covent Garden, while still a boy, and at the Royal Academy when he was just 15, becoming an Academician in his twenties. Marine scenes appealed to Turner throughout his life, and one of the finest examples in the Tate is *The Shipwreck*. Natural cataclysms also feature strongly in Turner's works, either for their own sake, as in *Deluge*, or as part of a grand historical painting like *Snow Storm: Hannibal and His Army Crossing the Alps*.

Turner's only known self-portrait (he had no pretensions as a portraitist and was rather ashamed of his ruddy complexion), is usually displayed alongside belongings such as his pocket watercolour kit and fishing rod, and his toothless death mask. From 1810 onwards, the works of the French painter Claude Lorrain became more and more important for Turner. His Claude-inspired canvases range from direct imitations, such as *The Decline of the Carthaginian Empire* and *Apullia in Search of Appullus*, to *Crossing the Brook*, in which a traditional English landscape is given the Claude treatment.

Canaletto was another of Turner's heroes, though pictures like *Venetian Festival* have only their geographical location in common with the earlier master. Rembrandt also exerted a powerful influence on Turner during the 1830s, most notably in works such as *Pilate*

Washing His Hands. In later life Turner painted at the country mansions of two devoted patrons: the architect John Nash, who had a neo-Gothic pile on the Isle of Wight, and the Earl of Egremont, who owned Petworth House and commissioned paintings such the light-suffused *Lake, Petworth*.

Turner's late works are great smudges of colour, and seem to anticipate Monet in their almost total abandonment of linear representation. *Snow Storm* is a classic late Turner, a symbolic battle between the steam age and nature's primeval force. It was criticized at the time as "soapsuds and whitewash", though Turner himself claimed he merely painted what he saw, having been "lashed to a mast" for four hours.

To use the Clore Gallery's study room phone ☎020/7887 8657.

The rest of the bequest is displayed floor to ceiling in the **reserve galleries** on the second floor, where free temporary exhibitions on various Turner themes are regularly staged. There is also a **study room** on the second floor, with monographs and books on all aspects of Turner's works and influences.

From Millbank to Queen Anne's Gate

The area to the south and west of Westminster Abbey – bounded by Millbank to the east and St James's Park to the north – is cut off from the noise and pollution which disfigure Parliament Square. The area's proximity to Parliament, and the various governmental ministries that have spread their departmental tentacles across it, mean that property prices are high. Nevertheless, it's a favourite place for MPs to have their London bases, and many of the restaurants and pubs in the area have "division bells", which ring eight minutes before the members are needed for a vote in the House of Commons. As for landmarks, the area boasts two of London's most unusual churches: the Baroque fancy of **St John's** in **Smith Square** and the exotic **Westminster Cathedral**, the capital's principal Roman Catholic church.

Smith Square to Vincent Square and beyond

Two blocks south of Westminster Abbey lies the fine early Georgian architectural ensemble of **Smith Square**, home to the Conservative Party headquarters and, more importantly, to the church of **St John** (*www.sjss.org.uk*), a rare slice of full-blown Baroque completed in 1728 by Thomas Archer. With its four distinctive towers topped by pineapples, it was dubbed the "footstool church" – the story being that Queen Anne, when asked how she would like the church to look, kicked over her footstool. Burnt in 1758 and gutted in 1941, it has since been restored as a concert venue, best known for its lunchtime recitals; if the church is not being used for rehearsals or performances, you can have a peek at the bare interior. To complete the

As well as the lunchtime classical music concerts, St John's has a good crypt restaurant called The Footstool.

Georgian experience, approach the square from Lord North Street, to the north, an almost perfect early eighteenth-century terrace that was built at the same time as the church and square.

From
Millbank to
Queen
Anne's Gate

Before heading west to Westminster Cathedral, continue two more blocks south and pick up **Page Street**, flanked by Edwin Lutyens' chequerboard council flats, erected in the 1920s – walking between the six-storey blocks is a surreal experience. Page Street brings you, almost, to the playing fields of **Vincent Square**, where the boys from Westminster School play sports, and where the **Royal Horticultural Society** (*www.rhs.org.uk*) – best known as the organizers of the Chelsea Flower Show (see p.623) – have one of their two exhibition halls (the second is round the corner down Elverton Street). Flower shows are still held here regularly, supplemented by exhibitions on model railways, vintage cars, stamps and so on. To the north of the RHS halls, on Horseferry Road, stands Richard Rogers' **Channel 4 TV headquarters**, a characteristic mass of shiny neo-industrial tubes, steel cables, external lifts and rust-red iron stanchions, its most striking innovation being the circular glazed pool that forms part of the entrance, as well as the roof of an underground studio.

While you're in these parts, be sure to check out the remarkable High Victorian church of **St James-the-Less**, designed by George Edmund Street in the 1860s, which lies to the south of Vincent Square, on the far side of Vauxhall Bridge Road, amidst an unprepossessing 1960s housing estate. The red and black brickwork patterning on the exterior is exceptional, but is nothing to the red, black, cream and magenta tiling on the interior walls. The capitals of the church's rounded pillars hide biblical scenes amidst the acanthus leaf foliage, and the font boasts similarly rich adornments, while above the chancel arch there's a wonderfully colourful fresco by G.F. Watts.

Westminster Cathedral

Mon–Fri & Sun 7am–7pm, Sat 8am–7pm; free. Campanile lift daily 9am–5pm; £2; ☎020/7798 9055; *www.westminsterdiocese.org.uk*. Victoria tube.

To the west of Vincent Square, just off Victoria Street, you'll find one of London's most surprising churches, the stripy neo-Byzantine concoction of the Roman Catholic **Westminster Cathedral**. Begun in 1895, it's one of the last and wildest monuments to the Victorian era: constructed from more than twelve million terracotta-coloured bricks, decorated with hoops of Portland stone, it culminates in a magnificent tapered campanile which rises to 274ft. A small piazza has been laid out to the north, from where you can admire the cathedral and the neighbouring mansions on Ambrosden Avenue, whose brickwork echoes that of the cathedral.

The **interior** is only half-finished, and the domed ceiling of the nave – the widest in the country – remains an indistinct blackened mass, free of all decoration. To get an idea of what the place will look like when it's finally completed, explore the series of **side chapels** –

in particular the All Souls Chapel, the first one in the north aisle – whose rich, multicoloured décor makes use of over one hundred different marbles from around the world. Be sure, too, to check out the striking baldachino (the canopy above the High Altar), held up by mustard yellow pillars, and the low-relief Stations of the Cross sculpted by the controversial Eric Gill during World War I. The view from the campanile is definitely worth taking in as well, especially as you don't even have to slog up flights of steps, but can simply take a lift; the entrance is in the north aisle.

North of Victoria Street

In the 1860s, Victorian planners ploughed their way through the slums of Westminster to create **Victoria Street**, a direct link between Parliament and the newly built Victoria train station. The bland 1960s blocks that now line the street give you some idea of what the rest of London might have looked like if the developers had got it all their own way in that iconoclastic decade. The best feature of the street these days, though, is the way in which it perfectly frames the Millennium Wheel. One tower block that deserves a special mention, however, is the headquarters of the Metropolitan Police, **New Scotland Yard**, on Broadway opposite the Strutton Ground market. The revolving sign alone should be familiar to many from countless TV detective serials and news reports.

Further down Broadway, at no. 55, is the austere **Broadway House**, home to London Transport and St James's Park tube station, and the tallest building in London when it was built in 1929 by Charles Holden. It gained a certain notoriety at the time for its nude statues by Jacob Epstein, in particular the boy figure in *Day*, whose penis had to be shortened to appease public opinion. Round the corner, standing on its own in Caxton Street, is the former **Blewcoat School** (Mon–Fri 10am–5.30pm), built in red brick in 1709 by a local brewer as a charity school for the poor and used as such until 1926. It now serves as a National Trust shop. A statue of a blue-coated charity boy stands above the doorway.

There's more delightful Queen Anne architecture just to the north in **Queen Anne's Gate**, an amalgamation of two exquisite streets, originally separated by a wall, whose position is indicated by a weathered statue of Queen Anne. The western half is the older and more interesting of the two, each of its doorways surmounted by a rustic wooden canopy with pendants in the shape of acorns. It's worth walking round the back of the houses on the north side to appreciate the procession of elegant bow windows that look out onto St James's Park.

Chapter 3

St James's, Piccadilly, Mayfair and Marylebone

S T JAMES'S, MAYFAIR and MARYLEBONE emerged in the late seventeenth century as London's first real suburbs. Sheep and cattle were driven off the land as small farms made way for London's first major planned development: a web of brick and stucco terraces and grid-plan streets feeding into grand, formal squares, with mews and stables round the back. This expansion set the westward trend for middle-class migration, which gradually extended to Kensington and Chelsea, and as London's wealthier consumers moved west, so too did a large section of the city's commerce, particularly the more upmarket shops and luxury hotels which are still a feature of the area.

Aristocratic **St James's**, the rectangle of land to the north of St James's Park, was one of the first areas to be developed, and remains the preserve of the seriously rich. Piccadilly, which forms the border between St James's and Mayfair, is no longer the fashionable promenade it once was, but a whiff of exclusivity still pervades **Bond Street** and its tributaries, whose windows display the wares of top couturiers, art dealers and jewellers. **Regent Street** was created as a new "Royal Mile", a tangible borderline to shore up these new fashionable suburbs against the chaotic maze of Soho and the City, where the working population still lived. Now, along with **Oxford Street**, it has become London's busiest shopping district, drawing in thousands of shoppers from all over the world, particularly during the Christmas rush.

Away from the shops, the streets of **Mayfair** are quieter and more residential in flavour, with pockets of well-preserved Georgian architecture here and there, particularly around Shepherd Market and Hanover Square. **Marylebone**, which lies to the north of Oxford Street, is another grid-plan Georgian development, elegant in parts, though several social and real-estate leagues below Mayfair. It preserves much of its original village high street, while nearby Manchester Square boasts one of the city's best art galleries, the

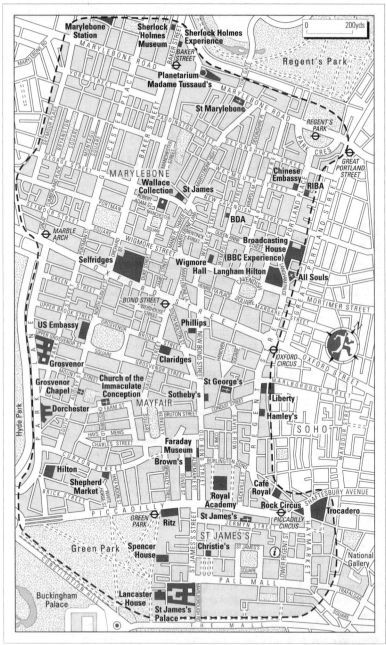

© crown copyright

Wallace Collection. In the northern fringes of Marylebone, you'll also find one of London's biggest tourist attractions, **Madame Tussaud's** – the oldest and largest wax museum in the world – and, beside it, London's **Planetarium**.

St James's

St James's, an exclusive little enclave sandwiched between The Mall and Piccadilly, was laid out in the 1670s close to St James's Palace. Royal and aristocratic residences predominate along its southern border, gentlemen's clubs cluster along Pall Mall and St James's Street, while jacket-and-tie restaurants and expense-account shops line Jermyn Street. Hardly surprising, then, that most Londoners rarely stray into this area, even though it contains some interesting architectural set pieces and a few of central London's scarce areas of real tranquillity.

If you're not in St James's for the shops, the best time to visit is on a Sunday, when the traffic is quieter, and the royal chapels, plus the one accessible Palladian mansion, are open to the public.

Haymarket

No prizes for guessing what **Haymarket** – which connects Piccadilly Circus with Pall Mall and marks the eastern border of St James's – was until 1830, despite numerous attempts to close it down and get rid of the smell. It was also, until early this century, an area where, in Dostoevsky's words, "thousands of whores swarm through the dark" servicing the wealthy gentlemen who frequented the street's two historic theatres, both of which survive to this day.

The Nash-built **Theatre Royal**, on the east side, with its handsome Corinthian portico and gilded acanthus leaves, is the more impressive. It was here that Oscar Wilde's plays *A Woman of No Importance* and *An Ideal Husband* were premiered, the latter closing down shortly after his arrest in 1895. **Her Majesty's Theatre**, opposite, has the finer pedigree, having played a leading part in London's musical life for over two centuries. It was the venue for numerous Handel premieres between 1711 and 1736, when the composer was joint-manager, and was effectively the city's royal opera house until Covent Garden rose to prominence this century. The present building, constructed in 1897, is only half the size of its predecessors, which were built on a scale with La Scala in Milan. Their scale is still suggested by the **Royal Opera Arcade**, which Nash placed round the back of the opera house, a short distance down Charles II Street on the left.

The nearest tube to Haymarket is Piccadilly Circus.

Lower Regent Street and Waterloo Place

Lower Regent Street, which runs parallel with Haymarket, was the first stage in John Nash's ambitious plan to link George IV's magnificent Carlton House with Regent's Park, though few of today's houses date from that period. Like so many of Nash's grandiose schemes, it never quite came to fruition, as George IV, soon after ascending the throne, decided that Carlton House – the most expensive palace ever to have been built in London – wasn't quite luxurious enough, and had it pulled down. Its Corinthian columns now support the main portico of the National Gallery.

The rest of Regent Street is described on p.114.

Lower Regent Street now opens up into **Waterloo Place**, which Nash was able to extend beyond Pall Mall once Carlton House had been demolished. At the centre of the square stands the **Guards' Crimean Memorial**, fashioned from captured Russian cannons, and commemorating the 2162 Foot Guards who died during the Crimean war – the horrors of battle were witnessed by Florence Nightingale, whose statue graces one of the monument's pedestals.

For more on Florence Nightingale, see p.306.

Having dodged the traffic hurtling down Pall Mall and cutting the square in two, you come face to face with the two grandest gentlemen's clubs in St James's (see box on p.108): the former **United Services Club**, to the east, and the **Athenaeum**, to the west. Their almost identical Neoclassical designs are the work of Nash's protégé

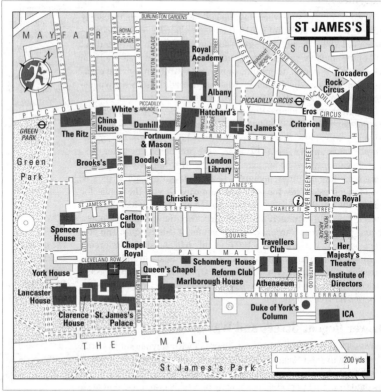

© crown copyright

Decimus Burton: of the two, the better-looking is the Athenaeum, its portico sporting a garish gilded statue of the goddess Athena and, above, a Wedgwood-type frieze inspired by the Elgin marbles, which had just arrived in London from Athens. The Duke of Wellington was a regular at the United Services Club, now the **Institute of Directors**, over the road, and the horse blocks – confusingly positioned outside the Athenaeum – were designed so the duke could mount his steed more easily.

Another inveterate club man, Edward VII – the "Gentleman of Europe", as he was known – sits permanently on his horse between the two clubs, while more statuary hides behind the railings of Waterloo Gardens, including one of Captain Scott, sculpted by the widow he left behind after failing to complete the return journey from the South Pole. Beyond, overlooking St James's Park, is the "Grand Old" **Duke of York's Column**, erected in 1833, ten years before Nelson's more famous one, and paid for by stopping one day's wages of every soldier in the army he marched "up the hill and down again", in the famous doggerel verse.

Having pulled his old palace down, George IV had Nash build **Carlton House Terrace**; the monumental facade now looks out onto St James's Park, but the rear is built on a much more human scale. It has long been a sought-after address: the **Royal Society**, the scientific body set up by Wren, among others, occupies no. 6; no. 4, by the exquisitely tranquil Carlton Gardens, was given to de Gaulle for the headquarters of the Free French during the last world war; while nos. 7–9, by the Duke of York steps, were the site of the German Embassy from 1849 (when it was the Prussian legation) until the outbreak of World War II. Albert Speer redesigned the interior, but the only external reminder of this period is a tiny grave for *ein treuer Begleiter* (a true friend) behind the railings near the column – it holds the remains of **Giro**, the Nazi ambassador's pet alsatian, accidentally electrocuted in February 1934.

Pall Mall and St James's Square

Running west from Trafalgar Square across Waterloo Place, **Pall Mall** is also renowned for its clubs, whose restrained Italianate and Neoclassical facades, fronted by cast-iron torches, still punctuate the street. It gets its bizarre name from the game of *pallo a maglio* (ball to mallet) – something like modern croquet – popularized by Charles II and played here and on The Mall. Crowds gathered here in 1807 when it became London's first gas-lit street – the original closely spaced lampposts (erected to reduce the opportunities for crime and prostitution) are still standing – but the heavy traffic that now pounds down it makes Pall Mall no fun to explore.

Instead, once you've passed Waterloo Place, head one block north to **St James's Square**, which had considerable cachet as a fashionable address when it was first laid out in the 1670s. Around the time

The gentlemen's clubs

The **gentlemen's clubs** of Pall Mall and St James's Street remain the final bastions of the male chauvinism and public-school snobbery for which England is famous. Their origins lie in the coffee and chocolate houses of the eighteenth century, though the majority were founded in the post-Napoleonic peace of the early nineteenth century by those who yearned for the life of the all-male officers' mess; drinking, whoring and gambling were the major features of early club life. **White's** – the oldest of the lot, and with a list of members that still includes numerous royals (Prince Charles held his stag party here), prime ministers and admirals – was renowned for its high gambling stakes, as was nearby **Brooks's**. Bets were wagered on the most trivial of things to relieve the boredom – "a thousand meadows and cornfields were staked at every throw" – and in 1755 one MP, Sir John Bland, shot himself after losing £32,000 in one night.

In their day, the clubs were also the battleground of sartorial elegance, particularly **Boodle's**, where the dandy-in-chief Beau Brummell set the fashion trends for the London upper class and provided endless fuel for gossip. It was said that Brummell's greatest achievement in life was his starched neckcloth, and that the Prince Regent himself wept openly when Brummell criticized the line of his cravat or the cut of his coat. More serious political disputes were played out in clubland, too. The **Reform Club**, from which Phileas Fogg set off on his trip "Around the World in Eighty Days", was the gathering place of the liberals behind the 1832 Reform Act, and remains one of the more "progressive" – it's one of the few to admit women as members. The Tories, led by Wellington, countered by starting up the **Carlton Club** for those opposed to the Act – it's still the leading Conservative club, and still men-only (Mrs Thatcher had to be made a special member). The **Travellers' Club** is the only one where there's even the remotest possibility of joining a guided tour; phone ☎020/7930 8688 for more details.

of George III's birth at no. 31, the square could boast no fewer than six dukes and seven earls, and over the decades it has maintained its exclusive air: no. 10 was occupied in turn by prime ministers Pitt the Elder, Lord Derby and Gladstone; at no. 16 you'll find the silliest sounding gentlemen's club, the East India, Devonshire, Sports and Public Schools Club; no. 4 was once home of Nancy Astor, the first woman MP to sit in the House of Commons, in 1919, while no. 31 was where Eisenhower formed the first Allied HQ. The narrowest house on the square (no. 14) is home to the **London Library**, the oldest and grandest private library in the country, founded in 1841 by Thomas Carlyle, who got sick of waiting up to two hours for books to be retrieved from the British Library shelves only to find he couldn't borrow them (he used to steal them instead). It's open only to fee-paying members.

Architecturally, the square is no longer quite the period piece it once was, but its proportions remain intact, as do the central **gardens**, which feature an equestrian statue of William III, depicted tripping over on the molehill that killed him at Hampton Court Palace. In the northeastern corner, across the road from the Astors' pad, there's a small memorial marking the spot where WPC Yvonne Fletcher was shot dead during the 1984 siege of what was then the Libyan Embassy, at no. 5. It has a quiet dignity that's lacking in most of London's public statuary to the great and (rarely) good.

Back on Pall Mall, the unusual seventeenth-century facade of **Schomberg House**, rebuilt in the 1950s, is one of the few to stand out, thanks to its Dutch-style red brickwork and elongated caryatids; it was here that Gainsborough spent the last years of his life. Next door, at no. 79 (now the P&O headquarters), Charles II housed Nell Gwynne, so that the two of them could chat over the garden wall, which once backed onto the grounds of St James's Palace. It was from one of the windows overlooking the garden that Nell is alleged to have dangled the 6-year-old future Earl of Burford, threatening to drop him if Charles didn't acknowledge paternity and give the boy a title; another, more tabloid-style version of the story alleges that Charles was persuaded only after overhearing Nell saying "Come here, you little bastard", then excusing herself on the grounds that she had no other name by which to call him.

St James's Square gardens are open to all.

St James's Palace

At the western end of Pall Mall stands **St James's Palace**, built on the site of a lepers' hospital which Henry VIII bought and demolished in 1532. It was here that Charles I chose to sleep the night before his execution, so as not to have to listen to his scaffold being erected, and when Whitehall Palace burnt down in 1698, St James's became the principal royal residence. In keeping with tradition, an ambassador to the UK is still known as "Ambassador to the Court of St James", even though the court moved down the road to Buckingham Palace when Queen Victoria came to the throne.

St James's Palace is closed to the public. The nearest tube is Green Park.

The main red-brick gate-tower, which looks out onto St James's Street, is the most conspicuous reminder of Tudor times, but the rest of the rambling, crenellated complex is the result of Nash's restoration and remodelling, and now provides a bachelor pad for Prince Charles and a home for the Duke and Duchess of Kent, as well as offices for various other royals and the Lord Chamberlain. Nash was also responsible for **Clarence House**, connected to the palace's southwest wing and barely visible from Cleveland Row. Built for William IV when he was the Duke of Clarence, it was the royal residence for the seven years of his reign, and is currently home to the Queen Mother, widow of George VI and the oldest star in the royal soap, having reached the age of 100 in the year 2000.

Prince Charles has his own Web site at www.prince ofwales.gov.uk.

St James's Palace is off limits to the public, with the exception of the **Chapel Royal**, which is open for services only. Access is from the Cleveland Row end of the palace, and gives you the chance to have a snoop around the complex and see Prince Charles's personal parking space. It was in the Chapel Royal that Charles I took Holy

The Chapel Royal is open for services on Sundays from October to Good Friday, at 8.30 and 11.15am.

Communion on the morning of his execution, and here, too, that the marriages of William and Mary, George III and Queen Charlotte, Victoria and Albert, and George V and Queen Mary, took place. One of the few remaining sections of Henry VIII's palace, it was redecorated in the 1830s, though the gilded strap-work ceiling matches the Tudor original erected to commemorate the brief marriage of Henry and Anne of Cleves (and thought to have been the work of Hans Holbein). The only other part of the palace you can explore is the partly arcaded **Friary Court** on Marlborough Road, assembly point for the Foot Guards marching to the Changing of the Guard ceremony at Buckingham Palace (see box on p.76).

The Queen's Chapel and Marlborough House

The Queen's Chapel is open for services on Sundays from Easter to July at 8.30 and 11.15am.

On the other side of Marlborough Road is the **Queen's Chapel**, once part of St James's Palace but now in the grounds of Marlborough House. A perfectly proportioned classical church, it was designed by Inigo Jones for the Infanta of Spain, the intended child bride of Charles I, and later completed for his French wife, Henrietta Maria, who was also a practising Catholic. A little further down Marlborough Road, and looking thoroughly forgotten, is the glorious Art Nouveau memorial to **Queen Alexandra** (wife of Edward VII), designed by Sir Alfred Gilbert (of Eros fame; see p.112), comprising a bronze fountain crammed with allegorical figures and flanked by robust lampposts.

Marlborough House (closed to the public) is hidden from Marlborough Road by a high, spiked, brick wall, and is only partly visible from The Mall. Queen Anne sacrificed half her garden in granting this land to her lover, Sarah Jennings, Duchess of Marlborough, in 1709. The duchess in turn told Wren to build her a "strong, plain and convenient" palace, and from the outside that's all it is; the interior, however, includes frescoes depicting the duke's famous victories at Blenheim, Ramillies and Malplaquet, along with ceiling paintings transferred from the Queen's House in Greenwich. The royals took over in 1817, though the last one to live here was Queen Mary, wife of George V, who died in 1953. The current residents are the Commonwealth Secretariat.

Green Park and Spencer House

To the west of St James's Palace lies **Green Park**, laid out on the burial ground of the old lepers' hospital by Henry VIII; it was left more or less flowerless – hence its name. Nowadays, apart from the springtime appearance of great swaths of daffodils and crocuses, it remains a moderately peaceful grassy spot, dominated by graceful London plane trees, but in its time it was a popular place for duels (banned from neighbouring St James's Park), ballooning and fireworks displays. Of the last, the most famous was the one immortalized by

Handel's *Music for the Royal Fireworks*, performed here on April 27, 1749 to celebrate the Peace of Aix-la-Chapelle, which ended the War of the Austrian Succession – over 10,000 fireworks were let off, setting fire to the custom-built Temple of Peace and causing three fatalities. The music was a great success, however.

St James's

Along the east side of the park runs the wide, pedestrian-only **Queen's Walk**, laid out for Queen Caroline, wife of George II, who had a little pavilion built nearby. At its southern end, there is a good view of **Lancaster House** (closed to the public), a grand Neoclassical palace built in rich Bath stone in the 1820s by Benjamin Wyatt, and used for government receptions and conferences since 1913. It was home to the London Museum (see p.236) until 1946, and it was here that the end of white rule in Southern Rhodesia was negotiated in the late 1970s.

Green Park extends from St James's Park and connects, via a subway, with Hyde Park. You can thus walk almost entirely over parkland as far as Notting Hill, a distance of some two and a half miles.

Spencer House

Feb–July & Sept–Dec Sun 11.30am–4.45pm; £6 (no admission for children under 10); ☎020/7499 8620. Green Park tube.

Two doors up from Lancaster House is Princess Diana's ancestral home, **Spencer House**, one of London's finest Palladian mansions, erected in the 1750s. Its best-looking facade looks out onto Queen's Walk, though access is from St James's Place. Inside, tour guides take you through nine of the state rooms, returned to something like their original state by their current owners, the Rothschilds. The Great Room features a stunning coved and coffered ceiling in green, white and gold, while the adjacent Painted Room is a feast of Neoclassicism, decorated with murals in the "Pompeian manner". The most outrageous décor, though, is to be found in Lord Spencer's Room, with its astonishing gilded palm-tree columns.

Jermyn Street

Jermyn Street (pronounced like "German"), which runs parallel with Piccadilly, has been, along with Savile Row, the spiritual home of English gentlemen's fashion since the advent of the clubs (see box on p.108). Its window displays and wooden panelled interiors still evoke an age when mass consumerism was unthinkable, and when it was considered that gentlemen "should either be a work of art or wear a work of art", in the words of Oscar Wilde. The kind of Englishmen for whom these shops originally catered are now a dying breed, and nowadays Americans and Japanese tend to make up the bulk of the customers.

The endurance of the cigar as a status symbol is celebrated at Davidoff, on the corner of St James's and Jermyn Street, with nothing so vulgar as a cigarette in the window. Further down Jermyn Street, on the corner with Bury Street, is Turnbull & Asser, who have placed shirts on the backs of VIPs from David Bowie to Ronald

Reagan, while *Wilton's*, at no. 55, is a truly Edwardian English restaurant where the main course alone costs £25, and ties and jackets are required Monday to Saturday (men can leave the tie at home on a Sunday).

Pipe smokers are a dying breed, but they can find solace at the **Dunhill shop** (*www.whitespot.co.uk*) on the corner of Jermyn and Duke streets, which has an enormous range of pipes (and cigars) for sale on the first floor, and a small **museum** in the circular basement. The best accessories on display are those made by Dunhill Motorities, gadget suppliers to Rolls Royce, whose slogan was "the smartness of the car is in the equipment". There are hip flasks disguised as books and "Bobby Finders" for detecting police cars, but sadly no sign of Mr Dunhill's greatest cigarette inventions: the in-car hookah and the motorist's pipe with a windshield for open-top toking.

Dunhill's museum is open Mon–Fri 9.30am–6pm, Sat 10am–6pm; free.

Antiquated epithets are part the street's quaint appeal: Taylor, at no. 74, still describe themselves as "Court hairdressers", Foster & Son, at no. 85, style themselves as "Bootmakers since 1840", while Geo. F. Trumper, at no. 20, is billed as a "Gentlemen's Perfumier". Floris, at no. 89, covers up the royal family's body odour with its ever-so-English fragrances, and Paxton & Whitfield, at no. 93, boasts an unrivalled selection of English and foreign cheeses. Lastly, at no. 21a, there's Bates the hatters, not quite as famous as Lock & Co at 6 St James's St, where the bowler hat was invented in 1850, but more memorable thanks to Binks, the stray cat who entered the shop in 1921 and never left, having been stuffed and displayed in a glass cabinet inside the shop, sporting a cigar and top hat. The shop has never had anything so vulgar as a sale.

Piccadilly Circus and around

Anonymous and congested it may be, but **Piccadilly Circus** is, for many Londoners, the nearest their city comes to having a centre. A much-altered product of Nash's grand 1812 Regent Street plan, and now a major traffic bottleneck, it's by no means a picturesque place, and is probably best seen at night, when the spread of illuminated signs (a feature since the Edwardian era) gives it a touch of Las Vegas dazzle, and when the human traffic flow is at its most frenetic.

The nearest tube is Piccadilly Circus.

As well as being the gateway to the West End, and a notorious spot for rent boys and drug dealers, this is also prime tourist territory, thanks mostly to Piccadilly's celebrated aluminium statue, popularly known as **Eros**. The fountain's archer is one of the city's top tourist attractions, a status that baffles all who live here – when it was first unveiled in 1893, it was so unpopular that the sculptor, Sir Alfred Gilbert, lived in self-imposed exile for the next thirty years. Despite the bow and arrow, it's not the god of love at all but the *Angel of Christian Charity*, erected to commemorate the Earl of

Shaftesbury, a Bible-thumping social reformer who campaigned against child labour.

Eros's plinth stands in front of the **Criterion**, one of London's more elegant theatres, with a sumptuous adjoining restaurant. This Art Nouveau building, with its ceiling of glittering gold mosaics, was, incredibly, covered over by plastic pizza-chain décor from the 1960s to the mid-1980s but is now back to its former glory. Next door to the Criterion theatre is Lillywhites, a long-established emporium for all things sporting, while another megastore – Tower Records' flagship UK outlet, open and crowded to midnight on weekdays – fronts no. 1 on the west side of the Circus.

Rock Circus

Mon, Wed, Thurs & Sun 10am–8pm, Tues 11am–8pm, Fri & Sat 10am–9pm; £8.25; ☎020/7734 7203; *www.rock-circus.com*. Piccadilly Circus tube.

If Eros's fame remains a mystery, the regular queue outside the nearby **Rock Circus** – on the top two floors of the old London Pavilion music hall, across Piccadilly Circus from the Criterion – is a good deal more perplexing. The "circus" of the title is a painful twenty-minute introductory show in a revolving theatre: the film is admirably narrated by Jools Holland, but the jerky animatronic "classic rock" performances by wax models are truly embarrassing. The rest of the attraction is little more than an array of Madame Tussaud's waxen rock legends, many of which are risible in the extreme: the Beatles look like a bunch of bank managers. There's a paltry collection of memorabilia – one of Elvis's less remarkable shirts, Paul Simon's diminutive Levi's – but virtually nothing on black music, dance music or the entire 1990s. The best bit is the graveyard of rock casualties, with headstones inscribed with "electrocuted by unearthed guitar", "choked on own vomit", "shot by his own father", "died from a tooth abscess" and so on. As for the so-called after-show party, it's a drugs-free zone and has clearly hardly got started.

Trocadero

Mon–Fri 10.30am–midnight, Sat & Sun 10.30am–1am; free; ☎020/7439 1791. Piccadilly Circus tube.

Next door to Rock Circus is the equally tacky **Trocadero**, site of another defunct nineteenth-century music hall. It's constantly being revamped and refurbished in an attempt to find a winning formula for what is, in reality, just a glorified amusement arcade with a surplus of escalators. The first sight that greets you is the *Free Fall Ride*, which relieves punters of £3 before making them feel like they've just fallen from a top-floor window. Trocadero's main offering at the moment, though, is *Funland*, a "back-to-basics" theme park, with dodgems, ten-pin bowling, mini-golf, go-karting, a ghost train, pool hall and sports bar, as well as the usual video games and virtual-reality thrill rides.

Regent Street

Drawn up by John Nash in 1812 as both a luxury shopping street, and a triumphal way between George IV's Carlton House and Regent's Park, **Regent Street** was the city's first attempt at dealing with traffic congestion, and was also the first stab at the slum clearance and planned social segregation which would later be perfected by the Victorians. Several unsavoury neighbourhoods were wiped off the map during its construction, and the completed street acted as a barrier separating the disreputable, immigrant Soho from the bourgeois quarters of Mayfair, St James's and Marylebone.

Despite the subsequent destruction of much of Nash's work and its replacement in the 1920s by what one critic has described as "neo-fascist Art Deco", it's still possible to admire the stately intentions of his original Regent Street plan, in particular the curve of the Quadrant, which swerves north from Piccadilly Circus. Sadly the Victorians, many of whom thought Nash's architecture monotonous, tore down the Quadrant's graceful colonnades in 1848 – shopkeepers claimed they obscured their window displays and encouraged prostitution.

Regent Street enjoyed eighty years as Bond Street's nearest rival, a place where "elegantly attired pedestrians evince the opulence and taste of our magnificent metropolis", as one Victorian observer put it. Redevelopment this century coincided with an increase in the purchasing power of the city's middle classes, bringing the tone of the street "down" and ushering in several heavyweight stores catering for the masses. The only truly bourgeois survivor in the Quadrant itself is the **Café Royal**, at no. 68, focus of the beau monde from the 1890s to the outbreak of World War I, when Oscar Wilde and Aubrey Beardsley presided, along with Walter Sickert, Max Beerbohm, Augustus John and George Bernard Shaw; later, Edward VIII and George VI hung out there (in their days as princes), though already it was a shadow of its former self. The present Grill Room, built in the 1920s, preserves some of the flavour of the café's halcyon days.

For a run-down on department-store shopping, see p.596.

Continuing northwards, the big stores are mostly on the right: recent recruits such as Gap, followed by more firmly established giants like **Hamley's**, the world's largest toy shop, and **Liberty**, the department store that popularized Arts and Crafts designs at the beginning of last century. The Liberty store is divided into two: the older part, which looks onto Regent Street, features a traditional, central roof-lit well, surrounded by wooden galleries carved from the timbers of two old naval battleships; an overhead walkway leads to the eye-catching mock-Tudor extension, added in the 1920s and stretching back along Great Marlborough Street as far as Carnaby Street (see p.147).

Piccadilly

Piccadilly apparently got its name from the ruffs or "pickadills" worn by the dandies who used to promenade here in the late seventeenth

century. Despite its fashionable pedigree, it is no place for prome-
nading in its current state, with traffic careering down it nose to tail
most of the day and night. Infinitely more pleasant places to window-
shop are the **nineteenth-century arcades**, originally built to protect
shoppers from the mud and horse dung on the streets, but now
equally useful for escaping exhaust fumes.

From Simpson's to the Ritz

With the exception of the modernist 1930s facade of the former
Simpson's department store (now Waterstone's flagship bookstore), there's nothing much to distract the eye along the south side
of Piccadilly until you reach **St James's Church**, Wren's favourite
parish church (he built it himself). The church has rich historical
associations – Pitt the Elder and William Blake were baptized here –
and rich furnishings, with the reredos, organ-casing and font all by
the master sculptor Grinling Gibbons. It's a traditional venue for big
society weddings, yet, like St Martin-in-the-Fields on Trafalgar
Square, it also ministers to the homeless (the church's heated interior is an unofficial daytime refuge). In addition, to generate some
extra income, St James's runs a daily craft market in the churchyard, and has a branch of the *Aroma* café chain at the west end of
the church; it also puts on top-class free lunchtime concerts.

*St James's is
another
London church
with a decent
café and
lunchtime
concerts.*

Piccadilly may not be the shopping heaven it once was, but there
are still several old firms here that proudly display their royal war-
rants. **Hatchard's Bookshop**, at no. 187, was founded in 1797, when
it functioned something like a cross between a gentlemen's club and
a library, with benches outside for customers' servants and daily
papers for the gentlemen inside to peruse. Today, Hatchard's is the
prestige branch of Waterstone's, elegant still, but with its old traditions marked most overtly by a large section on international royalty.

An even older institution, and a favourite with the twinset-and-
pearls contingent, is **Fortnum & Mason** (*www.fortnumandma-
son.com*), the food emporium at no. 181, which was established in
the 1770s by Charles Fortnum, one of George III's footmen.
Fortnum's intimate knowledge of the needs of a royal household,
together with his partner Hugh Mason's previous work at nearby St
James's Market (now defunct), helped make the shop an instant success. Fortnum's has been serving delicacies to the Royal Family and
slightly less exalted mortals ever since, watched over by the figures
of its founders, who bow to each other on the hour as the clock, over
the main entrance, clanks out the Eton school anthem – a rather
kitsch addition which dates only from 1964.

The store is most famous for its picnic hampers, an upper-class
institution, first introduced as "concentrated lunches" for hunting
and shooting parties, and now *de rigueur* for Ascot, Glyndebourne,
Henley and other society events. They are, of course, ludicrously
priced, but the food hall (there are upper floors for clothes and

accessories) has more affordable and individual treats to incite most visitors into opening their wallets. You can also take full English afternoon tea at the store's *Fountain* tearoom at around half the price of that offered in the big hotels.

Across St James's Street, with its best rooms overlooking Green Park, stands the **Ritz Hotel** (*www.theritzhotel.co.uk*), a byword for decadence since it first wowed Edwardian society in 1906; the hotel's design, with its two-storey French-style mansard roof and long arcade, was based on the buildings of Paris's Rue de Rivoli. For a prolonged look inside, you'll need to be in good appetite (and book in advance) for the famous afternoon tea in the hotel's *Palm Court* (see box on p.122).

*For more on
afternoon teas,
see box on
p.122.*

Further along Piccadilly, on the corner of Arlington Street, there's a superb Art Deco building that was built as a car showroom in the 1920s. The building is now, appropriately enough, a shop, bar and Chinese restaurant called **China House** (*www.chinahouse.co.uk*), and the interior is still pretty much intact, with zigzag inlaid marble flooring, Chinese-style painted woodwork and giant red lacquer columns among the most striking features.

The Royal Academy

Daily 10am–6pm, Fri until 8.30pm; £6–8; guided tours of the permanent collection Tues–Fri 1pm; free; ☎020/7300 8000; *www.royalacademy.org.uk*. Green Park or Piccadilly Circus tube.

*The RA hosts
some of
London's
major art
exhibitions –
as well as its
own summer
show.*

Across the road from Fortnum & Mason, the **Royal Academy of Arts** (RA) occupies the enormous Burlington House, one of the few survivors from the ranks of aristocratic mansions that once lined the north side of Piccadilly. Rebuilding in the nineteenth century destroyed the original curved colonnades beyond the main gateway, but the complex has kept much of its Palladian palazzo design from the early eighteenth century. The Academy itself was the country's first ever formal art school, founded in 1768 by a group of English painters including Thomas Gainsborough and Joshua Reynolds. Reynolds went on to become the academy's first president, and his statue now stands in the courtyard, palette in hand ready to paint the cars hurtling down Piccadilly.

The Academy's roll call of past members ranges from J.M.W. Turner and John Constable to Elisabeth Frink, though the college has always had a conservative reputation both for its teaching and its shows. More recently, the RA has deliberately courted the odd bit of controversy, as it did in 1997 with the "Sensation" show and again in 2000 with the "Apocolypse show". Nevertheless, the record-breaking crowds that flocked to the 1999 Monet exhibition are more typical, and little has changed at the **Summer Exhibition**, which opens in June each year. It's an odd event: a stop on the social calendar of upper-middle-class England, who are catered for, as at Wimbledon and Ascot, with a Pimm's bar (Pimm's being the classic English summer cocktail). And yet the show itself is, more or less, egalitarian. Anyone can enter paintings in any style, and the lucky winners get hung, in rather close proximity, and sold. Supposed gravitas is added by the RA "Academicians", who are allowed to display six of their own works – no matter how awful. The result is a bewildering display, which gets annually panned by highbrow critics.

As well as hosting exhibitions, the RA has a small **permanent collection**, featuring the heavyweights of its formative decades, plus the gallery's most valuable asset, Michelangelo's marble relief, the *Taddei Tondo*, displayed in the glass atrium of Norman Foster's Sackler Galleries.

The Albany and Burlington Arcade

Another palatial Piccadilly residence which has avoided redevelopment is the **Albany**, a plain, H-shaped Georgian mansion, neatly recessed behind its own iron railings and courtyard to the east of the Royal Academy. It was originally built for Lord Melbourne, but was divided in 1802 into a series of self-contained bachelor apartments. These are a classic address and have been occupied over the years by such literary figures as Lord Byron, J.B. Priestley, Aldous Huxley and Graham Greene; women have only recently been allowed to lease flats at the Albany in their own right.

Along the other side of the Royal Academy runs the **Burlington Arcade**, built in 1819 for Lord Cavendish, then owner of Burlington House, to prevent commoners throwing rubbish into his garden. Today it's London's longest and most expensive nineteenth-century arcade, lined with mahogany-fronted jewellers, gentlemen's outfitters and the like. Upholding Regency decorum, it is still illegal to whistle, sing, hum, hurry or carry large packages or open umbrellas on this small stretch, and the arcade's beadles (known as Burlington Berties), in their Edwardian frock coats and gold-braided top hats, take the prevention of such criminality very seriously.

Neither of Piccadilly's other two arcades can hold a torch to the Burlington, though they are still worth exploring if only to marvel at the strange mixture of shops. Of the two, the **Piccadilly Arcade** is the finer, an Edwardian extension to the Burlington on the south side of Piccadilly, its squeaky-clean bow windows displaying, among other items, Wedgwood porcelain, Russian icons, model soldiers and Eton collars.

Mayfair

Mayfair's rise to fame originated in the eighteenth century, when the area began to attract aristocratic London away from hitherto fashionable Covent Garden and Soho. Across rolling fields north of Piccadilly, the two big landowners, the Grosvenors and the Berkeleys, laid out magnificent squares, which remained at the heart of London's high society from the 1720s onwards. Offices,

Mayfair

embassies and luxury hotels now outnumber aristocratic pieds-à-terre – a process accelerated by the last war, which forced many businesses to relocate here away from the bomb-damaged City – though Mayfair's social cachet has remained much the same.

On the borders of Mayfair are London's prime shopping streets, catering to all classes and all purses. It's here that Londoners talk of "going shopping up the West End": to Piccadilly and Regent Street (described above), and to Bond Street and Oxford Street (described below). Piccadilly was already a fashionable place to shop by the eighteenth century, as was Bond Street, which runs through Mayfair. Regent Street was created in 1812 and took a while to catch on, while Oxford Street, to the north, didn't really come into its own until early last century, though it now surpasses the lot in the sheer mass of people who fight their way down it.

Bond Street

Bond Street runs more or less parallel with Regent Street, extending right the way from Piccadilly to Oxford Street. It is, in fact, two streets rolled into one: the southern half, laid out in the 1680s, is known as Old Bond Street; its northern extension, which followed less than fifty years later, is known as New Bond Street. In contrast to their international rivals, Rue de Rivoli or Fifth Avenue, they are both pretty unassuming architecturally – a mixture of modest Victorian and Georgian town houses – the shops that line them, however, are among the flashiest in London.

For a consumers' guide to London's fashion shops, see p.595.

Unlike its masculine counterpart, Jermyn Street (see p.111), Bond Street caters for both sexes, and though it also has its fair share of old established names, it's now dominated by foreign designer outlets like Prada, Versace, Donna Karan, Chanel, DKNY and so on. Versace's palatial premises, at 36 Old Bond St, are a sight worthy of any guidebook – the Versailles of consumerist London, spread over four floors and adapted from already opulent banking premises at a cost of over £12 million. Another grand emporium is the Nicole Farhi store at 158 New Bond St: 10,000 square feet of minimalist design and elegant, wearable clothes, plus a basement bar/restaurant.

Neighbouring **Conduit Street** has recently become something of a British fashion enclave. Vivienne Westwood was the first to spot the potential of this wide street, situated halfway down Bond Street. She has since been joined by Alexander McQueen, The Conran Shop and the ultra-discreet Connolly, as well as Issey Miyake, Yohji Yamamoto and Moschino. In the 1980s, it was pedestrianized **South Molton Street**, northwest off New Bond Street and surfacing on Oxford Street just behind Bond Street tube, that attracted the top designers. The only survivor from those days, though, is Browns, a honeypot of the trendier labels which occupies several premises in the street.

In addition to fashion, Bond Street is renowned for its **auction houses** and for its **fine art galleries**. Visiting the auction houses is free and can be fun (see box below), but even if you don't venture in, take a look at the doorway of Sotheby's, topped by an Egyptian statue dating from 1600 BC and thus the oldest outdoor sculpture in London. Bond Street's art galleries – exclusive mainstays of the street – are actually outnumbered by those on neighbouring **Cork Street**. The main difference between the two locations is that the Bond Street dealers are basically heirloom offloaders, whereas Cork Street galleries sell largely contemporary art. Both have impeccably

For art gallery listings, see p.588.

Auction houses

A very Mayfair-style entertainment lies in visiting the area's trio of **auction houses**: Christie's, at 8 King St in St James's (☎020/7839 9060; *www .christies.com*), which has attracted high society since the days of Garrick, Reynolds and Boswell; Sotheby's, at 34–35 New Bond St (☎020/7293 5000; *www.sothebys.com*), the oldest of the three, having been founded in 1745 (though its pre-eminence only really dates from the last war); and Phillips, a little more modest, at 101 New Bond St (☎020 /7629 6602; *www.phillips-auctions.com*).

Viewing takes place from Monday to Friday, and also occasionally at the weekend, and the galleries are open free of charge, though without a catalogue (costing £10 or more) the only information you'll glean is the lot number. Thousands of the works that pass through the rooms are of museum quality, and, if you're lucky, you might catch a glimpse of a masterpiece in transit between private collections, and therefore only ever on public display in the auction-house galleries. And of course anyone can attend the auctions themselves, though remember to keep your hands firmly out of view unless you're bidding.

Sotheby's is probably the least intimidating: staff run an excellent café, and offer free valuations, if you have an heirloom of your own to check out. There is always a line of people unwrapping plastic bags under the polite gaze of valuation staff, who call in the experts if they see something that sniffs of real money. The auction houses have all suffered from allegations of price-fixing recently, though so far business seems unaffected.

---

presented and somewhat intimidating staff, but, if you're interested, walk in and look around. They're only shops, after all.

Bond Street also has its fair share of perfumeries and **jewellers**, many of them long-established outlets that have survived the vicissitudes of fashion. A fine example is Asprey & Garrard, at the corner of New Bond Street and Grafton Street. Founded in 1781 by a family of Huguenot craftsmen, and now jewellers to the royals, the company is currently owned by Tommy Hilfiger, purveyors of hip streetwear. The facade of the company's Bond Street store features a wonderful parade of arched windows, picked out in fairy lights and flanked by slender Corinthian wrought-iron columns. Close by is a double statue of Winston Churchill and President Roosevelt enjoying a chat on a park bench.

One Bond Street institution you can feel free to walk into is **Smythson**, at no. 40 New Bond Street, the bespoke stationers, founded in 1887, who made their name printing Big Game books for colonialists to record what they'd bagged out in Africa and India. At the back of the shop is a small octagonal museum encrusted with shells and mirrors, and a few artefacts. There photos and replicas of the book of condolence Smythson created for JFK's funeral, and the cherry calf and vellum diary given to Princess Grace of Monaco as a wedding gift.

Smythson is open Mon–Fri 9.30am–6pm, Sat 10am–6pm; free.

Burlington Gardens, Savile Row and Hanover Square

For an interesting detour off Bond Street, head east along **Burlington Gardens**, which boasts an imposing nineteenth-century Italianate pile on its south side, built in the 1860s to house London University's administration and peppered with statues of international intellectuals. Until fairly recently, it was home to the **Museum of Mankind**, the ethnographic department of the British Museum, which is slowly returning to the museum's Bloomsbury site (see p.161).

At the end of Burlington Gardens, running parallel with New Bond Street, is another classic address in sartorial matters, **Savile Row**, still considered the place to go for made-to-measure suits for those with the requisite £2000 or so to spare. The number of bespoke tailors has declined, but several venerable businesses remain. Gieves & Hawkes, at no. 1, were the first tailors to establish themselves here back in 1785, with Nelson and Wellington among their first customers; more recently, they courted controversy by offering a suit made from hamster skin. Dege & Skinner, at no. 10, is strong on military tailoring (Prince Andrew's mess kit was made here), while Henry Poole & Co, at no. 15, has cut suits for the likes of Napoleon, Dickens, Churchill and de Gaulle.

Savile Row also has connections with the pop world at no. 3, where Apple, the record label set up by **The Beatles**, had its offices and recording studio from 1968 until the building's near physical collapse in 1972. In February 1969 The Beatles gave their last live gig on the roof here, stopping the traffic and eventually attracting the attentions of the local police – as captured on film in *Let It Be*.

The Row terminates at Conduit Street (see above), where the funnel-shaped St George's Street splays into **Hanover Square**, site of the old Hanover Square Rooms where Bach, Liszt, Haydn and Paganini all performed before the building's demolition in 1900. Halfway up St George's Street, and contemporaneous with the square, is the sooty Corinthian portico of **St George's Church**, much-copied since, but the first of its kind in London when it was built in the 1720s. Nicknamed "London's Temple of Hymen", it has long been Mayfair's most fashionable church for weddings: among those who tied the knot here are the Shelleys, George Eliot, Benjamin Disraeli and Teddy Roosevelt; Handel, a confirmed bachelor, was a regular here for many years and even had his own pew (see box on p.123).

Albemarle Street and Berkeley Square

On the west side of Old Bond Street, a garish orange and white plasterwork entrance announces the **Royal Arcade**, a full-blown High Victorian shopping mall with tall arched bays and an elegant glass roof, designed so that the wealthy guests of **Brown's** hotel in Albemarle Street could have a sheltered and suitably elegant approach to the shops on Bond Street. Apart from being a posh hotel (see box on p.122), *Brown's* was where the country's first telephone call was placed by Alexander Graham Bell in 1848, though initially he got a crossed line with a private telegraph wire, before finally getting through at around 3am to the hotel manager, who was installed at his home in Hammersmith. Also in Albemarle Street, at no. 50, are the offices of John Murray, the publishers of Byron and of the oldest British travel guides. It was here in 1824 that Byron's memoirs were tragically destroyed, after Murray managed to persuade Tom Moore, to whom they had been bequeathed, that they were too scurrilous to publish.

Further up Albemarle Street, at no. 21, is the weighty Neoclassical facade of the **Royal Institution**, a scientific body founded in 1799 "for teaching by courses of philosophical lectures and experiments the application of science to the common purposes of life"; its professors have included Humphrey Davy (inventor of the miner's lamp), Michael Faraday and Lord Rutherford. The building's basement has since been converted into a small **Faraday Museum**, featuring his original notebooks, equipment and a mock-up of the lab in which the "father of electricity" discovered the laws of electromagnetics. Faraday (who features on the current £20 note) was also instrumental in inaugurating the Royal Institution's six Christmas Lectures, a continuing tradition designed to popularize science among schoolchildren.

The Faraday Museum is open Mon–Fri 9am–6pm; £1; ☎020/7409 2992; www.ri .ac.uk.

Two blocks west of Albemarle Street lies **Berkeley Square**, where, according to the music-hall song, nightingales sing. Laid out in the 1730s, only the west side of the square has any surviving Georgian

---

Afternoon tea in Mayfair

Only the horribly rich can afford to stay in Mayfair's top hotels, but any-one – provided they are suitably attired – can enjoy their sumptuous décor by partaking in the ritual of a "traditional" **afternoon tea** (usually served between 3 and 6pm). At a cost of between £15 and £20 a head, this is no quick cuppa, but a high-cholesterol feast that kicks off with sandwiches, moves on to scones festooned with clotted cream and jam, and finishes up with assorted cakes, all washed down with innumerable pots of tea.

Tea in the (no-smoking) *Palm Court* at the *Ritz* is to most people's minds the ultimate in extravagance, and is consequently oversubscribed (you'll need to book several weeks in advance, and wear a jacket and tie to get in). For a more intimate, specifically English ambience, you might pre-fer the leather sofas and wooden panelling of *Brown's*, on Albemarle Street, or the Fortnum & Mason store on Piccadilly (see p.115). Other grand-hotel tea options in Mayfair include *Claridge's*, the Art Deco mas-terpiece on Brook Street, which has the most obsequious waiters, assisted by liveried footmen and a string quartet; the *Dorchester*, on Park Lane, built in the 1930s and now owned by the Sultan of Brunei, is rather more vulgar in its opulence; and the *Park Lane Hotel* on Piccadilly, again extravagantly revamped but featuring a wonderful grey and silver Jazz Age foyer from the 1920s.

Other grand hotels for a central London tea include the *Savoy* on the Strand and the *Waldorf* at Aldwych. And keep in mind that any of these hotels will do you a traditional **English breakfast**, wheeling out kippers, eggs, bacon and all manner of offal on silver platters, again for around £15 a head for the works. The *Savoy*, in particular, excels at this.

---

houses to boast of, and nowadays any nightingales would have trou-ble being heard over the traffic. However, the thing that saves the square is its wonderful parade of 200-year-old London plane trees. With their dappled, peeling trunks, giant lobed leaves and globular spiky fruits, these pollution-resistant trees are a ubiquitous feature of the city, and Berkeley Square's specimens are among the finest in the capital.

Shepherd Market

Strictly speaking, Mayfair is the area bordered by Regent Street, Piccadilly, Oxford Street and Park Lane, but its residential heart has been pushed further west towards Hyde Park. If you're coming from Green Park tube, head west down Piccadilly until you get to **Half Moon Street**, where the fictional Wooster and his faithful valet Jeeves of P.G. Wodehouse's novels lived, and where in 1763 the real James Boswell, newly arrived from Edinburgh, took lodgings and wrote his scurrilous diary.

At the end of the street, turn left into Curzon Street, site of **Crewe House**, now a company headquarters and one of the few eighteenth-century Mayfair mansions still standing. It was originally construct-ed by local builder Edward Shepherd, who also laid out nearby

Shepherd Market, a little warren of alleyways and passages now occupied by swanky cafés and restaurants, plus a couple of Victorian pubs, all extremely popular in summer. It was here that the infamous May Fair – which gives the area its name – took place until it was suppressed in the mid-eighteenth century because of

---

Handel and Hendrix in Mayfair

Born **Georg Friedrich Händel** (1685–1759) to a barber-surgeon in Halle, Saxony, Handel paid his first visit to London in 1711, where he marked his arrival by the composition of *Rinaldo*, which he wrote in fifteen days flat. The furore it produced – not least when Handel released a flock of sparrows for one aria – made him a household name. On his return in 1712 he was commissioned to write several works for Queen Anne, before becoming the court composer to George I, his one-time patron in Hanover.

London became Handel's spiritual home: he anglicized his name and nationality and lived out the rest of his life here, producing all the work for which he is now best known, including the *Water Music*, the *Fireworks Music* and his *Messiah*, which was composed in less than a month and failed to enthral its first audiences, but is now one of the great set pieces of Protestant culture. George III was so moved by the grandeur of the Hallelujah Chorus that he leapt to his feet and remained standing for the entire performance. Handel himself fainted during a performance of the work in 1759, and died shortly afterwards in his home at 25 Brook St; he is buried in Westminster Abbey.

Handel's birthday is celebrated with a concert of his music given at the Coram Foundation, site of the old Foundling Hospital (see p.180) which he helped to finance, and the London Handel Society organizes an annual Handel festival in April, centred on St George's Church, Hanover Square (see p.121). In addition, fans will be pleased to know that the composer's Mayfair house is due to open as the **Handel House Museum** during the course of 2001 (for more information phone ☎020/7495 1685).

Some two hundred years later, another ground-breaking musician, **Jimi Hendrix** (1942–70), lived on and off for eighteen months, in the neighbouring house of no. 23. Both men are currently honoured with blue plaques, Jimi receiving his in 1995 – a first for a rock musician, and only the third black person to be commemorated in such a way. Born Johnny Allen Hendrix in Seattle in 1942, he was persuaded to fly over to London in September 1966 after meeting Chas Chandler, manager and producer of The Animals. Shortly after arriving, he teamed up with two other British musicians, Noel Redding and Mitch Mitchell, and formed The Jimi Hendrix Experience. During the next two years, The Experience toured extensively, releasing three top-selling albums before splitting up in late 1968.

It was at the beginning of 1969 that Hendrix moved into Brook Street with his girlfriend, Kathy Etchingham; apparently he was much taken with the fact that it was once Handel's residence, ordering Kathy to go and buy the albums for him. It was also in London that Hendrix met his untimely death, on September 18, 1970. At around 7am, in the *Samarkand Hotel* in Notting Hill, after a final gig at *Ronnie Scott's* in Soho, Hendrix swallowed nine sleeping pills, later vomiting in his sleep, slipping into unconsciousness and suffocating. He died in the *Great Cumberland Hotel* on Oxford Street, and is buried in Seattle.

"drunkenness, fornication, gaming and lewdness". Appropriately enough, the market is still a well-known haunt for high-class prostitutes, and frequented by politicians and media folk. To complete the seedy picture, it was round the corner from Shepherd Market, at 9 Curzon Place, that Cass Elliot (aka Mama Cass) of The Mamas and Papas died in July 1974, and, four years later, Keith Moon, drummer with The Who, died of an overdose.

Around Grosvenor Square

Grosvenor Square, to the northwest, is the largest of the three Mayfair squares, and was known during World War II as "Little America" – General Eisenhower, whose statue now stands here, ran the D-day campaign from no. 20. The American presence is still pretty strong, thanks to the Roosevelt Memorial, which overlooks the square's central garden, and to the monstrously ugly **American Embassy**, which occupies the entire west side of the square. Completed in 1960 to designs by Eero Saarinen, the embassy is watched over by a giant gilded eagle plus a small posse of police, as most weeks there's some demonstration or other against US foreign policy – albeit nothing to rank with 1968's violent protests against US involvement in Vietnam. So the story goes, Mick Jagger was innocently signing autographs in his Bentley as the 1968 riot began, and later wrote *Street Fighting Man*, inspired by what he witnessed.

Eisenhower's initial pied-à-terre was a room painted "whorehouse pink" in **Claridge's**, the hotel for the rich and royal one block east of Grosvenor Square on Brook Street. *Claridge's* also served as the

Tea at Claridge's? See box on p.122.

The Cato Street Conspiracy

British history is disappointingly short on political assassinations: one prime minister, no royals and only a handful of MPs. One of the most dismal failures was the 1820 **Cato Street Conspiracy**, drawn up by a motley band of sixteen men in an attic off the Edgware Road. Their plan was to murder the entire Cabinet as they dined with Lord Harrowby at 44 Grosvenor Square. Having beheaded the Home Secretary and another of the ministers, they then planned to sack Coutts' Bank, capture the cannon on the Artillery Ground, take Gray's Inn, Mansion House, the Bank of England and the Tower, torching the barracks in the process, and proclaiming a provisional government.

As it turned out, one of the conspirators was an agent provocateur, and the entire mob were arrested in the Cato Street attic by a detachment of Coldstream Guards on the night of the planned coup, February 23. In the melee, one Bow Street Runner was killed and and eleven of the conspirators escaped. Eventually, the five ringleaders were hanged at Newgate, and another five were transported to Australia. Public sympathy for the uprising was widespread, so the condemned were spared from being drawn and quartered, though they did have their heads cut off afterwards. (The hangman was later attacked in the streets and almost castrated.)

---

wartime hang-out of the OSS, forerunner of the CIA, one of whose representatives held a historic meeting here in 1943 with Szmul Zygielbojm from the Jewish Board of the Polish government-in-exile. Zygielbojm was told that Roosevelt had refused his request to bomb the rail lines leading to Auschwitz; the following day he committed suicide.

American troops stationed over here used to worship at the **Grosvenor Chapel** on South Audley Street, a building reminiscent of early settlers' churches in New England. It's still a favourite with the American community in London, though its most illustrious occupant is radical MP John Wilkes ("Wilkes and Liberty" was the battle cry of many a riot in the mid-eighteenth century). Behind the chapel are the beautifully secluded **Mount Street Gardens**, dotted with 200-year-old plane trees and enclosed by nineteenth-century red-brick mansions. At the far eastern end of the gardens is the back entrance to the **Church of the Immaculate Conception**, on Farm Street, the Jesuits' London stronghold, built in ostentatious Neo-Gothic style in the 1840s. Every surface is covered in decoration, but the reredos of gilded stone by Pugin (of Houses of Parliament fame) is particularly impressive.

Oxford Street

As wealthy Londoners began to move out of the City during the eighteenth century in favour of the newly developed West End, so **Oxford Street** (*www.oxfordstreet.co.uk*) – the old Roman road to Oxford – gradually replaced Cheapside (see p.243) as London's main shopping street. Today, despite successive recessions and sky-high rents, this scruffy, two-mile hotchpotch of shops is still one of the world's busiest streets, its Christmas lights are still switched on by esteemed public figures, and its traffic controllers have to be equipped with loud-hailers to prevent the hordes of Christmas shoppers from losing their lives at the busy road junctions.

Oxford Street has four tube stations along its length, from west to east: Marble Arch, Bond Street, Oxford Circus and Tottenham Court Road.

East of Oxford Circus, the street forms the border between Soho and Fitzrovia (see Chapter 4), and is peppered with booths selling cheap gifts and policemen's hats, and auctioneers selling liquidated stock out of short-lease shops. There's a fair number of nationwide giants here as well, including the main HMV record store, the Virgin Megastore and Marks & Spencer, which started life in Leeds market in 1912 under the slogan "Don't ask the price – it's a penny."

The west end of Oxford Street is dominated by more upmarket stores, including the one great landmark, **Selfridge's** (*www .selfridges.co.uk*), a huge Edwardian pile fronted by giant Ionic columns, with the Queen of Time riding the ship of commerce and supporting an Art Deco clock above the main entrance. The store was opened in 1909 by Chicago millionaire Gordon Selfridge, who flaunted its 130 departments under the slogan, "Why not spend a day at Selfridge's?", but was later pensioned off after running into trouble

The nearest tube for Selfridge's is Bond Street.

with the Inland Revenue. We have Selfridge's to thank for the concept of the "bargain basement", the irritating "only ten more shopping days to Christmas" countdown, and the nauseous bouquet of perfumes from the women's cosmetics counters, strategically placed at the entrance to all department stores to entice customers in.

Marylebone

To the north of Oxford Street lies **Marylebone**, once the outlying village of St Mary-by-the-Bourne. Samuel Pepys walked through open countryside to reach its pleasure gardens in 1668 and declared it a "pretty place". During the course of the next century, the gardens were closed and the village was swallowed up as its chief landowners – among them the Portlands and the Portmans – laid out a mesh of uniform Georgian streets and squares, much of which has been left unaltered.

Sights in this part of town include the **BBC Experience** in Broadcasting House, the massively touristed **Madame Tussaud's** and the **Planetarium**, both on Marylebone Road, the low-key galleries of the **Wallace Collection**, and Sherlock Holmes' old stomping grounds around **Baker Street**. There is a pleasure, though, in just wandering the Marylebone streets, especially the village-like quarter around **Marylebone High Street**.

Langham Place

Regent Street and its accompanying shops stop abruptly at **Langham Place**, site of **All Souls**, Nash's simple and ingenious little Bath-stone church, built in the 1820s. The unusual circular Ionic portico and conical spire, which caused outrage in its day, were designed to provide a visual full stop to Regent Street and a pivot for the awkward twist in the triumphal route to Regent's Park. Behind All Souls lies the totalitarian-looking **Broadcasting House**, BBC radio headquarters since 1931, and now home to the interactive "BBC Experience" (see below). The figures of Prospero and Ariel (pun intended) above the entrance are by Eric Gill, who caused outrage by sculpting Ariel with overlarge testicles, and, like Epstein a few years earlier at Broadway House (see p.102), was forced in the end to cut the organs down to size.

Opposite Broadcasting House stands the **Langham Hilton**, built in heavy Italianate style in the 1860s, badly bombed in the last war and recently refurbished at a cost of millions. It features in several Sherlock Holmes mysteries, and its former guests have included Antonín Dvořák (who courted controversy by ordering a double room for himself and his daughter to save money), exiled emperors Napoleon III and Haile Selassie, and the once-famous Ouida (aka Marie Louise de la Ramée), who threw outrageous parties for young

Guards officers and wrote many of her best-selling romances in her
dimly lit hotel boudoir.

The BBC Experience

Mon 11am–4.30pm, Tues–Sun 10am–4.30pm; £7.50; ☎0870/603 0304;
www.bbc.co.uk/experience. Oxford Circus tube.

As part of its 75th anniversary celebrations in 1997, the BBC opened
its very own interactive museum, the **BBC Experience**, in its offices
on Langham Place. A word of warning is necessary to TV addicts,
however, as the museum is almost exclusively concerned with radio
(Broadcasting House is the home of BBC radio, but not television).
The museum is part guided tour, part hands-on experience, so visits
are carefully orchestrated, with tours setting off every thirty minutes
(every fifteen at peak times). The museum's initial waiting area contains an interesting and informative exhibition devoted to **Guglielmo
Marconi**, the Italian who came to Britain in order to develop "wire-
less" radio telegraphy, to make communication possible with ships at
sea, but ended up being instrumental in the birth of the radio as a
broadcasting medium in the 1920s.

The ten-minute "behind-the-scenes" audiovisual presentation, is a
typically entertaining, informative and educative "Beeb" production.
Much more fun, however, is the Interactive Radio Studio, where you
get to record a short radio play with your fellow visitors – an activity
guaranteed to break the ice. Unfortunately, instead of building on
this, you're then forced to sit through an overlong multimedia programme *Heritage and History* of BBC radio. Finally, you get to sit
in TV-dominated living rooms through the decades, and to play
around in the museum's interactive section, directing an episode of
Eastenders, fine-tuning your sports commentary and presenting the
weather. There are BBC CD-Roms and Web sites to surf, though the
snippets from the organization's sound archives are a lot more fun:
you can hear the ball burst in the 1947 FA Cup Final, relive
Churchill's funeral or listen to coverage of Kennedy's assassination.

Portland Place

After the chicane around All Souls, you enter **Portland Place**, laid out
by the Adam brothers in the 1770s and incorporated by Nash in his
grand route. Once the widest street in London, it's still a majestic
avenue, lined exclusively with Adam-style houses, boasting wonderful fanlights and iron railings. Several embassies occupy properties
here, including the Chinese legation at no. 49, where the exiled
republican leader **Sun Yat Sen** was kidnapped and held incognito for
several days in 1896, on the express orders of the Chinese emperor.
Eventually Sun managed to send a note to one of his British friends,
saying "I am certain to be beheaded. Oh woe is me!", though it was
only when the press got hold of the story that Sun was finally

Marylebone

The café at the RIBA is run by the superb Patisserie Valerie chain and is open Mon–Sat 8am–6pm; the bookshop is open Mon–Fri 9.30am–5.30pm, Sat 10am–5pm.

Regent's Park is covered on p.387.

released; he went on to found the Chinese Nationalist Party and became the first president of China in 1911.

Arguably the finest of all the buildings on Portland Place is the sleek Portland-stone facade of the **Royal Institute of British Architects** (RIBA; *www.architecture.com*), built in the 1930s amidst the remaining Adam houses. The highlight of the building is the interior, which you can view en route to the institute's first-floor café, to the excellent ground-floor bookshop, or during one of the frequent exhibitions and Tuesday-evening lectures held here. The main staircase remains a wonderful period piece, with its etched glass balustrades and walnut veneer, and with two large black marble columns rising up on either side.

At the far end of Portland Place, Nash originally planned a giant "circus" as a formal entrance to Regent's Park. Only the southern half – two graceful arcs of creamy terraces known collectively as **Park Crescent** – was eventually completed, and it is now cut off from the park by the busy thoroughfare of Marylebone Road.

The Wallace Collection

Mon–Sat 10am–5pm, Sun noon–5pm; free; ☎020/7563 9500; *www.wallace-collection.org.uk*. Bond Street tube.

Of the three squares immediately north of Oxford Street, only Manchester Square has kept its peaceful Georgian appearance, thanks to its position away from the main traffic arteries. At its head is Hertford House, a miniature eighteenth-century French chateau transplanted to central London, which holds the splendid **Wallace Collection**, a museum-gallery best known for its eighteenth-century French paintings and decorative art. In 2000, the museum had a clever makeover, courtesy of architect Rick Mather, who glassed over the central courtyard to create a swanky café. At the same time, a more hands-on approach has been adopted, with talks and demonstrations aimed at all ages.

The Wallace Collection was originally bequeathed to the nation in 1897 by Lady Wallace, widow of Sir Richard Wallace, an art collector who, as the illegitimate son of the fourth Marquess of Hertford, also inherited this elegant mansion and the family treasures. Despite its recent re-make, the museum remains, at heart, an old-fashioned institution, with exhibits piled high in glass cabinets and paintings covering every inch of wall space. However, it is the combined effect of the exhibits set amidst the period fittings – and a bloody great armoury – that makes the place so remarkable.

The courtyard and lower ground floor

On entering the house, pick up a plan at the main desk and march through the entrance hall and dining room and cross the glass bridge to the covered **courtyard**, now home to *Café Bagatelle*, which is a fully fledged French-run restaurant with airs and graces to match its setting, and not a place for a quick cuppa. If you're not partaking, head down the stairs to the **Porphyry Court**, named after the eighteenth-century vases displayed there. Off the court, you'll find the Meeting Room, where talks and demonstrations take place, the Education Studio for school groups, a lecture theatre and the museum toilets.

In the nearby **Conservation Gallery**, which reveals the construction techniques that lie behind the expensive furniture and armour in the collection, folk of all ages can also try on some medieval armour. Adjacent, the **Reserve Collection** houses second-division pictures and antique bits and bobs, but also has an interesting section on fakes and forgeries. Changing exhibitions of works by Richard Parkes Bonington, whose translucent watercolours of Italy and France were the sort of "pleasing pictures" which appealed to the fourth Marquess, are displayed in the **Watercolour Gallery**, beyond which is the museum's temporary exhibition space.

The ground floor

The best way to tour the ground-floor rooms is to start in the **Front State Room**, where the walls are hung with several mildly distracting paintings by Reynolds, and Lawrence's typically sensuous portrait of the author and society beauty, the Countess of Blessington, which went down a storm at the Royal Academy in 1822. In the **Back State Room**, you'll find the cream of the house's Sèvres porcelain, and, centre stage, a period copy of Louis XIV's desk, which was the most expensive piece of eighteenth-century French furniture ever made. In the **Sixteenth-Century Gallery**, there are several interesting medieval and Renaissance pieces, ranging from *pietro dure*, bronze and majolica to Limoges porcelain and Venetian glass.

In the **Smoking Room**, a small alcove at the far end survives to give an idea of the effect of the original Minton-tiled décor Wallace chose for this room. The next three rooms house the extensive armoury bought *en bloc* by Wallace around the time of the Franco-Prussian War; it was in recognition for the humanitarian assistance Wallace provided in Paris during that war that he received his baronetcy. A fourth room houses Oriental arms and armour, collected by the fourth Marquess of Hertford. The ground floor finishes in the **Housekeeper's Room**, with a group of fine nineteenth-century pictures including several oil paintings by Bonington, who exhibited alongside his close friend Delacroix, whose works also feature here.

The first floor

The most famous paintings in the collection are on the first floor, the tone of which is set by **Boucher**'s sumptuous mythological scenes over the main staircase. In the **Boudoir**, you'll find Reynolds' doe-eyed moppets and Greuze's soft-focus studies of kids. En route to the

Study, check out the decorative gold snuffboxes and the silver-gilt Augsburg toilet service for an eighteenth-century lady's *levée*. In the **Study** itself are several portraits by Elizabeth Vigée le Brun, one of the most successful portraitists of pre-revolutionary France. Meanwhile, in the **West Room**, there are more Boucher nudes – the soft porn of the *ancien régime* – and his gloriously florid portrait of Madame de Pompadour, Louis XV's mistress and patron of many of the great French artists of the period.

Among the Rococo delights in the **West Gallery** are some elegiac scenes by Watteau, such as *Halt During the Chase* and *Music Party*, and Fragonard's coquettes, one of whom flaunts herself to a smitten beau in *The Swing*. In addition to all this French finery there's a good collection of Dutch paintings in the **East Galleries** on the other side of the house: de Hooch's *Women Peeling Apples*, oil sketches by Rubens and landscapes by Ruisdael. And in the **Small Drawing Room**, there are contrasting vistas by Canaletto and Guardi, whose works were more or less souvenirs for eighteenth-century Brits doing the Grand Tour.

The **Great Gallery**, the largest room in the house, was specifically built by Wallace to display what he considered to be his finest paintings, including works by Murillo and Poussin, several vast Van Dyck portraits, Rubens' *Rainbow Landscape* and **Frans Hals'** *Laughing Cavalier*. Here, too, are *Perseus and Andromeda*, a late work by **Titian**, **Velázquez**'s *Lady with a Fan* and **Rembrandt**'s affectionate portrait of his teenage son, Titus, who was helping administer his father's estate after bankruptcy charges, and who died at the age of just 28. At one end of the room are three portraits of the actress Mary Robinson: one by Romney, one by Reynolds and, best of the lot, **Gainsborough**'s deceptively innocent portrayal, in which she insouciantly holds a miniature of her lover, the 19-year-old Prince of Wales (later George IV).

Doctors and dentists

Cavendish Square, just north of Oxford Street, marks the beginning of **Harley Street**, where doctors, dentists and medical specialists opened up shop in the mid-nineteenth century to serve the area's wealthy citizens. Private medicine survived the threat of the postwar National Health Service, and the most expensive specialists and hospitals are still to be found in the streets around here.

For the dentally inclined, the national dental body, the **British Dental Association**, or BDA (*www.bda-dentistry.org.uk*), has its headquarters at nearby 64 Wimpole St. Though dentistry is traditionally associated with pain, it was, in fact, a dentist who discovered the first anesthetic. The BDA used to run a museum, displaying the gruesome contraptions of early dentistry, and old prints of agonizing extractions, but the whole collection is currently under wraps.

Marylebone High Street

Marylebone High Street, which starts near Manchester Square and finishes at Marylebone Road, is all that's left of the village street that once ran along the banks of the Tyburn stream. It has become considerably more cosmopolitan and upmarket since those bucolic days, though the pace of the street is leisurely by central London standards, and its shops and cafés are mostly small, independent ventures, a pleasant contrast to the big stores on nearby Oxford Street. One or two shops, in particular, deserve mention: *Patisserie Valerie*, at no. 105, is decorated with the same mock-Pompeian frescoes that adorned it when it was founded in the 1920s (as *Maison Sagne*) by a Swiss pastry-cook; at no. 83 is Daunt, a purpose-built bookshop from 1910, which specializes in travel books, and has a lovely, long, galleried hall at the back, with a pitched roof of stained glass; finally, at the very top of the street, there's a branch of the Conran Shop, housed in an old tyre-depot and garage.

Bond Street is the best tube from which to begin an exploration of Marylebone High Street.

St James's Church, Spanish Place

Despite its name, **St James's Church**, Spanish Place, is actually tucked away on neighbouring George Street, just off Marylebone High Street. A Catholic chapel was built here in 1791 thanks to the efforts of the chaplain at the Spanish Embassy, though the present Neo-Gothic building dates from 1890. Designed in a mixture of English and French Gothic, the interior is surprisingly large and richly furnished, from the white marble and alabaster pulpit to the richly gilded heptagonal apse. The Spanish connection continues to this day: Spanish royal heraldry features in the rose window, and there are even two seats reserved for the royals, denoted by built-in gilt crowns high above the choir stalls.

St Marylebone Church

At the north edge of Marylebone High Street is **Marylebone Road**, an extension of Euston Road, built in the 1750s to provide London with its first bypass. The traffic that pounds down its six lanes unfortunately cuts off **St Marylebone Church**, built in 1813, from Nash's York Gate, which was designed as an alternative gateway to Regent's Park. The church crypt is now a counselling and healing centre with a vegetarian café attached; the rest of the interior is only open fitfully, but the church's most attractive feature – the gilded caryatids holding up the beehive cupola on top of the tower – is visible from the High Street. It was here in 1846 that Elizabeth Barrett and Robert Browning were secretly married; a facsimile of the certificate is displayed outside the church. Elizabeth – 40 years old, an invalid and a virtual prisoner in her father's house on Wimpole Street – returned home and acted as if nothing had happened. A week later the couple eloped to Italy, where they spent most of their married life.

St Marylebone Church has a café in its crypt.

Baker Street and around

Czech writer Karel Čapek was disappointed to find no trace of Sherlock Holmes on **Baker Street**, which cuts across Marylebone Road – "if we briefly touch upon its underground station, we have exhausted everything including our patience", he wrote in the 1930s. Happily, for those on the trail of English literature's languid supersleuth, who lived at 221b Baker St, London's tourist industry has now rectified all that. First of all, those arriving at Baker Street tube are now confronted with a statue of the pipe-smoking detective, sporting his trademark deerstalker and magnifying glass, as soon as they leave the station. Meanwhile, round the corner, the fans who flock here from all over the world now have a choice of museums dedicated to the man, though neither place has any real connection with the fictional character (no. 221b doesn't actually exist), nor his creator, Arthur Conan Doyle.

The Sherlock Holmes Museum is open daily 9.30am–6pm; £6; ☎020/7935 8866; www .sherlockholmes .co.uk.

The **Sherlock Holmes Museum**, at no. 239 (the sign on the door says 221b), is a competent exercise in period reconstruction, but there's no attempt to impart any insights (or even basic facts) about Holmes or Doyle. It's situated above *Hudson's Restaurant* (Mrs Hudson was Holmes' and Watson's opium-tolerant landlady). Much better value for money is the **Sherlock Holmes Experience**, situated on the opposite side of the street above a memorabilia shop at no.

The Sherlock Holmes Experience is open Mon–Sat 10am–5pm, Sun 11am–4pm; £1.50; ☎020/7486 1426; www .sh-memorabilia. co.uk.

230. The curator is a real enthusiast, and has re-created the study from the 1980s British TV series, starring Jeremy Brett, and filled it with artefacts from the show, plus an impressive collection of first editions. Devotees of the detective may also want to visit the *Sherlock Holmes* pub, off Northumberland Avenue, near Charing Cross Station.

One last curiosity in this area is **Marylebone Station**, hidden in the backstreets to the north of Marylebone Road on Melcombe Street, where a delicate and extremely elegant wrought-iron canopy links the station to the former *Great Central Hotel* (now *The Landmark*). The last and most modest of the Victorian terminals, this was intended to be the terminal for the Channel tunnel of the 1880s, a scheme abandoned after only a mile or so of digging, when Queen Victoria got nervous about foreign invasions. Marylebone now serves the commuter belt in Buckinghamshire.

Madame Tussaud's

Daily: June to mid-Sept 9am–5.30pm; mid-Sept to May 10am–5.30pm; £11.50; combined ticket with the Planetarium £13.95; information and advance booking ☎0870/400 3000; *www.madame-tussauds.com*. Baker Street tube.

Madame Tussaud's wax models have been pulling in the crowds ever since the good lady arrived in London in 1802 bearing the sculpted heads of guillotined aristocrats (she herself only just managed to escape the same fate – her uncle, who started the family business, was less fortunate). The entrance fee might be extortionate, the likenesses occasionally dubious and the automated dummies inept, but you can still rely on finding London's biggest queues here – to avoid queuing, book your ticket in advance over the phone or on the Internet.

The best photo opportunities come in the first section, an all-star garden party peppered with contemporary politicians, TV and sports personalities (some of them bafflingly unknown to non-British visitors). The next section, called **200 Years**, is more offbeat, with the dismembered heads and limbs of outdated personalities – Rudolf Nureyev, Sophia Loren, Nikita Khrushchev – ranged on a shelf as in a butcher's shop, along with a fire-damaged model of George IV with a melted eye. Close by is the very first Tussaud figure, Madame du Barry, Louis XV's mistress, who gently respires as Sleeping Beauty – in reality she was beheaded in the French Revolution.

A dull array of international screen stars leads down to the **Grand Hall**, lined with oil paintings and hung with chandeliers to lend a regal air to this po-faced gathering of statesmen, clerics, generals and British royalty stretching back to medieval times. The US presidents look like the bunch of crooks that several of them undoubtedly were, and Lenin looks diminutive enough, but elsewhere the veracity is a bit suspect. The Beatles, in particular, are virtually unrecognizable, and Princess Diana looks bug-eyed.

The **Chamber of Horrors**, the most popular section of all, is irredeemably tasteless, and includes a reconstruction of a foggy East End street strewn with one of Jack the Ripper's mutilated victims. All the "great" British serial killers are here, and it remains the murderer's greatest honour to be included: Dennis Nilsen, a gruesome killer of young gay men in the 1980s, begged to be allowed to pose for Tussaud's while in prison. There's a reconstruction of John Christie's hanging, a tableau of Marat's death in the bath, and guillotine chop just for good measure.

The tour of Tussaud's ends with the **Spirit of London**, a manic and irreverent five-minute romp through the history of London in miniaturized taxicabs. It begins well, dropping witty visual jokes as it careers through Elizabethan times, the Great Plague, the Great Fire, Wren and Dickens to Swinging London, ending in a postmodern heritage nightmare (not unlike much of London today) with a cacophony of punks and Beefeaters, before shuddering to a halt by a slobbering Benny Hill.

The London Planetarium

Mon–Fri 11.30am–5pm, Sat, Sun & school holidays 10am–5pm; £6.30; combined ticket with Madame Tussaud's £13.45; ☎0870/400 3000; *www .madame-tussauds.com*. Baker Street tube.

The adjoining and equally crowded **London Planetarium** has a permanent display featuring a giant revolving Earth circled by

Marylebone

satellites, as well as live weather satellite transmissions, images from the Hubble space telescope, touch-screen computers and information on the rest of the planets in the solar system. All this is just a taster, however, for a thirty-minute high-tech presentation, projected onto a vast dome in the auditorium upstairs. The latest show explores the possibilities of deep space travel in the year 2502, and takes you on journey through the universe, accompanied by new age music and a cosmic astro-babble commentary.

Chapter 4

Soho and Covent Garden

S OHO and **COVENT GARDEN** are very much the heart of London – and the centre's most characterful areas. It's here you'll find the city's street fashion on display, its more oddball shops, its opera houses, theatres, mega-cinemas and the widest variety of restaurants and cafés – where, whatever hour you wander through, there's always something going on. There always was a life to these neighbourhoods, of course, but their aspect today is very different to the recent past. Both started out as wealthy residential developments, then sunk into legendary squalor, until their revival over the past 25 years. Soho, uniquely, retains an unorthodox and slightly raffish air born of an immigrant history as rich as that of the East End, while Covent Garden's transformation from a fruit and vegetable market into a fashion-conscious quarter is one of the most miraculous and enduring developments of the 1980s. Both districts are worth making time for well beyond their ostensible "sights", both by day and, for Soho especially, by night.

Soho and Covent Garden provide a generous core of our café, pub and restaurant listings – see Chapters 15, 16 & 17.

Soho gives you the best and worst of London. The porn joints that made the district notorious in the 1970s are still in evidence, especially to the west of Wardour Street, as are the media folk who pushed up the rents in the 1980s. Soho transformed itself again in the 1990s, this time into one of Europe's leading gay centres, with bars and cafés bursting out from the Old Compton Street area. The area continues to boast a lively fruit and vegetable market on **Berwick Street**, and a nightlife that has attracted writers and ravers of every sexual persuasion to the place since the eighteenth century. The big movie houses on **Leicester Square** always attract crowds of punters, and the tiny enclave of **Chinatown** continues to double as a focus for the Chinese community and a popular place for inexpensive Chinese restaurants.

A little more sanitized and unashamedly commercial, **Covent Garden** today is a far cry from its heyday, when the Piazza was the great playground (and red-light district) of eighteenth-century London. The buskers in front of St Paul's Church, the theatres round about and the **Royal Opera House** on Bow Street are survivors in

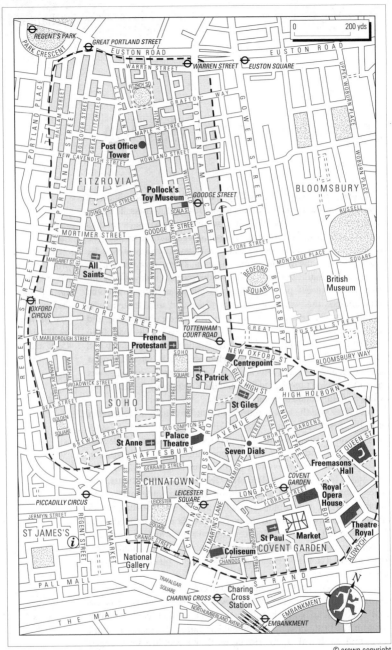

© crown copyright

THE CITY: CHAPTER 4

this tradition, and on a balmy summer evening, **Covent Garden Piazza** – the old marketplace – is still an undeniably lively place to be. Another positive side effect of the market development has been the renovation of the run-down warehouses to the north of the piazza, especially around the Neal Street area, which now boasts some of the trendiest fashion shops in the West End, selling everything from shoes to skateboards.

Soho

When **Soho** – named for the cry that resounded through the district when it was a hunting ground – was first built over in the seventeenth century, its streets were among the most sought-after addresses in the capital. Princes, dukes and earls built their mansions around Soho and Leicester squares, which became the centre of high-society nightlife, epitomized by Viennese prima donna Theresa Cornelys' wild masquerades, which drew "a riotous assembly of fashionable people of both sexes", a traffic jam of hackney chairs and a huge crowd of onlookers. By the end of the eighteenth century, however, the party was over, the rich moved west to Mayfair, and Soho began its inexorable descent into poverty and overcrowding.

Even before the last aristocrats left, Soho had become, along with the East End, the city's main dumping ground for immigrants, a place caricatured (albeit much later) by Galsworthy as "untidy, full of Greeks, Ishmaelites, cats, Italians, tomatoes, restaurants, organs, coloured stuffs, queer names, people looking out of upper windows". The first wave of refugees were the French Huguenots, who settled in Bateman Street after fleeing from Louis XIV's intolerant regime, followed later by more French, Italians, Irish and Jews. More recently, Asians, particularly the Chinese, took advantage of Soho's cheap postwar rents for their workshops and restaurants.

For many years, Soho had also been a favourite haunt of the capital's creative bohos and literati. It was at the *Turk's Head* coffee shop in 1764, in what is now Chinatown, that Joshua Reynolds founded "The Club", to give Dr Johnson unlimited opportunities for talking with the likes of Goldsmith, Burke and Boswell. Thomas de Quincey turned up in Soho in 1802, having run away from school, and was saved from starvation by a local prostitute, an incident later recalled in his *Confessions of an English Opium Eater*. Wagner arrived destitute in the neighbourhood in 1839, Marx ended up here after the failure of the upheavals of 1848, and Rimbaud and Verlaine escaped here after the fall of the Paris Commune in 1871.

Soho's reputation for tolerance also made it an obvious place of refuge from dour, postwar Britain. Jazz and skiffle clubs proliferated in the 1950s, folk and rock clubs in the 1960s, and punk-rock venues at the end of the 1970s. Throughout this period, the *Colony Club*, one of the area's many private drinking clubs, catered for Soho's

For listings of
Soho's music
clubs, see
p.554.

artistic (and alcoholic) clique, under the helm of Muriel Belcher,
who, according to *Colony* stalwart Daniel Farson, "presided over its
shabby bamboo-clad bar like a monarch over a small, tightly knit
kingdom, her strong Sephardic profile reminiscent of a canny,
watchful hawk". Other pubs and clubs provided – and provide – focal
points for political, literary and cultural circles: the satirical magazine *Private Eye* is based in Carlisle Street and the *Coach and
Horses* pub, while writers, publishers and artists hold court at the
members-only *Groucho Club* in Dean Street.

The area's creative energy is perhaps best expressed in its clubs
(both public and private), and the presence of Wardour Street, core
of the movie and advertising business in Britain, provides a clientele
on the doorstep. The attraction, though, remains in the unique mix

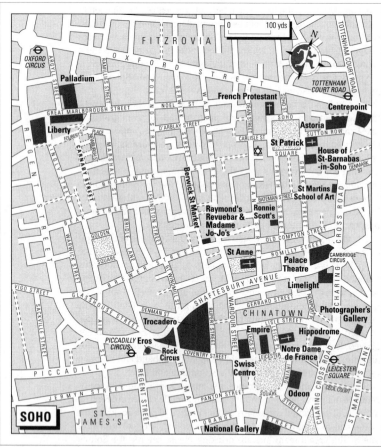

© crown copyright

of people who drift through Soho. There's nowhere else in the city where such diverse slices of London come face to face with each other: businessmen, clubbers, drunks, theatregoers, fashion victims, market-stallholders, pimps, prostitutes and politicians. Take it all in, and enjoy – for most of London is not like this.

Soho

Leicester Square

A short hop east of Piccadilly Circus, **Leicester Square** is a popular spot for London's myriad visitors to hang out, with the big cinemas and discos doing good business, and buskers entertaining the crowds. By night it is one of the most crowded places in London, particularly on a Friday or Saturday, when huge numbers of tourists and half the youth of the suburbs seem to congregate here. By day, queues form for half-price deals at the Society of West End Theatres booth at the south end of the square, while touts haggle with tourists over the price of dodgy tickets for the top shows, and clubbers hand out flyers to likely-looking punters.

The nearest tube is Leicester Square – which is actually on Charing Cross Road.

For the lowdown on buying theatre tickets, see p.580.

The small, smart patch of grass at the centre of the square is centred on a copy of the Shakespeare memorial in Westminster Abbey's Poets' Corner and a statue of Charlie Chaplin (neither of whom has any connection with the square); around the edge are busts of Sir Isaac Newton, William Hogarth, Joshua Reynolds and a Scottish surgeon, John Hunter – all of whom lived hereabouts in the eighteenth century.

At that time, the square was a kind of informal court for the fashionable "Leicester House set", headed by successive princes of Wales who didn't get on with their fathers at St James's. It wasn't until the mid-nineteenth century that the square began to emerge as an entertainment zone, with Turkish baths, accommodation houses (for prostitutes and their clients), oyster rooms and music halls such as the grandiose *Empire* and the *Hippodrome* (just off the square), edifices which survive today as cinemas and discos. Cinema moved in during the 1930s, a golden age evoked by the sleek black lines of the Odeon on the east side, and maintains its grip on the area. The Empire, at the top end of the square, is the favourite for the big royal premieres, and, in a rather half-hearted imitation of the Hollywood (and Cannes) tradition, there are hand prints visible in the pavement by the southwestern corner of the garden railings.

For listings of nightclubs, see p.554; for cinemas, p.585.

There are no sights as such on the square, though if you find yourself near the monumentally ugly Swiss Centre, you'll be assaulted – on the hour, every hour – by a five-minute medley played by the Centre's alpine peasants on a wall-mounted glockenspiel-clock. One little-known sight, just off the north side of the square, hidden away in Leicester Place, is the modern Catholic church of **Notre-Dame de France**. The church's unusual circular plan is derived from the Panorama, a rotunda 90ft in diameter originally built here and decorated with a scenic cylindrical painting by the Irish artist Robert

Barker in 1796. The main point of interest, however, is the church's Chapelle du St-Sacrement, which contains a series of simple frescoes by Jean Cocteau from 1960.

Chinatown

Chinatown, hemmed in between Leicester Square and Shaftesbury Avenue, is a self-contained jumble of shops, cafés and restaurants that makes up one of London's most distinct and popular ethnic enclaves. **Gerrard Street**, Chinatown's main drag, has been endowed with ersatz touches – telephone kiosks rigged out as pagodas and fake Oriental gates – but few of London's 60,000 Chinese actually live in the three small blocks of Chinatown. Nonetheless, it remains a focus for the community, a place to do business or the weekly shopping, celebrate a wedding or just meet up for meals, particularly on Sundays, when the restaurants overflow with Chinese families tucking into *dim sum*.

If you're in the city for Chinese New Year, check the listings magazine Time Out *for details of events.*

The **Chinese New Year** celebrations, instigated here in 1973, are a community-based affair, drawing in thousands of Chinese for the Sunday nearest to New Year's Day (late Jan or early Feb). To a cacophony of fireworks, huge papier-mâché lions dance through the streets devouring cabbages hung from the upper floors by strings pinned with money. The noise is deafening and, if you want to see anything other than the backs of people's heads, you'll need to

---

London's Chinese

London's first Chinese immigrants were sailors who arrived here in the late eighteenth and early nineteenth centuries on the ships of the East India Company. A small number settled permanently around the docks at Limehouse (see p.292), which became London's first **Chinatown**, boasting over thirty Chinese shops and restaurants by the turn of the century. Predominantly male, this closed community achieved a quasi-mythical status in Edwardian minds as a hotbed of criminal dives and opium dens, a reputation further enhanced by Sax Rohmer's novels (later made into films) featuring the evil Doctor Fu Manchu.

Wartime bomb damage, postwar demolition and protectionist union laws all but destroyed Limehouse Chinatown. At the same time, following the Communist takeover in China, a new wave of predominantly Cantonese refugees arrived via Hong Kong, and began to buy up the cheap and run-down property around Gerrard Street. Western interest in Chinese food provided the impetus for the boom in the catering industry, which to this day remains inexpensive, since it continues to provide for the Chinese community itself.

Soho's Chinatown has had to absorb a fresh wave of immigration from Hong Kong, which passed into the hands of Communist China in 1997. Hong Kong's current status has also strengthened the hand of the **Triads**, organized crime societies who have long been involved in drug dealing, gambling, protection rackets and other misdemeanours. Needless to say, as an outsider, it's easy to remain happily oblivious to all of this.

---

position yourself close to one of the cabbages around noon and stand your ground.

For the rest of the year, most Londoners come to Chinatown simply to eat – easy and inexpensive enough to do, though the choice is somewhat overwhelming, especially on Gerrard Street itself. Cantonese cuisine predominates, though there's a smattering of Shanghai and Szechuan outlets. You're unlikely to be disappointed wherever you go – watching where the Chinese themselves eat is the most obvious policy and, if you get offered local advice on what to eat and where, take it.

For reviews of Chinatown restaurants, see Chapter 16.

In addition to the restaurants, most of the shops in Chinatown are geared towards Chinese trade. If the mood takes you, you can while away several hours sorting through the trinkets, ceramics and ornaments in the various arts and crafts shops. Ying Hwa bookshop, on the corner of Macclesfield Street and Gerrard Street, is a good place to pick up Eastern newspapers in English or Cantonese. If you know what you're looking for, you can amass the right ingredients for a demon stir-fry – with exotic fruits to finish – in the supermarkets on Gerrard Street and Newport Place. Also worth checking out is the big Chinese medicine outlet, Tong Ren Tang, on the corner of Gerrard Place and Shaftesbury Avenue, its window display stuffed with teas, infusions and jars of unmentionables.

Charing Cross Road and Shaftesbury Avenue

The creation of **Charing Cross Road**, Soho's eastern border and a thoroughfare from Trafalgar Square to Oxford Street, was less disruptive than other Victorian "improvements", though slum clearance was part of its design. The street now boasts the highest concentration of **bookshops** anywhere in London, one of the first to open here being the chaotic, antiquated Foyles at no. 119, where De Valera, George Bernard Shaw, Walt Disney and Conan Doyle were all once regular customers. The street was later immortalized in Helene Hanff's biographical novel *84 Charing Cross Road*, based on her correspondence with Marks & Co, the now defunct bookshop at that address. The radical bookshop Colletts, founded by lefties in the 1920s, was equally well known in its day, but finally folded in 1992, giving way to an expansion of Waterstone's at no. 121, who have since been joined across the road by several other chain bookstores, such as Borders, Books Etc and Blackwell's. The street retains more of its original character south of Cambridge Circus, where you'll find the capital's main feminist bookshop, Silver Moon, along with a cluster of ramshackle secondhand bookshops, such as Quinto, and swankier outfits like Zwemmer, which has a shop on Charing Cross Road and an art books branch on Litchfield Street.

London's bookshops are detailed on p.602.

One of the nicest places for secondhand-book browsing is **Cecil Court** – the alleyway between the southern end of Charing Cross Road and St Martin's Lane. This short, civilized, paved street boasts

The
Photographers'
Gallery is open
Mon–Sat
11am–6pm,
Sun noon–
6pm; free;
☎020/7831
1772; www
.photonet.org.uk

specialist bookshops devoted to dance, Italy, New Age philosophies and the like, plus various antiquarian dealers selling modern first editions, old theatre posters, maps and stamps. Another place you shouldn't miss, just off Charing Cross Road, is the **Photographers' Gallery** at nos. 5 and 8 Great Newport St, established in 1971 as the first of its kind in London, and hosting free temporary exhibitions that are invariably worth a browse, as is the bookshop.

As well as being prime bookworm territory, Charing Cross Road is one of the main drags through the West End, flanked by **theatres, clubs** and **rock venues**. Further up Charing Cross Road is the *Hippodrome*, designed as a variety theatre by Frank Matcham in 1900, and now a hi-tech nightclub, where queues of eager punters begin to gather early in the evening. On Cambridge Circus, the huge terracotta Palace Theatre opened in 1891 as the Royal English Opera House, but folded the following year. Since then it has been a variety theatre, a cinema and, most recently, a popular venue for musicals; *Les Misérables* is the long-term resident. On the other side of Shaftesbury Avenue, you'll find the *Limelight*, one of London's more unusual nightclubs, converted from a Welsh Presbyterian Chapel. Meanwhile, just off Cambridge Circus, hidden away down West Street, is the record-breaking St Martin's Theatre; where Agatha Christie's *Mousetrap* has been on non-stop since 1952.

One last venue worth mentioning is the **Coliseum**, at the southern end of St Martin's Lane, parallel with Charing Cross Road, another extravagant work by Frank Matcham that was built in 1904 as a variety theatre (the illuminated globe on top of the building used to revolve). Still London's largest theatre; Lillie Langtry, Sarah Bernhardt and the Ballet Russe have all performed at the Coliseum; it's now home to the English National Opera (*www.eno.org*).

Sweeping northeast towards Bloomsbury from Piccadilly Circus, and separating Soho proper from Chinatown, the gentle curve of **Shaftesbury Avenue** is the heart of mainstream Theatreland, with theatres and cinemas along its entire length. Like Charing Cross Road, it was conceived in the late 1870s, ostensibly to relieve traffic congestion but with the dual purpose of destroying the slums that lay in its path. Ironically, it was then named after Lord Shaftesbury (of Eros fame), whose life had been spent trying to help the likes of those dispossessed by the road scheme.

For more on
the city's
theatres, see
p.580.

Central Soho

If Soho has a main drag, it has to be **Old Compton Street**, which runs parallel with Shaftesbury Avenue, linking Charing Cross Road and Wardour Street. The corner shops, peepshows, boutiques and trendy cafés here are typical of the area and a good barometer of the

Soho on record

As London's premier boho area, Soho has been a popular meeting point for the capital's up-and-coming pop stars since the late 1950s, when young hopefuls like Cliff Richard, Tommy Steele and Adam Faith used to hang out at the **2 i's coffee bar** at 59 Old Compton St, and perform at the rock-and-roll club in the basement. Marc Bolan, whose parents ran a market stall on Berwick Street, also worked at the café in the early 1960s. The Rolling Stones first met in a pub (since gone) on Broadwick Street in early 1962 and, by the mid-1960s, were playing Soho's premier rock venue, the now-defunct **Marquee**, at 90 Wardour St. David Bowie played there (as David Jones) in 1965, Pink Floyd played their "Spontaneous Underground" sessions the following year, Led Zeppelin played their first London gig there in 1968, and Phil Collins worked for some time as a cloakroom attendant.

In November 1975, the Sex Pistols played their first gig at **St Martin's School of Art** on Charing Cross Road, during which Sid Vicious (in the audience, and not the band, at the time) made his contribution to dance history when he began to "pogo". The classic venue during the heyday of punk in 1976, however, was the **100 Club** on Oxford Street, where the Pistols, The Clash, Siouxsie, The Damned and The Vibrators all played. The Pistols used to rehearse in the studios behind the music shops on **Denmark Street**, London's tame version of New York's Tin Pan Alley, off Charing Cross Road. The Rolling Stones, the Kinks and Genesis all recorded songs there, and Elton John got his first job at one of the street's music publishers in 1963.

---

latest Soho fads. One of the few places which has survived the vicissitudes of fashion on this short stretch is the original *Patisserie Valerie* (which now has several branches elsewhere), opened by Madame Valerie in 1926 and long a favourite with art students and other bohemian types. *Valerie*'s is now vastly outnumbered by mock-continental **cafés** whose pavement tables provide maximum posing potential, with the sprawling *Café Bohème* almost entirely open to the street in warm weather. Several other old stores remain embedded on Old Compton Street, most notably the Algerian Coffee Store, the Italian deli, I Camisa & Son, Capital newsagents and The Vintage House off-licence, which claims to stock over 700 malt whiskies.

The liberal atmosphere of Soho has also made it a permanent fixture on the **gay scene** for much of this century: gay servicemen frequented the *Golden Lion*, on Dean Street, from World War II until the end of National Service, while a succession of gay artists found refuge here (and in neighbouring Fitzrovia) during the 1950s and 1960s. Nowadays the scene is much more upfront, with gay bars, clubs and cafés jostling for position on Old Compton Street, and round the corner in Wardour Street. And it doesn't stop there: there's now a gay travel agency, a gay financial adviser and, even more convenient, a gay taxi service.

Full gay and lesbian listings start on p.563.

Greek Street, Frith Street and Soho Square

The streets off Old Compton Street are lined with Soho institutions past and present, starting in the east with **Greek Street**, named after the Greek church that once stood nearby. This and parallel **Frith Street** both lead north to Soho Square.

On Romilly Street, which runs between the two, just south of Old Compton Street, is one of London's landmark restaurants, *Kettner's*, founded back in the 1860s by Napoleon III's personal chef and favoured by Oscar Wilde. It's now part of the excellent Pizza Express chain, but retains a smidgen of faded Edwardian elegance in its décor – and a pianist in its champagne bar. Only a little younger is *Maison Bertaux*, opposite at 28 Greek St, founded in 1871; its windows are piled high with patisserie, and its owners resolutely refuse to serve any type of coffee other than *café au lait*. It's roomier than it looks, with a wonderful little salon upstairs.

Close by, and also on Greek Street, is the *Coach and Horses*, an ordinary sort of pub that was lorded over for years by the boozy gang of writer Jeffrey Bernard, painter Francis Bacon and jazz man George Melly, as well as the *Private Eye* crew. Jazz connections are in evidence on Frith Street, too, where *Ronnie Scott's (www.ronniescotts.co.uk)*, London's longest-running jazz club, was founded in 1958 and still pulls in the big names. Opposite is the *Bar Italia*, an Italian café with a big screen for satellite TV transmissions of Italian football games, and late-night hours that ensure its place as an espresso stop on every self-respecting clubber's itinerary. It was in this building, appropriately enough for such a media-saturated area, that John Logie Baird made the world's first public television transmission in 1926. Next door, a plaque recalls that the 7-year-old Mozart stayed here in 1763, having wowed George III and London society.

Soho Square is virtually the only patch of green amid the neighbourhood's labyrinth of streets and alleys. It began life as a smart address, surrounded by the houses of the nobility and centred on an elaborate fountain topped by a statue of Charles II. Charles survives, if a little worse for wear, and stands on one of the pathways, but the fountain has made way for an octagonal, mock-Tudor garden shed, which doubles as a ventilation shaft for the tube. As for the buildings around the square, they are a typical Soho mix: 20th Century Fox occupies one corner, with the Victorian Hospital for Sick Women now a walk-in health centre; Paul McCartney has his discreet corporate headquarters, mpl, in another corner, close to the British Board of Film Classification. There are also two square, red-brick churches: the Italianate **St Patrick's**, which serves the Irish, Italian and Chinese communities, and the **French Protestant Church**, sole survivor of London's 23 Huguenot churches, concealed on the north side of the square.

One of Soho's nicest pubs, the old Dog and Duck *Hotel, is a couple of doors up from* Ronnie Scott's. *For more Soho pub listings, see p.537.*

The nearest tube to Soho Square is Tottenham Court Road.

If you're finding it difficult to imagine Soho ever having been an aristocratic haunt, pay a visit to the **House of St Barnabas-in-Soho,** a Georgian mansion just south of the square on Greek Street. Built in the 1740s, the house retains some exquisite Rococo plasterwork on the main staircase and in the Council Chamber, which has a lovely view onto Soho Square. Since 1861 the building has been a Christian charity house for the destitute, so the rest of the interior is much altered and closed off. You can, however, visit the paved garden, whose plane trees inspired Dickens, and whose twisted and gnarled mulberry tree was planted by some silk-weaving Huguenots. On the south side of the garden is a cute little Byzantine-style chapel, built for the residents and used by the Serbian refugees during World War I.

Soho

The House of St Barnabas-in-Soho is open Wed 2.30– 4.30pm and Thurs 11am– 12.30pm; small donation expected; ☎ *020/7437 1894.*

Dean Street and Wardour Street

One block west of Frith Street runs **Dean Street**, home of the *Colony Club*, the heart of the postwar bohemian drinking scene, and of the *Groucho Club*, where London's literati and media types preen themselves. Neither is especially exclusive, but you need to find a member to sign you in. If your interest doesn't extend that far, there's an open-to-all bohemian landmark nearby in the form of *The French House*, at no. 49. This was just the plain old *York Minster* pub when it was bought by a Belgian, Victor Berlemont, in 1914 and transformed into a French émigré haunt. It was frequented by de Gaulle and the Free French forces during the last war, and has long had a reputation for attracting artists (Salvador Dalí, among others) and writers.

Soho's once-strong Jewish presence is now confined to Dean Street's synagogue. The most famous Jewish immigrant to live in Soho was **Karl Marx**, who in 1851 moved into two "evil, frightful rooms" across the street from here, on the top floor of no. 28, with his wife and maid (both of whom were pregnant by him) and four children, having been evicted from his first two addresses for failing to pay the rent. There's a plaque commemorating his stay, and the waiters at *Leoni's Quo Vadis* restaurant, the current occupants, will happily show diners round the rooms on request.

West again is **Wardour Street** – Soho's longest street, stretching from Coventry Street to Oxford Street, and a kind of dividing line between the trendier, eastern half of Soho and the sleazier western zone. Its southern end is now part of Chinatown (see p.140); north of Shaftesbury Avenue, there's a small park laid out on what used to be **St Anne's Church**, bombed in the last war, with only its tower now standing. The rest of the street is largely given over to the film industry – Warner Brothers is based here, along with numerous smaller companies.

Berwick Street to Poland Street

Despite the council's best efforts, the **vice and prostitution** rackets still have the area immediately west of Wardour Street well staked out. Straight prostitution in fact makes up a small proportion of what gets sold here (King's Cross and Mayfair are the places for that), and has been since Paul Raymond – now Britain's richest man – set up his Folies Bergères-style *Revue Bar* in the late 1950s off Brewer Street, now complemented by the transvestite floor show next door at *Madame Jo-Jo's*. These last two are paragons of virtue compared with the dodgy videos, short con outfits and rip-off joints that operate in the neighbouring streets. One of the most lucrative cons worked on punters in Soho is "clipping", whereby gullible men are asked to leave a deposit and meet at a nearby place; needless to say, their amour never arrives.

In amongst the video shops and triple-X-rated cinemas is the unlikely sight of **Berwick Street Market**, one of the capital's finest (and cheapest) fruit and vegetable markets. The street itself is no beauty spot, but the market's barrow displays are works of art in themselves. On either side of the stalls, you'll find some of London's best specialist pop record shops: Interface and Sister Ray cater for the indie/ambient crowd, Daddy Kool supplies reggae and ska, while the Music & Video Exchange trades in secondhand rock, soul and jazz.

For a full guide to London's record stores, see p.554.

Soho vice

Prostitution is nothing new to Soho. Way back in the seventeenth and eighteenth centuries, prince and prole alike used to come here (and to Covent Garden) for paid sex. Several prominent courtesans were residents of Soho, their profession recorded as "player and mistress to several persons", or, lower down on the social scale, "generally slut and drunkard; occasionally whore and thief". *Hooper's Hotel*, a high-class Soho brothel which the Prince of Wales frequented, even got a mention in a popular book of the late eighteenth century, *The Mysteries of Flagellation*. By Victorian times, the area was described as "a reeking home of filthy vice", where "the grosser immorality flourishes unabashed from every age downwards to mere children". And it was in Soho that Gladstone used to conduct his crusade to save prostitutes – managing "to combine his missionary meddling with a keen appreciation of a pretty face", as one perceptive critic observed.

By World War II, **organized gangs** like the notorious Messina Brothers from Malta controlled a huge vice empire in Soho, later taken over by one of their erstwhile henchmen, Bernie Silver, Soho's self-styled "Godfather". In the 1960s and 1970s, the sex trade threatened to take over the whole of Soho, aided and abetted by the police themselves, who were involved in a massive protection racket. The complicity between the gangs and the police was finally exposed in 1976, when ten top-ranking Scotland Yard officers were charged with bribery and corruption on a massive scale and sentenced to prison for up to twelve years (Silver himself was put inside in 1974). Since then, the combined efforts of the Soho Society and, more recently, Westminster Council, have reduced the number of sex establishments. Soho's vice days are by no means over – the sex shops and peepshows still dominate large parts of the neighbourhood – but they are well down on their all-time high of the mid-1970s.

The market stops at the crossroads with Broadwick Street, which features a replica of the water pump that caused the deaths of some five hundred Soho residents in the **cholera epidemic** of 1854. Dr John Snow, Queen Victoria's obstetrician, traced the outbreak to the pump, thereby proving that the disease was waterborne rather than airborne, as previously thought. No one believed him, however, until he removed the pump handle and effectively stopped the epidemic. The original pump stood outside the pub now called the *John Snow*, beside which there's a commemorative plaque and a red granite kerbstone.

This part of Soho has its fair share of **artistic associations** too. It was on Broadwick Street that William Blake was born in 1757, above his father's hosiery shop, and where from the age of 9 he had visions of "messengers from heaven, daily and nightly". He opened a print shop of his own next door to the family home, and later moved to nearby Poland Street, where he lived six years with his "beloved Kate" and wrote perhaps his most profound work, *The Marriage of Heaven and Hell*, among other poems. Poland Street was also Shelley's first halt after having been kicked out of Oxford in 1811 for distributing *The Necessity of Atheism*, while Canaletto ran a studio on Beak Street for a couple of years while he sat out the Seven Years' War in exile in London.

Carnaby Street and around

Until the 1950s, **Carnaby Street** (*www.carnaby.co.uk*) was a backstreet on Soho's western fringe, occupied, for the most part, by sweatshop tailors who used to make up the suits for nearby Savile Row. Then, sometime in the mid-1950s, Bill Green opened a shop called Vince, selling outrageous clothes to the gay men who were hanging out at the local baths. He was followed by John Stephen, a Glaswegian grocer's son, who, within a couple of years, owned a string of trendy boutiques which catered for the new market in flamboyant men's clothing. In 1964 – the year of the official birth of the Carnaby Street myth – Mods, West Indian Rude Boys and other "switched-on people", as the *Daily Telegraph* noted, began to hang out in Carnaby Street. By the time Mary Quant sold her first miniskirt here, the area had became the epicentre of Swinging Sixties' London, and its street sign the capital's most popular postcard.

The nearest tube to Carnaby Street is Oxford Circus.

A victim of its own hype, Carnaby Street quickly declined into an avenue of overpriced tack, and so it remained for the next twenty-odd years. More recently, things have started to pick up again, especially at the top end of the street, and round the corner in Foubert's Place and **Newburgh Street**, where contemporary London fashion now has a firm foothold. Elsewhere, cheap leather and jeans survive for the moment, along with the likes of Rugby Scene and Soccer Scene, and shops like Merc and The Face which continue to flog Mod clothes.

For fashion listings, see p.595.

Fitzrovia

Bounded by Gower Street to the east, Great Portland Street to the west and the shabbier eastern half of Oxford Street to the south, **Fitzrovia** is a northern extension of Soho. Like its neighbour, it has a raffish, cosmopolitan reputation, and Fitzrovia has attracted its fair share of writers and bohemians over the last hundred years or so, including the Pre-Raphaelites and members of the Bloomsbury Group (for more on whom, see p.178). That said, there's a lot less going on here than in Soho, and just two real sights you can visit – the Victorian church on Margaret Street and Pollock's Toy Museum – now that the landmark Post Office Tower is closed to the public.

All Saints, Margaret Street

Few London churches are as atmospheric as **All Saints**, built by William Butterfield in the 1850s, two blocks north of Oxford Street on Margaret Street. Patterned brickwork characterizes the entire ensemble of clergy house, choir school (Laurence Olivier sang here as a boy) and church, set around a small court that's entered from the street through a pointed arch. The church interior, one of London's gloomiest, is best visited on a sunny afternoon when the light pours in through the west window, illuminating the fantastic variety of coloured marble and stone which decorates the place from floor to ceiling. Several of the walls are also adorned with Pre-Raphaelite Minton tile paintings, the east window is a quasi-Byzantine iconostasis with saintly images nestling in gilded niches, and the elaborate pulpit is like the entire church in miniature. Surrounded by such iconographical clutter, you would be forgiven for thinking you were in a Catholic church – but then that was the whole idea of the High Church movement, which sought to re-Catholicize the Church of England without actually returning it to the Roman fold.

Charlotte Street and around

The nearest tube to Charlotte Street is Goodge Street.

After All Saints, the place to head for in Fitzrovia is **Charlotte Street**, where inexpensive Greek Cypriot restaurants compete for space with some very designer-conscious French places. Two restaurants here have illustrious literary associations: *The White Tower* (now *Bam Bou*), where Wyndham Lewis and Ezra Pound launched the vorticist magazine *Blast*; and *L'Étoile*, further up, which the likes of Dylan Thomas and T.S. Eliot used to patronize. The same crowd would get plastered in the nearby *Fitzroy Tavern* – from which the area got its sobriquet in the 1930s – along with rather more outrageous bohemians, like the hard-drinking Nina Hamnett, the self-styled "Queen of Bohemia", who used to boast that Modigliani once told her she had the best tits in Europe.

One block east, on Scala Street, is **Pollock's Toy Museum**, housed above a toy shop. Its collections include a fine example of the Victorian paper theatres popularized by Benjamin Pollock, who sold them under the slogan "a penny plain, twopence coloured". The other exhibits range from vintage teddy bears to rod and glove puppets, Red Army soldiers to wax dolls, filling every nook and cranny of the museum's six tiny, rickety rooms. There are occasionally Pollock Theatre performances in the basement; if you're seriously interested, it's best to phone ahead.

Exploring Fitzrovia, it's impossible to ignore the looming presence of the **Post Office Tower** (officially known as the BT Tower these days), a glass-clad pylon designed in the early 1960s by a team of bureaucrats in the Ministry of Works, that sits one block west of Fitzroy Street, the extension of Charlotte Street. It was the city's tallest building until the NatWest Tower topped it in 1981, and is still one of the most obvious landmarks north of the river. Sadly, following an anonymous bomb attack in 1971, the tower and its revolving restaurant have been closed to the public.

Soho

Pollock's Toy Museum is open Mon–Sat 10am–5pm; £3; ☎ *020/7 636 3452;* www .pollocks.cwc.net

Fitzroy Square and around

At the top of Fitzroy Street is **Fitzroy Square**, the only formal square in Fitzrovia, begun by the Adam brothers in the 1790s and faced, unusually, with light Portland stone rather than the ubiquitous dark Georgian brickwork. Traffic is now excluded, but few pedestrians come here either – yet it's a square with both Bloomsbury and Soho associations. Virginia Woolf's blue plaque is here: her Bloomsbury chums considered it a disreputable neighbourhood but she moved here with her brother in 1907, after taking the precaution of checking with the police. It had enjoyed an even dodgier reputation in the 1890s when the square was home to the International Anarchist School for Children, run by 60-year-old French anarchist Louise Michel. The police eventually raided the building and closed down the school after finding bombs hidden in the basement.

Fitzrovia's radical pedigree has a further presence in **Marie Stopes House**, nearby at 108 Whitfield St, originally opened as the pioneering Mother's Clinic for Constructive Birth Control in 1921 and kept functioning in the face of numerous legal battles. A qualified paleobotanist, Stopes courted controversy by advocating birth control as an aid to women's sexual pleasure, after her first marriage failed to be consummated in five years. However, her espousal of eugenics – she was keen to reduce the size of working-class families in order to improve the nation's stock, and even invented her own cervical cap called "Pro-racial" – has left a cloud over her reputation.

Tottenham Court Road

For the record, it's been centuries since there was a stately mansion – the original Tottenham Court – at the end of **Tottenham Court**

Road, which now makes a strong challenge for London's least pre-possessing central shopping street. A rash of stores at the southern end flogging discount-priced stereos, CD players, computers and all sorts of electrical equipment has pushed out the furniture makers, the street's original vendors, though a few shops – most notably Habitat and Heal's – survive at its northern end. The London listings magazine *Time Out* has its base here, too. Unless you're desperate for a Sega Megadrive or a pine bed-base, however, you won't lose much by giving this whole street a miss.

Covent Garden

Covent Garden has come full circle: what started out in the seventeenth century as London's first luxury neighbourhood is once more a highly desirable place to live, work and shop. Based around Inigo Jones's piazza – London's oldest planned square – the area had for years been a market centre for fruit and vegetables. But that closed in 1974 and for a while it looked as if the developers would move in on this prime central real estate and demolish it all for unwanted new office blocks. In the face of public protest, these plans collapsed and, instead, the elegant old market hall and its environs were restored to house shops, restaurants and arts-and-crafts stalls.

Covent Garden tube takes you to the heart of the area. Leicester Square tube is also close by.

Boosted by buskers and street entertainers, Covent Garden has since become one of London's major tourist attractions, its success prompting a wholesale gentrification of the streets to the north of the market, which now boast some of the trendiest clothes shops, cafés and restaurants in London. Alongside them – and saving the area from being too over-commercial – are a few odd pockets of mid-Seventies "alternative" culture, which established itself here, in squats and cheap rentals, when the whole area was threatened with destruction. London's tourism revenues owe them a considerable debt – it was only their demonstrations, and mass squats, that saved the area.

The intervening 350 years were rather less salubrious – if perhaps a lot more fun – but little or no trace of those bacchanalian days survives in the pricey bars and cafés around the piazza. The most enduring feature of Covent Garden has been its theatres and, of course, the internationally famous **Royal Opera House**, which has recently – and very expensively – been totally refurbished and expanded, so that it now overlooks the piazza.

The Piazza

Covent Garden's **Piazza** was laid out in the 1630s, when the Earl of Bedford commissioned Inigo Jones to design a series of graceful Palladian-style arcades based on the main square in Livorno, Italy,

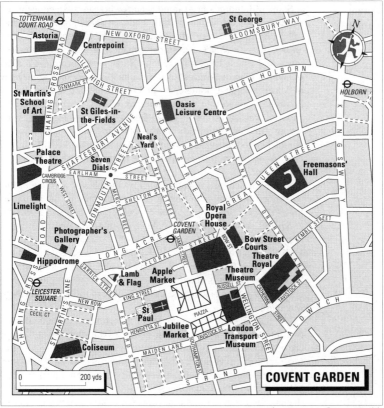

© crown copyright

where Jones had helped build the cathedral. Initially the development was a great success, its novelty value alone attracting a rich and aristocratic clientele, but over the next century the tone of the place fell as the fruit and vegetable market, set up in the Earl's back garden, expanded, and theatres and coffee houses began to take over the peripheral buildings. Macaulay evoked the following scene: "fruit women screamed, carters fought, cabbage stalks and rotten apples accumulated in heaps at the thresholds of the Countess of Berkshire and the Bishop of Durham."

By the early eighteenth century the area was known as "the great square of Venus", with dozens of gambling dens, bawdy houses and so-called "bagnios" in and around the piazza. Some bagnios were plain Turkish baths, but most doubled as brothels, where courtesans stood in the window and, according to one contemporary, "in the most impudent manner invited passengers from the theatres into the houses".

Some of London's most famous coffee houses were concentrated here, too, attracting writers such as Sheridan, Dryden and Aphra Behn. The rich and famous frequented places like the *Shakespeare's Head*, whose cook made the best turtle soup in town, and whose head waiter, John Harris, even produced a kind of "Who's Who of Whores", revised annually. London's great man of letters, Samuel Johnson, and his future biographer, James Boswell, bumped into one another by chance at Davies's bookshop on Russell Street in 1763. Boswell thought Johnson "very slovenly and most uncouth", but resolved to "mark what I remember of his conversation", which is precisely what he did for the next twenty years, thus compiling the material for his famous *Life of Johnson*.

Russell Street, which leads east from the piazza, was one of the most notorious streets in Covent Garden, and housed the infamous *Rose Tavern*, immortalized in a scene from Hogarth's *Rake's Progress*. This was one of the oldest brothels in Covent Garden – Pepys mentions "frigging with Doll Lane" at the *Rose* in his diary of 1667 – and specialized in "Posture Molls", who engaged in flagellation and striptease, and were deemed a cut above the average whore. Food at the *Rose* was apparently excellent, too, and despite the frequent brawls, men of all classes, from royalty to ruffians, made their way there.

The piazza's status as a centre of entertainment declined with the approach of the nineteenth century. The theatres still drew crowds but the market now occupied most of the area, and the few remaining taverns had become dangerous. In the 1830s the piazza was cleaned up, slums were torn down and a proper market hall built in the Greek Revival style. A glass roof was added in the late Victorian era, but otherwise the building stayed unaltered until the closure of the market in 1974 – when trade moved to Nine Elms in Vauxhall – and its early-1980s renovation as a shopping arcade.

St Paul's Church

Of Jones's original piazza, the only remaining parts are the two sections of north-side arcading (one part rebuilt by the Victorians, the other reinstalled by the Royal Opera House) and **St Paul's Church**, facing the west side of the market building. In a now famous exchange, the Earl of Bedford told Jones to make St Paul's no fancier than a barn, to which the architect replied, "Sire, you shall have the handsomest barn in England." The proximity of so many theatres has made it known as the "Actors' Church", and it's filled with memorials to international thespians from Boris Karloff to Gracie Fields. Several famous artists are buried here, too; among them Grinling Gibbons, Sir Peter Lely and satirist Samuel Butler.

The space in front of the church's Tuscan portico – where Eliza Doolittle was discovered selling violets by Henry Higgins in George Bernard Shaw's *Pygmalion* – is now a legalized venue for buskers and street performers, who must audition for a slot months in advance. Despite the vetting, the standard of the acts varies enormously, though comedy is the ultimate aim.

The piazza's history of entertainment actually goes back to May 1662, when the first recorded performance of Punch and Judy in England was staged by Italian puppeteer Pietro Gimonde, and witnessed by Pepys. This historic event is now commemorated every second Sunday in May by a **Punch and Judy Festival**, held in the gardens behind the church, in which numerous booths compete for audiences; for the rest of the year the churchyard provides a tranquil respite from the activity outside (access is from King Street, Henrietta Street or Bedford Street).

The piazza's markets and shops

The market stalls in the piazza are a victim of their own success, with a captive tourist market all too likely to pick up novelties and "craft" items. However, among the back-massage tools, the jokey duvet covers and the ceramic flying nuns, there are always a few worthwhile stalls – even the odd clothing designer (knitwear, especially) with imagination and style. And stallholders alternate, often operating on only one or two days, so if you come more than once you may find a different scene. There are in fact two separate market areas: the "Apple Market", inside the old market building, and the tackier Jubilee Hall market, on the south side of the piazza. The Apple Market specializes in arts and crafts, the Jubilee Hall sells mainly clothes, though both are given over largely to antiques on Mondays.

The market stalls are open daily 10am–7pm, later in summer.

As for the shops in the piazza complex, increased rents have edged out many of the odder and more interesting outlets of the early days in favour of blander fare, including a number of big-name stores – the Dr Marten's flagship is the most visible of these – exactly the reverse of the original development plans. A couple of more interesting, smaller outlets, in keeping with the idea of the place, are the Museum Shop, which stocks goods and reproductions from museums across Europe and America, and Mullins and Westley, a snuff and tobacco parlour with its own brands and a mighty selection of Cuban cigars.

London Transport Museum

Mon–Thurs, Sat & Sun 10am–6pm, Fri 11am–6pm; £5.50; ☎020/7836 8557; *www.ltmuseum.co.uk*. Covent Garden tube.

A former flower-market shed on the piazza's east side is now home to the over-popular **London Transport Museum**. A herd of old buses, trains and trams make up the bulk of the exhibits, though there's enough interactive fun – touch-screen computers and the odd costumed conductor and vehicles to climb on – to keep most children amused. The layout is pretty confusing, but the museum's survey begins with the 1820s, when the Thames was finally abandoned as the city's main thoroughfare. The easiest way to find your way around is to follow the fourteen clearly signposted KidZones, designed for little ones, but equally useful as orientational markers for adults.

To begin chronologically, climb aboard the "oldest" exhibit (it's actually a reconstruction), the 1829 Shillibeer's Horse Omnibus, which provided the city's first regular horse-bus service. Despite having the oldest underground system in the world, begun in 1863, London was still heavily reliant on horse power at the turn of the century – fifty thousand animals worked in the transport system, producing a thousand tons of dung a day. You can also clamber aboard several of the electric trams on display here, which, by the 1930s, formed part of the largest electric tram system in the world. By 1952 the whole network had been dismantled, to be superseded by trolleybuses, of which there are several examples – these, in turn, bit the dust in the following decade.

London Transport now has a reserve collection on display in the Depot Museum in Acton (p.456).

Upstairs, you can step into a lovely 1920s Metropolitan line tube, fitted out in burgundy and green with pretty, drooping lamps, and have a go at the tube driver's simulator, complete with Dead Man's Handle, the safety device introduced in 1903. The contemporary section quite rightly rails against the parlous state of public transport in a capital that has seen the average speed of traffic through central London slow to just 8mph. London Transport's stylish maps and posters, many commissioned from well-known artists, are displayed in their very own gallery, and you can buy reproductions, plus countless other LT paraphernalia, at the shop on the way out.

Theatre Museum

Tues–Sun 10am–6pm; £4.50; ☎020/7943 4700; *www.theatremuseum.org*. Covent Garden tube.

The rest of the old flower market now houses the **Theatre Museum**, an outpost of the V&A displaying three centuries of memorabilia from every conceivable area of the performing arts in the West (the entrance is on Russell Street). The corridors of glass cases cluttered with props, programmes and costumes are not especially exciting, and the portrait collection to the right of the gangway is dull – far better to head for the **study room**, which is lined with pull-out panels of engravings, photographs and letters. Among the hundreds of papers are a cable from Sarah Bernhardt cheerfully announcing the imminent amputation of her leg; eighteenth-century cartoons, including one of an overcrowded theatre, a chaos of fainting, vomiting and discarded clothing; and Victorian advertisements for "dog dramas", melodramas with canine heroes.

In addition to the permanent exhibits, two special areas host long-term displays, usually with a workshop or hands-on element. The *Wind in the Willows* exhibition, which traces the development of the National Theatre's production from day one to first performance, is currently the longest-running exhibit. The museum also recently acquired the last surviving complete troupe of Victorian marionettes, which are permanent display, and perform at least once a year. In addition, the museum offers a **booking service** for West End shows, has an unusually good selection of cards and posters and is a resource centre, with a theatre hosting performances, lectures and debates.

Bow Street and around

The area's high crime rate was no doubt the reason behind the opening of a new magistrates' office in **Bow Street** in 1748. The first two magistrates were Henry Fielding, author of *Tom Jones*, and his blind half-brother John – nicknamed the "Blind Beak" – who seem to have been exceptional in their honesty and the infrequency with which they accepted bribes (the only income a magistrate could rely on). Finding "lewd women enough to fill a mighty colony", Fielding also set about creating the city's first police force, known as the **Bow Street Runners**. Never numbering more than a dozen, they were employed primarily to combat prostitution, and they continued to exist a good ten years after the establishment of the uniformed Metropolitan Police in 1829. Before it was finally closed in 1989, Bow Street police station had the honour of incarcerating Oscar Wilde after he was arrested for "committing indecent acts" in 1895 – he was eventually sentenced to two years' hard labour. And, in 1928, Radclyffe Hall's lesbian novel *Well of Loneliness* was deemed obscene by magistrates at Bow Street and remained banned in this country until 1949.

The Royal Opera House

The Corinthian portico of the **Royal Opera House** (ROH; *www.royaloperahouse.org*) stands opposite Bow Street magistrates' court. First built as the Covent Garden Theatre in 1732, in a backstreet behind a fruit and vegetable market, it witnessed premieres of Goldsmith's *She Stoops to Conquer* and Sheridan's *The Rivals* before being destroyed by fire in 1809. To offset the cost of building the new theatre, ticket prices were increased; riots ensued for 61 consecutive performances until the manager finally backed down. In 1847 the theatre was renamed the Italian Royal Opera and soon became the city's main opera house; royal patronage ensured its success, and since the last war it has been home to both the Royal Ballet and Royal Opera.

The building has recently undergone a £220 million redevelopment, which has opened up the place to the public as never before.

Inigo Jones's arcading has been rebuilt in the northeast corner of the piazza, from which a covered passageway connects with Bow Street. The ROH box office occupies part of the passageway, from which the public are free to head upstairs into the beautifully renovated wrought-iron and glass **Floral Hall** (daily 10am–3pm), which now serves as the opera house's main foyer. Continuing upwards, you reach the *Amphitheatre* bar/restaurant, which has a glorious terrace overlooking the piazza. Unfortunately, a byproduct of all this redevelopment was the wanton demolition of the Georgian terrace on the north side of Russell Street.

Drury Lane

One block east of Bow Street runs **Drury Lane**, nothing to write home about in its present condition, but in Tudor and Stuart times a very fashionable address. During the Restoration, it became a

---

Theatre Royal, Drury Lane

It was at the original **Theatre Royal, Drury Lane**, built in 1663, that women were first permitted to appear on stage in England (their parts having previously been played by boys), but critics were sceptical about their abilities to portray their own gender, and thought their profession little better than prostitution – and, indeed, most had to work at both to make ends meet (as the actress said to the bishop). The women who sold oranges to the audience were even less virtuous, **Nell Gwynne** being the most famous, though she also trod the boards in comic roles. Eventually she became Charles II's mistress, the first in a long line of Drury Lane actresses who made it into royal beds. Sarah Siddons' theatrical success brought a degree of respectability to the female acting profession for the first time; the majority of her female contemporaries, however, were more in the vein of Nancy Dawson, who "danced the jigg to smutty songs" here.

It was at the Theatre Royal that **David Garrick**, as actor, manager and part-owner from 1747, revolutionized the English theatre. Garrick treated his texts with a great deal more reverence than had been customary, insisting on rehearsals and cutting down on improvisations. The rich and privileged, who had previously occupied seats on the stage itself, were confined to the auditorium, and the practice of refunding those who wished to leave at the first interval was stopped. However, an attempt to prevent half-price tickets being sold at the beginning of the third act provoked a riot by disgruntled punters and was eventually withdrawn. Despite Garrick's reforms, the Theatre Royal remained a boisterous and often dangerous place of entertainment: George II and George III both narrowly escaped attempts on their lives while here, and the orchestra often had good cause to be grateful for the cage under which they were forced to play. The theatre has one other unique feature: two royal boxes, instigated in order to keep George III and his son, the future George IV, apart, after they had a set-to in the foyer. **Backstage tours** of the theatre are great fun and take place daily, culminating with a mini-pantomime in which everyone has to get involved; for more details phone ☎020/7240 5357.

---

permanent fixture in London's theatrical and social life, when the first Theatre Royal (see box opposite) was built in 1663. (The current one dates from 1812 and faces onto Catherine Street.) Nell Gwynne was born close by, and Pepys recalls seeing "pretty Nelly standing at her lodgings door in Drury Lane in her smock-sleeves and bodice, looking upon one she seemed a mighty pretty creature". Like the rest of Covent Garden, Drury Lane had degenerated considerably by the eighteenth century, when Hogarth depicted it in *The Harlot's Progress*. Nowadays, it's something of a backwater, but business certainly prospered for the Sainsbury family, who opened their first shop in 1869 at no. 173, selling dairy products. Meanwhile, Brodie & Middleton, the "scenic colourmen" who established themselves here in the 1840s, are still selling glitters, glues, artificial cobwebs and skinheads from no. 68.

North of the piazza

The piazza itself is pleasant to stroll around, but the shops themselves are less interesting: they're either big flagship stores like *Dr Martens*, out-and-out tourist shops or ubiquitous franchises – in other words, the only ones who can afford piazza rents. By contrast, commercial life in the network of streets to the north of Covent Garden Piazza is still significantly more varied, with clusters of designer clothes outlets, plus the occasional oddball shop of the sort that once characterized the entire neighbourhood. Neal Street is the area's main street, with Floral Street, Long Acre, Shelton Street and Shorts Gardens all worth exploring, too.

Floral Street and Long Acre

The western half of **Floral Street** is dominated by three adjoining shops run by top-selling British designer Paul Smith, whose tongue-in-cheek window displays are always worth inspecting. Smith also runs outposts for jeans and workwear – marketed as R. Newbold – on adjoining Langley Court. Keeping him company are branches of Nicole Farhi and Jones, the ultimate fashion-victim bazaar, plus a few quirkier outlets, like a shop dedicated purely to Tintin, the Belgian boy detective. Meanwhile, squeezed beside a very narrow alleyway off the western end of Floral Street, is the **Lamb and Flag** pub, where the Poet Laureate, John Dryden, was beaten up in December 1679 by a group of thugs, hired most probably by his rival poet, the Earl of Rochester.

Though it originally specialized in coach manufacture, **Long Acre**, to the north of and parallel to Floral Street, was Covent Garden's main shopping street long before the market was converted into a glorified shopping mall. Nowadays, it's dominated by branches of big-name clothing chains, and continental-style cafés and bistros, but there are some survivors of earlier times, most notably Stanford's, the world's oldest and largest map shop (see p.20). Look out, too, for **Carriage Hall**, an old stabling yard, surrounded by cast-iron pillars and situated between Long Acre and Floral Street, which was originally used by coach makers and has now been converted into shops.

Freemasons' Hall

Mon–Fri 10am–5pm; free. Guided tours of the Grand Temple Mon–Fri hourly 11am–4pm; free. ☎020/7831 9811; *www.grand-lodge.org*. Covent Garden or Holborn tube.

Looking east down the gentle curve of Long Acre, it's difficult to miss the austere, Pharaonic mass of the **Freemasons' Hall**, built as a memorial to all the masons who died in World War I. Whatever you may think of this reactionary, secretive, male-only organization, which enjoys a virtual stranglehold over institutions like the police and judiciary, the interior is worth a peek for the Grand Temple alone, whose pompous, bombastic décor is laden with heavy symbolism – to see the Grand Temple, you must sign up for one of the **guided tours**. The masonically curious might also take a look at the shops opposite the temple, which sell mason merchandise: aprons, rings and all the essential accoutrements and souvenirs of the art.

Neal Street and Neal's Yard

North from Long Acre runs **Neal Street**, one of the most sought-after commercial addresses in Covent Garden, which features some fine Victorian warehouses, complete with stair towers for loading and shifting goods between floors. Neal Street used to be famous for single-theme shops like The Kite Store and the Oriental goods emporium Neal Street East. However, these are being edged out by multi-national fashion stores such as Mango, Diesel and O'Neill.

A decade or so ago, the feel of the street was a lot less moneyed and more alternative, but that ambience only really survives in *Food for Thought*, the veggie café that's been here since 1971, and **Neal's Yard**, a wholefood haven set in a tiny little courtyard off Shorts Gardens, prettily festooned with flower boxes and ivy. Here, you'll find the excellent Neal's Yard co-op bakery, several vegetarian cafés and takeaway outlets, a superb cheese shop, a herbalist and even a bit of therapy. The complex was set up in the early 1970s by Nick Saunders, one of the leading lights of "alternative London" and the campaign to rescue Covent Garden, and is endowed with a splendid water clock (above the Neal's Yard Wholefood Warehouse), which gave unwary customers a soaking on the hour, every hour, until the staff, tired of the joke, put up a canopy.

Still, there's enough in and around Neal's Yard to divert most visitors. Skateboarders pick their way through the wholefood to get to Slam City Skates, one of a number of cult shops in the area whose popularity is impenetrable to outsiders; its basement is home to Rough Trade records, haven of obscure indie produce. New Agers flock to The Astrology Shop on Neal Street and Mysteries round the corner on Monmouth Street, while 2000AD fans head for Comic Showcase at the top of Neal Street. Coffee addicts have a treat in store, too, in Monmouth Street Coffee Shop (another Saunders initiative), which roasts its own beans on the premises. Inevitably, amid all this innovative consumerism, there are one or two blemishes, most notably the **Thomas Neal Centre**, a sanitized shopping mall, housed in a former banana warehouse.

Seven Dials

West of Neal Street is **Seven Dials**, the meeting point of seven streets which make up a little circus, centred on a slender column topped by six tiny blue sundials (the seventh dial is formed by the column itself and the surrounding road). The column has had a chequered history: erected in 1693, it was torn down in 1773 when a rumour went about that treasure was hidden beneath it; it was re-erected in Weybridge fifty years later, and the replica which now stands in Covent Garden was built in 1989 as a sort of roundabout with seats. **Earlham Street**, which runs from Seven Dials into Charing Cross Road, harbours an old-fashioned ironmonger and a local butcher, and was once a flourishing market street, though only a handful of stalls remain. They include, however, one of London's very best cut-flower stalls – a visual treat at any time of year.

St Giles

"Women with scarcely the articles of apparel which common decency requires, with forms bloated by disease, and faces rendered hideous by habitual drunkenness – men reeling and staggering along – children in rags and filth – whole streets of squalid and miserable appearance whose inhabitants are lounging in the public road, fighting, screaming and swearing . . . "

Thus Dickens described the old **St Giles rookery**, the predominantly Irish slum area north of Covent Garden, which, less than a hundred years earlier, had provided the setting for Hogarth's *Gin Lane*. Even at its height, St Giles was by no means the most dangerous slum in London – parts of the East End were far worse. But it was the rookery's position at the heart of the West End that scared the daylights out of wealthy Londoners. Here were ten to twelve acres of densely populated hovels which provided "a convenient asylum for the offscourings of the night-world" – Dickens again. Even after the establishment of the police, few officers could expect to emerge from the maze of brothels and gin shops unscathed; on one occasion a foolhardy evangelist was ejected from the slums stripped and bound, his mouth stuffed with mustard powder.

In the end, the wide new roads of the Metropolitan Board of Works did what no police force or charity organization could manage, by "shovelling out the poor" as one critic put it. Virtually the only reminder of the rookery is the early eighteenth-century church of **St Giles-in-the-Fields** on the south side of the old St Giles High Street, last resting place of poet Andrew Marvell, and of the twelve Catholics denounced by Titus Oates as participants in a completely fictitious (as it turned out) Popish plot to murder Charles II. The rest of the slums were demolished to make way for New Oxford Street and the busy interchange of Shaftesbury Avenue, High Holborn and St Giles High Street at the top of Neal Street.

At the eastern end of the old high street is St Giles Circus, now a godforsaken spot skewered by the hideous 1960s skyscraper called **Centrepoint**. Designed by Richard Seifert (who was also responsible for the NatWest Tower on Bishopsgate), it was built by property tycoon Harry Hyams, who kept it famously empty for more than a decade, a profit-making venture whose cynicism transcended even the London norms of the time. The tower, which is now a listed building, stands on the site of the gallows where Sir John Oldcastle – the model for Shakespeare's Falstaff and leader of the heretical Lollards – was hanged and burnt in 1417.

Chapter 5

Bloomsbury

BLOOMSBURY gets its name from its medieval landowners, the
Blemunds, who were probably given the estate – described in
the Domesday Book as having vineyards and "wood for 100
pigs" – by William the Conqueror. Nothing was built here, though,
until the 1660s, when the Earl of Southampton laid out Bloomsbury
Square, which John Evelyn thought "a noble square or piazza – a little towne". Through marriage, the Russell family, the earls and later
dukes of Bedford, acquired much of the area, and established the
many formal, bourgeois squares which remain the main distinguishing feature of Bloomsbury. The Russells named the grid-plan streets
after their various titles and estates, and kept the pubs and shops to a
minimum to maintain the tone of the neighbourhood.

In the twentieth century, Bloomsbury acquired a reputation as the
city's most learned quarter, dominated by the dual institutions of the
British Museum and London University, and home to many of
London's chief book publishers, but perhaps best known for its literary inhabitants. Today, the **British Museum** is clearly the star attraction – it takes up half this chapter, and could occupy you for several
days or more – but there are other sights, such as the **Dickens House
Museum**, that are high on many people's itineraries.

In its northern fringes, the character of the area changes dramatically, becoming steadily more seedy as you near the two big main-line
train stations of **Euston** and **King's Cross**, where cheap B&Bs and
run-down council estates provide fertile territory for prostitutes and
drug dealers, and an unlikely location for the new **British Library**.

The British Museum

Mon–Sat 10am–5pm, Sun noon–6pm; free; ☎020/7636 1555; *www
.thebritishmuseum.ac.uk*. Café and restaurant Mon–Sat 10am–4.30pm, Sun
noon–5.30pm. Tottenham Court Road, Holborn or Russell Square tube.

One of the great museums of the world, the **British Museum** is Britain's
most popular tourist attraction after Blackpool, drawing more than six

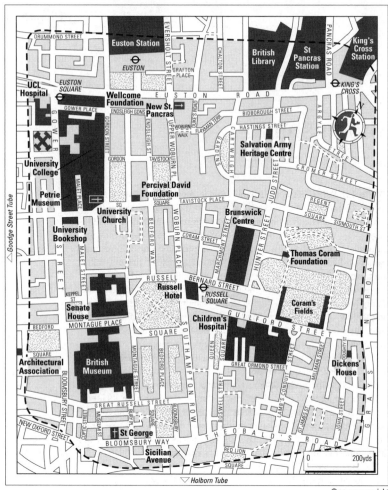

© crown copyright

million visitors a year. With over four million exhibits – a number increasing daily with the stream of new acquisitions, discoveries and bequests – ranged over two and a half miles of galleries, this is one of the largest and most comprehensive collections of antiquities, prints, drawings and books to be housed under one roof. Its assortment of Roman and Greek art is unparalleled, its Egyptian collection is the most significant outside Egypt and, in addition, there are fabulous treasures from Anglo-Saxon and Roman Britain, from China, Japan, India and Mesopotamia – not to mention an enormous collection of prints and drawings, only a fraction of which can be displayed at any one time.

The Great Court

The British Library's departure to St Pancras (see p.185) has allowed the British Museum to open up and redevelop the building's **Great Court**. Protected from the elements by a startling glass and steel curved roof, designed by Norman Foster, the court is now open to the public, and allows greater access between the museum's various wings. At the centre stands the copper-domed former **Round Reading Room**, built in the 1850s to house the British Library. It was here, at desk O7, that Karl Marx penned *Das Kapital*; Lenin also worked here, at desk L13, under his pseudonym of Jacob Richter in 1902. As part of the redevelopment, the Round Reading Room has now been transformed into a public study area, with a multimedia guide to the museum's collections.

The origins of the BM (as regular users call it) lie in the collection of over 80,000 curios – everything from plants and fossils to flamingo tongues and "maggots taken from a man's ear" – belonging to Hans Sloane, a wealthy Chelsea doctor who bequeathed them to the king in 1753, in return for £20,000. The king couldn't (or wouldn't) pay, so the collection was finally purchased by an unenthusiastic government to form the kernel of the world's first public secular museum, housed in a building bought with the proceeds of a dubiously conducted public lottery. Soon afterwards, the BM began to acquire the antiquities that have given it a modern reputation as the world's largest museum of stolen goods. The "robberies" of Lord Elgin are only the best known; countless others engaged in sporadic looting throughout the Empire – the Napoleonic Wars provided the victorious Brits with heaps of antiquities pilfered by the French in Egypt, and the BM itself sent out its own archeologists to strip classical sites bare.

The illuminated manuscripts, such as the Lindisfarne Gospels, are housed in the British Library (see p.186).

As early as 1820 it was clear that more space was needed for all this loot, hence the present structure, built piecemeal over the course of the next thirty years. The overall design was by Robert Smirke, whose giant Ionic colonnade and portico, complete with a pediment frieze, make this the grandest of London's Greek Revival buildings. Lack of space has continued to be a problem, however: the natural history collections were transferred to South Kensington as far back as the 1880s (see p.360), and the ethnographical department has only recently returned home. Over the next couple of years, more and more of what used to be known as the "Museum of Mankind" will be housed in new galleries in the BM's north wing.

The area south of the BM is good for bookshops, cafés and pubs, and the museum itself has a branch of the popular Milburns café chain.

Visiting the British Museum

The BM's fourteen-acre site is enough to tire even the most ardent museum lover. J.B. Priestley, for one, wished "there was a little room somewhere in the British Museum that contained only about twenty exhibits and good lighting, easy chairs, and a notice imploring you to

The British Museum

smoke." Short of such a place, the best advice is either to see the highlights (listed in the box below) and leave the rest for another visit, or to concentrate on one or two sections. Alternatively, you might consider one of the BM's daily **guided tours**: the highlights tour (1hr 30min) costs £7, while the focus tour (1hr) costs £5, though both, in fact, show you the highlights. The "eyeOpener" (50min) and Spotlight (20min) tours are free, but concentrate on just one of the BM's collections.

The BM has **two entrances** (both have cloakrooms): the main one, on Great Russell Street, brings you to the information desk and bookshop, while the smaller doorway on the north side of the building in Montague Place opens onto the Oriental galleries. The information desk will furnish you with a free museum plan, and the noticeboard close by announces which rooms are currently closed. Even equipped with a plan, it's easy enough to get confused, as the room numbering is complicated and many sections are spread over more than one floor – don't hesitate, however, to ask the museum staff, who are usually extremely helpful and knowledgeable. The BM can get crowded, too, so if you're heading for the major sights, try to get here as early in the day as possible, and avoid the weekends if you can, when the popular galleries are overrun. It's a far

---

WHERE TO FIND WHAT IN THE BRITISH MUSEUM

MAIN PERMANENT EXHIBITIONS:

Coins and medals: Upper floor, rooms 68 & 69a.

Egyptian antiquities: Ground floor, room 25; upper floor, rooms 60–66.

Ethnography: Ground floor rooms 33c & 33d.

Greek and Roman antiquities: Ground floor, rooms 1–15; basement, rooms 77–85; upper floor, rooms 69–73.

Medieval, Renaissance and Modern collections: Upper floor, rooms 41–48.

Oriental collections: Ground floor, rooms 33–34; upper floor, rooms 91–94.

Prehistoric and Romano-British collections: Upper floor, rooms 37, 49 & 50.

Prints and drawings: Upper floor, room 90.

Western Asiatic antiquities: Ground floor, rooms 16–26; basement, rooms 88–89; upper floor, rooms 51–59.

THE MOST POPULAR ITEMS:

Egyptian mummies: Upper floor, room 61.

Elgin Marbles: Ground floor, room 8.

Lewis chessmen: Upper floor, room 42.

Lindow Man: Upper floor, room 50.

Oxus Treasure: Upper floor, room 52.

Portland Vase: Ground floor, room 14.

Rosetta Stone: Ground floor, room 25.

Sutton Hoo Treasure: Upper floor, room 41

---

cry from the museum's beginnings in 1759, when it was open for just three hours a day, entry was by written application only, and tickets for "any person of decent appearance" were limited to ten per hour.

Because of the sheer volume of the BM's hoard of **prints and drawings**, everything from Botticelli to Bonnard, there is only space for temporary exhibitions in room 90, which change every three to four months. The same is true of the BM's collection of 500,000 **coins and medals**, of which only a fraction can be shown at any one time, usually in room 69a. The sensitive materials used in Japanese art mean that the **Japanese Galleries** in rooms 91 to 94 also host only temporary shows. And finally, the BM puts on regular **temporary exhibitions** (Tutankhamen was the most famous) on a wide range of themes in room 28, for which there is usually an entrance charge.

Temporary displays and exhibitions

Greek and Roman antiquities

Greek and Roman antiquities make up the largest section in the museum, spread over three floors. The ground floor (rooms 1–15) is laid out along broadly chronological lines, starting with the Bronze Age and finishing up in late Roman times; highlights include the Elgin Marbles and the Nereid monument. The basement (rooms 77–85) holds the chaotic Townley collection, while the upper floor (rooms 69–73) houses less spectacular finds, the exception being the Portland Vase.

From Prehistoric to Classical Greece

From the foyer, pass through the bookshop, ignore the alluring Assyrian sculpture to your right, and enter through the twin half-columns taken from one of the beehive tombs at Mycenae. Room 1 kicks off with Cycladic figures from the Aegean islands, whose meaning is still disputed, while room 2 contains Minoan artefacts (mainly from Knossos on Crete), the Aegina treasure of gold jewellery and a small selection of Mycenaean finds. Beyond lies the museum's excellent **café and restaurant**.

Rooms 1 & 2

The BM boasts an exhausting array of **Greek vases**, starting with the Geometric and early pictorial-style period (ninth and eighth centuries BC) in room 3, and moving on through the unusual Corinthian hybrid-animal vases to more familiar Athenian black-figure vases of the Archaic period (seventh and sixth centuries BC) in room 3. Among the later red-figure vases from Greece's Classical age (fifth century BC) in rooms 4 and 5, check out the satyrs balancing wine coolers on their erect penises. There are further hoards of early Greek vases in the basement of room 3, and later, mostly red-figure examples in room 9 and the mezzanine room 11, not to mention the various examples dotted about rooms 68–73 on the upper floor.

Greek vases

The British
Museum

Room 5

Room 6

Room 7

Room 8

The Harpy Tomb, Bassae frieze and Nereid monument

From room 5 onwards, the real highlights of the Classical section begin, starting with the marble relief from the **Harpy Tomb**, a huge imposing funerary pillar from Xanthos in western Turkey, which originally rose to a height of nearly 30ft. The tomb occupies centre stage in the room, its name derived from the pairs of strange bird-women that appear on two sides of the relief, carrying children in their arms.

In the purpose-built mezzanine (room 6) is the fifth-century BC marble frieze from the **Temple of Apollo at Bassae**, which would originally have been lodged 50ft up by the roof of the temple, barely visible and poorly lit. Here, you come face to face with naked Greeks battling it out with half-clad Amazons, and inebriated centaurs misbehaving at a Lapith wedding feast, all depicted vigorously in high relief.

Back down the stairs, in room 7, your eyes are drawn to the reconstructed fourth-century BC **Nereid monument**, a mighty temple-like tomb of a Lycian chieftain, fronted with Ionic columns interspersed with figures once identified as Nereids (sea nymphs), now thought to be Aurae or wind goddesses. The monument was the most important construction at Xanthos until 1842, when it was carried off by Charles Fellows on the HMS *Beacon*, along with the greater part of the site's movable art (including the aforementioned Harpy Tomb relief).

The Elgin Marbles

The large, purpose-built room 8 is devoted to the museum's most famous relics, the **Parthenon sculptures**, better known as the **Elgin Marbles**, after Lord Elgin, who removed them from the Parthenon in Athens in 1801. As British ambassador to Constantinople, Lord Elgin was able to wangle permission from the Turkish Porte (which then ruled Greece) to remove "any pieces of stone with figures and inscriptions". He interpreted this as a licence to make off with almost all of the reliefs of the Parthenon frieze and most of its pedimental sculptures, which he displayed in a shed in his Pall Mall garden until he eventually sold them to the BM in 1816 for £35,000.

There were justifications for Elgin's action – the Turks' tendency to use Parthenon stones in their lime kilns, and the fact that the building had already been partially wrecked in 1687 when a Venetian missile landed on the pile of gunpowder the Turks had thoughtfully stored there – though it was controversial even then and was opposed, notably by Byron. The Greek government has repeatedly requested the sculptures be returned, and has commissioned a special museum to house them near the Acropolis itself. The BM's argument that the marbles are in safer hands here in London was seriously undermined when it was disclosed that the gallery was available for party hire, and that a cleaning in the last century had actually damaged the sculptures.

Despite their grand setting (and partly due to all the hype), first impressions of the marble friezes, carved between 447 and 432 BC under the supervision of the great sculptor Pheidias, can be a little disappointing. After the vigorous high relief of the Bassae frieze, the Parthenon's sculptures can appear flat and lifeless, made up of long, repetitive queues of worshippers. To help prepare you for what you're about to see, first check out the museum's excellent interpretive rooms on either side of the main entrance.

In one room, a short, mercifully silent, video shows you where the marbles would originally have been situated, which, in the case of the main frieze, was high up and virtually out of sight behind the first set of columns. The video also demonstrates, with the help of computer-generated graphics, how ingeniously the sculptor dealt with the complex compositional problems of trying to carve groups of people and animals. In the opposite room are casts taken from the pieces of the frieze that remain in Athens, and a useful reminder that the frieze, like most of the classical sculptures in the BM, would originally have been vibrantly picked out by red, blue and gold paint.

The audioguide to the marbles, for which you're invited to donate £3, certainly helps focus your mind on the sculpture, though it's by no means essential listening, as the explanatory panels are good enough if you take the time to read them. It's now generally agreed that the main frieze depicts the Panathenaic festival, held every four years to glorify the goddess Athena. One of the most impressive sections is the traffic jam of horsemen on the north frieze, which is better preserved and exhibits superb compositional dexterity – it's worth remembering that the frieze is carved to a maximum depth of only 2in, yet manages to convey a much greater feeling of depth. Another superlative slice stands directly opposite, where the oxen are being led to the gods (said to have inspired Keats to write his *Ode on a Grecian Urn*).

At each end of the room are the free-standing pedimental sculptures: the figures from the east pediment, which depict the extraordinary birth of Athena – she emerged fully grown and fully armed from the head of Zeus – are the most impressive, though most are headless. The surrounding metopes, which vary enormously in quality, derive entirely from the south side of the Parthenon, and depict in high relief the struggle between centaurs and Lapiths.

The Tomb of Payava and the Mausoleum of Halicarnassus

Beyond the Nereid monument, in room 9, you come to two of Lord Elgin's less defensible appropriations, looking particularly forlorn and meaningless: a single column and one of the six caryatids from the portico of the **Erechtheion**, also on the Acropolis.

Room 9

Further on, in room 10, is another large relic from Xanthos, the **Tomb of Payava**, built during the incumbent's lifetime; the reliefs on

Rooms 10 & 11

the tomb's steep roof (particular to Lycia) would have been out of view of earthbound mortals, and are best viewed from the gallery, known as room 11, containing the reserve collection of Greek vases.

Room 12 contains fragments from one of the Seven Wonders of the Ancient World: two huge figures, an Amazonian frieze and a marble horse the size of an elephant from the self-aggrandizing tomb of **King Mausolus at Halicarnassus** (source of the word "mausoleum") from the fourth century BC. However, the real gem is the sculpted column drum from another Wonder of the World, the colossal **Temple of Artemis at Ephesus**, which is decorated in high relief with scenes from the underworld.

The drum lies in room 14 (there is no unlucky room 13), which is devoted to Hellenistic culture and features a fabulously delicate gold oak wreath with a bee and two cicadas. While you're here, don't miss the **Portland Vase**, made from cobalt-blue blown glass around the beginning of the first millennium, and decorated with opaque white cameos. The vase was smashed into over two hundred separate pieces by a young Irishman in 1845, for which he was fined £3.

The basement galleries: Greek and Roman sculpture

From room 12, steps lead down to the basement galleries. Room 77 is rather like a Classical builder's yard, piled high with bits of columns, architraves, entablatures and capitals, much of it gathered from the aforementioned Temple of Artemis, the Mausoleum of Halicarnassus and the Propylaea in Athens. Next comes a room full of Classical inscriptions, followed by room after room of Greek and Roman sculpture, arranged in the whimsical manner preferred by the eighteenth-century English collectors who amassed the stuff.

The best pieces come from the **Townley Collection**, bought from dealers in Rome and London between 1768 and 1791 by Charles Townley, for his London house in Queen Anne's Gate. In room 85, there are dozens of portrait busts of emperors and mythological heroes, while in the parallel room 83 there's a monumental marble foot (possibly) from a statue of the Egyptian god Serapis. But the final room (84) houses the most bewildering array of sculpture, much of it modified to Townley's own tastes. Here, you'll find two curiously gentle marble greyhounds, a claw-footed sphinx, a chariot-shaped latrine and one of Townley's last purchases, a Roman copy of the famous Classical Greek bronze of the Discobolus (the discus thrower).

The upper-floor galleries

The remainder of the Greek and Roman collection is situated on the **upper floor** (rooms 69–73), which you can approach either from the main stairs, or from the west stairs – the latter are lined with mosaic pavements from Halicarnassus. From the main stairs, turn immediately right and right again to get to room 69, whose "Daily Life" exhibition is one of the most user-friendly in the whole collection, with a variety of objects grouped under specific themes such as gladiators, music, women and so on.

There's a dazzling display of mostly third-century AD silverware from Roman Gaul in room 70, plus some fine seafood mosaics, and an intriguing, warty, crocodile-skin suit of armour worn by a Roman follower of the Egyptian crocodile cult. The last three rooms (71–73) of Etruscan artefacts, Cypriot antiquities and Apulian red-figure vases, which round off the Classical section, are of minor interest only, although the finely carved ostrich egg in room 71, discovered by Napoleon's brother, is worth a look.

Western Asiatic antiquities

The collections of the department of **Western Asiatic antiquities** cover all the lands east of Egypt and west of Afghanistan. The majority of exhibits on the ground floor come from the Assyrian Empire, which reached its height in the ninth and eighth centuries BC; upstairs you'll find the Nimrud ivories, rich pickings from Mesopotamia and the Oxus Treasure from ancient Persia.

Assyrian sculpture and reliefs

Through the bookshop, before you enter the Greek and Roman antiquities section, two attendant gods, their robes smothered in inscriptions, fix their gaze on you, signalling the beginning of the BM's remarkable collection of **Assyrian sculptures and reliefs**. Ahead of you lies the Egyptian Hall (room 25; see p.171), but to continue with Assyria, turn left and pass between the two awesome five-legged, human-headed winged bulls that once guarded the temple of Ashurnasirpal II (two larger ones stand in room 16). Beyond is a full-scale reconstruction of the colossal wooden **Balawat Gates** from the palace of Shalmaneser III (858–824 BC), which are bound together with bronze strips decorated with low-relief friezes (the originals are displayed close by) depicting the defeat and execution of Shalmaneser's enemies.

*Assyrian
artefacts*

All the above serves as a prelude to the Assyrian finds that are ranged in rooms 19 to 21, parallel to the Egyptian Hall. The **Nineveh reliefs**, which begin in room 19, were originally brightly coloured, appearing rather like stone tapestries. There are some great snapshots of Assyrian life – a review of prisoners, a bull hunt and so on – but the most memorable scene, located towards the middle of the room, is of the soldiers swimming across the sea on inflated animal bladders. At the centre of room 20 stands a small black obelisk carved with images of foreign rulers paying tribute to Shalmaneser III, interspersed with **cuneiform inscriptions** – discovered in 1846, these helped significantly in the decoding of this early form of writing. The reliefs in room 21 record the stupendous effort involved in transporting the aforementioned winged bulls from their quarry to the palace;

Rooms 19–21

they should be read from left to right, so start at the far end of the
room. Evidently the Assyrians moved these huge carved beasts in one
piece; not so the British, who cut the two largest winged bulls in the
BM into six pieces before transporting them – the joins are still visible on the pair in room 16, round the corner from room 20.

The partitioned galleries next door, known collectively as room
17, are lined with even more splendid friezes from Nineveh. On one
side is an almost continuous band portraying the chaos and carnage
during the Assyrian capture of the Judaean city of Lachish; the
Assyrian king Sennacherib's face was smashed by Babylonian soldiers when the Assyrian capital finally fell to its southern neighbours
in 612 BC. On the other side are depicted the **royal lion hunts** of
Ashurbanipal (668–627 BC), which involved rounding up the beasts
before letting them loose in an enclosed arena for the king's sport, a
practice which effectively eradicated the species in Assyria; the succession of graphic death scenes features one in which the king
slaughters the cats with his bare hands.

Mesopotamia, Ur and the Oxus Treasure

From room 17, it's a convenient trot down into the basement (room

89), where there are friezes, inscriptions and domestic objects,
including an iron bathtub decorated with wild goats which was found
reused as a coffin. All hail from the **Mesopotamian capital of Ur**,
thought to be the first great city on earth, dating from 2500 BC.

Up the west stairs, in room 56, are some of the BM's oldest artefacts, dating from Mesopotamia in the third millennium BC. The
most extraordinary treasures hail from Ur: the enigmatic **Ram in the
Thicket**, a deep-blue lapis lazuli and white shell statuette of a goat on
its hind legs, peering through gold-leaf branches; the equally mysterious **Standard of Ur**, a small hollow box showing scenes of battle on
one side, with peace and banqueting on the other, all fashioned in
shell, red limestone and lapis lazuli, set in bitumen; and the **Royal
Game of Ur**, one of the earliest known board games.

In room 55, a selection of tablets scratched with infinitesimal
cuneiform script includes the **Flood Tablet**, a fragment of the Epic
of Gilgamesh, perhaps the world's oldest story. Finally, there's the
Oxus Treasure, in room 52, a hoard of goldwork which appears to
have passed from one band of robbers to another until it was eventually bought from the bazaar at Rawalpindi by a British officer. The
pieces date from the fifth and fourth centuries BC and are executed
in a style used throughout the Persian Empire. The most celebrated
are the miniature four-horse chariot and the pair of armlets sprout-
ing fantastical horned griffins.

*There are
more Egyptian
antiquities in
the nearby
Petrie
Museum; see
p.184.*

Egyptian antiquities

The BM's collection of **Egyptian antiquities**, ranging from
Predynastic times to Coptic Egypt, is one of the finest in the world,

rivalled only by Cairo's and the New York Met's; the highlights are the Rosetta Stone, the vast hall of Egyptian sculpture and the large collection of mummies.

The Egyptian Hall

Beyond the bookshop on the ground floor, just past the entrance to the Assyrian section (see above), two black granite statues of Amenophis III guard the entrance to the **Egyptian Hall** (room 25), where the cream of the BM's Egyptian antiquities are on display. The name "Belzoni", scratched under the left heel of the larger statue, was carved by the Italian circus strongman responsible for dragging some of the heftiest Egyptian treasures to the banks of the Nile, prior to their export to England.

Rooms 25, 25a & 25b

Nearby, a crowd usually hovers around the **Rosetta Stone**, a black basalt slab found in the Nile delta in 1799 by French soldiers. It was surrendered to the Brits in 1801, but it was a French professor who finally unlocked the secret of Egyptian hieroglyphs, by comparing the stone's three different scripts – ancient hieroglyphs, demotic Egyptian and Greek. Beyond the stone are a series of **false doors**, richly decorated with hieroglyphs and figures of the deceased, through which, it was believed, the dead person's *ka* (soul) could pass to receive the food offerings laid outside the burial chamber.

Further on, a sombre trio of life-sized granite statues of **Sesotris III** make a doleful counterpoint to the pink-speckled granite head of the same ruler, and a colossal one of **Amenophis III**, whose enormous dislocated arm lies next to him. Further along are four seated statues of the goddess Sakhmet, the half lion, half-human bringer of destruction, who was much loved by Amenophis III – each sports solar discs and clutches the Egyptian symbol of life.

Glass cases in the central atrium display a fascinating array of smaller objects, from signet rings to eye-paint containers in the shape of hedgehogs, as well as figurines and religious objects, including a bronze of the cat goddess **Bastet**, with gold nose- and earrings – the subject of the museum's most popular reproduction. Further on still, another giant head and shoulders, made of two pieces of different coloured granite, still bears the hole drilled by French soldiers in an unsuccessful attempt to remove it from the Ramesseum, the mortuary temple of Rameses II. Moving towards the end of the room, past the red granite columns with palm leaf capitals, be sure to check out the colossal granite scarab beetle by the exit.

The mummies and other funerary art

Climbing the west stairs brings you to the popular **Egyptian mummy** collection. Room 60 looks set to be closed for some time, while room 61 houses an exhibition on Egyptian religion (for more on which, see below), so for the moment the mummies are on show in rooms 62 and 63. The sheer number of exhibits here is overwhelming, but the

explanatory panels do an excellent job of explaining the complex ritual of Egyptian mummification. The exhibits are arranged chronologically starting, confusingly, at the far end of room 63.

To attain the afterlife, it was necessary that the deceased's name
and body continued to exist, in order to sustain the *ka* or cosmic
double that was born with every person. At its height in the New
Kingdom (1567–1085 BC), **mummification** entailed removing the
brain (which was discarded) and the viscera (which were preserved
in jars); applying resin to the body and dehydrating the cadaver in
salts for about forty days; packing it to reproduce lifelike contours;
inserting artificial eyes and painting the face or entire body either red
(for men) or yellow (for women); wrapping it in gum-coated linen
bandages; and finally cocooning it in mummy-shaped coffins.

In room 62, you'll see numerous mummified corpses, embalmed
bodies and inner and outer **coffins** richly decorated with hieroglyphs.
In one display cabinet, there are even mummies of various animals,
including cats, apes, crocodiles, falcons and an eel, along with their
highly ornate coffins – the cobra's bronze coffin depicts the deceased
with a human head. Also on display are colourful funerary **amulets**
which were wrapped with the mummy, and **heart scarabs**, which
were placed on the chest of the mummy to prevent the deceased's
heart from bearing witness against him or her during the judgement
of Osiris, when the deceased's heart (believed to be the seat of intelligence) was weighed against Maat's feather of truth. The hearts of
the guilty were devoured by crocodile-headed Ammut, while the right-
eous were led into the presence of Osiris to begin their resurrection.

The tomb's contents (intended to satisfy the needs of the
pharaoh's *ka* in the afterlife) included food, drink, clothing, furniture, weapons and dozens of **shabti figures** designed to perform any
task that the gods might require. In room 63, there are miniature
boats to provide transport in the afterlife, beer brewers, butchers
and even an entire model granary. The last few rooms are less interesting, though the five-thousand-year-old sand-preserved corpse in
room 64 always comes in for ghoulish scrutiny.

The Prehistoric and Romano-British collections

The BM fulfils its less controversial role as national treasure house in
the (rather loosely defined) **Prehistoric and Romano-British collections** on the upper floor (rooms 36–40, 49 & 50), though even
here there have been calls for the items to be shared more with the
regional museums. The initial galleries (rooms 36–40) have been
undergoing refurbishment, which means that the majority of the collection is currently displayed in rooms 49 and 50. One of the most
famous exhibits in the collection, in room 49, is the 28-piece silver
tableware set known as the **Mildenhall Treasure** from the fourth
century AD. The Great Dish is an outstanding late Roman work,
weighing over 8kg and decorated with a mixture of Bacchic biblical

images in low relief. Several spectacular finds have been dragged out from the bottom of the River Thames, most notably a bronze head of the Roman emperor Hadrian. A whole load more are displayed in room 50, including the Battersea Shield, a bronze-faced Celtic shield from the first century BC.

Room 50 also houses one of the most sensational of the BM's recent finds, the leathery half-corpse **Lindow Man**. Clubbed and garrotted during a Druid sacrificial ceremony (or so it's reckoned), he lay in a hide-preserving Cheshire bog for some 2000 years. Also from Britain, there are fabulous heavy golden necklaces, a horned bronze helmet and fine decorative mirrors and shields. Best of all is the **Snettisham Treasure**, made up mostly of gold and silver torcs (neck-rings), the finest of which is made of eight strands of gold twisted together, each of which is in turn made up of eight wires. Brilliant displays of **Celtic craftwork** follow, two of the most distinctive objects being the French Basse-Yutz wine flagons, made from bronze and inlaid with coral. Showing Persian and Etruscan influences, they are supreme examples of Celtic art, with happy little ducks on the lip and rangy dogs for handles.

Room 50

The medieval, Renaissance and modern collections

The **medieval, Renaissance and modern collections** cover more than a millennium, from the Dark Ages to the interwar period. The first gallery (room 41) houses finds from all over Europe, but most visitors come here to see the Anglo-Saxon **Sutton Hoo Treasure**, which includes silver bowls, gold jewellery decorated with inset enamel and an iron helmet bejewelled with gilded bronze and garnets, all buried along with a forty-oar open ship in East Anglia around 625 AD. Discovered by accident in 1939, this enormous haul is by far the richest single archeological find ever made in Britain.

*Room 41:
Sutton Hoo
Treasure*

In the next room (42) are the thick-set **Lewis chessmen**, wild-eyed twelfth-century Scandinavian figures carved from walrus ivory, which were discovered in 1831 by a Gaelic crofter in the Outer Hebrides. There are more walrus ivories – mostly chess pieces and religious plaques – from France and Germany elsewhere in the room, as well as a smattering of medieval Russian and Byzantine icons. At the far end of the room is the richly enamelled, fourteenth-century French **Royal Gold Cup**, given by James I to the Constable of Castille, only to find its way back to England in later life.

Rooms 42–45

Room 43 displays tile mosaics and the largest tile pavement in the country, but you're likely to get more joy out of the adjacent room (44), which resounds to the tick-tocks and chimes of a hundred or more **clocks**, from pocket watches to grandfather clocks. These range in design from the very simple to the highly ornate, like the sixteenth-century gilded copper and brass clock from Strasbourg, based on the one that used to reside in the cathedral there; its series

Clocks

of moving figures includes the Four Ages of Man, who each strike one of the quarter-hours.

The purple-walled chamber beyond (room 45) contains the **Waddesdon Bequest**, amassed by Baron Rothschild in the nineteenth century: a mixed bag of silver gilt, enamelware, glassware and hunting rifles. The two finest works are a Flemish sixteenth-century boxwood altarpiece, which stands only 6in high and is carved with staggering attention to detail, and the Lyte Jewel, which contains a miniature of James I by Hilliard.

Rooms 46 and 47

Renaissance and Baroque art fill the long gallery of room 46, with a bafflingly wide range of works from all over Europe (though much of it is of British origin). Highlights to look out for are the Armada Service, a Tudor silver dining service, two pure gold ice pails that used to belong to Princess Di's family, the magic Aztec mirror and crystal ball used by Elizabethan alchemist John Dee, Cromwell's wax death mask and a collection of Huguenot silver. Room 47 brings you into the revamped **European nineteenth-century** section, and reflects the era's eclectic tastes, with almost every previously existing style – Chinese, Japanese, medieval Gothic, Classical and so on – being rehashed.

Room 48: the twentieth century

Before you leave, you must pay a visit to room 48, where a small selection of the museum's high-quality **twentieth-century exhibits** are displayed. There are stunning examples of Tiffany glass and Liberty pewter, a copper vase by Frank Lloyd Wright and a good selection of Bauhaus products. Perhaps the finest exhibit of all, though, is the chequered oak clock with a mother-of-pearl face, designed by the Scottish architect and designer Charles Rennie Mackintosh.

Coins and medals

Rooms 68 & 69a

To get to the BM's new **Money Gallery** (room 68), turn sharp right at the top of the main stairs. The displays trace the history of money from the use of grain in Mesopotamia around 2000 BC, to the advent of coins in around 625 BC in Greek cities in Asia Minor, to printed money in China in the tenth century AD. It's an attractive and informative gallery, which features pound-coin moulds and punches, a geometric lathe for old £1 notes and a wonderful turn-of-the-century National Cash Register till designed by Tiffany. The modern section has coins from all over the world, from Siberia to Papua New Guinea. The prize for the largest denomination bill goes to the 1993 500 thousand million Yugoslav dinar note, but perhaps the most unusual exhibit of all is the 1970s one million dollar note issued by the Hong Kong "Bank of Hell", featuring the face of Harold Wilson, and designed to be burnt as an offering to keep the deceased happy in the afterlife. Room 69a (tucked away under the mezzanine floor of room 69) hosts temporary exhibitions drawn from the BM's collection of over 500,000 coins and medals.

The ethnographic collections

The BM's **ethnography department** – what used to be the Museum of Mankind – is gradually returning to Bloomsbury from its temporary Mayfair home, and will be housed in the north wing, beginning at the Mexican and North American galleries (see below). Further galleries devoted to the Oceanic and Asian collections are due to open over the next few years. In the meantime, an ethnography showcase, in room 35, at the top of the main stairs, will continue to display a few tempting hors d'oeuvres from the collections.

The **Mexican Gallery** (room 33c) is a dramatically lit display, covering a huge period of Mexican art from the second millennium BC to the sixteenth century AD. As you enter, you're greeted by an Aztec fire serpent, Xiuhcoatl, carved in basalt. On one side is a collection of Huaxtec female deities in stone, sporting fan-shaped head-dresses; on the other are an Aztec stone rattlesnake cleverly lit and mirrored from below, the squatting figure of the sun-god, Xochipili, and the death-cult god, Mictlantecuhtli. A series of limestone Mayan reliefs from Yaxchilan, depicting blood-letting ceremonies, lines one wall. Elsewhere, there are some wonderful jade masks and figurines, and whatever you do don't miss the brilliant colours of the Mixtec painted screen-fold book made of deerskin.

Next door is the new **North American Gallery** (room 33d), whose precise exhibits are destined to change over the course of time due to the delicate organic nature of the materials used. However, you can be sure to find feather headdresses, basketry, artefacts carved from walrus ivory and zoomorphic stone pipes, plus intriguing items such as the skin map of Illinois and Indiana from 1775, which reveals the debt the first white cartographers owed to Native Americans. This is the first BM gallery to tackle a surviving ancient culture, so there are old and new examples of Native American art, and historic and contemporary photos to accompany them.

The Oriental collections

The **Oriental collections** cover some of the same geographical area as the museum's ethnography department, and also overlap with material in the V&A. The Chinese collection is, however, unrivalled in the West, and the Indian sculpture is easily as good as anything at the V&A. The easiest way to approach the Oriental galleries (rooms 33–34 & 91–94) is from the Montague Place entrance; from the Great Russell Street entrance, walk through the Library galleries, continue up the stairs past the 35-foot totem pole and pass along the temporary displays in room 33a.

Rooms 33-34 & 91-94: the Oriental collections

Chinese collection

The **Chinese collection** occupies the eastern half of room 33, which is centred on a wonderful marble well that allows you to look down

Room 33: the Hotung Gallery

The British Museum

onto the Montague Place foyer. The garish **"three-colour" statuary** occupying the centre and far end of the room is the most striking, particularly the central cabinet of horses and grotesque figures, but it's the smaller pieces that hold the attention the longest: for example, the central cabinet of miniature landscapes popular among bored Chinese bureaucrats during the Manchu Empire, or the incredible array of **snuff bottles** in the window cabinet, made from extremely diverse materials – lapis lazuli, jade, crystal, tortoiseshell, quartz and amber.

There's more Chinese porcelain on display at the Percival David Foundation; see p.184.

The Chinese invented **porcelain**, and it was highly prized both in China and abroad. The polychrome Ming and the blue-and-white Yuan porcelain became popular in the West from the fifteenth century onwards, as did the brightly coloured cloisonné enamelware, but it's the much earlier unadorned porcelain which steals the show, with its austere beauty and subtle pastel colours, as in the grey-green Ru porcelain and blue-green celadons from the Song dynasty.

Southeast Asian antiquities

The other half of room 33 starts with a beautiful gilt-bronze statue of the Bodhisattva Tara, who was born from one of the tears wept by Avalokiteshvara, a companion of the Buddha, who stands on the other side of the well. She heralds the beginning of the **Southeast Asian** antiquities, a bewildering array of artefacts from as far apart as India and Indonesia. There are so many cultures and countries covered (albeit briefly) in this section that it's impossible to do more than list some of **the highlights**: a cabinet of Tibetan musical instruments, with a conch-shell trumpet decorated with gilt and precious stones; two fearsome *dakinis*, malevolent goddesses with skull tiaras; a Nepalese altar screen with filigree work inset with bone, shell and semiprecious stones; and a jackfruit wooden door from a Balinese temple.

The classic Hindu image of **Shiva as Lord of the Dance**, trampling on the dwarf of ignorance, occupies centre stage halfway along the hall. Beyond are larger-scale **Indian stone sculptures**, featuring a bevy of intimidating goddesses such as Durga, depicted killing a buffalo demon with her eight hands. The showpiece of the collection, however, lies behind a glass screen in room 33a, a climatically controlled room of dazzling limestone reliefs, drum slabs and dome sculptures purloined from **Amaravati**, one of the finest second-century Buddhist stupas in southern India. The display is somewhat chaotic, however, and you'll have to consult the accompanying illustrations to get any idea of how it might have looked.

Room 33a

The Islamic gallery

Room 34

The museum's **Islamic** antiquities, ranging from Moorish Spain to southern Asia, are displayed in room 34, adjacent to the Montague Place entrance. The collection features thirteenth- to fifteenth-century

Syrian brass objects, inlaid with silver and gold and richly engraved with arabesques and calligraphy (figural representation being forbidden under Islamic law), Syrian and Egyptian enamelled glass mosque lamps and **Iznik ceramics** in greens, tomato-reds and no fewer than five shades of blue.

The best stuff is at the far end of the room, where Moorish lustre pottery resides alongside medieval astrolabes, celestial globes and a **geomantic instrument** from the seventh century, used to discover buried treasure and tell the future. Most unusual of all, though, is a naturalistic **jade terrapin**, discovered in Allahabad in 1600. Other curiosities include a falcon's perch, a back-scratcher, examples of modern Islamic calligraphy, and a couple of jade Mughal hookahs encrusted with lapis lazuli and rubies set in gold.

The rest of Bloomsbury

In comparison with the British Museum, the other sundry attractions of **Bloomsbury** are pretty lightweight, though no less enjoyable for that. The **Dickens Museum** in Doughty Street, at the edge of Holborn, is the most popular; the less well-known **Wellcome Foundation** building currently hosts temporary exhibitions; while the museum at the new **British Library**, near St Pancras, is a definite must. Then, of course, there are Bloomsbury's leafy squares, which, though no longer the set pieces of Georgian architecture they once were, still provide some of the nicest picnic spots in central London.

South of the British Museum

The grid of streets south of the BM has been threatened with demolition more than once, in order to make space for a more monumental approach to the museum. The future of this mostly Georgian "museum quarter" seems secure for the moment, however, and the parallel streets of Museum Street and Bury Place currently thrive on a mixture of antiquarian and secondhand print and bookshops, and cafés and sandwich shops.

Set back from busy Bloomsbury Way, three blocks south of the BM, is the Church of **St George's**, Bloomsbury, the westernmost of Hawksmoor's six London churches, built so that Bloomsbury's respectable residents wouldn't have to cross the St Giles rookery (see p.159) in order to attend services. Its main point of interest is the unusual steeple – a stepped pyramid based on Pliny's description of the tomb of Mausolus at Halicarnassus, fragments of which subsequently made their way to the BM – which is topped by London's only outdoor statue of the unpopular German-speaking monarch, George I, dressed, for reasons now obscure, in a Roman toga. Inside, it's tall and wide, decked out in sky blue and gold, with an unusual

For details of the pubs, cafés and restaurants in the area, see Chapters 15, 16 & 17.

St George's is open Mon–Fri 9.30am–5.30pm.

semi-circular apse complete with a gilded scallop-shell recess, which
served as the original altar until the church's internal realignment in
1781.

The Bloomsbury squares

A little further down Bloomsbury Way, past St George's, is
Bloomsbury Square, dating from 1665 and the first of the city's
open spaces to be officially called a "square". Little remains of its
original or later Georgian appearance, and the only reason to venture
down Bloomsbury Way is to see **Sicilian Avenue**, an unusually continental promenade sliced diagonally across the former slums on the
corner of Bloomsbury Way and Southampton Row. Separated from

The Bloomsbury Group

The **Bloomsbury Group** were essentially a bevy of upper middle-class
friends who lived in and around Bloomsbury, at that time "an antiquated,
ex-fashionable area", in the words of Henry James. The Group revolved
around Virginia, Vanessa, Thoby and Adrian Stephen, who moved into 46
Gordon Square in 1904, shortly after the death of their father, Sir Leslie
Stephen, editor of the *Dictionary of National Biography*. Thoby's
Thursday-evening gatherings and Vanessa's Friday Club for painters
attracted a whole host of Cambridge-educated snobs who subscribed to
Oscar Wilde's theory that "aesthetics are higher than ethics". Their diet of
"human intercourse and the enjoyment of beautiful things" was hardly revolutionary, but their behaviour, particularly that of the two sisters (unmar-
ried, unchaperoned, intellectual and artistic), succeeded in shocking
London society, especially through their louche sexual practices (most of
the group swung both ways).

All this, though interesting, would be forgotten were it not for their individual work. In 1922, Virginia declared, without too much exaggeration,
"Everyone in Gordon Square has become famous": Lytton Strachey had
been the first to make his name with *Eminent Victorians*, a series of
unprecedentedly frank biographies; Vanessa, now married to the art critic
Clive Bell, had become involved in Roger Fry's prolific design firm, Omega
Workshops; and the economist John Maynard Keynes had become an
adviser to the Treasury (he later went on to become the leading economic
theorist of his day). The Group's most celebrated figure, Virginia, now
married to Leonard Woolf and living in Tavistock Square, had become an
established novelist; she and Leonard had also founded the Hogarth Press,
which published T.S. Eliot's *Waste Land* in 1922.

Eliot was just one of a number of writers, such as Aldous Huxley,
Bertrand Russell and E.M. Forster, who were drawn to the interwar
Bloomsbury set, but others, notably D.H. Lawrence, were repelled by the
clan's narcissism and snobbish narrow-mindedness. (Virginia Woolf once
compared *Ulysses* to a "bell-boy at *Claridges*" scratching his pimples.)
Whatever their limitations, the Bloomsbury Group were Britain's most
influential intellectual coterie of the interwar years, and their appeal shows
little sign of waning – even now, scarcely a year goes by without the publication of the biography or memoirs of some Bloomsbury peripheral.

---

the main roads by slender Ionic screens, this simple but effective piece of town planning was created in 1910. It houses a couple of cafés and one of the city's largest secondhand bookshops, the palindromic Skoob Books.

The rest of Bloomsbury

The most handsome of the Bloomsbury squares is **Bedford Square**, to the west of the BM, up Bloomsbury Street. What you see now is pretty much as it was built in the 1770s by the Russells (who still own it), though the gates which sealed the square from traffic have unfortunately been removed, as have all but one of the mews that used to accommodate the coaches and servants of the square's wealthy inhabitants. Today, it's a perfect example of eighteenth-century symmetry and uniformity: each doorway arch is decorated with rusticated Coade stones, each facade is broken only by the white-stuccoed centre houses. The best way to get a look inside one of these Georgian mansions is to head for the **Architectural Association** (AA) at nos. 34–36, which puts on occasional exhibitions, and has a bookshop in the basement and a studenty café/bar on the first floor overlooking the square, with a roof terrace open in fine weather.

For a look inside a Bloomsbury mansion, head for the AA's café/bar, open Mon–Fri 9am–9pm.

The largest Bloomsbury square – indeed one of the largest in London – is **Russell Square**, to the northeast of the BM. Apart from its monumental scale, little remains of the Georgian scheme, though the gardens, with their gargantuan plane trees and defunct 1960s fountains, are good for a picnic; you can also grab a hot drink from the café in the northeastern corner. The figure most closely associated with this square is T.S. Eliot, who worked at no. 24, then the offices of Faber and Faber, from 1925 until his death. The only architectural curiosity is the *Russell Hotel*, on the eastern side; twice as high as everything around it, it's a no-holds-barred Victorian terracotta fancy, concocted in a bewildering mixture of styles in 1898 by Fitzroy Doll. The hotel's wood-panelled *King's Bar* is worth closer inspection, as are the main foyer and ballroom (the latter hosts a book fair on Sunday and Monday in the second week of each month) – though the nicest touch is the wonderfully incongruous *Virginia Woolf* burger, pasta and grill restaurant.

Gordon Square (Mon–Fri 8am–8pm), one block north of Russell Square, with its winding paths and summer profusion of roses, remains one of Bloomsbury's quietest sanctuaries, a favourite with students from the university departments hereabouts. Its one building of note is the strangely towerless neo-Gothic **University Church**, built in 1853 in the southwest corner of the square and looking like a miniature cathedral – the unbuilt tower was to have been nearly 300ft high. Gordon Square was once the centre of the Bloomsbury Group (see box opposite): on the east side, where the Georgian houses stand intact, plaques mark the residences of Lytton Strachey (no. 51) and John Maynard Keynes (no. 46), while another (no. 50) commemorates the Bloomsbury Group as a whole. At no. 53 is the Percival David Foundation of Chinese Art (see p.184).

One block east, and exhibiting almost identical proportions to Gordon Square, is **Tavistock Square**, laid out by Thomas Cubitt in the early part of the nineteenth century. Though the west side of the square survives intact, the house at no. 52, where the Woolfs lived from 1924 until shortly before Virginia's suicide in 1941, and from which they ran the Hogarth Press, is no longer standing. It was here that Woolf wrote her most famous novels – *To the Lighthouse*, *Mrs Dalloway*, *Orlando* and *The Waves* – in a little studio decorated by her sister Vanessa and Duncan Grant. At the centre of the square is a statue of Mahatma Gandhi; to the south stands the copper beech tree planted in honour of his compatriot Jawaharlal Nehru in 1953.

A short distance up Upper Woburn Place, to the northeast of the square, is the beautifully preserved Georgian terrace of **Woburn Walk**, designed in 1822 by Cubitt as London's first purpose-built pedestrianized shopping street. W.B. Yeats lived at no. 5 from 1895 to 1919, writing some of his greatest poetry while hobnobbing with the likes of Ezra Pound, T.S. Eliot and Rabindranath Tagore. The same address was later occupied by the unrequited love of Yeats's life, Irish nationalist Maud Gonne, reputedly the most beautiful woman in Ireland, with, in Yeats's own words, "the carriage and features of a goddess".

The Foundling Hospital and Coram's Fields

Halfway along Guilford Street, east off Russell Square, is the old entrance to the **Foundling Hospital**, founded in 1756 by Thomas Coram, a retired sea captain. Coram campaigned for seventeen years to obtain a royal charter for the hospital, having been shocked by the number of dead or dying babies left by the wayside on the streets of London. Papers in the archives of the Old Bailey relate the typical story of a mother who "fetched her child from the workhouse, where it had just been 'new-clothed', for the afternoon. She strangled it and left it in a ditch in Bethnal Green in order to sell its clothes. The money was spent on gin."

As soon as it was opened, the hospital was besieged, with many children being brought along half-dead just so they could be buried at the expense of the hospital, which soon became more like a morgue than a place of refuge. After less than four years, funding was cut off, since the open-door policy was deemed to encourage prostitution, and the hospital was forced to reduce its admissions drastically. After 1801 only illegitimate children were admitted, and even then only after the mother had filled in a questionnaire and given a verbal statement confirming that "her good faith had been betrayed, that she had given way to carnal passion only after a promise of marriage or against her will; that she therefore had no other children; and that her conduct had always been irreproachable in every other respect."

All that remains of the original eighteenth-century building – which was demolished when the foundation moved to the Home

Counties in the 1920s – is the whitewashed loggia which now forms the border to **Coram's Fields**, a wonderful inner-city **park for children**, with swings, slides, hens and horses, plus a whole host of sheep, pigs and rabbits. Adults are not allowed into the grounds unless accompanied by a child.

Just to the north of the fields, at 40 Brunswick Square, are the offices of the **Thomas Coram Foundation**. The foundation owns a collection of paintings donated by artists such as Gainsborough and Reynolds, on the suggestion of Hogarth, who was a governor and even fostered two of the foundlings; Hogarth's own *March of the Guards to Finchley* is the finest of the pictures. Handel was another of the hospital's early benefactors, giving annual charity performances of the *Messiah* and donating an organ for the chapel, the keyboard of which survives. Lastly, the Court Room, where the governors still hold their meetings, has been faithfully reconstructed, with all its fine stuccowork, to give some idea of the original eighteenth-century ambience.

To the south of Coram's Fields is the **Hospital for Sick Children** on Great Ormond Street, which was founded a hundred years after the Coram Foundation by Charles West, who (like Coram) was appalled by the infant mortality rate in London. Just as Handel had helped out Coram, so Great Ormond Street Hospital was assisted by J.M. Barrie, who donated the copyright (and thus the future royalties) of *Peter Pan* to the hospital in 1929. In 1987, fifty years after Barrie's death, the copyright expired, but the following year an Act of Parliament restored royalty income in perpetuity. With another four hospitals in close proximity, nearby **Queen Square** is more popularly known as "hospital square".

The rest of Bloomsbury

To find out about the possibility of visiting the Coram Foundation, call ☎ 020 /7278 2424.

Dickens' House

Mon–Sat 10am–5pm; £4; ☎020/7405 2127; *www.dickensmuseum.com*. Russell Square tube.

Despite the plethora of blue plaques marking the residences of local luminaries, the only Bloomsbury address that has been turned into a literary museum is **Dickens' House**, southeast of Coram's Fields at 48 Doughty St. Dickens moved here in 1837 – when it was practically on the northern outskirts of town – shortly after his marriage to Catherine Hogarth, and they lived here for two years, during which time he wrote *Nicholas Nickleby* and *Oliver Twist*. This is the only one of Dickens' fifteen London addresses to survive intact, but only the drawing room, in which Dickens entertained his literary friends, has been restored to its original Regency style. Letters, manuscripts and first editions, the earliest known portrait (a miniature painted by his aunt in 1830) and the annotated books he used during extensive lecture tours in Britain and the States are the rewards for those with more than a passing interest in the novelist.

Charles Dickens

Few cities are as closely associated with one writer as London is with **Charles Dickens** (1812–70). Though not born in London, Dickens spent much of his life here, and the recurrent motifs in his novels have become the clichés of Victorian London – the fog, the slums and alleys, the prisons and workhouses, and of course the stinking river. Drawing on his own personal experience, he was able to describe the workings of the law and the conditions of the poor with an unrivalled accuracy. He also lived through a time of great social change, during which London more than doubled in size, yet in his writing London remains a surprisingly compact place: only rarely do his characters venture east of the Tower, or west of St James's, with the centre of the city hovering somewhere around the Inns of Court, described in detail in *Bleak House*.

Born in Portsmouth to a clerk in the naval pay office, Dickens spent a happy early childhood in London and Chatham, on the Kent coast. This was cut short at the age of 12 when his father was imprisoned in Marshalsea debtors' prison, and Charles was forced to work in a rat-infested factory in the old Hungerford Market. The experience, though brief, scarred him for life – he was hurt further by his mother's attempt to force him to keep the job rather than return to school, even after his father's release. After two years as a solicitor's clerk at Gray's Inn, Dickens became a parliamentary reporter, during which time he wrote *Sketches by Boz* (Boz was Dickens' journalistic pen name). The publication of this propelled him to local fame and comparative fortune in 1836, and in the same year he married Catherine Hogarth and moved to the bourgeois neighbourhood of Doughty Street.

There followed nine children – "the largest family ever known with the smallest disposition to do anything for themselves", as Dickens later described them – and sixteen novels, each published in monthly instalments, which were awaited with bated breath by the Victorian public. Then in 1857, at the peak of his career, Dickens fell in love with an 18-year-old actress, Ellen Ternan. His subsequent separation from his wife, and his insistence that she leave the family house (while her sister Georgina stayed), scandalized society and forced the author to retreat to his country house in Rochester.

In the last decade of his life, Dickens found an outlet for his theatrical aspirations, and a way of supporting the three households for which he was now responsible, by touring Britain and America giving dramatic readings of his works. He died at his desk at the age of 58, while working on *The Mystery of Edwin Drood*. According to his wishes, there was no public announcement of his burial, though he was interred in Westminster Abbey (at Queen Victoria's insistence) rather than in Rochester (as he had requested). The twelve people present at the early-morning service were asked not to wear a black bow, long hatband or any other accessories of the "revolting absurdity" of mourning.

The University

London has more students than any other city in the world (over half a million at the last count), which isn't bad going for a city that only organized its own University (*www.lon.ac.uk*) in 1826, more than six hundred years after the likes of Oxford and Cambridge. The university started life in Bloomsbury, but it wasn't until after World War I that the institution really began to take over the area. Nowadays, its various colleges and departments have spread their tentacles to form an almost continuous wedge from the British Museum all the way to Euston Road, with plenty more outside this area. Despite this, the university's piecemeal development has left the place with no real focus, just a couple of landmarks in the form of Senate House and University College, plus two specialist art museums.

Senate House and University College

Looming behind the British Museum is the skyscraper of **Senate House**, a "bleak, blank, hideous" building according to Max Beerbohm. Completed by Charles Holden in 1932 and austerely clad in Portland stone, it's best viewed from Malet Street. During the war it served as the Ministry of Information, and George Orwell modelled *1984*'s Ministry of Truth on it. At the north end of Malet Street is another terracotta fantasy by Fitzroy Doll (architect of the *Russell Hotel*), erected in 1907 and now the university branch of the Waterstone's chain, strategically placed opposite the students' union.

The university's oldest building is William Wilkins' Neoclassical **University College** (*www.ucl.ac.uk*) near the top of Gower Street, nicknamed the "godless college" because it was founded for non-Anglican students, who were excluded from both Oxford and Cambridge at the time. In 1878 it also became the first university to accept women as equals. UCL has a fine courtyard, a handsome Corinthian portico, and is home to the most famous of London's art schools, the **Slade**, which puts on regular temporary exhibitions drawn from its collection of early works by former students, including Stanley Spencer, Augustus John and Percy Wyndham Lewis. These are held at the **Strang Print Room**, situated in the south cloister of the main quadrangle.

The Strang Print Room is open during term time Wed–Fri 1–5pm; free.

Also on display in the south cloisters is the philosopher **Jeremy Bentham** (1748–1832), one of the university's founders, who bequeathed his fully-clothed skeleton so that he could be posthumously present at board meetings of the University College Hospital governors, where he was duly recorded as "present, but not voting". Bentham's "auto-icon", topped by a wax head and wide-brimmed hat, is in "thinking and writing" pose as the philosopher requested, and can be seen in a hermetically sealed mahogany booth in the north cloister of the main building, close to the pair of watchful Egyptian lions, reconstructed from several thousand fragments belonging to the Petrie Museum (see p. 184).

On the other side of Gower Street stands the former **University College Hospital** (UCH), a typically striking terracotta and red-brick cruciform built by Alfred Waterhouse at the turn of last century.

Waterhouse designed the hospital with strictly segregated wards so as to prevent the miasma or "foul air" from passing from ward to ward – despite the fact that the discovery of bacterial infection in 1867 had made such precautions redundant. Eric Blair (aka George Orwell) died of tuberculosis here in 1950, shortly after getting married to his second wife in the hospital ward.

The Petrie Museum of Egyptian Archeology

Tues–Fri 1–5pm, Sat 10am–1pm; free; ☎020/7504 2884. Russell Square tube.

The **Petrie Museum of Egyptian Archeology**, on the first floor of the D.M.S. Watson building, down Malet Place, has a couple of rooms jam-packed with antiquities, the bulk of them from excavations carried out by Sir Flinders Petrie in the 1880s. To the non-specialist, the first room appears to contain little more than broken bits of pottery, but the second includes the Langton collection of miniatures of the cat goddess Bastet (some less than 1cm high), and several cabinets of smaller objects, ivories, *shabti*, toys and jewellery, not to mention the world's oldest dress, made from bead netting around 2400 BC.

The Percival David Foundation of Chinese Art

Mon–Fri 10.30am–5pm; free; ☎020/7387 3909. Goodge Street tube.

Tucked away in the southeast corner of Gordon Square, at no. 53, is the **Percival David Foundation of Chinese Art**, two floors of ceramics based around the collection of Sir Percival David, which was bequeathed to the university in 1950. The lower floor features delicate, pastel-coloured, unadorned Ru, Ding and Yue ware, striking purple and blue Jun ware and Guan ware, with its distinctive heavily cracked glaze. The most famous pieces are on the upper floor: the vivid blue and white porcelains, produced from the fifteenth century onwards, that have so influenced Western tastes in crockery, and some red and blue enamel Ming vases. Alongside these are even more colourful works in cobalt blue, coffee brown, copper red and a whole spectrum of primary colours.

Euston

The nearest tubes are Euston and Euston Square.

The northern boundary of Bloomsbury is defined by the **Euston Road**, laid out in 1756 as the city's first traffic bypass, and now a six-lane traffic jam moving slowly west into Marylebone Road and east towards Islington. Euston Road marked the northern limit of the city until the mid-nineteenth century, and it was here that the rival railway companies built Euston, King's Cross and St Pancras stations, the termini of the lines serving the industrial boom towns of the north of England. Since those days, Euston Road has had some of the city's worst office architecture foisted on it, which, combined with the volume of traffic, makes this an area for selective viewing.

Euston Road's oldest edifice is **St Pancras new church**, built in the 1820s on the corner of Upper Woburn Place. Designed in Greek Revival style, it is notable for the caryatids tacked onto the north facade, which are modelled on the Erechtheion on the Acropolis, and for its octagonal tower, based on another Athenian structure, the Tower of the Winds. The best time to visit the interior, which features a dramatically lit Ionic colonnade in the apse, is either in the mornings from Wednesdays to Saturdays, or during one of the free Thursday lunchtime recitals.

Amidst all the hubbub of Euston Road, it's easy to miss the depressing modernist hulk of **Euston Station**, descendant of the first of London's great train termini, which was built way back in 1840. All that remains of Philip Hardwick's original Neoclassical ensemble are the sad-looking lodge-houses, part of the Euston Arch, a much-loved landmark demolished in the face of fierce protests in the 1960s – British Rail claimed it needed the space in order to lengthen the platforms, which it never did.

On the other side of the road from Euston Station, at no. 183, stands the **Wellcome Building** (*www.wellcome.ac.uk*), a Neoclassical block erected in the 1930s by Sir Henry Wellcome, the American-born pharmacist, to accommodate his research laboratories and showcase his collections. The building is open to the public, and there are plans to open a new gallery dedicated to the arts and sciences, while in the basement there's a brief display on the history of the pharmaceutical company, which was the first to receive permission to conduct animal experiments (a practice it is still engaged in). The Wellcome Trust is currently in the process of building totally new headquarters designed by Michael Hopkins, in the next-door site above Euston Square tube.

The rest of Bloomsbury

St Pancras old church, just up Pancras Road, is described on p.393.

Euston's main appeal lies in some very good curry houses in Drummond Street.

The Wellcome Trust also funds several galleries in the Science Museum; see p.357.

The British Library

Mon & Wed–Fri 9.30am–6pm, Tues 9.30am–8pm, Sat 9.30am–5pm, Sun 11am–5pm; free. ☎020/7412 7332; *www.bl.uk*. King's Cross or Euston tube.

As the country's most expensive public building, it's hardly surprising that the £500 million **British Library** came under fire from all sides during its protracted construction. Few readers wanted to move out of the splendid Round Reading Room at the British Museum, where the library had been since the 1850s, while others argued that the whole idea of the book has been superseded by the computerized database. More critically, the number of extra readers' seats provided by the new library is negligible, and the shelving space is already inadequate, thus nullifying the building's original purpose of housing the entire British Library stock in one place.

Architecturally, the charge has been led, predictably enough, by Prince Charles, who compared it to an academy for secret policemen. Yet, while it's true that the architect, Colin St John Wilson, has a penchant for red-brick brutalism that's horribly out of fashion, and compares unfavourably with its cathedralesque red-brick neighbour, the former *Midland Grand Hotel*, the interior of the building has met with general approval, even from Prince Charles, and the new hi-tech exhibition galleries are an enormous improvement on the noisy, cramped conditions that prevailed in the British Museum.

The new piazza, in front of the library, is, it has to be said, redundant as a public space, due to the traffic roaring down Euston Road, though it does feature Paolozzi's giant statue of Sir Isaac Newton bent double over his protractor, inspired by William Blake – just one of a number of specially commissioned works of art on display in the library. Look out, too, for Bill Woodrow's *Book, Ball & Chain* sofa and R. B. Kitaj's unsettling giant tapestry, *If not, not*, both in the main foyer, and Patrick Hughes' optical illusion, *Paradoxymoron*, down by the cloakroom.

Visiting the library

With the exception of the reading rooms, the library is open to the general public. Orientation is relatively simple: the bookshop and the three exhibition galleries (described in detail below) are to the left as you enter; the library's café/restaurant and cloakroom are to the right; straight ahead, up the stairs by the information desk, is the spiritual heart of the BL, a multistorey glass-walled tower housing the vast **King's Library**, collected by George III, and donated to the museum by George IV in 1823; to the side of the King's Library, on the upper ground floor, is the philatelic collection. If you want to explore the parts of the building not normally open to the public, you must sign up for a **guided tour** (Mon, Wed, Fri & Sun 3pm, Sat 10.30am & 3pm; £4; or Tues 6.30pm & Sun 11.30am & 3pm if you want to see the reading rooms; £5). In addition to all the above, the library also puts on a wide variety of events, including talks, films and occasional live performances.

John Ritblat Gallery

The first of the three exhibition galleries to head for is the dimly lit **John Ritblat Gallery**, where a superlative selection of the BL's ancient manuscripts and precious books are displayed. Closest to the entrance are the library's old **maps**: a Benedictine monk's map of Britain from 1250; an extract from Mercator's world atlas from the 1560s, drawn by his own hand; a tiny little plan of New York, depicted shortly after its capture from the Dutch in 1664, and showing the original wall of Wall Street; and Heinrich Hammer's wishful pre-Columbus map, showing how easy it would be to sail west from Europe to Asia. Beyond are the **sacred texts**, kicking off with the richly illustrated **Lindisfarne Gospels**, begun in 698 AD, seen by many as the apotheosis of Anglo-Saxon art. The artistry displayed in the section and the sheer variety of exhibits is almost overwhelming: as well as numerous illuminated Bibles and Qur'ans, there are rules for Buddhist monks written on birch bark, a palm-leaf glorification of the Hindu goddess Devi and a Burmese folding book on the life of the Buddha, divided into 162 folds.

One of the exhibition's most appealing innovations is **Turning the Pages**, a small room off the main gallery, where you can turn the pages of six selected texts – the Lindisfarne Gospels, the Luttrell Psalter, the Golden Hagadah, Leonardo da Vinci's Notebooks, the Sforza Hours and the Diamond Sutra – "virtually" on a computer terminal, thus allowing you to see much more than the double page displayed in the glass cabinets. In the nearby section on printing, you can see the ninth-century **Diamond Sutra**, an Indian Buddhist text written in Chinese and the world's earliest dated printed document, along with the **Gutenberg Bible**, from 1454–55, the first Bible printed using movable type (and therefore capable of being mass-produced). Close by is Raoul le Fèvre's *History of Troy*, the first book to be printed in English in 1473 by William Caxton.

The most famous of the library's **historical documents** is probably King John's famous letter to his subjects in 1215, better known as the **Magna Carta**. Also displayed here are the 1601 death warrant for the Earl of Essex, Nelson's letter from the *Victory* setting out his plan for the Battle of Trafalgar, a letter from Mahatma Gandhi written during his 21-day prison fast in 1943, Scott's 1912 Polar Journal and a suffragette's scrapbook from 1911 to 1914, its cover decorated with the prison sentences suffered by its owner. Along the far wall is a selection of the library's **literary texts**, among them the collected works of Shakespeare from 1623, the original monthly instalments of Dickens' *David Copperfield* and the touchingly beautiful handwritten and illustrated copy of *Alice in Wonderland* given by Lewis Carroll to Alice Liddell. As well as examining James Joyce's maniacally scribbled *Finnegans Wake* – a chaotic contrast to Coleridge's fastidious *Kubla Khan* – you can also listen to Joyce (and several other authors) reading extracts from their works. Similarly, in the **music** section, you can listen to the works displayed, ranging from Bach to The Beatles.

The other galleries

Situated down the stairs from the John Ritblat Gallery is the spacious **Pearson Gallery of Living Words**, which houses temporary exhibitions (for which there is usually an entrance charge), employing more of the library's wonderful texts, supplemented by items on loan from the British Museum. To one side of the Pearson Gallery is the **Workshop of Words, Sounds and Images**, a hands-on exhibition of more universal appeal, where you can listen to Tchaikovsky's *1812 Overture* as it would have sounded over the course of the twentieth century, from mono wax-cylinder recording to CD. Visitors are also invited to try folding an eighteenth-century chapbook, and to explore a mock-up of a fifteenth-century scribe's studio, including a replica of the kind of wooden hand press used to produce the Gutenberg Bible.

Stamp lovers, meanwhile, should make their way up to the BL's gargantuan **Philatelic Collections**, made up of over eight million items, 80,000 of which are displayed in vertical pull-out drawers just outside the John Ritblat Gallery. The **Tapling Collection** kicks off the proceedings, as it did the collection when it was bequeathed in 1891, and in drawer number one you'll find the famous "Penny Black", the birthmark of modern philately. After that you get a world tour of stamps from long-forgotten mini-kingdoms such as Mecklenburg-Schwerin and Nowanugger. Those with a political interest should head for the **Bojanowicz Collection**, which covers Polish stamps from 1939 to 1946, including ones from the German and Russian occupations and even POW and DP camps. The **Kay Collection** consists of stamps from the colonies, but real boffins should head for the **Turner Collection** of railway letter stamps from the likes of the Pembroke & Tenby Railway.

St Pancras and King's Cross stations

The British Library has the misfortune of standing in the shadow of one of the most glorious of London's Victorian edifices, Sir George Gilbert Scott's **Midland Grand Hotel**. Completed in 1876, the hotel's majestic sweep of lancets, dormers and chimneypots forms the facade of **St Pancras Station**, terminus of the Midland Railway Company, which lies behind it. This masterpiece of Neo-Gothic architecture had its heyday in the 1890s when the ratio of staff to guests was 3:1, but with few private bathrooms and no central heating, the hotel couldn't survive long into the modern age. For fifty years from 1935, it languished under the name of **St Pancras Chambers**, as underused British Rail offices, but is due to reopen for business as a Marriott hotel in 2003. In the meantime, you can visit the foyer (Mon–Fri 11.30am–3pm; free), the grand staircase and the old coffee lounge, where there's an exhibition on the building, and a few remnants of its once lavish interior décor. For guided tours, lasting two hours, and costing £7.50, call ☎020/7304 3900.

The Salvation Army Heritage Centre is open Mon–Fri 9.30am– 3.30pm, Sat 9.30am– 12.30pm; free; ☎020/7332 0101; www .salvationarmy .org.uk.

Compared to St Pancras, **King's Cross Station**, opened in 1850 as the terminus for the Great Northern Railway, is a mere shed, though it was simple and graceful enough until British Rail added the modern forecourt. Legend has it that Boudicca's bones lie under platform 10 – the area used to be known as Battle Bridge, and was believed to have been the site of the final set-to between the Iceni and the Romans. More famously, the fictional Harry Potter and his wizarding chums leave for school on the Hogwarts Express each term from platform 9 3/4 – expect someone to milk that association in the near future.

Millions of pounds have been poured into King's Cross over the last decade – the local council has even produced a tourist map –

though little has changed on the surface. If and when St Pancras finally becomes the chief Channel Tunnel terminus, as has been mooted, King's Cross, and in particular the vast tracts of old sheds and neglected cobbled streets behind the station (described in more detail on p.393), may eventually be redeveloped. Until then, the area looks set to remain one of London's more notorious spots for drug pushing and prostitution. Perhaps it's appropriate, then, that the **Salvation Army Heritage Centre** should be situated close by at 117–21 Judd St. The exhibition here focuses mostly on the first forty years of the organization, which was founded by William Booth to help feed and house the poor in the East End (see p.277). There's a free audioguide to help you wade through the uniforms, press clipping, photos and badges.

Chapter 6

Strand, Holborn and Clerkenwell

The area covered in this chapter – **STRAND**, **HOLBORN** and **CLERKENWELL** – lies on the periphery of the entertainment zone of the West End and the financial district of the City. The **Strand**, as its name suggests, once lay along the river bank: it achieved its present-day form when the Victorians shored up the banks of the Thames to create the Embankment. One showpiece river palace, **Somerset House**, remains – the courtyard has been transformed into a public performance and exhibition space, and the chambers are now home to the Courtauld's superb collection of Impressionist paintings and a new museum of decorative arts.

Holborn, to the northeast, has long been associated with the law. Even today, every aspiring barrister must study at one of the four **Inns of Court** here in order to qualify. Secretive and typically old-fashioned (not to say reactionary) institutions, the Inns make for an interesting stroll, their archaic, cobbled precincts exuding the rarefied atmosphere of an Oxbridge college, and sheltering one of the city's oldest churches, the twelfth-century **Temple Church**. Close by the Inns, in Lincoln's Inn Fields, is the **Sir John Soane's Museum**, one of the most memorable and enjoyable of London's small museums, packed with architectural illusions and an eclectic array of curios.

Newly fashionable **Clerkenwell**, further to the northeast, is off the conventional tourist trail, yet contains a host of unusual sights, including vestiges of two pre-Fire-of-London priories, an old prison house, London's own "Little Italy" and the **Marx Memorial Library**, where the exiled Lenin plotted revolution. Clerkenwell's origins as a village are visible on Clerkenwell Green, and its long history as an artisanal adjunct to the City continues among the jewellers of Hatton Garden and the clockmakers of Clerkenwell Road. These days, though, the area is best known for the numerous designer bars and restaurants that cater for its new loft-dwelling residents.

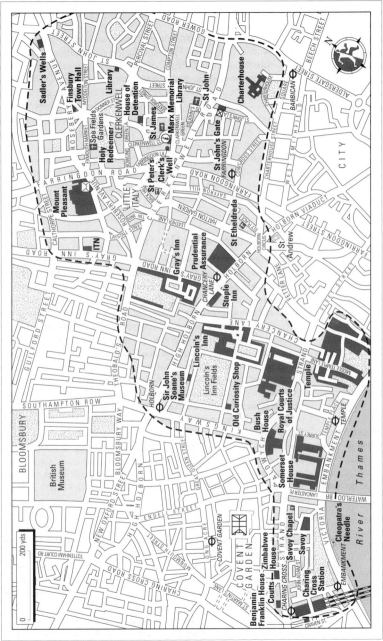

© crown copyright

Strand

The **Strand** – the main road connecting Westminster to the City – is a shadow of its former self. From the thirteenth century onwards, the street was famous for its riverside mansions, owned by bishops, noblemen and courtiers, while Nash's improvement to the western end, executed in the 1830s, prompted Disraeli to declare it "perhaps the finest street in Europe". In the 1890s, the Strand boasted more theatres than any other street in London, giving rise to the music-hall song *Let's All Go down the Strand*. The last to go of the Strand's aristocratic riverside mansions was Northumberland House, demolished in the 1870s to make way for Northumberland Avenue, which leads off Trafalgar Square; a hundred years later, the one surviving Nash terrace was chopped in two by the glass frontage of Coutts' Bank. Nowadays, the Strand is best known for the young homeless who shelter in the shop doorways at night.

Along the Strand to Aldwych

One of the few buildings worth a mention in the western section of the Strand is the Edwardian-era British Medical Association building – now **Zimbabwe House** – on the corner of Agar Street. Few passers-by even notice the eighteen naked figures by Jacob Epstein that punctuate the second-floor facade, but at the time of their unveiling in 1908, they caused enormous controversy – "a form of statuary which no careful father would wish his daughter and no discriminating young man his fiancée to see," railed the press. When the Southern Rhodesian government bought the building in 1937 they pronounced the sculptures to be "undesirable" and a potential hazard to passers-by, and proceeded to hack at the genitals, heads and limbs of all eighteen, which remain mutilated to this day.

Strand, from Aldwych eastwards, is described from p.199 onwards.

London's largest private bank, at no. 440, is the aforementioned **Coutts & Co** (*www.coutts.com*), whose customers include the Queen herself. It was founded in 1692 on the south side of the Strand by the Scottish goldsmith, John Campbell; a mock-up of Campbell's original premises stands behind a screen in the bank's concrete and marble atrium. Though Coutts is now owned by the Royal Bank of Scotland, today's male employees still sport anachronistic tail-coated suits, but the horse-drawn carriage which used to convey royal correspondence was taken out of service in 1993.

Some way further east on the opposite side of the Strand, the blind side street of Savoy Court – the only street in the country where the traffic drives on the right – leads to **The Savoy** (*www.savoy-group.co.uk*), London's grandest hotel, built in 1889 on the site of the medieval Savoy Palace. César Ritz was the original manager, Guccio Gucci started out as a dishwasher here, and the list of illustrious guests is endless: Monet painted the Thames from one of the south-facing rooms, Sarah Bernhardt nearly died here, and Strauss the Younger arrived with his own orchestra. It's worthwhile strolling up Savoy Court to check out the hotel's Art Deco foyer and the equally outrageous 1930s fittings of the adjacent **Savoy Theatre**, whose profits helped fund the hotel. The theatre was built in 1881 to stage Gilbert and Sullivan's operas, beginning with *Patience*, which was followed a couple of years later by their biggest hit, *The Mikado*.

Strand

Nothing remains of John of Gaunt's medieval Savoy Palace, which was burnt down in the Peasants' Revolt of 1381, though the late Perpendicular **Savoy Chapel**, hidden round the back of the hotel down Savoy Street, dates from the time when the complex was rebuilt as a hospital for the poor in 1505. The tall belfry has gone, as have most of the interior fittings, but the chapel enjoyed something of a revival as a fashionable venue for weddings when the hotel and theatre were built next door, and in 1890 it became the first place of worship in London to be lit by electricity.

The Savoy Chapel is open Tues–Fri 11.30am– 3.30pm.

Victoria Embankment

To get to the **Victoria Embankment**, head down Villiers Street, which slopes sharply down the flank of Charing Cross Station. The street marks the site of the old Hungerford Market, where Dickens was employed filling jars with boot polish from the age of 11, while his father began his slow descent to the debtors' prison. Terry Farrell's **Embankment Place** rises up above the train tracks. Built as the corporate headquarters of accountants Coopers & Lybrand, it's a deeply undistinguished 1990s postmodern building, the jokey Classical references doing little to relieve the repro-jukebox design.

The Victoria Embankment, built between 1868 and 1874, was itself the inspiration of French engineer Joseph Bazalgette, whose project simultaneously relieved congestion along the Strand, provided an extension to the underground railway and sewerage systems, and created a new stretch of parkland with a riverside walk – no longer much fun due to the volume of traffic. The 1626 **York Watergate**, in the Victoria Embankment Gardens to the east of Villiers Street, gives you an idea of where the banks of the Thames used to be; the steps through the gateway once led down to the river.

Less evidence remains of the Adam brothers' magnificent riverside development, known as the **Adelphi**, from the Greek for "brothers". Built between 1768 and 1772, this featured a terrace of eleven houses supported by massive arches and vaults which opened out onto a newly constructed wharf. The scheme was by no means a success – the houses wouldn't sell (despite having the actor David Garrick among their first residents), the wharf was prone to flooding, and the brothers ended up practically bankrupt – but it was a distinctive feature of the waterfront until 1936, when it was thoughtlessly demolished to make way for some nondescript office blocks. The only surviving Adam houses are between Victoria Embankment Gardens and the Strand: both 1–3 Robert St and 7 Adam St retain the

Adams' innovative stucco decoration on their pilasters, and the most elaborate of all, 6–8 John Adam St, is home to the **Royal Society of Arts** (*www.rsa.org.uk*), founded in 1754.

London's oldest monument, **Cleopatra's Needle**, languishes little-noticed on the Thames side of the busy Victoria Embankment, guarded by two Victorian sphinxes. In fact, the 60-foot-high, 180-ton stick of granite has nothing to do with Cleopatra – it's one of a pair erected in Heliopolis in 1475 BC (the other one is in New York's Central Park) and taken to Alexandria by the emperor Augustus fifteen years after Cleopatra's suicide. This obelisk was presented to Britain in 1819 by the Turkish viceroy of Egypt, but nearly sixty years passed before it finally made its way to London. It was erected in 1878 above a time capsule containing, among other things, the day's newspapers, a box of hairpins, a railway timetable and pictures of the country's twelve prettiest women.

For the latest on the Benjamin Franklin House, phone ☎020/7930 9121 or visit the Web site.

The **Benjamin Franklin House** at 36 Craven St, on the other side of Charing Cross Station, will probably attract more visitors than Cleopatra's Needle. Restored with help of, among others, the afore-mentioned Royal Society of Arts, the museum should be open by the time you read this, though the project won't be fully realized until 2002. The tenth son of a candlemaker, Benjamin Franklin (1706–90) had "genteel lodgings" here more or less continuously from 1757 to 1775. Whilst Franklin was espousing the cause of the British colonies (as the US then was), the house served as the first de facto American Embassy; eventually, he returned to America to help draft the Declaration of Independence, negotiate the peace treaty with Britain and frame the Constitution. Franklin was also, rather surprisingly, the inventor of the glass harmonica. At no. 32, two doors up from Franklin's house, a plaque commemorates the German poet **Heinrich Heine**, who stayed here for three unhappy months in 1827, complaining to his friends back home that "no one understands German."

Aldwych

The wide crescent of **Aldwych**, forming a neat "D" with the eastern part of the Strand, was driven through the slums of this zone in the last throes of the Victorian era. A confident ensemble occupies the centre, with the enormous Australia House and India House sandwiching **Bush House**, home of the BBC's World Service (*www.bbc.co.uk/worldservice*) since 1940. Despite its thoroughly British associations, Bush House was actually built by the American speculator Irving T. Bush, whose planned trade centre flopped in the 1930s. The giant figures on the north facade and the inscription, "To the Eternal Friendship of English-Speaking Nations", thus refer to the friendship between the US and Britain, and are not, as many people assume, the declaratory manifesto of the current occupants.

Not far from these former bastions of Empire, up Houghton Street, lurks that erstwhile hotbed of left-wing agitation, the **London School of Economics** (*www.lse.ac.uk*). Founded in 1895 by, among others, socialists Sidney and Beatrice Webb, the LSE gained a radical reputation in 1968, when a student sit-in ended in violent confrontations that were the closest London came to the heady events in Paris that year. Alumni include Carlos the Jackal, Cherie Booth (wife of Prime Minister Tony Blair) and Mick Jagger, but the place has been pretty quiet for the last three decades.

Somerset House

Courtyard and terrace: daily 7.30am–11pm; free. Interior: Mon–Sat 10am–6pm, Sun noon–6pm; free; ☎020/7845 4600; *www.somerset-house .org.uk*. Temple (Mon–Sat only) or Covent Garden tube.

South of Aldwych and the Strand stands **Somerset House**, sole survivor of the grandiose river palaces which once lined this stretch of the riverfront, its four wings enclosing a large courtyard rather like a Parisian *hôtel*. However, although it looks like an old aristocratic mansion, the present building was in fact purpose-built from 1776 onwards by William Chambers, to house governmental offices and learned societies. Over the course of the next two centuries, it served as home to, among others, the Navy Board, the Royal Academy of Arts, the Inland Revenue and the General Register of Births, Deaths and Marriages.

In 2000, after a £50 million refurbishment, Somerset House was reopened, its granite-paved courtyard freed of bureaucrats' cars and transformed into an exciting new public space for open-air performances, installations and a fab fountain. For the moment, the north wing remains home to the permanent collection of the **Courtauld Institute**, best know for its outstanding Impressionist and post-Impressionist paintings. The south wing, meanwhile, now houses the **Gilbert Collection** of silver and gold *objets d'art* and the **Hermitage Rooms** (*www.hermitagerooms.com*), featuring changing displays drawn from the Hermitage Museum in St Petersburg. In 2002, the Courtauld also plans to move its permanent collection into the south wing, leaving the north wing for large temporary exhibitions.

Visiting Somerset House

There are now **three entrances** to Somerset House: the Strand entrance to the north, the Terrace entrance off Waterloo Bridge and the Great Arch entrance on Victoria Embankment, where folk would once have sailed in off the Thames.

Centred on a 55-jet dancing fountain that spouts straight from the cobbles, the courtyard is now a lovely place to relax, away from the noise and fumes of the Strand. When the various galleries are open, you can gain access to the river terrace from the south side of the courtyard via the **Seamen's Waiting Hall**, originally used as an entrance to the Navy Board, and now containing several model ships and portraits of naval heroes. The river terrace itself features an open-air sculpture gallery and the alfresco *Admiralty* café/restaurant. To learn a bit more about the history of the site, head for the **Introductory Gallery**, just beyond the Great Arch entrance, where silent videos chart the development of the building. One floor below, at Thames' level, the Royal Naval Commissioners' gilded eighteenth-century barge languishes in the **King's Barge House**.

If you're interested in exploring more of the building, join one of the **guided tours** (1hr 10min; Tues, Thus & Sat 1.30pm; £6); alternatively, you can combine a tour of the building with a tour of the highlights of the collections described below (1hr 40min; Tues, Thus & Sat 1.30pm; £9).

Courtauld Institute

Mon–Sat 10am–6pm, Sun noon–6pm; £4; free Mon 10am–2pm; joint ticket with the Gilbert Collection £7; ☏020/7848 2526; *www.courtauld.ac.uk*. Temple (Mon–Sat only) or Covent Garden tube.

The first body in Britain to award degrees in Art History as an academic subject, the **Courtauld Institute** was founded in 1931 as part of the University of London. The Institute has a priceless art collection, whose virtue is quality rather than quantity. Chiefly known for its Impressionist and Post-Impressionist works, the Courtauld also owns a fine array of earlier works by the likes of Rubens, Van Dyck, Tiepolo and Cranach the Elder.

The displays currently start on the ground floor, beside the ticket office, with a small room devoted to medieval religious paintings from all over western Europe, including works by **Bernardo Daddi**, a pupil of Giotto, plus a few enamels and ivories. Next, you ascend the beautiful, semi-circular staircase to the first-floor galleries, whose exceptional plasterwork ceilings recall their original use as the learned societies' meeting rooms. In the first room (2), there's a large **Botticelli** altarpiece commissioned by a convent and refuge for former prostitutes; hence Mary Magdalene's pole position below the Cross. Amidst several splendid fifteenth-century Florentine *cassoni* (chests) and minor works by Tintoretto, Lotto and Veronese in room 3, you can admire the masterful handling of colour and light in **Giovanni Bellini**'s *The Assassination of St Paul Martyr*. Meanwhile, in room 4, **Lucas Cranach the Elder**'s *Adam and Eve* provides one of the highlights of the collection, with the Saxon painter revelling in the visual delights of Eden. Also on display here is a *grisaille* and a biblical landscape by **Pieter Brueghel the Elder**.

The Courtauld's large collection of works by **Rubens** fills room 5, ranging from oil sketches for church frescoes to large-scale late works and a winningly informal family portrait of the son of "Peasant Brueghel", Jan Brueghel. **Van Dyck**, a pupil of Rubens, shows his precocious skills in two early works in room 6, painted when the artist was just 20. Another painter who exuded confidence was **Tiepolo**, whose consummate draughtsmanship can be seen in the twelve preparatory paintings in room 7, which also contains an affectionate portrait by **Gainsborough** of his wife, painted in his old age.

The most popular section of the gallery, however, is the second floor, where some of the most famous Impressionist paintings in the world reside. In room 8, you'll find a small-scale version of **Manet**'s bold *Déjeuner sur l'herbe*, and **Renoir**'s *La Loge*, while the Great Hall (room 9) – purpose-built as the venue for the Royal Academy's Summer Exhibition (see p.116) – holds even more treasures. Among the best-known works here are **Degas**'s *Two Dancers* and Manet's atmospheric *Bar at the Folies-Bergère*, a nostalgic celebration of the artist's love affair with Montmartre, painted two years before his death. **Gauguin**'s Breton peasants *Haymaking* contrasts with his later Tahitian works, including the sinister *Nevermore*, while the most popular work by **Van Gogh** is his *Self-Portrait with Bandaged Ear*, painted shortly after his remorseful self-mutilation, following an attack on his flatmate Gauguin. Amidst paintings by Toulouse-Lautrec, Seurat and Sisley, there's a heap of **Cézanne**'s works, including one of his series of *Card Players*, and several magnificent, geometrical but lush landscapes.

Rounding off the collection are a couple of smaller galleries. Room 11 contains one of **Modigliani**'s celebrated nudes, an unusually dark, sylvan Fauvist landscape by Derain and a portrait by Bonnard of the young model he went on to marry some twenty years later. Next door, the focus is on **Roger Fry**, who organized the first Impressionist exhibitions in Britain, and went on to found the Omega Workshops in 1913 with Duncan Grant. Fry bequeathed many of the paintings displayed here, including several of his own works, such as his copy of the Cézanne painting he used as a model for a self-portrait and Sickert's depiction of Queensway Underground station.

Gilbert Collection

Mon–Sat 10am–6pm, Sun noon–6pm; £4; free Mon 10am–2pm; joint ticket with the Courtauld Institute £7; ☎020/7420 9400; *www.gilbert-collection.org.uk*. Temple (Mon–Sat only) or Covent Garden tube

The ground floor of the south wing is now given over to the **Gilbert Collection** a priceless private collection of silver and gold, micro-mosaics and snuffboxes, gifted to the nation by Arthur Gilbert. Born in London in 1913 of Polish Jewish ancestry, Gilbert made so much money in the rag trade that he was able to retire to Beverley Hills at the age of just 36, where he amassed even more wealth through real estate. Gilbert began collecting as a hobby in the 1960s, and while there's no denying the craftsmanship of the pieces that attracted his magpie-like attention, the sheer opulence and gaudiness of many of the exhibits may prove too much for some.

There's a free audioguide available at the ticket desk, where you can also borrow a magnifying glass.

The collection kicks off in room 1 with a whole series of cabinets, clocks, tables and pictures decorated with **Florentine hardstone mosaics** or *pietre dure*. An art form invented in the sixteenth century, hardstone mosaics are made from carefully chosen marbles and minerals, which are cut and fitted together like a stone collage. The technical achievement of the artists is phenomenal, but the pieces themselves verge on the kitsch, and the full-scale paintings of kids from the middle of the twentieth century are just plain mawkish. It comes as something of a relief, therefore, to reach the far end, where the shrine-like room 2 contains a small collection of **ecclesiastical silver**, including two pairs of spectacular silver-gilt Rococo gates which once formed the centrepiece of an iconostasis presented by Catherine the Great to a monastery in Kiev.

Room 3, on the mezzanine floor above, is a long gallery displaying the bulk of the **silver collection**, everything from flagons and cups to salvers, soup tureens, tea caddies, candelabra and plates. Among the most eye-catching items are a lovely little silver-gilt pomander, from around 1600, that divides into several spicy silver segments, and an outlandish Rococo "epergne", designed to hold fruit and desserts, and looking something like a miniature merry-go-round. Look out, too, for the Monteith bowl, an unusual piece featuring vigorous battle scenes in relief, and a couple of guys who appear to be fleeing the carnage and attempting to climb into the bowl.

Stairs lead up from the mezzanine to the four rooms of (modern, not ancient) **Roman micromosaics**, the collection of which clearly became one of Gilbert's chief obsessions. As with hardstone mosaics, Roman micromosaics were extremely popular with wealthy tourists on the Grand Tour in the late eighteenth and nineteenth centuries, and the majority of the exhibits here date from that period. Microcmosaics are made from tiny cubes of opaque glass or stone, and the detail achievable within the medium is awesome. Once again, though, it's the technique that fascinates rather than the end product. Faced with what appears to be a reasonable (though by no means perfect) copy of a tigress by George Stubbs, in room 7, it's only closer inspection that you can make out the fact that it's a mosaic, not an oil painting – remarkable, yes, and a staggering technical achievement, but not necessarily beautiful.

The most decadent objects in the whole collection are the **gold boxes** or snuff boxes, in room 8, which became a craze in aristocratic circles in eighteenth-century Europe. Fussily decorated with mother-of-pearl reliefs, enamel scenes or gaudy agate figures, the prevalent style is high-kitsch Rococo, and the most over-the-top of the lot are the six boxes made for Frederick the Great. The Prussian king is thought to have owned more than three hundred, each one encrusted in diamonds, rubies and emeralds, and costing as much as £1500 each (an absolute fortune at the time).

The "workshop gallery" (room 9) has occasional demonstrations, books to consult and a CD-Rom which allows you to put some of the collection under a computer microscope.

There are several more rooms of snuff boxes to wade through, plus a gallery of Georgian enamel portrait miniatures, before you can escape back through the mezzanine and downstairs to the final two rooms. First off, in room 16, there are several magnificently ornate **silver-gilt howdahs** (seats for riding elephants), a throne and a pair of doors, all built for Rajasthani rajas in the decadent days of the British Empire. Finally, room 17 concentrates on the sort of bizarre *objets d'art* that used to grace the "china closets" and *Kunstkammern* (art cabinets) of the European aristocracy: a silver-gilt boat on a stand, a cup made from an ostrich egg, another made from a turban shell and a partridge with mother-of-pearl feathers. And once you've reached the shop, you can start your own little collection of gewgaws.

St Mary-le-Strand to St Clement Danes

Next door to Somerset House, the ugly concrete facade of **King's College** conceals Sir Robert Smirke's much older buildings, which date from its foundation in 1829. Rather than entering the college itself, stroll down Surrey Street and turn right down Surrey Steps – in the middle of the old *Norfolk Hotel*, whose terracotta facade is well worth admiring. Follow the signs to the "**Roman Bath**", and you'll discover a fifteen-foot-long tub (probably dating from Tudor times) with a natural spring belching out two thousand gallons a day. The bath is visible all year round, but you can only get a closer look by appointment (☎020/7641 5264; May–Sept Wed 1–5pm; NT; 50p).

Two historic churches survived the Aldwych development, and are now stranded amid the traffic of the Strand. The first is James Gibbs's **St Mary-le-Strand**, his first commission, completed in 1724 in Baroque style and topped by a delicately tiered tower. Even in the eighteenth century, parishioners complained of the noise from the roads, and it's incredible that recitals are still given here. The entrance is flanked by two lovely magnolia trees, and the interior has a particularly rich plastered ceiling in white and gold. It was in this church that Bonnie Prince Charlie allegedly renounced his Roman Catholic faith and became an Anglican, during a secret visit to London in 1750.

St Mary-le-Strand is open Mon–Fri 11am–4pm, recitals Wed 1pm; free; ☎020/7836 3126.

In allusion to his own St Mary's, Gibbs placed a 115-foot tower on top of Wren's nearby **St Clement Danes**, whose bells play out the tune of the nursery rhyme "Oranges and Lemons" each day at 9am, noon, 3pm and 6pm – though St Clement's Eastcheap in the City is more likely to be the church referred to in the rhyme. Reduced to a smouldering shell during the Blitz, St Clement Danes was handed over to the RAF in the 1950s, and is now a very well-kept memorial to those killed in the air battles of the last war. Glass cabinets in the west end of the church contain some poignant mementos, such as a wooden cross carved from a door hinge in a Japanese POW camp. The nave and aisles are studded with over eight hundred squadron

St Clement Danes is open daily 8.30am–4.30pm.

and unit badges, while heavy tomes set in glass cabinets record the 120,000 RAF service personnel who died.

In front of the church, the statue of Gladstone and his four female allegorical companions is flanked by two air chiefs: to the right, Lord Dowding, the man who oversaw the Battle of Britain; to the left, Sir Arthur Harris, better known as "Bomber Harris", architect of the saturation bombing of Germany that resulted in the slaughter of thousands of German civilians (and over 55,000 Allied airmen now commemorated on the plinth). Although Churchill was ultimately responsible, most of the opprobrium was left to fall on Harris, who was denied the peerage all the other service chiefs received, while his forces were refused a campaign medal. The decision to honour Harris with this privately funded statue, unveiled by the Queen Mother on May 31, 1992 (the anniversary of the bombing of Cologne), drew widespread protests in Britain and from Germany.

Further east along the Strand are two more architectural curiosities. At no. 216 stands **Twinings** tea shop (Mon–Fri 9.30am–4.45pm), founded in 1706 by Thomas Twining, tea supplier to Queen Anne. Its slender Neoclassical portico features two reclining Chinamen, dating from the time when all tea came from China; there's a small tea museum at the back of the narrow shop. Several doors beyond, at no. 222, **Lloyd's Bank**'s Law Courts branch retains the extravagant décor of the short-lived *Royal Courts of Justice Restaurant*, which was built here in 1883. The foyer features acres of Doulton tiles, hand-painted in blues and greens, and a flying-fish fountain that was originally supplied with fresh water from an artesian well sunk 238ft below the Strand.

Holborn and the Inns of Court

Bounded by Kingsway to the west, the City to the east, the Strand to the south and Theobald's Road to the north, **Holborn** (pronounced "Ho-bun") is a fascinating area to explore. Strategically placed between the royal and political centre of Westminster and the mercantile and financial might of the City, this wedge of land became the hub of the English legal system in the early thirteenth century. Hostels, known as **Inns of Court**, were established where lawyers could eat, sleep and study English Common Law (which was not taught at the universities at the time).

Even today, every barrister in England must study (and eat a required number of dinners) at one of the four Inns – Inner Temple, Middle Temple, Lincoln's Inn and Gray's Inn – before being called to the Bar. It's an old-fashioned system of patronage (you need contacts to get accepted at one of the Inns) and one that has done much to keep the judiciary overwhelmingly white, male and Oxbridge-educated to this day.

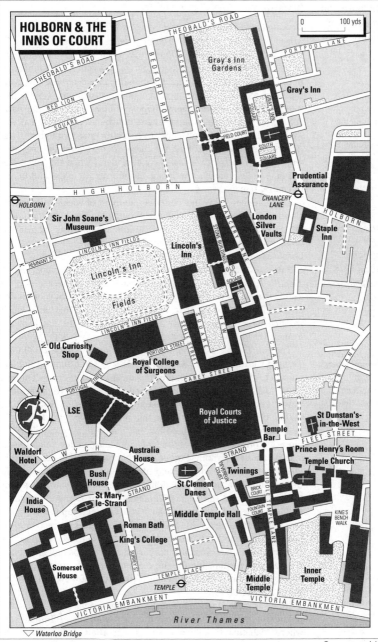

HOLBORN & THE INNS OF COURT

0   100 yds

THEOBALD'S ROAD

PORTPOOL LANE

Gray's Inn Gardens

Gray's Inn

THEOBALD'S ROAD

RED LION SQUARE

BEDFORD ROW

JOCKEY'S FIELD

GRAY'S INN SQUARE

GRAY'S INN ROAD

FIELD COURT

SOUTH SQUARE

Prudential Assurance

HIGH   HOLBORN

CHANCERY LANE

HOLBORN

HOLBORN

Sir John Soane's Museum

CHANCERY LANE

London Silver Vaults

Staple Inn

REMNANT ST

LINCOLN'S INN FIELDS

Lincoln's Inn

STONE BUILDINGS

Lincoln's Inn Fields

OLD SQUARE

NEW SQUARE

LINCOLN'S INN FIELDS

Old Curiosity Shop

PORTUGAL STREET

SERLE STREET

CHANCERY LANE

FETTER LANE

KINGSWAY

PORTUGAL STREET

Royal College of Surgeons

CAREY STREET

LSE

Royal Courts of Justice

St Dunstan's-in-the-West

Temple Bar

FLEET STREET

Waldorf Hotel

ALDWYCH

Australia House

STRAND

Prince Henry's Room

Temple Church

Bush House

STRAND

Twinings

DEVEREUX COURT

BRICK COURT

MIDDLE TEMPLE LANE

India House

St Mary-le-Strand

ARUNDEL STREET

St Clement Danes

FOUNTAIN COURT

KING'S BENCH WALK

Roman Bath

Middle Temple Hall

King's College

SURREY ST

Somerset House

TEMPLE PLACE

Middle Temple

Inner Temple

TEMPLE

VICTORIA EMBANKMENT

VICTORIA EMBANKMENT

River Thames

▽ Waterloo Bridge

© crown copyright

Temple

Temple is the largest and most complex of the Inns of Court, comprised of two Inns – **Middle Temple** (*www.middletemple.org.uk*) and **Inner Temple** (*www.innertemple.org.uk*) – both of which lie to the south of the Strand and Fleet Street, just within the boundaries of the City of London. The demarcation line between these two institutions is extremely convoluted, though most of Middle Temple lies west of Middle Temple Lane, with most of Inner Temple to the east. A few very old buildings survive here, but the overall scene is dominated by the soulless Neo-Georgian reconstructions that followed the devastation of the Blitz. Still, the maze of courtyards and passageways is fun to explore – especially after dark, when the Temple is gas-lit – and it's always a welcome haven from the noise and fumes of central London.

There are several points of access, simplest of which is Devereux Court, which leads south off the Strand. Medieval students ate, attended lectures and slept in the **Middle Temple Hall**, across the courtyard, still the Inn's main dining room. The present building was constructed in the 1560s and provided the setting for many great Elizabethan masques and plays – probably including Shakespeare's *Twelfth Night*, which is believed to have been premiered here in 1602. The hall is worth a visit for its fine hammerbeam roof, wooden panelling and decorative Elizabethan screen. The hall's small wooden table is said to have been carved from the hatch of Sir Francis Drake's ship, the *Golden Hind*.

*Middle Temple
Hall is open
Mon–Fri
10am–noon &
3–4pm.*

The two Temple Inns share use of the complex's oldest building, **Temple Church**, which was built in 1185 by the Knights Templar, an order founded to protect pilgrims on the road to Jerusalem that had its base here until 1312, when the Crown took fright at their power and handed the land over to the Knights of St John. An oblong chancel was added in the thirteenth century, and the whole building was damaged in the Blitz, but the original round church – modelled on the Church of the Holy Sepulchre in Jerusalem – still stands, with its striking Purbeck marble piers, recumbent marble effigies of medieval knights and tortured grotesques grimacing in the spandrels of the blind arcading. At the northwestern corner of the choir, behind the decorative altar tomb of Edmund Plowden, builder of the Middle Temple Hall, a stairwell leads up to a tiny cell, less than 5ft long, in which disobedient knights were confined. Much of the church was restored in 1682 by Wren (who married his first wife here), although only his carved oak reredos remains today. He was also responsible for the elegant red-brick buildings along the northern side of King's Bench Walk, south of the church in the Inner Temple Court.

*Temple Church
is open
Wed–Sun
11am–4pm.*

Inner Temple Hall, to the south of Temple Church, is a postwar reconstruction, as is clear from the brickwork. Inner Temple was where Mahatma Gandhi studied Law in 1888, living as a true

Englishman, dressing as a dandy, dancing, taking elocution lessons and playing the violin, while his close associate Jawaharlal Nehru spent two even wilder years here a decade or so later, gambling, drinking and running up considerable debts. If you're here at the right time, you can also explore the **Inner Temple Garden**, which slopes down to the Embankment.

Temple Bar and the Royal Courts of Justice

If you walk to the top of Middle Temple Lane, you'll hit the Strand right at **Temple Bar**, the latest in a long line of structures marking the boundary between Westminster and the City of London. Wren's triumphal arch was removed in 1878 to ease traffic congestion and now moulders away beyond the M25 just north of London. The heads of executed traitors (boiled in salt so that birds wouldn't eat them) were displayed on the arch until the mid-eighteenth century – one could even rent a telescope for a closer look. The monument which replaced the arch, topped by a winged dragon, marks the spot where the sovereign must ask for the Lord Mayor's permission to enter the City, a tradition that began when Elizabeth I passed through Temple Bar on her way to St Paul's to give thanks for the defeat of the Armada.

Occupying the north side of the last stretch of the Strand before it hits Temple Bar are the **Royal Courts of Justice**, home to the Court of Appeal and the High Court, where the most important civil cases are tried (criminal cases are heard at the Old Bailey; see p.232). The main portal and steps of this daunting Gothic Revival complex, designed by George Edmund Street in the 1870s, are familiar from innumerable news reports, since this is where many major appeals and libel suits are heard – it was from here that the Guildford Four and Birmingham Six walked to freedom, and it is where countless pop and soap stars have battled it out with the tabloids. The fifty-odd courtrooms are open to the public, though you have to go through stringent security checks first (no cameras allowed). Once through those, you're into the intimidating Main Hall, where bewigged barristers are usually busy on their mobile phones. The information desk here can equip you with a plan and a short guide to the complex, while the glass cabinets in the centre of the hall list which cases are being heard and where. In the minstrels' gallery, there's a small exhibition on the history of legal dress codes; if you continue heading north, you can leave via the Carey Street exit.

Lincoln's Inn Fields

On the north side of the Law Courts lies **Lincoln's Inn Fields**, London's largest square, laid out in the early 1640s; however, no. 59–60, on the west side, is the sole survivor from that period and is possibly the work of Inigo Jones. On the north side of the gardens is

Holborn and the Inns of Court

The Inner Temple Garden is open all year Mon–Fri noon–2pm.

Nearby Fleet Street is covered on p.219.

The Royal Courts of Justice are open Mon–Fri 8.30am–4.30pm: www .courtservice .co.uk.

a statue of Margaret MacDonald (wife of the first Labour prime minister Ramsay MacDonald, who lived for a time at no. 3) amid a brood of nine children, commemorating her social work among the young. Much of the south side of the square is occupied by the gigantic **Royal College of Surgeons**, containing several museums, including the **Hunterian**, a fascinating collection of pickled bits and bobs. On a different scale, to the southwest, is one of London's few surviving timber-framed buildings, the sixteenth-century **Old Curiosity Shop** in Portsmouth Street, which claims to be the inspiration for Dickens' cloyingly sentimental tale of the same name. This seems unlikely, but it is certainly London's oldest shop building.

Hunterian Museum

Mon–Fri 10am–5pm; free; 020/7973 2190; *www.rcseng.ac.uk*. Holborn tube.

Housed on the first floor of the Royal College of Surgeons building, the **Hunterian Museum** contains the unique specimen collection of the surgeon-scientist, John Hunter (1728–93). The museum first opened in 1813, but was badly damaged during the Blitz, so what you see now is a mere fraction of the original displays – and, sadly, the postwar architecture of the setting is not quite as grand. Since most of the exhibits are comprised of jars of pickled skeletons and body pieces – from the tibia of a young pig to the human tongue – it's certainly not a museum for the squeamish. Hunter's own tortoiseshell surgery tools occupy centre stage, along with one of the museum's prize exhibits, the skeleton of the Irish giant, O'Brien (1761–83), who was seven feet ten inches tall, and stands beside the Sicilian midget Caroline Crachami (1815–24), who stood at only one foot ten and a half inches when she died at the age of 9. In the museum's upstairs gallery, there's Lord Lister's examination couch and his cumbersome carbolic-acid spray machine, known as the "donkey engine". A room off the Hunterian houses the college's **Odontological Museum**, its glass cabinets filled with teeth, including some taken from the battlefield of Waterloo, and the instruments of dentistry.

Sir John Soane's Museum

Tues–Sat 10am–5pm; first Tues of the month also 6–9pm; free. Guided tour Sat 2.30pm; free. 020/7405 2107; *www.soane.org*. Holborn tube.

A group of buildings on the north side of Lincoln's Inn Fields house **Sir John Soane's Museum**, an unsung glory which many people consider their favourite museum in London – bar none. Soane (1753–1837), a bricklayer's son who rose to be architect of the Bank of England, gradually bought up three adjoining Georgian properties here, altering them to serve not only as a home and office, but also as a place to stash his large collection of art and antiquities. No. 13, the central house with the stone loggia, is arranged much as it was in his lifetime, with an ingenious ground plan and an informal, treasure-hunt atmosphere, with surprises in every alcove. Few of Soane's projects were actually built, and his home remains the best example of what he dubbed his "poetry of architecture", using mirrors, domes and skylights to create wonderful spatial ambiguities.

To the right of the hallway, you enter the **dining room**, which adjoins the **library**, bedecked in Pompeiian red and green to give it a Roman feel. Pass through Soane's tiny study and dressing room, little more than a corridor crammed with fragments of Roman marble and loads of cameos and miniatures, and you find yourself in the main colonnaded display hall, built over the former stables: all around are busts and more masonry; below you is the Egyptian sarcophagus (see below); above your head is the wooden chamber on stilts from which Soane used to supervise his students in other rooms. To your right is the **picture room**, whose false walls swing back to reveal another wall of pictures (including original Piranesi studies of the temples at Paestum and architectural drawings of Soane's projects), which itself opens to reveal a window and a balcony looking down onto the basement. The star paintings are **Hogarth**'s satirical *Election* series and his merciless morality tale *The Rake's Progress*.

A narrow staircase leads down into the flagstoned **crypt**, which features the "monk's parlour", a Gothic folly dedicated to a make-believe padre, Giovanni, complete with tomb (containing Soane's wife's dog, Fanny), cloister and eerie medieval casts and gargoyles. The hushed sepulchral chamber continues the morbid theme with its wooden mummy case, a model of an Etruscan tomb (complete with skeleton), and the tombstones of Soane's wife and son. You then emerge into another colonnaded atrium, where the alabaster **sarcophagus of Seti I**, rejected by the British Museum and bought by Soane, is watched over by rows and rows of antique statuary.

Soane's mausoleum lies in Old St Pancras graveyard; see p.393.

Back on the ground floor, make your way to the **breakfast parlour**, which features all of Soane's favourite architectural features: coloured skylights, a canopied dome and ranks of tiny convex mirrors. A short stroll up the beautiful cantilevered staircase brings you to the first-floor **drawing rooms**, whose airiness and bright colour scheme come as a relief after the ancient clutter of the downstairs rooms; there's also a startling view of the ground floor's numerous and varied skylights from the north drawing room.

Rather surprisingly, in 1999, the museum appointed the young Swiss curator, Hans Obrist, who is keen on peppering the collection with contemporary art. Perhaps it's just a phase. In the meantime, fascinating hour-long **free guided tours** continue, each Saturday at 2.30pm, taking folk round the museum and next door to no. 12, which holds an enormous research library of architectural drawings and books, and a room crammed with cork and wood models of Pompeiian and Paestum temples (some of these are also displayed in the basement of no. 13).

Lincoln's Inn

Mon–Fri 9am–6pm; Old Hall by appointment only; ☎020/7405 1393;
www.lincolnsinn.org.uk. Chapel and gardens Mon–Fri noon–2pm. Holborn
tube.

On the east side of Lincoln's Inn Fields lies **Lincoln's Inn**, the first
and in many ways the prettiest of the Inns of Court, having miraçu-
lously escaped the ravages of the Blitz; famous alumni include
Thomas More, Oliver Cromwell and Margaret Thatcher. As you might
guess, the oldest buildings are in the Old Buildings courtyard, starting chronologically with the fifteenth-century **Old Hall**, where the
lawyers used to live and where Dickens set the case Jarndyce versus
Jarndyce in *Bleak House*.

Beyond the Old Hall is the sixteenth-century **gatehouse**, impressive for its age and bulk, not to mention its faded diamond-patterned
brickwork, a decoration repeated elsewhere in the Inn. Adjacent to
the gatehouse is the early seventeenth-century **chapel**, with its
unusual fan-vaulted open undercroft and, on the first floor, its late
Gothic nave, hit by a zeppelin in World War I and much restored
since. To the north of the chapel, on the other side of Old Square, lie
the Palladian **Stone Buildings**, very different in style to the rest of
the Inn and best appreciated from the manicured lawns of the Inn's
garden; the strange miniature castle near the garden entrance is the
gardeners' tool shed, a creation of George Gilbert Scott, designer of
London's old red telephone boxes.

Chancery Lane and Gray's Inn

Running along the eastern edge of Lincoln's Inn is legal London's
main thoroughfare, **Chancery Lane**, home of the Law Society (the
solicitors' regulatory body) and lined with shops where barristers,
solicitors and clerks can buy their wigs, gowns, legal tomes, stationery and champagne. A confident piece of mock-Tudor Victorian
municipal architecture, opposite Lincoln's Inn's real Tudor gateway,
was built to house the Public Records Office, which has recently relocated to Kew (see p.467). A little further up on the same side of the
street are the **London Silver Vaults**, which began life as safe-deposit
vaults, but now house a strange, claustrophobic lair of subterranean
shops selling every kind of silverware – occasionally antique, mostly
tasteless.

*The London
Silver Vaults
are open
Mon–Fri
9am–5.30pm,
Sat 9am–1pm;
free;* ☎*020
/7242 3844.*

The last of the four Inns of Court, **Gray's Inn**, lies hidden to the
north of High Holborn, at the top of Chancery Lane; the entrance is
through an anonymous cream-coloured building next door to the
venerable *Cittie of Yorke* pub. Established in the fourteenth century,
the Inn took its name from the de Grey family, who owned the original mansion used as student lodgings; many more buildings were
added during the sixteenth century, but most of what you see today
was rebuilt after the Blitz. The **Hall**, with its fabulous Tudor screen

and stained glass, is thought to have witnessed the premiere of Shakespeare's *Comedy of Errors* in 1594. Unlike the south side, the north side of the Inn, taken up by the wide green expanse of **Gray's Inn Gardens**, is entirely and impressively visible through its wrought-iron railings from Theobald's Road; the gardens are open to the public weekday lunchtimes.

Holborn Circus

Heading east along High Holborn, it's worth pausing to admire two remarkable buildings. The first, on the right, is **Staple Inn**: not one of the Inns of Court, but one of the now defunct Inns of Chancery, which used to provide a sort of foundation course for those aspiring to the Bar. Its overhanging half-timbered facade and gables date from the sixteenth century and are the most extensive in the whole of London; they survived the Fire, which stopped just short of Holborn Circus, but had to be extensively rebuilt after the Blitz. The second building is the palatial, terracotta-red **Prudential Assurance Building** on the opposite side of Holborn, begun in 1879 by Alfred Waterhouse. You need to penetrate the inner courtyard to appreciate the magnificent scale of this fortress of Victorian capitalism, with its very own Bridge of Sighs and dramatic war memorial. From the Holborn entrance, you can peek through the windows at the original Doulton-tiled interior.

At **Holborn Circus** itself, the traffic swirls around London's politest statue, a cheerful equestrian figure of Prince Albert doffing his hat to passers-by. The nearby church of **St Andrew**, Wren's largest parish church, marks the beginning of the City (see Chapter 7), which lies to the south and east, over the Holborn Viaduct. Benjamin Disraeli was baptized here by his father, Isaac, in protest at being refused the office of warden at the Bevis Marks Synagogue (see p.251), and Thomas Coram (see p.180) lies at the west end of the church. Nowadays, St Andrew's serves as the headquarters of the Royal College of Organists (*www.rco.org.uk*), which means there's a good chance of hearing someone practising on the new organ.

Take the first left off Charterhouse Street, which runs northeast from the Circus, and you'll come to **Ely Place**, named after the Bishop of Ely, whose London residence used to stand here. Guarded by a beadle, lodge and wrought-iron gates, this patch is technically still outside the jurisdiction of the London authorities, but all that remains of the bishop's palace is its plain Gothic chapel, now **St Etheldreda's Church**, hidden halfway down this dead-end street on the left. Since 1874 this has been an exclusive Catholic stronghold, attracting a fair number of worshippers from the City during the week, and foreign diplomats at the weekend. The main body of the church, though much restored, dates back to 1300, and is lined with niches sheltering statues of English martyrs; the atmospherically gloomy crypt contains a model of the pre-Reformation church complex.

Holborn and the Inns of Court

Gray's Inn is open Mon–Fri 10am–4pm. The Hall is open by appointment only; ☎ *020 /7458 7800; www.graysinn .org.uk. The nearest tube is Chancery Lane (Mon–Sat only) or Holborn.*

St Andrew's Church is open Mon–Fri 8.15am– 5pm.

Clerkenwell

The hushed collegiate atmosphere of the Inns of Court comes to an abrupt end in **Clerkenwell**, one of inner London's up-and-coming quarters, which lies north and slightly uphill from the City. Along with Hoxton (see p.282), Clerkenwell is one of the areas in inner London currently enjoying something of a renaissance. Artists, photographers and other media folk have moved in, converting the area's spacious lofts, and bringing with them a rash of chic new bars and restaurants.

Clerkenwell began life in the twelfth century as a village serving the local monastic foundations (two of which survive to some extent). Following the Great Plague and the Great Fire, the area was settled by craftsmen, including newly arrived Huguenots, excluded by the restrictive practices of the City guilds. At the same time, the springs that give the place its name were rediscovered, and Clerkenwell became a fashionable spa resort for a century or so.

During the nineteenth century, the district's population trebled, mostly through Irish and Italian immigration; the springs and streams became cholera-infested sewers, and Clerkenwell became a slum area as notorious as the East End. "In its lanes and alleys the lowest debauch – the coarsest enjoyment – the most infuriated passions – the most unrestrained vice – roar and riot", in the words of one contemporary chronicler.

Victorian road schemes and slum clearances, wartime bombing and economic decline all took their toll, though Clerkenwell held on to a residual residential population, even before the latest influx of new blood. The area's traditional trades, such as lockmaking, clockmaking, printing and jewellery survive here and there, but the overall trend is now towards designer furniture, media companies and fashionable bars and restaurants.

Hatton Garden

For more on London's Hasidic Jewish community, see p.284.

No one would try to pretend that **Hatton Garden**, the street which connects Holborn Circus with Little Italy, is an attractive spot, but as the centre of the city's diamond and jewellery business, it's an intriguing place to visit during the week. As in Antwerp and New York, ultra-orthodox Hasidic Jews are heavily involved in the business here as middlemen. (They are catered for by a couple of kosher cafés on nearby Greville Street.) The diamond trade is, of course, strictly controlled by the all-powerful South African cartel led by De Beers (*www.adiamondisforever.com*), whose headquarters are on nearby Charterhouse Street.

Near the top of Hatton Garden, there's a plaque commemorating **Hiram Maxim**, who perfected the automatic gun named after him in the workshops at no. 57. To the east of Hatton Garden, off Greville Street, you'll find **Bleeding Heart Yard**, whose name refers to the gruesome murder of Lady Hatton in 1626 – her body was found torn limb from limb, while her heart was still bleeding and throbbing on the pavement. Parallel to Hatton Garden, be sure to take a wander through the **Leather Lane Market**, an old Cockney market open each weekday lunchtime, now revitalized thanks to the new office developments around Holborn, and selling everything from fruit and vegetables to clothes and electrical gear.

Little Italy

In the latter half of the nineteenth century, London experienced a huge influx of Italian immigrants who created their own **Little Italy** in the triangle of land now bounded by Clerkenwell Road, Rosebery Avenue and Farringdon Road; craftsmen, artisans, street performers and musicians were later joined by ice-cream vendors, restaurateurs and political refugees. Between the wars the population peaked at around 10,000 Italians, crammed into overcrowded, insanitary slums. The old streets have long been demolished to make way for council and other low-rent housing, and few Italians live here these days; nevertheless, the area remains a focus for a community that's now spread right across the capital.

The main point of reference is **St Peter's Italian Church**, built in 1863 and still the favourite venue for Italian weddings and christenings, as well as for Sunday Mass. It's rarely open outside of services, though you can view the memorial, situated in the main porch, to the seven hundred Anglo-Italian internees who died aboard the *Arandora Star*, a POW ship which sank en route to Canada in 1940.

St Peter's is the starting point of the annual Italian Procession, begun in 1883 and now a permanent fixture on the Sunday nearest July 16.

A few old-established Italian businesses survive here, too: the Scuola Guida Italiana driving school at 178 Clerkenwell Rd, and G. Gazzano & Son at 169 Farringdon Rd. There's also a plaque to **Giuseppe Mazzini**, the chief political theorist behind Italian unification, above the Italian barbers at 10 Laystall St. Mazzini lived in exile in London for many years and was very active in the Clerkenwell community, establishing a free school for Italian children in Hatton Garden.

Rosebery Avenue

Halfway up **Rosebery Avenue** – built in the 1890s to link Clerkenwell Road with Islington – stands the **Mount Pleasant Post Office**, the country's largest sorting office, built on the site of the Coldbath Fields prison. Over a third of all inland mail passes through this building, much of it brought by the post office's own underground railway network, **Mail Rail**. Built between the wars and similar in design to the tube, the railway is fully automatic, sending driverless trucks of mail between London's sorting offices at speeds of up to 35mph.

Mail Rail can be visited by appointment; ☎020/7239 2311.

Opposite Mount Pleasant is **Exmouth Market**, now at the epicentre of trendy Clerkenwell. The market has been reduced to a

Clerkenwell

*Exmouth
Market is open
Mon–Sat
9.30am–
4.30pm.*

raggle-taggle of tatty stalls, while the rest of the street is slowly being swamped by modish new bars and restaurants. The Grimaldi family of clowns lived in Exmouth Market in the nineteenth century, so it's appropriate that the street's Roman Catholic church of the **Holy Redeemer** should boast such an unusual Italianate campanile; the groin-vaulted interior is lined with big Composite pillars and a large baldachin occupies centre stage, but it is otherwise lightly decorated for a Catholic church.

At the end of the market, the Spa Field Gardens recall Clerkenwell's days as a fashionable spa, which began in 1683 when Thomas Sadler rediscovered a medicinal well in his garden and established a music house to entertain visitors. The well has recently made a comeback at the new **Sadler's Wells Theatre**, further up Rosebery Avenue, the fifth theatre on this site and one of the city's main venues for visiting opera and ballet companies. As part of the rebuilding, a new borehole has been sunk into the old well, and now provides all the theatre's non-drinking supplies, helps cool the building and produces 45 gallons of bottled drinking water a day for the punters.

Another building which catches the eye on Rosebery Avenue is the turn-of-the-century **Finsbury Town Hall**, whose name is spelt out in magenta glass on the delicate wrought-iron canopy that juts out into the street. The borough of Finsbury was subsumed into Islington in 1965, but the town hall building is still used as council offices. As the plaque outside states, the district was the first in the country to boast an Asian MP, **Dadabhai Nairoji**, who was elected (after a recount) as a Liberal MP in 1892 with a majority of five.

Clerkenwell Green and around

Izaak Walton lived on **Clerkenwell Green** – just to the north of Clerkenwell Road and east of Farringdon Road – while he wrote *The Compleat Angler*, but by the eighteenth century the Green had already lost its grass; by the nineteenth century, poverty and overcrowding were the main features of Clerkenwell – Oliver Twist learnt the tricks of the trade here in Dickens' tale. At this time the Green was known in the press as "the headquarters of republicanism, revolution and ultra-non-conformity" and became a popular spot for demonstrations. The most violent of these was the "Clerkenwell Riot" of 1832, when a policeman was stabbed to death during a clash between unemployed demonstrators and the newly formed Metropolitan Police Force; the "blue devils", as they were known, were at the height of their unpopularity, and the coroner reached a verdict of justifiable homicide.

The largest building on the Green is the Middlesex Sessions House, once the scene of many a political trial, now in the hands of the Freemasons. The oldest building, at no. 37a, is the former Welsh Charity School, built in 1737 and now home to the **Marx Memorial**

Lenin in Clerkenwell

Virtually every Bolshevik leader spent at least some time in exile in London at the beginning of last century, to avoid the attentions of the Tsarist secret police. **Lenin** (1870–1924), whose real name was Vladimir Ilyich Ulyanov, and his wife, Nadezhda Krupskaya, arrived in London in April 1902 and found unfurnished lodgings at 30 Holford Square, off Great Percy Street, under the pseudonyms of Mr and Mrs Jacob Richter (the house was destroyed in the war). The couple entertained numerous other exiles – including Trotsky, whom Lenin met for the first time at Holford Square in October 1902 – but the most important aspect of Lenin's life here was his editing of *Iskra* with Yuli Martov (later the Menshevik leader) and Vera Zasulich (one-time revolutionary assassin). The paper was set in Cyrillic script at a Jewish printer's in the East End and run off on the Social Democratic Federation presses on Clerkenwell Green.

In May 1903, Lenin and Krupskaya left to join other exiles in Geneva, but over the next eight years Lenin visited London on five more occasions, twice for research purposes, three times for party congresses. The first two congresses (the second and third overall) were held at secret locations, but the fifth, attended by 330 delegates including Trotsky, Gorky and Stalin, was held openly in the Brotherhood Church on Southgate Road in Islington (since destroyed). A blue plaque at the back of the hotel on the corner of Great Percy Street commemorates the site of 16 Percy Circus, where Lenin stayed in 1905 for the third congress.

Library (*www.marxmemoriallibrary.sageweb.co.uk*). Headquarters of the left-wing London Patriotic Society from 1872, and later the Social Democratic Federation press, this is where **Lenin** edited seventeen editions of the Bolshevik paper *Iskra* in 1902–03 (see box above). The library, situated on the first floor, was founded in 1933 in response to the book burnings taking place in Nazi Germany, and the poky little back room where Lenin worked is maintained as it was then, as a kind of shrine – even the original lino survives. You're free to view the Lenin Room, an original copy of *Iskra* produced there, and the library's workerist Hastings Mural from 1935, but to consult the unrivalled collection of books and pamphlets on the labour movement you need to become a library member.

The Marx Memorial Library is open Mon 1–6pm, Tues–Thurs 1–8pm, & Sat 10am–1pm; ☎020/7251 4706.

Clerkenwell's connections with **radical politics** have continued into this century: the modern-day Labour Party was founded at a meeting of socialists and trade unionists on Farringdon Road; the Communist Party had its headquarters at nearby St John Street for many years, and the Party paper, the *Daily Worker* (later the *Morning Star*), was printed on Farringdon Road, currently home to the *Guardian*, the country's only left-leaning daily broadsheet with a mass readership.

The area north of the Green was once occupied by the Benedictine convent of St Mary, founded in the twelfth century. The buildings have long since vanished, though the current church of **St James**, on Clerkenwell Close, is the descendant of the convent church. A plain, galleried eighteenth-century building decorated in Wedgwood blue

St James's is open Mon–Fri 11am–3pm.

and white, its most interesting feature is the twin staircases for the galleries at the west end, both of which were fitted with wrought-iron guards to prevent parishioners from glimpsing any ladies' ankles as they ascended.

The original **Clerk's Well**, which gives the area its name, flowed through the west wall of the nunnery and was "excellently clear, sweet and well tasted" even in 1720, and still in use until the mid-nineteenth century, by which time it had become polluted. It was rediscovered in 1924 and is now visible through the window of 14–16 Farringdon Lane; to get a closer look at it, you need to arrange a visit with the Finsbury Library on St John Street (☎020 /7527 7994).

House of Detention

Daily 10am–6pm; £4; ☎020/7253 9494. Farringdon tube.

Long before Clerkenwell became known for its "thieves' houses", it had been blessed with no fewer than four prison houses to take the overspill from the City jails. All have since been torn down, but the basement of the **House of Detention**, built in 1846 to relieve over-crowding at Bridewell Prison, and demolished in 1890, is now a museum on Clerkenwell Close, just north of St James's Church. Tickets are sold from the plush former warder's residence above ground; underground, the place has been left authentically dark and dank, enhanced by a theatrical use of sound and light. To begin with, the emphasis of the prison regime was on religious conversion through sensory deprivation – prisoners were made to wear masks and forbidden to talk, the penalty for which was three days and nights in the "dark cells" – but the death and insanity rate was so high the rules were eventually relaxed. The prison's greatest claim to fame, however, was as the target of Britain's first ever Irish Fenian bomb attack of 1867, which aimed to free two Fenian prisoners, but ended up destroying much of the prison and killing six people. It was "a colossal stupidity" according to Marx, as it "infuriated" the London masses who had shown much sympathy for Ireland, and thus marked the beginning of modern terrorism in the capital.

St John's Priory

Mon–Fri 10am–5pm, Sat 10am–4pm; free. Guided tours of Chapter Hall and the Grand Priory Church Tues, Fri & Sat 11am & 2.30pm; £4; ☎020/7253 6644. Farringdon tube.

Of Clerkenwell's three medieval religious establishments, remnants of two survive, hidden away to the southeast of Clerkenwell Green. The oldest is the priory of the Order of St John of Jerusalem, whose Knights Hospitaller, along with the Knights Templar, were responsible for the defence of the Holy Land against the heathens. The sixteenth-century **St John's Gate**, built in Kentish ragstone on the south side of Clerkenwell Road and originally forming the southern entrance to the complex, is the most visible survivor of the foundation. The twelfth-century priory was sacked by Wat Tyler's poll tax rebels in 1381, when the prior, Robert Hales, who was also responsible for collecting the tax, was dragged out and beheaded on Tower Hill. After the Reformation, the Gate housed the Master of Revels, the Elizabethan censor, and later it housed a coffee house run by Richard Hogarth, father of the painter, William.

Today, the gatehouse forms part of a **museum**, whose main room traces the development of the Order of St John of Jerusalem before its dissolution in 1540 by Henry VIII. Elsewhere, there are bits of masonry from the old priory, crusader coins and a small armoury salvaged from the Knights' armoury on Rhodes, where they were besieged and eventually expelled in 1523. In 1877, the **St John Ambulance** (*www.st-john-ambulance.org.uk*) was established, to provide a voluntary first-aid service to the public. It's in this field that the order is now best known in Britain, and a splendid new interactive gallery is now devoted to the history of the service. The cabinets of uniforms and pull-out drawers of cigarette cards, badges and medals are interspersed with touch screens with interviews from members past and present. And be sure to check out the Ashford litter, an early ambulance that was basically a stretcher on wheels with a protective hood.

To get to see the rest of the gatehouse, including the Chapter Hall, which was redesigned in mock-medieval style in the nineteenth century, and to visit the Grand Priory Church over the road, you must take a **guided tour**. Of the original twelfth-century church, all that remains is the **Norman crypt**, which contains two outstanding monuments: a sixteenth-century Spanish alabaster effigy of a Knight of St John, and the emaciated effigy of the last prior, who is said to have died of a broken heart in 1540 after hearing of the order's dissolution. Above ground, the curve of the church's walls – it was circular, like the Temple Church (see p.202) – is traced out in cobblestones on St John's Square.

Charterhouse

Guided tours only April–July Wed 2.15pm; £3; ☎020/7253 9503. Barbican tube.

A little to the southeast of St John's lies **Charterhouse**, founded in 1371 as a Carthusian monastery. The public school with which the foundation is now most closely associated moved out to Surrey in 1872, but forty-odd pensioners – known as "brothers" – continue to be cared for here. The Carthusians were one of the few religious bodies in London to put up any resistance during the Reformation, for which the prior was hanged, drawn and quartered at Tyburn, and his severed arm nailed to the gatehouse as a warning to the rest of the community, fifteen more of whom were later martyred. This gatehouse on

Charterhouse Square, which retains its fourteenth-century oak doors, is the starting point for the exhaustive two-hour **guided tours** that are the only way to visit the site.

The monastery was rebuilt as a private mansion in the Tudor period, which is why its architecture is reminiscent of an Oxbridge college rather than a religious institution. Very little remains of the original monastic buildings, which featured a large cloister surrounded by individual monks' cells, each with its own garden. The monks lived on a diet of fish and home-grown vegetables, and were only allowed to speak to one another on Sundays; three of their tiny self-contained cells can still be seen in the west wall of **Preachers' Court**.

The larger of the two enclosed courtyards, **Masters' Court**, which was badly gutted in World War II, retains the wonderful Great Hall, which boasts a fine Renaissance carved screen and a largely reconstructed hammerbeam roof, as well as the Great Chamber where Elizabeth I and James I were entertained. The **Chapel**, with its geometrical plasterwork ceiling, is half-Tudor and half-Jacobean, and contains the marble and alabaster tomb of **Thomas Sutton**, whose greyhound-head emblem crops up throughout the building. It was Sutton, deemed "the richest commoner in England" at the time, who bought the place in 1611 and converted it into a charity school for boys and an almshouse for gentlemen.

Chapter 7

The City

T HE CITY is where London began. Long established as the financial district, it stretches from Temple Bar in the west to the Tower of London in the east – administrative boundaries that are only slightly larger than those marked by the Roman walls and their medieval successors. However, in this Square Mile (as the City is sometimes referred to) you'll find precious few leftovers of London's early days, since four-fifths of the area burnt down in the Great Fire of 1666. Rebuilt in brick and stone, the City gradually lost its centrality as London swelled westwards, though it has maintained its position as Britain's financial heartland, home to banking, insurance and other services. What you see on the ground is mostly the product of three fairly recent building phases: the Victorian construction boom of the latter half of the nineteenth century; the overzealous postwar reconstruction following the Blitz; and the money-grabbing frenzy of the Thatcherite 1980s, in which nearly fifty percent of the City's office space was rebuilt, regardless of the lack of potential occupants.

When you consider what has happened here, it's amazing that so much has survived to bear witness to the City's two-thousand-year history. Wren's spires still punctuate the skyline here and there, and his masterpiece, **St Paul's Cathedral**, remains one of London's geographical and tourist pivots. At the eastern edge of the City, the **Tower of London**, begun shortly after the Norman Conquest, still stands protected by some of the best-preserved medieval fortifications in Europe. Other relics, such as the City's few surviving medieval alleyways, Wren's **Monument** to the Great Fire and London's oldest synagogue and church, are less conspicuous, and even the locals have problems finding the more modern attractions of the **Museum of London** and the **Barbican** arts complex.

It's also worth checking out some of the new architecture that has shot up within the Square Mile since the mid-1980s, most famously the **Lloyd's Building**, a mould-breaking modern construction designed by Richard Rogers, shortly to be joined by an equally arresting **Swiss Re** building by Norman Foster. There are obvious parallels

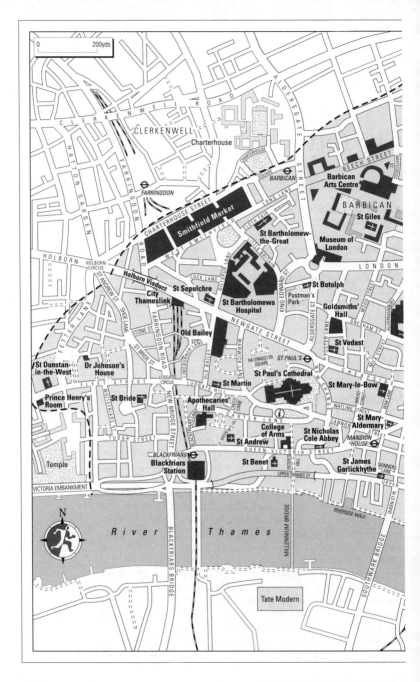

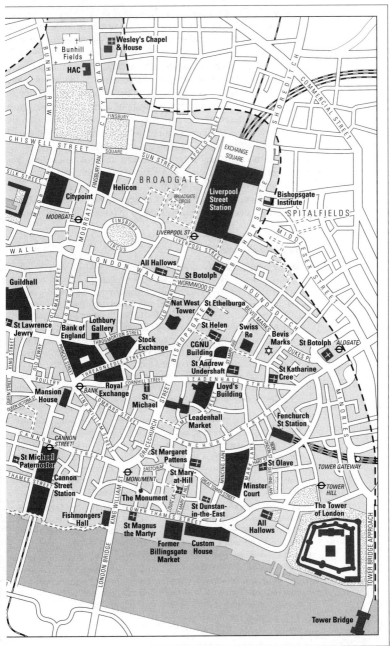

© crown copyright

between new City projects and the benighted Docklands development (see Chapter 8), but creations such as the vast **Broadgate** complex, up by Liverpool Street Station, have been more successful on balance.

Perhaps the biggest change of all, though, has been in the City's population. Up until the eighteenth century, the vast majority of Londoners lived and worked in or around the City; nowadays, while more than 300,000 commuters spend the best part of Monday to Friday here, only 5000 people remain at night and at weekends, most of them cooped up in the upmarket apartments of the Barbican complex. The result of this demographic shift is that the City is fully alive only during office hours. This means that weekdays are by far the best time to visit; many pubs, restaurants and even some tube stations and tourist sights close down at the weekend.

The one unchanging aspect of the City is its special status, conferred on the area by William the Conqueror and extended and reaffirmed by successive monarchs and governments ever since.

The City churches

The City of London is now overendowed with churches (*www.london-city-churches.org*) – well over forty at the last count, the majority of them built or rebuilt by Wren after the Great Fire. Prompted by the decline in the City's population, the Victorians demolished a fair few, but there are still far too many to be supported by the tiny resident population. The opening times given in the text should be taken with a pinch of salt, since most rely on volunteers to keep their doors open. As a general rule, weekday lunchtimes are the best time to visit the City's churches, many of which put on free lunchtime concerts for the local wage slaves.

On the surface, many of the City churches appear quite similar: plain, light-filled interiors, with white, gold and dark wood furnishings. Below is a list of six of the most varied and interesting churches within the area:

St Bartholomew-the-Great, Cloth Fair (see p.234). The oldest surviving church in the City and by far the most atmospheric; a fascinating building. St Paul's aside, if you visit just one church in the City, it should be this one.

St Mary Abchurch, Abchurch Lane, Cannon Street (see p.247). Uniquely for Wren's City churches, the interior features a huge painted domed ceiling, plus the only authenticated Gibbons reredos.

St Mary Aldermary, Queen Victoria Street (see p.243). Wren's most successful stab at Gothic, with fan vaulting in the aisles and a panelled ceiling in the nave.

St Mary Woolnoth, Lombard Street (see p.247). Hawksmoor's only City church, sporting an unusually broad, bulky tower and a Baroque clerestory that floods the church with light from its semicircular windows.

St Olave, Hart Street (see p.254). Built in the fifteenth century, and one of the few pre-Fire Gothic churches in the City.

St Stephen Walbrook, Walbrook (see p.246). Wren's dress rehearsal for St Paul's, with a wonderful central dome and plenty of woodcarving by Gibbons.

Nowadays, with its Lord Mayor, its Beadles, Sheriffs and Aldermen, its separate police force and its select electorate of freemen and liverymen, the City is an anachronism of the worst kind. The **Corporation of London** (*www.corpoflondon.gov.uk*), which runs the City like a one-party mini-state, is an unreconstructed old-boy network whose medievalist pageantry camouflages the very real power and wealth which it holds – the Corporation owns nearly a third of the Square Mile (and several tracts of land elsewhere in and around London). Its anomalous status is all the more baffling when you consider that the area was once the cradle of British democracy: it was the City that traditionally stood up to bullying sovereigns.

Fleet Street and Ludgate Hill

In 1500 a certain Wynkyn de Worde, a pupil of William Caxton, moved the Caxton presses from Westminster to **Fleet Street** to be close to the lawyers of the Inns of Court (who were among his best customers) and to the clergy of St Paul's, who comprised the largest literate group in the city. However, the street really boomed two hundred years later, when in 1702 the now defunct *Daily Courant*, Britain's first daily newspaper, was published here. By the nineteenth century, all the major national and provincial dailies had their offices and printing presses in the Fleet Street district, a situation that prevailed until 1985, when Eddy Shah set up Britain's first colour tabloid, *Today*, using computer technology that rendered the Fleet Street presses obsolete. It was then left to gutter-press baron Rupert Murdoch to take on the printers' unions in a bitter year-long dispute that changed the face of the newspaper industry for ever (see p.290 for details).

The nearest tube is Temple (closed Sun) or Blackfriars; buses #11, #15, #23 and #26 plough down Fleet Street.

All but one of the press headquarters that once dominated this part of town have now relocated, leaving a couple of architectural landmarks and the headquarters of Reuters to testify to nearly five hundred years of printing history. Nonetheless, Fleet Street offers one of the grandest approaches to the City, thanks to the view across to Ludgate Hill and beyond to St Paul's, the City's number one tourist sight.

Around Temple Bar

Since the Middle Ages, **Temple Bar** (see p.203), at the top of Fleet Street, has marked the western limit of the Square Mile's administrative boundaries. This western part of the street was spared by the Great Fire, which stopped at the junction with Fetter Lane, just short of **Prince Henry's Room**, a fine Jacobean house with timber-framed bay windows on the first floor, and the gateway to Inner Temple at street level. Originally a pub, later a waxworks, the first-floor room now contains material relating to the diarist Samuel Pepys (see box on p.220), who was born and baptized in the area. Even if you've no

Inner and Middle Temple lie within the City but are covered on p.202.

Fleet Street and Ludgate Hill

Prince Henry's Room is open Mon–Sat 11am–2pm; free; ☎020 /8294 1158.

interest in Pepys, the wood-panelled room is worth a look – it con-tains one of the finest Jacobean plasterwork ceilings in London and a lot of original stained glass.

Opposite Prince Henry's Room stands the church of **St Dunstan-in-the-West**, whose distinctive octagonal tower and lantern, built in Neo-Gothic style, dominate this top end of the street. To the side of the tower is the much earlier clock temple, erected by the parish-ioners in thanks for escaping the Great Fire; within the temple, Gog and Magog, in gilded loincloths, nod their heads and clang their bells on the hour. The statue of Queen Elizabeth I, in a niche in the vestry wall, dates from 1586 and is the oldest stone statue of the monarch in existence (it originally stood over the Ludgate entrance into the City and survived the Great Fire). The unusual, octagonal, Neo-Gothic interior, built in the 1830s, features a huge wooden iconostasis, for use during the church's regular Romanian Orthodox services.

St Dunstan-in-the-West is open Tues & Fri 9.30am–3pm, Sun 10am–4pm; ☎020/7405 1929.

On the other side of Fleet Street, at no. 37, is **Hoare's Bank**, the only surviving independent private bank in the City, founded in 1672. The layout of the Fleet Street branch hasn't changed since 1829, and it's worth peeking inside, past the doormen in their top hats and tails, to admire the flagstone floor and the smell of mahogany. Founded in 1671, **Child & Company**, at no. 1, was the first bank in Britain (though it's now merely an arm of the Royal Bank of Scotland). The interior retains many of its nineteenth-century fittings, including a case of muskets, kept as a safety measure by many City banks after the Gordon Riots of 1780.

Fleet Street and Ludgate Hill

Dr Johnson's House

May–Sept Mon–Sat 11am–5.30pm; Oct–April Mon–Sat 11am–5pm; £3; ☎020/7353 3745; *www.drjh.dircon.co.uk*. Temple, Chancery Lane (both Mon–Sat only) or Blackfriars tube.

Numerous narrow alleyways lead off the north side of Fleet Street beyond Fetter Lane, concealing legal chambers and offices. Two such alleys – Bolt Court and Hind Court – eventually open out into Gough Square, a newly cobbled courtyard surrounded, for the most part, by Neo-Georgian buildings. Gough Square's one authentic seventeenth-century building is **Dr Johnson's House**, where the great savant, writer and lexicographer lived from 1747 to 1759 while compiling the 41,000 entries for the first dictionary of the English language.

Johnson came to London from Lichfield with David Garrick, the pair taking it in turns to ride the one horse they could afford; Garrick had three halfpennies in his pocket, Johnson was richer by a penny. For several years Johnson lived on little more than bread and water in a garret on Exeter Street, before he finally rented the house on Gough Square, paid for with the £1500 advance he received for the dictionary. Despite his subsequent fame, though, Johnson continued to be in and out of debt all his life – his famous philosophical romance, *Rasselas*, was written in less than a week to raise funds for his mother's funeral.

The grey-panelled rooms of the house are peppered with period furniture and lined with portraits and etchings of Johnson, as well as pictures of Boswell, his biographer, and other members of their circle, including Johnson's black servant Francis Barber. Quirky memorabilia include Boswell's coffee cup, two first-edition copies of the great *Dictionary* and Johnson's gout chair from the *Old Cock Tavern*, a pub still standing on Fleet Street. The open-plan attic, in which Johnson and his six helpers put together the *Dictionary*, now looks a bit like a classroom, lined with explanatory panels on lexicography.

For details of Fleet Street's numerous pubs, see Chapter 17.

The press buildings and St Bride's

Two outstanding pieces of architecture bear witness to Fleet Street's heyday. First off, at no. 135, is the old headquarters of the **Daily**

Telegraph (dubbed the "Torygraph" for its entrenched conservatism), now occupied by the Credit Agricole bank. An adventurous building for such a conservative newspaper, it was one of London's first (and few) truly Art Deco edifices, built in a vaguely Egyptian style in 1930. It was upstaged a year later, however, by the sleek, black, former **Daily Express** building foyer (now home to Goldman Sachs), the city's first glass curtain-wall construction, with its remarkable chrome and gold foyer. Across the way, **Reuters** is the sole survivor of the old Fleet Street, still occupying the Portland-stone fortress designed in 1935 by Edwin Lutyens.

St Bride's is open Mon–Sat 9am–5pm, Sun for choral services only at 11am & 6.30pm; there are also frequent lunchtime concerts.

The best source of information about the old-style Fleet Street is the "journalists' and printers' cathedral", the church of **St Bride**, situated behind the Reuters building on the site of Wynkyn de Worde's sixteenth-century press. The church boasts Wren's tallest and most exquisite spire (said to be the inspiration for the traditional tiered wedding cake), but was extensively damaged in the Blitz. The Nazis' bombs did, however, reveal a crypt containing remains of Roman mosaics, medieval walls and seven previous churches on the site. Nestled among these relics, a little **museum** of Fleet Street history includes information on the *Daily Courant* and the *Universal Daily Register*, which later became *The Times*, claiming to be "the faithful recorder of every species of intelligence . . . circulated for a particular set of readers only".

Ludgate Circus and Ludgate Hill

The nearest tube is Blackfriars.

Fleet Street terminates at **Ludgate Circus**, which has held onto three of its four original segments, dating from the 1870s. The circus replaced the bridge crossing the River Fleet, which joins the Thames at Blackfriars Bridge. Buried under the roads in the 1760s after a drunken butcher got stuck in the river mud and froze to death, the Fleet marked the western boundary of the Roman city, and was an unmissable feature of the landscape, as the tanneries and slaughter-houses of Smithfield (see p.235) used to turn the water red with entrails. The western bank of the Fleet was the site of the notoriously inhumane **Fleet Prison**, whose famous incumbents included the poet John Donne, imprisoned here for marrying without his father-in-law's consent. Until the Marriage Act of 1754, Fleet Prison was famous for its clandestine "**Fleet Marriages**", performed by priests (or impostors) who were imprisoned there for debt. These marriages, in which couples could marry without a licence, attracted people of all classes, and took place in the prison chapel until 1710, when they were banished to the neighbouring taverns, the fee being split between clergyman and innkeeper.

St Martin-within-Ludgate is open Mon–Fri 11am–3pm; ☎020 /7248 6054.

Beyond the Circus, **Ludgate Hill** curves up to St Paul's, the view of the dome punctuated by the lead spire of the church of **St Martin-within-Ludgate**, which still rises above the housetops just as Wren intended. It was originally the church of Ludgate, one of the six City gates, which according to tradition was built by the mythical King Lud in the first century BC; the gate was eventually torn down in 1760. The cruciform interior of the church survived the Blitz intact and is now crisply maintained by several City guilds and masonic lodges, including the secretive Knights of the Round Table. Disney fans might like to note that Pocahontas stayed in a now demolished inn on the south side of Ludgate Hill in 1616–17.

St Paul's
Cathedral

St Paul's Cathedral

Mon–Sat 8.30am–4pm; £5; ☎ 020/7236 4128; *www.stpauls.co.uk*. St Paul's tube.

St Paul's Cathedral, topped by an enormous lead-covered dome that's second in size only to St Peter's in Rome, has been a London icon since the Blitz, when it stood defiantly unscathed amid the carnage (or so it appeared on the famous wartime propaganda photo). It remains a dominating presence in the City, despite the encroaching tower blocks of the financial sector; its showpiece west facade is particularly magnificent, fronted by a wide flight of steps, a double-storey portico and two of London's most Baroque towers, and is at its most impressive at night when bathed in sea-green arc lights. Westminster Abbey, St Paul's long-standing rival, has the edge when it comes to celebrity corpses, pre-Reformation sculpture, royal connections and sheer atmosphere. St Paul's, by contrast, is a soulless but perfectly calculated architectural set piece, a burial place for captains rather than kings, though it does contain more artists than Westminster Abbey, and continues to serve as a popular wedding church for the privileged few of the upper stratosphere: Charles and Di exchanged their vows here.

The City of London tourist office, to the south of St Paul's, is open April–Sept daily 9.30am–5pm; Oct–March Mon–Fri 9.30am–5pm, Sat 9.30am–12.30pm; ☎ 020/7332 1456; www .cityoflondon .gov.uk

Excluding the temple to Apollo that may have stood here in Roman times, the current building is the fifth church on this site, its immediate predecessor being Old St Paul's, a huge Gothic cathedral whose 489-foot spire was one of the wonders of medieval Europe. It was also the last resting place of the Saxon king of England, Ethelred the Unready, and of John of Gaunt, Duke of Lancaster, regent to Richard II and the deeply hated instigator of the medieval poll tax.

By all accounts, Old St Paul's was an unruly place, and home to some obscure cults devoted to the likes of the fictitious St Uncumber, a bearded virgin who could rid women of unwanted husbands in return for pecks of oats. Horse fairs took place here, ball games had to be banned in 1385, and by the close of the sixteenth century it had become a "common passage and thoroughfare . . . a daily receptacle for rogues and beggars however diseased, to the great offence of religious-minded people". During the Commonwealth, the nave became a cavalry barracks, with both men and horses living in the church, and shops were set up in the portico. By the Restoration things had become so bad that St Paul's was dubbed "a loathsome Golgotha" – and on one memorable occasion a circus horse named Morocco performed tricks here, including a quick trot up the stairs to the top of the bell tower.

The Great Fire caused irreparable damage to this unlikely centre of iniquity, and Christopher Wren was given the task of building a replacement – just one of over fifty church commissions he received in the wake of the blaze. The final design was a compromise solution after several more radical, European-style plans were rejected by the conservative clergy. Hassles over money plagued the project throughout – at one point Parliament withheld half of Wren's salary because they felt the work was proceeding too slowly. Wren remained unruffled and rose to the challenge of building what was, in effect, the world's first Protestant cathedral, completing the commission in 1711 during the reign of Queen Anne, whose statue still stands in front of the west facade.

Visiting the cathedral

Admission charges are nothing new at St Paul's – they were first introduced in 1709, before the cathedral was even finished. Once inside, simply pick up a free plan, and ask the vergers if you have any questions about a particular monument. Alternatively, you could hire an **audioguide** for an extra £3, or join one of the **guided tours** that set off regularly, take an hour and a half and cost £2.50. It's well worth attending one of the cathedral's **services**, if only to hear the choir, who perform during most evensongs (Mon–Sat 5pm), and on Sundays at 10am, 11.30am and 3.15pm. St Paul's is, strictly speaking, open for services only on Sundays, and consequently there's no admission charge. However, in between the services you're free to wander round the cathedral and the crypt (though not the OBE Chapel or the galleries).

The interior

Despite the hourly calls for prayer, St Paul's is now a major tourist business, with visitors funnelled through revolving doors towards the ticket booth. Before reaching the till you pass the **Chapel of All Souls** on the left, containing a memorial to Lord Kitchener, the moustachioed figure on the World War I "Your Country Needs You" posters, who was shipwrecked, along with his lover, Captain Fitzgerald (and most of the crew), off the Orkney Islands in 1916.

Once past the ticket office, you can take in the main body of the church for the first time. Queen Victoria thought it "dirty, dark and undevotional", though since the destruction of the stained glass in the Blitz it is once again light and airy, as Wren intended. Burials are confined to the crypt, and memorials were only permitted after 1790 when overcrowding at Westminster Abbey had become intolerable. With the onset of the Napoleonic Wars, it was decided to erect a series of expensive monuments to the military commanders who had sacrificed their lives. These overblown funerary monuments are difficult to stomach nowadays: some border on the ludicrous, like the virtually naked statue of Captain Burges, in the south aisle, holding hands with an angel over a naval cannon; others are mildly offensive, such as the nearby monument to Thomas Fanshaw Middleton, first Protestant Bishop of India, depicted baptizing "heathen" locals. The best of the bunch are Flaxman's Nelson memorial, in the south transept, with its seasick lion, and, in the north aisle, Alfred Steven's bombastic bronze and marble Duke of Wellington monument, begun in 1857 but only topped with the statue of the duke astride his faithful steed, Copenhagen, in 1912.

The best place from which to appreciate the glory of St Paul's is beneath the **dome**, which was decorated (against Wren's wishes) by Thornhill's trompe l'oeil frescoes, rather insipid but on a scale that can't fail to impress. The funerals of Nelson and Wellington took place at St Paul's, and Churchill lay in state here in 1965 – a memorial plaque, set into the monochrome marble flooring, indicates where his catafalque stood while several million paid their respects. St Paul's most famous work of art hangs in the north transept: the crushingly symbolic *Light of the World* by the Pre-Raphaelite painter **Holman Hunt**, depicting Christ knocking at the handleless, bramble-strewn door of the human soul, which must be opened from within. The original is actually in Keble College, Oxford, though this copy was executed by the artist himself, some fifty years later in 1900.

By far the most richly decorated section of the cathedral is the **chancel**, in particular the spectacular, swirling, gilded Byzantine-style mosaics of birds, fish, animals and greenery, dating from the 1890s. The intricately carved oak and limewood choir stalls, and the imposing organ case, are the work of Grinling Gibbons, who worked with Wren on many of his commissions. The north choir-aisle – used for temporary exhibitions on the history of the cathedral – contains Henry Moore's *Mother and Child* sculpture and allows you to admire Jean Tijou's pair of black-and-gold **wrought-iron gates** that separate the aisles from the high altar. The latter features an extravagant Baroque baldachin, held up by barley-sugar columns and wrapped round with gilded laurel, and is a postwar creation designed according to a pencil sketch by Wren. Behind the high altar stands the **American Memorial Chapel**, designed in the 1950s in honour of the 28,000 Americans based in Britain who lost their lives in World War II (check out the space rocket hidden in the carved wooden foliage of the far right-hand panel). To leave the chancel, you must pass through the south choir-aisle, where the upstanding shroud of **John Donne**, poet, preacher and one-time Dean of St Paul's, now resides, the only complete effigy to have survived from the previous cathedral.

The galleries

Beginning in the south transept, a series of stairs lead to the dome's three **galleries**, and they're well worth the effort of climbing, though none are recommended for anyone with a fear of heights. The initial 259 steps are relatively painless and take you as far as the internal **Whispering Gallery,** so called because of its acoustic properties – words whispered to the wall on one side are distinctly audible over 100ft away on the other, though the place is often so busy you can't hear very much above the hubbub except a ghostly murmur. Another 119 steps up, the broad exterior **Stone Gallery,** around the balustrade at the base of the dome, offers a great view of the City and along the Thames – you should be able to identify the distinctive white facade of Wren's London house, next door to the reconstructed Globe Theatre, from which he was able contemplate his masterpiece.

The final leg of the climb – 152 spiralling steel steps – takes you inside the dome's very complicated structure: the inner painted cupola is separated from the wooden, lead-covered outer dome by a funnel-shaped brick cone which acts as a support for the lantern, with its **Golden Gallery,** and ultimately the golden ball and cross which top the cathedral. The view from the Golden Gallery is unbeatable, but before you ascend the last flight of stairs be sure to take a look through the peephole in the floor, which looks down onto the monochrome marble floor beneath the dome, a truly terrifying sight.

The Blitz

The **Blitz** bombing of London in World War II began on September 7, 1940, and continued for 57 consecutive nights, then intermittently until the final and most devastating attack on the night of May 10, 1941, when 550 Luftwaffe planes dropped over 100,000 incendiaries and hundreds of explosive bombs in a matter of hours. The death toll that night was over 1400, bringing the total killed during the Blitz to between 20,000 and 30,000, with some 230,000 homes wrecked. Along with the East End, the City was particularly badly hit: in a single raid on December 29 (dubbed the "Second Fire of London"), 1400 fires broke out across the Square Mile. Some say the Luftwaffe left St Paul's standing as a navigation aid, but it came close to destruction when a bomb landed near the southwest tower; luckily this didn't go off, and was successfully removed to the Hackney marshes, where the 100ft-wide crater left by its detonation is still visible.

The authorities were ready to build mass graves for potential victims, but were unable to provide adequate air-raid shelters to prevent widespread carnage. The corrugated steel **Anderson shelters** issued by the government were of use to only one in four London households – those with gardens in which to bury them. Around 180,000 made use of the tube, despite initial government reluctance, by simply buying a ticket and staying below ground. The cheery photos of singing and dancing in the Underground which the censors allowed to be published tell nothing of the stale air, rats and lice that folk had to contend with. And even the tube stations couldn't withstand a direct hit, as occurred at Bank, when over a hundred died. In the end, the vast majority of Londoners – some sixty percent – simply hid under the sheets and prayed.

The crypt

Access to the **crypt** – reputedly the largest in Europe – is immediately on your left as you leave the south choir-aisle. The whitewashed walls and bright lighting, however, make this one of the least atmospheric mausoleums you could imagine – a far cry from the last century, when visitors were shown around the tombs by candlelight.

You're encouraged to turn right at the entrance to the crypt, thus bringing you to the southern aisle, popularly known as **Artists' Corner**, which boasts as many painters and architects as Westminster Abbey has poets. It became a popular resting place with the arrival of Wren himself; his son composed the famous inscription on his tomb – *"lector, si monumentum requiris, circumspice"* (reader, if you seek his monument, look around). Close to Wren are the graveslabs of Reynolds, Turner, Millais, Holman Hunt, Lord Leighton and Alma-Tadema; nearby there's a bust of Van Dyck, whose monument perished along with Old St Paul's.

To the north lies the former Chapel of St Faith, named after the parish church which disappeared when the choir of Old St Paul's was enlarged in the fourteenth century. It's now the most modern part of the cathedral, having been redesigned on and off since the 1960s, when it was designated the OBE Chapel, commemorating the state-honoured. In the north aisle is a modern plaque to the great church reformer John Wycliffe, and the grave of Alexander Fleming, the discoverer of penicillin.

The crypt's two star tombs are those of **Nelson** and **Wellington**, both occupying centre stage and both with more fanciful monuments upstairs. Wellington's porphyry and granite monstrosity is set in its own mini-chapel, surrounded by later illustrious British field marshals, while Nelson's embalmed body lies in a black marble sarcophagus originally designed for Cardinal Wolsey and later intended for Henry VIII and his third wife, Jane Seymour. As at Trafalgar Square, Nelson lies close to fellow admirals Jellicoe and Beatty – Beatty was the last person to be buried in St Paul's, in 1936. Nearby is a memorial to the hundreds of British soldiers who died in the **Falklands War**, listed alphabetically, without rank, in an unusually egalitarian gesture.

The **treasury**, situated in the north transept of the crypt, displays church plate, richly embroidered copes and mitres and bejewelled altar crosses; nearby are a couple of damaged marble effigies from the previous cathedral. At the western end of the crypt, you'll find a model of Old St Paul's, the cathedral shop, a Millburns café, a licensed restaurant, some toilets and, more importantly, the exit.

To get to the Millennium Bridge from St Paul's, head down Peter's Hill by the side of the City of London information centre.

The churchyard

St Paul's itself may have survived World War II relatively unscathed, but the area immediately surrounding it, still known optimistically as **St Paul's Churchyard**, was obliterated. From 1500 this district had been the centre of the London book trade; Wynkyn de Worde was among the first to set up shop here, though his main office was on Fleet Street. Another feature of the churchyard was Paul's Cross – also known as "Pol's Stump" – where proclamations and political speeches were made from a wooden pulpit. Heretics were regularly executed on this spot, and in 1519 Luther's works were publicly burnt here, before Henry VIII changed sides and demanded the "preaching down" of papal authority from the same spot. The cross was finally destroyed by Cromwell and his followers, and a memorial to it was erected to the northeast of the cathedral in 1910.

Blackfriars to Southwark Bridge

The combination of Victorian town planning, which created Queen Victoria Street, and postwar traffic schemes, which are responsible for the thundering dual carriageway and underpass of Upper Thames Street, are enough to put most people off venturing into the City south of St Paul's. Despite these handicaps, however, there are several fine Wren churches to explore in the backstreets and alleyways,

---

The City Livery Companies

London's hundred or so City Livery Companies are descended from the craft guilds of the Middle Ages, whose purpose was to administer apprenticeships and take charge of quality control, in return for which they were granted monopolies. As their powers and wealth grew, the guilds advertised their success by staging lavish banquets and building ever more opulent halls for their meetings and ceremonies. The wealthiest members of each company wore elaborate "livery" (or uniforms) on such occasions, and automatically received the Freedom of the City, entitling them to stand for election to the Court of Common Council, the Corporation's ruling body, and to be appointed to the Court of Aldermen.

Despite various attempts to introduce democracy over the centuries, the organization of the Livery Companies remains deeply undemocratic, but their prodigious wealth – together they own around fifteen percent of the City – has enabled them to fund almshouses, schools and a wide range of other charities, all of which has helped pacify their critics. As in masonic lodges (to which most liverymen belong), the elaborate ceremonies serve to hide the very real power which these companies still hold. For, in spite of the fact that many of the old trades associated with the Livery Companies have died out, liverymen still dominate the Court of Common Council and the Court of Aldermen. What's more, once elected, Aldermen remain in office for life, taking it in turns to be first a Sheriff, and eventually Lord Mayor – a knighthood is virtually guaranteed.

Anyone visiting the City can't fail to notice the numerous signs directing you to the Livery Company halls, many with enticing names such as the Tallow Chandlers and Cordwainers. Few medieval halls survived the Great Fire, fewer still the Blitz, but some are worth a look nonetheless for their ornate interiors. The problem is gaining admission. The City of London

---

and now that the old wharves are no longer in use, huge strides have been made to reclaim the riverfront for pedestrians. Nowadays, the **Riverside Walk** extends from Blackfriars railway bridge all the way to London Bridge, with only two short detours inland.

Blackfriars area

The streets to the north and east of **Blackfriars**, where a Dominican monastery stood until the Dissolution, see few tourists nowadays, yet in the seventeenth century this was a fashionable district – Ben Jonson had a house here, as did Shakespeare and, later, Van Dyck. Thoroughly destroyed in the Great Fire, the area suffered only peripheral damage from wartime bombing, leaving a warren of alleyways, courtyards and narrow streets, which, while holding few specific sights, manage to convey something of the plan of the medieval City before the Victorians, the German bombers and the 1960s brutalists did their worst.

To give some structure to your wanderings, head down Creed Lane and St Andrew's Hill, backstreets to the south of Ludgate Hill, to the least costly of Wren's churches, **St Andrew-by-the-Wardrobe**, so called because the royal depot for furniture and

St Andrew-by-the-Wardrobe is open Mon–Fri 8.30am–4.30pm; ☎020 /7248 7546.

---

tourist office (☎020/7606 3030) has free tickets to some halls; other halls will allow you to join a pre-booked group tour for around £3–5 per person. It's certainly not something you can do on the spur of the moment, though during the City of London Festival (late June to mid-July), many events do take place inside the Livery halls. Below is a selection of the most interesting of the City Livery halls to aim for; limited tickets are available from the tourist office for all except Apothecaries' Hall and Merchant Taylors' Hall.

Apothecaries' Hall, Blackfriars Lane (☎020/7236 1189). The seventeenth-century courtyard is open to the public, but entry to the magnificent staircase and the Great Hall – with its musicians' gallery, portrait by Reynolds and collection of pharmaceutical gear – is by prior appointment only.

Fishmongers' Hall, London Bridge (☎020/7626 3531). A prominent Greek Revival building on the riverfront, with a grand staircase and the dagger that killed Wat Tyler (see p.235).

Goldsmiths' Hall, Foster Lane (☎020/7606 7010). Features a sumptuous central staircase built in the 1830s. One of the easiest to visit, as there are occasional public exhibitions.

Merchant Taylors' Hall, 30 Threadneedle St (☎020/7450 4440). The fourteenth-century crypt chapel here contains more medieval masonry than in any other livery hall; entry by prior appointment only.

Skinners' Hall, 8 Dowgate Hill (☎020/7236 5629). Seventeenth-century courtroom and hall containing a splendid Russian chandelier.

Tallow Chandlers' Hall, 4 Dowgate Hill (☎020/7248 4726). Retains its seventeenth-century courtroom.

Vintners' Hall, 68 Upper Thames St (☎020/7236 1863). The oldest hall in the City, dating from 1676, with a magnificent staircase.

St Paul's Cathedral

The Black Friar, London's most ornate Arts and Crafts pub, stands near the site of the old monastery at 174 Queen St (see p.229).

armour was situated here before the Great Fire. The interior is usually locked, but you can look through from the vestry at the simple, light interior, with its oak wood-panelling and attractive white plasterwork. To the north, off **Carter Lane**, you'll find various unexpected little streets and courtyards – like Wardrobe Place – that present a slice of the pre-Blitz City. At the end of Carter Lane is Ludgate Broadway and the cobbles of Blackfriars Lane. Ahead is the wedding-cake spire of St Bride's (see p.222), viewed across bomb sites that have only recently been redeveloped; to the south is the Apothecaries' Hall, one of the prettiest of the City Livery Companies (see box on p.229), with a tiny doorway leading to a pastel-shaded seventeenth-century court.

East to Cannon Street

The College of Arms is open Mon–Fri 10am–4pm; free; ☎020 /7 248 2762.

A short way east along **Queen Victoria Street** stands the surprising little red-brick mansion of the **College of Arms**, which was built round a courtyard in the 1670s but subsequently opened up to the south with the building of the new road. The Earl Marshal's Court – featuring a gallery, copious wooden panelling and a modest throne – is the only one open to the public, unless you apply to trace your family or study heraldry in the college library. Wren's Dutch-looking church of **St Benet** (now a Welsh Church), opposite, completes this vignette of seventeenth-century London, despite the roar of traffic; it is only open for the Welsh-language services held every Sunday at 11am and 2.30pm. Further east stands another prominent Wren church, **St Nicholas Cole Abbey**, now used by the Free Church of Scotland.

St Nicholas Cole Abbey is open Tues–Thurs noon–2pm; ☎020/7248 5213.

Just down Lambeth Hill is the tower of St Mary Somerset, looking very forlorn, its main body having been destroyed in 1871. Further east still, along Upper Thames Street, is the elegant three-tiered steeple of yet another Wren church, **St James Garlickhythe**, named after the garlic that used to be sold from the nearby banks of the Thames. Badly damaged in the Blitz, and again in 1991 by a nearby crane which fell through the south rose window into the nave, the interior nevertheless remains much as Wren designed it, with the highest roof in the City after St Paul's, generously lit by clear arched windows in the clerestory, an arrangement which earned it the nickname of "Wren's Lantern".

St James Garlickhythe is open Mon–Fri 10am–4pm.

St Michael Paternoster Royal is open Mon–Fri 8am–5.30pm; ☎020/7248 5202.

Continue eastwards, along Skinner's Lane (which runs parallel to Upper Thames Street), to **St Michael Paternoster Royal**, another Wren church badly damaged in the war, less remarkable for its architecture than for its modern stained-glass windows, including one of the pantomine character Dick Whittington (see box opposite) with his knapsack and cat. Whittington, the only Mayor of London anyone has ever heard of, was buried in the church and lived next door on College Hill, still an evocative little cobbled street today.

Dick Whittington

The third son of a wealthy Gloucestershire family, **Dick Whittington** was an apprentice mercer, dealing in silks and velvets, who rose to become one of the richest men in the city by the age of just 21. He was an early philanthropist, establishing a library at Greyfriars' monastery and a refuge for single mothers at St Thomas's Hospital, and building one of the city's first public lavatories, a unisex 128-seater known as "Whittington's Night Soil House of Easement". On his death bed in 1423 he left money to pay half the costs of the Guildhall library, to repair St Bartholomew's Hospital, to refurbish Newgate Prison and to build various almshouses and a college of priests adjacent to St Michael's, who would pray for his soul.

The **pantomime** story appeared for the first time some two hundred years after Whittington's death, though quite how the wealthy Whittington became the fictional ragamuffin who comes to London after hearing the streets are paved with gold, no one seems to know. In the story, Whittington is on the point of leaving London with his knapsack and cat, when he hears the Bow bells ring out "Turn again, Whittington, thrice Lord Mayor of London" (he was, in fact, mayor on four occasions and was never knighted as the story claims). The theory on the cat is that it was a common name for a coal barge at the time, and Whittington is thought to have made much of his fortune in the coal trade.

Newgate to Smithfield

The area to the north of St Paul's is one of the most interesting parts of the City. The financial and business sectors play a more minor role here, the three most important institutions being the criminal court at the **Old Bailey**, which stands on the site of the old **Newgate Prison**; the hospital of **St Bartholomew's**, the only medieval hospital which occupies its original site to the present day; and the meat market at **Smithfield**, one of the last of the ancient London markets within the City.

Paternoster Square to Postman's Park

The Blitz destroyed the area immediately to the north of St Paul's, incinerating all the booksellers' shops and around six million books. In their place the City authorities built the brazenly modernist **Paternoster Square**, a grim pedestrianized piazza, surrounded by equally unprepossessing office blocks. In the 1980s it was decided to pull the buildings down and start again, but the new proposals provoked the first in a long line of architectural interventions from Prince Charles, who blamed planners and architects for having "wrecked the London skyline and desecrated the dome of St Paul's with a jostling scrum of office buildings". The Corporation took fright and initially opted for a gross pastiche of Neoclassical buildings by the prince's favourite architect, John Simpson. The Japanese group Mitsubishi, which now owns most of the five-acre site, has decided against Simpson's plan, and has gone instead for a restrained masterplan by William Whitfield, who is seen as a compromise choice in the modernism versus classicism debate. Construction of the new development was well under way as the book went to print.

To the north of Paternoster Square, on Newgate Street, is the hollowed-out shell of Wren's **Christ Church**, bombed in the last war and restored as a rose garden, with only the tower, now converted into an architect's office, standing entirely intact. Adjacent to the ruined church is the city's former General Post Office building on King Edward Street, opposite which lies **Postman's Park**, one of the most curious and little-visited corners of the City. Here, in 1900, in the churchyard of **St Botolph-without-Aldersgate**, the painter and sculptor George Frederick Watts paid for a national memorial to "heroes of everyday life", a patchwork of majolica tiles inscribed with the names of ordinary folk who had died in the course of some act of bravery. It exhibits the classic Victorian sentimental fascination with death, and makes for macabre but compelling reading: "Drowned in attempting to save his brother after he himself had just been rescued" or "Saved a lunatic woman from suicide at Woolwich Arsenal station, but was himself run over by the train".

*St Botolph-
without-
Aldersgate is
open Mon–Wed
& Fri
11am–3pm,
Thurs
12.45–2.30pm;
☎ 020/7606
0684.*

The Old Bailey, Newgate and St Sepulchre's

A short distance west along Newgate Street, you'll find the Central Criminal Court, more popularly known as the **Old Bailey** after the street on which it stands, which used to form the outer wall of the medieval city. The current, rather pompous Edwardian building is distinguished by its green dome, surmounted by a gilded statue of Justice, unusually depicted without blindfold, holding her sword and scales. The Old Bailey's fame, however, rests upon the fact that since 1834 virtually all the country's most serious criminal court cases have taken place here, including the trials of Oscar Wilde, the Nazi propagandist Lord Haw-Haw, the wrongly convicted Guildford Four and Birmingham Six "IRA bombers", and all Britain's multiple murderers. You can watch the proceedings from the visitors' gallery (no under 14s), but note that bags and cameras are not allowed in, and that there is no cloakroom. Even if you don't want to sit through a trial, it's worth venturing inside to see the Grand Hall, with its swirling marble floor and walls, succession of domes, and grandiloquent frescoes.

*The nearest
tube is St
Paul's.*

*The Old Bailey
is open
Mon–Fri
10.30am–1pm
& 2–4.30pm;
☎ 020/7248
3277.*

Until 1902 the Old Bailey was also the site of **Newgate Prison**, which began life as one of the prisons above the medieval gateways into the City and was burnt down during the Gordon Riots of 1780, only to be rebuilt as "a veritable Hell, worthy of the imagination of Dante", as one of its more famous inmates, Casanova, put it. Earlier well-known temporary residents included Sir Thomas Malory, who wrote *Le Morte d'Arthur* while imprisoned here for murder (among

Public executions and body snatchers

After 1783, when hangings at Tyburn were stopped, **public executions** drew the crowds to Newgate, with more than 100,000 turning up on some occasions. The last public beheading took place here in 1820 when the five Cato Street Conspirators were hung and then decapitated with a surgeon's knife. It was in hanging, however, that Newgate excelled, and its most efficient gallows could dispatch twenty criminals simultaneously. Public unease over the "robbery and violence, loud laughing, oaths, fighting, obscene conduct and still more filthy language" that accompanied public hangings drove the executions inside the prison walls in 1868. Henceforth, a black flag and the tolling of the bell of Old Bailey were the only signs that an execution had taken place. The night before an execution, a handbell was tolled outside the condemned's cell, while the jailer recited the Newgate verse, bellowing the last two lines: "And when St Sepulchre's bell tomorrow tolls/The Lord have mercy on your souls." The reference was to the "Great Bell of Old Bailey" in the church of St Sepulchre-without-Newgate (Tues 11am–3pm), which tolled the condemned to the scaffold at eight in the morning. The handbell and verse are now displayed inside the church, whose fifteenth-century tower stands diagonally opposite the Old Bailey on Holborn Viaduct.

The bodies of the executed were handed over to the surgeons of St Bartholomew's for dissection, but **body snatchers** also preyed on those buried in the St Sepulchre churchyard. Such was the demand for corpses that relatives were forced to pay a nightwatchman to guard over the graveyard in a specially built watch-house that still stands to the north of the church – in order to prevent the "Resurrection Men" from retrieving their quarry. The stolen stiffs would then be taken up Giltspur Street to the *Fortune of War* tavern, on Pie Corner, at the junction of Cock Lane, where the bodies were laid out for the surgeons. The pub has now gone, but Pie Corner is still marked by a gilded overfed cherub known as **Fat Boy**. He commemorates the "staying of the Great Fire", which, when it wasn't blamed on the Catholics, was ascribed to the sin of gluttony, since it had begun in Pudding Lane and ended at Pie Corner.

other things); Daniel Defoe, who was put inside for his *The Shortest Way with Dissenters*; Ben Jonson, who served time for murder; Christopher Marlowe who was on a charge of atheism; and the murderer Major Strangeways, who was "pressed" to death with piles of weights in the courtyard in 1658.

St Bartholomew's Hospital and churches

North of the Old Bailey on Giltspur Street stands the main building of **St Bartholomew's Hospital** – affectionately known as Bart's. This is the oldest hospital in London, and arguably the most respected, though it no longer has an accident and emergency section thanks to the myopic policies of the previous Tory government. Nevertheless, its remaining departments spread their tentacles across the surrounding area, creating a kind of open-plan medical village. With a couple of notable exceptions (detailed below) the buildings

themselves are unremarkable, but the history of the place is
fascinating. It began as an Augustinian priory and hospice in 1123,
founded by Rahere, court jester to Henry I, on the orders of St
Bartholomew, who appeared to him in a vision while he was in malarial delirium on a pilgrimage to Rome. The priory was dissolved by
Henry VIII, though in 1546, as a sick old man with just two weeks to
live, Henry agreed to refound the hospital.

There's a statue of Henry in the main gateway, built in 1702, looking out over Smithfield Market; a lame man and a melancholic man
sit above the broken pediment. Immediately on your left as you pass
through the gateway stands the church of **St Bartholomew-the-Less**
(daily 7am–8pm), sole survivor of the priory's four chapels, where
Inigo Jones was baptized. The tower is fifteenth-century, but the
octagonal interior was largely rebuilt in nineteenth-century Neo-
Gothic style and reconstructed after the last war. Beyond the church
lies three-quarters of the courtyard created for the hospital by James
Gibbs in the mid-eighteenth century, including the **Great Hall** and
the **staircase**, its walls decorated with biblical murals which were
painted free of charge by Hogarth, who was born and baptized nearby and served as one of the hospital's governors.

*Bart's Museum
is open
Tues–Fri
10am–4pm;
free. Guided
tours, including Bart's
Great Hall,
take place
April–Nov Fri
2pm; £4;
☎020/7601
8033. The
meeting point
is the hospital
gate.*

You can get a glimpse of the staircase from the new **Museum of St
Bartholomew's Hospital**, situated to the left just before you enter
the courtyard. The museum displays the charter granted by Henry
VIII on his deathbed, and other medieval documents dating back as
far as 1137, but first you get to watch a short video on the foundation of Bart's by Rahere. Among the medical artefacts, there are
some fearsome amputation instruments, a pair of leather "lunatic
restrainers", some great jars with labels such as "poison – for external use only", and a cricket bat autographed by W.C. Grace, who was
a student at Bart's in the 1870s. To see the Great Hall you must go
on one of the fascinating **guided tours**, which take in Smithfield and
the surrounding area as well.

St Bartholomew-the-Great

Mon–Fri 8.30am–4pm, Sat 10.30am–1.30pm, Sun 8am–8pm; ☎020/7606
5171; Barbican tube.

St Bartholomew-the-Great, hidden away in the backstreets to the
north of the hospital, is London's oldest and most atmospheric
parish church, and is much beloved of film companies (*Shakespeare
in Love* and *Four Weddings and a Funeral* both shot scenes here).
Begun in 1123 as the priory's main church, it was partly demolished
in the Reformation, and gradually fell into ruins: the cloisters were
used as a stable, there was a Nonconformist boys' school in the triforium, a coal and wine cellar in the crypt, a blacksmith's in the north
transept and a printing press (where Benjamin Franklin worked for
a while) in the Lady Chapel. From 1887, the architect Aston Webb
set about restoring what was left of the old church, patching up the

chequered patterning and adding the flintwork that now character-izes the exterior.

To get an idea of the scale of the original church, approach it through the half-timbered Tudor **gatehouse**, on Little Britain Street, which was discovered after a zeppelin raid in World War I. A wooden statue of St Bartholomew stands in a niche, holding the knife with which he was flayed; below is the thirteenth-century arch which once formed the entrance to the nave. The churchyard now stands where the nave itself would have been, and one side of the **cloisters** survives to the south of the church, immediately to the right as you enter. The rest of the church is a confusion of elements, including portions of the transepts and, most impressively, the **chancel**, where thick Norman pillars separate the main body from the ambulatory. There are various pre-Fire monuments, the most prominent being Rahere's tomb, which shelters under a fifteenth-century canopy to the north of the altar, with an angel at his feet and two canons kneeling beside him reading from the prophets. Beyond the ambulatory lies the Lady Chapel, mostly Webb's work, though with original stonework here and there; it's now dedicated to the City of London Squadron, hence the RAF standard that hangs here.

Smithfield

The ground was covered, nearly ankle-deep with filth and mire; a thick steam perpetually rising from the reeking bodies of the cattle, and mingling with the fog.

Charles Dickens, *Oliver Twist*

Blood and guts were regularly spilled at **Smithfield** long before the meat market was legally sanctioned here in the seventeenth century. This patch of open ground outside the City walls (its name is a corruption of "Smooth Field") was used as a horse fair in Norman times, and later for jousts and tournaments. In 1381, the poll tax rebels under Wat Tyler assembled here to negotiate with the boy king Richard II. Tyler's lack of respect towards the king gave Mayor Walworth the excuse to pull Tyler from his horse and stab him, after which he was bustled into Bart's for treatment, only to be dragged out by the king's men and beheaded on the spot.

The nearest tubes are Farringdon and Barbican.

Smithfield subsequently became a venue for **public executions**. The Scottish hero, William Wallace, was hanged, disembowelled and beheaded here in 1305, and the Bishop of Rochester's cook was boiled alive in 1531, but the local speciality was burnings. These reached a peak during the reign of "Bloody" Mary, when hundreds of Protestants were burnt at the stake for their beliefs, in revenge for the Catholics who had suffered a similar fate under Mary's father, Henry VIII; a plaque on the side of St Bartholomew's Hospital commemorates some of the Protestants who died.

Even more popular than the public executions was the **St Bartholomew's Fair**, a cloth fair established by Rahere in the twelfth

century in order to fund Bart's, and held over three days in late
August until the Victorians closed it down to protect public morals.
It was, of course, much more than just a cloth fair, with every kind of
debauchery and theatrical entertainment laid on: Rahere himself
used to perform juggling tricks, while Pepys reports seeing a horse
counting sixpences and, more reliably, a puppet show of Ben
Jonson's play *Bartholomew Fair*.

The **meat market** with which Smithfield is now synonymous grew
up as a kind of adjunct to the fair. Live cattle continued to be herded
into central London and slaughtered here until 1855, when the fair
was suppressed and the abattoirs moved out to Islington. A new covered market hall, designed by City architect Sir Horace Jones, was
erected in 1867, along with the "Winkle", a spiral ramp at the centre
of West Smithfield, linked to the market's very own tube station (now
a car park). Restored and redecorated in a rather nasty purple,
mauve and green combination, Smithfield remains London's main
market for TK (town-killed) meat, but if you want to see it in action,
you'll need to get here early – the action starts around 4am and is all
over by 9 or 10am. The compensation for getting up at this ungodly
hour are the early licensing laws which apply to certain local pubs,
where you can get a hearty breakfast and an early-morning pint.

*For details of
Smithfield's
pubs, see
p.540.*

North of London Wall

London Wall, a highway driven through the bomb sites in the north
of the City and lined by a phalanx of postwar architectural errors,
punctuated by Terry Farrell's monstrous Alban Gate, forms the
southern boundary of the Barbican complex, extending east as far as
Bishopsgate. As the name suggests, it follows the line of the **Roman
wall**, portions of which still stand on the north side in St Alphage's
Garden and by the Barber Surgeons' Hall; these surviving sections
formed part of the Roman fort that was incorporated into the wall
system at Cripplegate. If you're interested in tracing the line of the
old city walls, you can follow a trail that begins outside the nearby
Museum of London and extends a mile and a half to the Tower of
London, with explanatory panels displayed at intervals along the
way.

Museum of London

Mon–Sat 10am–5.50pm, Sun noon–5.50pm; £5 (tickets valid for a year); free
after 4.30pm; ☎020/7600 3699; *www.museumoflondon.org.uk*. St Paul's or
Barbican tube.

Despite London's long pedigree, very few of its ancient structures
are now standing, thanks to the Great Fire, the Blitz and the postwar
developers. However, numerous Roman, Saxon and Elizabethan
remains have been discovered during the City's various rebuildings,

and many of these finds are now displayed at the **Museum of London**, hidden above the western end of London Wall in the southwestern corner of the Barbican complex. The museum's permanent exhibition is basically an educational trot through London's past from prehistory to the present day. This is interesting enough (and understandably attracts a lot of school groups), but the real strength of the museum lies in the excellent temporary exhibitions, lectures, walks and videos it organizes throughout the year.

The newly revamped, and vastly improved, permanent displays start on the upper floor (where visitors enter), with sections on prehistoric and **Roman London**. Surviving Roman relics include marble busts from the Temple of Mithras (p.246), the Bucklersbury mosaic, discovered during the Victorian road-building projects and now displayed in a mock-up of a wealthy Roman dining room, and, from the windows of the museum, an impressive section of the Roman wall. The **Tudor London** and **Early Stuart London** sections contain some excellent models of the great buildings of pre-Fire London: the Royal Exchange, London Bridge, Whitehall Palace and the Rose Theatre. At the end of the upper floor there's a diorama accompanied by a loop-tape of Pepys' firsthand account of the Great Fire.

From here a ramp leads to the post-Fire section on the lower floor, set around a nursery garden filled with plants and flowers typical of various epochs. The most eye-catching item here is the **Lord Mayor's coach**, which rivals the Queen's in sheer weight of gold decoration. There are maps of the expanding capital and replicas of a wood-panelled, late-Stuart interior, featuring a four-poster "tester" bed, followed by a mock Newgate prison cell. The **Georgian London** section includes some very fine period dresses, which belonged to Princess Charlotte, only daughter of George IV, who died in childbirth at the age of just 21. Beyond are several reconstructed offices, pubs and shops from **Victorian London**, along with Dickens' chair, and the sort of hansom cab that Sherlock Holmes would have taken.

The highlight of the early twentieth-century gallery is undoubtedly the **Art Deco lift** from Selfridges, which precedes the museum's account of the Blitz, complete with obligatory Anderson shelter and gas masks. More intriguing is the model of the **1951 Festival of Britain** site on the South Bank, whose dome provided the inspiration for the Millennium Dome in Greenwich (see p.433). Finally, there's a small **London Now** section focusing on the problems facing present-day London, though the museum's temporary exhibitions on contemporary issues are usually much more enlightening than the random selection of exhibits on offer here.

The Barbican

The City's only large residential complex is the **Barbican**, a phenomenally ugly and expensive concrete ghetto built on the heavily bombed Cripplegate area. It's an upmarket urban

North of
London Wall

*The nearest
tube is
Barbican.*

dystopia, comprising a maze of pedestrian walkways and underground car parks, pinioned by three 400-foot, 42-storey tower blocks – the tallest residential accommodation in Europe when it was built in the 1970s. The great footballer and drinker George Best, a resident in the following decade, described it as "like living in Colditz. If I came home the worse for wear it was an achievement to find my own front door in that concrete wasteland and in all the months we were there I never even saw a neighbour, never mind spoke to one." Be warned.

The zone's solitary prewar building is the heavily restored sixteenth-century church of **St Giles Cripplegate**, where Oliver Cromwell was married in 1620 and where John Milton is buried. St Giles is now bracketed between a pair of artificial lakes, and lies directly opposite the sole reason for venturing into this depressing complex – the **Barbican Arts Centre** (*www.barbican.org.uk*), the "City's Gift to the Nation", which was formally opened in 1982, nearly thirty years after the first plans were drawn up.

*St Giles
Cripplegate is
open Mon–Fri
9.30am–
5.15pm, Sat
9am–noon,
Sun 8am–
4pm;* ☎*020
/7638 1997.*

Even the arts centre has its drawbacks, not least an obtusely confusing layout that continues to prove user-repellent; just finding the main entrance on Silk Street is quite a feat for most Londoners. Built on nine levels, three of them subterranean, the complex contains a huge concert hall (home of the London Symphony Orchestra), two theatres for the London chapter of the Royal Shakespeare Company, a good three-screen repertory cinema, a rooftop garden, a public library and a poorly designed exhibition space, as well as housing the **Guildhall School of Music and Drama** (*www.gsmd.ac.uk*).

Bunhill Fields and the HAC

Some way to the northeast of the Barbican, formerly just outside the administrative boundaries of the City, lie **Bunhill Fields**, once a plague pit and later the main burial ground for Dissenters or Nonconformists (practising Christians who were not members of the Church of England). Following bomb damage in the last war, most of the graveyard was fenced off from the public, though you can still stroll through on the public footpaths under a canopy of giant London plane trees. The three most famous graves have been placed in the central paved area: the simple tombstone of poet and artist William Blake stands next to a replica of writer Daniel Defoe's, while opposite lies the recumbent statue of John Bunyan, the seventeenth-century author of *The Pilgrim's Progress*.

*Bunhill Fields
is open
April–Sept
Mon–Fri
7.30am–7pm,
Sat & Sun
9.30am–4pm;
Oct–March
closes 4pm; the
nearest tube is
Old Street.*

The cricket field to the south belongs to the **Honourable Artillery Corps** (HAC), whose quasi-medieval barracks, built in 1737, face onto City Road. The HAC is a volunteer unit, formed by Henry VIII in 1537, which now performs ceremonial duties in the City, including the gun salutes which take place outside the Tower of London on Tower Wharf.

Wesley's Chapel and House

Mon–Sat 10am–4pm, Sun noon–2pm; £4; ☎020/7253 2262. Old Street tube.

Directly opposite the entrance to Bunhill Fields, the largely Georgian ensemble of **Wesley's Chapel and House**, set around a cobbled courtyard, strikes an unusual note of calm on City Road. A place of pilgrimage for Methodists from all over the world, the chapel was built in 1777 and heralded the coming of age of the followers of **John Wesley** (1703–91), who had started out in a small foundry to the east of the present building. The name "Methodist" was first coined as a term of abuse by Wesley's fellow Oxford students, but it wasn't until his "conversion" at a prayer meeting in Aldersgate (marked by a plaque outside the Museum of London) in 1738, and later expulsion from the Anglican Church, that he decided to become an independent field preacher. More verbal and even physical abuse followed – Wesley was accused of being a papist spy and an illegal gin distiller – but by the time of his death there were more than 350 Methodist chapels serving over 130,000 worshippers.

The chapel forms the centrepiece of the complex, though it is uncharacteristically ornate for a Methodist place of worship, with its powder-pink columns of French jasper and its superb, Adam-style gilded plasterwork ceiling, not to mention the colourful Victorian stained glass depicting, among other things, Wesley's night-time conversion, with his brother still in his dressing gown. The chapel has often attracted well-heeled weddings: one Margaret Hilda Roberts got married to divorcé Denis Thatcher here in 1951, and more recently paid for the new communion rail.

The **Museum of Methodism** in the basement tells the story of Wesley and Methodism, and there's even a brief mention of Mrs Mary Vazeille, the 41-year-old insanely jealous wealthy widow he married, and who eventually left him. Wesley himself lived his last two years in the Georgian **house** to the right of the main gates, and inside you can see bits of his furniture and his deathbed, plus an early shock-therapy machine which he used to treat members of his congregation. Wesley's **grave** is round the back of the chapel, in the shadow of a modern office block.

From Guildhall to Bank

Guildhall is the civic focus of the City, just as the **Bank of England** is its financial focus, making the area around and between these two institutions very much the City's hub. The architecture here is typical of much of the City: a mixture of the old and very new, scattered with Wren churches, the Livery halls and postwar tower blocks. Apart from **Guildhall Art Gallery** and the **Museum of the Bank of England**, the only really specific sights are the excellent **Lothbury**

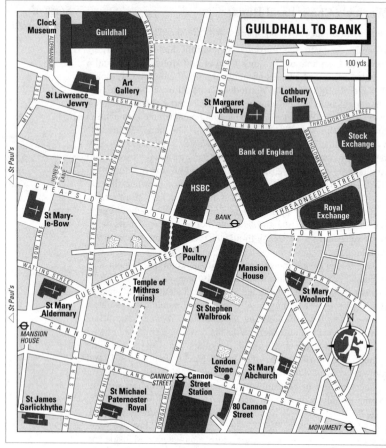

Gallery and the **churches**, in particular Wren's St Mary Aldermary and St Stephen Walbrook, and Hawksmoor's St Mary Woolnoth.

Guildhall

May–Sept daily 10am–5pm; Oct–April Mon–Sat 10am–5pm; free; ☎020/7606 3030 ext 1463; *www.cityoflondon.gov.uk*. St Paul's or Bank tube.

Situated at the geographical centre of the City, **Guildhall** has been the seat of the City administration for over eight hundred years. It remains the headquarters of the Corporation of London, and is still used for many of the City's formal civic occasions. Architecturally, however, it no longer exudes the municipal wealth it once did, having been badly damaged in both the Great Fire and the Blitz, and scarred by the early 1970s addition of a grotesque concrete cloister and wing.

Nonetheless, the quasi-medieval **Great Hall** is worth a visit and is more accessible than it looks – it's entered through the hideous modern extension, not the quasi-Indian porch, which was tacked on in the eighteenth century and is the most striking aspect of the exterior. Venue in 1556 for the high-treason trials of Lady Jane Grey, her husband, Lord Dudley, and Archbishop Cranmer, the Great Hall is still used for meetings of the Court of Common Council and for various state functions. The interior is basically a postwar reconstruction of the fifteenth-century original, complete with a minstrels' gallery from which statues of the pagan giants Gog and Magog look down. The hall is also home to a handful of vainglorious late eighteenth- and early nineteenth-century monuments, replete with lions, cherubs and ludicrous allegorical figures.

The only surviving part of the medieval Guildhall is the **crypt**, which dates from the thirteenth to the fifteenth centuries. Unfortunately, to visit the crypt, you must join up with a group booked in for a guided tour. To find out when the next tour will be, phone the Keeper's Office on the number quoted above.

Guildhall Art Gallery

Mon–Sat 10am–5pm; Sun noon–4pm; £2.50; ☎020/7606 1632; *www .corpoflondon.gov.uk*. St Paul's or Bank tube.

The City's newest attraction is the **Guildhall Art Gallery**, on the eastern side of Guildhall's main courtyard. More than fifty years have passed since the original gallery burnt down in the Blitz, but no expense has been spared in the eventual rebuilding, a safe Neo-Gothic pastiche by one of the Gilbert Scott family. Construction was delayed, however, by the discovery of a Roman amphitheatre six metres below the current street level, dating from around 120 AD; there's a small exhibition about it all in the basement.

Around 250 paintings are on show at any one time, though you can view the entire collection on the computer terminals dotted about the museum. As you might expect, there's plenty of pomp and pageantry, with paintings in the entrance depicting the opening of Tower Bridge and the Lord Mayor's Parade, and lots of dull, official portraits of royals, aldermen and mayors on the upper floor. The best place to start, though, is in the **undercroft galleries**, which are packed floor to ceiling with Victorian works by prosperous artists such as G.F. Watts, Alma-Tadema and Lord Leighton. A typical example is *Israel in Egypt* by E.J. Poynter (son of the architect), which was inspired by (and depicts) many exhibits from the British Museum. There are, however, one or two exceptional paintings worth seeking out: **Constable**'s full-sized oil sketch of *Salisbury Cathedral*, characterized by loose brushwork and an air of foreboding; **Holman Hunt**'s *The Eve of St Agnes* (inspired by Keats's poem), painted while he was still a student at the RA, and bought by the gallery's first director out of his own pocket; and **Rossetti's** *La Ghirlandata*, a typically lush portrait, in intense blues and greens, of a model who's a dead ringer for Jane Morris, with whom the artist was infatuated.

The centrepiece of the entire gallery is the gigantic and very dramatic *Defeat of the Floating Batteries, September 1782*, by **John Singleton Copley**, depicting the siege of Gibraltar, when the Spanish tried to dislodge the British from the Rock by firing incendiary devices from "unsinkable" floating barges. The picture shows the Brits magnanimously saving the drowning enemy from the flaming barques. The piece was commissioned by the Corporation in 1783, but poor old Copley had to redo the entire thing when the garrison officers insisted on having more prominence. Also in this main room are four paintings by Richard Paton, showing the same battle at four different stages from a wider perspective.

The gallery also owns a mixed bag of smaller works, hung in the **ground-floor galleries**, ranging from portraits by Reynolds and Lely to modern works by the likes of Leon Kossoff and William Roberts. On the whole, they're interesting as much for what they depict – bygone vistas of old London, postwar bomb sites and so on – as for their artistry.

Guildhall Clock Museum

Mon–Sat 10am–5pm, Sun noon–4pm; free; ☎020/7332 1868. St Paul's or Bank tube.

Round the corner on Aldermanbury hides the **Guildhall Clock Museum**, a collection of over six hundred timepieces that are rather unimaginatively displayed by the Worshipful Company of Clockmakers. You'll find just about every type of device from Jacobean pocket watches to grandfather clocks, which ring out in unison on the hour. Of particular interest is the collection of marine chronometers, belonging to John Harrison, including his personal pair-case watch, made under his instructions by one of the guild's apprentices, John Jefferys, and the prototype for the H4 clock that won him half the Longitude Prize money. Pride of place, though, goes to H5, which was tested by George III himself at Richmond observatory, and which won him a sum of money almost equivalent to the full prize money. Close by is the ghoulish skull watch, allegedly given by Mary Queen of Scots to her maid-of-honour. Next door to the clock museum is the Guildhall **library**, which has a small display of antique playing cards, and temporary exhibitions of London maps and prints, and the excellent Guildhall **bookshop**.

For more on John Harrison and the Longitude Prize, see the Old Royal Observatory (p.438).

St Lawrence Jewry

Mon–Fri 7.30am–2pm; organ recitals Mon & Tues 1pm; free; ☎020/7600 9478. St Paul's or Bank tube.

Directly south of Guildhall, across the courtyard, stands Wren's church of **St Lawrence Jewry**, the splendour of its interior perfectly suited to its role as the official church of the Corporation of London. Opened in 1677 in the presence of Charles II, but gutted during the Blitz, its handsome, wide, open-plan interior has been lovingly restored and is well worth a peek – the richly gilded plasterwork on the ceiling is particularly fine. As the name indicates, this was once the site of London's **Jewish ghetto**. Old Jewry, two blocks east, was the nucleus of the quarter, containing a synagogue that was confiscated by the City authorities in 1272, shortly before the expulsion of the entire community by Edward I.

From Guildhall to Bank

For more on London's Jewish community, see p.269.

Cheapside and Bow Lane

It's difficult to believe that **Cheapside**, a couple of blocks south of the Guildhall, was once the City's foremost medieval marketplace. Only the names of the nearby streets – Bread Street, Milk Street, Honey Lane, Poultry – recall its former prominence, which faded when the shops and their customers began to move to the West End from the seventeenth century onwards.

The nearest tube is St Paul's.

Nowadays, the only distinguishing feature on this otherwise bleak parade of postwar office blocks is Wren's church of **St Mary-le-Bow** (Mon–Fri 6.30am–6pm; ☎020/7248 5139), whose handsome tower features each of the five classical orders, a granite obelisk and a dragon weather vane. The tower also contains postwar replicas of the famous "Bow Bells", which sounded the 9pm curfew for Londoners from the fourteenth to the nineteenth centuries, and within whose earshot all true Cockneys are born. The church's interior was totally destroyed in the Blitz and, though rebuilt in the 1950s, contains little of interest.

The Place Below is a popular vegetarian café in the crypt of St Mary-le-Bow church.

Down the side of St Mary-le-Bow runs **Bow Lane**, narrow, pedestrianized and jam-packed at weekday lunchtimes with office workers heading for the sandwich bars, but also featuring a butcher's and barber's, not to mention several good pubs. At its southern end, just before you hit Queen Victoria Street, is the church of **St Mary Aldermary** (Mon, Thurs & Fri 11am–3pm; ☎020/7248 4906), whose pinnacled spire suggests a pre-Fire edifice, though it is, in fact, a rare foray into the Perpendicular style by Wren, based on the original church. The plasterwork fan-vaulting and saucer domes in the aisles are the highlight, best viewed during one of the church's free lunchtime concerts.

The nearest tube is Mansion House.

Lothbury

A couple of blocks east of Guildhall, Gresham Street leads into **Lothbury**, which runs along the back of the Bank of England. Tucked into the north side of the street is the tiny Wren church of **St Margaret Lothbury** (Mon–Fri 8am–4.30pm; ☎020/7606 8330), whose plain interior harbours some of the finest furnishings of any City church. The most eye-catching is the magnificent screen, designed by Wren

The nearest tube is Bank.

and comprised of delicate, intertwined spiral columns either side of the main entrance, which features a segmental pediment and a huge eagle. Also worth a closer look is the wonderful hexagonal pulpit and tester, laden with carved putti, birds, fruit and flowers.

Further along Lothbury, at no. 41, is the excellent **Lothbury Gallery**, where the banking corporation, NatWest Group, puts on a series of exhibitions drawn from its collection of over 1500 paintings, ranging from the seventeenth to the twentieth century (but with the emphasis firmly on the latter). Most of the City's banks own vast numbers of art works, but NatWest is the only one to have opened a public gallery in which to display them, for which it should be heartily congratulated. What's more, the Neoclassical former banking hall is a splendidly grandiose setting for an art gallery, and is generously flooded with natural light from the glass ceiling. The exhibitions change every few months, and each summer the country's biggest art competition, the NatWest Art Prize, is awarded, with shortlisted works on display in the gallery beforehand.

*Lothbury
Gallery is open
Mon–Fri
10am–4pm;
free;* ☎ *020
/7726 1642.*

Bank

*The nearest
tube is Bank.*

Bank is the finest architectural arena in the City. Heart of the finance sector and the busy meeting point of eight streets, it's overlooked by a handsome collection of Neoclassical buildings – among them, the Bank of England, the Royal Exchange and Mansion House – each one faced in Portland stone.

By far the most graceful of the trio is the **Royal Exchange**, twice destroyed by fire since it was first built in 1570. The current building, fronted by a massive eight-column portico, and a very convenient set of steps for lunching office workers, was built in the 1840s

---

The City's financial heart

The City has been London's **financial centre** since the Middle Ages, when business was conducted in the local streets, courtyards or taverns and, later, in coffee shops. In 1567, prompted by England's persistently bad weather and Antwerp's new stock exchange, Thomas Gresham, financial adviser to Elizabeth I, founded the Royal Exchange. Nevertheless, it wasn't until 1694 that the Bank of England came into existence; until then all of London's financial institutions were dominated by the accounting skills of the Italians, who inhabited nearby Lombard Street.

Today, all the key money markets and the City's five hundred foreign banks continue to be concentrated around Bank. By virtue of its position between New York and Tokyo, and the employment of a highly skilled workforce whose native tongue is the international language of finance, the City has remained in the triumvirate of top money markets. London's financial sector employs over 120,000 people in the City, dominates the European share and foreign-exchange markets and leads the world in futures and options. However, with the impact of the introduction of the Euro still hanging in the air, the City is having to fight hard to maintain its hegemony in the twenty-first century.

---

by Sir Edward Tite. Sadly, the arcaded inner courtyard no longer buzzes with the polyglot sound of Dutch, Spanish, Scottish, Irish and Jewish traders, as it once did. And for the moment, the general public are not allowed access to the interior to admire the original Turkish pavement and the late Victorian frescoes within.

Mansion House, the Lord Mayor's sumptuous Neoclassical lodgings during his or – on only one occasion so far – her term of office, is also only open to group tours. However, you might be able to join up with a group tour if there's space; to do so you'll need to phone several months in advance, and then apply in writing. The building was designed in 1753 by George Dance; highlights of the 45-minute tour are Dance's opulent Egyptian Hall, the Lord Mayor's insignia and the vast collection of gold and silver plate.

One magnificent building at Bank that's easy to gain access to is the former Midland Bank headquarters, now a branch of **HSBC** (Mon–Fri 8.30am–5pm), which has its main entrance on Poultry. Built between the wars by Edwin Lutyens, the public banking halls on the ground floor feature magnificent green African verdite square columns, walnut counters, flying-saucer hanging lights and really comfy sofas.

The one blot on Bank's otherwise homogenous surroundings is **No. 1 Poultry**, horizontally striped in sand and salmon colours, and topped by a Swatch-like clock tower, a prime example of 1990s postmodernism by James Stirling. Equally ugly in a very 1970s way is the modern **Stock Exchange** (*www.londonstockexchange.com*), a short way up Threadneedle Street from Bank. Its public gallery has been closed to the public since it was bombed by the IRA in 1990, though in any case the human scrum has now been largely replaced by computerized dealing, and the whole shebang looks set to merge with another European stock exchange.

From Guildhall to Bank

To enquire about the free guided tours of Mansion House, call ☎020/7626 2500.

Bank of England

Mon–Fri 10am–5pm; free; audio tour £1; ☎020/7601 5545; *www .bankofengland.co.uk*. Bank tube.

Established by William III in 1694 to raise funds for his costly war against France, the **Bank of England**, the so-called "Grand Old Lady

---

London's loos

> *Down gleaming walls of porc'lain flows the sluice*
> *That out of sight decants the kidney juice*
> *Thus pleasuring those gents for miles around*
> *Who, crying for relief, once piped the sound*
> *Of wind in alleyways . . .*

This celebratory ode was composed by Josiah Feable for the opening, in 1855, of the first public flush lavatories, which were situated outside the Royal Exchange. There was a charge of one penny (hence the euphemism) and the toilets were gents-only – ladies had to hold theirs in until 1911, when new lavatories were built.

---

of Threadneedle Street", wasn't erected on its present site until 1734. During the Gordon Riots of 1780, the bank was attacked by rioters, but successfully defended with the help of some of the bank's clerks who made bullets by melting down their ink wells. Subsequently a detachment of the Foot Guards, known as the Bank Picquet, was stationed outside every night until 1973. Security remains pretty tight at the bank, which, after all, still acts as a giant safe-deposit box, storing the official gold reserves of seventy or so central banks around the world, but not, ironically, of Britain itself. British gold reserves are kept in the Federal Reserve Bank of New York, where they moved during World War II. Since 1997, the bank has also been responsible for setting interest rates, in order to hit an inflation target determined by the government.

The windowless, outer curtain wall, which wraps itself round the 3.5-acre island site, is pretty much all that remains of the building design on which Sir John Soane spent the best part of his career from 1788 onwards. However, you can view a reconstruction of Soane's Bank Stock Office, with its characteristic domed skylight, in the **museum**, which has its entrance on Bartholomew Lane. The permanent exhibition traces the history of the bank, and includes a model of Soane's bank, a Victorian-style diorama of the 1780 siege and, beyond, a reconstruction of Herbert Baker's interwar rotunda (wrecked in the Blitz). Sadly most of the gold bars are fakes, but there are specimens of every note issued by the Royal Mint over the centuries, and a brain-straining computer on which you can play at being a foreign-exchange dealer.

Walbrook and the Temple of Mithras

Along the west wall of Mansion House runs Walbrook, named after the shallow stream which used to provide Roman London with its fresh water. On the eastern side of Walbrook, behind Mansion House, stands the church of **St Stephen Walbrook**, the Lord Mayor's official church and Wren's most spectacular after St Paul's. Faced with a fairly cramped site, Wren created a church of great space and light, with sixteen Corinthian columns arranged in clusters around a central dome, which many regard as a practice run for the cathedral. The modern beech-wood pews don't fit well with Grinling Gibbons' dark-wood furnishings; similarly awkward is Henry Moore's altar, an amorphous blob of stone, placed centrally right under the dome. The Samaritans were founded here in 1953, and their first helpline telephone now rests on a plinth in the southwest corner as a memorial.

*St Stephen
Walbrook is
open Mon–
Thurs
10am–4pm,
Fri 10am–
3pm;* ☎ *020
/7283 4444.*

Remains of a **Temple of Mithras**, which once stood on the river's western bank, were discovered in 1954 during the laying of the foundations for Bucklersbury House, the monstrosity set back from Queen Victoria Street. Mithraism was a male-only cult popular among the Roman legions before the advent of Christianity. Its Persian deity, Mithras, is always depicted slaying a cosmic bull, while a scorpion grasps its genitals and a dog licks its wounds – the bull's blood was seen as life-giving, and initiates to the cult had to bathe in it in subterranean tombs. The foundations of the third-century temple, which have been reassembled in the shadow of the office block, give very little impression of what the building would have been like – the rich finds and more substantial reconstruction in the Museum of London give a slightly better idea.

From Guildhall to Bank

St Mary Woolnoth to the London Stone

Hidden from the bustle of Bank itself, a short distance down King William Street, stands **St Mary Woolnoth**, one of Nicholas Hawksmoor's six idiosyncratic London churches. The main facade is very imposing, with its twin turrets, Doric pillars and heavy rustication. As the only City church to come through the war unscathed, the interior is also well worth inspecting. In a cramped but lofty space, Hawksmoor managed to cram in a cluster of three big Corinthian columns at each corner, which support an ingenious lantern lit by semicircular clerestory windows. The most striking furnishing is the altar canopy, held up by barley-sugar columns and studded with seven golden cherubic faces. The church's projecting clock gets a brief mention in T.S. Eliot's *The Waste Land*.

St Mary Woolnoth is open Mon–Fri 8am–5pm; ☎020/7626 9701.

To the north of St Mary Woolnoth, and running east, is **Lombard Street**, focus of London's financial community before the Royal Exchange was built, and named after the region of Italy from which most of the bankers and merchants originated. The street contains the head office of Lloyds Bank and also the sign of the golden grasshopper, emblem of Thomas Gresham, who used to live on the site of one of the oldest banks in the City, Martin's, founded in 1563. Lombard Street also boasts several old trade signs rehung for the coronation of Edward VII in 1902. Framed in iron and often as thick as paving stones, these were previously a feature of every commercial street in London, but were banned in 1762 after one fell down and killed four passers-by.

The nearest tubes are Cannon Street (closed Sat and Sun) and Monument.

A complete contrast to Hawskmoor's church is provided by Wren's **St Mary Abchurch**, set in its own courtyard (the paved-over former graveyard) on Abchurch Lane, south off King William Street. Nothing about the dour red-brick exterior prepares you for the interior, which is dominated by a vast dome fresco painted by a local parishioner and lit by oval lunettes, with the name of God in Hebrew centre stage. The lime-wood reredos, festooned with swags and garlands and decorated with gilded urns and a pelican, is one of the few authenticated works by Grinling Gibbons in the City.

St Mary Abchurch is open Mon–Thurs 10.30am–3pm, Fri 10.30am– noon; ☎020 /7626 0306.

A brief diversion west, via Cannon Street, will take you to one of London's most esoteric sights, the **London Stone**, a small block of limestone lodged behind an iron grille within the exterior wall of the Oversea Chinese Banking Corporation, 111 Cannon St, at the corner of St Swithin's Lane. To some it is London's omphalos, its geomantic centre; to the uninitiated, it looks more like a lump of Roman mason-ry. Whatever your reaction to this bizarre relic, it has been around for some considerable time, certainly since the 1450 peasants' revolt, when the Kentish rebel Jack Cade struck it, declaring himself "Lord of the City". Nearby, on the corner of Walbrook and Cannon Street, is a more recent arrival, a statue of a futures trader on his mobile phone.

Bishopsgate to the Tower

The largest number of pre-Fire churches are concentrated in the easterly section of the Square Mile between Bishopsgate and the Tower, but it's financial institutions that predominate, many of them housed in the brashest of the City's new architecture. Thus, the area's two most obvious landmarks are the controversial **Lloyd's Building** and the generally disliked **NatWest Tower**. These, plus the Victorian splendour of **Leadenhall Market**, the oldest **synagogue** in the country and Wren's famous **Monument** to the Great Fire, make for an especially interesting sector of the City to explore.

Broadgate

The **Broadgate** complex, to the north of Bank and west of Bishopsgate, is by far the largest and most ambitious of the "Big Bang" office developments of the late 1980s, and one of the most successful. The offices' proximity to Liverpool Street Station, and the new traffic-free piazzas, have proved very popular with City workers. The architecture is in the bland US corporate style, replete with secu-rity cameras and guards, but on the plus side Broadgate is adorned with a substantial crop of outdoor sculptures, which succeed in heightening the tone a bit. Another positive note has been the reno-vation of the City's busiest train terminal, **Liverpool Street**, which is now a bright and airy station, with vibrantly painted wrought-iron Victorian arches.

The easiest way to reach the Broadgate complex is to head west from Liverpool Street's main concourse until you come face to face with the rusting steel sheets of *Fulcrum*, an immense sculpture by Richard Serra. To the north lies **Broadgate Circle**, with its circular arena, used as an open-air ice rink in winter and as a performance space in summer. Cascading foliage thankfully obscures much of the architecture in this square, which is probably the most popular of all the piazzas. To the east, **Finsbury Avenue** is disappointing – only the sculptural commuters of *Rush Hour* are at all memorable.

Exchange Square, built above the rail tracks to the north of the station, is the most impressive of the new piazzas, but also the most remote – you're unlikely to come across it by chance. Its distin-guishing features include a cascading waterfall, a phalanx of

chestnut trees and a covered amphitheatre, the whole dominated by
the hi-tech Exchange House, which floats on eight piers spanned by
giant arches. However, it's the sculptures here that have thrust themselves into the public consciousness, in particular the hefty
Broadgate Venus by Fernando Botero and Xavier Corbero's *Broad
Family* of obelisks, one of whose "children" reveals a shoe. The last
word, though, goes to the headquarters of the European Bank for
Economic Development, on the east side of the square. Set up to
provide assistance to the old Eastern Bloc countries, it squandered
much of its budget on Italian marble and other luxury fittings.

Bishopsgate to the Baltic Exchange

The final and most visible stage of the Broadgate development is the
thirteen-floor office block that occupies a huge chunk of land on the
west side of **Bishopsgate**. It's an unoriginal and undistinguished
muddle of orders and motifs, and looks all the more so by contrast
with the imaginative faïence facade of the diminutive **Bishopsgate
Institute** across the road, a sort of proto Art Nouveau building
designed in 1894 by Harrison Townsend. The institute houses an
excellent reference library (Mon–Wed & Fri 9.30am–5.30pm, Thurs
11.30am–5.30pm; ☎020/7247 6844) specializing in works on the
nearby East End, and a Great Hall, used for exams, courses and
lunchtime concerts. Townsend also designed the Whitechapel Art
Gallery (p.274) and the Horniman Museum (p.427).

*Spitalfields
Market is a
couple of min-
utes walk east
of Bishopsgate
– see p.228.*

Back on the south side of the train station, the church of **St
Botolph-without-Bishopsgate**, where John Keats was christened,
used to stand just outside the city gates, and is named for the Anglo-
Saxon abbot who cared for travellers. Damaged in the 1993 IRA
bomb, it's been restored seven times since the current building was
erected in 1728. The church's coved ceiling, with its undersized
dome and lantern, added in 1828, now looks as good as new. A service in Japanese is held here on the second Thursday in the month.
The churchyard, with its fountain and tennis court, is a favourite picnic spot for City workers and contains an old charity school building,
decorated with a uniformed boy and girl, and a small ceramic and
terracotta Turkish bathhouse, now converted into an Indian
restaurant.

*St Botolph-
without-
Bishopsgate is
open Mon–Fri
8am–5.30pm;
☎020/7588
3388.*

Further south down Bishopsgate, the **NatWest Tower**, Britain's
tallest building until the completion of Canary Wharf in 1991, was
damaged in the IRA blasts of 1992 and 1993. This was regarded as
one of the few positive outcomes of the bombing campaign by those
who see Richard Seifert's colossus as the nadir of postwar City development. However, the tower has since been repaired, given a new
glass atrium round the back, and renamed Tower 42 (after the number of floors); there's a café on the ground floor, and a restaurant on
the twenty-fourth, called Twentyfour – the views are great, so if
you're dressed smartly enough not to arouse suspicion, have a drink

at the bar (Mon–Fri noon–11pm). Meanwhile, funds are currently being sought in order to rebuild the tiny pre-Fire church of **St Ethelburga**, hemmed in by office blocks on the opposite side of Bishopsgate, which was all but totally destroyed by the 1993 bomb. The idea is to rebuild the church as a centre for peace and reconciliation.

St Helen's is open Mon–Fri 9am–5pm. Access is via the church office; ☎020 /7281 2231.

Another pre-Fire church that suffered extensive damage in the IRA blasts is the late Gothic church of **St Helen**, to the east of Bishopsgate. With its undulating crenellations and Baroque bell turret, it's an intriguing building, which incorporates the original Benedictine nuns' church and contains five grand pre-Fire tombs. Its interior has been totally reorganized, the architect Quinlan Terry having raised the floor level, shifted the church screens, added a new organ gallery and rearranged the seating to focus on the pulpit, in keeping with the church's current evangelical bent. It is now by far the best-attended church in the City, with hundreds showing up for the regular Tuesday lunchtime and Sunday services, which feature a rock band on Sunday nights.

To the south of St Helen is the giant, bland **Commercial & General Union** skyscraper, which looks set to be upstaged when Norman Foster's "upside-down ice-cream cone" building for **Swiss Re** is completed on the site of the old Baltic Exchange. The medieval church of **St Andrew Undershaft**, to the south on St Mary Axe, miraculously survived the 1992 bomb. Though less remarkable than St Helen's, it does contain the tomb erected by the widow of John Stow, a humble tailor who wrote the first detailed account of the City in 1598. A memorial service is held here annually in April, during which the Lord Mayor replaces the quill pen in the tailor's hand; at other times, you must ring ahead to arrange a visit (☎020/7283 2231).

Lloyd's

Lloyd's is not open to the public.

To the south of the Commercial & General Union building, on Leadenhall Street, stands Richard Rogers' glitzy **Lloyd's Building** (*www.lloydsoflondon.co.uk*), completed in 1984. Thought to have been the intended target of the 1992 IRA bomb, it's the one building in the vicinity which came away relatively unscathed. A startling array of glass and blue-steel pipes – a vertical version of Rogers' own Pompidou Centre – this is easily the most popular of the new City buildings, at least with the general public. Its claims of ergonomic and environmental efficiency have, however, proved to be false, its open-plan trading floor remains extremely unpopular with the workers themselves, and the exterior piping is already in need of extensive repairs. The main portico of the company's previous building, dating from 1925, has been retained to the west of Rogers' building. It came as something of a surprise that one of the most conservative of all the City's institutions should have decided to build such an avant-garde edifice, which is still guarded by porters in waiters' livery, in recognition of the company's modest origins as a coffee house.

Bishopsgate to the Tower

Lloyd's started out in shipping (where it still has major interests) and is now the largest insurance market in the world. The company's famous Lutine Bell in the main office, brought here from a captured French frigate in 1799, is still struck – once for bad news, twice for good. Members of Lloyd's syndicates (known as "Names") pledge their personal fortunes in return for handsome and consistent premiums – that is, they did until the 1990s, when Lloyd's suffered record losses of over £1 billion. One result of the company's financial crisis was the sale of the building to a German financial institution, though it continues to rent the building from the new owners.

Leadenhall Market and Cornhill

Just south of the Lloyd's Building you'll find the picturesque **Leadenhall Market**, whose trading traditions reach back to its days as the centre of the Roman forum. Designed by Sir Horace Jones in 1881, the graceful Victorian cast-ironwork is richly painted in cream and maroon, and each of the four entrances to the covered arcade is topped by an elaborate stone arch. Inside, the traders cater mostly for the lunchtime City crowd, their barrows laden with exotic seafood and game, fine wines, champagne and caviar. The shops and bars remain open until the evening, but to catch the atmosphere, it's best to get here at breakfast or lunchtime.

Across Gracechurch Street from the market, and a short distance down Cornhill stands **St Michael's** – the second, and the more interesting, of the two churches on the street. Wren-designed, but drastically "restored" by George Gilbert Scott in the mid-nineteenth century, it's worth venturing inside simply to listen to the terrifyingly loud organ, which is put through its paces during the free Monday lunchtime recitals. Before you leave, make sure you clock the remarkable eighteenth-century sculpture of a pelican feeding its young, situated at the west end of the church. While on Cornhill, it's also worth peeking inside the **Union Discount Company of London's** headquarters, at no. 39, which has a superbly ornate coffered majolica ceiling.

St Michael's is open Mon–Fri 8.30am–5pm. Organ recitals Mon–Fri 1pm; free; ☎020 /7626 8841.

Bevis Marks Synagogue

Guided tours Mon, Wed, Fri & Sun noon, Tues 11.30am; £1; ☎020/7626 1274. Aldgate or Liverpool Street tube.

Hidden away behind a red-brick office block in a little courtyard off Bevis Marks, at the north end of St Mary Axe, is the **Bevis Marks Synagogue**. Built in 1701 by Sephardic Jews who had fled the Inquisition in Spain and Portugal, this is the country's oldest surviving synagogue, and its roomy, rich interior gives an idea of just how wealthy the community was at the time. Although it seats over six hundred, it is only a third of the size of its prototype in Amsterdam, where many Sephardic Jews initially settled. Past congregations have included some of the most successful Anglo-Jews, including the Disraeli family and Sir Moses Montefiore, whose family still has a special seat reserved for it in the front pew. Nowadays the Sephardic community has dispersed across London, and the congregation has dwindled, though the magnificent array of chandeliers makes it very popular for candle-lit Jewish weddings.

St Katharine Cree and St Botolph's

Close by, just past Creechurch Lane, stood the even larger Great Synagogue of the Ashkenazi Jews, founded in 1690 but bombed out of existence in 1941, and recalled now only by a plaque. At the south-

St Katharine Cree is open Mon–Fri 10.30am–4pm; ☎ 020/7236 5733.

ern end of Creechurch Lane is the church of **St Katharine Cree**, where Hans Holbein is supposed to have been buried after dying of the plague in 1543. Holbein's grave is now lost, but the church, which was rebuilt in the 1620s, survived the Great Fire, and remains a rare example of its period. It's a transitional building with Classical elements, such as the Corinthian columns, and above, a Gothic clerestory and ribbing. At the east end is a rare, and very lovely, seventeenth-century stained-glass Catherine-wheel window.

St Botolph-without-Aldgate is open Mon–Fri 10am–3pm; ☎ 020/7283 1950.

To the east along Aldgate, at the City's gates, is **St Botolph-without-Aldgate**, another unusual church, this time designed in 1741 by George Dance. Its bizarre interior, remodelled last century, features blue-grey paintwork, gilding on top of white plasterwork, some dodgy modern art, a batik reredos and a stunning, modern stained-glass rendition of Rubens' *Descent from the Cross* on a deep-purple background. At the very edge of the East End, this is a famous campaigning church, active on issues like gay priests, the headquarters of the society for promoting Jewish–Christian under-standing, and with a crypt used as a day centre for homeless men.

London Bridge and the Monument

The nearest tube is Monument.

Until 1750, **London Bridge** was the only bridge across the Thames. The Romans were the first to build a permanent crossing here, a structure succeeded by a Saxon version that was pulled down by the Danes in 1014, an event which gave rise to the popular nursery rhyme *London Bridge is Falling Down*. It was the medieval bridge, howev-er, that achieved world fame: built of stone and crowded with timber-framed houses, it became one of the great attractions of London. At the centre stood the richly ornate Nonsuch House, decorated with onion domes and Dutch gables, and a small chapel dedicated to Thomas à Becket; at the Southwark end was the Great Gatehouse, on which the heads of traitors were displayed, dipped in tar to preserve them. The houses were finally removed in the mid-eighteenth century,

The Great Fire

In the early hours of September 2, 1666, the **Great Fire** broke out at Farriner's, the king's bakery in Pudding Lane. The Lord Mayor refused to lose any sleep over it, dismissing it with the line "Pish! A woman might piss it out." Pepys was also roused from his bed, but saw no cause for alarm. Four days and four nights later, the Lord Mayor was found crying "like a fainting woman", and Pepys had fled: the Fire had destroyed some four-fifths of London, including 87 churches, 44 Livery halls and 13,200 houses. The medieval city was no more.

Miraculously, there were only nine recorded fatalities, but 100,000 people were made homeless. "The hand of God upon us, a great wind and a season so very dry", was the verdict of the parliamentary report on the Fire; Londoners preferred to blame Catholics and foreigners. The poor baker eventually "confessed" to being an agent of the pope and was executed, after which the following words, "but Popish frenzy, which wrought such horrors, is not yet quenched", were added to the Latin inscription on the Monument. (The lines were erased in 1831.)

and a new stone bridge erected in 1831; that one now stands in the middle of the Arizona desert, having been bought for $2.4 million in the late 1960s by a gentleman who, so the story goes, was under the impression he had purchased Tower Bridge. The present concrete structure, without doubt the ugliest yet, dates from 1972.

The only reason to go anywhere near London Bridge is to see the **Monument**, which was designed by Wren to commemorate the Great Fire of 1666 (see box above). Crowned with spiky gilded flames, this plain Doric column stands 202ft high, making it the tallest isolated stone column in the world; if it were laid out flat it would touch the bakery where the Fire started, east of Monument. The bas-relief on the base, now in very bad shape, depicts Charles II and the Duke of York in Roman garb conducting the emergency relief operation. The 311 steps to the gallery at the top – a favourite place for suicides until a cage was built around it in 1842 – once guaranteed an incredible view; nowadays it is dwarfed by the buildings around it.

Monument is open daily 10am–6pm; £1.50; ☎020 /7626 2717.

East to the Tower

Signs from the Monument will point you in the right direction for another Wren edifice, the church of **St Magnus-the-Martyr**, whose octagonal spire used to greet travellers arriving across old London Bridge. Now it stands forlorn and battered by the heavy traffic hurtling down Lower Thames Street, though the Anglo-Catholic interior holds, in T.S. Eliot's words, "an inexplicable splendour of Ionian white and gold". In addition, there's a wooden pier from an old Roman wharf in the porch, and a great model of the old London Bridge in the vestry. Access to the Thames from here is via HSBC Bank, which stands alongside the striking titanium-blue glass cubes of the Hong Kong and Shanghai Bank.

St Magnus-the-Martyr is open Tues–Fri 10am–4pm, Sun 10am–1pm; ☎020 /7626 4481.

Beyond is the old **Billingsgate Market**, London's chief wholesale fish market from Roman times until 1982, when it was moved out to Docklands. It's hard now to imagine the noise and smell of old Billingsgate, whose porters used to carry the fish in towers of baskets on their heads, and whose wives were renowned for their bad language even in Shakespeare's day: "as bad a tongue . . . as any oyster-wife at Billingsgate" (*King Lear*). The Victorian hall was successfully renovated in 1990 by Richard Rogers, but as an office it understandably has no atmosphere. From Billingsgate, the riverside walk is interrupted by the gates of **Custom House** (*www.hmce.gov.uk*), which has been collecting duties from incoming ships since around 1275. The present undistinguished Neoclassical structure dates from 1825.

As an alternative to the riverside walk, you could cut north from Lower Thames Street up **Lovat Lane**, one of the City's most atmospheric cobbled streets, once renowned for its brothels and known as Love Lane until 1939. Halfway up Lovat Lane, you come to **St Mary-at-Hill**, whose entrance is to the east, down a passageway in the parallel street of the same name. Having escaped the Blitz unscathed, the church was almost entirely destroyed by fire in 1988, but has since made a phoenix-like recovery. The white-stuccoed dome held up by four fluted columns is all there is so far, but the church's remarkable furnishings – box pews, pulpit and reredos – are still in storage.

St Mary-at-Hill eventually brings you out onto **Eastcheap**, site of the medieval meat market, along which several admirable Victorian Gothic facades have survived (no. 33 is particularly fancy). If you're looking for a secluded spot, however, you could do worse than the garden in the nave of the ruined church of **St Dunstan-in-the-East**, off St Dunstan's Hill, which retains its distinctive Wren-designed crown steeple. For a different scale of architecture, cross over Eastcheap and head down Mincing Lane. Occupying a vast site between here and Mark Lane is **Minster Court**, the new London Underwriting Centre, nicknamed "Munster Court" for its haunted, Hammer-horror Gothicisms. A stroll under the vast glass atrium guarded by three giant horses will bring you to Dunster Court, and then to **Fenchurch Street Station**, a modest little Victorian terminus with a scalloped canopy and a bow-shaped segmental pediment.

To the south of the station, down New London Street, is the ragstone Gothic church of **St Olave**, or "St Ghastly Grim", as Dickens called it, for the skulls and crossbones and vicious-looking spikes adorning the entrance to the graveyard on Seething Lane. Only the outside walls made it through the Blitz, though there are some interesting pre-Fire brasses and monuments. Samuel Pepys lived in Seething Lane for much of his life, and had his own seat in the church's Navy Office pew in the now-demolished galleries; he and his wife, Elizabeth, are both buried here – Elizabeth's monument was raised by Pepys himself, Pepys' own is Victorian.

*St Olave's is
open Mon–Fri
9am–5pm;
☎ 020/7488
4318.*

At the bottom of Seething Lane, on the other side of the noisy highway of Lower Thames Street, stands another pre-Fire church, **All-Hallows-by-the-Tower**. It too was reduced to a burnt-out shell by the Blitz, with only the red-brick tower (from which Pepys watched the Great Fire) remaining intact. The rest of the church, including the needle-sharp copper spine, is a personal reinterpretation of the Gothic style by the postwar architect Lord Mottistone. Don't miss the exquisitely carved Gibbons lime-wood font cover, sealed in a private chapel in the southwest corner of the church. Close by is an arch from the original church on this site, founded in 675 AD; even older remains of two Roman pavements can be found in the claustrophobic little crypt. If you want to learn more about the church, there's an audioguide available (Mon–Fri 11am–4pm, Sat & Sun 1–4pm; £2.50).

*The Tower
area*

All Hallows-by-the-Tower is open Mon–Fri 9am–5.45pm, Sat & Sun 10am–5pm; ☎020/7481 2928.

The Tower area

The area around the **Tower of London** is choked with tourists, traffic and office workers, while souvenir stalls and the dominating presence of London's most famous landmark, **Tower Bridge**, add further bustle to the scene. Yet, despite all the hype and heritage claptrap, the Tower remains one of London's most remarkable buildings, site of some of the goriest events in the nation's history and somewhere all visitors and Londoners should explore at least once.

The Tower of London

March–Oct Mon–Sat 9am–6pm, Sun 10am–6pm; Nov–Feb Mon & Sun 10am–5pm, Tues–Sat 9am–5pm; £11; ☎020/7709 0765; *www.hrp.org.uk*. Tower Hill tube.

The **Tower of London**, one of London's main tourist attractions, overlooks the river at the eastern boundary of the old city walls. Chiefly famous as a place of imprisonment and death, it has variously been used as a royal residence, armoury, mint, menagerie, observatory and – a function it still serves – a safe-deposit box for the Crown Jewels. Yet, amidst the crush of tourists and the weight of history surrounding the place, it's easy to forget that the Tower is, above all, the most perfectly preserved medieval fortress in the country.

Although you can explore the Tower complex independently, it's a good idea to get your bearings by joining up with one of the **guided tours**, given every thirty minutes by one of the forty-odd, eminently photographable **Beefeaters**. These ex-servicemen are best known for their scarlet-and-gold Tudor costumes, but unless it's a special occasion you're more likely to see them in dark-blue "undress". Formed by Henry VIII as a personal bodyguard, they're officially known as Yeoman Warders – the nickname "Beefeaters" was coined

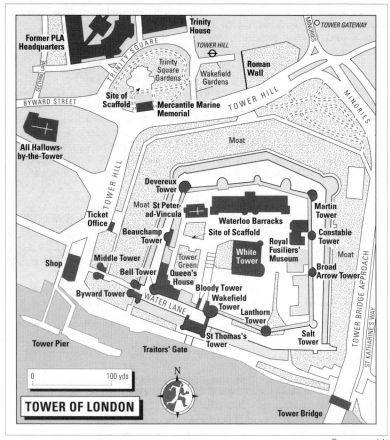

in the seventeenth century, when it was a common term of abuse for a well-fed domestic servant.

A brief history

Begun as a simple watchtower, built by **William the Conqueror** to keep an eye on the City, the Tower had evolved into a palace-fortress by 1100. The inner curtain wall, with its numerous towers, was built in the time of Henry III, and a further line of outer fortifications, plus an even wider moat, were added by Edward I, which means that most of what's visible today was already in place by 1307, the year of Edward's death.

The Tower's first prisoner, the Bishop of Durham, arrived in 1101 and escaped from the window of his cell by a rope, having got the guards drunk. Gruffyd, the last Welshman to be Prince of Wales, attempted a similar feat in 1244, with less success: "his head and neck were crushed between his shoulders . . . a most horrid spectacle". The most famous escapee from the Tower was the Earl of Nithsdale, imprisoned for his part in the 1715 Jacobite rebellion, who, despite his red beard, managed to get past the guards dressed as a woman, and lived on in exile for another thirty years. Richard II was the first king to be imprisoned here, though like the vast majority of Tower prisoners he was later set free.

Following the Restoration, guns were placed along the walls and a permanent garrison stationed in the Tower, which continued to be used as a state prison, the royal mint and an arsenal. At the same time, the general public were admitted for the first time to view the coronation regalia and the impressive displays of arms and armour. Under the Duke of Wellington, who was convinced revolution was around the corner, the Tower returned to a more military role and the public was excluded. Even long after its military obsolescence, it was used to hold German spies during both world wars; the last execution took place in the Tower on August 14, 1941, when a German spy, who had broken his ankle on landing by parachute, was given the privilege of being seated during his execution.

Traitors' Gate and the medieval palace

Two of the first victims of the Reformation – Sir Thomas More and John Fisher – were incarcerated near the main entrance and exit in the **Bell Tower**, which sports a dinky wooden belfry atop its battlements. More was initially allowed writing materials, but later they were withdrawn; Fisher was kept in even worse conditions ("I decay forthwith, and fall into coughs and diseases of my body, and cannot keep myself in health") and was so weak by the end that he had to be carried to the scaffold on Tower Hill. The 20-year-old future Queen Elizabeth I arrived here via Traitors' Gate in 1554, while her half-sister Queen Mary tried to find incriminating evidence against her. Roman Catholic Mass was performed daily in Elizabeth's cell for the two months of her imprisonment, but she refused to be converted.

Visitors today enter the Tower along Water Lane, but in times gone by most prisoners were delivered through **Traitors' Gate**, on the waterfront, having been ferried down the Thames from the courts at Westminster Hall. The gate forms part of **St Thomas's Tower**, which, along with the Wakefield Tower beyond, has been reconstructed to re-create the atmosphere of Edward I's **medieval palace**, with period-clad actors on hand to answer questions. The Aula, where the king ate and relaxed, has a beautiful little oratory in one of the turrets, while the Throne Room, in the Wakefield Tower, contains a gilded and colourful replica of the Coronation Chair (the battered original is in Westminster Abbey), and a huge crown-shaped candelabra depicting the twelve gates of the New Jerusalem. It was in the

Throne Room's oratory that the "saintly but slightly daft" Henry VI was murdered at prayer on the orders of Edward IV in 1471.

Bloody Tower

The main entrance to the Inner Ward is beneath a 3.5-ton, seven-hundred-year-old portcullis, which forms part of the **Bloody Tower**. Here the 12-year-old Edward V and his 10-year-old brother were accommodated "for their own safety" in 1483 by their uncle, Richard of Gloucester (later to be Richard III), after the death of their father, Edward IV. Of all the Tower's many inhabitants, few have so captured the public imagination as the "**Princes in the Tower**", due in part to Sir Thomas More's detailed account of their murder. According to More, they were smothered in their beds, and buried naked at the foot of the White Tower. In 1674, during repair work, the skeletons of two young children were discovered one on top of the other close to the Tower; they were subsequently buried in Innocents' Corner in Westminster Abbey. Some have contended that Richard III has been the victim of Tudor propaganda, and that several other people in high places were equally keen to dispose of the little dears; the jury is still out on this one.

The Bloody Tower's other illustrious inmate – even more famous in his time than the princes – was **Walter Ralegh**, who spent three separate periods in the Tower. His first stay was in 1592, when he incurred the displeasure of Elizabeth I for impregnating one of her ladies-in-waiting; his second and longest spell began in 1603, when his death sentence for suspected involvement in the Gunpowder Plot was commuted to life imprisonment. In the event, he spent thirteen years here growing and smoking tobacco (his most famous import), writing poetry, concocting various dubious potions in his distillery and completing the first volume of his History of the World, which in its day outsold even Shakespeare, despite being banned by James I for being "too saucy in censuring princes". Ralegh's study is recreated on the ground floor, while his sleeping quarters, built especially to accommodate his wife, children and three servants, are upstairs. When Ralegh complained that the noise of the portcullis kept him awake at night, he was moved to much worse accommodation. Ralegh was eventually released in 1616 and sent off to Guyana to discover gold, on condition that he didn't attack the Spanish. He broke his word and was sent straight back to the Tower on his return in 1618. For six weeks he was imprisoned in "one of the most cold and direful dungeons", before being beheaded at Westminster.

The White Tower

William the Conqueror's central hall-keep, known as the **White Tower**, is the original "Tower", begun in 1076 by the Bishop of Rochester. Whitewashed (hence its name) in the reign of Henry III, it was later returned to its Kentish ragstone exterior by Wren, who added the large windows. Of the tower's four turrets, topped by stylish Tudor cupolas, only three are square: the fourth is rounded in order to encase the main spiral staircase, and for a short while was used by Charles II's astronomer royal, Flamsteed, before he moved to Greenwich to escape the attentions of the Tower's ravens. The main entrance to the Tower is the original one, high up in the south wall, out of reach of the enemy, and accessed by a wooden staircase which could be removed during times of siege.

The three floors of arms and armour displayed within the tower represent a mere smidgen of the **Royal Armouries** (the majority of which is now in Leeds), which have been on almost permanent display since the time of Charles II. At the entrance, you have a choice of following the short or the long tour. The short tour only takes you through the ground floor and basement, so it's best to opt for the long tour, for even if you've no interest in military paraphernalia, you should at least pay a visit to the **Chapel of St John**, on the first floor of the White Tower, a beautiful Norman structure completed in 1080, making it the oldest intact church building in London. It was here that Henry VI's body was buried following his murder in 1471; that Henry VII's queen, Elizabeth of York, lay in state surrounded by eight hundred candles, after dying in childbirth; that Lady Jane Grey came to pray on the night before her execution; and that "Bloody Mary" was betrothed by proxy to King Philip of Spain. Today, the once highly decorated blocks of honey-coloured Caen limestone are free of all ecclesiastical excrescences, leaving the chapel's smooth curves and rounded apse perfectly unencumbered.

Among the most striking armour displayed on the first floor are the colossal Holbein-designed garniture of 1540 made for Henry VIII, the Japanese armour presented to King James I by the Shogun of Japan and Charles I's unusual gold-leaf suit. Temporary exhibitions are staged on the top floor, along with displays on the tower's role as an arms store – by around 1600, it housed the largest magazine in the country, comprising nearly 10,000 barrels of gunpowder. Back down on the ground floor, there's yet more weaponry, including the Spanish Armoury, said to have been taken from the Armada, and displayed on and off for the last three hundred years. Other items on show include the execution block used for the last public beheading (see box on p.233), the odd token instrument of torture, a suit of armour for a man six feet nine inches tall (thought to have been John of Gaunt) and one for Richard, Duke of York, who was just three feet, one and a half inches high at the time. The Line of Kings – a display first recorded in 1660, depicting the monarchs of England on horseback – is more like a Line of Horses, since only one of the wooden steeds carries a royal rider in full armour. Visitors exit via the basement, which contains the knarled, melted relics salvaged from the tower after the fire of 1841, some of which were sold to the public immediately afterwards and later made into candelabra and the like.

There's nowhere to get anything to eat or drink within the Tower, but there is the branch of Pret à Manger underneath Tower Bridge. You can obtain a re-entry pass as you leave the Tower.

Tower Green

Being beheaded at Tower Hill (as opposed to being hanged, drawn
and quartered) was a privilege of the nobility; being beheaded on
Tower Green, the stretch of lawn to the west of the White Tower, was
an honour conferred on just six (possibly seven) people, whose
names are recorded on a brass plate at the centre of the green. It was
an arrangement that suited both parties: the victim was spared the
jeering crowds and rotten apples of Tower Hill (see p.263), and the
monarch was spared bad publicity. The privileged victims were: Lord
Hastings, executed (near this spot) immediately after his arrest on the
orders of Richard III, who swore he wouldn't go to dinner until
Hastings was beheaded; Anne Boleyn (Henry VIII's second wife),
accused of incest and adultery, who was dispatched cleanly and swiftly with a French long sword rather than the traditional axe, at her own
insistence; Catherine Howard (Henry VIII's fifth wife and Anne's
cousin), convicted of adultery and beheaded along with her lady-in-
waiting, who was deemed an accomplice; the 70-year-old Countess of
Salisbury; the 17-year-old Lady Jane Grey; and the Earl of Essex, one-
time favourite of Elizabeth I. The bloody, headless corpses of these
"traitors", and those of an estimated 1500 other victims executed on
Tower Hill, including Sir Thomas More, were all hastily buried in the
plain Tudor **Chapel of St Peter-ad-Vincula**, to the north of the scaffold site, accessible only on the Beefeaters' tours.

Close by the chapel is the **Beauchamp Tower**, a relatively plush
place which accommodated only the most wealthy of prisoners. The

---

The Royal Menagerie and the ravens

The **Royal Menagerie** began in 1235 when the Holy Roman Emperor presented three leopards to Henry III; the leopard keeper was initially paid
sixpence a day for the sustenance of the beasts, and one penny for himself.
They were put on public display and joined three years later by an elephant
from the King of France and a polar bear from the King of Norway. James
I was particularly keen on the menagerie, which by then included eleven
lions, two leopards, three eagles, two owls, two mountain cats and a jackal. He used to stage regular animal fights on the green, but the practice
was stopped in 1609 when one of the bears killed a child. Even in the eighteenth century, visitors were still advised not to "play tricks" after an
orang-utan threw a cannonball at one and killed him.

The menagerie was transferred to the newly founded London Zoo in
1831, leaving the Tower with just its **ravens**, descendants of early scav-
engers attracted by waste from the palace kitchens. They have been protected by royal decree since the reign of Charles II, and have their wings
clipped so they can't fly away – legend says that the Tower (and therefore
the kingdom) will fall if they do, though the Tower was in fact briefly
raven-less during the war. While the ravens may appear harmless, they are
vicious, territorial creatures best given a wide berth. They live in coops in
the south wall of the Inner Ward, have individual names and even have
their own graveyard in the dry moat near the ticket barrier.

---

tower also boasts a better class of graffiti: Lord Dudley, husband of the aforementioned Lady Jane Grey, even commissioned a stonemason to carve the family crest on the first floor. On the far side of the green is the **Queen's House** (closed to the public), built in the last years of Henry VIII's reign and distinguished by its swirling timber frames. These were the most luxurious cells in the Tower, and were used to incarcerate the likes of Catherine Howard and Anne Boleyn, who had also stayed there shortly before her coronation. Lady Jane Grey was cooped up here in 1554 after just nine days as queen, and from here watched the headless torso of her husband, Lord Dudley, being brought back from Tower Hill, only hours before her own execution. In 1688, William Penn, the Quaker and founder of Pennsylvania, was confined to the Queen's House, where he penned his most popular work, *No Cross, No Crown*. The last VIP inmate was **Rudolf Hess**, Hitler's deputy, who flew secretly into Britain to sue for peace in 1941 and was held here for four days; he eventually died in Berlin's Spandau prison in 1987.

The Crown Jewels

The castellated **Waterloo Barracks**, built to the north of the White Tower during the Duke of Wellington's term as Constable of the Tower, now hold the **Crown Jewels**, perhaps the major reason so many people flock to the Tower. At least some of the Crown Jewels have been kept in the Tower since 1327, and have been on display since Charles II let the public have a look at them (there was a steep entrance charge even then). These days, the displays are efficient and disappointingly swift. While you are queuing, giant video screens inflict a three-minute loop of footage from the last coronation, plus close-up photos of the baubles. Finally, you get to view the actual Jewels, sped along on moving walkways which allow just 28 seconds' viewing during peak periods – at non-peak times, you can usually go back for a second look without queuing once again.

The vast majority of exhibits postdate the Commonwealth (1649–60), when many of the royal riches were melted down for coinage or sold off. The oldest piece of regalia is the twelfth-century **Anointing Spoon**; the most famous is the **Imperial State Crown**, sparkling with 2868 diamonds, a sapphire from a ring said to have been buried with Edward the Confessor, eleven emeralds, five rubies and 273 pearls. All in all, it's a stunning ensemble, though only a few of the exhibits – Queen Victoria's small diamond crown, for example – could be described as beautiful. Assertions of status and wealth are more important considerations, and the Jewels include the three largest cut diamonds in the world: the 530-carat Cullinan I, set into the Sceptre with the Cross, the 317-carat Cullinan II, in the aforementioned Imperial State Crown, and the **legendary Koh-i-Noor**, set into the Queen Mother's crown in 1937. Check out, too, the wine

cistern at the end, thought to be the heaviest surviving piece of
English plate at nearly a quarter of a ton.

The Salt Tower to the Martin Tower

Visitors can now walk along the eastern section of the Tower walls,
starting at the **Salt Tower**, which features more prisoners' graffiti,
including a stunningly detailed horoscope carved into the walls by
Hugh Draper, who was incarcerated in the Tower in 1561 on a
charge of sorcery. Further along the walls, the **Broad Arrow Tower**
is decked out as it would have been when Sir Simon de Burley – tutor
to Richard II and later to be beheaded on Tower Hill – took refuge
here during the 1381 Peasants' Revolt.

The **Martin Tower**, at the far end of the wall walk, was previously
the home of Henry Percy, the Earl of Northumberland, who moved in
here in 1605 having rejected another suite of cells because of their
smell and lack of shade. He had good reason to be choosy, since he
was serving a sentence of life imprisonment in the Tower for failing
to inform the king of the Gunpowder Plot. One of the richest men in
the country, Percy employed his own cook, and paid for a bowling
alley as well as for the walls near his cell to be paved for his daily
stroll. Like Walter Ralegh (held at the same time in the Bloody
Tower; see p.258), Percy brought a library with him, plus three eminent scholars to assist him with his astrological and alchemical studies. When he was finally released in 1621, he was given a royal salute
from the Tower guns.

The Martin Tower now houses an exhibition entitled **Crowns and
Diamonds**, featuring lots of royal crowns without their precious

---

Tower ceremonies

The **Ceremony of the Keys** is a 700-year-old, seven-minute floodlit ceremony which commences at 9.53pm daily. The Chief Yeoman Warder,
accompanied by the Tower Guard, locks the Tower gates, and the following exchange then takes place: "Halt. Who comes there?" "The Keys."
"Whose Keys?" "Queen Elizabeth's Keys." "Pass, Queen Elizabeth's Keys.
All's well." To obtain tickets to witness this long-running drama, you must
write several months in advance to the Resident Governor and Keeper of
the Jewel House, Queen's House, HM Tower of London, EC3.

Royal Gun Salutes are fired by the Honourable Artillery Company at 1pm
at Tower Wharf on royal birthdays and other special occasions.

The **Ceremony of the Lilies and Roses** takes place on May 21, the
anniversary of the murder of King Henry VI in 1471. It is carried out by the
provosts of Eton and King's College, Cambridge, who place white lilies
and roses (their respective emblems) in the Wakefield Tower.

The **Beating of the Bounds** ceremony takes place once every three years
on Ascension Day (forty days after Easter), outside the walls of the Tower.
The 29 stones that mark the limits of the Tower's jurisdiction are beaten
with willow wands by local children, while the Chief Yeoman Warder gives
the order "Whack it boys! whack it!"

stones or with replicas. The exhibition also relates the most famous attempt to steal the Crown Jewels, which took place in the Martin Tower. Shortly after the Crown Jewels were put on show during the reign of Charles II, "Colonel" **Thomas Blood**, an Irish adventurer, made an attempt to make off with the lot, disguised as a parson. He was caught on the point of escape with the crown under his habit, the orb in one of his accomplices' breeches and the sceptre about to be filed in half. Charles, good-humoured as ever, pardoned the felon, and even restored him to his estate in Ireland.

Tower Hill

Perhaps it's fitting that traffic-blighted **Tower Hill** should be such a god-awful place, for it was here that over one hundred "traitors" were executed after being held in the Tower. The first beheading took place in 1388; Sir Thomas More, the Earl of Stafford, Lord Dudley, the Duke of Monmouth, and the 80-year-old Jacobite Lord Lovat were among those who subsequently met their end here. The Duke of Monmouth is credited with suffering the most botched execution: it took five blows of the axe to sever his head, and even then the executioner had to finish the job off with a surgeon's knife. Lord Lovat – the last man to be publically beheaded in England, in 1747 – drew such a crowd that one of the spectators' stands close to the scaffold collapsed, killing several bystanders, at which Lovat is said to have exclaimed: "the more mischief, the better sport." Hangings continued on this spot for another thirty-odd years, ending with the execution of two prostitutes and a one-armed soldier arrested for attacking a Catholic-run pub in the Gordon Riots of 1780.

The actual spot for the executions, at what was the country's first permanent scaffold, is marked by a plaque in **Trinity Square Gardens**, to the northeast of the Tower. Close by stands the **Mercantile Marine Memorial**, a temple designed by Edwin Lutyens, smothered with the names of those who died at sea in World War I, and subsequently enlarged to commemorate the victims of the last war in a zigzagging sunken section to the north. The marine theme is continued in the buildings overlooking the gardens: the temple-like former headquarters of the **Port of London Authority**, a gargantuan Edwardian edifice with Neptune adorning the main tower; and, to the east, the elegant Neoclassical **Trinity House**, which oversees the upkeep of the country's lighthouses. Continuing east, you'll find perhaps the most impressive remaining section of the old **Roman walls** in Wakefield Gardens, close to Tower Hill tube station.

Tower Bridge

Daily: April–Oct 10am–6.30pm; Nov–March 9.30am–6pm. Guided tour £6.25; ☎020/7378 1928; *www.towerbridge.org.uk*; Engine Room only £3.25. Tower Hill tube.

Tower Bridge is just over one hundred years old, yet it ranks with Big Ben as the most famous of all London landmarks. Completed in 1894 to a design by Sir Horace Jones, its Neo-Gothic towers are clad in Cornish granite and Portland stone, but conceal a steel frame, which, at the time, represented a considerable engineering achievement, allowing a road crossing that could be raised to give tall ships access to the upper reaches of the Thames. The raising of the bascules (from the French for "see-saw") remains an impressive sight, and an event that takes place some five hundred times a year. The bridge is at its busiest in summer, so ring ahead to find out when the next opening is (☎020/7378 7700). The elevated walkways linking the summits of the towers (intended for public use) were closed from 1909 to 1982 due to their popularity with prostitutes and the suicidal; you can visit them now on the guided tour described below.

Exploiting the glut of people looking for things to do after leaving the Tower, the City of London Corporation has installed a touristy exhibition, the "Tower Bridge Experience", employing videos and an animatronic chirpy Cockney to describe the enormous opposition there was to the bridge's construction and talk you through a demonstration of the bascules. The tour takes around three-quarters of an hour, which is about twice as long as it need be, leaving many visitors so wearied that they don't bother with the Engine Room, on the south side of the bridge, where you can see the giant coal-fired boilers which drove the hydraulic system until 1976, and play some interactive engineering games. You can, in fact, skip the tour of the Tower – though, of course, you'll miss out on the overhead walkways – and get tickets for the Engine Room only.

Chapter 8

The East End and Docklands

The East End of London is the hell of poverty. Like an enormous, black, motionless, giant kracken, the poverty of London lies there in lurking silence and encircles with its mighty tentacles the life and wealth of the City and of the West End . . .

J.H. Mackay *The Anarchists* (1891)

Few places in London have engendered so many myths as the **EAST END** (a catch-all title which covers just about everywhere east of the City, but has its heart closest to the latter). Its name is synonymous with slums, sweatshops and crime, as epitomized by antiheroes such as Jack the Ripper and the Kray Twins, but also with the rags-to-riches careers of the likes of Harold Pinter and Vidal Sassoon, and whole generations of Jews who were born in the most notorious of London's cholera-ridden quarters and have now moved to wealthier pastures. Old East Enders will tell you that the area's not what it was – and it's true, as it always has been. The East End is constantly changing, as newly arrived **immigrants** assimilate and move out.

The East End's first immigrants were French Protestant Huguenots, fleeing from religious persecution in the late seventeenth century – the word "refugee", from the French, *réfugié*, entered the English language at this time. With anti-Catholic feeling running high in London, they were welcomed with open arms by all except the apprentice weavers whose work they undercut, and who attacked them on more than one occasion. Some settled in Soho, but the vast majority settled in Spitalfields, where they were operating an estimated twelve thousand silk looms by the end of the eighteenth century.

Within three generations the Huguenots were entirely assimilated, and the Irish became the new immigrant population. Traditionally engaged in the construction industry, Irish labourers, ironically enough, played a major role in building the area's many eighteenth-century

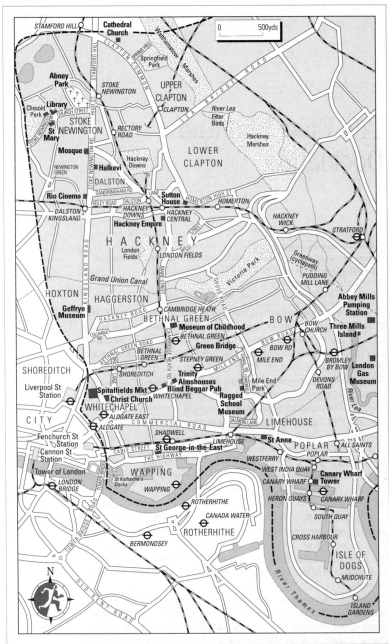

© crown copyright

Protestant churches, and later were crucial to the development of the docks. The perceived threat of cheap Irish labour provoked riots in 1736 and 1769, and their Catholicism made them easy targets during the Gordon Riots of 1780. Famine and disease in Ireland brought thousands more Irish over to London in the 1840s and 1850s, but it was the influx of Jews escaping pogroms in eastern Europe and Russia that defined the character of the East End in the second half of the nineteenth century.

Jewish immigration prompted the Bishop of Stepney to complain in 1901 that his churches were "left like islands in the midst of an alien sea". The same year, the MP for Stepney helped found the first organized racist movement in the East End, the British Brothers League, whose ideology foreshadowed that of the later British Union of Fascists, led by Sir Oswald Mosley and famously defeated at the Battle of Cable Street (see p.269).

The area's Jewish population has now dispersed throughout London, though the East End remains at the bottom of the pile. Even the millions poured into the **DOCKLANDS** development during the last two decades have failed to make much impression on the perennial unemployment and housing problems of the local population. Unfortunately, racism is still rife in the East End, and is directed, for the most part, against the extensive Bengali community, who came here from the poor rural area of Sylhet in Bangladesh in the 1960s and 1970s.

Most visitors to the East End come for its famous Sunday **markets**: **Petticoat Lane** for clothing, **Brick Lane** for bric-a-brac (and wonderful curry houses), **Columbia Road** for flowers and plants and **Spitalfields** for crafts and organic food. These apart, the area is not an obvious place for sightseeing, and certainly no beauty spot – Victorian slum clearances, Hitler's bombs and postwar tower blocks have left large areas looking pretty bleak. However, there are several specific points of interest, including a trio of **Hawksmoor churches**, three **museums** open to the public free of charge, and, further south in Wapping and Limehouse, a pleasant **riverside walk**. **Bengali culture** makes a strong impression in "Bangla Town", around Brick Lane, and, last but not least, there's the vast **Docklands** redevelopment, which has to be seen to be believed.

It's best to visit Whitechapel and Spitalfields on a Sunday, when the markets are buzzing (see p.268). By contrast, Docklands is ghostly quiet after dark and at weekends.

Whitechapel and beyond

The districts of **Whitechapel**, and in particular **Spitalfields**, within sight of the sleek tower blocks of the financial sector, represent the old heart of the East End, where the French Huguenots settled in the seventeenth century, where the Jewish community was at its strongest in the late nineteenth century, and where today's Bengali community eats, sleeps, works and prays. If you visit just one area in the East End, it should be this zone, which preserves mementos from

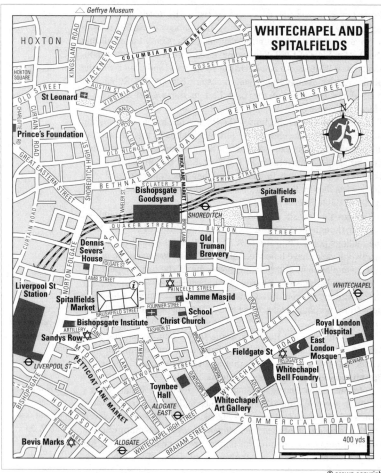

each wave of immigration. The further east you venture, the more the bomb damage inflicted on the area during World War II becomes apparent, and the more dispersed the sights, such as they are, become.

Petticoat Lane market runs throughout the week, but is at its busiest on Sundays.

Petticoat Lane (Middlesex Street)

Heavily bombed in the Blitz, **Petticoat Lane** is not one of London's prettiest streets, but it is, without a doubt, one of London's most famous street markets, and has been trading every Sunday for more than two hundred years. The Huguenots sold the petticoats that gave the market and the street its name; the authorities renamed it

London's Jews

It was William the Conqueror who invited the first **Jews** to England in
1066. Regarded with suspicion because of their financial astuteness, yet
exploited for these very qualities, Jews were banned from numerous pro-
fessions, but actively encouraged to pursue others, such as moneylending
(Christians themselves were banned from lending money for interest, a
practice considered sinful by the Church). After a period of relatively
peaceful coexistence and prosperity, the small community increasingly
found itself under attack, milked by successive monarchs and forced eventually to wear the distinguishing mark of the *tabula* on their clothing. The
Crusades whipped up further religious intolerance, the worst recorded
incident taking place in 1189, when thirty Jews were killed by a mob during the coronation of Richard I. In 1278 Edward I imprisoned the entire
community of around six hundred Jews on a charge of "clipping coins",
executing 267 and expelling the rest.

For nearly four centuries thereafter, Judaism was outlawed in England.
Sephardic (ie Spanish or Portuguese) Jews fleeing the Inquisition began
arriving from 1540 onwards, though they had to become, or pretend to be,
Christians until 1656, when Oliver Cromwell granted Jews the right to
meet privately and worship in their own homes. The Jews who arrived
immediately following this **Readmission** were in the main wealthy merchants, bankers and other businessmen. In contrast to conditions in the
rest of Europe, Jews in London were self-governing and subject to the
same restrictions as all other religious dissenters and foreigners. As a beacon of tolerance and economic prosperity, London quickly attracted further Jewish immigration by poorer Sephardi families and, increasingly,
Ashkenazi settlers from eastern and central Europe.

*London's two
Jewish
museums are
covered on
p.393 and
p.415.*

By far the largest influx of **Ashkenazi Jews** arrived after fleeing
pogroms that followed the assassination of Tsar Alexander II in 1881. The
more fortunate were met by relatives at the Irongate Stairs by Tower
Bridge; the rest were left to the mercy of the boarding-house keepers or,
after 1885, found shelter in the Jewish Temporary Shelter in Leman Street
(later moved to Mansell Street). They found work in the sweatshops of the
East End: cabinetmaking, shoemaking and, of course, tailoring – by 1901,
over 45 percent of London's Jews worked in the garment industry.

Perhaps the greatest moment in Jewish East End history was the **Battle
of Cable Street**, which took place on October 4, 1936, when Sir Oswald
Mosley and 3000 of his black-shirted fascists attempted to march through
the East End. More than twice that number of police tried to clear the way
for Mosley with baton charges and mounted patrols, but they were met
with a barrage of bricks and stones from some 100,000 East Enders chant-
ing the slogan of the Spanish Republicans: "*No pasaran*" (They shall not
pass). Barriers were erected along Cable Street and eventually the police
chief halted the march – and another East End legend was born. A mural
on the side of the old Shadwell town hall on Cable Street commemorates
the event.

After World War II, more and more Jews moved out to the suburbs of
north London, where the largest Orthodox Jewish communities are now to
be found in Golders Green (p.413) and Stamford Hill (p.284). The East
End Jewish population, which had peaked at around 130,000 in 1914, was
soon reduced to a handful of Jewish businesses.

*The nearest
tubes are
Liverpool
Street, Aldgate
and Aldgate
East.*

Middlesex Street in 1830 to avoid the mention of ladies' underwear (though the original name has stuck) and tried to prevent Sunday trading here until it was finally sanctioned by law in 1936. In the Victorian era the market grew into one of the largest in London, and by the turn of the century it stood at the heart of the Jewish East End, a "stronghold of hard-sell Judaism . . . into which no missionary dared to set foot", according to novelist Israel Zangwill. Nowadays, the kosher takeaway joint *Macabi* is the only high-profile Jewish business, but with over a thousand stalls on a Sunday, run mostly by Bengalis and Cockneys, this is still the city's number one cheap clothes market. A smaller lunchtime version runs throughout the week (though not on Saturdays) on neighbouring Wentworth Street.

To the north of Petticoat Lane are further reminders of the old Jewish community: the **Soup Kitchen for the Jewish Poor**, on Brune Street, which opened in 1902 and finally closed in 1992 (the undulating stone lettering is still clearly visible); the Jewish Free School, which functioned on the corner of Frying Pan Alley from 1821 to 1939, and boasted 4300 pupils at the turn of the century, making it the largest school in the country; and the **Sandys Row synagogue**, which now struggles to maintain a *minyan* (the minimum of ten male adults needed to perform a service).

The network of narrow streets around Sandys Row is fascinating to walk around – unique survivors that give a strong impression of the old East End. From Sandys Row, walk down Artillery Passage, a mixture of Bengali shops and new, City-type businesses, and on into **Artillery Row**, which boasts a superb eighteenth-century Huguenot shopfront at no. 56. Incidentally, the ballistic connection dates from the reign of Henry VIII, when the Royal Artillery used to hold gunnery practice here.

Old Spitalfields Market and around

*Tower Hamlets
information
centre is at 18
Lamb Street,
on the corner
of the market;
Mon, Tues,
Thurs & Fri
9.30am–
1.30pm &
2.30–4.30pm,
Wed 9.30am–
1pm, Sun
11.30am–
2.30pm; ☎020
/7364 4970.*

To the north of Petticoat Lane lies **Old Spitalfields Market**, once the capital's premier wholesale fruit and vegetable market. The old fruiterers' shops can still be seen throughout the area, though they closed down after the market moved out to Stratford in 1991. Even the strange-looking red-brick and green-gabled **market hall** building itself is now under threat from redevelopment (*www.spitalfields .co.uk*) – or at least half of it is. The gabled eastern half, built in 1893 by rags-to-riches speculator Robert Horner, is a listed building, and looks safe for the moment, but the current plan is to demolish the western half, which was added in the 1920s. A final decision has yet to be made, and in the meantime, the place remains a popular mix of shops, workshops, cafés, restaurants, stalls and five-a-side football pitches. It's quiet during the week, but absolutely mobbed for the Sunday market, which specializes in organic food, along with clothes and jewellery. If demolition plans go ahead, it looks likely that the shops will be relocated in the Bishopsgate Goodsyard (see p.273).

The dominant architectural presence in Spitalfields, facing the market halls, is **Christ Church**, built between 1714 and 1729 to a characteristically bold design by Nicholas Hawksmoor. Best viewed from Brushfield Street, the church's main features are its huge 225-foot-high broach spire and giant Tuscan portico, raised on steps and shaped like a Venetian window (a central arched opening flanked by two smaller rectangles), a motif repeated in the tower and doors. For thirty years the church lay derelict and under threat of demolition, but a £4 million restoration programme has returned it to something like its former glory. Inside, the church is a forest of giant columned bays, with a lion and a unicorn playing peekaboo on the top of the chancel beam and, opposite, London's largest Georgian organ.

Whitechapel and beyond

Christ Church is open Mon–Fri noon–2.30pm. Its seasonal concerts are among the finest in the capital.

The church hall, next door, was host in spring 1888 to meetings of the **Bryant & May match girls**, who personified the Dickensian stereotype of the downtrodden East End girl. Some 672 of them went on strike against their miserable wages and work conditions, which gave no protection against "phossy jaw", a deterioration of the jaw-bone caused by prolonged exposure to yellow phosphorus. Feminist Annie Besant organized a strike committee and galvanized public opinion, and within a fortnight the firm had backed down.

An outstanding feature of the Spitalfields area is its early Georgian terraced housing. First occupied by Huguenot silk-weavers and merchants, many of the houses in the streets around the market retain their weaving attics, identifiable by their long windows. The best examples are to be seen on **Fournier Street**, most of which have been restored over the last few decades by a fairly well-heeled wave of immigrants – a mix of artists, academics and, latterly, City workers.

Brick Lane and beyond

Crossing the eastern end of Fournier Street, **Brick Lane**, as its name suggests, was once the main location for the brick kilns

---

18 Folgate Street

You can, on occasion, visit **18 Folgate Street**, to the north of the market, home of the American Dennis Severs until his death in 1999. Severs created a theatrical experience which he described as "passing through a frame into a painting". The house is entirely candle-lit and log-fired, and decked out as it would have been over the course of the last two hundred years ago. Visitors are free to explore the ten rooms, and are left with the distinct impression that someone has literally just popped out. The house cat prowls, there is the smell of food, and the sound of horses' hooves on the cobbled street outside. "The Experience" takes place on the first Sunday of the month between 2pm and 5pm (admission £7); on the Monday following the first Sunday, the candlelit "Silent Night" takes place (April–Sept 8–11pm; Oct–March 6–9pm; £12). It's advisable to book ahead for the Monday evenings (☎020/7247 4013).

Whitechapel and beyond

Brick Lane has some of the best curry houses in London (see p.528), while for snacks there's a 24-hour bagel bakery at the Bethnal Green Road end.

which helped rebuild the City after the Great Fire. At the turn of the nineteenth century, many of the streets around here were 100 per-cent Jewish, making this the high street of the ghetto – nowadays, Brick Lane lies at the heart of the Bengali community, who first began to settle here in the 1960s. In the following decade, Brick Lane emerged as a kind of "front line" of defence against racist attacks on the community. The most publicized eruption of vio-lence occurred during a Sunday market in the summer of 1978, when 150 National Front skinheads went on the rampage smashing Bengali shop windows. The counter-demonstrations on subsequent Sundays succeeded in temporarily driving the NF out of Brick Lane. The relative lull of the 1980s was shattered in the early 1990s, when the extreme-right British National Party staged fur-ther confrontations at the Sunday market. Since then, there has been a nail-bomb attack by a lone racist, and continuing racist attacks. A further threat to the community are the developers who are moving steadily eastwards, eyeing up properties that are just a few minutes' walk from the City.

Bangla Town

The southern half of Brick Lane is the central focus of what is increasingly referred to as "**Bangla Town**". Here, bright-coloured sari fabrics line the clothes-shop windows, the heavy beat of bhangra music emanates from music shops and passing cars, and the smell of spices wafts from the numerous Bangladeshi cafés and restaurants, ranging from the new minimalist-style *Café Naz*, at no. 46, to the old-style *Café Bangla* at 128a, with its Lady Di Bollywood mural. For the outsider, it's a compelling scene, glimpsed en route to a cheap curry house; hidden behind this facade, though, are over-crowded flats and sweatshops that would not look out of place in Victorian times.

The changing ethnic make-up of this part of Brick Lane is most clearly illustrated in the **Jamme Masjid** (Great Mosque) on the cor-ner of Fournier Street. Established in 1743 as a Huguenot church, it became a Wesleyan chapel in 1809, the ultra-Orthodox Spitalfields Great Synagogue in 1897, and since 1976 has served as the main mosque for the area. A little further north is another example of the changing face of Brick Lane: **Christ Church primary school**, still nominally affiliated to the Church of England, though the vast major-ity of its pupils are Muslim; a hundred years ago they were mainly Jewish, as the Star of David on one of the drainpipes testifies. If you want to dig a bit deeper into the old Jewish presence here, try to arrange to see the wonderfully evocative disused **synagogue** hidden behind the Georgian facade of **19 Princelet Street**, built by Polish Jews in the 1860s (call ahead on ☎020/7247 0971), and a central theme in Rachel Lichtenstein and Iain Sinclair's book *Rodinsky's Room*.

The Old Truman Brewery

A red-brick chimney halfway up Brick Lane heralds the **Old Truman Brewery** (*www.trumanbrewery.com*), which is now a multimedia centre for music, fashion, art and IT. The brewery itself was founded in 1666, and was the largest in the world at the end of the nineteenth century, but closed down in 1989. It always acted as a kind of frontier post between the immigrant population to the south and the mostly white population to the north; redeveloped, it now forms the hub of Brick Lane's new creative enclave. You can pop into the brewery's popular *Vibe Bar* (*www.vibe-bar.co.uk*), which offers free Internet access, or head round the corner into **Dray's Lane**, where the old stables have been turned into shops for designers and artists, with snappy names like eatmyhandbagbitch.

Another new development worth keeping an eye out for is the **Bishopsgate Goodsyard**, a vast brick-vaulted space underneath the railway arches, to the north, that looks set to complement the Old Truman Brewery. Once a major freight depot, the goodsyard is currently being used as a venue for art exhibitions, but will eventually be turned over to shops, workshops and possibly a leisure centre. Watch this space.

Brick Lane and Columbia Road markets

North of the brewery and railway, among the cheap leather shops and bagel bakeries, are the streets that serve as the venue for **Brick Lane's Sunday market** of bric-a-brac. Its nucleus is the crossroads of Brick Lane and Cheshire Street; the further east you go down Cheshire Street, the tattier the stalls and the dodgier the deals; the further west you go down Sclater Street and beyond into Bethnal Green Road, the more desperate the stalls and cheaper the prices. The bulk of the action goes on in the morning, so get there early.

The East End is particularly richly endowed with city farms – for more details, see p.632.

Many people combine a visit with a browse round the lively Sunday **flower and plant market**, to the north, amid the small-scale Victorian terraces of **Columbia Road**. As well as seeds, bulbs, potted plants and cut flowers from the stalls, you can also buy every kind of gardening accessory from the chi-chi shops that line the street, listen to a busker or two and keep yourself sustained with bagels, cakes and coffee. Columbia Road's open-air flower market is the descendant of the market that once occupied a huge cathedralesque Gothic-Revival building financed in 1869 by Baroness Burdett-Coutts, who was appalled at the dishonesty of Cockney costermongers. The Archbishop of Canterbury and the Duke of Wellington were present at the grand opening, but the high-handed philanthropy behind the scheme – the great hall was daubed with uplifting inscriptions such as "Speak everyman truth with his neighbour" – was resented by the traders; the market flopped and was handed back to the baroness within five years, after which it was let out as workshops and finally pulled down in 1960.

In the nineteenth century, the streets between Columbia Road and Bethnal Green Road formed one of the East End's most notorious slum areas, known as "Old Nichol" or "Jago". On its northern fringe was – in the words of Engels – a "stagnant lake of thickened putrefying matter" which gave off "bubbles of pestilential exhalation". Poverty and disease were the distinguishing features of this slum, cleared away in the 1890s to make way for London's first big municipal housing development, the **Boundary Street Estate**, conceived by the newly formed London County Council. More people were displaced than were rehoused, and few of the original inhabitants could afford the new rents, but the five-storey blocks, centred around the raised garden and bandstand of **Arnold Circus**, became a model for municipal projects throughout Europe. To the modern eye, the rather gloomy red brickwork makes the estate look more like a slum than an ideal home.

The nearest tube is Aldgate East.

Whitechapel Road

Whitechapel Road – as Whitechapel High Street and the Mile End Road are collectively known – is still the East End's main street, shared by all the many races who live in the borough of Tower Hamlets. The East End institution that draws in more outsiders than any other is the **Whitechapel Art Gallery**, a little further up the High Street in a beautiful crenellated 1899 Arts and Crafts building by Charles Harrison Townsend, architect of the similarly audacious Horniman Museum (p.427). The gallery puts on some of London's most innovative exhibitions of contemporary art, as well as hosting the biennial Whitechapel Open, a chance for local artists to get their work shown to a wider audience; it also has a pleasant café overlooking Angel Alley.

Whitechapel Art Gallery is open Tues & Thurs–Sun 11am–5pm, Wed 11am–8pm; free; ☎020/7522 7888; www .whitechapel .org.

Like the library adjoining it, the gallery was founded by one of the East End's many Victorian philanthropists, **Samuel Barnett**, who was vicar in the worst parish in Whitechapel in the 1870s. His motives may have been dubious – "the principle of our work is that we aim at decreasing not suffering but sin" he once claimed – but the legacy of his good works is still discernible. Another of Canon Barnett's enduring foundations was **Toynbee Hall**, founded in 1884 as a residence for Oxbridge volunteers who wished to do social and educational work in the East End. The original nineteenth-century hall survives in a modern courtyard just off Commercial Street.

Barnett's wife, Henrietta, went as far as to propose moving into one of the infamous thieves' dens and brothels to the north of Toynbee Hall. Barnett put his foot down at the suggestion, but he helped set up the East End Dwellings Company, a scheme providing housing for the poor. The Rothschilds followed suit and founded the **Four Per Cent Dwellings Company**, which guaranteed a four percent dividend for the wealthy investors who backed it. The original arch of the latter scheme survives above the entrance to the modern

The Whitechapel murders

In the space of just eight weeks between August and November 1888, five prostitutes were stabbed to death in and around Whitechapel; all were found with their innards removed. Few of the letters received by the press and police, which purported to come from the murderer, are thought to have been genuine (including the one which coined the nickname **Jack the Ripper**), and the murderer's identity remains a mystery to this day. At the time, it was assumed by many that he was a Jew, probably a *shochet* (a ritual slaughterman), since the mutilations were obviously carried out with some skill. The theory gained ground when the fourth victim was discovered outside the predominantly Jewish Working Men's Club in Berner Street, and for a while it was dangerous for Jews to walk the streets at night for fear of reprisals.

Ripperologists have trawled through the little evidence there is to produce numerous other suspects, none of whom can be positively proven guilty. The most celebrated suspect is the Duke of Clarence, eldest son of Edward VII; an easy if improbable target, since he was involved in a scandal involving a male brothel and was a well-known homosexual. Other famous suspects include a scholarly cousin of Virginia Woolf, who, it was rumoured, had had an affair with Clarence, and was later committed to an asylum in 1892, and the painter Walter Sickert, who exhibited an unhealthy fascination with the murders during his lifetime. Equally fanciful are the likes of George Chapman, alias Severin Klosowski, a Polish immigrant who poisoned his wife and was hanged for the crime in 1903, and Dr Pedachenko, a junior surgeon from Russia with transvestite leanings who was allegedly sent over by the tsarist secret police to show up the defects in the British police system. The man who usually tops the lists, however, was a cricket-playing barrister named Druitt whose body was found floating in the Thames some weeks after the last murder, though, as usual, there is no evidence linking him with any of the murders.

The one positive outcome of the murders was that they focused the attention of the rest of London on the squalor of the East End. Philanthropist Samuel Barnett, for one, used the media attention to press for improved housing, streetlighting and policing to combat crime and poverty in the area. Today, the murders continue to be exploited in gory, misogynous detail by the likes of Madame Tussaud's, the London Dungeon and the *Ten Bells* pub on Commercial Road, near where the Ripper's first victim was found, which has a painted board detailing each of the victims and where their bodies were found.

---

red-brick Flower and Dean estate, to the north of Wentworth Street, which now stands in its place.

The most visible symbol of the new Muslim presence in the East End is the Saudi-financed **East London Mosque**, an enormous red-brick building, a short walk up Whitechapel Road from the art gallery; it stands in marked contrast to the tiny Great Synagogue, dating from 1899, which stands behind the mosque in Fieldgate Street. Neither of these buildings is open to the public, but you can pay a quick visit to the small exhibition in the nearby **Whitechapel Bell Foundry** (Mon–Fri 8am–5pm), part of which occupies the short

Guided tours of Whitechapel Bell Foundry take place Sat 10am; £7. You need to book in advance on ☎020/7247 2599.

*Whitechapel
Market is open
Mon–Wed, Fri
& Sat 8.30am–
5.30pm, Thurs
8.30am–1pm.*

terrace of Georgian houses on the corner of Fieldgate Street. Big Ben, the Liberty Bell, the Bow Bells and numerous English church bells (including those of Westminster Abbey) all hail from the foundry, established here in 1738.

Past Vallance Road, the street widens at the beginning of the daily **Whitechapel Market**, once one of the largest hay markets in London, now given over to the retail of everything from nectarines to net curtains, and including a large number of stalls catering for the Bengali and Somali communities. At the turn of the century, this was where casual workers used to gather to be selected for work in the local sweatshops, earning it the Yiddish nickname *Hazer Mark*, or "pig market". Nearby, on the other side of Vallance Road, stood the Pavilion Theatre, one of several East End theatres that used to put on Yiddish shows for the thousands of newly arrived Jews. Raucous and irreverent, Yiddish theatre was frowned upon by the Anglicized Jews, the *Jewish Chronicle* stating that Yiddish was "a language we should be the last to encourage any efforts to preserve". The sole reminder of those days is the Edward VII monument at the centre of the market, erected by the local Jewish community in 1911.

Anarchists in the East End

Founded in 1886, the **Freedom Press** (Mon–Fri 10.30am–6pm, Sat 11am–5pm), a small anarchist bookshop and printing press in Angel Alley, by the side of the Whitechapel Art Gallery, is the lone survivor of an East End tradition of radical politics that reached its height at the end of the nineteenth century. East End anarchism found a strong following among the Jewish community especially, and supporters of the *Arbeter Fraint* newspaper staged atheistic demonstrations outside Orthodox synagogues on the Sabbath, as well as making other gestures like ostentatiously smoking and eating ham sandwiches. In 1907, delegates to the Fifth Congress of the Russian Social Democratic Labour Party staged a meeting on the corner of Fulbourne Street attended by Lenin, Stalin, Trotsky, Gorky and Litvinov, and the Jubilee Street Anarchist Club later loaned £1700 to the Bolsheviks (paid back in full by the Soviet government after the revolution).

The event for which the anarchists are best remembered, however, is the **Siege of Sidney Street**, which took place in January 1911. The first gun battle occurred after a routine police enquiry at the back of a jeweller's on Houndsditch, and left one Russian anarchist and three policemen dead. Over the next few weeks, all but three of the anarchist gang were arrested; following a tip-off, they themselves were eventually cornered in a building on Sidney Street. A further gun battle ensued: a detachment of Scots Guards and two cannons were deployed, and the Home Secretary, Winston Churchill, arrived on the scene to give orders. By lunchtime the house was in flames, leaving two charred bodies in the burnt-out shell. However, the ringleader, nicknamed Peter the Painter, vanished without trace, to join the likes of Jack the Ripper as an East End legend.

It was on the Mile End Road that Joseph Merrick, better known as the **"Elephant Man"**, was discovered in a freak show by Dr Treves, and subsequently admitted as a patient to the **Royal London Hospital** on Whitechapel Road. He remained there, on show as a medical freak, viewed by the likes of Princess Alexandra, for four years until his death in 1890, at the age of just 27. The hospital still owns his skeleton (it's not on public display), despite an offer of several million pounds from Michael Jackson. There's a small section on Merrick in the **Hospital Museum**, housed beside the red-brick church of St Augustine with St Philip's (now the medical college library) on Newark Street. The museum also covers the history of the hospital and of nursing and medicine in general, with another section on Edith Cavell, who trained here before assisting Allied soldiers to escape from occupied Belgium; she was eventually arrested and shot by the Germans in 1915.

Whitechapel and beyond

Hospital Museum is open Mon–Fri 10am–4.30pm; free; ☎020 /7377 7608.

Just before the point where Whitechapel Road turns into Mile End Road stands the handsome gabled entrance to the former Albion Brewery (now a health centre), where the first bottled brown ale was produced in 1899. Next door lies the **Blind Beggar**, the East End's most famous pub since March 8, 1966, when Ronnie Kray walked into the crowded bar and shot gangland rival George Cornell for calling him a "fat poof". This murder spelt the end of the infamous Kray Twins, Ronnie and Reggie, both of whom were sentenced to life imprisonment, though their well-publicized gifts to local charities created a Robin Hood image that still persists in these parts of town.

Mile End Road

On Saturdays, the Whitechapel market extends beyond Cambridge Heath Road into the **Mile End Road**, the first section of which is known as the **Mile End Waste**. It's punctuated at one end by a bust, and at the other by a more dramatic statue, of the most famous of all the East End philanthropists, **William Booth**. It was here one late June evening in 1865 that Booth, moved by the sight of the crowds at the pubs and gin palaces, made his first impromptu public speech. Later on he set up a tent on Vallance Road and began in earnest the missionary work which eventually led to the foundation of the quasi-military Salvation Army in 1878. In contrast to many Victorian philanthropists, Booth never accepted the divisive concept of the deserving and undeserving poor – "if a man was poor, he was deserving". Booth preached a simple message of "Heaven in East London for everyone", railing against the laissez-faire economic policies of his era, while at the same time attending to the immediate demands of the poor, setting up soup kitchens and founding hostels, which, by the time of his death in 1912, had spread right across the globe.

William Booth is buried in Abney Park Cemetery; see p.284. The Salvation Army Heritage Centre is on Judd Street; see p.189.

Another East End philanthropist, **Frederick Charrington**, used to try his best to steer the local inhabitants away from their sinful ways at this very spot. Heir to the wealthy brewery, Charrington was, rather surprisingly, a tireless temperance campaigner, who in 1886 established a vast Assembly Hall on the Mile End Waste, capable of seating 5000, with a Coffee Palace and a "pure" book salon. He tried unsuccessfully to close down the neighbouring music hall by marching up and down outside with sandwich boards reading "The Wages of Sin is Death" and, more effectively, used to keep vigil outside brothels, threatening to publish the names of those who entered. The Assembly Hall was also used for some of the most famous political meetings of the era: the Bryant & May match girl strikers (see p.271), Eleanor Marx and anarchist Prince Kropotkin, who spoke out against racist trade union resolutions, and in support of the 1912 dock strikers.

There are two unusual architectural features worth mentioning on the Waste. The biggest surprise is the **Trinity Almshouses**, a quaint courtyard of cottages with a central chapel, built in 1695 for "Twenty-eight decay'd Masters and Commanders and the widows of such", and rebuilt after World War II as a home for the disabled. Further up, on the same side of the street, stands a large Neoclassical former department store, sporting a central domed tower, its facade sliced in two by a small two-storey shop that used to belong to a Jewish watchmaker called **Spiegelhalter**. This architectural oddity is the result of a dispute between Spiegelhalter and his affluent Gentile neighbour, Thomas Wickham, who was forced to build his new store around the watchmaker's shop after he refused to be bought out.

Stepney and Bow

*The nearest
tube is
Bromley-
by-Bow.*

Stepney, to the east of Whitechapel, was the site of Edward I's second parliament in 1299, but by Victorian times it was one of the most miserable and crowded districts in the East End. It was here that the first "Ragged School" for the poor was established in 1865 by Dr Barnardo, and today, the museum dedicated to the philanthropist is the area's principal sight. Close by the museum is the **Mile End Park** (*www.mileendpark.co.uk*), a park created from bomb sites which has recently had millions spent on it. The park certainly looks better for all its relandscaping, and now sports a remarkable "green bridge", designed by Piers Gough, which takes the park (complete with ten trees, a footpath and a cycle track) over the busy Mile End Road.

Further east still lies **Bow**, fringed by the River Lea, along which there developed a milling industry in medieval times. By the second half of the nineteenth century, the East End's relentless expansion had engulfed Bow, which became notorious for its slums and factories, among them the infamous Bryant & May match factory. This was the constituency of George Lansbury, who famously resigned his seat in 1912, in order to fight (and, as it turned out, lose) a by-election on the issue of women's suffrage. The following year, Sylvia Pankhurst moved to Bow and set up her radical East London Federation of Suffragettes (ELFS), holding frequent meetings in Victoria Park.

Ragged School Museum

Wed & Thurs 10am–5pm, first Sun of month 2–5pm; free; ☎020/8980 6405; *www.ics-london.co.uk/rsm*. Mile End tube.

To the south of the Mile End Road, on the bombed-out remains of Copperfield Road, the **Ragged School Museum** occupies a Victorian canalside warehouse. Accommodating more than one thousand pupils from 1877 to 1908, this was the largest of London's numerous Ragged Schools, institutions that provided free education and two free meals daily to children with no means to pay the penny a week charged by most Victorian schools. This particular Ragged School was just one of innumerable projects set up by the East End's most irrepressible philanthropist, the diminutive and devout **Dr Thomas Barnardo**, whose tireless work for the children of the East End is the subject of the ground-floor exhibition. Upstairs, there's a reconstructed Victorian schoolroom, where period-dressed teachers, cane in hand, take today's schoolkids through the rigours of a Victorian lesson. On the top floor you can learn to make a rag rug and take part in wash day; there are also further displays on the nearby docks and local sweatshops. There are plans to expand and renovate more of the building in the future.

Three Mills Island

The most remarkable vestige of Bow's past is the eighteenth-century architectural ensemble on **Three Mills Island**, an artificial island in the River Lea. Despite its name, there are now only two mills remaining, the most distinctive of which is the Clock Mill, with its conical oasts – kilns used to dry out grain – and its pretty white clock tower. Opposite stands the recently restored **House Mill** (May–Oct Sun 2–4pm; £2; ☎020/8980 4626), built in 1776 and now open for guided tours, which take you through the milling process and allow you to see the surviving mill wheels which were driven by the tidal flows from the nearby River Thames. On the first Sunday of the month, from March to December, the mill is open from 11am to coincide with the craft market that takes place on the island. Beyond the mills are later gin-distillery buildings, many of which have been converted into film studios, which you can occasionally visit on guided tours (call ☎020/7377 1154 for more details).

Visible to the northeast of the island is the brand new **Abbey Mills Pumping Station**, sporting a gleaming metal pitched roof, and, adjacent, its much more famous Victorian predecessor, a glorious Gothic-Italianate edifice nicknamed the "Cathedral of Sewage". The latter was built in the 1860s by Joseph Bazalgette and Edwin Cooper, and was originally flanked by two twin chimneys decorated in Moorish style, which were sadly demolished during World War II. Tours of this fantastic building are occasionally possible; call Thames Water on ☎020/8983 1121 for details. To the southeast of Three Mills stand seven ornate, Grade II-listed wrought-iron

*The London
Gas Museum is
open Mon–Fri
9am–4pm;
free; ☎020
/7538 4982.*

Victorian gas holders, built on the site of a rocket factory set up in the 1820s by William Congreve. If the gas holders quicken your pulse, phone ahead and make an appointment to visit the nearby London Gas Museum, on Twelve Trees Crescent, which boasts the world's largest collection of gas appliances.

Bethnal Green Museum of Childhood

Daily except Fri 10am–5.50pm; free; ☎020/8983 5200; *www.vam.ac.uk*. Bethnal Green tube.

The Bethnal Green Museum of Childhood, a branch of the V&A, is situated just across Cambridge Heath Road from Bethnal Green tube station. The elegant, open-plan wrought-iron hall was, in fact, part of the original V&A building, and was transported here from South Kensington in the late 1860s in order to bring art to the East End. The emphasis has changed since those pioneering days, and although the wide range of exhibits means that there's something here for everyone from the age of 3 to 93, the museum's most frequent visitors are children, and special kids' events are put on here at weekends and during school holidays.

The ground floor is best known for its unique collection of antique dolls' houses dating back to 1673. Among the jumble of curiosities on the mezzanine are model trains, cars and rocking horses, wooden models of carcass-hung nineteenth-century butcher's shops, and dolls made from found objects (including a little man made from a lobster claw). Remember to take a pile of 20p pieces with you to work the handful of automata – Wallace the Lion gobbling up Albert is always a firm favourite. Elsewhere, there are puppets and a vast doll collection including Native American representations of spirits, stylish flapper dolls carried by the bright young things of the Jazz Age and a macabre Shirley Temple. The top gallery is given over to excellent temporary exhibitions, as well as antique accessories for babies – from eighteenth-century baby-walkers to Victorian metal nipple shields – and educational toys for toddlers.

Victoria Park

The Victorians were firm believers in parks as instruments of moral and physical improvement, particularly for the working classes. As "sanitary reformer" William Farr maintained, the use of parks would "diminish deaths by several thousands and add years to the lives of the entire population". Victoria Park, London's first public park (as opposed to royal park), was opened in the heart of the East End in 1845, after a local MP presented Queen Victoria with a petition of 30,000 signatures.

The only large open space in the area, "Viccy Park" immediately became a favourite spot for political rallies: Chartists congregated here in their thousands in 1848, George Bernard Shaw and William

Morris addressed demonstrations, and Suffragette supporters of the ELFS gathered here, under the leadership of Sylvia Pankhurst, who was described by Shaw as "the most ungovernable, self-interested, blindly and deadly wilful little rapscallion-condottiera that ever imposed itself on the infra-red end of the revolutionary spectrum". In 1978, over 100,000 people turned up for an open-air concert organized by the Anti-Nazi League.

The park is divided in two unequal halves by Grove Road. The smaller western section has the largest and nicest of the lakes, complete with a fully functioning fountain, not to mention the **Dogs of Alcibiades**, two snarling sculpted beasts presented by Lady Regnart in 1912. The much larger eastern section contains an extraordinarily lavish Gothic-cum-Moorish **drinking fountain**, decorated with oversized cherubs and paid for by Baroness Burdett-Coutts in 1861 – it hasn't functioned for years. The Old **English Garden**, laid out to the northeast of the fountain, provides a pleasant haven of flowers and shrubs; next door there's a small deer enclosure, and a much larger children's playground; the park's **model boat club** meets on most Sunday mornings. To get to the park by public transport, take bus #277 from Mile End tube or bus #8 from Liverpool Street tube.

Hackney

The borough of **Hackney** stretches from the thoroughly East End districts of Hoxton, **Shoreditch** and **Dalston** in the south, to the north London suburbs of Stoke Newington and **Stamford Hill**. With the city's largest Afro-Caribbean community after Brixton, a sizeable Hasidic Jewish population and an even greater number of Turkish/Kurdish inhabitants, this is one of the most ethnically diverse of all London boroughs. It's hardly surprising, then, that the country's longest-serving black woman MP, Diane Abbott, has her constituency in Hackney, or that this was one of the infamous "loony left" councils of the 1980s that the Thatcherite press loved to hate. The fact that the borough has tourist signposts comes as a surprise to many visitors, yet Hackney repays selective visits: **Ridley Road** boasts one of London's most vibrant multi-ethnic markets, the red-brick Tudor mansion of **Sutton House** hides away on the fringes of Homerton, **Stoke Newington** is a haven of inexpensive Turkish and Indian restaurants and trendy laid-back cafés, and there are more **art galleries** (and resident artists) in enclaves like **Hoxton** than anywhere else in London.

Shoreditch and Hoxton

Until recently, **Shoreditch**, on the northeastern edge of the City, was a none-too-savoury slice of London, an unpleasant amalgam of wholesale clothes and shoe shops, striptease pubs and roaring traffic. It still is, in many ways, but over the last few years it has been colonized by, in the words of one journalist, "designers and architects and beautiful people with studs all over, mangled aubergine hair and me-and-my-genius portfolios". Moreover, it has been rejacketed: what was once Shoreditch is now **Hoxton**, previously a much smaller neighbourhood confined to the north of Old Street. Whatever its real name, the area is, in actual fact, rich in literary and artistic associations. It was here that James Burbage established the country's first public theatre – called simply the Theatre – in 1576 (he subsequently took it down and reassembled it on Bankside as the Globe). The area became something of an entertainment district, and the subject of a poem, written at the beginning of the seventeenth century, entitled *'Tis a mad world at Hogsdon*.

The geographical focus of the area's current transformation is **Hoxton Square**, a strange and not altogether happy mixture of light industrial units and artists' studios arranged around a leafy, formal square. Despite the lack of aesthetic charm, the area has become an increasingly fashionable place to live and work. The BFI's fancy new **Lux arts cinema** (see p.585), with a gallery and trendy bar and restaurant, is the most obvious new arrival, though several leading West End **art galleries** have opened up premises here since, among them Victoria Miro, Jay Jopling's White Cube and Sadie Coles' Hoxton House. Other than cruising the bars (listed on p.542), and art galleries (see p.590), there are no real sights as such, though you might want to take a peek at the **Prince's Foundation** (*www .princes-foundation.org*), the institute of architecture set up by Prince Charles, which has opened new headquarters on Charlotte Road. The Foundation runs courses on everything from building arts to Islamic calligraphy, and, inside, there's a gallery, a bookshop and, naturally, an organic café.

Geffrye Museum

Tues–Sat 10am–5pm, Sun noon–5pm; free; ☎020/7739 9893; *www .geffrye-museum.org.uk*. Bus #67, #149 or #242 from Liverpool Street tube.

In terms of conventional sights, Shoreditch has just one to offer: the **Geffrye Museum**, housed in a peaceful little enclave of eighteenth-century ironmongers' almshouses, set back from Kingsland Road. Sold to the London County Council in 1911 at a time when the East End furniture trade was centred on Shoreditch, the almshouses were converted into a museum for the "education of craftsmen". The Geffrye remains, essentially, a furniture museum, with the almshouses rigged out as period living rooms, ranging from the oak-panelled seventeenth century, through refined Georgian to cluttered Victorian. As you pass through the rooms, be sure to take time to admire the original central Georgian **chapel**, with its tiny Neoclassical apse and archetypal stone-coloured wood panelling;

round the back of the chapel, an enclosed balcony overlooking the garden serves as a coffee bar.

The museum has recently expanded considerably, with building of the fabulous **New Gallery Extension**, hidden behind the almshouses. Here, four new "snapshots in time" from the twentieth century have been added, beginning with an Edwardian drawing room in understated Arts and Crafts style, and finishing off with a minimalist 1990s loft conversion of the type you might well see in today's Hoxton or Clerkenwell. Also on this level, there's a room where you can play on the museum's CD-Rom, while on the lower ground floor, the Geffrye puts on excellent temporary exhibitions and houses a **Design Centre**, where predominantly local artists' work is displayed (and can be bought). Back upstairs, there's a very pleasant licensed **café-restaurant**, serving inexpensive British food. Out the back, a series of "outdoor rooms" show the transition in horticultural tastes from the seventeenth-century knot gardens to today's patio garden, culminating in a pungent walled **herb garden** (April–Oct only).

Dalston

In the late 1940s **Dalston** was the scene of battles between Mosley's fascists and supporters of the 43 Club, an organization set up by Jewish ex-servicemen to combat the resurgence of fascism in Britain. Nowadays the different communities of this area have a strong enough presence not to feel threatened by the residual white racism of the borough's southern fringes. The ethnic diversity of Dalston is best expressed in the **Ridley Road Market**: between the Cockney market-stallholders at the High Street end and the Turkish/Kurdish supermarket that marks the eastern end (its railings still displaying the Star of David from its original occupants), you'll find West Indian grocers and fishmongers, halal butchers and the Ridley Bagel Bakery, fairy lights announcing its fame as a 24-hour refuelling point. Across the road from the market at 41 Kingsland Rd is the *Shanghai* restaurant, formerly *F. Cooke*, London's best-preserved **eel and pie shop**, founded in 1862 by the Cooke family, its 1910 décor of tiles, marble and glass miraculously intact.

The nearest train station is Dalston Kingsland on the North London Line.

A little further north up Kingsland High Street stands Dalston's only remaining cinema, the Art Deco **Rio**, recently given a much-needed face-lift. In the good old days there were four cinemas on Kingsland (later, Stoke Newington) High Street alone – the northernmost of these, the Moorish Alhambra, has, by a judicious twist of fate, been turned into a mosque. The mosque lies at the heart of the local Turkish/Kurdish community, whose exclusively male cafés, named after Turkish football clubs, line the street. The various left-wing factions to which most of the community belong join together annually for London's largest May Day march, down the High Street, while the Kurdish New Year (April) is celebrated in grand style at

Halkevi, the Turkish/Kurdish community centre housed in a disused factory built by Simpson's of Piccadilly.

Stoke Newington

Stoke Newington is best reached on the #73 bus from Angel, King's Cross or Euston tubes, or on the train to Stoke Newington station from Liverpool Street.

Predominantly rural until the middle of the last century, **Stoke Newington** was something of a haven for Nonconformists, who were denied the right to live in the City. When Bunhill Fields (see p.238) became overcrowded, **Abney Park Cemetery**, to the north of Church Street, which feeds off west from the High Street, became the "Campo Santo of English non-Conformists", in the words of the 1903 brochure. The only really famous grave is that of William Booth, founder of the Salvation Army, by the Church Street entrance, but the romantically overrun cemetery was originally planted as an arboretum, and is now something of an inner-city wildlife reserve (not to mention a gay cruising area). If you want to know more about Abney Park, head for the **visitors' centre** (Mon–Fri 9.30am–4.30pm, Sun noon–3pm) housed in one of the Egyptian-style lodges at the main entrance to the east, at the very top of Stoke Newington High Street.

The most famous Dissenter to live in the village was **Daniel Defoe**, who wrote *Robinson Crusoe* in a house on the corner of what is now Defoe Road and Church Street; his gravestone is displayed in the local library opposite – stolen from Bunhill Fields in the 1870s, it was discovered in Southampton in 1940. The two local churches, both dedicated to St Mary, reflect the changes wrought on this area: the sixteenth-century village church stands on the north side of the road, opposite a more urbane structure built by George Gilbert Scott in the 1850s, with a spire that outreached all others in London in its day. This pair mark the entrance to **Clissold Park**, founded in 1899 and centred on a porticoed mansion that was built in 1790 as a country house for the Quaker Hoare banking family, and which now contains an inexpensive vegetarian café. The clay pits dug to make bricks for the house serve as duck ponds, and are used by a wide variety of birds, terrapins, hens, goats and even deer. To the north, you can just make out the bizarre quasi-medieval turrets and towers of the Stoke Newington pumping station, built in 1856, closed in 1946 and redesigned in the 1990s by Nicholas Grimshaw as an indoor rock-climbing centre called **The Castle**.

Church Street and the High Street are great for cheap ethnic eating, with several Turkish charcoal grills and South Indian vegetarian places.

Clissold Park is open daily 7.30am–dusk.

Stamford Hill and the Lea Valley

Stamford Hill, the area northeast of Clissold Park, is home to a tight-knit Yiddish-speaking community of ultra-orthodox Hasidic Jews, one of Hackney's oldest immigrant populations. The Hasidic movement originated in Poland in the eighteenth century under the charismatic leadership of Baal Shem Tov (often known as the "Besht"), who preached a message of joyful worship, influenced by the mystical teachings of the cabbala. The movement has since rigidified into a much more conservative one, made up of individual dynasties, each of which follows a particular *rebbe* or wise man, whose authority is passed from father to son. As such, they have more in common with their brethren in New York and Israel than they do with their Gentile neighbours or even other less orthodox Anglo-Jews. The most celebrated aspect of Stamford Hill's Hasidic Jews is their attire – frock coats, white stockings and elaborate headgear – which derives from that worn by the Polish nobility of the period.

The shops on Dunsmure Road and Stamford Hill are where the Hasidim buy their kosher goods, and on Sundays, large families take the air at Clissold Park, and at **Springfield Park**, a beautifully landscaped space opened in 1905 "to change the habits of the people and to keep them out of the public houses". To get to the park from Stamford Hill, walk across the remnants of Clapton Common, and down Spring Hill. En route, be sure to check out the four winged beasts (characters from Revelation) who sit around the base of the spire of the **Cathedral Church of the Good Shepherd**, on the corner of Rookwood Road. Six thousand people gathered outside the church in September 1902 to throw rotten tomatoes at the womanizing local vicar who had declared himself the Second Messiah. The park itself boasts an attractive **hothouse** (daily 11am–2.30pm) near the entrance, and an awesome view east across the Lea Valley. The best café is the one down by the River Lea marina, in the park's northernmost tip.

On the other side of the Lea lie the **Walthamstow Marshes**, a valuable stretch of wetland that's alive with bumble bees and warblers in the summer. If you follow the river southwards, you will eventually reach the **Middlesex Filter Beds**, originally built in 1852 on the south side of Lea Bridge Road. Today, drained of most of their water, the filter beds serve as a nature reserve – in the summer check out the noisy frogs in the pond by the main culvert. Beyond, to the south, lie the **Hackney Marshes**, best known as the venue for Sunday League football matches.

The Filter Beds are open Sat & Sun: Easter–Sept 10am–6pm; Oct–Easter 10am–4pm; summer holidays also Mon–Fri 10am–5pm; free.

Mare Street

The old parish of **Hackney** (as opposed to the modern borough) lies to the east of Dalston, around **Mare Street**, whose main claim to fame is the ornate terracotta **Hackney Empire**, one of the last surviving variety theatres in London, built in typically extravagant style by Frank Mitcham in 1899. Next door, set back from Mare Street, stands **Hackney Town Hall**, built in the 1930s in a very restrained Art Deco style. Opposite stands the equally austere Central Hall, built between the wars as a two-thousand-seater Methodist meeting place, and now a new music venue called, rather mysteriously, *Ocean*. The old library, meanwhile, has moved next door, and is due to be reopened in 2001 as a "technology and learning centre", which will

The nearest train station is Hackney Central on the North London Line.

also house the reborn **Hackney Museum** (☎020/8986 6914; *www.hackney.gov.uk/hackneymuseum*). Visitors to the latter used to be able to view Marc Bolan's leather hat from *Born to Boogie* (Bolan was born in Stoke Newington), but will now have to make do with the Anglo-Saxon log boat and eighteenth-century fire engine, instead. On the north side of the railway bridge, Mare Street is still discernibly a village high street, overlooked by the dumpy fifteenth-century tower of the former parish church of **St Augustine**.

Sutton House

House: Feb–Nov Wed & Sun 11.30am–5.30pm; NT; £2.10. Café and art gallery: open all year Wed–Sun 11.30am–5pm; ☎020/8986 2264. Hackney Central train station.

Head east across the graveyard behind the tower and down the Georgian terrace of Sutton Place and you'll come to **Sutton House**, Hackney's prime tourist attraction. In the mid-1980s this mansion was just one of the borough's numerous squats; since then it has been painstakingly restored to a condition that does some justice to its status as the oldest house in the entire East End. Built in 1535 for Ralph Sadleir, a rising star at the court of Henry VIII, it takes its name from Thomas Sutton, founder of Charterhouse (p.213), who lived in an adjacent building. (He is buried at Charterhouse, minus his entrails, which you've just walked over in the graveyard.) The National Trust have done their best to adapt to unfamiliar surroundings and have preserved not just the exquisite Elizabethan "linenfold" wooden panelling, but also a mural left by squatters in 1986. In addition to the rambling complex of period rooms, the house puts on contemporary art exhibitions and classical concerts, and even runs a veggie café.

Docklands

The architectural embodiment of Thatcherism, a symbol of 1980s smash-and-grab culture according to its critics or a blueprint for inner-city regeneration to its free-market supporters – the **Docklands** redevelopment continues to provoke extreme reactions. Despite its catch-all name, however, Docklands is far from homogeneous. Canary Wharf, with its Manhattan-style skyscrapers, is only its most visible landmark, and is by no means typical of the area; pseudo-warehouse architecture, industrial-estate sheds, left-over council housing and yuppie flats in a whole variety of styles are more indicative. **Wapping**, the most easily accessible district, has retained and restored much of its old Victorian warehouse architecture, as has Bermondsey on the south bank (covered in Chapter 9), while the Royal Docks, further east and yet to be fully redeveloped, remain a relatively undisturbed wasteland. Travelling through on the overhead railway, Docklands comes over as a fascinating open-air design museum, not a place one would choose to live or work – most people stationed here see it as a bleak business-oriented outpost – but a spectacular sight nevertheless.

A brief history

From the sixteenth century onwards the **Port of London** was the key to the city's wealth. The "legal quays" – roughly the area between London Bridge and the Tower – were crowded with as many as 1400 seagoing vessels forced to wait for up to six weeks to be unloaded, with some 3500 cutters, barges and punts jostling between their hulls. It was chiefly to relieve such congestion, which worsened with the increased trade from the Empire, that from 1802 onwards London began to construct the largest enclosed cargo-dock system in the world. Each dock was surrounded by forty-foot-high walls, patrolled by its own police force and geared towards a specific type of cargo. Casual dockers gathered at the dock gates each morning for the "call-on", a human scrummage to get selected for work. This mayhem was only stopped after World War II, when the Dock Labour Scheme was introduced, and by then it was too late. Since the mid-nineteenth century, competition from the railways had been eroding the river traffic, and with the development of container ships and the movement of the port to Tilbury in the 1960s, the city docks began to close.

For almost two decades, the quaysides and the surrounding areas were a wasteland, beset with high unemployment and a dwindling population, until the **London Docklands Development Corporation** (LDDC) was set up in 1981, with its unfortunate slogan of "Looks like Venice, works like New York". One hundred percent tax relief on capital expenditure, no business rates for ten years and freedom from planning controls were just some of the ploys used to kickstart the project, and were the conditions which allowed Canary Wharf and the Enterprise Zone to be built. No one thought the old docks could ever be rejuvenated; the LDDC, on the other hand, predicted a resident population of over 100,000 and a working population twice that, all by the end of the millennium.

In 1998, the LDDC was wound up, having achieved more than many thought possible, and less than it had promised. It's certainly easy to criticize its approach: ad hoc planning; a lack of basic amenities, of open green spaces, of civic architecture or public buildings, and of consultation with the local community. The real shot in the foot, though, was the government's negligence over basic public transport infrastructure: the Tories refused to foot more than half the bill and the new **Jubilee Line Extension** only opened late in 1999 (see p.40). In the end, however, the market-led bubble was burst by the economic reality of the early 1990s recession: the developers went bust and virtually all construction was halted. The economic situation has since picked up, and construction is once more continuing apace, but the end result is still destined to be, as one critic aptly put it, "a chain of highly polarized ghettos epitomizing the gulf between the rich and poor, home-owner and tenant".

Visiting Docklands

Nothing will convey to the stranger a better idea of the vast activity and stupendous wealth of London than a visit to these warehouses, filled to overflowing with interminable stores of every kind of foreign and colonial products; to these enormous vaults, with their apparently inexhaustible quantities of wine; and to these extensive quays and landing-stages, cumbered with huge stacks of hides, heaps of bales, and long rows of casks . . . Those who wish to taste the wines must procure a tasting-order from a wine merchant. Ladies are not admitted after 1pm. Visitors should be on their guard against insidious effects of "tasting" in the heavy, vinous atmosphere.

Baedeker 1905

Sadly, visits to the docks are no longer so intoxicating. You can, however, view Docklands from a distance on one of the pleasure boats that course up and down the Thames (see p.44). For a close-up you should take the driverless, overhead **Docklands Light Railway** (DLR; ☎020/7363 9700; *www.dlr.co.uk*), which sets off from Bank in the City, or from Tower Gateway, close to Tower Hill tube and the Tower of London. Travelcards are valid on the DLR, or you can get an off-peak Docklander ticket for £3.10, giving you unlimited travel on the network after 9.30am Monday to Friday and all day on the weekend. Tour guides give a free running commentary on DLR trains that set off on the hour from Tower Gateway (daily 10am–2pm), and Bank (Mon–Fri 11am–2pm, Sat & Sun 10am–2pm) as far as Crossharbour. The DLR now extends south of the river to Lewisham via Greenwich, but if you're heading for Greenwich, and fancy taking a boat back into town, it might be worth considering a Sail & Rail ticket (£7.80), which gives you an off-peak Docklander ticket, plus a boat trip between Greenwich and Westminster piers. Alternatively, *Remember that* you can now walk from Wapping to Canary Wharf along, or close to, *Canary Wharf* the river bank, by following the Thames Path; there are also several *is office-land:* pedestrian bridges linking the different quays around Canary Wharf. *dead in the* Further south, however, walking is not much fun, and you're proba-*evenings and* bly best off exploring by bike – unfortunately bicycles are not *at weekends.* allowed on the DLR, though they are allowed to use the Greenwich Foot Tunnel.

Wapping

Once famous for its boatyards and its 36 riverside pubs (a handful of which remain), **Wapping** changed forever with the construction of the enclosed docks in the early nineteenth century. Cut off from the

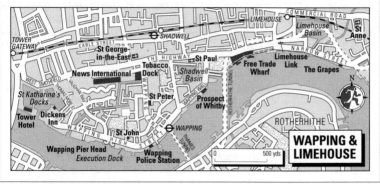

© crown copyright

rest of the East End by the high walls of the docks, its inhabitants crowded into insanitary housing, the area became notorious for its thieves, attracted by the opportunities of rolling-drunk sailors and poorly guarded warehouses. With the demise of the docks, Wapping became an early victim of gentrification, though restoration and renovation of existing property rather than demolition and redevelopment has been the rule. Thus something of Wapping's Victorian atmosphere has been preserved, and as it lies just a short walk east of the Tower, this is one of the easiest parts of Docklands to explore.

St Katharine's Docks

St Katharine's Docks were built in the late 1820s immediately east of the Tower – in the process some 11,300 people were made homeless, and the medieval foundations of St Katharine's hospital and church were demolished. Having specialized in luxury goods such as ivory, spices, carpets and cigars, St Katharine's became the first phase of the Docklands renewal scheme in the early 1970s, when it was turned into a luxury yacht marina by Taylor Woodrow, who also raised the phenomenally ugly *Tower Hotel* and the neo-warehouse World Trade Centre (now defunct), which backs onto Tower Bridge Road. Taylor Woodrow's latest offering is **Europe House**, which is currently being rebuilt in the docks' northeastern corner to a typically high-tech design by Richard Rogers.

The nearest tube is Tower Hill; the nearest DLR station is Tower Gateway.

St Katharine's proximity to the Tower makes it a popular destination for tour groups and wandering tourists, who tend to head for the *Dickens Inn*. Originally an eighteenth-century timber-framed brewery warehouse, situated several hundred yards east of its present site, much of the current building, including the weatherboarding and galleries, is, in fact, fake. Roughly at the centre of the docks is the ugly **Coronarium chapel** (now a coffee shop), built for Queen Elizabeth II's silver jubilee, and situated as near as possible to the old church of St Katharine's, which was itself owned by the Queen.

The docks' redeeming qualities are the old swing bridges (including a Telford footbridge from 1828), the boats themselves, often beautiful old sailing ships, and the **Ivory House** warehouse, with its clock tower, at the centre of the three basins. Built in 1854, at its peak this warehouse received over 200 tons of ivory annually (that's 4000 dead elephants), plus hippopotamus and walrus teeth and even mammoth tusks from Siberia. On the corner of West Smithfield and Thomas More Street, you can also see the remains of the original dock wall, and the main entrance to the former London Docks, with two Neoclassical Customs and Excise offices from 1805.

News International to St George-in-the-East

The nearest tube and DLR station is Shadwell.

East down the busy Highway lies the headquarters of Rupert Murdoch's **News International**, a complex known colloquially as "**Fortress Wapping**", on account of its high walls, barbed wire and security cameras. Murdoch was one of the first capitalist barons to give Docklands his blessing, sacking his entire workforce of printers and journalists when he moved his newspapers – the *Times*, *Sunday Times*, *Sun* and *News of the World* – out here in 1986, thus sparking one of the most bitter trade union disputes of the Thatcher era. Mounted police engaged in violent skirmishes with protesters for nearly a year – no prizes for guessing who won.

Close by stands **Tobacco Dock**, a huge warehouse built in 1814 and initially used to store tobacco and wine (sheepskin, cork and molasses came later). A fascinating combination of timber and early cast-iron framing, it was converted into a kitsch shopping complex in the late 1980s by postmodernist Terry Farrell. Dreams of the East End's answer to Covent Garden, though, evaporated within a matter of years, and the latest attempt to establish discount factory shopping here has also failed. The locals would probably prefer another superstore, while the rest of London wouldn't dream of coming out here.

St George-in-the-East is open daily 9am–5pm; ☎020/7481 1345.

Tobacco Dock is a short distance south of Nicholas Hawksmoor's church of **St George-in-the-East**, built in 1726 on the north side of the busy Highway. As bold as any of Hawksmoor's buildings, it boasts four "pepperpot" towers above the nave and a hulking west-end tower topped by an octagonal lantern. Within, it comes as something of a shock to find a miniature modern church squatting in the nave, but that's all the parish could come up with following the devastation of the Blitz.

A pleasant feature of this area, which will take you effortlessly back to Wapping High Street, is the tree-lined **canal walk** which begins south of Tobacco Dock, where two "pirate" sailing ships are moored. The canal – all that remains of the huge Western Dock that once stood here – runs through the Dutch-gabled Thomas More housing estate, some of which is now council housing, a policy change which prompted legal action against the developers from some of the yuppie residents.

Wapping High Street to Shadwell Basin

If you arrive on **Wapping High Street** expecting the usual parade of shops, you're in for a big surprise. Traditionally, the business of Wapping took place on the river; thus tall brick-built warehouses, most now tastefully converted into yuppie flats, line the Thames side of the street, while to the north, in a stark contrast typical of Docklands, lie the council estates of the older residents. Deterred by the private riverside housing developments in between, few tourists make it out here, but it's only a ten-minute walk from St Katharine's Dock, and well worth the effort.

The nearest tube is Wapping.

Walk about five minutes along the High Street and you'll come to **Wapping Pier Head**, the former entrance to the London Docks, now grassed over but still flanked by grand curvaceous Regency terraces built for the officials of the Dock Company. Further east is the unusual Neo-Gothic former tea warehouse, **Oliver's Wharf**, a trail-blazing apartment conversion from 1972, with a couple of preserved overhead gangways crossing the High Street just beyond. You'll also find one of the few surviving stairs down to the river beside the nearby *Town of Ramsgate* pub.

Just east of the Pier Head, up Scandrett Street is the eighteenth-century **St John's Old School**, with Coade stone figures of a boy and girl set in niches. It and its Victorian extension, which features wonderfully exuberant stone swags over the doorways, have been sensitively converted into housing, as has the adjacent parish church, whose tower alone survived the bombs of World War II. Back on the High Street, **Wapping Police Station** is the headquarters of the world's oldest uniformed police force, the marine police, founded in the 1790s and now a subdivision of the Met. Down by the riverside here, at the low-water mark, was **Execution Dock**, where pirates and mutineers were hanged in the conventional manner, after which their bodies were left until three tides had washed over them. The most famous felon to perish here was Captain Kidd, pirate-catcher-turned-pirate, hanged in 1701; the last victims were executed for murder and mutiny in 1830.

If you don't want to continue east, you could take a short cut up Wapping Lane from Wapping tube station in order to get to Tobacco Dock (see above); en route, have a peek at **St Peter's Church**, a classic Victorian church with a mock-Tudor timber-framed ceiling and attractive red-brick patterning. Meanwhile, further east, along **Wapping Wall**, you'll find the finest collection of nineteenth-century warehouses left in the whole of Docklands, beginning with the gargantuan Metropolitan Wharf, its wrought-iron pulleys still clearly in evidence. At the far end of Wapping Wall is the ivy-clad red-brick **Pumping Station**, built in 1890s, and once chief supplier of hydraulic power to the whole of central London, powering the likes of the bascules of Tower Bridge.

Wapping has several old riverside taverns, most famously The Prospect of Whitby on Wapping Wall; see p.542.

Shadwell Basin, over the swing bridge to the north of the Pumping Station, is one of the last remaining stretches of water that

Docklands once comprised three interlocking docks, known simply as London Docks and first opened in 1805. Now a yachting and canoeing centre, it's enclosed on three sides by new housing finished off in primary reds and blues, a gimmicky touch characteristic of Docklands projects. Rising up majestically behind the houses to the north is **St Paul's Church** (closed except for services), the "sea captains' church", with a Baroque tower.

Limehouse

The nearest DLR stations are Limehouse and Westferry. East of Wapping, **Limehouse** was a major shipbuilding centre in the eighteenth and nineteenth centuries, hub of London's canal traffic and the site of the city's first Chinatown, a district sensationalized in Victorian newspapers and popular fiction as a warren of opium and gambling dens, viz Dickens: "Down by the docks the shabby undertaker's shop will bury you for next to nothing, after the Malay or Chinaman has stabbed you for nothing at all." Wartime bombing and postwar road schemes have all but obliterated Limehouse; the only remnants of the Chinese community are the street names.

If you're heading east from Wapping to Limehouse, you can avoid the Highway by taking the Thames Path, which passes below the Legoland ziggurat of **Free Trade Wharf**, a deplorable bit of specula-*There are a couple of good pubs on Narrow Street, by the river (see p.542).*tive apartment building, eventually bringing you out on **Narrow Street**, Limehouse's sleepy main thoroughfare. Just to the north is one of the playful postmodern portals of the mile-long Limehouse Link tunnel (rumoured to be the world's most expensive piece of road), whose strange sculpture, *Restless Dream*, by Zadok Ben-David, can be admired from the top of Spert Street.

East down Narrow Street, past the giant herring-gull sculpture, several excellent pubs and the entrance to the packed Limehouse Basin, stands Nicholas Hawksmoor's **St Anne's Church**, which was begun in 1714. Dominated by a gargantuan west tower, topped by an octagonal lantern and boasting the highest church clock in London, the interior was badly damaged by fire in 1850, though it does contain a superb organ built for the Great Exhibition the following year. In the graveyard Hawksmoor erected a strange pyramidal structure carved with Masonic symbols, now hopelessly eroded; opposite is a war memorial with relief panels depicting the horrors of trench warfare.

While you're here it's worth walking down Newell Street, to the west, which retains several Georgian houses, while Three Colt Street, to the east, is home to the wonderful Art Nouveau **Limehouse Church Institute**, now converted into private flats. Back on the waterfront, the Thames Path continues inexorably towards the Isle of Dogs. A new pedestrian bridge carries the path over the entrance to the tidal inlet of **Limekiln Dock**, overlooked to the north by a picturesque gaggle of listed warehouses, and to the south by the gargantuan Dundee Wharf development, which sports a huge grey free-standing pylon of balconies, which can be accessed by the neighbouring flats. Beyond lies the Egyptian-style development that houses the *Four Seasons Hotel*. The Thames Path will eventually plough its way right round to Island Gardens, but for now it stops just past Cascades (see below).

Isle of Dogs

The Thames begins a dramatic horseshoe bend at Limehouse, thus creating the **Isle of Dogs**, a marshy peninsula on which cattle were once fattened for City banquets. The unusual name has prompted various theories as to its origin, from dead dogs washed up on the shore to old royal kennels, though the most plausible is that it's a corruption of the Flemish *dijk* (dyke). In 1802 the peninsula became an island, when a canal was cut to form London's first enclosed trade dock, built to accommodate rum and sugar from the West Indies. With the opening of the Millwall Docks further south, the population rose to 21,000 by the turn of the century. The demise of the docks was slow in coming, but rapid in its conclusion: 8000 jobs in 1975 dwindled to just 600 following the closure of both docks in 1980.

Without doubt, the Isle of Dogs is the geographical and ideological heart of the new Docklands, which reaches its apotheosis in Canary Wharf, home to Britain's tallest building and the busiest bit of the Isle of Dogs. The rest of the island remains surreally lifeless, an uneasy mix of drab high-rises, council estates, warehouses converted into expensive apartments and a lot of new architecture – some of it startling, some of it crass. The area's long-term residents see the new developments as a threat rather than a blessing, and a section of them have voiced their discontent in the not too distant past by voting for the far-right British National Party.

Canary Wharf

Canary Wharf – the strip of land in the middle of the former West India Docks, previously a destination for rum and mahogany, later tomatoes and bananas (from the Canary Islands, hence the name) – is one of the most cohesive and complete Dockland complexes. To the east of the landmark tower, several more skyscrapers have recently gone up, as have the final pieces in the jigsaw around **Westferry Circus**, the double-decker roundabout park at the western end of the tree-lined West India Avenue. The largest project undertaken by a single developer in Europe, Canary Wharf ran into the ground in the early 1990s, but has since restarted with a vengeance. The Jubilee Line tube extension has finally arrived, with its station, and the nearby headquarters of Citibank, both designed by Norman Foster.

Canary Wharf has both a tube and a DLR station.

Canary Wharf's most famous building is Cesar Pelli's landmark tower, officially known as **One Canada Square**, but usually referred to as Canary Wharf Tower, which at 800ft is the highest building in

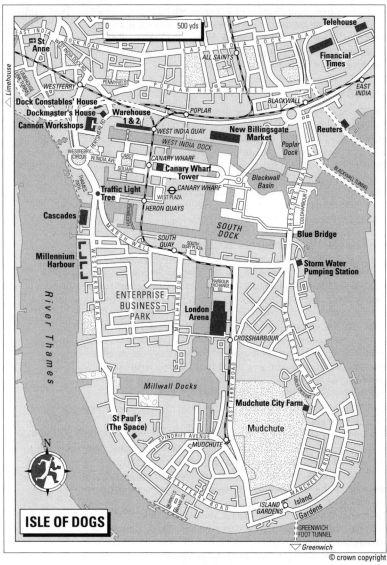

Labels on the map: Telehouse, Financial Times, St Anne, ALL SAINTS, EAST INDIA, Limehouse, WESTFERRY, PENNYFIELDS, POPLAR HIGH STREET, BLACKWALL, Dock Constables' House, Dockmaster's House, Warehouse 1 & 2, POPLAR, Cannon Workshops, WEST INDIA QUAY, New Billingsgate Market, Reuters, WESTFERRY CIRCUS, W.INDIA AVE, CABOT SQUARE, WEST INDIA DOCK, CANARY WHARF, Poplar Dock, BLACKWALL TUNNEL, Canary Wharf Tower, CANARY WHARF, Blackwall Basin, Traffic Light Tree, WEST PLAZA, HERON QUAYS, SOUTH DOCK, Cascades, SOUTH QUAY, SOUTH QUAY PLAZA, Blue Bridge, Millennium Harbour, Storm Water Pumping Station, HARBOUR EXCHANGE SQ, ENTERPRISE BUSINESS PARK, London Arena, River Thames, CROSSHARBOUR, Millwall Docks, Mudchute City Farm, St Paul's (The Space), Mudchute, SPINDRIFT AVENUE, MUDCHUTE, WESTFERRY ROAD, ISLAND GARDENS, Island Gardens, GREENWICH FOOT TUNNEL, Greenwich, ISLE OF DOGS

0   500 yds

© crown copyright

the country. The world's first skyscraper to be clad in stainless steel, it's an undeniably impressive sight, both from a distance (its flashing pinnacle is a feature of the horizon at numerous points in London – and out as far as Kent and Essex) and close up. Unless you work here, however – residents include the *Daily Telegraph*, *Daily Mirror* and *Independent* newspapers – there is no public access except to the marble atrium. The best view of the tower close up is from the forest of public clocks on West Plaza, to the south, outside Foster's sting ray-like entrance to the tube.

Arriving by DLR at Canary Wharf is quite spectacular, with the rail line cutting right through the middle of the office buildings, and arriving under a parabolic steel and glass canopy. The station platforms straddle a shopping mall: Cabot Square East features a glass-domed atrium through which you get a great view of Pelli's tower; Cabot Street West is nondescript but gives access to **Cabot Square** proper, centred on a graceful fountain.

West India Quay

From Fisherman's Walk, to the north side of Cabot Square, you can cross over a floodlit floating bridge to **West India Quay**, where the last surviving Georgian warehouses of the **West India Docks** have recently been converted into flats, and, on the ground floor, dockside bars and restaurants. To the west five floors of **Warehouse No. 1**, built in 1803 for storing rum, sugar, molasses, coffee and cotton, have been given over to the **Museum in Docklands** (☎020/7515 1162), scheduled to open in 2001. To the east, beyond the multi-story Horizon Building, is the striking tubular link between West India Quay and Poplar DLR stations and, beyond that, the **New Billingsgate Market**, a hangar-like building housing the fish market which moved here from the City in 1982 (see p.254).

The nearest DLR station is West India Quay.

Immediately to the west of the warehouses is the old entrance to the West India Docks, heralded by the **Ledger Building**, which sports a dinky Doric portico, and, round the corner, a splendidly pompous plaque from 1800. Opposite, across Hertsmere Road, stands a small, circular, domed building, the surviving one of two guardhouses which flanked the main entrance to the docks; behind it lies the docks' former cooperage, converted in the early 1980s into the **Cannon Workshops**.

To the northeast, behind the Ledger Building, are more little-known remnants of the old docks, among them the stately **Dockmaster's House**, built in 1809 as the Excise Office, later a pub, and now an Indian restaurant, with its smart white balustrade. Behind here, on Garford Street, there's a prim row of **Dock Constables' Cottages**, built in pairs in 1802, with the one for the sergeant slightly detached. Before you reach them, you'll pass **Grieg House**, a lovely yellow and red-brick building, built in 1903 as part of the Scandinavian Seamen's Temperance Home, with a little cupola and lovely exterior mouldings.

Heron Quays and beyond

Mackenzie Walk, on the south side of Cabot Square, is the best place to admire the view over to **Heron Quays**, the thin slip of quayside to the south of Canary Wharf. The modest, low-rise, Swedish-style

The nearest DLR station is Westferry.

clapboard buildings which occupy the western section were completed way back in 1986, and turned out to be fairly untypical of what was to follow in the rest of the Isle of Dogs. The roundabout to the west sports one of Docklands' more playful monuments: the **Traffic Light Tree**, which features a cluster of traffic signals all flashing madly – a strangely confusing sight for drivers after dark. Impossible to miss, to the southwest, is **Cascades**, a strange wedge of high-rise triangular apartments, erected by CZWG that has also become something of a Docklands landmark. Equally unavoidable is **Millennium Harbour**, whose weatherboarded top-floor penthouses jut out like air-traffic control towers.

A curved steel footbridge with leaning masts and cables links Heron Quays with **South Quay**, where rebuilding work continues more than five years after the IRA bomb which marked the end of the terrorist organization's eighteen-month-old ceasefire of the mid-1990s. If you follow dockside walk east from South Quay, you'll eventually reach the **Blue Bridge** that spans the entrance to the South Dock, and gives an unparalleled view of the Millennium Dome (see p.433). You can contemplate the view at more leisure from *The Gun*, an old pub on nearby **Coldharbour**, a street which still retains one or two early nineteenth-century buildings from old Docklands.

Mudchute, Island Gardens and around

Apart from Canary Wharf and its environs, the only other slice of the Isle of Dogs that repays exploration on foot is around Mudchute. The **Mudchute** itself is a large grassy expanse formed by silt dumped here after the dredging of the nearby Millwall Docks. In the northeastern corner of "The Muddie", as it's known locally, is **Mudchute Farm**, the largest and most rural of all the city farms, and a strange place from which to view Canary Wharf.

Mudchute Farm is open daily 8am–5pm; free (see p.632).

The DLR makes a slow descent to the new terminus at **Island Gardens**, before heading under the Thames to Greenwich (see p.428), and eventually to Lewisham. Island Gardens, though, is still the place to get out if you want to explore the 1902 **Greenwich Foot Tunnel** (open 24hr), or stand at Christopher Wren's favourite Thames-side spot, from which he could contemplate his masterpieces across the river, the Royal Naval College and the Royal Observatory.

If you'd rather explore a little more of Docklands, head west along the river or Westferry Road until you come to **Burrell's Wharf**, a residential development based around the industrial relics of the old Millwall Ironworks, built in the 1830s. The boiler-house chimney survives, as does the Italianate Plate House, where the steel plates for Isambard Kingdom Brunel's *Great Eastern* steamship were manufactured in the 1850s. Built at a cost of £1 million, the *Great Eastern* was the largest ship in the world at the time, but enjoyed a working life of just sixteen years as a passenger liner and cable layer. The timber piles of the ship's launching site can still be seen, a little further upstream from Burrell's Wharf.

Further up Westferry Road stands the Presbyterian church of **St Paul**, built in the 1850s for the Scottish shipbuilders working at Millwall Docks, and one of the few old churches to survive on the Isle of Dogs. Its Neo-Romanesque facade of blind stone arcading and polychrome brick patterning is remarkable, and has recently been restored and sensitively converted into an arts centre known as **The Space**, with the *Hubbub* café attached.

The Hubbub is open Mon–Fri 5–11pm, Sat 11am–11pm, Sun 11am–10.30pm.

Chapter 9

Lambeth and Southwark

I n Tudor and Stuart London, the chief reason for crossing the
Thames, to what is now **LAMBETH** and **SOUTHWARK**, was to
visit the disreputable Bankside entertainment district around the
south end of London Bridge. Four hundred years on, Londoners have
rediscovered the habit of heading for the South Bank, thanks to the
wealth of new attractions – with the charge led by the spectacular
London Eye and the mighty **Tate Modern** – that now pepper the
riverside from Lambeth Bridge to Tower Bridge and beyond. What's

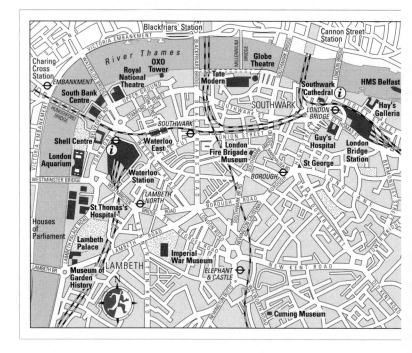

more, you can happily explore the whole area – predictably enough, it's been dubbed the "millennium mile" – on foot, free from the traffic noise and fumes that blight so much of central London.

Over the years, various attempts have been made at regenerating the South Bank, which was a grimy jungle of warehouses, slums and overhead railways for much of the last two centuries. In 1951, a slice of **Lambeth**'s riverside was used as a venue for the Festival of Britain, and the site eventually evolved into the **South Bank Centre** by the 1970s. More recently, **County Hall** has been slowly transformed into a massive leisure complex, with the London Eye towering over it; the British Film Institute have built a state-of-the-art **IMAX cinema**; and the distinctive **Oxo Tower** has been turned into flats, workshops and restaurants. In fact, it's the South Bank Centre itself that's now in most need of redevelopment.

An excellent Web site for the area, which gives a daily update of events taking place on the South Bank, is www.london-se1 .co.uk.

There are more sights downriver in **Southwark**, once the cradle of Elizabethan theatre, where a reconstruction of **Shakespeare's Globe Theatre** has been built in the shadow of the giant Tate Modern. At this point, the **Millennium Bridge**, central London's first new river crossing for over a century, provides a means of escape to the City and St Paul's. Alternatively. you can continue east, past **Vinopolis**, an excellent new museum devoted to wine, and the area's two maritime

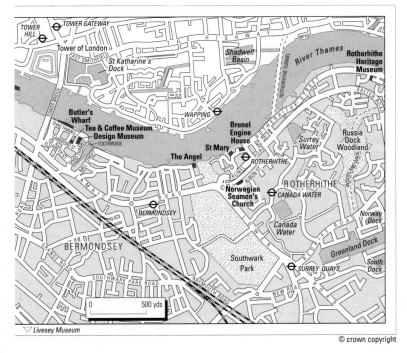

© crown copyright

sights – the wartime frigate **HMS Belfast** and a replica of the Tudor galleon, the **Golden Hinde** – to the likes of the ever-popular **London Dungeon** on Tooley Street.

Southwark also marks the beginning of the Docklands' south bank development around **Bermondsey**, which, though less well known than Canary Wharf, contains some interesting warehouse conversions, including a number of commercial art galleries and some of the developers' better stabs at new architecture. **Butler's Wharf**, in particular, is a thriving little warehouse development, centred on the excellent **Design Museum**. Further east, **Rotherhithe** clings onto its old seafaring identity despite the demise of the nearby docks and its subsequent new housing developments.

The South Bank

In 1951, the South Bank Exhibition, held on derelict land south of the Thames, formed the centrepiece of the nationwide **Festival of Britain**, an attempt to revive postwar morale by celebrating the centenary of the Great Exhibition (when Britain really did rule over half the world). The most striking features of the site were the ferris wheel (which has since returned to the South Bank as the London Eye), the saucer-shaped Dome of Discovery (inspiration for today's Millennium Dome) and the cigar-shaped Skylon tower. The great success of the festival provided the impetus for the eventual creation of the **South Bank Centre** (see below), though this failed to capture the imagination of the public in the same way. Instead, the South Bank Centre became London's much unloved culture bunker, a mess of "weather-stained concrete, rain-swept walkways, urine-soaked stairs", as one critic put it.

The nearest tube is Waterloo, but the best way to approach the South Bank is via Hungerford railway and foot bridge from Embankment or Charing Cross tube.

The South Bank Centre has very precise parameters, but when most Londoners talk about the South Bank, they're referring to a much wider area that includes the likes of **County Hall**, now home to the London Aquarium, Dalí Universe and Namco Station, plus several hotels and restaurants. Meanwhile, the area between the South Bank Centre and County Hall looks set to be redeveloped in the near future, once all the funding has been found. The idea, put forward by architect Rick Mather, is to expand and re-landscape the **Jubilee Gardens**, originally laid out during the Queen's silver jubilee in 1977, so that they slope upwards away from the river, and link up with the new **Hungerford footbridges**, which have recently been constructed on either side of the Hungerford railway bridge.

The South Bank Centre

The **South Bank Centre** (*www.sbc.org.uk*) reached its nadir in the 1980s, when its concrete undercroft and the neighbouring railway arches and "Bull Ring" subway became "**Cardboard City**", home to

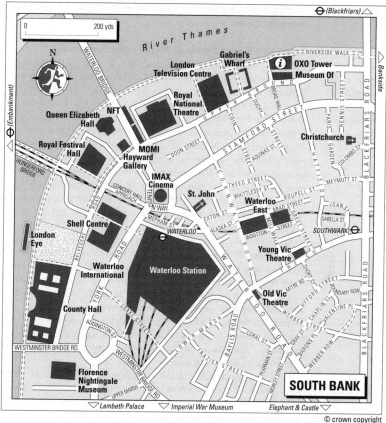

hundreds of homeless **people** sleeping out in cardboard boxes. The
population of Cardboard City peaked in the Thatcher years, when the
homeless were considered little more than people you had to step
over on the way to the opera (to paraphrase one of her housing ministers). The situation has improved, but shelter provided by the
South Bank looks likely to remain popular as long as homelessness
in London continues.

On the plus side, the South Bank Centre is currently under
inspired artistic direction and stands very much at the heart of the
capital's arts scene. Its unprepossessing appearance is softened,
too, by its riverside location, its avenue of trees, its fluttering banners, its occasional buskers and skateboarders and the second-
hand bookstalls and café outside the National Film Theatre. There
have been considerable improvements, too, such as better sign-
posting and plans of the area, to help punters get around. Further

redevelopment looks likely, too, as part of the overall plans described above.

From the Royal Festival Hall to the National

*For classical
concert details,
see Chapter 20.*

The only building left over from the 1951 Festival of Britain is the **Royal Festival Hall** (RFH), one of London's main concert venues. Uniquely, the auditorium is suspended above the open-plan foyer – its curved roof is clearly visible above the main body of the building.

*For theatre
details, see
Chapter 21.*

The interior furnishings are still appealingly 1950s, and will hopefully stay that way even after the current renovation programme. The English National Ballet puts on regular seasons here, and exhibitions and events in the foyer are generally excellent, making this one of the most pleasant South Bank buildings to visit. You also get a pleasant view from the terrace café across the Thames to (from right to left) the Shell-Mex building with its giant clock face, Terry Farrell's postmodern development above Charing Cross Station, and the stripy brickwork and pepper pots of Gilbert Scott's New Scotland Yard.

Architecturally, the most depressing part of the South Bank Centre is the **Queen Elizabeth Hall** (QEH) and the more intimate **Purcell Room**, which share the same foyer and are built in uncompromisingly brutalist 1960s style. These two look set to be either seriously redesigned or replaced when the centre is finally redeveloped. The **Hayward Gallery** (*www.hayward-gallery.org.uk*), which sits behind and on top of all this concrete garbage, is equally repellent from the outside – with the exception of its strange rooftop neon sculpture – but has an uncluttered gallery space that hosts major contemporary art exhibitions.

*The NFT is the
centre of the
London Film
Festival each
November (see
p.627).*

Tucked underneath Waterloo Bridge is the **National Film Theatre** (NFT), which screens London's most esoteric films – some 2000 of them each year – and hosts a variety of talks, lectures and mini-festivals. Straddling the underside of Waterloo Bridge, behind the NFT is the site of the popular, interactive **Museum of the Moving Image**, affectionately known as MOMI, which closed for major refurbishment in 1999. The plan is for the museum to reopen in 2002, but both the NFT and MOMI may, instead, move to new premises underneath the Jubilee Gardens, if the current redevelopment plans go ahead.

On the far side of the bridge, looking like a multistorey car park, is Denys Lasdun's **Royal National Theatre** (*www.nt-online.org*) – popularly known as "the National" or NT – an institution first mooted in 1848 but only finally realized in 1976. It contains three separate theatres: the large open-stage Olivier (named after the famous actor, who was also the theatre's first director), the more traditional Lyttelton and the Cottesloe studio theatre. Again, it tends to receive flak from architectural critics, though the theatres themselves are superb, and, in fairness to Lasdun, nobody told him that the concrete exterior would receive a zero maintenance budget. The National offers **backstage tours** around all three theatres (Mon–Sat 10.15am, 12.15 & 5.15pm; £4.25; ☎020/7452 3400) lasting about an hour.

Gabriel's Wharf and the OXO Tower

Beyond the National Theatre, the riverside promenade takes you past another Denys Lasdun building, London Television Centre offices and studios, bringing you eventually to **Gabriel's Wharf**, a laid-back collection of lock-up craft shops, brasseries and bars that has a small weekend craft market. It's a pleasant extension to the South Bank Centre's own, rather limited facilities, and one for which the Coin Street Community Builders must be thanked. With the population in this bomb-damaged stretch of the South Bank down from 50,000 at the beginning of the century to 4000 in the early 1970s, big commercial developers were keen to step in and build hotels and office blocks galore. They were successfully fought off, and instead the emphasis has been on projects that combine commercial and community interests.

Coin Street's most high-profile project has been the restoration of the landmark **OXO Tower**, an old power station that was converted into a meat-packing factory in the 1930s by Liebig Extract of Meat Company, best known in Britain as the makers of OXO stock cubes. To get round the local council's ban on illuminated advertisements, the company cleverly incorporated the letters into the windows of the main tower, and then illuminated them from within. The building now contains an information centre and contemporary art gallery on the ground floor, plus flats for local residents, sandwiched between a series of retail-workshops for contemporary designers on the first and second floors (Tues–Sun 11am–6pm), and a very swanky restaurant and brasserie on the top floor. To enjoy the view, however, you don't need to eat or drink here: you can simply take the lift to the eighth-floor **public viewing gallery** (daily until 10pm).

Coin Street information centre, on the ground floor of the OXO Tower, is open daily 11am–6pm; ☎020/7401 2255.

Funds are currently being sought to try and renovate the warehouse immediately behind the OXO Tower, known as the **Bargehouse**. It got its name way back in Tudor times, when the Royal Barge was stored here, and the plan is to turn the building into a Thames Discovery Centre. In the meantime, however, it's being used for a series of quirky, light-hearted, free exhibitions or temporary "museums": the Museum of Collections was followed by the Museum of Me and the Museum of Love – known collectively as the **Museum Of**.

Beyond the OXO Tower stands the Seacontainers House, a grotesque 1970s speculative hotel which never came about, now used as offices, and the similarly ugly **Doggett's Coat and Badge** pub. The latter is named after the rowing race from London Bridge to Chelsea, begun in 1715 by an Irish comedian called Thomas Doggett to celebrate the beginning of the Hanoverian dynasty. The race is still held every year in late July, and the winner gets to wear a

The Museum Of is open Wed–Sun noon–7pm; free; ☎020 /7401 2255.

comical red Hanoverian costume as his prize; for more information, see p.625.

IMAX and Waterloo Station

At the southern end of Waterloo Bridge, the eye-catching glass-drum of the high-tech **BFI London IMAX Cinema** rises up from the old "Bull Ring" underneath the roundabout. Boasting the largest screen in the country, it's definitely worth experiencing a 3D film here at least once, but as with all IMAX cinemas, it suffers from the fact that very few movies are shot on 70mm film.

A short walk along the river beyond Blackfriars Bridge will bring you to Bankside; see p.315.

Hidden away behind the Stalinist-looking Shell Centre (officially and poetically entitled the Downstream Building), is **Waterloo Station**, originally built in 1848, its grandiose Edwardian facade now lost behind the railway bridge on Mepham Street. Along the western edge of the old station is **Waterloo International**, the main arrival and departure point for Channel Tunnel trains. The extraordinarily long, curving platforms are only accessible for passengers about to embark, but you can view the station's snake-like, curving roof, designed by Nicholas Grimshaw, from the York Road and from the main station concourse. It was hailed as a major architectural success when it was first unveiled in 1993, but the glass panels have proved unable to withstand the heat, and look like they are going to have to be modified.

London Eye

Daily: April–Sept 9am–late evening; Oct–March 9am–5.30pm; £8.50; ☎0870/500 0600; *www.ba-londoneye.com*. Waterloo or Westminster tube.

South of the South Bank Centre proper, beside County Hall, is London's most prominent new landmark, the Millennium Wheel or **London Eye**, British Airways' magnificently graceful observation

The London Eye ticket office is in the northernmost riverside entrance to County Hall.

wheel which spins slowly and silently over the Thames. Designed by David Marks and Julia Barfield, and standing an incredible 443ft high, it's the largest observation wheel ever built, weighing over 2000 tonnes, yet as simple and delicate as a bicycle wheel. It's constantly in slow motion, which means a full-circle "flight" in one of its 32 pods should take around thirty minutes. That may seem a long time, though in fact it passes incredibly quickly; a "flight attendant" in each capsule will point out the major landmarks if you ask them. Not surprisingly, you can see right out to the very edge of the city, where the suburbs slip into the countryside – on a good day you can see as far out as Windsor – making the wheel one of the few places (apart from a plane window) from which London looks a manageable size. Due to the Eye's popularity, it is a bit risky to simply turn up and queue, as the pods may be booked solid. Instead, phone up and book in advance; on arrival, you'll still have to queue to be loaded on, but at least it'll only take twenty minutes maximum.

County Hall

The colonnaded crescent of **County Hall** is the only truly monumental building in this part of town. Designed to house the London County Council, it was completed in 1933 and enjoyed its greatest moment of fame as the headquarters of the GLC (Greater London Council), under the leadership of Ken Livingstone, or "Red Ken" as the Thatcherite press loved to call him. The Tories moved in swiftly, abolishing the GLC in 1986, and leaving London as the only European city without an elected authority. In May 2000, Livingstone had the last laugh when he was successfully elected to become the city's first mayor, and head of the new Greater London Authority (GLA), which will eventually be housed in a new building near Tower Bridge (see p.263).

County Hall, meanwhile, is now in the hands of a Japanese property company, and its vast floor space is home to, among other things, two hotels, several restaurants, a giant aquarium, a glorified amusement arcade called Namco Station, a museum devoted to Salvador Dalí, and the charity set up in the wake of Princess Diana's death. None of the slightly ad hoc attractions that have gravitated here is an absolute must, but they have certainly succeeded in pulling in the crowds, and there are more projects in the pipeline for the near future.

London Aquarium

Daily 10am–6pm or later; £8.50; ☎020/7967 8000; *www.londonaquarium .co.uk*. Westminster or Waterloo tube.

The basement of County Hall is now home to the **London Aquarium**, laid out across three floors. With some super-large tanks, and everything from dog-face puffers to piranhas, this is an attraction that's pretty much guaranteed to please younger kids. The Touchpool, where children can handle hermit crabs and starfish, and the Beach, where they can actually stroke the (non-sting) rays, are particularly popular. Impressive in scale, the aquarium is fairly conservative in design, though, with no walk-through tanks and only the very briefest of information on any of the fish. Ask at the main desk for the times of the daily presentations.

Dalí Universe

Daily 10am–6pm (later in the summer); £7; ☎020/7620 2420; *www .daliuniverse.com*. Westminster or Waterloo tube.

Three giant surrealist sculptures outside County Hall help to advertise the building's latest attraction, **Dalí Universe**, whose entrance lies between the London Eye box office and the London Aquarium. With two museums (in the US and Spain) already devoted to the Catalan artist, Salvador Dalí (1904–89), some might question the need for a third. On the other hand, Dalí's popularity shows no sign of waning, and as a supreme self-publicist himself – even his moustache was a work of art – he would definitely have approved of the project. The museum has certainly gone out of its way to appear as wacky as its star, but you can't help feeling that Dalí himself would have done something altogether more outrageous.

There's no denying Dalí was an accomplished and prolific artist, but you'll be disappointed if you come expecting to see his "greatest hits" – those are scattered across the globe. The majority of the works displayed here are little-known bronze and glass sculptures, and various drawings from the many illustrated books which he published, ranging from Ovid to the Marquis de Sade. That said, all his trademark themes are here: melting clocks, lots of Freudian allusions, phalluses and naked Venuses. Aside from these, there's one of the numerous Lobster Telephones, which Edward James commissioned for his London home, a copy of his famous Mae West lips sofa and the oil painting from the dream sequence in Hitchcock's movie *Spellbound*. You can even buy a Dalí print from the shop here from as little as £350.

Lambeth

South of Westminster Bridge, you leave the South Bank proper behind (and at the same time lose the crowds). Nevertheless, there are a few minor sights worth considering, such as **Lambeth Palace** or the **Museum of Garden History**. It's also from this stretch of the river bank that you get the best views of the Houses of Parliament. Inland, housed in a former lunatic asylum, lies London's most even-handed military museum, the **Imperial War Museum**, which now has a very moving permanent exhibition devoted to the Holocaust.

Florence Nightingale Museum

Mon–Fri 10am–5pm, Sat & Sun 11.30am–4.30pm; £4.80; ☎020/7620 0374; *www.florence-nightingale.co.uk*. Westminster or Waterloo tube.

On the south side of Westminster Bridge, a series of red-brick Victorian blocks and modern accretions make up **St Thomas's Hospital**, which moved here after being ejected from its Georgian premises in 1862, when the railway came sweeping through Southwark. At the northeastern corner of the hospital, on Lambeth Palace Road, is the **Florence Nightingale Museum**, celebrating the woman who revolutionized the nursing profession by establishing the first school of nursing at St Thomas's in 1859. The exhibition gives a strictly orthodox and uncritical account, but hits just the right note by putting the two years she spent in the Crimea in the context of a lifetime of tireless social campaigning. Exhibits include the white lantern that earned her the nickname "The Lady with the Lamp", a reconstruction of a Crimean military hospital ward and an overlong slide show.

Lambeth Palace

April–Oct Tues–Sat 10am–5pm; £6; ☎020/7898 1198; *www.archbishopof canterbury.org*. Westminster or Lambeth North tube.

A short walk south of St Thomas's stands **Lambeth Palace**, London residence of the archbishop of Canterbury since 1197. Opened to the general public for the first time ever in the new millennium, its hour-long guided tours have proved so popular that they look set to becoming a permanent feature; however, it's worth phoning ahead beforehand just to make sure. Sadly, the public don't get to enter via the imposing red-brick Tudor Gate, but through the Oil Gate to the north, up Lambeth Palace Road.

Parts of the newly renovated crypt chapel date back to the original medieval palace, but the most impressive room on the tour is, without doubt, the **Great Hall** (now the library), with its oak hammer-beam roof, built after the Restoration by Archbishop Juxon, who made his money in the slave trade, hence the negro heads on his coat of arms (and on the bookshelves). On display here are some of the library's most valuable books – a Gutenberg Bible, the Nuremberg Chronicle, "mad" King George III's medical reports – and the grubby leather gloves allegedly handed to Juxon by Charles I on the scaffold. Upstairs, the **Guard Room** boasts an even older, arch-braced timber roof from the fourteenth century, and is the room where Thomas More was brought for questioning before being sent to the Tower (and subsequently beheaded).

Lastly, you get to see the **palace chapel**, where the religious reformer and leader of the Lollards, John Wycliffe, was tried (for the second time) in 1378 for "propositions, clearly heretical and depraved". The door and window frames date back to Wycliffe's day, but the place is somewhat overwhelmed by the ceiling frescoes added in the 1980s, telling the story of the Church of England. Best of all is the fact that you can see the choir screen and stalls put there in the 1630s by Archbishop Laud, and later used as evidence against him at his trial (and execution) in 1645.

Museum of Garden History

March to mid-Dec daily except Sat 10.30am–5pm; free; ☎020/7261 1891. Westminster or Lambeth North tube.

Just to the south of Lambeth Palace is the Kentish ragstone church of **St Mary-at-Lambeth**, which retains its fourteenth-century tower but is otherwise a Victorian re-creation. Deconsecrated in 1972, the church now contains a café and an unpretentious little **Museum of Garden History**, which puts particular emphasis on John Tradescant, gardener to James I and Charles I. A tireless traveller in his search for new species, Tradescant set up a museum of curiosities known as "Tradescant's Ark" in Lambeth in 1629. Among the many exhibits were the "hand of a mermaid . . . a natural dragon,

---

London by Balloon

If the London Eye hasn't given you enough of a lift, you can go even high-er, to over 500ft (weather permitting), in the **hot air balloon** situated behind Vauxhall tube station in Spring Gardens. Though the Skyview Balloon (daily 10am–dusk; £9.95; *www.skyviewballooning.com*) is the largest tethered helium balloon in the world, it remains to be seen whether it can withstand the competition from the wheel.

---

above two inches long . . . blood that rained on the Isle of Wight . . . and the Passion of Christ carved very daintily on a plumstone". The less fantastical pieces formed the nucleus of Oxford's Ashmolean Museum, while here you can see a few scant examples: the toothed jaw of a sawfish, and a copy of king of Virginia, Powhatan's habit, embroidered with shells.

A section of the graveyard has been transformed into a small and visually subdued **seventeenth-century garden**, where two interest-ing sarcophagi lurk among the foliage. The first, which features a sculpted eternal flame, is the resting place of one-time Lambeth res-ident **Captain Bligh**, the commander of the *Bounty* in 1787 when it set off to transport breadfruit trees from Tahiti to the West Indies for transplanting. On the way home the crew mutinied and set Bligh and eighteen others adrift in a small open boat, with no map and few pro-visions. Using just a sextant, Bligh navigated the craft 3600 miles to the Indonesian island of Timor, a journey of 48 days. He later became governor of New South Wales, where his subjects once again rebelled, after which he was promoted to vice admiral. The **Tradescant memorial** is more unusual, depicting a seven-headed griffin contemplating a skull, and several crocodiles sifting through sundry ruins flanked by gnarled trees.

Imperial War Museum

Daily 10am–6pm; £5.50; free after 4.30pm; ☎020/7416 5000; *www.iwm .org.uk*. Lambeth North or Elephant and Castle tube.

From 1815 until 1930, the domed building at the east end of Lambeth Road was the infamous lunatic asylum of Bethlehem Royal Hospital, better known as **Bedlam**. (Charlie Chaplin's mother was among those confined here – the future comedian was born and spent a troubled childhood in nearby Kennington.) When the hospi-tal was moved to Beckenham on the southeast outskirts of London, the wings of the 700-foot-long facade were demolished, leaving just the central building, now home to the **Imperial War Museum**, by far the best military museum in the capital.

The treatment of the subject is impressively wide-ranging and fair-ly sober, with the main hall's militaristic display of guns, tanks, fight-er planes and a giant V-2 rocket offset by the lower-ground-floor array of documents and images attesting to the human damage of the last century of war. Less enlightening is the disappointingly uncritical Secret War gallery on the first floor, pandering to the popular fascination with the clandestine activities of MI5, MI6 and the SOE, and with an unrealistically glowing account of the SAS operations in the Gulf War.

In addition to the static displays, a good deal of stagecraft is used to convey the misery of combat, with walk-through World War I trenches, and a re-creation of the Blitz in which you wander from an air-raid shelter through bomb-ravaged streets, accompanied by blaring sirens and human voices. Also worth exploring are the museum's art galleries on the second floor, which display some harrowing works by war artists such as Paul Nash, whose desolate images faithfully depict the living hell of World War I.

The Holocaust Exhibition

Many people come to the Imperial War Museum specifically to see the new **Holocaust Exhibition**, which you enter from the third floor, and for which you must obtain a separate (free) timed ticket from the ground-floor box office either on arrival, or by booking ahead over the phone (☎020/7416 5439; last entry 5pm). On the whole, the curators have taken a conventional approach to the exhibition, creating a solemn mood without resorting to theme-park style reconstructions. The museum has also made a valiant attempt to avoid depicting the victims of the Holocaust as nameless masses by focusing on individual cases, and interspersing the archive footage with eye-witness accounts from contemporary survivors.

The Holocaust Exhibition is not recommended for children under 14.

The exhibition pulls few punches, bluntly stating that the pope failed to denounce the anti-Jewish Nuremberg Laws, that writers such as Eliot and Kipling expressed anti-Semitic views, and that the Evian Conference of European powers in 1938 refused to accept any more Jewish refugees. Despite the restrictions of space, there are sections on the extermination of the gypsies, Nazi euthanasia, pre-Holocaust Yiddish culture and the persecution of the Slavs. The genocide, which began with the *Einsatzgruppen* and ended with the gas chambers, is catalogued in painstaking detail, while the problem of "proving" the Final Solution is also addressed, in a room that emphasizes the complexity of the Nazi bureaucracy, which, allied to an ideology of extermination, made the Holocaust not just possible but inevitable.

The centrepiece of the museum is a vast scale model of (what is, in fact, only a very small slice of) Auschwitz-Birkenau, showing what happened to the 2000 Hungarian Jews who arrived at the camp from the town of Berehovo in May 1944. The significance of this transport is that, uniquely, photographs, taken by the SS, of the selection process meted out on these particular arrivals, managed to survive the war. In the alcoves overlooking the model, which has a pile of discarded possessions from the camps as its backdrop, survivors

Lambeth

describe their first impressions of Auschwitz. This section is especially harrowing, and it's as well to leave yourself enough time to listen to the reflections of camp survivors at the end, as they attempt to come to terms with the past.

Southwark

Southwark – originally the name of the area around the southern end of London Bridge, but now a vast borough reaching as far south as Dulwich – has a history as long as that of the City. It started out as a Roman red-light district, and its brothels continued to do a thriving illegal trade until 1161, when they were licensed by royal decree. This measure imposed various rules and restrictions on the prostitutes, who could now be fined three shillings for "grimacing to passers-by", but were given Sunday mornings off in order to attend church. The women wore red-and-white striped caps and white aprons, and were known as "Winchester Geese", since the land was owned by the Bishop of Winchester, and the church made a small fortune out of the rent until Henry VIII, of all people, closed the bawdy houses down (they returned soon after his death). Under the bishop's rule, bull- and bear-baiting, drinking, cockfighting and gambling were also rife, especially on Bankside, to the west. After 1556 Southwark came under the jurisdiction of the City, but it was still not subject to its regulations on

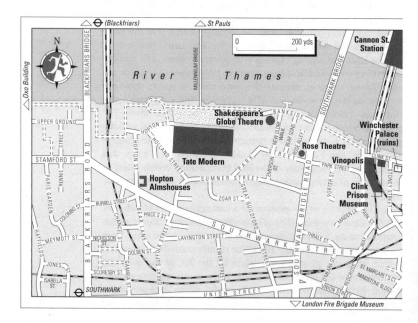

entertainment, and the area remained the pleasure quarter of Tudor and Stuart London, where brothels and other disreputable institutions banned in the City – most notably theatres – continued to flourish until the Puritan purges of the 1640s. With the Restoration, the focus of the theatre scene, and its accompanying vices, moved to Covent Garden, and Southwark faded from the limelight.

By the nineteenth century, warehouses and factories had occupied much of the land closest to the river, while countless houses were demolished during the construction of the new London Bridge and the laying of the train tracks. As a result, little remains above ground to remind you of Southwark's most interesting pre-industrial period. The **Clink Prison Museum** and the rebuilt **Globe Theatre** (where most of Shakespeare's plays had their first performances) go some way towards remedying this, as do **Southwark Cathedral** and the *George Inn*, London's last surviving galleried coaching inn, but the area's biggest attraction by far is the new **Tate Modern** gallery, which is housed in the former Bankside power station.

Tate Modern

Mon–Thurs & Sun 10am–6pm, Fri & Sat 10am–10pm; free; ☎020/7887 8000; *www.tate.org.uk*. Southwark or Blackfriars tube.

Architecturally dominating Bankside, the awesome new **Tate Modern** is an absolutely must for anyone visiting or living in London.

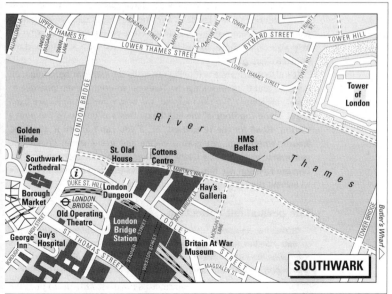

Originally designed as a oil-fired power station by Giles Gilbert Scott, this austere, brick-built "cathedral of power" was up and running for just sixteen years, before being closed down in 1980. In the late 1990s, it was transformed by the Swiss architectural duo Herzog & de Meuron into the world's largest modern art gallery, displaying works by all the major artists of the twentieth century, including Dalí, Duchamp, Giacometti, Matisse, Mondrian, Picasso, Pollock, Rothko and Warhol.

Visiting Tate Modern

Tate Modern is worth visiting for its architecture alone, so to appreciate it fully, approach from the north bank, since the river crossing gives you an unhindered view of the building. The best way to enter is via the **ramp** at the west side of the building, allowing you to fully appreciate the stupefying enormity of the main **turbine hall**, which sits below the level of the Thames yet rises to a height of 115ft, and is now used to display large-scale works of art. It's also where you'll find the **information desk**, and, on the opposite side, the museum's giant **bookshop** and **cloakroom**.

Escalators from this floor lead straight up to Level 3, which, along with Level 5, contains the permanent collection; Level 4, between the two, is used for large-scale temporary exhibitions, for which there is an entrance fee. **Audioguides** to the permanent collection are available for £1. The galleries themselves are pleasingly varied in size, lighting and colour scheme (though the majority are white). Be warned, however, that you've got to have stamina to wade through more than one or two levels in any one visit, so if there's something you really want to see, go there first before you run out of energy. To help you relax, there are several little alcoves with seating and art books to look at.

It's also worthwhile venturing out on to the **outdoor balconies**, on Levels 4 and 6, overlooking the Thames (where it's even possible to have a cigarette). For the moment, the best views of the lot are from Level 7, the top floor of the lightbeam that sits on top of the power station. Head for the restaurant, or, if you can't afford it, the **East Room**, where you can grab a coffee and get a great 270-degree panoramic view over the Globe and the City in one direction, and the London Eye and Big Ben in the other. Eventually, you should be able to ascend the building's 325ft-high central **chimney**.

The permanent collection

"Museums: cemeteries! ....Identical, surely, in the sinister promiscuity of so many bodies unknown to one another. Museums: public dormitories where one lies forever beside hated or unknown beings. Museums: absurd abattoirs of painters and sculptors ferociously slaughtering one another..."

Marinetti's *Futurist Manifesto* of 1909.

With such criticisms very much in the forefront of their minds, the Tate Modern's curators have eschewed the old chronological approach, and gone instead for hanging works according to (very broad) themes. Within these, the odd room is devoted to an "-ism" or an individual artist, and, after a short time, you're likely to have forgotten the original theme. The gallery is aiming to rehang bits of the collection every six months, so it's impossible to say what will be on display; the account below is therefore very selective. The themes, however, are here to stay.

Level 3

Landscape/Matter/Environment, on Level 3, is as good a place as any to start. The Tate's huge expansion has allowed many works, hitherto seldom seen, to escape from the vaults, but there are also plenty of old favourites, like **Mark Rothko**'s abstract "Seagram Murals". Commissioned by the swanky *Four Seasons* restaurant in New York, they were first exhibited at the Tate shortly after Rothko's suicide, having been withheld by the artist, who decided he didn't wish his art to be a mere backdrop to the recreation of the wealthy. Also in this section are several early Cubist works by **Picasso** and **Braque**, a jaunty paper collage by **Matisse**, executed towards the end of his life, and a smattering of works by the major Surrealists: **Ernst**, **Miró** and **Dalí**. One of the tallest rooms is given over to **Joseph Beuys**, whose bizarre choice of materials derives directly from his wartime experiences, when his plane crashed in the Crimea and he was saved by local Tartars, who cocooned him in felt and fat.

If there is a problem with the Tate's mix-and-match approach, it is that the early twentieth-century paintings, some still in their old-fashioned gilded frames, struggle to compete with the attention-grabbing installations; **Monet**'s *Water-Lilies*, in particular, would probably be happier back in the National Gallery. The captions, curators' notes and, occasionally, other artists' eulogies that accompany the paintings are by turns revealing, irritating and unintentionally hilarious. Confronted by **Lucio Fontana**'s *Spatial Concept "Waiting"*, we are told (without a hint of irony) that "Fontana first slashed his canvases with a razor blade in 1958, although he had been making holes in them since 1949".

Over in **Still Life/Object/Real Life**, there's a replica of **Marcel Duchamp**'s seminal *Fountain*, a urinal signed "R. Mutt, 1917" which was the first "readymade", a non-art object which becomes "art" only because it sits in a museum. Taking this idea one stage further, **Karl Schwitters** put together works such as an "assemblage of discarded rubbish and printed ephemera", for as he himself said, "everything the artist spits is art." One look at **Tony Cragg**'s "stack sculptures" of flotsam and jetsam reveals the durability of Dadaism. However, Fischli and Weiss, who re-created a room as it was before the builders moved out, caused possibly the biggest stir when the gallery first opened.

Level 5

If anything, on first hanging, Level 5 has the edge over Level 3. **History/Memory/Society** kicks off with Marinetti's aforementioned Futurist manifesto, and the revolutionary leap away from reality taken by **Malevich** in his Suprematist paintings. These, and works such as David Bomberg's severely geometric *The Mud Bath*, no longer have quite the same ability to shock. (When Bomberg hung his painting outside a King's Road art gallery in 1914, the horses pulling the no. 29 bus shied away from it.) Not so, **George Grosz**, whose hideous depiction of *Suicide* still succeeds in graphically illustrating the artist's "disgust of life". Other highlights in this section include the utopian abstract works of **Mondrian** and the De Stijl movement, Picasso's *Weeping Woman*, which is both a portrait of his lover Dora Maar and a heartfelt response to the Spanish Civil War, minimalist **Carl André**'s famous "pile of bricks" and several works by the leading protagonists of **Pop Art**, Andy Warhol and Roy Lichtenstein.

Several rooms in **Nude/Action/Body** are given over to video installations by contemporary artists Steve McQueen and Sam Taylor-Wood, which succeed in proving that the only truly unexplored taboo left is the male penis on film. Elsewhere, you'll stumble over **Degas'** bronze *Dancer*, **Jackson Pollock**'s drip paintings and Giacometti's spindly sculptures. **Francis Bacon** is represented by one of his best-known works, *Three Studies for Figures at the Base of a Crucifixion*, painted in 1945, and as unsettling as ever more than half a century on. There's some top-class sculptures here, too: Matisse's largest-ever sculptural works, *Backs I–IV*, an early Cubist bust by Picasso and **Modigliani**'s African-style carved heads. **Stanley Spencer**'s *Double Nude* remains shockingly explicit – had it been publicly exhibited when it was painted, in 1937, would have almost certainly have resulted in criminal prosecution. Equally unsparing in their depiction of the human body are the nude portraits of Britain's leading living painter, **Lucien Freud**.

Millennium Bridge

Though by no means the only millennial project to run into problems, the sleek, stainless-steel **Millennium Bridge** was the only one to have literally a rocky start. Having failed to finish in time for the official opening by the Queen, the bridge was closed indefinitely shortly after opening to the public in June 2000, due to the worrying way in which it (and the pedestrians crossing it) bounced up and down. All of which was just a little bit embarrassing to the high-profile triumvirate who'd helped design it: sculptor Anthony Caro, architect Norman Foster and engineers Ove Arup. Assuming such teething problems have been sorted out, you should – by the time you read this – be able to cross the Thames from the steps of Peter's Hill, below St Paul's Cathedral, to the Tate Modern, on London's first bridge across the Thames since Tower Bridge opened in 1894, and its first ever designed for pedestrians only.

In Elizabethan times, **Bankside** was the most nefarious street in London, known as "Stew's Bank" for its brothels or "stewhouses", and studded with **bull and bearpits**. Pepys recalls seeing "some good sport of the bulls tossing of the dogs; one into the very boxes", but opinion was by then inclining towards Evelyn's description of the sport as a "rude and dirty pastime"; in 1682 the last bear garden was closed down. In James I's reign, Bankside also boasted no fewer than four thriving **theatres**: the Swan, built in 1587, with Edward Alleyn (founder of Dulwich College) as the lead actor and Christopher Marlowe as its main playwright; the **Rose**, built in 1595, its foundations still visible on Park Street; the Hope, built in 1613, which doubled as a bear garden and theatre; and the **Globe**, the Burbages' theatre (originally built in Shoreditch in 1576, and dismantled in 1599 and erected on Bankside, on the south side of Park Street), where Shakespeare put on his greatest plays. The theatres lasted barely half a century before being closed down by the Puritans, who considered them "chapels of Satan".

Shakespeare's Globe Theatre

Daily: May–Sept 9am–noon; Oct–April 10am–5pm; £7.50; ☎020/7902 1500; *www.shakespeares-globe.org*. Southwark or Blackfriars tube.

Seriously dwarfed by the Tate Modern, but equally spectacular in its own way, **Shakespeare's Globe Theatre** is a more or less faithful 1990s reconstruction of the polygonal playhouse where most of the Bard's later works were first performed (the original Bankside site of the Globe is on Park Street – see p.316) The theatre, which boasts the first new thatched roof in central London since the Great Fire, uses only natural light and the minimum of scenery. The season runs from mid-May to mid-September, and plays tend to be performed uncut, often with men playing all the parts, and with short intervals between each of the five acts (you can pick up a "groundling", or standing, ticket for £5). Also on site are a pricey restaurant and café, and, inevitably, a shop selling lots of Bard merchandise. Eventually, there will be an indoor theatre, made to designs by Inigo Jones, for use during the winter season.

For theatre details on the Globe, see p.584.

To find out more about Shakespeare and the history of Bankside, the Globe's pricey but stylish new **exhibition**, to the west of the theatre, is well worth a visit. It begins by detailing the long campaign by the single-minded American actor Sam Wanamaker (1919–93) to have the Globe rebuilt, but it's the imaginative hands-on exhibits that really hit the spot. You can have a virtual play on period musical instruments such as the crumhorn or sackbut, prepare your own edition of Shakespeare and feel the thatch, hazelnut shell and daub used to build the theatre. There are even booths in which you can record and compare your own rendition of key speeches with those of the stage greats, and, more or often than not, the odd live demo on the exhibition's stage. Visitors also get taken on an informative **guided tour** round the theatre itself, except in the afternoons during the summer season, when you can only visit the exhibition (for a reduced entrance fee).

Rose Theatre Exhibition

Daily 10am–5pm; £3; ☎020/7593 2600; *www.rdg.ac.uk/rose*. Southwark, Blackfriars or London Bridge tube.

The discovery of the remains of the **Rose Theatre**, underneath an office block on Park Street in 1988, helped enormously in the reconstruction of the Globe. After an exhausting campaign to save the site, the finds have been successfully preserved in the basement of the new building. The outline of the theatre can be clearly traced in the foundations, but they are currently flooded to preserve them until sufficient funds can be found for a full excavation. In the meantime, to raise money, there's an excellent twenty-minute *son et lumière* on the history of Southwark, Bankside and the Rose.

Close by the Rose exhibition, there's a plaque showing where the Globe actually stood, before it was destroyed in a fire started by a spark from a cannon during a performance of Shakespeare's *Henry VIII*.

Vinopolis

Daily 10am–5.30pm or later; £11.50 (discount for booking in advance on ☎0870/444 4777); ☎020/7940 8300; *www.evinopolis.com*. London Bridge tube.

The latest big-money venture to hit this up-and-coming area is **Vinopolis**, discreetly housed in the former wine vaults under the railway arches on Clink Street. The focus of the complex is the "Wine Odyssey", a light-hearted trot through the world's wine regions, equipped with a CD audioguide. There are plenty of visual gags – you get to tour round the Italian vineyards on a Vespa – and, half way round, an art gallery which stages exhibitions of contemporary art from the private collection of the Swiss-born Donald Hess. Ticket prices for the "Wine Odyssey" are certainly pricey, but they do include five generous wine tastings – from champagne to vintage port – with the option of buying another five for a mere £2.50 extra. In many ways, this is the most appealing and educative aspect of the whole tour. The well-informed and enthusiastic staff diligently use spittoons, but most visitors seem quite happy to get slowly inebriated. At the end, you can buy a crate of the wines you enjoyed from the branch of Majestic Wines, or head into the brick-vaulted *Cantina* for glass or two more and a bite to eat.

Clink Street

Round the corner from Vinopolis, in the suitably dismal confines of dark and narrow Clink Street, is the **Clink Prison Museum**, built on the site of the former Clink Prison, and the origin of the expression "in the clink". The prison began as a dungeon under the Bishop of **Winchester's Palace** for disobedient clerics – the rose window of the palace's Great Hall has survived just east of the museum – and later it became a dumping ground for heretics, debtors, prostitutes and a motley assortment of Bankside lowlife, before being burnt to the ground during the Gordon Riots of 1780. The exhibition features a handful of prison-life tableaux and dwells on the torture and grim conditions within, but, given the rich history of the place, it's a disappointingly lacklustre display.

Further east down Clink Street, at the back of Southwark Cathedral, an exact replica of the **Golden Hinde**, the galleon in which Sir Francis Drake sailed around the world from 1577 to 1580, nestles in St Mary Overie Dock. This version was launched in 1973, and circumnavigated the world for the next twenty years or so, before eventually settling on a permanent mooring here in Southwark. The ship is surprisingly small and, with a crew of eighty-plus, must have been cramped, to say the least. There's a refreshing lack of interpretive panels, so it's worth paying the little bit extra and getting a guided tour from one of the folk in period garb. They will show you the ropes, so to speak, and demonstrate activities such as firing a cannon or using the ship's toilet.

The Clink Museum is open daily 10am–6pm; £4; ☎020/7378 1558; www.clink .co.uk. *London Bridge tube.*

The Golden Hinde is open daily 10am–dusk; £2.50; £3 including a guided tour; ☎0870/011 8700; www .goldenhinde .co.uk. *London Bridge tube.*

Southwark Cathedral

Daily 8am–6pm; free; ☎020/7367 6734. London Bridge tube.

To the west of London Bridge tube, and the bridge itself, stands **Southwark Cathedral**, built in the thirteenth and fourteenth centuries as the Augustinian priory church of St Mary Overie. It's a minor miracle that the church survived the nineteenth century, which saw the east-end chapel demolished to make way for London Bridge, railways built within a few feet of the tower and some very heavy-handed Victorian restoration. As if in compensation, the church was given cathedral status in 1905, and recently it has begun to gain the upper hand – an entirely new chapterhouse has been built to the north, funded by a *Pizza Express* franchise inside, and a new refectory and library are currently being constructed.

The cathedral's **interior**, too, has had a lot of money spent on it, its walls now a warm honeyed hue. Of the original church, which was rebuilt after a devastating fire in 1212, only the choir and retrochoir now remain, separated by a beautiful high stone Tudor screen; they are probably the oldest Gothic structures left in London. The nave was entirely rebuilt in the nineteenth century, though several of the bosses from the original wooden ceiling are displayed against the west wall; among the most interesting is the pelican drawing blood from its breast to feed its young (a symbol of Christ's sacrifice).

The cathedral contains numerous **monuments**: from a thirteenth-century oak effigy of a knight, to one dedicated to the 51 people who died when the *Marchioness* pleasure boat collided with a barge on the Thames in 1989. Others include the brightly painted tomb of poet John Gower, Chaucer's contemporary, in the north aisle, his head resting on the three books he wrote – one in Latin, one in French and one in English. The quack doctor Lionel Lockyer has a humorous epitaph in the north transept, and, nearby, there's a chapel dedicated to John Harvard, who was baptized here in 1607. In the south aisle, an early twentieth-century memorial to Shakespeare (his brother is buried here) depicts the Bard in green alabaster lounging under a stone canopy. Above the memorial is a stained-glass window featuring a whole cast of characters from the plays.

The Borough

Medieval Southwark, also known as **The Borough**, was London's first suburb, clustered round the southern end of London Bridge, London's only bridge over the Thames from Roman times until 1750, and thus the only route south. The Borough was the most obvious place for the Kent farmers to sell their goods to the City grocers, and there's been a thriving market here since medieval times. The present **Borough Market** (*www.londonslarder.org.uk*) is squeezed beneath the railway arches between the High Street and the cathedral. It's one of the few wholesale fruit and vegetable markets still trading under its original Victorian wrought-iron shed, which is little changed since Dickens' time (if you ignore the fork-lift trucks), and it puts on a bit of a show, with luscious displays to attract small shopkeepers and market traders rather than bulk-buyers. In addition, the surrounding area has recently undergone a transformation from scruffy obscurity to a small foodie haven, with a weekly Saturday market for traders and customers, a glass-roofed branch of *Fish!* (see p.529) in the market itself, and, nearby, outlets for Neal's Yard Dairy and Konditor & Cook, among others.

Good times to visit the market are Tuesday and Friday mornings (4–9am), though there's something going on every morning except Sunday.

As the main road south out of the City, Borough High Street was for centuries famous for its coaching inns. Chaucer's Canterbury pilgrims set off from the *Tabard* (in Talbot Yard), but by Dickens' time "these great rambling queer old places", as he called them, were closing down. The only extant coaching inn is the **George Inn**, situated in a cobbled yard east off the High Street, dating from 1677 and now owned by the National Trust. Unfortunately, the Great Northern Railway demolished two of the three original galleried fronts, but the lone survivor is a remarkable sight nevertheless, and is still run as a pub (see p.544).

Opposite Borough tube station, at the southernmost end of Borough High Street, is **St George the Martyr**, built in the 1730s, where Little Dorrit got married in the Dickens novel of the same name, much of which is set in the area. St George's has four clock faces: three white and illuminated at night; one black and pointing towards Bermondsey, whose parishioners refused to give money for the church. Beyond St George's, a wall survives from the **Marshalsea**, the city's main debtors' prison, where Dickens' father was incarcerated for six months in 1824 (it, too, features in *Little Dorrit*).

Old Operating Theatre Museum and Herb Garret

Daily 10am–4pm; £3.25; ☎020/7955 4791; *users.aol.com/museumweb /chr.htm*. London Bridge tube.

The most educative and strangest of Southwark's museums is the **Old Operating Theatre Museum and Herb Garret** on St Thomas Street. Built in 1821 at the top of a church tower, where the hospital apothecary's herbs were stored, this women's operating theatre was once adjacent to the women's ward of St Thomas's Hospital, which has since moved to Lambeth. Despite being entirely gore-free, the museum is as stomach-churning as the London Dungeon (see p.321), for this theatre dates from the pre-anaesthetic era.

The surgeons who used this room would have concentrated on speed and accuracy (most amputations took less than a minute), but there was still a thirty percent mortality rate, with many patients simply dying of shock, and many more from bacterial infection (about which very little was known). This much is clear from the design of the theatre itself, which has no sink and is made almost entirely of mahogany and pine, which would have harboured bacteria even after vigorous cleaning. Sawdust was sprinkled on the floor to soak up the blood and prevent it dripping onto the heads of the worshippers in the church below.

Opposite the museum stands **Guy's Hospital**, founded in 1726 by Sir Thomas Guy, a governor of St Thomas's Hospital, with the money he made on the City money markets. The hospital still occupies some of its original eighteenth-century buildings, in particular the courtyard on St Thomas Street. Guy's also retains its pretty little **Hospital Chapel**, built in the 1770s on the west side of the courtyard, with raked balconies on three sides, and cheerful light-blue paintwork throughout. You can wander in to admire the giant marble and alabaster tomb of the founder, who's depicted welcoming a new patient to the hospital, though in fact Guy died a year before the first patients were admitted.

London Fire Brigade Museum

Mon–Fri by appointment; £3; ☎020/7587 2894; Borough tube.

The **London Fire Brigade Museum**, housed in the old LFB headquarters on Southwark Bridge Road, is a short walk from Borough tube. Fire-fighting enthusiasts from all over the world descend on the museum, but you've really got to have some kind of interest in the subject to get a lot out of it. Tours start off in the appliances hall, which has only a modest range of old engines, and then proceed to the museum proper, ranged over two floors of the neighbouring Regency mansion which was home to the second LFB superintendent in the mid-nineteenth century. Expect to see silver-plated chiefs' helmets, a mock-up of a Victorian firemen's waiting room, breathing apparatus and lots of uniforms, but ring first before turning up, as the guided tours are by appointment only.

The London Bridge area

There is a tourist office by the Southwark Needle at the southern end of London Bridge, open Easter–Oct Mon–Sat 10am–6pm, Sun 10.30am–5.30pm; Nov–Easter Mon–Sat 10am–4pm, Sun 11am–4pm; ☎020 /7403 8299.

From 1651 onwards, the stretch of river frontage between London Bridge and Tower Bridge was occupied by Hay's Wharf, the largest of the "sufferance wharves" that were built to ease the volume of shipping trying to dock at the "legal quays" on the north bank. So much of the city's food – in particular teas, wines, grain, butter, bacon and cheese – was stored here that the area became known as "London's Larder". Badly bombed in the Blitz, the wharf never recovered.

However, the area's proximity to the City made this one of the first targets of the Docklands development, aimed at transforming the wharves and warehouses into a buzzing new business environment tagged "**London Bridge City**". Phase One of the complex, which went up extremely quickly in the mid-1980s, begins inauspiciously with the pink granite monstrosity of No. 1 London Bridge, a typically uncompromising piece of Big Bang architecture. Adjacent to this, emblazoned with "Hay's Wharf" in giant gold lettering, is **St Olaf House**, a 1930s Art Deco warehouse which points up the lack of imagination in its neighbour. From Tooley Street (see below) you can view the building's wonderful black and gold mosaic of the Norwegian king, St Olaf, who assisted Ethelred the Unready in his defence of London against the Danes.

Beyond is the Cottons Centre, another spectacularly ugly office development, with mustard-coloured cladding, and **Hay's Galleria**, a new shopping precinct built over what used to be Hay's Dock. The idea of filling in the curvaceous dock and covering it with glass and steel barrel-vaulting, while retaining the old Victorian warehouses on three sides, is an effective one. The pastiche of phoney market barrows, gravel underfoot and red phone boxes and the gimmicky kinetic sculpture at the centre, however, is less successful.

After adverse criticism from the likes of Prince Charles, the developers had a crisis of confidence about London Bridge City's Phase Two, east to Tower Bridge. The revised plan for John Simpson's "Venice-on-Thames", featuring a grand arcaded piazza and campanile à la St Mark's, has now been shelved. Alternative plans are currently being drawn up, the centrepiece of which will be Norman Foster's new **GLA headquarters**, a startling glass-encased building that looks like a giant car headlight. In the meantime, you can walk along the riverside from London Bridge all the way to Tower Bridge, and beyond into Bermondsey and Rotherhithe.

London Dungeon

Daily: April–Sept 10am–6pm; Oct–March 10.30am–5.30pm; £9.50; ☎0990 /160 0066; *www.thedungeons.com*. London Bridge tube.

The vaults beneath the railway arches of London Bridge train station, on the south side of Tooley Street, are now occupied by the Gothic horrors of the **London Dungeon**, one of the city's major crowd-pleasers – to avoid the inevitable queue, buy your ticket from the Southwark tourist office (see margin comment opposite). Young teenagers and the credulous probably get the most out of the life-sized waxwork tableaux of folk being hanged, drawn, quartered and tortured, the general hysteria being boosted by actors dressed as top-hatted Victorian vampires pouncing out of the darkness. Visitors are then herded into a court room, condemned to the "River of Death" boat ride and forced to endure the "Jack the Ripper Experience", an exploitative trawl through post-mortem photos and wax mock-ups of the victims, followed by the "Great Fire of London", in which visitors get to experience the heat and the smell of the plague-ridden city, before being forced to walk through a revolving tunnel of flames.

Britain at War Experience

Daily: April–Sept 10am–5.30pm; Oct–March 10am–4.30pm; £5.95; ☎020 /7403 3171; *www.britain-at-war.co.uk*. London Bridge tube.

A little further east along Tooley Street is **Winston Churchill's Britain at War Experience**, which, despite its jingoistic name, is an illuminating insight into the stiff-upper-lip London mentality during the Blitz. It begins with a rickety elevator ride down to a mock-up of a tube air-raid shelter (minus the stale air and rats), in which a con-temporary newsreel cheerily announces "a great day for democracy" as bombs drop indiscriminately over Germany. This is just a prelude to the museum's hundreds of sometimes bizarre wartime artefacts, such as a child's gas mask designed to look like Mickey Mouse. You can sit in an Anderson shelter beneath the chilling sound of the V-1 "doodlebugs", tune in to contemporary radio broadcasts and, as a grand finale, walk through the chaos of a just-bombed street – pitch-dark, noisy, smoky and chokingly hot.

HMS Belfast

Daily: March–Oct 10am–6pm; Nov–Feb 10am–5pm; £4.70; ☎020/7407 6434; *www.iwm.org.uk*. London Bridge tube.

Permanently moored opposite Southwark Crown Court, the camou-flage-painted **HMS Belfast** was a World War II cruiser in the Royal Navy. Armed with six torpedoes, and six-inch guns with a range of over fourteen miles, the *Belfast* spent over two years of the war in the Royal Naval shipyards, after being hit by a mine in the Firth of Forth at the beginning of hostilities. It later saw action in the Barents

A ferry service runs April–Sept daily every 15min from the ship to Tower Pier.

Sea and assisted in the D-Day landings before being decommissioned after the Korean War, becoming an outpost of the Imperial War Museum.

The ship, which could accommodate a crew of up to eight hundred, is low on info or high-tech gadgetry, so head for the Exhibition Flat in Zone 5, to find out about its history. The fun bit, though, is exploring the maze of cabins and scrambling up and down the vertiginous ladders of the ship's seven confusing decks. Be sure to check out the punishment cells, in the most uncomfortable part of the ship, and to make it down to the airlocked Boiler Room, a spaghetti of pipes and valves, from which there was no chance of escape in the event of the boat being hit.

Bermondsey

Famous in the Middle Ages for its Cluniac abbey, and later frequented for its pleasure gardens and spa, **Bermondsey** changed enormously in the nineteenth century. In 1836, the London and Greenwich Railway – the city's first – was built through the district, supported by 878 brick arches stretching for four miles. Teeming riverside wharves and overcrowded tenements brought some of the worst social conditions in Victorian London, as Charles Kingsley discovered: "O God! What I saw! People having no water to drink but the water of the common sewer which stagnates full of . . . dead fish, cats and dogs."

The most recent change came with the closure of the docks in the 1960s. The area to the north of Jamaica Road was designated part of the Docklands regeneration scheme. Some areas, like the **Butler's Wharf** warehouse development, were developed pretty quickly, before the money ran out at the end of the 1980s; other sections have only recently been redeveloped. The area's prime attraction is the excellent **Design Museum** in Butler's Wharf, along with the Friday-morning Bermondsey **antique market**, also known confusingly as the New Caledonian Market, since this is the descendant of the prewar flea market that used to take place off Islington's Caledonian Road.

Butler's Wharf

The nearest tubes are Tower Hill and Bermondsey.

In contrast to the brash offices of London Bridge City, the new developments to the east of Tower Bridge have attempted to retain some semblance of the historical character of the area. This is particularly true of **Butler's Wharf**, one of the densest networks of Victorian warehousing in London, where the policy has been one of restoring the old buildings where possible, while subtly enhancing the area with new modernist and postmodernist constructions. This approach is infinitely preferable to the old scorched-earth policy, and makes this one of the most enjoyable parts of Docklands to explore.

The best place to start is on Tower Bridge itself, the only place from where you can get a really good view of the old **Anchor Brewhouse**, which produced Courage ales from 1789 until 1982. A cheery, ad hoc sort of building, with a boiler-house chimney at one end and malt mill tower and cupola at the other, it has been sensitively converted into apartments. Next door is the original eight-storey **Butler's Wharf warehouse**, which gives its name to the surrounding area. The upper floors have again been converted into yuppie accommodation, while the ground-floor shops and restaurants form part of Terence Conran's commercial empire and cater for a moneyed clientele. However, the wide promenade on the riverfront is open to the public.

Shad Thames, the narrow street at the back of Butler's Wharf, has kept the wrought-iron overhead gangways by which the porters used to transport goods from the wharves to the warehouses further back from the river; it's one of the most atmospheric alleyways in the whole of Docklands, and was used by David Lynch as a Victorian backdrop for *The Elephant Man*. For a totally different ambience, head for **Horsleydown Square**, to the south of Shad Thames, where terracotta-rendered flats, with striking blue balconies, overlook a kind of continental piazza centred on a fountain, encrusted with naked women, whose belongings are sculpted around the edge. Also worth a look, two blocks south on Queen Elizabeth Street, is the **Circle**, CZWG's modern take on the Victorian "circus", its street facades smothered in shiny cobalt blue tiles.

Design Museum

Mon–Fri 11.30am–6pm, Sat & Sun 10.30am–6pm; £5.50; ☎020/7378 6055; *www.designmuseum.org*. Tower Hill or Bermondsey tube.

The big attraction of Butler's Wharf is Terence Conran's superb riverside **Design Museum**, at the eastern end of Shad Thames. The stylish white edifice, a Bauhaus-like conversion of an old 1950s warehouse, is the perfect showcase for an unpretentious display of mass-produced industrial design from classic cars to Tupperware. The first floor hosts temporary exhibitions on important designers, movements or single products, while the constantly evolving Collections Gallery, displaying everything from chairs and radios to telephones and kettles, is on the top floor, along with the Review Gallery, which acts as a showcase for new ideas, including success-ful prototypes and failures. The small coffee bar in the foyer serves snacks and is a great place to relax, and there's a superb but pricey Conran restaurant, the *Blue Print Café*, on the top floor.

Bramah Tea and Coffee Museum

Daily 10am–6pm; £4; ☎020/7378 0222; *www.bramahmuseum.co.uk*. Tower Hill or Bermondsey tube.

The **Bramah Tea and Coffee Museum**, housed in an old tea ware-house, Tamarind House, behind the Design Museum on Maguire

Street, is not quite in the same league as its neighbour. Nevertheless, it's a fun museum, and well worth a visit. Tea arrived in London only a decade or two after coffee, but it quickly established itself as the national drink, and remained unchallenged until the 1950s, when the espresso arrived in Soho's trendy cafés. At the same time, the South American coffee producers foisted instant coffee on the unsuspecting public. The tea companies retaliated with tea bags, and the end result is that the British drink the worst tea and coffee in the world.

The museum itself was founded in 1992 by Edward Bramah, whose family have been in the tea business for nearly 250 years. It's not surprising then that the story of tea occupies the larger part of the museum, while the coffee section is housed in a separate building down Gainsford Street. There's a wealth of information, and an incredibly impressive array of teapots, from Wedgwood and Chinese porcelain to Clarice Cliff and novelty ones in the shape of planes, camels and even car radiators; ditto, coffee machines, from huge percolator siphons to espresso contraptions spanning the twentieth century. Since Mr Bramah is quite religious about his mission to try and convert the British public to proper tea and coffee, you can be sure of enjoying a good cup of either beverage at the end of your visit.

St Saviour's Dock and beyond

To the east of the Design Museum, a bright, new stainless-steel footbridge takes you across **St Saviour's Dock**, a tidal inlet overlooked by swanky new warehouse offices. Incredible though it may seem, it really is still possible to smell the spices – cinnamon, nutmeg and cloves, mostly – which were once stored here, especially in the last section of Shad Thames after a shower of rain. The footbridge takes you over to **New Concordia Wharf** on Mill Street, one of the first warehouse conversions in the area, completed in 1984. Next door stands **China Wharf**, designed by CZWG and one of the most photographed postmodernist buildings in Docklands, with its stack of semicircular windows picked out in red.

The area to the east of **Mill Street** was dubbed by the Victorian press "the very capital of cholera". In 1849, the *Morning Chronicle* described it thus: "Jostling with unemployed labourers of the lowest class, ballast heavers, coal-whippers, brazen women, ragged children, and the very raff and refuse of the river, [the visitor] makes his way with difficulty along, assailed by offensive sights and smells from the narrow alleys which branch off." This was the location of Dickens' fictional Jacob's Island, a place with "every imaginable sign of desolation and neglect", where Bill Sikes met his end in *Oliver Twist*.

Much of the riverfront from St Saviour's Dock to Rotherhithe has yet to be attacked by the developers, who have only just got going again after the recession of the early 1990s. If you want to continue east on foot to Rotherhithe, you can follow a route alongside the river, stopping en route at **The Angel** (see p.544), a pub once frequented by Pepys and Captain Cook, on Bermondsey Wall, with great views over to Wapping. Close by are the foundations of Edward III's moated manor house, begun in 1353.

Rotherhithe

Rotherhithe, the thumb of marshy land jutting out into the Thames east of Bermondsey, has always been slightly removed from the rest of London. It was a thriving shipbuilding centre even before the construction of the Surrey Commercial Docks in the nineteenth century, and remained busy until the eve of the last war. No other set of London dockyards took such a hammering in the Blitz, however, and the decades until their closure in 1970 were years of inexorable decline. Most of the docks, which took up almost the entire peninsula, have now been reclaimed for new housing estates and more upmarket accommodation. The lack of any relationship between the old Rotherhithe communities, which face the street, and the new ones, which face the water, give the whole area a strange, dislocated feeling that's typical of the new Docklands.

Around St Mary's

The area of Rotherhithe most worthy of a visit is the heart of the eighteenth-century seafaring village around **St Mary's Church**, which stands in its own little leafy square just northwest of the tube station. The church itself is unremarkable, but it has rich maritime associations: several of the furnishings are made from the timber of the *Fighting Téméraire*, the veteran of Trafalgar which ended its days in a Rotherhithe breaker's yard (Turner's painting of its last voyage is in the National Gallery), and the master of the *Mayflower* was buried here. The *Mayflower* was pretty much Rotherhithe-owned and crewed, and set off from its mooring outside the *Mayflower* pub in 1620 to transport the Pilgrim Fathers to the New World (via Plymouth). The pub, to the north of the church, is a rickety white weatherboarded building, badly damaged in the last war, and a minor pilgrimage site for Americans.

To the east of the church are a couple of old timber-framed warehouses that now house the **Rotherhithe Picture Research Library**, a friendly place that's happy for anyone at all to go in and browse through the collection. To the south of the church is a slip of a Georgian house; the figures of a blue-coated boy and girl sheltering in the niches of the facade recall its former use as a charity school. To squeeze the last ounce of atmosphere from Rotherhithe, check out the narrow alleyway called Waterside, to the northwest of the church, still flanked by old wharves featuring overhead gangways. At

The Rotherhithe Picture Research Library is open Mon–Fri 10.30am–4pm; free; ☎020 /7231 2209.

the western end rises the new **Princes Tower**, its whitewashed modernism harking back to Le Corbusier.

Brunel Engine House

April–Oct Sat & Sun 1–5pm; Nov–March Sun 1–5pm; £2; ☎020/7231 3840; *www.museumweb.freeserve.co.uk/brunel.htm*. Rotherhithe tube.

To the east of St Mary's, down Tunnel Street, you'll find the **Brunel Engine House**, a brick-built shed that marks the site of the Thames Tunnel, the world's first under-river tunnel. It was begun in 1825 by Marc Brunel and his more famous son, Isambard, to link Rotherhithe with Wapping, using technology which was invented by Brunel senior and whose basic principles have been used for all subsequent tunnelling. Plagued by periodic flooding, labour unrest, fatalities and lack of funds, the tunnel took eighteen years to construct and was nicknamed "The Great Bore" by the press.

The circular working shaft, which housed an engine to pump water out of the tunnel, survives to the east of the engine house, but funds ran out before the spiral ramps, which would have allowed horse-drawn vehicles actually to use the tunnel, could be built. Instead, in 1843, the tunnel was opened to pedestrians as a tourist attraction. It was visited by Queen Victoria herself, who knighted Brunel junior, but soon became the haunt of whores and "tunnel thieves". Since 1869 it has formed part of the East London Railway (now a tube line) and remains the most watertight of all the rail tunnels under the Thames. Don't be put off by the weekend-only opening hours of the engine house; this is an interesting museum, with a short video on the tunnel and a functioning pumping engine from Chatham Docks.

Scandinavian seamen's missions

The nearest tubes are Rotherhithe, Canada Water and Surrey Quays.

One of the more unusual legacies of Rotherhithe's seafaring past is the trio of Scandinavian seamen's missions – a reminder of the former dominance of the timber trade in the nearby Surrey Docks (see below) – which survive to the south of the tube station, around Albion Road. The most prominent is the **Norwegian Seamen's Church**, by the approach road to the Rotherhithe Tunnel, which flies the Norwegian flag and features a longboat atop its weather vane. Albion Road itself still has a Scandinavian bent – even the nearby public toilets are bilingual – and further down you'll find the well-maintained **Finnish Seamen's Mission**, built in modernist style in 1958, with a freestanding belfry that looks more like a fire station practice tower. The 1960s **Swedish Seamen's Church**, further south at 120 Lower Rd, completes the trio but is architecturally undistinguished.

Rotherhithe Street and Surrey Docks

The once marshy land of Rotherhithe peninsula, to the east of the old village, was chosen as the site for London's first wet dock, built in

1696 to take on any extra repair work and refitting emanating from the Royal Dockyards in nearby Deptford. Later renamed Greenland Dock, the Rotherhithe docks became part of the network known as **Surrey Commercial Docks**. The main trade was timber, which was piled into stacks up to 80ft high by porters nicknamed "Flying Blondins" (after the tightrope walker), who wore distinctive leather pads on their heads and shoulders to protect them from splinters. The docks took a pounding in the Blitz, and on one particular occasion, 350,000 tons of timber was set ablaze in the largest fire ever seen in Britain.

Rotherhithe Street, which hugs the river bank, is the longest street in London at around a mile and a half. For the most part, it's residential, a mixture of new Docklands private flats and council housing, but the Thames Path, which runs parallel to it for most of the way, is pleasant enough to walk or cycle along, with great views over to Limehouse and Canary Wharf. Halfway along the street, you can learn more about the area's history from the **Rotherhithe Heritage Museum**, which is housed in the old Lavender Pumphouse on Lavender Street. Further along, by the new *Holiday Inn* hotel, there's a three-masted sailing ship (now a restaurant) built in the 1950s as a training ship for the French navy, and close by, **Nelson House**, a beautiful Georgian house built for one of the wealthy owners of the nearby Nelson Dock.

The Heritage Museum is open Mon–Fri 10am–3pm; free; ☎020 /7231 2976.

The only large expanse of water remaining is **Greenland Dock** itself, now used by the local sailing club; the most imaginative new housing is around **Norway Dock** – dubbed "The Lakes" – just to the north beyond Finland Street, where the houses sit in the water on timber decks. The **Russia Dock Woodland Walk** now wends its way over a large part of the old docks, and, though not very well maintained, offers an inland alternative from Lavender Pier or Nelson Dock to Greenland Dock. If you continue along the Thames Path from Greenland Dock, you'll eventually reach Deptford (see p.441).

Elephant and Castle and around

No one can quite agree about the derivation of Elephant and Castle, which either comes from the sign of the Cutlers' Company, which dealt in ivory, or from the Infanta of Castile, who was once engaged to Charles I. Despite its comical name, however, the place is not much fun at all. A notorious traffic bottleneck since the eighteenth century, it's also a supremely ugly spot, distinguished by its red shopping centre and serviced by a network of graffiti-riddled subways. It's unlikely, therefore, that many will shed a tear if plans to tear the whole lot down, and redesign it according to a plan by Norman Foster, go ahead.

To complete the happy picture, to the southeast, you'll find one of the most depressing roads in London, the **Old Kent Road**, justifiably the cheapest property on the Monopoly board. Lying along the old Roman Watling Street to Dover, it runs dead straight for more than two miles from Borough to Deptford, lined with numerous boarded-up shops and other delights such as one of the city's first drive-through *McDonald's*.

Cuming Museum

Tues–Sat 10am–5pm; free; ☎020/7701 1342. Elephant and Castle tube.

The only conceivable reason to pay homage to the Elephant and Castle is to take a short stroll down the Walworth Road to the **Cuming Museum**, on the first floor of the local library, which houses a remarkable collection of curiosities. The museum's treasure-trove of objects was collected by two wealthy local gentlemen, Richard Cuming (1777–1870) and his son Henry Cuming (1817–1902), who together amassed over 130,000 objects. Opened in 1906 as a "British Museum in miniature", this single-room collection contains an incredible range of exhibits: everything from a mummified leg from ancient Egypt to a pair of Queen Victoria's satin shoes, as well as a host of fake figures from a "lost civilization" and other pseudo-antiques.

Livesey Museum

Tues–Sat 10am–5pm; free; ☎020/7639 5604. Bus #53, #63 or #172 from Elephant and Castle tube.

Wending your way down the Old Kent Road for a mile or two will bring you to the **Livesey Museum**, at no. 682, housed in a beautiful late Victorian red-brick library that was gutted in World War II. Aimed principally at kids, the Livesey is one of London's liveliest local museums. There are no permanent displays; instead, the Livesey stages temporary exhibitions drawn from the collections of a wide range of other museums, on topics such as dinosaurs, rubbish and robots. Ring before you set out to check that there's an exhibition on.

Chapter 10

Hyde Park, Kensington, Chelsea and Notting Hill

Londoners tend to see their city as grimy and built-up, but most visitors are amazed at how green and pleasant so much of the centre is. The three royal parks – St James's, Green Park and Hyde Park – form a continuous green belt that stretches for four miles. **HYDE PARK**, together with its westerly extension, **Kensington Gardens**, is the largest of the trio, covering a distance of two miles from Speakers' Corner in the northeast to Kensington Palace in the southwest. In between, you can jog, swim, fish, sun-bathe or mess about in boats on the Serpentine, cross the park on horseback or mountain bike, or view the latest in modern art at the Serpentine Gallery. At the end of your journey, you've made it to one of London's most exclusive districts, the Royal Borough of Kensington and Chelsea, which makes up the bulk of this chapter.

Other districts go in and out of fashion, but **KENSINGTON**, to the west of Hyde Park, has been in vogue ever since royalty moved into Kensington Palace in the late seventeenth century. Aside from the shops around Harrods in Knightsbridge, however, the popular tourist attractions lie in **South Kensington**, where three of London's top museums – the **Victoria and Albert**, **Natural History** and **Science museums** – stand on land bought with the proceeds of the Great Exhibition of 1851. The following half-century saw the entire borough transformed from fields, farms and private estates into street after street of ostentatious Italianate terraces, grandiose red-brick mansions and mews houses. This is prime London real estate and heartland of the privately educated, wealthy and vacuous off-spring of the middle and upper classes.

CHELSEA, bordering the river, also has royal connections, though these date mostly from Tudor times and have left few tangible remains. Since the nineteenth century, when artists and writers began to move here in significant numbers, Chelsea's character has been more bohemian than its neighbours. In the 1960s, the **King's Road** carved out its reputation as London's catwalk, while in the late

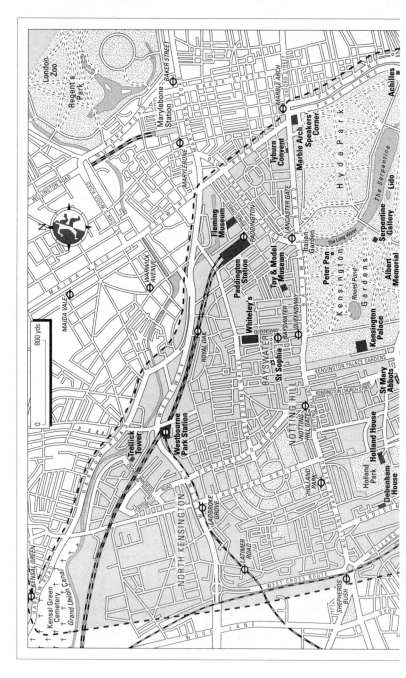

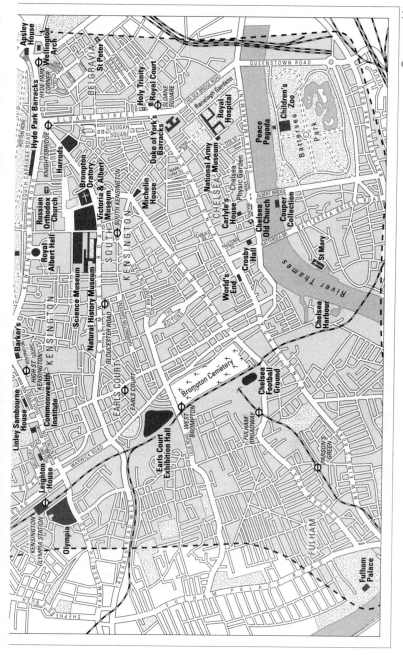
© crown copyright

1970s it was the epicentre of the punk explosion. Nothing so risqué goes on in Chelsea now, though its residents like to think of themselves as rather more artistic and intellectual than the purely moneyed types of Kensington.

Once slummy, now swanky, **Bayswater** and **NOTTING HILL**, to the north of Hyde Park, were for many years the bad boys of the borough, dens of vice and crime comparable to that of Soho. Gentrification has changed them immeasurably over the last thirty years, though they remain the borough's most cosmopolitan districts, with a strong Arab presence and vestiges of the African-Caribbean community who initiated and still run the city's (and Europe's) largest street **carnival**, which takes place every August Bank Holiday weekend.

Hyde Park and Kensington Gardens

Seized from the Church by Henry VIII to satisfy his desire for yet more hunting grounds, **Hyde Park** was first opened to the public by James I, when refreshments available included "milk from a red cow". Under Charles II, the park became a fashionable gathering place for the beau monde, who rode round the circular drive known as the Ring, pausing to gossip and admire each other's equipages. Its present appearance is mostly due to Queen Caroline, an enthusiast for landscape gardens, who spent a great deal of George II's money creating the park's main feature, the **Serpentine lake**.

The park and gardens are open daily dawn–dusk; www.royalparks .co.uk.

Hangings, muggings and duels, the Great Exhibition of 1851 and numerous public events have all taken place in Hyde Park – and it's still a popular gathering point or destination for political demonstrations, as well as the location of **Speakers' Corner**, of which more below. For most of the time, however, Hyde Park is simply a leisure ground – a wonderful open space which allows you to lose all sight of the city beyond a few persistent tower blocks.

The more tranquil half of the park, to the west of Victoria Gate and the Ring, is known as **Kensington Gardens** and is, strictly speaking, a separate entity from Hyde Park, though you hardly notice the change. These gardens were first opened to the public in George II's reign, but only on Sundays and only to those in formal dress, and that didn't include sailors, soldiers or liveried servants. Unrestricted access was only granted in Victoria's reign, by which time, in the view of the Russian ambassador's wife, the park had already been "annexed as a middle-class rendezvous. Good society no longer [went] there except to drown itself."

The nearest tube is Marble Arch.

Marble Arch and Speakers' Corner

Marble Arch, located at the treeless northeastern corner of the park and the west end of Oxford Street, is the most historically charged spot in Hyde Park, as it marks the site of **Tyburn gallows**, the city's main public execution spot until 1783, when the action moved to Newgate (see box on p.233). There's a plaque on the traffic island at the bottom of Edgware Road/Bayswater Road marking the approximate site of the gallows, where around 50,000 lost their lives. Of these, some 105 were Catholics, martyred during the Reformation, in whose memory the **Tyburn Convent** (daily 6.30am–8.30pm) was established at 8 Hyde Park Place in 1902. It's run by a group of French Benedictine nuns who are happy to show visitors round the basement shrine (10am, 3.30pm & 5.30pm; free), which contains a

Hyde Park and Kensington Gardens

Tyburn Gallows

For nearly five hundred years, **Tyburn** was the capital's main public execution site, with around fifteen victims a month swinging, some of them dispatched for the most petty of crimes (there were 156 capital offences in eighteenth-century England). "Hanging Matches", as they were known, usually drew huge crowds – up to 200,000 for the execution of a noted criminal – and became something of a show of working-class solidarity, with numerous side-stalls and a large permanent grandstand known as "Mother Proctor's Pews". Dressed in their best clothes, the condemned were processed through the streets in a cart (the nobility were allowed to travel in their own carriage) from Newgate Prison, three miles away, often with the noose already looped in place. They received a nosegay at St Sepulchre, opposite the prison, and then at St Giles-in the-Fields, and at various taverns along the route they were given a free pint of ale, so that many were blind drunk by the time they arrived at the three-legged gibbet known as the "Tyburn Tree" or the "Triple Tree", which could dispatch over twenty people at one go.

The condemned were allowed to make a speech to the crowd and were attended by a chaplain, though according to one eighteenth-century spectator he was "more the subject of ridicule than of serious attention". The same witness then goes on to describe how the executioner, who drove the cart, then tied the rope to the tree: "This done he gives the horse a lash with his whip, away goes the cart and there swings my gentleman kicking in the air. The Hangman does not give himself the trouble to put them out of their pain but some of their friends or relations do it for them. They pull the dying person by the legs and beat his breast to dispatch him as soon as possible."

Not all relatives were so fatalistic, however, and some would attempt to support the condemned in the hope of a last-minute reprieve, or of reviving the victim when they were cut down. Fights frequently broke out when the body was cut down, between spectators hoping to touch the corpse in the belief it had miraculous medicinal qualities, and between relatives and surgeons who were allowed ten corpses a year for dissection. The executioner, known as "Jack Ketch" after the famous London hangman who botched the Duke of Monmouth's beheading (see p.263), was allowed to take home the victim's clothes, and made further profit by selling the hanging rope inch by inch. Altogether, an estimated 50,000 were hanged at Tyburn, but following the 1780 Gordon Riots, the powers-that-be took fright at unruly gatherings like Tyburn, and demolished the Tyburn Tree in 1783.

mock-up of the Tyburn gibbet over the main altar, and various pictures and relics of the martyrs.

Marble Arch itself has a long and dismal history, and is now stranded on a ferociously busy traffic island. It was designed in 1828 in white Carrara marble by John Nash as a triumphal arch (after the Arch of Constantine in Rome) and was originally positioned in front of Buckingham Palace, for the exclusive use of royalty. The sculpted friezes intended to adorn it ended up on Buck House, while the equestrian statue of George IV, intended to surmount it, was carted off to Trafalgar Square. When the palace was extended in the 1840s, the arch was moved to form an entrance to Hyde Park, its upper chambers used as a police observation post. During the 1855 riot (described below), a detachment of police emerged, like the Greeks from the Trojan Horse, much to the surprise of the demonstrators.

In 1855 an estimated 250,000 people gathered in the section of the park directly across the road from Marble Arch to protest against the Sunday Trading Bill (Karl Marx was among the crowd and thought it was the beginning of the English Revolution), and ever since then it has been one of London's most popular spots for political demos. Riots in 1866 eventually persuaded the government to license free assembly at **Speakers' Corner**, once an entertaining and peculiarly English Sunday tradition, featuring an assembly of characterful speakers and hecklers – sadly, it's now degenerated into a forum for soapbox religious extremists.

Hyde Park Corner

*The nearest
tube is Hyde
Park Corner.*

A better place to enter the park is at **Hyde Park Corner**, the southeast corner, where **Wellington Arch** stands in the midst of another of London's busiest traffic interchanges. Designed by a youthful Decimus Burton in 1828 to commemorate Wellington's victories in the Napoleonic Wars, the arch originally served as the northern gate into Buckingham Palace grounds.

Positioned opposite Burton's delicate Hyde Park Screen, which was intended as a formal entrance into the park, the arch once formed part of a fine architectural ensemble with Apsley House, Wellington's London residence, and St George's Hospital to the west. Unfortunately the symmetry was destroyed when it was repositioned in 1883 to line up with Constitution Hill – whose name derives not from a written constitution, which England has never had, but from the "constitutional" walks that Charles II used to take there. The arch's original statue, an enormous equestrian portrayal of the "Iron Duke", was taken down the same year, and was eventually replaced by Peace and her four-horse chariot, erected incongruously in the summer of 1914.

The replacement statue for the Iron Duke is much smaller, and stands opposite his erstwhile residence, **Apsley House** (see below). He is depicted seated astride his faithful steed, Copenhagen, who carried the field marshal for sixteen hours during the Battle of Waterloo; the horse eventually died in 1836 and was buried with full military honours at the Duke's country pile in Hampshire. Close by are two powerful war memorials erected in 1925: the first, the **Machine Gun Corps Memorial**, features the naked figure of David leaning on Goliath's sword and the chilling inscription, "Saul hath slain his thousands, but David his tens of thousands"; the larger of the two, the **Artillery Memorial**, includes a 9.2-inch howitzer rendered in Portland stone, realistic relief depictions of the brutality of war, and the equally blunt epitaph, "Here was a royal fellowship of death."

Apsley House: the Wellington Museum

Tues–Sun 11am–5pm; £4.50; ☎020/7499 5676; *www.vam.ac.uk*. Hyde Park Corner tube.

Known during the Iron Duke's lifetime as No. 1, London, **Apsley House** was once an immensely desirable residence, but nowadays, with traffic roaring past at all hours of the day and night, it would be poor reward for any national hero. The interior isn't what it used to be either, but in this case it's Wellington himself who was to blame. The house was built and exquisitely decorated by Robert Adam in 1771, but after buying the place from his brother in 1817 the duke ordered Benjamin Wyatt to reface the house in Bath stone and replace or modify virtually all of the Adam interiors. As a result, however, the house is very much as it would have been in Wellington's day, and the current duke still lives in the attic.

Since 1952 most of the house has been preserved as a **Wellington Museum**, and is currently run by the V&A; tickets for the latter cover entry here, and there's a free audioguide available. Unless you're a keen fan of the Duke (or Wyatt), the highlight of the museum is the **art collection**, much of it belonging to the King of Spain, but captured from Napoleon's brother after the Battle of Vitoria (1813). The best pieces, including works by de Hooch, Van Dyck, Goya, Rubens and Murillo, cover the red walls of the Waterloo Gallery on the first floor. The most prized of all are a trio by Diego Velázquez – *The Water-Seller of Seville*, *Portrait of a Gentleman* and *Two Young Men Eating at a Humble Table* – though Wellington preferred Correggio's *Agony in the Garden*, the key for which he used to carry round with him, so he could take the picture out of its frame and dust it fondly.

The room itself was originally hung with yellow satin, which, as one of the Duke's friends lamented, "is just the very worst colour he can have for the pictures and will kill the effect of the gilding". It was here that Wellington held his annual Waterloo banquet, using the 1000-piece silver-gilt Portuguese service, now displayed in the rather lugubrious Dining Room at the other end of the house. Most of the Waterloo portraits are, in fact, hung in the adjacent Striped

Hyde Park and Kensington Gardens

The Iron Duke

Perhaps if the **Duke of Wellington** had died, like Nelson, at his moment of greatest triumph, he too would enjoy an unsullied posthumous reputation. Instead, he went on to become the epitome of the outmoded reactionary conservative, earning his famous nickname, the "Iron Duke", not from his fearless military campaigning, but from the iron shutters which he had installed at Apsley House after his windows had twice been broken by demonstrators rioting in favour of the 1832 Reform Bill, which gave the vote to almost all members of the middle class, and to which the Duke was vehemently opposed.

Born Arthur Wellesley in Dublin in 1769 – the same year as Napoleon – he was educated at Eton and the French military academy at Angiers. "Aloof and rather aggressive as a boy", according to one of his contemporaries, he was, by all accounts, a fairly terrifying personality, who barked rather than spoke. He scored his first military victories out in India, defeating Tippoo Sahib, and becoming governor of Mysore. After continued military success in his Napoleonic campaigns, he eventually became Duke of Wellington in 1814, shortly before achieving his most famous victory of all at Waterloo.

Though he had been MP for Trim in Ireland since 1806, and held various political posts throughout his life, it was only with great reluctance that he became prime minister in 1828, "a station, to the duties of which I am unaccustomed, in which I was not wished, and for which I was not qualified . . . I should have been mad if I had thought of such a thing." Despite his own misgivings, his government passed the Catholic Relief Bill – allowing Catholics to sit in parliament – thus avoiding civil war in Ireland, but splitting the Tory ranks. Accused of popery by the Earl of Winchelsea, Wellington challenged him to a duel in Battersea Park; the Duke fired and missed, while the Earl shot into the air and apologized for the slur.

Wellington's opposition to the Reform Bill brought down his government and allowed the Whigs to form a majority government for the first time in sixty years. Despite retiring from public life in 1846, he was on hand to organize the defence of the capital against the Chartists in 1848, and strolled across to the Great Exhibition every day in 1851. Something approaching two million people lined the streets for his funeral in 1852 (more than for anyone before or since), and he has more outdoor statues (and pubs named after him) in London than any other historical figure. Despite this, his greatest legacy is, of course, the Wellington boot, originally made of leather, now rubber.

Drawing Room, which is decorated like a military tent in the manner of Napoleon's Loire chateau Malmaison.

The famous, more than twice life-size, nude statue of Napoleon by Antonio Canova stands at the foot of the main staircase, having been bought by the Prince Regent in 1816 and presented to the Duke for services rendered. It was disliked by the sitter, not least for the tiny figure of Victory in the emperor's hand, which appears to be trying to fly away. In the Plate and China Room, also on the ground floor, you can view numerous gifts to the Duke, including a 400-piece dinner service decorated with scenes of Wellington's life that was presented by the King of Prussia, and the bizarre Egyptian service, which was originally a divorce present from Napoleon to Josephine; unsurprisingly she rejected it and Louis XVIII ended up giving it to the Duke. In the basement there are various personal effects, medals and a goodly selection of cruel, contemporary caricatures.

Hyde Park and Kensington Gardens

Achilles and Rotten Row

Behind Apsley House, a pair of frothy new silvery gates – installed in 1993 as a birthday present to the Queen Mother – marks the Queen Elizabeth Gate, and the beginning of the park proper. Close by the entrance, overlooking the back of Apsley House, is the 33-ton bronze **Achilles statue**, designed by Sir Richard Westmacott and cast from captured French cannon. It was erected in 1822 on behalf of "the women of Great Britain" who acted as fundraisers for the statue, which commemorates the Duke's achievements. As the country's first public nude statue it caused outrage, especially since many thought it a portrait of the Duke himself. In actual fact, it isn't meant to represent either the Duke or Achilles, but is a copy of one of the horse-tamers from the Monte Catallo in Rome. William Wilberforce led a campaign to have the statue removed for decency's sake; a fig leaf was eventually placed in the appropriate place as a compromise.

From the gates, two roads set off west to Kensington: South Carriage Road, which is open to cars, and **Rotten Row**, thought to be a corruption of *route du roi*, since it was established by William III as a bridle path linking Westminster and Kensington. William had three hundred lamps hung from the trees to try to combat the increasing number of highwaymen active in the park, thus making Rotten Row the first road in the country to be lit at night. The measure was only partly successful – George II himself was later mugged here. To the south of Rotten Row, the **Hyde Park Barracks** are difficult to miss, thanks to Basil Spence's hideous high-rise design. Early in the morning, you might catch sight of the Household Cavalry exercising in the park, and at around 10.30am daily (Sun 9.30am) they set off for Horse Guards Building in Whitehall for the Changing of the Guard (see p.71).

At noon on Feb 6, April 21, June 2 & 10, Aug 4 and other special occasions, the Royal Horse Artillery wheel out cannons and the park resounds to a 41-round Royal Gun Salute.

The Serpentine and the Long Water

Rotten Row remains a bridle path, so pedestrians should wander through the pretty flower gardens to the north instead. Beyond lies the **Serpentine Lake**, created in 1730 by damming the Westbourne, a small tributary of the Thames, in order that Queen Caroline might have a spot for the royal yachts to mess about on. A miniature re-enactment of the Battle of Trafalgar was staged here in 1814, and two years later Shelley's pregnant wife, Harriet Westbrook, drowned herself in the Serpentine after Shelley had eloped with the

The nearest tube is Lancaster Gate.

16-year-old Mary Wollstonecraft. The popular **Lido** (June–Sept daily 10am–6pm; £2.70; ☎ 020/7298 2100) is situated on the south bank, alongside a café, and rowboats can be rented (March–Oct daily 10am–6.30pm or dusk; £4 per hour) from the boathouse on the north bank.

To the north of the lake is Jacob Epstein's monument, a relief of **Rima**, the naked spirit of nature, which provoked such hostility when it was unveiled in 1925 that it was tarred and feathered on two separate occasions. The dedicatee of the monument is the naturalist **W.H. Hudson**, and the area around it is supposed to be a bird sanctuary, though its dribbling fountain and manicured lawn are not the most obvious spot for birds to seek refuge.

The upper section of the Serpentine – beyond the bridge – is known as **Long Water**, and is by far the prettiest section of the lake. It narrows until it reaches a most unlikely sight in an English park: a group of four fountains, laid out symmetrically in front of an Italianate summerhouse designed by Wren. To the east, by Victoria Gate, lies the odd little **Pet Cemetery**, begun in the 1880s when Mr & Mrs J. Lewis Barnes buried their Maltese terrier, Cherry, here. When the Duke of Cambridge buried his wife's pet hound at the same spot after it had been run over on Bayswater Road, it became the place to bury your pooch; three hundred other miscellaneous cats and dogs followed, until the last burial in 1967. The cemetery – "perhaps the most horrible spectacle in Britain", according to George Orwell – is no longer open to the public, though you can peep over the wall.

There's some **outdoor sculpture** worth attention to the west of Long Water: the rough-hewn muscleman struggling with his horse is G.F. Watts' *Physical Energy*, a copy of the Rhodes memorial in Cape Town; to the north is a granite obelisk raised to John Hanning Speke, who was the first non-African to find the source of the Nile, and who died in 1864 after accidentally shooting himself rather than the partridge he was aiming at. Finally, perhaps the best known of all Hyde Park's outdoor monuments is *Peter Pan*, erected in 1912 in the northwest corner of the park, with funds provided by the book's author, J.M. Barrie, who used to walk his dog here; fairies, squirrels, rabbits, birds and mice are sculpted scampering round the pedestal, while close by, there's a top-quality children's playground built in memory of Princess Diana.

*The Serpentine
Gallery is open
daily 10am–
6pm; free;
☎ 020/7402
6075; www
.serpentine
gallery.org.*

To the south of all this statuary, on the west side of the Ring (the road that splits the park in half), stands the **Serpentine Gallery**, built as a tearoom in 1908 because the park authorities thought "poorer visitors" might otherwise cause trouble if left without refreshments. Since the 1960s, the tearoom has served as an art gallery, which has a reputation for lively, and often controversial, contemporary art exhibitions, and contains an excellent art bookshop.

The Albert Memorial

Hyde Park and Kensington Gardens

Guided tours Sun 2 & 3pm; £3; ☎020/7495 0916; South Kensington tube.

Completed in 1876 by George Gilbert Scott, the **Albert Memorial**, on the south side of Kensington Gardens, is as much a hymn to the glorious achievements of Britain as to its subject, Queen Victoria's husband (who died of typhoid in 1861), though he occupies its central canopy, clutching a catalogue for the Great Exhibition (see box below). The pomp of the monument is overwhelming: the spire, inlaid with semi-precious stones and marbles, rises to 180ft, a marble frieze around the pediment is cluttered with 169 life-sized figures (all men) in high relief, depicting poets, musicians, painters, architects and sculptors from

For the Albert Hall and the museums and institutions to the south, see p.344 and p.346.

The Great Exhibition and the Crystal Palace

East of the Albert Memorial, opposite Prince of Wales Gate, was the site of the **Great Exhibition of the Works and Industry of All Nations**, held between May 1 and October 15, 1851. The idea originated with Henry Cole, a minor civil servant in the Record Office, and was taken up enthusiastically by Prince Albert despite much opposition from snooty Kensington residents, who complained that it would attract an "invasion of undesirables who would ravish their silver and their serving maids". A competition to design the exhibition building produced 245 rejected versions, until Joseph Paxton, head gardener to the Duke of Devonshire, offered to build his "**Crystal Palace**", a wrought-iron and glass structure some 1848ft long and 408ft wide. The acceptance of Paxton's radical proposal was an act of faith by the exhibition organizers, since such a structure had never been built, and their faith was amply rewarded – a team of two hundred workers completed the building in just four months, and more than six million people came to visit it.

The exhibition was primarily designed to show off the achievements of the British Empire but, with over a third of all the exhibits coming from outside Great Britain, it was also a unique opportunity for people to enjoy the products of other cultures. Thousands of exhibits were housed in the Crystal Palace, including the Koh-i-Noor diamond (displayed in a bird-cage), an Indian ivory throne, a floating church from Philadelphia, a bed which awoke its occupant by ejecting him or her into a cold bath, false teeth designed not to be displaced when yawning, a fountain running with eau de Cologne, and all manner of china, fabrics and glass. To everyone's surprise, the exhibition was even profit-making and the surplus was used to buy 87 acres of land to the south of Kensington Road, for the creation of a "Museumland" where "the arts and sciences could be promoted and taught in a way which would be of practical use to industry and make Britain the leading country of the industrialized world". Much to most people's dismay, the Crystal Palace itself was dismantled after the exhibition and rebuilt in southeast London in 1854, where it served as a concert hall, theatre, menagerie and exhibition space, only to be entirely destroyed by fire in 1936. Its loss has been lamented by Londoners for decades, but so far plans to resurrect the palace – either a full-scale replica (with hotels and other mod cons) at Sydenham or a one-third-size model in Hyde Park itself – have come to nothing.

---

ancient Egypt onwards; the pillars are topped with bronzes of Astronomy, Chemistry, Geology and Geometry; mosaics show Poetry, Painting, Architecture and Sculpture; four outlying marble groups represent the four continents; and other statuary pays homage to Agriculture, Commerce and other aspects of imperial economics.

For most of the 1990s the entire memorial was obliterated by scaffolding, a fact which might have pleased Albert, who claimed that "I can say, with perfect absence of humbug, that I would rather not be made the prominent feature of such a monument . . . it would upset my equanimity to be permanently ridiculed and laughed at in effigy." The most surprising aspect of the £13-million restoration was that Albert emerged gilded from head to toe for the first time since the original gilding was removed in 1915, amid fears that the German zeppelins would use the gaudy statue as a marker for bombing nearby Kensington Palace.

Kensington Palace

April–Sept daily 10am–6pm; Oct–March Wed–Sun 10am–5pm; £9.50; ☎020/7937 9561; *www.hrp.org.uk*. High Street Kensington or Queensway tube.

On the western edge of Kensington Gardens stands **Kensington Palace**, a modestly proportioned Jacobean brick mansion bought by William and Mary in 1689 because the king's asthma and bronchitis were aggravated by Whitehall's damp and fumes. Wren, Hawksmoor and later William Kent were all called in to overhaul and embellish the place, though in the end the palace was the chief royal residence for barely fifty years. The most handsome facade faces south, behind a flamboyant statue of William III, given to Edward VII by the Kaiser. Most people, however, approach from the Round Pond to the east, where George I used to keep his edible turtles, and which is now overlooked by a flattering statue of Queen Victoria sculpted by her daughter, Princess Louise. The nearby Broad Walk is now a favourite spot for rollerblading.

KP, as it's fondly known in royal circles, is, of course, best known today as the place where Princess Diana lived up until her death in 1997. It was, in fact, the official London residence of both Charles and Di until the couple formally separated, and Charles moved out to bachelor accommodation in St James's Palace. In the weeks following Diana's death, literally millions of flowers, mementos, poems and gifts were deposited at the Crowther Gates, to the south of the palace. Kensington Palace has certainly found itself much busier than it ever used to be, with crowds of Di fans paying through the nose to visit the modest state apartments on the east side of the complex (the entrance, however, is to the north). Visitors do not get to see Diana's apartments, which were situated on the west side of the palace, where the likes of Princess Margaret, the Duke and Duchess of Kent and the Duke and Duchess of Gloucester all still live.

Royal Ceremonial Dress Collection

Entrance tickets are purchased in the gloomy **Red Saloon** on the ground floor, where the 18-year-old Victoria held her first Privy Council meeting, just hours after hearing of William IV's death on June 20, 1837. Visitors are given personal audioguides, lasting just over an hour, and starting with the **Royal Ceremonial Dress Collection**. The one-time star exhibit, Diana's wedding dress, is now on show at the Spencer family home of Althorp, and only passing reference is made to the fact that Diana lived here from 1981 to 1997.

Unfortunately, the exhibition isn't laid out chronologically, so you get little impression of the historical development of court dress; the earliest exhibits, from the eighteenth century, are, in fact, displayed last. This was the era of the ludicrous mantua dress with side hoops, which were eventually dispensed with during the reign of George IV. Certain elements, however, such as the ostrich-feather headdress and the lace lappets or veil, persisted right up until World War II, after which debutantes were invited to "coming out" parties instead. The whole charade finally came to an official end in 1958, though court dress is still worn by the royals and their minions during big state occasions.

The tour kicks off with a tableau of a 1920s debutante getting ready to be presented at court, and an ambassador getting kitted out in full court dress. Later on, there's an Edwardian court scene, with the women clothed in flamboyant cream silk dresses designed to accentuate their bust, and the men buttoned up in stiff, military garb. You then get to see a few of the Queen's zillion dresses: from the glamorous 1950s ball gowns, smothered in sequins and pearls, to her more suspect later penchant for apricot- and peach-coloured dresses. After a room dominated by purple and ermine coronation robes, you get to go round the state apartments proper on the first floor.

State apartments

Little of Wren's work survives in the **King's Apartments**, and the most interesting rooms are mostly designed by William Kent, beginning with the **King's Staircase**, with its Tijou wrought-iron balustrade and trompe l'oeil crowds of courtiers and yeomen. Another great Kent creation is the "grotesque" style painting on the ceiling of the **Presence Chamber**, which also features a lovely pear-wood Gibbons overmantle with weeping putti. Two rooms further on, the **Cupola Room**, with its monstrously ugly clock occupying centre stage, features another wonderful trompe l'oeil fresco, which gives the effect of a coffered dome. Another two rooms on, the **King's Bedroom** is a bit of a shocker, since it was totally redecorated in 1836 for the Duchess of Kent and her daughter, the future Queen Victoria. Victoria was born in the decaying palace in 1819, and spent her dull, sad childhood cooped up here with her strict mother, who even slept in the same room as her. According to her diary, her best friends were the palace's numerous "black beetles", though it's clear from the Indian clubs, that she was also into keep-fit. The grandest room in the palace is the **King's Gallery**, whose red damask walls are hung with paintings by, among others, Tintoretto (the equestrian portrait of Charles I is not an original Van Dyck). Also of interest is the wind dial above the fireplace, connected to the palace weather vane and still fully functioning.

The **Queen's Apartments**, which follow, are, by contrast, much more modest, wood-panelled rooms hung with Dutch works reflecting the tastes of William and Mary – they are also the most dull, since they contain little furniture, and what decoration there was disappeared in the bomb damage of the last war. The best room is the **Queen's Bedchamber**, decked out in deep blue velvet, with a four-poster bed that belonged to Queen Mary of Modena, James II's second wife, brought here from St James's Palace. It was here that the diminutive Queen Anne died of apoplexy after overeating; the toilet on which George II died of a heart attack, brought on by constipation, is, however, no longer in existence. The last room on the tour is the **Queen's Gallery**, once magnificently decorated with 154 pieces of oriental porcelain, now reduced to a mere handful, and lined with royal portraits. At the far end is one by Peter Lely, of Anne Hyde, mistress and later wife of the future James II; they officially married after she was already pregnant, causing something of a royal scandal even in the libidinous Restoration period.

Around the palace

Before you leave the palace grounds, take a look at the Sunken Garden, created to the east of the palace in 1909 in emulation of the formal gardens laid out by William and Mary. Dwarf cypresses punctuate the garden's oblong pond, with terraced flowerbeds surrounding it, but the prettiest feature is the lime walk. To the north is Nicholas Hawksmoor's exquisite **Orangery** (daily: Easter–Oct 10am–6pm; Nov–Easter 10am–5pm), built for Queen Anne as a summer dining room, where you can now enjoy expensive coffee and snacks while taking in carving and statues by Grinling Gibbons.

Kensington Palace Gardens, the leafy avenue which runs along the edge of Kensington Gardens, was the Millionaires' Row of the Victorian period, flanked by a succession of ostentatious detached mansions set within their own grounds and built by some of the most successful architects of the day, such as Decimus Burton and Sidney Smirke. It remains a private road and an expensive piece of real estate, with most of the houses adopted as embassies or ambassadorial residences.

Nearby High Street Kensington is covered on p.363.

South Kensington: Museumland

To everyone's surprise, the 1851 Great Exhibition (see box on p.339) was not only an enormous success, but actually yielded a profit of £186,000, with which Prince Albert and his committee bought 87 acres of land in **South Kensington**. Institutions and museums, whose purpose was to "extend the influence of Science and Art upon Productive Industry", were to be established here to form a kind of "Museumland". Albert died of typhoid in 1861 at the age of just 41, and never saw his dream fully realized, but "Albertopolis", with its remarkable cluster of **museums and colleges**, plus the vast Albert Hall, now stands as one of London's most enlightened examples of urban planning.

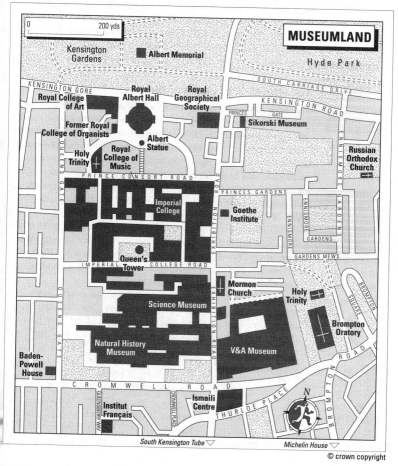

© crown copyright

The nearest
tube is South
Kensington,
from which
there is a long,
tiled foot tun-
nel leading to
the museums.

With the founding of "Museumland", the surrounding area was transformed almost overnight into one of the most fashionable in town – which it remains. The multistorey mansions around the Royal Albert Hall and the grand Italianate houses along Queen's Gate, and further south around Onslow Square, date from this period. South Ken, as it's called, has acquired further cachet thanks to its **French connections**, with a French school, crèche, bookshop and several genuine patisseries and brasseries clustered around the **Institut Français**, on Queensbury Place, which maintains an interesting programme of theatre, cinema and exhibitions. Over on nearby Exhibition Road, rival German cultural offerings emanate from the **Goethe Institute**, while the Islamic world is represented by the **Ismaili Centre**.

A further French sight – and one not to be missed while in this part of town – is the gorgeous Art Deco **Michelin House**, a short walk to the south down Brompton Road. Faced in white faïence and deco-rated with tyres and motoring murals by French artists in 1911, its ground floors now house the shop, café, oyster bar and restaurant of *Bibendum*, all run by Terence Conran (see p.530).

The Albert Hall and around

The fresh funds raised to commemorate the Prince Consort on his death in 1861 were squandered on the Albert Memorial (see p.339), and it took considerable effort by Henry Cole, his collaborator on the Great Exhibition, to get funding to complete the **Royal Albert Hall**, on Kensington Gore. Plans for this splendid iron-and-glass-domed auditorium had been drawn up during the prince's lifetime, with an exterior of red brick, terracotta and marble that was already the hallmark of South Ken architecture. The hall was finally completed in 1871 by selling seats on 999-year leases – an "ownership" that persists today, though this is also the venue for Europe's most demo-cratic music festival, the Henry Wood Promenade Concerts. Better known as the **Proms** (*www.bbc.co.uk/proms*), these top-flight clas-sical concerts take place from July to September, with standing-only (or sit-on-the-floor) tickets for as little as £3.

For informa-
tion on tickets
to the Proms,
see p.576.

Behind the hall, flanked by the monumental South Steps, is a memorial to the Great Exhibition, once more featuring the Prince Consort. Predating the Royal Albert Hall (which Albert turns his back on), it originally stood amid the gardens and pavilions of the Royal Horticultural Society, which were replaced in the 1880s by the colos-sal **Imperial Institute** building. Of this only the 280-foot **Queen's Tower** remains, stranded amid Imperial College, London University's science faculty. On the north side of this complex is the Neo-Gothic **Royal College of Music**, whose students have included Ralph Vaughan Williams and Benjamin Britten. The college also houses a museum containing a collection of nearly six hundred instruments, mostly European, dating from the fifteenth to the twentieth centuries.

The Royal
College of
Music's mu-
seum is open
term time Wed
2–4.30pm; £3;
☎020/7589
3643; www.
rcm.ac.uk.

Several other educational institutions congregate near the Albert Hall, as was Albert's intention. The most striking is the former **Royal College of Organists**, to the west of the Albert Hall, a strange Neo-Jacobean confection, designed for free in 1875 by Henry Cole's eldest son and laced with cream, maroon and sky-blue sgraffito. Also on the west side of the Albert Hall is the headquarters of the **Royal College of Art**, a seven-storey 1960s block which belies its foundation by Prince Albert; student art exhibitions are held during term time on the ground floor (daily 10am–6pm; *www.rca.ac.uk*).

To the east is the **Royal Geographical Society**, a wonderful brick-built complex in the Queen Anne style, with statues of two of the society's early explorers, David Livingstone and Ernest Shackleton, occupying niches along the outer wall. The society hosts exhibitions and lectures, and maintains a remarkable library, open to non-members by appointment only.

There are strong Polish connections in the South Ken area, as exemplified by the **Sikorski Museum** in the Polish Institute, a little to the east of the Royal Geographical Society at 20 Princes Gate. This was founded after the war by disgruntled Polish exiles, whose contribution to the Allied cause was significant, particularly in the RAF, and World War II militaria forms the bedrock of the museum, along with the personal effects of General Władysław Sikorski, the prewar prime minister who fled to London in 1939, only to die in a mysterious plane accident over Gibraltar in 1943. The absence of a non-Communist leader of Sikorski's standing after the war has been lamented by exiled Poles ever since.

Another East European connection is contained within the **Westminster Synagogue**, a couple of blocks west of the Sikorski Museum in Rutland Gardens. In 1964 this received 1564 Torah scrolls, gathered from all over Czechoslovakia by the Nazis for their planned "Museum of an Extinct Race". Hundreds have since been restored and sent out to Jewish communities in America, Israel and throughout Europe, but the remainder are displayed here.

South Kensington: Museumland

The Royal Geographical Society is open Mon–Fri 9am–5pm by appointment only; call ☎020/7591 3040; www .rgs.org.

The Sikorski Museum is open Mon–Fri 2–4pm, also first Sat of month 10am– 4pm; free; ☎020/7589 9249.

Westminster Synagogue is open Tues & Thurs 10am– 4pm; free; ☎020/7584 3741.

Brompton Oratory and other South Ken churches

London's most flamboyant Roman Catholic church, the **Brompton Oratory**, stands just east of the V&A. The first large Catholic church to be built since the Reformation, it was begun by the young and unknown Herbert Gribble in 1880 and modelled on the Gesù church in Rome, "so that those who had no opportunity of going over to Italy to see an Italian church had only to come here to see a model of one". The ornate Italianate interior, financed by the Duke of Norfolk, contains some genuine Italian Baroque fittings from the Gesù church and Siena cathedral, notably the seventeenth-century apostles in the nave and the main altar, and reredos of the Lady Chapel. The pulpit is a superb piece of Neo-Baroque from the 1930s, with a high cherub count on the tester. And true to its architecture, the church practises a "rigid, ritualized, smells and bells Catholicism", as one journalist put it, with a sung Mass in Latin every Sunday, and some very high-society weddings throughout the year.

The Victoria and Albert Museum

Daily 10am–5.45pm (Wed also 6.30–9.30pm); £5; free after 4.30pm; ☎020/7942 2000; *www.vam.ac.uk*. South Kensington tube.

In terms of sheer variety and scale, the **Victoria and Albert Museum** (popularly known as the V&A) is the greatest museum of applied arts in the world. The range of exhibits on display here means that, whatever your taste, there is almost bound to be something to grab your attention: the world's largest collection of Indian art outside India,

---

VISITING THE V&A

As Baedeker noted in 1905: "it can hardly be claimed that the arrangements of the [museum] are specially perspicuous." Beautifully but haphazardly displayed across a seven-mile, four-storey maze of halls and corridors, the V&A's treasures are impossible to survey in a single visit. Floor plans from the information desks at the **main entrance** on Cromwell Road and the **side entrance** on Exhibition Road can help you decide on which areas to concentrate – we've listed some of the highlights below. Even equipped with a plan, it's easy to get lost – the room numbering is confusing – so you may prefer to sign up for one of the museum's hourly, free introductory **guided tours**. Those with children in tow should ask about the "Trails for Kids", and watch out for the touch-screens and "touch objects" strewn about the galleries. If you're flagging, head for the licensed café-restaurant in the basement of the Henry Cole Wing, or the more snacky café in the glorious Gamble Room, and, in summer only, in the grassy main courtyard of the Pirelli Garden.

HIGHLIGHTS

Raphael Cartoons: Level A, room 48a.
European Dress Collection: Level A, room 40.
Indian Art: Level A, room 41.
Photography Gallery: Level A, room 38.
Plaster Casts: Level A, rooms 46a & 46b.
Poynter, Morris and Gamble Rooms: Level A, off rooms 13–15.
Twentieth-Century Galleries: Level B, rooms 70–74.
Glass Gallery: Level B, room 131.
Frank Lloyd Wright Gallery: Henry Cole Wing, Level 2, room 202.
Constable Paintings: Henry Cole Wing, Level 6, room 603.

SEASON TICKETS

If you can see yourself making more than one visit in the coming year to the Natural History, Science or V&A museums, it's worth buying a **Season Ticket**, which costs £29 and provides unlimited access for a year to all three sights; for more details call ☎020/7942 4455.

plus huge Chinese, Islamic, Japanese and Korean galleries; the country's largest dress collection; a gallery of twentieth-century *objets d'art* to rival the Design Museum; more Constable paintings than the Tate, plus seven Raphael masterpieces and sizeable collections of miniatures, watercolours and medieval and Renaissance sculpture. As if all this were not enough, the V&A's temporary shows are among the best in Britain, ranging over vast areas of art, craft and technology.

South Kensington: Museumland

The V&A began life in 1852, under the directorship of Henry Cole, as the Museum of Manufactures, a gathering of objects from the Great Exhibition and a motley collection of plaster casts – it being Albert's intention to rekindle Britain's industrial dominance by inspiring factory workers, students and craftspeople with examples of excellence in applied art and design. This notion disappeared swiftly as ancient and medieval exotica poured in from other international exhibitions and from the far corners of the Empire and beyond. By the turn of the century, it was clear that Thomas Cubitt's cast-iron and glass sheds, in which the exhibits were temporarily housed, would have to be replaced with something bigger.

In the 1980s the V&A famously advertised itself as "A great café with a museum attached"; the café is, in fact, run by Millburns, who run several of London's museum and gallery cafés.

Queen Victoria laid the foundation stone of the present deeply colonial building in 1899 (the last major public engagement of her life); ten years later Aston Webb's imposing main entrance, with its octagonal cupola and flying buttresses and pinnacles, was finished. The side entrance on Exhibition Road into the Henry Cole Wing, originally built in 1873 for the School of Naval Architects and more in the South Ken style, is equally ornate, with its terracotta arcading and Minton tiles. Like all London's major museums, the V&A has big plans for the new millennium, with a £75-million multifaceted extension, known as the "**Spiral**" and designed by the controversial Polish-born architect, Daniel Libeskind, due to open in 2004.

The Raphael Cartoons

The most famous of the V&A's many exhibits are the **Raphael Cartoons** (room 48a), to the left of the main entrance, beyond the museum shop. The cartoons comprise seven vast, full-colour paintings, which are, in fact, designs for tapestries ordered by Pope Leo X for the Sistine Chapel. The pictures – based on episodes from the lives of SS Peter and Paul during the foundation of the early Christian Church (as described in Acts) – were bought by the future Charles I in 1623. They were reproduced in countless tapestries and engravings in the seventeenth and eighteenth centuries, and during this period were probably more familiar and influential than any of the artist's paintings. Alongside the paintings is an example of one of the tapestries woven at Mortlake in the 1630s, which are considered to be more faithful to the original colours as intended by Raphael than those woven in Brussels for the Vatican.

Room 48a

At the far end of room 48a stands the **Retable of St George**, a huge fifteenth-century gilded altarpiece from Valencia, centred on a depiction of James I of Aragon defeating the Moors at the Battle of Puig in 1237. More alarming, though, are the bloodthirsty side panels, which feature the gross tortures endured by St George, which ended with him having nails driven through his body, being placed in a cauldron of molten lead, dragged naked through the streets and finally beheaded and sawn in half.

The Dress Collection and Musical Instruments

Directly opposite the Cartoons room is the dimly lit domed hall of Costume Court, which houses the excellent European section of the

Room 40

Dress Collection (room 40). The exhibition starts with examples of Jacobean doublet and breeches, from the days when real men wore lace, and proceeds chronologically, though you need to consult the plan at the entrance as the layout is confusing. The more contemporary stuff changes with current fashions, but usually includes a catwalk video of a recent collection by top British designers such as Paul Smith, Alexander McQueen and Vivienne Westwood.

A central flight of stairs in this hall leads up to the museum's (strangely silent) collection of **Musical Instruments** (room 40a), chosen for their decorative rather than musical qualities (you can't actually get to hear any of them being played). Among the more amazing exhibits are sixteenth-century Italian harpsichords, a three-stringed giant double bass, various lutes inlaid with ivory and shell, the dauphin's very own pocket violin and a bizarre wind instrument called a serpent, a distant relative of the tuba.

India and Islam

Back on the ground floor, east of the Costume Court, there follows a string of superb Eastern galleries, kicking off with the Nehru Gallery

Room 41

of **Indian Art** (room 41), which shows only a fraction of this world-class collection, much of it derived from the city's old East India Company Museum. The most popular exhibit, and always on display, is **Tippoo's Tiger**, a life-sized wooden automaton of a tiger mauling an officer of the East India Company; the innards of the tiger feature a miniature keyboard which simulates the groans of the dying soldier. It was made for the amusement of the Sultan of Mysore, who was killed when the British took Seringapatam in 1799, and whose watch, telescope, brooch and sword are also displayed here.

One particular exhibit that is highly revered by the Sikh community is the **Golden Throne**, which belonged to **Ranjit Singh**, the last Sikh emperor, and was taken by the British when they annexed the Punjab in 1849. Other treasures at the heart of the gallery include several panels inset with *jalis* (sandstone window screens) and a superb white nephrite-jade wine cup, carved in the shape of a shell, made for the Mogul emperor Shah Jahan.

Rooms 47a, 47b & 42

Outside the Nehru Gallery is a long corridor (rooms 47a & 47b) lined with big basalt sculptures from India and Nepal, plus copper artefacts such as a superb Nepalese mask of the wrathful Shiva, studded with skulls and snakes. Next comes the **Islamic Gallery** (room 42), a dramatic gathering of vivid blue tiles, colourful earthenware and a carved wooden *mimbar* (pulpit), dominated by the stupendous sixteenth-century Ardabil Persian carpet bought on the advice of William Morris, and the exquisite **Chelsea Carpet**, bought in Chelsea but of unknown origin.

The Medieval Treasury, China, Japan and Korea

The gallery straight ahead of you as you enter the museum is the darkened **Medieval Treasury** (room 43), lit through fragments of stained glass. Among the many reliquaries, sculptures and other devotional items are the **Eltenberg Reliquary** (a miniature Byzantine church wrought in a mixture of bronze, oak, gilt copper, enamel and walrus ivory), and the **Gloucester Candlestick**, a Norman masterpiece of gilt bronzework with tiny figures and animals wrapped like ivy round its stem.

Next door, the T.T. Tsui Gallery of **Chinese Art** (room 44) has been imaginatively redesigned around themes rather than in chronological sequence, with bilingual labelling and touch-screen computers on hand to elucidate. The range of materials, from jade to rhino horn, lacquer to lapis lazuli, is more striking than any individual piece, though the pair of top-hatted gentlemen carved in marble stand out in the parade of Buddhas near the entrance – they are thought to represent Korean envoys.

At the main entrance to the atmospheric adjacent Toshiba Gallery of **Japanese Art** (room 45) is an incredible bronze incense burner, decorated with life-size peacocks – it was bought by the V&A in 1883 and the price tag of over £1500 was a record at the time. The most intriguing objects, which stand out among a wealth of silk, lacquer and samurai armour, are the tiny, elaborately carved, jade and marble *netsuke* (belt toggles) portraying such quirky subjects as "spider on aubergine" and "starving dog on a bed of leaves". Look out, too, for the articulated wrought-iron eighteenth-century snake.

Room 45

Hidden in a slightly obscure corridor, along from the Japanese gallery, is the Samsung Gallery of **Korean Art** (room 47g), which ranges from simple stoneware and ceramics from the first millennium to ornate red-lacquered chests made for the nineteenth-century royal court of the Choson dynasty, and a modern silk patchwork "flower shoe", designed by a contemporary Korean artist.

Room 47g

Sculpture and architecture

Turn right at the main information desk and you'll reach the airy gallery of **Sculpture and Architecture** (rooms 50a and 50b), which is guarded at the entrance by four larger-than-life heraldic beasts. Beyond lies Antonio Canova's *Three Graces*, bought jointly by the V&A and the National Gallery of Scotland in 1994 for an absolute

Rooms 50a & 50b

fortune. There's more Neoclassical soft porn, in the form of Canova's *Sleeping Nymph*, nearby, plus the sculptor's *Theseus and the Minotaur*, another version of which sits on the main staircase of Vienna's Kunsthistorisches Museum. Much of the sculpture here is portraiture, and the most famous of the lot is the marble statue of Handel, created in 1738 by Roubiliac. The first statue in Europe to a living artist, it originally stood in the then-fashionable Vauxhall Gardens in South London, and caused a great stir in its day, with the composer depicted as Apollo slouching in inspired disarray, one shoe dangling from his foot.

Beyond the gallery's giant rood loft (from 'sHertogenbosch cathedral) is a collection of predominantly Italian sculpture and architectural fragments. At the centre stands Bernini's magnificent *Neptune and Triton*, initially brought to this country by Joshua Reynolds. Around the edges are bits and pieces from the churches and palaces of northern Italy, the most impressive being the towering equestrian funerary monument of the soldier, Marchese Spinetta Malaspina, from the fifteenth century. There's also a whole array of glazed terracotta works by Della Robbia, including a superb *Last Supper* based on Leonardo's famous composition.

Rooms 62–64

Upstairs, among smaller-scale **sculpture and carvings** (room 64) are some remarkable wax sculptures, mostly portraits, but including one or two entire scenes: *Death of Voltaire* and an *Adoration of the Shepherds*. The ivory pieces range from Carolingian portable altars to scenes of love-making on medieval Italian combs, and from an utterly ridiculous, staggeringly intricate Rococo depiction of the Immaculate Conception to a walrus ivory nude by Eric Gill.

For the moment, while the British galleries (rooms 52–58 & 118–126) are being redesigned, the highlights of those rooms are displayed as the "**Best of British**" (rooms 62 & 63).

Fakes and forgeries and plaster casts

*Plaster casts;
rooms 46a &
46b*

The gallery (room 46) between the two Cast Courts (see below) is fascinating; it is lined with **fakes and forgeries**, among them a "fourteenth-century" wooden oratory which the museum purchased in good faith in 1912, only to be informed by the craftsman's son that it was a fake, and two busts, which were made and sold in the nineteenth century as copies of a bust by the fifteenth-century Florentine sculptor, Desiderio da Settignano in the Louvre (which is now thought to be a nineteenth-century copy itself).

On either side are the two enormous Cast Courts filled with **plaster casts**; genuine fakes, as it were, created so that ordinary Londoners would be able to experience the glories of classical and ancient art. Still with their barrel-vaulted glass roofs and heavy Victorian décor, these little-visited rooms are an astonishing sight, and hark back to the origins of the museum. In the Victorian Court, to the west, a copy of the colossal Trajan's Column from the Forum in Rome, sliced in half to fit in the room, towers over the rest of the South Kensington: Museumland plaster casts, which include the Brunswick Lion, Prague's St George and a full-scale painted replica of the entire portal of the cathedral of Santiago de Compostela, set around the ill-fitting doors of Hildeheim cathedral. In the Italian Court, opposite, a life-sized replica of Michelangelo's *David* stands opposite Verrocchio's smaller bronze of the same subject in the company of the pulpits of Pisa cathedral and baptistry, and Ghiberti's celebrated bronze doors from the baptistry in Florence, which are framed by the central doorway of Bologna's San Petronio.

Photography and Northern Europe

The V&A now has an entire room, the Canon **Photography Gallery** *Room 38* (room 38), devoted to the art form. Given the limited space available, the exhibitions here are likely to be changed fairly frequently, and are drawn from the museum's vast collection, which was begun by Sir Henry Cole as long ago as 1856 and now numbers over 300,000 works.

Close by are the rooms used for the V&A's special exhibitions, but if you're heading for the Poynter, Gamble and Morris rooms (see p.352) you need to pass through a whole series of rooms displaying works from **Northern Europe** (rooms 25–29), including a German *Room 25–29* copper tankard designed like a miniature fairy-tale castle.

European Art and Sculpture 1100–1900

Weaving its way around much of the ground floor is a typical V&A potpourri that goes under the catch-all title of **European Art and** *Rooms 21 & 24* **Sculpture** (rooms 21–24 & 1–9), with the earliest works just beyond the Medieval Treasury (see p.349).

At the eastern end (room 24), there's an incredible altarpiece from Hamburg, featuring apocalyptic seven-headed beasts, frog-eating dragons and lots of slaughter and miracles. At the opposite end of the gallery (room 21), you'll find two masterpieces from the Italian Renaissance: Giambologna's marble statue *Samson Slaying a Philistine* (not to be confused with Foggini's nearby, much later version, *Samson Slaying Two Philistines*) and Michelangelo's two tiny wax models, one for a figure on the tomb of Pope Julius II, the other for a Medici tomb.

Meanwhile **Europe 1600–1800** (rooms 1–7) continues in the base- *Rooms 1–7* ment, where the first room is filled with treasure cabinets in a variety of materials from Limoges enamel to ebony, walnut and bone; there's also a sixteenth-century Italian spinet inlaid with nearly two thousand precious and semiprecious stones. Beyond lies a collection of large cabinets, a painted wood-panelled room from a provincial manor house near Alençon, Meissen porcelain, gilded leather panels in "Chinese" style, exhibits reflecting the sickly tastes of the French nobility in the eighteenth century and finally a polygonal mirrored cabinet from Italy.

The chronological sequence continues on the other side of the main entrance with **Europe and America 1800–1900** (rooms 8 & 9). The first room is given over to the kind of over-the-top stuff that packed out the international exhibitions of the 1860s and 1870s – cumbersome Neo-Gothic furniture and the like. The small green room at the end contains works from the 1900 Paris Exhibition, which heralded the emergence of Art Nouveau. Tiffany glassware, furniture by Adolf Loos and Otto Wagner and posters by Toulouse-Lautrec, Hector Guimard and Alfons Mucha are thrown in for good measure.

Rooms 8 & 9

The Poynter, Morris and Gamble Rooms

Whatever you do, don't miss the museum's original refreshment rooms at the back of the main galleries. Embellished by Edward Poynter with a wash of decorative blue tiling depicting the months and seasons of the year, the eastern **Poynter Room**, where hoi polloi ate, was originally known as the Grill Room – the grill, also designed by Poynter, is still in place and was in use until 1939. On the other side, the dark green **Morris Room** – one of Morris & Co's first public commissions – accommodated a better class of diner. The decorative detail is really worth taking in: gilded Pre-Raphaelite panels and Burne-Jones stained glass, embossed olive-branch wallpaper and a running cornice frieze of dogs chasing hares.

The largest and grandest of the rooms lies between the two. The **Gamble Room**, which is now open as a café once more, was designed by the museum's own team of artists and boasts dazzling, almost edible décor, with mustard, gold and cream-coloured Minton tiles covering the walls and pillars from floor to ceiling. Fleshy Pre-Raphaelite nudes hold up the nineteenth-century chimneypiece from Dorchester House, while a ceramic frieze of frolicking cherubs accompanies a quote from Ecclesiastes, spelt out in decorative script around the cornice.

Italy 1400–1500

The Poynter, Gamble and Morris rooms lie off the sprawling, L-shaped series of galleries devoted to **Italy 1400–1500** (rooms 12–20), in other words the Renaissance. The collection begins, confusingly, in room 16, which is devoted to Donatello and contains, among other reliefs, the sculptor's *Ascension*, illustrating his "squashed relief" technique. Room 13 features lots of glazed terracotta works from the workshop of Della Robbia, as does room 12, which has a lovely series of roundels depicting the months/labours of the year, which once decorated the Medici palace in Florence. Room 17 boasts an entire eighteenth-century ceiling fresco, while, two rooms on, is the Fairfax Cup, an early sixteenth-century Venetian opaque turquoise glass, decorated with enamel scenes from Ovid. The collection ends in room 20, with an amazing sixteenth-century

Rooms 12–20

pear-wood crucifixion scene. Two of the finest works from the period are, in fact, displayed in room 21 (see p.351).

Britain 1500–1900

If you go up to the first floor from the main entrance, follow the long dark corridor of stained glass and turn left along a gallery of iron-work, you should arrive at a series of rooms covering **Britain 1500–1750** (rooms 52–58). These galleries are being redesigned and will be open from the end of 2001, though the contents outlined below should stay pretty much the same. In the intervening time, the highlights of the galleries will be shown in the "Best of British" collection in room 62.

Rooms 52–58

The galleries begin with Holbein's miniature of Anne of Cleves and the sixteenth-century Howard Grace Cup, made from ivory and sil-ver-gilt and crowned by a tiny St George and the dragon. At the other end of the scale is the **Great Bed of Ware**, a king-sized Elizabethan oak four-poster in which 26 butchers and their wives are said to have once spent the night. Among the Spitalfields silks, Huguenot silver and lime-wood carving by Gibbons are a number of period interiors saved in their entirety from buildings that have since been demol-ished. These include an Elizabethan wood-panelled room from Sizeburgh Castle in the Lake District, the Music Room from Norfolk House on St James's Square and a pine-panelled room from Hatton Garden.

There are more works from **Britain 1750–1900** (rooms 118–126) one floor up, including a Chippendale four-poster made for David Garrick, Adam bookcases and paintings by Gainsborough and Angelica Kauffmann. Again, period interiors are a big feature of the collection: Adam's Venetian-red Glass Drawing Room from Northumberland House, his ceiling from Garrick's house in the Adelphi Terrace and the fan-vaulted entrance to Lee Priory library in Kent. You'll also find plenty of outpourings from the **Arts and Crafts movement**, from William Morris wallpaper to Burne-Jones tiles. Other highlights include an almost Jazz Age piano by Baillie-Scott, a screen by Lawrence Alma-Tadema, William Burges's original furni-ture from his Tower House (see p.365), Charles Rennie Mackintosh panels from the Willow Tea Rooms and a Neo-Jacobean piano by Edwin Lutyens.

Rooms 118–126

Twentieth-Century Galleries

Beyond these British rooms, the attractively designed **Twentieth-Century Galleries** (rooms 70–74) make a diffident attempt to address contemporary questions of art and design (the original purpose of the V&A). The collection itself is impressive, beginning confusingly with room 74, the first and largest of the galleries, which takes up where the Arts and Crafts room left off. The shift into mod-ernist gear is smoothly effected with furniture by Otto Wagner,

Rooms 70–74

Bauhaus and the Wiener Werkstätte co-op. Constructivist fabrics and crockery follow, alongside a range of works by Finnish modernist supremo Alvar Aalto. Populist touches are provided by the odd cabinet of old advertisements and packaging from the likes of Vimto and Brylcreem, and the whole parade ends up with a mad melange of Olivetti typewriters, Swatch watches and a bubble-gum-pink vacuum cleaner from Japan, yours in the shops for a mere £1000.

Jewellery, Textiles, Silver and Glass

The remaining galleries in the main building used to be known as the **Study Collection**, or "Materials and Techniques Collection", and were intended for specialist study rather than for public consumption. All that is slowly changing as the V&A gradually redesigns the galleries – so far, the Glass Gallery and Silver Collection have been overhauled. The top-floor galleries of ceramics, pottery and porcelain are often closed in the summer; similarly, the twentieth-century study collection (rooms 103–106) is only infrequently open.

Rooms 91–94

Despite its presentational shortcomings, the heavily guarded **Jewellery Collection** (rooms 91–93) is well worth a visit, with over six thousand extremely valuable items on display, ranging from ancient Egyptian amulets and Celtic chokers to perspex bangles from the 1960s. One of the most treasured pieces is the brooch-sized Armada Jewel, which contains a delicate Hilliard portrait miniature of Elizabeth I, who is believed to have given the jewel to Sir Francis Drake. Look out, too, for the grandiose **Leighton Frescoes**, which have been cleaned eleven times since the last war in an effort to combat the effects of the damp English climate. They used to look down onto the Cast Courts from on high; now, stuck in the corridor between rooms 107 and 109, you can at least see them close up. Another gallery of more general interest is the darkened chamber in the far northeastern corner of the museum, which is hung with precious medieval **Tapestries** (room 94), among them the famous Devonshire Hunts.

The best approach to the museum's dazzling **Silver Galleries** (rooms 65–69) is via the spectacular **ceramic staircase**, its Minton tile decoration designed by Frank Moody, and intended to be just one of many such stairwells within the museum. Note the ceramic memorial to Sir Henry Cole, the work of his niece, who has rendered her uncle in mosaic with "Albertopolis" (or Museumland) in relief above. The galleries beyond originally displayed ceramics, and were lined with ceramic-clad pillars, of which just two remain, in room 65. The Silver Galleries house the national collection of English silver from 1300 to 1800, as well as contemporary works such as a chic chain-mail Bolero jacket. The centrepiece, though, is the giant **Jerningham Wine Cooler**, which is smothered with Bacchic revelry and imagery. It is, in fact, a Victorian copy of an eighteenth-century wine cooler – the world's largest – which took four years to make and now resides in the Hermitage. The nearby "Discovery Area" is the fun section, where you can rub or stamp a hallmark, and flick through the museum's photostore of contemporary artists working in silver. Before you leave, don't miss the three, virtually life-size silver lions, at the far end of the room.

South Kensington: Museumland

Lastly, there's the hi-tech **Glass Gallery** (room 131) on the second floor, with touch-screen computers and a spectacular modern glass staircase and balustrade. The staggering beauty and variety of the glass on display is only slightly tarnished by the lack of any extensive twentieth-century perspective, though there are some *objets d'art* by contemporary artists.

Room 131

The Henry Cole Wing

The **Henry Cole Wing** is easily overlooked, as it's only accessible from the northwest corner of the ground floor, or via the Exhibition Road entrance. Highlights here include the **Frank Lloyd Wright Gallery** (Level 2), whose centrepiece is a complete office interior created by the architect in the 1930s for a Pittsburgh department-store owner – a typically organic design in luxuriant wood. Also on this floor is the **European Ornament Gallery**, demonstrating the influences and fashions in decoration of all kinds: antiquities, Rococo figurines and architectural plans share space with 1920s cotton hangings inspired by Howard Carter's discovery of Tutankhamen's tomb, and kitsch 1950s china ornaments.

The Henry Cole Wing closes daily at 5.30pm.

Level 3 will eventually become home to the RIBA collection of architectural drawings.

Portrait miniatures, by Holbein, Hilliard and others, feature on Level 4, the rest of which is taken up with nineteenth-century oil paintings, densely hung in the manner of their period. The largest collection of Swiss landscape paintings outside Switzerland and sentimental Victorian genre works are of pretty specialist appeal, but persevere and you'll discover paintings by Landseer, the Barbizon School, an Arts and Crafts piano and a Burne-Jones sideboard. There are also minor works by Degas, Delacroix, Rembrandt and Botticelli, an Ingres nude, a Tiepolo sketch, some Fantin-Latour flowers and several Pre-Raphaelite works, the best of which is Rossetti's verdant, emerald-green *The Day Dream*, one of his last great works. At the far end, you may have to ask to see Carracciolo's 360-degree *Panorama of Rome*, which was displayed in the Rotunda off Leicester Square (see p.139).

Level 6 is almost wholly devoted to the paintings of **John Constable**, four hundred of whose works were left to the museum by his daughter. The finished paintings include famous views of Salisbury Cathedral and Dedham Mill, and there are full-size preparatory oil paintings for the *Hay Wain* and *The Leaping Horse*, plus a whole host of his alfresco cloud studies and sketches. There are also several works by **Turner**, including a dreamy view of East Cowes Castle, painted for the castle's owner, John Nash. Also on this level is a goodly collection of sculptures by **Auguste Rodin**, mostly donated to the V&A by the sculptor himself in 1914. They range from fairly straightforward portraits, such as the bust of Balzac, to more expressive and vigorous sculptures like *The Fallen Angel*, a swirling mass of rippling bronze, and the sensuous *Cupid and Psyche*, in which the lovers emerge half-hewn from the white marble.

The Science Museum

Daily 10am–6pm; £6.95; free after 4.30pm; ☎020/7942 4000; *www .sciencemuseum.org.uk*. South Kensington tube.

The **Science Museum**, on Exhibition Road, is undeniably impressive, filling seven floors with items drawn from every conceivable area of science, including space travel, telecommunications, time measurement, chemistry, computing, photography and medicine. The Science Museum also spent much of the 1990s updating many of its galleries with more interactive displays, culminating in 2000 with the opening of the spectacular, high-tech **Wellcome Wing**, which aims to keep its displays up to date with the latest in digital technology. Other parts of the museum remain rather like a sort of history of science museum, though they're no less enjoyable for all that.

Once you've paid your entrance fee, head for the **information desk** in "Power: the East Hall", where you can pick up a museum plan and find out what events and demonstrations are taking place; you can also sign up for a free **guided tour** on a specific subject. Most people will want to head for the new Wellcome Wing, past the info desk; note, however, that to go on a virtual reality ride or to see IMAX presentations in the Wellcome Wing, you have to pay extra. The wing is connected to the old museum at each level; touch-screen computers can show you exactly how to get from one section to the other. There's a simple café off the East Hall, and the very funky *Deep Blue Café* in the Wellcome Wing.

Power, Space and the Making of the Modern World

The museum unsurprisingly gives a lot of space to British innovation during the Industrial Revolution, beginning with its **Power** exhibition in the East Hall, which traces the story from James Watts' pioneering steam engines, first used in the late eighteenth century to pump water out of mine shafts, to the arrival of the combustion engine. The size of these machines is in itself quite a wonder. The largest exhibit is the bright-red Burnley Mill Engine, whose enormous wheel used to drive 1700 looms and worked *in situ* until as late as 1970; you can see it in action most days. And if you've ever wondered what **Foucault's Pendulum** is, check out the one by the stairs at the far end of the hall on the right-hand side.

Beyond lies the **Space** exhibition, which follows the history of rockets from Congreve's early nineteenth-century efforts through the V-1 and V-2 wartime bombs to the Apollo landings. There's a full-size replica of the Apollo 11 landing craft, which deposited US astronauts on the moon in 1969, and one of the Viking Lander that reached Mars in the mid-1970s. However, it's obvious, from the section on the Hubble Space Telescope on the mezzanine, that this gallery is a good decade – and more – old.

The old Transport hall is now the **Making of the Modern World**, a display of iconic inventions of modern science and technology. These include some of the museum's best-loved exhibits: *Puffing Billy*, the world's oldest surviving steam train, used for hauling coal in 1815, Robert Stephenson's *Rocket* of 1829 and his *Columbine* of 1845, used on the world's first passenger railway. Other groundbreaking inventions on display include a Ford Model T, the world's first mass-produced car, and a gleaming aluminium Lockheed 10A Electra Airliner from 1935, which signalled the birth of modern air travel. Less glamorous discoveries, such as the brain scanner, occupy the sidelines, along with disasters such as the thalidomide drug.

The Wellcome Wing

The darkened, ultra-purple **Wellcome Wing** beckons you on, its ground floor dominated by the floating, sloping underbelly of the state-of-the-art **IMAX cinema**. If you're interested in visiting the cinema (£6.75), or taking a **virtual reality ride** (£3.50), you need to buy a ticket from the desk to your right as you enter the wing; combined tickets for both cost £9.75. To one side is the **Deep Blue Café**, with its enticing underlit perspex tables and flashing pagers to tell you when your table is ready.

The two displays on the ground floor, **Antenna** and **Talking Points**, are specifically designed to be changed regularly in order to cover contemporary science issues while they are topical. **Pattern Pod**, meanwhile, is for under-8s only, and is basically a lot of interactive high-tech fun. Kids can experiment with water ripples, footprints, the Penrose tessellation and groove away in the multicoloured human shadow box.

On the first floor, **Who am I?** is a guaranteed winner, as it concentrates on humans themselves. The gallery features a series of "bloids", large blobs fitted with computers at different levels, where you can morph yourself into the opposite sex, watch a sperm race, and test the gender of your brain. Down the middle of the gallery are traditional static displays and reading matter, which delve more deeply into the issues raised in the bloids.

The second floor is home to **Digitopolis**, which attempts to explain the basics of how digital technology works, and its importance in the modern world. Whether it succeeds or not, this is the gallery with the most sophisticated computerized high-jinks – a Sony robot dog, that can actually learn behaviour, is the resident pet. You can make yourself sound like an alien opera singer, give yourself a leopard-print skin via a 3D face scanner and save the results on your very own Web page. The inner workings of these sophisticated tools are on display close by, and there are touch-screen quizzes, snippets of poetry and works of art to keep arts-inclined visitors happy.

Finally, on the third (and uppermost) floor of the Wellcome Wing, **In Future** is a small interactive gallery where several people can gather round and play a series of frivolous but fun multi-player educational games, and vote on contemporary scientific and moral questions, such as "should you be able to choose the gender of your child?".

The basement: hands-on galleries

Throughout the 1990s, the most popular section for those with children was the museum's **Launch Pad**. This lively play area has since been moved to the basement of the Wellcome Wing, and remains riotously popular with kids, though perhaps less successful in actually imparting any basic scientific principles.

There are two more hands-on galleries and a family picnic area in the rest of the basement. The misleadingly entitled **Garden** is aimed at 3- to 6-year-olds, and there's no denying that they will enjoy themselves – donning waterproofs to experiment with lock gates, and hard hats to play with pulleys.

Beyond the Garden, there's another hands-on gallery, imaginatively entitled **Things**, aimed at the natural curiosity of 7- to 11-year-olds about unidentifiable objects. A longer attention span and a fair bit of reading are involved, and there are the usual problems with crowds at the weekend, and with the durability of the exhibits. Lastly, the basement also houses the **Secret Life of the Home**, a static but interesting collection of domestic appliances from the last hundred years, displayed in glass cabinets.

First floor

The **Challenge of Materials**, ranged around the balcony on the first floor, is an extremely stylish exhibition – the glass-floored suspension bridge is particularly cool – covering the use of materials ranging from aluminium to zerodur (used for making laser gyroscopes). As well as the excellent hands-on displays, there are aesthetically pleasing displays of such diverse products as a Bakelite coffin to an Axminster-carpet morning gown designed by Vivienne Westwood.

Passing swiftly through the dated **Telecommunications** section, head for the section tracing the history of **Gas**, from its commercial exploitation in the early eighteenth century to the 1960s when coal-based gas was finally replaced by natural gas, much of it derived from the North Sea. On the opposite side of the gallery, **Agriculture** takes you swiftly from horse power to tractors. Along with displays on surveying, wind measurement and compasses, you'll also find **Time Measurement**, which stretches from Egyptian water clocks to quartz watches; the medieval clock mechanism from Wells Cathedral booms out over the entire hall every quarter of an hour.

Vastly more educative than the Launch Pad is the **Food for Thought** exhibition at the far end of the first-floor galleries. Interactive displays on nutrition, an exercise bicycle for kids who need to pedal off excess energy and a series of period kitchens and pantries bring you to possibly the healthiest branch of *McDonald's* in the world (it doesn't serve food). The sponsors, Sainsbury's, get their plug, of course, with a reconstruction of one of their 1920s shops displayed opposite a modern supermarket scanner till.

South Kensington: Museumland

Second floor

Much of the **second floor** is very heavy going: if you find yourself struggling through the forests of myoglobin in the **Chemistry** section, you'll need a PhD to understand the **Nuclear Physics** bit, which is sponsored by British Nuclear Fuels Limited. There's sobering film footage of Hiroshima, but very little about the numerous subsequent disasters within the nuclear industry. The nearby gallery on **Printing** concentrates mostly on hot metal and the paper industry, while the exhibitions on **Lighting** and **Weighing and Measuring** fail to inspire with their dull array of gas lamps, bulbs and sets of scales, ancient and (almost) modern.

If you crave a bit of peace and quiet, you're sure to find it in the **Picture Gallery**, a small room displaying original artworks with a scientific bent. Beyond, the sections on **Computing** and **Mathematics** have been rightly renamed "histories", which is to say, they are extremely out of date; computing, for example, begins with Charles Babbage and stops abruptly with the pocket calculators of the mid-1970s. Finally, you reach another little-visited area of the museum, the **Ships** section, with its interminable glass cabinets of model vessels from the *Great Harry* and the *Mayflower* to the *Great Eastern* and the *Cutty Sark*, not to mention Townsend Thoresen's ill-fated *Spirit of Free Enterprise*, which sank in the Zeebrugge disaster of 1987.

Third floor

The exquisitely made **eighteenth-century scientific instruments**, chiefly created by George Adams for **George III**, provide aesthetic relief on the **third floor**, especially the ornate Grand Orrery and Philosophical Table. Close by, the design influence of the Wellcome Institute is evident in the excellent, hi-tech **Health Matters**, which dwells on more modern medical history from the introduction of mass vaccination to the new challenge of finding a cure for HIV.

In **On Air**, you can make a five-minute radio programme in the mock-up studio. Beyond is another popular hands-on section called **Flight Lab**, teaching the basic principles of flight – check out the Bernoulli Blower. To have a go on the inevitable flight simulator, you have to have a strong stomach and another £2.50. The Flight Lab, in turn, leads into the giant hangar of the **Flight** exhibition, festooned with aircraft of every description from a Spitfire to a DC3. Be sure to check out the full-size model of the flimsy contraption in which the Wright brothers made their epoch-making power-assisted flight in 1903, and Vickers "Vimy", which completed the first transatlantic flight in 1919.

The fourth and fifth floors

On the floor above is a much older Wellcome-sponsored gallery called **Glimpses of Medical History**, a fairly undemanding series of dioramas of medical operations, and larger mock-ups of dentists, chemists and surgeries, finishing up with the gore-free spectacle of an open-heart operation, accompanied by a bleeping monitor.

The best section here – and arguably of the whole museum – is Wellcome's **Science and Art of Medicine** gallery, all too easily missed on the top floor. Using an anthropological approach, this is a visual and cerebral feast, galloping through ancient medicine, medieval and Renaissance pharmacy, alchemy, quack doctors, royal healers, astrology and military surgery. Offbeat artefacts include African fetish objects, an Egyptian mummified head, an eighteenth-century Florentine model of a female torso giving birth and George Washington's dentures.

Natural History Museum

Mon–Sat 10am–5.50pm, Sun 11am–5.50pm; £7.50; free Mon–Fri after 4.30pm, Sat & Sun after 5pm. Free guided tours daily. ☎020/7942 5000; *www.nhm.ac.uk*. South Kensington tube.

Alfred Waterhouse's purpose-built mock-Romanesque colossus ensures the **Natural History Museum**'s status as London's most handsome museum. Its vast collections – and there is much more hidden away in the vaults – derive from a bequest by Sir Hans Sloane to the British Museum, and it was separated off in the 1860s after a huge power struggle. Charles Darwin, notably, opposed the move, in part for the separation of science from the other arts, in part due to his hatred of the founding director, Richard Owen, an amazing figure who arranged expeditions around the globe to provide everything from butterflies to dinosaurs for the museum's cabinets.

The museum underwent massive redevelopment in the 1990s, and is now, by and large, imaginatively designed, though there are still one or two sections that have changed little since the museum's opening in 1881. To be fair, the museum is caught in a real conundrum, for while its dinosaur collection is a real hit with the kids, its collections are also an important resource for serious zoologists. The **main entrance** is in the middle of the 675-foot terracotta facade; but if the queues are long (as they can be at the weekend and during school holidays), you're better off heading for the **side entrance** on Exhibition Road. This brings you into what used to be the old Geology Museum, which is now incorporated into the Natural

History Museum and is called the **Earth Galleries**. The original Natural History Museum building houses the Life Galleries, though this division between the two collections is now less than clear-cut, as a few rocks and minerals have sneaked into the Life Galleries.

Life Galleries

The main entrance brings you straight into the **Central Hall**, which is dominated by the plaster cast of a **Diplodocus** skeleton, 85ft in length from tip to tail. The "side chapels" are filled with "wonders" of the natural world – the largest egg, a model of a sabre-tooth tiger and so on – which are changed fairly regularly. It's worth pausing here to take in the architecture of this vast "nave", whose walls are decorated with moulded terracotta animals and plants.

The redesigning and marketing of the new **Dinosaur** gallery, to the west of the central hall, was a stroke of a genius by the museum curators. A raised walkway leads straight to the highlight – the grisly life-sized animatronic tableau of carnivorous reptiles tearing apart a tenontosaurus, with much roaring, slurping and blood. The rest of the displays are less theatrical and more informative, with massive-jawed skeletons and models, plus a stimulating exhibition on *Tyrannosaurus rex* and his pea-brained cronies.

The other firm favourite with kids is the insect and arthropod room on the other side of the central hall, now known as **Creepy-Crawlies** (room 33). Definitely not for arachnophobes, the gallery is filled with giant models of bugs, arachnids and crustaceans, plus displays on the life cycle of the wasp and other unlovely creatures. You can hear the noise of the male deathwatch beetle, listen to pistol shrimps, and watch a mantis shrimp spearing its prey. It's here that you'll find the only live exhibits in the entire museum, a colony of leaf-cutter ants from Trinidad, who feed on a fungus which they grow on the leaves they've gathered.

A small thicket of reconstructed rainforest, situated opposite the Creepy-Crawlies, forms the entrance to the new **Ecology** gallery (room 32), a glass corridor, crisscrossed with overhead walkways, taking you through the basics of green politics: the food chain, recycling, the ozone layer and the greenhouse effect. It's a hi-tech, child-friendly exhibition, with a serious message, only slightly marred by the fact that it's sponsored by British Petroleum.

Down in the basement is an excellent new futuristic gallery called **Investigate**, aimed at children aged 7 to 14, for which you need to obtain a timed ticket when you enter the museum. Kids get to choose a tray of specimens and then play at being scientists, using microscopes, scales, a computer, and various tools of the trade to examine and catalogue the items before them. There are one or two simpler hands-on exhibits, too, as well as several plant species to look at.

The old-fashioned **Mammals** gallery (rooms 23 and 24), back on the ground floor, is dominated by a full-size model of a blue whale

South Kensington: Museumland

juxtaposed with its skeleton, and filled with stuffed animals and plastic models. It usually goes down well enough with younger children, but it's showing its age somewhat. Upstairs, on the first floor, the story of mammals continues with an investigation into the emergence of bipeds among the primates. This, in turn, is a natural lead-in to the section on Darwin's **Origin of Species** (room 105), which rocked the Victorian world of science shortly before this museum got off the ground.

On the same floor is the old-style **Minerals** gallery (room 102), regimented rows of glass cabinets culminating in a darkened chamber on meteorites – all of which really belongs in the Earth Galleries. If you've made it this far, don't miss the 1300-year-old slice of **Giant Sequoia**, on the second floor, a mere youngster compared to other members of the species that are still standing after more than 3200 years. While you're here, admire the view down onto the central hall and the moulded monkeys clinging to the arches.

Earth Galleries

The museum's **Earth Galleries** have been totally redesigned over the last few years. Coming from Exhibition Road, you enter a vast, darkened hall, with the solar system and constellations writ large on the walls, then walk past statues of Medusa, Atlas, Cyclops and an astronaut, before boarding an escalator which takes you through a partially formed globe to **The Power Within**, a big exhibition on volcanoes and earthquakes. The most popular section is the Kobe earthquake simulator, where you enter a mock-up of a Japanese supermarket and see the soy-sauce bottles wobble, while watching an instore video of the real event. Given that the earthquake is relatively recent, the whole thing seems in very poor taste. On the other side of the same floor is **Restless Surface**, an interactive display on the earth's elements, soil and rock erosion and, of course, global warming.

To get to the Earth Galleries from the central hall, head east along the wiggly "Waterhouse Way", past the stuffed birds.

Down one floor is **From the Beginning**, which covers the geological history of the planet from the Big Bang to the present day. The display ends with a crystal ball, which predicts the earth's future (bleak, but probably not within our lifetime). Perhaps the most alluring of the new galleries is the **Earth's Treasury**, a dimly lit display of lustrous minerals and crystals, gemstones and jewels. Exhibits include rocks that shine in UV light, carved artefacts such as a lapis lazuli necklace and a few serious gems, including a 17-carat diamond worth at least £1 million and an emerald the size of a lemon.

Finally, the **Earth Today and Tomorrow** (on the ground floor) is a depressing look at how we are running down the earth's non-renewable natural resources, and polluting the planet in the process. Ironically, one of the chief sponsors is Rio Tinto, the distinctly environmentally unfriendly mining company. More positively, the gallery also explains how the museum dug its own borehole to provide its washrooms and labs with up to half a gallon of water a second.

Kensington, Holland Park and Earl's Court

Despite the smattering of aristocratic mansions and the presence of royalty in Kensington Palace, **Kensington** remained little more than a village surrounded by fields until well into the nineteenth century, when the rich finally began to seek new stamping grounds away from the West End. The Great Exhibition and its legacy of museums brought further cachet to the area and prompted a building frenzy that boosted the borough's population to over 175,000 by 1901. The main draw nowadays are the shops along Kensington High Street, the wooded **Holland Park** and the former artists' colony clustered around the exotically decorated Leighton House.

Kensington High Street

Shopper-thronged **Kensington High Street** is dominated architecturally by the twin presences of George Gilbert Scott's Neo-Gothic church of **St Mary Abbots**, whose 250-foot spire makes it London's tallest parish church, and the Art Deco colossus of **Barkers** department store, remodelled in the 1930s.

The nearest tube is High Street Kensington.

A little-known feature of the High Street is Europe's largest **roof garden**, which tops what used to be Derry & Toms department store, another 1930s colossus, situated next door to Barkers. To gain access to the garden, you need to sign yourself in at the side entrance on Derry Street and then take the lift to the sixth floor. The nightclub at the centre of the garden is pretty tacky, as are the pink flamingos, but the mock-Spanish convent, the formal gardens and the views across the rooftops are surreal.

Kensington Square

On the south side of the High Street lies **Kensington Square**, an early piece of speculative building laid out in 1685. Luckily for the developers, royalty moved into Kensington Palace shortly after its construction, and the square soon became so fashionable that it was dubbed the "old court suburb". By the nineteenth century, the courtiers had moved out and more bohemian residents had moved in: Thackeray wrote *Vanity Fair* at no. 16; the Pre-Raphaelite painter Burne-Jones lived at no. 41 for a couple of years; the actress Mrs Patrick Campbell, with whom George Bernard Shaw was obsessed for most of his life, lived at no. 33; and composer Hubert Parry (of *Jerusalem* fame) gave music lessons to Vaughan Williams at no. 17. John Stuart Mill, philosopher and champion of women's suffrage, lived next door, and it was here that the first volume of Thomas Carlyle's manuscript of *The French Revolution* was accidentally used by a maid to light the fire.

The Commonwealth Institute

Tues–Sun 10am–5pm; free; ☎020/7603 4535; *www.commonwealth.org.uk.*
High Street Kensington tube.

Kensington's sights are mostly hidden away in the backstreets, the one exception being the **Commonwealth Institute**, housed in a bold 1960s building on the High Street – it's heralded by a forest of flag-poles. The building's tent-shaped Zambian copper roof is a startling sight, but neither the exterior nor the interior has worn well, and the whole place is currently undergoing a massive refurbishment pro-gramme. The new Commonwealth Resource Centre is due to open fully in 2002, and will profile each of the 54 member countries. In the meantime, the institute is staging an impressive series of large-scale exhibitions on specific areas of the Commonwealth.

Holland Park and around

Two paths pass along the east side of the Commonwealth Institute towards the densely wooded **Holland Park**, a spot popular with the neighbourhood's army of nannies and au pairs, who take their charges to the excellent adventure playground. The park is laid out in the former grounds of Holland House – only the east wing of the Jacobean mansion could be salvaged after the last war, but it gives a fairly good idea of what the place must have looked like. A youth hos-tel is linked to the east wing, while a concert tent to the west stages theatrical and musical performances throughout the summer months, continuing a tradition which stretches back to the first Lady Holland, who put on plays here in defiance of the puritanical laws of the Commonwealth. Several formal gardens are laid out before the house, drifting down in terraces to the arcades, Garden Ballroom and Ice House, which have been converted into a café, a restaurant and an art gallery. The most unusual of the formal gardens, which are now peppered with modern sculpture, is the Kyoto Garden, a Japanese-style sanctuary to the northwest of the house.

Leighton House

Daily except Tues 11am–5.30pm; free; ☎020/7602 3316; *www.rbkc.gov.uk.*
High Street Kensington tube.

In the second half of the nineteenth century, several of the wealthier artists of the Victorian era rather self-consciously founded an artists' colony around the fringes of Holland Park, and a number of their highly individual mansions are still standing. First and foremost is **Leighton House**, 12 Holland Park Rd, the "House Beautiful" built by the architect George Aitchison for Frederic Leighton, President of the Royal Academy from 1878 until his death in 1896 and the only artist ever to be made a peer (albeit on his deathbed). "It will be opu-lence, it will be sincerity", the artist opined before starting work on the house in the 1860s.

The big attraction is its domed Arab Hall, built in 1877: based on the banqueting hall of a Moorish palace in Palermo, it has a central black marble fountain, and is decorated with Saracen tiles, gilded mosaics and latticework drawn from all over the Islamic world. The other rooms are less spectacular but, in compensation, are hung with excellent paintings by Lord Leighton and his Pre-Raphaelite friends, Edward Burne-Jones, Lawrence Alma-Tadema and John Everett Millais. Skylights brighten the upper floor, which contains Leighton's vast studio, where his tradition of holding evening concerts continues to this day.

Around Leighton House

Leighton's neighbours included artists G.F. Watts and Holman Hunt, Marcus Stone, illustrator of Dickens, and, in the most outrageous house of all, architect William Burges, who designed his own medieval folly, the **Tower House**, at 29 Melbury Rd. Further afield, at 8 Addison Rd, is the Arts and Crafts **Debenham House**, designed by Halsey Ricardo in 1906 for the millionaire department store Debenham family (both closed to the public). The exterior is covered with peacock-blue and emerald-green tiles and bricks; the interior, which features a wonderful Neo-Byzantine domed hall, decorated with a lavish mosaic that features portraits of the Debenham family, and 28 individually tiled fireplaces, is even more impressive.

On the east side of the Commonwealth Institute, two blocks north of the High Street at 18 Stafford Terrace, is **Linley Sambourne House**, where the highly successful *Punch* cartoonist lived until his death in 1910. A grand, though fairly ordinary, stuccoed terrace house by Kensington standards, it's less a tribute to the artist (though it does contain a huge selection of Sambourne's works) and more a showpiece for the Victorian Society, which maintains the house in all its cluttered, late Victorian excess, complete with stained glass, heavy furnishings and lugubrious William Morris wallpaper. Unfortunately, the society is experiencing difficulties keeping the place going, and the house may well close indefinitely in 2001, so ring ahead to check.

Linley Sambourne House is open March–Oct Wed 10am–4pm, Sun 2–5pm; £3.50; phone the Victorian Society ☎020/8994 1019.

Earl's Court

Despite displaying the same ostentatious architecture as the rest of Kensington, **Earl's Court** itself is a less moneyed area, with many houses providing cheap bedsits and hotels for young Australians and New Zealanders, earning it the nickname "Kangaroo Valley". In the late 1970s, Earl's Court also became the gay capital of London, a position now challenged by trendier Soho. It's the (male) leather crowd that predominate here, epitomized by *The Coleherne* on Old Brompton Road, London's oldest leather pub, and by its most famous former resident, **Freddie Mercury**, the flamboyant queen of Queen, whose house, Garden

Lodge, 1 Logan Place, has remained a shrine for fans since his AIDS-related death in 1991.

The Earl's Court area is also well known for its two giant exhibition halls. The earlier of the two is the **Olympia Exhibition Hall**, built in 1884 as the National Agricultural Hall, and now hidden behind a severe 1930s facade at the western end of Kensington High Street. It later made its name as a circus venue, but is now firmly established as a show centre, hosting annual events like the Ideal Home Exhibition, and rock concerts by dry-ice dinosaurs. Even larger shows are put on at the **Earl's Court Exhibition Hall**, erected in 1937 to the south of Olympia, down Warwick Road. Both halls were used during the last war as internment centres for Germans and Italians, many of whom had themselves fled Fascist persecution.

Brompton Cemetery

Close by *The Coleherne* (and consequently a popular cruising area) is **Brompton Cemetery**, the least overgrown of London's Victorian graveyards. It was laid out in a grid plan in 1840 and is now overlooked by the east stand of Chelsea Football Club. The cemetery's leafy central avenue, which leads south to an octagonal chapel, contains the more interesting graves, most notably that of Frederick Leyland, president of the National Telephone Company: designed by Edward Burne-Jones, it's a bizarre copper-green jewel box on stilts, smothered with swirling wrought-ironwork. Before you reach the chapel, eerie colonnaded catacombs, originally planned to extend the full length of the cemetery, open out into the Great Circle, a forest of tilted crosses.

*Brompton
Cemetery is
open daily:
summer
9am–7pm;
winter
9am–4pm.*

Few famous corpses grace Brompton, but enthusiasts might like to seek out Suffragette leader Emmeline Pankhurst; Samuel Sotheby, who founded the famous auction house; Sir Henry Cole, the man behind the Great Exhibition and the V&A; Fanny Brawne, the love of Keats's life; and John Snow, Queen Victoria's anaesthetist, whose chloroform fixes the monarch described as "soothing, quieting and delightful beyond measure". Long Wolf, a Sioux Indian chief, was a temporary resident here, after he died while on tour entertaining the Victorian masses with Colonel "Buffalo Bill" Cody. His body has since been returned to his descendants in America.

Knightsbridge and Belgravia

Knightsbridge and Belgravia contain some of the most expensive real estate in London. **Knightsbridge** is irredeemably snobbish, revelling in its reputation as the swankiest shopping area in London, largely through Harrods, one of London's most popular tourist attractions. **Belgravia**, over to the east, and strategically placed behind Buckingham Palace Gardens, is London's chief embassyland, with at least 25 scattered amongst the grid-plan stuccoed streets.

Harrods and Knightsbridge

Most people come to Knightsbridge for just one thing: to shop or gawp at **Harrods** on Brompton Road. Without doubt the most famous department store in London, it started out as a family-run grocery store in 1849, with a staff of two. The current 1905 terra-cotta building, which turns into a palace of fairy lights at night, is now owned by the Egyptian Mohamed Al Fayed, *bête noire* of the Establishment, and employs in excess of 3000 staff, including several ex-army bagpipers who perform daily in the store. Harrods occupies four acres, and is made up of more than 300 departments, a dozen bars and restaurants, and even its own pub, all spread over seven floors.

Tourists flock to Harrods – it's thought to be the city's third top tourist attraction – with some 30,000 customers passing through each day. Most Londoners limit their visits to the annual sales, with more than 300,000 arriving on the first day of the Christmas give-away bonanza, though the store also has its regular customers, drawn from the so-called "Tiara Triangle" of this very wealthy neigh-bourhood, who would think nothing of buying dog food at cordon bleu prices. To help keep out the non-purchasing riffraff, a dracon-ian dress code has been introduced: no shorts, no ripped jeans, no vest T-shirts and no backpacks.

In truth, you can buy much of what the shop stocks a great deal more cheaply if you can do without the Harrods carrier bag, but the store does have a few sections that are architectural sights in their own right. Chief among these are the Food Hall, with its exquisite Arts and Crafts tiling and tempting oyster counter, and the Egyptian Hall, with its pseudo-hieroglyphs and sphinxes, both of which are on the ground floor. The Egyptian escalators in the centre of the build-ing are an added attraction, now that the Di and Dodi fountain is in place, but don't bother taking them to the first-floor "washrooms" unless you want to pay £1 for the privilege of relieving yourself.

Around Knightsbridge

If you want more window-shopping, or you have a wallet equipped for top-range designer clothing shops, **Sloane Street**, which runs due south of Knightsbridge tube, is the obvious next stop. Right on the corner of the street, facing the tube, is **Harvey Nichols**, another palatial department store, whose reputation has spiralled in recent years. Like Harrods, it has a wonderful food hall and a panoply of designer sections, while its fifth-floor café/restaurant is the in place to lunch for career shoppers. Ranging down Sloane Street, the names read like a fashion directory, including Giorgio Armani, Prada, Gucci, Christian Lacroix and Katharine Hamnett.

For the shopping-surfeited, Knightsbridge's mews and squares are good for a quick stroll. Having been built to house servants and sta-bles, converted mews houses, like those in **Pont Street Mews** immediately behind Harrods, are now among the most sought-after properties in the area. Built on a completely different scale, the red-brick four-, five- and six-storey mansions that flaunt their high Dutch gables off Pont Street proper gave rise to the architectural term "Pont Street Dutch". The most extreme examples of the style are in fact in **Harrington** and **Collingham Gardens**, to the west of South Kensington tube. They were built by Ernest George, who was fired up after a visit to Holland in the 1870s.

Belgravia

Belgravia does have some nice pubs; see p.544.

Despite its spacious streets of crisp white stucco, **Belgravia** is a soulless place, and not one in which you're likely to want to spend much time. If curiosity leads you here, the best approach is to take the tube to Hyde Park Corner and walk along Grosvenor Crescent, which curves round into Belgrave Square, a grandiose nineteenth-century set piece with detached villas positioned at three of its four corners. With royalty ensconced in nearby Buckingham Palace and Queen Victoria's mother temporarily living in the square, the area immediately attracted exactly the sort of clientele that property developer and architect Cubitt had hoped for, with three dukes, thirteen peers and thirteen MPs in residence by 1860. Nowadays, the place bristles with security cameras and police in bulletproof jackets guarding the numerous embassies; few can afford whole houses here, with short-lease apartments alone fetching millions of pounds.

Chelsea, Battersea and Fulham Palace

Until the sixteenth century, **Chelsea** was nothing more than a tiny fishing village on the banks of the Thames. It was Thomas More who started the upward trend by moving here in 1520, followed by members of the nobility, including Henry VIII himself (51 Glebe Place was for a long time thought to be his former hunting lodge). In the eighteenth century, Chelsea acquired its riverside houses along Cheyne Walk, which gradually attracted a posse of literary and intellectual types.

However, it wasn't until the latter part of the nineteenth century that Chelsea began to earn its reputation as London's very own Left Bank, a bohemianism formalized by the foundation of the Chelsea Arts Club in 1891 and entrenched in the 1960s, when Chelsea was at the forefront of "Swinging London", with the likes of David Bailey, Mick Jagger, George Best and the "Chelsea Set" hanging out in continental style-boutiques and coffee bars. The King's Road was also a fashion parade for hippies, as well as the birthplace of punk.

These days, Chelsea has a more subdued feel, with high rents and house prices keeping things staid, and interior-design shops rather than avant-garde fashion the order of the day. The area's other aspect, oddly enough considering its boho reputation, is a military one, with Chelsea Barracks (central London's main army barracks), the Royal Hospital (home of old soldiers known as the Chelsea Pensioners) and the National Army Museum.

Chelsea, Battersea and Fulham Palace

Further west, Chelsea becomes rather more down-to-earth, a transition signalled by the presence of the local football ground, beyond which lies **Fulham**, whose main point of interest is **Fulham Palace**, at the very end of the King's Road. To the south, across the river, Chelsea aspirants have, over the past decade or so, colonized previously working-class **Battersea**, an area dominated by the brooding presence of the disused Battersea Power Station – familiar to many visitors from its appearance, with floating pig, on Pink Floyd's *Animals* album cover.

Sloane Square

Sloane Square, a leafy nexus on the very eastern edge of Chelsea, takes its name from the wealthy eighteenth-century local doctor Sir Hans Sloane, whose "noble cabinet" of curios formed the basis of the British Museum. More recently, the square gave its name to the debutantes of the 1980s, the Sloane Rangers, whose most famous specimen was Princess Diana herself. The term has since gone out of fashion, but Sloanes, whose natural habitat is actually further north in Kensington and Knightsbridge, still exist, and are easily identifiable by their dress code: blue-and-white pinstriped shirts, cords and brogues for the men; flicked-back hair, pearls and flat shoes for the women; and waxed cotton Barbour jackets for all.

The nearest tube is Sloane Square.

At the head of the square, by the tube, stands the newly refurbished **Royal Court Theatre**, bastion of new theatre writing since John Osborne's *Look Back in Anger* sent tremors through the establishment in 1956, and still going strong. At the opposite end is **Peter Jones**, a popular department store for upper middle-class wedding lists, housed in London's finest glass-curtain building, built in the 1930s, which curves its way seductively into King's Road.

Round the corner in Sloane Street is another architectural masterpiece, **Holy Trinity** – created in 1890, and probably the finest Arts and Crafts church in London. The east window is the most glorious of the furnishings, a vast, 48-panel extravaganza designed by Edward Burne-Jones, and the largest ever made by Morris & Co. As with All Saints Margaret Street(see p.148), Holy Trinity is very High Church, filled with the smell of incense and statues of Mary, and even offering confession. Sadly it's only open before and after services (Mon–Fri 9.30am & 5.30pm, Sat 10.30am & 4.30pm, Sun 8.45 & 11am).

The King's Road

The **King's Road**, Chelsea's main artery, was designed as a royalty-only thoroughfare by Charles II, in order – so the story goes – to

Buses #11 and
#22 run the
length of the
King's Road;
bus #19 runs
down King's
Road and then
south across
Battersea
Bridge.

avoid carriage congestion en route to Nell Gwynne's house in Fulham, but more likely as a short cut to Hampton Court. George III used the road to get to Kew, but lesser mortals could do so only on production of a special copper pass – it was finally opened to the public in 1830. This prompted a flurry of speculative building that produced the series of elegant, open-ended squares – Wellington, Markham, Carlyle and Paultons – which still punctuate the road.

King's Road's household fame, however, came through its role as the unofficial catwalk of the Swinging Sixties. While Carnaby Street (see p.147) cashed in on its past long after its glory days were over, King's Road managed to move with the times, through the hippie era, punk and beyond. The "Saturday Parade" of fashion victims is not what it used to be, but posey cafés, boutiques (and antiques) are still what King's Road is all about. And the traditional "Chelsea Cruise", when every flash Harry in town parades his customized motor, still takes place at 8.30pm on the last Saturday of the month, though nowadays on the Battersea side of the Chelsea Bridge.

Chelsea's split personality is evident as soon as you head off down King's Road in search of fashion, and immediately come face to face with the **Duke of York's Barracks**, headquarters of the Territorial Army. A little further down on the same side is **Royal Avenue**, the first of the squares which open out onto the King's Road, where James Bond, Ian Fleming's spy hero, had his London address. Unlike the other squares off the King's Road, this one is rather like a Parisian *place*, with plane trees and gravel down the centre, and was originally laid out in the late seventeenth century as part of William III's ambitious (and unrealized) scheme to link Kensington Palace with the Royal Hospital to the south (see below).

Perhaps the most striking premises along King's Road is **The Pheasantry**, a fine red-brick mansion set back slightly from the road behind an archway flanked by bronze caryatids and topped by a mini-quadriga. After the pheasants who gave the building its name flew the nest, and the French upholsterers, whose wares are still advertised from the stonework, upped and left, the house was used by the Russian-born ballet dancer and teacher Princess Stephanie Astafieva as a ballet school. Later it became a drinking club, frequented by the likes of Dylan Thomas and Augustus John; Eric Clapton lived here briefly in the 1960s and, somewhat inevitably, it has now become a branch of *Pizza Express*.

The most famous address of all on the King's Road is **no. 430**, a modest little shop about a mile away from Sloane Square, where the designer Vivienne Westwood and her then-boyfriend Malcolm McLaren opened a teddy-boy revival store called Let It Rock, located, with a neat sense of decorum, right next door to the Chelsea Conservative Club. In 1975 they changed tack and renamed the shop Sex, stocking it with proto-punk fetishist gear, with simulated burnt limbs in the window. It became a magnet for the likes of John Lydon and John Simon Ritchie, better known as Johnny Rotten and Sid Vicious – the rest, as they say, is history. Now known as World's End, the shop, with its landmark backward-clock, continues to flog Westwood's eccentric, designer clothes.

The Royal Hospital

Mon–Fri 9am–noon & 2–4.30pm, Sat & Sun closes 3pm; free; ☎020/7730 5282. Sloane Square tube.

Among the most nattily attired of all those parading down the King's Road are the scarlet- or navy-blue-clad Chelsea Pensioners, the army veterans who live in the nearby **Royal Hospital**, founded by Charles II in 1681. Until the Civil War, England had no standing army and therefore no need to provide for its old soldiers; by the time of Charles's reign, all that had changed. Prompted by Nell Gwynne's encounter with a begging ex-serviceman on the King's Road, or – more likely – by Louis XIV's Hôtel des Invalides in Paris, Charles II commissioned Wren to provide a suitably grand almshouse for the veterans. The end result – plain, red-brick wings and grassy court-yards, which originally opened straight onto the river – became a blueprint for institutional and collegiate architecture all over the English-speaking world.

The **central courtyard** is centred on a bronze statue of the founder in Roman attire by Grinling Gibbons; on Oak Apple Day (May 29), the Pensioners, wearing their traditional tricorn hats, festoon the statue with oak leaves to commemorate the day after the Battle of Worcester in 1651, when Charles hid in Boscobel Oak to escape his pursuers. On the north side of the courtyard, below the central lantern, a giant Tuscan portico leads to an octagonal vestibule. On one side is the austere **hospital chapel**, with a huge barrel vault and a splash of colour in the apse provided by Sebastiano Ricci's *Resurrection*, in which Jesus patriotically bears the flag of St George. Opposite lies the equally grand, wood-panelled **dining hall**, where the four hundred or so Pensioners still eat under portraits of the sovereigns and a vast allegorical mural of Charles II and his hos-pital by Antonio Verrio. In the Secretary's Office, designed by Sir John Soane, on the east side of the hospital, there's a small **museum** (Mon–Fri 9am–noon & 2–4.30pm; free), with Pensioners' uniforms, medals and two German bombs.

The playing fields to the south, from which you get the finest view of the hospital, are the venue for the annual **Chelsea Flower Show**, organized by the Royal Horticultural Society, which takes place dur-ing the last week of May (☎0870 534 4444; *www.rhs.org.uk*). To the east is the last remnant of London's pleasure gardens, **Ranelagh Gardens**, now a pleasant little landscaped patch used mostly by the Chelsea Pensioners, but open to the general public too. A couple of information panels in the gardens' Soane-designed shelter show what the place used to look like when Canaletto painted it in 1751.

The main feature was a giant rotunda, modelled on the Pantheon in Rome, where the beau monde could promenade to musical accompaniment – the 8-year-old Mozart played here. Shortly after it opened in 1742, Walpole reported that "you can't set your foot without treading on a Prince or Duke." Fashion is fickle, though, and the rotunda was eventually demolished in 1805.

National Army Museum

Daily 10am–5.30pm; free; ☎020/7730 0717; *www.national-army-museum .ac.uk*. Sloane Square tube.

The concrete bunker next door to the Royal Hospital, on Royal Hospital Road, houses the **National Army Museum**. The militarily obsessed are unlikely to be disappointed by the succession of uniforms and medals, but there is very little here for non-enthusiasts. The temporary exhibitions staged on the ground floor are, without a doubt, the museum's strong point, but overall it's disappointing – you're better off visiting the infinitely superior Imperial War Museum (see p.308).

To follow the museum chronologically, you need to start in the basement with the **Rise of the Redcoat** (1415–1792), which takes

---

Wilde about Chelsea

John Singer Sargent, Augustus John, James Whistler and Bertrand Russell all lived at one time or another in Tite Street, which runs alongside the Army Museum, but by far the street's most famous resident was wit and writer **Oscar Fingal O'Flahertie Wills Wilde** (1856–1900), who moved into no. 1 with an old Oxford chum, Frank Miles, in 1880, only to be asked to leave the following year by the latter (under pressure from his father, Canon Miles), after the hostile reception given to Wilde's recently published poetry. Four years later, in 1885, Wilde moved back into the street, to no. 34, with his new bride, Constance Lloyd. By all accounts he was never very good at "playing husband", though he was happy enough to play father to his two boys (when he was there). It was in Tite Street, in 1891, that Wilde first met Lord Alfred Douglas, son of the Marquis of Queensberry, known to his friends as "Bosie", who was to become his lover, and eventually to prove his downfall.

At the height of Wilde's fame, just four days after the first night of *The Importance of Being Earnest*, the marquis left a visiting card for Wilde, on which he wrote "To Oscar Wilde, posing as a somdomite [sic]". Urged on by Bosie, Wilde unsuccessfully sued Queensberry, losing his case when the marquis produced incriminating evidence against Wilde himself. On returning to the *Cadogan Hotel* on Sloane Street, where Bosie had rooms, Wilde was arrested by the police, taken to Bow Street police station, charged with homosexual offences and eventually sentenced to two years' hard labour. Bankrupt, abandoned by Bosie and separated from his wife, he served his sentence in Pentonville, Wandsworth and later Reading jail. On his release he fled abroad and travelled under the pseudonym of Sebastian Melmoth; he died three years later from a syphilitic infection and was buried in Paris's Père Lachaise cemetery.

---

you from Agincourt to the American Revolution, before heading for the **Road to Waterloo**, where you can see the skeleton of Marengo, Napoleon's charger at the battle, and an audiovisual played out over a large spotlit model of the battlefield on which 48,000 lost their lives. There's a none-too-critical look at the British Empire in the adjacent **Victorian Soldier**, after which you should head across to the **Nation in Arms** (1914–45), covering both world wars, and featuring a World War I dugout and a mock-up Burmese swamp.

The new postwar section on the top floor, taking you as far as Bosnia, features slightly more imaginative, interactive displays, though it's really little more than a propaganda exercise for the armed forces. Next door in the Art Gallery, there are some excellent military portraits by the likes of Reynolds, Gainsborough, Romney and Lawrence, not to mention a suave self-portrait by a uniformed Rex Whistler, who died in action shortly after D-day.

Chelsea Physic Garden

April–Oct Wed noon–5pm, Sun 2–6pm; £4; ☎020/7352 5646; *www .cpgarden.demon.co.uk*. Sloane Square tube.

The **Chelsea Physic Garden** lies at the western end of Royal Hospital Road. Founded in 1673 by the Royal Society of Apothecaries, this is the oldest botanical garden in the country after Oxford's: the first cedars grown in this country were planted here in 1683; cotton seed was sent from here to the American colonies in 1732; England's first rock garden was constructed here in 1773; and the walled garden contains Britain's oldest olive tree. At the entrance (on Swan Walk) you can pick up a map of the garden with a list of the month's most interesting flowers and shrubs, whose labels are slightly more forthcoming than the usual terse Latinate tags. A statue of Sir Hans Sloane, who presented the Society with the freehold, stands at the centre of the garden; and behind him there's an excellent teahouse, serving tea and delicious home-made cakes, with exhibitions on the floor above.

Cheyne Walk

The Chelsea Physic Garden marks the beginning of **Cheyne Walk** (pronounced "chainy"), whose quiet riverside locale and succession of Queen Anne and Georgian houses, drew artists and writers here in great numbers during the nineteenth century. Since the building of the Embankment and the increase in the volume of traffic, however, the character of this peaceful haven has been lost. Novelist Henry James, who lived at no. 21, used to take "beguiling drives" in his wheelchair along the Embankment; today, he'd be hospitalized in the process. An older contemporary of James, Mary Ann Evans (better known under her pen name George Eliot), moved into no. 4 – the first blue plaque you come to – in December 1880, five months after marrying an

American banker 21 years her junior. Three weeks later she was dead. In the 1960s, Mick Jagger and Keith Richards graced this section of Cheyne Walk with their presence, at no. 48 and no. 3 respectively.

Perhaps the most famous of all Cheyne Walk's bohemian residents, however, were the trio who lived at the Queen's or Tudor House (no. 16): painter and poet **Dante Gabriel Rossetti**, poet Algernon Charles Swinburne and writer George Meredith. Rossetti moved in shortly after the death of his first wife and model, Elizabeth Siddall, from an overdose of laudanum in 1862. The "tiny, gesticulating, dirty-minded" Swinburne, as one of his many critics described him, was habitually drunk, but it was Rossetti's back-garden menagerie that really got his neighbours' backs up – an amazing array that included owls, wombats, wallabies, parrots, salamanders, a Brahmin bull, burrowing armadillo, braying jackass and screeching, belligerent peacocks. In 1872 Rossetti tried to commit suicide as his wife had done, but survived to live a progressively more debauched and withdrawn existence until his death in 1882.

Chelsea Old Church and Crosby Hall

At the end of Cheyne Walk's gardens, there's a garish, gilded statue of **Thomas More**, "Scholar, Saint, Statesman", who lived hereabouts and used to worship in nearby **Chelsea Old Church** (daily 9.30am–1pm & 2–4.30pm), where he built his own private chapel in the south aisle (the hinges for the big oak doors are still visible). The church was badly bombed in the last war, but an impressive number of monuments were retrieved from the rubble and continue to adorn the interior. Chief among them is Lady Cheyne's memorial, and More's simple canopied memorial to his first wife, Jane, in which he himself hoped to be buried. In the event, his headless body ended up in the Tower chapel, while his head was secretly buried in Canterbury by his daughter, Margaret Roper. More's second wife, Alice, is buried here too.

Thomas More is best known for his martyrdom in 1535, brought about by his refusal to swear the Oath of Succession, which declared Henry VIII's marriage to Anne Boleyn valid, and their children as heirs. However, More was no shy flower himself when it came to punishing heretics – he even had some tied to a tree in his Chelsea back garden and flogged - and his zeal in dealing with such matters is perhaps another reason why the Catholic Church canonized him in 1935.

More's house on Cheyne Walk was destroyed in 1740 by Sir Hans Sloane, but in the 1920s **Crosby Hall**, part of a fifteenth-century wool merchant's house once owned by More, was transferred bit by bit from Bishopsgate in the City and incorporated into the International Hostel of the British Federation of University Women, on the corner of Danvers Street, to the west of the church. Sadly, it's now a private residence and its fine hammerbeam roof can no longer be viewed. If you're wondering what the twenty-storey pagoda in the distance to the west is, it belongs to Chelsea Marina, an exclusive (in a very literal sense) marina and apartment complex completed in 1987, and already dying on its feet.

Beyond Crosby Hall

The western half of Cheyne Walk, beyond Crosby Hall, is no less rich in cultural associations. Mrs Gaskell was born in 1810 at no. 93, while the Brunels, Marc and Isambard, both lived at no. 99. The painter James Whistler, who lived at ten different addresses in the 41 years he spent in Chelsea, lived for a time at no. 96, the house where, in July 1972, the Provisional IRA and the British government met secretly to discuss peace, some five months after the "Bloody Sunday" massacre. The Brunels' and Whistler's old residences form part of **Lindsey House**, the oldest and finest house on Cheyne Walk, built in 1674 on the site of Thomas More's farm. The house was divided into separate homes in 1775, but if you're really keen to have a look inside, it is possible to visit the entrance hall, garden room and gardens by written appointment on roughly six specified afternoons of the year; phone the National Trust on ☎01494/528051 for more details. Last, but not least, the reclusive J.M.W. Turner lived at no. 118 for the last six years of his life under the pseudonym Booth, and painted many a sunset over the Thames.

Carlyle's House

April–Oct Wed–Sun 11am–5pm; NT; £3.30; ☎020/7352 7087. Sloane Square tube.

A short distance inland from Cheyne Walk, at 24 Cheyne Row, is **Carlyle's House**, the Queen Anne house where the historian Thomas Carlyle set up home with his wife, Jane Welsh Carlyle, having moved down from his native Scotland in 1834. Carlyle's full-blooded and colourful style, best illustrated by his account of the French Revolution, brought him great fame during his lifetime – a statue was erected to the "Sage of Chelsea" on Cheyne Walk less than a year after his death in 1881, and the house became a museum just fifteen years later. That said, the intellectuals and artists who visited Carlyle – among them Dickens, Tennyson, Chopin, Mazzini, Browning and Darwin – were attracted as much by the wit of his strong-willed wife, with whom Carlyle enjoyed a famously tempestuous relationship. The house itself is a typically dour Victorian abode, kept much as the Carlyles would have had it – the historian's hat still hanging in the hall, his socks still in the chest of drawers – and you're positively encouraged to lounge around on the sofas by the live-in curator. The top floor contains the garret study where Carlyle tried in vain to escape the din of the street and the neighbours' noisy roosters in order to complete his final magnum opus on Frederick the Great.

Fulham Palace

March–Oct Wed–Sun 2–5pm; Nov–Feb Thurs–Sun 1–4pm; £1; ☎020/7736
3233. Putney Bridge tube.

One last sight worth visiting in this part of town is **Fulham Palace**,
stuck in the middle of Bishop's Park, at the far end of the New King's
Road by Putney Bridge. Once the largest moated site in England, it
was the residence of the Bishop of London – third in the Church of
England hierarchy – from 704 to 1973. The oldest section of the
present-day complex is the modestly scaled Tudor courtyard, patterned with black diamonds; the most recent is William Butterfield's
Neo-Gothic chapel, which, with the other period interiors, can only
be seen on the **guided tours** that take place on the second – and, in
the summer, fourth – Sunday of the month at 2pm (£2). At other
times, you have to make do with the small **museum**, which traces the
complex history of the building and displays a motley collection of
archeological finds, including a mummified rat. In the palace
grounds there's a lovely herb garden, with a Tudor gateway and a
maze of miniature box hedges, but sadly no sign of a moat, since it
was filled in 1921.

Battersea

*The Children's
Zoo is open
Easter–Sept
daily
10am–5pm;
Oct–Easter
Sat & Sun
11am–3pm;
adults £1.80,
children 90p;
☎020/8871
7540.*

In the property boom of the 1980s, aspiring Chelsea types began
to colonize the cheaper terraces and mansions across the river in
Battersea, which duly earned itself the nickname "South Chelsea".
For the best part of last century, however, Battersea was a
staunchly working-class enclave, which in the 1920s returned
Shapurji Saklatvala as its MP – first for the Labour Party, then as
a Communist. Saklatvala was always in the news: he was banned
from entry into the US and even to his native India, and was the
first person to be arrested during the 1926 General Strike, after a
speech in Hyde Park urging soldiers not to fire on striking workers, for which he received a two-month prison sentence.

The poverty in the area was one of the main reasons behind the
establishment of **Battersea Park**, opened in 1853 as the capital's
second non-royal public park after Victoria Park in the East End
(see p.280). It is connected to Chelsea by the Albert Bridge, one
of the prettiest to span the Thames, especially when lit at night.
The park itself is best known nowadays for its two-tier **Peace
Pagoda**, erected in 1985 by Japanese Buddhists. Made from a
combination of reconstituted Portland stone and Canadian fir

*The Couper
Collection is
open Fri & Sat
2–6pm; £3;
☎020/8871
7572.*

trees, the pagoda shelters four large gilded Buddhas in its niches.
To the southeast, there's a small **Children's Zoo**, established during the 1951 Festival of Britain, with monkeys, reptiles, birds,
otters and mongooses.

If you're in the vicinity of the park towards the end of the week, it's
probably worth strolling over to inspect the **Couper Collection**, a

new permanent floating art museum located within several convert-ed Thames barges, just to the west of Albert Bridge. On board, twen-ty years' artwork by Max Couper, the Thames-based artist and mariner, is displayed.

The old village of Battersea was originally centred on **St Mary's Church**, half a mile or so further west, hard by the river. In 1775, when the current church was built, Battersea was a peaceful place with fewer than two thousand inhabitants, among them Catherine Butcher, who went on to marry the poet and visionary William Blake in the church some seven years later. Another painter associated with St Mary's is Turner, who used to sit in the oriel vestry window and paint the clouds and sunsets (his favourite chair is now rever-ently preserved in the chancel).

Among most Londoners, though, Battersea is known for just two things: its **Dogs' Home**, which moved to 4 Battersea Park Rd in 1871, and **Battersea Power Station**, Giles Gilbert Scott's awesome cathedral of power. Closed in 1983, it's now in a shocking condi-tion, its innards ripped out and its exterior walls looking precarious. There is currently talk of turning the place into some kind of leisure and entertainment complex, but as yet there is little sign of progress.

Bayswater and Notting Hill

It wasn't until the removal of the gallows at Tyburn (see box on p.333) that the area to the **north of Hyde Park** began to gain respectability. The arrival of the Great Western Railway at Paddington in 1838 further encouraged development, and the gentrification of **Bayswater**, the area immediately north of the park, began with the construction of an estate called Tyburnia. These days Bayswater is mainly residential, and a focus for London's widely dispersed Arab community, who are catered for by some excellent Lebanese restaurants and cafés along the busy Edgware Road.

Much more tangible attractions lie to the west in **Notting Hill**, where London's most popular market, **Portobello Road**, takes place each Saturday, and where the August Bank Holiday weekend sees West Indian London out in force for the **Notting Hill Carnival**, Europe's largest. The area is now one of the city's trendiest and most affluent multicultural neighbourhoods. Back in the 1950s, when it was among London's poorest neighbourhoods, it was, along with Brixton in South London, settled by Afro-Caribbean immigrants, invited over to work in the public services. Gentrification in the last two decades has changed the population greatly, but there's still a significant black presence, especially in the northern fringes.

Bayswater and Paddington

Bayswater's combination of classic urban squares, big stuccoed terraces and grand tree-lined avenues gives the district a wealthy and almost continental feel, but the volume of traffic, as usual, spoils much of the effect. The area's main focus is **Paddington Station** on Praed Street, one of the world's great early train stations; designed by Isambard Kingdom Brunel in 1851, the cathedral-scale wrought-iron sheds replaced a wooden structure that was the destination of Victoria and Albert's first railway journey. The train travelled from Slough (near Windsor) at an average speed of 44mph, which the prince considered excessive – "Not so fast next time, Mr Conductor", he is alleged to have remarked.

The nearest tube is Paddington.

The Fleming Laboratory is open Mon–Thurs 10am–1pm; £2; ☎ 020 /7725 6528.

One block east of Paddington is St Mary's Hospital, home of the **Fleming Laboratory**, on the corner of Norfolk Place, where the young Scottish bacteriologist Alexander Fleming accidentally discovered penicillin in 1928. A short video, a small exhibition and a reconstruction of Fleming's untidy lab tell the story of the medical discovery that has saved more lives than any other last century. Oddly enough, it aroused little interest at the time, until a group of chemists in Oxford succeeded in purifying penicillin in 1942. Desperate for good news in wartime, the media made Fleming a celebrity, and he was eventually awarded the Nobel Prize, along with several of the Oxford team.

Bayswater's main drag is **Queensway**, whose rash of cafés, clothes shops and French patisseries keeps buzzing until late in the evening. The renewed prosperity here is due, in large part, to the resurgent Arab community, but to add to the cosmopolitan atmosphere, Queensway also boasts the largest concentration of Chinese restaurants outside Soho's Chinatown. A short distance up Moscow Road, you'll find **St Sophia**, London's ornate Greek Orthodox Cathedral, boasting mosaics by Boris Anre.

One whole block of Queensway is taken up by **Whiteley's**, established in 1863 as the city's first real department store. The present building opened in 1912 with the boast that they could supply "anything from a pin to an elephant", and had the dubious distinction of being Hitler's favourite London building – he planned to make it his HQ once the invasion was over. Nowadays it houses an indoor shopping mall with several restaurants and a multi-screen cinema.

Notting Hill

The urbanization of **Notting Hill**, the area to the north of Holland Park Avenue, began in the first half of the nineteenth century, when the leafy avenues and majestic crescents of the Norland and Ladbroke estates were laid out. In those days, the area was still known as the Potteries (after the gravel pits and pottery works on Walmer Road) or the Piggeries (after the district's three-to-one ratio

Notting Hill Carnival

When it emerged in the 1960s, **Notting Hill Carnival** (*www
.nottinghillcarnival.net.uk*) was little more than a few church-hall events
and a carnival parade, inspired by that of Trinidad – home to many of the
area's immigrants. Today the carnival, held over the August Bank Holiday
weekend, still belongs to West Indians (from all parts of the city), but there
are participants, too, from London's Latin American and Asian communities, and, of course, Londoners of all descriptions turn out to watch the
bands and parades, and hang out.

The main sights of the Carnival are the **costume parades**, which take
place on the Sunday (for kids) and Monday (for adults) from around 10am
until just before midnight. The parade makes its way around a three-mile
route, starting at the top end of Ladbroke Grove, heading south under the
Westway, then turning into Westbourne Grove, before looping north again
via Chepstow Road, Great Western Road and Kensal Road. The procession
consists of "big trucks", which carry the sound systems and *mas* (masquer-
ade) bands, behind which dance the masqueraders in outrageous costumes.

Most of the *mas* bands play a variety of soca music, while others feature
steel bands – the "pans" of the steel bands are one of the chief sounds of
the Carnival and have their own contest on the Saturday at Horniman's
Pleasance. In addition to those playing *mas*, there are three or four **stages
for live music** – Portobello Green and Powis Square are regular venues –
and numerous **sound systems** where you can catch reggae, ragga, drum
'n'bass, jungle, garage, house and much more. A lot of people just mill
around the sound systems, dancing as the day progresses, fuelled by cans
of Red Stripe, curried goat and Jamaican patties, which are sold by a multitude of weekend entrepreneurs.

Over the last few years, the Carnival has been fairly relaxed, considering the huge numbers of people it attracts. However, this is not an event
for you if you are at all bothered by crowds – you can be wedged station-
ary during the parades – and very loud music. It is worth taking more than
usual care with your belongings too: leave expensive cameras and jewellery at home, and bring only enough money for the day, as pickpockets
turn up from all over. As far as safety goes, don't worry unduly about the
media's horror stories (a perennial feature, along with pictures of police
being kissed by large Caribbean women), as you're in plentiful company.
However, the static sound systems are switched off at 7pm each day, and
if there's going to be any trouble it tends to come after that point. If you
feel at all uneasy, head home early.

Getting to and from the Carnival is quite an event in itself. Ladbroke
Grove tube station is closed for the duration, while Notting Hill Gate and
Westbourne Park are open only for incoming visitors. The nearest fully
operative tube stations are Latimer Road and Royal Oak. Alternatively,
there's a whole network of buses running between most points of London
and Notting Hill Gate.

of pigs to people). Even forty years ago Notting Hill was described as
"a massive slum, full of multi-occupied houses, crawling with rats
and rubbish", and populated by offshoots of the Soho vice and crime
rackets. These insalubrious dwellings – many owned by the infamous
vice king and slum landlord Peter Rachman – became home to a

large contingent of West Indian immigrants, who had to compete for jobs and living space with the area's similarly downtrodden white residents.

For four days in August 1958, Pembridge Road became the epicentre of the country's first **race riots**, when busloads of whites attacked West Indian homes in the area. The **Notting Hill Carnival** began unofficially the next year as a response to the riots; in 1965 it took to the streets and has since grown into the world's biggest street festival outside Rio, with an estimated two million revellers turning up on the last weekend of August for the two-day extravaganza of *mas* (costume) parades, steel bands, live music stages and deafening sound systems. Strenuous efforts have been made in recent years to ease the tension between the black community and the police, but there are still plenty of doubters among the area's wealthier and mostly white residents, most of whom switch on the alarm system and leave town for the weekend.

The rest of the year, Notting Hill is a lot quieter, though its cafés and restaurants are cool enough places to pull in media folk from all over, and, of course, thanks to the myths spun about the area in the film, *Notting Hill*, there are now significantly more overseas visitors than before (and even higher house prices). The busiest day of the week is always Saturday, when big crowds of Londoners and tourists alike descend on the mile-long **Portobello Road Market**.

Portobello Road Market

*The nearest
tubes are
Notting Hill
Gate and
Ladbroke
Grove.*

Portobello Road kicks off at the intersection of Chepstow Road, though this initial stretch, lined with rather junky antique stalls and classier antique shops, is overpriced and geared very much to tourists. The **market** gets a lot more fun and funky after a brief switch to fruit and veg around the old Electric cinema, on the corner of Blenheim Crescent, which opened in 1911, had serial killer John Christie as its projectionist during the last war and is currently undergoing restoration. Continuing along Portobello Road, you reach an area under the Westway flyover, where the emphasis of the market switches to street clothes and jewellery, odd trinkets, records and books.

There are some interesting shops in a complex under the Westway, and many more in the streets around. A wander through the grid between Elgin Crescent and Lancaster Road will take you past art galleries and shops selling contemporary ceramics, old jukeboxes and all manner of exotics and essentials. Blenheim Crescent and adjoining Talbot Road are a good place to start, with the excellent Travel Bookshop and Books for Cooks on the former, and Rough Trade records on the latter.

*For more on
Ernö
Goldfinger, see
p.405.*

Across the Westway, the stalls get progressively cheaper as they swing east into Golborne Road, which sits in the shadow of the awesome **Trellick Tower**, the tallest block of flats in the country when it was built by Ernö Goldfinger in 1973, and despite appearances still popular with its residents. Golborne Road is a market of its own, really, with a constellation of bric-a-brac stalls, and Portuguese and Moroccan cafés and shops, giving the road some of the bohemian feel of old Notting Hill, and making it the perfect place to wind up a visit to the market.

Bayswater and Notting Hill

Kensal Green Cemetery

Daily: April–Sept 8am–6pm; Oct–March 9am–5pm; free. Guided tours of cemetery Sun 2pm, including catacombs (bring a torch) first and third Sun of month; £4. ☎020/8960 1030. Kensal Green tube.

Within easy walking distance of Portobello Road, on the other side of the railway tracks, gasworks and canal, is **Kensal Green Cemetery**, the first of the city's commercial graveyards, opened in 1833 to relieve the pressure on overcrowded inner-city churchyards. It's still owned by the founding company and still a functioning cemetery, with services conducted daily in the central Greek Revival chapel.

The nearest tube and train station is Kensal Green.

Graves of the more famous incumbents – Thackeray, Trollope and the Brunels – are less interesting architecturally than those arranged on either side of the Centre Avenue, which leads from the easternmost entrance on Harrow Road. Vandals have left numerous headless angels and irreparably damaged the beautiful Cooke family monument. Look out, though, for Major-General Casement's bier, held up by four grim-looking turbaned Indians, and circus manager Andrew Ducrow's conglomeration of beehive, sphinx and angels. Other interesting characters buried here include Charles Wingfield, who invented lawn tennis; Charles Blondin, the famous tightrope walker; Carl Wilhelm Siemens, the German scientist who brought electric lighting to London; and "James" Barry, Inspector-General of the Army Medical Department, who, it was discovered during the embalming of the corpse, was in fact a woman. The Queen singer, Freddie Mercury, was cremated here but his ashes were scattered in Bombay.

Chapter 11

North London: Camden, Regent's Park, Hampstead and beyond

Everything north of the Marylebone and Euston roads was, for the most part, open countryside until the mid-nineteenth century, and is now largely residential right the way up to the "green belt", created in the immediate postwar period to try and limit the continuing urban sprawl. The area of the city covered in this **NORTH LONDON** chapter is necessarily much smaller, concentrating on just a handful of the satellite villages, now subsumed into the general mass of London. Almost all the northern suburbs are easily accessible by tube from the centre; in fact, it was the expansion of the tube which encouraged the forward march of bricks and mortar in many of the outer suburbs.

The first section of the chapter traces the route of the **Regent's Canal**, which skirts what was, at the beginning of the nineteenth century, the city's northern periphery. Along the way, the canal passes one of London's finest parks, **Regent's Park**, framed by Nash-designed architecture and home of London Zoo. The canal forces its way into Londoners' consciousness only at **Camden**, whose weekend market is one of the city's big attractions – a warren of stalls with an alternative past still manifest in its offbeat wares, street fashion, books, records and ethnic goods.

Far fewer visitors to the capital bother to check out neighbouring **Islington**, thus missing out on one of North London's defining areas, endowed with its own flourishing antiques trade. The real highlights of North London, though, for visitors and residents alike, are **Hampstead** and **Highgate**, elegant, largely eighteenth-century developments which still reflect their village origins. They have the added advantage of proximity to one of London's wildest patches of greenery, **Hampstead Heath**, where you can enjoy stupendous views, kite-flying and nude bathing, as well as outdoor concerts and

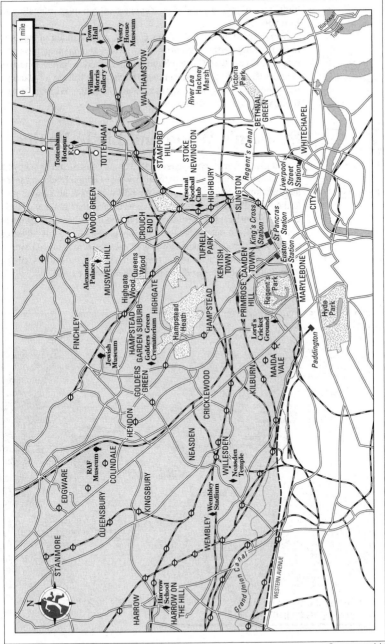

© crown copyright

high art in and around the Neoclassical country mansion of **Kenwood House**.

Also covered, at the end of this chapter, are a handful of sights in more far-flung northern suburbs. They include the nineteenth-century utopia of **Hampstead Garden Suburb**; the Orthodox Jewish suburb of **Golders Green**; the **RAF Museum** at Hendon; the "village" of **Harrow**; the exhibition halls of **Alexandra Palace**; and the **William Morris Gallery**, way out in Walthamstow.

St John's Wood and Little Venice

The **Regent's Canal**, completed in 1820, was constructed as part of a direct link from Birmingham to the newly built London Docks. Its seemingly random meandering, from the Grand Junction Canal at Paddington to the River Thames at Limehouse, traces the fringe of London's northernmost suburbs at the time. After an initial period of heavy usage it was overtaken by the railway, and never really paid its way as its investors had hoped. By some miracle, however, it escaped being covered over or turned into a rail or road route, and its nine miles, 42 bridges, twelve locks and two tunnels stand as a reminder of another age.

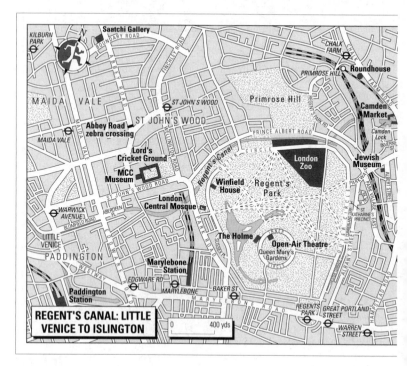

REGENT'S CANAL: LITTLE VENICE TO ISLINGTON

0 400 yds

The lockless run of the canal **between Little Venice and Camden Town** is the busiest, most attractive stretch, tunnelling through to Lisson Grove, skirting Regent's Park, slicing London Zoo in two, and passing straight through the heart of Camden Market. It's also the one section that's served all year round by narrowboats (see box on p.386). Alternatively you can cycle, walk or jog along the towpath.

St John's Wood

The Regent's Canal starts out from the west in the smart, residential district of **St John's Wood**, which was built over in the nineteenth century by developers hoping to attract a wealthy clientele with a mixture of semi-detached Italianate villas, multi-occupancy Gothic mansions and white stucco terraces. Edwin Landseer (of Trafalgar Square lions fame), novelist George Eliot and Mrs Fitzherbert, the uncrowned wife of George IV, all lived here, while current residents include knights Richard Branson and Paul McCartney.

To catch a canal boat to Camden through the southern borders of this neighbourhood, head for the triangular leafy basin known as **Little Venice**, a nickname coined by the one-time resident, poet Robert Browning. The title may be far-fetched, but the willow-tree

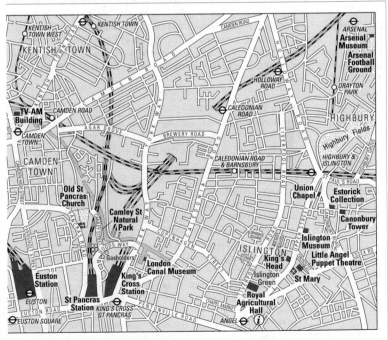

© crown copyright

St John's Wood and Little Venice

To book for the Puppet Theatre Barge shows, call ☎020/7249 6876.

Regent's Canal by boat

Three companies run boat services on the Regent's Canal between Little Venice (Warwick Avenue tube) and Camden (Camden Town tube), passing through the Maida Hill tunnel and stopping off at London Zoo on the way. Jason's crafts start off at Little Venice, the *Jenny Wren* starts off at Camden, and the London Waterbus Company sets off from both places. Whichever company you choose, you can board at either end; journey time is 35–45 minutes one way, and tickets cost £5–6 return. The times given below are approximate and depend slightly on the weather, so ring first to check.

Jason's Trip ☎020/7286 3428. Narrowboat from Little Venice to Camden Lock and back; Easter–Oct daily 10.30am–2.30pm, Sat & Sun until 4.30pm.

Jenny Wren ☎020/7485 4433. Narrowboat from Camden Lock to Little Venice and back; Easter–Oct daily 10.30am–2.30pm, Sat & Sun until 4.30pm.

London Waterbus Company ☎020/7482 2660. Boats between Little Venice and Camden Lock via London Zoo; April–Oct daily 10am–5pm; Nov–March Sat & Sun only.

---

island is one of the prettiest spots on the canal, and the houseboats and barges moored hereabouts are brightly painted and strewn with tubs of flowers. If you're here between October and May, be sure to try and catch a traditional marionette performance on the **Puppet Theatre Barge**, moored on the Blomfield Road side of the basin, a unique and unforgettable experience; performances, for both kids and adults, take place every weekend and daily throughout the school holidays.

Lord's Cricket Ground

Guided tours daily (except match days) 10am, noon & 2pm; £6; ☎020/7432 1033; *www.lords.org.uk*. St John's Wood or Maida Vale tube.

The building of the Regent's Canal was bad news for Thomas Lord, who had only recently been forced to shift his cricket ground due to the construction of what is now Marylebone Road. Once more he upped his stumps and relocated, this time to St John's Wood Road, where **Lord's**, as the ground is now known, remains to this day. The ground is owned by the **MCC (Marylebone Cricket Club)**, which was founded in 1787 and is the most hallowed institution in the game, boasting a very long waiting list (unless you're exceptionally famous or rich). Its politics were neatly summed up by Viscount Monckton, who said, "I have been a member of the Committee of the MCC and of a Conservative cabinet, and by comparison with the cricketers, the Tories seem like a bunch of Commies." The MCC only agreed to allow women membership at the end of 1998, after lottery funding was withheld because of the club's exclusively male status – though, of course, the Committee denied that this had any effect on their decision.

The Beatles in London

Since the Fab Four lived in London for much of the 1960s, it's hardly surprising that the capital is riddled with Beatle associations. The prime
Beatles landmark is, of course, the **Abbey Road** zebra crossing featured on
the album cover, located near the EMI studios, where the group recorded
most of their albums. To get there, walk up Grove End Road, which runs
along the west side of Lord's cricket ground, until you come to the junction where it turns into Abbey Road – and remember to bring three other
friends and someone to take the photos. Incidentally, Paul McCartney still
owns the house at 7 Cavendish Ave, two blocks east of the zebra crossing,
which he bought in 1966.

One other nearby curiosity, which existed for only a brief time, was the
Apple Boutique, opened by the Beatles at 94 Baker St in December 1967
as a "beautiful place where you could buy beautiful things". The psychedelic murals that covered the entire building were whitewashed over after
a lawsuit by the neighbours, and eight months later the Beatles caused
even more pandemonium when they gave the shop's entire stock away free
in the closing-down sale.

The other main Beatles location in London is the old Apple headquarters in Savile Row, where the 1969 rooftop concert took place (see p.120),
while Macca has his current office on Soho Square (see p.144). Real devotees of the group, however, should get hold of a copy of *The Beatles'
England* by David Heron and Norman Maslov, which covers every conceivable association. Alternatively, sign up for a Beatles tour, run by The
Original London Walks (☎020/7624 3978).

A match ticket will allow you free access to the **MCC museum**,
which traces the history of modern cricket, and features the minuscule pottery urn containing the Ashes (along with the complex tale
of this odd trophy), numerous historic balls, bats and bails, and a
sparrow which was "bowled out" by Jehangir Khan at Lord's in
1936. If you take one of the tours, you'll also get to see the famous
Long Room (from which the players walk onto the pitch), which is
otherwise off limits to non-members. The tours set off from the
Grace Gates at the southwest corner of the ground, and, in addition
to the museum and Long Room, you'll get endless cricketing anecdotes, a tour round Lord's Real Tennis Court and a quick look at the
dazzling Mound Stand, designed by Michael Hopkins in the late
1980s, and the new futuristic Media Centre, cruelly nicknamed
"Cherie Blair's Smile".

Regent's Park

As with almost all of London's royal parks, we have Henry VIII to
thank for **Regent's Park**, which he confiscated from the Church for
yet more hunting grounds. However, it wasn't until the reign of the
Prince Regent (later George IV) that the park began to take its current form. According to the master plan, devised by John Nash in

Regent's Park
is open daily
5am–dusk; the
nearest tubes
are Great
Portland
Street,
Regent's Park,
Baker Street
and Camden
Town;
www.royalparks
.co.uk.

1811, the park was to be girded by a continuous belt of terraces, blessed with two grand circuses and sprinkled with a total of 56 villas, including a magnificent pleasure palace for the prince himself, which would be linked by Regent Street to Carlton House in St James's (see p.107). Work was halted in 1826 due to lack of funds, and the plan was never fully realized, but enough was built to create something of the idealized garden city that Nash and the Prince Regent envisaged.

The eastern terraces

To appreciate the special quality of Regent's Park, you should take a closer look at the architecture, starting with the Nash terraces, which form a near-unbroken horseshoe of cream-coloured stucco around the Outer Circle. Each one is in a slightly different Neoclassical style, but by far the most impressive is **Cumberland Terrace**, built in 1826–28 and intended as a foil for George IV's private tea pavilion, which never materialized. Its 800-foot-long facade, hidden away on the eastern edge of the park, is punctuated by Ionic triumphal arches, peppered with classical statues and centred on a Corinthian portico with a pediment of sculptures set against a vivid sky-blue background. In 1936 an angry crowd threw bricks through the windows of no. 16, which belonged to American divorcée Mrs Wallis Simpson, whose relationship with Edward VIII was seen as a national calamity.

The nearest
tube is
Camden Town.

Fifty-two more statues depicting British worthies were planned for the even longer facade of **Chester Terrace**, to the south, but Nash decided the ridicule they provoked was "painful to the ears of a professional man" and ditched them. Nevertheless, Chester Terrace is worth walking down if only to take in the splendid triumphal arches at each end, which announce the name of the terrace in bold lettering; the northern one features a bust of Nash. Still further south, facing east onto Albany Street, is Cambridge Gate, built some fifty years later in Bath stone to replace the "**Colosseum**", a rotunda built by Decimus Burton in 1829 in the style of the Pantheon. Inside, visitors were treated to a 360-degree view of London, spread out on an acre of canvas, drawn from sketches made by Thomas Hornor from the top of St Paul's Cathedral. A million people visited the panorama in the first year, and further attractions were added, including a hall of mirrors, stalactite caverns and even roller-skating, but it fell into decline and was finally demolished in 1875.

The Inner Circle and the western periphery

The nearest
tubes are
Regent's Park
and Baker
Street.

Of the numerous villas planned for the park itself, only eight were built, and of those just two have survived around the **Inner Circle**: St John's Lodge, in its own private grounds to the north, and **The Holme**, Decimus Burton's first ever work (he was 18 at the time), picturesquely sited by the Y-shaped **Boating Lake**. Designed by

Nash, and a haven for waterfowl, the lake is fed by the waters of the Tyburn, one of London's "lost" – that is, underground – rivers. Within the Inner Circle is the Open Air Theatre, which puts on summer performances of Shakespeare, opera and ballet, and **Queen Mary's Gardens**, by far the prettiest section of the park. A large slice of the gardens is taken up with a glorious rose garden, featuring some four hundred varieties, surrounded by a ring of ramblers.

On the western edge of the park, the curved end wings and quirky octagonal domes of **Sussex Place** stand out among the other more orthodox Nash terraces (see below). A further surprise breaks the skyline to the north – the shiny copper dome and minaret of the **London Central Mosque**, an entirely appropriate addition given the Prince Regent's taste for the Orient (as expressed in Brighton Pavilion). Non-Muslim visitors are welcome to look in at the information centre, and glimpse inside the hall of worship, which is packed out with a diversity of communities for the lunchtime Friday prayers.

A little further up the Outer Circle, Quinlan Terry has added a trio of Neo-Nash villas that reflect the conservative tastes of the current Prince of Wales. On the opposite side of the road is **Winfield House**, built in the 1930s by heiress to the Woolworth chain Countess Haugwitz-Reventlow (better known as Barbara Hutton), who married Cary Grant in 1942; it's now the US ambassador's residence.

St Katharine's Precinct and Park Village West

To the north of Cumberland Terrace, the Neo-Gothic **St Katharine's Precinct** provides a respite from the Grecian surroundings, though not one Nash was at all happy with. The central church now serves the Danish community, who have erected a copy of the imposing tenth-century **Jelling Stone** in an alcove to the right. The original was erected in memory of King Gorm by his son, Harald Bluetooth, the first Danish ruler to convert to Christianity, as the colourful runic inscription and image of Christ hewn into the granite testify.

For proof that Nash could build equally well on a much more modest scale than the Regent's Park terraces, take a stroll round **Park Village West**, which lies in a secluded network of winding streets and culs-de-sac just off Albany Street, on the other side of Gloucester Gate. The houses, Nash's last work for Regent's Park, feature copious ornamental urns and black lattice pergolas, and range from mock-Athenian cottages to Tudor and Italianate villas.

London Zoo

Daily: March–Oct 10am–5.30pm; Nov–Feb 10am–4pm; £9; ☎020/7722 3333; *www.londonzoo.co.uk*. Camden Town tube.

The northeastern corner of the park, beyond acres of football pitches, is occupied by **London Zoo**, founded way back in 1826. Over the last decade, after a major financial crisis, the zoo has sought to redefine itself as an eco-conscious place whose prime purpose is to save species under threat of extinction. It's still not the most uplifting spot for animal-lovers, though the enclosures are as humane as any inner-city zoo could make them, and kids usually love the place. Most are particularly taken by the children's enclosure, where they can actually handle the animals, and the regular "Animals in Action" live shows. The new invertebrate house, known as the Web of Life, is also a guaranteed winner, as it has lots of creepy-crawlies, much more hands-on stuff and strong green credentials.

The zoo boasts some striking architectural features, too, such as the 1930s modernist, spiral-ramped concrete penguin pool (where Penguin Books' original colophon was sketched), designed by the Tecton partnership, led by Russian émigré Berthold Lubetkin, who also made the zoo's Round House. The Giraffe House, by contrast, was designed in Neoclassical style by Decimus Burton, who was also responsible for the mock-Tudor Clock Tower. Other landmark features are the mountainous Mappin Terraces, dating from just before World War I, and the colossal tetrahedral aluminium-framed tent of Lord Snowdon's Aviary.

Prince Albert Road and Primrose Hill

Nash intended the Regent's Canal to run right through the middle of the park, but potential residents objected to lower-class canal-faring families ploughing through their well-to-do neighbourhood. Instead, the canal curves its way along the northern periphery, passing right through London Zoo, with the Snowdon Aviary to one side and giraffes and camels to the other. Equally visible from the canal are the millionaire apartment buildings of **Prince Albert Road**, which boast unrivalled views across the park. Nash left the park's north side open so folk might enjoy "the many beautiful views towards the villages of Hampstead and Highgate", and it was left to twentieth-century architects to fill in the gaps with a wild variety of high-rise flats, some clad in Edwardian pomp, others with package-tour balconies.

Halfway along Prince Albert Road, the mansions stop to reveal the small northern extension of Regent's Park, known as **Primrose Hill**, which commands a superb view from its modest summit. In the sixteenth century, Mother Shipton prophesied that "When London surrounds Primrose Hill, the streets of the Metropolis shall run with blood", and in May 1829 a Mr Wilson proposed turning the hill into a necropolis, with a lift running down the core of the hill to give access to the various levels. Neither of these calamities came about, and the most unusual thing you're likely to witness is the Neo-Druidic ceremony which takes place here every autumn equinox. To the east is the much-sought-after residential area of Primrose Hill, which continues to attract successful literati and artists: H.G. Wells, W.B.

Yeats, Friedrich Engels, Ted Hughes, Sylvia Plath and Morrissey have all lived here, and you might catch the present denizens such as Noel Gallagher or Sam Mendes browsing the bookshops and galleries on **Regent's Park Road**, which skirts Primrose Hill park to the east.

Camden Town

Until the canal arrived, **Camden Town** wasn't even a village, but by Victorian times it had become a notorious slum area, an image that it took most of last century to shed. Over the years, however, it has attracted a fair share of artists, most famously the Camden Town Group formed in 1911 by Walter Sickert, later joined by the likes of Lucien Freud, Frank Auerbach and Leon Kossoff. These days, you're more likely to bump into young foreign tourists heading for the market, and as-yet-unknown bands on the lookout for members of the local music industry.

For all the gentrification of the last twenty years, Camden retains a seedy air, compounded by the various railway lines that plough through the area, the canal and Europe's largest dosshouse on Arlington Road. Its proximity to three main-line stations has also made it an obvious point of immigration over the years, particularly for the Irish, but also for Greek Cypriots during the 1950s. The **market**, however, gives the area a positive lift on the weekends, and is now the district's best-known attribute.

Camden Market and High Street

Camden Market was confined to Inverness Street until the 1970s, when the focus began to shift towards the disused timber wharf and warehouses around Camden Lock. The tiny crafts market which began in the cobbled courtyard by the lock has since mushroomed out of all proportion, with everyone trying to grab a piece of the action on both sides of Camden High Street and Chalk Farm Road. More than 100,000 shoppers turn up here each weekend and parts of the market now stay open all week long, alongside a similarly oriented crop of shops, cafés and bistros.

The nearest tube is Camden Town.

Camden Market

Camden's overabundance of cheap leather, DM shoes and naff jewellery is compensated for by the sheer variety of what's on offer: from bootleg tapes to furniture and mountain bikes, along with a mass of street fashion that may or may not make the transition to mainstream stores. For all its tourist popularity, this is a market that remains a genuinely offbeat place.

To avoid the crowds, which can be overpowering on a summer Sunday afternoon, you'll need to come either early (before 10am) or late – say, after 4pm – when many of the stalls will be packing up to

Camden market is busiest on Saturday and Sunday; at peak times such as these, Camden Town tube is exit-only.

go. The oldest part of the market is the fruit and vegetable stalls of **Inverness Street**, which have been set up every day except Sunday since the nineteenth century. Opposite, the covered section known as **Camden Market**, which backs onto Buck Street, is now Thursday to Sunday and sells mostly records and clothes.

The three-storey Victorian **Market Hall**, just past the canal bridge on the left, is home to numerous small shops, studios and stalls, which are open seven days a week. Behind the hall are the three cobbled yards of **Camden Lock**, enclosed by arty-crafty shops, most of which are open Tuesday to Sunday, and densely packed with jewellery and clothing stalls at the weekend. Further up Chalk Farm Road, the weekend-only stalls in the **Stables** feature household accessories, furniture and cheap clothes. Another adjunct to the market, which is often overlooked, is the weekend **Camden Canal Market**, across the High Street from the Market Hall; it is a riot of stalls selling everything from wrought iron to china miniatures.

Camden Lock to the Roundhouse

For more on canal rides between Camden, Regent's Park and Little Venice, see box on p.386.

If you've seen enough jangly earrings for one day, stand on the bowed iron footbridge by **Camden Lock** itself, and admire the castellated former lock-keeper's house, to the west, and the flight of three locks to the east, which begin the canal's descent to Limehouse. For the boat ride down to Little Venice, you buy tickets on board; the boats leave from the lock inlet, on the north side of the canal. Here too are the covered basins of the Interchange Warehouse, which in turn are linked by a disused railway line to the **Camden Catacombs**, built in the nineteenth century as stables for the pit ponies once used to shunt railway wagons.

The stabling extended as far north as the brick-built **Roundhouse**, on Chalk Farm Road, built by Robert Stephenson in 1847 to house 23 goods engines arranged around a central turntable. Within fifteen years the engines had outgrown the building, and for the next century it was used for storing booze. In 1966, on the initiative of Arnold Wesker, the Roundhouse became a centre for political theatre, rock gigs and other nonconformist happenings, opening with a launch party for the *International Times*, at which Pink Floyd and Soft Machine both performed, and later hosting a Dialectics of Liberation conference organized by R.D. Laing, not to mention performances by the anarchist Living Theatre, which featured a naked cast, and a regular spot for London's premier psychedelic club *UFO*. The Roundhouse closed down in 1983, and has been the subject of numerous abortive plans from a black arts centre to an architectural library. One-off events and shows are still staged here – the latest scheme is to turn the place into a creative arts complex.

Camden Town also boasts a few architectural curiosities, from Piers Gough's **Glass Building**, with its undulating bile-green façade on Jamestown Road, to Terry Farrell's corrugated steel-clad former

TV-AM Building, over the High Street on Hawley Crescent. TV-AM, which was the country's first breakfast TV station, has long since been replaced by MTV, but the building's best feature, the giant blue-and-white egg cups on the canal façade, remain. Further along the canal are the technologically astonishing **canalside flats** designed by Farrell's former partner, Nicholas Grimshaw. The upper floors feature curved aluminium vertical sliding doors, which allow the dining room to become alfresco; the south side, by contrast, is windowless to cut out noise from the adjacent car park of the Camden Road **Sainsbury's** supermarket, another modernist structure by Grimshaw.

The Jewish Museum

Mon–Thurs & Sun 10am–4pm; £3; ☎020/7284 1997; *www.jewmusm.ort*
.org. Camden Town tube.

Despite having no significant Jewish associations, Camden is home to London's **Jewish Museum**, at 129 Albert St, just off Parkway. The purpose-built premises are smartly designed, but the conventional style and contents of the museum are disappointing. The collection of *Judaica* includes treasures from London's Great Synagogue, burnt down by Nazi bombers in 1941, and a sixteenth-century Venetian Ark of the Covenant. There's also a video and exhibition explaining Jewish religious practices and the history of the Jewish community in Britain. Look out, too, for the occasional cultural event or concert. More challenging temporary exhibitions are held in the museum's Finchley branch on East End Road (see p.415).

Old St Pancras to Camley Street Natural Park

By tradition the first parish church built in London, **Old St Pancras Church** lies hidden and neglected behind iron railings on raised ground above Pancras Road, a few minutes' walk east of the bottom of Camden High Street. Parts of the church date from the eleventh century – most notably the north and south doorways – but the rest was rebuilt in the nineteenth. Unfortunately, since Satanists attacked the church in 1985, access has been difficult outside of services.

The nearest tubes are Mornington Crescent and King's Cross.

Its churchyard, which backs onto the railway lines and the lugubrious Victorian Hospital for Tropical Diseases, was turned into a public garden in 1877, with the majority of graves being heaped around an ash tree, though it's all now rather melancholic, with crumbling verges and cracking pathways. Only **Sir John Soane's mausoleum** from 1816 – the inspiration for Giles Gilbert Scott's traditional red phone box – designed initially for his wife, is still standing in its original location, to the north of the church. Also buried here was Britain's great protofeminist, Mary Wollstonecraft Godwin, who died a few days after giving birth to her daughter, Mary. At the age of 16, the younger Mary was spotted visiting her mother's grave by the poet

Sir John Soane's Museum is covered on p.204.

Percy Bysshe Shelley, who immediately declared his undying love, before eloping with her to Italy – both Marys are now buried in Bournemouth. A list of the graveyard's most prominent dead is inscribed on the monumental sundial erected by Baroness Burdett-Coutts.

If you continue down Pancras Road until you come to the collection of railway bridges, and then turn left, you'll come out on the desolate Goods Way, a backwater of the King's Cross red-light district. On either side rise the brooding skeletal **King's Cross Gasholders**, framed by wrought-iron Doric pillars and embellished with red triglyphs. These Victorian monsters are still in use, and hark back to an era when nothing was too lowly to be given Neoclassical decoration; they're listed buildings but are currently under threat from the new Channel Tunnel train tracks into St Pancras.

*Camley Street
Natural Park
is open
summer
Mon–Thurs
9am–5pm, Sat
& Sun
11am–5pm;
winter Sat &
Sun only; free;
☎020/7833
2311.*

Up Camley Street, past the gasholders, is **Camley Street Natural Park**, transformed from a rubbish dump into a canalside wildlife haven, and run by the London Wildlife Trust. Pond, meadow and woodland habitats have been re-created and provide a natural environment for birds, butterflies, frogs, newts, toads and even the odd heron, plus a rich variety of plantlife.

London Canal Museum

Tues–Sun 10am–4.30pm; £2.50; ☎020/7713 0836; *www.canalmuseum.org .uk*. King's Cross tube.

An insight into life on the canals can be gained from the **London Canal Museum**, on the other side of York Way, down New Wharf Road. The museum testifies to the hard life boat families had to endure and includes a 1924 film of life on the Regent's Canal. Other exhibits relate to the building itself, which was built as an ice house by Swiss-Italian entrepreneur Carlo Gatti, London's main ice trader in the nineteenth century. Gatti single-handedly popularized ice cream in London, supplying most of the city's vendors, who became known as "Hokey-Pokey Men" – a corruption of the street cry *Ecco un poco*, "Just try a little". Also on view are a restored "butty" (an engineless narrowboat used for extra storage) and some of the unusual Measham Ware pottery that was popular with canal-boat families.

The Canal Museum stands alongside the **Battlebridge Basin**, which is just about the end of the road if you're walking along the towpath, for under the next road bridge the canal enters the Nash-built **Islington Tunnel**, 1000ft long and hard work for the boatmen, who would lie on their backs and push the boat through with their feet. In 1826, a miniature steamboat took over the job, emerging into the light between Vincent Terrace and Noel Road, on the other side of Upper Street.

Islington

Islington has acquired something of a reputation as the home of what the British media like to call "the chattering classes" – the liberal, *Guardian*-reading middle class. Local Labour MP Chris Smith is openly gay and the Prime Minister, Tony Blair, lived in the borough before moving into no. 10. Parts of Islington have certainly come a long way up the social ladder in the last thirty years, since low house prices in the 1960s and 1970s encouraged a lot of arty professionals to buy and renovate the area's dilapidated Regency and early Victorian squares and terraces. In the 1980s this process was accelerated by an influx of far-from-left-leaning yuppies, who snapped up properties in an area attractively convenient for the City.

The impact of this gentrification has been relatively minor on the district as a whole, which stretches as far north as Highgate Hill, and Islington remains one of the poorest boroughs in England. On the other hand, the main drag, Upper Street, has changed enormously: the arrival of its antique market, confusingly known as Camden Passage, coincided with the new influx of cash-happy customers, and its trendy pubs and ethnic restaurants, from Turkish to Thai, Japanese to Lebanese, reflect the wealth of its new residents. For entertainment, there are more pub-theatres in Islington than anywhere else, the oldest established being the *King's Head*, whose better productions transfer to the West End; in addition to these, there's the Almeida – a top fringe theatre that has attracted the likes of

For more on London's theatre and comedy scene, see Chapter 21.

Orton in Islington

Playwright **Joe Orton** and his lover **Kenneth Halliwell** lived together for sixteen years, spending the last eight years of their lives in a top-floor bedsit at 25 Noel Rd, to the east of Upper Street, where the Regent's Canal emerges from the Islington tunnel. It's ironic that the borough council has seen fit to erect a plaque on the house commemorating the couple, when it was instrumental in pressing for harsh prison sentences after both men were found guilty of defacing local library books in 1962. (The wittily doctored books are now among the most prized possessions of Islington Central Library, on Fieldway Crescent; the books themselves are now too delicate to handle, but colour photocopies can be viewed on request.)

Six months in prison worked wonders for Orton's writing, as he himself said: "Being in the nick brought detachment to my writing." It also brought him success, with irreverent comedies like *Loot, Entertaining Mr Sloane* and *What the Butler Saw* playing to sell-out audiences in the West End and on Broadway. Orton's meteoric fame and his sexual profligacy drove Halliwell to despair, however, and on August 9, 1967, Halliwell finally cracked – beating Orton to death with a hammer and then killing himself with a drug overdose. Their ashes were mixed together and scattered over the grass at Golders Green Crematorium (see p.414). Apart from the local public toilets, Orton's favourite hang-out was the appropriately entitled *Island Queen* pub, at the end of Noel Road.

Juliette Binoche, Ralph Fiennes, Kevin Spacey and Liam Neeson – and several comedy and live-music venues. All of which makes Islington one of the liveliest areas of north London in the evening – a kind of off-West End.

Upper Street and around

Looking at the traffic fighting its way along **Upper Street**, it's hard to believe that "merry Islington", as it was known, was once a spa resort to which people would flock from the City to drink the pure water and breathe the clean air. Today, the district has fewer green spaces than any other London borough – one of the few being the minuscule **Islington Green**, a short distance along Upper Street from Angel tube. At the apex of the green stands a weathered statue of Sir Hugh Myddelton, the Welsh jeweller to James I, who revolutionized London's water supply by drawing fresh water direct from springs in Hertfordshire via an aqueduct known as the New River. From 1612 until the late 1980s Myddelton's New River continued to supply most of north London with its water – the succession of ponds to the northeast of Canonbury Road is a surviving fragment of the scheme.

To the east of the Green, a black glass canopy provides shelter for the antique stalls of the **Camden Passage market** (Wed & Sat), which began in the 1960s. The antique shops in the market's narrow namesake and the surrounding streets stay open all week, as do the lockups in "The Mall" – in fact a converted tramshed – to the south of the passage. Since many of the locals are prepared to pay through the nose for antiques, you're unlikely to find bargains here. The perfect antidote, however, is to walk along **Chapel Street market** (Tues–Sun), a short distance up Liverpool Road, on the other side of Upper Street. Selling cheap clothes, fruit and veg and Arsenal football memorabilia, it's a salutary reminder of Islington's working-class roots.

Royal Agricultural Hall and Liverpool Road

On the other side of the Green from Camden Passage, the ugly modern glass frontage of the Business Design Centre hides the former **Royal Agricultural Hall**, built in 1862 and known locally as the "Aggie". As well as hosting annual agricultural and livestock exhibitions, it was in many ways a precursor to the later exhibition halls of Earl's Court and Olympia, hosting the World's Fair, the Grand Military Tournament, Cruft's Dog Show and such marvels as Urbini's performing fleas. During World War II, however, it was requisitioned by the government for use by the Post Office, who remained in residence until 1971. The interior is still magnificent, but the best exterior view is now from **Liverpool Road**, where two large brick towers rise up either side of the roof, rather like a Victorian train station.

Walking along these sections of Upper Street and Liverpool Road, it's impossible not to be struck by one of the quirky architectural features of Islington – the raised pavements which protected pedestrians from splattered mud. Such precautions were especially necessary in Islington, which was used as a convenient grazing halt for livestock en route to the City markets. The residential streets on either side of Liverpool Road, developed shortly after the completion of the Regent's Canal, are also worth exploring for their wonderful Georgian and early Victorian squares. The earliest examples, like Cloudesley Square and Myddelton Square, further south, are in plain Georgian style with early Neo-Gothic churches as their centrepieces; Lonsdale Square, with its Tudor styling, and Milner Square, with its parade of giant pilasters, are slightly later Victorian variations on the same theme.

From St Mary's to Highbury Fields

Back on Upper Street, past the Green, is **St Mary's Church**, originally built in the 1750s. Only the steeple survived the Blitz, though the light, spacious 1950s interior is an interesting period piece, with six fluted Egyptian-style columns framing the sanctuary. The churchyard opens out into Dagmar Passage, where in 1961 a former temperance hall was converted into the **Little Angel Puppet Theatre**, London's only permanent puppet theatre. The archway at the end of Dagmar Terrace brings you out onto **Cross Street**, Islington's loveliest street, with eighteenth-century houses sloping down to Essex Road and raised pavements on both sides. If you've a penchant for Deco-style buildings, head north up much less lovely Essex Road, where the former **Carlton Cinema** (now a bingo club) was built in 1929 in mock-Egyptian style, using brightly coloured Hathernware tiles.

For Little Angel bookings, call ☎ 020/7226 1787.

Back on Upper Street, heading north, you pass **Islington Town Hall**, a handsome 1920s Neoclassical Portland Stone building, whose southernmost entrance is now home to the tiny **Islington Museum** (Wed–Sat 11am–5pm, Sun 2–4pm), which puts on exhibitions with a local theme. Continuing north, Upper Street is flanked to the east by Compton Terrace, a standard late Georgian terrace, interrupted halfway along by the fancifully extravagant **Union Chapel**, built in 1888 at the height of the Congregationalists' popularity. The spacious octagonal interior is designed like a giant auditorium, with raked seating and galleries capable of holding the 1600 rapt worshippers who used to come and listen to the sermons of the local pastor. The number of chapelgoers has since dwindled, and the chapel now doubles as an innovative concert venue. To the north of Highbury Corner, at the top of Upper Street, lies the largest open space in the entire borough, **Highbury Fields**, where over 200,000 people gathered in 1666 to escape the Great Fire.

Canonbury Square

East of Compton Terrace is Islington's most perfect Regency set piece, **Canonbury Square**, centred on a beautifully kept flower garden sadly blighted by traffic ploughing up Canonbury Road. In the northeast corner of the square stands the last remaining relic of Islington's bygone days as a rural retreat, the red-brick **Canonbury Tower**, originally part of a Tudor mansion and once no doubt providing a wonderful view down to the City. Part of the building is used by the Tower Theatre Company, but the very top floor, which boasts three panelled Elizabethan interiors, is currently looked after by the nearby Canonbury Academy, who will occasionally show visitors round the tower (☎020/7359 6888).

Estorick Collection of Modern Italian Art

Wed–Sat 11am–6pm, Sun noon–5pm; £3.50; ☎020/7704 9522; *www .estorickcollection.com*. Highbury & Islington tube.

Islington's most popular attraction is the **Estorick Collection of Modern Italian Art**, housed in a large converted Georgian mansion at 39a Canonbury Square, though the entrance is on Canonbury Road. The collection is the legacy of Eric Estorick, an American sociologist who married Salome Dessau, the wealthy daughter of a Nottingham textile magnate, and became an art dealer. The most exciting works in the gallery are those of the early Italian Futurists, though of course it's impossible to escape the irony of having a museum to a movement whose founding manifesto of 1909, by Filippo Marinetti, urged its followers to "divert the canals to flood the museums!" Marinetti, a rich boy with a penchant for crashing fast cars, was Futurism's mouthpiece and, as evidenced by the photos, had an eye for natty waistcoats, complete with appliqué hands patting the pockets.

The works, spread out over several floors, range from Russolo's rainbow-coloured *Music*, which is firmly Futurist, to a couple of portraits by Modigliani, and a typically melancholic canvas by Surrealist painter, Giorgio de Chirico. One of the strangest works is Medardo Rosso's wax sculpture *Woman with a Veil*, from 1893, which had a profound influence on several of the movement's artists. Other highlights include Umberto Boccioni's *Dynamism of a Cyclist*, a classic Futurist paean to speed, and Carlo Carrà's *Boxer*, which is a more-or-less standard Cubist deconstruction. The gallery also features works by lesser-known Italian artists such as Giorgio Morandi, Massimo Campigli, Mario Sironi and Zoran Music, as well as works by Italy's two leading postwar sculptors, Emilio Greco and Marino Marini. Temporary exhibitions are also held here, and there's a pleasant Italian café that spills out into the back courtyard in good weather.

Hampstead

Perched on a hill to the west of Hampstead Heath, **Hampstead** village developed into a fashionable spa in the eighteenth century, and was not much altered thereafter. Its sloping site, which deterred Victorian property speculators and put off the railway companies, saved much of the Georgian village from destruction. Later, it became one of the city's most celebrated literary *quartiers* and even now it retains its reputation – just ahead of Islington – as a bolt hole of the high-profile intelligentsia. You can get some idea of its tone from the fact that the local Labour MP is currently the actor-turned-politician Glenda Jackson.

The steeply inclined High Street, lined with trendy clothes shops and arty cafés, flaunts the area's ever-increasing wealth without completely losing its picturesqueness, though the most appealing area is the precipitous network of alleyways, steps and streets north of the tube and west of Heath Street. Proximity to the Heath is, of course, the real joy of Hampstead, for this mixture of woodland, smooth pasture and landscaped garden (see below) is quite simply the most exhilarating patch of greenery in London.

Hampstead has some fine pubs, which are especially pleasant in summer; see p.546 for listings.

Holly Bush to the Admiral's House

Whichever route you take north of Hampstead tube, you will probably end up at the small triangular green on **Holly Bush Hill**, where the white weatherboarded **Romney House** stands (closed to the public). In 1797, painter George Romney converted the house and stables into London's first purpose-built studio house, though he spent only two years there before returning to the Lake District and the wife he had abandoned thirty years earlier. Later, it served as Hampstead's Assembly Rooms, where Constable used to lecture on landscape painting. Several houses are set grandly behind wrought-iron gates, on the north side of the green – the one you can hardly see at all, is the late seventeenth-century **Fenton House**, now a museum of musical instruments (see p.400).

The nearest tube is Hampstead.

Beyond Fenton House, up Hampstead Grove, is Admiral's Walk, so-called after its most famous building, **Admiral's House**, a whitewashed Georgian mansion with nautical excrescences. Once painted by Constable, it was later lived in by Victorian architect Sir George Gilbert Scott, of Albert Memorial fame. Until his death in 1933 John Galsworthy lived in the adjacent cottage, **Grove Lodge** – "[it] wasn't cheap, I can tell you", he wrote to a friend on arrival – where he completed *The Forsyte Saga* and received the 1932 Nobel Prize, which was presented to him here since he was too ill to travel abroad. Opposite is **The Mount**, a gently sloping street descending to Heath Street, which has changed little since it was depicted in *Work* by Pre-Raphaelite artist (and local resident) Ford Madox Brown – a reproduction is on display in Burgh House (see below).

Hampstead

Fenton House

April–Oct Wed–Fri 2–5pm, Sat & Sun 11am–5pm; NT; £4.20; ☎020/7435 3471. Hampstead tube.

All three floors of **Fenton House** are decorated in the eighteenth-century taste and currently house a collection of European and Oriental ceramics bequeathed by the house's last private owner, Lady Binning. More interestingly, the house also contains the superb Benton-Fletcher collection of **early musical instruments**, chiefly displayed on the top floor – from which you can see right across the Heath. Among the many spinets, virginals and clavichords is an early English grand piano, an Unverdorben lute from 1580 (one of only three in the world) and, on the ground floor, a harpsichord from 1612, owned by the Queen Mother, on which Handel is thought to have played, though DNA tests have failed to back this up. Experienced keyboard players are sometimes let loose on some of the instruments during the day; **concerts** are also given occasionally

---

A Hampstead who's who

Hampstead has more blue plaques commemorating its residents than any other London borough. Here's a by-no-means-exhaustive selection of Hampstead figures past and present, focusing mainly on writers, artists and politicos. For full details of where everyone lived and when, check out the local history society's pamphlet, available at Hampstead bookshops.

Cecil Beaton in the 1910s

William Blake in the 1820s

Dirk Bogarde born here 1920

Richard Burton in the 1950s

John le Carré in the 1980s & 1990s

Agatha Christie in the 1940s

John Constable in the 1820s

Edward Elgar in the 1910s

Ian Fleming in the 1960s

Michael Foot in the 1980s & 1990s

Sigmund Freud in the 1930s

Hugh Gaitskell died here 1963

John Galsworthy in the 1920s

Charles de Gaulle during World War II

Boy George in the 1980s & 1990s

Walter Gropius in the 1930s

Barbara Hepworth in the 1920s & 1930s

Gerard Manley Hopkins in the 1850s

Barry Humphries in the 1980s

Mohammed Ali Jinnah in the 1930s

John Keats in the 1820s

Oskar Kokoschka during World War II

Ramsey MacDonald in the 1920s & 1930s

A.A. Milne in the 1880s

Piet Mondrian in the 1930s

Henry Moore in the 1930s

Paul Nash in the 1930s

Ben Nicholson in the 1930s

George Orwell in the 1930s & 1940s

Peter O'Toole in the 1980s

Peter Sellers in the 1960s

Walter Sickert in the 1880s

Edith Sitwell in the 1960s

Robert Louis Stevenson in the 1870s

Twiggy in the 1960s

Sid Vicious and Johnny Rotten in the 1970s

---

in the drawing room on Thursday evenings, though tickets tend to sell out months in advance; alternatively, sign up for one of the monthly **demonstration tours** (April–Oct first Thurs of month 2pm; £10). There's very little information within the house, so it's worth buying the briefer of the guides at the entrance. Don't neglect to take a stroll in the beautiful formal **garden**, which features some top-class herbaceous borders, and is open for free whenever the house is open.

St John's-at-Hampstead and Hampstead Cemetery

The Georgian terraces of **Church Row**, at the southern end of Heath Street, are the nearest Hampstead comes to an architectural set piece, and the street was where City gents would stay for the week when Hampstead was a thriving spa. Church Row also forms a grand approach to the eighteenth-century church of **St John's-at-Hampstead**, which has an attractive Georgian interior and a romantically overgrown cemetery. The clockmaker John Harrison is buried in the church; John Constable is buried in the southeastern corner of the cemetery; Hugh Gaitskell, the Labour Party leader from 1955 to 1963, lies in the Churchyard Extension to the northeast. If you continue up Holly Walk past the Extension, you'll come to **St Mary's Church**, whose Italianate facade is squeezed into the middle of a row of three-storey cottages. As this was one of the first Roman Catholic churches to be built in London after the Reformation, the original facade from 1816 was much less conspicuous.

Further Hampstead luminaries are buried in the rather more neatly maintained **Hampstead Cemetery**, founded in 1876 when the Churchyard Extension was full, and situated half a mile to the west, on the other side of Finchley Road. The pioneer of antiseptic surgery Joseph Lister, music-hall star Marie Lloyd, children's book illustrator Kate Greenaway, Hollywood actress Lilli Palmer and the Hungarian Laszlo Biro, who invented the ballpoint pen in 1938, are among those buried here. The full-size stone organ monument to the obscure Charles Barritt is the most unusual piece of funerary art, while the most unlikely occupant is Grand Duke Michael Michaelovitch of Russia, uncle to the last tsar, Nicholas II.

Freud Museum

Wed–Sun noon–5pm; £4; ☎020/7435 2002; *www.freud.org.uk*. Finchley Road tube.

One of the most poignant of London's house museums is the **Freud Museum**, hidden away in the leafy streets of south Hampstead at 20 Maresfield Gardens. Having fled Vienna after the Nazi invasion, Sigmund Freud arrived in London in the summer of 1938, and was immediately Britain's most famous Nazi exile. He had been diagnosed as having cancer way back in 1923 (he was an inveterate

Freud was cremated at nearby Golders Green Crematorium; *see p.414.*

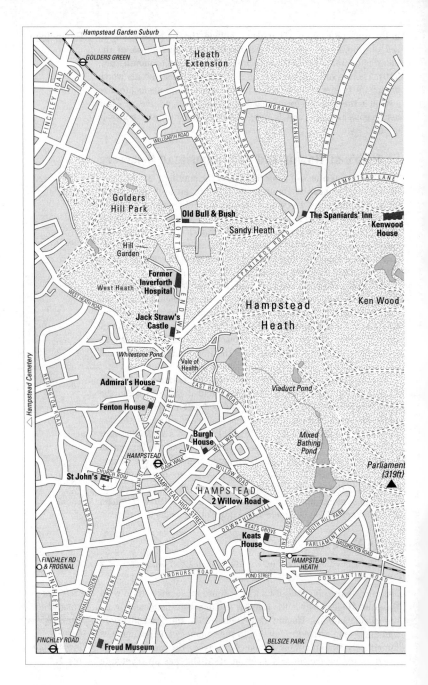

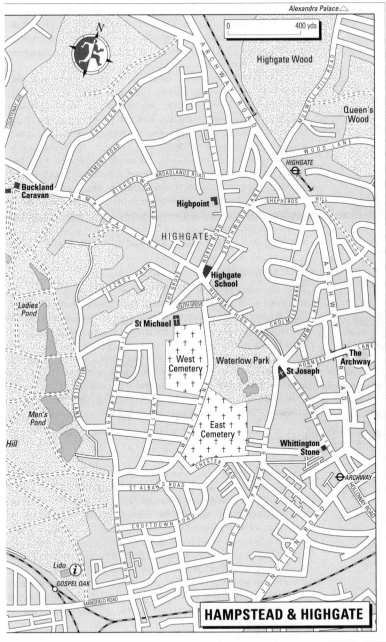

Alexandra Palace △

0   400 yds

Highgate Wood

Queen's Wood

ARCHWAY ROAD

MUSWELL HILL ROAD

WOOD LANE

HIGHGATE

COURTLANE

SHELDON AVENUE

STORMONT ROAD

BISHOPSWOOD ROAD

BROADLANDS ROAD

NORTH ROAD

SOUTHWOOD LANE

SHEPHERDS

HILL

Buckland Caravan

HAMPSTEAD LANE

Highpoint

HIGHGATE

CHOLMELEY PARK

ARCHWAY

FITZROY PARK

THE GROVE

Highgate School

'Ladies' Pond

HIGHGATE HIGH STREET

SOUTH GROVE

St Michael ✝

✝ ✝
✝ ✝ ✝
✝ **West** ✝
Cemetery ✝
✝ ✝

HORNSEY LANE

The Archway

Waterlow Park

HORNSEY

✝ **St Joseph**

HIGHGATE HILL

MILLFIELD LANE

HIGHGATE WEST HILL

SWAINS LANE

East ✝
Cemetery ✝
✝ ✝

CROMWELL AVE

Men's Pond

Whittington Stone

Hill

CHESTER ROAD

⊖ ARCHWAY

HOLLOWAY ROAD

ST ALBANS ROAD

DARTMOUTH PARK HILL

JUNCTION ROAD

CROFTDOWN ROAD

HIGHGATE ROAD

Lido ⓘ

GOSPEL OAK

MANSFIELD ROAD

HAMPSTEAD & HIGHGATE

© crown copyright

cigar-smoker) and given just five years to live. He lasted sixteen, but was a semi-invalid when he arrived in London, and rarely left the house except to visit his pet dog, Chun, who was held in quarantine. On September 21, 1939, Freud's doctor fulfilled their eleven-year-old pact and gave his patient a lethal dose of morphine.

The ground-floor study and library look exactly as they did when Freud lived here (they are modelled on his flat in Vienna); the large collection of antiquities and the psychiatrist's couch, sumptuously draped in opulent Persian carpets, were all brought here from Vienna in 1938. Upstairs, where the Freud archive now resides, home movies of the doctor's family life in Vienna are shown continually, while another room is dedicated to his favourite daughter, Anna, herself an influential child analyst, who lived in the house until her death in 1982. Sigmund's architect son, Ernst, designed a loggia at the back of the house so that Freud could sit out and enjoy the garden; it has since been enclosed and serves as the museum shop, which flogs Freudian merchandise such as a "Brainy Beanie" – Freud himself as a cuddly childhood toy – and stocks a superb range of books.

Hampstead Wells

When the healing properties of Hampstead's waters were discovered at the end of the seventeenth century, Hampstead was rapidly transformed from a quiet village into a thriving spa. The assembly rooms and pump room, the standard institutions of any self-respecting spa, have long since been demolished, but there are a few scattered reminders of the days of **Hampstead Wells**, as it was briefly known. Threepenny containers of spring water were sold close to the High Street in the pedestrianized alleyway of **Flask Walk** (hence its name), which opens out into **Well Walk**, where the Victorian Chalybeate Well commemorates the springs.

Bottling of spa water took place at The Flask, on Flask Walk, now one of Hampstead's most popular pubs.

Burgh House

Wed–Sun noon–5pm; free; 020/7431 0144.

The nearby Queen Anne mansion of **Burgh House**, on New End Square, off Well Walk, dates from the halcyon days of Hampstead Wells, and was at one time occupied by Dr Gibbons, the physician who discovered the spring's medicinal qualities. Surrounded by council housing, its ground floor now serves as an exhibition space, and there's a modest museum upstairs, with special emphasis on such notable locals as Constable and Keats. Other curiosities include a reproduction of Ford Madox Brown's painting *Work* (see p.399), a modernist Isokon plywood chair by Hungarian Bauhaus designer Marcel Breuer, found in a Hampstead skip by a local councillor, and the hat from Stanley Spencer's portrait of the artist Daphne Charlton, which was painted at the Charltons' house at 40 New End Square, and now belongs to the Tate. The *Buttery* tearoom in the basement has outdoor seating in the summer on a lovely terrace surrounded by plants.

2 Willow Road

Guided tours April–Oct every 45min Thurs–Sat noon–5pm; NT; £4.20; ☎020/7435 6166. Hampstead tube.

Hampstead's newest attraction is **2 Willow Road**, a modernist red-brick terraced house, built in the 1930s by the Hungarian-born architect Ernö Goldfinger, best known for his controversial Trellick Tower (see p.380). When Goldfinger moved in, in 1937, this was a state-of-the-art house, its open-plan rooms flooded with natural light and much of the furniture designed by Goldfinger himself. Strangely for a modernist, Goldfinger changed little in the house in the following sixty years, so what you see is a 1930s avant-garde dwelling preserved in aspic, a house at once both modern and old-fashioned. An added bonus is that the rooms are packed with *objets trouvés* and works of art by the likes of Max Ernst, Marcel Duchamp, Henry Moore and Man Ray. Incidentally, James Bond's adversary is indeed named after Ernö, as Ian Fleming lived close by and had a deep personal dislike of both Goldfinger and his modernist abode.

Keats' House

April–Nov Tues–Sun noon–5pm; £3; ☎020/7435 2062; *www.keatshouse.org.uk*. Hampstead tube.

Hampstead's most lustrous figure is celebrated at **Keats' House**, an elegant, whitewashed Regency double villa on Keats Grove, a short walk south of Willow Road. The consumptive poet moved here in 1818 shortly after his brother Tom had died of the same illness. Inspired by the peacefulness of Hampstead and by his passion for girl-next-door Fanny Brawne (whose house is also part of the museum), Keats wrote some of his most famous works here before leaving for Rome, where he died in 1821. In the pretty front garden, as you approach the house, you pass a deeply uninspiring plum tree, which replaces a much larger specimen in whose shade Keats is said to have sat for two or three hours before composing *Ode to a Nightingale*. The neat, rather staid interior contains books and letters, an anatomical notebook from Keats' days as a medical student at Guy's Hospital, Fanny's engagement ring and the four-poster bed in which the poet first coughed up blood, confiding to his companion, Charles Brown, "that drop of blood is my death warrant." The house is currently run by the Corporation of London, and there are regular events – poetry readings, performances and talks – on Wednesday evenings.

Hampstead Heath

Hampstead Heath, north London's "green lung", is the city's most enjoyable public park. Though it may not have much of its original

*The Heath
information
centre is by the
Lido and is
open Wed–Fri
1–5pm Sat &
Sun 10am–
5pm; ☎020
/7482 7073.*

*If you're in
London for
Guy Fawkes
night (Nov 5),
Parliament
Hill is one of
the best loca-
tions to watch
the fireworks
at a safe
distance.*

heathland left, it packs in a wonderful variety of bucolic scenery from the formal **Hill Garden** and rolling green pastures of **Parliament Hill** to the dense woodland of **West Heath** and the landscaped grounds of **Kenwood**. As it is, the Heath was lucky to survive the nineteenth century intact, for it endured more than forty years of campaigning by the Lord of the Manor, Sir Thomas Maryon Wilson, who introduced no fewer than fifteen parliamentary bills in an attempt to build over it. It wasn't until after Wilson's death in 1871 that 220 acres of the Heath passed into public ownership. The Heath now covers over 800 acres, and is currently in the relatively safe hands of the Corporation of London.

Parliament Hill and the Ponds

Parliament Hill, the Heath's southernmost ridge, is perhaps better known as **Kite Hill**, since this is north London's premier spot for kite-flying, especially busy at weekends when some serious equipment takes to the air. The parliamentary connection is explained in various ways by historians, so take your pick: a Saxon parliament is thought to have met here; Guy Fawkes' cronies are said to have gathered here with the hope of watching the Houses of Parliament burn; the Parliamentarians placed their cannon here during the Civil War to defend London against the Royalists; and the Middlesex parliamentary elections took place here in the seventeenth century. Whatever the reason for the name, the view over London is rivalled only by the one from Kenwood (see p.408).

The Heath is the source of several of London's lost rivers – the Tyburn, Westbourne and Fleet – and home to some 28 natural ponds, of which the most extensive are the eight **Highgate and Kenwood Ponds**, arranged in steps along a shallow valley on the eastern edge of the Heath. The Highgate Men's Pond (daily 7am–9pm or dusk; free), second from the bottom, is a secluded sylvan spot, popular with nudists, including a strong gay contingent; two ponds up is the cleanest of the lot, the Kenwood Ladies' Pond (times as above), with enough foliage to provide relaxed topless bathing, and similarly popular with lesbians. The Corporation is none too happy with either pond's reputation, but both are preferable to the Mixed Bathing Pond (times as above), on the Hampstead side of the Heath.

To the Vale of Health

To the northwest of Parliament Hill is a fenced-off tumulus known as **Boudicca's Mound**, where, according to one tradition, Queen Boudicca (Boadicea) was buried after she and 10,000 other Brits had been massacred at Battle Bridge; another legend says that she's buried in King's Cross Station (see p.188). Due west lies the picturesque **Viaduct Pond**, named after its red-brick bridge, which is also known as Wilson's Folly. It was built as part of Sir Thomas Maryon Wilson's abortive plans to drive an access road through the middle of the Heath to his projected estate of 28 villas.

Below, to the west, beyond the Viaduct Pond, an isolated network of streets nestles in the **Vale of Health**, an area that was, in fact, a malarial swamp until the late eighteenth century. Literary lion Leigh Hunt moved to this quiet backwater in 1816, after serving a two-year prison sentence for libel, having called the Prince Regent "a fat Adonis of fifty", among other things. Hunt was instrumental in persuading Keats to give up medicine for poetry, and introduced him to Shelley, Byron and other members of his literary circle. Other artistic residents have included Indian poet and Nobel prizewinner Rabindranath Tagore, who lived here in 1912, and Stanley Spencer, who stayed here with the Carline family and married their daughter Hilda in the 1920s. D.H. Lawrence spent a brief, unhappy period here in 1915: in September of that year his novel *The Rainbow* was banned for obscenity, and by December Lawrence and his wife, Frieda von Richthofen, whose German origins were causing the couple immense problems with the authorities, had resolved to leave the country.

West of Spaniards Road

The section of the Heath to the northwest of the Vale of Health misses out on the wonderful views of Parliament Hill and Kenwood, but makes up for it with some of the park's best-kept secrets. The place to start is the busy road junction around **Whitestone Pond**, which marks the highest point in north London (440ft). This former horse pond is overlooked by the cream-coloured weatherboarding and castellations of *Jack Straw's Castle*, a pub which, despite appearances, was entirely rebuilt in the 1960s.

The nearest tube is Golders Green.

To the west of Whitestone Pond is **West Heath**, a densely wooded, boggy area with a thick canopy of deciduous trees sloping down towards Childs Hill; it's a very peaceful place for a stroll and a popular cruising area for gay men. A track leads northwest from *Jack Straw's Castle* across West Heath past **The Hill Garden**, the Heath's most secretive and romantic little gem. It was built as an extension to the grounds of nearby Hill House (formerly the Inverforth Hospital, now converted into flats), and the formal gardens eventually became public property in 1960. Their most startling features are the eccentric balustraded terraces, which look out over West Heath and west to Harrow-on-the-Hill. All along the L-shaped terrace Doric columns support a ruinous pergola, which has been lovingly restored along with the bridge which Lord Lever (who bought the house in 1906) had to build over the public footpath in order to link his two gardens.

The path across West Heath eventually leads to the more formal landscaped gardens of **Golders Hill Park**. The central section of the park is taken up by animal enclosures containing pygmy goats and fallow deer, and a series of impeccably maintained aviaries, home to flamingos, cranes and other exotic birds; to the north, closer to the entrance, is a beautifully kept walled garden and pond. Before you leave the park, make sure you try some of the café's wonderful Italian ice cream. Beside the park entrance on North End Road stands **Ivy House**, where the great Russian ballerina Anna Pavlova lived from 1912 until her death in 1931.

Back up North End Road, past the *Old Bull & Bush* pub, a rough track curves its way through another secluded patch of woodland. Halfway along you'll come across a stranded red-brick archway that leads through into **Pitt's Garden**, originally the grounds of Pitt House (destroyed in the last war), home of eighteenth-century statesman William Pitt the Elder. Pitt retreated here on several occasions, most famously in 1767, when "gout in the head", as his bouts of insanity were euphemistically called, rendered him catatonic, upon which he shut himself away and received meals through a hatch.

Past the archway, the track turns into North End Avenue, which joins up with North End, which in turn backs onto Hampstead's sole remaining farmstead, the weatherboarded seventeenth-century **Wyldes Farm**. In the first decade of this century, the adjacent farmland was bought from Eton College by Henrietta Barnett to provide land for Hampstead Garden Suburb (see p.413) and also for an eighty-acre addition to the Heath, now known as the **Heath Extension**. Its origins as agricultural pastureland are evident in the surviving hedgerow boundaries, and the Corporation is considering reintroducing sheep, last seen here in the 1930s.

Spaniards Road runs along the eastern edge of **Sandy Heath**, a triangle of oak and beech woodland to the south of the Extension. At the northern end of Spaniards Road, cars struggle to avoid oncoming traffic as the road squeezes between the old tollhouse and the **Spaniards Inn**, an eighteenth century coaching inn thought to have been used by the highwayman Dick Turpin as a hiding place and vantage point for sizing up the coaches leaving town. The aforementioned Barnetts lived in the white weatherboarded house by the side of the *Spaniards Inn*.

Kenwood House

Daily: April–Sept 10am–6pm; Oct 10am–5pm; Nov–March 10am–4pm; EH; free; ☎0181/348 1286. Bus #210 from Highgate tube.

The Heath's most celebrated sight is **Kenwood House**, which is most enjoyably approached via the winding path from the Highgate Ponds. Set in its own magnificently landscaped grounds, the house dates from the seventeenth-century, but was later remodelled by Robert Adam for the Earl of Mansfield, Attorney-General, Lord Chief Justice and the most powerful jurist in the country. Mansfield, who had sent 102 people to the gallows and sentenced another 448 to transportation, was a deeply unpopular character and one of the prime targets of the Gordon rioters in 1780, who ransacked his Bloomsbury house. A crowd also made their way towards Kenwood, but they were waylaid by the canny landlord of the nearby *Spaniards Inn* (an ex-butler of Mansfield's), who plied them with free drink until soldiers arrived to disperse the mob.

Hampstead

Thanks to Kenwood's last private owner, the Earl of Iveagh (head of the Guinness family), the house is now open to the public and home to the **Iveagh Bequest**, a collection of seventeenth- and eighteenth-century art from the English, Dutch and French schools. You pass some good examples of Boucher's slightly sickly, flirtatious pastoral scenes, before coming to the Music Room, where you'll find several masterful portraits by Gainsborough, including the diaphanous *Countess Howe*, caught up in a bold, almost abstract landscape, plus a whimsical Reynolds painting, *Venus Chiding Cupid for Learning to Cast Accounts*. In the Dining Room, a superb Rembrandt self-portrait shares space with Franz Hals's *Man with a Cane* and Vermeer's delicate *Guitar Player*, plus works by Van Dyck, Guardi and, once again, Reynolds. Elsewhere, there are canvases by Cuyp, Turner, Romney and Landseer and several new, long-term loans, among them works by Botticelli and Memlinc.

Of the house's many wonderful period interiors, the most spectacular is Adam's sky-blue and gold **Library**, its book-filled apses separated from the central entertaining area by paired columns. The *pièce de résistance* is a tunnel-vaulted ceiling, decorated by Antonio Zucchi, who fell in love with and married Kenwood's other ceiling painter, Angelica Kauffmann. Adam was also responsible for landscaping the grounds of Kenwood, creating views across the Heath to St Paul's Cathedral and the Palace of Westminster – vistas that are now obscured by trees. Kenwood has splendid gardens of azaleas and rhododendrons to the west, and a huge grassy amphitheatre to the south, which slopes down to a lake where outdoor **classical concerts** are held on summer evenings – Handel's *Fireworks Music* has a regular spot on July 4. The grassy lawn is also a favourite picnic spot (and a good place to catch the afternoon rehearsals for free), while the provisionless can head for the excellent coach-house café.

A last and little-known attraction, hidden in a purpose-built hut to the northeast of Kenwood House, is the Romany-style **Buckland Caravan** (Sat & Sun: April–Sept 1–4pm; Oct–March 11am–3pm; free), last used in the 1920s and now beautifully restored. From the nearby sheltered viewpoint you'll get one of the finest views across the Heath to the City and West End, with the Crystal Palace TV tower on the horizon.

The grounds of Kenwood are open daily: summer 8am–8pm; winter 8am–4pm. For details of the Kenwood concerts, see p.624.

Highgate

Northeast of the Heath, and fractionally lower than Hampstead (appearances notwithstanding), **Highgate** lacks the literary cachet of Hampstead, but makes up for it with London's most famous cemetery, resting place of, among others, Karl Marx. It also retains more of its village origins, especially around **The Grove**, Highgate's finest

The nearest tube is Highgate.

row of houses. Set back from the road in pairs overlooking the village green, they date as far back as 1685 and have been occupied by such luminaries as J.B. Priestley and Yehudi Menuhin. The most famous one-time resident, however, is Samuel Taylor Coleridge, who lived at no. 3 from 1819, with a certain Dr Gillman and his wife. With Gillman's help, Coleridge reduced his dosage of opium and enjoyed the healthiest, if not necessarily the happiest, period of his life.

Coleridge was initially buried in the local college chapel, but in 1961 his remains were reburied in **St Michael's Church**, in South Grove. Its spire is a landmark, but St Michael's is much less interesting architecturally than the grandiose late seventeenth-century Old Hall next door, or the two tiny ramshackle cottages opposite, which were built for the servants of one of the luxurious mansions that once characterized Highgate. Arundel House, which stood on the site of the Old Hall, was where Sir Francis Bacon, the seventeenth-century philosopher and statesman, is thought to have died, having caught a chill while trying to stuff a chicken full of ice during an early experiment in refrigeration.

One of Highgate's best pubs, The Flask, is on South Grove; see p.546.

North and south of the High Street

Highgate gets its name from the tollgate – the highest in London and the oldest in the country – which stood where the *Gate House* pub now stands on **Highgate High Street**. The High Street itself, though lined with swanky Georgian shops, is marred by heavy traffic, as is its northern extension, North Road.

If you persevere with North Road, you'll pass **Highgate School**, founded in 1565 for the local poor but long established as an exclusive fee-paying public school, housed in suitably impressive Victorian buildings. Famous alumni, known as Cholmleians after the founder Sir Roger Cholmley, include Gerard Manley Hopkins, John Betjeman and Clive Sinclair, creator of the first mass-produced pocket calculator and other less successful inventions. Further on up North Road, on your left, are the whitewashed high-rises of **Highpoint 1 and 2**, seminal essays in modernist architecture designed by Berthold Lubetkin and his Tecton partnership in the late 1930s. The caryatids that support the entrance to Highpoint 2 are Lubetkin's little joke at the expense of his anti-modernist critics.

In the other direction, Highgate High Street slopes down into **Highgate Hill**, with still more amazing views down towards the City. The steep gradient of Highgate Hill caused enormous problems for horse-drawn vehicles, and in 1813 a tunnel was attempted through neighbouring Hornsey. It collapsed and was replaced by a stone viaduct designed by Nash, in its turn usurped by the current cast-iron **Archway** on Hornsey Lane, a favourite spot for suicide attempts. For the record, you'll find the **Whittington Stone**, with cat, marking the spot where Dick Whittington miraculously heard the Bow Bells chime, towards the bottom of Highgate Hill outside the hospital named after the eponymous mayor (see p.231 for more on Whittington).

The other ecclesiastical landmark in Highgate is the copper dome of "Holy Joe", the Roman Catholic church which stands on Highgate Hill beside **Waterlow Park**. The park is named after Sir Sydney Waterlow, who donated it in 1889 as "a garden for the gardenless", and also bequeathed **Lauderdale House**, a much-altered sixteenth-century building, which is thought to have been occupied at one time by Nell Gwynne and her infant son. The house, which backs onto the park, is now used to stage children's shows and other events, and contains a decent café and restaurant that spill out into its western terraced gardens. The park itself, occupying a dramatic sloping site, is an amalgamation of several house gardens, and is one of London's finest landscaped parks, providing a through-route to Highgate Cemetery.

Highgate Cemetery

Ranged on both sides of Swain's Lane and receiving far more visitors than Highgate itself, **Highgate Cemetery** is London's most famous graveyard. Opened in 1839, it quickly became the preferred resting place of wealthy Victorian families, who could rub shoulders here with numerous intellectuals and artists. As long as prime plots were available, business was good and the cemetery could afford to employ as many as 28 gardeners to beautify the place. But as the cemetery filled, funds dried up and the whole place fell prey to vandals. In 1975, the old (west) cemetery was closed completely and was taken under the wing of the Friends of Highgate Cemetery. Unfortunately, the Friends see all visitors as potential vandals, and rarely allow unsupervised wandering, the chief joy of visiting graveyards. You can still wander freely in the newer east cemetery, the less dramatic of the two sites, though even here a small entrance fee is now charged.

West Cemetery

Guided tours Mon–Fri noon, 2pm & 4pm, Sat & Sun hourly 11am–4pm; £3, no children under 8; ☎020/8340 1834. Archway tube.

The old, overgrown **West Cemetery** is the ultimate Hammer-horror graveyard, and one of London's most impressive sights, with its huge vaults and stunning array of statuary. It's a shame you have to follow a tour around it, but even so it's not to be missed, and it must be said that things were pretty seedy before the Friends took over.

Dickens could have been the most famous corpse here, but only his estranged wife and daughter lie in the family tomb – despite the author's wishes to be buried privately and without ostentation, he was posthumously overruled by Queen Victoria, who insisted on his being buried in Westminster Abbey. Other famous names here are

Charles Chubb (of the locks), Charles Cruft (of the Dog Show) and Michael Faraday, who as a member of the obscure Sandemanian sect is buried along the unconsecrated north wall. There's no guarantee your tour will cover these tombs, but you're more than likely to be shown the **Rossetti family tomb**, initiated on the death of Gabriel Rossetti, professor of Italian at King's College, London. Next in the family vault was Elizabeth Siddall, the Pre-Raphaelites' favourite model and wife of Rossetti's artistic son, Dante Gabriel, who buried the only copy of his many love poems along with her. Seven years later he changed his mind and had the poems exhumed and published. The poet Christina Rossetti, Dante's sister, is also buried in the vault.

The cemetery's spookiest section is around **Egyptian Avenue**, entered through an ivy-covered portal flanked by pillars and obelisks, known as the "Gateway to the City of the Dead". Despite the restrictions of access, the tomb of the lesbian novelist Radclyffe Hall is regularly strewn with flowers and tributes (her lover, Mabel Batten, is also buried here). The avenue, in turn, leads to the Circle of Lebanon, above which are the **Terrace Catacombs**, with views out across the cemetery and far beyond. Gathered together here are the most ostentatious mausoleums, some of which accommodate up to fifteen coffins; the largest – based on the tomb of Mausolus at Halicarnassus – is that of Julius Beer, one-time owner of the *Observer* newspaper.

Bram Stoker was cremated at Golders Green Crematorium; see p.414.

This section of the cemetery provided inspiration for Bram Stoker's *Dracula*, and was at the centre of a series of bizarre incidents in the early 1970s. Graves were smashed open, cadavers strewn about, and the High Priest of the British Occult Society, Allan Farrant, was arrested here, armed with a stake and crucifix with which he hoped to destroy "the Highgate Vampire". He was eventually sentenced to four years' imprisonment, after being found guilty of damaging graves, interfering with corpses and sending death-spell dolls to two policemen.

East Cemetery

Daily: April–Sept 10am–5pm; Oct–March 10am–4pm; £1.

What the **East Cemetery** lacks in atmosphere is in part compensated for by the fact that you can wander at will through its maze of circuitous paths. The most publicized occupant is, of course, **Karl Marx**, who spent more than half his life in London, much of it in bourgeois Hampstead. Marx himself asked for a plain and simple grave topped by a headstone, but by 1954 the Communist movement had decided to move his tomb to a more prominent position and erect the vulgar bronze bust that now surmounts a granite plinth bearing the words "Workers of all lands, unite", from *The Communist Manifesto*. He has been visited here by Khrushchev, Brezhnev and just about every postwar Communist leader in the world.

Buried along with Marx are his grandson, wife and housekeeper, Helene Delmuth, whom he got pregnant. Engels accepted paternity to avoid a bourgeois scandal and only told Marx's daughter, Eleanor, on his deathbed in 1895. Eleanor committed suicide a few years later after discovering her common-law husband had secretly married someone else. Her ashes were finally placed in the family vault in 1954, having been seized from the Communist Party headquarters in London by the police in 1921.

Lesser-known Communists such as Yusef Mohamed Dadoo, chairman of the South African Communist Party until his death in 1983, cluster around Marx. Not far away is **George Eliot**'s grave and, behind it, that of her lover, George Henry Lewes.

Golders Green, Hendon and Neasden

North and west of Hampstead is suburbia good and proper, but there are one or two specific reasons for venturing so far into residential London: **Hampstead Garden Suburb**, an offshoot of Golders Green, is the city's original garden suburb; the **RAF Museum** in Hendon has probably the country's finest collection of military aircraft; and the **Hindu temple** in Neasden – the largest outside India – has to be seen to be believed.

Golders Green

If the East End is the spiritual home of working-class Jews, **Golders Green**, to the northwest of Hampstead, is its middle-class equivalent. Less than a hundred years ago this whole area was open countryside but, like much of suburbia, it was transformed overnight by the arrival of the tube in 1907. Before and after World War II, the area was heavily colonized by Jews moving out of the old East End ghetto around Spitalfields or fleeing as refugees from Europe ahead of the Nazis. Nowadays, Golders Green, along with Stamford Hill, is one of the most distinctively Jewish areas in London. The Orthodox community has a particularly strong presence here: *yarmulkas* (skullcaps) are commonplace, and there's a profusion of kosher shops beyond the railway bridge on Golders Green Road, at their busiest on Sundays.

Hampstead Garden Suburb

Much of Golders Green is architecturally bland, the one exception being **Hampstead Garden Suburb**, begun in 1907 to the north of the Hampstead Heath Extension. This model housing development was a product of the utopian dream of Henrietta Barnett, wife of the philanthropist who established Toynbee Hall in the East End (see p.274). In the Barnetts' view, the only long-term solution to social

The nearest tube is Golders Green, whence it's a fair walk.

reform was to create a mixed social environment where "the poor shall teach the rich, and the rich, let us hope, shall help the poor to help themselves". Yet from the start the suburb was socially segregated, with modest artisan dwellings to the north, middle-class houses to the west and the wealthiest villas overlooking the Heath to the south. As a social engineering experiment it was a failure – the area has remained a thoroughly middle-class ghetto – but as a blueprint for suburban estates it has been enormously influential.

The formal entrance to the suburb is the striking Arts and Crafts gateway of shops and flats on Finchley Road; from here, ivy-strewn houses, each with its own garden encased in privet hedges, fan out eastwards along tree-lined avenues towards the deliberately "non-commercial" **Central Square**, laid out by Edwin Lutyens in a Neo-Georgian style he dubbed "Wren-aissance". (Pubs, shops, cinemas and all commercial buildings were, and still are, excluded from the suburb.) Lutyens also designed the square's twin churches: the Nonconformist Free Church, sporting an octagonal dome, and the Anglican St Jude's, the finer of the two with its steeply pitched roof and spire, and its unusual 1920s murals within. East of the central green is the Lutyens-designed **Institute**, now occupied by an adult education centre and Henrietta Barnett Girls' School. From the square, you could walk south along cherry-tree-lined Heathgate, which ends at the Heath Extension (see p.408).

Golders Green Crematorium and the Jewish Cemetery

To the east of Hampstead Garden Suburb, down Meadway and then Hoop Lane, is the **Golders Green Crematorium**, where over 280,000 Londoners have been cremated since 1902. More famous names have been scattered over the crematorium's unromantically named Dispersal Area than have been buried at any single graveyard: Anna Pavlova, T.S. Eliot, Sean O'Casey, Enid Blyton, Charles Rennie Mackintosh, Kipling, Shaw, Alexander Fleming, Ralph Vaughan Williams, Peter Sellers, Peggy Ashcroft, Joyce Grenfell, Marc Bolan, Keith Moon, Bram Stoker and Freud, to name but a few. Finding a particular memorial plaque among this complex of serene red-brick chapels and arcades is no easy task, and if you're keen to trace someone or wish to visit one of the columbaria you should enquire at the office in the main courtyard. The Ernst George Columbarium is where you'll find the ashes of Anna Pavlova, sealed in an urn draped with a pair of her pink ballet shoes, while Freud, his wife Martha and his daughter Anna, are contained within one of Freud's favourite Greek urns in an adjacent room.

On the opposite side of Hoop Lane is a **Jewish Cemetery**, founded in 1895 before the area was built up. The eastern section, to your right, is for Orthodox Sephardic Jews, whose tombs are traditionally laid flat with the deceased's feet pointing towards Jerusalem. To the left are the upright headstones of Reform Jews, including the great

Golders Green Crematorium is open daily 9am–5pm.

The Jewish Cemetery is open daily except Sat 8.30am–5pm or dusk.

cellist Jacqueline du Pré, who died tragically young of multiple sclerosis, and Lord Hore-Belisha, Minister of Transport in the 1930s, who gave his name to "Belisha beacons" (the yellow flashing globes at pedestrian crossings).

Golders Green, Hendon and Neasden

Jewish Museum

Mon–Thurs 10.30am–5pm, Sun 10.30am–4.30pm; closed Sun during Aug; £2; ☎020/8349 1143; *www.jewmusm.ort.org.* Finchley Central tube.

To the north of Golders Green, on the other side of the North Circular Road, is the Finchley branch of London's **Jewish Museum**. Housed within the Sternberg Centre for Judaism, at 80 East End Rd, the museum puts on exceptionally good temporary shows, and has a permanent exhibition on the social history of London's Jews, with particular emphasis on life in the old East End. Another of the long-term exhibitions focuses on the moving personal account of Londoner Leon Greenman, the only member of his family to survive Auschwitz. There's an excellent Jewish bookshop within the centre.

London's main Jewish Museum is in Camden; see p.393.

Hendon: the RAF Museum

Daily 10am–6pm; £7.50; ☎020/8205 2266; *www.rafmuseum.org.uk.* Colindale tube.

One of the most impressive collections of historic military aircraft in the world is lodged at the **RAF Museum**, in a godforsaken part of Hendon beside the M1 motorway. The site was an airfield from as early as 1910, and was venue for the RAF Hendon Air Pageants until the 1960s. In the **Main Aircraft Hall**, start your tour at the flimsy biplanes of World War I, with their wooden frames and wicker armchairs. The vast 1920s Southampton reconnaissance flying boat dominates the space ahead, but be sure to check out the Hoverfly, the first really effective helicopter, and, of course, the most famous British plane of all time, the Spitfire. By the exit you'll find a Harrier jump jet, the world's first vertical takeoff and landing aircraft, labelled with a text extolling its role in the Falklands War.

The most chilling section is the adjacent **Bomber Command Hall**, where you're greeted by a colossal Lancaster bomber, a modified version of which was used in Operation Upkeep, the mission carried out by Squadron 617 (and immortalized in the film *The Dambusters*), about which there's a ten-minute documentary. To the museum's credit, the assessment of Bomber Command's wartime policy of blanket-bombing Germany into submission gives both sides of the argument. The video of the so-called "precision bombing" conducted during the Gulf War is given rather less even-handed treatment. Two other exhibits deserve special mention: the crumbling carcass of a Halifax bomber, recovered from the bottom of a Norwegian fjord, and the clinically white Valiant, the first British aircraft to carry thermonuclear bombs.

Those with children should head for the new hands-on **Fun 'n'
Flight** gallery, which teaches the basic principles of flight and air-
plane construction. Those without children should explore the often
overlooked **Display Galleries**, ranged around the edge of the Main
Aircraft Hall, which contain an art gallery and an exhibition on the
history of flight, accompanied by replicas of some of the deathtraps
in which the first aviators risked their lives. Across the car park is the
Battle of Britain Hall, which contains a huge Sunderland flying
boat, a V1 flying bomb and a V2 rocket. The focus of the hall, though,
is now *Our Finest Hour*, an unashamedly jingoistic fifteen-minute
audiovisual of the battle for the skies above Britain fought between
the RAF and the Luftwaffe during the autumn of 1940.

Neasden: the Swaminarayan temple

Daily 9–11am & noon–6.30pm; free; ☎020/8965 2651; *www.swaminarayan
-baps.org.uk*. Stonebridge Park or Neasden tube.

> *The lotus blooms in splendour, but its roots lie in the dirt.*
> Hindu proverb

Perhaps the most remarkable building in the whole of London lies just
off the North Circular, in the glum suburb of Neasden. Here, rising
majestically above the dismal semi-detached houses of the inter-war
period like a mirage, is the **Shri Swaminarayan Mandir**, a traditional
Hindu temple topped with domes and shikharas, erected in 1995 in a
style and scale unseen outside of India for over a millennium. The
building's vital statistics are incredible: 3000 tons of Bulgarian limestone and 2000 tons of Carrara marble were shipped out to India,
carved by over 1500 sculptors, and then shipped back to London and
assembled in a matter of weeks. Even more surprising is the fact that
Lord Swaminarayan (1781–1830), to whom the temple is dedicated,
is a relatively obscure and very recent Hindu deity. There are no more
than 10,000 followers in Britain, mostly from Gujarat, and no more
than a million worldwide, yet they have dug deep into their pockets
and, at an estimated cost of £10 million, erected this fantastic edifice.

To reach the temple, you must enter through the adjacent **Haveli**, or
cultural complex, with its carved wooden portico and balcony, and its
twin covered, carpeted courtyards. Shoes are the only thing that are sex-
ually segregated inside the temple, so, having placed yours in the appropriate alcove, you can then proceed to the **Mandir** (temple) itself, carved
entirely out of light-grey Carrara marble from the floor to the dome, with
every possible surface transformed into a honeycomb of arabesques,
flowers and seated gods. The pillars are intricately decorated with figures of gods and goddesses, while on three sides are alcoves sheltering
serene life-sized **Murti** (gods), garish figures in resplendent clothes representing Rama, Sita, Ganesh the elephant god, Hanuman the monkey
god, and, of course, Shri Swaminarayan himself. The Murti are only on
display from 9am to 11am, and from 4pm to 6.30pm.

Beneath the Mandir, an **exhibition** (Mon–Fri 9am–6pm, Sat & Sun 7am–7pm; £2) explains the basic tenets of Hinduism through dioramas, extolls the virtues of vegetarianism and details the life of Lord Swaminarayan, who became a yogi at the age of eleven, and stood naked on one leg for three months amidst snowstorms and "torturing weather". At the end, there's a short video about the history of the building.

Wembley Stadium

Closed until summer 2003. ☎020/8795 5733; *www.wembleynationalstadium.com*. Wembley Park tube.

A shrine of a different sort – **Wembley Stadium** – lies west of the Neasden temple. However, it's currently closed, and in the process of being entirely rebuilt as part of a £250 million redevelopment programme. The old stadium was, in fact, the sole survivor of a much larger complex, constructed in 1924 for the British Empire Exhibition, which later served as the main focus for the 1948 Olympic Games. The stadium's famous "twin towers" – giant domes that were meant as a mute reference to the old Raj – were only added in 1963, to celebrate the 100th anniversary of the Football League. However, they are forever associated with England's historic victory here in the 1966 World Cup Final. The new design, by Norman Foster, will do away with the twin towers, but will, with any luck, provide slightly better sight-lines than the old behemoth. The FA Cup Final, held in May, still provides the highlight of Wembley's annual calendar of events, and the new stadium is due to be completed in time for the 2003 final. Unless you're going to a sporting event (or a gig in the neighbouring Wembley Arena), there's little reason to come here.

Harrow-on-the-Hill

Harrow-on-the-Hill, in the northwestern reaches of London, is one of the three main heights north of the river, along with Highgate and Hampstead. Less than a century ago, it would have been surrounded by green fields; nowadays, the village looks down, in every sense and in every direction, on amorphous suburbs. The village actually predates the school, but the latter – which has educated the likes of Churchill, Byron and Nehru – now dominates the place and is the main reason most visitors come here. Consequently, it's best to visit during term time, since without the blue-blazered boys in their straw hats, the place is utterly lifeless.

St Mary's and Harrow School

Approaching from Harrow-on-the-Hill tube, the first building you come across is the church of **St Mary**, whose needle spire is visible

Harrow-on-the-Hill

There is a tourist office in the Civic Centre, Station Road, open Mon–Fri 9am–5pm; ☎020/8424 1103.

for miles around. It's worth penetrating the flint exterior in order to see the thirteenth-century Purbeck marble font, the Jacobean pulpit and the numerous brasses, including that of John Lyon, the Elizabethan landowner who founded Harrow as a free grammar school for local boys. (It's now a very expensive fee-paying school.) Outside, in the graveyard, is the **Peachey Stone**, now protected by an iron grille and inscribed with a verse from Byron's "Lines written beneath an elm in the churchyard of Harrow, September 2, 1807". This was the poet's "favourite spot", though the pastoral view he enjoyed has now been replaced by a thoroughly depressing overview of suburbia.

To the south and east of the church lies **Harrow School**, whose buildings are dotted about the hillside and on either side of the High Street. The oldest of the lot is the red-brick **Old School** building, distinguished by its pretty crow-stepped gables, bay windows and dinky clock cupola, though in fact all these seemingly Jacobean details were added in the 1820s. The only portion of the building which dates from the seventeenth century is the west wing, containing the wood-panelled **Fourth Form Room**, which has changed little since its construction. Sadly, this and most of the rest of the school's buildings are only open to the public on a guided tour, for which you must contact the school in advance (☎020/8423 1524; £3.25).

The Old Speech Room Gallery is open term time: daily except Wed 2.30–5pm; free; ☎020/8872 8205.

The **Old Speech Room Gallery**, which forms part of the Old School building, can, however, be visited. As well as staging surprisingly interesting temporary exhibitions, the gallery has an eclectic permanent collection, based on gifts from old boys. Fifth-century Greek red- and black-figure vases and Egyptian funerary figures fill the ground floor, while upstairs, amidst British butterflies and moths, are skeletons of puffer fish, turkey vultures, baboons, sundry rocks and crystals and more Egyptian artefacts. Inevitably, there's a portrait of Byron, but also, more intriguingly, several works by old boy and later Vorticist, Victor Pasmore.

Alexandra Palace and Walthamstow

For all its unrealized potential, **Alexandra Palace** is one of the great landmarks of North London, and worth a visit if only for its splendid position and extensive grounds. **Walthamstow**, by many people's reckoning – and by virtue its postcode – is strictly speaking part of East London, and is included here mainly for its excellent William Morris Gallery.

Highgate Wood and the Parkland Walk

If you're heading for Alexandra Palace, and want to make a day of it, explore the **Parkland Walk**, a disused railway line which gives great views out over London, and allows you to walk all the way from Highgate to the Palace – a distance of around one and a half miles – without touching tarmac. The best place to start is at **Highgate Wood**, one of two remaining slices of the Great Forest of Middlesex, to the north of Highgate tube. Carefully managed by the Corporation of London, this lovely deciduous patch of woodland boasts the excellent *Oshobasho Café* at its heart, overlooking a cricket and football pitch. Close by, on the other side of Muswell Hill Road, lies **Queen's Wood**, which has kept rather more of its ancient woodland character.

Alexandra Palace

Built in 1873 on the commanding heights of Muswell Hill, **Alexandra Palace** is now London's only surviving example of a Victorian "People's Palace", since its more famous rival, Crystal Palace, burnt down in 1936. However, the history of "Ally Pally" is almost as tragic as that of Crystal Palace. Sixteen days after the official opening, the whole place burnt down and, despite being rebuilt within two years and boasting a theatre, a reading room, an exhibition hall and a concert room with one of the largest organs in the world, it was a commercial failure. During World War I more than 17,000 German POWs passed through its gates, and in 1936 the world's first television transmission took place here.

The nearest train station is Alexandra Palace, accessible from King's Cross.

After another devastating fire in 1980 the palace was again rebuilt, and is currently trying to reinvent itself as a multipurpose conference and exhibition venue. In addition to the annual round of shows, there's a pub with great views, a garden centre and an indoor ice rink open daily, as well as a funfair at Easter, Whitsuntide and throughout the summer holidays. To the west of the palace, there's also a vegan café, *Popcorn in the Park*, which sells wonderful sorbet, among other things.

Walthamstow

The northeastern suburb of **Walthamstow**, east of the River Lee, is on few tourists' itineraries, but it's somewhere you could easily spend an afternoon, especially if you've an interest in the work of William Morris, who was born here in 1834. In addition, if you come on a Tuesday, Thursday, Friday or Saturday, you can also visit **Walthamstow Market**, which claims to be the longest street market in the country, stretching for well over a mile along the old High Street. And for a traditional East End snack, head for *Manzes*, at no. 76, one of London's finest pie-and-mash shops, with its traditional tiled walls and lincrusta ceiling.

The nearest tube is Walthamstow Central.

The Vestry House Museum is open Mon–Fri 10am–1pm & 2–5.30pm, Sat closes 5pm; free; ☎020 /8509 1917.

From the tube, head east down St Mary Road, then Church End, which will take you to the heart of the old village conservation area, a surprising oasis of calm. On your right as you reach the end of Church End is the **Vestry House Museum**, built in 1730 and at one time the village workhouse. Later on, it became the police station, and a reconstructed police cell from 1861 is one of the museum's chief exhibits. The prize possession, however, is the tiny Bremer Car, Britain's first ever automobile, designed in 1894 by local engineer Fred Bremer. Victorian times are comprehensively covered, but there's precious little on the area's postwar immigrants. The other point of interest here is the fifteenth-century half-timbered **Ancient House**, a short walk up Church Lane.

Walthamstow's two other sights are a five-minute walk north past the concrete-encased church of St Mary's, and up The Drive and its continuation, Hurst Road. First is the local **Civic Centre**, set back from Forest Road around a huge open courtyard. Designed in an unusual Scandinavian style in the 1930s, it is, without doubt, London's grandest town hall complex. Indeed, there's a touch of Stalinism about the severe classicism of the centre's central portico and in the exhortation above the adjacent Assembly Hall: "Fellowship is life and the lack of fellowship is death." Sadly, construction of the law courts that would have completed the ensemble was interrupted by the war, but this remains one of the most startling public buildings in London.

William Morris Gallery

Tues–Sat & first Sun of month 10am–1pm & 2–5pm; free; ☎020/8527 3782; *www.lbwf.gov.uk/wmg*. Walthamstow Central tube.

To the west of the Civic Centre, along Forest Road, stands a lovely Georgian mansion with two big bay windows, now known as the **William Morris Gallery**, which became the Morris family home in 1848 after the death of William Morris's father, a successful businessman in the City. Poet, artist, designer and socialist, William Morris (1834–96) was one of the most fascinating characters of Victorian London. He was closely associated with both the Pre-Raphaelite and Arts and Crafts movements, and went on to set up Morris & Co, whose work covered all areas of applied art: glasswork, tiles, metalwork, curtains, furniture, calligraphy, carpets, book illumination and (perhaps most famously) wallpaper.

You can see several works by Morris elsewhere in London: at the V&A (p.346), Holy Trinity Church, off Sloane Square (p.369), and the Red House (p.447).

The ground floor of the museum contains a modest array of every kind of work with which Morris got involved, and also hosts temporary exhibitions. Disappointingly, there are only passing references to Morris's stormy personal life: he married Jane Burden, a working-class girl whom Rossetti picked up at the theatre in Oxford and later reclaimed as his lover. Upstairs, there's a small collection of paintings by his later followers and Pre-Raphaelite chums. Edward Burne-Jones shows his mastery of gouache in *St George and the Dragon*, while Ford Madox Brown does the same for pure watercolour in his richly textured portrait, *Jacopo Foscari in Prison*. As is clear from his *Portrait of Alexa Wilding*, Rossetti was so obsessed with Jane Burden that just about every woman's portrait he subsequently drew looked like her.

As well as being a successful capitalist – the company's flagship store was on Mayfair's Hanover Square – Morris also became one of the leading political figures of his day, active in the Socialist League with Eleanor Marx, and publishing several utopian tracts, most famously *News from Nowhere*, which you can buy in the bookshop for the tube journey home.

Chapter 12

Southeast London: Brixton to Greenwich and beyond

Boats run daily from Westminster, Charing Cross and Tower Bridge to Greenwich – one of the most popular and enjoyable river trips.

Aside from the Royal Palace at Greenwich and the Royal Dockyards at Deptford and Woolwich, **SOUTHEAST LONDON** was a confirmed part of rural Kent until the late eighteenth century. Now largely built up into a patchwork of Victorian terraces, one area stands head and shoulders above all the others in terms of sightseeing, and that is **Greenwich**, once home to the Tudor court. Its nautical associations are trumpeted by the likes of the *Cutty Sark* and the National Maritime Museum; its architecture, especially the Old Royal Naval College and the Queen's House, is some of the finest on the river; and its Observatory is renowned throughout the world.

The rest of this chapter is really just a hotchpotch of scattered suburban sights, where, given the distances involved and the dire lack of tube lines south of the river, it pays to be selective. A few areas do, however, stand out: **Dulwich**, whose public art gallery is even older than the National Gallery, and, way out on the very edge of London, the **Chislehurst Caves** and **Down House**, the home of Charles Darwin.

Our account begins with **Brixton** – south London's liveliest neighbourhood, with its large African-Caribbean community and market – which pedants might claim is more southwest than southeast, though its borders actually span both postal districts.

Brixton

Brixton is a classic Victorian suburb, transformed from open fields into bricks and mortar in a couple of decades following the arrival of the railways in the 1860s. The viaducts still dominate the landscape of central Brixton, with shops and arcades hidden under their arches,

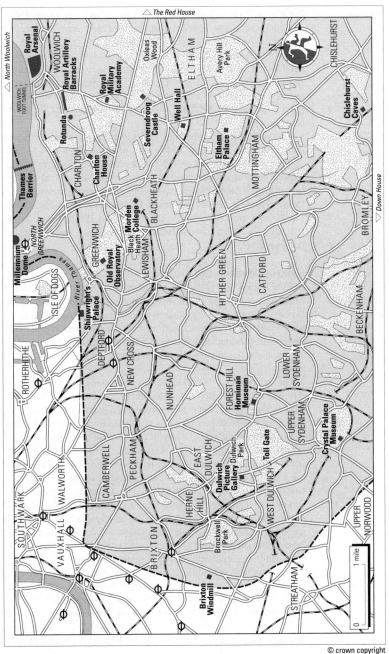

but it's the West Indian community, who arrived here in the 1950s and 1960s, who now define the character of the place – Notting Hill may have the Carnival, but it's Brixton that has the most upfront African-Caribbean consciousness. It is regarded as a pretty cool neighbourhood by a large slice of white Londoners, too – youthful types, who like a bit of "street grit" in their lives. Despite popular perceptions of Brixton as a black ghetto, the area is in fact seventy percent white, and distinctly middle-class over towards Streatham and Herne Hill.

For those who don't know the place, however, Brixton is still best known for the 1981 and 1985 riots, when tensions between the police and the locals (not only the black community) came to a head. Various government initiatives have since attempted and failed to get to the root of local discontent, racism and unemployment, though the visual fabric of the place has definitely improved in the 1990s. The council, through much of the 1970s and 1980s, had a "loony left" image second to none in Britain, but has since cleaned up its act immeasurably.

Brixton Market and around

The nearest tube station is Brixton.

Brixton's main axis is the junction of Brixton Road, Acre Lane and Coldharbour Lane, overlooked by the slender clock tower of the Edwardian town hall; the dinky Neo-Renaissance Tate Library; the Ritzy multiplex arts cinema; and, on the triangular traffic island, the Neoclassical church of **St Matthew**, with its grandiose Doric portico, its crypt now converted into a trendy bar, restaurant and theatre space.

The commercial lifeblood of Brixton, however, pulses most strongly through **Brixton Market** (Mon, Tues & Thurs–Sat 8am–5.30pm, Wed 8am–1pm), whose stalls spread out through the warren of streets and arcades east of Brixton Road. **Electric Avenue** – the market's main drag – which runs behind the tube station, is solidly fruit and veg (most of it West Indian), and was one of the first London shopping streets to be lit by electricity in the 1880s, hence the name. A network of appealingly shabby interwar arcades runs parallel with the avenue, culminating in the **Granville Arcade**, where you can buy bold African and Asian fabrics, jewellery, all manner of exotic fruit and meat, amazing wigs and much more besides. On the far side of the railway tracks, the market veers eastwards along Brixton Station Road, with stalls flogging cheap secondhand clothes to rap and reggae soundtracks from Crystal Records.

The crossroads of Atlantic Road and Coldharbour Lane, to the south-east of the market, marks the beginning of Brixton's so-called "**Front Line**", which, with nearby Railton Road, was the epicentre of the 1981 riots, and still has a drug-dealing reputation. The former *Atlantic* pub on the corner once prided itself on its especially mean reputation, but has since been resurrected as a trendy drinking hole called the *Dog*.

Brixton Windmill, at the end of Blenheim Gardens, a few stops up Brixton Hill by bus, is a surprising sight. This is about the last place in London that you'd expect to find a windmill, but with its blades intact and a fetching weatherboarded "hood", the 1816 mill makes a splendid sight in a deeply depressing municipal space. Brixton also has a very fine green lung in **Brockwell Park** (daily 8am–dusk), half a mile or so up Effra Road. The park is made up of the former grounds of Brockwell House, a handsome Regency lodge, built by a local glass merchant, that occupies the park's heights and now houses an unremarkable tearoom. There's also a popular **lido** (mid-May to mid-Sept Mon–Fri 6.45–10am & noon–7pm, Sat & Sun 11am–7pm; £1.50–3), and a beautiful walled garden with yew-hedge snugs and shady arbours.

Dulwich, Forest Hill and Crystal Palace

Dulwich Village is just two stops from Brixton on the overland railway, but light years away in every other respect. This affluent, middle-class enclave is one of southeast London's prettier patches, cut off from most of its suburban neighbours by parkland, playing fields, woods and golfing fairways. The leafy streets boast handsome Georgian houses and even a couple of weatherboarded cottages, while the Soane-designed **Picture Gallery** is one of London's finest small museums. If Dulwich has a fault, it's the somewhat cloying self-consciousness about its "village" status, with its rather twee little shops, rural signposts and fully functioning tollgate – the only one remaining in London.

Nonetheless, Dulwich makes for a pleasant day out south of the river, and can be combined with a visit to the nearby **Horniman Museum**, an enjoyable ethnographic collection, and, for the very curious, the remnants of the old **Crystal Palace**, further south. The green spaces between these sights are also worth exploring. **Dulwich Park**, opposite the Picture Gallery, is a pleasant enough public park, but **Sydenham Hill Wood**, a London Wildlife Trust nature reserve on the other side of Dulwich Common, is the one to head for. Incidentally, the disused railway line that runs through the woods once took folk to the Crystal Palace, and was committed to canvas by Camille Pissarro (the picture now hangs in the Courtauld Institute).

Dulwich Village

Dulwich came to prominence in the 1610s when its lord of the manor, actor-manager Edward Alleyn, founded the **College of God's Gift** as almshouses and a school for poor boys on the profits of his whorehouses and bear-baiting pits on Bankside. The college has long

Dulwich, Forest Hill and Crystal Palace

since outgrown its original buildings, which still stand to the north of the **Picture Gallery**, and is now housed in a fanciful Italianate complex designed by Charles Barry (son of the architect of the Houses of Parliament), south of Dulwich Common; Alleyn is buried in the college chapel. The college is now a fee-paying public school, with an impressive roll call of old boys, including Raymond Chandler, P.G. Wodehouse and World War II traitor Lord Haw-Haw, though they tend to keep quiet about the last of the trio.

Dulwich Picture Gallery

Tues–Fri 10am–5pm, Sat & Sun 11am–5pm; £4, free on Fri; ☎020/8693 5254; *www.dulwichpicturegallery.org.uk*. West Dulwich train station, from Victoria.

Dulwich Picture Gallery, on College Road, is the nation's oldest public art gallery. Designed by Sir John Soane in 1814, it houses, among other bequests, the collection assembled in the 1790s by the French dealer Noel Desenfans on behalf of King Stanislas of Poland, who planned to open a national gallery in Warsaw. In 1795, Poland disappeared from the map of Europe, Stanislas was forced to abdicate and Desenfans was left with the paintings. Having failed to persuade either the British government or the Russian tsar to purchase the collection, Desenfans proposed founding a national gallery. In the end it was left to his friend, the landscape painter Francis Bourgeois, and Desenfans' widow, to complete the task and open the gallery in 1817.

Soane, who worked for no fee, created a beautifully spacious building, awash with natural light, and added a tiny **mausoleum** at the centre for the sarcophagi of the Desenfans family and of Francis Bourgeois. Thought to be based on an Alexandrian catacomb, it's suffused with golden yellow light from the mausoleum's coloured glass – a characteristic Soane touch. Originally, Soane had intended to create a new quadrangle, using the old college building to the north. The gallery's gentle new extension by Rick Mather has gone some of the way to realizing that plan, by completing three sides of the courtyard with a glass cloister walk that connects the gallery with the education department and the new café by the entrance.

The gallery itself is crammed with superb paintings – elegiac landscapes by **Cuyp**, one of the world's finest **Poussin** series and splendid works by Hogarth, Murillo and Rubens. There's an unusually cloudy **Canaletto** of Walton Bridge on the Thames, **Rembrandt**'s tiny *Portrait of a Young Man*, a top-class portrait of poet, playwright and Royalist, the future Earl of Bristol, by **Van Dyck**, and a moving one of his much lamented kinswoman by marriage, Venetia Stanley, on her deathbed. Among the gallery's fine array of **Gainsborough** portraits are his famous *Linley Sisters*, sittings for which were interrupted by the elopement of one of them with the playwright Sheridan, and a likeness of Samuel Linley that's said to have been painted in less than an hour.

Horniman Museum

Mon–Sat 10.30am–5.30pm, Sun 2–5.30pm; free; ☎020/8699 1872; *www .horniman.ac.uk*. Forest Hill train station, from Victoria or London Bridge.

Dulwich, Forest Hill and Crystal Palace

To the southeast of Dulwich Park, on the busy South Circular, is the wacky **Horniman Museum**, purpose-built in 1901 by Frederick Horniman, a tea trader with a passion for collecting, and principally a monument to its creator's freewheeling eclecticism. The building itself is a striking edifice designed in warm Doulting stone by Charles Harrison Townsend, architect of the Whitechapel Gallery (see p.274). Its most striking features are the massive clock tower, with its smoothly rounded bastions and circular cornice, and the polychrome mosaic of allegorical figures in classical dress on the main facade.

Inside, the first gallery to greet you is the **Living Waters Aquarium**, a didactic display of (mostly native) fish, which flank the stairs leading to the main top-floor gallery. Upstairs, the main gallery houses the museum's vast **natural history** collection of stuffed birds – everything from a half-dissected pigeon to an ostrich – stuffed animals and their skeletons. Pride of place goes to the Horniman Walrus, who occupies centre stage on a mocked-up iceberg. Beyond lies the new **African World** gallery, but the rest of the museum is likely to remain closed until at least 2002. That includes the Horniman's timber-clad "centre for understanding the environment", known as **"cue"**, which overlooks the museum's lovely **park** (daily 8am–dusk), around the back. Here, you'll find turkeys, geese, hens and rabbits, a sunken water garden and a graceful Victorian conservatory, brought here from the Horniman family's mansion in Croydon.

Crystal Palace

In the 1850s, the **Crystal Palace** from the 1851 Great Exhibition (see p.339) was re-erected on the commanding heights of Sydenham Hill, to the south of Dulwich, a site affording spectacular views over London, Kent and Surrey. A fantastic pleasure garden was laid out around this giant glasshouse, with a complex system of fountains, some of which reached a height of 250ft. Exhibitions, funfairs, ballooning, a miniature railway and a whole range of events, including, from 1894 to 1924, the FA Cup Final, were staged here. Despite its initial success, though, the Palace soon became a financial liability – then, in 1936, the entire structure burnt to the ground overnight.

The nearest train station is Crystal Palace, accessible from Victoria.

All that remains now are the stone terraces, the triumphal staircase, a few sphinxes and a small, uninspiring **museum** on Anerley Hill (Sun 11am–5pm; free; ☎020/8676 0700) that tells the history of the place. Though there are plans afoot to redevelop on this site, the **park** remains open (daily 7.30am–dusk) – dominated by the TV transmitter, visible from all over London, and the National Sports

Centre, which, with its attendant car parks, takes up much of the available space. There are further reminders of the park's heyday in and around **Lower Lake**, in the southeast corner of the park, whose islands feature around thirty life-sized dinosaurs lurking in the undergrowth, built out of brick and iron by Waterhouse Hawkins in the 1850s and now given the status of listed buildings. Nearby, the old zoo is currently being transformed into a super new **city farm**, but won't be open until 2002.

Greenwich

*The nearest
DLR station is
Cutty Sark; the
nearest train
stations are
Greenwich and
Maze Hill.*

"The most delightful spot of ground in Great Britain", according to Daniel Defoe, **Greenwich** is still one of London's most beguiling places, and the one place in southeast London that draws tourists out from the centre in considerable numbers. At its heart is the outstanding architectural set piece of the **Old Royal Naval College** and the **Queen's House**, courtesy of Christopher Wren and Inigo Jones respectively. Most visitors, however, come to see the **Cutty Sark**, the **National Maritime Museum** and the **Royal Observatory** in Greenwich Park, though Greenwich also pulls in an ever-increasing volume of Londoners in search of bargains at its weekend market. With the added attractions of its riverside pubs and walks – plus startling views across to Canary Wharf and Docklands – it makes for one of the best weekend trips in London. Greenwich is, of course, also famous as the "home of time", thanks to its status as the **Prime Meridian of the World** from where time all over the globe is measured. It's partly for this reason that Greenwich was chosen as the centrepiece of the country's millennium celebrations, though the **Millennium Dome** is, in fact, situated in the industrial wasteland of North Greenwich, a mile or so northeast of Greenwich town centre.

Visiting Greenwich

Greenwich is still most quickly reached from central London by **train** from Charing Cross, Waterloo East or London Bridge (every 30min), although taking a **boat** from one of the piers between Westminster and Tower Bridge is more scenic (and more expensive). Another possibility is to take the **Docklands Light Railway** (DLR) from Bank or Tower Gateway direct to Cutty Sark. For the best view of the Wren buildings, though, get out at Island Gardens to admire the view, and then take the Greenwich Foot Tunnel under the Thames.

The local **tourist information office** (daily 10am–5pm; ☎0870/608 2000), the grandly named Greenwich Gateway Visitor Centre, is located in the Pepys Building by the side of the *Cutty Sark*. Staff there can answer most queries and tell you the latest information on the Dome; there's also a little exhibition area, giving a brief outline of the area's history.

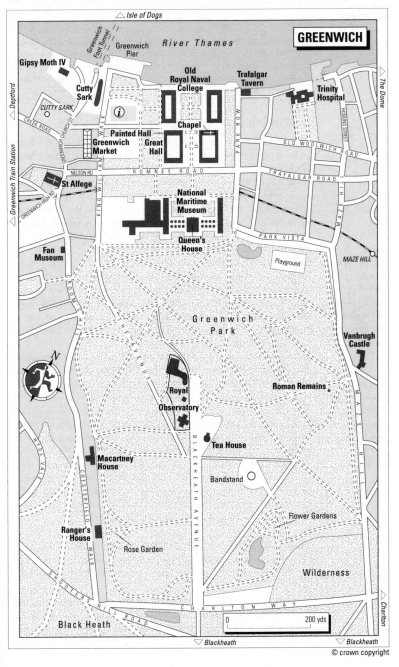

Greenwich town centre

Greenwich town centre was laid out in the 1820s, hence the Nash-style terraces of Nelson Road, College Approach and King William Walk, now a one-way system plagued with heavy traffic. At the centre of these busy streets, filled with nautical knick-knack shops and bookshops, stands the old covered market, which sold mostly fruit and veg until the late 1980s; you can still see the wonderfully Victorian inscription on one of the archways: "A false balance is abomination to the Lord, but a just weight is his delight." The old market and flanking stables are now part of the new **Greenwich Market**, a lively antique, crafts and clothes market which has spread far beyond the perimeters of its predecessor, spilling out up the High Road, Stockwell Road and Royal Hill. The best sections are the indoor secondhand book markets, flanking the Central Market on Stockwell Road; the antiques hall (actually a very mixed bag of goods), further down on Greenwich High Road; and the flea market on Thames Street.

Greenwich Market runs Wed–Sun 9am–5pm, but is at its busiest and biggest on Saturday and Sunday.

A short distance in from the old covered market, on the opposite side of Greenwich Church Street, rises the Doric portico and broken pediment of Nicholas Hawksmoor's **St Alfege's Church**. Built in 1712–18 to replace a twelfth-century structure in which Henry VIII was baptized and Thomas Tallis, the "father of English church music", was buried, the church was flattened in the Blitz, but it has been magnificently repaired. Alfege is an unusual saint, in that he wasn't really martyred for his religion. As Archbishop of Canterbury he was captured in 1011 by the marauding Danes, and carried off to Greenwich, where they demanded a ransom for him. Alfege refused to allow any ransom to be paid, at which the furious Danes pelted him to death with ox bones. Thorkell the Tall, the one Dane who took pity on him, got an axe in the head for his pains.

St Alfege's Church is open Mon–Sat 10am–4pm, Sun 1–4pm; www.st-alfege.org.

The Cutty Sark and Gipsy Moth

Cutty Sark: April–Sept Mon–Sat 10am–6pm, Sun noon–6pm; Oct–March closes 5pm; £3.50; ☎020/8858 3445; *www.cuttysark.org.uk*. Cutty Sark DLR station.

Wedged in a dry dock by the Greenwich Foot Tunnel is the majestic **Cutty Sark**, the world's last surviving tea clipper, which was launched from the Clydeside shipyards in 1869. The *Cutty Sark* lasted just eight years in the China tea trade, and it was as a wool clipper that it actually made its name, returning from Australia in just 72 days. The vessel's name comes from Robert Burns's *Tam O'Shanter*, in which Tam, a drunken farmer, is chased by Nannie, an angry witch in a short Paisley linen dress, or "cutty sark"; the clipper's figurehead shows her clutching the hair from the tail of Tam's horse. Inside, there's little to see beyond the exhibition in the main hold which tells the ship's story from its inception to its arrival in Greenwich in 1954. Before you disembark, don't miss the colourful parade of buxom figureheads in the lower hold.

A mast's length from the *Cutty Sark*, and dwarfed by the bulk of its neighbour, is the tiny **Gipsy Moth IV**, the 54-foot boat in which, at the age of 66, Francis Chichester became the first person to sail solo around the world in 1965–66 (for which he was knighted on this very spot).

Old Royal Naval College

Mon–Sat 10am–5pm, Sun 12.30–5pm; £3; free after 3.30pm & all day Sun; ☎0800/389 3341; *www.greenwichfoundation.org.uk*. Cutty Sark DLR station.

It's entirely appropriate that the one London building that makes the most of its river-bank location should be the **Old Royal Naval College**, a majestic Baroque ensemble which opens out onto the Thames. Despite the symmetry and grace of the four buildings, which perfectly frame the Queen's House beyond (see p.435), the whole complex has a strange and piecemeal history. John Webb, Inigo Jones's assistant and nephew, began the first of the four blocks in the 1660s as a replacement palace for Charles II, but the money ran out after just five years. William and Mary eschewed the unfinished palace for Hampton Court and decided to turn the Greenwich building into a hospital for disabled seamen, along the lines of Royal Hospital in Chelsea (see p.372). Wren, working for nothing, then had his original designs vetoed by the queen, who insisted the new development must not obscure the view of the river from the Queen's House – what you see now is Wren's revised plan, augmented by, among others, Hawksmoor and Vanbrugh.

The population of the hospital swelled to over 2500 in the aftermath of the Napoleonic Wars, but charges of cruelty and corruption, coupled with dwindling numbers, forced a move to new premises in 1869. Four years later the vacated buildings were taken over by the Royal Naval College, which later moved to Dartmouth, though specialist training for senior officers continued here until the 1990s. Initially, the government attempted to sell off the historic buildings, but the sale was hampered by the presence of a thirty-year-old nuclear reactor – affectionately known as Jason – in the basement. The buildings now house the University of Greenwich and the Trinity College of Music.

The two grandest rooms, situated underneath Wren's twin domes, are well worth visiting, Approaching from King William Walk, you enter via the West Gate, whose gateposts are each topped by a globe:

celestial to the left, terrestrial to the right. Visitors must buy their tickets in the entrance to the **RNC Chapel**, in the east wing. The current chapel was designed by James "Athenian" Stuart (so called because of his espousal of the Greek Revival style), after a fire in 1779 destroyed its predecessor. However, it is Stuart's assistant, William Newton, whom we have to thank for the chapel's exquisite pastel and sky-blue plasterwork and spectacular decorative detailing, among the finest in London. The altarpiece, by Benjamin West, depicts St Paul wrestling with the viper that leapt out of the fire after he was shipwrecked off Malta.

From here, you descend to the temporary exhibition room, and along the underground Chalk Walk to the licensed café, and then up to the magnificent **Painted Hall**, in the west wing. The hall is dominated by James Thornhill's gargantuan allegorical ceiling painting, which took him nineteen years to complete, and spans several reigns. It depicts William and Mary handing down Peace and Liberty to Europe, with a vanquished Louis XIV clutching a broken sword below them. Equally remarkable are Thornhill's trompe l'oeil fluted pilasters and decorative detailing, while on the far wall, behind the high table, Thornhill himself appears beside George I and family, with St Paul's in the background. Designed to be the sailors' dining hall, it was considered far too splendid for plebs and lay more or less empty and unused until Nelson's lying-in-state in 1806.

The riverside

A fine vantage point for viewing the Old Royal Naval College is the **Five-Foot Walk**, which squeezes between the college railings and the river bank. It was here that George I landed to take the throne on September 18, 1714, though it was estimated that 57 other cousins had a better claim. His wife was not with him, having been incarcerated, on George's orders, in a castle in Germany for adultery; she remained there for 32 years. If you're in need of refreshment, drop into the Regency-style **Trafalgar Tavern**, at the east end of the walk. The pub was frequented by Whig politicians and the Victorian literary set – its legendary whitebait suppers inspired Dickens to use the pub as the setting for the wedding breakfast in *Our Mutual Friend*.

Just beyond the pub down Crane Street is the **Trinity Hospital**, founded in 1613 by the Earl of Northampton for 21 pensioners; the entry requirements declared the hospital would admit "no common beggar, drunkard, whore-hunter, nor unclean person . . . nor any that is blind . . . nor any idiot". The cream-coloured mock-Gothic facade and chapel (which contains the Earl's tomb) were rebuilt in the nineteenth century, but the courtyard of almshouses remains much as it was at its foundation. Beyond the Trinity Hospital, the Thames Path continues past some unprepossessing properties and emerges at the *Cutty Sark* pub, another great riverside halt. You can continue along the river all the way to the Dome (see box opposite).

The Millennium Dome

*[A] yellow-spiked Teflon tent....a genetically modified mol-
lusc....The Dome is a blob of correction fluid, a flick of Tipp-Ex to
revise the mistakes of nineteenth-century industrialists....a
poached egg designed by a committee of vegans.*

Iain Sinclair, *Sorry Meniscus*

London's controversial **Millennium Dome** is located on contaminated
land (formerly one of Europe's largest gasworks) downstream at North
Greenwich, and is clearly visible from the riverside at Greenwich and
from Greenwich Park. Built at a cost approaching £800 million, and
designed by Richard Rogers (of Lloyd's Building and Pompidou Centre
fame), it is by far the world's largest dome – over half a mile in circumference and 160ft in height – held up by a dozen, 300-foot-tall
yellow steel masts. In 2000, it housed the nation's chief millennium
extravaganza: an array of high-tech sponsor-dominated zones set
around a stage, on which a circus-style performance took place to
music by Peter Gabriel.

Like most grand projects, the Dome had a rough ride from the press
right from the beginning. The hiccups and headaches continued into the
year 2000, with bad reviews and over-optimistic estimates of visitor numbers forcing the government to pump in around £150 million of public
money to keep it open. Nevertheless, millions paid up £20 each to visit,
and millions went away happy. Nobody quite knows what the future holds
for the Dome, and as this book went to print, no decision had been made.

The easiest way to get to the Dome is to take the tube, as the Dome has
its very own, very large, very fancy Jubilee line tube station designed by
Norman Foster; there are also boat services which stop at the Dome's
Millennium Pier. It's also possible to walk or cycle the mile and a half along
the riverside pathway from Greenwich, or take bus #188 from Greenwich
town centre.

National Maritime Museum

Daily 10am–5pm; £7.50; ☎020/8858 4422; *www.nmm.ac.uk*. Cutty Sark
DLR, Greenwich or Maze Hill train station.

The **National Maritime Museum**, which occupies the west wing of
the former Naval Asylum, has recently undergone a lengthy £20 million redevelopment programme. The main entrance is now on
Romney Road, and brings you out into the spectacular glass-roofed
central courtyard, designed by Rick Mather. The various themed galleries are ranged over three floors, and are imaginatively designed to
appeal to visitors of all ages, with plenty of hands-on stuff to keep
children amused. The courtyard, meanwhile, has a new building slap
bang in the centre, and several "streets" along the sides, which house
some of the museum's largest artefacts, among them the splendid
63ft-long gilded **Royal Barge**, a gilded Rococo confection designed
by William Kent for Prince Frederick, the much-unloved eldest son of
George II.

Greenwich

Level 1: Explorers, Passengers & Cargoes

Explorers, on Level 1, takes you from the Vikings to Franklin's attempt to discover the Northwest Passage; on display are the relics recovered from the Arctic by John Rae in 1854, many of which had to be bought from the local Inuit. In the central building, you get to view some of the museum's most highly prized artefacts, such as **Captain Cook**'s sextant and K1 marine clock, Shackleton's compass and **Captain Scott**'s furry reindeer-hide sleeping bag and sledging goggles. There's also footage of the **Titanic**, a ticket belonging to a lucky guy who couldn't go at the last minute and a pocket watch, stopped at 3.07am, retrieved from one of the drowned.

In **Rank & Style**, you can inspect various marine get-ups from naval uniforms to the survival suit that saved Tony Bullimore's life when his yacht capsized – each one is hidden within a cupboard and accompanied by a brief audioguide. **Maritime London** has displays on the Thames Barrier (see p.443), and gives Lloyds of London a nice opportunity to plug its services as the world's largest marine insurer. **Passengers** re-lives the glory days of transatlantic shipping, which officially came to an end in 1957 when more people went by air than by sea. To their credit, the displays also touch on the role of shipping in immigration and in transporting refugees. Sponsors P&O get to display their wares at the end, with several huge models of P&O's *Grand Princess*, built in 1998 and, at 109,000 tons and over 950ft in length, the largest passenger vessel ever built. **Cargoes**, meanwhile, concentrates on the less glamorous, modern face of shipping: sea containerization, which is still responsible for transporting 95 percent of the world's goods.

Level 2: Art, the Empire and Green issues

On Level 2, there's a large maritime art gallery, **Art & the Sea**, which displays a wide range of works from eighteenth-century oils of historic naval encounters to Art Deco lithographs of submarine life by Admiralty war artist Eric Ravilious. **Trade & Empire** is a gallery devoted to the legacy of the British Empire, warts and all, from the slave trade to the opium wars. In the eco-conscious, arty section on the **Future of the Sea**, by the café, you can have a look inside a Greenpeace survival pod, while the nearby **Global Garden** touches on biodiversity. The only gallery left from the old days of the museum is **Seapower**, which focuses on twentieth-century trade and naval prowess. Among the numerous military portraits, there's a full-size cutaway submarine, a video war game and a section justifying the sinking of the *Belgrano* during the Falklands War.

Level 3: Hands-on galleries and Nelson

Level 3 is the place to head if you've got children, as it boasts two excellent hands-on galleries. **The Bridge** is aimed at all ages, as it really does take some skill to navigate a catamaran, a paddle steamer and a rowing boat to shore. **All Hands** is aimed at a younger audience, and gives kids a taste of life on the seas over the last millennium, loading miniature cargo, firing a cannon, learning to use Morse code and so forth.

The **Nelson Gallery**, meanwhile, contains the museum's vast collection of Nelson memorabilia, including his grog jug, Bible and the diminutive "undress coat" worn during the Battle of Trafalgar, with a tiny bullet hole made by the musket shot that killed him. Another prize possession is Turner's *Battle of Trafalgar, 21st October, 1805*, his largest work and only royal commission, which was intended for St James's Palace; there's a good audio commentary on the canvas, with synchronized spotlighting to enhance the effect. Other quirky features include a virtual-reality video re-enactment of Trafalgar and a computer pin-up gallery of Lady Hamilton. Lastly, there's a wonderful cabinet of Nelson kitsch produced in the nineteenth century: pipes, vinaigrettes, souvenirs made from the timber of HMS *Victory* and, best of all, a set of toy bricks depicting Nelson's funeral procession from Whitehall to St Paul's.

Queen's House

Inigo Jones's **Queen's House**, originally built on a cramped site amidst the Tudor royal palace, is now the focal point of the Greenwich ensemble. As royal residences go, it's an unassuming little Palladian country house, "solid . . . masculine and unaffected" in Jones's own words. Its significance in terms of British architecture, however, is immense. Begun in 1616, it is the earliest example of Renaissance architecture in Britain, and the first Neoclassical building in the country since Roman times, signifying a clear break with all that preceded it.

The interior, exterior and setting of the Queen's House have all changed radically since Jones's day, making it difficult to imagine the impact the building must have had when it was built. The house is linked to its neighbouring buildings by open colonnades, added in the early part of the nineteenth century, when the entire complex was converted into a school for the children of seamen. The colonnades follow the course of the muddy road which the H-shaped block originally straddled, thus enabling the queen to pass from the formal gardens to the royal park without sullying her shoes.

The interior is currently used by the National Maritime Museum for temporary exhibitions. Nevertheless, one or two features survive (or have been reinstated) from Stuart times. The **Great Hall**, a perfect cube, is galleried and decorated with computer-enhanced copies of Orazio Gentileschi's panel paintings, which were removed to Marlborough House by the Duchess of Marlborough herself during the reign of Queen Anne. The southeastern corner of the hall leads to the beautiful **Tulip Staircase**, Britain's earliest cantilevered spiral staircase, whose name derives from the floral patterning in the wrought-iron

Royal Greenwich

The history of Greenwich is replete with royal connections. Edward I appears to have been the first of the English kings to have stayed here, though there was nothing resembling a palace until Henry V's brother, the Duke of Gloucester, built Bella Court in 1426. Henry VI honeymooned here with his new wife, Margaret of Anjou, and eventually took over the place and rebuilt it in her honour. However, it was under the Tudors that Greenwich enjoyed its royal heyday. Henry VII took over the place and rebuilt it from 1500 onwards, renaming it **Palace of Placentia**. Henry VIII, who was born in Greenwich, made this his main base, pouring even more money into it than he did at Hampton Court (see p.477). He added armouries, a banqueting hall and a huge tiltyard, hunted in the extensive grounds and kept a watchful eye over proceedings at the nearby Royal Dockyards in Deptford. His children, Mary and Elizabeth, were both born here.

Edward VI came to Greenwich in 1553 to try to restore his frail health, but died shortly afterwards. Mary came here rarely as queen, and on one of her few visits had the wall of her personal apartment blasted away by a cannonball fired in salute. For Elizabeth, Greenwich was the chief summer residence, and it was here in 1573 that she revived the Maundy Ceremony, washing the feet of 39 poor women (though only after three others had washed them first). The royal palace fell into disrepair during the Commonwealth, when it was turned into a biscuit factory, and was finally torn down by Charles II to make way for a new edifice, which eventually became the Royal Naval College.

balustrade. The only other significant interior decoration is upstairs, in the room intended as the bedchamber of Charles I and Henrietta Maria, which retains its ceiling decoration from the 1630s.

Greenwich Park and the Royal Observatory

Greenwich Park is the starting point for the annual London Marathon, the world's biggest road race, which takes place on a Sunday in mid-April.

Greenwich Park (daily dawn–dusk; *www.royalparks.co.uk*) is one of the city's oldest royal parks, having been enclosed in the fifteenth century by the Duke of Gloucester, who fancied it as a hunting ground (its royal title actually came later). Henry VIII was particularly fond of the place, to which he characteristically introduced deer in 1515, as well as archery and jousting tournaments, and sword-fighting contests. André le Nôtre, Louis XIV's gardener at Versailles, seems to have had a hand in redesigning the park after the Commonwealth, though he never actually set foot in Greenwich.

The park was finally opened to the public in the eighteenth century, and after the arrival of the railway in 1838 it began to attract Londoners in great numbers. In 1894 Greenwich Park witnessed one of the more bizarre incidents in London's long history of terrorism: Martial Bourdin, a young French anarchist, was killed when the bomb he was carrying in a brown paper bag exploded. The questions of whether he was planning to blow up the observatory, and whether he was a police informer, remain unresolved. Joseph Conrad used the episode as the basis of his novel *The Secret Agent*.

The park's chief delight is the view from the steep hill crowned by the Royal Observatory (see below), from which you can see Canary Wharf and the Millennium Dome. The most popular place from which to take in the panorama is the statue of **General James Wolfe** (1727–59), who lived at Macartney House at the top of Croom's Hill, close to the Ranger's House (see p.440), and is buried in St Alfege (see p.430). Wolfe is famed for the audacious campaign with which he captured Quebec in 1759, a battle in which he and his opposite number, the French General Montcalm, were both mortally wounded. Victory celebrations took place throughout England, but were forbidden in Greenwich out of respect for Wolfe's mother, who had also lost her husband only a few months previously.

Greenwich Park is also celebrated for its rare and ancient trees, the most famous of which, **Queen Elizabeth's Oak** – not, in fact, an oak, but a sweet chestnut – finally toppled in 1992. For over a hundred years the tree had been reduced to an ivy-covered dead stump, albeit a stump so big that the hollowed-out trunk was at one time used as a lockup by the park police. It was around this oak tree that Henry VIII and Anne Boleyn (whom he later accused of adultery and had beheaded) are said to have danced. Queen Elizabeth was fond of playing in the tree, and it was at a lodge gate close by that, according to tradition, Walter Ralegh earned his knighthood by gallantly throwing down his cloak into the mud for the queen to walk over.

The descendants of Henry's deer are now safely enclosed within "**The Wilderness**", a fenced area in the southeast corner where they laze around "tame as children", in Henry James's words; close by is the **Flower Garden**, actually more impressive for its exotic trees than its flowers. If you're in this part of the park, don't miss **Vanbrugh Castle**, halfway down Maze Hill, England's first mock-medieval castle, designed by the architect John Vanbrugh as his private residence in 1726. If you're heading for the Ranger's House (see p.440), the best approach is via the semicircular **Rose Garden**, laid out in front of it, which is worth a visit itself from June to August.

Royal Observatory

Daily 10am–5pm; £5; ☎020/8858 4422; *www.rog.nmm.ac.uk*. Cutty Sark DLR or Greenwich train station.

The **Royal Observatory** is the longest-established scientific institution in Britain. Built on the foundations of a medieval outpost of Greenwich Palace, it was established by Charles II in 1675 to house the first Astronomer Royal, John Flamsteed. Flamsteed's chief task was to study the night sky in order to discover an astronomical method of finding the longitude of a ship at sea, the lack of which was causing enormous problems for the emerging British Empire. Astronomers continued to work here at Greenwich until the postwar smog forced them to decamp to Herstmonceux Castle and the clearer skies of Sussex (they've since moved to the Pacific); the observatory, meanwhile, is now a very popular museum.

Greenwich's other great claim to fame is of course as the home of **GMT** and the **Prime Meridian** – a meridian being any north–south line used as a basis for astronomical observations, and therefore also for the calculation of longitude and time. By the mid-nineteenth century, it was clear that an internationally agreed system of timekeeping was needed. In 1852, Britain adopted "London time", which meant, in effect, Greenwich Mean Time (GMT), though, in fact, this wasn't formally acknowledged until 1880. Three years later the US also adopted Greenwich as the Prime Meridian, and in 1884 persuaded an international convention in Washington DC to agree to make Greenwich the Prime Meridian of the World – in other words, zero longitude. As a result, the entire world sets its clocks in relation to GMT.

The red strip in the main courtyard lies along the Greenwich Prime Meridian, which is still used as an absolute today. However, what the Royal Observatory don't tell you is that, as a result of communications problems encountered during the Vietnam War, the Americans starting using satellites to work out longitude in the 1980s. The global standard for air navigation, and used widely by the military, is now the **Global Positioning System** or GPS, which bases its calculations on the centre of the earth not the surface, and places the meridian approximately 336ft to the east of the red strip.

Flamsteed House

The oldest part of the observatory is **Flamsteed House**, built by Wren (himself a trained astronomer) "for the observator's habitation and a little for pompe". The northeastern turret sports a bright-red Time-Ball that climbs the mast at 12.58pm and drops at 1pm GMT precisely; it was added in 1833 to allow ships on the Thames to set their clocks. On the house's balcony overlooking the Thames, you can take a look at a **Camera Obscura**, of the kind which Flamsteed used to make safe observations of the sun – the current model gives a you a panorama of Greenwich, with the Isle of Dogs beyond. Beyond the displays of globes, astrolabes and quadrants, and the restored apartments in which the cantankerous Flamsteed lived, you eventually reach the **Octagon Room**, containing a single eighteenth-century telescope – though, in fact, this room was never used to map the movement of the stars, acting instead as a reception room in which the king could show off. The ceiling plasterwork is all that remains of the original décor, and there are replicas of the precision clocks installed behind the original walnut panelling in 1676, which boast 13-foot-long pendulums with a two second-swing.

Longitude

The next gallery focuses on the search for longitude. The displays show you how to use a quadrant in order to measure latitude, and explains lunar distance method of calculating longitude. However, before the invention of the seagoing clock, which could tell travellers what time it was back home and therefore how far east or west they'd travelled, longitude was impossible to measure at sea in cloudy weather. The displays reveal some of the crazy ideas that were put forward in order to try to measure longitude and win the £20,000 **Longitude Prize**. Much the most bizarre involved stabbing a number of dogs with the same knife, then taking them off to different countries; at noon in England a man would jab the knife into a mysterious substance called "powder of sympathy", at which point, supposedly, all the dogs would bark simultaneously, thus revealing the time differentials.

The exhibition then progresses to more successful experiments, including the first four marine chronometers designed by **John Harrison**, three of which are still in working order today. Harrison eventually went on to win the prize in 1763 with his giant pocket watch, H4 – the only one that no longer functions – after much skulduggery against his claims, most notably by the Astronomer Royal at the time, Nevil Maskelyne. The story of how Harrison finally won the prize is the subject of the best-selling book *Longitude* by Dava Sobel. The downstairs rooms contain an eclectic collection of timepieces from around the world, including the electrical contacts that used to provide the hourly six pips for the BBC. Among the more unusual exhibits are a delicate Chinese Fire Clock in the shape of a dragon, which uses a burning incense stick, and an alarm clock from the Cultural Revolution, in which the seconds tick away against a background of women waving Mao's *Little Red Book*.

The Meridian Building and the Telescope Dome

Flamsteed carried out more than thirty thousand observations – "nothing can exceed the tediousness and ennui of the life" was his dispirited description of the job – in the Quadrant House, which now forms part of the **Meridian Building**, but was originally little more than a brick shed in the garden. Flamsteed's meridian line is a brass strip in the floor, though it was originally formed by the west wall of his shed. Edmond Halley, who succeeded Flamsteed as Astronomer Royal in 1720, bought more sophisticated quadrants, sextants, spyglasses and telescopes, which are among those displayed in the **Quadrant Room**. With the aid of his eight-foot iron quadrant he charted the comings and goings of the famous comet – though he never lived to see its return – and worked out his own version of the meridian. Next door, the **Bradley Meridian Room** reveals yet another meridian, standard from 1750 to 1850 and still used for Ordnance Survey maps. Finally, you reach a room that's sliced in two by the present-day Greenwich Meridian, fixed by the cross hairs in Airy's "Transit Circle", the astronomical instrument that dominates the room.

En route to the **Telescope Dome** of the octagonal Great Equatorial Building, built in 1857, you can find out facts about the universe on the observatory's "Astroweb", look at several antique (and a working) orreries, which plot the movements of the solar system like a clock, and a series of astrolabes used by Islamic astronomers. The building is also home to Britain's largest telescope, a Victorian 28-inch refractor which weighs over one and a half tons. The soothing videos of space images are supplied courtesy of NASA. In addition, there are half-hourly presentations in the **Planetarium** (Mon–Fri 2.30pm; £2), housed in the adjoining South Building.

Ranger's House

April–Sept daily 10am–6pm; Oct–March Wed–Sun 10am–4pm; EH; £2.80; ☎020/8853 0035; *www.english-heritage.org.uk*. Greenwich DLR and train station.

Southwest of the observatory, and backing onto Greenwich Park's Rose Garden, is the **Ranger's House**, a red-brick Georgian villa which looks out over Blackheath (see p.441). Built as a private residence in the early eighteenth century, it was bought in 1815 by the Crown and became the official residence of the park ranger (hence its name), a sort of top-notch grace-and-favour home. Entrance to the house is either from Croom's Hill, or from the doorway in the wall by the park's Rose Garden. However, the house is likely to be closed until 2002, so phone ahead before you set out.

In the foyer, there's a wonderful portrait by John Singer Sargent of the nineteenth countess of Suffolk, who donated the collection of paintings which now fill the ground-floor rooms. The high points of the collection are William Larkin's full-length portraits of a Jacobean wedding party, which line the splendid main gallery with its three bow windows and duck-egg-green coffered ceiling; among the most striking of the portraits are the twin bridesmaids in slashed silver brocade dresses, and the arrogant Richard Sackville, a dissolute aristocrat resplendent in pompom shoes.

Temporary exhibitions take place on the first floor, but make sure you also take time to explore the Architectural Study Centre in the old coach house across the stableyard, which is filled with all manner of bits and bobs: plaques, mantels, fireplaces and chimneys saved from London's historic buildings, some hidden in pull-out drawers. The cast-iron spiral staircase snaking through the centre of the room was retrieved from the old Covent Garden market hall.

The Fan Museum

Tues–Sat 11am–5pm, Sun noon–5pm; £3.50; ☎020/8305 1441; *www .fan-museum.org*. Cutty Sark DLR or Greenwich train station.

At the bottom of Croom's Hill, the twisting road that runs along the western edge of the park and which boasts some of Greenwich's finest seventeenth- and eighteenth-century buildings, you'll find the

Down in Deptford

Deptford, just west of Greenwich, is not an area that immediately springs
to mind when thinking of places to visit in London. However, it does have
a very rich history, due, in part, to the presence of the **Royal Naval
Dockyards** here from 1513 until 1869. It was at Deptford that Drake
moored the *Golden Hinde* (see p.317), in 1581, after circumnavigating
the globe, had Elizabeth I on board for dinner, and was knighted for his
efforts. All that remains of the old dockyards today are a few officers' quarters hidden in the Pepys housing estate, and the **Shipwright's Palace**
(phone for times; ☎020/8692 5836), at the bottom of Watergate Street,
fifteen minutes' walk west of Cutty Sark DLR or five minutes' walk north
of Deptford train station. Originally constructed in Tudor times, the last
rebuild, in 1708, was deemed so ridiculously expensive that the building
became known as a palace, though in fact, it's nothing of the sort. Opened
up to the public for the first time in 2000, the house is in a terrible state,
and is currently used for exhibitions and art shows, though the idea is to
restore it eventually. In the meantime, it's an intriguing slice of history,
and a most unlikely find in Deptford. You can get an idea of how prosperous the area once was just off the High Street at **St Paul's Church**, the
local architectural gem, designed by Thomas Archer in 1720, whose interior Pevsner described as "closer to Borromini and the Roman Baroque
than any other English church". Things are looking up, too, if the new
Laban Centre for contemporary dance at Creekside, east of the High
Street, designed by Tate Modern duo Herzog and de Meuron, is a sign of
things to come.

Fan Museum at no. 12. It's a fascinating little place (and an
extremely beautiful house), revealing the importance of the fan as a
social and political document. The permanent exhibition on the
ground floor traces the history of the materials employed, from peacock feathers to straw, while temporary exhibitions on the first floor
explore conditions of production, the fan's link with the Empire and
changing fashion. Outside in the garden, there's a kitsch, hand-
painted Orangery.

Blackheath

Immediately south of Greenwich Park lies the well-to-do suburb of
Blackheath (so called because of the colour of the soil), whose
bleak, windswept heath, crisscrossed with busy roads, couldn't be
more different from the royal park. Nonetheless, with its pair of
century-old pubs, the *Princess of Wales* and *Hare and Billet*, each
set beside a pond (on the south side of the heath), it can be quite
pleasant on a summer afternoon. The odd fair takes place here on
public holidays, and it's south London's premier kite-flying spot.

Blackheath has its historic connections, too, most famously as a
plague burial ground – a role which perhaps slowed development.
Lying on the main road to Dover, it was a convenient spot on which

to pitch camp, as the Danes did in 1011, having kidnapped St Alfege. Their example was followed during the 1381 Peasants' Revolt by Wat Tyler's rebels, who were treated to a rousing revolutionary sermon by John Bull, which included the famous lines "When Adam delved and Eve span, who was then the gentleman?" The victorious Henry V was welcomed back from the Battle of Agincourt here in 1415, while Henry VII fought a pitched battle on this spot against Cornish rebels in 1497. It was at Blackheath, also, that Henry VIII was so disappointed on meeting his fourth wife, Anne of Cleves, in 1540; he didn't fancy her and filed for divorce after just six months.

The heath's chief landmark is **All Saints' Church**, which nestles in a slight depression in the south corner. Built in rugged Kentish ragstone in 1859, it's at odds with the rest of the architecture bordering the heath, which dates mostly from the area's development in the late eighteenth and early nineteenth century. One of the earliest residential developments was **The Paragon**, a crescent of four-storey Georgian mansions linked by Doric colonnades. An even earlier foundation, set in its own grounds to the east, is **Morden College** (not open to the public), the aristocrat of almshouses, built in 1695 not for the deserving poor but for "decayed Turkey merchants" who had lost their fortunes. The quadrangular red-brick building, built by Wren's favourite mason, possibly to a design by the master himself, reflects the lost status of its original inhabitants and is now an old people's home.

Age Exchange Reminiscence Centre

Mon–Sat 10am–5pm; free; ☎ 020/8318 9105.

It's worth venturing down the charmingly named Tranquil Vale into the village-like centre of Blackheath, if only to visit the **Age Exchange Reminiscence Centre**, situated opposite the train station. A favourite with the older folks of Blackheath, the centrepiece is an old-fashioned shop counter, whose drawers are filled with two-pin plugs, wooden clothes pegs, chalk powder and a whole host of everyday objects now rarely seen. Ask for a demonstration of the shop's rare surviving example of a rapid-wire cash system, via which banknotes could be whizzed from cashier to till worker. Out the back, you can get a cuppa from the museum's period tuck shop, and, if you're lucky, you might even catch an impromptu piano recital.

Woolwich

The chief reason to journey out to **Woolwich** is to visit the **Thames Barrier**, an awesome piece of modern engineering and the largest movable flood barrier in the world. A boat trip from Greenwich is the best way to take this in, but if you have a fascination for military history you may want to explore the arsenal and dockyards, dating from

Tudor times, and the military museums and architecture. As for the rest of Woolwich, it's difficult to disagree with the visitor who commented in 1847 that it was the "dirtiest, filthiest and most thoroughly mismanaged town of its size in the kingdom". With its docks and factories defunct, this is one of the poorest parts of the old Docklands, and is only now beginning to be regenerated.

Thames Barrier

The brief boat trip from Greenwich passes drab industrial landscapes before gliding towards the gleaming fins of the **Thames Barrier**. London has been subject to flooding from surge tides since before 1236, when it was reported that in "the great Palace of Westminster men did row with wherries in the midst of the Hall". One of the worst recorded floods took place as recently as 1953, when more than three hundred people were drowned in the Thames Estuary alone. A flood barrier had been advocated as far back as the 1850s, but it wasn't until global warming and rising tides, coupled with the fact that southeast England is sinking slowly into the sea, that the Greater London Council finally agreed to build the present barrier. Built from 1972 to 1984, it's a mind-blowing feat of engineering, with its ten moveable steel gates weighing from 400 to 3700 tons each.

For information on boat services from Greenwich to the Thames Barrier, call ☎020/8305 0300.

The **Thames Barrier Visitors' Centre**, on Unity Way, is little more than a handful of glossy models, macho videos and dull statistics, though it does explain the basic mechanism of the barrier (something which is by no means obvious from above the water). By far the most interesting way to see the Thames Barrier, however, is from the river bank on the one day a month when it is raised for tests (phone for dates and times). Alternatively, there are thirty-minute cruises from the nearby pier which take you much closer to the barrier gates.

The Visitors' Centre is open Mon–Fri 10am–4pm, Sat & Sun 10.30am– 4.30pm; £3.40; ☎020/8854 1373; www .environment- agency.gov.uk.

Military Woolwich

Woolwich, like Deptford, owes its existence to the **Royal Dockyards**, which were established here in 1513 by Henry VIII. The great men-of-war that established England as a world naval power were built in these dockyards, starting with the *Great Harry*, the largest ship in the world when it was launched from here in 1514, and Sir Walter Ralegh and Captain Cook set out from Woolwich on their voyages of discovery. Despite costly modernization in the early nineteenth century to enable the dockyards to build and repair steamships, their capacities were quickly outstripped by the much larger iron-clad vessels, and they finally closed in 1869.

The closest train station is Charlton, from Charing Cross, Waterloo East and London Bridge stations.

Royal Arsenal

The **Royal Arsenal**, for which the area is now famous, grew up alongside the Tudor dockyards. Charles II fortified the area with a sixty-gun battery and sunk several ships in the river in preparation for an

Woolwich

The nearest train station is Woolwich Arsenal, from Charing Cross, Waterloo East and London Bridge stations.

Woolwich was the birthplace of Arsenal Football Club, now located in Highbury, Islington; see p.397.

attack by the Dutch fleet that never materialized. In 1695 the Royal Laboratory for the manufacture of fireworks and gunpowder moved here, and was joined, in 1717, by the main government brass foundry. Formally entitled the Royal Arsenal in 1805, the complex grew during the following century, reaching its heyday during World War I, when it employed nearly 80,000 people. After the armistice, there was a half-hearted attempt to convert the arsenal to nonmilitary production, paring the workforce down to just 20,000, and then another boom period during the last war. However, the ordnance factories were closed altogether in 1967, and much of the site was then given over to council housing.

During the course of the 1990s, the Ministry of Defence gradually pulled out of the arsenal altogether, and the fine collection of mostly eighteenth-century buildings is now set to be restored as part of an ambitious programme to turn the whole area into a mixed commercial and residential district. The **Beresford Gateway**, built in 1829 as the arsenal's main entrance, is now freestanding on Beresford Square and separated from the rest of the complex by Beresford Street/Plumstead Road. With the help of the plan visible through the iron gates of the main complex, you can identify the Guardhouse, Royal Brass Foundry, Royal Laboratory and Verbruggen's House, which all overlook Dial Square. From 2001, the public should be able to gain access to this area, which is due to house a new Greenwich borough heritage museum and a high-tech **Museum of Artillery**, which used to reside in the Rotunda (see below). For the latest on the museum, visit the Web site: *www.firepower.org.uk*.

Royal Artillery Barracks and around

Britain's first two artillery regiments were founded at the arsenal in 1716, and are now housed in the **Royal Artillery Barracks**, completed in 1802 by James Wyatt. This stands half a mile to the south of the arsenal, up Grand Depot Road. Its three-storey Georgian facade, interrupted by stucco pavilions and a central triumphal arch, runs for an amazing 1080ft, making it one of the longest in Europe.

The barracks face south onto the grassy parade ground, to the east of which lies the abandoned **Garrison Church of St George**, built in Neo-Romanesque style in 1863. Gutted in the last war, it's now an attractive husk, with fragments of its colourful interior décor still surviving. Further south still, on the other side of Woolwich Common, is Wyatt's only slightly less imposing **Old Royal Military Academy**, built in mock-Tudor style as a foil to the Royal Artillery Barracks. The 720-foot facade faces north onto a parade ground, with an imitation of the Tower of London's White Tower as its centrepiece. The Academy is set to be restored by English Heritage and will eventually be opened to the public.

To the west of the Royal Artillery Barracks, off Repository Road, stands John Nash's bizarre Chinese-style **Rotunda**. Originally designed for the gardens of Charlton House, the Rotunda was damaged by a gas explosion, repaired and re-erected on its present site. It used to house the Museum of Artillery, which has since moved to the old Royal Arsenal (see opposite), and is now likely to be used to house the museum's reserve collection.

North Woolwich

If Woolwich itself looks dismal, **North Woolwich**, on the north bank of the Thames, is worse – little more than an industrial wasteland. For nine hundred years it was a geographical anomaly, an island of Kent in Essex, claimed as such by the Sheriff of Kent way back in the eleventh century. The current name and the first real habitation came with the arrival of the Eastern Counties and Thames Junction Railway in 1847. In 1965 it was submerged into the East End borough of Newham, and over the next twenty years most of the area's factories closed down, as did the Royal Docks (not to be confused with the militarily inclined Royal Dockyards, described on p.443) that had been its life-support system. Apart from the presence of London City Airport, the DLR and the Tate & Lyle sugar factory, the whole area is awaiting development – and shows it.

North Woolwich Old Station

Jan–Nov Sat & Sun 1–5pm; school holidays also Mon–Wed 1–5pm; free; ☎020/7474 7244. North Woolwich train station.

The railway still reaches as far as North Woolwich, where a modern station serves as the terminus of the North London Line from Richmond. Meanwhile, the original station has been restored in all its Victorian glory and opened as the **North Woolwich Old Station**, a museum which recounts the impact of the railways on this part of London, and displays several restored steam engines outside, which are put through their paces on the first Sunday of each month in the summer. To reach the museum, you can either walk through the **Woolwich Foot Tunnel**, which opened in 1912, or take the **Woolwich Free Ferry**, established in perpetuity by an Act of Parliament in 1889.

Charlton to Chislehurst and beyond

This final section is a real miscellany of sights, spread between **Charlton** and **Chislehurst** and beyond, across considerable tracts of suburbia and countryside. Unless you are driving, you'll need to be selective in your choices; top targets are the Tudor **Eltham Palace**; the amazing **Chislehurst Caves**; and Charles Darwin's home, **Down House**.

Charlton House to Eltham

A little to the west of Woolwich, on Charlton Road, stands **Charlton House**, the finest Jacobean mansion in or around London, completed in 1612 as a "nest for his old age" by Adam Newton, tutor to the eldest son of James I, Prince Henry, who died in the same year. It was designed by John Thorpe, architect of Holland House in Kensington, though the Orangery to the north (now a public lavatory) is thought to be the work of Inigo Jones. The house as a whole is currently used as a community centre, which means you're free to roam the place, as long as there are no events going on – call ☎020/8856 3951 to check. Take the wonderful oak staircase to the left of the Great Hall, to appreciate the beautifully carved bulb- and plant-shaped newels and grotesque faces on the balusters. Off the wood-panelled Long Gallery on the top floor, with its strapwork ceiling, is the White Room, which harbours the finest of the house's period fireplaces, adorned with a relief of Perseus and several biblical scenes. The best of the strapwork ceilings, however, is to be found in the Grand Salon, featuring lovely drooping pendants.

*Bus #53 from
Elephant &
Castle tube (or
Woolwich
Arsenal) runs
to Charlton
House via the
south end of
Greenwich
Park.*

A mile or so southeast of Charlton, up Shooters Hill, are a series of ancient woodlands, the most famous of which is the easternmost, **Oxleas Wood**, through which the Tory government were keen to drive a motorway. Coppicing has helped keep the woodland floor a rich floral haven, as well as home to over 200 species of fungi. Jack Wood and Castle Wood, to the west, also feature the odd bit of more formal parkland, and the one point of specific interest, **Severndroog Castle** (closed to the public), a triangular tower erected in 1784 by Lady James of Eltham in memory of her husband, William, who once attacked a pirate stronghold in the island fortress of Severndroog, off the west coast of India. A mile or so to the south, across Shepherdleas Wood and the odd golf course and playing field, is **Avery Hill Park**, whose Victorian domed Winter Garden (Mon–Sat 10am–noon & 1–4pm) is, without a doubt, southeast London's finest greenhouse.

Eltham Palace

Wed–Fri & Sun: April–Sept 10am–6pm; Oct 10am–5pm; Nov–March 10am–4pm; £5.90; gardens only £3.50. ☎020/8294 2548. Eltham train station, from Victoria, London Bridge or Charing Cross.

A mile or so to the south of Oxleas Wood, at the end of Court Yard, lies **Eltham Palace**, which was one of the country's foremost medieval royal residences and even a venue for Parliament for some two hundred years from the reign of Edward II. All that remains of Eltham's medieval glory now is the fifteenth-century bridge across what used to be the moat and the **Great Hall**, built by Edward IV in 1479, with a fine hammerbeam roof hung with pendants, and two fan-vaulted stone oriels at the far end. The hall's two original fireplaces are now in Eltham's pubs; the best one, with its sixteenth-century Chinese tiles intact, can be seen in *The Greyhound* on the High Street.

Somewhat incredibly, in the 1930s, the millionaire Stephen Courtauld (of art-collecting fame) got permission to build his own "Wrenaissance" style **house** onto the Great Hall, and convert the moat into landscaped gardens. Courtauld lavished a fortune on the place, creating a sort of movie star's party palace for his glamorous half-Italian, half-Hungarian wife, Virginia (who sported a risqué tattoo of a snake above one ankle). The house was designed by the duo Seely and Paget, furnished by the best Swedish and Italian designers, and kitted out with all the latest mod cons, including underfloor heating, a centralized vacuum cleaner, a tannoy system and ten ensuite bedrooms. Then, shortly before the end of the war, the family left for Rhodesia, taking most of the house's furniture with them.

Until 1993, the Ministry of Defence used and abused the place; since then, English Heritage have restored the entire house and gardens and replaced lost furnishings. There's acres of exotic veneer, an onyx and gold-plated bathroom, and lots of quirky little Art Deco touches – check out the Alice in Wonderland relief above the door in the circular entrance hall, which is flooded with light from a spectacular glazed dome. The audiotours fill visitors in on the family's various eccentricities, which included keeping a pet ring-tailed lemur called Mah-Jongg, who had his own centrally heated bedroom approached by a bamboo ladder and was notorious for biting disliked male visitors.

Red House

Guided tours, which must be booked ahead, run May–Oct on first Sat & Sun of month at 2pm, 2.45pm & 3.30pm; £4; ☎020/8331 8138. Bexleyheath train station, from Victoria, London Bridge and Charing Cross.

Two miles east of Oxleas Wood, in Bexleyheath on the very outskirts of London, lies the **Red House**, a wonderful red-brick country house designed by Philip Webb in 1860 for his friend William Morris, following Morris's marriage to Pre-Raphaelite heart-throb Jane Burden. The details, such as the turreted well-house and the pointed brick arches, are Gothic, but the whole enterprise stands as a landmark in English architecture, and the beginning of the Arts and Crafts movement with which Morris is most closely associated. Much of the interior has been altered beyond recognition, but here and there the designs of Morris and his chief collaborator, Edward Burne-Jones, remain. If you're interested in signing up for a **guided tour**, then make sure you book early as they often sell out in advance. To get to the house, walk south from Bexleyheath station down Avenue Road, cross over into Upton Road; Red House Lane is the third street on your right.

Chislehurst Caves

Wed–Sun 10am–4pm (daily during school holidays); £3. Long tour Sun & Bank
Holidays 2.30pm; £5. ☎020/8467 3264. Chislehurst train station, from
Charing Cross or London Bridge.

Five miles southwest of Bexleyheath is one of London's more unusual tourist attractions, the **Chislehurst Caves**, prehistoric underground tunnels which stretch for miles and have been used over the
centuries by everyone from the Romans, who set up chalk mines, to
the locals, who came here to shelter from wartime bombs. **Guided
tours** set off on the hour and take around 45 minutes, with longer
tours on Sundays and bank holidays. Either way, the experience is
pretty spooky and claustrophobic as the caves have no lighting and
you are taken around by a guide with a lamp. The caves are a short
walk north of the train station, off Old Hill.

Down House

Wed–Sun: April–Oct 10am–6pm; Oct 10am–5pm; Nov, Dec, Feb & March
10am–4pm; EH; £5.50; ☎01689/859119 *www.english-heritage.org.uk*. Bus
#R2 from Orpington train station, accessible from Victoria, London Bridge
and Charing Cross.

Down House, home of the scientist Charles Darwin, is situated
another five miles south of Chislehurst in the village of Downe, overlooking the southeastern suburbs of London. Born in Shrewsbury in
1809, Darwin showed little academic promise at Cambridge. It was
only after returning from his five-year tour of South America aboard
the HMS *Beagle* – in which he stopped off at the Galapagos Islands
– that he began work on the theory he would eventually publish in
1859 as *On the Origin of Species*. Darwin moved to Down House in
1842, shortly after his marriage to his cousin Emma Wedgwood, who
nursed the hypochondriac scientist here until his death forty years
later. The house itself is set in lovely grounds, and is stuffed with
Darwin memorabilia, though there's no sign (nor smell) of the bar-
nacles which Darwin spent eight years dissecting – he later moved on
to the study of orchids, to the relief, no doubt, of his wife and children. Note that parking is very limited, so English Heritage is trying
to encourage folk arriving by car to **pre-book** timed-entry tickets. If
you come by public transport, it's worth knowing that the bus from
Orpington station runs once an hour only, with no service on
Sundays; ring first to check your connections.

Chapter 13

Out West: Chiswick to Kew, Hampton Court and Windsor Castle

C HISWICK to WINDSOR – a distance of some fifteen miles overland (considerably more by the river) – takes you from the traffic-clogged western suburbs of London to the heavily touristed royal outpost of **Windsor Castle**. In between, London and its satellites seem to continue unabated, with only fleeting glimpses of the countryside, in particular the fabulous **Kew Gardens** and the two old royal hunting parks, **Richmond** and **Bushy Park** – though, as one nineteenth-century visitor observed, they are "no more like the real untrimmed genuine country than a garden is like a field". Running through the chapter, and linking many of the places described, is the **River Thames**, once known as the "Great Highway of London" and still the most pleasant way to travel in these parts during the summer.

Aside from the river and the parks, the chief attractions are the numerous royal palaces and lordly mansions that pepper the river banks: textbook Palladian style at **Chiswick House**, unspoilt Jacobean splendour at **Ham House**, Tudor and Baroque excess (and the famous maze) at **Hampton Court**, and medieval ramparts at **Windsor** itself, which is also home to **Eton College**.

We actually kick off this chapter at **Hammersmith** – London's gateway to the west, by road or tube – which, with neighbouring **Chiswick**, and **Kew**, **Richmond** and **Twickenham** beyond, has the additional appeal of its riverside walks and pubs.

River transport

Westminster Passenger Services (☎020/7930 4721; *www.wpsa.co.uk*) runs two to three **boats** between Westminster and Hampton Court daily from April to September, calling at Kew and Richmond; the full trip takes 3–4hr one way, and costs £10 single, £14 return.

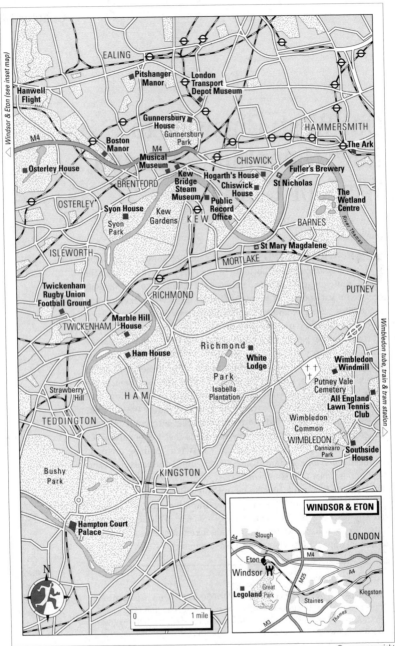

Chiswick to Pitshanger

Most people experience the five-mile stretch of west London between Chiswick and Osterley en route to or from Heathrow airport, either from the confines of the train or tube (which runs overground at this point) or from the M4, which was driven through areas of parkland in the 1960s. The sights here – former country retreats now surrounded by suburbia – are among the most neglected in this part of the city, receiving nothing like the number of visitors of Kew and Richmond, on the south bank of the Thames.

The Palladian villa of **Chiswick House** is perhaps the best known of these attractions, but you'll never see a crowd there and, though nearby Syon Park draws in the locals, most come for the garden centre rather than for the splendid **Syon House**, a showcase for the talents of Robert Adam and Capability Brown. There's yet more of Adam's work at **Osterley House**, another Elizabethan conversion now owned by the National Trust, while **Pitshanger Manor** is a must for fans of Sir John Soane's architecture. The latest attraction in these parts is the remarkable **Wetland Centre**, a newly landscaped haven for rare wildfowl, across the river from Hammersmith in the sleepy suburb of Barnes.

Hammersmith Bridge to Chiswick Mall

This chapter starts in the hellhole of **Hammersmith**, for several reasons: the nearby tube station, the riverside walk to Chiswick and easy access to Barnes' Wetland Centre. Hammersmith's heart was ripped out in the 1960s when the Hammersmith Flyover was built to relieve congestion on the Broadway, the main shopping street. This had the simultaneous effect of making the adjacent roundabout one of the busiest traffic intersections in London, and cutting off Hammersmith from the nearby river. The tube, which lies at the middle of the roundabout, is now enveloped on three sides by a shopping mall and an ugly office building that's home to Coca-Cola's UK headquarters.

Squeezed between the Flyover and the railway line is another 1990s landmark, Ralph Erskine's **London Ark**, a ship-shaped office block that's been trumpeted as the city's first ecologically sound building. Inside, the building is flooded with natural light, while triple glazing helps to keep energy in and noise out; from the outside, the result is less laudable, particularly for local residents, as noise from the trains bounces off the building.

The Wetland Centre

Mon–Sat: summer 9.30am–6pm; winter 9.30am–5pm; £6.50; open Sun for WWT members only; ☎020/8409 4400; *www.wetlandcentre.org.uk*. Bus #283 from Hammersmith tube, or walk from Barnes train station.

For anyone even remotely interested in wildlife, the new **Wetland Centre** in well-to-do Barnes is an absolute must. On the site of four disused reservoirs, across the river from Hammersmith, the Wildfowl & Wetland Trust (WWT) has created a high-tech 105-acre mosaic of wetland habitats, a stone's throw from central London. On arrival – unless it's raining – you might as well skip the (albeit superbly produced) introductory audiovisual in the theatre, and head straight out to the ponds, which are peppered with all-weather touch-screen computers and information sheets. If the weather's bad, or you've children with you, however, it's definitely worth visiting the **Discovery Centre**. After a child-centred journey through the virtues of wetlands, kids can head upstairs to take part in a swan identification parade, or take a duck's-eye view of the world, while their minders check out the WWT Web site. You can also look out over the wetlands from the glass-walled **Bird Airport Observatory** next door, or from the tables of the *Water's Edge Café*.

The centre basically serves a dual function: to attract native species of bird to its watery lagoons, and to assist in the WWT's programme of breeding rare wildfowl in captivity. Heading north from the visitor centre, you enter **World Wetlands**, where a network of paths leads you past a variety of extremely rare wildfowl – from White-faced Whistling Ducks to the highly endangered Blue Duck – whose wetland habitats have been re-created in miniature. Beyond, in the **Wildside**, are the reedbeds and pools that attract native species, such as lapwing, tufted ducks, grebes and swans, all of which you can view from a moss-roofed hide. **Waterlife**, east of the visitor centre, includes a sustainable garden, a chance for younger children to get near some domesticated wildfowl, and, best of all, to do some pond-dipping with a WWT volunteer. At the far end, is the mother of all hides: a triple-decker octagonal one with a lift, allowing views over the whole of the reserve.

The riverside walk to Chiswick

This riverside walk may not be possible during very high tides.

The best aspect of Hammersmith is the **riverside walk**, which begins a short way southwest of the roundabout, down Queen Caroline Street. First off, you must pass underneath **Hammersmith Bridge**, a graceful suspension bridge from the 1880s which the IRA first bombed in 1939, as part of their attempt to disrupt the British war effort. They tried to destroy the bridge again in 1996; the splinter group, the Real IRA, is thought to have been behind the latest attack, which took place in June 2000. From the bridge, you can walk all the way to Chiswick along the most picturesque stretch of river bank in the whole of London, much of it closed to traffic.

The University Boat Race, a London institution since 1845, takes place in late March or early April; see p.623.

Lower Mall, the section closest to the bridge, is a mixture of Victorian pubs, boathouses, Regency verandas and modern flats. An interesting array of boats huddles around the marina outside the *Dove*, a seventeenth-century riverside pub (see p.548). This started out as a coffee house and has the smallest back bar in the country, copious literary associations – regulars have included Graham

Greene, Ernest Hemingway and William Morris – and a canopied balcony overlooking the Thames (one of the best places from which to view the annual University Boat Race).

Chiswick to Pitshanger

Kelmscott House is open Thurs & Sat 2–5pm; free; ☎ *020/8741 3735.*

It's strange to think that this genteel part of the Thames was once a hotbed of radicals, who used to congregate at **Kelmscott House**, beyond the *Dove* at 26 Upper Mall, where William Morris lived and worked from 1878 until his death in 1896. (Morris used to berate the locals from a soapbox on Hammersmith Bridge.) The basement now houses the original Kelmscott Press and the offices of the William Morris Society, who hold meetings in the adjacent Coach House. From 1885 onwards, the Hammersmith Branch of the Socialist League and later the Hammersmith Socialist Society used to meet here on a Sunday evening. Keir Hardie (first leader of the parliamentary Labour Party), anarchist Prince Kropotkin, George Bernard Shaw and Fabian founders the Webbs were among the speakers, and their photos now line the walls.

Chiswick Mall

A modern, pedestrianized section of the embankment connects the Upper Mall with **Hammersmith Terrace**, a line of tall Georgian houses built facing the river sometime before 1755. **Chiswick Mall**, which marks the end of Hammersmith, continues for another mile or so to the riverside village of Chiswick. A riotous ensemble of seventeenth- and eighteenth-century mansions lines the north side of the Mall, which cuts them off from their modest riverside gardens. Halfway along, a particularly fine trio ends with **Walpole House**, once the home of Barbara Villiers, Duchess of Cleveland, Countess of Castlemaine and mistress of Charles II.

Chiswick Mall terminates at the church of **St Nicholas**, built mostly in the last century, but retaining its original fifteenth-century ragstone tower. The church lay at the heart of the riverside village of **Chiswick** from medieval times until the nineteenth century, when the action moved north to Chiswick High Street, its modern heart. Lord Burlington and his architect friends William Kent and Colen Campbell are all buried in the graveyard, as is the aforementioned Barbara Villiers, though only the painters William Hogarth and James Whistler are commemorated by gravestones, the former enclosed by wrought-iron railings.

Church Lane was the medieval village high street. Its oldest building today is the *Old Burlington*, originally a sixteenth-century inn, and now a private residence. Beyond it lies the huge **Fuller's Brewery**, dating back to the seventeenth century and still going strong. You can book yourself onto a guided tour, which includes the inevitable tasting session, and also gives visitors the chance to see the country's oldest wisteria, which has clung to the brickwork for over 180 years. To continue on to Chiswick House, head across Powell's Walk (behind the church),

Guided tours of Fuller's take place Mon & Wed–Fri, but you must pre-book; £5; ☎ *020/8996 2000;* www .fullers.co.uk.

to Burlington Lane, which runs along the southeastern edge of
the house gardens.

Chiswick House and around

April–Sept daily 10am–6pm; first three weeks of Oct daily 10am–5pm; late
Oct–March Wed–Sun 10am–4pm; EH; £3.30; ☎020/8995 0508. Chiswick
train station, from Waterloo.

Chiswick House is a perfect little classical villa, designed by Richard
Boyle, third Earl of Burlington, in the 1720s, and set in one of the
most beautifully landscaped gardens in London. Like its prototype,
Palladio's Villa Rotonda near Vicenza, the house was purpose-built as
a "temple to the arts" – here, amid his fine art collection, Burlington
used to entertain such friends as Swift, Handel and Alexander Pope,
who lived in nearby Twickenham.

Guests and visitors (who could view the property on payment of an
admission fee even in Lord Burlington's day) would originally have
ascended the quadruple staircase and entered the *piano nobile*
(upper floor) through the magnificent Corinthian portico. The public entrance today is via the **lower floor**, where the earl had his own
private rooms and kept his extensive library. Here, you can pick up
an audioguide from the main desk, watch a short video on the house,
and peruse an exhibition on the history of the house and grounds, a
trio of Roman statues brought back from Hadrian's villa at Tivoli and
a bronze sphinx.

Entertaining took place on the **upper floor**, a series of cleverly
interconnecting rooms, each enjoying a wonderful view out onto the
gardens – all, that is, except the Tribunal, the domed octagonal hall
at the centre of the villa, where the earl's finest paintings and sculptures would have been displayed. The Tribunal and other rooms are
largely empty, but retain much of their rich décor, in particular the
ceilings, designed by William Kent. The most sumptuous is the Blue
Velvet Room, decorated in a deep Prussian blue with eight pairs of
heavy gilded brackets holding up the ceiling. The finest views onto
the garden are from the Gallery, a series of interconnecting rooms,
all enclosed in deference to the English climate.

The gardens

*Admission to
the gardens is
free; daily
8am–dusk.*

If you're a bit lost by the finer points of classical architecture, you'll
probably get more pleasure from the house's extensive **gardens**, an
intriguing mixture of earlier, formal elements and more "natural"
features added under Kent's direction. The gardens span the period
in the history of English gardening when tastes fluctuated from the
geometrical Versailles-like style to the freer – but equally well-
orchestrated – designs perfected by the likes of Capability Brown.

To do a quick circuit of the gardens, head south from the front
entrance of the house and cross the once-straight canal that was transformed into an irregular "natural" shape by Kent. It served as the

prototype for other artificial lakes, like the Serpentine in Hyde Park, and is the setting for England's first mock ruin, the Kent-designed cascade.

To the west of the lake is one of two *pattes d'oie* – designs made up of straight-hedged alleyways radiating from a central focal point, in this case the obelisk, at the far end of the nearby terrace. The other goosefoot lies to the northeast of James Wyatt's elegant stone bridge from 1774, and is made up of a network of narrow yew-hedge avenues, each one ending at some diminutive building or statue. Neither goosefoot survives in its original form, however, as winding paths were reintroduced in the 1780s when the vogue for informality returned. One of the most remarkable focal points is the grassy amphitheatre, by the side of the lake, centred on an obelisk in a pond and overlooked by an Ionic temple.

A great place from which to admire the northwest side of the house is from the stone benches of the exedra, a set of yew-hedge niches harbouring lions and copies of Roman statuary, and overlooking a smooth carpet of grass, punctuated by urns and sphinxes, that sit under the shadow of two giant cedars of Lebanon.

To the north of the villa, beside a section of the gardens' old ha-ha, stands a grand stone gateway designed by Inigo Jones (one of Burlington's heroes); it was bequeathed by Burlington's doctor, Hans Sloane, and brought here from Beaufort House in Chelsea in 1736. Beyond the gateway lies a large conservatory which looks out onto the formal **Italian Garden**, laid out in the early nineteenth century by the sixth Duke of Devonshire, who also established a zoo (now sadly gone) featuring an elephant, giraffe, elks and emus.

Hogarth's House

April–Oct Tues–Fri 1–5pm, Sat & Sun 1–6pm; Nov–March closes one hour earlier; closed Jan; free; ☎020/8994 6757.

If you leave Chiswick gardens by the northernmost exit, beyond the conservatory, it's just a short walk (to the right) along the thunderous A4 road to **Hogarth's House**, where the artist spent each summer with his wife, sister and mother-in-law from 1749 until his death in 1764. Nowadays it's difficult to believe Hogarth came here for "peace and quiet", but in the eighteenth century the house was almost entirely surrounded by countryside. After Chiswick House, which epitomized everything Hogarth loathed the most, the domesticity here comes as some relief. Among the scores of Hogarth's engravings, you can see copies of his satirical series – *An Election, Marriage à la Mode, A Rake's Progress* and *A Harlot's Progress* – and compare the modern view from the parlour with the more idyllic scene in *Mr Ranby's House*.

Gunnersbury Park and around

An even earlier Palladian villa, built by Inigo Jones's son-in-law, John Webb, once stood in **Gunnersbury Park**, a mile or so to the

*The museum is
open April–Oct
Mon–Fri
1–5pm, Sat &
Sun 1–6pm;
Nov–March
closes one
hour earlier;
free;* ☎ *020
/8992 1612.
Acton Town
tube.*

northwest of Chiswick House. In 1801 the villa was demolished and the estate divided (hence the park's two adjacent mansions), only to be reunited under the wealthy Rothschild family in the late nineteenth century. The larger of the mansions is now the **Gunnersbury Park Museum**, with interesting temporary exhibitions on the local boroughs of Ealing and Hounslow, a fully restored set of Victorian kitchens (only viewable at the weekend), and a permanent collection of historical vehicles, including a tandem tricycle and the Rothschilds' own Victorian "chariot". The park itself has been largely given over to sports pitches, but overlooking the boating pond to the west of the museum there's a fine relic of the park's previous existence: a Neoclassical temple erected by George II's daughter Amelia, who used to spend her summers at the aforementioned Palladian villa. It was later used as a private synagogue by the Rothschilds.

Adjoining the park's southeast corner is a section of **Kensington Cemetery**, which contains a black marble obelisk erected in 1976 to the 14,500 Polish POWs who went missing in 1940, when the Nazi–Soviet Pact carved up Poland. A mass grave containing 4500 was later discovered by the advancing Nazis at Katyn, near Smolensk, but responsibility for the massacre was denied by the Russians until fifty years later, as a new plaque bitterly records. Fifty yards to the south is the grave of General Komorowski, leader of the Polish Home Army during the ill-fated 1944 Warsaw Uprising, who lived in exile in Britain until his death in 1966. Also buried here is the film director Carol Reed, best known as the director of *The Third Man*. There's no direct access to the graveyard from the park; the main entrance is quarter of a mile further south down Gunnersbury Avenue.

London Transport Depot Museum

Open days Sun 11am–5pm; £6.95; ☎ 020/7379 6344; *www.ltmuseum.co.uk*. Acton Town tube.

*The main
London
Transport
Museum is in
Covent
Garden, see
p.153.*

The London Transport Museum houses its reserve collection in the purpose-built **Depot Museum**, beside the Piccadilly Track & Signal Operation Centre opposite Acton Town tube. It's a hangar-like building, stuffed full of unlabelled bits and bobs, from old signs and maps to fog repeater signals and the insides of old engines – in other words, a specialist's paradise. However, along with the usual parade of buses and trains, there are one or two sections that have wider appeal, such as the Poster Store, which holds around 16,000 examples of tube artwork, and the LT films shown in the cinema. Also of interest are the various prototypes of projects now consigned to the historical dustbin, like CrossRail, which was supposed to become a high-speed rail link between mainline stations. The museum is only open by guided tour or on open days, during which there are usually various train and bus-spotting stalls and one or two other activities laid on.

Kew Bridge Steam Museum

Daily 11am–5pm; Mon–Fri £3; Sat & Sun £4; ☎020/8568 4757; *www.kbsm
.org.uk*. Kew Bridge train station, from Waterloo; or bus #237 or #267 from
Gunnersbury tube.

Difficult to miss thanks to its stylish Italianate standpipe tower, yet
largely overlooked as a tourist attraction, **Kew Bridge Steam
Museum** occupies the former Grand Junction Water Works pumping
station, on the corner of Kew Bridge Road and Green Dragon Lane,
100yd west of the bridge itself. At the heart of the museum is the
Steam Hall, which contains a triple expansion steam engine, similar
in date and construction to the one used by the *Titanic*, and four
gigantic nineteenth-century Cornish beam engines (one of which was
only decommissioned in 1983), while two adjoining rooms house the
pumping station's original beam engines, including the world's
largest.

The steam engines may be things of great beauty, but they are primarily of interest to enthusiasts. Not so the museum's state-of-the-art
"Water for Life" gallery, devoted to the history of the capital's water
supply. Situated in the basement and overlooked by a vast bank of
ancient boilers, baths, sinks, taps and kettles, the exhibition employs
plenty of hands-on features to enliven the subject. The section on rats
and cockroaches goes down particularly well with kids, while the tales
of the Victorian "toshers", who had to work the sewers in gangs of
three to protect themselves from rat attacks, will make adults' stom-
achs turn. The best time to visit is at weekends, when each of the
museum's industrial dinosaurs is put through its paces, and the small
narrow-gauge steam railway runs back and forth round the yard.

Musical Museum

April–Oct Sat & Sun 2–5pm; July & Aug also Wed 2–4pm; £3.50; ☎020/8560
8108. Kew Bridge train station, from Waterloo; or bus #237 or #267 from
Gunnersbury tube.

Five minutes' walk west of the Steam Museum along a bleak section
of Brentford High Street is the superb **Musical Museum**, a converted ragstone church packed with fully functioning musical automata
and run by wildly enthusiastic and engaging volunteers. During the
noisy ninety-minute demonstrations, you get to hear – and often lend
a hand with – every kind of mechanical music-making machine from
cleverly crafted music boxes, through badly tuned barrel organs, to
the huge orchestrions that were once a feature of London cafés. The
museum also boasts one of the world's finest collections of player-
pianos, including a "Duo-Art" grand, which can reproduce live performances of the great pianists. In addition, there are fortnightly
concerts on Saturday evenings throughout the summer, performed
on the museum's enormous Art Deco Wurlitzer, which once graced
the Regal cinema in Kingston-upon-Thames.

Syon Park

Syon Park, directly across the Thames from Kew Gardens (see p.464), was once one of the richest monasteries in the country. Established by Henry V after the Battle of Agincourt, it was dissolved by Henry VIII, who incarcerated his fifth wife, Catherine Howard, here shortly before her execution in 1542. Half a century later Queen Elizabeth I granted the **Syon** estate to the Percys, earls (later dukes) of Northumberland, whose property it remains. These days, however, it's more of a working commercial concern than a family home, embracing a garden centre – the country's first when it opened in 1965 – a wholefood shop, a trout fishery, an aquatic centre stocked with tropical fish, a mini-zoo and a butterfly house, as well as the old mansion.

The House

March–Oct Wed, Thurs & Sun 11am–5pm; £6, including entry to the gardens; ☎020/8560 0881; *www.syonpark.co.uk*. Bus #237 or #267 from Gunnersbury tube or Kew Bridge train station, or fifteen minutes' walk from Syon Lane train station.

From its rather plain Elizabethan exterior, with corner turrets and rigid castellations, you'd never guess that **Syon House** contains the most opulent eighteenth-century interiors in the whole of London. The splendour of Robert Adam's refurbishment is immediately revealed, however, in the pristine **Great Hall**, where you can pick up the excellent free audioguide. An apsed double cube with a screen of Doric columns at one end and classical statuary dotted around the edges, the chequered marble floor of the Great Hall cleverly mirrors the pattern of the coffered ceiling. It was here – or rather, in the hall's Tudor predecessor – that Henry VIII's body lay in state en route to Windsor, and was discovered the next morning surrounded by a pack of hounds happily lapping the blood seeping from the coffin.

From the austerity of the Great Hall you enter the lavishly decorated **Ante Room**, with its florid scagliola floor (made from a mixture of marble-dust and resin) and its green-grey Ionic columns topped by brightly gilded classical statues. Here, guests could mingle before entering the **Dining Room**, a compromise between the two preceding rooms, richly gilded but otherwise calm in its overall effect. The remaining rooms are warmer and softer in tone, betraying their Elizabethan origins much more than the preceding ones. The **Red Drawing Room** retains its original red silk wall hangings from Spitalfields, upon which are hung portraits of the Stuarts by Lely, van Dyck and others, and features a splendid ceiling studded with over two hundred roundels set within gilded hexagons. Off the Red Drawing Room, you can now glimpse the Duke's Study.

Beyond, the **Long Gallery** – 136ft by just 14ft – stretches the entire width of the house, decorated by Adam's busy pink and gold plasterwork and lined with 62 individually painted pilasters. It was in the Long Gallery that Lady Jane Grey was formally offered the crown by her father-in-law, John Dudley, the owner of Syon at the time; nine days later they were arrested and later beheaded by "Bloody Mary". At the end of the Long Gallery, you can step into the richly decorated **Turret Room**, nicknamed the birthday cake room, which has a mechanical singing bird in a gilded cage. Off the **Print Room**, containing yet more works by Lely and Van Dyck, plus a couple by Gainsborough and Reynolds, are the Duchess's Sitting Room, and, more strikingly, the **Green Drawing Room**, still used by the family, with its superb Adam fireplace, ornate fan-patterned ceiling and portraits by Holbein and Reynolds. Off the narrow Oak Passage is the **Private Dining Room**, with its spectacular chandelier, now hired out by the family for private functions.

At the foot of the modest principal staircase stands a monster golden **Sèvres vase**, a present to the first duke from Charles X of France for having attended his coronation in 1825. At the top of the staircase is a much more delicate **Sèvres dinner service** with sufficient pieces to serve a thousand guests. Along the passage, the old nursery has been turned into an Edwardian gentleman's bedroom, and further along is an elegant lady's boudoir of the same period. Round the corner past the bathroom, two more bedrooms face each other, refurbished in 1832 for Princess Victoria and her mother, the Duchess of Kent, with magnificent canopied beds, blue silk outside and yellow within. At the end of the passage is the **State Bedroom**, where visiting royals were put up in a red four-poster with an exquisitely embroidered gold bedspread.

The gardens

Daily 10am–5.30pm; £3, or free with ticket to the house.

While Adam beautified Syon House, Capability Brown laid out its **gardens** around an artificial lake, surrounding it with oaks, beeches, limes and cedars. Since then, the gardens have been further enhanced by still more exotic trees, ranging from an Indian bean tree to a pagoda tree. Beside the lake, there's a stretch of lawn overlooked by a Doric column topped by a fibreglass statue of Flora, but the gardens' real highlight is the crescent-shaped **Great Conservatory**, an early nineteenth-century addition which is said to have inspired Joseph Paxton, architect of the Crystal Palace. Those with young children will be compelled to make use of the **miniature steam train** which runs through the park at weekends from April to October, and on Wednesdays during the school holidays.

The London Butterfly House

Daily: April–Sept 10am–5pm; Oct–March 10am–3.30pm; £3.30; *www .butterflies.org.uk*. ☎020/8560 7272.

Another plus point for kids (and adults) at Syon is the **Butterfly House**, across the car park from the house and gardens. Here, in a small, mesh-covered hothouse, you can walk amid hundreds of exotic butterflies from all over the world, as they flit about the foliage. The largest inhabitant is the Giant Atlas Moth, which only flies at night, but can be admired from close quarters as it sleeps. Displays show the butterfly in its stages of metamorphosis, and an adjoining room houses a collection of iguanas, millipedes, tarantulas and giant hissing Tanzanian cockroaches.

London Aquatic Experience

Daily 10am–5pm; £3.50; ☎020/8847 4730; *www.aquatic-experience.org*.

If your kids show more enthusiasm for life-threatening reptiles than delicate insects, then you could skip the Butterfly House entirely and head for the **London Aquatic Experience** instead. The small purpose-built centre, which is adjacent to the Butterfly House, contains a modest but mixed range of aquatic creatures from the mysterious basilisk, which can walk on water, to the perennially popular piranhas, both vegetarian and carnivorous. Other favourites include several lethal snakes, a few crocodiles, a small falconry and some charming, tiny, brightly coloured tree frogs. There's also a mini-farm next door to the building.

Osterley Park

Daily 9am–7.30pm or dusk; free. Osterley tube.

Robert Adam redesigned another colossal Elizabethan mansion three miles northwest of Syon at **Osterley Park** – one of London's largest surviving estate parks, which still gives the impression of being in the middle of the countryside, despite the presence of the M4 to the north of the house. The main approach is along a splendid avenue of sweet chestnuts to the south, past the National Trust-sponsored farmhouse (whose produce you can buy all year round). From the car park, the driveway curves past the southernmost of the park's three lakes, with a Chinese pagoda at one end. Cedars planted in the 1820s and oaks planted in Victorian times stand between the lake and the house, and to the north are the grandiose Tudor stables of first owner Thomas Gresham, now converted into a café.

Osterley House

April–Oct Wed–Sun 1–4.30pm; NT; £4.20; ☎020/8568 3164.

Unlike Syon, **Osterley House** was built with mercantile rather than aristocratic wealth – it was erected in 1576 by Thomas Gresham, the brains behind the City's Royal Exchange. Two hundred and fifty years later it was bought by yet another City gent, the goldsmith and banker Francis Child, who appears to have used it merely as a kind of giant safe-deposit box – it was his grandsons who employed Robert Adam to create the house as it is today.

From the outside, Osterley bears some similarity to Syon, the big difference being Adam's grand entrance portico, with a broad flight of steps rising to a tall, Ionic colonnade, which gives access to the central courtyard. From here, you enter Adam's characteristically cool **Entrance Hall**, a double-apsed space decorated with grisaille paintings and classical statuary. The finest rooms are the so-called State Rooms of the south wing, where the *nouveaux riches* Childs hoped, vainly, to entertain royalty as Gresham had once done. The **Drawing Room** is splendid, with Reynolds portraits on the damask walls and a coffered ceiling centred on a giant marigold, a theme continued in the lush carpet and elsewhere in the house. The **Tapestry Room** is hung with Boucher-designed Gobelin tapestries, while the silk-lined **State Bedchamber** features an outrageous domed bed designed by Adam. Lastly, there's the **Etruscan Dressing Room**, in which every surface is covered in delicate painted trellis-work, sphinxes and urns, a style that Adam (and Wedgwood) dubbed "Etruscan", though it is in fact derived from Greek vases found at Pompeii.

The **Long Gallery** is much broader, taller and plainer than the one at Syon and, like much of the house, features Adam-designed furniture, as well as some fine chinoiserie. Sadly, the Childs' collection of Rubens, Van Dyck and Claude pictures no longer hangs here, having been transported to the family's new home in the Channel Islands (where they were destroyed by fire), and replaced instead by second-rank works from the V&A.

The north wing is disappointing after the State Rooms, though the whitewashed Library is worth a quick peek. The Neoclassical **Great Staircase**, stuck rather awkwardly halfway along the north wing, has a replica Rubens ceiling painting, the original having been destroyed by fire while being removed by the last owner in 1949. Only a few rooms are open on the first floor, each one pleasant enough but by no means essential viewing.

The Hanwell Flight and Boston Manor

The **Grand Union Canal** skirts Osterley Park to the north, linking up with the River Brent, which in turn flows into the Thames at Brentford. You can walk along the towpath at any point, but the most interesting section is the sequence of five manually operated locks known as the **Hanwell Flight**, a mile or so up from where the M4 crosses the canal near Boston Manor tube. Here, the canal drops over fifty feet in less than a quarter of a mile and, though few boats now use the canal, you're quite likely to see some action most weekends.

To the southeast of Boston Manor tube, down Boston Gardens, is the seventeenth-century **Boston Manor House**. With magnificent cedar trees and ornamental flowerbeds, the grounds are well worth a visit, even though the M4 cuts right through the middle. If you come on a weekend afternoon in summer you can also visit the house, the

Chiswick to Pitshanger

If you arrive by public transport, you get a £1 reduction off the price of your ticket (or £1 off the guidebook if you're an NT member); car drivers must pay £2.50 to park.

The nearest tube is Boston Manor.

Boston Manor House is open April–Oct Sat & Sun 2.30–5pm; free; ☎ 020/8560 5441.

highlight of which is the extraordinarily elaborate Jacobean ceiling of the first-floor Drawing Room.

Pitshanger Manor

Tues–Sat 10am–5pm; free; ☎020/8567 1227. Ealing Broadway tube.

One last west London country house worth a mention is **Pitshanger Manor**, a couple of miles north of Boston Manor, southwest of Ealing Broadway on Mattock Lane. Built in 1770, it was later bought and remodelled by Sir John Soane, who in 1811 sold up and moved to Lincoln's Inn Fields (see p.204). In time Pitshanger became the local library, but in the late 1980s the house was superbly restored. The balustraded main facade, though small, is magnificent, its bays divided by Ionic pillars topped by terracotta statues. As soon as you enter the narrow vestibule, Soane stops you short with some spatial gymnastics by taking a section of the ceiling up through the first floor. To the right is the now bookless Library, which features a cross-vaulted ceiling, decorated with an unusual trelliswork pattern. Soane's masterpiece, though, as at Lincoln's Inn Fields, is the **Breakfast Room**, with caryatids in the four corners and lush red porphyry and grey marbling on the walls.

An unexpected bonus is the **Martinware gallery**, a display of the idiosyncratic stoneware pottery produced around the turn of the century by the four Martin brothers from the nearby Southall Pottery. Its centrepiece is their Moorish ceramic fireplace, made for the billiard room at Buscot Park, Oxfordshire. The rest of the ware, including face mugs and bird jars, is more of an acquired taste.

The manor's south wing is all that survives from the original house by George Dance (Soane's architectural teacher), the remainder of which Soane demolished. The rooms here are on a much larger scale, providing an interesting contrast to Soane's intimate and highly wrought style, while the Monk's Dining Room in the basement is the precursor of the Monk's Parlour in Lincoln's Inn Fields.

Richmond and Kew

Richmond and Kew, on the south bank of the Thames, basked for centuries in the glow of royal patronage. Plantagenet kings and Tudor monarchs frequented the riverside palace of Shene, as Richmond Palace was then called, while the Hanoverians favoured the royal estates to the north – now the **botanical gardens** of Kew, which manages to be a world leader in botanical research and an extraordinarily beautiful park at the same time. In the eighteenth century Richmond enjoyed a brief life as a spa, and its agreeable locale began to attract City merchants, as well as successful artists, actors and writers: Pope, Gainsborough, Garrick and Reynolds are just some of the plaque-worthy names associated with the place.

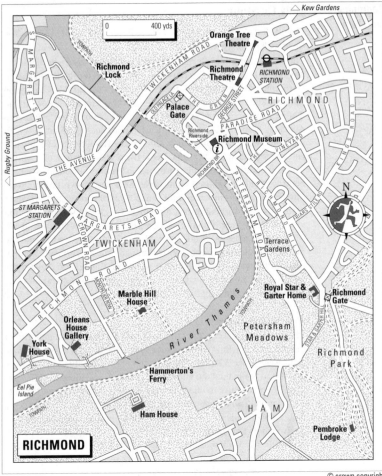

Although most of the courtiers and aristocrats have gone, as has the Tudor palace on Richmond Green, **Richmond** is still a wealthy district, with two theatres and highbrow pretensions. In reality, though, it's been a commuter town since the arrival of the railway in the 1870s. To appreciate its attractions fully, you need to visit the old village green, walk along the riverside to one of the nearby stately homes of Ham (see p.473) or Marble Hill (see p.474), take in the glorious view from **Richmond Hill** and pay a visit to the vast acreage of **Richmond Park**, the old royal hunting grounds, still wild and replete with deer.

Kew Gardens

Daily 9.30am–7.30pm or dusk; £5; ☎020/8332 5000; *www.kew.org*. Kew
Gardens tube and train station.

The **Royal Botanical Gardens** started out as a pleasure garden, created in 1731 by Prince Frederick, eldest son of George II and Queen
Caroline, who considered their offspring "the greatest ass, the
greatest liar, the greatest canaille and the greatest beast in the
whole world". But it was the widow of "Poor Fred", Princess
Augusta, who established Kew's first botanical gardens in 1759,
with the help of her paramour, the Earl of Bute. Some of the earliest specimens were brought back from the voyages of Captain
Cook, instantly establishing Kew as a leading botanical research
centre. From its original eight acres Kew has grown into a three-
hundred-acre site in which more than 33,000 species are grown in
plantations and glasshouses, a display that attracts over a million
visitors every year, most of them with no specialist interest at all.
The only drawbacks with Kew are the prohibitive entry fee, and the
fact that flights to Heathrow occasionally pass overhead. Though
there's always something to see whatever the season, to get the
most out of the place, visit sometime between spring and autumn,
bring a picnic and stay for the day.

The glasshouses

There are four entry points to the gardens, but the vast majority of
people arrive at Kew Gardens tube and train station, a few minutes'
walk east of the **Victoria Gate**, at the end of Lichfield Road. Here
you'll find the main shop and visitor centre, with videos and displays
about Kew. Be sure to check out the Kew Mural as you pass through
– it's an unattractive piece of art, but it's made from 23 varieties of
wood, and stands as a testimony to the thousand trees damaged or
destroyed at Kew in the 1987 storm. If at any point you're trying to
find your way back to the Victoria Gate, look out for the **Campanile**
that stands right next to it and originally served as the chimney for
the furnaces below the Palm House.

Beyond lies the Pond, home to a handful of black swans and two
ten-ton Ming lions, and the best vantage point from which to appreciate the **Palm House**, the first and most famous of Kew's magnificent array of glasshouses. A curvaceous mound of glass and wrought
iron, the Palm House was designed by Decimus Burton in the 1840s,
predating the Crystal Palace by some three years. Its drippingly
humid atmosphere nurtures most of the known palm species, while
in the basement there's a small but excellent tropical aquarium (signposted "Marine Display"). You can turn the heat up further by going
to the diminutive **Waterlily House** (north of the Palm House), where
a canopy of plants and creepers overhangs a circular pond boasting
spectacular giant waterlilies.

To cool off, head for the **Princess of Wales Conservatory**, a rather less graceful glasshouse a little further to the north. Opened in 1987, it nurtures plants from ten distinct climatic zones, ranging from cactus-infested desert to cloud forest. Giant koi fish swim stealthily beneath the pathways, while giant waterlilies and visitors alike benefit from intermittent artificial rainfall; an ecological slide show takes place in the underground exhibition hall.

The largest of all the glasshouses is the **Temperate House**, another of Decimus Burton's innovative structures, twice the size of the Palm House and almost forty years in the making. It contains plants from every continent, including one of the largest indoor palms in the world, the sixty-foot Chilean Wine Palm, first planted in 1846 and currently approaching the roof – and therefore the end of its life.

The eighteenth-century gardens

Almost nothing survives of William Chambers' landscape gardening at Kew, but some of the buildings he created in the 1760s for the amusement of Princess Augusta remain dotted about the gardens. The **Orangery** was one of the earliest, and the largest hothouse in the country when it was built; it now houses a restaurant and shop. The most famous is his ten-storey, 163-foot-high **Pagoda**, Kew's most distinctive landmark, though disappointing close up, having lost the eighty enamelled dragons that used to adorn it. More fun close up is the ornate **Japanese Gateway**, a legacy of the 1911 Japanese Exhibition, built in cedar wood and topped by a copper roof, which stands nearby in a sort of miniature tea garden.

To the north of the Pagoda, you can walk through Chambers' **Ruined Arch**, purpose-built with sundry pieces of Roman masonry strewn about as if tossed there by barbarian hordes. Close by is Kew's tallest object, a 225-foot-high flagpole fashioned from a single Canadian fir tree and erected in 1959. The rest of Chambers' works are all classical temples, the most picturesque being the **Temple of Aeolus**, situated close to Cumberland Gate on one of Kew's few hillocks, surrounded by a carpet of bluebells and daffodils in the spring.

Capability Brown's work on the gardens at Kew has proved more durable than Chambers': his lake remains a focal point of the Syon vista from the Palm House, and the **Rhododendron Dell** he devised survives to the south of it. This more thickly wooded, southwestern section of the park is the bit to head for if you want to lose the crowds, few of whom ever make it to **Queen Charlotte's Cottage**, a tiny thatched summerhouse built in brick and timber in the 1770s as a royal picnic spot for George III's wife. There's very little to see inside, beyond a room of Hogarth prints and a trompe l'oeil pergola, but the surrounding native woodland is a peaceful haven, carpeted with bluebells in spring.

The Cottage is open April–Sept Sat & Sun 10.30am–4pm; free.

Kew Palace

Clearly visible to the west of the Orangery stands the country's smallest royal residence, **Kew Palace**, a three-storey red-brick mansion measuring a mere 70ft by 50ft, and commonly known as the "Dutch House", after its fancy Flemish-bond brickwork and its curly Dutch gables. It's the sole survivor of the three royal palaces that once stood at Kew and was bought by George II as a nursery for his umpteen children. The only king to live here, though, was George III, who was confined here from 1802 onwards and subjected to the dubious attentions of two doctors who attempted to find a cure for his "madness" by straitjacketing him and applying poultices of mustard and Spanish fly. The palace, and the secluded Queen's Garden behind it, have recently been restored and are both worth a peek (there is a separate entrance charge for the palace).

Museum No. 1

Despite its rather unpromising title, Kew's newly restored **Museum No. 1**, on the other side of the Pond from the Palm House, provides another excellent wet-weather retreat. Inside is an exhibition entitled "Plants and People", which shows the myriad uses to which humans have put plants, from food and medicines to clothes and tools. Along with the usual static glass-case displays, there are also touch-screen computers to hand, a scent station and various hands-on exhibits which should keep younger visitors happy.

The art galleries

Kew also boasts two little-known art galleries, some distance from one another along the eastern edge of the gardens. **Kew Gardens Gallery**, the larger of the two, is in the northeastern corner of the gardens in Cambridge Cottage, originally the Earl of Bute's residence but rebuilt in Queen Anne style in 1867. The gallery puts on temporary exhibitions on a wide variety of horticultural themes. To the south of Victoria Gate stands the **Marianne North Gallery**, purpose-built in 1882 to house the prolific output of the self-trained artist Marianne North. Over eight hundred paintings, completed in fourteen years of hectic world travel, are displayed end to end, filling every single space in the gallery.

Kew Green and the Public Record Office

Decimus Burton's majestic **Main Gates** fulfilled their stated function until the arrival of the railway at Kew. Nowadays, you only get to see them if you're walking from Kew Bridge or exploring **Kew Green**, which rivals Richmond's for the accolade of London's prettiest village green. Lined with Georgian houses, the green is centred on the delightful church of **St Anne**, an unusual building sporting a Victorian polygonal clock turret at one end and a peculiar Georgian octagonal cupola at the other. The light, barrel-vaulted interior is lined with Tuscan columns and sports a royal gallery at the west end; the painters Gainsborough and Zoffany lie in the churchyard.

Richmond and Kew

Hidden in the residential backstreets of Kew is the **Public Record Office** (*www.pro.gov.uk*), which moved wholesale into new, rather nasty-looking beige and green premises in the late 1990s. Its research library is full of historians consulting primary source materials, while its **education and visitor centre** displays some fascinating artefacts ranging from the Domesday Book and the trial record of Charles I, to Queen Victoria's 1851 census return and Elton John's Deed Poll certificate changing his name (wisely) from Reginald Kenneth Dwight. In addition, you can listen to extracts from the record books through headphones, from Churchill's "Finest Hour" speech to an account of child slavery from the 1770s.

The Public Records Office museum is open Mon, Wed & Fri 9am–5pm, Tues 10am–7pm, Thurs 9am–7pm, Sat 9.30am–5pm; free; ☎020 8392 5202.

Richmond Green and Palace

On emerging from the station at Richmond, you'd be forgiven for wondering why you're here, but the procession of chain stores spread out along the one-way system is only half the story. To see Richmond's more interesting side, take one of the narrow pedestrianized alleyways off busy George Street, a few minutes' walk west of the station. Lined with arty shops and tea rooms, these will bring you to the wide open space of **Richmond Green**, one of the finest village greens in London, and no doubt one of the most peaceful before it found itself on the main flight path into Heathrow. Handsome seventeenth- and eighteenth-century houses line the southwest and southeast sides of the green, with the most striking building of all, the flamboyant Richmond Theatre, designed by the great Frank Matcham in terracotta and brick in 1899, on Little Green, to the northeast of its larger neighbour.

Richmond tourist office is open Mon–Sat 10am–5pm; Easter–Sept also Sun 10.15am–1.30pm; ☎020 /8940 9125.

The southwest side of the green is the site of medieval **Richmond Palace**, built originally in the twelfth century (when it was known as Shene Palace) and acquired by Henry I in 1125. The first king to frequent the place was Edward III, who lay dying here in 1377 while his mistress urged the servants to prise the rings from his fingers. Seventeen years later a grief-stricken Richard II razed the place to the ground after his wife, Anne of Bohemia, died here of plague. Henry V had it restored and Edward IV held jousting tournaments on the green, but it was Henry VII, in an untypical burst of extravagance, who constructed the largest complex of all, renaming it Richmond after his Yorkshire earldom. Henry VIII later granted the palace to his fourth wife, Anne of Cleves, as part of their surprisingly amicable divorce settlement. Queen Mary and Philip of Spain spent part of their honeymoon here and Elizabeth I came here to die in 1603.

Very little of Richmond Palace survived the Commonwealth and even less is visible now. The most obvious relic is the unspectacular

Tudor Gateway, on the south side of the green; to the left, the building calling itself Old Palace incorporates some of the Tudor brickwork of the outer wall. The gateway, which once led into the palace's outer courtyard, now takes you into **Old Palace Yard,** a sort of miniature village green, and Crown property even today. The palace's furnishings, and over two thousand dresses belonging to Elizabeth I, were once stored in the building on the left – a trio of houses known collectively as the **Wardrobe.**

Richmond Riverside

From April to October you can rent row-boats from the nearby jetties, or take a boat trip to Hampton Court or Westminster.

Neglected for many years, the main river-frontage of **Richmond Riverside** was pedestrianized, terraced and redeveloped by Quinlan Terry in the late 1980s. To the untrained eye, the Georgian buildings initially look convincing enough, but closer inspection reveals them to be a sham: the cupolas conceal air vents, the chimneys are decorative and the facades hide offices and flats. A few of the original Georgian and Victorian buildings do remain, though, like **Heron House,** a narrow three-storey building where Lady Hamilton and her daughter Horatia came to live shortly after Trafalgar, the battle in which the girl's father died. Steps lead through the house's ground-level arch to the desolate space of Heron Square, which looks like a film set without the extras.

The museum is open Tues–Sat 11am–5pm; May–Oct also Sun 1–4pm; £2; ☎020 /8332 1141.

The old town hall, set slightly back from the new development, to the north, now houses the **tourist office** (*www.guidetorichmond .co.uk*), a library and, on the second floor, the **Richmond Museum.** The museum contains a small permanent exhibition on the history of the town, plus the lowdown on (and a model of) the royal palace; temporary displays tend to focus on Richmond's past luminaries. However, the real joy of the waterfront is **Richmond Bridge** to the south – an elegant span of five arches made from Purbeck stone in 1777, and cleverly widened in the 1930s, thus preserving London's oldest extant bridge. If you continue along the towpath beyond Richmond Bridge, you will eventually come to Ham House – for more on this riverside walk, see p.473.

Richmond Hill

If you're still wondering what's so special about Richmond, take a hike up **Richmond Hill.** To get there, head up Hill Rise from the top of Bridge Street, passing Nathan's the tobacconist, and between the eighteenth-century antique shops and tearooms on your left, and the small sloping green on your right. Eventually you come to **Terrace Gardens,** which stretch right down to the river. The gardens are worth exploring but are most celebrated for the view from the top terrace out across the thickly wooded Thames valley. Turner, Reynolds, Kokoschka and countless other artists have painted this view, which takes in six counties from Windsor to the North Downs.

Richmond's wealthiest inhabitants have flocked to the hill's commanding heights over the centuries. The future George IV is alleged to have spent his secret honeymoon at 3 **The Terrace**, after marrying Mrs Fitzherbert; twice divorced and a Catholic to boot, she was never likely to gain official approval, though she bore the prince ten children. Further along, on the opposite side of the street, William Chambers built **Wick House** in 1772 as a summer residence for the enormously successful Joshua Reynolds. The building currently houses the nurses who work at the nearby **Royal Star & Garter Home**, a rest home for war veterans built shortly after World War I, and now the dominant feature of the hillside.

Richmond Park

Daily March–Sept 7am–dusk; Oct–Feb 7.30am–dusk; free; ☎020/8948 3209; *www.royalparks.co.uk*. Richmond tube.

Richmond's greatest attraction is the enormous **Richmond Park**, at the top of Richmond Hill – 2500 acres of undulating grassland and bracken, dotted with coppiced woodland and as wild as anything in London. Royal hunting ground since the thirteenth century (when it was known as Shene Chase), this is Europe's largest city park – eight miles across at its widest point. It's famous for its red and fallow deer, which roam freely – and breed so successfully, they have to be culled twice a year – and for its ancient oaks. Though for the most part untamed, there are a couple of deliberately landscaped plantations which feature splendid springtime azaleas and rhododendrons.

Walking or cycling are the two best ways of getting around the park. You can rent bikes from Supercycles, 219 Lower Mortlake Rd; ☎020/8940 3717.

Charles I was the first to formally establish the royal park, appropriating land willy-nilly against the counsel of his advisers, and enclosing his "New Park" with a high wall nine miles long (still in existence) to keep out trespassers. Equally unpopular with the locals was **Princess Amelia**, youngest daughter of George II, who closed the park off to all but her closest friends shortly after being appointed ranger in 1747. Local opposition – in particular from a Richmond brewer **John Lewis**, who sued the gatekeeper, Martha Gray, for assault – eventually succeeded in forcing through public access, prompting Amelia's resignation, after which she moved to Gunnersbury (see p.455). Lewis became a local hero, though he was bankrupted by the legal costs and the subsequent flooding of his brewery and died in poverty.

From Richmond Gate, at the top of Richmond Hill, it's a short walk south along the crest of the hill to **Pembroke Lodge** (originally known as The Molecatcher's), enlarged in 1788 by Sir John Soane, childhood home of the philosopher Bertrand Russell, and now a teahouse with outdoor seating affording yet more spectacular views across the Thames valley. Close by, to the north, is the highest point in the park, known as **King Henry VIII's Mount**, where tradition has it the king waited for the flare launched from the Tower of London, which signalled the execution of his second wife, Anne Boleyn, though historians believe he was in Wiltshire at the time.

For a much longer stroll through the park, head east from Pembroke Lodge into **Sidmouth Wood**, whose sweet chestnuts, oaks and beeches were planted during the nineteenth century. Originally established as pheasant cover, the wood is now a bird sanctuary, and walkers must keep to the central path, known as the Driftway. A little further east lie the **Pen Ponds**, the largest stretches of water in the park; it's a good spot for birdwatching, and it's also possible to fish here, if you have a permit. To the south is by far the most popular section of the park, the **Isabella Plantation**, a carefully landscaped woodland park created in 1951, with a little rivulet running through it, two small artificial ponds, and spectacular rhododendrons and azaleas in the spring. The round trip from Richmond Gate is about four miles.

The two most important historic buildings in the park are sadly both closed to the public. Of the two, the **White Lodge**, to the east of the Pen Ponds, is the more attractive, a Palladian villa commissioned by George II, and frequented by his wife, Queen Caroline, and their daughter, the aforementioned Amelia. Much altered over the years, it was also the birthplace of the ill-fated Edward VIII, and home to the Duke and Duchess of York (later George VI and the Queen Mother); it currently houses the Royal Ballet School. The **Thatched House Lodge**, in the southernmost corner of the park, was built in the 1670s for the park's rangers, and gets its name from the thatched gazebo in the garden. General Eisenhower hung out in the lodge during World War II, and it's now home to Princess Alexandra and her hubby, Angus Ogilvy.

Wimbledon

Wimbledon is a dreary, high, bleak, windy suburb, on the edge of a threadbare heath.

Virginia Woolf

Nowadays, of course, **Wimbledon** is best known for its tennis tournament, the Wimbledon Championship, held every year in the last week of June and the first week of July, on the grass courts of the All England Lawn Tennis and Croquet Club – to give the ground its official title. For the rest of the year, though, Wimbledon's vast **common** is its most popular attraction, worth a visit for its windmill alone, and, in the first half of the year, for the remarkable living museum of **Southside House**.

Wimbledon Lawn Tennis Museum

Daily 10.30am–5pm, Sun 2–5pm; £2.50; during the championship open for ticket-holders only; ☎020/8946 6131; *www.wimbledon.org*. Bus #39, #93 or #200 from Southfields tube.

If you've missed the tournament itself (see p.616), the next best thing for tennis fans is a quick spin around the **Wimbledon Lawn Tennis Museum**, situated by Gate 4, on the east side of the All England grounds, on Church Road. The museum traces the history of the game, which is descended from the *jeu de paume* played by the French clergy from the twelfth century onwards. The modern version, though, is considered to have been invented by a Victorian major, who called it "Sphairstike", a name that not surprisingly failed to stick. The new sport was initially seen as a genteel pastime, suitable for both gentlemen and ladies, and its early enthusiasts hailed almost exclusively from the aristocracy and the clergy – the museum's Edwardian dressing room is the epitome of upper-class masculinity. As well as the historical and fashion angles, there's also plenty of opportunity for watching hours of vintage game-footage.

Wimbledon Common

Another reason to visit Wimbledon is **Wimbledon Common**, to the southwest of Richmond Park, which with neighbouring Putney Heath covers an area more than three times the size of the better-known North London rival, Hampstead Heath. True, it doesn't have the views of Hampstead and, after Richmond Park, Wimbledon can appear rather bleak: mostly rough grass and bracken punctuated by playing fields and golf courses, and cut through by the busy A3. As at Richmond, the common has been under threat periodically from its blue-blooded landlords, most recently the Spencer family (ancestors of Princess Di), who in 1865 tried unsuccessfully to get a bill through Parliament allowing them to sell off part of the common and enclose the rest. Historically, the common was a popular venue for duelling from at least the seventeenth century. Several prime ministers are recorded as having fought here, including George Canning, who was shot in the leg by another ex-minister, and William Pitt the Younger, who faced the local MP in 1798 – neither was a seasoned marksman, and after two attempts and two misses the duel was called off. The last recorded duel took place (illegally) in 1840.

The chief landmark is the **Wimbledon Windmill**, situated at the end of Windmill Road in the northern half of the common, with a conveniently placed café nearby. Built in 1817, the mill was closed down in 1864 as part of the Spencer family's plans to sell off part of the common, and converted into cottages, one of which was home to Baden-Powell when he began writing his *Scouting for Boys* in 1908. The windmill has since been restored and turned into a museum, which helps to elucidate the significance of this, the last remaining hollow-post flour mill in the country; you can also climb into the first section of the wooden cap and see the giant chain wheel.

The nearby pool of **Queen's Mere**, just to the west of the windmill, is one of the common's most appealing spots, overhung with beech and oak, and home to numerous toads, coots and the odd heron.

The windmill is open April–Oct Sat 2–5pm Sun 11am–5pm; £1; ☎020/8947 2825. Bus #93 from Wimbledon tube.

Beyond the pond lies **Putney Vale Cemetery**, which is also worth a visit for its wonderful array of Victorian angels and its peaceful Gardens of Remembrance, at their best in early summer. The cemetery's most illustrious incumbent is Alexander Kerensky, leader of the Russian Revolution of February 1917, which overthrew the tsar. Kerensky's downfall was his failure to bring an end to the war, and he was forced to flee disguised as a Serbian officer when the Bolsheviks rose to power in the October Revolution.

If the common is too vast and bleak for you, head for **Cannizaro Park**, in the southeastern corner of the common. This small, sheltered, wooded park is made up of the grounds of Cannizaro House (now a hotel frequented by the tennis glitterati), and can only be entered from West Side Common. Within its walls are a lovely stretch of lawn for picnicking, a maze of paths, an aviary, an Italian garden, occasional student art shows and an open-air theatre and jazz festival every summer. Another intriguing sight is the **Buddhapadipa Temple**, a richly decorated red and gold Thai Buddhist complex east off the common, on Calonne Road.

The temple is open Sat & Sun 1–6pm; free; ☎020 /8946 1357. Bus #93 from Wimbledon tube.

Southside House

Guided tours Jan–mid-June Tues, Thurs & Sat 2, 3 & 4pm; £5; ☎020/8946 7643. Wimbledon tube and train station.

Hidden away behind high walls just round the corner from Cannizaro Park in Woodhayes Road is the Dutch-Baroque mansion of **Southside House**, built in the late seventeenth century, and now hemmed in by Wimbledon's King's College School. The house is currently the headquarters of the School Teachers' Cultural Foundation, and sees few visitors. Yet it's an unforgettable experience, not least because you're guided round, and fed with anecdotes, by the eccentric descendants of the Pennington family who first built the house – several of whom still live here in a kind of time warp, using only candles for light and open fires for warmth, surrounded by the house's rich and slowly disintegrating décor, and the family's ancestral hangings, many of which are extremely valuable.

Inside, the house has a ramshackle feel, partly because at heart it's still an old Tudor farmhouse, onto which a Dutch facade has been added, and partly because of bomb damage. Nevertheless, virtually every room is stuffed to the rafters with artworks and other sundry treasures. In the Dining Room alone, there are no fewer than 34, mostly full-length, portraits, including three by Van Dyck, one each by Hogarth and Goya and a depiction of St George by Burne-Jones. Other treasures on show include the sapphire worn by the last king of Serbia on the day of his assassination, and, in a cabinet of curiosities in the royal bedroom upstairs, you can see the pearl necklace worn by Marie Antoinette on the day of her execution. Finally, in the Music Room, there's a portrait of Angelica Kauffmann, a self-portrait

Tramlink

Wimbledon's newest attraction is its **Tramlink** (*www.tramlink.net*), London's first tram since the 1950s when the whole network was dismantled. The hub of the new system is the much maligned southern suburb of Croydon, from which eighteen miles of track – much of it on old railways – fans out to destinations as unlikely as Beckenham, Addington and Wimbledon. A day on the trams might seem a nice idea, especially for those with children; unfortunately, however, there are few conventional sights along the way. The award-winning **Croydon Clocktower** (Mon–Sat, Sun noon–5pm; £2; ☎020/8253 1030) is a museum worth visiting, which puts on excellent interactive exhibitions, and there's a city farm and bit of National Trust meadowland over in Morden, where Tramlink connects with the tube. However, it's probably the journey itself rather than any particular destination that's the attraction – and, of course, you can visit the **Tramlink shop** at Unit 5, Suffolk House, George St, Croydon (Mon–Fri 9am–5pm; ☎020/8681 8300). Travelcards are valid on the trams, or you can buy tickets from the automatic machines at the stops. It's worth knowing that off-peak, trams run only every thirty minutes to and from Wimbledon.

by Reynolds, a Fragonard and one of George Romney's famous portraits of Emma, Lady Hamilton, who used to strike her "attitudes" in that very room.

Ham and Twickenham

Ham and **Twickenham** lie on either side of the Thames to the south of Richmond. **Ham House**, off the beaten track and rarely visited, is one of the most appealing of all the historic houses along the river. Twickenham, best known for its rugby – there's a museum if you're really keen (see p.476) – also conceals a cluster of lesser-known sights close to the river, all of which repay a brief visit. The banks are connected all year round by ferry, or, weather permitting, it's a pleasant mile-long walk from Richmond Riverside.

Ham House

House: April–Oct Mon–Wed, Sat & Sun 1–5pm. Gardens: open all year Mon–Wed, Sat & Sun 10.30am–6pm; house & gardens £5; gardens only £1.50; ☎020/8940 1950. Bus #65 from Richmond tube.

The best approach to **Ham House** is on foot from Richmond Riverside, heading south along the towpath, which eventually leaves the rest of London far behind. On either side are the wooded banks of the Thames; to the left cows graze on Petersham Meadows, while hidden in the woods some way beyond lies Ham House, home to the earls of Dysart for nearly three hundred years. The first Earl of Dysart was Charles I's childhood whipping boy (he literally received the punishment on behalf of the prince when the latter misbehaved), who was granted a peerage and the estate of Ham for his pains, but it was his ambitious daughter, Elizabeth – at one time Oliver Cromwell's lover – who is most closely associated with the place. With the help of her second husband, the Earl of Lauderdale, one of the most powerful ministers to Charles II, she added numerous extra rooms, "furnished like a great Prince's" according to diarist John Evelyn, and succeeded in shocking even Restoration society with her extravagance.

Elizabeth's profligacy left the family heavily in debt, and the later earls of Dysart could afford to make few alterations, prompting Horace Walpole (who lived across the river at Strawberry Hill) to describe Ham as a "Sleeping Beauty". Restoration has only enhanced this period piece, which boasts one of the finest Stuart interiors in the country. The Great Staircase, to the east of the Central Hall, is stupendously ornate, featuring huge bowls of fruit at the newel posts and trophies of war carved into the balustrade. The rest of the house is equally sumptuous, with lavish plasterwork, silverwork and parquet flooring, Verrio ceiling paintings and rich hangings, tapestries, silk damasks and cut velvets. The Long Gallery, in the west wing, features six "Court Beauties" by Peter Lely, and elsewhere there are works by Van Dyck and Reynolds.

Another bonus are the formal seventeenth-century **gardens**, now restored to something like their former glory. The first feature to be appreciated on entering the grounds from the river are the stone pineapples (looking more like pine cones) set at intervals along the railings. To the east lies the Cherry Garden, laid out with a pungent lavender parterre, and surrounded by yew hedges and pleached hornbeam arbours. To the south, there's a "Wildernesse", where the Lauderdales would display their orange trees, considered the height of luxury at the time. Finally, to the west, you'll find the original kitchen garden (now a rose garden), overlooked by the Orangery, which currently serves as a tearoom.

Marble Hill House

April–Sept daily 10am–6pm; Oct daily 10am–5pm; Nov–March Wed–Sun 10am–4pm; EH; £3.30; ☎020/8892 5115. St Margaret's train station, from Waterloo.

Hammerton's Ferry takes people (and bicycles) across the Thames daily 10am–6pm; £1.

On the Twickenham side of the river, not far from Hammerton's Ferry, is **Marble Hill House**, a stuccoed Palladian villa set in rolling green parkland. Unlike Chiswick, this is no architectural exercise, but a real house, built in 1729 for Henrietta Howard, Countess of Suffolk, mistress of George II for some twenty years and, conveniently perhaps, also a lady-in-waiting to his wife, Queen Caroline (apparently "they hated one another very civilly"). Her wit and intelligence – though not her beauty – were renowned and she entertained literary figures of the day, such as Alexander Pope, John Gay and Horace Walpole. Another royal mistress, Mrs Fitzherbert, the Prince Regent's unofficial wife, later occupied the house in 1795.

Nothing remains of the original furnishings, alas, and though some period furniture has taken its place the house feels barren. The principal room is the Great Room on the *piano nobile*, a perfect cube whose coved ceiling carries on up into the top-floor apartments. Copies of Van Dyck decorate the walls as they did in Lady Suffolk's day, and a further splash of colour is provided by Panini's Roman landscapes above each of the five doors, two of which are purely decorative in order to complete the symmetry. The other highlight is Lady Suffolk's Bedchamber, which features an Ionic columned recess – a classic Palladian device. Enquire about the summer evening open-air concerts.

Orleans House Gallery

April–Sept Tues–Sat 1–5.30pm, Sun 2–5.30pm; Oct–March closes 4.30pm; free; ☎020/8892 0221; *www.guidetorichmond.co.uk/orleans.html*. St Margaret's or Twickenham train stations from Waterloo.

Set in a small adjacent wood to the west of Marble Hill House is the **Orleans House Gallery**, in what began life as a villa built in 1710 for James Johnston. It was most famously occupied in 1815–17 by the exiled Duc d'Orléans (later to become King of France), and subsequently all but entirely demolished in 1926 – all, that is, except for the **Octagon**. Designed by James Gibbs in 1720 as a garden pavilion, the Octagon was added to the original house by Johnston in honour of a visit by the aforementioned Queen Caroline (see p.474). The exhibitions staged in the old stables and the modern extension are interesting enough, but it's the Octagon that steals the limelight, an unusually exuberant Baroque confection celebrated for its masterly Italian stucco decoration.

York House and Eel Pie Island

A little further west, towards Twickenham town centre, is **York House**, an early seventeenth-century mansion which now belongs to the local council, though the gardens, laid out by the last private owner, the Indian prince Sir Ratan Tata, are open to the public. The bit to head for is the riverside section – a great picnic spot – which lies beyond the sunken garden, on the other side of the delicate arched bridge spanning the road. Here, you'll find the gardens' celebrated "naked ladies", seven larger-than-life marble nymphs frolicking in the waters of an Italian fountain, above which Venus rises up at the head of a double-headed winged horse.

A few yards offshore, near York House, lies **Eel Pie Island**, the only inhabited island in the tidal Thames. Tea dances began at the island's Eel Pie Hotel back in the 1920s; bawdy jazz nights were the staple diet in the 1950s; rock and rhythm and blues followed in the

1960s. The hotel burned down in 1972, and the island is now better
known for its eccentric community of independent-spirited artisans,
among them Trevor Baylis, inventor of the clockwork radio.

Twickenham Museum of Rugby

Tues–Sat 10am–5pm, Sun 2–5pm; £3; guided tours £5; ☎020/8892 2000;
www.rfu.com.

Sports tourism is a growing industry, and the rugby fan's number
one pilgrimage site is the English national stadium at Twickenham.
The ground's new **Museum of Rugby**, in the East Stand, is, predictably enough, full of video footage and lots of memorabilia from
the sport that was famously invented in 1823, when W.W. Ellis
picked up and ran with the ball during a game of football at Rugby
School. There's not much here for the non-specialist, however, save
for the Calcutta Cup, which is an object of supreme beauty, having
been made from 270 silver rupees, with great cobra handles and an
elephant lid. The "Twickenham Experience" **guided tour** is the only
way to get to see the dressing rooms and onto the pitch itself. Note
that on match days the museum is open from 11am until an hour
before kickoff (free of charge to ticket-holders), and that there are
no guided tours two days either side of a match.

Strawberry Hill

Easter–Oct Sun 2–4.30pm; rest of the year by appointment; ☎020/8240 4114.

One last oddity well worth making the effort to visit is **Strawberry
Hill**, to the south of Twickenham and upriver from Eel Pie Island, the
Gothic fantasy home of writer, wit and fashion queen Horace
Walpole, youngest son of former prime minister, Sir Robert Walpole.
In 1747 Walpole bought this "little play-thing house . . . the prettiest
bauble you ever saw . . . set in enamelled meadows, with filigree
hedges", renamed it Strawberry Hill and set about inventing the most
influential building in the Gothic Revival. Walpole appointed a
"Committee of Taste" to embellish his project with details from other
Gothic buildings: screens from Old St Paul's and Rouen cathedrals,
and fan-vaulting from Henry VII's Chapel in Westminster Abbey.

The house quickly became the talk of London, a place of pilgrimage for royalty and foreign dignitaries alike. Walpole was forced to
issue tickets to cut down the number of visitors, whom he used to
greet dressed in a lavender suit and silver-embroidered waistcoat,
sporting a cravat carved in wood by Grinling Gibbons and an enormous pair of gloves that once belonged to James I. When he died in
1797, he left the house to his friend, the sculptor Anne Damer, who
continued to entertain in the same spirit, giving lavish garden parties
dressed in a man's coat, hat and shoes. The house is now owned and
carefully maintained by St Mary's University College.

Hampton Court Palace

Mid-March to mid-Oct Mon 10.15am–6pm; Tues–Sun 9.30am–6pm; mid-Oct to mid-March closes 4.30pm; £10.50; ☎020/8781 9500; *www.hrp.org.uk*. Hampton Court train station, from Waterloo.

Hampton Court Palace, a sprawling red-brick ensemble on the banks of the Thames, thirteen miles southwest of London, is the finest of England's royal abodes. The present building began life, however, as an ecclesiastical palace, built in 1516 by the upwardly mobile **Cardinal Wolsey**, Henry VIII's high-powered, fast-living Lord Chancellor. The good times which rolled at Hampton prompted Henry to enquire why the cardinal had built such an extravagant home for himself. Wolsey, in a vain attempt to win back the king's favour, made the fatal reply "to show how noble a palace a subject may offer to his sovereign". In 1529, when Wolsey failed to secure a papal annulment for Henry's marriage to Catherine of Aragon, Henry took him at his word, sacked him and moved into Hampton Court.

Like Wolsey, **Henry VIII** spent enormous sums of money on the palace, enlarging the kitchens, rebuilding the chapel and altering the rooms to suit the tastes of the last five of his six wives. Under Elizabeth I and James I, Hampton Court became renowned for its masques, plays and balls; during the Civil War, it was a refuge and then a prison for Charles I. The palace was put up for sale during the Commonwealth, but, with no buyers forthcoming, Cromwell decided to move in and lived here until his death in 1658. Charles II laid out the gardens, inspired by what he had seen at Versailles, but it was **William and Mary** who instigated the most radical

---

Visiting Hampton Court

Tickets to the Royal Apartments cover entry to the rest of the sites in the grounds. Those who don't wish to visit the apartments are free to wander around the grounds, with the exception of the South Gardens and the courtyards; separate tickets can be bought to enter the Maze (£2.50), the Royal Tennis Courts (50p) and the Privy Garden (£2.50).

The **Royal Apartments** are divided into six thematic walking tours, which are numbered and colour-coded. There's not a lot of information in any of the rooms, but guided tours, each lasting half an hour or so, are available at no extra charge for the state apartments; all are led by period-costumed historians, who do a fine job of bringing the place to life. In addition, the King Henry VIII's Apartments, the Tudor Kitchens, the King's Apartments and the Georgian Rooms are served by an audioguide, available (again at no extra charge) from the information centre on the east side of Clock Court.

If your energy is lacking – and Hampton Court is a huge complex – the most rewarding sections are **Henry VIII's State Apartments** (aka the Tudor Rooms), the **King's Apartments** (remodelled by William III) and the **Tudor Kitchens**. And be sure not to miss out on the **Maze**.

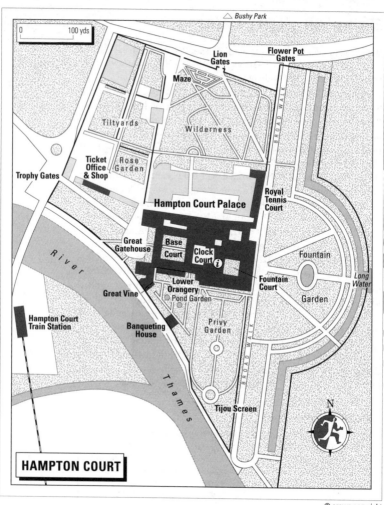

Bushy Park

Lion Gates

Flower Pot Gates

Maze

Tiltyards

Wilderness

BROAD WALK

Ticket Office & Shop

Rose Garden

Trophy Gates

Hampton Court Palace

Royal Tennis Court

River

Great Gatehouse

Base Court

Clock Court *i*

Fountain

Great Vine

Lower Orangery

Pond Garden

Fountain Court

Garden

Long Water

Hampton Court Train Station

Banqueting House

Privy Garden

Thames

Tijou Screen

N

HAMPTON COURT

alterations, hiring Christopher Wren to remodel the buildings. Wren intended to tear down the whole palace and build a new Versailles, but contented himself with rebuilding the east and south wings, adding the Banqueting House on the river and completing the chapel for Queen Anne.

George III eschewed the place, apparently because he associated it with the beatings he received here from his grandfather. Instead, he established grace-and-favour residences for indigent members of the royal household, which still exist today. The rest of the palace was opened to the public by Queen Victoria in 1838. In March 1986, extensive damage was sustained in a fire started by one such elderly grace-and-favour resident, Lady Gale, who ignited the silk hangings with a bedside candle and died in the blaze.

The Palace

From the train station, it's a short walk across the river to the **Trophy Gates**, designed for William III as the main approach to the palace, but not completed until the reign of George II, when the frisky-looking lion and unicorn were added. The ticket office and main shop are housed in the former Cavalry Barracks on the left. Ahead lies the Tudor west front, no longer moated but prickling with turrets, castellations, chimneypots and pinnacles. The **Great Gatehouse**, the main entrance to the palace courtyards, would have been twice its present height in Wolsey's day.

Before you get stuck into the Royal Apartments, it's worth getting your bearings by walking through the three main courtyards. The first and largest quadrangle, **Base Court**, is reminiscent of an Oxbridge college and features another Tudor gateway known as Anne Boleyn's Gateway, though it too dates from the time of Wolsey. Beyond lies **Clock Court**, which has none of the uniformity of the other two courtyards: to the north rises the Tudor Great Hall (see below), to the south Wren's colonnade, announcing the new State Apartments, and to the east a fairly convincing mock-Tudor gateway by William Kent. Originally centred on a large fountain which was equipped by Elizabeth I with a nozzle that soaked innocent passers-by, the courtyard gets its current name from the astronomical clock on the inside of the Anne Boleyn Gateway, made in 1540 for Henry VIII, which was used to calculate the high tide at London Bridge (and thus the estimated time of arrival of palace guests travelling by boat). The last and smallest of the three courtyards is Wren's **Fountain Court**, which crams in more windows than seems possible and does actually have a fountain at its centre.

Henry VIII's State Apartments

Henry VIII lavished more money on Hampton Court than any other palace except Greenwich (which no longer exists). That said, the only major survival from Tudor times is his **Great Hall**, which was completed with remarkable speed in 1534, Henry having made the builders work day and night – a highly dangerous exercise in candle-light. The double hammerbeam roof is exceptionally ornate, and would have originally featured a louvre to allow the smoke to escape from the central hearth. Under Elizabeth I and James I the hall served as the palace theatre, where theatrical troupes, among them Shakespeare's, entertained royalty. Even Cromwell had an organ installed here so that he and his family could enjoy recitals by John Milton, an accomplished musician as well as poet.

The entrance to Henry VIII's State Apartments is beneath Anne Boleyn's Gateway.

Passing through the Horn Room, where dishes from the kitchens below were given their final touches before being served, you enter the **Great Watching Chamber**. The gilded oak-ribbed ceiling is studded with leather-mâché Tudor insignia, and hung with tapestries which were part of Wolsey's collection. In these surroundings up to eighty yeomen would be stationed at any one time, guarding the principal entrance to the king's private chambers, which William and Mary found "old-fashioned and uncomfortable" and consequently demolished.

From here you come to the **Haunted Gallery**, built by Wolsey to connect his apartments to the chapel, and home to the ghost of Henry's fifth wife, 19-year-old Catherine Howard. The night before her arrest for high treason in November 1541, Catherine is alleged to have run down the gallery in an attempt to make a final plea for mercy to the king, who was praying in the chapel. Henry refused to see her, and she was dragged kicking and screaming back to her chambers – or so the story goes, for it's since been proved that Catherine could not, in fact, have reached the chapel from her rooms via the gallery.

The Haunted Gallery leads into the Royal Pew in the chapel gallery, which was decorated for Queen Mary but has been a feature since Wolsey's day – it was here that Henry VIII was passed the note alleging that Catherine Howard was not in fact a virgin when he married her. From here, you can look down on the **Chapel Royal**, and admire the colourful false timber vaulting wrought in plaster, heavy with pendants of gilded music-making cherubs – one of the most memorable sights in the whole palace.

The entrance to the Queen's Apartments is in the passageway between Clock and Fountain courts.

The Queen's State Apartments

The **Queen's Apartments** were intended for Queen Mary II, but were completed some years after her death in 1694. The main approach is via the grandiose **Queen's Staircase**, splendidly decorated with trompe l'oeil reliefs and a coffered dome by William Kent. This, in turn, leads to the **Queen's Guard Chamber**, where larger-than-life marble yeomen guard the main chimneypiece.

The Queen's state rooms continue in the east wing of Fountain Court, overlooking Fountain Garden and Long Water. One of the finest is the **Queen's Drawing Room**, decorated top to bottom with trompe l'oeil paintings depicting Queen Anne's husband, George of Denmark – in heroic naval guise, and also, on the south wall, riding naked and wigless on the back of a dolphin. Queen Anne takes centre stage on the ceiling as Justice, somewhat inappropriate given her habit of not paying her craftsmen, including Verrio, the painter of this room. After Anne's death in 1714, the Prince and Princess of Wales (later George II and Queen Caroline) took over the Queen's Apartments, until they fell out with the king in 1717 and moved to Kew. The ceiling painting in the **Queen's Bedroom** by James

Thornhill predates the quarrel, with four portraits of a seemingly happy Hanoverian family staring at one another from the coving.

The **Queen's Gallery** features one of the finest marble fireplaces in the palace – originally intended for the King's Bedchamber – with putti, doves and Venus frolicking above the mantelpiece; the walls, meanwhile, are hung with Gobelin tapestries depicting Alexander the Great's exploits. This route ends with **Queen Mary's Closet**, so called because the walls were once hung with needlework by the queen and her ladies, though Mary herself never set foot in the place.

The Georgian Rooms

The **Georgian Rooms** route begins with the three small rooms of the **Cumberland Suite**, lived in by George II before his accession, then by his eldest son, Prince Frederick, and lastly by Frederick's brother, the Duke of Cumberland, better known as "Butcher Cumberland" for his ruthless suppression of the Jacobites in Scotland. The rooms were decorated by Kent, who added Gothic touches to the first two rooms and a grandiose Neoclassical alcove in the bedchamber.

The entrance to the Georgian Rooms is in the passageway between Clock and Fountain courts.

Beyond here you'll find the tiny **Wolsey Closet**, the only remnant of Wolsey's apartments, and a tantalizing glimpse of the splendour of the original palace. It's a jewel of a room – though at 12ft square it's easily missed – with brightly coloured fifteenth-century paintings set above exquisite linen-fold panelling and a fantastic gilded ceiling of interlaced octagons.

Next is the **Communication Gallery**, constructed to link the King's and Queen's apartments, now lined with Lely's flattering portraits of the mistresses of Charles II. The **Cartoon Gallery** itself, designed by Wren for the Raphael cartoons now in the V&A (see p.346), is hung with seventeenth-century copies – tapestries made from the cartoons are scattered around the Queen's and King's apartments.

The next sequence of small rooms is of minor interest, though they do include a gaming room, a couple of marble wall basins and the Gibbons overmantle in the King's Private Chamber. Last of all, you enter the **Queen's Private Chapel**, completed for Queen Caroline in 1728 – it's one of the few windowless rooms, hence the octagonal dome and skylight.

The King's Apartments

William III's state apartments are approached via the **King's Staircase**, the grandest of the lot thanks chiefly to Verrio's busy, militaristic trompe l'oeil paintings glorifying the king, depicted here as Alexander the Great. The **King's Guard Chamber** is notable chiefly for its three-thousand-piece display of arms, arranged as they were laid out in the time of William III. William's rather modest throne still stands in the **King's Presence Chamber**, under a canopy of crimson damask. The magnificent sixteenth-century Brussels tapestries in the room were originally commissioned by Henry VIII for Whitehall Palace.

The entrance to the King's Apartments is in the south wing of Clock Court.

Further on, in the **Privy Chamber**, is a much grander throne used by William, with a canopy that still retains its original ostrich feathers. The most impressive room is the **Great Bedchamber**, which boasts a superb vertical Gibbons frieze and ceiling paintings by Verrio – just as you're leaving this floor, you'll catch a glimpse of the splendidly throne-like velvet toilet. Ground-floor highlights include the **Orangery**, built to house the king's orange trees during the winter, and the only room in the palace lockable solely from the inside (a tryst room – highly unusual for the royals' very public life). Past here is the **King's Private Dining Room**, its table laden with pyramids of meringues and fruit. Its chief interest is a series of eight full-length portraits of Queen Mary's favourite ladies-in-waiting (known as the "Hampton Court Beauties") for which the German-born painter Godfrey Kneller received a knighthood.

The Wolsey Rooms and the Renaissance Picture Gallery

The entrance to the Wolsey Rooms is in the south wing of Clock Court.

The **Wolsey Rooms** comprise four early Tudor rooms, where the only reminders of Wolsey's day are the striking linen-fold panelling of the walls and the original gilded strapwork ceilings. The suite now houses the palace's **Renaissance Picture Gallery**, which is chock-full of treasures from the vast Royal Collection. There's a wonderfully vibrant *Portrait of a Young Man in Red* by an unknown Tudor artist, and a very serious portrait of Johannes Froben, Erasmus's publisher, by Holbein. Tintoretto's portrait of the Venetian goldsmith Girolamo Pozzo is a masterly study of old age, while the striking, highly finished, almost photographic *Portrait of a Lady in Green* is possibly by Bronzino. Among the portraits in the next room by, among others, Lotto, Titian and Joos van Cleve, Bellini's terrific, late *Portrait of a Young Man* stands out, as does Raphael's self-portrait, painted at the age of just 23, and presented to George III in 1781. In Cranach's *Judgement of Paris*, the startled Paris looks as though he's been accosted by three naked women whilst riding in the woods, while Pieter Brueghel the Elder's *Massacre of the Innocents* looks more like a village fete, though it was intended as an allegory for the contemporary atrocities committed by the Spanish troops of the Duke of Alba in Holland.

The Tudor Kitchens

After a surfeit of opulent interiors, the workaday **Tudor Kitchens** come as something of a relief. Henry VIII quadrupled the size of the kitchens, large sections of which have survived to this day and have been restored and embellished with historical reconstructions. To make the most of this route, you really do need to use the audioguide, which helps to evoke the scene with contemporary accounts. Past the Boiling Room and Flesh Larder (not for squeamish vegetarians) you come to the **Great Kitchen**, where a fire is still lit in the main hearth every day. This kitchen is only one of three Henry built to cope with the prodigious consumption of the royal court – six oxen, forty sheep and a thousand or more larks, pheasants, pigeons and peacocks were an average daily total.

The tour ends in Henry's vast **Wine Cellar**, where the palace's Rhineland wine was stored. At each main meal, the king and his special guests would be supplied with eight pints of wine; courtiers had to make do with three gallons of beer, which was very weak and drunk as a substitute for what was then a very dodgy water supply.

The Gardens

The 669-acre **Palace Gardens** were largely the creation of three monarchs: Henry VIII, Charles II and William III. If you're coming from the Royal Apartments, you'll probably emerge onto the magnificent **Broad Walk**, which runs for half a mile from the Thames past Wren's austere east front to the putti-encrusted Flower Pot Gate and is lined with some of the country's finest herbaceous borders. Halfway along the Broad Walk lies the indoor **Royal Tennis Court**, established here by Henry VIII (a keen player of Real Tennis himself), but extensively restored by Charles II – you might even catch a game of this arcane precursor of modern tennis.

The Palace Gardens are open daily 7am–dusk; free.

Fanning out from the Broad Walk is William's **Fountain Garden**, a grand, semicircular parterre, which in William's day featured box hedges, thirteen fountains and dwarf yew trees pruned to look like obelisks. A fair number of these "black pyramids", as Virginia Woolf called them, have been reduced to chubby cone shapes, while a solitary pool stands in place of the fountains, and the box hedges have become plain lawns. A semicircular canal separates the Fountain Garden from the Home Park beyond, its waters feeding Charles II's **Long Water**, Hampton Court's most Versaillean feature, which slices the Home Park in two.

To the south of the palace lie the **South Gardens**, the first of which is the **Privy Garden**, now restored to the stifling formality that prevailed under William III; the twelve magnificent wrought-iron panels at the river end of the garden are the work of Jean Tijou. Further west, you can peek into the **Pond Gardens**, which were originally constructed as ornamental fish ponds stocked with freshwater fish for the kitchens, and feature some of the gardens' most spectacularly colourful flowerbeds. Further along, protected by glass, is the palace's celebrated **Great Vine**, grown from a cutting in 1768 by Capability Brown and averaging about seven hundred bunches of Black Hamburg grapes per year. The grapes are sold at the palace each year in September.

The South Gardens are open at the same times as the palace, but can be viewed separately; £2.10.

Close by stands the **Lower Orangery**, built for William and Mary by Wren and used as a dimly lit gallery for Andrea Mantegna's heroic canvases, *The Triumphs of Caesar*, bought by Charles I in 1629 and kept here ever since. Painted around 1486 for the Ducal Palace in Mantua, Mantegna's home town, these nine richly coloured paintings, depicting the general's victory parade, are among his best works, characterized by his obsessive interest in archeological and historical accuracy.

Hampton
Court Palace

Beyond the South Gardens, beside the river, is William III's dinky little red-brick **Banqueting House**, built for intimate riverside soirées, with castellations and mouldings by Gibbons and paintings by Verrio.

The Maze

To the north of the palace, Henry VIII laid out a **Tiltyard** with five towers for watching jousting tournaments, one of which survives near the garden restaurant. William III transformed the tiltyard into a "**Wilderness**" – a formal garden of evergreens – which now contains the most famous feature of the palace gardens, the deceptively tricky **Maze**, laid out in 1714. Originally, there were four mazes, and there are plans to restore the other three over the next decade or so. Mazes, or labyrinths as they were called at the time, were all the rage among the eighteenth-century nobility, though their origins lie in the Middle Ages, when they were used by pilgrims who used to crawl along on hands and knees reciting prayers, as penance for not making a pilgrimage to the Holy Land. On the north side of the Maze stand the **Lion Gates**, built as a new grand approach to Wren's planned north front, which was never realized.

Bushy Park

Beyond the Lion Gates, and across Hampton Court Road, lies **Bushy Park**, the palace's semi-wild enclosure of over a thousand acres, which sustains copious herds of fallow and red deer. Wren's mile-long royal road, Chestnut Avenue, cuts through the park, and is at its best in May when the horse chestnuts are in blossom. The main architectural feature of the park is the **Diana Fountain**, situated a third of the way along the avenue to help break the monotony. The statue – which, in fact, depicts Arethusa – was commissioned by Charles II from Francesco Fanelli and originally graced the Privy Garden; stranded in the centre of this vast pond, she looks ill-proportioned and rather isolated.

Off to the west, a little further up the avenue, you'll come upon the **Waterhouse Woodland Gardens**, created in 1949, and at their most colourful each spring when the rhododendrons, azaleas and camellias are in bloom. The crowds are fairly thin even here, compared with the crush around the palace, but if you really want to seek out some of the park's abundant wildlife head for the wilder western section of the park, where few visitors venture.

Windsor and Eton

Every weekend, trains from Waterloo and Paddington are packed with people heading for **Windsor**, the royal enclave 21 miles west of London, where they join a human conveyor belt round **Windsor Castle**. Towering above the town on a steep chalk bluff, the castle is an undeniably awesome sight, its chilly grey walls, punctuated by mighty medieval bastions, continuing as far as the eye can see. Once there, the small selection of State Rooms open to the public are unexciting, though the magnificent St George's Chapel and the chance to see another small selection of the Queen's private art collection make the trip worthwhile. On a fine day, it pays to put aside some time for exploring Windsor Great Park, which stretches for several miles to the south of the castle.

Though almost as famous as Windsor, **Eton** – the exclusive and inexcusably powerful school founded by Henry VI directly across the river from the castle in 1440 – receives a mere fraction of the tourists. True, there's not so much to see here, but the guided tours give an eye-opening glimpse of life as lived by the offspring of Britain's upper classes, and the Gothic chapel is definitely worth a visit.

Windsor Castle

Daily: March–Oct 9.45am–5.15pm; Nov–Feb 9.45am–4.15pm; £10.50; ☎01753/868286; *www.royal.gov.uk*.

Windsor Castle began its life as a wooden keep built by William the Conqueror, and numerous later monarchs had a hand in its evolution. Henry II tore down the wooden buildings and rebuilt the castle in stone, much as you see it now – in plan at least – though George IV was mainly responsible for today's rather over-restored appearance.

The ticket office is next to St George's Gate, up Castle Hill.

The most significant event to have befallen the castle in recent years was the devastating **fire** of November 20, 1992, which gutted a good number of the State Apartments. Having ignored the advice of various fire officers, and failed to insure the place, the royal family found itself faced with a repair bill of around £50 million – or rather, the taxpayers did. In an attempt to assuage public opinion, the Queen subsequently offered to foot half the bill, and set about

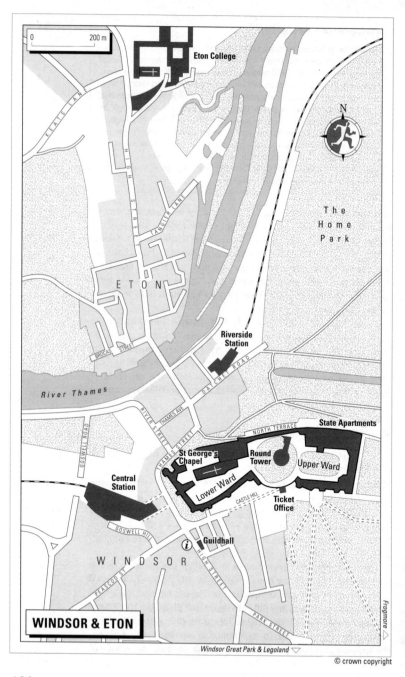

© crown copyright

Visiting the castle

Tickets to Windsor Castle include entry to the castle precincts, the St
George's and Albert Memorial chapels, the State Apartments, the Gallery
and Queen Mary's Dolls' House. Occasionally, the State Apartments and/or
other parts of the castle are closed to the public, in which case the admission will be reduced to reflect this. In addition, St George's Chapel is
always closed on Sundays, except for those attending one of the services;
note, too, that the chapel closes at 4pm on weekdays, in order to prepare
for the daily evensong at 5.15pm.

raising some of the money by opening up Buckingham Palace to the
public.

The Middle and Upper wards

Leaving the ticket office, you find yourself in the **Middle Ward**,
where the flagpole of the **Round Tower** flies the Royal Standard
when the Queen is in residence, and the Union Flag at other times.
Constructed out of Caen stone in 1170 and heightened 30ft by
George IV, the tower is the direct descendant of William the
Conqueror's fortress and stands on the original motte-hill; despite its
name, the moat below the tower has never held water, as its chalky
soil is highly porous.

If you're running late, it's best to head for St George's Chapel first,
as it closes at 4pm. If you're here relatively early in the day, head
straight for the State Apartments before the tour groups get into
their stride – to do so, walk around the Round Tower and pass under
the **Norman Tower**. Three kings have been imprisoned in the pris-
onhouse above the gate: David of Scotland, John of France and
James I of Scotland, whose only compensation for his eleven years'
incarceration was a glimpse of his future wife, Jane Beaufort, from
his cell window.

From here you enter the **Upper Ward** or Quadrangle, where an
equestrian statue of Charles II looks across the manicured stretch of
lawn where the **Changing of the Guard** takes place when the Queen
is at home (April–June Mon–Sat 11am; rest of year on alternate
days). The south and east wings contain the Queen's private apartments, where she still hangs out occasionally at the weekend, Easter
and in June during Ascot. The State Apartments lie to the north: the
official State entrance is immediately to your left, but plebs must trot
down the passageway and enter from the North Terrace, after admiring the splendid view across to Eton College Chapel, the Mars chocolate factory at Slough and the Chiltern Hills beyond.

The Gallery and Queen Mary's Dolls' House

Before entering the State Apartments, most folk pay a quick visit to
Queen Mary's Dolls' House, a palatial micro-residence designed by
the eminent architect Edwin Lutyens for the wife of George V and

situated in a dimly lit chamber beneath the royal apartments. The three-storey Neoclassical house features a fully plumbed-in toilet and working electric lights, and contains paintings by eminent artists and handwritten books by Kipling, Hardy and Conan Doyle. If the queue looks bad, however, you may decide to skip the pleasure and walk straight into the **Gallery**, to the left of the main entrance, where you can see exhibitions of prints and drawings culled from Windsor's slice of the royal art collection (which includes the world's finest collection of sketches and notebooks by Leonardo da Vinci).

The State Apartments

The **State Apartments** – originally created for Charles II and his wife, Catherine of Braganza, but much altered since then – receive over a million visitors a year, so it can get crowded in high season. Visitors enter via the **Grand Staircase**, a quasi-medieval stairwell lit by a polygonal lantern – until the 1820s this area was an open courtyard, which once served as the herb garden. To the east lies George III's **Grand Vestibule**, featuring a smaller octagonal lantern, pseudo-Gothic fan-vaulting, and floor-to-ceiling patterned displays of arms. There are also several Victorian showcases displaying such treasures as a locket containing the bullet which killed Nelson at Trafalgar, and some wonderful armoury seized from Tippoo Sultan of Mysore when the British took Seringapatam in 1799.

The **Waterloo Chamber**, built to celebrate the defeat of Napoleon, is lined with portraits of wartime worthies and royals, mostly the work of Sir Thomas Lawrence. More interesting is the room's seamless Indian carpet, woven in Agra for the Empress of India, Queen Victoria. Most visitors just gape in awe at the monotonous, gilded grandeur of the state rooms, while the real highlights – the paintings from the Royal Collection that line the walls – are rarely given a second glance. In the **King's Drawing Room**, for example, there are no fewer than three works by Rubens over by the fireplace, while the **King's Bed Chamber** features numerous Canalettos and a couple of very fine Gainsborough portraits; the French eighteenth-century domed bed is also rather splendid. The **King's Dressing Room**, meanwhile, despite its small size, contains a feast of art treasures, including a dapper Rubens self-portrait, Van Dyck's famous triple portrait of Charles I, and *The Artist's Mother*, a perfectly observed portrait of old age by Rembrandt.

Only three of Verrio's thirteen ceiling paintings have survived the whims of the royals, the first and finest of which is the *Banquet of the Kings* in the rather lush **King's Dining Room**, which is further embellished by fish and fruit festoons courtesy of Grinling Gibbons. The two other surviving works by Verrio are located beyond the Queen's Ballroom, itself lined with portraits of the royals by Van Dyck. Sadly the Baroque décor and colourful Gobelin tapestries of these few rooms, which dates back to the days of Charles II, gives way to yet more Neo-Gothicisms in the Queen's Guard Chamber, from which you now enter the part of the palace which suffered most from the 1992 fire.

The **St George's Hall**, in which monarchs from Edward III onwards held banquets for the Knights of the Garter, has been restored more or less to its original 1820s design, though the roof is more steeply pitched and now features brand-new oak hammerbeams. At the far end of the hall you can admire the armour of the Royal Champion, who used to ride into Westminster Hall during the coronation banquet and challenge anyone present to dispute the sovereign's right to the throne. The octagonal **Lantern Lobby**, beyond, is an entirely new room, replacing Queen Victoria's private chapel which was gutted in the fire – predictably enough, the royals have again opted for a safe Neo-Gothic design.

At this point, those visiting during the winter season are given the privilege of seeing the **Semi-State Rooms**, which are still used in the summer months by the Royal Family. The set of four rooms (and a corridor) were created in the 1820s for George IV, and reflect the monarch's penchant for heavily gilded, pompous décor. If the Semi-State Rooms are closed, visitors pass straight into the **Grand Reception Room**, easily the most stunning of the rooms created by George IV, though the rich helpings of French gilded stuccowork might be a bit much for some. The fantastic chinoiserie clock on the mantelpiece, topped by a peacock and flanked by a Chinese gentleman and lady, was brought here from the Brighton Pavilion, while the huge malachite vase managed to survive the fire virtually unscathed, despite being too heavy to move.

The Lower Ward and St George's Chapel

You leave the castle via the sloping **Lower Ward**, site of **St George's Chapel**, a glorious Perpendicular structure ranking with Henry VII's Chapel in Westminster Abbey (see p.89), and the second most important resting place for royal corpses after the Abbey. The chapel was founded by Edward III in 1348 as the spiritual centre for the Order of the Knights of the Garter, the chivalric elite established in the same year; the present edifice, however, was begun by Edward IV but not completed until 1528. If you're interested in visiting only the chapel, you can enter free of charge for the daily services; the 5.15pm evensong is particularly atmospheric thanks to the chapel's excellent boys' choir.

The chapels are closed to the public on Sundays.

Entrance to the chapel is via the south door, and a one-way system operates; it's worth buying a plan as you enter to locate the graves, which aren't always obvious. What strikes you at once is the superb fan-vaulting of the chapel ceiling, the final flowering of English Gothic architecture. The first tomb you come to is the white marble sarcophagus of **Prince Napoleon** (son of Napoleon III), who was speared to death in 1879 during the Zulu War, at the age of just 23.

In the Unswick Chantry in the north aisle is the extravagant white marble monument to George IV's only child and heiress to the throne, **Princess Charlotte**, who died in childbirth in 1817. Shrouded female figures mourn the body of the princess, whose hand emerges dramatically from the folds; meanwhile, her spirit flies heavenwards attended by angels, one of whom is holding her stillborn son. Nearby is a statue of her husband, Leopold, a particularly vile colonial monarch, after his accession as king of Belgium. **George V** and **George VI** are both buried in the north aisle, the latter in his own memorial chapel with a space ready and waiting for his wife, the Queen Mother.

Continuing up the north choir aisle, it's worth peeking into the tiny **Hastings Chantry**, decorated with brightly coloured sixteenth-century paintings of St Stephen's martyrdom. More architectural glories lie within the choir itself, with its intricate fifteenth-century three-tier stalls and two exquisite oriel windows side by side: the Gothic **Royal Gallery**, built in wood for Catherine of Aragon; the other in Renaissance style and carved in stone. Underneath the floor of the choir is the **Queen's Closet**, built for the burial of Jane Seymour, Henry VIII's third wife, who died giving birth to Edward VI; it also contains Henry himself, Charles I and one of the children born to Queen Anne. Edward IV, Henry VI and Edward VII lie either side of the high altar.

The **Albert Memorial Chapel**, which adjoins St George's Chapel to the east, was built by Henry VII as a burial place for Henry VI, completed by Cardinal Wolsey for his own burial, but eventually converted for Queen Victoria into a memorial to her husband, Prince Albert. Albert himself now lies alongside his wife in the equally extravagant mausoleum in Frogmore (see p.492). Decorated in the High Victorian style, the vaulted ceiling boasts gold Italian mosaic infill, while the walls are lined with biblical murals in marble. Albert's now-empty memorial is actually upstaged by the centrepiece of the chapel: the extraordinary, heavy-duty wrought-iron grille surrounding the tomb of "Eddy", Duke of Clarence and eldest son of Edward VII, who was as dissolute as his father but differed in his sexual preference; he died in 1892, officially from pneumonia, probably from syphilis. Beneath the chapel lies the **Royal Vault**, where George III and Queen Charlotte are buried along with six of their sons, including George IV and William IV.

*The Changing
of the Guard
takes place
April–June
Mon–Sat at
11am;
July–March
alternate days.*

The foot of the Lower Ward is occupied by the Guard Room, where the Changing of the Guard takes place when the Queen is not in residence. More interesting is the **Horseshoe Cloister**, hidden away to the west of the chapel. These medieval timber-framed houses form an arresting piece of domestic architecture in the otherwise frigid surroundings of the castle, and provide accommodation for members of the chapel choir. When you leave the Lower Ward, be sure to admire the **King Henry VIII Gate**, the castle's main gate: built in 1511, its outer arch is decorated with a panel carved with the Tudor rose and the pomegranate emblem of Henry's first wife, Catherine of Aragon.

Windsor town and Windsor Great Park

Once you've seen the castle, you've covered just about everything worth seeing in Windsor, with the exception of the park (see below). The small network of cobbled streets to the south of the castle is too busy scrambling for every tourist pound to retain any quaintness, and the other so-called "attractions" are well worth skipping. More appealing is the town's **Guildhall**, with a delicate arcaded loggia designed by Wren. The story goes that the town authorities insisted that Wren's initial version, which was supported by only one line of columns, was unstable, so Wren duly added the central row, but placed a one-inch gap at the tops of the columns to prove his point.

Windsor Great Park

Most tourists are put off going to **Windsor Great Park** by its sheer scale. Covering nearly five thousand acres, fifteen miles in circumference and accessible from central Windsor only via the three-mile Long Walk, in actual fact the Great Park is a mere fraction of the whole estate, since the Home Park, nearer to the castle, is off limits to the public, with the exception of Frogmore (see below).

Windsor Great Park is open daily 10am–6pm or dusk; free.

At the far end of the Long Walk stands the gargantuan equestrian statue of George III, known as the **Copper Horse**, sculpted by Westmacott and erected by George IV – so the story goes, sixteen people had lunch inside the horse before it was placed on the plinth. It was here at Windsor that George III lived out his last years, racked by "madness", subsequently diagnosed as porphyria, a rare metabolic disorder, which gets its name from the port-coloured urine that characterizes it. It was during one of his attacks at Windsor that George famously leapt from his carriage and addressed an oak tree, believing it to be the King of Prussia.

If you need a focus for your wandering, head for **Savill Garden**, a 35-acre patch of woodland on the park's southeastern boundary, a mile or so from the Copper Horse. Begun in 1932, this is one of the finest floral displays in and around London, with magnolias, rhododendrons and camellias galore, plus many other more unusual trees and shrubs. Adjacent, to the southwest, is **Smith's Lawn**, home of the Guards' Polo Club, where you can watch the upper classes at leisure most weekends from May to September.

Savill Garden is open daily: March–Oct 10am–6pm; Nov–Feb 10am–4pm; £4.

Frogmore House

Open on at least three days in May, including the Wed closest to Queen Victoria's birthday (May 23), plus a few days in Aug; £5; ☎01753/743900.

At the centre of the Home Park is the secluded whitewashed mansion of **Frogmore House**, which can be visited on a few days each year, along with its gardens and the Royal Mausoleum, the latter built by Queen Victoria as a shrine to her husband, Albert. The house was built around 1680, but was bought by Queen Charlotte in the 1790s and converted for use as a royal retreat by architect James Wyatt. With the exception of the Green Pavilion, the décor of the rooms dates from the mid-nineteenth century, when the house was used by the Duchess of Kent, Victoria's crabby mother. The last royal to use the place to any great extent was Queen Mary (of Dolls' House fame), who established a sort of family souvenir and bygones museum.

On the opposite side of the lake from Frogmore House lies the ornate, Neo-Romanesque **Royal Mausoleum**, its interior awash with inlaid marble and gilded frescoes after Raphael. Centre stage is Baron Carlo Marochetti's grey granite double sarcophagus, topped by the recumbent marble figures of Victoria and Albert (both carved shortly after Albert's death in 1861). To the southwest of the mausoleum is a royal burial ground containing the graves of three of Victoria's children, plus sundry other royals, including the Duke and Duchess of Windsor (Edward VIII and Mrs Simpson).

Legoland

Easter to mid-July daily 10am–6pm; mid-July to Aug daily 10am–8pm; Sept–Easter daily 10am–6pm or dusk; adults £18, under-15s £15, under 3s free; ☎0990/040404; *www.legoland.co.uk*. Shuttle bus departs from the High Street; £2 return.

Among younger kids, the attractions of Windsor Castle are overshadowed by the town's **Legoland** theme park aimed at pre-teenage children (the perfect age is around 5–8). The entrance charges are enough to put off most people, but if you've got the money, and several small kids in tow, it's one way of keeping them happy for a day. Whatever you do, though, try not to go at the weekend or during the school holidays, when the queues for the various rides become grievously long.

On arrival, a funicular railway takes visitors down into the park, disgorging them close to Miniland, the *raison d'être* of the whole show. Model InterCity trains scoot about from LegoEngland to LegoWales and LegoScotland, while a Eurostar train speeds off to LegoFrance. Other featured countries include Germany, Belgium, Italy and, of course, Denmark, where Lego was invented in 1932 by Ole Kirk Christiansen.

The rest of the park is really just a series of rides, most of them very gentle. The biggest queues are for the Driving School, the mildly scary (and very wet) Pirate Falls and the Dragon, a ghost train and helter-skelter rolled into one, so it's not a bad idea to head for those at the beginning, or the end, of the day, when the queues are usually at their shortest. There are numerous places to eat, though it makes sense to take a picnic and save yourself some money.

Eton College

College and chapel: Easter, July & Aug daily 10.30am–4.30pm; after Easter to
June & Sept daily 2–4.30pm; £2.70; guided tours daily 2.15 & 3.15pm; £4;
☎01753/671177; *www.etoncollege.com.*

Crossing the bridge at the end of Thames Avenue in Windsor brings
you to **Eton**, a one-street village lined with bookshops and antique
dealers, but famous all over the world for **Eton College**, a ten-minute
walk from the river. When this, Britain's most aristocratic public
school, was founded in 1440 by Henry VI, its aim was to give free
education to seventy poor scholars and choristers – how times have
changed. It would be easier to list Establishment figures who haven't
been to Eton than vice versa – Percy Bysshe Shelley, George Orwell
and Tony Benn are rare rebels in the roll call. This is the old school
of many a Conservative cabinet – it recently educated Prince
William, and still receives his little brother, Harry.

Within the rarefied complex, the original fifteenth-century **schoolroom**, gnarled with centuries of graffiti, survives to the north of the
first courtyard, but the real highlight is the **College Chapel**, a wonderful example of English Perpendicular architecture completed in
1482. The fan-vaulting, which was destroyed in the last war, has
been completely reconstructed in concrete (though you'd never
know from looking at it), but the most remarkable feature of the
place is its medieval grisaille wall paintings, the finest in the country,
which were whitewashed over by the Victorians and only uncovered
in 1923. The small self-congratulatory **Museum of Eton Life** is well
worth missing unless you have a fascination with flogging, fagging
and bragging about the school's facilities and alumni. If you're thinking of going on a guided tour, ring ahead to make sure the school
isn't closed for some special reason.

The Listings

Chapter 14

Accommodation

There's no getting away from the fact that **accommodation** in London is expensive. Compared with most European cities, you pay over the odds in every category. The city's hostels are among the most expensive in the world, while venerable institutions such as the *Ritz*, the *Dorchester* and the *Savoy* charge guests the very top international prices – up to £300 and more per luxurious night.

The cheapest places to stay are the city's **campsites**, some of which also have dormitories, charging as little as £6 a night. A dorm bed in one of the numerous independent **hostels** will cost you double that, while official YHA hostels can charge up to £20. Even the most basic **B&Bs** struggle to bring their tariffs below £40 for a double with shared facilities, and you're more likely to find yourself paying £50 or more.

Most B&Bs and hotels are housed in former residential properties, which means that rooms tend to be on the small side, and only the more upmarket hotels have lifts. That said, even the most basic rooms tend to have TVs, tea- and coffee-making facilities and telephones, and breakfast is nearly always included in the price.

Although many of the places listed below can be booked out months in advance, the sheer size of London means that there is little chance of failing to find a room, even in midsummer, and the tube network makes accommodation in most of the satellite boroughs a feasible option.

We've given phone numbers and Web sites or email addresses where available for all our listed accommodation, but if you fail to find a bed in any of the places we've recommended, you could turn to one of the various **accommodation agencies**. All London tourist offices (listed on p.38) operate a room-booking service, which costs £5 (they also take the first night's fee in advance); you can book over phone with a credit card, too (☎020/7604 2890; *www .londontown.com*).

In addition, **Thomas Cook** has accommodation desks at Charing Cross (☎020/7976 1171), Euston (☎020/7388 7435), Gatwick Airport (☎01293/ 529372), King's Cross (☎020/7837 5681), Paddington (☎020/7837 5681) and Victoria (☎020/7828 4646) train stations, plus Earl's Court (☎020/7244 0908) and South Kensington (☎020/7581 9766) tubes and at the British Visitor Centre on Lower Regent Street (see p.38). Most (though not all) of these are open daily from 7am till 11pm, and will book anything from youth hostels (£2 fee) through to five-star hotels (£5 fee).

There are also **British Hotel Reservation Centre** (BHRC; *www.bhrc .co.uk*) desks at Heathrow arrivals terminal, and at both Heathrow underground stations (☎020/8564 8808 or ☎020/8564 8211), and both terminals of Gatwick Airport (☎01293/502433); there

Accommodation

are also four desks in and around Victoria: at the train station (☎020/7828 1027), coach station (☎020/7824 8232), underground (☎020/828 2262) and at 13 Grosvenor Gardens, SW1 (☎020/7828 2425). Most offices are open daily from 6am till midnight and most charge a £5 fee. The Victoria coach station and Heathrow underground offices offer their services free of charge, and will book accommodation for free over the phone.

You can also book hotels and B&Bs online via **Web sites** such as *www .lastminute.com*, which almost always offer discounts, or through *www .hotelsengland.com*.

Hostels, student halls and camping

London's seven **Youth Hostel Association (YHA) hostels** are generally the cleanest, most efficiently run hostels in the capital. However, they charge around fifty percent more than most private hostels, and tend to get booked up several months in advance. Curfews and character-building daily chores may have been abolished in YHA hostels, but they still exude an institutionalized wholesomeness that isn't to everyone's taste: dorms are segregated, and drinking and smoking are discouraged or forbidden. Members of any association affiliated to Hostelling International have automatic membership of the YHA; non-members can join at any of the hostels. Note that you can book a bed in advance with a credit card either by ringing individual hostels or by logging on to the main Web site, *www.yha.org.uk*. At peak periods, or to get an immediate overview of the availability of beds, and to make an immediate booking, contact the **YHA central reservations** (☎020/7373 3400; *lonres@yha.org.uk*).

At best, **independent hostels** offer facilities commensurate with those of the YHA places at a lower price and in a less restrictive atmosphere; on the whole, however, they tend to be a little tattier with facilities that are less reliable. Still, a lot of people find the more

relaxed atmosphere ample compensation for the less than salubrious environment. The most promising newcomer is the **St Christopher's Inn** chain, more often than not attached to a *Belushi's* bar. A more hippyish brand of hostel is the **Astor chain**, which now runs five hostels in the capital, exclusively for the under-30s.

Outside term time, you also have the option of staying in **student halls of residence**. Prices are slightly higher than hostels because you usually get a room to yourself, and some locations are very central and attractive. The quality of the rooms varies enormously, but tends to be fairly basic. Rooms get booked up quickly, especially in July, and can be had on a B&B or self-catering basis – the quads are particularly good value for families. Finally, London's **campsites** are all out on the perimeters of the city and for committed campers only. Pitches cost around £2–4, plus a fee of around £3–4 per person per night, with reductions for children and during the low season. Throughout this hostels section, all prices quoted are per person for the cheapest beds available in high season.

YHA hostels

City of London, 36 Carter Lane, EC4 ☎020/7236 4965; *city@yha.org.uk*. 200-bed hostel in great situation opposite St Paul's Cathedral; some twins at £50 a room, but mostly four- and five-bed dorms for £22.95 per person, or triple bunks in larger dorms for £20.50. No groups. St Paul's tube.

Earl's Court, 38 Bolton Gardens, SW5 ☎020/7373 7083; *earlscourt@yha.org .uk*. Better than a lot of accommodation in Earl's Court, but only offering dorms of mostly 10 beds – the triple bunks take some getting used to. Kitchen, café and patio garden. No groups. £19.95. Earl's Court tube.

Hampstead Heath, 4 Wellgarth Rd, NW11 ☎020/8458 9054; *hampstead @yha.org.uk*. One of the biggest and best-appointed YHA hostels, with its own garden and the wilds of Hampstead

Heath nearby. Rooms with 3–6 beds cost £19.70; family rooms with 2–5 beds are also available, starting at £35 for one adult and one child or £45 for two adults. Golders Green tube.

Holland House, Holland Walk, W8 ☎020/7937 0748; hollandhouse@yha .org.uk. Idyllically situated in the wooded expanse of Holland Park and fairly convenient for the centre, this extensive hostel offers a decent kitchen and an inexpensive café, but tends to be popular with school groups. Dorms only, at £19.95 per person. Holland Park or High Street Kensington tube.

Oxford Street, 14 Noel St, W1 ☎020 /7734 1618; oxfordst@yha.org.uk. The unbeatable West End location and modest size (75 beds in rooms of 2, 3 and 4 beds) mean that this hostel tends to be full even out of high season. No children under 6, no groups, no café, but a large kitchen. £20.55 per person or £21.80 in a twin room. Oxford Circus or Tottenham Court Road tube.

Rotherhithe, Island Yard, Salter Rd, SE16 ☎020/7232 2114; rotherhithe @yha.org.uk. London's largest purpose-built hostel is located in a Docklands area that has little going for it compared to the location of other London YHAs, but it's only a 20min tube ride from the West End and often has space. Rooms have 2, 4, 5 or 10 beds and cost from £22.95; the twins cost £50. Rotherhithe or Canada Water tube.

St Pancras, 79–81 Euston Rd, NW1 ☎020/7388 9998; stpancras@yha.org .uk. Housed on six floors of a former police station, directly opposite the new British Library, on the busy Euston Road. Beds costs £22.95 per person, and rooms are very clean, bright, triple-glazed and air-conditioned – some even have en-suite facilities. There are a few en-suite doubles and family rooms available, all with TVs, for £50. No groups. King's Cross or Euston tube.

Windsor, Edgeworth House, Mill Lane, Windsor ☎01753/861710; windsor@yha .org.uk. Staying out in Windsor may not be everyone's idea of the best way to enjoy London, but it is easy enough to commute between the two, and beds here are half the price of the city hostels: £10.85 in 4- to 22-bed dorms. The hostel is housed in an attractive early eighteenth-century house, with a nice garden and a kitchen. Windsor & Eton Central train station from Paddington.

Accommodation

Private hostels

Albert Hotel, 191 Queen's Gate, SW7 ☎020/7584 3019; thealbertx@aol.com. Battered budget accommodation right next door to the luxury Gore Hotel. It's a long walk from the nearest tube, but very close to Hyde Park and the South Kensington museums. Dorm beds from £13–17, twins from £50. There's no kitchen, but breakfast is included, and there's a communal laundry and TV room. South Kensington, Gloucester Road or High Street Kensington tube.

Ashlee House, 261–265 Gray's Inn Rd, WC1 ☎020/7833 9400; info @ashleehouse.co.uk. 140-bed dorm in a converted office block near King's Cross Station. Dorms, which vary in size from 2 to 16 beds, can get a bit cramped, but the place is clean enough, and there's a laundry and kitchen for guests' use. Dorm beds start at £15; there's also a few private rooms with bunk bed at £48; breakfast is included. King's Cross tube.

Curzon House Hotel, 158 Courtfield Gardens, SW5 ☎020/7373 6745; www.curzonhousehotel.co.uk. Shared rooms from just £16, including continental breakfast and use of a small kitchen and TV lounge. Twins are available from £42; doubles from £48; discounts for longer stays. Gloucester Road tube.

Generator, Compton Place, off Tavistock Place, WC1 ☎020/7388 7666; www.the-generator.co.uk. A huge, funky hostel in a converted police barracks, hidden away down a cobbled street. The neon and UV lighting and post-industrial décor may not be to everyone's taste, but the youthful clientele certainly enjoy the cheap bar that's open daily until 2am. Over eight hundred beds, prices varying from £38

Accommodation

for a single, to £26 per person for a double, £22 per person for a triple, £20 for shared room and £15 for a dorm bed. Russell Square or Euston tube.

Hyde Park Hostel, 2–6 Inverness Terrace, W2 ☎020/7229 5101; *www.scoot.co.uk /astorhostels*. This grandiose stucco mansion in Bayswater is the latest acquisition by the Astor chain. They've got big plans which will no doubt one day come to fruition – in the meantime, it's £12.50–14 a night in five- to eight-bed dorms. Queensway tube.

Kagyu Samyé Dzong London, Carlisle Lane, SE1 ☎020/7928 5447; *www .samye.org/london*. Hostel-style accommodation for £15 per person in a small Tibetan Buddhist Centre, hidden away behind Waterloo station, off Royal Street. The perfect haven if you want to go to bed early (curfew is 9pm) in a meditative, smoke-free, alcohol-free environment; tea is free. Waterloo tube.

Leinster Inn, 7–12 Leinster Square, W2 ☎020/7229 9641; *www.scoot.co.uk /astorhostels*. The biggest and liveliest of the Astor hostels, with a party atmosphere, and two bars open until the small hours. Dorm beds (3–7 per room) £14–17 per person, singles £30, doubles £40. Queensway or Notting Hill Gate tube.

Museum Inn, 27 Montague St, W1 ☎020/7580 5360; *www.scoot.co.uk /astorhostels*. In a lovely Georgian house by the British Museum, this is the quietest of the Astor hostels. There's no bar, though it's still a sociable, laid-back place, and well situated. Dorms with 4–10 beds per room from £14–17, including breakfast. Small kitchen, TV lounge, and baths as well as showers. Russell Square tube.

Quest Hotel, 45 Queensborough Terrace, W2 ☎020/7229 7782; *www.scoot.co.uk /astorhostels*. Small, well-worn, but lively Astor hostel. Dorms with 4 to 5 beds per room from £15, including breakfast. The kitchen is fine for the hostel's capacity and there's also a TV lounge. Queensway tube.

St Christopher's Village, 161–165 Borough High St, SE1 ☎020/7407 1856; *www.st-christophers.co.uk*. Flagship of a chain of independent hostels, with no fewer than three properties on Borough High Street (and branches in Camden and Greenwich). The décor is upbeat and cheerful, the place is efficiently run and there's a party-animal ambience, fuelled by the neighbouring bar and the rooftop sauna and pool. London Bridge tube.

Tonbridge Club, 120 Cromer St, WC1 ☎020/7837 4406. This is a real last resort, but if you're desperate (and a non-British passport-holder), you can sleep on a mattress on the floor for £5 per person. Hot showers, TV room. Check-in 9pm to midnight. King's Cross tube.

Victoria Hotel, 71 Belgrave Rd, SW1 ☎020/7834 3077; *www.scoot.co.uk /astorhostels*. Another of the Astor hostels for the under-30s, with the usual lively atmosphere. Dorms with six to eight beds start at £12.50. Victoria tube.

Student halls

City University

City University (*www.city.ac.uk/ems*) offers rooms in two of its halls of residence to the general public all year round. You're best off either booking online or contacting the halls direct. **Francis Rowley Court**, 16 Briset St, EC1 ☎020/7505 5500 8822 (Farringdon tube), is a modern building in trendy Clerkenwell, with self-catering singles from £30, with TVs in every room and shared facilities throughout. The equally modern **Walter Sickert Hall**, Graham St, N1 ☎020/7477 8822 (Angel tube), just off the City Road, has single rooms with shared facilities from £26, plus en-suite twins from £55. Rates here include breakfast.

Imperial College ☎020/7594 9507; *www.ad.ic.ac.uk/conferences*. Three halls of residence are available through Imperial College: *Evelyn Gardens*, a Victorian terrace just off the Fulham Road in South Kensington; *Pembridge*

Gardens, stucco mansions in Notting Hill; and Prince's Gardens, in the main, modern campus in South Kensington, close to the college facilities. You can book online, and singles start at around £30, twin rooms from around £50, including breakfast. Easter & July to late Sept.

International Students House, 229 Great Portland St, W1 ☎020/7631 8300; www.ish.org.uk. Hundreds of beds in a vast complex at the southern end of Regent's Park. Dorm beds from £10, quads at £17.50 per person, twins at £22 per person, singles at £30. Open all year. Great Portland Street tube.

John Adams Hall, 15–23 Endsleigh St, WC1 ☎020/7387 4086. A hall of residence belonging to the Institute of Education, set in a Georgian terrace in Bloomsbury. Singles from £24, doubles from £40, including breakfast; discounts for students and longer stays. Open Easter & July–Sept. Euston Square tube.

King's College ☎020/7928 3777; www.kcl.ac.uk. King's College has a wide range of accommodation available from July to September. You can either contact the Vacation Bureau by phone or book online. **Great Dover Street apartments** (165 Great Dover St, SE1; Borough tube) is a Victorian building not far from Bankside, with en-suite singles at £30, and a few twins at £47; discounts for students, and a shared kitchen. **Hampstead Campus** (Kidderpore Ave, NW3; Finchley Road tube) is the cheapest and tattiest of the lot, and gets booked up quickly. It's located in a nice Victorian building on a tree-lined avenue, in walking distance from the Heath. Singles at £17 and twins at £29, all with shared facilities. **Stamford Street apartments** (127 Stamford St, SE1; Waterloo tube) is a new purpose-built block close to the South Bank, with smart en-suite single rooms, and a shared kitchen. All rooms are around £30. **Wellington Hall** (71 Vincent Square, SW1; Victoria tube) has singles from £26 and twins from £40, all with shared facilities; breakfast is included in the price.

London School of Economics (LSE) ☎020/7955 7370; www.lse.ac.uk /vacations. The LSE offers singles, twins, triples and quads in various halls across London, en suite or with shared facilities, and either on a bed-and-breakfast or self-catering basis. To find out about availability, you can ring the central office or contact the individual halls listed below; on the Web site, you can find out about prices, location and facilities, and then fill in a booking form online. Individual locations are: **Bankside House** (24 Sumner St, SE1 ☎020/7633 9877; open July–Sept; Southwark tube) has singles from £28; **Carr-Saunders Hall** (18–24 Fitzroy St, W1 ☎020/7323 9712; open Easter & July–Sept; Warren Street tube) has singles from £27; **High Holborn** (178 High Holborn, WC1 ☎020/7379 5589; open July–Sept; Holborn tube) has singles from £34; **Passfield Hall** (1–7 Endsleigh Place, WC1 ☎020/7387 3584; open Easter & July–Sept; Euston Square tube) has singles from £22.50; **Rosebery Avenue Hall** (90 Rosebery Ave, EC1 ☎020/7278 3251; open Easter & July–Sept; Angel tube) has singles from £26.

Campsites

Abbey Wood, Federation Rd, Abbey Wood, SE2 ☎020/8311 7708. Enormous, and well-equipped Caravan Club site, ten miles southeast of central London. Open all year. Abbey Wood train station from Charing Cross.

Crystal Palace, Crystal Palace Parade, SE19 ☎020/8778 7155. All-year Caravan Club site, with maximum stays of two weeks in summer, three weeks in winter. Crystal Palace train station from Victoria or London Bridge.

Lea Valley Leisure Centre Caravan Park, Meridian Way, N9 ☎020/8803 6900. Well-equipped site, situated behind the leisure centre at Pickett's Lock, backing on to a vast reservoir. Ponders End train station from Liverpool Street.

Tent City Hackney Camping, Millfields Rd, Hackney Marshes, E5 ☎020/8985 7656. The cheapest beds in London:

Accommodation

Accommodation

dorm tents for £5 a night, plus tent pitches. Big, but very inconvenient, way over in the east of the city with poor transport connections. Open June–Aug. Bus #38 from Victoria to Hackney Central, then #236 or #276.

Hotels and B&Bs

The following listings indicate some of London's best-value **hotels and B&Bs**, from palatial establishments patronized by royalty, statesmen and other celebrities to budget-bracket B&Bs. The bulk of the recommendations cost between £50 and £100 a double, though a few are considerably more expensive. During the week, the plush hotels tend to charge £300 and over, exclusive of VAT and breakfast. However, when the business types have gone home at the weekend, these same places slash their advertised rates to around £200, sometimes even less, with breakfast thrown in, too.

Most places take all major **credit cards**, particularly Visa and Access/MasterCard, so in the listings we've simply noted those that don't.

Victoria

The streets south and west of **Victoria Station** harbour dozens of very inexpensive B&Bs – notably along Belgrave Road and Ebury Street. This area is pretty dead in the evening, but it's generally better value than Earl's Court, is within easy striking distance of the West End, and is very convenient for those taking continental trains, or buses around Britain. Unless otherwise stated, Victoria is the nearest tube.

Cartref House & James House, 129 & 108 Ebury St, SW1 ☎020/7730 6176; *www.jamesandcartref.co.uk*. Two clean Georgian B&Bs situated opposite one another, and run by the same owners; en-suite rooms and ones with shared facilities available. ④.

Dover Hotel, 44 Belgrave Rd, SW1 ☎020/7821 9085; *www.rooms.demon .co.uk*. One of the best B&Bs in this area. All rooms are tastefully decorated, and have a shower, toilet, telephone and TV. ③.

The Goring, 15 Beeston Place, SW1 ☎020/7396 9000; *www.goringhotel .co.uk*. This Edwardian hotel, owned and run by the Goring family for three generations, succeeds in creating an atmosphere of elegance and tranquillity despite its position amid busy roads. Afternoon tea is served on the delightful private garden terrace in fine weather; doubles start at £210 (breakfast not included). ⑨.

Luna & Simone Hotel, 47–49 Belgrave Rd, SW1 ☎020/7834 5897; fax 7828 2474. Inexpensive B&B beyond Warwick Square, with a stylish foyer, friendly owner and plain, but very well-maintained rooms with TVs and telephones, some en suite, some with shared facilities. ④.

Melbourne House Hotel, 79 Belgrave Rd, SW1 ☎020/7828 3516; fax 7828 7120. One of the best B&Bs along Belgrave Road: family run, well furnished, offering clean and bright rooms, excellent communal areas and friendly service. All doubles have en-suite facilities, but there are a couple of very cheap singles without (£30). Victoria or Pimlico tube. ⑤.

Accommodation price codes

All hotel accommodation has been graded on a scale of 1 to 9 for the minimum nightly charge you can expect to pay for a double room in high season (breakfast is generally included in the price). The prices signified by these categories are as follows:

① under £40	④ £60–70	⑦ £110–150
② £40–50	⑤ £70–90	⑧ £150–200
③ £50–60	⑥ £90–110	⑨ over £200

Oxford House Hotel, 92–94 Cambridge St, SW1 ☎020/7834 6467; fax 7834 0225. Victoria tube. Probably the best-value rooms you can get in the vicinity of Victoria station. Showers and toilets are shared, but kept pristine. Full English breakfast is included in the price. ②.

Sanctuary House, 33 Tothill St, SW1 ☎020/7799 4044; *sanctuary@fullers .demon.co.uk*. Run by Fuller's Brewery, situated above a Fuller's pub, and decked out like one, too, in smart, pseudo-Victoriana. Breakfast is extra, and is served in the pub, but the location right by St James's Park is very central. Ask about the weekend deals. St James's Park tube. ⑥.

Topham's Hotel, 26 Ebury St, SW1 ☎020/7730 8147; *www.tophams.co.uk*. Charming family-owned hotel in the English country-house style, just a couple of minutes' walk from the Victoria stations. Sumptuously furnished en-suite twins or doubles from £120, including full English breakfast. ⑦.

Winchester Hotel, 17 Belgrave Rd, SW1 ☎020/7828 2972; fax 7828 5191. Exemplary B&B, one of the best medium-range places in Victoria. All rooms have en-suite facilities and TV, and are freshly decorated. ⑤.

Windermere Hotel, 142–144 Warwick Way, SW1 ☎020/7834 5163; *www .windermere-hotel.co.uk*. Situated at the western end of Warwick Way, this is a tastefully decorated and quietly stylish place, with a couple of good-value doubles with shared facilities and en-suite doubles for considerably more. There's a tasty restaurant downstairs, too. Sloane Square, Pimlico or Victoria tube. ④–⑦.

Woodville House & Morgan House, 107 & 120 Ebury St, SW1 ☎020/7730 1048, or 7730 2384; *www.woodvillehouse .co.uk*. Two above-average B&Bs, run by the same vivacious couple. Great breakfasts, patio garden and an iron and a fridge for guests to use. All rooms at *Woodville* are with shared facilities; some at *Morgan* are en suite. ③.

St James's, Mayfair and Marylebone

St James's and **Mayfair** contain few choices for mere mortals. **Marylebone** is more mixed, with a range of places on and around Gloucester Place, a convenient but traffic-clogged street running between Regent's Park and Oxford Street.

Brown's, 30–34 Albemarle St, W1 ☎020/7493 6020; *www.brownshotel .com*. An ever-popular, traditionally English hotel dating from the coronation of Queen Victoria, *Brown's* is renowned as one of the best in its class. Rosewood, antiques, stained glass and other fine period details set the tone, and the rooms are individually decorated. Without air conditioning. Nothing under £300. Green Park tube. ⑨.

Claridge's, Brook Street, W1 ☎020/7629 8860; *www.savoygroup.com*. This famous and glamorous Mayfair hotel is the chosen abode of visiting heads of state and media megastars. Twins or doubles cost over £350, but for this you get wardrobes bigger than most bathrooms, shower-heads the size of dinner plates and décor as plush as any vacationing potentate could wish for. Bond Street tube. ⑨.

The Dorchester, 54 Park Lane, W1 ☎020/7629 8888; *www.dorchesterhotel .com*. Rooms here cost over £300 (not including tax and breakfast), for which you get luxuries such as individual buzzers for valet, waiter or maid, and huge bathrooms. Most of the suites overlook Hyde Park, but the hotel won't guarantee park views. Superb European cuisine in the *Grill Room*, with the *Oriental* restaurant featuring Thai, Chinese and Indian food, and the *Bar* providing light Italian meals, cocktails and jazz in the evenings. There is also a fabulously equipped spa and gym. Hyde Park Corner tube. ⑨.

Dorset Square Hotel, 30–40 Dorset Square, NW1 ☎020/7723 7874; *www .firmdale.com*. Beautifully appointed on a Marylebone garden square, this relaxing hotel has cheery Regency town-house

Accommodation

style décor, comfortable doubles and a restaurant in the basement. Breakfast not included. Baker Street or Marylebone tube. ⑧.

Durrants Hotel, George St, W1 ☎020/7935 8131; *www.durrantshotel .co.uk*. Just round the corner from the Wallace Collection and Oxford Street, this Georgian terrace hotel first opened in 1790, and has been run by the same family since 1921. Inside, it's a great exercise in period-piece nostalgia, with lots of wood panelling, old prints and doormen. Bond Street tube. ⑦.

Edward Lear Hotel, 28–30 Seymour St, W1 ☎020/7402 5401; *www.edlear.com*. Great location close to Oxford Street and Hyde Park, lovely flower boxes and a plush foyer. Rooms themselves need a bit of a makeover, but the low prices reflect both this and the fact that most only have shared facilities. Kids free at the weekend. Marble Arch tube. ④.

Hotel La Place, 17 Nottingham Place, W1 ☎020/7486 2323; *www .hotellaplace.com*. Just off the busy Marylebone Road, this is a small, good-value place; rooms are all en suite, equipped with all the gadgets usually found in grander establishments and are comfortably furnished. Baker Street tube. ⑦.

The Landmark, 222 Marylebone Rd, NW1 ☎020/7631 8000; *www .landmarklondon.co.uk*. The location is hardly fashionable, but this hotel can stand comparison with almost any luxury establishment in London. Once inside the magnificently bright atrium, with its huge cast-iron pillars (a great spot for afternoon teas), all external distractions can be forgotten. The rooms are notably bigger than average, and cost over £300 for the least expensive of the three grades. In addition to bars and restaurants, there's a fitness centre and pool. Marylebone tube. ⑨.

The Langham Hilton, 1 Portland Place, W1 ☎020/7636 1000; *www.langham .hilton.com*. Built in 1865 as London's first grand hotel, the *Langham* has

rejoined the elite following a refurbishment that has painstakingly re-created the Victorian atmosphere of well-padded luxury. Standard twins cost nearly £350. Oxford Circus tube. ⑨.

Leonard, 15 Seymour St, W1 ☎020/7935 2010; *www.theleonard .com*. Very efficient place, elegantly decorated with a mixture of repro and real antiques, plus a touch of gilded pomp. Rooms, which start at around £235, have everything you'd expect, including a stereo system. The bar is open 24hr. Marble Arch tube. ⑨.

Lincoln House Hotel, 33 Gloucester Place, W1 ☎020/7486 7630; *www .lincoln-house-hotel.co.uk*. New wood panelling gives this B&B a ship's cabin feel. All rooms are en suite and well equipped, but rates vary according to the size of the bed and room itself. Marble Arch or Baker Street tube. ⑤.

The London Hilton, 22 Park Lane, W1 ☎020/7493 8000; *www.hilton.com*. From the outside, the *Hilton* may look dated, but the quality of the service, décor and furnishings makes it clear that the hotel is not sitting on its five-star laurels. The hotel boasts the finest views in Mayfair – especially from the *Windows* restaurant on the 28th floor. Rooms cost from around £290; those preferring a more intimate, town-house setting could stay at the popular *Hilton London Mews* behind the main building in Stanhope Row (☎020/7493 7222), where weekend room rates start at just £160, including breakfast. Green Park tube. ⑨.

The Metropolitan, Old Park Lane, W1 ☎020/7447 1000; *www.metropolitan .co.uk*. Run by Christina Ong, this terrifyingly trendy hotel near the *Hilton* adheres to the 1990s fad for pared-down minimalism. The staff are kitted out in DKNY clothes, the Japanese restaurant is outstanding, and the *Met* bar is members- and residents-only in the evenings. Green Park or Hyde Park Corner tube. ⑨.

Palace Hotel, 31 Great Cumberland Place, W1 ☎020/7262 5585; *palacehotel@compuserve*. Small but luxurious hotel which oozes class, from the hand-painted friezes of the staircase to the four-poster beds in many of the rooms. Breakfast included. Marble Arch tube. ⑦.

The Ritz, 150 Piccadilly, W1 ☎020/7493 8181; *www.theritzhotel.co.uk*. In a class of its own among London's hotels, with its extravagant Louis XVI interiors and overall air of decadent luxury. Rooms, which start at around £350 for a double, maintain the opulent French theme, with the west-facing accommodation, over-looking Green Park, in greatest demand. Ask about the special weekend pack-ages, including breakfast and cham-pagne, available throughout the year. Green Park tube. ⑨.

The Stafford, St James's Place, SW1 ☎020/7493 0111; *www .thestaffordhotel.co.uk*. Tucked in a quiet backstreet off St James's Street, with views of Green Park, the *Stafford* pro-vides high-class rooms in the main building from around £300, with more expensive accommodation in the unique *Carriage House*, a row of eighteenth-century stables luxuriously converted to large guest rooms. The hotel also offers the usual refined dining rooms, while the sporty *American Bar* and its courtyard terrace make a welcome change from the gentlemen's-club norm. Green Park tube. ⑨.

22 Jermyn Street, 22 Jermyn St, SW1 ☎020/7734 2353; *www.22jermyn.com*. Discreet hotel just off Piccadilly, providing well-appointed and traditionally decorat-ed studios from £240, and suites at just over £300. Small enough to offer a genuinely personal service, although there is no bar or dining room – break-fast is extra and is served in the rooms. Piccadilly Circus tube. ⑨.

Wigmore Court Hotel, 23 Gloucester Place, W1 ☎020/7935 0928; *www .wigmore-court-hotel.co.uk*. The relentless-ly pink décor may not be to everyone's taste, but this Georgian town house is a better than average B&B, boasting a high tally of returning clients. Comfortable

rooms with en-suite facilities, plus two doubles with shared facilities for just £70. Unusually, there's also a laundry and basic kitchen for guests' use. Marble Arch or Baker Street tube. ⑤.

Soho, Covent Garden and Strand

Booking into a hotel in **Soho** or **Covent Garden** puts you right in the centre of the West End. Hotels tend to be pricey, with just one or two choice places com-ing in at under £100 a double. The **Strand** is very busy with traffic, and chock-a-block with luxury hotels.

Covent Garden Hotel, 10 Monmouth St, WC2 ☎020/7806 1000; *www.firmdale .com*. Stylish conversion of a former French hospital in the heart of the West End, just off Shaftesbury Avenue. Rooms, which start at around £260 a double, are all stylishly and individually decorated in luxurious and striking fur-nishings. All mod cons including stereo, video, fax and voice mail. Bar and brasserie on the ground floor. Covent Garden tube. ⑨.

The Fielding Hotel, 4 Broad Court, Bow Street, WC2 ☎020/7836 8305; *www .the-fielding-hotel.co.uk*. Quietly and per-fectly situated on a traffic-free and gas-lit court, this excellent hotel is one of Covent Garden's hidden gems. Its en-suite rooms are a firm favourite with vis-iting performers, since it's just a few yards from the Royal Opera House. Breakfast is extra. Covent Garden tube. ⑥.

Hazlitt's, 6 Frith St, W1 ☎020/7434 1771; *reservations@hazlitts.co.uk*. Located off the south side of Soho Square, this early eighteenth-century building is a hotel of real character and charm, offering en-suite rooms decorated and furnished as close to period style as convenience and comfort allow. There is no dining room (although some of London's best restaurants are a stone's throw away), and continental breakfast (served in the rooms) is available, but isn't included in the rates. Tottenham Court Road tube. ⑨.

Accommodation

Accommodation

Manzi's, 1–2 Leicester St, WC2 ☎020/7734 0224; *manzis @netscapeonline.co.uk*. Set over the Italian and seafood restaurant of the same name, *Manzi's* is one of very few West End hotels in this price range, although noise might prove to be a nuisance. Continental breakfast is included in the price. Leicester Square tube. ⑤.

One Aldwych, 1 Aldwych, WC2 ☎020/7300 1000; *www.onealdwych .co.uk*. On the outside, this is one of London's few vaguely Art Nouveau buildings, built in 1907 for the *Morning Post*. However, little survives from those days, as the interior of this desperately fashionable luxury hotel firmly follows the 1990s minimalist trend. The draws now are the underwater music in the hotel's vast pool, the oodles of modern art about the place and the TVs in the bathrooms of the £300-plus rooms. Covent Garden or Temple tube. ⑨.

St Martin's Lane. 45 St Martin's Lane, WC2 ☎020/7300 5500 or ☎0800/634 5500; *stmartinslane@compuserve.com*. So cool you wouldn't know it was a hotel, this self-consciously chic "boutique hotel" from the New York-based Ian Schrager chain has proved an immediate hit with the media crowd. From the fluorescent yellow and white minimalist lobby to the large Portuguese limestone bathrooms, the interior has been designed throughout by the mischievous Philippe Starck. The *Light Bar* and the sushi *Sea Bar* are the most startling of the hotel's numerous eating and drinking outlets. Rooms currently start at around £250 a double, but rates come down at the weekend. Leicester Square tube. ⑨.

Sanderson, 50 Berners St, W1 ☎020/7300 1400; *sanderson.isuk @virginnet.co.uk*. This second collaboration by Schrager and Starck is set in a listed 1960s Fitzrovia office block. The usual assemblage of *objets d'art* peppers the white and magnolia lobby, where the black-clad staff flit about like silhouettes. The *Long Bar* is all translucent backlit onyx, but like the restaurant, is ludicrously overpriced. 3D "space" lifts take you to the equally bright white rooms (starting at around £250 a double), decked out with light wooden floors and billowing curtains. There's a large gym, steam room, sauna and health club on site. Tottenham Court Road or Oxford Circus tube. ⑨.

The Savoy, 1 Savoy Hill, Strand, WC2 ☎020/7836 4343; *www.savoy-group .co.uk*. Popular with businesspeople and politicians, the *Savoy* is a byword for luxury and service, though in some respects the charisma of the place is what keeps it ahead of many of its rivals. Rooms, which start at around £400 a double (weekend rates are considerably less) are decorated in the Deco style of the hotel's heyday or in a more classical vein. Guests have the use of the new Fitness Gallery and small pool on the third floor. *The Grill* is justly famed for its excellent cuisine, while the *American Bar* features jazz most evenings. Breakfasts and afternoon teas are served on the Thames Foyer, which peers through trees onto the river. Charing Cross tube. ⑨.

Strand Continental Hotel, 143 Strand, WC2 ☎020/7836 4880, fax 7379 6105. Almost opposite the *Waldorf*, this tiny Indian-run hotel offers very basic rooms with shared facilities, plus continental breakfast. Rooms have had a lick of paint in the not too distant past, but nothing too drastic, making this an unbeatable central London bargain. Temple or Covent Garden tube. Cash only. ②.

Waldorf, Aldwych, WC2 ☎020/7836 2400; *www.lemeridien-hotels.com*. A stay in the serenely luxurious Edwardian-era *Waldorf* is a memorable experience. The hotel's centrepiece is the Palm Court, which still stages tea dances every Sunday. The rooms have every comfort you'd want, though are by no means quite as spectacular. Published rates start at over £300, but pick a quiet weekend and you could pay as little as £100. Holborn or Temple tube. ⑨.

Bloomsbury

Bloomsbury is handy for the British Museum and the West End – Oxford

Street and Covent Garden are no more than ten minutes' walk away. Unfortunately, the main area for B&Bs is Gower Street, which is plagued by traffic, so make sure you get a room overlooking the gardens at the back. Cartwright Gardens, further north and east, is a much quieter Georgian crescent, and all the B&Bs here have use of the nearby tennis courts. Virtually all the hotels in the seedy neighbourhood opposite **King's Cross Station**, north of Bloomsbury, cater for the homeless on welfare.

Academy Hotel, 17–25 Gower St, WC1 ☎020/7631 4115; *www .etontownhouse.com*. Very, very smart place popular with business folk. Service is excellent, all rooms are air-conditioned, with luxurious bathrooms, and there are two lovely patio gardens to enjoy. Goodge Street or Tottenham Court Road tube. ⑧.

Arosfa Hotel, 83 Gower St, WC1 ☎ & fax 7636 2115. Well-maintained, simple B&B in the former home of Pre-Raphaelite painter John Everett Millais, with modern, plain furnishings, TVs and sinks in all the rooms and a small garden. Goodge Street or Euston Square tube. ③.

Hotel Cavendish, 75 Gower St, WC1 ☎020/7636 9079; *www.hotelcavendish .com*. A real bargain, with lovely owners, two beautiful overrun gardens and some quite well-preserved original features. All rooms have shared facilities, and there are some good-value family rooms, too. Goodge Street tube. ③.

Crescent Hotel, 49–50 Cartwright Gardens, WC1 ☎020/7387 1515; *www .crescenthoteloflondon.com*. Very comfortable and tastefully decorated B&B – definitely a cut above the rest, with a lovely blacked-up range in the breakfast room. All doubles are en suite, but there are a few bargain singles with shared facilities. Euston, King's Cross or Russell Square tube. ⑤.

Harlingford Hotel, 61–63 Cartwright Gardens, WC1 ☎020/7387 1551; fax 7387 4616. Another good option in this fine Georgian crescent. All rooms are en suite with TV, the lounge has a real fire, and the breakfast room is bright and cheery. Euston or Russell Square tube. ⑤.

Jenkins Hotel, 45 Cartwright Gardens, WC1 ☎020/7387 2067; *www .jenkinshotel.demon.co.uk*. Smartly kept, family-run place with just 14 fairly small, but well-equipped rooms, half of which are en suite. The lovely in-house black labrador is a big hit with visitors. ④.

myhotel, 11–13 Bayley St, WC1 ☎020/7667 6000; *www.myhotels.co.uk*. The aquarium in the lobby is the tell-tale sign that this is a feng shui hotel. Despite the positive vibes, and Conran-designed look, the double-glazed, air-conditioned rooms are on the small side for the price. Still, there's a gym, a very pleasant library, a restaurant attached and the location is great for the West End. Tottenham Court Road tube. ⑧.

Ridgemount Hotel, 65–67 Gower St, WC1 ☎020/7636 1141, fax 7636 2558. Old fashioned, family-run place, with small rooms, mostly with shared facilities, a garden, free hot-drinks machine and a laundry room. Cash only, but a reliable, basic bargain for Bloomsbury. Goodge Street tube. ②.

Hotel Russell, Russell Square, WC1 ☎020/7837 6470; *www .principalhotels.co.uk*. From its grand 1898 exterior to its opulent interiors of marble, wood and crystal, this late-Victorian landmark fully retains its period atmosphere in all its public areas. The rooms have less character but all are well appointed and decorated in a homely manner. Expensive, but various deals are available subject to availability. Breakfast is not included. Russell Square tube. ⑨.

Clerkenwell, the City & Docklands

Hotels are few and far between in **Clerkenwell** and, until recently, nonexistent in the **City** and **Docklands**. However, with areas on the edge of the City, like Clerkenwell, Hoxton and Brick Lane, now

Accommodation

Accommodation

replete with bars and restaurants, this is not a bad place to stay. More luxury hotels are in the pipeline for the City.

City Hotel, 12 Osborn St, E1 ☎020 /7247 3313; info@cityhotellondon.co.uk. Spacious, clean and modern inside, this hotel stands on the eastern edge of the City, in the heart of the Bengali East End at the bottom of Brick Lane. The plainly decorated rooms are all en suite, and many have kitchens, too; four-person rooms are bargain if you're a family or in a small group. Aldgate East tube. ⑦.

Four Seasons Hotel, 46 Westferry Circus, E14 ☎020/7510 1999; www .fourseasons.com. If you have to stay in Docklands (and someone else is paying), then stay here in style. Begun by Starck, but all the better for not having been finished off by him, the architecture is bizarre and the lobby a funkily open space, while several of the rooms (which start at £280) have superb Thames views. There's also the option of taking the boat into town. Canary Wharf tube and DLR. ⑨.

Great Eastern Hotel, Liverpool St, EC2 ☎020/7618 5000; www .great-eastern-hotel.co.uk. Without doubt, the place to stay if you need or wish to be near the City. This venerable late-nineteenth-century station hotel has had a complete Conran makeover, yet manages to retain much of its club-by flavour. The George pub boasts a superb mock-Tudor ceiling; the fabulous old lobby is now the Aurora restaurant, and the rooms themselves are impeccably well-appointed and tastefully furnished – to maximize your natural light, get a room facing out. Doubles start from around £250, but rates are cut at the weekend. Liverpool Street tube. ⑨.

International Hotel, Marsh Wall, E14 ☎020/7712 0100; www.britanniahotels .co.uk/internat.htm. Within walking distance of Canary Wharf, and one tube stop from the Dome, this is a classic, anonymous, mid-range business hotel.

Weekday rates are over £160, but at the weekend and on standby, you can get rooms for under £100. Canary Wharf tube or South Quay DLR. ⑤.

Jurys Inn, 60 Pentonville Rd, N1 ☎020/7282 5500; www.jurys.com. This modern Irish chain hotel is not a pretty sight on the busy Pentonville Road, but it's close to the tube, and equally convenient for the City and for Islington and Clerkenwell's trendy bars and restaurants. Service is very friendly, and the fixed room-rate is a bargain for three adults sharing or for those with kids. Angel tube. ⑤.

The Rookery, Peter's Lane, Cowcross Street, EC1 ☎020/7336 0931. Rambling Georgian town house on the edge of the City in trendy Clerkenwell that makes a fantastically discreet little hideaway. The rooms start at around £225 a double; each one has been individually designed in a deliciously camp, modern take on the Baroque period, and all have super bathrooms with lots of character. Farringdon tube. ⑧.

The South Bank

With the resurgence of the **South Bank**, thanks to the London Eye and the Tate Modern, various chain hotels have moved in, but there's not much else to choose from so far. Location is everything here.

Holiday Inn Express, 103–109 Southwark St, SE1 ☎020/7401 2525; www.hiexpress.com/lon-southwark. Unbeatable location just a stone's throw from the Tate Modern, and a relative bargain if you can stomach the motorway service station feel of the place. Southwark or Blackfriars tube. ⑤.

London Bridge Hotel, 8–18 London Bridge St, SE1 ☎020/7855 2200; www .london-bridge-hotel.co.uk. Perfectly placed for Southwark and Bankside or the City, this is a tastefully smart new hotel right by the station. As it attracts a mainly business clientele, rates do go down considerably at the weekend. London Bridge tube. ⑧.

London County Hall Travel Inn, Belvedere Rd, SE1 ☎020/7902 1619; *www.travelinn.co.uk*. Don't expect river views at these prices, but the location in County Hall itself is pretty good if you're up for a bit of sightseeing. Décor and ambience are functional, but for those with kids, the flat-rate rooms are a bargain. Waterloo or Westminster tube. ④.

London Marriott Hotel, County Hall, The County Hall, SE1 ☎020/7928 5200; *www.marriott.com/marriott/lonch*. If you want river views from County Hall, you'll need to book in here. Over three quarters of the rooms overlook the Thames, and many have little balconies, too, with prices hovering between £200 and £250. It's all suitably pompous inside, and there's a full-size indoor pool. Waterloo or Westminster tube. ⑨.

Mad Hatter, 3–7 Stamford St, SE1 ☎020/7401 9222; *madhatter@fullers .co.uk*. Situated above a Fuller's pub on the corner of Blackfriars Road, and run by the Fuller's brewery. Breakfast is extra, and is served in the pub, but this is a great location, a short walk from the Tate Modern and the South Bank. Ask about the weekend deals. Southwark or Blackfriars tube. ⑤.

Knightsbridge, Kensington and Chelsea

Adjoining Victoria to the west, the fashionable areas of **Belgravia**, **Knightsbridge** and **Kensington** are full of hotels catering for the sort of customers who can afford to shop in Harrods and other local stores, but there is a scattering of small, independent hotels offering good value for this exclusive neighbourhood. Average prices are slightly lower in **South Kensington** (site of the Victoria and Albert, Natural History and Science museums), and further south in **Chelsea**.

Abbey House, 11 Vicarage Gate, W8 ☎020/7727 2594. Inexpensive Victorian B&B in a quiet street just north of Kensington High Street, maintained to a very high standard by its attentive owners. Rooms are large and bright – prices are kept down by sharing facilities rather than fitting the usual cramped bathroom unit. Full English breakfast, with free tea and coffee available all day. High Street Kensington tube. Cash only. ⑤.

Aster House, 3 Sumner Place, SW7 ☎020/7581 5888; *www .welcome2london.com*. Pleasant, non-smoking B&B in a luxurious South Ken white-stuccoed street; there's a lovely garden at the back and a large conservatory, where breakfast is served. Singles with shared facilities start at a bargain £70 a night. South Kensington tube. ⑧.

Basil Street Hotel, 8 Basil St, SW3 ☎020/7581 3311; *www.thebasil.com*. Welcoming privately owned hotel in the heart of Knightsbridge, boasting a variety of idiosyncratically decorated rooms for just over £200. The women-only *Parrot Club* is a welcome riposte to the stuffy masculine bars of many traditional-style hotels. ⑨.

Blakes, 33 Roland Gardens, SW7 ☎020/7370 6701; *www.smallchichotels .com*. Blakes' dramatic interior – designed by Anouska Hempel – and glamorous suites have long attracted visiting celebs. A faintly *Raffles*-esque flavour pervades, with bamboo furniture and old travelling trunks mixing with unusual objects, tapestries and prints. Doubles from £220 are smart but small; fully equipped suites are spectacular, as they should be for £495. The restaurant and bar are excellent, and service is of a very high standard. Gloucester Road tube. ⑨.

Eden Plaza Hotel, 68–69 Queen's Gate, SW7 ☎020/7370 6111, fax 7370 0932. Part of a fast-growing budget-hotel chain catering for business and leisure clients. Rooms (sleeping up to four) are small, modern, en suite and brightly furnished, and there's a bistro and bar on the ground floor; breakfast is included. Gloucester Road tube. ⑤.

Five Sumner Place, 5 Sumner Place, SW7 ☎020/7584 7586; *www .sumnerplace.com*. Discreetly luxurious B&B in one of South Ken's prettiest

Accommodation

Accommodation

white-stuccoed terraces. All rooms are en suite and breakfast is served in the house's lovely conservatory. South Kensington tube. ⑧.

The Gore, 189 Queen's Gate, SW7 ☎020/7584 6601; *www.gorehotel.com.* Popular, privately owned century-old hotel, awash with oriental rugs, rich mahogany, walnut panelling and other Victoriana. A pricey but excellent bistro restaurant adds to its allure, and it's only a step away from Hyde Park. South Kensington, Gloucester Road or High Street Kensington tube. ⑧.

The Halkin, 5 Halkin St, SW1 ☎020/7333 1000; *www.halkin.co.uk.* A luxury hotel that spurns the chintzy country-house theme: elegant, Italian-influenced minimalism prevails in each of the 41 rooms, which cost from £300. The contemporary Italian theme is continued in the cuisine of the restaurant, which overlooks a private garden. Hyde Park Corner tube. ⑨.

Hotel 167, 167 Old Brompton Rd, SW5 ☎020/7373 0672; *www.hotel167.com.* Small, stylishly furnished B&B with en-suite facilities, double glazing and a fridge in all rooms. Continental buffet-style breakfast is served in the attractive morning room/reception. Gloucester Road tube. ⑥.

The Lanesborough, Hyde Park Corner, SW1 ☎020/7259 5599; *www .lanesborough.com.* A former hospital, this early nineteenth-century building has been meticulously restored in Regency style, with all mod cons discreetly hidden amid the ornate décor. Double rooms cost over £350, service is formal and the overall ambience conservative, in keeping with the tone of the diplomatic neighbourhood. Hyde Park Corner tube. ⑨.

Number Sixteen, 16 Sumner Place, SW7 ☎020/7589 5232; *www .numbersixteenhotel.co.uk.* Equally discreet B&B opposite *Five Sumner Place,* but this time larger and even more luxurious. Real fires, a conservatory and a charming garden. South Kensington tube. ⑧.

Sloane Hotel, 29 Draycott Place, SW3 ☎020/7581 5757; *www.premierhotels .com.* Understated hotel hidden in a terrace of red-brick mansions a short stroll from Sloane Square, and sumptuously stuffed full of antiques, which you can buy. There's also a fab roof terrace where you can take breakfast (which costs extra). Sloane Square tube. ⑧.

Strathmore Hotel, 41 Queen's Gate Gardens, SW7 ☎020/7584 0512; *www .grangehotels.co.uk.* Huge, old-fashioned and grandiose hotel close to the Kensington museums, recently overhauled by Grange Hotels. All double rooms have en-suite facilities and are nice and spacious, and rates include breakfast. Gloucester Road tube. ⑧.

Vicarage Hotel, 10 Vicarage Gate, W8 ☎020/7229 4030; *www .londonvicaragehotel.com.* Ideally located B&B a step away from Hyde Park. Clean rooms with shared facilities, and a full English breakfast included in the rates. Cash/travellers cheques only. ④.

Earl's Court

Tariffs take a drastic dive to the west of Kensington in **Earl's Court**, a network of Victorian terraced streets that's become a recognized backpackers' ghetto. Here you'll find a huge concentration of B&Bs, some offering dormitory-style accommodation. Earl's Court Road, which bisects this area, is a lively place, full of late-night supermarkets, cheap cafés, gay bars, fast-food joints, money-exchange booths and laundries. The nearest tube for all the following places is Earl's Court.

Amsterdam Hotel, 7 Trebovir Rd, SW5 ☎020/7370 5084; *www .amsterdam-hotel.com.* Just off Earl's Court Road, this presentable B&B has bright, clean en-suite rooms with TV. Continental breakfast is included; full English breakfast is an optional extra. ⑤.

Half Moon Hotel, 10 Earl's Court Square, SW5 ☎020/7373 9956, fax 7373 8456. Small, friendly B&B with clean rooms, some with en-suite facilities, all with TVs, and all at very keen prices. ②.

Kensington Court Hotel, 33 Nevern Place, SW5 ☎020/7370 5151. Situated near a quiet square, this modern hotel offers comfortable en-suite rooms with satellite TV, as well as an attractive lounge/bar area. Continental breakfast is included; English breakfast is extra. There's also a small car park. ⑤.

Merlyn Court Hotel, 2 Barkston Gardens, SW5 ☎020/7370 1640; *www .smoothhound.co.uk/hotels/merlyn.html*. Well-appointed and popular B&B in a quiet street close to the tube. Some rooms with en-suite facilities; English breakfast is included. ③.

Philbeach Hotel, 30–31 Philbeach Gardens, SW5 ☎020/7373 1244; *www .philbeachhotel.freeserve.co.uk*. Friendly, long-running gay/transvestite hotel, with basic and en-suite rooms, a pleasant TV lounge area, late bar and popular *Wilde About Oscar* garden restaurant. ④.

Rushmore Hotel, 11 Trebovir Rd, SW5 ☎020/7370 3839; fax 7370 0274. A cut above the average in this often dreary area, with colourful murals and imaginative Italianate room décor. The attic rooms are especially spacious and comfortable. Full continental breakfast is included. ⑥.

Paddington, Bayswater and Notting Hill

There's a lot of inexpensive accommodation in and around **Paddington** Station, especially along Sussex Gardens and in Norfolk Square, where small hotels and B&Bs outnumber residential homes. Proximity to Hyde Park is an added bonus here and in **Bayswater**, further west. Prices begin to rise, and places are few and far between, in neighbouring **Notting Hill**, which harbours a faintly bohemian community, as exemplified by the Portobello Road market.

Ashley Hotel, 15 Norfolk Square, W2 ☎020/7723 3375; *www.smoothhound .co.uk/hotels/ashley.html*. Three long-established hotels joined into one, just a couple of minutes' walk from Paddington Station. Most doubles have en-suite

facilities, though a few basic singles survive. English breakfast included. Paddington tube. ⑤.

The Columbia, 95–99 Lancaster Gate, W2 ☎020/7402 0021; *www .columbiahotel.co.uk*. Spacious public lounge, well-worn décor and useful 24-hour bar make this a rock-band favourite. All rooms are en suite. Lancaster Gate tube. ⑤.

Garden Court Hotel, 30–31 Kensington Garden Square, W2 ☎020/7229 2553; *www.gardencourthotel.co.uk*. Presentable, family-run B&B close to Portobello market; half the rooms are with shared facilities, half are en suite. English breakfast included. Bayswater or Queensway tube. ②.

The Gresham Hotel, 116 Sussex Gardens, W2 ☎020/7402 2920; *www .the-gresham-hotel.co.uk*. B&B with a touch more class than many in the area. Rooms are small but tastefully kitted out, and all have TV. Continental breakfast included. Paddington tube/train station. ⑤.

The Halcyon, 81 Holland Park, W11 ☎020/7727 7288; *www.thehalcyon .com*. This small and discreet hideaway is popular with paparazzi-dodging stars and anyone else with £280 or more to spare for a room (weekend rates come down to £200). For your money you get unrivalled personal service, lavish classical décor and cuisine to match. Holland Park tube. ⑨.

The Hempel, 31–35 Craven Hill Gardens, W2 ☎020/7 298 9000; *www .hempelhotel.com*. Deeply fashionable minimalist hotel, designed by Anouska Hempel, with a huge and very empty atrium entrance. White-on-white rooms start from around £290 for a double, and there's an excellent postmodern Italian/Thai restaurant called *I-Thai*. Lancaster Gate or Queensway tube. ⑨.

Mornington Hotel, 12 Lancaster Gate, W2 ☎020/7262 7361; *www .mornington.com*. Large Swiss-owned hotel with rooms decorated in Scandinavian style; the exception to the

Accommodation

Accommodation

Nordic theme is the bar/lounge, fitted out like a gentlemen's club with book-crammed shelving. A Swedish buffet or cooked breakfast is included. Lancaster Gate tube. ⑦.

Pavilion Hotel, 34–36 Sussex Gardens, W2 ☎020/7262 0905; *www.eol.net.mt /pavilion*. The successful rock star's home from home, with outrageously over-the-top décor and every room individually themed. Paddington tube/train station. ⑦.

Pembridge Court Hotel, 34 Pembridge Gardens, W11 ☎020/7229 9977; *www .pemct.co.uk*. Attractively converted town house close to Portobello Market, with spacious, fully equipped rooms. Two cats add to the homely feel, as does the lively *Caps Restaurant and Bar*. Notting Hill Gate or Holland Park tube. ⑧.

The Portobello Hotel, 22 Stanley Gardens, W11 ☎020/7727 2777; *www .portobello-hotel.co.uk*. Elegant Victorian hotel with individually designed double rooms, of varying sizes and prices, the most expensive overlooking the private gardens. Breakfast is included and there's a restaurant and 24-hour bar. Notting Hill Gate or Holland Park tube. ⑧.

St David's & Norfolk Court Hotel, 16–20 Norfolk Square, W2 ☎020/7723 4963; fax 7402 9061. A friendly welcome at this inexpensive B&B, famed for its substantial English breakfast. Most rooms share facilities. Paddington tube/train station. ④.

Hampstead

Hampstead is without doubt one of the most beguiling London suburbs, with a real village feel and the Heath close by, yet it's just 20min by tube to the West End.

Hampstead Village Guesthouse, 2 Kemplay Rd, NW3 ☎020/7435 8679; *hvguesthouse@dial.pipex.com*. Lovely B&B in an old house set in a quiet back-street between Hampstead Village and the Heath. Rooms (some en suite, all non-smoking) have "lived-in" clutter, which makes a change from anodyne hotels and spartan B&Bs. Meals to order. Hampstead tube. ⑤.

The House Hotel, Rosslyn Hill, NW3 ☎020/7431 3873. Spacious Victorian mansion on a busy junction. This place has lots of potential, and great things are promised. All rooms are en suite, and are gradually being upgraded. Hampstead or Belsize Park tube. ⑤.

La Gaffe, 107–111 Heath St, NW3 ☎020/7435 4941; *la-gaffe@msn.com*. Small, warren-like hotel situated over an Italian restaurant and bar in the heart of Hampstead Village. All rooms are en suite and there's a roof terrace for use in fine weather. Hampstead tube. ⑤.

Langorf Hotel, 20 Frognal, NW3 ☎020/7435 9055; *www.langorfhotel .com*. Pristinely maintained, tastefully decorated hotel in a trio of red-brick Victorian mansions, with a walled garden. There are also apartments, sleeping four or five for £130–150. Finchley Road or Hampstead tube. ⑥.

Chapter 15

Cafés and snacks

This short chapter covers **cafés, coffee bars, ice-cream parlours** and **tearooms**, all of which you'll find open during the day for light snacks or just a drink. Some of them also provide full evening meals, and, as they make little pretence to being full-blown restaurants, you can use them for an inexpensive or quick bite before going out to a theatre, cinema or club.

The listings here cover the range, from unreconstructed caffs, where you can get traditional **English breakfasts** (usually served until 11am), fish and chips, pies and other calorific treats, to the refined salons of London's top hotels, good for a teatime splurge. We have divided the listings in two: "Snacks, sandwiches, cakes and coffee", where you won't get much beyond that, and "Breakfasts, lunches and quick meals", where you can fill yourself up. Also featured are boxes on **afternoon tea**, cafés in parks, Internet cafés and a checklist of the best museum cafés and restaurants – some of which are almost worth a trip in their own right.

Snacks, sandwiches, cakes and coffee

As well as the places we've listed below, there are several London-wide chains that are well worth checking out. **EAT** (*www.eatcafe.co.uk*) is a promising new-comer, and makes up excellent sandwiches on its own-baked bread; **Pret à Manger** also does ready-made sandwiches (though it helps if you like mayo),

as well as hot stuffed croissants and sushi selections; **Caffè Nero** serves terrific coffee, a range of Italian cakes and pasta, calzone and pizza. As far as other coffee chains go; there's **Costa Coffee**, the train station favourite, which serves some of the best coffee in town, as does **Starbucks** (*www.starbucks.com*), the infamous clean-cut Seattle coffee company – **Coffee Republic** is a slightly less memorable replica; the only draw-back to **Aroma**, with its bright Aztec colours, designer sandwiches and Portuguese pastries, is that the whole chain is now owned by McDonalds. Also worth bearing in mind are the **Häagen-Dazs** outlets scattered around the capital, which offer cakes, sundaes, shakes and coffee alongside ice creams in a huge range of flavours.

The establishments listed below will just serve you a coffee if that's all you want. However, you'd be missing out to stick with just a drink, as our selection criterion lies in the quality of their cakes, sandwiches or snacks.

Mayfair and Marylebone
La Madeleine, 5 Vigo St, W1
☎020/7734 8353. Authentic French patisserie and café with mountains of tempting patisserie from which to indulge yourself while seated at the tables towards the front of the café; those at the back are for punters who want more substantial bistro fare. Green Park or Piccadilly Circus tube. Mon–Sat 8am–8pm, Sun 11am–7pm.

Cafés and snacks

Patisserie Valerie at Sagne, 105 Marylebone High St, W1 ☎020/7935 6240; *www.patisserie-valerie.co.uk.* Founded as *Maison Sagne* in the 1920s, and preserving its wonderful décor from those days, the café is now run by Soho's fab patisserie makers, and is without doubt Marylebone's finest. Bond Street tube. Mon–Fri 7.30am–7pm, Sat 8am–7pm, Sun 9am–6pm.

Regent Milk Bar, 362 Edgware Rd, W9 ☎020/7723 8669. A genuine 1950s milk bar, with the original chrome and pistachio- and vanilla-coloured formica in place. Caff food, lots of ice cream and knickerbocker glories. Edgware Road tube. Daily 9am–5.30pm.

Soho

Bar Italia, 22 Frith St, W1 ☎020/7437 4520. A tiny café that's a Soho institution, serving coffee, croissants and sandwiches more or less around the clock – as it has been since 1949. Popular with late-night clubbers and those here to watch the Italian-league soccer on the giant screen. Leicester Square tube. Nearly 24hr; closed Mon–Thurs 5–7am.

Beetroot, 92 Berwick St ☎020/7437 8591. Useful little veggie café in the heart of Soho's fruit and veg market. It's basically best as a takeaway place, so take your purchases over to St Anne's Gardens and enjoy them there. Piccadilly Circus, Oxford Circus or Tottenham Court Road tube. Mon–Sat 9am–7pm.

Maison Bertaux, 28 Greek St, W1 ☎020/7437 6007. Long-standing, old-fashioned, downbeat Soho patisserie, with tables on two floors (and one or two outside) and a loyal clientele that keeps them busy. You'll be tempted in by the window full of elaborate cakes, but be warned: when it comes to coffee, they only do *café au lait.* Leicester Square tube. Mon–Sat 9am–8pm, Sun 9am–1pm & 3–8pm.

Patisserie Valerie, 44 Old Compton St, W1 ☎020/7437 3466; *www .patisserie-valerie.co.uk.* Popular coffee, croissant and cake emporium dating from the 1920s and attracting a loud-talking, arty, people-watching Soho crowd. The same outfit now run *Maison Sagne* in Marylebone (see above) and the café inside the RIBA building, on Portland Place (see box on p.522). Leicester Square or Piccadilly Circus tube. Mon–Fri 7.30am–10pm, Sat & Sun 9.30am–7pm.

Covent Garden and Bloomsbury

M.J. Bradley's, 9 King St, WC2 ☎020/7240 5178. You'd have to go a long way to find designer sandwiches as good as these. Seats inside and out; takeaway, too. Covent Garden tube. Mon–Fri 8am–9pm, Sat & Sun 9am–10pm.

Coffee Gallery, 23 Museum St, WC1 ☎020/7436 0455. An excellent, if a little small, café close by the British Museum, serving mouthwatering Italian sandwiches and more substantial dishes at lunchtime. Get there early to grab a seat. Tottenham Court Road tube. Mon–Fri 8.30am–5.30pm, Sat 10am–5.30pm, Sun noon–6pm.

Mode, 57 Endell St, WC2 ☎020/7240 8085. The best things about this stylish Covent Garden café are the Italian sandwiches, the cheeses from nearby Neal's Yard Dairy and the laid-back, funky atmosphere. Covent Garden tube. Mon–Fri 8am–10pm, Sat 9am–9pm.

Monmouth Coffee Company, 27 Monmouth St, WC2 ☎020/7836 5272. The marvellous aroma is the first thing you notice here. Pick and mix your coffee from a fine selection (or buy the beans to take home), then settle into one of the cramped wooden booths and flick through daily newspapers on hand. No smoking. Covent Garden or Leicester Square tube. Mon–Sat 9am–6pm.

Poetry Café, 22 Betterton St, WC2 ☎020/7420 9888; *www.poetrysoc.com.* The ground-floor café is a pleasant place to relax, with salads, quiche and cakes on offer; the basement has had some fine poets grace its stage. You get four free visits before you're asked to join the in-house Poetry Society. Covent Garden

Cafés and snacks

INTERNET CAFÉS

If you just need to send a quick email to someone, or go online, head for a branch of *easyEverything* (*www.easyeverything.com*), the no-frills Internet café chain – there's a 24-hour branch just up the Strand, off Trafalgar Square; Net access starts at £1. Alternatively, the Internet cafés listed below are worth a visit in their own right.

The Buzz Bar, 95 Portobello Rd, W11 ☎020/7460 4906 (*mikebell @globalnet.co.uk*). Snug room above a pub, from which you can buy your drinks and snacks; there's an open fire burning in winter. Internet access is £3 per 30min. Notting Hill Gate or Ladbroke Grove tube. Mon–Sat 11am–8pm.

Global Café, 15 Golden Square, W1 ☎020/7287 2242; *www.globalcafe.net*. A pleasant, roomy central Soho café, with helpful staff, and a choice of

bagels, double-decker sandwiches, coffee, tea and beer. Access to one of the seven terminals costs around £5 an hour. Piccadilly Circus tube. Mon–Sat 11am–11pm.

The Vibe Bar, Truman Brewery, 91 Brick Lane, E1 ☎020/7247 3479; *www .vibe-bar.co.uk*. Head for "Room Service", a row of terminals in the corner of this trendy bar in a former East End brewery; Internet access is free of charge. Aldgate East tube. Mon–Sat 11am–11pm.

---

or Holborn tube. Mon–Fri 11am–11pm, Sat 6.30–11pm.

Clerkenwell & the East End

Brick Lane Beigel Bake, 159 Brick Lane, E1 ☎020/7729 0616. Classic bagel takeaway shop in the heart of the East End – unbelievably cheap, even for fillings such as smoked salmon and cream cheese. Whitechapel tube. Daily 24hr.

Feast, 86 St John St, EC1 ☎020/7253 7007. Delicious tortilla-wrapped sandwiches made to order; take away or eat in at this small, trendy, designer Clerkenwell café. Farringdon or Barbican tube. Mon–Fri 7.30am–4.30pm.

Ridley Bagel Bakery, 13–15 Ridley Rd, E8 ☎020/7923 0666. Fairy lights announce this bagel bakery as an oasis among the mean streets of Hackney. Dalston Kingsland train. Daily 24hr.

Lambeth and Brixton

Café Portugal, 6a Victoria House, South Lambeth Rd, SW8 ☎020/7587 1962. One of several Portuguese places stuck out on a limb beyond the traffic nightmare of Vauxhall. Still, this *pastelaria* is worth the trek. Vauxhall tube. Daily 10am–11.30pm.

Lounge, 88 Atlantic Rd, SW9 ☎020/7335 5229. Groovy little coffee bar a short way up towards Railton Road, with comfy sofas and Net surfing possibilities. Brixton tube. Mon–Sat 8am–late, Sun 10am–late.

Konditor & Cook, Young Vic Theatre, 66 The Cut, E1 ☎020/7729 0616. A cut above your average theatre café, this place gets its cakes and so forth made by the fabulous *Konditor & Cook* bakery, round the corner in Cornwall Road. You can also get snacks, organic ice creams and sorbets, and, of course, drinks at the bar. Waterloo tube. Mon–Fri 8.30am–11pm, Sat 10.30am–11pm.

Notting Hill

Books for Cooks, 4 Blenheim Crescent, W11 ☎020/7221 1992; *www .booksforcooks.com*. Tiny café/restaurant within London's top cookery bookshop. Conditions are cramped, but this is an experience not to be missed. Just wander in and have a coffee while browsing, or ring ahead to book a table for lunch. No smoking. Ladbroke Grove or Notting Hill Gate tube. Mon–Sat 9.30am–6pm.

Coins Coffee Store, 105–107 Talbot Rd, W11 ☎020/7221 8099. Spacious,

Cafés and snacks

Over the last few years, lunchtime catering in London has gone liquid, with an explosion of diminutive **soup and juice bars**. Below is a small selection to choose from:

Crussh, 48 Cornhill, EC3 ☎020/7626 2175. Tiny, unusually funky, City juice bar selling wraps, salads, sushi and, of course, fresh juices. Bank tube. Mon–Fri 7am–4pm.

Farmacia, 169 Drury Lane, EC3 ☎020/7831 0830. As the name suggests, this is a pharmacy dispensing organic juice to boost Covent Garden's unhealthy clubbers. Covent Garden or Holborn tube. Mon–Fri 8.30am–7pm.

Soup, 18 Cowcross St, EC1 (no phone). Tiny eat-in or takeaway soup outlet for the New Covent Garden Soup company, who make those nice cartons you can

buy in the supermarket. Farringdon tube. Mon–Fri 9am–5pm.

Soup Works, 9 D'Arblay St ☎020/7439 7687. Noodles served here as well as every type of soup from chicken to chilled borsht. Branches in Monmouth St, WC1, and Moor St, W1. Oxford Circus tube. Mon–Fri 8am–5pm, Sat noon–5pm.

Squeeze, 27 Kensington High St, W8 ☎020/7376 9786. Fruit smoothies, wraps, salads, sushi and muffins as well as fresh juices at this healthy pitstop. Mon–Fri 8am–7pm, Sat 9am–7pm, Sun 10am–7pm.

unpretentious café/diner just off the Portobello Road, offering all-day breakfasts, with tables outside in summer. Notting Hill Gate or Westbourne Park tube. Mon–Sat 8am–6pm, Sun 10am–4pm.

Lisboa Patisserie, 57 Golborne Rd, W10 ☎020/8968 5242. Authentic and friendly Portuguese *pastelaria*, with the best custard tarts this side of Lisbon – also coffee, cakes and a friendly atmosphere. The *Oporto* at no. 62a Golborne Road is a good fall-back if this place is full. Ladbroke Grove tube. Daily 8am–8pm.

Maison Blanc, 102 Holland Park Ave, W11 ☎020/7221 2494. French patisserie (with other branches in St John's Wood, Hampstead, Chelsea and Richmond) where you can guarantee you'll get the real thing when it comes to croissants and the like. Holland Park tube. Mon–Sat 8am–7pm, Sun 8.30am–6pm.

Kensington and Chelsea

Baker & Spice, 46 Walton St, SW3 ☎020/7589 4734. Absolutely spectacularly good Californian/French bread on offer, and patisserie, too. Only has a few tables out on what is a quiet backstreet,

right by the South Ken museums. South Kensington tube. Mon–Sat 7am–7pm, Sun 8.30am–2pm.

Patisserie Gloriette, 128 Brompton Rd, SW3 ☎020/7589 4750. Long-established Austrian *konditorei* serving mouth-wateringly delicious cakes, pastries and ice creams, a stone's throw from Harrods and the V&A. Knightsbridge tube. Mon–Sat 7am–7pm, Sun 9am–6pm.

Raison d'Être, 18 Bute St, SW7 ☎020/7584 5008. Smack in the middle of South Kensington's French quarter, this is a top-notch patisserie/boulangerie, serving excellent coffee. South Kensington tube. Mon–Fri 7.30am–6pm, Sat 9.30am–4pm.

North London

Café Delancy, 3 Delancy St, NW1 ☎020/7387 1985. Still probably the best French-style café in Camden, tucked away down a side road off Camden High Street; coffee, croissants, snacks and full meals. Camden Town or Mornington Crescent tube. Daily 9am–midnight.

Café Mozart, 17 Swains Lane, N6 ☎020/8348 1384. Viennese café – the food and cakes, that is – that's usefully

Cafés and snacks

Brew House, Kenwood, Hampstead Lane, NW3 ☎ 020/8341 5384. Everything from full English breakfast to lunches, cakes and teas, all served in the old laundry at Kenwood, or enjoyed on the terrace overlooking the lake. Highgate tube or bus #210 from Highgate. Daily: April–Sept 9am–6pm; Oct–March 9am–4pm.

Burlington's Café, Chiswick House, Burlington Lane, W4 ☎ 020/8742 7336. Chiswick House (see p.454) is one of West London's hidden gems, as is its park café, which offers delicious cakes and filling main courses that change daily. Chiswick train station or Turnham Green tube. Easter–Sept daily 10am–5pm; Oct–Easter Sat & Sun 10am–4pm.

Clissold Park Café, Stoke Newington Church St, N16 ☎ 020/7249 0672. Basic, no-nonsense, cheap café in the Georgian mansion of Stoke Newington's Clissold Park. Bus #73 from King's Cross or Angel tube. Daily: summer 10am–7pm; winter 10am–5pm.

Lauderdale House, Waterlow Park, Highgate Hill, N6 ☎ 020/8341 4807. Lovely café with a terrace overlooking the park, offering full meals as well as outrageous strawberry-and-cream scones on summer weekends. Archway tube. Tues–Sun 8am–7pm.

The Orangery, Kensington Palace, Kensington Gardens, W8 ☎ 020/7376 0239. Very swish café in Hawksmoor's Orangery, currently open year round. High Street Kensington or Notting Hill Gate tube. Daily: Easter–Sept 10am–6pm; Oct–Easter 10am–4pm.

Oshobasho Café, Highgate Wood, Muswell Hill Rd, N10 ☎ 020/8444 1505. Licensed veggie café in a former cricket pavilion, with great daily specials plus all the usual cakes and coffees. Highgate tube. Tues–Fri 9.30am–dusk, Sat & Sun 8.30am–dusk.

Popcorn in the Park, Alexandra Park, N10 ☎ 020/8883 0720. Unusual vegan café with an exquisite range of fresh-fruit sorbets. Alexandra Park train station from King's Cross. Daily 10am–5pm.

---

close to the southeast side of the Heath. They also serve a few hearty Austrian dishes. Gospel Oak train, or bus #C2. Daily 9am–10pm.

Louis Patisserie, 32 Heath St, NW3 ☎ 020/7435 9908. Popular Central European tearoom serving sticky cakes to a mix of Heath-bound hordes and elderly locals. (There's another branch at 12 Harben Parade, Finchley Rd, NW3.) Hampstead tube. Daily 9am–6pm.

Marine Ices, 8 Haverstock Hill, NW3 ☎ 020/7485 3132. Situated halfway between Camden and Hampstead, this is a splendid and justly famous old-fashioned Italian ice-cream parlour; pizza and pasta are served in the adjacent restaurant. Chalk Farm tube. Mon–Sat 10.30am–11pm, Sun 11am–10pm.

Primrose Patisserie, 136 Regent's Park Rd, NW1 ☎ 020/7722 7848. Very

popular pastel-pink and sky-blue patisserie in fashionable Primrose Hill, offering superb East European cakes and pastries. Chalk Farm tube. Daily 8am–9/10pm.

Greenwich

Pistachio's Café, 15 Nelson Rd, SE10 ☎ 020/8853 0602. Just about the only good sandwich café in the centre of Greenwich, serving excellent coffee, and with a small garden out back. (There's another branch at 43 Montpelier Vale, Blackheath, SE3.) Greenwich train station from London Bridge. Daily 10am–6pm.

Breakfasts, lunches and quick meals

There are cafés and small, basic restaurants all over London that can rustle up an **inexpensive meal**. You should be

Cafés and snacks

able to fill up at all of the places listed in this section for under £10, including tea or coffee.

Most of these cafés also feature big **English breakfasts** – fried egg, bacon, sausage and chips, usually available till 11am, but sometimes served all day and always very filling. A huge number of London's cafés are run by Anglo-Italians, which means you're guaranteed good coffee and ciabatta sandwiches. Several of the places listed are also open in the evening, but the turnover is fast, so don't expect to linger; they're best seen as fuel stops before – or in a few cases, after – a night out.

A few London-wide chains are worth checking out: the white and blue Art Deco-ish **Café Flo** does decent French brasserie fare, as does the red-clad **Café Rouge**; **Crank's**, the original veggie café, is making a bid for world domination, losing its character and flavour en route; **Ed's Easy Diner** is a 1950s-theme fast-food joint dishing up some of the city's best

burgers and fries for middling prices; and **Stockpot** serves big portions at rock-bottom prices.

Mayfair and Marylebone

Ayoush, 58 Wigmore St, W1 ☎020/7935 9839. Arab-style café off Oxford Street, with pungent hookahs for hire, and North African snacks and mint tea to sample. Bond Street tube. Daily noon–midnight.

Love, 62–64 Weymouth St, W1 ☎020/7487 5683. Laid-back organic café attached to the Aveda natural cosmetics shop, serving mostly veggie fare and fresh juices. Baker Street or Bond Street tube. Mon–Sat 8am–7pm.

Mô, 25 Heddon St, W1 ☎020/7434 4040. The ultimate Arabic pastiche, but a successful one at that. The restaurant is pricey, but the tearoom serves delicious snacks and is a great place to hang out, with tables and hookahs spilling out onto the pavement of this little Mayfair

---

AFTERNOON TEA

The classic **afternoon tea** – assorted sandwiches, scones and cream, cakes and tarts and, of course, lashings of tea – is available all over London. Best venues are the capital's top hotels and most fashionable department stores; a selection is picked out below. To avoid disappointment it's best to book ahead. Expect to spend around £20 a head, and leave your jeans and trainers at home – most hotels will expect men to wear a jacket of some sort, though only the *Ritz* insists on jacket and tie. For more on the ambience of the following listings, see pp.503–6.

Brown's, 30–34 Albemarle St, W1 ☎020/7493 6020; *www.brownshotel .com*. Green Park tube. Daily 3–6pm.

Claridge's, Brook Street, W1 ☎020/7629 8860; *www.savoy-group .co.uk*. Bond Street tube. Daily 3–5.30pm.

The Dorchester, 54 Park Lane, W1 ☎020/7629 8888; *www.dorchesterhotel .com*. Hyde Park Corner tube. Daily 3–6pm.

Fortnum & Mason, *The Fountain*, 181 Piccadilly, W1 ☎020/7734 8040; *www .fortnumandmason.com*. Green Park tube. Mon–Sat 3–5pm.

The Lanesborough, Hyde Park Corner, SW1 ☎020/7259 5599; *www .lanesborough.com*. Hyde Park Corner tube. Daily 3.30–6pm.

The Ritz, Piccadilly, W1 ☎020/7493 8181; *www.theritzhotel.co.uk*. Green Park tube. Daily 2–6pm.

The Savoy, Strand, WC2 ☎020/7836 4343; *www.savoy-group.co.uk*. Charing Cross tube. Daily 3–5.30pm.

The Waldorf, Aldwych, WC2 ☎020/7836 2400; *www.forte-hotels .com*. Holborn or Temple tube. Mon–Fri 3–5.30pm; tea dances Sat 2.30–5pm, Sun 4–6.30pm.

alleyway behind Regent Street. Piccadilly Circus tube. Mon–Sat noon–1pm, Sun noon–5pm.

Sotheby's, 34–35 New Bond St, W1 ☎020/7293 5077. As you might expect, Sotheby's café is by no means cheap, but the lunches are exquisitely prepared, and the excellent afternoon teas are a fraction of the price of the nearby hotels. Bond Street tube. Mon–Fri 9.30–11.30am & noon–4.45pm.

Soho

Bar du Marché, 19 Berwick St, W1 ☎020/7734 4606. A weird find in the middle of raucous Berwick Street market: a French café serving quick snacks, brasserie staples, fried breakfasts and set meals for under £10. Leicester Square or Tottenham Court Road tube. Mon–Sat 10am–11pm.

Centrale, 16 Moor St, W1 ☎020/7437 5513. Tiny, friendly Italian café that serves up huge plates of steaming, garlicky pasta as well as omelettes, chicken and chops for around £5. You'll almost certainly have to wait for – or share – a formica-topped table. Bring your own booze; there's a 50p–£1 corkage charge. Leicester Square tube. Mon–Sat noon–9.45pm.

Lee Ho Fook 4 Macclesfield St, W1 ☎020/7734 0782. A genuine Chinese barbecue house – small, spartan and cheap – that's very difficult to find. Firstly, it is not the larger, grander, more tourist-friendly Lee Ho Fook around the corner in Gerrard Street. Macclesfield Street runs from Shaftesbury Avenue to Gerrard Street; on the west side is Dansey Place, and on the corner with a red and gold sign in Chinese and a host of ducks hanging on a rack is this place. Leicester Square tube. Daily 11.30am–11pm.

Pollo, 20 Old Compton St, W1 ☎020/7734 5917. You won't find much haute cuisine at Pollo, but you do get value for money. As at neighbouring *Centrale* (see above), we're talking comfort food, Latin style. Devotees return time and again for the cheap platefuls of

filling pasta dishes, and friendly prompt service. Alcohol is served. Leicester Square tube. Daily noon–midnight.

Tokyo Diner 2 Newport Place, WC2 ☎020/7287 8777. Providing conclusive proof that you don't need to take out a second mortgage to enjoy Japanese food in London, this friendly eatery on the edge of Chinatown shuns elaboration for fast food, Tokyo style. Minimalist décor lets the sushi and sumo do the talking, which – if the number of Japanese who frequent the place is anything to go by – it does fluently. Leicester Square tube. Daily noon–midnight.

Fitzrovia

Diwana Bhel Poori House, 121 Drummond St, NW1 ☎020/7387 5556. Unlicensed, South-Indian restaurant, specializing in *dosas, bhel poori* and vegetarian *thalis*. Not a place for a night out, but the food and prices usually manage to please. Euston or Euston Square tube. Daily noon–11.30pm.

Indian YMCA, 41 Fitzroy Square, W1 ☎020/7387 0411. Don't take any notice of the signs saying the canteen is only for students – this place is open to the public; just press the bell and pile in. The entire menu is portioned up into pretty little bowls; go and collect what you want and pay at the till. The food is great and the prices unbelievably low. Warren Street tube. Mon–Fri 8–9.15am, 12.30–1.45pm & 8–9.15pm, Sat & Sun 8.30–9.30am, 12.30–1.45pm & 8–9.15pm.

Covent Garden and the Strand

Café in the Crypt, St Martin-in-the-Fields, Duncannon St, WC2 ☎020/7839 4342. The self-service buffet food is nothing special, but there are regular veggie dishes, and the handy location – below the church in the crypt – makes this an ideal spot to fill up before hitting the West End. Charing Cross tube. Mon–Sat 10am–8pm, Sun noon–8pm.

Cafés and snacks

Cafés and snacks

Food for Thought, 31 Neal St, WC2 ☎020/7836 0239. Long-established but minuscule bargain veggie restaurant and takeaway counter – the food is good, with the menu changing twice daily, plus regular vegan and wheat-free options. Expect to queue and don't expect to linger at peak times. Covent Garden tube. Mon–Sat 9.30am–8.30pm.

Frank's Cafe, 52 Neal St, WC2 ☎020/7836 6345. Classic Anglo-Italian café/sandwich bar with easy-going service. All-day breakfasts and plates of pasta and omelettes on offer; come either side of lunch to make sure of a table. Covent Garden tube. Mon–Sat 7.30am–8pm.

Gaby's, 30 Charing Cross Rd, WC2 ☎020/7836 233. Busy café and takeaway joint serving a wide range of home-cooked veggie and Middle Eastern specialities. Hard to beat for value, choice or long hours. It's licensed, too, and the takeaway falafel is a central London bargain. Leicester Square tube. Mon–Sat 9am–midnight, Sun 11am–9pm.

India Club, 143 Strand, WC2 ☎020/7836 0650. There's a faded period charm to this long-established, inexpensive Anglo-Indian eatery, sandwiched between floors of the cheap *Strand Continental Hotel* (see p.506). The chilli bhajis are to be taken very seriously. Covent Garden or Temple tube. Mon–Sat noon–2.30pm & 6–10pm.

Neal's Yard Bakery and Tearoom, 6 Neal's Yard, WC2 ☎020/7836 5199. Ramshackle first-floor room above superb co-operative organic bakery. Order your food downstairs before heading for the rickety seats upstairs. Covent Garden tube. Mon–Sat 10.30am–4.30pm.

Porky's Pantry, 49 Chandos Place, WC2 ☎020/7836 0967. Cracking little early-opening diner/sandwich bar diagonally opposite Charing Cross post office, with all-day breakfasts or super fry-ups for well under a fiver. Charing Cross tube. Mon–Sat 6am–5.30pm.

Wagamama 4 Streatham St, WC1 ☎020/7323 9223; *www.wagamama.com*. Austere, minimalist, canteen-style place where the waiters take your orders on hand-held computers. Diners share long benches and slurp huge bowls of noodle soup or stir-fried plates. You may have to queue, however, and the rapid turnover means it's not a place to consider for a long, romantic dinner. Tottenham Court Road tube. Mon–Sat noon–11pm, Sun 12.30–10pm.

World Food Café, 14 Neal's Yard, WC2 ☎020/7379 0298. First-floor veggie café that comes into its own in summer, when the windows are flung open and you can gaze down upon trendy humanity as you tuck into pricey but tasty dishes from all corners of the globe. Bring your own booze, or stick to the fruit juices. Covent Garden tube. Mon–Sat noon–5pm.

Clerkenwell & the City

Al's Café Bar, 11–13 Exmouth Market, EC1 ☎020/7837 4821. This is a trendy little spot – a designer greasy spoon with a local media-luvvie clientele, who are served up Italian breads, Mediterranean dishes, nachos, decent coffee and good soups alongside the chips and grills. Angel or Farringdon tube. Mon & Tues 8am–midnight, Wed–Fri 8am–2am, Sat & Sun 9.30am–2am.

Clark & Sons, 46 Exmouth Market, EC1 ☎020/7837 1974. Exmouth Market has undergone something of a trendy transformation, so it's all the more surprising to find this genuine eel and pie shop still going strong – this is the most central one in the capital. Angel or Farringdon tube. Mon–Thurs 10.30am–4pm, Fri 10.30am–5.30pm, Sat 10.30am–5pm.

Lunch, 60 Exmouth Market, EC1 ☎020/7278 2420. In style and ambience, the minimalist *Lunch* is typical of nouveau Clerkenwell. However, the food is good, salads fresh, the specials worth looking out for, and, in fine weather, there's often a barbie out the back. Angel or Farringdon tube. Mon–Fri 8.30am–4pm, Sat 10am–4pm.

The Place Below, St Mary-le-Bow, Cheapside, EC2 ☎020/7329 0789. Something of a find in the midst of the City – a café serving imaginative (albeit slightly pricey) vegetarian dishes. Added to that, the wonderful Norman crypt makes for a very pleasant place in which to dine. St Paul's or Bank tube. Mon–Fri 7.30am–2.30pm.

Ponti's Polo Bar, 176 Bishopsgate, EC2 ☎020/7283 4889. There's nothing in any way special about the Ponti's chain of cafés, but they're cheap, filling, vaguely Italian, and this particular branch is open round the clock. Liverpool Street tube. Daily 24hr.

East End & Docklands

Arkansas Café Unit 12, Old Spitalfields Market, E1 ☎020/7377 6999. American barbecue fuel stop, using only the very best ingredients. Try chef Bubb's own smoked beef brisket and ribs, and be sure to taste his home-made barbie sauce (made to a secret formula). Liverpool Street tube. Mon–Sat noon–2.30pm, Sun noon–4pm.

F. Cooke, 9 Broadway Market, E8 ☎020/7254 6458. Great little East End pie and mash shop serving meat or veggie-mince versions with mash, and fresh eels too. Bus #55 from Old Street tube. Mon–Sat 10.30am–7pm.

Hubbub, 269 Westferry Rd, E14 ☎020/7515 5577. A real oasis in the desert of Docklands, this café is housed in a former church, now arts centre, and does decent fry-ups, sandwiches and a few fancier dishes. Mudchute DLR or bus #D7 from Westferry DLR. Daily 11am–11pm.

Huong-Viet, 12–14 Englefield Rd, N1 ☎020/7249 0877. Tip-top Vietnamese food from this community café, a couple of stops before you reach Dalston. No licence, but home-made lemonade on offer. Bus #149 or #242 from Liverpool Street tube. Mon–Fri & Sun noon–3.30pm, Sat noon–4pm.

E. Pellicci, 332 Bethnal Green Rd, E2 ☎020/7739 4873. Famous East End caff with original 1940s décor intact, serving great fry-ups and good Anglo-Italian grub at low prices. Bethnal Green tube. Mon–Sat 6.30am–5pm.

Notting Hill

Costas Fish Restaurant, 18 Hillgate St, W8 ☎020/7727 4310. One of the best fish and chips experiences in London can be had at this old-fashioned Greek-Cypriot caff. Notting Hill tube. Tues–Sat noon–2.30pm & 5.30–10.30pm.

Sausage and Mash Café, 268 Portobello Rd, W11 ☎020/8968 8898. Pricier-than-usual bangers and mash W11-style, with retro furnishings and cheap booze. Ladbroke Grove tube. Tues–Sun 11am–10pm.

Victoria, South Ken and Chelsea

Daquise 20 Thurloe St, SW7 ☎020/7589 6117. This old-fashioned Polish café right by the tube is something of a South Ken institution, serving Polish home cooking or simple coffee, tea and cakes depending on the time of day. South Kensington tube. Daily 11.30am–11pm.

Jenny Lo's Teahouse 14 Ecclestone St, SW1 ☎020/7259 0399. Bright, bare and utilitarian yet somehow stylish and fashionable, too, Jenny Lo's serves good Chinese food at low prices. Be sure to check out the therapeutic teas. Victoria tube. Mon–Fri 11.30am–3pm & 6–10pm, Sat noon–10pm.

New Culture Revolution 305 King's Rd, SW3 ☎020/7352 9281. Great name, great concept – big bowls of freshly cooked noodles in sauce or soup, or dumplings and rice dishes, all offering a one-stop meal at bargain prices in simple, minimalist surroundings. Not a place to linger. Sloane Square tube. Daily noon–11pm.

Greenwich

Tai Won Mein, 49 Greenwich Church St, SE10 ☎020/8858 1668. Good-quality fast-food noodle bar that gets very busy at weekends. Décor is functional and minimalist; choose between rice, fried or soup noodles and *ho fun* (a flatter,

Cafés and
snacks

Cafés and snacks

Most museums in London have a café of some description, several run by the ubiquitous and perfectly pleasant Millburns chain. Others are a bit more special and are worth planning your visiting times around. The best of the bunch include:

Design Museum, Butlers Wharf, SE1 ☎020/7378 6055; see p.323. The ground-floor café is a simple coffee and cake affair; if you're feeling flush, though, book a table at Conran's *Blue Print Café*, above the museum.

Estorick Collection, 39a Canonbury Square, N1; see p.398. *Café Panini* does great ciabatta sandwiches and salads, and has a quiet little gravel terrace.

ICA Café, The Mall, SW1 ☎020/7930 8754; see p.70. Great Italian and more international fare at the avant-garde HQ.

National Gallery, Trafalgar Square, WC2 ☎020/7747 2869; see p.53. The NG's new café-restaurant, *Crivelli's Garden*, in the Sainsbury Wing, is better than ever before.

National Portrait Gallery, St Martin's Place, WC2 ☎020/7312 2490; see p.65. The NPG's pricey new café-restaurant, *The Portrait*, has an unusual roof-top view over Trafalgar Square.

RIBA, 66 Portland Place, W1 ☎020/7631 0467; see p.128. The architects' HQ has a branch of the wonderful *Patisserie Valerie* on its first floor.

Science Museum, Exhibition Rd, SW7 ☎020/7938 8080; see p.356. The funky-looking *Deep Blue Café* is situated in the museum's new Wellcome Wing, and serves pizza, pasta and rotisserie chicken on long, underlit tables.

Tate Modern, Sumner St, SE1 ☎020/7401 5020; see p.311. *Café Level Seven* is often booked out, but get there early and you may have a chance – the views are terrific. *Café Level Two* is more ordinary, as are the views, but the food is just as good.

Wallace Collection, Manchester Square, W1 ☎020/7935 0687; see p.128. The Wallace Collection's *Café Bagatelle* is situated in the new covered courtyard, and serves classy, pricey Modern European food.

softer, ribbon-like noodle). Cutty Sark DLR or Greenwich DLR and train station. Daily 11.30am–11.30pm.

North London

Blue Legume, 101 Stoke Newington Church St, N16 ☎020/7923 1303. Buzzy atmosphere, arty décor, mosaic tables and delicious chocolate cakes, teas and coffee. Good breakfasts too – smoked fish, wild mushrooms on toast and the like. Bus #73 from King's Cross or Angel tube. Tues & Wed 9.30am–6.30pm, Thurs & Fri 9.30am–11pm, Sat 10.30am–11pm, Sun 10.30am–6.30pm.

L Manze, 76 Walthamstow High St, E17 ☎020/8520 2855. No longer run by the Manze family, but still boasting its original 1929 décor, this is probably London's finest pie and mash shop,

architecturally speaking. Walthamstow Central tube. Mon–Wed 10am–4pm, Thurs–Sat 10am–5pm.

Sauce barorganicdiner, 214 Camden High St, NW1 ☎020/7482 0777. *Sauce* offers food free of chemicals, pesticides and preservatives in a bright, colourful diner, with a juice and cocktail bar attached. Burgers, sandwiches and wraps are on the menu, and it's also fine to go just for a coffee or a beer. Camden Town tube. Mon–Sat noon–11pm Sun noon–4.30pm.

Upper Street Fish Shop, 324 Upper St, N1 ☎020/7359 1401. Probably the best budget fill-up in Islington, takeaway and sit-down fresh fish and chips, plus fancier fare such as oysters and halibut. Angel tube. Mon 6–10pm, Tues–Sat noon–2pm & 6–10pm.

Chapter 16

Restaurants

London is a great place in which to eat. You can sample more or less any kind of cuisine here, and – wherever you come from – you should find something new and possibly unique. The list of positive recommendations is wide and ever-expanding. London is home to some of the best **Cantonese** restaurants in the whole of Europe, is a noted centre for **Indian and Bangladeshi** food, and has numerous French, Greek, Italian, Japanese, Spanish and Thai restaurants. And within all these cuisines you can choose anything from simple meals to gourmet spreads. Traditional and modern **British** food is available all over town, and some of the best venues are reviewed below.

There are plenty of places to eat around the main tourist drags of the West End – **Soho** has long been renowned for its eclectic and fashionable restaurants – and new eateries appear every month – while **Chinatown**, on the other side of Shaftesbury Avenue, offers value-for-money eating right in the centre of town. Further west, upmarket areas like **Kensington** and **Chelsea** feature many *haute cuisine* restaurants.

To sample the full range of possibilities, it's worth taking time to explore quarters away from the core of the city. Try the Indian, Pakistani and Bangladeshi restaurants of Brick Lane in the **East End** or around **Wembley** and **Southall**, for example, or the bistros and brasseries of **Camden** and **Islington**, a short tube ride away to the north.

Many of the restaurants we've listed will be busy on most nights of the week, particularly on Thursday, Friday and Saturday. You're best advised to **reserve a table** wherever you're headed, and with the most renowned places you'll probably be disappointed unless you plan at least a week ahead; don't be surprised to be asked for a contact number and for your table reservation to be confirmed by the restaurant nearer the date. If you can't make your reservation, let the restaurant know.

We've given the **opening hours** for all the restaurants listed in this chapter, but it's always worth calling to check, as things change and some proprietors have a creative attitude towards timekeeping. Most places take all major credit cards, particularly Visa and Access/MasterCard – in the listings, we've simply noted those that don't.

As for **prices**, you can pay an awful lot for a meal in London, and if you're used to North American portions you're not going to be particularly impressed by the volume in most places. In the listings, we've quoted the minimum you can get away with spending (one main course and a drink) to the amount you can expect to pay for a full blowout. For really cheap eats, see the previous chapter.

At most places, **service** is discretionary, but restaurants tend to take no chances, emblazoning their bills with reminders that "Service is NOT included", or even including a ten to fifteen percent service charge on the bill, which they

Restaurants

have to announce on the menu, by law. Normally you should, of course, pay service – it's how most of the staff make up their wages – but check to ensure you're not paying twice.

In addition, if you're paying by credit card and service is already included, check that the "total" box on the card slip is not left blank, thereby encouraging you to leave another tip. If this happens, complain to the management.

St James's and Mayfair

The Criterion, 224 Piccadilly, W1 ☎020/7930 0488. One of the city's most beautiful restaurants, right by Piccadilly Circus. Refurbishment has made the huge dining room sparkle, and the menu has been devised by scourge of the faint-hearted, Marco Pierre White. Piccadilly Circus tube. Mon–Sat noon–2.30pm & 6–11pm, Sun noon–3pm & 6–10.30pm. £20–45.

L'Oranger, 5 St James's St, SW1 ☎020/7839 3774. From the outside, this place looks like a very expensive French restaurant dedicated to expense account diners. However, while it's not cheap, the inclusive menus bring serious French cooking within reach. At lunch you pay £20 for two courses and around £25 for three. Green Park tube. Mon–Fri noon–2.30pm & 6–11pm, Sat 6–11pm. £23–65.

Mirabelle, 56 Curzon St, W1 ☎020/7499 4636. Elegant, beautifully presented *haute cuisine* at occasionally reasonable prices – go for the set lunches and avoid the wine list and you could eat for under £20. Green Park tube. Mon–Fri noon–2.30pm & 6–11.30pm, Sat & Sun 6–10.30pm. £22–90.

Momo, 25 Heddon St, W1 ☎020/7434 4040. Hip and fashionable Moroccan restaurant where you need to book at least a fortnight in advance. Décor is "harem-meets-style-police"; ambience is noisy and clubbish; food is excellent. Piccadilly Circus tube. Mon–Fri noon–2.30pm & 7–11.30pm, Sat 7–11.30pm, Sun 7–10pm £28–45.

Quaglino's, 16 Bury St, SW1 ☎020/7930 6767; *www.conran.com*. Huge 1930s ballroom revived by Terence Conran as one of the capital's busiest and most fashionable eating spots. Tourists are more in evidence than the glitterati these days, but you still need to book well in advance. Dishes don't always work but the splendid surroundings and an unmistakable buzz are the reward. Green Park tube. Mon–Sat noon–3pm & 5.30pm–midnight, Sun 5.30–11pm. £22–50.

Marylebone

Abu Ali, 136–138 George St, W1 ☎020/7724 6338. Honest Lebanese fare from the *tabbouleh* to the kebabs that's terrific value for money – wash it all down with fresh mint tea. Marble Arch tube. Daily 9.30am–midnight. Cash only. £7–25.

Caravan Serai, 50 Paddington St, W1 ☎020/7935 1208. Afghan restaurant set up in 1975 and little changed since then, with a menu that reveals strong links between Afghan, Indian and Middle Eastern cuisines. You'll see a good many familiar spices, healthy dollops of yoghurt, and a tandoor in the kitchen. Baker Street tube. Mon–Sat noon–3pm & 6–11pm, Sun noon–3pm & 6–10.30pm. £14–27.

Ibla, 89 Marylebone High St, W1 ☎020/7224 3799. If possible, ask for a table in the back room, a pretty yet functional square space painted beetroot-red, and settle down for some excellent Italian food. Baker Street or Regent's Park tube. Mon–Sat noon–2.30pm & 7–10.15pm. £18–35.

La Spighetta, 43 Blandford St, W1 ☎020/7486 7340. Not a spaghetti house, in fact, but a pizza and pasta joint – *spighetta* means "wheat" – and a very good one at that. Bond Street tube. Mon–Fri noon–2.15pm & 6.30–10.30pm, Sat until 11pm, Sun 6.30–10.30pm. £25–40.

Mandalay, 444 Edgware Rd, W2 ☎020/7258 3696; *www.bcity.com*

/mandalay. Pure and unexpurgated Burmese cuisine – a melange of Thai, Malaysian and a lot of Indian. The portions are huge, the service friendly and the prices low. Edgware Road tube. Mon–Sat noon–2.30pm & 6–10.30pm. £6–16.

Orrery, 55 Marylebone High St, W1 ☎020/7616 8000; *www.conran.com*. Another Conran enterprise, and a very good French restaurant indeed, driven by a passion for food. The service is slick and friendly, the dining room is beautiful, and the cheeseboard has won prizes. Baker Street or Regent's Park tube. Mon–Sat noon–3pm & 7–11pm, Sun 7–10.30pm. £25–90.

Chinatown

China City, White Bear Yard, 25a Lisle St, WC2 ☎020/7734 3388. Large restaurant tucked into a little courtyard off Lisle Street; fresh and bright, with *dim sum* that's up there with the best, service that is "Chinatown brusque", and a menu with eminently reasonable prices. Leicester Square tube. Mon–Sat noon–midnight. £10–25.

Fung Shing, 15 Lisle St, W1 ☎020/7437 1539. You can eat very cheaply in Chinatown, but if you want to splash out for some serious Chinese cooking, *Fung Shing* offers really good value. The food here has that earthy, robust quality which you only encounter when the chef is absolutely confident of his flavours and textures. Leicester Square tube. Daily noon–11.30pm. £15–40.

Mr Kong, 21 Lisle St, WC2 ☎020/7437 7923. One of Chinatown's finest, with a chef-owner who pioneered many of the modern Cantonese dishes now on menus all over town. You may have to be firm with staff if you want the more unusual dishes – order from the "Today's" and "Chef's Specials" menu and don't miss the mussels in black-bean sauce. If you want to avoid the rather grungey basement, book ahead. Leicester Square tube. Daily noon–3am. £7–20.

New World, 1 Gerrard Place, W1 ☎020/7734 0396. Another reasonable stab at an overblown Hong Kong dining palace – all red, gold and dragons. Best deal here is the lunchtime *dim sum*, served by indefatigable trolley-pushers. Leicester Square tube. Daily 11am–midnight. £6–18.

Soho

French House Dining Room, 49 Dean St, W1 ☎020/7437 2477. Small room above the *French House* pub which, despite its name, excels in traditional British meat dishes and ingredients. Choosing is made easy by the short, sharp menu which changes daily. Leicester Square tube. Mon–Sat noon–3pm & 6–11.15pm. £22–45.

Kettner's, 29 Romilly St, W1 ☎020/7734 6112. Despite the expensive-looking Baroque décor and the pianist, this place serves cheap pizzas and the like. You can't book and might be forced to hang out a while in the noisy *Champagne Bar* – no great hardship. Leicester Square tube. Daily noon–midnight. £12–30.

Kulu Kulu, 76 Brewer St, W1 ☎020/7734 7316. Small, friendly, *kaiten* (or conveyor belt) sushi restaurant which pulls off the unlikely trick of serving really good sushi without being intimidating. Piccadilly Circus tube. Mon–Fri noon–2.30pm & 5–10pm, Sat noon–3.45pm & 5–10pm. £10–30.

Mezzo, 100 Wardour St, W1 ☎020/7314 4000; *www.conran.com*. *Mezzo* has remained popular ever since Terence Conran opened this 600-seater in 1995. There's a bar, an informal *Mezzonine* restaurant upstairs, and, down the sweeping staircase, the full-on *Mezzo* with a space for performers. This is not a place for a quiet night out, but considering the numbers served here, the French/Med food is pretty good. There's a £5 "music cover charge" after 8pm. Piccadilly Circus or Tottenham Court Road tube. Mon–Thurs noon–3pm & 6pm–midnight, Fri & Sat until 1am, Sun 12.30–3pm & 6–11pm. £15–50.

Restaurants

Restaurants

Randall and Aubin, 16 Brewer St, W1 ☎020/7287 4447. Converted butcher's, now a champagne-oyster bar, rotisserie, sandwich shop and charcuterie – in the summer, this is a wonderfully airy place to eat. Piccadilly Circus tube. Mon–Sat noon–11pm, Sun 4–10.30pm. £12–38.

Soho Soho, 11–13 Frith St, W1 ☎020/7437 3091. Provençal restaurant with a lunchtime rotisserie on the ground floor, a more serious restaurant upstairs, and a cheaper brasserie in the basement; good cooking with judicious use of spices and seasoning, and friendly service. Leicester Square or Tottenham Court Road tube. Mon–Fri noon–3.30pm & 5.30–11.30pm, Sat 5.30–11.30pm. £15–40.

Spiga, 84–86 Wardour St, W1 ☎020/7734 3444. A pleasantly casual Italian affair, with a lively atmosphere, a serious wood-fired oven and a cool look about it. Leicester Square tube. Mon, Tues & Sun noon–3pm & 6–11pm, Wed–Sat noon–3pm & 6pm–midnight. £14–30.

Sugar Club, 21 Warwick St, W1 ☎020/7437 7776. Stylish, elegant place, run by irreverent Antipodean chefs who serve up passionate, eclectic and well-executed "Pacific Fusion" food. Piccadilly Circus tube. Daily noon–3pm & 6–11pm. £32–60.

Yo! Sushi, 52–53 Poland St, W1 ☎020/7287 0443; *www.yosushi.co.uk*. Much-hyped *kaiten* (or conveyor belt) sushi restaurant, with a robot drinks trolley, colour-coded plates and video screens. Oxford Circus or Piccadilly Circus tube. Daily noon–midnight. £8–25.

Covent Garden

Bank, 1 Kingsway, WC2 ☎020/7234 3344; *www.bankrestaurant.co.uk*. The closest London gets to recreating the all-day buzz and unfussy cuisine of the big Parisian brasseries. You can have a power breakfast here, and whatever time of the day, the Modern British food is impressive, if overpriced. Covent Garden or Temple tube. Mon–Fri 7–11.30am,

noon–3pm & 5.30–11.30pm, Sat & Sun 11.30am–3.30pm & 5.30–11.30pm (Sun closes at 10pm). £18–60.

Belgo Centraal, 50 Earlham St, WC2 ☎020/7813 2233; *www.belgo-restaurants.com*. Massive metal-minimalist cavern off Neal Street, serving excellent kilo buckets of moules marinière, with frites and mayonnaise, a bewildering array of Belgian beers to choose from, and waffles for dessert. The £5 lunchtime specials are a bargain for central London. Covent Garden tube. Mon–Thurs noon–11.30pm, Fri & Sat noon–midnight, Sun noon–10.30pm. £5–30.

Café Pacifico, 5 Langley St, WC2 ☎020/7379 7728. The salsa is hot here – both types – and the menu includes all the favourites, such as fajitas, flautas and tacos. Portions are generous and spicy, and there are nine varieties of Mexican beer and more than sixty types of tequila. The place is very popular and lively in the evening – in fact, you're advised to book. Covent Garden tube. Mon–Sat noon–midnight, Sun closes 11pm. £15–30.

The Ivy, 1 West St, WC2 ☎020/7836 4751. Regency-style restaurant built in 1928 that's been a theatreland and society favourite throughout the last century – and never more so than today. The only problem is getting a table; either book months ahead or try at very short notice, make do with a table in the bar area, or go for the bargain £18 three-course weekend lunch, with valet parking thrown in. Leicester Square tube. Daily noon–3pm & 5.30pm–midnight. £25–60.

Livebait, 21 Wellington St, WC2 ☎020/7836 7161; *www.sante-gcg.com*. Innovative, irrepressible restaurant, with a large, bustling, black-and-white-tiled dining room, and fish and crustacea so fresh you expect to see them flapping on the slab. Covent Garden tube. Mon–Sat noon–3pm & 5.30–11.30pm. £20–50.

J. Sheekey, 28–32 St Martin's Court, WC2 ☎020/7240 2565. J. Sheekey's pedigree goes back to World War I, but the place has recently been totally redesigned and refurbished. The menu is still focused on fish, but in addition to traditional fare such as grilled Dover sole, you're just as likely to find modernist dishes like grilled cuttlefish with creamed brandade. The weekend lunches, costing £10–15, are great value. Leicester Square tube. Mon–Sat noon–3pm & 5.30pm–midnight, Sun noon–3.30pm & 5.30pm–midnight. £17–55.

Fitzrovia and Bloomsbury

Chez Gérard, 8 Charlotte St, W1 ☎020/7636 4975; *www.sante-gcg.com*. Original premises of what is now something of a chain. Still, when the inner prompting shouts for steak frites, you can't do better than come here. Goodge Street tube. Mon–Fri noon–3pm & 6–10.30pm, Sun noon–3pm & 6–10.30pm. £20–45.

Great Nepalese, 48 Eversholt St, NW1 ☎020/7388 6737. An old-fashioned place, but one of very few in London serving genuine spicy Nepalese dishes. Euston tube. Mon–Sat noon–2.45pm & 6–11.30pm, Sun noon–2.30pm & 6–11.15pm. £8–22.

Ikkyu, 67a Tottenham Court Rd, W1 ☎020/7636 9280. Busy basement Japanese restaurant, good enough for a quick lunch or a more elaborate dinner. Either way, prices are infinitely more reasonable than elsewhere in the capital, and the food is tasty and authentic. Goodge Street tube. Mon–Fri noon–2.30pm & 6–10.30pm, Sun 6–10.30pm. £10–40.

The Kerala, 15 Great Castle St, W1 ☎020/7580 2125. Friendly Keralan restaurant, just behind Oxford Circus, that's a contender for bargain of the age. The menu is divided into a number of sections – Syrian Christian specialities, coastal seafood dishes, Malabar *biryanis*, vegetable curries and special *dosas* – all well judged and well spiced. Oxford Circus tube. Daily noon–3pm & 5.30–11pm. £6–18.

Mandeer, 8 Bloomsbury Way, WC1 ☎020/7242 6202. London's one and only Ayurvedic vegetarian restaurant, this place dishes up very cheap, very good, very worthy Gujarati food to everyone from penniless students to religious devotees. Holborn or Tottenham Court Road tube. Mon–Sat noon–3pm & 5–10pm. £8–15.

Mash, 19–21 Great Portland St, W1 ☎020/7637 5555. Buzzy modern bar/café/restaurant, with its own microbrewery, that offers an eclectic roster of dishes from pizza to sea bass from its wood-fired oven and grill. Oxford Circus tube. Mon–Sat noon–3pm & 6–11.30pm. £15–35.

Passione,10 Charlotte St, W1 ☎020/7636 2833. Superb Italian restaurant, simple and unpretentious. Look out for the special breads, including chef Gennaro Contaldo's fabled focaccio. Goodge Street tube. Mon–Fri 12.30–2.30pm & 7–10.30pm. £24–50.

Rasa Samudra, 5 Charlotte St, W1 ☎020/7637 0222. The food served at *Rasa Samudra* would be more at home in Bombay than in London, consisting as it does of sophisticated Southern Indian fish dishes – a million miles from curryhouse staples. *Rasa* also has an exclusively vegetarian branch at 6 Dering St, W1 ☎020/7629 1346 (Bond Street tube). Goodge Street tube. Mon–Sat noon–3pm & 6–11pm. £18–40.

R.K. Stanley, 6 Little Portland St, W1 ☎020/7462 0099; *www.rkstanley.co.uk*. Sausages from all over the globe, served in modern surroundings, and washed down with ale, lager, stout or porter. Oxford Circus tube. Mon–Fri noon–11.30pm, Sat 6–11.30pm. £10–25.

Clerkenwell, Hoxton & the City

Cantaloupe, 35 Charlotte Rd, EC3 ☎020/7613 4411. *Cantaloupe* is proof positive that something special is going on in Hoxton. The bar is noisy and serves passable tapas, but the Spanish-influenced restaurant round the back is several degrees quieter and better. Old

Restaurants

Restaurants

Street tube. Mon–Fri 12.30–3pm & 6.30–11pm, Sat 7–11.30pm. £20–90.

Cicada, 132 St John St, EC1 ☎020/7608 1550. Part bar, part restaurant, *Cicada* offers an unusual Thai-based menu that allows you to mix and match from small, large and side dishes ranging from fishy *tom yum* to ginger noodles or sushi. Farringdon tube. Mon–Fri noon–11pm, Sat 6–11pm. £17–37.

Moro, 34–36 Exmouth Market, EC1 ☎020/7833 8336. Modern, spartan restaurant that typifies the new face of Clerkenwell and attracts a clientele to match. *Moro* is a place of pilgrimage for disciples of the wood-fired oven and those who love food that is both Moorish and more-ish. Farringdon or Angel tube. Mon–Fri 12.30–2.30pm & 7–10.30pm. £18–48.

Moshi Moshi Sushi, Unit 24, Liverpool Street Station, EC2 ☎020/7247 3227; *www.moshimoshi.co.uk*. *Kaiten* (conveyor belt) sushi bar situated above the platforms. Just pluck whatever dish you like – the pattern on your plate determines your bill at the end – and wash it down with the free green tea. Liverpool Street tube. Mon–Fri 11.30am–9pm. £7–20.

Real Greek, 15 Hoxton Market, N1 ☎020/7739 8212. Yes, it's run by a real Greek, but this is nothing like your average London Greek-Cypriot joint. Small, modern and comfortable, the menu shows off the authentic dishes of Greece, and the service is excellent. Set lunch and early doors dinner are a bargain. Old Street tube. Mon–Sat noon–3pm & 5.30–10.30pm. £15–40.

St John, 26 St John St, EC1 ☎020/7251 0848; *www.stjohnrestaurant.co.uk*. This minimalist former smokehouse is now a decidedly English restaurant, only a stone's throw from Smithfield meat market and specializing in offal. All those strange and unfashionable cuts of meat that were once commonplace in rural England – brains, bone marrow, meat from a cow's sternum – are on offer, making this no place for vegetarians. That said, the food is terrific and the

service is attentive and informed. Farringdon tube. Mon–Fri noon–3pm & 6–11pm, Sat 6–11pm. £20–40.

Singapura, 1–2 Limeburner Lane, EC4 ☎020/7329 1133; *www .singapura-restaurants.co.uk*. Beautiful, large, modern restaurant off Ludgate Hill specializing in *Nonya* cuisine – a sort of fusion of Malayan and Chinese traditions – from Singapore. The food is spicy, garlicky and delicious. Blackfriars or St Paul's tube. Mon–Fri 11.30am–3.30pm & 5.30–10pm. £20–40.

Smiths, 67–77 Charterhouse St, EC1 ☎020/7236 6666; *www .smithsofsmithfield.co.uk*. An ambitious warehouse conversion with a bar and café on the ground floor serving sensible food from breakfast to bedtime; above are the "Dining Room" and the "Fine Dining" areas. The food is Modern British and the nearby meat market has a strong influence over the dishes. Farringdon tube. Mon–Fri 7am–5pm & 6–11pm, Sat 10.30am–5pm & 6–11pm, Sun 10.30am–5pm. £15–40.

Viet Hoa Café, 72 Kingsland Rd, E2 ☎020/7729 8293. Large, light and airy Vietnamese café in Hoxton, serving splendid "meals in a bowl", soups and noodle dishes with everything from spring rolls to tofu. Be sure to try the *Pho* soup, a Vietnamese staple that's eaten at any and every meal. Old Street tube. Daily noon–3.30pm & 5.30–11.30pm. £8–18.

East End & Docklands

Café Naz, 46–48 Brick Lane, E1 ☎020/7247 0234. Self-proclaimed contemporary Bangladeshi restaurant that cuts an imposing modern figure on Brick Lane. The menu has all the standards plus a load of "baltis", the kitchen is open-plan, and the prices keen. Aldgate East tube. Mon–Fri noon–midnight, Sat 6pm–midnight, Sun noon–3pm & 6pm–midnight. £9–22.

Café Spice Namaste, 16 Prescott St, E1 ☎020/7488 9242; *www.booktoeat.com*. Very popular East End Indian, where the menu is a touch more varied than in many of its rivals – Goan and Kashmiri dishes are often included, and you're as likely to find squid or potato cakes as your usual favourites. Weekday lunchtimes are particularly busy. Tower Hill tube. Mon–Fri noon–3pm & 6.15–10.30pm, Sat 6.30–10.30pm. £12–30.

Lahore Kebab House, 2 Umberstone St, E1 ☎020/7481 9737. Despite refurbishment, the food is still good and spicy, the prices low, and the service brusque – bring your own booze. Whitechapel or Aldgate East tube. Daily noon–midnight. Cash only. £4–14.

Mem Saheb on Thames, 65–67 Amsterdam Rd, E14 ☎020/7538 3008. Decent Indian restaurant in the cultural wasteland that is Docklands, with a superb view over the river to the Dome. Crossharbour DLR. Mon–Fri noon–2.30pm & 6–11.30pm, Sat & Sun 6–11.30pm. £12–28.

New Tayyab, 83 Fieldgate St, E1 ☎020/7247 9543. Twenty-five years in business, the *Tayyab* has now expanded into an evening joint, serving straightforward Pakistani food at unbelievably cheap prices. Service is without pretension – this is not a place to dither over the menu. Aldgate East or Whitechapel tube. Daily 5pm–midnight. Cash only. £3–10.

Tabla, Hertsmere Rd, E14 ☎020/7345 0345. Stylish Indian restaurant located within the Regency Dockmaster's House, an easy walk from Canary Wharf (if you know where you're going). The food is good, modern and authentic, and uses fish fresh from nearby Billingsgate. West India Quay DLR. Mon–Fri noon–3pm & 6–11pm. £20–50.

Taja, 199a Whitechapel Rd, E1 ☎020/7247 3866; *www.cuisinenet.co.uk /taja*. A genuine rarity – an ultra-modern Bangladeshi restaurant in a converted toilet, with a menu that's as rich in veggie dishes as it is in meat ones. Prices are low and standards high. Whitechapel tube. Mon–Wed & Sun 11am–midnight, Thurs–Sat 11am–12.30am. £5–12.

Lambeth and Southwark

Blue Print Café, Design Museum, Shad Thames, SE1 ☎020/7378 7031; *www .conran.com*. The oldest and best of Terence Conran's gastrodomes – expect to pay higher than average prices for a higher than average meal, and a fabulous view from the terrace windows (for which you must book ahead). Tower Hill tube. Mon–Sat noon–3pm & 6–11pm, Sun noon–3pm. £22–45.

Delfina Studio Café, 50 Bermondsey St, SE1 ☎020/7357 0244; *www.delfina.org .uk*. This adjunct to the Delfina art gallery is a serious restaurant and a great place to go for lunch if you're in the area. The cooking is Modern British, and the prices have moved well beyond café norms, but the quality justifies a bit of a splurge. London Bridge tube. Mon–Fri noon–3pm. £19–55.

Fina Estampa, 150 Tooley St, SE1 ☎020/7403 1342. This may be London's only Peruvian restaurant, but it also happens to be the very best, bringing a little of downtown Lima to London Bridge. The menu is traditional Peruvian, with a big emphasis on seafood. London Bridge tube. Mon–Sat noon–2.30pm & 6.30–10.30pm. £5–15.

Fish!, Cathedral St, SE1 ☎020/7234 3333; *www.fishdiner.co.uk*. Busy, buzzy, tank-like restaurant, with huge windows and a glass ceiling, right in the middle of Borough Market. Choose your fish, decide how you want it cooked, and with what sauce, and then sit back and wait. Portions are huge, and the fish is as good and fresh as you'd expect. London Bridge tube. Mon–Sat 11.30am–3pm & 5.30–11pm. £20–50.

Little Saigon, 139 Westminster Bridge Rd, SE1 ☎020/7207 9747. Great Vietnamese spring rolls, grilled squid-cake and crystal pancakes, all served with a wonderful array of sauces, plus great crispy fried noodles. Waterloo tube. Mon–Fri noon–3pm & 5.30–11.30pm, Sat & Sun 5.30–11.30pm. £15–35.

RSJ, 13a Coin St, SE1 ☎020/7928 4554; *www.rsj.uk.com*. Regularly high standards

Restaurants

Restaurants

of Anglo-French cooking make this a good spot for a meal after or before an evening at a South Bank theatre or concert hall. The set meals for around £15 are particularly popular. Waterloo tube. Mon–Fri noon–2.30pm & 5.30–11pm, Sat 5.30–11pm. £18–45.

Tas, 33 The Cut, SE1 ☎020/7928 1444. Bright, bustling and inexpensive Turkish restaurant with an almost baffling choice, and frequent live music. If lively is what you like, then *Tas* will do just fine. Southwark tube. Mon–Sat noon–11.30pm, Sun noon–10.30pm. £8–35.

Kensington and Chelsea

Bibendum Oyster House, Michelin House, 81 Fulham Rd, SW3 ☎020/7589 1480; *www.bibendum.co.uk*. A glorious tiled affair built in 1911, this former garage is the best place to eat shellfish in London. If you're really hungry, try the "Plateau de Fruits De Mer", which has crab, clams, langoustine, oysters, prawns, shrimps, whelks and winkles. South Kensington tube. Mon–Sat noon–10.30pm, Sun noon–10pm £12–30.

Boisdale, 15 Ecclestone St, SW1 ☎020/7730 6922; *www.boisdale.co.uk*. Owned by Ranald MacDonald, son of the Chief of Clanranald, this restaurant offers the best of Scottish, in a clubby atmosphere. Victoria tube. Mon–Sat noon–1am. £15–50.

Hunan, 51 Pimlico Rd, SW1 ☎020/7730 5712. Probably England's only restaurant serving Hunan food, a relative of Sichuan cuisine with the same spicy kick to most dishes, and a fair wallop of pepper in those that aren't actively riddled with chillis. Most people opt for the £25 "leave-it-to-us feast" which lets the chef, Mr Peng, show what he can do. Sloane Square tube. Mon–Sat noon–2.30pm & 6–11.30pm. £25–40.

O Fado, 45–50 Beauchamp Place, SW3 ☎020/7589 3002. Probably the oldest Portuguese restaurant in London, which speaks volumes for its authenticity. It can get rowdy, what with the live *fado* ballads and the family parties, but that's

half the enjoyment. You'll need to reserve a table. Knightsbridge tube. Daily noon–3pm & 6.30pm–1am. £18–35.

Organic Veg, 8 Egerton Gardens Mews, SW3 ☎020/7584 7007. Non-smoking, vegetarian Sichuan restaurant, tucked away in a quiet little mews in South Kensington. For a tête-à-tête, book one of the two cubbyholes. South Kensington tube. Mon–Sat noon–2.30pm & 6–11.15pm, Sun noon–2.30pm & 6–11pm (winter only). Cash only. £10–25.

Roussillon, 16 Barnabas St, SW1 ☎020/7730 5550; *www.roussillon.co.uk*. Brave restaurant that's single-minded in its pursuit of top-of-the-range French cooking with a very bright and very young chef, whose three menus (vegetarian, fish and meat) are season- and market-driven. Set lunches (£25–30) are a treat. Victoria or Sloane Square tube. Mon–Fri noon–2.30pm & 6–10.45pm, Sat 6.30–10.45pm. £30–70.

Wódka, 12 St Albans Grove, W8 ☎020/7937 6513. The food here is cooked with a little imagination, which makes the smart *Wódka* the place to go if you want to experience the best that Polish cuisine has to offer. It's not an expensive place to eat until you start ladling out the ice-cold, flavoured vodkas. High Street Kensington or Gloucester Road tube. Mon–Fri 12.30–2.30pm & 7–11pm, Sat & Sun 7–11.15pm. £14–35.

Zafferano, 15 Lowndes St, SW1 ☎020/7235 5800. Booking ahead is essential for this popular Italian restaurant, which is fashionably minimalist in its décor, and deliciously simple in its cooking. It's pricey, but the lunchtime fixed-price menus are pretty good value at around £20. Knightsbridge tube. Mon–Sat noon–2.30pm & 7–11pm, Sun noon–2.30pm & 7–10.30pm. £25–45.

Bayswater and Notting Hill

Al Waha, 75 Westbourne Grove, W2 ☎020/7229 0806. Arguably London's best Lebanese restaurant; meze-obsessed, but also painstaking in its preparation of the main-course dishes. Bayswater or Queensway tube. Daily noon–midnight. £10–35.

Alounak, 44 Westbourne Grove, W2 ☎020/7229 0416. Don't be put off by the dated sign outside – this place turns out really good, really cheap Iranian food. Bayswater tube. Daily noon–midnight. £8–20.

Khan's, 13–15 Westbourne Grove, W2 ☎020/7727 5420. Long-established, huge and crowded Indian restaurant, with palms, high ceilings and blue murals – unadventurous curries, perfunctory service, but great atmosphere. Bayswater or Queensway tube. Mon–Thurs noon–3pm & 6–11.45pm, Fri, Sat & Sun noon–midnight. £6–20.

Mandarin Kitchen, 14–16 Queensway, W2 ☎020/7727 9012. In a western outpost of Chinatown, this large and very classy Cantonese is renowned for its fish and seafood, all of which are sparklingly fresh. Service is brusque. Bayswater or Queensway tube. Daily noon–11.30pm. £15–35.

The Mandola, 139 Westbourne Grove, W11 ☎020/7229 4734. Strikingly delicious "urban Sudanese" food at sensible prices, served by extremely laid-back staff. Check out the Sudanese spiced coffee at the end. Notting Hill Gate tube. Mon 6–11pm, Tues–Sun noon–11pm. £12–22.

Offshore, 148 Holland Park Ave, W11 ☎020/7221 6090; *www.offshore.uk .com*. Mauritian fish restaurant, with a dauntingly long menu: a seasonal à la carte, l'arrivage de la semaine, plus catch of the day and set luncheons. The dishes are precisely judged, with a cheerful Franco-Chinese anarchy about the saucing. Holland Park tube. Daily noon–3pm & 6.30–11pm. £18–60.

Rodrizio Rico, 111 Westbourne Grove, W11 ☎020/7792 4035. No menu, no prices, but no problem either as this Brazilian eatery specializes in smoky, grilled meat. Carvers come round and lop off chunks of freshly grilled meats, while you prime your plate from the salad bar

and hot buffet. Notting Hill Gate or Queensway tube. Mon–Fri 6.30pm–midnight, Sat 12.30–4.30pm & 6.30pm–midnight, Sun 12.30–11pm. £18–25.

Xios, 47 Moscow Rd, W2 ☎020/7243 0606. Situated in a small Greek enclave just off Queensway, this is a small, patriotically blue and white family restaurant, where the food is unfussy and has Greek rather than Cypriot roots. Go for the daily specials. Bayswater or Queensway tube. Mon–Sat 6pm–midnight, Sun noon–midnight. £15–30.

St John's Wood and Camden

El Parador, 245 Eversholt St, NW1 ☎020/7387 2789. Small, no-frills Spanish restaurant a stone's throw from Camden High Street, serving up tasty *tapas* at very reasonable prices. Service is friendly and laid-back and there's a lovely garden, with tables for alfresco eating, though you need to book in advance. Mornington Crescent tube. Mon–Thurs noon–3pm & 6–11pm, Fri noon–3pm & 6–11.30pm, Sat 6–11.30pm, Sun 7–10.30pm. £8–20.

Harry Morgan's, 245 Eversholt St, NW1 ☎020/7722 1869. The salt beef on rye with horseradish is as good as it was when Harry Morgan first opened a restaurant on this site in 1962. Other Jewish medicines available at this newly revamped and airy eatery include chicken noodle soup, chopped liver and a whole range of pickled cucumbers. St John's Wood tube. Daily 11.30am–10pm. £7–20.

Mango Rooms, 10 Kentish Town Rd, NW1. An engaging, laid-back, Camden-cool Caribbean place whose cooking is consistent and whose presentation is first class. Camden Town tube. Mon 6pm–midnight, Tues–Sun noon–3pm & 6pm–midnight. £10–35.

The Salt House, 63 Abbey Rd, NW8. *The Salt House* combines corner pub, bar, restaurant and flower stall; there is even a paved area set back from the road for those rare alfresco dining days. The food is carefully cooked, well presented and

Restaurants

Restaurants

unfussy, and the menu is market-driven. St John's Wood tube. Mon–Fri noon–3pm & 6.30–10.30pm, Sat & Sun noon–4pm & 7–10.30pm. £20–45.

Hampstead and Golders Green

Base, 71 Hampstead High St, NW3 ☎020/7431 2224. In a wealthy suburb strangely short on decent placers to eat, this stylish café/restaurant, serving Modern British cuisine, is a real god-send, and consequently very popular. Hampstead tube. Mon–Sat noon–2.30pm & 7–10.30pm, Sun noon–2.30pm. £14–50.

Cucina, 45a South End Rd, NW3 ☎020/7483 3765. Brightly painted, wooden-floored, roof-lit first-floor restaurant that's very contemporary, very fashionable and very Hampstead. The Modern British menu changes every two weeks or so, and darts about a bit from cuisine to cuisine, but wherever you alight, each dish is well presented. Belsize Park or Hampstead tube. Mon–Thurs noon–2.30pm & 7–10.30pm, Fri & Sat noon–2.30pm & 7–11pm, Sun noon–2.30pm. £16–35.

Czech & Slovak National House, 74 West End Lane, NW6 ☎020/7372 5251. Meat-and-dumpling-dominated meals in a restaurant complete with flock wallpaper and Gambrinus on draught. Set in a lovely house with a garden out back, and very popular with Czech expats – book ahead if you want to come for Sunday lunch. West Hampstead tube. Tues–Fri 6–9pm, Sat & Sun noon–3pm & 6–10pm. Cash/cheque only. £12–26.

L'Artista, 917 Finchley Rd, NW11 ☎020/8731 7501. Under the railway arches opposite Golders Green tube, this is a lively and local Italian serving a range of dishes from *fegato Veneziana* to thin-crust pizzas. Golders Green tube. Daily noon–midnight. £15–24.

New End, 102 Heath St, NW3 ☎020/7431 4423; www.thenewend.co .uk. *New End* is a spiffing restaurant, much loved by Hampsteadians. The dining room is pleasantly unfussy, the

service is friendly, and the Modern European food is very good indeed. Hampstead tube. Tues 6–11pm, Wed–Sat noon–3pm & 6–11pm, Sun 6–10.30pm. £18–50.

Solly's, 146–150 Golders Green Rd, NW11 ☎020/8455 2121. Downstairs is a small kosher restaurant and deli spe-cializing in epic felafel; *Solly's Exclusive*, upstairs, is a huge, bustling kosher restaurant. Golders Green tube. Mon–Thurs & Sun 6.30–10.30pm, Sat 8pm–1am. £16–35.

Wembley

Chetna's, 420 High Rd, Middlesex ☎020/8900 1466. Busy, cheap, vegetari-an Indian restaurant that's a firm favourite with Wembley's considerable Afro-Asian population. Best value has to be the vast *Delhi Darbar thali*, a complete meal in itself for around £6. Wembley Central tube. Tues–Fri noon–3pm & 6–10.30pm, Sat & Sun 1–10.30pm. £4–10.

Sakoni's, 127–129 Ealing Rd, Alperton Middlesex ☎0181/903 9601. Topnotch vegetarian meal factory, crowded with Asian families and serving terrific food, especially good *dosas*, great *farari* cut-lets, deep-fried delights and wonderful juices. Alperton or Wembley Central tube. Mon–Thurs & Sun 11am–11pm, Fri & Sat 11am–midnight. £4–10.

Islington and Stoke Newington

Granita, 127 Upper St, N1 ☎020/7226 3222. Fashionably minimalist, this is one of Islington's most favoured restaurants, with a wide-ranging Med-influenced menu; booking essential. Angel tube. Tues 6.30–10pm, Wed–Sat 12.30–2.30pm & 6.30–10.30pm, Sun 12.30–3pm & 6.30–10pm. £16–45.

Maremma, 11–13 Theberton St, N1 ☎020/7226 9400. In the heart of Blairite Islington, this is a top-class, child-friendly Italian restaurant, whose menu is littered with chic favourites that hit just the right note. Angel or Highbury & Islington tube. Tues–Fri 6–11pm, Sat & Sun noon–3pm & 6–11pm. £18–30.

Pasha, 301 Upper St, N1 ☎020/7226 1454. *Pasha* looks nothing like a traditional Turkish restaurant, with only the odd brass pot hinting at its Ottoman origins. Food is fresh, light and authentic, and the menu easy to decipher. Angel or Highbury & Islington tube. Mon–Fri noon–3pm & 6–11.30pm, Sat & Sun noon–midnight. £15–30.

Primos Lounge, 54 Islington Park St, N1 ☎020/7954 5717. Genial and lively Italian restaurant, with excellent, authentic pizzas and interesting innovations such as champagne and strawberry risotto; regular live jazz in the evenings. Angel tube. Daily noon–11pm. £7–12.

Rasa, 55 Stoke Newington Church St, N16 ☎020/7249 0344. Splendid no-smoking South Indian vegetarian restaurant with unusual, delicate Keralan taste sensations, and staff that take the time to explain what's what; booking essential. Stoke Newington train station or bus #73 from King's Cross or Angel tube. Mon–Fri 6–11pm, Sat & Sun noon–2.30pm & 6pm–midnight. £12–27.

Brixton

Bah Humbug, The Crypt, St Matthew's Church, Brixton Hill, SW2 ☎020/7738 3184; *www.bahhumbug.co.uk.* Atmospheric vaulted crypt underneath Brixton's landmark church, serving innovative, mostly veggie dishes (plus the odd fish). Serious brunches served up at the weekend. Brixton tube. Mon–Fri 5pm–midnight, Sat 11am–midnight, Sun 11am–11.30pm. £13–20.

Satay Bar, 450 Coldharbour Lane, SW9 ☎020/7326 5001. Lively, up-for-it bar and restaurant tucked away behind the Ritzy cinema, that plays loud music, serves good Indonesian food and doubles as a local art gallery. Brixton tube. Mon–Thurs noon–3pm & 6–11.30pm, Fri & Sat noon–2am, Sun 1pm–midnight. £12–25.

Greenwich and Blackheath

Time, 7a College Approach, SE10 ☎020/8305 9767; *www.timerestaurant .com.* Floating elegantly above tourist Greenwich, *Time* is a small, appealing restaurant, with roomy tables and a sophisticated clientele. The menu is not long, but it offers plenty of choice, celebrating flavours borrowed from around the world. Cutty Sark DLR. Mon–Fri noon–2.30pm & 7–10.30pm, Sat 7–11pm. £22–40.

Lawn, 1 Lawn Terrace, SE3 ☎020/8355 1110; *www.lawnrestaurant.co.uk.* Former print works, with industrial décor, high ceilings and a trendy buzz. The menu is Modern European, fishy, and has echoes of *Bank* (see p.526), which is run by the same owners. Blackheath train station from London Bridge. Mon–Thurs 6–12.30pm, Fri 6–11pm, Sat 11am–2.30pm & 6–11pm, Sun 11.30am–5.30pm. £18–35.

Southall

Gifto's Lahore Karahi, 162–164 The Broadway, Southall, Middlesex ☎020 /8813 8669. *Gifto's* specializes in freshly grilled, well-spiced meats and exceptionally good breads, backed up by a few curries and one or two odd dishes from Lahore, all done superbly well. Southall train station from Paddington. Mon–Thurs noon–11.30pm, Fri–Sun noon–midnight. £7–14.

Omi's, 1 Beaconsfield Rd, Southall, Middlesex ☎020/8571 4831. *Omi's* is a small, no-frills eatery with a kitchen as spacious as the dining area. It may not be prepossessing, but you'll get tasty Punjabi/Kenyan-Asian dishes, lots of rich flavours and great value. Southall train station from Paddington. Mon–Thurs 11am–9pm, Fri & Sat 11am–9.30pm. £18–30.

Chiswick to Richmond

Chez Lindsay, 11 Hill Rise, Richmond, Surrey ☎020/8948 7473. Small, bright, authentic Breton creperie, with a loyal local following, and fixed-price lunchtime menus for under £10. Choose between galettes, crepes or more formal French main courses, including lots of fresh fish and shellfish, and wash it all down with Breton cider in traditional earthenware *bolées.* Richmond tube. Mon–Sat 11am–11pm, Sun noon–10pm. £7–27.

Restaurants

Restaurants

The Glasshouse, 14 Station Parade, Kew, Surrey ☎020/8940 6777. Clean-cut, modern restaurant by Kew Gardens tube, with blissfully comfortable chairs. The menu changes daily, with set-menu prices hovering around the £20 mark. The cooking is imaginative and straight-forward, and owes much to genuine French food. Kew Gardens tube. Mon–Sat noon–2.30pm & 7–10.30pm, Sun noon–3pm. £20–50.

Grano, 162 Thames Rd, W4 ☎020/8995 0120. Award-winning neighbourhood Italian restaurant situated a few yards from the Thames in Strand on the Green. The chef's strengths are fish, game and pasta: two courses cost around £20, three courses around £25. Gunnersbury tube. Mon–Fri noon–2.30pm & 6–11pm, Sat 6–11pm. £18–30.

Pallavi, 1st floor, 3 Cross Deep Court, Heath Rd, Twickenham, Middlesex ☎020/8892 2345. Southwestern outpost of a South Indian restaurant empire, *Pallavi* has moved into smart new premises, but is the simplest and cheapest of the lot. Twickenham train station from Waterloo. Tues–Sun noon–3pm & 6–11pm. £10–23.

Patio, 5 Goldhawk Rd, W12 ☎020/8743 5194. At *Patio*, you get good, solid Polish food in a friendly comfortable atmos-phere, for a relatively small amount of money. The set menu for around £11 – for a starter, main, petits fours, fruit and a vodka – is the trump card. Goldhawk Road or Shepherd's Bush tube. Mon–Fri noon–3pm & 6pm–midnight. £10–25.

Springbok Café, 42 Devonshire Rd, W4 ☎020/8742 3149. Small, informal, authentic South African restaurant, with an open-plan barbie-oriented kitchen. Many of the ingredients are imported, so there's plenty of biltong, smoked ostrich and the like to please expats. Turnham Green tube. Mon–Sat 6.30–11pm. £20–30.

Chapter 17

Pubs and bars

Pubs are one of England's most enduring social institutions, and have outlived the church and marketplace as the focal points of communities, with London's fringe theatre, alternative comedy and live-music scenes still largely pub-based. At their best, pubs can be as welcoming as their full name, "public house", suggests, offering a fine range of drinks and filling food. At their worst, they're dismal rooms with surly bar staff and rotten snacks. One thing you can be sure of, however, is that most pubs and bars remain smoke-filled places where drinking alcohol is the prime activity.

Older-style inns, with oak beams, open fires and polished-brass fittings survive here and there, but they're not a great feature of the capital. London's great period of pub building took place in the Victorian era, to which many pubs still pay homage; genuine Victorian interiors, however, are increasingly difficult to find, as indeed are genuinely individual pubs. **Chain pubs** can now be found all over the capital: branches of All Bar One, Pitcher & Piano and the Slug & Lettuce are the most obvious, as they all share the chain name, whereas J.D. Wetherspoon and Fuller's pubs do at least vary theirs. Even the Firkin chain, which began with honourable intentions − to promote real ale through its own micro-breweries − has since been sold off and simply become another marketing device.

Some pubs are owned by, or "tied" to, the large breweries, and sell mainly their own brand of **beers** and **lagers**, along with a few "guest beers", all dispensed by the pint or half-pint. From a beer-drinking point of view, the most interesting places are "free houses", pubs that are unattached to breweries and free to sell whatever beers they like, often including a good range of real ales (see the "Beers" box, p.536); they are often more characterful places, too. **Wines** sold in pubs are still, generally speaking, appalling, and if you're after a decent bottle, you're nearly always better off in a fully fledged wine bar, the best of which are located in the claret-swilling City.

Pub food, on the whole, is a lunchtime affair, although "gastropubs", which put more effort into their cooking, are increasingly offering meals in the evening, too. The traditional image of London pub food is dire − a pseudo "ploughman's lunch" of bread and cheese, or a murky-looking pie and chips − but the last couple of decades have seen plenty of improvements. You can get a palatable lunchtime meal at many of the pubs listed in this chapter, and at a few of them, you're looking at cooking worthy of high, restaurant-standard praise.

Though pubs may be constantly changing hands (and names), the quickest turnover is in **bars**, which go in and out of fashion with incredible speed. These are very different places to your average pub, catering to a somewhat cliquey, often youngish crowd, with

This chapter covers pubs, bars and wine bars that are good for drinking − and, sometimes, eating − in. It doesn't include pubs and bars that are primarily music venues, which you'll find in Chapter 18, nor gay pubs and bars, which are covered in Chapter 19.

Pubs and bars

Beers

The classic English beer is **bitter**, an uncarbonated and dark beverage that should be pumped by hand from the cellar and served at room temperature. In the last two decades, **lager** has overtaken bitter in popularity, and every pub will have at least two draught lagers on offer, plus innumerable foreign bottled brands, which go in and out of fashion very quickly.

English beer drinkers go almost exclusively for bitter, and take the various brews extremely seriously. A moving force in this camp is **CAMRA** – the Campaign for Real Ale – which worked hard to keep local beers from dying out amid the big brewery takeovers of the 1970s. Some of the beer touted as good English ale is nothing of the sort (if the stuff comes out of an electric pump, it isn't the real thing), but these days even the big breweries distribute some very good beers – for example, Directors, produced by the giant Courage group, is a very classy strong bitter.

Smaller operations whose fine ales are available over a wide area include Young's and Fuller's – the two main London breweries – and Wadworth, Adnams, Greene King, Flowers and Samuel Smith's. Regional concoctions from other independent breweries are frequently available, too, at free houses, and London also has a number of brew-pubs, which produce their own peculiar brand on the premises, the most famous being the Firkin chain.

Guinness, a very dark, creamy Irish stout, is also on sale virtually everywhere, and is an exception to the high-minded objection to electrically pumped beers – though purists will tell you that the stuff the English drink does not compare with the home variety.

Standard pub opening hours are Mon–Sat 11am–11pm, Sun noon–10.30pm. Our listings only specify the exceptions.

designer interiors and drinks; they also tend to be more expensive. We've listed a fair few, while leaving those more like (or in some cases attached to) clubs and dance places for the "Live Music and Clubs" chapter, which follows.

England's **licensing laws** are likely to have changed by the time you read this, as after more than a century of draconian restrictions, the government has finally caved in and liberalized English opening hours. This should allow pubs and bars to stay open way beyond the standard 11pm last-orders without charging an entrance fee, so the times listed below may well have changed significantly since this book went to press.

Whitehall and Westminster

Albert, 52 Victoria St, SW1 ☎020/7222 5577. Roomy High Victorian pub, with big bay windows and glass partitions, good food, with an excellent upstairs carvery. St James's Park tube.

ICA Bar, 94 The Mall, SW1 ☎020/7930 2402; www.ica.org.uk. You have to be a member to drink at the *ICA Bar* – but

anyone can join on the door (Mon–Fri £1.50; Sat & Sun £2.50). It's a cool drinking venue, with a *noir* dress code observed by the arty crowd and staff. Piccadilly Circus or Charing Cross tube. Mon noon–11pm, Tues–Sat noon–1am, Sun noon–10.30pm.

Lord Moon of the Mall, 16 Whitehall, SW1 ☎020/7839 7701. Huge, high-ceilinged former bank, now a popular Weatherspoon pub serving decent grub and real ales on Whitehall of all places. Embankment or Charing Cross tube. Mon–Sat 11am–11pm, Sun noon–7pm.

Paviour's Arms, Page St, SW1 ☎020/7834 2150. A unique survivor, this large, stylish 1930s Art Deco pub, in the backstreets close to the Tate Britain gallery, has much of its original décor intact; you can also get decent Thai food with your beer. Pimlico tube. Closed Sat & Sun.

Red Lion, 48 Parliament St, SW1 ☎020/7930 5826. Good old pub, convenient for Westminster Abbey and Parliament. Popular with MPs, who are called to votes by a division bell in the bar. Westminster tube. Mon–Sat 11am–11pm, Sun noon–7pm.

St James's

Red Lion, 23 Crown Passage, SW1 ☎020/7930 4141. Not to be confused with the nearby pub of the same name (see below), this is a small, local, wood-panelled pub hidden away in a passageway off Pall Mall. Green Park tube.

Red Lion, 2 Duke of York St, SW1 ☎020/7930 2030. Genuine old Victorian gin palace with elegant etched mirrors, polished wood and a great ceiling. Piccadilly Circus tube. Mon–Sat 11.30am–11pm.

Sports Café, 80 Haymarket, SW1 ☎020/7839 8300. A long way from upper-crust St James's, this very central sports-theme bar is guaranteed to be showing whatever televised sport event is taking place. Piccadilly Circus tube. Mon noon–1am, Tues–Thurs noon–2am, Fri & Sat noon–3am, Sun noon–10.30pm.

Mayfair

Audley, 41 Mount St, W1 ☎020/7499 1843. A grand Mayfair pub, with original Victorian burgundy lincrusta ceiling, chandeliers and clocks. Green Park, Hyde Park Corner or Marble Arch tube.

Guinea, 30 Bruton Place, W1 ☎020/7409 1728. Pretty, tiny, old-fashioned, flower-strewn mews pub, serving good Young's bitter and excellent steak-and-kidney pies. Bond Street or Green Park tube. Mon–Fri 11am–11pm, Sat 6.30–11pm.

Mulligans, 13–14 Cork St, W1 ☎020/7409 1370. A fine Irish pub with an odd mix of clientele – Cork Street gallery staff and Irish lads – and the best Guinness in London. Also has a high-class restaurant downstairs, with fine Modern British cooking. Green Park or Piccadilly tube. Mon–Sat 11am–11pm.

Woodstock, 11 Woodstock St, W1 ☎020/7408 2008. Small, traditional pub off Oxford Street, with Abbot ales,

Theakston and guest beers – an oasis of calm in this area. Green Park or Hyde Park Corner tube.

Ye Grapes, 16 Shepherd Market, W1 ☎020/7499 1563. Victorian free house, with a good selection of beers and an open fire – a great local in the heart of Mayfair. Green Park or Hyde Park Corner tube.

Marylebone

Barley Mow, 8 Dorset St, W1 ☎020/7935 7318. This local pub tucked away in the backstreets of Marylebone has pawnbrokers' snugs and serves a range of real ales. Baker Street tube. Mon–Sat 11am–11pm.

Devonshire Arms, 21a Devonshire St, W1 ☎020/7935 8327. Beautiful interior with lots of brass, frosted mirrors and original tiling, plus newspapers to read. Baker Street or Regent's Park tube. Mon–Fri 11am–11pm, Sat noon–11pm.

Dover Castle, 43 Weymouth Mews, W1 ☎020/7580 4412. A traditional boozer down a quiet, labyrinthine Marylebone mews. Green upholstery, dark wood and a nicotine-stained lincrusta ceiling. Regent's Park or Oxford Circus tube. Mon–Fri 11.30am–11pm, Sat noon–11pm.

O'Conor Don, 88 Marylebone Lane, W1 ☎020/7935 9311. Stripped bare anti-theme Irish pub with table service, excellent Guinness and a pleasantly measured pace. Bond Street tube. Mon–Fri 11am–11pm, Sat noon–11pm.

William Wallace, 44 Blandford St, W1 ☎020/7935 5963. Scottish pub with stained glass and a mock-Tudor theme, but more importantly, 80/- and 70/- and Deuchars Caledonian IPA on offer. Baker Street or Bond Street tube.

Soho

Coach & Horses, 29 Greek St, W1 ☎020/7437 5920. Long-standing – and, for once, little-changed – haunt of the ghosts of old Soho, *Private Eye* staff, nightclubbers and art students from nearby St Martin's College. 1950s

Pubs and bars

Club-bars and lesbian and gay bars are covered on p.559 and pp.568–9 respectively.

Pubs and bars

red plastic stools and black formica tables guaranteed. Leicester Square tube.

Dog & Duck, 18 Bateman St, W1 ☎020/7437 4447. Tiny Soho pub that retains much of its old character, beautiful Victorian tiling and mosaics, and a loyal clientele that often includes jazz musicians from nearby *Ronnie Scott's* club. Leicester Square or Tottenham

Court Road tube. Mon–Fri noon–11pm, Sat 6–11pm, Sun 7–10.30pm.

French House, 49 Dean St, W1 ☎020/7437 2799. This tiny French pub has been a Soho institution since Belgian Victor Berlemont bought the place shortly before World War I. Free French and literary associations galore (see p.145), half-pints only at the bar (no real ale) and a fine little restaurant upstairs. Leicester Square tube. Mon–Sat noon–11pm, Sun noon–10.30pm.

The Toucan, 19 Carlisle St, W1 ☎020/7437 4123; www.thetoucan.co .uk. Small bar serving excellent Guinness and a wide range of Irish whiskies, plus cheap, wholesome and filling food. So popular it can get mobbed. There's another branch, *Toucan Two*, in Marylebone (94 Wimpole St, W1; Bond Street or Oxford Circus tube). Tottenham Court Road tube. Mon–Sat 11am–11pm.

Two Floors, 3 Kingly St, W1 ☎020/7439 1007. Laid-back, designer-style Soho bar, laid out, unsurprisingly, on two floors, attracting a mixed media crowd – quite a find in what is otherwise a dire part of West Soho. Oxford Circus tube. Mon–Sat 11am–11pm.

Fitzrovia

Bradley's Spanish Bar, 42–44 Hanway St, W1 ☎020/7636 0359. Appealingly unpretentious backstreet bar with a bizarre but faithful clientele. Tottenham Court Road tube. Mon–Sat 11am–11pm.

The Hope, 15 Tottenham St, W1 ☎020/7637 0896. Chiefly remarkable for its sausage (veggie ones included), beans and mash lunches, and its real ales. Goodge Street tube.

Newman Arms, 23 Rathbone St, W1 ☎020/7636 1127. What *The Hope* is to sausages, the *Newman Arms* is to pies, with every sort from gammon to steak and kidney. Tottenham Court Road tube. Mon–Fri 11.30am–11pm.

Sevilla Mia, 22 Hanway St, W1 ☎020/7637 3756. Another Fitzrovia Spanish bar, more Spanish and often more fun than *Bradley's*, with impromptu flamenco and a good range of *tapas*. Tottenham Court Road tube. Mon–Sat 7pm–1am, Sun 7pm–midnight.

Covent Garden

Africa Centre, 38 King St, WC2 ☎020/7836 1976. Occasionally noisy, convivial basement bar, attracting Africans and Africa-philes. The beer's

awful, but that's missing the point. Covent Garden tube. Mon–Thurs 5.30–11pm, Fri & Sat until 3am.

The Angel, 61 St Giles High St, WC2 ☎020/7240 2876. A friendly local in the centre of town, popular with musos. Small garden, open fires and a loyal crowd. Tottenham Court Road tube.

The Chandos, 29 St Martin's Lane, WC2 ☎020/7836 1401. If you can get one of the booths downstairs, or the leather sofas upstairs in the Opera Room, then you'll find it difficult to leave, especially given the cheap Sam Smith's beer. Leicester Square tube.

Cross Keys, 31 Endell St, WC2 ☎020/7836 5185. A wonderfully cluttered old pub, with a good blend of older Covent Garden residents and new young workers. Leicester Square tube.

Freedom Brewing Company, 41 Earlham St, WC2 ☎020/7240 0606; www .freedombrew.com. Busy, brick-vaulted basement bar with wrought-iron pillars, lots of brushed steel and pricey, strong brews, made on the premises – in particular, there's a very fine organic honey wheat beer. Covent Garden tube.

Lamb & Flag, 33 Rose St, WC2 ☎020/7497 9504. Busy, tiny and highly atmospheric pub, tucked away down an alley between Garrick Street and Floral Street, where John Dryden was attacked in 1679 for writing scurrilous verses about one of Charles II's mistresses. Leicester Square tube.

Opera Tavern, 23 Catherine St, WC2 ☎020/7836 7321. Cosy Victorian pub opposite Drury Lane Theatre, so relatively quiet while the show's going on; the beer's good, too, and there's a real fire in winter. Covent Garden tube.

Opera Terrace Bar, Covent Garden Piazza, WC2 ☎020/7379 0666. A little hard to find, but worth the effort, this upstairs bar overlooks the piazza and has an outdoor terrace open in summer. Covent Garden tube.

Salisbury, 90 St Martin's Lane, WC2 ☎020/7836 5863. One of the most

Pubs and bars

Pubs and bars

beautifully preserved Victorian pubs in the capital, with cut, etched and engraved windows, bronze figures and a lincrusta ceiling. Overzealous doormen and overcrowding are the only drawbacks. Leicester Square tube.

Bloomsbury

Lamb, 94 Lamb's Conduit St, WC1 ☎020/7405 0713. Pleasant Young's pub with a marvellously well-preserved Victorian interior of mirrors, old wood and "snob" screens. Russell Square tube.

Museum Tavern, 49 Great Russell St, WC1 ☎020/7242 8987. Large and characterful old pub, right opposite the main entrance to the British Museum, and once the erstwhile drinking hole of Karl Marx. Tottenham Court Road or Russell Square tube.

Princess Louise, 208 High Holborn, WC1 ☎020/7405 8816. Old-fashioned Sam Smith's pub, with highly decorated ceilings and lots of glass, brass and mahogany. Holborn tube. Mon–Fri 11am–11pm, Sat noon–11pm.

Strand

Coal Hole, 91 Strand, WC2 ☎020/7836 7503. Very popular former coal-heavers' hangout, next to the *Savoy* hotel. There's a nice gallery upstairs, a cellar bar below and good real ales. Charing Cross or Embankment tube.

Gordon's, 47 Villiers St, WC2 ☎020/7930 1408. A claustrophobic, cave-like wine bar specializing in ports, right next door to Charing Cross Station. The excellent and varied wine list, decent buffet food and genial atmosphere make this a favourite with local office workers. Charing Cross or Embankment tube. Mon–Sat 11am–11pm.

Holborn

Cittie of Yorke, 22 High Holborn, WC1 ☎020/7242 7670. Upstairs is the grand quasi-medieval wine hall, with cubicles once the preserve of lawyers and their clients; below is the more down-to-earth cellar. Chancery Lane tube. Mon–Sat 11.30am–11pm.

Na Zdrowie, 11 Little Turnstile, WC1 ☎020/7831 9679. Great new Polish bar hidden in an alleyway behind Holborn tube, with a wicked selection of flavoured vodkas and cheap Polish food. Mon–Fri noon–11pm, Sat 6–11pm.

Ye Olde Mitre, 1 Ely Court, off Ely Place, EC1 ☎020/7405 4751. Rickety eighteenth-century two-bar pub, popular with City wage-slaves. Farringdon tube. Mon–Fri 11am–11pm.

Clerkenwell

Café Kick, 43 Exmouth Market, EC1 ☎020/7837 8077. Stylish take on a smoky, local French-style café/bar in the heart of fashionable Exmouth Market, with three busy table-football games to complete the retro theme. Farringdon or Angel tube. Mon–Sat noon–11pm.

Clerkenwell House, 23–27 Hatton Wall, EC1 ☎020/7404 1113. One of a whole host of new bars that have opened on and off the Clerkenwell Road. The retro 1970s furniture includes some wickedly comfy semi-circular sofas, the Med food is good, and there are four American pool tables in the basement bar. Farringdon tube. Mon–Sat 11am–2am, Sun noon–10.30pm.

Eagle, 159 Farringdon Rd, EC1 ☎020/7837 1353. The first of London's pubs to go foody, this place is heaving at lunch and dinner times, as *Guardian* and *Observer* workers tuck into Med dishes, but you should be able to find a seat at other times. Farringdon tube. Mon–Sat noon–11pm, Sun noon–5pm.

Fox & Anchor, 115 Charterhouse St, EC1 ☎020/7253 4838. Handsome Smithfield market pub famous for its early opening hours and huge breakfasts (served 7–10am). Farringdon or Barbican tube. Mon–Fri 7am–11pm.

Jerusalem Tavern, 55 Britton St, EC1 ☎020/7490 4281. Cosy little converted Georgian parlour, stripped bare and slightly "distressed", serving tasty food at lunchtimes, along with an excellent range of draught beers from St Peter's Brewery in Suffolk. Farringdon tube. Mon–Fri 9am–11pm.

Match, 45–47 Clerkenwell Rd, EC1 ☎020/7250 4002. If you like cocktails, this cool, dark bar is a great place to drink them: noisy, often packed, but nice with it. Farringdon tube. Mon–Fri 11am–midnight, Sat 6pm–midnight.

O'Hanlon, 8 Tysoe St, EC1 ☎020/7837 4112. Small Irish pub serving its own brews, including the best stout in London, plus great Irish food. Angel tube. Mon–Sat noon–11pm.

The City: Fleet Street & Blackfriars

Blackfriar, 174 Queen Victoria St, EC4 ☎020/7236 5650. A gorgeous, utterly original pub, with Art Nouveau marble friezes of boozy monks and a wonderful highly decorated alcove – all original, dating from 1905. Blackfriars tube. Mon–Fri 11.30am–11pm.

Old Bank of England, 194 Fleet St, EC4 ☎020/7430 2255. Not the actual Bank of England, but the former Law Courts' branch, this imposing High Victorian banking hall is now a magnificently opulent ale and pie pub. Temple or Chancery Lane tube. Mon–Fri 11am–11pm.

Old Bell Tavern, 95 Fleet St, EC4 ☎020/7583 0070. Built in 1678 by Wren as his masons' local boozer, and for years the printers' favourite. Now a listed building with characteristic triangular oak stools. Temple or Blackfriars tube. Mon–Fri 11.30am–11pm, Sun noon–4pm.

Old Cheshire Cheese, Wine Office Court, 145 Fleet St, EC4 ☎020/7353 6170. A famous seventeenth-century watering hole, with several snug, dark-panelled bars and real fires. Popular with tourists, but by no means exclusively so. Temple or Blackfriars tube. Mon–Fri 11.30am–11pm, Sat noon–9.30pm, Sun noon–4pm.

The City: St Paul's to Bishopsgate

The Counting House, 50 Cornhill, EC2 ☎020/7283 7123. Another Fuller's bank conversion, with fantastic high ceilings, a glass dome, chandeliers and a central oval bar. Naturally enough, given the location, it's wall-to-wall suits. Bank tube. Mon–Fri 11am–11pm.

The George, Bishopsgate, EC2 ☎020/7618 7310. *The George* – the pub on the corner of Liverpool Street – is a much more relaxing place to have a drink than the nearby *Hamilton Hall*. It's part of Conran's smoothly-run refurbished *Great Eastern Hotel*, and retains its wonderful original mock-Tudor décor. Liverpool Street tube.

Hamilton Hall, Liverpool Street Station, EC2 ☎020/7247 3579. Cavernous former ballroom of the *Great Eastern* hotel, adorned with gilded nudes and chandeliers. Packed-out with City commuters tanking up before the train home, but a great place nonetheless. Liverpool Street tube.

Jamaica Wine House, St Michael's Alley, EC3 ☎020/7626 9496. An old City institution tucked away down a narrow alleyway. Despite the name, this is really just a pub, divided into four large "snugs' by high wooden-panelled partitions. Bank tube. Mon–Fri 11am–11pm.

Lamb, Leadenhall Market, EC3 ☎020/7626 2454. A great pub right in the middle of Leadenhall Market, serving pricey but excellent roast beef sandwiches at lunchtime. Monument tube. Mon–Fri 11am–10pm.

Twentyfour, Tower 42 (NatWest Tower), Old Broad St, EC2 ☎020/7877 2424. Bar on the 24th floor of the old NatWest Tower, with one of the best views in all London. Dress smart and tuck into the cocktails. Bank or Liverpool Street tube. Mon–Fri noon–11pm.

Viaduct Tavern, 126 Newgate St, EC1 ☎020/7606 8476. Glorious gin palace built in 1869 opposite what was then Newgate Prison and is now the Old Bailey. The walls are adorned with oils of faded ladies representing Commerce, Agriculture and the Arts. St Paul's tube.

Ye Olde Watling, 29 Watling St, EC4 ☎020/7653 9971. Low oak-beamed

Pubs and bars

Pubs and bars

ceiling and a dark, wood-panelled interior, rebuilt in 1666 by Wren as an office and inn for the St Paul's workmen. Mansion House tube. Mon–Fri 11am–11pm.

Whitechapel and Wapping

Dickens Inn, St Katharine's Way, E1 ☎020/7488 2208. Eighteenth-century timber-framed warehouse transported on wheels from its original site, and then much altered. Still, it's a remarkable building, with a great view, but very firmly on the tourist trail. Tower Hill tube.

Grapes, 76 Narrow St, E14 ☎020/7987 4396. The *Grapes'* fame is assured thanks to a possible connection with Dickens' *Our Mutual Friend*; it has a riverside balcony out back, standard bar meals and an expensive fish restaurant upstairs. Westferry DLR. Mon–Fri noon–3pm & 5.30–11.30pm, Sat 7–11pm, Sun noon–3pm & 7–10pm.

Hoop & Grapes, 47 Aldgate High St, EC3 ☎020/7265 5171. A very old pub before the developers got at it, but the choice of real ales is good, the food is quite passable, and it's roomy. Aldgate tube. Mon–Wed 11am–10pm, Thurs & Fri 11am–11pm.

Prospect of Whitby, 57 Wapping Wall, E1 ☎020/7481 1095. London's most famous riverside pub, with a flagstone floor, a cobbled courtyard and great views. Wapping tube. Mon–Fri 11.30am–3pm & 5.30–11pm, Sat 11.30am–11pm, Sun noon–10.30pm.

Town of Ramsgate, 62 Wapping High St, E1 ☎020/7264 0001. Dark, narrow, medieval pub located by Wapping Old Stairs, which once led down to Execution Dock. Captain Blood was discovered here with the Crown Jewels under his cloak, "Hanging" Judge Jeffreys was arrested trying to flee, and Admiral Bligh and Fletcher Christian were regular drinking partners in pre-mutiny days. Wapping tube. Mon–Sat noon–11pm, Sun noon–10.30pm.

Hoxton and Hackney

Bar Lorca, Stoke Newington Church St, N16 ☎020/7254 2266. Lively Spanish salsa bar, with tapas on offer – it gets busier and louder the later it gets. Admission £3 Fri & Sat after 10pm. Bus #73. Mon–Thurs noon–1am, Fri & Sat noon–2am, Sun noon–midnight.

Bricklayer's Arms, 63 Charlotte Rd, EC2 ☎020/7739 5245. An appealingly ramshackle Shoreditch pub that predates the area's trendification, and is therefore all the more popular with its new arty residents. Old Street tube.

Home, 100–106 Leonard St, EC2 ☎020/7684 8618. It may not be your idea of home, but this Hoxton basement bar, below the restaurant of the same name, is an attractively laid-back living room in which to chill out. Old Street tube. Mon–Fri noon–midnight, Sat 6pm–midnight.

The Pool, 104–108 Curtain Rd, EC2 ☎020/7739 9608. The three pool tables looking out onto busy, busy Curtain Road give this bar its name; big bean bags add a retro touch. Old Street tube. Daily noon–11pm.

Pub on the Park, 19 Martello St, E8 ☎020/7275 9586. Good food, mixed company and a great place to take kids – as it is, as the name suggests, right on the edge of London Fields, by the playground. London Fields train station. Mon–Thurs 11am–11pm, Fri & Sat 11am–midnight, Sun noon–10.30pm.

Shoreditch Electricity Showrooms, 39a Hoxton Square, N1 ☎020/7739 6934. Kitsch, retro bar that is one of the flagships of new, arty, trendy Hoxton. Old Street tube. Tues & Wed noon–11pm, Thurs noon–midnight, Fri & Sat noon–1am, Sun noon–10.30pm.

Isle of Dogs

The Gun, 27 Cold Harbour, E14 ☎020/7987 1692. An old dockers' pub with lots of maritime memorabilia, and – the main attraction – an unrivalled view of the Millennium Dome. South Quay or Blackwall DLR.

RIVERSIDE, CANALSIDE AND DOCKLAND PUBS

In summer, the most popular pubs in London are those with a **riverside, canalside or dockland view**. You can sit outside at any of the places listed below (see main text for reviews); another option is to drink on one of the old **naval and merchant boats** moored on the north bank of the Thames, between Westminster and Blackfriars bridges – there's little to distinguish these, so stroll down and take your pick.

Pubs and bars

East End and Docklands

Grapes (see opposite)
The Gun (see opposite)
Henry Addington (see below)
Prospect of Whitby (see opposite)
Tollesbury Thames Barge (see below)
Town of Ramsgate (see opposite)
Via Fossa (see below)

Lambeth and Southwark

Anchor Bankside (see below)
Angel (see p.544)
Founders Arms (see below)

Mayflower (see p.544)
Spice Island (see p.544)

Greenwich

Cutty Sark (see p.547)
Trafalgar Tavern (see p.547)

Hammersmith and Chiswick

Black Lion (see p.548)
Dove (see p.548)

Richmond and Twickenham

Fox & Grapes (see p.548)
White Cross Hotel (see p.548)

Henry Addington, 20–28 MacKenzie Walk, E14 ☎020/7513 0921. Named after the prime minister who sanctioned the original Canary Wharf, this is the simplest choice when it comes to having a pint in this area, since it's big and has a nice dockside terrace. Canary Wharf DLR/tube. Mon–Fri 11am–11pm, Sat & Sun noon–4pm.

Tollesbury Thames Barge, Marsh Wall, E14 ☎020/7363 1183. For the ultimate Docklands experience, climb aboard this old Thames barge and enjoy a pint, while surveying the old Millwall Docks. South Quay DLR. Mon–Fri 11.30am–11pm.

Via Fossa, West India Quay, E14 ☎020/7515 8549. Housed in a nineteenth-century warehouse, and accessible from Canary Wharf via a footbridge. If the weather's warm, the south-facing terrace is great to sit out on. West India Quay DLR. Mon–Sat noon–11pm, Sun noon–7pm.

The South Bank and Bankside

Anchor Bankside, 34 Park St, SE1 ☎020/7407 1577. While the rest of Bankside has changed almost beyond all

recognition, this pub still looks much as it did when first built in 1770 (on the inside, at least). Good for alfresco drinking by the river. London Bridge tube.

Fire Station, 150 Waterloo Rd, SE1 ☎020/7620 2226. This gloriously red former fire station is a step away from Waterloo, and therefore a popular place for an after-work pint. The restaurant at the back is good, too. Waterloo tube.

Founders Arms, 52 Hopton St, SE1 ☎020/7928 1899. A modern pub, undistinguished except for its position by the river, with outside tables and great views across to the City. Blackfriars tube.

NFT Bar, South Bank, SE1 ☎020/7928 3535. The National Film Theatre's bar is the only riverfront bar on the South Bank between Westminster and Blackfriars bridges – worth checking out not only for the views, but also for the food and the congenial crowd. Waterloo tube. Mon–Sat noon–11pm, Sun noon–10.30pm.

Southwark

George Inn, 77 Borough High St, SE1 ☎020/7407 2056. London's only

Pubs and bars

surviving coaching inn (see p.318), dating from the seventeenth century and now owned by the National Trust; it also serves a good range of real ales. Borough or London Bridge tube.

Market Porter, 9 Stoney St, SE1 ☎020/7407 2495. Handsome semi-circular pub with early opening hours for workers at the Borough Market, and a seriously huge range of real ales. London Bridge tube. Mon–Sat 6–8.30am & 11am–11pm, Sun noon–10.30pm.

Old Thameside Inn, Pickfords Wharf, 1 Clink St, SE1 ☎020/7403 4243. Another undistinguished pub whose only virtue is its riverside terrace, right by the *Golden Hinde*. London Bridge tube. Mon–Fri 11am–11pm, Sat & Sun noon–6pm.

Royal Oak, 44 Tabard St, SE1 ☎020/7357 7173. Beautiful, lovingly restored Victorian pub that eschews jukeboxes and one-armed bandits and opts simply for serving real ales. Borough or London Bridge tube. Mon–Fri 11am–11pm.

Bermondsey and Rotherhithe

Anchor Tap, 20a Horselydown Lane, SE1 ☎020/7403 4637. The former tap of the old Anchor brewery – itself now converted to yuppie flats – is now a Sam Smith's pub, with a surprisingly down-to-earth clientele for these parts. Tower Hill tube. Mon–Sat 11.30am–11pm, Sun noon–10.30pm.

Angel, 101 Bermondsey Wall East, SE16 ☎020/7237 3608. Ancient and enjoyable riverside inn, stranded in no-man's-land between Bermondsey and Rotherhithe, with good river views. Bermondsey tube. Mon–Sat 11.30am–11pm, Sun noon–10.30pm.

Mayflower, 117 Rotherhithe St, SE16 ☎020/7237 4088. A postwar reconstruction, but this pub, in the heart of old Rotherhithe, is steeped in history and has a good view out onto the Thames. Rotherhithe tube. Mon–Sat noon–11pm, Sun noon–10.30pm.

Spice Island, 163 Rotherhithe St, SE16 ☎020/7394 7108. Huge, converted

wooden warehouse, with great beers, good food and fine views across the Thames. Rotherhithe tube.

Knightsbridge and Belgravia

Antelope, 22–24 Eaton Terrace, SW1 ☎020/7730 7781. Old-fashioned, posh pub that predates Belgravia itself; high-class pub food downstairs, real restaurant upstairs. Sloane Square tube. Mon–Sat 11.30am–11pm, Sun noon–10.30pm.

Grenadier, 18 Wilton Row, SW1 ☎020/7235 3074. Wellington's local (his horse block survives outside) and his officers' mess; the original pewter bar survives, and the Bloody Marys are special. Hyde Park Corner or Knightsbridge tube. Mon–Sat noon–11pm, Sun noon–10.30pm.

Paxton's Head, 153 Knightsbridge, SW1 ☎020/7589 6627. Wonderful Edwardian pub, with lincrusta ceiling tiles, mahogany bar and etched mirrors; very unpretentious given the locale. Avoid the bar food. Knightsbridge tube.

Star Tavern, 6 Belgrave Mews West, SW1 ☎020/7235 3019. Quiet two-storey mews pub, built for the large local servant population. Fine beer and classy food. Hyde Park Corner or Knightsbridge tube. Mon–Fri 11.30am–11pm, Sat 11.30am–3pm & 6.30–11pm, Sun noon–3pm & 7–10.30pm.

South Kensington

Blenheim, 27 Cale St, SW3 ☎020/7349 0056. Large Georgian pub, with lots of lovely wood, an unusual menu, excellent beers and cheap grub. South Kensington tube.

Bunch of Grapes, 207 Brompton Rd, SW3 ☎020/7589 4944. This popular High Victorian pub, complete with snob screens, is the perfect place for a post-museum pint. Opposite the Brompton Oratory. South Kensington tube.

The Crescent, 99 Fulham Rd, SW3 ☎020/7225 2244. Designer, minimalist, air-conditioned wine bar with a staggering range of over two hundred wines (over twenty by the glass), and tasty, but expensive food. South Kensington tube.

Chelsea

Front Page, 35 Old Church St, SW3 ☎020/7352 2908; *www.frontpagepubs .com*. Centre of boho Chelsea and infinitely preferable to anything on offer on the King's Road. Sloane Square tube.

Mason's Arms, 169 Battersea Park Rd, SW8 ☎020/7622 2007. Renovated, trendy bare-boards and sofas pub directly opposite the train station. Battersea Park train station. Mon–Sat noon–11pm, Sun noon–10.30pm.

Orange Brewery, 37 Pimlico Rd, SW1 ☎020/7730 5984. The area may be posh, but this is a fairly down-to-earth boozer with its very own micro-brewery. Sloane Square tube.

Sporting Page, 6 Camera Place, SW10 ☎020/7376 3694; *www.frontpagepubs .com*. Great place for a bit of Sloane-watching – it sells more Bollinger than any other pub in London. Sloane Square tube.

Notting Hill

The Cow, 89 Westbourne Park Rd, W2 ☎020/7221 5400. Owned by Tom Conran, son of gastro-magnate Terence, this pub pulls in the beautiful W11 types, thanks to its spectacular food, including a daily supply of fresh oysters. Westbourne Park tube. Mon–Sat noon–11pm, Sun noon–10.30pm.

Elbow Room, 103 Westbourne Grove, W2 ☎020/7221 5211; *www.elbow-room .co.uk*. With seven purple-baize tables, funky loud music and a trendy crowd, this is the pool pub of the future. Book ahead to be sure of a table. Bayswater tube. Mon–Sat noon–11pm, Sun noon–10.30pm.

Ground Floor, 186 Portobello Rd, W11 ☎020/7243 8701. A good bet for a relaxed drink on Portobello Road, this colourful place is no ordinary boozer, specializing instead in cocktails and a straightforward but excellent bar menu. Ladbroke Grove tube.

Ion, 161–165 Ladbroke Grove, W10 ☎020/8960 1702. Retro 1960s feel to this Mean Fiddler-run bar situated under the Westway. There's food available on the mezzanine, and DJs on some nights. Ladbroke Grove tube. Mon–Fri 5pm–midnight, Sat & Sun noon–midnight.

Liquid Lounge, 209 Westbourne Park Rd, W11 ☎020/7243 0914. Another essential stop on any Notting Hill designer bar crawl, this symphony in blue has a useful late licence, though it can get loud and large. Mon–Fri 5pm–midnight, Sat 10am–midnight, Sun 10am–11.30pm.

Market Bar, 240a Portobello Rd, W11 ☎020/7229 6472. Self-consciously bohemian pub with gilded mirrors and weird *objets* – all very Notting Hill. Ladbroke Grove tube. Mon–Fri noon–11pm, Sat noon–midnight, Sun noon–10.30pm.

The Westbourne, 101 Westbourne Park Villas, W2 ☎020/7221 1332. One of a trio of bare-boards Notting Hill gastro-pubs, serving top-notch Brit-Med food. Westbourne Park tube. Mon 5–11pm, Tues–Fri noon–11pm, Sat 11am–11pm, Sun noon–10.30pm.

St John's Wood and Maida Vale

Crocker's Folly, 24 Aberdeen Place, NW8 ☎020/7286 6608. Gloriously over-the-top Victorian pub with oodles of marble and mahogany and coffered ceilings; built as a railway hotel by Frank Crocker, who committed suicide (by throwing himself off the roof of the pub) when an alternative location was announced for Marylebone Station. Warwick Avenue tube.

Prince Alfred, 9 Formosa St, W9 ☎020/7286 3027. Another fantastic period-piece Victorian pub with all its original 1862 fittings intact, right down to the glazed snob screens. The beer and Thai food are good, too. Warwick Avenue tube.

Warrington Hotel, 93 Warrington Crescent, W9 ☎020/7286 2929. Yet another architectural gem in an area replete with them. This one's a former

Pubs and bars

Pubs and bars

Edwardian hotel lobby done out in flamboyant Art Nouveau, with a useful Thai restaurant upstairs. Maida Vale tube.

Camden Town

Bartok, 78–79 Chalk Farm Rd, NW1 ☎020/7916 0595. Mean Fiddler-run bar where punters can sink into one of the sofas and sup beer or wine while listening to classical music instead of the usual muzak. Chalk Farm or Camden Town tube. Mon–Thurs 5pm–midnight, Fri 5pm–1am, Sat noon–1am, Sun noon–midnight.

Camden Brewing Co., 1 Randolph St, NW1 ☎020/7267 9829. Old pub totally transformed inside into a boldly colourful designer interior, with comfy sofas, real fires and good Thai food. Camden Town tube. Mon–Thurs & Sun noon–11pm, Fri & Sat noon–midnight.

The Engineer, 65 Gloucester Ave, NW1 ☎020/7722 0950. Smart, grandiose Victorian pub for the Primrose Hill posse – the food is exceptional though pricey, and it's advisable to book if you're intending to nosh. Chalk Farm tube. Mon–Sat 9am–11pm, Sun 9am–10.30pm.

Lansdowne, 90 Gloucester Ave, NW1 ☎020/7483 0409. Big, bare-boards minimalist pub with comfy sofas, in elegant Primrose Hill. Pricey, tasty food. Chalk Farm tube. Mon 7–11pm, Tues–Sat noon–11pm, Sun noon–4pm & 7–10.30pm.

Queens, 49 Regent's Park Rd, NW1 ☎020/7586 0408. A light and airy, posh Young's pub in Primrose Hill, with a green and magnolia colour scheme. Above average food for above average prices. Chalk Farm tube.

Islington

Bierdorome, 173–174 Upper St, N1 ☎020/7226 5835; *www.belgo-restaurants.com*. A designer-pubby branch of the Belgo restaurant chain, where the Belgian beers and schnapps hog the limelight, but where you can also tuck into mussels and chips. Angel tube. Daily noon–11pm.

Camden Head, 2 Camden Walk, N1 ☎020/7359 0851. Confusingly, not in Camden at all, but in the midst of Islington's antique market. The pub itself is something of an antique, with engraved glass fittings and mirrors. Angel tube.

Compton Arms, 4 Compton Ave, N1 ☎020/7359 6883. Nice little local, hidden away down a sort of mews near Canonbury Square, that likes to pretend it's standing right by the village green. Highbury & Islington tube.

Duke of Cambridge, 30 St Peter's St, N1 ☎020/7359 3066; *www.singhboulton .co.uk*. Not just a gastropub, but an organic one – and that goes for the beers and wines as well as the (pricey) food. Angel tube. Mon–Fri noon–11pm, Sun noon–10.30pm.

King's Head, 115 Upper St, N1 ☎020/7226 0364. Busy pub-theatre in the heart of Islington with regular live music, a useful late licence and a bizarre affectation of quoting prices in pre-decimal money. Angel tube. Mon–Thurs 11am–midnight, Fri & Sat 11am–2am, Sun noon–midnight.

Hampstead and Highgate

Bar Room Bar, 48 Rosslyn Hill, NW3 ☎020/7435 0808. Self-consciously clubby, pared-down pub that does decent lunches (daily noon–4pm), and has a nice conservatory out back. Handy for the Heath. Hampstead tube.

Flask, 14 Flask Walk, NW3 ☎020/7435 4580. Convivial Hampstead local which retains its original Victorian snob screen. Serves good food and fine ale. Hampstead tube.

Flask, 77 Highgate West Hill, N6 ☎020/8340 7260. Ideally situated at the heart of Highgate village green, with a rambling, low-ceilinged interior and a summer terrace. Highgate tube.

Freemason's Arms, 32 Downshire Hill, NW3 ☎020/7433 6811. Big, smart pub close to the Heath, of interest primarily for its large beer garden and its basement skittle alley. Hampstead tube.

Mon–Sat noon–11pm, Sun noon–10.30pm.

Holly Bush, 22 Holly Mount, NW3 ☎020/7435 2892. A lovely old gas-lit pub, tucked away in the steep back-streets of Hampstead village, which can get a bit too mobbed on the weekend. Hampstead tube. Mon–Sat noon–11pm, Sun noon–10.30pm.

Jack Straw's Castle, North End Way, NW3 ☎020/7435 8885. Named after the Peasants' Revolt leader who was executed outside the pub, the present building is a 1960s pastiche, popular with tourists and Heath-walking types. Hampstead tube.

Sir Richard Steele, 97 Haverstock Hill, NW3 ☎020/7483 1261. Cluttered, oddball décor and clientele, and live jazz, folk or flamenco several nights a week. Belsize Park or Chalk Farm tube.

Spaniard's Inn, Spaniards Rd, NW3 ☎020/8731 6571. Big sixteenth-century coaching inn, frequented by everyone from Dick Turpin to John Keats. Aviary, pergola and roses in the garden. Hampstead tube or bus #210 from Highgate tube.

Brixton, Clapham and Dulwich

Bread & Roses, 68 Clapham Manor St, SW4 ☎020/7498 1779. One good reason for venturing into resolutely residential Clapham, this Workers' Beer Company pub serves fine ales, holds political events upstairs and is very welcoming to those with kids. Clapham Common tube.

Brixtonian Havana Club, 11 Beehive Place, SW9 ☎020/7924 9262. Funky, quirky attic bar, hidden away off Brixton Station Road (near the Rec), serving Caribbean food, lots of rum and a few bottled beers. Brixton tube. Tues & Wed noon–1am, Thurs–Sat noon–2am.

Crown & Greyhound, 73 Dulwich Village, SE21 ☎0181/693 2466. Grandiose Victorian pub, convenient for the Picture Gallery, with an ornate plasterwork ceiling and a nice summer beer garden. North Dulwich train station.

Hope & Anchor, 123 Acre Lane, SW2 ☎020/7274 1787. A very pleasant local (not a phrase you'd use about most pubs in Brixton), with Young's beer, decent food and a kids' play area in the back garden. Brixton tube.

Trinity Arms, 45 Trinity Gardens, SW2 ☎020/7274 4544. Brixton's most attractive pub, hidden in the backstreets off Acre Lane. Crowds spill out into the nearby square in summer. Brixton tube.

Greenwich

Cutty Sark, Ballast Quay, off Lassell St, SE10 ☎0181/858 3146. The nicest riverside pub in Greenwich, yet much less touristy than the *Trafalgar Tavern* (it's a couple of minutes' walk further east, following the river). Cutty Sark DLR or Maze Hill train station.

Richard I, 52–54 Royal Hill, SE10 ☎0181/692 2996. Popular Greenwich local tucked away off the main drag. Good beer and a garden make it an ideal post-market retreat – and if it's too crowded, the *Fox & Hounds* next door is good too. Greenwich DLR & train station.

Trafalgar Tavern, 5 Park Row, SE10 ☎0181/858 2437. Great riverside position and a mention in Dickens' *Our Mutual Friend* have made this Regency-style inn a firm tourist favourite. Good whitebait and other snacks. Cutty Sark DLR or Maze Hill train station. Mon–Sat 11.30am–11pm, Sun noon–10.30pm.

Blackheath

The Crown, 49 Tranquil Vale, SE3 ☎0181/852 0326. Not on the heath, but in the village, this is a nice old-fashioned pub, serving up traditional ale and pies. Blackheath train station.

Hare & Billet, 1a Eliot Cottages, SE3 ☎0181/852 2352. A small heathside pub, with drinkers drifting outside in summer, and cut-price four-pint jugs on offer. Blackheath train station.

Princess of Wales, 1a Montpelier Row, SE3 ☎0181/297 5911. Another old heathside pub, on a fine Georgian terrace. Extremely popular in summer, when

Pubs and bars

Club-bars and gay and lesbian bars are covered on p.559 and pp.568–9 respectively.

Pubs and bars

it's hard to move on the grass outside. Blackheath train station. Mon–Sat noon–11pm, Sun noon–10.30pm.

Hammersmith and Chiswick

Black Lion, 2 South Black Lion Lane, W6 ☎0181/748 2639. Congenial local, slightly set back from the river, with an indoor skittle alley, and a bouncy castle in summer. Stamford Brook tube.

Blue Anchor, 13 Lower Mall, W6 ☎0181/748 5774. First of Hammersmith's riverside pubs, with a boaty theme and a beautiful pewter bar; most people sit outside and enjoy the river, however. Hammersmith or Ravenscourt Park tube.

Dove, 19 Upper Mall, W6 ☎0181/748 5405. Old, old riverside pub with literary associations, the smallest back bar in the UK (4ft by 7ft), and Thai food in the evening. Ravenscourt Park tube.

Richmond, Twickenham and Wimbledon

Fox & Grapes, 9 Camp Rd, SW19 ☎0181/946 5599. Right on the edge of Wimbledon Common, and great in summer, when you can sit outside on the grass. Wimbledon tube.

White Cross Hotel, Water Lane, Richmond ☎0181/940 6844. With a longer pedigree and more character than its rivals, the *White Cross* is also closer to the river, has a garden out back and serves filling pub food. Richmond tube.

White Swan, Riverside, Twickenham ☎0181/892 2166. Decent food and beer and a quiet riverside location – with a beer pontoon overlooking Eel Pie Island if you want to get even closer to the water. Twickenham train station from Waterloo.

Chapter 18

Live music and clubs

Don't believe the Cool Britannia hype: as far as London is concerned, there's been a bewildering range of places to go after dark – to hear bands, dance or club – for at least the last twenty years. The live music scene remains amazingly diverse, encompassing all variations of **rock and blues music**, from big names on tour at the city's main venues, through to a network of indie and pub bands in more immediate surroundings. The popularity of multicultural festivals such as Notting Hill Carnival (see p.379) has increased demand for **world music**, too – especially African, Latin and Caribbean bands, many of whom are based in London. There is a fine scattering of clubs and pubs devoted to **Celtic music** and **English roots**, and although London's **jazz clubs** aren't on a par with those in the big American cities, there's a highly individual scene of home-based artists, which is supplemented by top-name visiting players.

If you're looking for **dance music**, then you've come to the right place. After dark, London is thriving, with diverse scenes championing everything from hip-hop to house, techno to trance, samba to soca and drum'n'bass to R&B on virtually any night of the week. Venues once used exclusively by performing bands now pepper the week with club nights, and you often find dance sessions starting as soon as a band has stopped playing. Dance music has taken London by storm and, after a few hiccup years when bad drugs and

bad attitude threatened the very essence of the scene, London is once again party capital of Europe – and that's no hype.

Bear in mind that there's an overlap between "live music venues" and "clubs" in the listings below; we've indicated which places serve a double function. Proposed changes to England's licensing laws seem likely to finally take effect in 2001, and the already relaxed attitude to late-night bars should become even more liberal in the near future. So far, though, the main consequence of the previous restrictions on late-night drinking laws has been the rapid growth and diversity of **club-bars**, places which are essentially bars, but cater for a clubby crowd – funky décor, DJs, late opening hours and ridiculously overpriced foreign beers.

The dance and club scene is, of course, pretty much in constant flux, with the hottest items moving location, losing the plot or just cooling off. Weekly **listings magazines** like *Time Out* and *7*, as well as the bi-weekly *DJ*, give up-to-date details of prices and access, plus previews and reviews.

Live music

Major bands on world tours always stop off in London, despite there being no decent venue for the biggest names to play: Wembley Arena and Earl's Court have all the atmosphere of shopping malls, while the Royal Albert Hall is overly decorous. But London is nonetheless

Exclusively gay clubs and discos are covered in Chapter 19.

Live music and clubs

hard to beat for its musical mix: whether you're into **jazz**, **indie rock**, **R&B**, **blues** or **world music**, you'll find something worth hearing on almost any night of the week. Entry prices for gigs run from a couple of pounds for an unknown band thrashing it out in a pub, to around £30 for the likes of U2, but £10–15 is the average price for a good night out – not counting expenses at the bar. It's often cheaper to book tickets in advance with a credit card via the Internet, from sites such as *www.ticketweb.co.uk*, *www.tickets-online.co.uk* or *www.gigsandtours.com*. We've listed Web sites for all venues that have them.

The mega-venues

Earl's Court, Warwick Rd, SW5 ☎020/7385 1200; *www.eco.co.uk*. Singers like Ricky Martin, and bands such as the Spice Girls and Oasis play here on their world tours; most smaller outfits would have difficulty filling this soulless hangar. Earl's Court tube.

London Arena, Limeharbour, Isle of Dogs, E14 ☎020/7538 1212; *www.londonarena.com*. Another huge mainstream venue. Average in every aspect other than the prices, which are outrageous. Crossharbour DLR.

London Hammersmith Apollo, Queen Caroline St, W6 ☎020/7416 6080; *www.tickets-direct.co.uk*. The former *Hammersmith Odeon* is a cavernous, theatre-style venue which tends to host safe, middle-of-the-road bands. Frustratingly, you can only buy drinks during the interval, which leads to horrendous queues at the bar. Hammersmith tube.

Royal Albert Hall, Kensington Gore, SW7 ☎020/7589 8212; *www.royalalberthall.com*. Colossal Victorian concert hall, visited by the big boys from time to time – Massive Attack played here in 1998, while the ever-exuberant Afro Cuban All Stars resplendently hit the stage at the beginning of 2000, as did ageing Mod icon Paul Weller. South Kensington tube.

Wembley Arena, Empire Way, Wembley, Middlesex ☎020/8902 0902; *www.wembleyticket.com*. The main indoor venue for mega-bands, be they Steps or Simply Red. Rip-off prices, poor sound quality and a severe shortage of atmosphere make for a generally disappointing experience. Wembley Park or Wembley Central tube.

General venues

Astoria, 157 Charing Cross Rd, WC2 ☎020/7434 0403. One of London's best and most central medium-sized venues, this large, balconied one-time theatre tends to host slightly alternative bands (from underground US hip-hop to thrashing rock), usually from Monday to Thursday, and club nights on Friday and Saturday. More adventurous than most other big venues. Tottenham Court Road tube.

Brixton Academy, 211 Stockwell Rd, SW9 ☎020/7771 2000. The *Academy* has seen them all – mods and rockers, punks and hippies. Its refurbished Victorian hall, complete with Roman decorations, can hold four thousand and usually does, but still manages to seem small and friendly, probably because no one is forced to sit down. Hosts mainly mid-league bands. Brixton tube.

Forum, 9–17 Highgate Rd, NW5 ☎020/7344 0044; *www.meanfiddler.com*. This is one of the capital's best medium-sized venues – large enough to attract established bands, and with great views and good bars. It was always keen to promote newer talent, but seems to rely more and more on safer, established acts. Kentish Town tube.

The Grand, Clapham Junction, St John's Hill, SW11 ☎020/7385 0834. Another grand old theatre now dedicated to music. Good acoustics and not so big that the band gets lost – if you're feeling really decadent, book a royal box. Saturday is 1970s club night. Clapham Junction train station, from Waterloo or Victoria.

LA2, 157 Charing Cross Rd, WC2 ☎020/7434 0403. Next door to the

Astoria and becoming more popular with bands who have just made it or are just about to. Usually a cheap venue, but it's primarily a club and the raised central dancefloor makes for poor viewing of bands. Tottenham Court Road tube.

Shepherds Bush Empire, Shepherds Bush Green, W12 ☎020/8740 7474. Yet another grand old theatre, the *Empire* now plays host to probably the finest cross-section of mid-league UK and US bands in the capital, from R&B siren Kelis to Irish singer-songwriter David Gray. Intimate with a great atmosphere downstairs. Upstairs, balconies provide some of the best stage views around. Shepherd's Bush tube.

Rock and blues clubs and pubs

12 Bar Club, 22–23 Denmark Place, WC2 ☎020/7916 6989; *www.12barclub.com*. A combination of live blues and contemporary country seven nights a week. Tottenham Court Road tube.

Amersham Arms, 388 New Cross Rd, SE14 ☎020/8692 2047. Students from nearby Goldsmiths' College pack out this indie-oriented venue. New Cross tube.

Borderline, Orange Yard, off Manette St, W1 ☎020/7734 2095; *www .borderline.co.uk*. Intimate basement joint with a diverse musical policy, and a good place to catch new bands. Tottenham Court Road tube.

Bull & Gate, 389 Kentish Town Rd, NW5 ☎020/7485 5358. Basic pub venue for currently obscure, but soon to be big, indie bands. Kentish Town tube.

Dover Street Wine Bar, 8–9 Dover St, W1 ☎020/7629 9813. An enjoyable, central brasserie hosting blues, R&B, jazz and soul bands. Green Park tube.

Dublin Castle, 94 Parkway, NW1 ☎020 /7485 1773. Music pub with a diverse booking policy. Camden Town tube.

The Falcon, 234 Royal College St, NW1 ☎020/7482 4884. Grubby, one-hundred-capacity pub showcasing loud indie bands. Camden Town tube.

Fitz and Firkin, 240 Great Portland St, W1 ☎020/7388 0588. A stone's throw from Regent's Park, this charismatic pub venue plays host to some of the best up-and-coming rock and indie bands. Great Portland Street Tube.

The Garage, 20 Highbury Corner, N1 ☎020/7607 1818. Intimate, mainly indie place with a good reputation for up-and-coming talent which makes the occasional excursion into jazz and funk. Highbury & Islington tube.

Half Moon Putney, 93 Lower Richmond Rd, SW15 ☎020/8780 9383; *www .halfmoon.co.uk*. Well-respected pub venue – good for blues at the weekend and rock during the week – catering for a younger crowd. Putney Bridge tube.

Hope and Anchor, 207 Upper St, N1 ☎020/7354 1312. This cramped venue is popular with indie acts, many playing their first gig here. Angel tube.

The Mean Fiddler, 24–28a Harlesden High St, NW10 ☎020/8961 5490; *www .meanfiddler.com*. An excellent – if inconveniently located – small venue with a main hall and smaller acoustic room. The music veers from rock to world to folk to soul (and even, occasionally, gospel). Good sound. Willesden Junction tube.

Monarch, 48 Chalk Farm Rd, NW1 ☎020/7916 1049. Great Camden pub-venue to catch punk-influenced rock bands. Chalk Farm Tube.

Roadhouse, 35 The Piazza, WC2 ☎020/7240 6001; *www.roadhouse.co .uk*. American food, 1950s US-style decor and a lineup of mainly blues and rock'n'roll bands performing to a mature, nostalgic crowd. Covent Garden tube.

Rock Garden, 35 The Piazza, WC2 ☎020/7240 6001; *www.rockgarden .co.uk*. Loud, central joint where you can get in free if you dine at the attached burger place first. Live music tends towards conventional rock, but the venue hosts a garage and R&B club night on Saturdays. Covent Garden tube.

Live music and clubs

Live music and clubs

The Social, 5 Little Portland St, W1 ☎020/7636 4992. Industrial and often bacchanalian club-bar-cum-music venue run by the Heavenly record label (*St Etienne, Beth Orton, Monkey Mafia*) that hosts emerging pop-rock-folk bands on varying week nights. Free entry. Oxford Circus Tube.

Station Tavern, 41 Bramley Rd, W10 ☎020/7727 4053. Arguably London's best blues venue, with free – and occasionally great – blues six nights a week. Latimer Road tube.

Subterania, 12 Acklam Rd, W10 ☎020/8960 4590; *www.meanfiddler .com*. One of the original live music/club crossover venues in an arch under a flyover. The crowd is as trendy as the music, which is often dance-oriented. Ladbroke Grove tube.

Swan, 215 Clapham Rd, SW9 ☎020/7978 9778. Celtic-style rock'n'roll seven nights a week in this large pub. Stockwell tube.

Underworld, 174 Camden High St, NW1 ☎020/7482 1932. Labyrinthine venue that's good for new bands, and has sporadic club nights. Camden Town tube.

The Venue, 2a Clifton Rise, New Cross, SE14 ☎020/8692 4077. Indie bands on a tiny stage, with a club afterwards. New Cross tube/train, from Charing Cross.

Water Rats, 328 Grays Inn Rd, WC1 ☎020/7284 0077. Loud and brash punk, rock and indie bands trying to make it big in the biz can be found thrashing it out in this notoriously high-spirited pub venue. Kings Cross Tube.

Jazz

Bull's Head Barnes, Barnes Bridge, SW13 ☎020/8876 5241. This riverside alehouse – with pub prices to boot – attracts Britain's finest jazz musicians, though it's now a little shabby around the edges. Bus #9 from Hammersmith tube or Barnes Bridge train station from Waterloo.

Dingwalls (Camden Jongleurs), Camden Lock, NW1 ☎020/7267 1577. This *Jongleurs* comedy venue becomes a top-ranking jazz club on Mondays and Wednesdays. Also worth checking for the occasional indie, pop and world music bands. Camden Town tube.

Dover Street, 8–9 Dover St, W1 ☎020/7629 9813. London's largest jazz restaurant has music and dancing every night until 3am, plus Modern British food. Green Park tube.

Jazz after Dark, 9 Greek St, W1 ☎020/7734 0545. Diverse selection of jazz – often fusing Latin, blues or funk into the equation. Tottenham Court Road tube.

Jazz Café, 5 Parkway, NW1 ☎020/7916 6060; *www.jazzcafe.co.uk*. Futuristic, white-walled venue with an adventurous booking policy exploring Latin, rap, funk, hip-hop and musical fusions. Die-hard trad-jazz fans won't be happy, despite the fact that there's a rather good restaurant upstairs with a few prime tables overlooking the stage (book ahead if you want one). Camden Town tube.

Le Méridien Waldorf, Aldwych WC2 ☎020/7836 2400. Sunday brunch jazz at the *Waldorf* hotel. You'll need to book ahead for this event. Holborn tube.

100 Club, 100 Oxford St, W1 ☎020/7636 0933. After a brief spell as a stage for punk bands, the *100 Club* is once again an unpretentious and inexpensive jazz venue. Tottenham Court Road tube.

Pizza Express, 10 Dean St, W1 ☎020/7437 9595. Enjoy a good pizza, then listen to the resident band or highly skilled guest players. There's also a late night session on Saturdays which starts at 9pm and finishes in the early hours of Sunday. Oxford Street tube.

Pizza on the Park, 11 Knightsbridge, Hyde Park Corner, SW1 ☎020/7235 5273. Spacious restaurant with upmarket ambience and mainstream jazz acts. Hyde Park Corner tube.

Ronnie Scott's, 47 Frith St, W1 ☎020/7439 0747; *www.ronniescotts.co.uk*. The most famous jazz club in London: small and smoky and still going strong, even though the great man himself has passed away. The place for top-line names, who play two sets – one at around 10pm, the other after midnight. Book a table, or you'll have to stand. Leicester Square tube.

606 Club, 90 Lots Rd, SW10 ☎020/7352 5953. A rare all-jazz venue, located just off the less trendy end of the King's Road. You can book a table, and the licensing laws dictate that you must eat if you want to drink, but there's no cover charge. Fulham Broadway tube.

Vortex, Stoke Newington Church St, N16 ☎020/7254 6516. Cheap, cheerful and hugely enjoyable jazz club that attracts a youngish crowd. Often showcases local and up-and-coming musicians. Bus #73 or Stoke Newington train from Liverpool Street.

West One Four, 3 North End Crescent, W14 ☎020/7381 0444 (answerphone outside office hours). Pub-like venue for serious-minded jazz-funkers. There are also club nights (nights vary). West Kensington tube.

World music and roots

Africa Centre, 38 King St, WC2 ☎020/7836 1973; *www.africacentre.org.uk*. The packed old hall was once the venue that launched Soul II Soul; these days, it hosts African bands and nights like Saturday's P-Funk heavy *Funkin Pussy*, but still draws a vibrantly enthusiastic crowd. Covent Garden tube.

Barbican Centre, Silk St, EC2 ☎020/7638 8891; *www.barbican.org.uk*. The expansive Barbican is fast becoming a focal point for great world music bands and orchestras, recently hosting brilliant shows from Japan's Kodo Drummers and Istanbul's Musafir. Barbican tube.

Blackheath Halls, 23 Lee Rd, SE3 ☎020/8463 0100; *www.blackheathhalls.com*. It may be some distance from the centre of town, but this medium-sized venue hosts some of the best world, roots and African bands when they come to the capital. Blackheath train.

Cecil Sharp House, 2 Regent's Park Rd, NW1 ☎020/7485 2206. A centre for British folk music: singing, dancing and a folk-music shop. Camden Town tube.

Halfway House, 142 The Broadway, West Ealing, W5 ☎020/8567 0236. Regular roots bands, from Cajun to Irish folk. Bus #207 from Ealing Broadway tube.

Jazz Café, 5 Parkway, NW1 ☎020/7916 6060; *www.jazzcafe.co.uk*. Hosts regular Latin, jazz-funk, hip-hop and world acts. Camden Town tube.

The Mean Fiddler, 24–28a Harlesden High St, NW10 ☎020/8961 5490; *www.meanfiddler.com*. A long trek out, but well worth it for the excellent Irish and other roots bands. Willesden Junction tube.

The Rhythmic, 89–91 Chapel Market, Islington, N1 ☎020/7713 5859. Large, stylish venue with a daytime café at the front. Latin, jazz, soul and roots music. Angel tube.

South Bank Centre, SE1 ☎020/7960 4242. On the south bank of the Thames, the all-seater Queen Elizabeth Hall, Purcell Rooms and Royal Festival Hall host imaginative programmes of world music, jazz acts and folk music, as well as classical. Waterloo tube.

Swan, 215 Clapham Rd, SW9 ☎020/7978 9778. Live Irish music nightly in this huge pub. Stockwell tube.

Union Chapel, Compton Ave, N1 ☎020/7226 1686. A wonderfully idiosyncratic old chapel that hosts an array of world-fusion nights. Highbury & Islington tube.

Live music
and clubs

Live music
and clubs

Weavers Arms, 98 Newington Green Rd, N1 ☎020/7226 6911. Intimate pub venue with folk, blues or country bands nightly. Highbury & Islington tube.

Clubs

More than a decade after the explosion of acid-house, London remains *the* place to come if you want to party after dark. The sheer diversity of dance music has enabled the city to maintain its status as **Europe's dance capital** – and it's still a port of call for DJs from around the globe. The relaxation of late-night licensing has encouraged many venues to keep serving alcohol until 6am or even later, and this resurgence of alcohol in clubland (much to the relief of the breweries) has been echoed by the meteoric rise of the club-bar (see p.559 for club-bar listings). Drug culture has long since been associated with clubbing, and these days anything seems to go – from marijuana and alcohol through ecstasy, cocaine and speed – along with a wider divide between the generations and a

call for more education and information from users.

While dance music has evolved to now encompass a multitude of sub-genres, London clubs are currently embracing nights which provide a variety of electronic sounds to their punters. That said, house still dominates – but the term now covers anything from US garage, deep house and European tech-no to the home-grown styles of hard house and progressive trance. Drum'n'bass has cut out a niche, though it is UK garage that has really taken London by storm in the last few years – a mixture of American garage and jungle basslines that's grown into a chart-topping genre all of it's own – two step. It's also given birth to a core clientele who are consciously dressy and have a penchant for drinking champagne and flashing expensive labels. Look out for DJs like The Dreem Teem, Tuff Jam, Norris "Da Boss" Windross and M.J. Cole if you want to check out what all the fuss is about. The jazz and acid-jazz scene still

---

thrives, too, though Brazilian bossanova now also commands a passionate following, thanks to the support of influential DJs like Gilles Peterson. In addition, reggae, ragga and the US-led fusion of swing and hip-hop still command a loyal following. Latin, African, Indian and world-music fans have their own clubs too, some of them veering off into modern fusion, whether it be with the chilled sounds of ambient or catalytic distortions of drum'n'bass.

Nearly all **dance clubs** open their doors between 10pm and midnight, with most favouring the 11pm slot. Some are open six or seven nights a week; some keep irregular days; others just open at the weekend – and very often a venue will host a different club on each night of the week; bear in many of London's best nights take place during the week, especially Wednesdays and Thursdays. Sunday clubs are also increasingly popular; some starting in the wee hours to catch the Saturday night crew who can't face going home, some featuring a chilled downtempo and mellow Sunday afternoon vibe, while others are still geared towards the total hedonists who party on until Monday morning.

Admission charges vary enormously, with small midweek nights starting at around £3 and large weekend events charging as much as £25; around £10 is the average for a Friday and Saturday night, but bear in mind that profit margins at the bar are even more outrageous than at live music venues, especially for water, which costs £1–2 for a small bottle. However, clubs are finally getting more clued-up, and many now operate free water fountains or give free water from behind the bar (check with staff). Most also now have air conditioning, chill-out areas and even paramedic staff on duty should the worst occur.

Club venues

Aquarium, 256 Old St, EC1 ☎020/7251 6136. The place with the pool – when all the beautiful young things get hot and sweaty, they can dive in and cool

off. Popular for two-step garage nights on Sundays. Old Street tube.

The Arches, 53 Southwark St, SE1 ☎020/7207 2980. A good place to head if you like your music retro. Soul, funk and disco from the 1970s and 80s every weekend, courtesy of the long-running *Starsky & Hutch* night. London Bridge tube.

Bagley's, King's Cross Goods Yard, off York Way, N1 ☎020/7278 2171. Vast warehouse-style venue with a 2500-capacity, located in a post-apocalyptic industrial estate. The perfect place for enormous raves, with a different music – normally including drum'n'bass, garage and old-school house in each of the three rooms, and a chill-out bar complete with sofas. King's Cross tube.

Bar Rumba, 36 Shaftesbury Ave, W1 ☎020/7287 2715; www.barrumba.co.uk. Fun, smallish West End venue with an adventurous mix of nights ranging from the future-jazz of *That's How It Is* on Mondays to the deep house vibes of *Space* on Wednesdays, and top-notch house and R&B at weekends. Pop in during the early evening (when it's free) to sample some cocktails on the cheap during happy hour. Piccadilly Circus tube.

Café de Paris, 3 Coventry St, W1 ☎020/7734 7700. Following several dark years the elegant *Café* ballroom has been restored to its former glory and plays house, garage and disco to a smartly dressed, trendy crowd of wannabes – no jeans or trainers. Leicester Square tube.

Camden Palace, 1 Camden High St, NW1 ☎020/7387 0428. A key venue for the New Romantics back in the early 1980s, now home to popular UK garage nights on Saturdays with DJs such as Spoony and Matt "Jam" Lamont; great lights, great sound, heaving crowds. Hard house dominates Fridays at the long-running *Peach* club, hosted by DJ Graham Gold. Camden Town tube.

The Clinic, 13 Gerrard St, W1. Small, minimally designed venue in the heart of

Live music
and clubs

Live music and clubs

the West End which plays host to good-quality soul, jazz and house nights at the weekends. Leicester Square or Piccadilly Circus tube.

Cloud 9, 67–68 Albert Embankment, SE1 ☎01249 783 262. Friendly venue, under the arches near Vauxhall bridge. One arch for full-on house and techno and the other for the chill-out. Vauxhall tube.

The Colosseum, 1 Nine Elms Lane, SW8 ☎020/7720 9200. Huge stamping ground, popular for hard house through to garage. Weekends only. Vauxhall tube.

The Cross, Goods Way Depot, off York Way, N1 ☎020/7837 0828. Hidden underneath the arches, the favourite flavours of this renowned club are hard-house, house and garage. It's bigger than you imagine, but always rammed with chic clubby types, and there's a cool garden – perfect for those chill-out moments. King's Cross tube.

Cuba, 11–13 Kensington High St, W8 ☎020/7938 4137. Grab a cocktail upstairs in the sociable bar before heading below for club nights that focus around Latin, salsa and Brazilian bossanova. High Street Kensington tube.

Dingwalls (Camden Jongleurs), Camden Lock, NW1 ☎020/7267 1577. This once top club venue (the original home of jazz-fusion night *Talkin' Loud Saying Something*) is now an essential stop-off for drum'n'bass fans: every Sunday it's home to Goldie's furious *Metalheadz* sessions. Camden Town tube.

Electric Ballroom, 184 Camden High St, NW1 ☎020/7485 9006; *www .electricballroom.co.uk*. Attracts a truly mixed crowd of Camden regulars from punks to b-boys, who come for the wide range of sounds: rock, hip-hop, jazz and house. Camden Town tube.

The End, 18 West Central St, WC1 ☎020/7419 9199; *www.the-end.co.uk*. Owned by Mr C (ex-Shamen MC), this club has been designed for clubbers by clubbers – the DJ box is on the same level as the dancefloor, the dry ice is a

substance that doesn't damage your lungs and the club itself is large and spacious with chrome minimalist decor. And it also has one of the best sound systems in the world. Well known for its focus on tech-house (thanks to resident DJs Layo and Matthew "Bushwacka" B) and drum'n'bass at weekends, and well worth checking for monthly nights hosted by other clubs or record labels, and for Sunday's infamous UK garage mecca, *Twice As Nice*. Holborn tube.

Fabric, 77a Charterhouse St, EC1 ☎020/7490 0444; *www.fabric-london .com*. If you're a serious dance music fan then there really isn't a better weekend venue in London than the newly opened *Fabric*, a cavernous, underground, brewery-like space with three rooms, holding 2500 people, as well as a devastating sound system in the main room. Fridays alternate between hard-house and hip-hop/drum'n'bass (and often feature live acts – check *Fabric Live*), while Saturdays concentrate on the most cutting-edge house sounds around, played by the best of the big-name DJs from around the globe, as well as UK DJ talent like Tyrant (aka Craig Richards and Lee Burridge) and Terry Francis. Get there early to avoid a night of queuing. Farringdon tube.

Fridge, Town Hall Parade, Brixton Hill, SW2 ☎020/7326 5100; *www.fridge.co .uk*. Weekends alternate between pumping mixed/gay nights like *Love Muscle* and trance favourites like the monthly *Escape From Samsara*, a Friday night with a psychedelic vibe, a hippy market and plenty of lightstick-waving action. Brixton tube.

Gardening Club, 4 The Piazza, WC2 ☎020/7497 3154. A popular choice for house and garage, but it's lost the plot somewhat since its early 1990s heyday. Be warned – you could well find yourself sharing the dancefloor with beer-boys and bemused tourists. Open till the dawn chorus. Covent Garden tube.

Gossips, 69 Dean St, W1 ☎020/7434 4480. Cave-like basement club that seems to have been around aeons. Located deep in the heart of Soho, it's a popular stop for swing and hip-hop fans. Tottenham Court Road tube.

Hanover Grand, 6 Hanover St, W1 ☎020/7499 7977; www.hanovergrand .com. A former Masonic hall that's now a cool and extravagant club, with £100,000 light and sound system, a fine dancefloor, lots of alcoves – and air conditioning. Popular with the glammed-up, glittery and beautiful crew who like chart-bound house'n'garage. Tottenham Court Road tube.

Heaven, Under The Arches, Craven St, WC2 ☎020/7930 2020. London's best-known gay club, the vast *Heaven* is clawing back its reputation as home to some of the best straight nights too, thanks to DJ John Digweed's massively popular monthly progressive house shindig, *Bedrock* (Thursdays). Charing Cross tube.

Home, 1 Leicester Square, WC2 ☎020/7909 0000; www.homecorp.com. The recently opened central London rival to Fabric, this multi-floored superclub may often feel like a leisure complex, but with some of the best resident DJs in Britain and one of the finest sound systems around, it's hard to feel too depressed. The VIP bar on the sixth floor boasts spectacular panoramic views, but unless you're on the guest list you'll have to make do with the club rooms below. Piccadilly Circus or Leicester Square tube.

HQs, West Yard, Camden Lock, NW1 ☎020/7485 6044. Smallish venue by the canal with a range of nights, though the emphasis is on hip-hop and jazz-fusion. Friendly vibe, good cocktails and free entry if you arrive early on week-days. Camden Town tube.

ICA, The Mall, SW1 ☎020/7930 3647; www.ica.org.uk. The Institute of Contemporary Arts may not seem the perfect setting for a great club night, but weekends play host to some of the most cutting-edge audiovisual

collaborations in town. If you're into Latin music, then the once a month, Friday night *Batmacumba*, with DJ Cliffy, is a must. There's also a great bar and excellent modern European food. Piccadilly Circus tube.

LA2, 157 Charing Cross Rd ☎020/7434 0403. Tacky but fun nineties-house-meets-disco place with gay and straight nights. Come Saturday, it's home to the legendary 1970s disco night, *Carwash*. But remember, you'll have to dress up to get in. Tottenham Court Road tube.

Legends, 29 Old Burlington St, W1 ☎020/7437 9933. Weekend house nights are the star attraction at this two-floored, style-conscious club. Green Park or Oxford Circus tube.

The Leisure Lounge, 121 Holborn, EC1 ☎020/7242 1345. This sparsely deco-rated venue has had its share of the big-name nights, such as *Clockwork Orange*, and remains a good place to check out the latest grooves, despite having somewhat fallen off the Richter scale in the past few years. Two dancefloors – one a full-on dance zone, the other a more relaxed bar area. Chancery Lane or Farringdon tube.

Limelight, 136 Shaftesbury Ave, WC2 ☎020/7434 0572. Housed in a hi-tech converted church; super-trendy in the 1980s, now overpriced and rarely visited by Londoners. Popular at the weekend. Leicester Square tube.

Loughborough Hotel, corner of Loughborough and Evandale roads, SW9 (no phone). Massively popular jazz/funk/Latin venue which is more about having a good time than worrying about what label you're flashing or how many style bibles you've consumed that week. Brixton tube or bus #3 or #159.

Mars, 12 Sutton Row, W1 ☎020/7439 4655. When this intimate club was called the *Milk Bar* it played host to some of the best club nights of the time (Danny Rampling's *Glam* and Lisa Loud's *FUBAR*), but it's now only a pale shadow

Live music
and clubs

Live music and clubs

of its former self. Still host to the occasionally intriguing night, but check press for details. Tottenham Court Road tube.

Mass, The Brix, St Matthew's Church, SW2; www.massclub.co.uk. Located inside a colossal church in the centre of Brixton (opposite the Ritzy Cinema), this is one of the best new venues to spring up in the capital over the past five years. Drawing one of the friendliest, most unpretentious, up-for-it crowds around, *Mass* holds nights that champion dance music across house, dub, break-beat and almost anything else in between. *Funkt* is especially recommended for acid-house era casualties, while if the jackin' house grooves of folks like Chicago's Derrick Carter are your thing, then check the monthly *Daytona* (on Fridays). Brixton tube.

Ministry of Sound, 103 Gaunt St, SE1 ☎020/7378 6528; www .ministryofsound.co.uk. A vast, state-of-the-art club based on New York's legendary *Paradise Garage*, with an exceptional sound system and the pick of visiting US and Italian DJs like Erick Morillo (who holds a monthly residency called *Subliminal Sessions*) and Claudio Coccoluto. Corporate clubbing and full of tourists (as well as Sega games machines), but it still draws the top talent, especially for Saturday's *Rulin*, when you can party through to 9am. Look out for their excellent, hedonistic Bank Holiday parties – go early or buy a ticket to ensure you get in. Elephant & Castle tube.

Notting Hill Arts Club, 21 Notting Hill Gate, W11 ☎020/7460 4459. Basement club that's popular for everything from Latin-inspired funk, jazz and disco through to soul, house and garage, and famed for (Everything But The Girl member) Ben Watt's Sunday night deep-house session, *Lazy Dog*.

Office, 3–5 Rathbone Place, W1 ☎020/7636 1598. Various music styles (among them 1980s revival nights), often focusing on swing, TLC-style R&B and hip-hop, but best known as home to a midweek session where you can play

games like Ker-Plunk, Buckaroo, Operation and Twister. Booking a table in advance is advised. Tottenham Court Road tube.

Open, 144 Charing Cross Rd, WC2 ☎020/7692 2010. Large-scale venue located just around the corner from Soho that's been somewhat forgotten with the media furore surrounding the launch of new clubs *Fabric* and *Home*. Though relatively soulless in atmosphere and often incredibly hot, *Open* does draw some superior house and R&B nights at weekends. Tottenham Court Road tube.

Plastic People, 147–149 Curtain Rd, EC2 ☎020/7739 6471. Slightly larger version of the original Oxford Street venue, with a state-of-the-art sound system and a blend of musical nights that fuse Latin, house, soul and percussive disco. If you like the house-fusion sound of Nuphonic Records, then this is the venue for you. Old Street tube.

The Rocket, 166–220 Holloway Rd, N7 ☎020/753 3200. Part of North London University, and so has a studenty edge. Some good and inexpensive raves in a huge vaulted main room, which can lack atmosphere if it's not full. Holloway Road or Highbury & Islington tube.

Salsa! 96 Charing Cross Rd, WC2 ☎020/7379 3277. Funky and fun salsa-based club-cum-restaurant that's a popular choice for birthday bookings: you can book a table to eat as you mambo. Leicester Square tube.

Scala, 278 Pentonville Rd, N1 ☎020/7833 2022; www.scala-london .co.uk. Once a cinema (it was forced to shut down after illegally showing Kubrick's *Clockwork Orange*), the *Scala* is now one of London's best clubs, holding unusual and multifaceted nights that take in film, live bands and music ranging from quirky hip-hop to drum'n'bass and deep house. Club night *Sonic Mook Experiment*, which fuses genres as disparate as postmodern rock and leftfield dub, is a must for the open-minded. King's Cross tube.

Subterania, 12 Acklam Rd, W10
☎020/8960 4590; *www.meanfiddler .com*. Just off the Portobello Road, Subterania is worth a visit for its diverse club nights at weekends. The superior hip-hop and R&B-heavy *Rotation* is every Friday. The venue also plays host to emerging hip-hop and R&B acts from both the US and Europe during club nights. Ladbroke Grove tube.

333, 333 Old St, EC1 ☎ 020/7630 5949. One of London's best clubs for new dance music, in the heart of trendy-as-hell Hoxton. Three floors of drum'n'bass, twisted disco and break-beat madness. Old Street tube.

Turnmills, 63 Clerkenwell Rd, EC1 ☎020/7250 3409; *www.turnmills.com*. The place to come if you want to sweat from dusk till dawn, with an alien-invasion-style bar and funky split-level dancefloor in the main room. Trance and house with top-name guest DJs rule Fridays (especially at the bi-weekly *Gallery*, where Tall Paul is resident), but it's rightly famed for the awesomely glorious gay extravaganza, *Trade*, which begins on Sunday morning at 4 am. Farringdon tube.

The Velvet Room, 143 Charing Cross Rd, WC2 ☎020/7439 4655. Very chic, velvet-dripping interior, with house, techno and drum'n'bass nights. The ever-engaging Carl Cox resides at *Ultimate Base* on Thursdays. Tottenham Court Road tube.

The Wag Club, 35 Wardour St, W1 ☎020/7437 5534. The rare-groove shrine of the 1980s, and now in need of an overhaul, though the two floors of sounds still pack 'em in on Eighties revival nights. The pick of the club nights, *Blow Up* (Saturdays) offers a 1960s-schmooze meets jazz-funk soundtrack flavour. Leicester Square or Piccadilly Circus tube.

Club-bars

The most notable event in the clubbing world in the past few years has been the rapid growth of **club-bars**: essentially a bar with modern decor, dance music and a club clientele. However, club-bars are more than just more aesthetically pleasing British pubs – DJs (unknown and otherwise) are given a platform on which to make more of their individual tastes and the punters are given free (or cheap) music of a more experimental nature than what's often on offer at regular clubs. Perhaps most importantly, the club-bar is a more social environment than a club – there's no denying it gets tedious when you have to yell. Yet already the boundaries between club and club-bar are beginning to fade, and it's therefore difficult to categorize all the places around. *Bar Rumba*, for example, is a club, and yet has an early-evening happy hour; similarly, *The Social* (run by Heavenly Records) is a bar, but with DJs and/or live music every night of the week, and it's as hedonistic an atmos-phere as any club. Some of the places listed are more like bars – not all of them have DJs, although the majority have music of some form. Music varies from deep house, hip-hop, big beats and disco to pop-rock.

Prices for **drinks** can be outrageous, although with a little forethought a night out need not bankrupt you. Many places hold happy hours, where drinks are about half price (phone and check) – and when you consider that you are get-ting good music into the early hours, it's not a bad deal. The list below is by no means exhaustive: club-bars are opening all the time. Soho and Hoxton in particu-lar are areas where you could happily wander for hours and not visit them all. Indeed, much of the appeal of club-bars is stumbling across them, music pump-ing and drinks flowing; alcohol is well and truly an integral part of the current London clubbing scene, and club-bars, if not entirely responsible, are certainly mir-roring this trend.

A.K.A, 18 West Central St, WC1 ☎020/7836 0110; *www.the-end.co.uk*. Minimalist, twenty-first-century-style bar, next door to (and owned by) *The End*. A chrome balcony overlooks the main floor, which includes a well-stocked bar

Live music and clubs

Live music and clubs

where you can also eat such delights as chive and butternut squash soup. Tottenham Court Road tube.

Alphabet, 61–63 Beak St, W1 ☎020/7439 2190. *Alphabet* has the feel of two places: upstairs is light and spacious with decadent leather sofas and a great choice of European beers and mouthwatering food; downstairs, the dimmed coloured lights and car seats strewn around make for an altogether seedier atmosphere. Oxford Circus tube.

Atlantic, 20 Glasshouse St, W1 ☎020/7734 4888. Still a popular choice for the glitzy, cash-hungry crowd. Three bars designed in the Art Deco style attract a mixed clientele of those that have money and those that want it. Still, *Jack's Bar* just about retains some authentic atmosphere. Oxford Circus tube.

Bar Rumba, 36 Shaftesbury Ave, W1 ☎020/7287 2715. A club with early sessions (Mon–Fri 5–8pm), including happy hours, DJs in the bar (usually playing jazz, funk, Latin or smooth house grooves) and half-price drinks. Piccadilly Circus tube.

Bar Vinyl, 6 Inverness St, NW1 ☎020/7681 7898. Tiny, funky glass-bricked place complete with a record shop downstairs and a breakbeat and trip-hop vibe. Camden Town tube.

Bug Bar, St Matthew's Church, Brixton Hill, SW2 ☎020/7738 3184. Set in a church crypt, this place certainly has character, and remains a popular stop before the *Fridge*, playing reggae, drum'n'bass and house. Brixton tube.

Detroit, 35 Earlham St, WC2 ☎020/7240 2662. Cavernous underground venue with an open-plan bar area, secluded, Gaudíesque booths and a huge range of spirits. DJs take over at the weekends, with underground house on Saturdays. Covent Garden tube.

Dog House, 187 Wardour St, W1 ☎020/7434 2118; *www.doghouse.co .uk*. Colourful basement bar, popular for

hip-hop, funk and acid jazz, that draws a friendly mix of office types, students and film runners. Leicester Square tube.

Dog Star, 389 Coldharbour Lane, SW9 ☎020/7733 7515. At weekends especially, this large wooden pub becomes more like a club complete with full-on techno, house or disco. The vibe is mellower during the week, but with nights like Monday's *Stoned Asia* (with DJ Pathaan) and Tuesday's hip-hop hoedown *The Bullitt*, the music quality is just as good. A great place to hear some of London's best DJs on the cheap, if not for free. Brixton tube.

Dragon Bar, 5 Leonard St, EC2 ☎020/7490 7110. Trendy two-floored place, with bare-brick walls and crumbling leather sofas, that attracts a camouflage-trouser-wearing mix of locals and pre-clubbers at weekends. The DJ plays whatever takes his fancy, which normally includes house, breakbeat and the odd hip-hop classic. Old Street tube.

Dust, 27 Clerkenwell Rod, EC1 ☎020/7490 5120. The ultimate Clerkenwell bar – this modernist space (with silver walls) was once a watchmaker's premises. It's now a thriving club-bar serving the area's trendy twentysomethings. Farringdon tube.

The Elbow Room, 89–91 Chapel Market, N1 ☎020/7278 3244. Newly opened venue, co-owned by New York Electropioneer Arthur Baker (who now lives in London), *The Elbow Room* provides great new music from resident DJs in stylish surrounds, with the added bonus of pool tables for when the drinking and dancing get too much. Angel tube.

Embassy, 119 Essex Rd, Islington N1 ☎020/7226 9849. Art-school posturing meets pub debauchery in this charismatic, darkened bar a million miles removed from the twee trendy-left respectability of nearby Upper Street. Great music – dub to drum'n'bass – from the resident DJs; the Sunday-night *They Do Play Records Don't They* (where band members from the likes of Primal Scream or Cabaret

Voltaire play their favourite classic tunes) is especially recommended. Angel tube.

Fridge Bar, 1 Town Hall Parade, Brixton Hill, SW2 ☎020/7326 5100; www.fridge .co.uk. Packed at weekends (when there's free entry in the early evening), the two-floored *Fridge Bar* is a real melting pot, with a multi-tribal clientele grooving to R&B, house and drum'n'bass in the intimate, pitch-black downstairs club, or slamming shots in the bright upstairs bar. There are tables and chairs outside in the summer. Brixton tube.

Great Eastern Dining Room, 54–56 Great Eastern St, EC2 ☎020/7613 4545. Wonderful Modern European restaurant and smart bar area upstairs, and the laid-back bar-club *Below 54* downstairs – all sofas, cinema screens, dim lighting, great cocktails and future-leaning electronic sounds. Get there early, if you want to get in – it stays open until 2am. Old Street tube.

Home, 100–106 Leonard St, EC2 ☎020/7684 8618. Hoxton's original club-bar still looks more like a shabby sixth-form common room than a trendy watering hole, but it still attracts a hip, friendly crowd. No DJs, but plenty of comfy leather sofas and good vibes. Old Street tube.

Hoxton Square Bar and Kitchen, 2–4 Hoxon Square, N1 ☎020/7613 0709. Next door to the Lux cinema, this *Blade Runner*-esque concrete bar attracts the area's artists, writers and wannabes with its mix of modern European food, kitsch-to-club soundtracks, worn leather sofas and temporary painting and photography exhibitions. Best in the summer, when the drinking spills into the square in a carnival-like spirit. Old Street tube.

Jerusalem, 33–34 Rathbone Place, W1 ☎020/255 1120. Décor is all chandeliers and velvet drapes, and there's an especially good mix of music on Thursday nights, though it does attract a large proportion of local office workers. Tottenham Court Road tube.

Lab, 12 Old Compton St, W1 ☎020/7437 7820; www.lab-bar.co.uk. Chic, multicoloured former strip joint that stirs up some of the best cocktails in town for its style-conscious crowd of beautiful Soho-ites. Tottenham Court Road tube.

Match Bar, 37–38 Margaret St, W1 ☎020/7499 3443. Plenty of tasty cocktails up for grabs in this leather-sofa-adorned, wooden-floored bar, tucked away only a stone's throw from the organized chaos of Oxford Street. Oxford Circus tube.

Medicine, 181 Upper St, N1 ☎020/7704 8056. Very nice if you can get in; it's members-only at the weekends. Inside, comfy couches abound, while DJs spin the latest tunes. Angel tube.

O Bar, 83–85 Wardour St, W1 ☎020/7437 3490. The zebra-print fur sofa and the spiral staircase are at home here; the dancer's cage is a bit more suspect. Wide selection of music from disco to soul and garage caters to a youngish crowd of tourists and students. Monday's happy hour lasts all night. Leicester Square tube.

The Pool, 104–108 Curtain Rd, EC2 ☎020/7739 9608. Popular two-floored bar that boasts three American pool tables downstairs. DJs play a mix of upfront house and garage at the weekends. Old Street tube.

Pop, 14 Soho St, W1 ☎020/7734 4004. Alternating between club nights and free-to-enter club-bar sessions, this multicoloured basement venue is one of the hippest spots in town, thanks to its fashion-conscious crowd and exclusive door policy. If you want to strike a pose, then *Pop* is for you. Also home to London's first-ever female urinal. Tottenham Court Road tube.

Shoreditch Electricity Showrooms, 39A Hoxton Square, N1 ☎020/7739 6934. One of the many trendy haunts in and around Hoxton Square, the two-floored Electricity Showrooms (yes, it was converted) is better value than most. Free to

Live music and clubs

Live music and clubs

enter, the upstairs bar mixes kitsch art-work with digital boards flashing ironic weather and text messages, while the intimate club downstairs hosts weekend parties. Good Modern European food available too, although the choice is limited. Old Street tube.

The Social, 5 Little Portland St, W1 ☎020/7636 4992. Bacchanalian, industri-al club-bar run by the Heavenly record label – home to bands such as St Etienne and folk singer-songwriter Beth Orton. The bar has great DJs playing everything from rock to rap, a truly hedonistic-cum-alcoholic crowd and the ultimate snacks – beans on toast and cosy soup in a

mug – for when you get an attack of the munchies. Fab music on the upstairs jukebox too. Oxford Circus tube.

Tea Room des Artistes, 697 Wandsworth Rd, SW8 ☎020/7652 6526. Wonderful veggie restaurant which holds an unpretentious, chilled-out Sunday session (*Sunday Best*) that is justly famed and often hosts DJs like Harvey or Groove Armada. Clapham Common tube.

WKD, 18 Kentish Town Rd, NW1 ☎020/7267 1869. A laid-back café and a groovy club. Saturday daytime features jazz, rare-groove and hip-hop, while the evenings are a fusion of soul, reggae and funky vibes. Camden Town tube.

Chapter 19

Lesbian and gay London

London's **lesbian and gay scene** is so huge, diverse and well established that it's easy to forget just how much – and how fast – it has grown over the last few years. Pink power has given rise to the pink pound, gay liberation to gay lifestyle, and the ever-expanding Soho – now firmly established as the homo heart of the city – is vibrant, self-assured and unashamedly commercial. As a result of all this high-profile activity, straight Londoners tend to be a fairly homo-savvy bunch and, on the whole, happy to embrace and even dip into the city's queer offerings.

The wider picture is also positive – though the notorious Clause 28 (which forbids the promotion of homosexuality by schools and local authorities) is yet to be repealed, equality before the law is slowly and surely becoming a reality under the New Labour government. Gay men finally enjoy the same age of consent (16) as heterosexuals, the long-standing ban on homosexuals in the armed forces has at last been lifted, and lesbians and gay men occupy public positions with increasing confidence.

Having said this, however, the recent terrorist bombing of a gay Soho pub is still fresh and raw in people's minds. The largest and most viciously calculated of three nailbomb attacks targeting the city's black, Asian and gay communities, the blast claimed several lives, left scores of casualties and served as a terrible reminder that none of us is yet safe from hatred. But it was also heartening to witness the spontaneous and unanimous condemnations from police, politicians and community leaders. Never before had the words "homophobia must not be tolerated" crossed so many politicians' lips.

Soho is the obvious place to start exploring London's gay and lesbian scene, and **Old Compton Street** is, so to speak, its main drag. Here, traditional gay pubs rub alongside café/bars selling expensive designer beers and lattés, while hairdressers, letting agencies, sex boutiques and spiritual health centres offer a range of gay-run services. There are clubs to cater for just about every musical, sartorial and sexual taste and, while the bigger ones tend to cluster around the West End, there are equally well-established venues all over the city. Gay men still enjoy the best permanent facilities London-wide, but today's **lesbian scene** is bigger and more eclectic than ever, and the cruisey girl bars which took up prize pitches on the boys' Soho turf a few years ago look like they're there to stay.

You can also find pockets of queer activity away from the centre in the city's funkier residential areas, most notably Brixton, Islington and (especially for dykes) Hackney. Open anti-gay hostility is rare in London, although it's probably wise not to hold hands or smooch too obviously in areas you don't know well, just in case you've stumbled into a gay-bashing backwood.

Lesbian and gay London

The two big **outdoor events** of the year are Mardi Gras and Summer Rites, in early July and early September respectively. A colourful, whistleblowing march through the city streets followed by a huge, ticketed party in Finsbury Park, **Mardi Gras** is the up-for-it carnival child of Pride, which finally outgrew itself a few years ago and collapsed in spectacular fashion just a week before its own big day. The newly branded event, now managed by a consortium of gay businesses, is no longer free, but continues to draw people from all over the country for the largest queer party of the year. For up-to-date information, festival plans and transport information, call ☎020 /7494 2225 or visit the Web site: *www .londonmardigras.com*. The ticketed **Summer Rites** in Brixton's Brockwell Park

---

LESBIAN AND GAY MEDIA

PRINT

If you can't find it here, try GAY to Z (www.gaytoz .com), a comprehensive online directory of gay, lesbian, bisexual and TV/TS-friendly organizations and businesses. A print version (£3 in UK; £10 from overseas) is also available from Gay to Z Directories, 41 Cooks Rd, London SE17 3NG.

Though they carry excellent entertainment listings, lesbian- and gay-oriented **newspapers and magazines** are pretty poor at present, offering little by way of groundbreaking news, political analysis or cultural critique. The titles listed below can be picked up at most major newsagents, in many bookshops (gay and straight), and in the cafés and bars of Soho. In addition to these, consumerist freesheets like *Boyz*, *Fluid*, *qx* and *DNT* abound in clubs and bars. They're pretty vacuous, but they'll give you up-to-date club listings, gossip and the odd feisty feature.

Attitude (monthly; £2.50). Glossy gay men's lifestyle magazine with crossover appeal to style-conscious straight boys and the odd dyke reader. Occasional well-written, offbeat arts pieces and investigative features make it the best of the bunch.

Axiom (monthly; £2.50). Monthly men's glossy with an emphasis on health, plus arts features, interviews and reviews.

Axiom News (weekly; free). Recently launched, this promising news and entertainment weekly tries hard but struggles to find the stories, and can be hard to find.

Diva (monthly; £2). Glossy national lifestyle magazine for lesbians, with a middle-brow range of features, news pieces, interviews and arts reviews which aim, perhaps unwisely, to please everyone.

Gay Times (monthly; £2.50). Long-established glossy national aimed primarily at gay men, but also read by lesbians, offering news, arts and features, listings, reviews and community information.

The Pink Paper (weekly; free). Once respectable weekly forum for community debate, and the only gay paper to address lesbians, but too many redesigns have meant that it's now useful principally for Russell Grant's horoscopes and the extensive "personals" section.

ONLINE

The following are the most useful Web sites, and the only ones to offer more than just an online version of printed publications.

www.rainbownetwork.com
Well-designed lifestyle e-zine for boys and girls, including reviews of the latest events, interviews with scene faces, news, listings and information on a wealth of topics.

www.sonow.com
Not so great to look at, but with a useful lesbian section, *www.dykesnow.com*, offering up-to-date listings and reviews of bars, clubs and events.

offers a similar menu of dance, music, performance and stalls, but dispenses with the long walk and the whistles, and has so far managed to remain a more relaxed and relaxing affair. For more information on Summer Rites, check *Time Out* and the queer press (see box opposite)

London also boasts several queer-oriented annual arts events. In March, the National Film Theatre (see p586) hosts the annual **Lesbian and Gay Film Festival**; in the last two weeks of June, the **Mardi Gras Arts Festival**, staged at venues throughout London, leads the run-up to Mardi Gras itself; and in mid-June, there's the unmissably camp **National Lesbian Beauty Contest**, currently held at the *Scala* in King's Cross; for information, call ☎07932 046938; for tickets, call ☎0870 6060204.

Elsewhere, queer theatre and arts events take place all year round in the city's many fringe theatres, arts centres, galleries and clubs. If none of this is up your street, there are also a huge number of **gay groups and organizations** which offer everything from ballroom dancing to spanking seminars. Details of most events appear in *Time Out* and in the gay press.

Hotels

Below is a small selection of London's best-known gay accommodation options. They cater mostly for gay men, though all are lesbian-friendly, and a full breakfast is almost always included in the price.

If you'd prefer a **self-catering** apartment, try Outlet Gay Accommodation, 32 Old Compton St, W1 ☎020/7287 4244; *www.outlet.co.uk*; or London Holiday Accommodation, 16 Chalk Farm Rd, NW1 ☎020/7485 0117; fax 020/7495 0117; *www.londonholiday.co.uk*. Both are gay-run; London Holiday Accommodation will even throw in a free tour of the London scene.

New York Hotel, 32 Philbeach Gardens, SW5 ☎020/7244 6884; fax 020/7370 4961; *www.newyorkhotellondon.co.uk*. This quiet hotel in Earl's Court offers decent-sized, comfortable rooms, is

frequented more by couples than singles, and was voted best gay hotel two years running by US magazine *Out & About*. Earl's Court tube. ⑤.

Noël Coward Hotel, 111 Ebury St, SW1 ☎020/7730 2094; fax 020/7730 8697; *www.noelcowardhotel.com*. Elegant-fronted hotel in the heart of Belgravia, the home of Noël Coward between 1917 and 1930. The comfortable rooms are en suite, there's an attractive patio garden, and theatre or club package deals are available. Sloane Square or Victoria tube. ④.

Number Seven Guesthouse, 7 Josephine Ave, SW2 ☎020/8674 1880; fax 020/8671 6032; *www.no7.com*. Voted Best UK Gay Hotel two years running by *The Pink Paper*, this small, friendly Victorian guesthouse in a leafy part of Brixton is well away from the hubbub of Soho, but easily accessible by tube. All rooms are well cared for and have en-suite bathrooms. Brixton tube. ⑤.

Philbeach Hotel, 30–31 Philbeach Gardens, SW5 ☎020/7373 1244; fax 020/7244 0149; *www.philbeachhotel .freeserve.co.uk*. London's busiest gay hotel, large and friendly, with room-only or en-suite options, Internet and TV lounge, *Appleby's Bar*, and the *Wilde About Oscar* conservatory restaurant. Earl's Court tube. ④.

Prince William Hotel, 42–44 Gloucester Terrace, W2 ☎020/7724 7414. Cheap, friendly place close to the West End. Most rooms are en suite, and the *Pearl of India* restaurant is on site. Paddington or Lancaster Gate tube. ③.

Russell Lodge Apartments, 20 Little Russell St, WC1 ☎020/7430 2489 or ☎07967 /440942; fax 020/7681 7604; *russell.lodge @virgin.net*. This seventeenth-century listed building in the heart of serene Bloomsbury actually houses two separate lodgings. No. 20 is a four-bedroom house which can be rented complete, while no. 21 houses one two-bedroom and one three-bedroom apartment. All the rooms feature original period detail. Tottenham Court Road tube. ③.

Lesbian and gay London

GAY to Z (see opposite) has comprehensive accommodation listings.

Lesbian and gay London

Cafés, bars and pubs

There are loads of lesbian and gay **eating and watering holes** in London, many of them operating as cafés by day and transforming into drinking dens by night. Lots have **cabaret or disco nights** and are open until the early hours, making them a fine alternative to the more expensive clubs.

The places below represent a selective list of the best and most central, from self-consciously minimalist eateries to shabby old pubs. Bear in mind that, as ever, "mixed" tends to mean mostly men.

Mixed cafés, bars and pubs

The Admiral Duncan, 54 Old Compton St, W1 ☎020/7437 5300. Unpretentious, traditional-style gay bar in the heart of Soho, popular and busy with a post-work crowd, and now fully restored after the blast that ripped through it in 1999. Leicester Square tube.

Balans, 60 Old Compton St, W1 ☎020/7437 5212. This relaxed, fashionable, but fairly pricey café/bar-cum-brasserie is quintessential queer Soho, always packed, open late during the week and until the small hours at weekends, and often with a singer or cabaret after 11pm. *Balans'* breakfasts are already an institution. Leicester Square tube.

Balans West, 293 Old Brompton Rd, SW5 ☎020/7244 8838. Same scene as its sister branch, without the singing. Earl's Court tube.

Bar Aquda, 13–14 Maiden Lane, Covent Garden WC2 ☎020/7557 9891. Bright, modern and fashionable café/bar with good food. Mixed, but mostly boys. Leicester Square or Covent Garden tube.

Bar Fusion, 45 Essex Rd, N1 ☎020/7688 2882. Friendly Islington café/bar with a pool table, comfy chairs at the back and a local, laid-back crowd. Angel tube.

BJ's White Swan, 556 Commercial Rd, E14. ☎020/7780 9870. Busy, late-night East End local with nightly drag, cabaret,

trashy disco, amateur stripping contests and a Sunday tea dance (see p.570). Mixed during the week, mostly men at the weekend. Aldgate East tube, Limehouse DLR or bus #15 from Oxford Circus.

The Black Cap, 171 Camden High St, NW1 ☎020/7428 2721. Venerable North London institution offering cabaret of wildly varying quality almost every night. Laugh, sing and lip-synch along, and then dance drunkenly to 80s tunes until the early hours. The upstairs *Mrs Shufflewick's Bar* is quieter, and opens onto a lush and lovely roof garden in the summer. Camden Town tube.

The Box, 32–34 Monmouth St, WC2 ☎020/7240 5828. Popular, bright café/bar serving good food for a mixed gay/straight crowd during the day, and becoming queerer as the night draws in. Mon–Sat 11am–11pm, Sun noon–10.30pm. Covent Garden or Leicester Square tube.

Café Goya, 85 Acre Lane, SW2 ☎020/7274 3500; goya@cybermax .dircon.co.uk.Gay-friendly, relaxed and attitude-free bar and grill serving up a fresh cosmopolitan menu against the backdrop of a strictly mellow CD jazz collection. At weekends you can revive yourself over serious hangover breakfasts, coffees and cocktails. Brixton tube.

Due South, 35 Stoke Newington High St, N16 ☎020/7249 7543. Large, friendly gay pub with food, regular quizzes, karaoke and cabaret. There's a pool table, and a busy beer garden in summer. Thursdays is the packed and popular women-only night. Dalston or Stoke Newington train, or buses #73 from Victoria or #76 from Waterloo.

The Edge, 11 Soho Square, W1 ☎020/7439 1313. Busy, style-conscious and pricey Soho café/bar spread over several floors, although this doesn't seem to stop everyone ending up on the pavement, especially in summer. Food daily, interesting art exhibitions and DJs most nights. Tottenham Court Road tube.

First Out, 52 St Giles High St, WC2 ☎020/7240 8042. The West End's original gay café/bar, and still permanently packed, serving good veggie food at reasonable prices. Upstairs is airy and non-smoking, downstairs dark and foggy. *Girl Friday* (Fri) is a busy pre-club session for grrrls; gay men are welcome as guests. Tottenham Court Road tube.

Freedom, 60–66 Wardour St, W1 ☎020/7734 0071. Hip, busy, late-opening café/bar, popular with a mixed straight/gay Soho crowd. Great juices and healthy food in the daytime, cocktails and overpriced beer in the evening. The theatre space downstairs occasionally transforms itself into a funky basement club, and there are some intriguing art installations, too. Leicester Square or Piccadilly tube.

Fridge Café/Bar, 1 Town Hall Parade, Brixton Hill, SW2 ☎020/7326 5100. Bang next door to the club of the same name (and with similarly late weekend hours), this hip café/bar lets you lurch from pint to party in one fell swoop and attracts a trendy, straight/gay crowd. Closed Sun. Brixton tube.

The Gloucester, 1 King William Walk, SE10 ☎020/8293 6131. Right at the gates of Greenwich Park and featured in the hit coming-out movie *Beautiful Thing*, this friendly local offers regular cabaret, discos and theme nights for a mostly male crowd. Greenwich tube or train.

Halfway 2 Heaven, 7 Duncannon St, WC2 ☎020/7930 8312. Friendly, traditional pub just off Trafalgar Square, featuring occasional cabaret. Charing Cross tube.

Joiners' Arms, 116–118 Hackney Rd, E2. ☎020/7729 9180. Mixed bar with regular DJs and funky dancefloor, open late at weekends. Bethnal Green tube or buses #26 from London Bridge, or #48 and #55 from New Oxford Street.

Kazbar, 50 Clapham High St, SW4 ☎020/7622 0070. Modern, mostly boyzy split-level bar from the team who brought you *Kudos* in the West End, with a video screen playing happy, poppy hits. Clapham Common tube.

King Edward VI, 25 Bromfield St, N1. ☎020/7704 0745. Busy, mostly boyzy pub with café upstairs and a pleasant beer garden. Angel tube.

King William IV, 77 Hampstead High St, NW3 ☎020/7435 5747. Relaxed, traditional and friendly pub with an older crowd of regulars. Great food at lunchtimes. Hampstead tube.

Ku Bar, 75 Charing Cross Rd, WC2 ☎020/7437 4303. Trendy bar serving a young, scene-conscious clientele. There's candlelight upstairs for those who want to canoodle. Leicester Square tube.

Kudos, 10 Adelaide St, WC2 ☎020/7379 4573. Busy venue, popular amongst smart, besuited post-work boys, with ground-floor café and a basement video bar. Charing Cross tube.

Matrix, 125 Cleveland St, W1. ☎020/7637 5352. Stylish new West End club-bar on two floors, with DJs most nights. *Sunday Girlz* (Sun) plays twenty-first-century tunes for girlz and their gay boyfriends. Bond Street tube.

The Oak, 79 Green Lanes, N16 ☎020/7354 2791. Friendly, spacious local pub with a dancefloor and pool table, recently refurbished and with much improved loos. Hosts a range of mixed and women-only club nights and special events, including the wildly popular *Liberté*. Manor House tube or buses #73, #171A or #141 from Angel tube.

Old Compton Café, 34 Old Compton St, W1 ☎020/7439 3309. This enduringly busy Soho institution never closes. Strong coffee and a range of cakes and snacks make it the obvious solution to mid- or post-party wooziness. Tottenham Court Road or Leicester Square tube.

Popstarz Liquid Lounge, 275 Pentonville Rd, N1 (no phone). Happy-go-lucky weekend dance bar with DJs and reliably cheap beer, popular with a young, indie-minded crowd. Thursdays is *Club Deb*, with Curve and Echobelly guitarist Debbie Smith playing indie, big beat, retro and funk for girlz and boyz. Kings Cross tube.

Lesbian and gay London

Lesbian and gay London

Retro Bar, 2 George Court, Adelphi Terrace (off the Strand), WC2 ☎020/7321 2811. Friendly, indie/retro bar playing 70s, 80s, goth and alternative sounds and featuring regular DJs and karaoke. Charing Cross tube.

The Royal Oak, 73 Columbia Rd, E2 ☎020/7739 8204. In the heart of the famous Columbia Road flower market, this old, comfortable market pub caters for a mixed gay/straight crowd, and offers Sunday breakfasts or Tex Mex meals at the upstairs restaurant; occasionally hosts live gigs. Old Street tube.

The Royal Vauxhall Tavern, 372 Kennington Lane, SE11 (no phone). A London institution with late opening hours, this huge, disreputable and divey drag and cabaret pub is facing possible redevelopment as a sports centre. In the meantime, all the attention has shoved it up a notch in the queer performance world, with artists such as the Divine David and Neil Bartlett putting in the odd appearance. Vauxhall tube.

Rupert Street, 50 Rupert St, W1 ☎020/7734 5614. Trendy, busy, glass-doored Soho bar; very boyzy, very stylish. Piccadilly Circus tube.

The Spiral Staircase, 138 Shoreditch High St, E1 ☎020/7613 1351. This notorious two-level dive attracts a mixed gay/straight, up-for-it crowd of drinkers. Comfy sofas upstairs, a singing, dancing basement area, and open until 4am at the weekends. Old Street tube.

Ted's Place, 305a North End Rd, W14 ☎020/7385 9359. Friendly, late-opening local with a gay/lesbian/bi and TV/TS clientele, long-running lesbian "Blind Date" contest and assorted outbreaks of frivolity. Cheap drinks, too. West Kensington or West Brompton tube.

Two Brewers, 114 Clapham High St, SW4 ☎020/7622 3621. Long-established and popular South London drag pub, with nightly cabaret in the front bar and a more cruisey dancefloor in the back. Clapham Common tube.

Village Soho, 81 Wardour St, W1 ☎020/7434 2124. Elegant split-level café/bar attracting more pretty boyz than girlz. Leicester Square or Piccadilly Circus tube.

The Yard, 57 Rupert St, W1 ☎020/7437 2652. Attractive café/bar with courtyard and loft areas. Good food, weekly cabaret and regular fortune tellers. Piccadilly Circus tube.

Lesbian cafés, bars and pubs

Candy Bar, 23–24 Bateman St, W1 (corner of Frith and Bateman streets) ☎020/7437 1977. The UK's first seven-day all-girl bar will have moved into these new, bigger and better premises by the time you read this. No previews were available, but we've been promised lots more space with the same crucial, cruisey vibe that made its original Soho home just around the corner such a hit. Tottenham Court Road tube.

The Drill Hall, 16 Chenies St, WC1 ☎020/7637 8270. This lesbian-run arts centre offers good, mixed queer and international theatre all year round, but has been opening its bar, restaurant and workshops to women only on Monday nights since time began. Goodge Street tube.

Due South, 35 Stoke Newington High St, N16 ☎020/7249 7543. Hackney is the lesbian capital of London, and Thursday nights are a women-only fixture at this large, friendly mixed pub. Packed, beery, leery and fun, with a pool table and a beer garden open in summer. Dalston or Stoke Newington train or bus #73 from Victoria.

Duke of Clarence, 140 Rotherfield St, N1 ☎020/7226 6526. This traditional local has an untraditional separate women's bar with pool table and its own beer garden. Angel or Highbury & Islington tube or buses #38, #73, #56, #277 or #171a from Angel tube.

Fried Green Tomatoes, upstairs at *Café Goya*, 85 Acre Lane, SW2 ☎020/7274 3500. Fortnightly on Wednesdays, this new, late-opening women-only bar and social club above the restaurant has a laid-back vibe, mood music, free olives and easy conversation. Brixton tube.

The Glass Bar, West Lodge, Euston Square Gardens, 190 Euston Rd, NW1 ☎020/7387 6184; www.glassbar.ndo .co.uk. Difficult to find, (and hard to forget), this friendly and intimate late-opening women-only members bar (membership is automatic once you're inside) is housed in a listed building and features a wrought-iron spiral staircase which becomes increasingly perilous as the night goes on. Knock on the door to get in. No admission after 11.30pm. Euston tube.

Sister George, basement of *St George's Tavern*, 14 Belgrave Rd, SW1 (corner of Belgrave and Hugh streets) ☎020/7592 9911. Long-running women's basement bar with DJs and drinks promotions; gay men are welcome as guests. Victoria tube.

Sylvia's Piano Bar, Stoke Newington High St, N16 ☎020/7249 0616. Women-only piano bar with eats and a no-smoking area. Ring for opening times. Dalston or Stoke Newington train from Liverpool Street or bus #73 from Victoria or #76 from Waterloo.

Vespa Lounge, upstairs at *The Conservatory*, Centrepoint House, 15 St Giles High St, WC1 ☎020/7836 8956; vespalounge@aol.com. London's newest girl bar sets up shop in this prime location at weekends, and it gets busy. Pool table, video screen, cute bar staff and a predominantly young crowd. Gay men welcome as guests. Tottenham Court Road tube.

Gay men's cafés, bars and pubs

The Artful Dodger, 139 Southgate Rd, N1 ☎020/7226 0841. Rather louche men-only cruising dive with two bars and various uniformed theme nights. Angel or Highbury & Islington tube.

BarCode, 3–4 Archer St, W1. ☎020/ 7734 3342. Busy, stylish cruise and dance bar on two floors. Piccadilly Circus tube.

Brief Encounter, 41–43 St Martin's Lane, WC2 ☎020/7240 2221. One of the oldest men's bars in London, recently given a facelift and still hard at it. A popular pre-*Heaven* or post-opera hangout (it's

next door to the *Coliseum*); the front bar is bright, the back bar dark, and both are busy. Leicester Square tube.

Brompton's, 294 Old Brompton Rd, SW5 ☎020/7370 1344. Long-established, leathery and immensely popular late-opening bar-cum-club that's packed at weekends, and features regular cabarets and PAs. Earl's Court tube.

Central Station, 37 Wharfdale Rd, N1 ☎020/7278 3294. Award-winning, late-opening community pub on three floors (one of them non-smoking), offering cabaret, cruisey club nights in the *Underground* basement area, and the UK's only gay sports bar. Not strictly men-only, but mostly so. King's Cross tube.

The Champion, 1 Wellington Terrace, Bayswater Rd, W2 ☎020/7229 5056. Longstanding, unpretentious local, with basement bar *Ruby's* and a beer garden. Notting Hill Gate or Queensway tube.

Chariots Café Bar, Chariots House, Fairchild St, EC2 ☎020/7247 5222. This large, stylish and friendly café/bar adjoins Chariots Sauna and offers regular late-licence extensions, cabaret and good-value food. Liverpool Street tube.

City of Quebec, 12 Old Quebec St, W1 ☎020/7629 6159. Long-established and busy homo haunt with downstairs disco and a late licence at weekends. Especially popular with an older crowd. Marble Arch tube.

The Coleherne, 261 Old Brompton Rd, SW5 ☎020/7244 5951. Famous and permanently packed leather and denim bar, bristling with history, muscles and moustaches. Earl's Court tube.

Compton's of Soho, 53 Old Compton St, W1 ☎020/7479 7961. This large, traditional-style pub is a Soho institution, always busy with a youngish crowd, but still a relaxed place to cruise or just hang out. Leicester Square or Piccadilly Circus tube.

The Orange, Orange Place, 118 Lower Rd, SE16 ☎020/7237 2224. Large, friendly, very cruisey pub-cum-club hosting regular late-night queercore and

Lesbian and gay London

Lesbian and gay London

Most of the major chains (Waterstone's, Dillons, Books Etc) now have respectable lesbian and gay sections, but it's always worth going to the experts listed below.

Gay's the Word, 66 Marchmont St, WC1 ☎020/7278 7654; *www.gaystheword.co.uk*. Famed for the weekly lesbian discussion groups and readings held in the back of the shop, and offering an extensive collection of lesbian and gay classics, pulps, contemporary fiction and non-fiction, plus cards, calendars etc. Russell Square tube.

Silver Moon Women's Bookshop, 64–68 Charing Cross Rd, NW1 020/7836 7906; mail order ☎020/7836 6849; *www.silvermoonbookshop.co.uk*. Large, well-stocked women's bookshop on two floors, boasting the biggest lesbian department in the country, knowledgeable staff and a good selection of magazines, periodicals, cards, T-shirts and other peripherals, too. Leicester Square tube.

For a guaranteed harassment-free drive home, Freedom Cabs, next door to the Rupert Street bar, 50 Rupert St, W1 (☎020/7734 1313) offers a conveniently located and reasonably priced, 24-hour gay-run cab service.

fetish nights and post-weekend chill-outs. Surrey Quays tube.

79CXR, 79 Charing Cross Rd, WC2 ☎020/7734 0769. Busy, cruisey men's den on two floors, with industrial décor, late licence and a no-messing atmosphere. Leicester Square tube.

Substation Soundshaft, behind *Heaven*, Hungerford Lane, WC2 ☎020/7278 0995. The original late-night cruising pit, open until 5am daily. Steamy, cruisey and sleazy, offering a diverse seven-day menu of sartorial and musical preferences. Sister venue *Substation South* (9 Brighton Terrace, SW9 ☎020/7732 2095; Brixton tube) offers more of the same. Embankment tube.

Tea dances

Somewhere between a café and a club is the institution of the **tea dance**, a fun and friendly place to try out old-fashioned partner dancing. Traditionally, tea dancing happens on a Sunday, which means you're unlikely ever to get a serious tea dance habit – although be warned, it has happened. It's best to arrive early, especially if you need a class: ring in advance for details.

Gay Tea Dance at the *Limelight*, 136 Shaftesbury Ave, W1 ☎020/7439 0572. A smorgasbord of 70s, 80s and 90s pop for gay boys and their girlfriends, hosted by Miss Dusty O. Sundays 6–11pm. Leicester Square tube.

Original Sunday Tea Dance at *BJ's White Swan*, 556 Commercial Rd, E14 ☎020/7780 9870. Hosted by the legendary tea-dancing maestro Jo Purvis, and playing ballroom, cheesy disco and everything in between. Sundays 5.30pm–midnight (tea and sandwiches until 7pm). Aldgate East tube.

Pink Jukebox, *Warren Bar* at the *Grafton Hotel*, 130 Tottenham Court Rd, W1 ☎0374 443627. Lesbian and gay Latin and ballroom dancing club, with friendly classes for beginners and intermediates. Second and fourth Sunday of each month, 6–11pm. Tottenham Court Road tube.

Ruby's Tea Dance at *Ruby's*, 49 Carnaby St, W1 ☎020/8302 6651. Ballroom, Latin and line dancing, with free afternoon tea. Profits go to the Lesbian & Gay Switchboard. Sundays from 5.30pm (4.30pm for beginners). Oxford Circus tube.

Waltzing with Hilda at Jackson's Lane Community Centre, 269a Archway Rd, N6 ☎079390 72958. Women-only Latin and ballroom dancing club – with a dash of country & western thrown in to keep you on your toes. Beer at pub prices and classes for beginners. Monthly on Saturdays, 7.45pm–midnight. Highgate tube.

Clubs

London's **clubs** tend to open up and shut down with surreal frequency, only to pop up again a few months later somewhere entirely different, or in the same place but with a different name. Unless otherwise specified, we've detailed only the longest-running and most popular nights here – check the gay press, listings mags and individual Web sites for up-to-date times and prices before you plan your night out.

We've listed places by club name where that's best known and long-lived, and by venue where there's a variety of changing theme nights, and have tried to give a London-wide sample of what's on offer (usually clubs are significantly cheaper once you're out of the West End). **Entry charges** start at £3–4, but are more often between £6 and £10, rising to around £35 or even £50 for special events like New Year's Eve extravaganzas. Some places offer concessions for students and those on benefits, and some extend discounts if you've managed to pick up the right flyer. Some clubs, especially the men's, stipulate **dress codes** – mainly leather, rubber, uniform and other fetishwear. We've specified such sartorial regulations, but it's best to check before setting out in your finery.

Most clubs kick off at around 11pm (although some don't get going until the small hours) and close between 3am and 5am, sometimes later. A few of the cafés, bars and pubs listed above (pp.566–70) provide a good, cheap alternative to the fully fledged clubs, though they usually close earlier. Lastly, bear in mind that "mixed" tends to mean mostly men.

Mixed clubs

Addiction to DTPM at *Fabric*, 77a Charterhouse St, EC1 ☎020/7251 8778. This long-running Sunday-nighter can now be found in *Fabric's* chic surroundings, with three dancefloors offering soul, jazz, funk, R&B, hip-hop, Latino house and progressive to hard house. Farringdon Road tube.

Club Kali at *The Dome*, 1 Dartmouth Park Hill, N19 (no phone). Held on the third Friday of every month, *Kali* is a huge multi-ethnic extravaganza offering bhangra, Bollywood, Arabic, swing, Hindi

and house flavours for a friendly, attitude-free crowd. Tufnell Park tube.

Club Travestie Extraordinaire at *Stepney's Nightclub*, 373 Commercial Rd, E1 (club entrance on Aylward Street, off Jubilee Street) ☎020/8788 4154. Long-running and popular Saturday night club for TVs/TSs and their pals. Aldgate East tube or Shadwell DLR.

Club V, upstairs at *The Garage*, 20–22 Highbury Corner, N5 ☎020/7607 1818. Every other Saturday, this mock-Tudored venue reverberates to the sounds of queercore and indie tunes spinning for a big, happy, well-lubricated crowd. Regular bands and cheap beer. Highbury & Islington tube.

Crash, Arch 66, Goding St, SE11 ☎020/7278 0995. Four bars, two dancefloors, chillout areas and hard bodies make this weekly Saturday nighter busy, buzzy, sexy and mostly boyzy. Vauxhall tube.

Duckie at the *Royal Vauxhall Tavern*, 372 Kennington Lane, SE11 ☎020/7737 4043; *www.duckie.co.uk. Duckie's* modern, rock-based hurdy gurdy provides a creative and cheerfully ridiculous antidote to the dreary forces of gay techno domination. Regular live art performances, occasional bouncy castles and theme nights. Vauxhall tube.

Exilio Latino, 229 Great Portland St, W1 ☎0956/983230 or 07931 374391; *gexilio@aol.com.* Every other Saturday night, *Exilio* erupts in a lesbian & gay Latin frenzy, spinning salsa, cumbias and merengue, and also featuring live acts. Great Portland Street tube.

Fist at *Imperial Gardens*, 299 Camberwell New Rd (entrance in Medlar Street), SE5 (no phone). This famously depraved monthly Saturday sleaze pit offers a porn cinema, cruising gallery and chill-out area, presumably to escape the hardcore techno. Live action and strict leather /rubber/uniform/military/jockstrap dress code. Oval tube.

G.A.Y. at the *Astoria* (*LA1* & *LA2*), 157 & 165 Charing Cross Rd ☎020/7434 9592 or 0171/734 6963. Of the *Astoria's*

Lesbian and gay London

Despite their illegality, dance drugs remain an integral part of London's queer clubbing scene. Help and advice on recreational or problematic drug use is available from Project LSD (see box on p.573).

Lesbian and gay London

neighbouring venues, *LA1* hosts huge, unpretentious and fun-loving dance nights for a young crowd on Fridays and Saturdays, often featuring big name PAs. There are lots of cheap entry deals to be had at *LA2*, including the famous *G.A.Y. Pink Pounder* trash bash – just £1 for a Wednesday night on the tiles. Tottenham Court Road tube.

Hamam at *Çema*, 129 Stoke Newington High St, N16 ☎020/7249 0213. This friendly, funky, low-ceilinged basement club offers a mix of pop, oriental, salsa and Asian music for an eclectic, attitude-free gay crowd on the first Saturday of the month, and soul, swing, reggae and garage vibe on each third Saturday. Dalston or Stoke Newington train from Liverpool Street or buses #73 from Victoria or #76 from Waterloo.

Heaven, under the Arches, Villiers St, WC2 ☎020/7930 2020; *www .heaven-london.com*. Widely regarded as the UK's most popular gay club, this legendary, 2000-capacity venue continues to reign supreme. Big nights are Mondays (*Popcorn*), Wednesdays (*Fruit Machine*) and Saturdays (just *Heaven*), all with big-name DJs, PAs and shows. More Muscle Mary than Diesel Doris. Charing Cross or Embankment tube.

Love Muscle at *The Fridge*, Town Hall Parade, Brixton Hill, SW2 ☎020/7326 5100; *www.fridge.co.uk*. A regular Saturday night workout for oiled torsos, disco dykes and fag-hag friends, this sweaty, eight-year-old all-nighter offers everything from fluffy techno to hard house via Europop. Big stage shows, stunning lights, go go dancers and a chill-out zone top off the party madness. Brixton tube.

Madame Jo-Jo's, 8–10 Brewer St, W1 ☎020/7734 2473. Lush, louche, newly refurbished cabaret club offering a variety of club nights and spectacular drag shows for office girls, gay boys and everyone in between. It's not cheap, though – make it a special occasion. Piccadilly Circus tube.

Popstarz at the *Scala*, 27 Pentonville Rd, N1 ☎020/7738 2336. Groundbreaking Friday night indie club, now in its fifth year and its sixth venue, and with a still-winning formula of alternative toons, 70s and 80s trash, cheap beer and no attitude. King's Cross tube.

Queer Nation at *Substation South*, 9 Brighton Terrace, SW9 ☎020/7732 2095. Long-running and popular New York-style house and garage nights for funksters. Brixton tube.

Shakti at *The Dome*, 1 Dartmouth Park Hill, N19 (no phone). Every first Friday of the month, this long-running, mixed club plays the best in bhangra, Arabic and jungle sounds for Asian queers and their friends. Tufnell Park tube.

Trade at *Turnmills*, 63b Clerkenwell Rd, EC1 ☎020/7250 3409; *www.turnmills.com*. This legendary Saturday all-nighter (business kicks off at 4am and carries on until Sunday lunchtime) is still going strong. Expect techno and hard house from some of the best DJs in the country, lots of lasers and special effects, and some very sweaty hard bodies – of all genders and flavours, but mostly boyz. Farringdon tube.

The Tube, 1–6 Falconberg Court, W1 ☎020/7287 3726. Late-night, cruisey club behind the *Astoria* with a range of nights catering for every taste (mainly male) from goth indie to funk, via Saturday night's *Wig Out*, a very, very trashy disco. Tottenham Court Road tube.

WayOut Club at *Charlie's*, 9 Crosswall, off Minories, EC3 ☎020/8363 0948. Long-established Saturday night for gays, straights, crossdressers, drag queens, TVs, TSs and friends offers a warm welcome, changing rooms, video screen and regular cabaret. Aldgate or Tower Hill tube.

Lesbian clubs

Ace of Clubs, 52 Piccadilly, W1 ☎020/7408 4457. A veritable institution, this weekly Saturday night women-only club for all ages, styles and musical tastes has been packing 'em in for years and shows no sign of losing its appeal. Piccadilly Circus tube.

Lesbian and gay London

HELPLINES AND INFORMATION

All the following services provide information, advice and counselling, but the **Lesbian & Gay Switchboard** is the one to turn to first; its volunteers have details on all the capital's resources and can point you in the direction of specific organizations and community or support groups.

Bisexual Helpline ☎ 020/8569 7500. Tues & Wed 7.30–9.30pm, Sat 10.30am–12.30pm. Advice, support and information for bisexuals.

Lesbian Line ☎ 020/7251 6911, or minicom 020/7253 0924. Mon & Fri 2–10pm, Tue–Thurs 7–10pm. Advice, support and information for lesbians and those who think they might be, or who are questioning their sexuality.

London Friend ☎ 020/7837 3337. Daily 7.30–10pm. Confidential information and support for lesbians and gay men. The women-only service (☎ 020/7837 2782; 7.30–10pm) is from Sunday to Thursday.

London Lesbian & Gay Switchboard ☎ 020/7837 7324. Huge database on everything you might ever want to know, plus legal advice, good counselling skills and good humour. Lines are 24hr; keep trying if you can't get through.

National AIDS Helpline ☎ 0800/567 123. Freephone 24-hour service for anyone worried about HIV and AIDS-related issues.

Project LSD ☎ 020/7439 0717; *projectlsd@hungerfordII.freeserve.co .uk.* Wed 6–9pm. The UK's only lesbian, gay and bisexual drugs project, offering information, advice and counselling.

Terrence Higgins Trust ☎ 020/7242 1010. Daily noon–10pm. Information and advice on HIV and AIDS. For self-referrals to the counselling unit, call ☎ 020/7835 1495.

Babi Lotion at *Electraworks, 7* Torrens St, N1 ☎ 020/7387 6184). Monthly Friday nighter playing uplifting house for Islington girlz. First fifty women get through the door for free. Angel tube.

Cheekies at the *Jaque of Clubs, 47* Ossory Rd, SE1 ☎ 020/7252 0007. Long-running and popular women-only Saturday night club, with guest DJs, pub prices and a happy hour. Elephant & Castle tube.

Club K at *The Aristocrat,* 88–90 George St, W1. Dancing, drinking and eating on the last Saturday of the month with the ladies of this long-established lesbian social club. Marble Arch tube.

Flirt! at the *Sauna Bar,* 29 Endell St, WC2 ☎ 020/7836 2236 or ☎ 020/7437 1977. This'll get you sweating: the return of the lesbian sauna/club night (Mondays 6pm–midnight) from the successful *Candy Bar* crew, boasting a jacuzzi with room for 20. Covent Garden tube.

4 U Girl at *The Seen,* 93 Dean St, W1 ☎ 0956 514574; *www.wowbar.dircon .co.uk.* A funky, glamour-dyke dive in the heart of Soho, playing house, soul and garage. Men welcome as guests. Tottenham Court Road tube.

Galore at Waterman's Arts Centre, 40 High St, Brentford, Middlesex ☎ 020/8658 1176. Successful and well-established, this big, brash, fun monthly club night proves that you don't have to live in Soho to know how to party. No attitude, no posing, just a good time every third Saturday of the month. Brentford train from Waterloo.

Girlfriend and **Liberté** at *The Oak,* 79 Green Lanes, N16 ☎ 020/7354 2791. This late-night watering hole offers women-only *Girlfriend* (Fri), with live cabaret, commercial dance, R&B, rare groove, house and garage; or the hugely popular, busy *Liberté* (last Sat in each month) spinning soulful grooves, reggae and garage for girls who like to smile

---

Lesbian and gay London

when they're swinging. Manor House tube or buses #73, #171 or #141a from Angel tube.

Gia at *Shillibeers*, Carpenters Mews, North Road, N7 ☎020/7607 0519. Monthly Saturday-nighter for North London grrrls and their gay male friends in a huge, multi-level venue with a restaurant, cocktail and champagne lounge and a summer-only barbecue courtyard. Live PAs, celebrity guests, R&B, soul and NRG. Caledonian Road tube.

Hamam at *Çema*, 129 Stoke Newington High St, N16 ☎020/7249 0213. This friendly, funky, low-ceilinged basement club stages the lesbian-oriented *Harem* each second Saturday, with a music policy of soul, swing, reggae and garage. Dalston or Stoke Newington train or buses #73 from Victoria or #76 from Waterloo.

Loose at *Sunset Strip*, 30 Dean St, W1 ☎020/7494 4041. This Tuesday-night is the only lesbian strip joint in the country. Sit back, get a shot when the tequila girl comes round, order your dollars from the MC and tuck them in where you dare. Tottenham Court Road tube.

Precious Brown at the *Candy Bar*, 23–24 Bateman St, W1 (corner of Frith and Bateman streets) ☎020/7437 1977. This friendly monthly Sunday-nighter in the *Candy Bar's* tiny basement has quite a reputation. Serious music and serious sweating: jungle, funk, Nuyorican, African and the occasional Latin beat to drive you wild. Gay men welcome as guests. Tottenham Court Road tube.

Rumours at *Minories*, 64–73 Minories, EC3. There's room for 500 grrrls at this

bi-weekly, women-only Saturday night, with two bars, quiet lounges and two dancefloors. Tower Hill or Aldgate tube.

Gay men's clubs

Backstreet, Wentworth Mews, off Burdett Rd, E3 ☎020/8980 8557 or 8980 7880 outside club hours. Long-running, traditional leather and rubber club with a strict, *very* butch dress code. Mile End tube.

The Block, 28 Hancock Rd, Bow E3 ☎020/8983 4233. Notorious late-night cruising haunt; the dress code is leather, rubber, uniform, skinhead, construction and industrial wear. Phone for membership details. Bromley-by-Bow tube.

Chariots Roman Baths, 201–207 Shoreditch High St, EC1 ☎020/7247 5333. London's largest and most fabulous gay sauna features everything you could wish for in the way of clearing out pores (and much else), and is open late all week and all night at weekends. Liverpool Street tube.

The Hoist, Railway Arch 47c, South Lambeth Rd, SW8 ☎020/7735 9972. Weekend men's cruise bar with a leather/rubber/industrial/uniform dress code. Hosts *SM Gays* every third Thursday. Vauxhall tube.

Underground at Central Station, 37 Wharfdale Rd, N1 ☎020/7278 3294. The basement of this friendly, three-tiered pub yields sleazy late-night cruising seven nights a week and is also host to *Gummi*, Europe's only rubber-only club, every second Sunday of the month. Equally picturesque theme nights take place on other nights: ring for details. Kings Cross tube.

Chapter 20

Classical music, opera and dance

With the South Bank, the Barbican and the Wigmore Hall offering year-round appearances by generally first-rank musicians, and numerous smaller venues providing a stage for less established or more specialized performers, the capital should satisfy most devotees of **classical music**. What's more, in the annual Promenade Concerts at the Royal Albert Hall, London has one of Europe's greatest, most democratic music festivals – see box on p.576.

While the English National Opera (ENO) quietly continues to try and demolish the elitist stereotypes of **opera**, the Royal Opera House (ROH) continues to grab the headlines. After a long, costly and painful period of rebuilding and refurbishment, the ROH finally reopened at the end of 1999. Embarrassing technical hitches meant that part of the initial programme of events had to be cancelled, and ticket prices are still far too high, but the new Floral Hall development has generally been well received.

The more modest economics of **dance** mean that you'll often find ambitious work on offer, with several adventurous companies appearing sporadically, while fans of classicism can revel in the Royal Ballet – as accomplished a company as any in Europe.

Classical music

London is spoilt for choice when it comes to **orchestras**. On most days

you'll be able to catch a concert by either the London Symphony Orchestra, the London Philharmonic, the Royal Philharmonic, the Philharmonia or the BBC Symphony Orchestra, or a smaller-scale performance from the English Chamber Orchestra, London Sinfonietta or the Academy of St Martin-in-the-Fields. Unless a glamorous guest conductor is wielding the baton, or one of the world's high-profile orchestras is giving a performance, full houses are a rarity, so even at the biggest concert halls you should be able to pick up a ticket for around £12 (the usual range is about £8–20).

The Proms provide a feast of music at bargain-basement prices (see box on p.576), and during the week, there are also **free lunchtime concerts** by students or professionals in many of London's churches, particularly in the City; performances in the Royal College of Music and Royal Academy of Music are of an amazingly high standard, and the choice of work a lot riskier than the commercial venues can manage.

Concert venues

Barbican Centre, Silk St, EC2 ☎020/7638 8891 or 7638 4141; *www.barbican.org.uk*. Home to the London Symphony Orchestra and the English Chamber Orchestra, and the

Classical music, opera and dance

The Royal Albert Hall's **BBC Henry Wood Promenade Concerts** – known to Brits as the "Proms" – tend to be associated primarily with the raucous "Last Night", when the flag-waving audience sings its patriotic heart out. This jingoistic nonsense completely misrepresents the Proms, however, which from July to September feature at least one concert daily in an exhilarating melange of favourites and new or recondite works. You can book a seat as you would for any other concert, but that would be to miss the essence of the Proms, for which the stalls are removed to create hundreds of standing places costing just £3. The upper gallery is similarly packed with people sitting on the floor or standing, and tickets there are even cheaper. The acoustics aren't the world's best, but the performers are usually outstanding, the atmosphere is great, and the hall is so vast that the likelihood of being turned away if you turn up on the night is slim. The annual Proms Guide, available at most bookshops from May, gives information on every concert; you can also call the Albert Hall direct on ☎ 020/7589 8212, or visit the Web site: *www.royalalberthall.com*.

BOC Covent Garden Festival, venues in and around Covent Garden, WC2 ☎ 020/7379 0870; *www.cgf .co.uk*. Three-week festival of music, opera and dance in late May/early June, held in some unusual venues in and around Covent Garden. Covent Garden tube.

City of London Festival, Barbican Centre and many venues in and around the City ☎ 020/7377 0540; *www.colf .org*. International soloists, chamber groups, orchestras and choirs perform in various City churches and livery halls at this month-long festival in late June/July. Barbican or St Paul's tube.

Greenwich & Docklands Festival, various venues, Greenwich, SE10 & Docklands, E14 ☎ 020/8305 1818; *www.festival.org*. Classical music plays its part in this combined ten-day arts festival in July, housed in venues ranging from the Royal Naval College Chapel to nearby pubs. Greenwich or Maze Hill train station, from Charing Cross.

Kenwood Lakeside Concerts, Kenwood House, Hampstead Lane, NW3 ☎ 020/7973 3427; *www.picnicconcerts .com*. The grassy amphitheatre in front of Kenwood House is the venue for alfresco classical concerts every Saturday evening from July to early September. The programme is conservative and crowd-pleasing, but executed with real panache and often ending with a fireworks display. Bus #210 from Archway tube; shuttle bus from East Finchley tube on concert nights.

Meltdown, South Bank Centre, SE1 ☎ 020/7960 4242; *www.meltdown.co .uk*. A short festival of avant-garde offerings, held in various parts of the South Bank complex in June, and one of the most stimulating musical events on the London calendar. Waterloo tube.

Spitalfields Festival, Christ Church, Spitalfields, E1 ☎ 020/7377 0287; *www.spitalfieldsfestival.org.uk*. Classical music recitals in Hawksmoor's mighty Christ Church, during the area's June arts shindig. Liverpool Street, Aldgate or Aldgate East tube.

regular haunt of big-name soloists, programming at the Barbican has become much more adventurous recently, and free music in the foyer is often very good. Unfortunately, however, it's a difficult place to find and to find your way around. Barbican or Moorgate tube.

Blackheath Concert Halls, 23 Lee Rd, SE3 ☎ 020/8463 0100; *www .blackheathhalls.com*. Often a venue for excellent solo recitals – even top-of-the-bill performers from the Met have sung here. Blackheath train station, from Charing Cross.

BMIC (British Music Information Centre), 10 Stratford Place, W1 ☎020/7499 8567; *www.bmic.co.uk*. Low-price recitals most Tuesday and Thursday evenings, usually of freshly minted British music (good, bad and ugly). Bond Street tube.

St John's, Smith Square, SW1 ☎020/7222 1061; *www.sjss.org.uk*. This charming but empty, deconsecrated Baroque church is situated behind Westminster Abbey, and presents a musical menu dominated by chamber music and solo recitals. The restaurant in the crypt is good for before or after. Westminster tube.

South Bank Centre, South Bank, SE1 ☎020/7960 4242; *www.sbc.org.uk*. The South Bank Centre has three concert venues: the Royal Festival Hall (RFH) is a gargantuan space, tailor-made for large-scale choral and orchestral works. It plays host to some soloists as well, though few can fill it nowadays. The Queen Elizabeth Hall (QEH) is the prime location for chamber orchestras and big-name soloists, but by no means an exclusively classical venue; while the Purcell Room is the most intimate venue, excellent for chamber music and solo recitals by future star instrumentalists and singers. All concerts, other than the occasional performance in the foyer, are fee-paying. Waterloo tube.

Wigmore Hall, 36 Wigmore St, W1 ☎020/7935 2141; *www.wigmore-hall .org.uk*. With its nigh-perfect acoustics, the Wigmore is a favourite with artists and audiences alike. An exceptional venue for chamber music, it is renowned for its song recitals by rising young instrumentalists. Stages very popular, fee-paying mid-morning concerts on a Sunday. Bond Street or Oxford Circus tube.

Free lunchtime concerts

Royal Academy of Music, Marylebone Rd, NW1 ☎020/7873 7373; *www .ram.ac.uk*. During term time, you can catch three lunchtime concerts each week (1pm; days vary), and an early-evening recital, for which there's some-times an entry charge. Regent's Park or Baker Street tube.

Royal College of Music, Prince Consort Rd, SW7 ☎020/7589 3643; *www.rcm .ac.uk*. Concerts are staged at London's top music college (and occasionally at nearby St Mary Abbots Church, Kensington High Street) every lunchtime at around 1pm during term time (free), as well as on occasional evenings (for which there's sometimes an entry charge). South Kensington tube.

St Anne and St Agnes, Gresham St, EC2 ☎020/7606 4986. As well as lunchtime recitals (Mon & Fri), this Lutheran place of worship is big on Bach as part of its Sunday service, and has a mini-festival in July. St Paul's tube.

St Bride, Fleet St, EC4 ☎020/7353 1301. Lunchtime concerts every week (Tues & Fri), often by professional musicians; occasional organ recitals (Wed). Blackfriars tube.

St Giles Cripplegate, Fore St, Barbican, EC2 ☎020/7638 1997. Lurking in the midst of the Barbican, this church pro-vides the complex with an extra perfor-mance space. Barbican or Moorgate tube.

St James, Piccadilly, W1 ☎020/7381 0441. The emphasis is on Baroque music in this beautiful Wren church. Piccadilly Circus tube.

St Lawrence Jewry, Guildhall, EC2 ☎020/7600 9478. Piano recitals on Mondays and organ-playing on Tuesdays. Bank or St Paul's tube.

St Magnus the Martyr, Lower Thames St, EC3 ☎020/7626 4481. Recitals each Tuesday and Wednesday, with music often used in the services, too. Monument tube.

St Margaret, Lothbury, EC2 ☎020/7606 8330. Thursday lunchtime recitals make great play of the nearly 200-year-old church organ. Bank tube.

Classical music, opera and dance

Classical music, opera and dance

St Martin-in-the-Fields, Trafalgar Square, WC2 ☎020/7839 8362; www.stmartin-in-the-fields.org. Free lunchtime recitals on Mondays, Tuesdays and Fridays, plus a few fee-charging candle-lit concerts in the evenings, sometimes featuring the top-notch orchestra of the Academy of St Martin-in-the-Fields. Charing Cross or Leicester Square tube.

St Martin-within-Ludgate, Ludgate Hill, EC4 ☎020/7248 6054. A fantastically spired Wren church with a varied Wednesday lunchtime recital programme. St Paul's or Blackfriars tube.

St Mary Abchurch, Abchurch Lane, EC4 ☎020/7626 0306. Tuesday-lunchtime concerts under St Mary Abchurch's wonderful frescoed dome. Cannon Street or Monument tube.

St-Mary-le-Bow, Cheapside, EC2 ☎020/7248 5139. An excellent Thursday programme of medieval and Renaissance recitals. St Paul's tube.

St-Mary-le-Strand, Strand, WC2 ☎020/7836 3126. Wednesday recitals battle it out with the traffic that swishes past on either side of the church. Covent Garden or Temple tube.

St Michael, Cornhill, EC3 ☎020/7626 8841. Bracing organ recitals that lift the spirits of wage slaves every Monday. Bank tube.

St Olave, Hart St, EC3 ☎020/7488 4318. Chamber pieces on Wednesday and Thursday. Tower Hill tube.

St Sepulchre-without-Newgate, Holborn Viaduct, EC1 ☎020/7248 1660. The so-called "Musicians' Church" holds regular piano recitals on Tuesdays. Chancery Lane or St Paul's tube.

St Stephen Walbrook, Walbrook, EC4 ☎020/7283 4444. Friday-lunchtime organ recitals at the earlier-than-normal time of 12.30pm. Bank tube.

Opera

Despite enjoying an increase in popularity, opera remains an elitist genre and has had a bad press in London, largely owing to the travails of the **Royal Opera House**, which was expensively – and, it has to be said, impressively – refurbished in 1999. In contrast to public perception of the ROH, the **English National Opera**, based at the London Coliseum, has worked hard to bring exciting, entertaining opera to the masses.

Opera companies and venues

Almeida Theatre, Almeida St, N1 ☎020/7359 4404; www.almeida.co.uk. The Almeida Opera festival, held in July, is a showcase for new works and a highlight of the music year in London. Angel or Highbury & Islington tube.

English National Opera, Coliseum, St Martin's Lane, WC2 ☎020/7632 8300; www.eno.org. Home of the English National Opera, the Coliseum tends to employ more radical producers, put on a more ambitious and populist programme and offer way more democratic prices than its Royal Opera House rival. Ticket prices start at as little as £5, rising to just over £50; day seats are also available to personal callers after 10am on the day of the performance, with balcony seats going for just £2.50. Three hours before the performance, standbys go on sale (subject to availability) at a maximum price of £18 to students, senior citizens and the unemployed. All works are sung in English. Leicester Square or Charing Cross tube.

Holland Park, Holland Park, Kensington High St, W8 ☎020/7602 7856; www.operalondon.com. Opera, as well as dance and theatre, takes to the great outdoors in green and pleasant Holland Park during the summer months. There's a canopy to cover you in case of rain. High Street Kensington or Holland Park tube.

Royal Opera House, Bow St, WC2 ☎020/7304 4000; www.royaloperahouse.org. The ROH is attempting to make itself more accessible – the new Floral Hall foyer is open to the public during the day, there's the odd free lunchtime recital, and a new studio theatre, tickets for which are more modestly priced. However, the ROH still has a deserved reputation for snobbery, conservative productions and ludicrous seat prices (over £100 for the best seats). A small number of day seats (for £30 or under) are put on sale from 10am on the day of a performance – these are restricted to one per person, and you need to get there by 8am for popular shows. Four hours before performances, low-price standbys (subject to availability) can be bought for around £15 by students, senior citizens etc. In summer, some performances are occasionally relayed live to a large screen in Covent Garden Piazza. All operas are performed in the original language but are discreetly subtitled. Covent Garden tube.

Dance

From the time-honoured showpieces of the **Royal Ballet** to the offbeat acts of kinetic surrealism on show at the ICA, there's always a **dance performance** of some kind afoot in London, and the city also has a good reputation for international dance festivals showcasing the work of a spread of ensembles. The biggest of the annual events is the **Dance Umbrella** (☎020/8741 5881; www.danceumbrella.co.uk), a six-week season (Oct–Nov) of new work from bright young choreographers and performance artists at venues across the city.

Dance companies and venues

Chisenhale Dance Space, 64–84 Chisenhale Rd, E3 ☎020/8981 6617; www.chisenhale.demon.co.uk. Showcases the work of new choreographers and student performers. Mile End tube.

ICA, Nash House, The Mall, SW1 ☎020/7930 3647; www.ica.org.uk. Experimental performance-cum-dance shows dominate at the small-scale venue of the avant-garde Institute of Contemporary Arts. Charing Cross tube.

London Coliseum, St Martin's Lane, WC2 ☎020/7632 8300; www.eno.org. The English National Ballet performs on and off at this beautiful venue throughout the year (with regular spots in the summer and at Christmas), interspersed by

occasional touring companies. Leicester Square or Charing Cross tube.

The Place, 17 Duke's Rd, WC1 ☎020/7387 0031; www.theplace.org.uk. Home to the Richard Alston Dance Company, this small theatre also plays host to the finest in performance art and contemporary dance from across the globe. Euston tube.

Riverside Studios, Crisp Rd, W6 ☎020 /8237 1111; www.riversidestudios.co.uk. Two performance spaces used for small-scale productions, often on the border between dance and performance art. Hammersmith tube.

Royal Ballet, Royal Opera House, Bow St, WC2 ☎020/7304 4000; www .royaloperahouse.org. The Royal Ballet is one of the world's finest classical companies, although its repertoire isn't all tutus and swans. Prices are considerably lower than for the opera – you should be able to get tickets for around £25 if you act quickly, though sell-outs are frequent (see Royal Opera House, opposite, for details of day tickets and standbys). Covent Garden tube.

Sadler's Wells Theatre, Rosebery Ave, EC1 ☎020/7863 8000; www.sadlers-wells.com. A diverse and exciting range of British and international dance goes on at the newly rebuilt Sadler's Wells in Islington, including productions from the Rambert Dance Company, which is usually resident here in spring and autumn. The Lilian Baylis theatre, tucked around the back, puts on smaller-scale shows, while Sadler's Wells continues to stage more populist dance at the Peacock Theatre in the West End. Angel tube.

South Bank Centre, South Bank, SE1 ☎020/7960 4242; www.sbc.org.uk. The resident company here is the English National Ballet, which performs The Nutcracker to capacity audiences every winter and has a three- to six-week summer season in the Royal Festival Hall. The South Bank also regularly hosts dance performances by some of Europe's most adventurous groups. Waterloo tube.

Classical music, opera and dance

Chapter 21

Theatre, comedy and cinema

For more on all London theatre productions, check www.albemarle -london.com.

London has enjoyed a reputation for quality **theatre** since the time of Shakespeare, and despite the increasing prevalence of fail-safe blockbuster musicals and revenue-spinning star vehicles, the city still provides a platform for innovation. The **comedy** scene in London goes from strength to strength, so much so that the capital now boasts more comedy venues than any other city in the world, while comedians who have made the transition to television also stage shows in major theatres.

Cinema is rather less healthy, for London's repertory theatres are a dying breed, edged out by the multiscreen complexes which show mainstream Hollywood fare some months behind America. There are a few excellent independent cinemas, though, including the National Film Theatre, which is the focus of the richly varied **London International Film Festival** in November.

Current details of **what's on** in all these areas can be found in a number of publications, the most comprehensive being the weekly *Time Out.* The *Guardian's The Guide* section (free with the paper on Saturdays) and Friday's *Evening Standard* are other good sources.

Theatre

At first glance it might seem that London's **theatreland** has become a province of the Andrew Lloyd Webber global empire, but in fact few cities in the world can match the variety of the London scene. Many of the **West End** theatres have been hijacked by long-running musicals or similarly unchallenging shows (see box on p.583), but others offer more intriguing productions. The government-subsidized **Royal Shakespeare Company** and the **National Theatre** often put on extremely original productions of mainstream masterpieces. while some of the most exciting work is performed in what have become known as the **Off West End** theatres, which consistently stage interesting and often challenging productions. Further down the financial ladder still are the **fringe theatres**, more often than not pub venues, where ticket prices are low, and quality variable.

Unfortunately, theatre-going doesn't come cheap in this city. **Tickets** under £10 are very thin on the ground for any of the major theatres; the box-office average is closer to £15, with £30 the usual top whack. Tickets for the durable musicals and well-reviewed plays are like gold dust.

The Society of London Theatres' (SOLT) **half-price ticket booth**, in Leicester Square (Mon–Sat 2.30–6.30pm; Sun noon–3pm; noon–2.30pm matinées only), sells tickets for that day's performances of all the West End

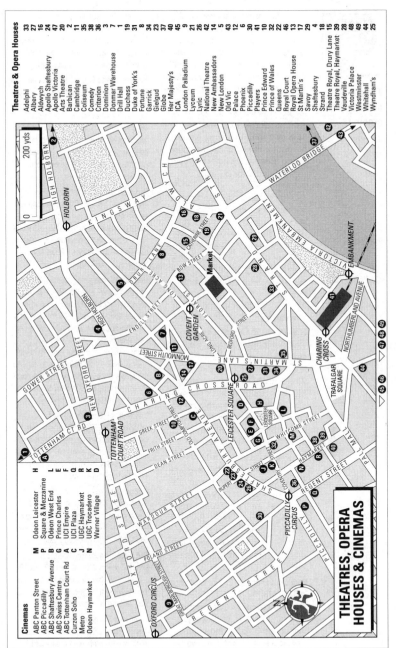

Cinemas

ABC Panton Street	H
ABC Piccadilly	
ABC Shaftesbury Avenue	
ABC Swiss Centre	L
ABC Tottenham Court Rd	F
Curzon Soho	Q
Metro	R
Odeon Haymarket	K

Odeon Leicester	M
Square & Mezzanine	P
Odeon West End	B
Prince Charles	G
UCI Empire	A
UCI Plaza	J
UGC Haymarket	I
UGC Trocadero	N
Warner Village	D

THEATRES, OPERA HOUSES & CINEMAS

Theatres & Opera Houses

Adelphi	33
Albery	27
Aldwych	16
Apollo Shaftesbury	24
Apollo Victoria	47
Arts Theatre	20
Barbican	2
Cambridge	11
Coliseum	35
Comedy	38
Criterion	36
Dominion	3
Donmar Warehouse	7
Drill Hall	1
Duchess	19
Duke of York's	31
Fortune	8
Garrick	34
Gielgud	23
Globe	37
Her Majesty's	40
ICA	45
London Palladium	9
Lyceum	21
Lyric	26
National Theatre	42
New Ambassadors	14
New London	5
Old Vic	43
Palace	12
Phoenix	6
Piccadilly	30
Players	41
Prince Edward	10
Prince of Wales	32
Queens	22
Royal Court	46
Royal Opera House	13
St Martin's	17
Savoy	29
Shaftesbury	4
Strand	18
Theatre Royal, Drury Lane	15
Theatre Royal, Haymarket	39
Vaudeville	28
Victoria Palace	48
Westminster	49
Whitehall	44
Wyndham's	25

©crown copyright

Theatre, comedy and cinema

shows, but they tend to have only the top end of the price range. Tickets are sold for cash (or theatre tokens) only, are restricted to four per person, and carry a service charge of up to £2 per ticket. If the SOLT booth has sold out, you could turn to agencies such as Ticketmaster (☎020/7344 4444; www.ticketmaster.co.uk) or First Call (☎020/7497 9977; www.firstcalltickets.com), who can get seats for all West End shows, but add a ten percent mark-up on the ticket price. Bear in mind that if you buy from touts, there's no guarantee the tickets are genuine.

Students, senior citizens and the unemployed can get **concessionary rates** on tickets for many shows, and nearly all theatres offer reductions on standby tickets to all these groups. The SOLT runs a very busy Student Theatre Line (☎020/7379 8900), which lists all the student standby tickets available and their prices.

The venues

What follows is a list of those West End theatres that offer a changing roster of good plays, along with the most consistent of the Off West End and fringe venues. This by no means represents the full tally of London's stages, as there are scores of fringe places that present work on an intermittent basis – *Time Out* provides the most comprehensive and detailed up-to-the-minute survey.

Almeida, Almeida St, N1 ☎020/7359 4404; www.almeida.co.uk. A deservedly popular Off West End venue which premieres excellent new plays and excitingly reworked classics, and has attracted some big Hollywood names. The Almeida also puts on productions in other venues, including theatres in the West End. Angel or Highbury & Islington tube.

Barbican Centre, Silk St, EC2 (box office ☎020/7638 8891 or 7638 4141; www.barbican.org.uk). After a season in the company's HQ at Stratford, Royal Shakespeare Company productions move to one of the Barbican's two

venues: the excellently designed Barbican Theatre and the much smaller Pit. A wide range of work is produced, though the writings of the Bard predominate. Barbican or Moorgate tube.

Battersea Arts Centre, 176 Lavender Hill, SW11 ☎020/7223 2223; www.bac.org.uk. The BAC is a triple-stage building, housed in an old town hall in south London, and has acquired a reputation for excellent fringe productions, from straight theatre to comedy and cabaret. Clapham Junction train station from Victoria or Waterloo.

Bush, Shepherd's Bush Green, W12 ☎020/8743 3388. This minuscule above-pub theatre is London's most reliable venue for new writing after the Royal Court, and it has turned out some real crackers. Goldhawk Road or Shepherd's Bush tube.

Donmar Warehouse, Thomas Neal's, Earlham St, WC2 ☎020/7369 1732; www.theambassadors.com. A performance space that's noted for new plays and top-quality reappraisals of the classics, and which has enticed several Hollywood stars – most notably Kevin Spacey and Nicole Kidman – to take to the stage. It's currently run by the young Oscar-winning director Sam Mendes. Covent Garden tube.

Drill Hall, 16 Chenies St, WC1 ☎020/7637 8270. This studio-style venue specializes in gay, lesbian, feminist and all-round politically correct new work. Monday evenings are women only. Goodge Street tube.

Finborough, The Finborough Arms, 118 Finborough Rd, SW10 ☎020/7373 3842. A pub-theatre presenting a challenging range of high-minded new pieces. Earl's Court tube (Warwick Road exit).

The Gate, The Prince Albert, 11 Pembridge Rd, W11 ☎020/7229 0706. A small pub-theatre noted for its excellent revivals of neglected European classics. Notting Hill Gate tube.

Hampstead Theatre, Swiss Cottage Centre, Avenue Rd, NW3 ☎020/7722 9301; www.hampstead-theatre.co.uk. A

LONDON'S LONG-RUNNERS

Most overseas visitors to the West End theatres come to see one of the city's big musicals, which have been so successful in recent years that serious theatre has been all but squeezed off these stages. On any given night in the West End there are more people watching musicals than all other forms of theatre put together, and the trend shows no sign of abating, despite the odd well-publicized flop. Below is a list of the established songfests, along with the two plays that have attained comparable landmark status. All of the shows below are listed on *www.albemarle-london.com*.

Theatre, comedy and cinema

Blood Brothers, Phoenix Theatre, 110 Charing Cross Rd, WC2 ☎ 020/7369 1733. Willy Russell and Bob Thomson's sentimental, decade-old musical about Scouse (Liverpool) twins separated at birth. Tottenham Court Road or Leicester Square tube.

Buddy, Strand Theatre, Aldwych, WC2 ☎ 020/7930 8800. All the old favourites resurrected in the story of Buddy Holly's brief life. Covent Garden or Holborn tube.

Cats, New London Theatre, Parker Street, WC2 ☎ 020/7405 0072. Lloyd Webber's most popular musical, and London's longest-running, with all-singing, all-dancing feline favourites from T.S. Eliot's *Old Possum's Book of Practical Cats*. Holborn or Covent Garden tube.

Chicago, Adelphi Theatre, Strand, WC2 ☎ 020/7344 0055. Cynical tale of two murderesses who escape Death Row for fame and stardom thanks to their scheming lawyer. Charing Cross tube.

Les Misérables, Palace Theatre, Shaftesbury Ave, W1 ☎ 020/7434 0909. Trevor Nunn's sanitized adaptation of Victor Hugo's classic. Alluring peasants, vicious villains and heart-wrenching musical numbers. Leicester Square or Tottenham Court Road tube.

Lion King, Lyceum Theatre, Wellington Street, WC2 ☎ 0870/243 90.

A guaranteed winner with the kids, this stage adaptation of the Oscar-winning Disney film is better than you might fear. Covent Garden or Charing Cross tube.

The Mousetrap, St Martin's, West St, WC2 ☎ 020/7836 1443. Run-of-the-mill Agatha Christie murder mystery that's been running for nearly fifty years – a world record. Leicester Square tube.

The Phantom of the Opera, Her Majesty's Theatre, Haymarket, SW1 ☎ 020/7494 5400. Extravagant Lloyd Webber production about a physiognomically challenged subterranean who falls for a beautiful young opera singer. Piccadilly Circus tube.

Starlight Express, Apollo Victoria Theatre, 17 Wilton Rd, SW1 ☎ 020/7416 6070. Lloyd Webber on wheels. Fast-moving rollerskating extravaganza, with an innovative set circling the audience above and below. Victoria tube.

Whistle down the Wind, The Aldwych, WC2 ☎ 020/7416 6003. Another Lloyd Webber musical, this time set in the 1950s, panned by the critics, but still pulling them in. Covent Garden tube.

The Woman in Black, Fortune Theatre, Russell Street, WC2 ☎ 020/7836 2238. Susan Hill's ghost tale is the longest-running play in this theatre's history. Covent Garden tube.

shed-like but comfortable theatre in Swiss Cottage (not in Hampstead proper) whose productions often move on to the West End. Such is its prestige that the likes of John Malkovich have been enticed into performing here. Swiss Cottage tube.

ICA, Nash House, The Mall, SW1 ☎ 020/7930 3647; *www.ica.org.uk*. The Institute of Contemporary Arts attracts the most innovative practitioners in all areas of performance. It also attracts a fair quantity of modish junk, but the hits

Theatre, comedy and cinema

generally outweigh the misses. Piccadilly Circus or Charing Cross tube.

King's Head, 115 Upper St, N1 ☎020/7226 1916. The oldest and probably most famous of London's thriving pub-theatres (with a useful late licence). Adventurous performances in a pint-sized room at lunchtimes and in the evening. Angel or Highbury & Islington tube.

National Theatre, South Bank Centre, South Bank, SE1 ☎020/7452 3000; *www.nt-online.org.uk*. The Royal National Theatre, as it's now officially known, consists of three separate theatres: the 1100-seater Olivier, the proscenium-arched Lyttelton and the experimental Cottesloe. Standards set by the late Lawrence Olivier, founding artistic director, are maintained by the country's top actors and directors in a programme ranging from *Wind in the Willows* to the work of Arthur Miller. Some productions sell out months in advance, but a few discounted tickets go on sale on the morning of each performance – get there by 8am for the popular shows. Waterloo tube.

New End Theatre, 27 New End, NW3 ☎020/7794 0022; *www.newendtheatre .com*. Cosy neighbourhood venue in literary-minded Hampstead that offers a reliable programme of fringe-like fare. Hampstead tube.

Open Air Theatre, Regent's Park, Inner Circle, NW1 ☎020/7486 2431. If the weather's good, there's nothing quite like a dose of alfresco drama. This beautiful space in Regent's Park hosts a tourist-friendly summer programme of Shakespeare, musicals, plays and concerts. Baker Street tube.

Orange Tree, 1 Clarence St, Richmond, Surrey ☎020/8940 3633. Consistently good low-budget, period dramas for the wealthy denizens of Richmond and Kew. Richmond tube.

Richmond Theatre, The Green, Richmond, Surrey ☎020/8940 0088. Suburban theatre with an excellent record of classic dramas, from Aristophanes to the present century. Richmond tube.

Royal Court, Sloane Square, SW1 ☎020/7565 5000; *www .royalcourttheatre.com*. The Royal Court has recently undergone a massive refurbishment programme, but its long-standing tradition of presenting the finest in new writing looks set to continue. Smaller-scale and often more radical work gets its chance in the Theatre Upstairs. Sloane Square tube.

Shakespeare's Globe, New Globe Walk, SE1 ☎020/7902 1500; *www .shakespeares-globe.org*. This thatch-roofed Elizabethan theatre uses only natural light and the minimum of scenery, and currently puts on solid, fun shows from mid-May to mid-September, with "groundling" tickets (standing-room only) for a mere £5. The new indoor Inigo Jones

---

THE DRAMA SCHOOLS

The London drama schools each mount as many as ten productions per term, giving you a chance to indulge in a bit of talent-spotting for very little outlay – indeed, Guildhall plays are free. The following are the main schools.

Central School of Speech and Drama, 64 Eton Ave, NW3 ☎020/7722 8183; *www.cssd.ac.uk*. Swiss Cottage tube.

Guildhall School of Music and Drama, Silk Street, Barbican, EC2 ☎020/7628 2571; *www.gsmd.ac.uk*. Barbican or Moorgate tube.

London Academy of Music and Dramatic Art, Tower House, 226 Cromwell Rd, SW5 ☎020/7373 9883; *www.lamda.org.uk*. Gloucester Road tube.

Royal Academy of Dramatic Art, 62–64 Gower St, WC1 ☎020/7636 7076; *www.rada.org.uk*. Goodge Street tube.

Theatre is set to continue the season throughout the winter months. London Bridge, Blackfriars or Southwark tube.

Tricycle Theatre & Cinema, 269 Kilburn High Rd, NW6 ☎020/7328 1000. One of London's most dynamic fringe venues, showcasing a mixed bag of new plays, with an emphasis on black and Irish issues, and international productions of the core repertoire. Kilburn tube.

Young Vic, The Cut, SE1 ☎020/7928 6363; www.youngvic.org. A large "in-the-round" space, perfect for Shakespeare, which is something of a speciality, as well as a studio for variable fringe productions. Big names have appeared on the main stage over the years – Vanessa Redgrave's version of Ibsen's *Ghosts* is near-legendary. Waterloo tube.

Comedy and cabaret

The **comedy scene** continues to live up to its media-coined status as the new rock'n'roll, with the leading funnypersons catapulted to unlikely stardom on both stage and screen. The **Comedy Store** is the best-known venue on the circuit, but even in the lowliest suburbs you can often find a local pub giving a platform to young hopefuls (again, *Time Out* gives full listings). Note that many venues operate only on Friday and Saturday nights, and that August is a lean month, as much of London's talent then heads north for the Edinburgh Festival. **Tickets** vary in price, but average around £5; in the more established places, you're looking at more like £12.

Backyard Comedy Club, 231 Cambridge Heath Rd, E2 ☎020/7739 3122; www.leehurst.com. Purpose-built club in Bethnal Green established by comedian Lee Hurst, who has successfully managed to attract a consistently strong lineup. Fri & Sat. Bethnal Green tube.

Banana Cabaret, *The Bedford*, 77 Bedford Hill, SW12 ☎020/8673 8904. This double-stage pub has become one of London's finest comedy venues – well worth the trip out from the centre of town. Fri & Sat from 9pm. Balham tube.

Canal Café Theatre, The Bridge House, Delamere Terrace, W2 ☎020/7289 6054. Perched on the water's edge in Little Venice, this venue is good for improvisation acts and is home to the *Newsrevue* team of topical gagsters; there's usually something going on from Thursday to Sunday. Warwick Avenue tube.

Comedy Café, 66 Rivington St, EC2 ☎020/7739 5706. Long-established club on the edge of the City, often with impressive lineups, and free admission for the new-acts slot on Wednesday nights. Wed–Sat. Old Street tube.

Comedy Store, Haymarket House, 1 Oxendon St, SW1 ☎020/7344 0234; www.thecomedystore.co.uk. Widely regarded as the birthplace of alternative comedy, though no longer in its original venue, the Comedy Store has catapulted many a stand-up onto primetime TV. Improvisation by in-house comics on Wednesdays and Sundays, in addition to a stand-up bill; Thursday night offers try-out spots for those brave enough to handle the hecklers, while Friday and Saturday are the busiest nights, with two shows, at 8pm and midnight – book ahead. Piccadilly Circus tube.

Jongleurs Battersea, The Cornet, 49 Lavender Gardens, SW11 (Clapham Junction train station); **Jongleurs Bow**, 221 Grove Rd, E3 (Mile End tube); and **Jongleurs Camden Lock**, Dingwalls Building, 36 Camden Lock Place, Chalk Farm Road, NW1 (Camden tube); ☎0870 /7870707; www.jongleurs.com. Jongleurs is a top-ranking chain of venues; there's a spot of post-revelry disco-dancing included in the ticket price on Fridays at Camden, two shows on Saturdays at Camden and Battersea, and one show on Fridays and Saturdays at Bow. Book well in advance. Camden Town tube.

Cinema

There are an awful lot of **cinemas** in the West End, but only a very few places committed to non-mainstream movies, and even fewer repertory cinemas

Theatre, comedy and cinema

Theatre, comedy and cinema

programming serious films from the back catalogue. November's **London Film Festival** (*www.lff.org.uk*), which occupies half a dozen West End cinemas, is now a huge event, and so popular that most of the films sell out within a couple of days of the publication of the festival's programme.

Tickets for regular showings tend to cost upwards of £7 at the major screens in the West End, although afternoon shows are usually discounted. The suburban screens run by the big companies (see *Time Out* for full listings) tend to be a couple of pounds cheaper, as do independent cinemas. Students, senior citizens and the unemployed can get concessionary rates for some shows at virtually all cinemas, usually all day Monday or at off-peak times on all weekdays.

First-run cinemas

The cinemas here are the pick of the bunch for first-run movies, with decent-sized screens and auditoriums.

Odeon Leicester Square, 22-24 Leicester Square, WC2 ☎0870/5050 007; *www.odeon.co.uk*. London's largest cinema, and thus a favourite for celeb-packed premieres. There's just one screen here, but the adjacent Odeon Mezzanine crushes five into a far smaller space (one reason why it's been voted London's worst). Leicester Square tube.

Odeon Marble Arch, 10 Edgware Rd, W2 ☎0870/5050 007; *www.odeon.co.uk*. Blockbuster specialist, on account of possessing the city's biggest (normal format) screen, with a sound system to match. Marble Arch tube.

UCI Empire, Leicester Square, WC20870/6034567; *www.uci-cinemas.co.uk*. The huge, expensive, hi-tech main auditorium here is London's second largest, and is the place where blockbusters tend to premiere, and royalty occasionally turn up. Leicester Square tube.

Repertory

These are the places you're most likely to catch back-catalogue and foreign

movies, often as part of a themed programme lasting a week or more.

Barbican, Silk St, EC2 ☎020/7382 7000; *www.barbican.org.uk*. Tiny screens, but a regular rota of obscure classics, plus the odd mini-festival. Barbican tube.

Ciné Lumière, 17 Queensberry Place, SW7 ☎020/7838 2144. Predominantly, but by no means exclusively, French films, both old and new (sometimes with subtitles), put on by the Institut Français. South Kensington tube.

Everyman, Hollybush Vale, NW3 ☎020/7431 1777; *www.everymancinema.com*. The city's oldest repertory cinema, and still one of its best, with strong programmes of classics, cultish crowd-magnets and directors' seasons. Very hot in summer. Hampstead tube.

Goethe Institut, 50 Princes Gate, Exhibition Rd, SW7 ☎020/7596 4000; *www.goethe.de/london*. Sporadic showings of German cinematic masterpieces. South Kensington tube.

ICA Cinema, Nash House, The Mall, SW1 ☎020/7930 3647; *www.ica.org.uk*. Vintage and underground movies shown on one of two tiny screens in the avantgarde HQ of the Institute of Contemporary Arts. Piccadilly Circus or Charing Cross tube.

BFI London Imax Centre, South Bank, SE1 ☎020/7902 1234; *www.bfi.org.uk*. The British Film Institute's remarkable glazed drum has the largest screen in Europe. It's stunning, state-of-the-art stuff alright, showing 2D and 3D films on a massive screen, but like all IMAX cinemas, it suffers from the paucity of good material that's been shot on the format. Waterloo tube.

Lux Cinema, 2-4 Hoxton Square, N1 ☎020/7684 0201; *www.lux.org.uk*. Relatively new arts cinema in trendy Hoxton, showing an eclectic mix of films and with an art gallery on the first floor. Old Street tube.

National Film Theatre, South Bank, SE1 ☎020/7928 3232; *www.bfi.org.uk/nft*. Known for its attentive audiences and an exhaustive, eclectic programme that includes directors' seasons and thematic series. Around six films daily are shown in the vast NFT1 and the smaller NFT2. Waterloo tube.

Prince Charles, 2–7 Leicester Place, WC2 ☎020/7734 9127. The bargain basement of London's cinemas (entry for some shows is just £2.50), with a programme of new movies, classics and cult favourites – *Sing-along-a-Sound of Music* is a regular. Leicester Square or Piccadilly Circus tube.

Riverside Studios, Crisp Rd, W6 ☎020 /8237 1111; *www.riversidestudios.co.uk*. There's often very good work on show in this converted film studio (often a different film each day). Hammersmith tube.

Waterman's Arts Centre, 40 High St, Brentford, Middlesex ☎020/8568 1176. Inventive programming at this theatre's rep cinema, but it's a long way from the centre of town. Kew Bridge train or bus #237 or #267 from Gunnersbury tube.

Theatre, comedy and cinema

Chapter 22

Galleries

The vast permanent collections of the **National Gallery** and the two **Tates**, the fascinating miscellanies of the Victoria and Albert Museum, and the select holdings of such institutions as the Courtauld and the Wallace Collection, make London one of the world's great repositories of Western art. However, the city is also a dynamic creative centre, with young artists such as Rachel Whiteread, Sarah Lucas and Steve McQueen maintaining the momentum established by the likes of Hockney, Caro, Auerbach and Freud. In the environs of Cork Street, behind the Royal Academy, you'll find various **commercial galleries** showing the best of what's being produced in the studios of Britain and further afield, while numerous other private showcases are scattered all over London, from the superb Saatchi Gallery in St John's Wood to the consistently challenging place run by Flowers East over in the East End.

London fails to compete with Berlin, Paris and New York in only one respect – it doesn't have a special **exhibition space** good enough to handle the blockbuster shows. That looks set to change with the ongoing expansion of both Tates, but until then London will continue to miss out on some of the really big touring shows. Nevertheless, at any time of year, the city's public galleries will be offering at least one absorbing exhibition, on anything from the art of the apocalypse to Soviet supremacists.

Annual fixtures include the **Royal Academy's Summer Exhibition**, when hordes of amateur artists enter their efforts for sale, and November's controversial **Turner Prize**, which is preceded by a month-long display of work by the shortlisted artists at the Tate Britain. More exciting than these, however, are the art school **degree shows** in late May and June, when the current crop of student talent puts its work on display. The Royal College, the Royal Academy, Slade and St Martin's are all good, but Goldsmiths', which has produced some of the most celebrated artists of the last ten years, is the one likeliest to thrill devotees of the avant-garde. Pick up a copy of *Time Out* in mid-May for the times and locations of the student shows.

Major galleries and exhibition spaces

Expect to pay around £7 for entry to one of the big exhibitions at the Barbican or Hayward. Similar prices are charged for special shows at the National Gallery, the Tates, Royal Academy and V&A (see above). Students, senior citizens and the unemployed are eligible for concessionary rates. Hours vary so it's always best to check *Time Out* or ring the gallery before setting off.

Barbican Gallery, Level 3, Barbican Centre, Silk Street, EC2 ☎020/7638 8891; *www.barbican.org.uk*. The

Barbican's two-floor gallery is badly designed, but its thematic exhibitions – ranging from African bush art to the latest photography – are often well worth the entrance fee. Barbican or Moorgate tube.

Camden Arts Centre, corner of Arkwright and Finchley roads, NW3 ☎020/7435 5224. Showcases the work of both new and established artists. Finchley Road tube.

Crafts Council, 44a Pentonville Rd, N1 ☎020/7278 7700; *www.craftscouncil .org.uk*. Showcases the work of contemporary artists working in the applied arts. Work by those shortlisted for the annual Jerwood Prize is displayed here in September. Angel tube.

Hayward Gallery, South Bank Centre, Belvedere Rd, SE1 ☎020/7960 5226; *www.hayward-gallery.org.uk*. Part of the huge South Bank arts complex, the Hayward is one of London's most prestigious venues for major touring exhibitions, with the bias towards twentieth-century work. Waterloo tube.

ICA Gallery, Nash House, The Mall, SW1 ☎020/7930 3647; *www.ica.org.uk*. The Institute of Contemporary Arts has two gallery spaces, in which it displays works that are invariably characterized as "challenging" or "provocative" – occasionally, they are. To visit, you must be a member of the ICA; a day's membership costs £1.50 (Mon–Fri) or £2.50 (Sat & Sun). Piccadilly Circus or Charing Cross tube.

Riverside Studios, Crisp Rd, W6 ☎020/8237 1000;*www.riversidestudios .co.uk*. A wide range of exciting new work is shown at this multifunctional West London arts centre. Hammersmith tube.

Royal Academy, Burlington House, Piccadilly, W1 ☎020/7300 8000; *www .royalacademy.org.uk*. The Royal Academy is best known for its major one-off exhibitions – its recent Monet extravaganza was the most popular art exhibition of all time. From early June to mid-August, the RA stages its Summer

Exhibition, when the public can submit work to be displayed (and sold) alongside the work of Academicians. Tasteful landscapes, interiors and nudes tend to predominate, but there's the odd splash of experimentation. For the most popular shows here, you're advised to pre-book a ticket. Green Park or Piccadilly Circus tube. See p.116.

Royal Institute of British Architects (RIBA), 66 Portland Place, W1 ☎020/7307 3770; *www.riba.net*. Regular architectural exhibitions by the leading lights, housed in a beautiful 1930s building, with an excellent café. Oxford Circus tube. See p.128.

Serpentine Gallery, Kensington Gardens, Hyde Park, W2 ☎020/7402 6075; *www .serpentinegallery.org.uk*. This fine gallery displays dynamic work by new and established modern artists, as well as hosting interesting Sunday-afternoon lectures, and a performance-art festival in the summer. It's free, too. Lancaster Gate tube.

Whitechapel Gallery, Whitechapel High St, E1 ☎020/7522 7888. The Whitechapel is a consistently excellent champion of contemporary art, housing major shows by living or not-long-dead artists. It's also the focal point of the Whitechapel Open, a biennial summer survey (the next one is in 2002) of the work of artists living in the vicinity of the gallery; the show spreads into several local studios, too. Aldgate East tube.

Commercial galleries

The galleries listed below are at the hub of London's modern art market. Most are open Monday to Friday 10am to 6pm, plus a few hours on Saturday morning, and many are closed throughout August, but you'd be best advised to ring to check the latest hours, as rehangings or private viewings often interrupt the normal pattern of business. Some of these places can seem as intimidating as designer clothes shops, but at least they're all are free.

Galleries

Galleries

Below is a list of London's principal permanent art collections, with a brief summary of their strengths and, where relevant, a cross-reference to the page of the guide where you'll find more detailed coverage.

British Museum, Great Russell St, WC1 ☎020/7636 1555; *www .thebritishmuseum.ac.uk*. The BM owns a stupendous collection of drawings and prints, part of which is always on show in room 90; it also has excellent one-off exhibitions, sometimes with free entry. Russell Square or Tottenham Court Road tube. See p.161.

Courtauld Institute, Somerset House, The Strand, WC2 ☎020/7873 2526; *www.courtald.ac.uk*. Excellent collection of Impressionists and Post-Impressionists. Covent Garden or Temple (Mon–Sat only) tube. See p.196.

Dalí Universe, Riverside Building, County Hall, SE1 ☎020/7620 2420; *www.daliuniverse.com*. Permanent collection of works by Dalí, mostly little-known bronzes and illustrated books, but there are one or two classics. See p.305.

Dulwich Picture Gallery, College Rd, SE21 ☎020/8693 8000; *www .dulwichpicturegallery.org.uk*. London's oldest public art gallery has recently been refurbished, and houses a small but high-quality selection, with notable work from Poussin and Gainsborough to Rembrandt. West Dulwich train station from Victoria. See p.426.

Estorick Collection, 39a Canonbury Square, N1 ☎020/7704 9522; *www .estorickcollection.com*. Georgian

mansion with a small but interesting collection of twentieth-century Italian art, including Modigliani, di Chirico and the Futurists. Highbury and Islington tube. See p.398.

Guildhall Art Gallery, Gresham St, EC2 ☎020/7332 1632; *collage.nhil.com*. New purpose-built gallery housing the Corporation of London's collection, which contains one or two exceptional Pre-Raphaelite works by the likes of Rossetti and Holman Hunt. Bank or St Paul's tube. See p.241.

Iveagh Bequest, Kenwood House, Hampstead Lane, NW3 ☎020/8348 1286. Stately home overlooking Hampstead Heath that's best known for its pictures by Rembrandt, Gainsborough, Reynolds and Vermeer. Free entry. Bus #210 from Archway tube, or walk from Hampstead or Archway tube. See p.408.

Leighton House, 12 Holland Park Rd, W14 ☎020/7602 3316. The house itself is a work of art, but it also contains several works from Leighton himself and his Pre-Raphaelite chums. Free entry. High Street Kensington tube. See p.364.

Lothbury, 41 Lothbury, EC2 ☎020/7762 1642. Changing exhibitions from NatWest Bank's vast art collection, which is especially strong on twentieth-century British art. Free entry. Bank tube. See p.244.

Annely Juda, 4th Floor, 23 Dering St, W1 ☎020/7629 7578; *www.annelyjudafineart .co.uk*. One of the city's best modernist galleries, specializing in early twentieth-century avant-garde works, but equally strong on contemporary painting and sculpture. Oxford Circus or Bond Street tube.

Anthony d'Offay, 9, 21, 23 & 24 Dering St, W1 ☎020/7499 4100; *www.doffay.com*.

Several galleries on Dering Street, and a new one round the corner in the delightfully named Haunch of Venison Yard, all run by one of the real powerbrokers in the world of art politics. Works exhibited here range from recently dead greats to Pop Art and pieces by leading contemporary artists such as Rachel Whiteread. Oxford Circus or Bond Street tube.

National Gallery, Trafalgar Square, WC2 ☎ 020/7839 3321; *www .nationalgallery.org.uk*. The country's premier collection; it's difficult to think of a major artist born between 1300 and 1850 who isn't on show here. Charing Cross or Leicester Square tube. See p.53.

National Portrait Gallery, 2 St Martin's Place, WC2 ☎ 020/7306 0055; *www.npg.org.uk*. Interesting faces, but few works of art of a quality to match those on display in the neighbouring National Gallery, despite the NPG's snazzy redevelopment. Free entry. Leicester Square or Charing Cross tube. See p.65.

Queen's Gallery, Buckingham Palace, Buckingham Palace Rd, SW1 ☎ 020/7839 1377. Frequently changing displays from the royal hoard of old masters (not due to reopen until spring 2002). St James's Park or Victoria tube. See p.73.

Saatchi Gallery, 98a Boundary Rd, NW8 ☎ 020/7624 8299. First-rate exhibition space owned by Charles Saatchi, the Mr Big of Britain's art (and advertising) world. Shows change two or three times a year, and a couple of Saatchi's youngsters always hit the headlines straight after the opening. Thurs–Sun noon–6pm; £5. Kilburn High Road tube.

Tate Britain, Millbank, SW1 ☎ 020/7887 8000; *www.tate.org.uk*. The old Tate is now devoted to British art from the sixteenth century onwards (the British tag is fairly loosely applied), with several galleries permanently given over to Turner. Free entry. Pimlico tube. See p.96.

Tate Modern, Bankside, SE1 ☎ 020 /7887 8000; *www.tate.org.uk*. Housed in a spectacularly converted power station on the South Bank, the new Tate is the largest modern art gallery in the world, and displays the cream of the gallery's international modern art collection. Free entry. Southwark tube. See p.311.

Victoria and Albert Museum, Cromwell Rd, SW7 ☎ 020/7942 2000; *www.vam.ac.uk*. The city's principal applied arts museum boasts a scattering of European painting and sculpture, a fine collection of English statuary, two remarkable collections of casts, Raphael's famous tapestry cartoons, works by Constable, Turner and Rodin and a photography gallery. South Kensington tube. See p.346.

Wallace Collection, Hertford House, Manchester Square, W1 ☎ 020/7935 0687; *www.wallace-collection.org.uk*. A country mansion just off Oxford Street, with a small, eclectic collection; fine paintings by Rembrandt, Velázquez, Hals, Gainsborough and Delacroix. Free entry. Bond Street tube. See p.128.

William Morris Gallery, Forest Rd, E17 ☎ 020/8527 3782; *www.lbwf.gov .uk/wmg*. Covers every aspect of Morris & Co's work, and there's a small gallery of Pre-Raphaelite works by Morris and his colleagues upstairs. Walthamstow Central tube. See p.420.

Galleries

BCA (Boukamel Contemporary Art), 9 Cork St, W1 ☎ 020/7734 6444; *www .bca-gallery.com*. Exceptional work by figurative painters and sculptors, with a pan-European scope. Green Park tube.

Entwistle, 6 Cork St, W1 ☎ 020/7734 6440. Box-like space often featuring small shows by major figures in the British and American art scenes. Green Park tube.

Flowers East, 199–205 & 282 Richmond Rd, E8 ☎ 020/8985 3333; *www .flowerseast.com*. This outstanding, ever-expanding East End gallery shows a huge variety of work, generally by young British artists. London Fields train station from Liverpool Street.

Galleries

Frith Street, 59–60 Frith St, W1 ☎020/7494 1550; www.frithstreetgallery .co.uk. Good shows are held six times a year in this fine old Soho building. Tottenham Court Road tube.

Helly Nahmad, 2 Cork St, W1 ☎020/7494 3200. A gallery where you're guaranteed to glimpse some very expensive works by very famous artists, from Monet to Picasso. Green Park tube.

Lisson, 67 Lisson St & 52–54 Bell St, NW1 ☎020/7724 273; www.lisson.co .uk. An extremely important gallery whose regularly exhibited sculptors – among them Anish Kapoor and Richard Deacon – are hugely respected on the international circuit. Edgware Road tube.

Marlborough Fine Art, 6 Albemarle St, W1 ☎020/7629 5161; www .marlboroughfineart.com. This is where you'll find the latest work of many of Britain's most celebrated artists, many in one-person shows. Essential viewing for anyone interested in modern British art. Green Park tube.

Paton, 282 Richmond Rd, E8 ☎020/8986 3409. Relocated from the ruinously expensive West End site he occupied for years, Graham Paton now has far more space in which to display his bright young (generally figurative) artists. London Fields train station from Liverpool Street.

Sadie Coles HQ, 35 Heddon St, W1 ☎020/7434 2227; www.sadiecoles.com. New work is displayed in Hoxton House, 34 Hoxton St, N1 (Old Street tube). Sadie Coles's artists include Sarah Lucas, Jim Lambie and Nicola Tyson. Green Park tube.

Victoria Miro, 21 Cork St, W1 ☎020/7734 5082. Spartan gallery with a penchant for minimalist abstraction, with the likes of Chris Ofili and Andreas Gursky in the stable. Has a second gallery in – where else? – Hoxton (16–18 Wharf Rd, N1; Old Street tube). Green Park tube.

Waddington's, 11, 12 & 34 Cork St, W1 ☎020/7437 8611; www.waddington-galleries.com. No. 11 is the largest of three Cork Street premises owned by Leslie Waddington, and tends to concentrate on the established greats of the twentieth century. At the others you'll find newer international stars and younger upcoming artists, whose fame will probably spread beyond these shores now that Waddington is backing them. Green Park tube.

White Cube, 44 Duke St, W1 ☎020/7930 5373; www.whitecube.com. A gallery that likes to grab the headlines, representing folk like Damien Hirst, Tracey Emin and various other Turner Prize artists display here. The second gallery, White Cube2, is in trendy Hoxton (48 Hoxton Square, N1; Old Street tube). Green Park tube.

Photography

The Barbican and the Hayward both host photographic exhibitions from time to time. The galleries listed below are places you can guarantee will always have photos on show. Apart from at the V&A, entry is free.

Hamilton's, 13 Carlos Place, W1 ☎020/7499 9493; www .hamiltonsgallery.com. Classy Mayfair exhibition space for the most famous and fashionable contemporary photographers. Loads of pricey prints for sale as well. Bond Street or Green Park tube.

The Lux Centre, 2–4 Hoxton Square, N1 ☎020/7684 2785; www.lux.org.uk. Housed above the Lux arts cinema foyer, this new photography space stages challenging new photo and video work. Old Street tube.

National Portrait Gallery, 2 St Martin's Place, WC2 ☎020/7306 0055; www.npg .org.uk. The NPG has lots of exceptional photos in its collection, with a fair sampling on permanent display; it also regularly holds special (fee-charging) exhibitions on internationally famous photo-portraitists. Leicester Square or Charing Cross tube.

Photofusion, 17a Electric Lane, SW9 ☎020/7738 5774; www.photofusion .org. Community-based photo co-op, situated in the heart of Brixton, that concentrates on social documentary. Brixton tube.

Photographers' Gallery, 5 & 8 Great Newport St, WC2 ☎020/7831 1772; *www.photonet.org.uk*. The capital's premier photography gallery shows work by new and established British and international photographers, often with a couple of exhibitions running concurrently. The prints are often for sale. Leicester Square tube.

Special Photographers Company, 21 Kensington Park Rd, W11 ☎020/7221 3489; *www.specialphotographers.com*. Great Notting Hill gallery that shows a whole range of stuff, from abstract and landscape to social documentary. Notting Hill Gate tube.

Victoria and Albert Museum, Cromwell Road, SW7 ☎020/7942 2000; *www .vam.ac.uk*. The V&A now has a permanent gallery devoted to photography, but it's way too small to do justice to its vast collection. There's an admission charge for the museum. South Kensington tube.

Zelda Cheatle, 99 Mount St, W1 ☎020/7408 4448. A good little gallery with shows by names and unknowns alike; specially strong on documentary and landscape work. Green Park tube.

Galleries

Chapter 23

Shops and markets

Whether it's time or money you've got to burn, London is one big **shopper's playground**. And although chains and superstores predominate along the high streets, you're still never too far from the kind of oddball, one-off establishment that makes shopping an adventure rather than a routine. As befits a city of villages, London's **shopping districts** all have their own particular style and flavour, with some known for their specialisms and others simply for their geography. From the folie de grandeur that is Harrods to the frantic street markets of the East End, there's probably nothing you can't find in some corner of the capital. A full flavour and history of the main shopping districts can be found in earlier chapters, but the brief taster below should help you plan your bag-carrying expeditions. In the sections which follow, we've listed shops according to what they sell.

Where to shop

In the centre of town, **Oxford Street** is the city's frantic chain-store mecca, and, together with **Regent Street**, offers pretty much every mainstream clothing label you could wish for. Just off Oxford Street you can find pricier designer outlets in **St Christopher's Place** and **South Molton Street**, and even pricier designers and jewellers on the very chic **Bond Street**.

Tottenham Court Road is the place to go for hi-fi, computers, electrical goods and, further along, furniture and

design shops. **Charing Cross Road** is the centre of London's book trade, both new and second-hand. At its north end, and particularly on **Denmark Street** (known as **Tin Pan Alley**, and once the heart of Britain's music industry), you can find music shops selling everything from instruments to sound equipment and sheet music. On the other side of **Charing Cross Road** and stretching down to Piccadilly, **Soho** offers an offbeat mix of sex boutiques, specialist record shops and fabric stores, while the streets surrounding **Covent Garden** yield art and design shops, mainstream fashion chains, designer wear and camping gear.

Just off Piccadilly, **St James's** is the natural habitat of the quintessential English gentleman, with **Jermyn Street** in particular harbouring shops dedicated to his grooming. **Knightsbridge**, further west, is home to Harrods, and the big-name fashion stores of **Sloane Street** and **Brompton Road**.

Less central and well-trodden, there are a few idiosyncratic shopping streets and areas not mentioned elsewhere which are worth a detour just to sample the flavour. **Hampstead**, in a luxurious and leafy world of its own, is a great place to spend an afternoon browsing. Just about every upmarket clothing chain has an outlet here, as do designers like Nicole Farhi and Agnès B. Weaving in and out of the fashion stores are deliciously posh delicatessens and patisseries, antiquarian booksellers and shops stocking tasteful accessories, interior fripperies and the like.

Marylebone High Street is a similar story in the middle of town: a pretty village oasis where you can get all your label gear, treats and gifts away from the bustle and in one gentle amble.

South of the river, a stroll along the South Bank east of the National Theatre will bring you to the pleasant craft market of **Gabriel's Wharf** and the cutting-edge design shops of the **OXO Tower**. Less well known, and just a stone's throw from the ugly bustle of Waterloo, **Lower Marsh** harbours a fantastic variety of one-off shops, studios and cafés on either side of the daily local street market, with retro clothes, collectors' records, organic food and designer jewellery rubbing happily along with the fruit and veg, cheap jumpers and greasy-spoon cafes. The essential vintage memorabilia store Radio Days is here, next door to a funky fetish parlour and not far from the off-beat fashion and cultish ephemera of the Last Chance Saloon.

When to shop

Opening hours for central London shops are generally Monday to Saturday 9.30am to 6pm, although some stores stay open later, especially on Thursdays and in the weeks leading up to Christmas. Many shops now also open on Sundays, although opening hours tend to be shorter, from around noon to 5pm. If in doubt, it's wise to phone ahead to check.

The cheapest time to shop in London is during one of the two big annual **sale seasons**, centred on January and July, when prices are routinely slashed by anything between twenty and fifty per cent. In addition, some shops offer one-off discount events throughout the year: the best place to find details of these is in *Time Out*'s "Sell Out" section.

How to pay

Credit cards are almost universally accepted by shops (notable exceptions are Marks & Spencer and John Lewis,

Shops and markets

although both accept certain debit cards), and department stores and chain stores often run their own credit schemes as well. Travellers' cheques, whether in sterling or other currency, are rarely accepted; change them into local currency before hitting the shops. Market stalls tend to take cash only, or personal cheques (supported by a guarantee card) for more expensive items. Always keep your receipts: whatever the shop may tell you, the law allows a full refund or replacement on purchases which turn out to be faulty. There's no such legal protection if you just decide you don't like something, but most retailers will offer a credit note.

Finally, non-UK visitors can sometimes claim back the value added tax (VAT) that applies to most goods sold in British shops, although you will need to spend well over £100 for this to be worthwhile. On request, participating stores will issue you with a form which you should hand in to Customs on your way out of the country. There's a six-week wait for reimbursement.

Clothes and shoes

The listings below concentrate on the home-grown rather than the ubiquitous international names, but if it's **designer wear** you're after, bear in mind that nearly all the department stores listed on p.596 now stock lines from both major and up-and-coming names. For designer-style fashion at lower prices, try the more upmarket high-street **chain**

Shops and markets

DEPARTMENT STORES

Although all of London's **department stores** offer a huge range of high-quality goods under one roof, most specialize in fashion and food. Many of them are worth visiting just to admire the scale, architecture and interior design, and most have cafés or restaurants on one floor or another.

Fortnum & Mason, 181 Piccadilly, W1 ☎ 020/7734 8040; *www fortnumandmason.com*. This beautiful and eccentric store features heavenly ceiling murals, gilded cherubs, chandeliers and fountains as a backdrop to its perfectly English offerings. Justly famous for its fabulous, gorgeously presented and pricey food, it also specializes in the best and most upmarket designer clothes, furniture and stationery. Green Park or Piccadilly Circus tube.

Harrods, Knightsbridge, SW1 ☎ 020/7730 1234; *www.harrods.com*. Put an afternoon aside to visit this enduring landmark of quirks and pretensions – but don't wear jeans, a vest or a backpack, or you may fail the bizarre dress code. Harrods has everything, but is most notable for its fantastic Art Nouveau tiled food hall, the obscenely huge toy department and its extensive range of designer labels. Knightsbridge tube.

Harvey Nichols, 109–125 Knightsbridge, SW1 ☎ 020/7235 5000. Absolutely fabulous, darling, with all the latest designer collections on the scarily fashionable first floor, where even the shop assistants look like catwalk models. The cosmetics department is equally essential, and frequented by the famous and aspiring alike while the food hall offers irresistibly frivolous goodies at high prices. Knightsbridge tube.

John Lewis, 278–306 Oxford St, W1 ☎ 020/7629 7711; *www.johnlewis.co .uk*. Famous for being "never knowingly undersold", this reliable institution can't be beaten for basics. Every kind of

button, every kind of stocking, every kind of pen and rug can be found here, along with reasonably priced and well-made clothes, furniture and household goods. The staff are knowledgeable and friendly, too. Oxford Circus tube.

Liberty, 210–220 Regent St, W1 ☎ 020/7734 1234; *www.liberty-of-london.com*. A fabulous emporium of luxury, this exquisite store, with its mock-Tudor exterior and tastefully polished interior, is most famous for its fabrics, design and accessories, but is also building an excellent reputation for both mainstream and new fashion. The perfume, cosmetics and household departments are also commendable. Oxford Circus tube.

Marks & Spencer, 458 Oxford St, W1 ☎ 020/7935 7954; *www.marks-and-spencer.com*. The flagship store of this everyday British institution offers a huge range of own-brand clothes, food, homeware and furnishings. The underwear is essential (and the selection here is far larger than at local branches), the ready-made meals good value, and the clothes well made and reliable. Marble Arch tube.

Selfridge's, 400 Oxford Street, W1 ☎ 020/7 629 1234; *www.selfridges .co.uk*. This huge, airy mecca of clothes, food and furnishings was London's first great department store and remains one of its best. The menswear department is more fashion-conscious than that of its contemporaries, and the womenswear floor offers mainstream designers and casual lines alongside hipper, younger names and labels. The food hall is impressive, too. Bond Street tube.

stores: there are branches of Gap, French Connection, Karen Millen, Jigsaw, Monsoon, Kookai, Warehouse, Hobbs,

Whistles and Next all over the capital. Marks & Spencer and BHS are a good bet for even cheaper versions of the same styles. For street, clubwear, second-hand and vintage gear, London's **markets** (see p.610) also have plenty to offer.

Designer

Amazon, 1–22 Kensington Church St, W8 ☎020/7937 4692. With several sites close together, Amazon's busy outlets offer both designer and quality brand-name gear at huge discounts, with one store stocking a great range of strictly designer labels. A must if you want to look the part but don't have the budget to suit. High Street Kensington tube.

Browns, 23–27 South Molton St, W1 ☎020/7514 0016. London's biggest, range of designer wear, with big international names under the same roof as the hip young things, and catering equally well for women and men. Browns' Labels for Less, at 50 South Molton St, W1 (☎020/7514 0052) could save you precious pennies. Bond Street tube.

Burberry, 165 Regent St, W1 ☎020/7734 4060. The quintessential British outdoors label has relaunched itself as a fashion essential, with its classic trenchcoat now available in silk – rather less waterproof, but obviously a must-have. Get the traditional stock at a huge discount from Burberry's Factory Shop (29–53 Chatham Place, E9 ☎020/8985 3344 Hackney Central train from Liverpool Street). Oxford Circus or Piccadilly tube.

Christa Davies, 35 All Saints Rd, W11 ☎020/7727 1998. Imaginative, unique and often recycled one-off separates, with lots of cashmere, chiffon and crêpe. Ladbroke Grove or Westbourne Park tube.

Ghost, 36 Ledbury Rd, W11 ☎020/7229 1057; www.ghost.co.uk. Romantic, floaty and hugely popular modern Victoriana in pastel shades. If you ever regretted chucking out your mum's dirndl skirt, this is where to replace it. Notting Hill Gate tube.

Jean Paul Gaultier, Galerie Gaultier, 171–175 Draycott Ave, SW3 ☎020/7584 4648. Silly, outrageous, extravagant and fun, JPG's designs continue to raise a smile among those who can afford them and those who just like to watch. Here you can get the mid-price (which still doesn't mean cheap) range, too. South Kensington tube.

Jones, 13 & 15 Floral St, WC2 ☎020/7240 8312. Formal, casual and street-style menswear from all the big names and some of the smaller ones, as well as sharp tailoring, jeans and everything in between. Covent Garden tube.

Joseph, 23 Old Bond St, W1 ☎020/7629 3713 and many other branches. Classic cuts in imaginative styles, and the only place to go for perfect trousers for both men and women. The Joseph Sale Shop at 23 Avery Row, SW3; ☎010/7730 7562 (Sloane Square tube) offers good discounts on womenswear. Bond Street tube.

Katharine Hamnett, 20 Sloane St, SW1 ☎020/7823 1002. The only slogans you'll find on Hamnett's T-shirts these days are in diamanté. Lots of denim, prints, sequins and accessories. Knightsbridge tube.

Koh Samui, 65 Monmouth St, WC2 ☎020/7240 4280. The leading promoter of young British designers, this one-stop boutique offers a highly selective range of womenswear with an elegant, eclectic and urban feel. Leicester Square or Covent Garden tube.

Nicole Farhi, 158 New Bond St, W1 ☎020/7499 8368. Classic designs and cuts for women, invariably in the shades of a chameleon resting on a sandy rock, but no less elegant and popular for that. Bond Street tube.

Paul Smith, Westbourne House, 122 Kensington Park Rd, W11 ☎020/7727 3553 (Notting Hill Gate tube); and 40–44 Floral St, WC2 ☎020/7379 7133 (Covent Garden tube); www.paulsmith .co.uk. The Covent Garden store is more accessible, but the Notting Hill shop-in-a-house is worth a visit: ever so English in Smith's quirky way, and selling the whole range of his well-tailored clothes

Shops and markets

Shops and markets

for men, women and children. The Smith Sale Shop, at 53 Avery Row, W1 ☎020/7493 1287 (Bond Street tube) offers huge discounts.

Vivienne Westwood, 6 Davies St, W1 ☎020/7629 3757. Revered by the international fashion pack, this quintessentially English maverick is still going strong. The historic World's End branch, at 430 King's Rd, SW10 ☎020/7352 6551 (Sloane Square tube) is the best place to pick up her famous print jeans. Bond Street tube.

Street & clubwear

AdHoc/Boy, 10–11 Moor St, W1 ☎020/7287 0911. Party gear for exhibitionists: plenty of PVC, lycra, feathers and spangles, with fairy wings and magic wands to set your basics off nicely. There's a body-piercing studio downstairs. Leicester Square tube.

Burro, 19a Floral St, WC2 ☎020/7240 5120. Funky but with an air of studied nonchalance, this is for boys who really want to look cool but don't want to admit it. Covent Garden tube.

Cyberdog, 9 Earlham St, WC2 ☎020/7836 7855. Club ambience for club gear. Funky T-shirts, combat-style ski pants and glowing accessories like UV chokers to show you the way home. Covent Garden tube.

Diesel, 43 Earlham St, WC2 (☎020/7497 5543), and 24 Carnaby St, W1 (☎04688 06827); www.diesel.com. Still cool despite the hype, this trippy, industrial-looking store for label-conscious men and women continues to offer the retro-denim look in a dazzling variety of colours and styles. Covent Garden tube.

Dockers, Unit 8, North Piazza, Covent Garden Market, WC2 ☎020/7240 7908. Butch, fashionable American-style workwear for both sexes, featuring basic khakis, a range of heavy-duty, technologically enhanced fabrics and classic white T-shirts and vests. Covent Garden tube.

Duffer of St George, 29 Shorts Gardens, WC2 ☎20/7379 4660. Covent Garden

tube. Covetable own-label boys' casuals and streetwear, plus a range of other hip labels in the land of jeans, shoes, jackets and so on.

Home, 28a Floral St, WC2 ☎020 /7240 7077; www.paulfrankisyourfriend .com. The silly, cheeky monkey you've seen featured on some of the capital's cooler streetwear accessories originated here. Jeans, shirts, trainers, shoes, bags, wallets and hats make up a one-stop style combo. Covent Garden tube.

Mambo, 2–3 Thomas Neal Centre, 37 Earlham St, WC2 ☎020/7379 6066; www.mambo.com.au. Surf, skate and graffiti gear, including a range of books, mugs and hats. Covent Garden tube.

Vintage, retro & second-hand

Annie's Vintage Costume & Textiles, 10 Camden Passage, N1 ☎020/7359 0796. A tiny and well-stocked shop, draped in shimmering fabrics and specializing in fabulous pre-war glamour, from party dresses to handmade shoes or suitcases. Angel tube.

The Emporium, 330–332 Creek Rd, SE10 ☎020/7305 1670. Elegant retro store specializing in 1940s to 1960s clothes for men and women, and featuring kitsch and well-preserved bras, stockings, compacts and cigarette-holders in its beautiful glass-fronted cases. You can find well-kept bargains here for a tenner, or pay as much as you dare for that must-have tailored gent's suit. Greenwich tube and train.

Humana, 128 Uxbridge Rd, W12 ☎020/8740 0140. Retro chic is in abundance at this well-organized and friendly charity shop. You could easily get yourself a whole funky new wardrobe here for £20. Shepherd's Bush tube.

Modern Age Vintage Clothing, 65 Chalk Farm Rd, NW1 ☎020/7482 3787. Splendid clobber (mostly menswear) for lovers of 1940s and 1950s American-style gear. The best bargains are on the rails outside: inside, the very lovely cashmere and leather coats are a bit pricier. Chalk Farm tube.

162 Holloway Road, 162 Holloway Rd, N7 ☎ 020/7700 2354. Cheap, enormous and unmissable if your idea of heaven is American-style jeans, shirts, frocks, army surplus, sportswear or shoes for less than a fiver. Holloway Road tube.

Oxfam Originals, 26 Ganton St, W1 ☎ 020/7437 7338. Oxfam's well-kept retro branch offers cleaned-up clothes which appeal to hip, clubby bargain-hunters. There's another branch at 22 Earlham St, WC2 (☎ 020/7836 9666; Covent Garden tube). Oxford Circus tube.

Uniform & surplus

Laurence Corner, 62–64 Hampstead Rd, NW1 ☎ 020/7813 1010. London's oldest and most eccentric army surplus shop, which also stocks catering uniforms, thermals, military greatcoats, heavy-duty waterproofs and many kinds of hats. Upstairs are floors and floors of theatrical costumes for hire, to suit any conceivable fancy dress theme. Warren Street tube.

Surplus UK, 32 Chapel Market, N1 ☎ 020/7833 4805. Huge and to the point, this is *the* place to get your combats, boots and camping gear, with stock from every army anywhere. Angel tube.

Underwear

Agent Provocateur, 6 Broadwick St, W1 ☎ 020/7439 0229 (Oxford Circus tube), and 16 Pont St, SW1 ☎ 020/7235 0229 (Knightsbridge tube); *www .agentprovocateur.com*. Essential for any girl with an interest in the kitsch, sexy and glamorous. Offering a beautifully displayed range of lingerie and shoes, this is the only place to get the leopardskin-print bra and panties you've always wanted, or those Hollywood-style fluffy mules with the marabou trim.

Design Also, 101 St Paul's Rd, N1 ☎ 020/7354 0035. Lingerie, hosiery and corsetry galore, not to mention hats and accessories to die for, are all packed into this wonderful one-woman Islington enterprise. Owner Yvonne Lyddon can tell you your correct bra size before you're

even entered the shop, and offers an excellent fitting service. Highbury & Islington tube.

Knickerbox, 219 Oxford St, W1 ☎ 020/7734 4395, and many other branches. Whether it's plain, good-quality vests and pants or frilly nightwear you're after, Knickerbox has something for everyone, all at sensible prices. Particularly good on small sizes. Oxford Circus tube.

La Senza, 162 Oxford St, W1 ☎ 020/7580 3559, and many other branches; *www.lasenza.com*. Lingerie and swimwear in up-to-the-minute styles, from the practical to the gorgeous, available in every shape, size and colour. Oxford Circus tube.

Sh!, 39 Coronet St, N1 ☎ 020/7613 5458; *www.sh-womenstore.com*. The only women's sex boutique in London is always a good day out, offering the full range of fun and fantasy lingerie frills, from open-plan silk panties to more hardcore leather and PVC gear. Men welcome with female accompaniment. Old Street tube.

Shoes

Birkenstock, 37 Neal St, WC2 ☎ 020/7240 2783. Comfortable, classic sandals and shoes in leather, suede, nubuk and vegan styles. Covent Garden tube.

Buffalo Boots, 47–49 Neal St, WC2 ☎ 020/7379 1051; *www.buffalo-boots .com*. Everything from the practical to the clubby via spike-heeled boots and platform shoes. Covent Garden tube.

Dr Marten Department Store, 1–4 King St, WC2 ☎ 020/7497 1460. Five floors to bounce around on in those famous air-cushioned soles, stocking every kind of Dr Marten for every kind of Doc-lover, from traditional black and oxblood to metallic, pastel and playground colours. Covent Garden tube.

Holt's Footwear, 5 Kentish Town Rd, NW1 ☎ 020/7485 8505. Small, old-fashioned but essential shoe shop with a devoutly unfashionable window

Shops and markets

Shops and markets

display featuring every kind of sensible shoe, and all of them at sensible prices. Camden Town tube.

Natural Shoe Store, 21 Neal St, WC2 ☎020/7836 5254. Well-made, stylish, comfortable and sometimes strange shoes. Good value, although not cheap. Covent Garden tube.

Office, 57 Neal St, WC2 ☎020/7379 1896, and many other branches. Good, broad range of basics, including many own-label creations, at reasonable prices, and some more frivolous fashion moments, too. Covent Garden tube.

Pied à Terre, 31 Old Bond St, W1 ☎020/7629 0686, and many other branches. Elegant but pricey women's footwear, with an interesting combina-tion of classic and modern styles. Green Park tube.

Shellys, 266–270 Regent St, W1 ☎020/7287 0939, and many other branches. Offering pretty much everything from the sensible to the silly and with a good deal in between, this madly busy store has a huge range over several floors and at every price, for both men and women. Oxford Circus tube.

Hairdressers

Haircuts can be a risky business, but the following tried-and-tested suggestions should help eliminate the possibility of bad haircut trauma. Bear in mind that as these are the more central and popular crop spots in town, you're unlikely to get seen on spec: usually you'll need to make an **appointment** a week or so in advance. Unless otherwise stated, all cater for both men and women. Bear in mind that most **barber shops** will also cut women's hair if it's short and simple enough – and for a fraction of the price of a salon cut.

Antenna, 27a Kensington Church St, W8 ☎020/7938 1866. Once patronized by fashion luminaries like Boy George and Jean Paul Gaultier, this still-hip salon continues to specialize in hair extensions as well as offering an all-round cutting and styling service. Cuts from around

£30, extensions from £90. High Street Kensington tube.

Basecuts, 252 Portobello Rd, W11 ☎020/7727 7068. Funky, popular salon with prices starting from £18 for men, £23 for women. All styles, all colours. Ladbroke Grove tube.

Bladerunners, 158 Notting Hill Gate, W11 ☎020/7229 2255. Excellent, well-established Afro/Euro salon offering cuts, colours and extensions for all. Students receive a twenty percent discount with ID. Notting Hill Gate tube.

Fish, 30 D'Arblay St, W1 ☎020/7494 2398. Once a fishmonger's, now a high-fashion hair emporium catering for twenty-something Soho sophisticates. Good-quality cuts, starting from £25 for men and £30 for women. Oxford Circus or Tottenham Court Road tube.

Hair by Fairy, 8–10 Neal's Yard, WC2 ☎020/7497 0776. No appointments necessary in this hip and happening young salon. Cuts will set you back a mere tenner; colour, dreadlocks and extensions (Fairy's speciality) anything up to £200. Covent Garden tube.

John Frieda, 75 New Cavendish St, W1 ☎020/7636 1401, and other branches. Good, classic and stylish cuts from a well-established, well-regarded salon; cuts are around £50. Great Portland Street or Oxford Circus tube.

Lounge, 26 Peter St, W1 ☎020/7437 3877. This stylish multimedia establish-ment, complete with Sony Playstations for your enjoyment, also happens to be a fine salon. £30 for a cut and blow-dry. Piccadilly Circus tube.

Sadlers Wells Barbers Shop, 110 Rosebery Ave, EC1 ☎020/7833 0556. This good, old-fashioned, no-messing barber's will sort you out a good-quality short-back-and-sides, or any variation thereof, for a mere £6.50. Angel tube.

Terry Jacques, 31 The Pavement, SW4 ☎020/7627 4446. Equally good at Afro and Euro styling, this busy and popular salon has won the title of Afro Hairdresser of the Year three times in the ten years since it opened. Cut and blow-dry from £27; extensions from £185. Clapham Common tube.

Toni & Guy, 34 Southampton St, WC2 ☎020/7240 7342, and many other branches. Reputable and fashionable chain offering good-value, manageable cuts from around £35. Covent Garden tube.

Trevor Sorbie, 27 Floral St, WC2 ☎020/7379 6901. Not as pricey as you might imagine: £40 or so will get you a professional and stylish cut from one of this client-oriented salon's highly trained stylists. Covent Garden or Leicester Square tube.

G.F. Trumper, 9 Curzon St, W1 ☎020/7499 1850. Gentlemen's gentlemen offering a Victorian barbershop experience. They'll even teach you how to shave yourself properly. Shampoo and cut from £24. Green Park tube.

Pharmacies and cosmetics

As well as dispensing a large range of over-the-counter drugs and offering everything from photographic developing to ear piercing, London's **pharmacies** are major retailers of **perfumes and cosmetics** – in fact Boots (Britain's main high-street pharmacy chain) accounts for the lion's share of UK cosmetics sales. The big **department stores** – especially Harvey Nichols, Selfridges and Harrods –

also house excellent ranges of perfumes and cosmetics.

Boots the Chemist, 44 Regent St, W1 ☎020/7734 6126, and many other branches. The UK's main high-street supplier of pharmaceuticals, cosmetics, perfumes, toiletries, photographic equipment and often much more. This branch opens until 8pm daily. Piccadilly Circus tube.

The Body Shop, 374 Oxford St, W1 ☎020/7409 7868, and many other branches. One of the first to pioneer and market cruelty-free products, and still going strong after all these years, with new flavours, aromas and raw materials emerging regularly alongside old favourites. The make-up range is good, too. Bond Street tube.

Crabtree & Evelyn, 30 James St, WC2 ☎020/7379 0964. Several branches. The cosmetic equivalent of Laura Ashley: soaps and scents in pretty (and pricey) floral packages, all cruelty-free. Covent Garden tube.

MAC Cosmetics, 109 King's Rd, SW3 ☎020/7349 0601 (Sloane Square tube), and 28 Foubert's Place, W1 ☎020/7534 9222 (Oxford Circus tube). The UK's first professional make-up range, aimed mostly at models, but promoting a nicely subversive take on fashion and beauty, and offering some genuinely excellent products to back up the hype.

Shops and markets

Neal's Yard Remedies, 15 Neal's Yard, WC2 ☎020/7379 7222. Several branches. Fabulously scented, beautifully presented, entirely efficacious herbal cosmetics, toiletries and therapies, plus a whole range of holistic reference books and accessories. Covent Garden tube.

Nelson Pharmacy, 73 Duke St, W1 ☎020/7629 3118. This famous Victorian homeopathic pharmacy dispenses its own reputable range of highly effective lotions and potions for every ailment imaginable, as well as a full range of aromatherapy products, essential oils and Bach flower remedies. Bond Street tube.

Pak Cosmetic Centre, 27 Stroud Green Rd, N4 ☎020/7263 2088; www .afrohairandbeauty.com. All the Afro hair and skincare products you might ever need, plus a huge range of cosmetics, accessories and appliances. Finsbury Park tube or train.

Penhaligon's, 41 Wellington St, WC2 ☎020/7 581 0922 (South Kensington tube), and 16–17 Burlington Arcade, W1 ☎020/7629 1416 (Piccadilly Circus or Green Park tube). Several other branches. Wonderfully traditional old perfumery carrying a great range of colognes, potions and powders – including the famous Penhaligon's Love Potion No. 9. Great for (rather pricey) gifts and special occasions.

Books

As well as the big-name chain bookstores, most of which have branches throughout the city, London is blessed with a wealth of local, independent and specialist bookshops. Listed below are some of the most central, best known or just most interesting.

General interest

Blackwell's, 100 Charing Cross Rd, WC2 ☎020/7292 5100; www.bookshop .blackwell.co.uk. The London flagship of Oxford's best academic bookshop is bigger than it looks and has a much wider range than you might expect. Its

academic stock is unsurprisingly excellent, but so is its range of computing, travel and fiction titles. Tottenham Court Road or Leicester Square tube.

Books Etc, 120 Charing Cross Rd, WC2 ☎020/7379 6838, and many other branches. Large, laid-back and user-friendly, with a wide and well-stocked range of mainstream and specialist titles. Especially good on contemporary fiction. Several branches, including this one, have an on-site coffee shop. Tottenham Court Road tube.

Borders Books & Music, 203–207 Oxford St, W1 ☎020/7292 1600, and other branches; www.borders.com. Enormous London flagship of the American import, boasting four floors of books alongside a huge range of CDs and magazines. Good range of titles, with staff recommendations and reviews, a solid children's section, regular readings and a coffee bar. Oxford Circus or Tottenham Court Road tube.

Foyles, 113–119 Charing Cross Rd, WC2 ☎020/7437 5660. Endearingly and sometimes irritatingly antiquated, this huge and famous bookshop is best avoided if you're short of time. Pretty much everything you might want is here, but finding it is one adventure and paying for it another. You have to queue twice: once to part with your money, and again to pick up the book. Tottenham Court Road tube.

Waterstone's, 121–123 & 127–129 Charing Cross Rd, WC2 ☎020/7434 4291, and other branches. Neighbouring flagship stores of the huge, quality book chain, with technical and travel titles in the first branch, mostly fiction in the second. Tottenham Court Road tube.

Independent & specialist

Africa Book Centre, Africa Centre, 38 King St, WC2 ☎020/7240 6649; www .africabookcentre.com. Wide variety of African and Caribbean fiction, non-fiction and poetry in a tiny room above the Africa Centre. Covent Garden tube.

Al-hoda, 76–78 Charing Cross Rd, WC2
☎020/7240 8381. Specializing in
Islamic art and culture, with a strong
Arabic section. Leicester Square tube.

**Arthur Probsthain Oriental & African
Bookseller**, 41 Great Russell St, WC1
☎020/7636 1096. Connected to the
nearby School of Oriental and African
Studies, this impressive academic store
covers all relevant aspects of art, history,
science and culture. Tottenham Court
Road tube.

Atlantis Bookshop, 49a Museum St,
WC1 ☎020/7405 2120; *www
.atlantisbookshop.demon.co.uk*. Splendid
occult-oriented place, with the perfect
ambience for browsing through books
and magazines covering spirituality, psy-
chic phenomena, witchcraft and so on.
Tottenham Court Road tube.

Books for Cooks, 4 Blenheim Crescent,
W11 ☎020/7221 1992. Anything and
everything to do with food can be found
on the drooling shelves of this wonderful
new and second-hand, which also has a
tiny café (see p.515) offering cookery
demonstrations, coffee for browsers and
lunch (ring ahead to book). Ladbroke
Grove tube.

Bookmarks, 1 Bloomsbury St, WC1
☎020/7637 1848. Leftist and radical
fare in the heart of Bloomsbury, with a
wide range of political biography, history,
theory and assorted political ephemera.
There's even a children's section.
Tottenham Court Road tube.

European Bookshop, 5 Warwick St, W1
☎020/7734 5259; *www.eurobooks.co
.uk*. An excellent range of European
language books, with helpful staff.
Piccadilly Circus tube.

Forbidden Planet, 71–75 New Oxford St,
WC1 ☎020/7 836 4179. Two
permanently packed floors of all things
science-fiction and fantasy related, ranging from comics and graphic novels to
books, games and ephemera. Tottenham
Court Road tube.

Golden Square Books, 16 Golden
Square, W1 ☎020/7434 3337. World
religions, spirituality, healing, philosophy

and mythology over two floors, with
dedicated and knowledgeable staff.
Piccadilly Circus tube.

Gosh!, 39 Great Russell St, WC1
☎020/7636 1011. All kinds of comics
for all kinds of readers, whether you're
the casually curious or the serious collector. Check out the Cartoon Gallery in
the basement. Tottenham Court Road
tube.

Helter Skelter, 4 Denmark St, WC2
☎020/7836 1151; *www.skelter.demon
.co.uk*. Every kind of music book, but
especially strong on rock history and
biogs. Plenty of printed ephemera, too.
Tottenham Court Road tube.

Housmans, 5 Caledonian Rd, N1
☎020/7837 4473. Old, dilapidated and
friendly store specializing in black, lesbian and gay fiction, plus socialism,
anarchism and ecology. A good second-
hand basement lurks at the bottom of
creaky, dusty stairs. King's Cross tube.

ICA Bookshop, Nash House, The Mall,
SW1 ☎020/7925 2434. Worth a visit
whether you're exploring the rest of the
ICA's offerings or not. Hip and artsy, with
a strong style bent and lots of funky
zines, postcards and book imports.
Piccadilly Circus or Charing Cross tube.

Index Bookcentre, 10–12 Atlantic Rd,
SW9 ☎020/7274 8342. Small but
packed and friendly bookseller with
some general stock, but specializing in a
good range of black-oriented fiction and
non-fiction. Brixton tube.

Intermediate Technology Bookshop,
103–105 Southampton Row, WC1
☎020/7436 9761; *www.oneworld.org
/itdg/publications.html*. Everything connected with Third World issues, from
agriculture to health care and beyond,
plus a small selection of gifts and crafts.
Russell Square tube.

Murder One, 71–73 Charing Cross Rd,
WC2 ☎020/7734 3485. As you'd
expect: crime fiction galore, from the
traditional murder mystery to modern
urban noir, with the odd foray into other
genres. Tottenham Court Road tube.

Shops and markets

*Lesbian- and
gay-oriented
bookshops are
listed in the
box on p.570.*

Shops and markets

Offstage Theatre & Cinema Bookshop, 37 Chalk Farm Rd, NW1 ☎020/7485 4996. Excellent, well-stocked shop covering all aspects of stage and screen craft, plus theory, criticism, scripts and biographies. Camden Town or Chalk Farm tube.

Politico's, 8 Artillery Row, SW1 ☎020/7828 0010; *www.politicos.co.uk*. Mainstream political fare, both new and second-hand, with plenty of big biographies. A cosy café, board games and irreverent window displays give it a more frivolous edge. St James's Park tube.

Souls of Black Folks, 407 Coldharbour Lane, SW9 ☎020/7738 4141. Dedicated black bookshop specializing in African, Caribbean and African-American literature, with regular readings, a buzzing café and late opening hours. Brixton tube.

Stanford's Map and Travel Bookshop, 12–14 Long Acre, WC2 ☎020/7836 1321. The world's largest specialist travel bookshop, this features pretty much any map of anywhere, plus a huge range of books and guides. Leicester Square or Charing Cross tube.

Waterstone's Arts Bookshop, 8 Long Acre, WC2 ☎020/7836 1359. The future of this excellent store, covering all aspects of the graphic and fine arts, media and music, is currently in doubt, despite holding the best selection of its kind in central London. Leicester Square or Covent Garden tube.

Zwemmer Media Arts, 80 Charing Cross Rd, WC2 ☎020/7240 4157, and other branches; *www.zwemmer.com*. Specialist art bookstore with a fantastic and expert selection across several neighbouring branches. This branch specializes in film, design and photography. Leicester Square tube.

Second-hand and antiquarian

Any Amount of Books, 56 & 62 Charing Cross Rd, WC2 ☎020/7240 8140; *www .anyamountofbooks.com*. Wonderful, sprawling second-hand bookshop spread over two neighbouring sites and stocking everything from obscure 50p

bargains to rare and expensive first editions. Especially strong on fiction, the arts and literary biography. Leicester Square tube.

Fisher & Sperr, 46 Highgate High St, N6 ☎020/8340 7244. A little out of the way but well worth a visit, this fabulous old building at the top of Highgate Hill is a literary tardis. Several rooms, one entirely dedicated to books about London, plus a few expensive antiquarian jewels and a wide range of titles covering travel, literature, history and philosophy. Archway or Highgate tube.

Magpie Bookshop, 53 Brushfield St, E1 ☎020/7247 4263. Inside Spitalfields Market, this well-stocked, vaguely cultish store has a great stock of London-oriented titles, plus lesbian and gay fiction, occult writings, crime and a whole section on Jack the Ripper. Comics and graphic novels too. Liverpool Street tube.

Skoob Books, 15 Sicilian Ave, WC1 ☎020/7404 3063; *www.skoob.com*. Skoob ("books" backwards) is great for cut-price current and recent academic titles, and also offers an excellent range of modern fiction, poetry, travel and more. Staff are friendly and expert, and the atmosphere bookishly hectic. Students get a ten percent discount. Holborn tube.

Unsworths Booksellers, 12 Bloomsbury St, WC1 ☎020/7436 9836. Good for bargains, including recent and just-out-of-print novels and academic titles. Specializes in the arts and humanities, and features an interesting antiquarian selection. Tottenham Court Road tube.

Woburn Bookshop, 10 Woburn Walk, WC1 ☎020/7388 7278. This eclectic and intriguing bookshop lures you in with bargain stalls outside, and yields even more surprises inside. Chartism, Modernism, Marxism, modern art, fiction, poetry, Caribbean literature and much more besides. Euston or Russell Square tube.

Crafts and design

London has a huge number of young craft designers whose work you can find

Second-hand books are also available at Riverside Walk; see under Markets, p.612.

in shops and workshops all over the capital. There are also hundreds of shops which cater for craft-type hobbies, and plenty of places specializing in unusual gifts or homewares. What follows is a small selection of places to start.

The Bead Shop, 21a Tower St, WC2 ☎020/7240 0931. Every shape and size of bead, in wood, plastic, glass and any other material you can think of, plus wire, accessories and a range of semi-precious stones. Covent Garden tube.

Ceramica Blue, 10 Blenheim Crescent, W11 ☎020/7727 0288; www.ceramica-blue.co.uk. A vast and colourful array of multi-ethnic, hand-painted ceramics, at some surprisingly affordable prices. Ladbroke Grove tube.

Combined Harvest, 128 Talbot Rd, W11 ☎020/7221 4870. Eclectic shop full of work by young designers, with everything from mirrors and bedspreads to ceramics, marquetry and second-hand books. Ladbroke Grove or Notting Hill tube.

Contemporary Ceramics, William Blake House, 7 Marshall St, W1 ☎020/7437 7605. You can get anything and everything by and for ceramicists at this fascinating gallery-cum-shop, which is also the showcase and retail outlet for the Craft Potters' Association. Oxford Circus tube.

The Muse, Unit 71, The Catacombs, Stables Yard, Camden Market, NW1 ☎020/8965 8706. Beautiful, mostly North African artefacts and crafts at hugely discounted prices. Camden Town or Chalk Farm tube.

Neal Street East, 5 Neal St, WC2 ☎020/7240 0135/0136. A huge treasure trove of all things even vaguely oriental, ranging from the cheap and tacky to the expensive and beautiful. Jewellery, clothes, home furnishings, knick-knacks, kitchenware, books, cards and much, much more. Covent Garden or Leicester Square tube.

Eccentricities

The listings below are a small selection of shops which don't really fit into any particular category, or which are just interesting to visit.

Anything Left-Handed, 57 Brewer St, W1 ☎020/7437 3910; www.anythinglefthanded.co.uk. As the name suggest, the place to go for all kinds of left-handed tools, implements and gifts. Piccadilly Circus tube.

The Elvis Shop, 400 High St North, E12 ☎020/8552 7551; www.elvisshop.demon.co.uk. A little off the beaten track, but essential for any serious disciple of the King. Anything and everything to do with Elvis is sold in this majestically obsessive and splendid shop: CDs, vinyl, videos, books, magazines, postcards and international memorabilia, dating from the 1950s right up to yesterday. East Ham tube.

Flying Duck Enterprises, 320–322 Creek Rd, SE10 ☎020/8858 1964. Kitsch aplenty, whether it's tacky 1970s board games, Elvis soap or a full 1950s polka-dotted dinner service; you may get lost in here for some time. Greenwich tube or train, or Island Gardens DLR, then foot tunnel.

Last Chance Saloon, 88 Lower Marsh, SE1 ☎020/7771 7466; www.lastchancesaloon.demon.co.uk. Shop-cum-gallery selling whatever the owners like without regard for regular shopping conventions – you might find twisted T-shirts next to a fine range of Vince Ray knick-knacks, plus lots of erotica, exotica, beat and pulp fiction – in short, punk, junk and the odd bit of art. Waterloo tube.

The Museum Store, 4a–5a Perrin's Court, NW3 ☎020/7431 7156. Not actually attached to any one museum, but featuring a wonderful collection of items from museum shops around the world and well worth a visit. Hampstead tube.

Mysteries, 9–11 Monmouth St, WC2 ☎020/7836 4679. This huge, crowded, lurid and compulsive shop stocks just

Shops and markets

The Crafts Council is an excellent information centre for all matters craft- and design-related. You can find them at 44a Pentonville Rd, N1 ☎020 /7278 7700; www .craftscouncil .org.uk.

Shops and markets

about every occult-related book, magazine, accessory, crystal and piece of ephemera you can imagine, for the serious esoteric shopper as well as the casual browser.

Radio Days, 87 Lower Marsh, SE1 ☎020/7928 0800. A fantastic collection of memorabilia and accessories from the 1930s to the 1970s, including shoes, shot-glass collections, cosmetics and vintage magazines. A huge stock of well-kept ladies' and menswear from the same period fills the back room. Waterloo tube.

G. Smith & Sons, 74 Charing Cross Rd, WC2 ☎020/7836 7422. Exactly what an old English tobacconist's ought to look and smell like. Every variety of tobacco, including some of the shop's own creations, plus a huge range of snuff and a walk-in humidor featuring some very classy cigars. Leicester Square tube.

Food and drink

London is a great place to buy good food. In the centre of town, **Soho and Covent Garden**, in particular, are a gourmand's delight: the former replete with Chinese supermarkets and Italian delicatessens, the latter harbouring **Neal's Yard**, a haven of all that's best in health-conscious nutrition. For more basic requirements, there are numerous **supermarkets** in the high street of nearly every residential area: Safeway, Tesco, Sainsbury and Waitrose are the biggest, with all of them offering a good range of groceries and fresh foods, plus an increasingly impressive selection of upmarket gourmet fare. **Marks & Spencer** food halls are also an excellent source of both fresh foods and good-quality ready-meals. But although the supermarkets are hard to beat for convenience, and many now have late (if not 24-hour) opening hours, you still can't beat the satisfaction of food shopping in **specialist stores**, and in London's many local **food markets** (see Markets, p.610).

Bakeries and patisseries

Berwick Street Bread Stall, Berwick St, W1 (no phone). Fresh, good-quality breads at bargain prices, supplied by bakers all over London; Italian breads, bagels and croissants are the speciality. Oxford Circus tube.

Louis of Hampstead, 32 Heath St, NW3 ☎020/7435 9908. This fabulous-looking Hungarian patisserie doesn't seem to have changed much since it opened in 1963. Breads, pastries and creamy European cakes galore, plus a very splendid tearoom in the back of the shop. Hampstead tube.

Cheese

International Cheese Centre, 21 Goodge St, W1 ☎020/7631 4191. Several branches. A huge and frequently changing stock of cheeses from all over Europe and Scandinavia, with an especially good selection of French and English varieties. Goodge Street tube.

Neal's Yard Dairy, 17 Shorts Gardens, WC2 ☎020/7379 7646. Quality British and Irish cheeses, and plenty of them; taste as much as you like before you buy. Covent Garden tube.

Paxton & Whitfield, 93 Jermyn St, SW1 ☎020/7930 0259. Quintessentially English, 200-year-old cheese shop offering a very traditional range of English and European varieties, plus a good range of fine wines and ports. Green Park or Piccadilly tube.

Coffee & tea

Algerian Coffee Stores, 52 Old Compton St, W1 ☎020/7437 2480. Every kind of coffee, every kind of coffee-making apparatus and every kind of coffee connoisseur's accessory, all crammed into this great and abiding Soho institution. Leicester Square tube.

Monmouth Coffee Company, 27 Monmouth St, WC2 ☎020/7836 5272. A wonderful range of coffees, all roasted on the premises, and served up with delicious chocolate-coated coffee beans in the strictly non-smoking sampling room at the back of the shop. Covent Garden or Leicester Square tube.

Confectionery

Charbonnel et Walker, 1 The Royal Arcade, 28 Old Bond St, W1 ☎020/7491 0939. It might sound French, but this is a very English affair, dating from 1875, offering beautifully presented chocolates, truffles and peppermint creams. Green Park or Piccadilly Circus tube.

Godiva, 247 Regent St, W1 ☎020/7495 2845, and many other branches. Upmarket chain offering seriously sexy Belgian chocolates – at a price. Oxford Circus or Piccadilly Circus tube.

Delicatessens

Butlers Wharf Gastrodome, 36d & 36e Shad Thames, SE1 ☎020/7403 4030. This upmarket old warehouse complex, just behind the waterfront, holds both the Oil & Spice Shop, stocking a beautifully presented and mouthwatering range of oils, vinegars and spices, and, next door, the Pont de la Tour, offering an excellent range of deli fare. Tower Hill or London Bridge tube or Tower Gateway DLR.

Villandry, 170 Great Portland St, W1 ☎020/7631 3131. Fresh bread, fruit, veg and fish vie with the groceries for attention in this appealing store. An international range of fare, but with an emphasis on the French. Great Portland Street tube.

Health & organic

Brixton Wholefoods Transatlantic, 59 Atlantic Rd, SW9 ☎020/7737 2210. A splendid institution, offering everything you'd expect from a funky local wholefood store: fresh bread, groceries, organic fruit and veg and a wonderful range of herbs and spices. Brixton tube.

Freshlands, 49 Parkway, NW1 ☎020/7428 7575. Excellent range of fresh organic fruit, veg and wine, plus herbs, spices, fresh breads, organic and vegetarian cheeses, a wild variety of

organic deli-type groceries and basics and a very well-stocked section of cosmetics and herbal medicines. You can get juices, soups and salads to take away or eat in. Camden Town tube.

Chinese

Loon Fung Supermarket, 42–44 Gerrard St, W1 ☎020/7437 7332. This warren of a supermarket in the heart of Chinatown offers every kind of Chinese food item you can imagine, and probably some you can't. You can also find a huge range of foods and groceries in the shops of neighbouring Newport Street, Newport Place and Lisle Street. Piccadilly Circus tube.

Wing Yip, 395 Edgware Rd, NW2 ☎020/8450 0422. A Chinese superstore offering everything you could reasonably wish for under one roof, and all helpfully labelled in English. Kilburn tube.

French

Fileric, 12 Queenstown Rd, SW8 ☎020/7720 4844. A beautiful French food shop without the extravagant prices you might imagine. Oils, preserves, meats, terrines, cheeses and wines, plus dishes to take away. Clapham Common tube.

The House of Albert Roux, 229 Ebury St, SW1 ☎020/7730 4175. This very chichi Gallic enterprise has luxury and extravagance written over every ham, foie gras terrine and marron glacé in the place. Pricey but lovely. Sloane Square tube.

Indian

London Oriental Foods, 122 Drummond St, NW1 ☎020/7387 3740. Excellent Bengali food store in London's most central Asian shopping and eating enclave; check out the rest of the street for more good Indian food stores. Euston or Euston Square tube or train.

Taj Stores, 112 Brick Lane, E1 ☎020/7377 0061. Big South Asian food store offering everything from halal meats and herbs and spices to fish, fruit

Shops and markets

Shops and markets

and vegetables, and all under one roof. Aldgate East tube.

Italian

Fratelli Camisa, 53 Charlotte St, W1 ☎020/7255 1240. Old-style, rather old-fashioned establishment offering a wide and upmarket range of foodstuffs, wines and liqueurs. Goodge Street tube.

I. Camisa & Son, 61 Old Compton St, W1 ☎020/7437 7610. The whole classic Italian deli range packed into one small Soho space. Excellent cheeses, salamis, pastas and dried foods, plus all the essential wines and spirits. Leicester Square tube.

G. Gazzano & Son, 167–169 Farringdon Rd, EC1 ☎020/7837 1586. This fabulous Clerkenwell establishment has been keeping the area in Italian fare for a century, and the old wooden cabinets are still holding up under the weight of all that good-quality food. Farringdon tube or train.

Wine, beer & spirits

The specialist beer, wine and spirits outlets listed below are the pick of central London's numerous retailers, but you'll also find ever-improving ranges in the main **supermarkets**, for whom budget wine is a highly competitive area. Relaxed **licensing laws** mean that outlets no longer have to close between 3pm and 7pm on Sundays, although some – usually local, family-run places – still do.

The Beer Shop, 14 Pitfield St, N1 ☎020/7739 3701. Beers from all over the world in bottles and barrels, and everything you need to make your own. Old Street tube or train.

Berry Bros & Rudd, 3 St James's St, SW1 ☎020/7396 9600. This well-stocked, 300-year-old establishment houses a huge range of fine wines, and the friendly and helpful staff know pretty much everything there is to know on the subject. Green Park tube.

Bibendum, 113 Regent's Park Rd, NW1 ☎020/7916 7706. Splendid, modern

and unstuffy wine emporium with a great global selection. Chalk Farm tube.

Gerry's, 74 Old Compton St, W1 ☎020/7734 4215. The best, most eclectic and sometimes downright weird range of spirits you'll find anywhere in London; vodka is a speciality. Leicester Square tube.

Oddbins, 23 Earlham St, WC2 ☎020/7836 6331, and many other branches. This unswervingly excellent chain offers great wines at good prices, and is especially strong on New World names. There are plenty of good beers too. Staff are enthusiastic, unpretentious and always ready to help. Leicester Square or Covent Garden tube.

The Vintage House, 42 Old Compton St, W1 ☎020/7437 2592. Wines, brandies and more than seven hundred whiskies line the shelves of this family-run drinker's paradise. To add to the pleasure, the staff know their stuff inside out. Leicester Square tube.

Music

There are hundreds of mainstream, independent and specialist **music shops** in London, catering equally well for the CD bulk-buyer and the obsessive rare-vinyl collector. This is a selection of the best and best known. Bear in mind that London's markets, especially Camden, are also good sources of vinyl (see Markets, p.610).

Megastores

HMV, 150 Oxford St, W1 ☎020 /7631 3423; www.hmv.co.uk. All the latest releases, as you'd expect, but also an impressive backlist, a reassuring amount of vinyl and a good classical section downstairs. Dance music is also a strength. Oxford Circus tube.

MDC Classic Music, 437 Strand, WC2 ☎020/7240 2157, and many other branches. Big and brassy, this central chain store has an impressive range of stock, but specializes in special offers and cut-price CDs. Charing Cross or Embankment tube.

Tower Records, 1 Piccadilly Circus, W1
☎020/7439 2500; *www.towerrecords .co.uk*. Fantastic range, although it's not always easy to find what you're looking for, and the genre classifications sometimes seem a little random. Still, everything is here somewhere, and the jazz, folk and world music department upstairs is especially impressive. Piccadilly Circus tube.

Virgin Megastore, 14–16 Oxford St, W1
☎020/7631 1234. The mainstream floor here is better stocked than the specialist sections: the bias is rock-heavy, but there's a little of everything else, and plenty of books, magazines, T-shirts and assorted music ephemera. Tottenham Court Road tube.

Independent & specialist

Caruso & Company, 10 Charlotte Place, W1 ☎020/7636 6622. Comfortable, well-stocked shop specializing in opera, but with much else besides. Goodge Street tube.

Daddy Kool, 12 Berwick St, W1 ☎020 /7494 10181. Lots of collectable reggae vinyl, most of it classic roots and Studio One, but also with some up-to-the-minute ragga and drum'n'bass. Oxford Circus or Tottenham Court Road tube.

Dub Vendor, 274 Lavender Hill, SW11
☎020/7223 3757, and 150 Ladbroke Grove, W10 ☎020/8969 3375 (Ladbroke Grove tube). Essential reggae outlet, with up-to-the-minute imports and good advice. Clapham Junction train from Victoria or Waterloo.

EBL Latin Music Shop, 5a Goodge Place, W1 ☎020/7636 8349. Salsa, rhumba, merengue, and whatever else shakes your Latin tailfeather – it's all here. Except perhaps Ricky Martin. Goodge Street tube.

Gramex, 25 Lower Marsh, SE1
☎020/7401 3830. A splendid find for classical music lovers, this new and second-hand record store features both CDs and vinyl, and offers comfy leather armchairs to sample or discuss your finds at leisure. Waterloo tube.

Honest Jon's, 276 & 278 Portobello Rd, W10 ☎020/8969 9822. Jazz, soul, funk, R&B, rare groove, dance and much more: a DJ essential and a browser's delight, with current releases, second-hand finds and reissues on vinyl and CD. Ladbroke Grove tube.

Mole Jazz, 311 Gray's Inn Rd, WC1
☎020/7278 8623. CDs, vinyl, books and ephemera for the jazz purist, with a good range of recent and classic vinyl and CDs and some nice collector's items. King's Cross tube.

Mr Bongo, 44 Poland St, WC1
☎020/7287 1887; *www.mrbongo.com*. Good on 12" singles, and on hip-hop, jazz, funk, Latin American and Brazilian sounds. Oxford Circus tube.

Ray's Jazz Shop, 180 Shaftesbury Ave, WC2 ☎020/7240 3969. Essential jazz territory, lovingly curated and full of collectors and browsers poring happily over its well-stocked bins. New and old releases on CD, plus an extensive vinyl collection, a good blues basement, some choice world and folk music and expert, helpful staff. Leicester Square or Tottenham Court Road tube.

Rhythm Records, 281 Camden High St, NW1 ☎020/7267 0123. This small, manic shop has a huge range of better- and lesser-known indie CDs upstairs (no vinyl), with staff who know exactly what you're asking for. Downstairs is a calmer affair, with rock, folk, soul and R&B vinyl treasures and a pretty hip selection of jazz CDs. Camden Town tube.

Rough Trade, 130 Talbot Rd, W11
☎020/7229 8541 (Ladbroke Grove or Westbourne Park tube), and 16 Neal's Yard, WC2 ☎020/7240 0105 (Covent Garden tube); *www.roughtrade.com*. Indie specialist with knowledgeable, friendly staff and a dizzying array of wares, from electronica to hardcore and beyond.

Sister Ray, 94 Berwick St, W1 ☎020 /7287 8385; *www.sisterray.co.uk*. Up-to-the minute indie sounds, with lots of electronica and some forays into the

Shops and markets

Shops and markets

current dance scene, most on vinyl as well as CD. Oxford Circus or Piccadilly Circus tube.

Stern's African Record Centre, 293 Euston Rd, NW1 ☎020/7387 5550. World famous for its global specialisms, this expert store has an unrivalled stock of African music and excellent selections from pretty much everywhere else in the world, too. Euston Square tube.

Second-hand

Cheapo Cheapo Records, 53 Rupert St, W1 ☎020/7437 8272. Not everything here is totally cheapo cheapo – but there's a lot that is. CDs, vinyl and most musical tastes catered for. Piccadilly Circus tube.

Music & Video Exchange, 38 Notting Hill Gate, W11 ☎020/7243 8573, and other branches. This enduring, expanding and always busy second-hand and collectors' chain almost always has some unexpected treasure in store. Notting Hill Gate tube.

Reckless Records, 26 & 30 Berwick St, W1 ☎020/7434 3362 or 7437 4271. Neighbouring, famously hip second-hand CD and vinyl emporia in the heart of Soho. Good-quality stock, though not always as cheap as you might hope. Piccadilly Circus tube.

Markets

London's markets are more than just a cheap alternative to high-street shopping: many of them are significant remnants of communities endangered by the heedless expansion of the city. You haven't really got to grips with London unless you've rummaged through the junk at Brick Lane on a Sunday morning, or haggled over a leather jacket at Camden. Do keep an eye out for pickpockets: the weekend market provide them with easy pickings.

Bermondsey (New Caledonian) Market, Bermondsey Square, SE1. Fri 5am–2pm. Huge, unglamorous but highly regarded antique market offering everything from obscure nautical instruments to attractive

but pricey furniture. The real collectors arrive at dawn to pick up the bargains, and you need to get here at least before midday to ensure you don't go home empty handed. Borough or London Bridge tube.

Berwick Street, Berwick St and Rupert St, W1. Mon–Sat 8am–6pm. This famous and chaotic fruit and veg market is a piece of living London history, with ferociously fast vendors working the crowds like showmen. There's fish, cheese and herbs, too, and you can pick up produce for next to nothing after 4pm. You'll also find cheap clothes, tapes and CDs aplenty along neighbouring Rupert Street. Piccadilly Circus tube.

Brick Lane, Brick Lane, Cygnet St, Sclater St, E1; Bacon St, Cheshire St, Chilton St, E2. Sun 8am–1pm. Huge, sprawling, cheap and frenzied, this famous East End market is well worth getting up early for. Fruit and veg, household goods, clothes, antique furniture, scratched records, bicycles and broken spectacles – it's hard to say what you can't find here, and most of it is going for a song. Aldgate East, Shoreditch or Liverpool Street tube.

Brixton, Electric Ave, Pope's Rd, Brixton Station Rd, Atlantic Rd, SW9. Mon–Tue & Thurs–Sat 8am–6pm; Wed 8am–3pm. Based in the arcades just off Atlantic Row, but spilling out along nearly all of the neighbouring streets, this huge, energetic market is the centre of Brixton life, offering a vast range of African and Caribbean foods, hair and beauty products, records, clothes, a dazzling range of African fabrics and even triple-fast-action spiritual cleanser-cum-floor-wash. Brixton tube.

Camden, Camden High St to Chalk Farm Rd, NW1. A conglomeration of markets, all with a different emphasis. Camden Market (Camden High Street, on the junction of Buck Street; Thurs–Sun 9.30am–5.30pm) offers a good mix of new, second-hand, retro and young designer clothes, as well as records and ephemera, while the Electric Market

(Camden High Street, just before the junction of Dewsbury Terrace; Sun 9am–5.30pm) and Camden Canal Market (just over Camden Lock bridge; Sat & Sun 10am–6pm) offer cheap fashion, hippywear, smoking paraphernalia and souvenir knick-knacks. Camden Lock (Camden Lock Place, off Chalk Farm Road; daily 10am–6pm) offers mainly arts, crafts and clothes stalls, with the shops (Wed–Sun, 10am–6pm) adding a few hip designers, antique dealers and booksellers to the mix. The Stables Yard (leading off from Camden Lock or from Chalk Farm Road; Sat & Sun 10am–6pm) is a sprawling adventure of clubwear, more young designers, furniture, retro design, trinkets and antiques. Camden Town tube.

Columbia Road, Columbia Rd, E2. Sun 8am–1pm. Fabulous flower market in the heart of the East End, with bargains galore for the serious plantlover. Get here early, have breakfast in one of the many traders' street cafés, and take the time to check out the increasingly funky shops while you're at it. Buses #26, #48 or #55 from New Oxford Street.

Covent Garden, Apple Market, The Piazza; and Jubilee Market, off Southampton St, WC2. Daily 9am–5pm. The Apple Market offers handmade, rather twee craft stalls most days, while Jubilee Market offers endless cheap T-shirts, jewellery, souvenirs and so on. On Mondays, Jubilee is taken over by an antiques market which has some more enjoyable stalls. Whichever day you visit there are street performers to distract you in the piazza, and it's an amiable area to wander about in. Covent Garden tube.

Greenwich, Greenwich High Rd, Stockwell St, and College Approach, SE10. Another conglomeration, but in a rather more scenic setting than Camden, and offering a relaxing day out. The covered crafts market on College Approach sells mostly twentieth-century antiques on a Thursday (7.30am–5pm) and hand-made goods, clothes and gifts from Friday to Sunday (9.30am–5.30pm),

while the Central Market off Stockwell Street hosts funky second-hand clothes, bric-a-brac and furniture. The surrounding streets, and the shops inside the covered market, offer obscure maritime devices, new and old, plus lots of second-hand books and retro clothes. Greenwich tube and train or Island Gardens DLR.

Petticoat Lane, Middlesex St and around, E1. Sun 9am–2pm. Cheap, cheerful and heaving, this famous clothes and bric-a-brac market is much like any other local offering – but much, much bigger. Worth checking out for the cheap underwear, make-up, leather and electronic goods. Liverpool Street or Aldgate East tube.

Portobello Road, Portobello Rd and Golborne Rd, W10 and W11. Antique market Sat 7.30am–6.30pm; general market Mon–Wed 8am–6pm, Thurs 9am–1pm, Fri & Sat 7am–7pm; organic market Thurs 11am–6pm; Golborne Road market Mon–Sat 9am–5pm. Still a great day out, probably the best way to approach Portobello is from the Notting Hill end, working your way through the antiques and bric-a-brac down to the fruit and veg stalls, and then under the Westway to the seriously hip new and second-hand clothes stalls and shops, around which local style vultures circle and swoop. Friday is better than Saturday to pick up a bargain here. Still further up again, beyond Portobello Green, the second-hand becomes pure boot-sale material, laid out on rugs on the road. The Golborne Road market is cheaper and less crowded, with some very attractive antique and retro furniture and bits and pieces. Ladbroke Grove or Notting Hill Gate tube.

Ridley Road, Ridley Rd, E8. Mon–Sat 8.30am–6pm. A great food and clothes market at the everyday heart of Hackney, Ridley Road, like Brixton Market, is worth travelling to for the sheer diversity of goods on display. African and Caribbean fruit, veg and fish predominate, but there are also Turkish and Asian staples and a long line of shops offering fabrics, hair and beauty products, old gospel albums,

Shops and markets

Shops and markets

cheap shoes and clothes, and much else. Dalston Kingsland train or buses #30 from Marble Arch tube, #38 or #242 from New Oxford Street or #67, #76, #149 and #236 from Old Street tube.

Riverside Walk, beneath Waterloo Bridge on the South Bank, SE1. Sat & Sun 10am–5pm, and occasionally midweek. An attractive book market by the Thames, offering everything from current and recent fiction to obscure psychology textbooks, film theory, modern European poetry and pulp science fiction – most of it reasonably priced, although rarely a complete bargain. Waterloo or Embankment tube.

Spitalfields, Commercial St, between Brushfield St and Lamb Streets, E1. The East End's historic old fruit and veg hall, this beautiful Victorian building now houses an organic food, crafts and second-hand goods market. A hippy delight, and fun for kids and local office workers alike, with a miniature railway, a mini-football pitch and lots of tasty food stalls. Liverpool Street tube.

Chapter 24

Sport

As a quick glance at the national press will tell you, **sport** in Britain is a serious matter, with each international defeat being taken as an index of the country's slide down the scale of world powers. Many of the crucial international fixtures of the **football**, **rugby and cricket** seasons take place in the capital, and London also hosts one of the world's greatest tennis tournaments, the **Wimbledon** championships, as well as top-flight athletics at **Crystal Palace**. On the domestic front, several of the city's football (soccer) teams can easily match the star quality of northern England's best sides, and every Saturday (and occasionally Sunday or Monday) there's a chance to see Premier League action here. The rest of the sporting calendar is chock-full of other quality events, ranging from the sedate pleasures of **county cricket** to the thrills of **horse racing** on Epsom Downs.

For those who'd rather compete than spectate, London offers all the facilities you'd expect from a city of this size. Council-run leisure centres and parks provide inexpensive access to **swimming pools**, **gyms**, **aerobics classes**, **tennis courts** and so forth, while a host of private establishments cater for everyone from the pool-hall shark to the amateur canoeist – even **golfing** enthusiasts can find a course within the city limits.

For up-to-the-minute details of sporting events in London, check the *Evening Standard* or *Time Out,* or ring the London Sportsline on ☎020/7222 8000. For exhaustive **listings** of the capital's sports facilities, get hold of a copy of Sports England's *Directory of Sport in London* (☎0870/5210255; *www.english.sports .gov.uk*).

Spectator sports

In this section we've listed details of each of the main **spectator sports** in London, including a run-through of venues. For the top international events, it can be almost impossible to track down a ticket without resorting to the services of a grossly overcharging ticket agency, but for many fixtures you can make credit-card bookings by ringing the numbers we've given.

Should you be thwarted in your attempts to gain admission, you can often fall back on **TV or radio coverage**. BBC Radio 5 Live has live commentaries on most major sporting events, while one of the TV channels nearly always carries live transmission of the big international rugby and cricket matches. To watch live Premier League (and some international) football, you'll need to find a TV that has the Sky satellite stations – many pubs offer Sky games (sometimes on big screens) to draw in custom.

Football

English **football** (or **soccer**) is passionate, and if you have the slightest interest in the game, then catching a league or FA Cup fixture is a must. The season runs

Sport

from mid-August to early May, when the **FA Cup Final** at Wembley rounds things off. There are four league divisions: one, two, three, and, at the top of the pyramid, the twenty-club Premier League. There are London clubs in every single division, with around five or six in the Premiership at any one time.

London's top club at the moment is **Arsenal**, who won the double (league and FA Cup) in the 1997–98 season. Meanwhile, in west London, **Chelsea** waltzed away with the last-ever European Cup Winners' Cup in 1999. Nevertheless, the team with the most money, the largest support and the most impressive run of success over the last decade is **Manchester United**, and tickets for United games in London are consequently like gold dust, but well worth the hunt. Nevertheless, it's reasonably easy to get **tickets**, if booked in advance, for most London Premier League games, unless two London sides are playing each other. The biggest of these "derby" fixtures are the meetings of North London rivals **Arsenal** and **Tottenham Hotspur**. Tickets for Premiership matches don't come cheap, with most charging a minimum of £12–15.

The highlights of the day's best games are shown on BBC TV's *Match of the Day* on Saturday nights (due to switch to ITV for the 2001–2002 season). Most Premiership fixtures kick off at 3pm on Saturday, though there are always a few midweek games (usually 7.30pm on Wednesday), and one or two each Sunday (kick-off between 2 and 4pm) and Monday (kick-off around 8pm), broadcast live on Sky TV.

Since the introduction of all-seater Premiership stadiums, top-flight games have lost their reputation for tribal violence, and there's been a striking increase in the number of women and children watching the "beautiful game". Nonetheless, it's an intense business, with a lot of foul language, and being stuck in the middle of a few thousand West Ham supporters as their team goes down is not one of life's most uplifting experiences.

MAJOR FOOTBALL STADIUMS AND CLUBS

Arsenal, Highbury Stadium, Avenell Rd, N5 ☎020/7704 4000; *www.arsenal .co.uk*. Arsenal tube.

Charlton Athletic, The Valley, Floyd Rd, SE7 ☎020/8333 4010; *www.charlton -athletic.co.uk*. Charlton train station from Charing Cross.

Chelsea, Stamford Bridge, Fulham Rd, SW6 ☎020/7386 7799; *www.chelseafc .co.uk*. Fulham Broadway tube.

Tottenham Hotspur, White Hart Lane Stadium, High Street, N17 ☎020/8365 5000; *www.spurs.co.uk*. White Hart Lane train station from Liverpool Street.

Wembley Stadium, Wembley Way, Middlesex ☎020/8795 5733; *www .wembleynationalstadium.com*. Traditional venue for the FA Cup and England's home internationals, but currently being rebuilt and only due to re-open in time for the 2003 FA Cup. Wembley Park or Wembley Central tube.

West Ham United, Upton Park, Green St, E13 ☎020/8548 2748; *www.whufc .co.uk*. Upton Park tube or Stratford train station from Liverpool Street, then bus #104.

Cricket

In the days of the Empire, the English took **cricket** to the colonies as a means of instilling the gentlemanly values of fair play while administering a sound thrashing to the natives. These days, the former colonies – such as Australia, the West Indies and India – all beat England on a regular basis, and to see the game at its best you should try to get into one of the **Test matches** between England and the summer's touring team. These international matches are played in the middle of the cricket season, which runs from April to September. Two of the matches are played in London: one at **Lord's**, the home of English cricket (and the MCC – see p.386) in St John's Wood, the other at **The Oval** in Kennington. In tandem with the full-blown five-day Tests, there's also a series of one-day internationals, two of which are usually held in London.

Getting to see England play one of the big teams can be difficult unless you book months in advance. If you can't wangle your way into a Test, you could watch it live on television, or settle down to an inter-county match, either in the **county championship** (these are four-day games) or in one of the fast and furious one-day competitions. Two county teams are based in London: **Middlesex**, who play at Lord's, and **Surrey**, who play at The Oval.

CRICKET GROUNDS

Lord's, St John's Wood, NW8 ☎020 /7289 1611; *www.lords.org.uk*. St John's Wood tube.

The Oval, Kennington Oval, SE11 ☎020 /7582 6660; *www.surreyccc.co.uk*. Oval tube.

Rugby

Rugby gets its name from Rugby public school, where the game mutated from football (soccer) in the nineteenth century. A rugby match may at times look like a bunch of weightlifters grappling each other in the mud – as the old joke goes, rugby is a hooligan's game played by gentleman, while football is a gentleman's game played by hooligans – but it is in reality a highly tactical and athletic sport. England's rugby teams tend to represent the country with rather more success than the cricket squad, though they can't quite match the power and attacking panache of the sides from the southern hemisphere.

There are two types of rugby played in Britain: fifteen-a-side **Rugby Union**, which has upper-class associations (though the game is also very strong in working-class Wales) and only became a professional sport in 1995; and thirteen-a-side **Rugby League**, which has long been a professional game played almost exclusively in the north of England (though the final of its knockout trophy is played at Wembley), and which has recently moved into a new era with the formation of a Super League, featuring the big-name northern clubs, Paris and

one London club, the **London Broncos**, which shares a ground with Charlton Athletic football club. Games traditionally take place on Sundays at 3pm, but there are also matches on Friday and Saturday nights. The season runs from March to September, thus enabling players to play Union in the winter.

In London virtually all rugby clubs play Rugby Union, with the two biggest clubs being **Harlequins** and the **London Wasps**. The Premier League season runs from September until May, finishing off with the **Tetley Bitter Cup**, rugby's equivalent of the FA Cup, and the Europe-wide Heineken Cup. The Tetley Bitter Cup final and England's home international matches are played at **Twickenham**, in southwest London. Unless you are affiliated to one of the two thousand clubs of the Rugby Union, or willing to pay well over the odds at a ticket agency, it is tough getting a ticket for one of these big Twickenham games. A better bet is to go and see a Harlequins or Wasps league game, where there's bound to be an international player or two on display – you can usually get in for under £12.

MAJOR RUGBY STADIUMS AND CLUBS

Harlequins, Stoop Memorial Ground, Craneford Way, Twickenham ☎020 /8410 6000; *www.quins.co.uk*. Twickenham train station from Waterloo.

London Broncos, The Valley, Floyd Rd, SE7 ☎020/8410 5000; *www.londonbroncos.co.uk*. Charlton train station from Charing Cross.

Twickenham Stadium, Whitton Rd, Twickenham ☎020/8892 2000; *www.rfu.com*. Twickenham train station from Waterloo.

Wasps, Rangers Stadium, South Africa Rd, W12 ☎020/8902 4220; *www.wasps.co.uk*. White City tube.

Tennis

Tennis in England is synonymous with **Wimbledon**, the only Grand Slam tournament to be played on grass, and for many players the ultimate goal of their

Sport

Sport

careers. The Wimbledon championships last a fortnight, in the last week of June and the first week of July. Most of the **tickets**, especially seats for the main show courts (Centre and No. 1), are allocated in advance to the Wimbledon tennis club's members, other clubs and corporate "sponsors" – as well as by public ballot (see below) – and by the time these have taken their slice there's not a lot left for the general public.

On tournament days, queues for tickets start to form around dawn – if you arrive by around 7am, you have a reasonable chance of securing one of the limited number of Centre and No. 1 court tickets held back for sale on the day. If you're there by around 9am, you should get admission to the outside courts (where you'll catch some top players in the first week of the tournament). Either way, you then have a long wait until play commences at noon – and if it rains you don't get your money back.

If you want to see big-name players in London, an easier opportunity is the Stella Artois men's championship at **Queen's Club** (☎020/7385 3421) in Hammersmith, which finishes a week before Wimbledon. Many of the male tennis stars use this tournament to acclimatize themselves to British grass-court conditions. As with Wimbledon, you have to apply for tickets in advance, although there is a limited number of returns on sale at 10am each day.

For the unlucky, there's the consolation of TV coverage, which is pretty all-consuming for Wimbledon.

TENNIS CLUBS

All England Lawn Tennis and Croquet Club, Church Rd, Wimbledon SW19 5AE ☎020/8946 2244; *www.wimbledon.org.* For public-ballot tickets, you have to send a stamped addressed envelope to the club for an application form (available from September preceding the championship) and return it by December 31. Southfields or Wimbledon Park tube.

Queen's Club, Palliser Rd, W14 9EQ ☎020/7385 3421. For public-ballot tickets to the Stella Artois championships, phone Queen's Club for the address you need in order to apply for an application form – this needs to be done by September 30 at the latest. Barons Court tube.

Horse racing

There are five **horse racecourses** within easy reach of London: **Kempton Park**, near Sunbury-on-Thames; **Sandown Park**, near Esher in Surrey; and **Windsor**, in Berkshire, which hold top-quality races on the flat (April–Sept) and over jumps (Aug–April). There're also **Ascot**, in Berkshire, and **Epsom**, in Surrey, which are the real glamour courses, hosting major races of the flat-racing season every June.

Thousands of Londoners have a day out at Epsom on Derby Day, which takes place on the first or second Saturday in June. **The Derby**, a mile-and-a-half race for three-year-old thoroughbreds, is the most prestigious of the five classics of the April to September English flat season, and is preceded by another classic, **the Oaks**, which is for fillies only. The three-day Derby meeting is as much a social ritual as a sporting event, but for sheer snobbery, nothing can match the **Royal Ascot** week in mid-June, when the Queen and selected members of the royal family are in attendance, along with half the nation's bluebloods. The best seats are the preserve of the gentry, who get dressed up to the nines for the day; but, as is the case at most racecourses, the rabble are allowed into the public enclosure for a mere £5.

RACECOURSES

Ascot, High St, Ascot, Berkshire ☎01344 /622211; *www.ascot.co.uk.* The jewel in the crown of English racecourses. The week-long Royal Meeting in mid-June is the one to attend, and to dress up for – especially on Ladies' Day, when media attention turns to the extravagant headgear sported by the more flamboyant female spectators. The racecourse hosts less glamorous meetings throughout the rest of the year. Ascot train station from Waterloo.

Epsom, Epsom Downs, Surrey ☎01372/726311; www.epsomderby .co.uk. Derby week, in the first week of June, is when Epsom really comes alive. There are very few meetings at other times: evening meetings at the end of June and July, and a two-day event at the end of August. Epsom Downs train station from Waterloo, Charing Cross or Victoria.

Kempton Park, Staines Rd East, Sunbury-on-Thames ☎01932/782292; www .kempton.co.uk. This popular course has excellent facilities, including covered enclosures for inclement meetings. The majority of fixtures are run on the flat. Racing takes place all year, however, with evening meetings in April and from June to August. A highlight is the very popular two-day Christmas Festival, which starts on Boxing Day with the King George VI Stakes. Kempton Park train station from Waterloo.

Sandown Park, The Racecourse, Esher Station Rd, Esher ☎01372/463072; www.sandown.co.uk. Hugely popular, well-equipped venue that has been frequently voted Racecourse of the Year. The annual highlight is the Whitbread Gold Cup towards the end of April, and the Coral-Eclipse Stakes in early June. Esher train station from Waterloo.

Windsor, Maidenhead Road, Windsor ☎01753/865234; www.windsorracing .co.uk. Great location by the Thames, with Windsor Castle in view, a shuttle-boat service from central Windsor, and an unusual figure-of-eight-course. Windsor & Eton Riverside train station from Waterloo or Windsor Central from Paddington (change at Slough).

Greyhound racing

A night out at the **dogs** is still a popular pursuit in London. It's an inexpensive,

cheerful and comfortable spectacle: a grandstand seat costs less than £5, and all six London stadiums have one or more restaurants, some surprisingly good. Indeed, the sport has become so popular that you'd be best advised to book in advance if you want to watch the races from a restaurant table, particularly around Christmas. Meetings usually start around 7.30pm and finish at 10.30pm, and usually include around a dozen races. The two easiest stadiums to get to are **Catford** and **Wimbledon**, both in south London.

GREYHOUND TRACKS

Catford, Adenmore Rd, SE26 ☎020 /8690 8000; www.thedogs.co.uk. Catford Bridge train station from Charing Cross or Catford train station from Victoria.

Walthamstow, Chingford Rd, E4 ☎020/8531 4255; www.wsgreyhound .co.uk. Walthamstow tube, then bus #97.

Wimbledon, Plough Lane, SW17 ☎020 /8946 8000; www.wimbledondogs.co.uk. Wimbledon Park tube or Haydons Road train station from Blackfriars.

Athletics

In the age of multiple sponsorships, multi-million-pound TV deals and huge appearance fees, Britain is beginning to lag behind in the ranks of **athletics** venues. There are ambitious plans to build a huge stadium at Pickett's Lock in the Lea Valley in northeast London, but until then, any international athletic meetings held in London will continue to take place at the **Crystal Palace National Sports Centre**. If you want to attend one of the big meetings, don't leave it too late to apply for a ticket – the pulling power of these events is such that as many as six thousand extra seats have to be added to the stadium's sixteen thousand permanent capacity.

Crystal Palace National Sports Centre, Ledrington Rd, off Anerley Hill, SE19 ☎020/8778 0131; www.crystalpalace .co.uk. Crystal Palace train statio, from Victoria.

Sport

Sport

Motorsport

The only forms of motorsport in London itself are stock-car and banger races at Wimbledon stadium (see "Greyhound tracks", p.617), held every other Sunday from late August to May. The nearest track for top-class motorsport is **Brands Hatch** in Kent, which holds about eighteen big meetings between February and December, usually on Sundays and bank holidays. Brands Hatch hasn't held a Formula One race since 1986 and is unlikely to do so in future, as the regulations appear to have ruled the circuit out of contention. Brands Hatch is, however, host to the **World Superbikes** series, and three rounds of the **British Touring Car Championships**, which attract crowds of some thirty-five thousand, second only to the British Grand Prix at Silverstone (near Northampton).

Brands Hatch, Fawkham, Longfield, Kent ☎0990/125250; *www.brands-hatch .co.uk*. Swanley train station from Charing Cross then taxi.

Participating

The following section lists most of the **sporting activities** possible in the capital. As a rule, the most reasonably priced facilities are provided by council-run leisure and sports centres, all of which have membership schemes that give discounts to regular users. A year's membership tends to cost around £30, a bargain for Londoners (private clubs charge around twenty times more), but if you're only here for a short time it's unlikely to be a sensible investment, unless you intend using the gym or swimming pool twice every day.

Golf

Not the most obvious urban sport, it is, nevertheless, quite possible to have a round of **golf** within the city limits. At most places, you don't need to be a member – a pay-and-play round usually costs in the region of £15 – it's often advisable to book ahead if you're playing at the weekend. There are also a few places closer to

the city centre, where you can hone your driving and putting for considerably less. In addition, two of the country's most famous golf courses lie within easy reach of London: **Sunningdale**, near Ascot, and **Wentworth**, in Surrey.

Airlinks, Southall Lane, Hounslow, Middlesex ☎020/8561 1418. Eighteen-hole course. Hayes & Harlington train station from Paddington, then bus #195.

Lee Valley Golf Course, Picketts Lock Lane, N9 ☎020/8803 3611. Eighteen-hole course. Ponders End train station from Liverpool Street.

Regent's Park Golf School, Outer Circle, Regent's Park, NW1 ☎020/7724 0643. Driving range, putting practice, plus lessons with the club pro. Baker Street tube.

Richmond Park, Roehampton Gate, Richmond Park, SW15 ☎020/8876 3205. Two eighteen-hole courses. Barnes train station from Waterloo, bus #371 or #65 from Richmond tube or bus #85 from Putney Bridge tube.

Sunningdale, Ridgemount Rd, Sunningdale, Ascot, Berkshire ☎01344 /621681; *www.linksnet.co.uk*. Sunningdale train station from Waterloo.

Wentworth, Wentworth Drive, Virginia Water, Surrey ☎01344/842201; *www .wentworthclub.com*. Virginia Water train station from Waterloo.

Ice-skating

London has just one centrally located indoor ice rink, plus the outdoor Broadgate rink – located in the heart of the City near Liverpool Street station. Session times tend to vary quite a lot, but generally last for around two to three hours.

Alexandra Palace Ice Rink, Wood Green, N22 ☎020/8365 2121. Great location high above the city in Ally Pally. Admission £4.50 (including skates). Alexandra Palace train station from King's Cross.

Broadgate Ice Rink, Broadgate Circus, Eldon St, EC2 ☎020/7505 4068 www.broadgateestates.co.uk/ice/frameset.htm. A little circle of ice open from October to March. It's fun (in fine weather), but can get crowded during the weekend. Wednesday evenings are for "broomball" matches. Admission £5; skate rental £2. Liverpool Street tube.

Lee Valley Ice Centre, Lea Bridge Rd, E10 ☎020/8533 3154; www.leevalleypark.com. Excellent ice rink in the Walthamstow Marshes. Admission £4.50; skate rental £1. Clapton train station from Liverpool Street.

Leisurebox, 17 Queensway, W2 ☎020/7229 0172. The whole family can skate at this rink, which has ice-discos on Friday and Saturday evenings. Admission £5; skate rental £1. Queensway or Bayswater tube.

Sobell Leisure Centre, Hornsey Rd, N7 ☎020/7609 2166. Without doubt the cheapest ice rink in the capital. Admission £3 (including skate rental). Holloway Road or Finsbury Park tube.

Streatham Ice Rink, 386 Streatham High Rd, SW16 ☎020/8769 7771. South London's only ice rink. Admission £5; skate rental £1.50. Streatham train station, from Charing Cross.

Pool and snooker

Pool has replaced darts as the most popular pub sport in London. There are scores of pubs offering small-scale pool tables, even in the centre of the city, where space is at a premium. In some places you may find it hard to get a game, as the regulars tend to monopolize the tables, but in theory the way to get a game is to lay down the fee, usually £1, on the side of the table, and then wait your turn. Some pubs operate a "winner stays on" policy, which generally means you end up paying for the privilege of being slaughtered by the local champ. Generally more pleasurable is to go to one of the city's trendy new pool bars, where you can hire a much larger **American pool** table by the hour (£6–9). There are also, much more serious **snooker halls**, which usually have

both American pool and **snooker** tables, the equivalent British game. Below are a couple of friendly pool halls, plus one central establishment where the subtle skills of snooker still prevail.

Centrepoint Snooker Club, New Oxford St (corner of Charing Cross Rd), WC1 ☎020/7240 6886. Very central, licensed snooker club (with just one pool table). It's a membership club (£30 a year), but you can get in for £2 if the place isn't full. Tables are around £5 per hour (American pool £6 per hour). Daily 11am–6am. Tottenham Court Road tube.

Elbow Room, 103 Westbourne Grove, W2 ☎020/7221 5211; www.elbow-room.co.uk. Bayswater or Notting Hill Gate tube. Mon–Sat noon–11pm, Sun noon–10.30pm. The city's trendiest pool club by far, with designer décor, purple-baize American pool tables and better-than-average grilled fast food and beer. No membership fee: you simply pay £6–9 per hour for use of the tables, depending on the time of day. There's a larger **Islington branch** at 89–91 Chapel Market, N1 ☎020/7278 3244. Angel tube. Mon–Wed noon–2am, Thurs–Sat noon–3am, Sun noon–10.30pm.

The Pool, 104–108 Curtain Rd, EC2 ☎020/7739 9608. There are three pool tables at this retro Hoxton bar on busy, busy Curtain Road. Table hire is £10 an hour. Old Street tube. Daily noon–11pm.

Ritzy's Pool Shack, 16 Semley House, Semley Place, SW1 ☎020/7823 5817. Situated behind Victoria coach station, Ritzy's was exclusively a snooker hall, but has now added seventeen pool tables to its facilities and become one of the city's trendier pool clubs, with a cocktail bar and American-style diner. Day membership for the downstairs snooker club is £5; for pool you just pay the £6–9 fee per table per hour – the later the hour, the pricier it gets. Mon–Sat 11am–11pm, Sun noon–10.30pm. Victoria tube.

Horse riding

Strange though it might seem, there are places in the metropolis where you can

Sport

Sport

saddle up, though at quite a price – £25 per hour is the average. It is usually possible to borrow a hard hat, but you must wear shoes or boots with a heel.

Hyde Park Stables, 63 Bathurst Mews, W2 ☎020/7723 2813. The only stables in Central London, situated on the north side of Hyde Park. An hour's ride or lesson in a group costs £30, or you can pay around £60 for a private lesson at their Kensington Stables (☎020/7589 2299). Closed Mon. Lancaster Gate tube.

Suzanne's Riding School, Brooks Hill Drive, Harrow Weald, Middlesex ☎020/8954 3618. Only 12 miles from the West End, this place has 200 acres of grassland to hack over, as well as three all-weather arenas and an indoor school. There is a showjumping course and a cross-country course if you wish to polish your skills. Prices from £18 for an hour-long group hack or lesson; £25 for a private lesson. Closed Mon. Harrow & Wealdstone train station, from Euston.

Wimbledon Village Stables, 24 High St, SW19 ☎020/8946 8579. Hack over the wilds of Wimbledon Common and Richmond Park for £20–25 per hour. Private lessons available from British Horse Society-approved instructors at £26–30 per hour. Closed Mon. Wimbledon tube.

Boating and watersports

Although the Thames is a dangerously tidal river, and can look unappealingly dirty to boot (despite being one of the cleanest metropolitan rivers in the world), the city does offer a few opportunities for messing around on the water. You can rent a variety of rowing **boats** upstream at Richmond, where you'll find slightly calmer river waters. Local parks with lakes, such as Hyde Park, Regent's Park and Battersea Park, also rent out small boats during the summer. Quite close to the centre of town, there are also non-tidal basins in the former docks, where you can indulge in a surprising variety of **watersports**. During the summer, these

places can get very busy – it's always best to book ahead rather than just turn up.

Docklands Sailing & Watersports Centre, Millwall Docks, E14 ☎020/7537 2626. Dinghy sailing, canoeing, rowing and dragon-boat racing within sight of Canary Wharf. Closed Sat. Crossharbour DLR.

Docklands Watersports Club, Gate 16, King George V Dock, Woolwich Manor Way, E16 ☎020/7511 7000. Jetskiing at a price: £30 per half-hour, or £55 per hour. Closed Mon & Tues. Gallion's Reach DLR or North Woolwich train station.

Lee Valley Watersports Club, Banbury Reservoir, Harbet Rd, E14 ☎020/8531 1129; *www.leevalleypark.com*. Dinghy sailing, waterskiing and windsurfing on a 90-acre reservoir. Northumberland Park or Angel Road train station, from Liverpool Street.

Royal Docks Waterski Club, Gate 16, King George V Dock, E16 ☎020/7511 2000. Waterskiing or wake-boarding while watching the planes land at London City Airport. Closed Mon. North Woolwich train station.

Tennis courts

The most reasonably priced **tennis courts** in London are those in council-run parks, which should cost around £5 an hour; the downside is that they are rarely maintained to perfect standard. If you want to book a court in advance, you usually have to join the local borough's registration scheme, which is priced between £10 and £20 per year; we've given the phone numbers for the courts in the main central London parks. However, during the day it is generally possible to simply turn up and get a court within half an hour or so, except during July and August, when the Wimbledon tournament spurs a mass of couch potatoes into ill-advised activity. For those who want a better class of facilities, or to keep on playing when the rain pours, there are a few private indoor tennis centres which grant admission to

the public and charge between £10 and
£20 an hour.

COUNCIL COURTS

Battersea Park, and other courts in
Wandsworth ☎020/8871 7542.

Bishop's Park, and other courts in
Hammersmith and Fulham ☎020/7736
1735.

Highbury Fields, N1 ☎020/7226 2334.
Highbury & Islington tube.

Holland Park, and other courts in
Kensington and Chelsea ☎020/7602
2226.

Hyde Park ☎020/7262 3474. Lancaster
Gate tube.

Islington Tennis Centre, Market Rd, N7
☎020/7700 1370. Outdoor and indoor
courts. Caledonian Road tube.

Market Sports, 65 Brushfield St,
Spitalfields, EC1 ☎020/7377 1300.
Liverpool Street tube.

Paddington Recreation Ground, W2
☎020/7641 3642.

Regent's Park ☎020/7486 4216.
Regent's Park or Baker Street tube.

Swimming pools, gyms and fitness centres

Below is a selection of the best-
equipped, most central of London's
multi-purpose **fitness centres**. We
haven't given the addresses of the city's
many council-run **swimming pools**, virtually all of which now have fitness classes and gyms. Wherever you go, a swim
will usually cost you around £2.50.

Ironmonger Row Baths, Ironmonger
Row, EC1 ☎020/7253 4011. An old-
fashioned kind of place that attracts all
classes, with a steam room, sauna, small

plunge pool, masseurs, a lounge area
with beds, and a large pool. Admission
for a 3hr session is a bargain at £10.
Men: Tues & Thurs 9am–9.30pm, Sat
9am–6pm. Women: Mon, Wed & Fri
9am–9.30pm, Sun 10am–6pm. Old
Street tube.

Oasis Sports Centre, 32 Endell St, WC2
☎020/7831 1804. The Oasis has two
pools, one of which is the only heated
outdoor pool in central London; the
indoor pool is open Mon–Fri
6.30am–5pm, Sat & Sun 9.30am–
4.30pm; the outdoor pool opens Mon–
Fri 7.30am–9pm, Sat & Sun 7.30am
–4.30pm. Other facilities include a gym, a
health suite with sauna and sunbed,
massage and badminton and squash
courts. Covent Garden tube.

Porchester Spa, 225 Queensway, W2
☎020/7792 3980. Built in 1926, the
Porchester is one of only two Turkish
baths in Central London, and is well
worth a visit for the Art Deco tiling alone.
Admission is around £20, and entitles
you to use the saunas, steam rooms,
plunge pool, jacuzzi and swimming pool.
Men: Mon, Wed & Sat 10am–10pm.
Women: Tues, Thurs & Fri 10am–10pm,
Sun 10am–4pm. Mixed: Sun 4–10pm.
Bayswater or Queensway tube.

The Sanctuary, 11–12 Floral St, WC2
☎020/7420 5151. For a serious day of
self-indulgence, this women-only club in
Covent Garden is a real treat: the interior
is filled with lush tropical plants and you
can swim naked in the pool. It's a major
investment at £50 a day, but your
money gets you unlimited use of the
pool, jacuzzi, sauna and steam room,
plus one sunbed session. Mon, Tues &
Sun 10am–6pm, Wed–Fri 9.30am–6pm,
Sat 10am–8pm. Covent Garden tube.

Sport

*If you fancy an
alfresco dip,
Hampstead
Heath is your
place; see
p.406.*

Chapter 25

Festivals and special events

This chapter is simply a rundown of the principal **festivals** and **annual events** in the capital, ranging from the upper-caste rituals of Royal Ascot to the sassy street party of the Notting Hill Carnival, plus a few oddities like Horseman's Sunday. Our listings cover a pretty wide spread of interests, but they are by no means exhaustive; London has an almost endless roll call of ceremonials and special shows, and for daily information, it's well worth checking *Time Out* or the *Evening Standard*.

JANUARY 1
London Parade To kick off the new year, a procession of floats, marching bands, clowns, American cheerleaders and classic cars wends its way from Parliament Square at noon, through the centre of London, to Berkeley Square, collecting money for charity from around one million spectators en route. Information ☎020/8566 8586; *www.londonparade.co.uk*. Admission charge for grandstand seats in Piccadilly, otherwise free.

LAST SUNDAY IN JANUARY
Commemoration of Charles the Martyr
In a ceremony marking the execution of Charles I in 1649, a platoon of royalists in period costume from the Civil War Society retraces the monarch's final steps from St James's Palace to Banqueting House,

placing a wreath on the spot once occupied by the scaffold (see p.51).

LATE JANUARY
London International Mime Festival
Annual mime festival which takes place in the last two weeks of January on the South Bank, and in other funky venues throughout London. It pulls in some very big names in mime, animation and puppetry. Information ☎020/7637 5661; *www.mimefest.co.uk*.

LATE JANUARY OR EARLY FEBRUARY
Chinese New Year Celebrations Soho's Chinatown explodes in a riot of dancing dragons and firecrackers on the night of this vibrant annual celebration, and the streets and restaurants are packed to capacity. See p.140.

SECOND SUNDAY IN FEBRUARY
Clowns Service Special church service for clowns, commemorating the great Joey Grimaldi, at Holy Trinity Church, Beechwood Road, Dalston, E8 (Dalston Kingsland train), with a clown show afterwards in the church hall. Information ☎020/7254 5062.

SHROVE TUESDAY (LATE FEBRUARY OR EARLY MARCH)
Great Spitalfields Pancake Day Race
Erstwhile Spitalfields wholesale fruit and veg market is the arena for this annual

bout of absurd athleticism, when anyone armed with frying pan and pancakes is allowed to run the short but frantic course. Information ☎020/7375 0441.

MARCH

Head of the River Race Less well known than the Oxford and Cambridge race, but much more fun, since there are over four hundred crews setting off at ten-second intervals and chasing each other from Mortlake to Putney. Information ☎01932/220401; *www.horr.co.uk*.

LATE MARCH OR EARLY APRIL

Oxford and Cambridge Boat Race Since 1845 the rowing teams of Oxford and Cambridge universities have battled it out on a four-mile, upstream course on the Thames, from Putney to Mortlake. It's as much a social as a sporting event, and the pubs at prime vantage points pack out early. Alternatively, you can catch it on TV. The best source of information is the current sponsor's Web site: *www .aberdeen-asset.com*.

EASTER MONDAY (MARCH OR APRIL)

London Harness Horse Parade Heavy horses pull a variety of old carriages and carts around Battersea Park, from 10am onwards; there's a bank holiday funfair, too. Information ☎020/7223 6241.

THIRD SUNDAY IN APRIL

London Marathon The world's most popular marathon, with some thirty-five thousand masochists sweating the 26.2 miles from Greenwich Park to Westminster Bridge. Only a handful of world-class athletes enter each year; most of the competitors are club runners and obsessive flab-fighters. There's always someone dressed up as a gorilla, and you can generally spot a fundraising celebrity or two. Information ☎020/7620 4117; *www.london-marathon.co.uk*

LAST SUNDAY IN APRIL

Tyburn Walk Silent procession led by a Catholic bishop, starting at 3pm from

Newgate Prison (now the Old Bailey) and ending up at the Tyburn Convent (see p.333) near Marble Arch some two hours later. Information ☎020/8947 2598.

MAY BANK HOLIDAY WEEKEND

IWA Canal Cavalcade Lively celebration of the city's inland waterways, held at Little Venice (near Warwick Avenue tube), with scores of decorated narrow boats, Morris dancers and lots of children's activities. Information ☎020/8874 2787.

SUNDAY NEAREST TO MAY 9

May Fayre and Puppet Festival The garden of St Paul's Church in Covent Garden is taken over by puppet booths to commemorate the first recorded sighting of a Punch and Judy show, by diarist Samuel Pepys in 1662. Information ☎020/7375 0441.

SUNDAY NEAREST TO MAY 11

Chestnut Sunday Parade of antique bicycles and carriages along Chestnut Avenue, with the trees in full blossom, held in Bushy Park, near Hampton Court Palace (see p.484). Information ☎020 /8979 1586.

MID-MAY
FA Cup Final

This is the culmination of the football (soccer) year: the premier domestic knockout competition, traditionally played to a packed house at Wembley Stadium. However, the final will not be played at Wembley until 2003 at the earliest, due to the rebuilding of Wembley. The game is also shown live on television. Information ☎020/8795 5733; *www .wembleynationalstadium.com*.

THIRD OR FOURTH WEEK IN MAY

Chelsea Flower Show Run by the Royal Horticultural Society, the world's finest horticultural event transforms the normally tranquil grounds of the Royal Hospital in Chelsea for four days, with a daily inundation of up to fifty thousand

Festivals
and special
events

Festivals and special events

gardening gurus and amateurs. It's a solidly bourgeois event, with the general public admitted on the last two days only, and charged an exorbitant fee for the privilege. Information ☎020/7834 4333; www.rhs.org.uk.

LAST WEEK OF MAY

Festival of Mind, Body and Spirit New Agers and the cosmically inclined gather at the Royal Horticultural Halls for this hippie happening. Massage, aromatherapy, Chinese medicine, tarot readings and masses of other alternative options are on offer. Information ☎020/7938 3788; www.mbsfestival.com.

MAY 29

Oak Apple Day The Chelsea Pensioners of the Royal Hospital (see p.371) honour their founder, Charles II, by wearing their posh uniforms and decorating his statue with oak leaves, in memory of the oak-tree in which the king hid after the Battle of Worcester in 1651. Information ☎020 /7730 5282.

JUNE TO EARLY SEPTEMBER

Kenwood Lakeside Concerts Classical concerts every Saturday from June to early September, held in the grounds of Kenwood House (see p.408). Information ☎020/7973 3427; www.picnicconcerts .com.

FIRST OR SECOND SATURDAY IN JUNE

Derby Day Run at the Epsom racecourse in Surrey, the Derby is the country's premier flat race – the beast that gets its snout over the line first is instantly worth millions. Admission prices reflect proximity to the horses and to the watching nobility. The race is always shown live on TV. Information ☎01372/726311; www.epsomderby.co.uk.

EARLY JUNE

Greyhound Derby Wimbledon Stadium, Plough Lane, SW17. This evening meeting is the culmination of the greyhound racing year with optional posh black tie

dinner afterwards. Information 020/8946 8000 ext.281; www.wimbledondogs .co.uk.

JUNE

Fleadh Pronounced "flaa", this is a raucous (by no means exclusively) Irish music festival in Finsbury Park, North London. Van Morrison has pitched up here on more than a few occasions, but then so too have Bob Dylan and the briefly re-formed Sex Pistols. Information ☎020/8963 0940; www.meanfiddler .com.

EARLY JUNE TO MID-AUGUST

Royal Academy Summer Exhibition Thousands of prints, paintings, sculptures and sketches, most by amateurs and nearly all of them for sale, are displayed at one of the city's finest galleries (see p.116). Information ☎020/7300 8000; www.royalacademy.org.uk.

JUNE TO AUGUST

Coin Street Festival Hugely varied free festival that takes place in and around the OXO Tower (see p.303), just east of the South Bank Centre. Information ☎020/7620 0544; www.oxotower.co.uk.

JUNE

Spitalfields Festival Classical music recitals in Hawksmoor's Christ Church, the parish church of Spitalfields, and other events in and around the old Spitalfields Market for a fortnight or so. Information ☎020/7377 0287; www .spitalfieldsfestival.org.uk.

SECOND SATURDAY IN JUNE

Trooping of the Colour This celebration of the Queen's official birthday (her real one is on April 21) features massed bands, gun salutes, fly-pasts and crowds of tourists and patriotic Britons paying homage. Tickets for the ceremony itself (limited to two per person) must be applied for well in advance; phone ☎020/7414 2479. Otherwise, the royal procession along the Mall lets you glimpse the nobility for free, and there are rehearsals (minus Her Majesty) on the two preceding Saturdays.

MID-JUNE

Royal Ascot A highlight of the society year, held at the Ascot racecourse in Berkshire, this high-profile meeting has the Queen and sundry royals completing a crowd-pleasing lap of the track in open carriages prior to the opening races. The event is otherwise famed for its fashion statements, and there's TV coverage of both the races and the more extravagant headgear of the female racegoers. Information ☎01344/622211; *www.ascot.co.uk*.

MID-JUNE

Stoke Newington Midsummer Festival A couple of weeks of events featuring the large local artistic community in this part of Hackney; it kicks off with a street festival on the Sunday, held on Church Street. Information ☎020/7254 3735.

LAST WEEK IN JUNE AND FIRST WEEK IN JULY

Wimbledon Lawn Tennis Championships This Grand Slam tournament attracts the cream of the world's professionals and is one of the highlights of the sporting and social calendar. Tickets are hard to get hold of, but as they are valid for the whole day you could always hang around outside in the hope of gleaning an early leaver's cast-off. Don't buy from touts, even if you can afford to, as the tickets may well be fakes. Information ☎020/8946 2244; *www.wimbledon.org*. See also p.616.

LATE JUNE TO MID-JULY

City of London Festival For nearly a month, churches (including St Paul's Cathedral), livery halls and corporate buildings around the City play host to classical and jazz musicians, theatre companies and other guest performers. Information ☎020/7377 0540; *www.colf.org*.

EARLY JULY

Mardi Gras A colourful, whistleblowing march through the city streets followed by a huge, ticketed party in Finsbury Park. For up-to-date information, festival plans and transport information, call ☎020/7494 2225 or visit the Web site: *www.londonmardigras.com*.

MID-JULY

Greenwich & Docklands International Festival Ten-day festival of fireworks, music, dance, theatre, art and spectacles at venues on both sides of the river, plus a village fayre in neighbouring Blackheath. Information ☎020/8305 1818; *www.festival.org*.

JULY TO AUGUST

Test Cricket Matches The English cricket team plays a series of five international Test matches at home over the summer, and the second match always takes place at Lord's, in north London. The match is most exciting – and most crowded – when either Australia or the West Indies is playing. The best views are from the award-winning Mound Stand, but this is generally the domain of blazer-wearing MCC (Marylebone Cricket Club) members; the less decorous, more entertaining enthusiasts tend to occupy the open stands. The other four Tests take place at a variety of venues – The Oval, in south London, being used for the last Test. There's always live TV coverage of all summer Tests. For more information, see p.614.

MID-JULY TO MID-SEPTEMBER

BBC Henry Wood Promenade Concerts Commonly known as the Proms, this series of nightly classical concerts at the Royal Albert Hall is a well-loved British institution. See p.344. Information ☎020/7765 5575; *www.bbc.co.uk/proms*.

MID-JULY

Doggett's Coat and Badge Race World's oldest rowing race from London Bridge to Chelsea, established by Thomas Doggett,

Festivals
and special
events

Festivals and special events

an eighteenth-century Irish comedian, to commemorate George I's accession to the throne. The winner receives a Hanoverian costume and silver badge. Information ☎020/7626 3531.

SUNDAY NEAREST JULY 16

Italian Procession (Festival of Our Lady of Mount Carmel) Big, boisterous Italian Catholic parade, which starts from St Peter's Italian Church on Clerkenwell Road and roams the streets of what used to be London's very own Little Italy (see p.209). Information ☎020/7837 1528.

THIRD WEEK IN JULY

Swan Upping Five-day scramble up the Thames, from Sunbury to Pangbourne, during which liveried rowers search for swans, marking them (on the bill) as belonging to either the Queen, the Dyers' or the Vintners' City liveries. At Windsor, all the oarsmen stand to attention in their boats and salute the Queen. Information ☎020/7236 1863.

LATE JULY OR EARLY AUGUST

Cart Marking Recalling a 1681 Act which restricted to 421 the number of horse-drawn carts allowed in the City, this arcane ceremony involves vintage vehicles congregating at 11am in Guildhall Yard in a branding ceremony organized by the Worshipful Company of Car Men. Information ☎020/7489 8287.

EARLY AUGUST

Great British Beer Festival A five-day binge at Olympia hosted by the Campaign for Real Ale (CAMRA). With five hundred brews to sample, the entrance fee is a small price to pay to drink yourself silly. Information ☎01727/867201; www.camra.org.uk.

LAST BANK HOLIDAY WEEKEND IN AUGUST

Notting Hill Carnival The two-day free festival in Notting Hill Gate is the longest-running, best-known and biggest

street party in Europe. Dating back 35 years, Carnival is a tumult of imaginative-ly decorated floats, eye-catching cos-tumes, thumping sound systems, live bands, irresistible food and huge crowds. See p.379. Information ☎020/8964 0544; www.nottinghillcarnival.net.uk.

SEPTEMBER

Summer Rites. The ticketed Summer Rites in Brixton's Brockwell Park offers a menu of dance, music, performance and stalls, and has so far managed to remain a relaxed and relaxing affair. For more information on Summer Rites, check *Time Out* and the queer press (see p.564).

SATURDAY IN EARLY TO MID-SEPTEMBER

Great River Race Hundreds of boats are rowed or paddled from Ham House, Richmond, down to Island Gardens on the Isle of Dogs. Starts are staggered and there are any number of weird and won-derful vessels taking part. Information ☎020/8398 9057.

THIRD SUNDAY IN SEPTEMBER

Horseman's Sunday In an eccentric 11.30am ceremony at the Hyde Park church of St John and St Michael, a vicar on horseback blesses a hundred or so horses; the newly consecrated beasts then parade around the neighbourhood before galloping off through the park, and later taking part in showjumping. Information ☎020/7262 1732.

THIRD WEEKEND IN SEPTEMBER

Open House A once-a-year opportunity to peek inside over four hundred build-ings around London, many of which don't normally open their doors to the public. You'll need to book in advance for some of the more popular places. Information ☎0891/600061; www .londonopenhouse.org.

LATE SEPTEMBER TO EARLY OCTOBER

Soho Jazz Festival Headed by Ronnie Scott's, this is a week-long celebration of

one of Soho's most famous attributes –
its jazz culture. Information ☎020/7437
6437.

LATE SEPTEMBER OR EARLY OCTOBER

Horse of the Year Show Dressage,
fence-jumping and other equine exercises whip a genteel audience into a frenzy
at this Wembley Arena event. Tickets
need to be booked well in advance.
Information ☎020/8902 0902; *www
.wembleyticket.com.*

FIRST SUNDAY IN OCTOBER

**Costermongers' Pearly Harvest Festival
Service** Cockney fruit and vegetable festival at St Martin-in-the-Fields Church. Of
most interest to the onlooker are the
Pearly Kings and Queens who gather at
around 3pm in their traditional pearl-
button studded outfits (see p.52).
Information ☎020/7930 0089.

SUNDAY NEAREST OCTOBER 21

Trafalgar Day Parade Parade of sea
cadets and marching bands at 11am, to
commemorate the 1805 Battle of
Trafalgar, culminating in wreath-laying at
the foot of Nelson's Column. Information
☎020/7928 8978; *www.sea-cadets.org.*

LATE OCTOBER OR EARLY NOVEMBER

State Opening of Parliament The Queen
arrives by coach at the Houses of
Parliament at 11am accompanied by the
Household Cavalry and gun salutes. The
ceremony itself takes place inside the
House of Lords and is televised; it also
takes place whenever a new government is sworn in. Information
☎020/7219 3000; *www.parliament.uk.*

NOVEMBER

London Film Festival A three-week cinematic season with scores of new international films screened at the National
Film Theatre and some West End
venues. Information ☎020/7928 3232;
www.bfi.org.uk or (nearer the time)
www.lff.org.uk.

EARLY NOVEMBER

London Jazz Festival Big ten-day jazz
fest held in all London's jazz venues,
large and small. Information ☎020/7405
5974.

FIRST SUNDAY IN NOVEMBER

London to Brighton Veteran Car Run In
1896 Parliament abolished the Act that
required all cars to crawl along at 2mph
behind someone waving a red flag. Such
was the euphoria in the motoring community that a rally was promptly set up
to mark the occasion, and a century later
it's still going strong. Classic cars built
before 1905 set off from Hyde Park at
7.30am and travel the 58 miles to
Brighton along the A23 at the heady
maximum speed of 20mph. Information
☎01753/681736.

NOVEMBER 5

Bonfire Night In memory of Guy
Fawkes – executed for his role in the
1605 Gunpowder Plot to blow up King
James I and the Houses of Parliament –
effigies of the hapless Fawkes are
burned on bonfires all over Britain.
There are council-run fires and firework
displays right across the capital;
Parliament Hill in Hampstead provides a
good vantage point from which to take
in several displays at once. Information
☎020/7971 0026.

SECOND SATURDAY IN NOVEMBER

Lord Mayor's Show The newly appointed Lord Mayor begins his or her day of
investiture at Westminster, leaving there
at around 9am for Guildhall. At 11.10am,
the vast ceremonial procession, headed
by the 1756 State Coach, begins its journey from Guildhall to the Law Courts in
the Strand, where the oath of office is
taken at 11.50am. From there the coach
and its train of 140-odd floats make their
way back towards Guildhall, arriving at
2.20pm. Later in the day there's a fireworks display from a barge tethered
between Waterloo and Blackfriars
bridges, and a small funfair on
Paternoster Square, by St Paul's

Festivals
and special
events

Festivals and special events

Cathedral. Information ☎020/7606 3030; *www.corpoflondon.gov.uk.*

NEAREST SUNDAY TO NOVEMBER 11

Remembrance Sunday A day of nation-wide commemorative ceremonies for the dead and wounded of the two world wars and other conflicts. The principal ceremony, attended by the Queen, various other royals and the prime minister, takes place at the Cenotaph in Whitehall, beginning with a march-past of veterans and building to a one-minute silence at the stroke of 11am.

MID-NOVEMBER TO EARLY JANUARY

Christmas lights Assorted celebrities flick the switches, and Bond, Oxford and Regent streets are bathed in festive illumination from dusk to midnight until January 6. The lights along Oxford Street are invariably tacky, but Regent Street usually puts on a tasteful show, and there are other, less ostentatious displays in St Christopher's Place, Kensington High Street and Carnaby Street. Shop windows are dressed up for the occasion, too, with the automated displays of the big stores, such as Selfridge's and Liberty, a major seasonal attraction.

Also, each year since the end of World War II Norway has acknowledged its gratitude to the country that helped liberate it from the Nazis with the gift of a mighty spruce tree that appears in Trafalgar Square in early December. Decorated with lights, it becomes the focus for carol singing versus traffic noise each evening until Christmas Eve.

DECEMBER 31

New Year's Eve The New Year is welcomed en masse in Trafalgar Square as thousands of inebriated revellers stagger about and slur to *Auld Lang Syne* at midnight. For the millennium, there was a big firework display along the Thames, and it remains to be seen whether the show will be repeated or if the crowds will once more return to their traditional haunt. Whatever happens, London Transport runs free public transport all night, sponsored by various public-spirited breweries.

Chapter 26

Kids' London

On first sight, London seems a hostile place for children, with its crowds, incessant noise and intimidating traffic. English attitudes can be discouraging as well, particularly if you've experienced the more indulgent approach of the French or Italians – London's restaurateurs, for example, tend to regard children as if they were one step up the evolutionary scale from rats. Yet, if you pick your place carefully, even central London can be a delight for the pint-sized, and it needn't overly strain the parental pocket.

Covent Garden's buskers and jugglers provide no-cost entertainment in a car-free setting, and there's always the chance of being plucked from the crowd to help out with a trick. Right in the thick of the action, you'll find plentiful green spaces, such as **Hyde Park** and **Regent's Park**, providing playgrounds and ample room for general mayhem, as well as a diverting array of city wildlife. If you want something more unusual than ducks and squirrels, head for one of London's several **city farms**, which provide urbanites with a taste of country life.

Don't underestimate the value of London's **public transport** as a source of fun, either. The mere idea of an underground train gives a buzz to a lot of kids, and you can get your bearings while entertaining your offspring by installing them on the panoramic top deck of a red double-decker bus. The old-fashioned #11 double-decker from

Victoria, for instance, will trundle you past the Houses of Parliament, Trafalgar Square and the Strand on its way to St Paul's Cathedral for 40p per child – about one-eighth of what you'd pay for a ride on one of the capital's tour buses, and you don't have to endure a mind-numbing commentary either. The driver-less **Docklands Light Railway** is another source of amusement, too – grab a seat at the front of the train and pretend to be driver; at Island Gardens, you can take the foot tunnel under the river to Greenwich. Another alternative is to have a ride on one of London's new trams (see p.473).

Museums are another, more obvious diversion. The good news is that kids' admission charges for the national museums have been abolished, making it much cheaper to visit the likes of the **Science Museum**, the **Natural History Museum** and the **National Maritime Museum**. These, and other museums, have hi-tech, hands-on sections that will keep young kids busy for hours, and they might even learn something while they're at it. There are museums, too, devoted to childhood and toys – while teenage horror fans will, of course, demand to visit the **London Dungeon** and **Madame Tussaud's** Chamber of Horrors, among the most expensive sights in the entire city (see p.132).

The spread of **shows** on offer – from puppet performances to specially commissioned plays – is at its best during school holidays, when even the biggest

Time Out has weekly listings of kids' events, and also produces Kids Out, *a monthly listings magazine aimed at those with children.*

Kids' London

theatres often stage family entertainments. This is also the case at Christmas, when there's a glut of traditional British pantomimes, stage shows based on folk stories or fairy-tales, invariably featuring a showbiz star or two, and often with an undercurrent of innuendo aimed at the adults. If that's too passive for you, there are plenty of indoor play centres where children can burn off some excess energy.

Lastly, be warned that London is pretty hot on **toy shops**. The panoply is headed by Hamleys, the world's largest toy emporium, while other stores cater for kids of all temperaments and ages, from the studious to the computer-addicted.

Major attractions

Listed below are the sights that will most appeal to children. In addition, you'll find that most London museums contain at least something of interest for kids; the ones we've picked should evoke more than just the usual enthusiasm, and all are covered in more detail in the main part of the guide. Most offer child-oriented programmes of workshops, educational story trails, special shows and suchlike during school holidays.

Major sights

Kew Gardens, Richmond, Surrey ☎020/8332 5000; *www.kew.org*. Go here for the edifying open spaces, though the glasshouses usually go down well, too, and there's a small aquarium in the basement of the Palm House. The new Museum No. 1 has hands-on stuff. Kew Gardens tube. Daily 9.30am–7.30pm or dusk; adults £5, children £2.50. See p.464.

Legoland, Windsor, Berks ☎0870/5040404; *www.legoland.co.uk*. Very expensive but enjoyable and relatively tasteful theme park with gentle rides – perfect for five- to eight-year-olds. Windsor & Eton Central train station from Paddington (change at Slough), or Windsor & Eton Riverside from Waterloo. Daily 10am–6pm or dusk; adults £17.50, children £14.50. See p.492.

London Aquarium, County Hall, SE1 ☎020/7967 8000; *www .londonaquarium.co.uk*. London's largest aquarium is situated on the South Bank, and is very popular with kids, especially the bit where they get to stroke the (non-sting) rays. Westminster or Waterloo tube. Daily 10am–6pm or later; adults £8.50, children £5. See p.305.

London Eye, South Bank, SE1 ☎0870/5000 600; *www.ba-londoneye .com*. Don't be put off by the hassle of advance booking, nor the thought of being cooped up with the kids for forty minutes. Most children will love the new observation wheel – take some binoculars. Waterloo tube. Daily 9am–late evening; £8.50, children £5. See p.304.

London Zoo, Regent's Park, NW1 ☎020/7722 3333; *www.londonzoo .co.uk*. Smaller kids love the children's enclosure, where they can actually handle the animals, and the regular "Animals in Action" live shows. The new invertebrate house, known as the Web of Life, is also a guaranteed winner, as it has lots of creepy-crawlies, and much more hands-on stuff. Bus #274 from Camden Town or Baker Street tube. Daily: March–Oct 10am–5.30pm; Nov–Feb 10am–4pm; adults £9, children £7. See p.389.

Syon Park, Brentford, Middlesex ☎020/8560 7272; *www.syonpark.co.uk*. Good place for a day out, with the Butterfly House, an Aquatic House full of fish, reptiles and amphibians, plus a miniature steam railway in the house's lovely gardens. Snakes and Ladders, an indoor children's play area with impressive apparatus, is also in the park (☎020/8847 0946; daily 10am–6pm; adults free, under-5s £3.55, over-5s £4.65, with reductions on weekdays. Bus #237 or #267 from Gunnersbury tube. See p.458.

Big museums

London Transport Museum, 39 Wellington St, WC2 ☎020/7836 8557; *www.ltmuseum.co.uk*. The buses, trams, and tubes might be enough for some kids, though others may be frustrated that they can't clamber over absolutely everything. Following the Kidzone trail is a fun way for over-5s to get round the place. Covent Garden tube. Mon–Thurs, Sat & Sun 10am–6pm, Fri 11am–6pm; adults £5.50, children £2.95. See p.153.

National Maritime Museum, Romney Rd, SE10 ☎020/8858 4422; *www.nmm.ac .uk.* The newly revamped Maritime Museum has galleries that are superbly designed to appeal to visitors of all ages. In addition, Level 3 boasts two hands-on galleries, "The Bridge" and "All Hands", both specifically aimed at kids. Cutty Sark DLR. Daily 10am–5pm; adults £7.50, children free. See p.433.

Natural History Museum, Cromwell Rd, SW7 ☎020/7942 5000; *www.nhm.ac .uk.* Animated and skeleton dinosaurs, stuffed animals, live ants, a "rainforest", an earthquake simulator and lots of rocks, fossils, crystals and gems. South Kensington tube. Mon–Sat 10am–5.50pm, Sun 11am–5.50pm; adults £7.50, children free: Mon–Fri all free after 4.30pm, Sat & Sun all free after 5pm. See p.360.

RAF Museum, Grahame Park Way, NW9 ☎020/8205 2266; *www.rafmuseum.org .uk.* Colindale tube. Most kids will enjoy the vast collection of planes here, as well as the hands-on Fun 'n' Flight gallery; those without might prefer to explore the often overlooked display galleries, ranged around the edge of the Main Aircraft Hall, which contain an art gallery and an exhibition on the history of flight, accompanied by replicas of some of the death-traps of early aviation. Daily 10am–6pm; adults £7.50, children free. See p.415.

Science Museum, Exhibition Rd, SW7 ☎020/7942 4455; *www.nmsi.ac.uk.* The new Wellcome Wing is very high-tech and a guaranteed winner, as are the other hands-on galleries such as the Launch Pad, and the excellent daily demonstrations. South Kensington tube. Daily 10am–6pm; adults £6.95, children free; all free after 4.30pm. See p.356.

Smaller museums

Bethnal Green Museum of Childhood, Cambridge Heath Rd, E2 ☎020/8983 5200; *www.vam.ac.uk.* The museum itself, with its collection of historic dolls' houses and toys, is not that great for kids, but they put on lots of weekend/holiday events and activities. Bethnal Green tube. Daily except Fri 10am–5.50pm; free. See p.280.

Horniman Museum, London Rd, SE23 ☎020/8699 1872; *www.horniman.ac.uk.* An ethnographic museum, but with lots to interest kids, including an aquarium, a natural history section and lovely grounds. Forest Hill train station from Victoria or London Bridge. Mon–Sat 10.30am–5.30pm, Sun 2–5.30pm; free. See p.427.

Kew Bridge Steam Museum, Green Dragon Lane, Brentford, TW8. ☎020 /8568 4757; *www.kbsm.org.uk.* Best visited at weekends, when the beam engines are in steam and the miniature steam railway is in operation. Kew Bridge train station from Waterloo or bus #237 or #267 from Gunnersbury tube. Daily 11am–5pm; Mon–Fri adults £3, children £1; Sat & Sun adults £4, children £2. See p.457.

Livesey Museum, 682 Old Kent Rd, SE15 ☎020/7639 5604. A series of child-centred exhibitions are put on at this small museum; in between times, it's closed, so phone ahead to check it's open. Bus #53 or #63 from Elephant & Castle tube. Tues–Fri 10am–5pm; free. See p.328.

Pollock's Toy Museum, 1 Scala St, W1 ☎020/7636 3452; *www.pollocks.cwc .net.* Housed above a toy shop, the museum's impressive toy collection includes a fine example of the Victorian paper theatres sold by Benjamin Pollock. Goodge Street tube. Mon–Sat 10am–5pm; adults £3, children £1.50. See p.149.

Ragged School Museum, Copperfield Rd, E3 ☎020/8980 6405; *www.ics-london .co.uk/rsm.* The reconstructed Victorian schoolroom here makes kids realize what an easy life they have these days. Mile

Kids'
London

Kids' London

End tube. Wed & Thurs 10am–5pm, first Sun in month 2–5pm; free. See p.279.

Parks

Battersea Park, Albert Bridge Rd, SW11 ☎020/8871 7540 (zoo) or 8871 6374 (playground). The park has an excellent free adventure playground and a children's zoo with monkeys, reptiles, birds, otters and mongooses, and lots of open space. Every August the free 'Teddy Bears' Picnic" draws thousands of children and their plush pals. Battersea Park or Queenstown Road train station from Victoria. Zoo: Easter–Sept daily 10am–5pm; Oct–Easter Sat & Sun 11am–3pm; adults £1.80, children 90p. Playground: term time Tues–Fri 3.30–7pm; holidays and weekends 11am–6pm. See p.376.

Coram Fields, 93 Guilford St, WC1 ☎020/7837 6138. Very useful, centrally

---

CITY FARMS

College Farm, 45 Fitzalan Rd, N3 ☎020/8349 0690. Former dairy farm with horses, donkeys, Highland cattle, pigs, sheep and rabbits. Finchley Central tube. Daily: April–Oct 10am–6pm; Nov–March 10am–5pm; adults £1.50, children 75p, under-3s free.

Crystal Palace Farm, Crystal Palace Park, Anerley Hill, SE19 ☎020/8778 4487. Small farm with rare farm animals and birds. Crystal Palace train, from Victoria or bus #3. Due to reopen in 2002.

Freightliners Farm, Sheringham Rd, N7 ☎020/7609 0467. Small farm with pigs, goats, hens, ducks and sheep. Highbury & Islington or Holloway Road tube. Tues–Sun 9am–1pm & 2–5pm; free.

Hackney City Farm, 1a Goldsmith's Row, E2 ☎020/7729 6381. Converted brewery that's now a small city farm, with sheep, pigs, hens, turkeys, rabbits and butterflies; also has an organic garden. Bethnal Green tube. Tues–Sun 10am–4.30pm; free.

Kentish Town City Farm, 1 Cressfield Close, Grafton Rd, NW5 ☎020/7916 5421. Five acres of farmland with horses, pigs, goats and chickens. Chalk Farm or Kentish Town tube. Tues–Sun 9.30am–5pm; free.

Mudchute City Farm, Pier St, E14 ☎020/7515 5901. Covering some 35 acres, this is London's largest city farm, with farmyard animals, llamas, pets' corner, study centre and café. Mudchute or Island Gardens DLR. Daily 9am–5pm; free.

Newham City Farm, King George Ave, E16 ☎020/7476 1170. Horses, goats, pigs, sheep and a llama. Prince Regent DLR. Summer Tues–Sun 10am–5pm; winter 10am–4pm.

Spitalfields Community Farm, Weaver St, E1 ☎020/7247 8762. Another tiny East End farm with sheep, cows, donkeys, goats, pigs, rabbits and guinea pigs. Shoreditch tube. Tues–Sun 10.30am–5pm.

Stepping Stones Farm, Stepney Way, E1 ☎020/7790 8204. A rural haven in the East End, with cows, pigs, goats, sheep, rabbits, ferrets, donkeys and guinea pigs. Stepney Green tube. Tues–Sun 9.30am–6pm.

Surrey Docks Farm, Rotherhithe St, SE16 ☎020/7231 1010. A corner of southeast London set aside for goats, sheep, donkeys, chickens, pigs, ducks and bees in hives. Surrey Quays tube. School term time Tues–Fri 10am–5pm, Sat & Sun 10am–1pm & 2–5pm; school holidays Tues–Thurs & Sat & Sun 10am–1pm & 2–5pm; free.

Vauxhall City Farm, Tyers St, SE11 ☎020/7582 4204. Little city farm with sheep, pigs and ducks, plus ponies and donkeys to ride if you become a member (£8 adults, £4 children). Tues–Thurs, Sat & Sun 10.30am–5pm.

---

located playground plus mini-farm with ducks, sheep, rabbits, goats and chickens. Adults admitted only if accompanied by a child. Russell Square tube. Daily 9am–dusk/8pm; free. See p.180.

Hampstead Heath, NW3 ☎020/7485 4491. Nine hundred acres of grassland and woodland, with superb views of the city. Excellent kite-flying potential, too. Hampstead tube, or Gospel Oak or Hampstead Heath train station. Open daily 24hr. See p.405.

Holland Park, Abbotsbury Rd, W11 ☎020/7603 2838 (for information on playgroups). Much-loved, well-tended park with a "One o' Clock" club for under-8s and a playgroup for under-5s; the former is a free drop-in facility, but you must register in advance for the latter, which costs £4.20 per week. Holland Park tube. One o' Clock club Mon–Fri 1–4pm. Playgroup Mon–Fri 9.30am–noon. See p.363.

Hyde Park/Kensington Gardens, W8 ☎020/7298 2100; *www.royalparks.co .uk*. Hyde Park is central London's main open space; in Kensington Gardens, adjoining its western side, you can find the famous Peter Pan statue (near the Long Water), a groovy new playground dedicated to Princess Diana and a pond that's perfect for toy boat sailing. Hyde Park Corner, Knightsbridge, Lancaster Gate or Queensway tube. Daily dawn–dusk. See p.332.

Richmond Park, Richmond, Surrey ☎020/8948 3209; *www.royalparks .co.uk*. A fabulous stretch of countryside, with opportunities for duck-feeding and deer-spotting. Richmond tube or train station from Waterloo. Daily 8am–dusk; free. See p.469.

Shops

Benjamin Pollock's Toy Shop, 44 The Market, Covent Garden, WC2 ☎020/7379 7866; *www.pollocks-coventgarden.co.uk*. Beautiful, old-fashioned toys, for grown-ups as well as children: toy theatres, glove puppets, jack-in-the-boxes and so on.

Covent Garden tube. Mon–Sat 10.30am–6pm.

Children's Book Centre, 237 Kensington High St, W8 ☎020/7937 7497; *www .childrensbookcentre.co.uk*. Huge bookstore for kids, with an excellent range of fiction and non-fiction, lots of gift ideas, a toy basement and a huge multimedia section. High Street Kensington tube. Mon, Wed, Fri & Sat 9.30am–6.30pm, Tues 9.30am–6pm, Thurs 9.30am–7pm, Sun noon–6pm.

Davenport's Magic Shop, 7 Charing Cross Underground Arcade, Strand WC2 ☎020/7836 0408. The oldest family magic business in the world, stocking magic tricks for amateurs and professionals alike, and offering good, practical advice. Charing Cross or Embankment tube. Mon–Fri 9.30am–5.30pm, Sat 10.15am–4.30pm.

Early Learning Centre, Unit 8, Ealing Broadway Centre, The Broadway, W5 ☎020/78567 7076, and several other branches. Toys, puzzles and books to educate and entertain. Good value and great fun: just what early learning should be about. Ealing Broadway tube.

Eric Snook's Toyshop, 32 Covent Garden Market, WC2 ☎020/7379 7681. Eschewing movie merchandise and cheap tat, this shop sells only the most tasteful, meticulously crafted playthings. Covent Garden tube. Mon–Sat 10am–7pm, Sun 11am–6pm.

Hamleys, 188–196 Regent St, W1 ☎020/7494 2000; *www.hamleys.com*. Probably the most famous toystore in the world, spread over five floors and stocking everything from cuddly toys to executive (and junior) board games, via the humble Slinky and the rather less humble, scaled-down, petrol-driven Porsches. Oxford Circus tube. Mon–Fri 10am–8pm, Sat 9.30am–8pm, Sun noon–6pm.

The Kite Store, 69 Neal St, WC2 ☎020/7836 1666. Kites of all kinds for the beginner and stunt master alike, plus a few other fun little things. Covent Garden tube. Mon–Wed & Fri

Kids' London

Kids' London

10am–6pm, Thurs 10am–7pm, Sat 10.30am–6pm.

Skate Attack, 95 Highgate Rd, NW5 ☎020/7267 6961; *www.skateattack .com.* Europe's largest retailer of roller skates, rollerblades and equipment. Roller rental, with protective equipment, is £10 a day, £15 a weekend or £20 a week, plus £100 deposit. Tufnell Park tube. Mon–Fri 9.30am–6pm, Sat 9am–6pm, Sun 10am–1.30pm.

Playin' Games, 33 Museum St, WC1 ☎020/7323 3080. Two floors of traditional board games (Scrabble, Cluedo etc), plus backgammon, war games, fantasy games and more. Tottenham Court Road tube. Mon–Sat 10am–6pm, Sun 11–4pm.

Cinema clubs

Barbican Children's Cinema, Barbican Centre, Silk St, EC2 ☎020/7382 7000; *www.barbican.org.uk.* Films for kids at 11am on a Saturday; children must become members, which costs £4 a year and entitles them to bring up to three guests. Adults £3, Children £2.50. Barbican or Moorgate tube.

Clapham Picture House, 76 Venn St, SW4 ☎020/7498 2242. Saturday Morning Kids' Club with membership at £3 for the first child, £5 for two and so on, and films at 11.45am. Tickets £2.50. Clapham Common tube.

Junior NFT, National Film Theatre, South Bank, SE1 ☎020/7928 3232; *www.bfi .org.uk/nft.* NFT2 puts on matinees at around 3–4pm on Saturday and Sunday. Adults £4.75, children £1. Waterloo tube.

Rio Saturday Morning Picture Club, 107 Kingsland High St, E8 ☎020/7249 2722. Movies for minors at 11am on Saturdays. Adults £2.50, children £1.50. Dalston Kingsland train.

Ritzy Cinema, Brixton Oval, Coldharbour Lane, SW2 ☎020/7737 2121. Bargain-basement kids' films on Saturday mornings at 10.30am. Adults £2, children £1. Brixton tube.

Theatre

Battersea Arts Centre (BAC), 176 Lavender Hill, SW11 ☎020/7223 2223; *www.bac.org.uk.* Children's theatre shows at 2.30pm on Saturdays, and occasionally at other times. Adults £5, children £4. Clapham Junction train station from Waterloo or Victoria.

The Bull, 68 High St, Barnet ☎020/8449 0048. Children's theatre with an excellent reputation for dependably good shows – way out in North London, but easily accessible by tube. Adults £5, children £4. High Barnet tube.

Little Angel Theatre, 14 Dagmar Passage, off Cross St, N1 ☎020/7226 1787. London's only permanent puppet theatre, with shows on Saturdays and Sundays at 11am and 3pm; the mornings are for 3- to 6-year-olds, the afternoons for older kids. No babies are admitted. Additional shows during the holidays and occasionally in the evenings. Adults £5.50, children £5. Angel tube.

Lyric Theatre Hammersmith, King St, W6 ☎020/8741 2311. Children's shows at 11am and 1pm on Saturdays – plays, puppetry, clowns and more. Tickets £5 and upwards. Advance booking essential. Hammersmith tube.

Polka Theatre, 240 The Broadway, SW19 ☎020/8543 4888; *www.polkatheatre .com.* Aimed at kids aged up to around 12, this is a specially designed junior arts centre, with two theatres, a playground, a café and a toy shop. Storytellers, puppeteers and mimes make regular appearances. Tickets £5–8 for children and adults alike. Wimbledon or South Wimbledon tube.

Puppet Theatre Barge, Little Venice, W2 ☎020/7249 6876 or 0836/202745; *www.movingstage.co.uk.* Wonderfully imaginative marionette shows on a fifty-seater barge moored in Little Venice from November to May, then at various points along the Thames (including Richmond). Shows usually start at 2.30pm at weekends and in the holidays. Adults £6.50, children £6. Warwick Avenue tube.

Tricycle Theatre, 269 Kilburn High Rd, NW6 ☎020/7328 1000. High-quality children's shows most Saturdays at 11.30am and 2pm. Budding thespians can also attend drama and dance workshops after school and during the holidays. Tickets £3.50. Kilburn tube.

Unicorn Theatre, ☎020/7700 0702; *www.unicorntheatre.com*. The Unicorn is the oldest professional children's theatre in London, and is currently performing in several venues across the capital. Shows run the gamut from mime and puppetry to traditional plays.

Indoor adventure play centres and swimming pools

Bramley's Big Adventure, 136 Bramley Rd, W10 ☎020/8960 1515. Indoor play centre with sophisticated equipment suitable for older and younger children, and magazines for bored adults. Sessions of 1hr 30min: over-5s around £4, under-5s around £3. Latimer Road or Ladbroke Grove tube. Daily 10am–6pm.

Discovery Zone, First Floor, The Junction, Clapham Junction, SW11 ☎020/7223 1717. Vast, popular play area, located in a shopping centre – admission (£3–5) allows for unlimited play. Clapham Junction train station from Victoria or Waterloo. Mon–Fri 10am–6pm, Sat & Sun 10am–7pm.

The Playhouse, The Old Gymnasium, Highbury Grove School, Highbury Grove, N1 ☎020/7704 9424. Smallish play area, but fairly centrally located, with a maze of tunnels and slides. Children £3 or under. Highbury & Islington tube. Mon–Thurs 10am–6pm, Fri–Sun 10am–7pm.

Snakes & Ladders, Syon Park, Brentford, Middlesex ☎020/8847 0946; *www .syonpark.co.uk*. Indoor play centre, with a giant play frame, that forms part of the great Syon Park commercial extravaganza (see p.458). Unlimited play for around £4. Bus #237 or #267 from Gunnersbury tube. Daily 10am–6pm.

Spike's Madhouse, Crystal Palace National Sports Centre, Anerley Hill, Upper Norwood, SE19 ☎020/8778 9876. Indoor play centre/creche within the Crystal Palace sport complex. £2.50 per 1hr session. Crystal Palace train from Waterloo. Sat & Sun noon–5pm; daily noon–5pm in the school holidays.

Waterfront Leisure Centre, High St, Woolwich, SE18 ☎020/8317 5000. Massive Wild and Wet adventure swimming pool with 100ft-plus slide, wave machine, waterfall and all the usual aquatic high-jinks. Woolwich Arsenal train station from Waterloo, or North Woolwich train station, then foot tunnel. Mon–Fri 7.15am–11pm, Sat 9am–10pm, Sun 9am–9.30pm.

Kids' London

For sports listings, see p.613.

Chapter 27

Directory

AIDS Helpline ☎0800/567123.

Airlines Aer Lingus ☎0645/737747 (*www.aerlingus.ie*); Aeroflot ☎020/7355 2233 (*www.aeroflot.co.uk*); Air France ☎0845/0845111 (*www.airfrance.com*); Alitalia ☎0870/5448259 (*www.alitalia .co.uk*); American Airlines ☎0845 /7789789 (*www.aa.com*); British Airways ☎0845/7222111 (*www.britishairways .com*); Buzz ☎0870/2407070 (*www .buzzaway.com*); Canadian Airlines ☎020/8577 7722 (*www.cdnair.ca*); Delta ☎0800/414767 (*www.delta-air .com*); Easyjet ☎0870/600 0000 (*www.easyjet.com*); Go ☎0845/605 4321 (*www.go-fly.com*); KLM ☎0870 /5750900 (*www.klm.com*); Lufthansa ☎0845/7737747 (*www.lufthansa .co.uk*); Qantas ☎0845/7747767 (*www.qantas.com*); Ryanair ☎0541 /569569 (*www.ryanair.com*); United Airlines ☎0845/8444777 (*www.ual .com*); Virgin ☎01293/747747 (*www.fly .virgin.com*).

Airport enquiries Gatwick ☎01293 /535353 (*www.baa.co.uk*); Heathrow ☎0870/0000123 (*www.baa.co.uk*); London City Airport ☎020/7646 0000 (*www.londoncityairport.com*); Luton ☎01582/405100 (*www.london-luton .com*); Stansted ☎01279/680500 (*www.baa.co.uk*).

American Express 30–31 Haymarket, SW1 ☎020/7484 9600 (and other branches); *www.americanexpress.com*. Mon–Fri 9am–5.30pm, Sat 9am–4pm, Sun 10am– 1pm & 2–4pm. Piccadilly Circus tube.

Car rental Avis ☎0870/6060100 (*www.avis.com*); Global Leisure Cars ☎0870/241 1986 (*www .globalleisurecars.com*); Hertz ☎0870 /5996699 (*www.hertz.com*); Holiday Autos ☎0870/5300400 (*www .holidayautos.com*); Thrifty ☎0990 /168238; www.thrifty.co.uk.

Consulates and embassies Australia, Australia House, Strand, WC2 ☎020/7379 4334 (*www.australia .org.uk*); Canada, MacDonald House, 1 Grosvenor Square, W1 ☎020/7258 6600 (*www.canada.org.uk*); Ireland, 17 Grosvenor Place, SW1 ☎020/7235 2171; New Zealand, New Zealand House, 80 Haymarket, SW1 ☎020/7930 8422 (*www.newzealandhc.org.uk*); South Africa, South Africa House, Trafalgar Square, WC2 ☎020/7451 7299 (*www.southafricahouse.com*); US, 24 Grosvenor Square, W1 ☎020/7499 9000 (*www.usembassy.org.uk*).

Cultural institutes French Institute, 17 Queensbury Place, SW7 ☎020/7838 2144; Goethe Institute, Prince's Gate, Exhibition Rd, SW7 ☎020/7596 4000 (*www.goethe.de/london*); Italian Cultural Institute, 39 Belgrave Square, SW1 ☎020/7235 1461 (*www.italcultur .org.uk*).

Dentists Emergency treatment: Guy's Hospital, St Thomas St, SE1 ☎020 /7955 4317 (Mon–Fri 8.45am–3.30pm).

Electricity Electricity supply in London conforms to the EU standard of approximately 230V.

Emergencies For police, fire and ambulance services, call ☎999.

Hospitals For 24hr accident and emergency: Charing Cross Hospital, Fulham Palace Rd, W6 ☎020/8846 1234; Chelsea & Westminster Hospital, 369 Fulham Rd, SW10 ☎020/8746 8000; Royal Free Hospital, Pond St, NW3 ☎020/7794 0500; Royal London Hospital, Whitechapel Rd, E1 ☎020/7377 7000; St Mary's Hospital, Praed St, W2 ☎020/7886 6666; University College Hospital, Grafton Way, WC1 ☎020/7387 9300; Whittington Hospital, Highgate Hill, N19 ☎020/7272 3070.

Laundry There are self-service launderettes all over London. Duds'n'Suds is a good central outfit with TV, pool and pinball: 49–51 Brunswick Shopping Centre, WC1 ☎020/7837 1122 (Mon–Fri 8am–9pm, Sat & Sun 8am–8pm; Russell Square tube).

Left luggage

AIRPORTS Gatwick: North Terminal ☎01293/502013 (daily 6am–10pm); South Terminal ☎01293/502014 (24hr). Heathrow: Terminal 1 ☎020/8745 5301 (daily 6am–11pm); Terminal 2 ☎020 /8745 4599 (daily 6am–10.30pm); Terminal 3 ☎020/8759 3344 (daily 5.30am–10.30pm); Terminal 4 ☎020 /8745 7460 (daily 5.30am–11pm). London City Airport ☎020/7646 0000 (daily 6.30am–10pm). Stansted Airport ☎01279/680500 (24hr).

TRAIN STATIONS Charing Cross ☎020 /7839 4282 (daily 7am–11pm); Euston ☎020/7320 0528 (Mon–Sat 6.45am–11.15pm, Sun 7.15am–11pm); Victoria ☎020/7928 5151 ext 27523 (daily 7am–10.15pm, plus lockers); Waterloo International ☎020/7928 5151 (Mon–Fri 4am–11pm, Sat & Sun 6am–11pm).

Library Westminster Central Reference Library, 35 St Martin's St, WC2 ☎020 /7641 4634; *www.westminster .gov.uk*. Leicester Square tube. Mon–Fri 10am–8pm, Sat 10am–5pm.

Lost property

AIRPORTS Gatwick ☎01293/503162 (daily 7.30am–5.30pm); Heathrow

☎020/8745 7727 (Mon–Fri 8am–5pm, Sat & Sun 8am–4pm); London City Airport ☎020/7646 0000 (Mon–Fri 6am–9.30pm, Sat 6am–1am, Sun 10.30am–9.30pm); Stansted ☎01279 /680500 (daily 5.30am–11pm).

BUSES ☎020/7222 1234.

HEATHROW EXPRESS ☎020/8745 7727.

TAXIS (black cabs only) ☎020/7833 0996.

TRAIN STATIONS Euston ☎020/7922 6477 (Mon–Sat 6.45am–11pm); King's Cross ☎020 /7922 9081 (daily 8am–7.45pm); Liverpool Street ☎020/7928 9158 (Mon–Fri 7am–7pm, Sat & Sun 7am– 2pm); Paddington ☎020/7313 1514 (Mon–Fri 9am–5.30pm); Victoria ☎020 /7922 9887 (Mon–Fri 7.30am–10pm); Waterloo ☎020/7401 7861 (Mon–Fri 7.30am–8pm).

TUBE TRAINS London Regional Transport ☎020/7486 2496.

Motorbike rental Scootabout, 1–3 Leeke St, WC1 ☎020/7833 4607; *www .hgbmotorcycles.co.uk*. Mon–Fri 9am–6pm, Sat 9am–1pm.

Police Central police stations include: Charing Cross, Agar St, WC2 ☎020/7240 1212; Holborn, 70 Theobalds Rd, WC1 ☎020/7404 1212; King's Cross, 76 King's Cross Rd, WC1 ☎020/7704 1212; Tottenham Court Road, 56 Tottenham Court Rd, W1 ☎020/7637 1212; West End Central, 10 Vine St, W1 ☎020/7437 1212; City of London Police, Bishopsgate, EC2 ☎020/7601 2222.

Postal services The only late-opening post office is the Trafalgar Square branch at 24–28 William IV St, WC2 4DL ☎020/7484 9304 (Mon–Fri 8am–8pm, Sat 9am–8pm); it's also the city's poste restante collection point. For general postal enquiries phone ☎0845 /7740740, or visit the Web site: *www .royalmail.co.uk*.

Rape crisis ☎020/7837 1600.

Samaritans ☎0345/909090.

Directory

Directory

Time Greenwich Mean Time (GMT) is used from October to March; for the rest of the year the country switches to British Summer Time (BST), one hour ahead of GMT.

Train enquiries For national rail enquiries, call ☎0845/7484950.

Travel agents Campus Travel, 52 Grosvenor Gardens, SW1 ☎0870/240 1010 (*www.usitcampus.co.uk*); Council Travel, 28a Poland St, W1 ☎020/7437 7767 (*www.destination-group.com*); STA Travel, 86 Old Brompton Rd, SW7 ☎020/7361 6161(*www.statravel.co.uk*); Trailfinders, 42–50 Earl's Court Rd, SW5 ☎020/7938 3366 (*www.trailfinders.co.uk*).

The Contexts

A brief history

Two thousand years of compressed history – featuring riots and revolutions, plagues, fires, slum clearances, lashings of gin, Mrs Thatcher and the London people.

Roman Londinium

There is evidence of scattered **Celtic settlements** along the Thames, but no firm proof that central London was permanently settled by the Celts before the arrival of the Romans. Julius Caesar led several small cross-Channel incursions in 55 and 54 BC, but it wasn't until nearly a century later, in **43 AD**, that a full-scale invasion force of some forty thousand Roman troops landed in Kent.

Britain's rumoured mineral wealth was certainly one motive behind the Roman invasion, but the immediate spur was the need of the emperor Claudius, who owed his power to the army, for an easy military triumph. The Romans defeated the main Celtic tribe of southern Britain, the Catuvellauni, on the Medway, southeast of London, crossed the Thames and then set up camp to await the triumphant arrival of the emperor Claudius, his elephants and the Praetorian Guard.

It is now thought that the site of this first Roman camp was, in fact, in Westminster – the lowest fordable point on the Thames – and not in what is now the City. However, around 50 AD, when the Romans decided to establish the permanent military camp of **Londinium** here, they chose a point further downstream, building a bridge some 50 yards east of today's London Bridge. London became the hub of the Roman road system, but it was not the Romans' principal colonial settlement, which remained at **Camulodunum** (modern Colchester) to the northeast.

In 60 AD, the East Anglian people, known as the Iceni, rose up against the invaders under their queen **Boudicca** (or Boadicea) and sacked Camulodunum, slaughtering most of the legion sent from Lindum (Lincoln) and making their way to the ill-defended town of Londinium. According to archeological evidence, Londinium was burnt to the ground and, according to the Roman historian, Tacitus, whose father-in-law was in Britain at the time (and later served as its governor), the inhabitants were "massacred, hanged, burned and crucified". The Iceni were eventually defeated, and Boudicca committed suicide (62AD).

In the aftermath, Londinium emerged as the new commercial and administrative (though not military) capital of Britannia, and was endowed with an imposing basilica and forum, a governor's palace, temples, bath houses and an amphitheatre. To protect against further attacks, fortifications were built, three miles long, 15ft high and 8ft thick, with a large fort, whose ragstone walls can still be seen near today's Museum of London (see p.236), home to many of the city's most significant Roman finds.

Archeological evidence suggests that Londinium was at its most prosperous and populous from around 80 AD to 120 AD, during which time it is thought to have evolved into the empire's fifth largest city north of the Alps. Between 150 AD and 400 AD, however, London appears to have sheltered less than half the number of people, probably due to economic decline. Nevertheless, it remained strategically and politically important, and as an imperial outpost, actually appears to have benefited from the chaos that engulfed the rest of the empire during much of the third century. From 260 AD it formed part of the breakaway "Empire of the Gauls", while from 287 AD to 296 AD it became the capital of the short-lived British Empire, first under Emperor Carausius, and then by his assassin, Allectus.

In the fourth century, London found itself, once more, at the heart of various military revolts by would-be emperors, most notably Magnus Maximus, who in 383 AD led a rebellion in Britain, and marched off to eventual defeat some five years later. In 406 AD, the Roman army in Britain mutinied for the last time and invaded Gaul under the self-proclaimed Emperor Constantine III. The empire was on its last legs, and the Romans were never in a position to return, officially abandoning the city in 410 AD (when Rome was sacked by the Visigoths), and leaving the country and its chief city at the mercy of the marauding Saxon pirates, who had been making increasingly persistent raids on the coast since the middle of the previous century.

Saxon Lundenwic and the Danes

Roman London appears to have been more or less abandoned from the first couple of decades of the fifth century until the ninth century. Instead, the **Anglo-Saxon** invaders, who controlled most of southern England by the sixth century, appear to have settled, initially at least, to the west of the Roman city. When Augustine was sent to reconvert Britain to Christianity, the Saxon city of **Lundenwic** was considered important enough to be granted a bishopric, in 604, though it was Canterbury, not London, that was chosen as the seat of the Primate of England. Nevertheless, trade flourished once more during this period, as attested by the Venerable Bede, who wrote of London in 730 as "the mart of many nations resorting to it by land and sea".

In 841 and 851 London suffered Danish Viking attacks, and it may have been in response to these raids that the Saxons decided to reoccupy the walled Roman city. By 871 the **Danes** were confident enough to attack and established London as their winter base, but in 886 Alfred the Great, King of Wessex, recaptured the city, rebuilt the walls and formally re-established London as a fortified town and a trading port. After a lull, the Vikings returned once more during the reign of Ethelred the Unready (978–1016), attacking unsuccessfully in 994, 1009 and 1013. The

following year, the Danes, under Swein Forkbeard, finally recaptured London, only for Ethelred to reclaim it later that year, with help from King Olaf of Norway. In 1016, following the death of Ethelred, and his son, Edmund Ironside, the Danish leader Cnut (or Canute), son of Swein, became King of All England, and made London the national capital (in preference to the Wessex base of Winchester), a position it has held ever since.

Danish rule lasted only 26 years, and with the death of Cnut's two sons, the English throne returned to the House of Wessex, and to Ethelred's exiled son, **Edward the Confessor** (1042–66). Edward moved the court and church upstream to Thorney Island (or the Isle of Brambles). Here he built a splendid new palace so that he could oversee construction of his "West Minster" (later to become Westminster Abbey). Edward was too weak to attend the official consecration and died just ten days later: he is buried in the great cathedral he founded, where his shrine has been a place of pilgrimage for centuries. Of greater political and social significance, however, was his geographical separation of power, with royal government based in **Westminster**, while the **City of London** remained the commercial centre.

1066 and all that

On his deathbed in the new year of 1066, the celibate Edward made Harold, Earl of Wessex, his appointed successor. Having crowned himself in the new abbey, thus establishing a tradition that continues to this day, Harold went on to defeat his brother Tostig (who was in cahoots with the Norwegians), but was himself defeated by **William of Normandy** (aka William the Conqueror) and his invading army at the Battle of Hastings. On Christmas Day of 1066, William crowned himself king in Westminster Abbey. Elsewhere in England, the Normans ruthlessly suppressed all opposition, but in London William granted the City a charter guaranteeing to preserve the privileges it had enjoyed under Edward. However, as an insurance policy, William also built three forts in the city, of which the sole remnant is the White Tower, now the nucleus of the **Tower of London**. As a further precaution, he also established another castle, a day's march away at **Windsor**, and, like his predecessor, Edward, based the court at Westminster.

Over the next few centuries, the City waged a continuous struggle with the monarchy for a degree of self-government and independence. After all, when there was a fight over the throne, the support of London's wealth and manpower could be decisive, as **King Stephen** (1135–54) discovered, when Londoners attacked his rival for the throne, Mathilda, daughter of Henry I, preventing her from being crowned at Westminster. Again, in 1191, when the future **King John** (1199–1216) was tussling with William Longchamp over the kingdom during the absence of Richard the Lionheart (1189–99), it was the Londoners who made sure Longchamp remained cooped up in the Tower. For this particular favour, London was granted the right to elect its own sheriff, or **mayor**, an office that was officially acknowledged in the Magna Carta of 1215.

Occasionally, however, Londoners backed the wrong side, as they did with Simon de Montfort, who was engaged in civil war with **Henry III** (1216–72) during the 1260s. As a result, the City found itself temporarily stripped of its privileges. In any case, London was chiefly of importance to the medieval kings as a source of wealth. Traditionally, it was to the Jewish community, which arrived in 1066 with William the Conqueror, that the sovereign turned for a loan. By the second half of the thirteenth century, however, the Jews had been squeezed dry, and in 1290, after a series of increasingly bloody attacks, **London's Jews** were expelled by Edward I (1272–1307), who turned instead to the City's Italian merchants for financial assistance.

From the Black Death to the Wars of the Roses

London backed the right side in the struggle between Edward II (1307–27) and his queen, Isabella, who, along with her lover Mortimer, succeeded in deposing the king. The couple's son Edward III (1327–77) was duly crowned, and London enjoyed a period of relative peace and prosperity, thanks to the wealth generated by the wool trade. All this was cut short, however, by the arrival of the Europe-wide bubonic plague outbreak known as the **Black Death** in 1348. This disease, carried by black rats and transmitted to humans by flea bites, wiped out something like half the capital's population in the space of two years. Other epidemics followed in 1361, 1369 and 1375, creating a volatile

economic situation that was worsened by the financial strains imposed on the capital by having to bankroll the country's involvement in the Hundred Years' War.

Matters came to a head with the introduction of the poll tax, a head tax imposed in the 1370s on all men regardless of means. During the ensuing **Peasants' Revolt** of 1381, London's citizens opened the City gates to Wat Tyler's Kentish rebels and joined in the lynching of the archbishop, plus countless rich merchants and clerics. Tyler was then lured to meet the boy-king Richard II at Smithfield, just outside the City, where he was murdered by Mayor Walworth, who was subsequently knighted for his treachery. Tyler's supporters were fobbed off with promises of political changes that never came, as Richard unleashed a wave of repression and retribution.

Parallel with this social unrest were the demands for clerical reforms made by the scholar and heretic **John Wycliffe**, whose ideas were keenly taken up by Londoners. His followers, known as **Lollards**, made the first translation of the Bible into English in 1380. Another sign of the elevation of the common language was the success enjoyed by **Geoffrey Chaucer** (c.1340–1400), a London wine merchant's son, whose *Canterbury Tales* was the first major work written in English and was later one of the first books to be printed.

After the Peasants' Revolt, the next serious disturbance was **Jack Cade's Revolt**, which took place in 1450. An army of twenty-five thousand Kentish rebels – including gentry, clergy and craftsmen – defeated King Henry VI's forces at Sevenoaks, marched to Blackheath, withdrew temporarily and then eventually reached Southwark in early July. Having threatened to burn down London Bridge, the insurgents entered the City and spent three days wreaking vengeance on their enemies before being ejected. A subsequent attempt to enter the City via London Bridge was repulsed, and the army was dispersed with yet more false promises. The reprisals, which became known as the "harvest of heads", were as harsh as before – Cade himself was captured, killed and brought to the capital for dismemberment.

A decade later, the country was plunged into more widespread conflict during the so-called **Wars of the Roses**, the name now given to the strife between the rival noble houses of Lancaster and York. Londoners wisely tended to sit on the fence throughout the conflict, only committing themselves in 1461, when they opened the gates to the Yorkist king **Edward IV** (1461–70 and 1471–83), thus helping him to depose the mad Henry VI (1422–61 and 1470–71). In 1470, Henry, who had spent five years in the Tower, was proclaimed king once more, only to be deposed again a year later, following Lancastrian defeats at the battles of Barnet and Tewkesbury.

Tudor London

The **Tudor** family, which with the coronation of **Henry VII** (1485–1509) emerged triumphant from the mayhem of the Wars of the Roses, reinforced London's pre-eminence during the sixteenth century, when the Tower of London and the **royal palaces** of Whitehall, St James's, Richmond, Greenwich, Hampton Court and Windsor provided the backdrop for the most momentous events of the period. At the same time, the city's population, which had remained constant at around fifty thousand since the Black Death, increased dramatically, trebling in size during the course of the century.

One of the crucial developments of the century was the English **Reformation**, the separation of the English Church from Rome, a split initially prompted not by doctrinal issues, but by the failure of Catherine of Aragon, first wife of **Henry VIII** (1509–47), to produce a male heir. In fact, prior to his desire to divorce Catherine, Henry, along with his lord chancellor, Cardinal Wolsey, had been zealously persecuting Protestants. However, when the Pope refused to annul Henry's marriage, Henry knew he could rely on a large amount of popular support, as anti-clerical feelings were running high. By contrast, Henry's new chancellor, Sir Thomas More, wouldn't countenance divorce, and resigned in 1532. Henry then broke with Rome, appointed himself head of the English Church and demanded both citizens and clergy swear allegiance to him. Very few refused, though More was among them, becoming the country's first Catholic martyr with his execution in 1535.

Henry's most far-reaching act, by far, though, was his **Dissolution of the Monasteries**, a programme commenced in 1536 in order to bump up the royal coffers. The Dissolution changed the entire fabric of both the city and the country: previously dominated by its religious institutions,

London's property market was suddenly flooded with confiscated estates, which were quickly snapped up and redeveloped by the Tudor nobility.

Henry may have been the one who kickstarted the English Reformation, but he was, in fact, a religious conservative, and in the last ten years of his reign he succeeded in executing as many Protestants as he did Catholics. Religious turmoil only intensified in the decade following Henry's death. First, Henry's sickly son, **Edward VI** (1547–53), pursued a staunchly anti-Catholic policy. By the end of his short reign, London's churches had lost their altars, their paintings, their relics and virtually all their statuary. After an abortive attempt to secure the succession of Edward's Protestant cousin, Lady Jane Grey, the religious pendulum swung the other way for the next five years with the accession of **"Bloody Mary"** (1553–58). This time, it was Protestants who were martyred with abandon at Tyburn and Smithfield.

Despite all the religious strife, the Tudor economy remained in good health for the most part, reaching its height in the reign of **Elizabeth I** (1558–1603), when the piratical exploits of seafarers Walter Raleigh, Francis Drake, Martin Frobisher and John Hawkins helped to map out the world for English commerce. London's commercial success was epitomized by the millionaire merchant Thomas Gresham, who erected the **Royal Exchange** in 1572, establishing London as the premier world trade market.

The 45 years of Elizabeth's reign also witnessed the efflorescence of a specifically **English Renaissance**, especially in the field of literature, which reached its apogee in the brilliant careers of **Christopher Marlowe**, **Ben Jonson** and **William Shakespeare**. The presses of **Fleet Street**, established a century earlier by William Caxton's apprentice Wynkyn de Worde, ensured London's position as a centre for the printed word. Beyond the jurisdiction of the City censors, in the entertainment district of Southwark, whorehouses, animal-baiting pits and theatres flourished. The carpenter-cum-actor James Burbage designed the first purpose-built playhouse in 1574, eventually rebuilding it south of the river as the **Globe Theatre**, where Shakespeare premiered many of his works (the theatre has since been reconstructed; see p.315).

From Gunpowder Plot to Civil War

On Elizabeth's death in 1603, James VI of Scotland became **James I** (1603–25) of England, thereby uniting the two crowns and marking the beginning of the **Stuart dynasty**. His intention of exercising religious tolerance after the anti-Catholicism of Elizabeth's reign was thwarted by the public outrage that followed the **Gunpowder Plot** of 1605, when Guy Fawkes and a group of Catholic conspirators were discovered attempting to blow up the king at the state opening of Parliament. James, who clung to the medieval notion of the divine right of kings, inevitably clashed with the landed gentry who dominated Parliament, and tensions between Crown and Parliament were worsened by his persecution of the Puritans, an extreme but increasingly powerful Protestant group.

Under James's successor, **Charles I** (1625–49), the animosity between Crown and Parliament came to a head. From 1629 to 1640 Charles ruled without the services of Parliament, but was forced to recall it when he ran into problems in Scotland, where he was attempting to subdue the Presbyterians. Faced with extremely antagonistic MPs, Charles attempted unsuccessfully to arrest several of their number at Westminster. Acting on a tip-off, the MPs fled by river to the City, which sided with Parliament. Charles withdrew to Nottingham, where he raised his standard, the opening military act of the **Civil War**.

London was the key to victory for both sides, and as a Parliamentarian stronghold it came under attack almost immediately from Royalist forces. Having defeated the Parliamentary troops to the west of London at Brentford in November 1642, the way was open for Charles to take the capital. Londoners turned out in numbers to defend their city, some twenty-four thousand assembling at Turnham Green. Charles hesitated and in the end withdrew to Reading, thus missing his greatest chance of victory. A complex system of fortifications was thrown up around London, but was never put to the test. In the end, the capital remained intact throughout the war, which culminated in the execution of the king outside Whitehall's Banqueting House in January 1649.

For the next eleven years England was a **Commonwealth** – at first a true republic, then, after 1653, a Protectorate under **Oliver Cromwell**, who was ultimately as impatient of Parliament and as arbitrary as Charles had been. London

found itself in the grip of the **Puritans'** zealous laws, which closed down all theatres, enforced observance of the Sabbath and banned the celebration of Christmas, which was considered a papist superstition.

Plague and fire

Just as London proved Charles I's undoing, so its ecstatic reception of **Charles II** (1660–85) helped ease the **Restoration** of the monarchy in 1660. The "Merry Monarch" immediately caught the mood of the public by opening up the theatres, and he encouraged the sciences by helping the establishment of the **Royal Society** for Improving Natural Knowledge, whose founder members included **Christopher Wren**, **Isaac Newton** and **John Evelyn**.

The good times that rolled in the early period of Charles's reign came to an abrupt end with the onset of the **Great Plague** of 1665. Epidemics of bubonic plague were nothing new to London – there had been major outbreaks in 1593, 1603, 1625, 1636 and 1647 – but the combination of a warm summer and the chronic overcrowding of the city proved calamitous in this instance. Those with money left the city (the court moved to Oxford), while the poorer districts outside the City were the hardest hit. The extermination of the city's dog and cat population – believed to be the source of the epidemic – only exacerbated the situation. In September, the death toll peaked at twelve thousand a week, and in total an estimated hundred thousand lost their lives.

A cold snap in November extinguished the plague, but the following year London had to contend with yet another disaster, the **Great Fire** of 1666 (see p.253). As with the plague, outbreaks of fire were fairly commonplace in London, whose buildings were predominantly timber-framed, and whose streets were narrow, allowing fires to spread rapidly. So it was that between September 2 and September 5 some eighty percent of the City was razed to the ground, including 87 churches, 44 livery company halls and 13,200 houses; the death toll did not even reach double figures, but more than a hundred thousand were left homeless.

Within five years, nine thousand houses had been rebuilt with bricks and mortar (timber was banned), and fifty years later **Christopher Wren** had almost single-handedly rebuilt all the City churches and completed the world's first

Protestant cathedral, **St Paul's**. Medieval London was no more, though the grandiose masterplans of Wren and other architects had to be rejected due to the legal intricacies of property rights within the City. The **Great Rebuilding**, as it was known, was one of London's most remarkable achievements – and this despite a chronic lack of funds, a series of very severe winters and continuing wars against the Dutch.

Religious differences once again came to the fore with the accession of Charles's Catholic brother, **James II** (1685–88), who successfully put down the Monmouth Rebellion of 1685, but failed to halt the "Glorious Revolution" of 1688, which brought the Dutch king William of Orange to the throne, much to most people's relief. **William** (1689–1702) and his wife **Mary** (1689–95), daughter of James II, were made joint sovereigns, having agreed to a Bill of Rights defining the limitations of the monarch's power and the rights of his or her subjects. This, together with the Act of Settlement of 1701 – which among other things barred Catholics or anyone married to one from succession to the throne – made Britain the first country in the world to be governed by a **constitutional monarchy**, in which the roles of legislature and executive were separate and interdependent. A further development during the reign of **Anne** (1702–14), second daughter of James II, was the Act of Union of 1707, which united the English and Scottish parliaments.

Georgian London

When Queen Anne died childless in 1714 (despite having given birth seventeen times), the Stuart line ended, though pro-Stuart or Jacobite rebellions continued on and off until 1745. In accordance with the Act of Settlement, the succession passed to a non-English-speaking German, the Duke of Hanover, who became **George I** (1714–27) of England. As power leaked from the monarchy, the king ceased to attend cabinet meetings (which he couldn't understand anyway), his place being taken by his chief minister. Most prominent among these chief ministers or "prime ministers", as they became known, was **Robert Walpole**, the first politician to live at **10 Downing Street**, and effective ruler of the country from 1721 to 1742.

Meanwhile, London's expansion continued unabated. The shops of the newly developed

West End stocked the most fashionable goods in the country, the volume of trade more than tripled, and London's growing population – it was by now the largest city in the world, with a population rapidly approaching one million – created a huge market for food and other produce, as well as fuelling a building boom. In the City, the **Bank of England** – founded in 1694 to raise funds to conduct war against France – was providing a sound foundation for the economy. It could not, however, prevent the mania for financial speculation that resulted in the fiasco of the **South Sea Company**, which in 1720 sold shares in its monopoly of trade in the Pacific and along the east coast of South America. The "bubble" burst when the shareholders took fright at the extent of their own investments, and the value of the shares dropped to nothing, reducing many to penury and almost wrecking the government, which was saved only by the astute intervention of Walpole.

Wealthy though London was, it was also experiencing the worst mortality rates since records began in the reign of Henry VIII. Disease was rife in the overcrowded immigrant quarter of the East End and other slum districts, but the real killer during this period was **gin**. It's difficult to exaggerate the effects of the gin-drinking orgy which took place among the poorer sections of London's population between 1720 and 1751. At its height, gin consumption was averaging two pints a week for every man, woman and child, and the burial rate exceeded the baptism rate by more than 2:1. The origins of this lay in the country's enormous surplus of corn, which had to be sold in some form or another to keep the landowners happy. Deregulation of the distilling trade was Parliament's answer, thereby flooding the urban market with cheap, intoxicating liquor, which resulted in an enormous increase in crime, prostitution, child mortality and general misery among the poor. Eventually, in the face of huge vested interests, the government was forced to pass an act in 1751 that restricted gin retailing and brought the epidemic to a halt.

Policing the metropolis was an increasing preoccupation for the government. It was proving a task far beyond the city's three thousand beadles, constables and nightwatchmen, who were, in any case, "old men chosen from the dregs of the people who have no other arms but a lantern and a pole", according to one French visitor. As a result, crime continued unabated throughout the eighteenth century, so that, in the words of Horace Walpole, one was "forced to travel even at noon as if one was going into battle". The government imposed draconian measures, introducing capital punishment for the most minor misdemeanours. The prison population swelled, transportations began, and 1200 Londoners were hanged at Tyburn's gallows.

Despite such measures, and the passing of the Riot Act in 1715, rioting remained a popular pastime among the poorer classes in London. Anti-Irish riots had taken place in 1736; in 1743 there were further riots in defence of cheap liquor; and in the 1760s there were more organized mobilizations by supporters of the great agitator **John Wilkes**, calling for political reform. The most serious insurrection of the lot, however, were the **Gordon Riots** of 1780, when up to fifty thousand Londoners went on a five-day rampage through the city. Although anti-Catholicism was the spark that lit the fire, the majority of the rioters' targets were chosen not for their religion but for their wealth. The most dramatic incidents took place at Newgate Prison, where thousands of inmates were freed, and at the Bank of England, which was saved only by the intervention of the military – and John Wilkes, of all people. The death toll was in excess of three hundred, 25 rioters were subsequently hanged, and further calls were made in Parliament for the establishment of a proper police force.

Nineteenth-century London

The **nineteenth century** witnessed the emergence of London as the capital of an empire that stretched across the globe. The world's largest enclosed **dock system** was built in the marshes to the east of the City, Tory reformer **Robert Peel** established the world's first civilian **police force**, and the world's first public transport network was created, with horse-buses, trains, trams and an underground railway.

The city's population grew dramatically from just over one million in 1801 (the first official census) to nearly seven million by 1901. **Industrialization** brought pollution and overcrowding, especially in the slums of the East End. Smallpox, measles, whooping cough and scarlet fever killed thousands of working-class families, as did the cholera outbreaks of 1832 and 1848–49. The **Poor Law** of 1834 formalized **workhouses** for the destitute, but these failed to

alleviate the problem, in the end becoming little more than prison hospitals for the penniless. It is this era of slum life and huge social divides that Dickens evoked in his novels.

Architecturally, London was changing rapidly. **George IV** (1820–30), who became Prince Regent in 1811 during the declining years of his father, George III, instigated several grandiose projects that survive to this day. With the architect **John Nash**, he laid out London's first planned processional route, Regent Street, and a prototype garden city around **Regent's Park**. The Regent's Canal was driven through the northern fringe of the city, and Trafalgar Square began to take shape. The city already boasted the first secular public museum in the world, the **British Museum**, and in 1814 London's first public art gallery opened in the suburb of Dulwich, followed shortly afterwards by the National Gallery, which was founded in 1824. London finally got its own university, too, in 1826.

The accession of **Queen Victoria** (1837–1901) coincided with a period in which the country's international standing reached unprecedented heights, and as a result Victoria became as much a national icon as Elizabeth I had been. Though the intellectual achievements of Victoria's reign were immense – typified by the publication of Darwin's *The Origin of Species* in 1859 – the country saw itself above all as an imperial power founded on industrial and commercial prowess. Its spirit was perhaps best embodied by the great engineering feats of Isambard Kingdom Brunel and by the **Great Exhibition** of 1851, a display of manufacturing achievements from all over the world, which took place in the Crystal Palace, erected in Hyde Park.

Despite being more than twice the size of Paris, London did not experience the political upheavals of the French capital – the terrorists who planned to wipe out the cabinet in the **1820 Cato Street Conspiracy** were the exception (see p.124). Mass demonstrations and the occasional minor fracas preceded the passing of the **1832 Reform Act**, which acknowledged the principle of popular representation (though few men and no women had the vote), but there was no real threat of revolution. London doubled its number of MPs in the new parliament, but its own administration remained dominated by the City oligarchy.

The **Chartist movement**, which campaigned for universal male suffrage (among other things), was much stronger in the industrialized north than in the capital, at least until the 1840s. Support for the movement reached its height in the revolutionary year of 1848. In March, some ten thousand Chartists occupied Trafalgar Square and held out against the police for two days. Then, on April 10, the Chartists organized a mass demonstration on Kennington Common. The government panicked and drafted in eighty thousand "special constables" to boost the capital's four thousand police officers, and troops were garrisoned around all public buildings. In the end, London was a long way off experiencing a revolution: the demo took place, but the planned march on Parliament was called off.

The birth of local government

The first tentative steps towards a cohesive form of metropolitan government were taken in 1855 with the establishment of the **Metropolitan Board of Works** (MBW). Its initial remit only covered sewerage, lighting and street maintenance, but it was soon extended to include gas, fire services, public parks and slum clearance. The achievements of the MBW – and in particular those of its chief engineer, Joseph Bazalgette – were immense, creating an underground sewer system (much of it still in use), improving transport routes and wiping out some of the city's more notorious slums. However, vested interests and resistance to reform from the City hampered the efforts of the MBW, which was also found to be involved in widespread malpractice.

In 1888 the **London County Council** (LCC) was established. It was the first directly elected London-wide government, though as ever the City held on jealously to its independence. The arrival of the LCC coincided with an increase in working-class militancy within the capital. In 1884, 120,000 gathered in Hyde Park to support the ultimately unsuccessful London Government Bill, while a demonstration held in 1886 in Trafalgar Square in protest against unemployment ended in a riot through St James's. The following year the government banned any further demos, and the resultant protest brought even larger numbers to Trafalgar Square. The brutality of the police in breaking up this last demonstration led to its becoming known as "Bloody Sunday".

In 1888 the Bryant & May matchgirls won their landmark **strike action** over working conditions, a

victory followed up the next year by further successful strikes by the gasworkers and dockers. Charles Booth published his seventeen-volume *Life and Labour of the People of London* in 1890, providing the first clear picture of the social fabric of the city and shaming the council into action. In the face of powerful vested interests – landlords, factory owners and private utility companies – the LCC's Liberal leadership attempted to tackle the enormous problems, partly by taking gas, water, electricity and transport into municipal ownership, a process that took several more decades to achieve. The LCC's ambitious housing programme was beset with problems, too. Slum clearances only exacerbated overcrowding, and the new dwellings were too expensive for those in greatest need. Rehousing the poor in the suburbs also proved unpopular, since there was a policy of excluding pubs, traditionally the social centre of working-class communities, from these developments.

While half of London struggled to make ends meet, the other half enjoyed the fruits of the richest nation in the world. Luxury establishments such as *The Ritz* and Harrods belong to this period, which was personified by the dissolute and complacent Prince of Wales, later **Edward VII** (1901–10). For the masses, too, there were new entertainments to be enjoyed: music halls boomed, public houses prospered, and the circulation of populist newspapers such as the *Daily Mirror* topped one million. The first "Test" cricket match between England and Australia took place in 1880 at the Kennington Oval in front of twenty thousand spectators, and during the following 25 years nearly all of London's professional **football clubs** were founded.

From World War I to World War II

Public patriotism peaked at the outbreak of **World War I** (1914–18), with crowds cheering the troops off from Victoria and Waterloo stations, convinced the fighting would all be over by Christmas. In the course of the next four years London experienced its first aerial attacks, with Zeppelin raids leaving some 650 dead, but these were minor casualties in the context of a war that destroyed millions of lives and eradicated whatever remained of the majority's respect for the ruling classes.

At the war's end in 1918, the country's social fabric was changed drastically as the voting franchise was extended to all men aged 21 and over and to women of 30 or over. The tardy liberalization of women's rights – largely due to the radical **Suffragette** movement led by Emmeline Pankhurst and her daughters – was not completed until 1928, the year of Emmeline's death, when women were at last granted the vote on equal terms with men.

Between the wars, London's population increased dramatically, reaching close to nine million by 1939, and representing one-fifth of the country's population. In contrast to the nineteenth century, however, there was a marked shift in population out into the **suburbs**. Some took advantage of the new "model dwellings" of LCC estates in places such as Dagenham in the east, though far more settled in "Metroland", the sprawling new suburban districts that followed the extension of the Underground out into northwest London.

In 1924 the British Empire Exhibition was held, with the intention of emulating the success of the Great Exhibition. Some 27 million people visited the show, but its success couldn't hide the tensions that had been simmering since the end of the war. In 1926, a wage dispute between the miners' unions and their bosses developed into the **General Strike**. For nine days, more than half a million workers stayed away from work, until the government called in the army and thousands of volunteers to break the strike.

The economic situation deteriorated even further after the crash of the New York Stock Exchange in 1929, with unemployment in Britain reaching over three million in 1931. The Jarrow Marchers, the most famous protesters of the Depression years, shocked London on their arrival in 1936. In the same year thousands of British fascists tried to march through the predominantly Jewish East End, only to be stopped in the so-called **Battle of Cable Street** (see p.269). The end of the year brought a crisis within the Royal Family, too, when Edward VIII abdicated following his decision to marry Wallis Simpson, a twice-divorced American. His brother, **George VI** (1936–52), took over.

There were few public displays of patriotism with the outbreak of **World War II** (1939–45), and even fewer preparations were made against the likelihood of aerial bombardment. The most significant step was the evacuation of six hundred thousand of London's most vulnerable citizens (mostly children), but around half that number

had drifted back to the capital by the Christmas of 1939, the midpoint of the "phoney war". The Luftwaffe's bombing campaign, known as the **Blitz**, began on September 7, 1940, when in one night alone some 430 Londoners lost their lives, and over 1600 were seriously injured. For 57 consecutive nights the Nazis bombed the capital until the last raid on May 10, 1941. Further carnage was caused towards the end of the war by the pilotless V-1 "doodlebugs" and V-2 rockets, which caused another twenty thousand casualties. In total, thirty thousand civilians lost their lives in the bombing of London, with fifty thousand injured and some 130,000 houses destroyed.

Postwar London

The end of the war in 1945 was followed by a general election, which brought a landslide victory for the Labour Party under **Clement Attlee**. The Attlee government created the **welfare state**, and initiated a radical programme of **nationalization**, which brought the gas, electricity, coal, steel and iron industries under State control, along with the inland transport services. London itself was left with a severe accommodation crisis, with some eighty percent of the housing stock damaged to some degree. In response, prefabricated houses were erected all over the city, some of which were to remain occupied for well over forty years. The LCC also began building huge housing estates on many of the city's numerous bomb sites, an often misconceived strategy which ran in tandem with the equally disastrous New Towns policy of central government.

To lift the country out of its gloom, the **Festival of Britain** was staged in 1951 on derelict land on the south bank of the Thames, a site that was eventually transformed into the **South Bank Arts Centre**. Londoners turned up at this technological funfair in their thousands, but at the same time many were abandoning the city for good, starting a slow process of population decline that has continued ever since. The consequent labour shortage was made good by mass **immigration** from the former colonies, in particular the Indian subcontinent and the West Indies. The first large group to arrive were the 492 West Indians aboard the SS *Empire Windrush*, which docked at Tilbury in June 1948. The newcomers, a large percentage of whom settled in London, were given small welcome, and within ten years were subjected to race riots, which broke out in Notting Hill in 1958.

The riots are thought to have been carried out, for the most part, by "Teddy Boys", working-class lads from London's slum areas and new housing estates, who formed the city's first postwar youth cult. Subsequent cults, and their accompanying music, helped turn London into the epicentre of the so-called **Swinging Sixties**, the Teddy Boys being usurped in the early 1960s by the "Mods", whose sharp suits came from London's Carnaby Street. Fashion hit the capital in a big way, and, thanks to the likes of the Beatles, the Rolling Stones and Twiggy, London was proclaimed hippest city on the planet on the front pages of *Time* magazine.

Life for most Londoners, however, was rather less groovy. In the middle of the decade London's local government was reorganized, the LCC being supplanted by the **Greater London Council** (GLC), whose jurisdiction covered a much wider area, including many Tory-dominated suburbs. As a result, the Conservatives gained power in the capital for the first time since 1934, and one of their first acts was to support a huge urban motorway scheme that would have displaced as many people as did the railway boom of the Victorian period. Luckily for London, Labour won control of the GLC in 1973 and halted the plans. The Labour victory also ensured that the Covent Garden Market building was saved for posterity, but this ran against the grain. Elsewhere whole swaths of the city were pulled down and redeveloped, and many of London's worst tower blocks were built.

Thatcherite London

In 1979 **Margaret Thatcher** won the general election for the Conservatives, and the country and the capital would never be quite the same again. Thatcher went on to win three general elections, steering Britain into a period of ever greater social polarization. While taxation policies and easy credit fuelled a consumer boom for the professional classes (the yuppies of the 1980s), the erosion of the manufacturing industry and weakening of the welfare state created a calamitous number of people trapped in long-term unemployment, which topped three million in the early 1980s. The Brixton riots of 1981 and 1985 and the Tottenham riot of 1985 were reminders of the price of such divisive policies, and of the long-standing resentment and feeling of social exclusion rife among the city's black youth.

Nationally, the Labour Party went into sharp decline, but in London the party won a narrow victory in the GLC elections on a radical manifesto that was implemented by its youthful new leader **Ken Livingstone**, or "Red Ken" as the tabloids dubbed him. Under Livingstone, the GLC poured money into projects among London's ethnic minorities, into the arts and most famously into a subsidized fares policy which saw thousands abandon their cars in favour of inexpensive public transport. Such schemes endeared Livingstone to the hearts of many Londoners, but his popular brand of socialism was too much for the Thatcher government, who in 1986 abolished the GLC, leaving London as the only European capital without a directly elected body to represent it.

Abolition exacerbated tensions between the poorer and richer boroughs of the city. Rich Tory councils like Westminster proceeded to slash public services and sell off council houses to boost Tory support in marginal wards. Meanwhile in impoverished Labour-held Lambeth and Hackney, millions were being squandered by corrupt council employees. **Homelessness** returned to London in a big way for the first time since Victorian times, and the underside of Waterloo Bridge was transformed into a "Cardboard City", sheltering up to two thousand vagrants on any one night. Much greater efforts have been made since to alleviate homelessness, not least the establishment of a weekly magazine, the *Big Issue*, which is sold by the homeless right across London, earning them a small wage.

At the same time as homelessness and unemployment were on the increase, the so-called "**Big Bang**", which abolished a whole range of restrictive practices on the Stock Exchange, took place. The immediate effect of this deregulation was that foreign banks began to take over brokers and form new, competitive conglomerates. The side effect, however, was to send stocks and shares into the stratosphere, shortly after which they inevitably crashed, ushering in a recession that dragged on for the best part of the next ten years.

The one great physical legacy of the Thatcherite experiment in the capital is the **Docklands** development, which came about as a direct result of the Big Bang. Aimed at creating a new business quarter in the derelict docks of the East End, Docklands was hampered from the start by the Tories' blind faith in "market forces" and their refusal to help fund proper public transport links. Unable to find tenants for more than fifty percent of the available office space in the Canary Wharf development, the Canadian group Olympia & York had to call in the receivers just as the recession began to bite. Docklands finally got its tube in 1999, and, with the recession over, is now gradually being completed (see p.293).

Thatcher's greatest folly, however, was the introduction of the **Poll Tax**, a head tax levied regardless of means, which hit the poorest sections of the community hardest. The tax also highlighted the disparity between the city's boroughs. In wealthy, Tory-controlled Wandsworth, Poll Tax bills were zero, while those in the poorer neighbouring Labour-run Lambeth were the highest in the country. In 1990, the Poll Tax provoked the first full-blooded riot in Central London for a long, long time, and played a significant role in Thatcher's downfall later that year.

Millennium London

On the surface at least, twenty-first-century London has come a long way since the bleak Thatcher years. Redevelopment has begun again apace, partly fuelled by money from the National Lottery, which has funded a series of prestigious new **millennium projects** that have changed the

face of the city. A new pedestrian bridge now spans the Thames, leading to the new Tate Modern gallery, spectacularly housed in a converted power station. Numerous other national institutions have transformed themselves, too; among them the British Museum, the Royal Opera House, the Science Museum, Somerset House and the National Maritime Museum. And last, but not least, there's the controversial Millennium Dome, built and stuffed full of gadgetry for £750 million, but which failed to achieve the sort of success predicted by its backers.

The most significant political development for London, however, has been the creation of the new **Greater London Assembly** (GLA), along with an American-style **Mayor of London**, both elected by popular mandate. The New Labour government, which came to power on a wave of enthusiasm in 1997, did everything it could to prevent the election of the former GLC leader Ken Livingstone. Yet despite being forced to leave the Labour Party and run as an independent, Livingstone won a resounding victory in the elections of May 2000. It remains to be seen whether Ken can make any impact on the biggest problems facing the capital: transport, crime and racism within the Metropolitan Police Force.

London in film

As early as 1889 Wordsworth Donisthorpe made a primitive motion picture of Trafalgar Square, and since then London has been featured in countless films.

The selection given below ranges from studio recreations of a city that never existed, to films shot on locations from Soho to the suburbs. The cinema may not always have reflected London's diversity, but it has been capable of giving fresh life to some old myths, and of showing some of the lesser-known sides and unexpected sights of the city.

Broken Blossoms (D.W. Griffith, 1919). Limehouse melodrama about a peace-loving Chinaman (Richard Bathelemess), the girl who loves him (Lillian Gish) and her brutal prizefighter father (Donald Crisp). Remarkable for its display of Griffith's technique and for Gish's incandescent performance.

The Lodger (Alfred Hitchcock, 1926). "The first true Hitchcock movie" (according to Hitchcock), and one of the first of many variations on a Jack the Ripper theme, here given the "wrong man" twist much favoured by the director.

Piccadilly (E.A. Dupont, 1929). British potboiler made with Germanic style, with Anna May Wong caught in the East–West divide as she moves from Chinatown poverty to clubland luxury.

Underground (Anthony Asquith, 1929). Technically innovative pre-talkie, set on and around the Northern Line and culminating with a fight in Battersea Power Station.

Die Dreigroschenoper (G.W. Pabst, 1931). An un-Brechtian treatment of Brecht and Weill's update of *The Beggar's Opera,* featuring the legendary Lotte Lenya and a stylized re-creation of turn-of-the-century London. The film retained enough political bite to be banned on its initial British release.

Dr Jekyll and Mr Hyde (Rouben Mamoulian, 1931). Still the best version of this oft-filmed story, with Fredric March in the title parts. Set in Paramount's chiaroscuro re-creation of a repressive Victorian London, and made with an assured cinematic style.

Death at Broadcasting House (Reginald Denham, 1934). A conventional but clever whodunit given curiosity value on account of being set at the heart of the BBC.

The Man Who Knew Too Much (Alfred Hitchcock, 1934). Witty and pacy thriller about assassination-plotting anarchists, with Peter Lorre in fine, villainous form, and a nice use of settings (an East End mission house, the Royal Albert Hall). Hitchcock directed a glossier remake in 1956.

Drôle de Drame (Marcel Carné, 1936). A French attempt to poke fun at the British love of detective stories, set in a peculiar London designed by art director Alexander Trauner. Also known, appropriately enough, as *Bizarre, Bizarre.*

They Drive by Night (Arthur Woods, 1938). An atmospheric quota-quicky set in a world of Soho clubs and Great North Road transport caffs. Emlyn Williams stars as a petty thief on the run; Ernest Thesiger excels as a sinister sex-murderer.

The Adventures of Sherlock Holmes (Alfred Werker, 1939). The Baker Street Detective has made countless screen appearances, but Basil Rathbone remains the most convincing incarnation. Here Holmes and Watson (Nigel Bruce) are pitted against Moriarty (George Zucco), out to steal the Crown Jewels.

Dark Eyes of London (Walter Summers, 1939). Moody British chiller from an Edgar Wallace story, with Bela Lugosi orchestrating a series of murders at a home for the blind and disposing of the bodies in the Thames.

Fires Were Started (Humphrey Jennings, 1942). A re-creation of a day in a firefighter's life during the Blitz. One of several vivid and highly individual films documenting English life in wartime, made by Jennings in his too-brief career.

This Happy Breed (David Lean, 1944). Interwar saga of Clapham life taken from Noël Coward's play, with the emphasis on community values and ordinary, British decency. Enormously popular in its day.

Waterloo Road (Sidney Gilliatt, 1944). Worried about his wife's infidelity, a soldier goes AWOL. South-of-the-river melodrama with realist touches, and John Mills and Stewart Grainger literally fighting out their differences.

Hangover Square (John Brahm, 1945). Not an address listed in the streetfinder, and having next to nothing to do with the Patrick Hamilton novel it was nominally based on, but an atmospheric Hollywood thriller, in which Laird Cregar plays a schizophrenic composer living in gas-lit Chelsea.

London Town (Wesley Ruggles, 1946). A big-budget Technicolor musical that brought music-hall comedian Sid Field to the screen and aimed to bring Hollywood style to postwar Britain. It ended up a commercial and critical disaster.

Hue and Cry (Charles Crichton, 1947). Boys' Own adventure story featuring Jack Warner as a dubious Covent Garden trader, Alistair Sim as a timid writer of blood-and-thunder storie, and hoards of juvenile crime-fighters. Good use is made of the bomb-damaged locations.

It Always Rains on Sunday (Robert Hamer, 1947). An escaped convict (John McCallum) hides out in the Bethnal Green home of his former girlfriend (Googie Withers). Tense, fatalistic drama with a strong sense of place.

Oliver Twist (David Lean, 1948). An effective distillation of key elements of the Dickens novel, featuring Alec Guinness as a caricaturist's Fagin and a stylized re-creation of early nineteenth-century London from art director John Bryan.

Passport to Pimlico (Henry Cornelius, 1948). The quintessential Ealing Comedy, in which the inhabitants of Pimlico, discovering that they are actually part of Burgundy, abolish rationing and closing time. Full of all the usual eccentrics,

among them Margaret Rutherford in particularly fine form as an excitable history don.

Spring in Park Lane (Herbert Wilcox, 1948). One of a series of refined romances directed by Wilcox, and pairing his real-life wife Anna Neagle (austerity Britain's most popular star) with Michael Wilding, here playing an impoverished nobleman who takes a job as a footman.

The Blue Lamp (Basil Dearden, 1949). Metropolitan police drama introducing genial PC Dixon (Jack Warner) and charting the hunt for his killer (bad boy Dirk Bogarde). Now seems to come from another world, but its location photography was ground-breaking at the time.

Dance Hall (Charles Crichton, 1950). An evocative melodrama centred round the life and loves of four working-class women who spend their Saturday nights at the Chiswick Palais dancing to the sound of Ted Heath and his music.

Night and the City (Jules Dassin, 1950). London-set film noir, with Richard Widmark as a hustler on the run in an expressionistic city. Made when Dassin was himself escaping from McCarthyite America, and probably his best film.

Seven Days to Noon (Robert Boulting, 1950). Nightmares about the arms race lead a scientist (Barry Jones) to threaten to blow up London. Tense Cold War drama that gives an eerie view of the evacuated city.

Limelight (Charles Chaplin, 1952). Chaplin's final American film was a return to his London roots – a sentimental re-creation of poverty and music-hall life. Claire Bloom features as the ballerina whose career is promoted by Calvero (Chaplin), and there's a cameo from Buster Keaton.

The Ladykillers (Alexander Mackendrick, 1955). Delightfully black comedy set somewhere at the back of King's Cross (a favourite location for filmmakers). Katie Johnson plays the nice old lady getting the better of Alec Guinness, Peter Sellers and assorted other crooks.

Every Day Except Christmas (Lindsay Anderson, 1957). Short, lyrical and somewhat idealized documentary about work and the workers at Covent Garden.

Nice Time (Claude Goretta, Alain Tanner, 1957). An impressionistic view of Piccadilly Circus on a Saturday night, made by two Swiss film-makers and released, like Anderson's film, under the banner of "Free Cinema".

Expresso Bongo (Val Guest, 1959). A musical "comedy" in which smooth-talking agent Johnny Jackson (Laurence Harvey) takes "Bongo Herbert" (Cliff Richard) all the way from the coffee bars of Soho to the dizzy heights of fame.

Sapphire (Basil Dearden, 1959). A body discovered on Hampstead Heath is revealed to be that of a black woman passing for white. A worthy but fascinating "problem picture" that takes on rather more (black subculture, white racism and sexual repression) that it can deal with.

Beat Girl (Edmond Gréville, 1960). Also known as *Wild for Kicks*, this dated drama of teen rebellion marks Adam Faith's film debut and contains an early glimpse of Oliver Reed's smouldering skills. Notable for a wild party scene in Chislehurst Caves.

Peeping Tom (Michael Powell, 1960). A timid London cameraman (Carl Boehm) films women as he murders them. A discomforting look at voyeurism, sadism and watching movies; reviled on its original release, but latterly recognized as one of the key works of British cinema.

The Day the Earth Caught Fire (Val Guest, 1961). London swelters as the earth edges towards the sun following nuclear tests. A solidly British science-fiction film based around the (then) Fleet Street headquarters of the *Daily Express*.

Gorgo (Eugene Lourié, 1961). A creature from the ocean floor is exhibited at Battersea Funfair, until its mother comes to take it home, knocking down assorted London monuments on her way. An enjoyably tacky variation on the old monster-in-the-city theme.

One Hundred and One Dalmatians (Wolfgang Reitherman, Hamilton S. Luske, Clyde Geronimi, 1961). Disney's classic of animal liberation, in which the eponymous dogs do Scotland Yard's work, unmasking an unfriendly plot to turn puppies into fur coats. Villainess Cruella De Vil still manages to steal the show.

It Happened Here (Kevin Brownlow, Andrew Mollo, 1963). A shoestring production, filmed in and around London, that imagines Britain in 1944 after a successful German invasion. An anti-fascist film that refused to see people in terms of simple heroes and villains.

The Pumpkin Eater (Jack Clayton, 1964). Pinter-scripted story of middle-class, midlife crisis

unravelling in St John's Wood, Regent's Park Zoo and Harrods. Anne Bancroft is excellent as the mother of eight cracking under the strain.

Bunny Lake is Missing (Otto Preminger, 1965). Laurence Olivier plays a policeman searching the city for Carol Lynley's daughter. An accomplished psychological thriller with a creepy cameo from Noël Coward.

Four in the Morning (Anthony Simmons, 1965). This film started out as a documentary about the Thames, but evolved into a low-key drama about relationships and marital breakdown in the small hours of the morning.

The Ipcress File (Sidney J. Furie, 1965). An attempt to create a more down-to-earth variety of spy thriller, with Michael Caine as bespectacled Harry Palmer, stuck in a London of offices and warehouses rather than the exotic locations of the Bond films.

Repulsion (Roman Polanski, 1965). A study of the sexual fears and mental disintegration of a young Belgian woman left alone in a Kensington flat. Polanski's direction and Catherine Deneuve's performance draw the audience into the claustrophobic nightmares of the central character.

Alfie (Lewis Gilbert, 1966). Cockney wide boy Alfie Elkins (Michael Caine) has assorted affairs, and talks about them straight to the camera. An un-feminist comedy taken from Bill Naughton's play.

Blow-Up (Michelangelo Antonioni, 1966). Swinging London and some less obvious backgrounds (notably Maryon Park, Charlton) feature in this metaphysical mystery about a photographer (David Hemmings) who may unwittingly have recorded evidence of a murder.

The Deadly Affair (Sidney Lumet, 1966). Downbeat adaptation of a John Le Carré novel concerning an investigation into the supposed suicide of a Foreign Office diplomat. One of a number of thrillers portraying London as a city of repressed secrets.

Georgy Girl (Silvio Narizzano, 1966). A comedy of mismatched couples enlivened by excellent performances from Lynn Redgrave (as plain but loveable Georgy) and Charlotte Rampling (as her beautiful but cold flatmate).

Morgan, A Suitable Case for Treatment (Karel Reisz, 1966). A schizophrenic artist (David Warner) with a gorilla fixation attempts to win back his divorced wife (Vanessa Redgrave). The "madman as hero" message is rather swamped by the modish, 1960s humour.

Tonite Let's All Make Love in London (Peter Whitehead, 1967). Documentary on the "Swinging London" phenomenon, including music from The Animals, an interview with Allen Ginsberg and a happening at Alexandra Palace. Of its time.

Up the Junction (Peter Collinson, 1967). Middle-class Polly (Suzy Kendall) moves from Chelsea to ungentrified Battersea. Adapted from Nell Dunn's novel, this well-intentioned attempt to put working-class London on the big screen lacked the commitment and vitality of Ken Loach's earlier television version.

One Plus One (Jean-Luc Godard, 1968). A deliberately disconnected mix of footage of the Rolling Stones, assorted Black Power militants in a Battersea junkyard and "Eve Democracy" talking about culture and revolution. Also released as *Sympathy for the Devil*, with a complete version of the Stones number; Godard wasn't pleased.

The Strange Affair (David Greene, 1968). Made at the sour end of the 1960s, and set in a London of office blocks and multistorey car parks, this effectively gloomy police thriller stars Michael York as an innocent policeman in a corrupt world.

Leo the Last (John Boorman, 1969). Whimsical, sometimes striking fantasy set in a crumbling Notting Hill terrace, where stateless prince Marcello Mastroianni gradually begins to identify with his neighbours.

Performance (Nicolas Roeg, Donald Cammell, 1969). A sadistic gangster (James Fox) finds shelter and begins to lose his identity in another Notting Hill residence, this one belonging to a reclusive rock star (Mick Jagger). An authentic piece of psychedelia, and a cult movie that just about lives up to its reputation.

Deep End (Jerzy Skolimowski, 1970). At the public baths a naive teenager (John Moulder-Brown) becomes obsessed by his older workmate (Jane Asher). Excellent bleak comedy: set in an unglamorous London, made by a Polish director, and mainly shot in Munich.

A Clockwork Orange (Stanley Kubrick, 1971). A violent satire about violence, recently shown on British screens for the first time since the 1970s, which used some stylized sets and Thamesmead

locations to convey Kubrick's vision of a soulless near-future.

Death Line (Gary Sherman, 1972). Effectively seedy horror film about cannibalistic ex-navvies lurking in the tunnels around Russell Square Underground station. Most of the sympathy is reserved for the monsters.

Frenzy (Alfred Hitchcock, 1972). Hitchcock's final return to London, adapted from the novel *Goodbye Piccadilly, Farewell Leicester Square*, and filmed in and around Covent Garden. Displays all his old preoccupations (violence, sex, food) with added graphic detail.

The Satanic Rites of Dracula (Alan Gibson, 1973). At one point known as *Dracula is Alive and Well and Living in London*, this Hammer Horror uses the neat premise of a vampire property developer, but is otherwise unremarkable.

Punk in London (Wolfgang Büld, 1977). An earnest piece of German anthropology, featuring performances and interviews with the likes of The Sex Pistols, The Jam and X-Ray Specs.

Jubilee (Derek Jarman, 1978). Jarman's angry punk collage, in which Elizabeth I finds herself transported to the urban decay of late twentieth-century Deptford. Features Jordan as Amyl Nitrate, Little Nell as Crabs, Adam Ant as Kid and Jenny Runacre as the Queen.

The Long Good Friday (John Mackenzie, 1979). An East End gang boss (Bob Hoskins) has plans for the Docklands but finds himself fighting the IRA. A violent, contemporary thriller, looking towards the Thatcherite 1980s.

Babylon (Franco Rosso, 1980). Attempting to win a sound-system contest, Blue (Brinsley Forde) finds himself up against street crime, racism and police brutality. A sharp South London drama with a fine reggae soundtrack.

The Elephant Man (David Lynch, 1980). The story of John Merrick (John Hurt), exhibited as a fairground freak before being lionized by society. Freddie Francis's black and white photography brings out the beauty and horror of Victorian London. Much of the film was shot in Shad Thames, on the south side of Tower Bridge.

The Falls (Peter Greenaway, 1980). Long, strange, ornithologically obsessed pseudo-documentary, supposedly setting out to provide 92 biographies for the latest edition of the *Standard Dictionary of the Violent Unexplained*

Event. The locations include Goldhawk Road and Birdcage Walk.

An American Werewolf in London (John Landis, 1981). Comic horror movie with state-of-the-art special effects about an innocent abroad who gets bitten. Required viewing for all American backpackers.

Dance with a Stranger (Mike Newell, 1984). A well-groomed re-creation of the repressive 1950s, carried by Miranda Richardson's intense impersonation of Soho nightclub hostess Ruth Ellis, the last woman to be hanged in Britain.

Defence of the Realm (David Drury, 1985). Political thriller about state secrecy and newspaper ethics. With Gabriel Byrne, the always excellent Denholm Elliott and some atmospheric London locations.

My Beautiful Laundrette (Stephen Frears, 1985). A surreal comedy of Thatcher's London, offering the unlikely combination of an entrepreneurial Asian, his ex-National Front boyfriend and a Launderette called Powders. Frears and scriptwriter Hanif Kureishi worked together again on *Sammy and Rosie Get Laid* (1987): set in riot-torn Ladbroke Grove, it lacked the magic of their first collaboration, but was at least better than *London Kills Me* (1991), which Kureishi directed.

Absolute Beginners (Julien Temple, 1986). Musical version of the Colin MacInnes book, attempting to create a bold, stylized version of late 1950s Soho and Napoli (Notting Hill), but ending up as a confused mix of pastiche and pop promo.

Mona Lisa (Neil Jordan, 1986). A small-time crook (Bob Hoskins) falls for a high-class call-girl (Cathy Tyson) and helps search for her missing friend. Strikingly realized story of vice and betrayal, with great performances from the leads, and a view of King's Cross at its most infernal.

Hidden City (Stephen Poliakoff, 1987). Interesting piece of paranoia about an ill-matched couple (Charles Dance and Cassie Stuart) literally delving beneath the surface of the city. The plot treads fairly familiar territory, but the subterranean locations reveal a decidedly unfamiliar aspect of London.

Little Dorrit (Christine Edzard, 1987). Two-part adaptation (running to 6hr in total) of Dickens' novel of Victorian greed and deprivation. Faithful

to the complexities of the original, but put together with almost too much loving care.

Dealers (Colin Buckley, 1989). A risk-taking city trader with a private plane discovers that there's more to life than making money. A film as slick and empty as the characters it portrays.

Melancholia (Andi Engel, 1989). Intelligent thriller about a London-based German art critic (Jeroen Krabbe) whose radical past is brought back to him when he's asked to assassinate a Chilean torturer. An effective portrait of urban angst.

Queen of Hearts (Jon Amiel, 1989). Family life and troubles in Little Italy, London. This genial mix of fantasy and realism comes complete with a talking pig, a beautifully shiny espresso coffee machine and a jumbled sense of time and place.

I Hired a Contract Killer (Aki Kaurismäki, 1990). Jean-Paul Léaud decides to end it all by hiring a hitman, and then changes his mind. A typically wry film from this Finnish director, featuring such lesser-known landmarks as the *Honolulu* (a Docklands bar) and *Vic's Café* (in Hampstead Cemetery).

The Krays (Peter Medak, 1990). A chronicle of the life of Bethnal Green's gangland twins (Gary and Martin Kemp) that portrays them both as violent antiheroes and as damaged mother's boys. With Billie Whitelaw as the strong-willed mother.

Life is Sweet (Mike Leigh, 1990). Comic, poignant and acutely observed picture of suburban life and eating habits, with Leigh's semi-improvisational approach drawing fine performances from Alison Steadman, Jim Broadbent, and just about everyone else.

Riff-Raff (Ken Loach, 1990). A young Glaswegian works on a dodgy East End building site and shares a squat with a hopeful singer from Belfast. Less didactic and more comic than much of the director's work, Loach's film is good at conveying the camaraderie of the workers, but less convincing in its story of love found and lost.

Naked (Mike Leigh, 1993). David Thewlis is brilliant as the disaffected and garrulous misogynist who goes on a tour through the underside of what he calls "the big shitty" – life is anything but sweet in Leigh's darkest but most substantial film.

London (Patrick Keillor, 1994). Paul Scofield is the sardonic narrator of this "fictional documentary", describing three pilgrimages to little-visited tourist sights: the first to Strawberry Hill, Twickenham, the second in search of Edgar Allan Poe's old school in Stoke Newington, and the third along the River Brent. A witty, erudite and highly original film essay that looks at both London's literary past and its political present.

The Madness of King George (Nicholas Hytner, 1994). Excellent film version of the play by Alan Bennett, with Nigel Hawthorne in the lead role, Helen Mirren as his long-suffering consort and Rupert Everett as the Prince Regent. Cleverly shot in various locations in and around London, including Syon House, Windsor and Eton.

Beautiful Thing (Hettie MacDonald, 1996). Feel-good film, set, somewhat surprisingly, on the grim Thamesmead housing estate in southeast London. Glen Berry leads a cast of newcomers as teenager Jamie, coming to terms with his sexuality, starting with a crush on his best friend.

Restoration (Michael Hoffman, 1996). Flawed but atmospheric evocation of life in London under Charles II, seen through the eyes of a young doctor (Robert Downey Jr), whose career takes off after he restores the monarch's dog to health.

Richard III (Richard Loncraine, 1996). 1930s Britain, torn by civil war and sliding into fascism, is the setting for this pared-down and fast-paced version of Shakespeare's play, in which Ian McKellen gives a compelling performance in the title role. The inventively used locations include St Pancras Station (standing in as the entrance to the Royal Palace) and Bankside Power Station (as the exterior of the Tower of London).

Secrets and Lies (Mike Leigh, 1996). Palme d'Or-winning, heart-rending tale of young black woman who sets off in search of her natural mother, who turns out to be a sad, white, alcoholic woman, living a miserable life with her catatonic daughter.

Mojo (Jez Butterworth, 1997). Film adaptation of the critically acclaimed Royal Court play of the same name, featuring Tarantino-style gangsters, murder and rock'n'roll in 1950s Soho.

Mrs Dalloway (Marleen Goris, 1997). Very straightforward film version of Virginia Woolf's bivocal book, intertwining a day in the life of a society hostess, played by Vanessa Redgrave, and the paranoid thoughts of a World War I shell-shock victim.

Sliding Doors (Peter Howitt, 1997). Tricksy romantic comedy of parallel realities, set in London. Helen, played by Gwyneth Paltrow, discovers her boyfriend in bed with her best friend and dumps him; meanwhile, in an alternative reality, she remains blissfully ignorant of his misdemeanour.

Shooting Fish (Stefan Schwarz, 1997). Light, quirky romantic comedy, featuring two con men living in a London gasholder, who see themselves as modern-day Robin Hoods.

Spice World (Bob Spiers, 1997). The famous five (as they were then) cavort around London in a Union Jack double-decker. The plot is wafer thin, but there are lots of panoramic shots of London and plenty of cameos by famous actors and musicians. Of its time, already.

Babymother (Julian Henriques, 1998). Laudable attempt to deal with the breakdown of the traditional marriage within black British society, in which single mother Anita battles against the odds to try and find a man, make a success of her singing career and look after the kids.

Lock, Stock & Two Smoking Barrels (Guy Ritchie, 1998). Mostly famous for being directed by Madonna's beau, and featuring the acting debut of Vinnie Jones, former Wimbledon footballing hard man, this is a quick-fire Cockney rebel film about four lads hoping to make some fast money (to pay off their gambling debts) through a drugs deal.

End of the Affair (Neil Jordan, 1999). Not entirely successful film version of wartime Graham Greene novel about a passionate affair between a writer (Ralph Fiennes) and a civil servant's wife (Julianne Moore). Fiennes fans won't be disappointed, however, and there's lots of Catholic guilt to lap up.

Notting Hill (Roger Michell, 1999). Predictable but slick (and occasionally funny) romantic comedy in which Hugh Grant plays a posh and slightly useless bookshop owner, while Julia Roberts pretends to be a famous film actress, and the myth of happy, multicultural Notting Hill is fed to the Americans.

Wonderland (Michael Winterbottom, 1999). A long, lively weekend in the life of a typically dysfunctional 1990s south London family, featuring runaway sons, single mums and children born out of wedlock.

Gangster No. 1 (Paul McGuigan, 2000). Story of a young thug called Gangster, who becomes right-hand man to London crime king Freddy Mays in the late 1960s, only to betray him and see him sent to prison for thirty years. Violent, rather nasty piece of work (the film that is), starring Malcolm McDowell and David Thewlis.

24 Hours in London (Alexander Finbow, 2000). Another London gangster movie: the year is 2009, and a bunch of criminals controls the city (so what's changed?). Convoluted plot, over-the-top acting, led by Gary Olsen, and intentionally comic set pieces.

Books

Given the enormous number of books on London, the list below is necessarily a selective one. Most of the recommendations we've made are in print and in paperback – those that are out of print (o/p) should be fairly easy to track down in secondhand bookshops (see p.604). Publishers are detailed with the British publisher first, separated by an oblique slash from the US publisher, in cases where both exist. Where books are published in only one of these countries, UK or US follows the publisher's name; where the book is published by the same company in both countries, the name of the company appears just once. UP designates University Press.

London's bookshops are covered in detail on p.602, or for the real bibliophile, there's a well-indexed guide by Matt Jackson, *The Bookshops of London* (Mainstream, UK). The best known online bookshop is *www.amazon.co.uk* (for the UK), or *www.amazon.com* (for the US), but if you're looking for a particular book, *www.bookbrain.co.uk* will tell you which online bookshop is selling it for the cheapest price.

Travel, journals and memoirs

Paul Bailey (ed), *The Oxford Book of London* (Oxford UP). Big anthology of musings on London, arranged in chronological order from twelfth-century monks via Dostoevsky and Van Gogh to Hanif Kureishi and Angela Carter.

Julian Barnes, *Letters from London* (Picador/Vintage). Letters written between 1990 and 1995 for a regular column in the *New Yorker* magazine.

John Betjeman, *Betjeman's London* (John Murray, UK). A selection of writings and poems by the Poet Laureate, who spearheaded the campaign to save London's architectural heritage in the 1960s.

James Boswell, *London Journal* (Edinburgh UP). Boswell's diary, written in 1792–3 when he was lodging in Downing Street, is remarkably candid about his frequent dealings with the city's prostitutes, and is a fascinating insight into eighteenth-century life.

John Evelyn, *The Diary of John Evelyn* (Boydell & Brewer). In contrast to his contemporary, Pepys, Evelyn gives away very little of his personal life, but his diaries cover a much greater period of English history and a much wider range of topics.

Ford Madox Ford, *The Soul of London* (Everyman). Experimental, impressionist portrait of London, published in 1905 by the grandson of the famous Pre-Raphaelite painter, Ford Madox Brown.

Helene Hanff, *84 Charing Cross Road* (Warner /Moyer Bell). A touching autobiographical record of the letters between the author and a now-defunct Charing Cross Road bookshop.

Louis Heron, *Growing Up Poor in London* (Indigo, UK). Well-written account of growing up in an East End slum in 1919, by a man who later became Foreign Editor of *The Times*.

Irma Kurtz, *Dear London* (Fourth Estate). An affectionate, but not uncritical, eye is cast by an American who came to live in London in 1963 and stayed to write for *Cosmopolitan*.

Doris Lessing, *Walking in the Shade 1949–62* (Fontana). The second volume of Lessing's autobiography, set in London in the 1950s, deals with the writing and theatre scene and party politics, including her eventually disenchanted association with the Communist Party.

George Orwell, *Down and Out in Paris and London* (Penguin). Orwell's tramp's-eye view of the 1930s, written from firsthand experience. The London section is particularly harrowing.

Samuel Pepys, *The Shorter Pepys* (Penguin); *The Illustrated Pepys* (Unwin/University of California). Pepys kept a voluminous diary while he was living in London from 1660 until 1669, recording the fall of the Commonwealth, the Restoration, the Great Plague and the Great Fire, as well as describing the daily life of the nation's capital. The unabridged version is published in eleven volumes; Penguin's *Shorter Pepys* is abridged (though still massive); Unwin's is made up of just the choicest extracts accompanied by contemporary illustrations.

Iain Sinclair, *Lights Out for the Territory* (Granta/Penguin). Sinclair is one of the most original (and virtually unreadable) London writers of his generation. *Lights Out* – a series of ramblings across London starting in Hackney – is without a doubt his most accessible yet.

Peter Vansittart, *London: A Literary Companion* (John Murray). A rambling guide to the city, sprinkled with large chunks of literary quotes from everyone from Marx to P.G. Wodehouse.

Izaak Walton, *The Compleat Angler* (Oxford UP). Light-hearted seventeenth-century fishing guide set on London's River Lea, sprinkled with poems and songs. It has gone through more reprints than any other book apart from the Bible.

A.N. Wilson (ed), *The Faber Book of London/The Norton Book of London* (Faber/Norton). A voluminous collection of writings on all aspects of the capital by writers as diverse as Dostoevsky and Joe Orton.

History, society and politics

Peter Ackroyd, *Dickens* (Mandarin); *Blake* (Minerva/Ballantine); *Sir Thomas More* (Chatto & Windus, UK). Few writers know quite as much about London as Ackroyd does, and London is central to all three of his biographical subjects – the result is scholarly, enthusiastic and eminently readable.

James Boswell, *Life of Samuel Johnson* (Penguin). London's most famous man of letters has his sycophantic Scottish biographer, thirty years his junior, to thank for the longevity of his reputation.

E.J. Burford, *The Bishop's Brothels*; *Wits, Wenchers and Wantons*; *London: The Synfulle Citie* (all Hale, UK). Burford has written numerous somewhat prurient books on the sexual practices of Londoners through the ages. *The Bishop's Brothels* discusses the medieval whorehouses of Southwark, while *Wits, Wenchers and Wantons* is a bawdy history of post-Restoration Covent Garden. *London: The Synfulle Citie* covers the capital's bumping and grinding from Roman times to the eighteenth century.

Angus Calder, *The Myth of the Blitz* (Pimlico /Trafalgar Square). A timely antidote to the backs-against-the-wall, "London can take it" tone of most books on this period. Calder dwells instead on the capital's internees – Communists, conscientious objectors and "enemy aliens" – and the myth-making processes of the media of the day.

Hugh Clout, *London History Atlas* (Times Books, UK). This history atlas is packed full of illustrations and maps, which accompany a detailed account of the city's development from Londinium to Docklands.

Clive Emsley, *The Newgate Calendar* (Wordsworth, UK). Grim and gory account of the most famous London criminals of the day – Captain Kidd, Jack Sheppard, Dick Turpin – with potted biographies of each victim, ending with an account of his execution. First published in 1828, it was second in popularity only to the Bible at the time of publication.

William J. Fishman & Nicholas Breach, *The Streets of East London* (Duckworth, UK). Accessible social history of the East End, from

Victorian times to the present day, by a Jewish East Ender and scholar. Accompanied by black and white photos, old and new.

Stephen Inwood, *A History of London* (Carroll & Graf, UK). Weighty one-volume general history of the city from the Romans to the post-GLC mess, with more than half given over to the last two centuries.

Rachel Lichtenstein and Iain Sinclair, *Rodinsky's Room* (Granta, UK). A fascinating search into the Jewish past of the East End, centred on the nebulous figure of David Rodinsky.

Peter Linebaugh, *The London Hanged* (Cambridge UP). Superb Marxist analysis of crime and punishment in the eighteenth century, drawing on the history of those hanged at Tyburn.

Henry Mayhew, *London Labour and the London Poor* (Penguin). Mayhew's pioneering study of Victorian London, based on research carried out in the 1840s and 1850s.

Nick Merriman (ed), *The Peopling of London* (Museum of London/Reaktion Books). A large illustrated history of immigration to the capital, from the French Huguenots to the Somalis of the 1990s, with a separate section tracing the progress of each community.

Roy Porter, *London: A Social History* (Penguin /Harvard UP). This immensely readable history is one of the best books on London published since the war. It is particularly strong on the continuing saga of the capital's government and includes an impassioned critique of the damage done by Mrs Thatcher.

Winston G. Ramsey (ed), *The East End Then and Now* (After the Battle, UK). Massive tome full of black and white photos of the East End before and after the Blitz – covers all the legends from the Ripper to the Krays.

Maude Pember Reeves, *Round About a Pound a Week* (Virago, UK). From 1909 to 1913, the Fabian Women's Group, part of the British Labour Party, recorded the daily budget of thirty families in Lambeth living in extreme poverty. This is the accompanying comment, which is both enlightening and enlightened.

Donald Rumbelow, *The Complete Jack the Ripper* (Penguin). Of all the books exploiting this sordid tale of misogyny, Rumbelow's stands head and shoulders above the rest, trashing most previous accounts as sensationalist, and

concluding that there is insufficient evidence to pin the crime on any suspect.

John Stow, *A Survey of London* (Alan Sutton). Stow, a retired tailor, set himself the unenviable task of writing the first ever account of the city in 1598, for which he is now revered, though at the time the task forced him into penury.

Donald Thomas, *The Victorian Underworld* (John Murray/New York UP). A scholarly trawl through the sewers of Victorian London life, its prison houses, slums and criminal fraternity.

Judith R. Walkowitz, *City of Dreadful Delight: Narratives of Sexual Danger in Late-Victorian London* (Chicago UP). Weighty feminist tract on issues such as child prostitution and the Ripper murders, giving a powerful overview of the image of women in the fiction and media of the day.

Ben Weinreb & Christopher Hibbert, *The London Encyclopaedia* (Papermac/St Martin's Press). More than a thousand pages of concisely presented information on London past and present, accompanied by the odd illustration. The most fascinating book on the capital.

Philip Ziegler, *London at War 1939–45* (Mandarin, UK). A wide-ranging and even-handed account of life in the capital during the war years, from the Phoney War to the doodlebugs.

Art, architecture and archeology

Ken Allinson & Victoria Thornton, *A Guide to London's Contemporary Architecture* (Butterworth /Heinemann). Comprehensive gazetteer to the new buildings, great and small, erected all over Greater London in the 1980s and 1990s, with a black and white photo for each entry.

Felix Barker & Jason Hawkes, *London from the Air* (Ebury Press). The best of the aerial photo albums, with some intriguing arty shots of the city's more unusual landscapes.

Felix Barker & Ralph Hyde, *London As It Might Have Been* (John Murray, UK). A richly illustrated book on the weird and wonderful plans that never quite made it from the drawing board.

Felix Barker & Peter Jackson, *The History of London in Maps* (Barrie & Jenkins/Abbeville Press). A beautiful volume of maps, from the earliest surviving chart of 1558 to the new Docklands, with accompanying text explaining the history of the city and its cartography.

Bill Brandt, *London in the Thirties* (Herbert Press, UK). Brandt's superb black and white photos bear witness to a London lost in the Blitz.

Joe Friedman, *Inside London* (Phaidon). Beautiful colour illustrations of London's most ostentatious and opulent interiors, many of which are out of bounds to the public, though details of accessibility appear at the end of the book.

Samantha Hardingham, *London: A Guide to Recent Architecture* (Ellipsis London /Knickerbocker Press). Wonderful pocket guide to the architecture of the last ten years or so, with a knowledgeable, critical text and plenty of black and white photos.

Elaine Harwood & Andrew Saint, *London* (HMSO, UK). Part of the excellent Exploring England's Heritage series, sponsored by English Heritage. It's highly selective, though each building is discussed at some length and is well illustrated.

Edward Jones & Christopher Woodward, *A Guide to the Architecture of London* (Seven Dials, UK). Straightforward illustrated catalogue of London's 1920s buildings, each one accompanied by a black and white photo, and with useful maps at the beginning of each chapter.

Derek Kendall, *The City of London Churches* (Trafalgar Square, UK). A beautifully illustrated book, comprised mostly of colour photos, covering the remarkable City churches, many of them designed by Wren after the Great Fire.

Steven Parissien, *Regency Style*; *Adam Style*; *Palladian Style* (all Phaidon). Glossy coffee-table books with arty photographic illustrations. The Regency volume is particularly strong on Sir John Soane's work.

Nikolaus Pevsner and others, *The Buildings of England* (Penguin). Magisterial series, started by Pevsner, to which others have added, inserting newer buildings but generally respecting the founder's personal tone. The latest of the London volumes (there are now five in the series) is a paperback edition devoted to London Docklands.

Ann Saunders, *The Art and Architecture of London* (Phaidon). Weighty, well-illustrated and clearly presented rundown of just about every significant building in and around the capital.

John Schofield, *The Building of London* (British Museum Press, UK). A copiously illustrated architectural and archeological guide to pre-Fire

London, stretching from the Norman Conquest to the Great Fire.

Mary Ann Staples, *Fire Over London* and *Churchill's People* (Corgi, UK). Family stories set in London during the Blitz, with the emphasis on a determination to endure.

John Summerson, *Georgian London* (o/p). Scholarly treatise on the architecture of the capital from 1714 to 1830, which still predominates in areas like Mayfair, Marylebone and Bloomsbury. The Trafalgar volume is richly illustrated.

Richard Trench & Ellis Hillman, *London under London* (John Murray, UK). Fascinating book revealing the secrets of every aspect of the capital's subterranean history, from the lost rivers of the underground to the gas and water systems.

Ben and Matthew Weinreb, *London: Portrait of a City* (Phaidon). Historian and photographer combine to produce wonderful photos of often unnoticed details of London's architecture.

London in fiction

Peter Ackroyd, *English Music* (Penguin/ Ballantine); *Hawksmoor* (Penguin, UK); *The House of Doctor Dee* (Penguin, UK); *The Great Fire of London* (Penguin/Chicago UP); *Dan Leno and the Limehouse Golem* (Minerva, UK). Ackroyd's novels are all based on arcane aspects of London, wrapped into thriller-like narratives, and conjuring up kaleidoscopic visions of various ages of English culture. *Hawksmoor*, about the great church architect, is the most popular and enjoyable.

Dirian Adebayo, *Some Kind of Black* (Abacus, UK). Prizewinning 1996 novel portraying the London exploits of likeable but feckless student Dele and his sister Dapo.

Bruce Alexander *Blind Justice; Murder in Grubb Street; Watery Grave* (all Putnam). Whodunits set in the eighteenth century, featuring the blind magistrate Sir John Fielding, founder of the Bow Street Runners.

Martin Amis, *London Fields* (Vintage/Random House). "Ferociously witty, scabrously scatological and balefully satirical", it says on the back cover, though many regard Amis Jr's observation of lowlife London as pretentious drivel, written by a man who lives in comfortable old Notting Hill.

J.G. Ballard, *Concrete Island* (Vintage/Farrar Straus Giroux); *High Rise* (Vintage/Carroll & Graf); *The Drowned World* (Indigo, UK). Wild stuff. In *Concrete Island*, a car crashes on the Westway, leaving its driver stranded on the central reservation, unable to flag down passing cars. In *High Rise* the residents of a high-rise block of flats in East London go slowly mad. *The Drowned World*, Ballard's first novel, is set in a futuristic, flooded and tropical London – if only.

Neil Bartlett, *Mr Clive and Mr Page* (Serpent's Tail, UK). Strange, erotic and romantic story which ranges from the 1920s to the 1950s and reveals the homophobia of those years.

Samuel Beckett, *Murphy* (Jupiter, UK). Nihilistic, dark-humoured vision of the city, written in 1938, and told through the eyes of antihero Murphy.

Maeve Binchy, *Victoria Line, Central Line* (Arrow, UK). Gentle and compassionate tale, interweaving the lives of several people travelling on the Underground.

Elizabeth Bowen, *The Heat of the Day* (Penguin). Bowen worked for the Ministry of Information during the war, and witnessed the Blitz first-hand from her Marylebone flat; this novel perfectly captures the dislocation and rootlessness of wartime London.

Anthony Burgess, *A Dead Man in Deptford* (Vintage, UK). Playwright Christopher Marlowe's unexplained murder in a tavern in Deptford provides the background for this historical novel, which brims over with Elizabethan life.

Peter Carey, *Jack Maggs* (Faber). Set in 1837, this is the dark tale of a convict who returns secretly from Australia and gets involved in mystery and mesmerism.

Angela Carter, *The Magic Toyshop; Wise Children* (both Virago, UK). *The Magic Toyshop* was Carter's most celebrated 1960s novel, about a provincial woman moving to London, while *Wise Children* was published in 1992, the year of her untimely death.

G.K. Chesterton, *The Napoleon of Notting Hill* (Wordsworth). Written in 1904, but set eighty years in the future, in a London divided into squabbling independent boroughs – something prophetic there – and ruled by royalty selected on a rotational basis.

Liza Cody, *Bucket Nut; Monkey Wrench; Musclebound* (all Bloomsbury/Warner Books).

Feisty, would-be female wrestler of uncertain sexuality, with a big mouth, in thrillers set in lowlife London.

Sir Arthur Conan Doyle, *The Complete Sherlock Holmes* (Penguin). Deerstalkered sleuth Sherlock Holmes and dependable sidekick Dr Watson penetrate all levels of Victorian London, from Limehouse opium dens to millionaires' pads. *A Study in Scarlet* and *The Sign of Four* are based entirely in London.

Joseph Conrad, *The Secret Agent* (Penguin). Conrad's wonderful spy story, based on the botched anarchist bombing of Greenwich Observatory in 1894, and exposing the hypocrisies of both the police and the anarchists.

Daniel Defoe, *Journal of the Plague Year* (Penguin). An account of the Great Plague seen through the eyes of an East End saddler, written some sixty years after the event.

Thomas De Quincey, *Confessions of an English Opium Eater* (Penguin). Tripping out with the most famous literary drug-taker after Coleridge, and one of the greatest of all English prose stylists.

Charles Dickens, *Bleak House; A Christmas Tale; Little Dorrit; Oliver Twist* (all Penguin). The descriptions in Dickens' London-based novels have become the clichés of the Victorian city: the fog, the slums and the stinking river. *Little Dorrit* is set mostly in the Borough and contains some of his most trenchant pieces of social analysis. Much of *Bleak House* is set around the Inns of Court that Dickens knew so well.

Nell Dunn, *Up the Junction; Poor Cow* (both Virago, UK). Perceptive and unsentimental account of the downside of South London life in the 1950s after the hype of the Festival of Britain.

Buchi Emecheta, *Second-Class Citizen; Head above Water* (both Heinemann). Based on her own experiences in the 1960s, these tell the story of a young Nigerian woman struggling to survive in North London.

George Gissing, *New Grub Street* (Oxford UP/Everyman). Classic 1891 story of intrigue and jealousy among London's Fleet Street hacks.

Graham Greene, *The Human Factor; It's a Battlefield; The Ministry of Fear; The End of the Affair* (all Penguin). Greene's London novels are all fairly bleak, ranging from *The Human Factor*, which probes the underworld of the city's spies, to *The Ministry of Fear*, which is set during the Blitz.

Patrick Hamilton, *Hangover Square* (Penguin /Amereon); *Twenty Thousand Streets Under the Sky* (Vintage, UK). The first is a story of unrequited love and violence in Earl's Court in the 1940s, while the latter is a trilogy of stories set in seedy 1930s London.

Alethea Hayter, *A Sultry Month* (Faber/Robin Clark). Based on contemporary letters and newspapers, this deftly evokes the emotional temperature in London's literary circles in 1846.

Nick Hornby, *High Fidelity* (Orion). Hornby's extraordinarily successful second book focuses on the loves and life of a thirty-something bloke who lives near the Arsenal. . . rather like Hornby himself.

Aldous Huxley, *Point Counter Point* (Penguin). Sharp satire of London's high-society wastrels and dilettantes of the Roaring Twenties.

Robert Irwin, *Exquisite Corpse* (Vintage). Tale of obsessive love set in the Surrealist circles of postwar London (and elsewhere).

Henry James, *The Awkward Age* (Penguin). Light, ironic portrayal of London high society at the turn of the century.

P.D. James, *Original Sin*; *A Certain Justice* (both Penguin). Crime novels set in atmospheric locations in London's Docklands and law courts.

Hanif Kureishi, *The Buddha of Suburbia*; *The Black Album*; *Love in a Blue Time* (all Faber). *The Buddha of Suburbia* is a raunchy account of life as an Anglo-Asian in late 1960s suburbia, and the art scene of the 1970s. *The Black Album* is a thriller set in London in 1989, while *Love in a Blue Time* is a collection of short stories set in 1990s London.

John Lawton, *Black Out* (Orion). Thriller set in wartime London which begins with the discovery of a German found murdered in the bomb-torn East End.

Rosamond Lehmann, *The Weather in the Streets* (Virago, UK). Tragic sequel to *Invitation to the Waltz*, in which the heroine, Olivia Curtis, finds herself in boho London trying to breathe life into a doomed love affair.

Jack London, *The People of the Abyss* (Pluto/L. Hill Books). London's classic London novel.

Alison Lurie, *Foreign Affairs* (Vintage/Avon). A view from across the Atlantic: two American academics, sent to a wet, cold London to research in the British Library (the old one), find love in middle age.

Colin MacInnes, *Absolute Beginners*; *Omnibus* (both Allison & Busby, UK). *Absolute Beginners*, a story of life in Soho and Notting Hill in the 1950s (much influenced by Selvon – see below), is infinitely better than the film of the same name. *Omnibus* is set in 1957, in a Victoria station packed with hopeful black immigrants; white welfare officer meets black man from Lagos with surprising results.

Somerset Maugham, *Liza of Lambeth* (Vintage/Reed Consumer). Maugham considered himself a "second-rater", but this book on Cockney lowlife is packed with vivid local colour.

Timothy Mo, *Sour Sweet* (Vintage). Very funny and very sad story of a newly arrived Chinese family struggling to understand the English way of life, written with great insight by Mo, who is himself of mixed parentage.

Michael Moorcock, *Mother London* (Scribner, UK). A magnificent rambling novel by a once-fashionable but now very much underrated writer.

Iris Murdoch, *Under the Net*; *The Black Prince*; *An Accidental Man*; *Bruno's Dream*; *The Green Knight* (all Penguin). *Under the Net* was Murdoch's first, funniest and arguably her best novel, published in 1954 and starring a hack writer living in London. Many of her subsequent works are set in various parts of middle-class London and span several decades of the second half of the twentieth century. *The Green Knight*, her last novel, is a strange fable mixing medieval and modern London, with lashings of the Bible and attempted fratricide.

George Orwell, *Keep the Aspidistra Flying* (Penguin). Orwell's 1930s critique of Mammon is equally critical of its chief protagonist, whose attempt to rebel against the system only condemns him to poverty, working in a London bookshop and freezing his evenings away in a miserable rented room.

Jonanthan Raban, *Soft City* (Harvill Press). An early work from 1974 that's both a portrait of, and paean to, metropolitan life.

Derek Raymond, *Not till the Red Fog Rises* (Warner, UK). A book which "reeks with the pervasive stench of excrement" as Iain Sinclair (see below) put it, this is a lowlife spectacular set in the seediest sections of the capital.

Jay Rayner, *Day of Atonement* (Black Swan, UK). Traces the lives of two bright Jewish boys in northwest London in the 1960s, selling chicken-soup machines, whose association ends in tragedy in later life.

Ruth Rendell, *The Keys to the Street* (Arrow). The mystery centres on the homeless who are being spiked on the railings around rich Regent's Park.

Edward Rutherford, *London* (Arrow/Fawcett). A big, big novel (perhaps too big) which stretches from Roman times to the present and deals with the most dramatic moments of London's history. Masses of historical detail woven in with the story of several families.

Geoff Ryman, *253: The Print Remix* (Flamingo/St Martin's Press). First written on the Internet and now downloaded into book form. 253 characters appear, each on a separate page, as they journey on the Bakerloo Line between Embankment and Elephant & Castle. Great novelty value, but not great art.

Will Self, *The Quantity Theory of Insanity*; *My Idea of Fun*; *Grey Area* (all Penguin); *How the Dead Live* (Bloomsbury). Along with Martin Amis, Self is the current darling of the London literary world. Incisive social commentator or self-indulgent smartarse? Judge for yourself.

Samuel Selvon, *The Lonely Londoners* (Longman, UK). "Gives us the smell and feel of this rather horrifying life. Not for the squeamish", ran the quote from the *Evening Standard* on the original cover. This is, in fact, a wry and witty account of the Afro-Caribbean experience in London in the 1950s.

Iain Sinclair, *White Chappell, Scarlet Tracings* (Granta, UK); *Downriver* (Paladin/Random House); *Radon Daughters* (Cape/Random House). Sinclair's idiosyncratic and richly textured novels are a strange mix of Hogarthian caricature, New Age mysticism and conspiracy-theory rant. Deeply offensive and highly recommended.

Gillian Slovo, *Death by Analysis*; *Death Comes Staccato*; *Catnap* (all Women's Press/St Martin's Press). Private detective Kate Beier is generally sleuthing round Hackney, but sometimes finds herself in richer haunts.

Stevie Smith, *Novel on Yellow Paper* (Virago/New Directions). Poet Stevie Smith's first novel takes place in the publishing world of 1930s London.

John Sommerfield, *May Day* (o/p). Set in the revolutionary fervour of the 1930s, this novel is "as if *Mrs Dalloway* was written by a Communist Party bus driver", in the words of one reviewer.

Muriel Spark, *The Bachelors*; *The Ballad of Peckham Rye* (both Penguin). Two London-based novels written one after the other by the Scots-born author, best known for her *Prime of Miss Jean Brodie*.

William Sutcliffe, *New Boy* (Penguin). Funny and clever tale of the adolescent angst of Jewish boy growing up in northwest London.

Graham Swift, *Last Orders* (Picador/Vintage). Four friends recall the East End as it was during the war. Unsentimental view of Cockney life.

Paul Theroux, *The London Embassy* (o/p, but available on audio cassette). Not Theroux at his best, though fans of *The Consul's File* may be interested in the hero's posting to the London of the 1980s.

Evelyn Waugh, *Vile Bodies* (Penguin). Waugh's target, the "vile bodies" of the title, are the flippant rich kids of the Roaring Twenties, as in Huxley's *Point Counter Point* (see p.663).

Patrick White, *The Living and the Dead* (Vintage, UK). Novel set in 1930s London by the Australian Nobel prizewinner.

Angus Wilson, *The Wrong Set* (Penguin). A collection of short stories written in 1949 satirizing contemporary upper-middle-class characters in Knightsbridge and Kensington.

P.G. Wodehouse, *Jeeves Omnibus* (Hutchinson). Bertie Wooster and his stalwart butler, Jeeves, were based in Mayfair, and many of their exploits take place with London showgirls and in the Drones gentlemen's club.

Virginia Woolf, *Mrs Dalloway* (Penguin). Woolf's novel relates the thoughts of a London society hostess and a shell-shocked war veteran, with her "stream-of-consciousness" style in full flow.

Specialist guides

Felix Barker & Denise Silvester-Carr, *The Black Plaque Guide to London* (Constable, UK). An alternative to the official Blue Plaque Guide, cataloguing dens of vice, abodes of love and the homes of the disreputable.

Judi Culbertson & Tom Randall, *Permanent Londoners* (Robson Books/Walker & Co). An illustrated guide to the finest of London's cemeteries, from Westminster Abbey and St Paul's to the Victorian splendours of Highgate and Kensal Green. Very good on biographical histories of the deceased, too.

Andrew Duncan, *Secret London* (New Holland, UK). With boundless enthusiasm, Duncan takes you along the lost rivers, unmasks the property tycoons, exposes dead tube stations and just about uncovers every undiscovered nook and cranny in the city.

Bob Gilbert, *The Green London Way* (Lawrence & Wishart, UK). This hundred-mile walk (also cyclable) circles the capital, taking in favourites like Greenwich and Kew Gardens, but also covering more unusual urban landscapes such as the Northern Outfall Sewerway. Politically astute and ecologically sound text, too.

The Handbook Guide, *Rock & Pop London* (Handbook Publishing, UK). Rock and pop tourism is on the increase, though this unimaginative, rather dry book is unlikely to inspire too many folk, even if it casts its net fairly wide.

Ian McAuley, *Guide to Ethnic London* (Passport Books). A fine, accessible outline of the major ethnic communities in present-day London, with useful practical tips and a good all-round bibliography.

Glossary of architectural terms

Aedicule Small decorative niche formed by two columns or pilasters supporting a gable.

Aisle Clear space parallel to the nave of a church, usually with lower ceiling than the nave.

Altar Table at which the Eucharist is celebrated, at the east end of a church. (When the church is not aligned to the geographical east, the altar end is still referred to as the "east" end.)

Ambulatory Passage behind and around the chancel.

Apse The curved or polygonal east end of a church.

Arcade Row of arches on top of columns or piers, supporting a wall.

Ashlar Dressed building stone worked to a smooth finish.

Bailey Area enclosed by castle walls.

Baldachin Canopy over an altar.

Barbican Defensive structure built in front of main gate fortress.

Barrel vault Continuous rounded vault, like a semi-cylinder.

Boss A decorative carving at the meeting point of the lines of a vault.

Box pew Form of church seating in which each bench is enclosed by high, thin wooden panels.

Broach spire Octagonal spire rising straight out of a square tower.

Buttress Stone support for a wall; some buttresses are wholly attached to the wall, others, known as "flying buttresses" take the form of a tower with a connecting arch.

Capital Upper section of a column or pier, usually carved.

Chancel Section of a church where the altar is located.

Chantry Small pre-Reformation chapel in which masses were said for the soul of the person who financed its construction.

Choir Area in which the church service is conducted; next to or same as chancel.

Clerestory Upper storey of nave, containing a line of windows.

Coffering Regular recessed spaces set into a ceiling.

Corbel Jutting stone support, often carved.

Crenellations Battlements with square indentations.

Crossing The intersection of a church's nave and transepts.

Decorated Middle Gothic style; about 1280–1380.

Dogtooth Form of early Gothic decorative stonework, looking like raised "X"s.

Dormer Window raised above the main roof.

Early English First phase of Gothic architecture in England; about 1150–1280.

Fan vault Late Gothic form of vaulting, in which the area between walls and ceiling is covered with stone ribs in the shape of an open fan.

Finial Any decorated tip of an architectural feature.

Flushwork Kind of surface decoration in which tablets of white stone alternate with pieces of flint; very common in East Anglia.

Gallery A raised passageway.

Gargoyle Grotesque exterior carving, usually a decorative form of waterspout.

Hammerbeam Type of internal roofing in which horizontal beams support vertical timbers that connect to and support the roof.

Keep Main structure of a castle.

Lady chapel Chapel dedicated to the Virgin, often found at the east end of major churches.

Lancet Tall, narrow, plain window with pointed arch.

Lantern Structure on top of a dome or tower, often glazed to let in light.

Lunette Window or panel shaped like a half-moon.

Misericord Carved ledge below a tip-up seat, usually in choir stalls.

Motte Mound on which a castle keep stands.

Mullion Vertical strip between the panes of a window.

Nave The main part of a church on the other (usually western) side of the crossing from the chancel.

Ogee Double curve; distinctive feature of Decorated style.

Oriel Projecting window.

Palladian Eighteenth-century classical style adhering to the principles of Andrea Palladio.

Pediment Triangular space above a window or doorway.

Perpendicular Late Gothic style; about 1380–1550.

Pier Massive column, often consisting of several fused smaller columns.

Pilaster Flat column set against a wall.

Reredos Painted or carved panel at the back of an altar.

Rood screen Wooden screen supporting a crucifix (or rood), separating the choir from the nave; few survived the Reformation.

Rose window Large circular window, divided into vaguely petal-shaped sections.

Sedilia Seats for the participants in the church service, usually on south side of the choir.

Stalls Seating for clergy in the choir area of a church.

Tracery Pattern formed by narrow bands of stone in a window or on a wall surface.

Transept Sections of the main body of a church at right angles to the choir and nave.

Tympanum Panel over a doorway, often carved in medieval churches.

Vault Arched ceiling.

Index

Stay in touch with us!

ROUGHNEWS is Rough Guides' free newsletter. In three issues a year we give you news, travel issues, music reviews, readers' letters and the latest dispatches from authors on the road.

ROUGH GUIDES: Travel

Alaska
Amsterdam
Andalucia
Argentina
Australia
Austria

Bali & Lombok
Barcelona
Belgium &
  Luxembourg
Belize
Berlin
Brazil
Britain
Brittany &
  Normandy
Bulgaria
California
Canada
Central America
Chile
China
Corsica
Costa Rica
Crete
Croatia
Cuba
Cyprus
Czech & Slovak
  Republics

Dodecanese &
  the East Aegean
Devon &
  Cornwall
Dominican
  Republic
Dordogne & the
  Lot
Ecuador
Egypt
England
Europe
Florida
France
French Hotels &
  Restaurants
  1999
Germany
Goa
Greece
Greek Islands
Guatemala
Hawaii
Holland
Hong Kong &
  Macau
Hungary

Iceland
India
Indonesia
Ionian Islands
Ireland

Israel & the
  Palestinian
  Territories
Italy
Jamaica
Japan
Jordan
Kenya
Lake District
Languedoc &
  Roussillon
Laos
London
Los Angeles
Malaysia,
  Singapore &
  Brunei
Mallorca &
  Menorca
Maya World
Mexico
Morocco
Moscow
Nepal
New England
New York
New Zealand
Norway
Pacific
  Northwest
Paris
Peru
Poland
Portugal
Prague
Provence & the
  Côte d'Azur
The Pyrenees
Romania
St Petersburg
San Francisco

Sardinia
Scandinavia
Scotland
Scottish
  highlands and
  Islands
Sicily
Singapore
South Africa
South India
Southeast Asia
Southwest USA
Spain
Sweden
Switzerland
Syria

Thailand
Trinidad &
  Tobago
Tunisia
Turkey
Tuscany &
  Umbria
USA
Venice
Vienna
Vietnam
Wales
Washington DC
West Africa
Zimbabwe &
  Botswana

AVAILABLE AT ALL GOOD BOOKSHOPS

ROUGH GUIDES:
Reference and Music CDs

REFERENCE

Blues:
   100 Essential CDs
Classical Music
Classical:
   100 Essential CDs
Country Music
Country:
   100 Essential CDs
Drum'n'bass
House Music
Hip Hop
Irish Music
Jazz

Music USA
Opera
Opera:
   100 Essential CDs
Reggae
Reggae:
   100 Essential CDs
Rock
Rock:
   100 Essential CDs

Soul:
   100 Essential CDs
Techno
World Music

World Music:
   100 Essential CDs
English Football
European Football
Internet
Money Online
Shopping Online
Travel Health

ROUGH GUIDE MUSIC CDs

Music of the Andes
Australian Aboriginal
Bluegrass
Brazilian Music
Cajun & Zydeco
Music of Cape Verde
Classic Jazz
Music of
   Colombia
Cuban Music
Eastern Europe

Music of Egypt
English Roots Music
Flamenco
Music of Greece
Hip Hop
India & Pakistan
Irish Music
Music of Jamaica
Music of Japan
Kenya & Tanzania
Marrabenta
   Mozambique
Native American
North African
Music of Portugal
Reggae
Salsa
Samba
Scottish Music
South African Music
Music of Spain
Sufi Music
Tango

Tex-Mex
West African Music
World Music
World Music Vol 2
Music of Zimbabwe

Will you have enough stories to tell your grandchildren?

©2000 Yahoo! Inc.

Yahoo! Travel

Do You YAHOO!?

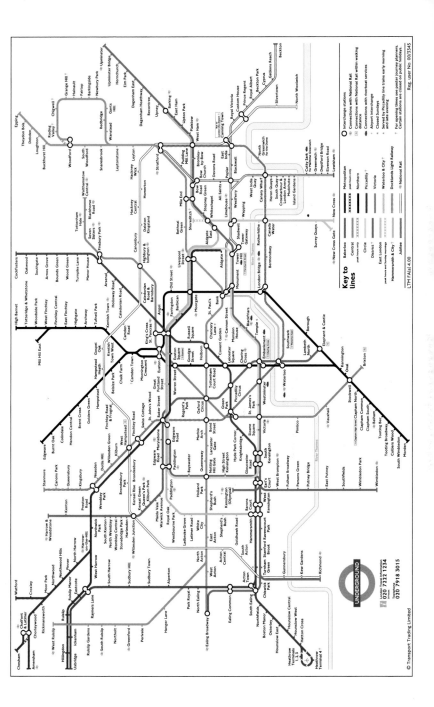

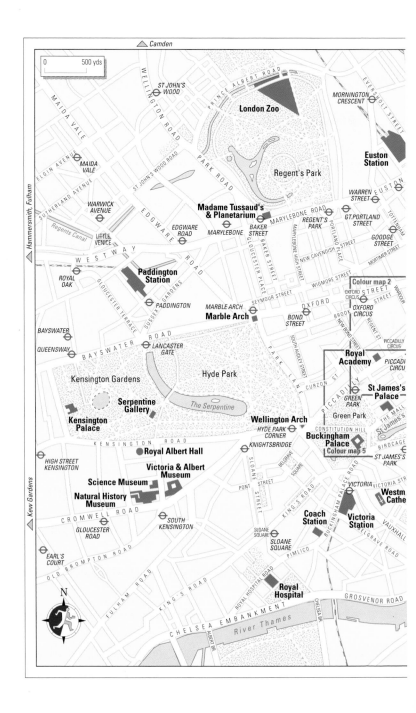

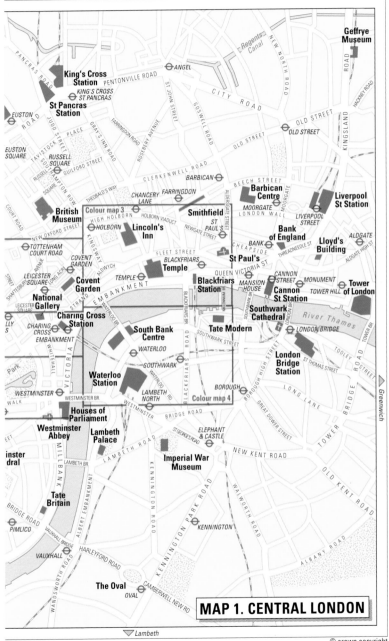

MAP 1. CENTRAL LONDON

© crown copyright

▽ Lambeth

▷ Greenwich

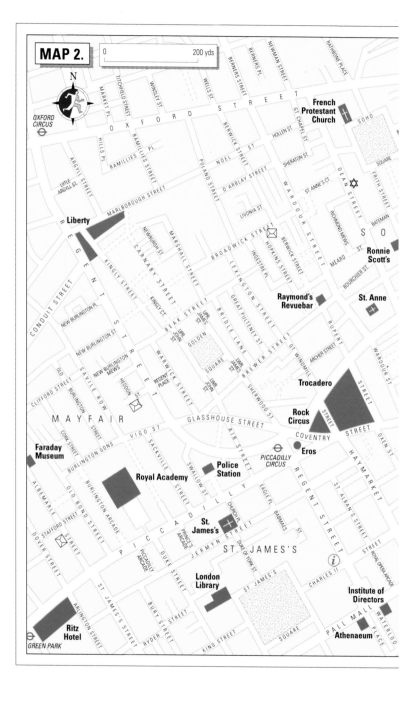